Job Seekers Guide to Silicon Valley Recruiters

Christopher W. Hunt

Scott A. Scanlon

John Wiley & Sons, Inc.
New York · Chichester · Weinheim · Brisbane · Singapore · Toronto

Copyright © 1998 by Hunt-Scanlon Publishing Company.
All rights reserved.
Published by John Wiley & Sons, Inc.

Published simultaneously in Canada.

Chapters 1, 2, and 3 consist of material adapted from
the following books by Richard H. Beatty: *The Resume Kit*,
The Perfect Cover Letter, and *The Five Minute Interview*.

This publication is designed to provide accurate and authoritative
information in regard to the subject matter covered. It is sold with
the understanding that the publisher is not engaged in rendering
professional services. If professional advice or other expert assistance
is required, the services of a competent professional person should be
sought.

Library of Congress Cataloging-in-Publication Data:

Hunt, Christopher W.
    Job seekers guide to Silicon Valley recruiters / Christopher W.
Hunt, Scott Scanlon.
        p.   cm.
    Includes index.
    ISBN 0-471-23993-3 (pbk. : alk. paper)
    1. Job hunting—California—Santa Clara County.   2. Information
technology—Vocational guidance—California—Santa Clara County.
I. Scanlon, Scott A.   II. Title.
HF5382.75.U62C224   1998
650.14'09794'73—dc21   97-44931
                                                            CIP

Printed in the United States of America

10 9 8 7 6 5 4 3 2 1

Contents

Introduction

No other field offers the range and number of opportunities to be found in information technology. And no area is so change-driven. The pace of technology and the rush of all types of businesses to keep up with it means that job definitions are being reformulated every day. The key to success in your job search is staying ahead of the curve, knowing how generational changes in infotech reshape established jobs—and create new ones. Your search should be regarded as a full-time job in itself—and fortune, as always, favors the prepared. You must highlight the skills and experience that will make you attractive to the companies you are targeting, and pursue your objectives energetically, imaginatively—and patiently. But the odds are in your favor. *Forbes* recently reported that "the top ten semiconductor companies have 12,000 open positions. Pay of computer engineers has risen two-thirds over the last decade. Over the next decade industry will need 730,000 computer engineers and systems analysts/developers." And the Internet opens up vistas that were undreamed of even two years ago. As Charles Polachi of Fenwick Partners, a leading infotech recruiting specialist, points out, only 3 percent of the world's population has personal computer (PC) access to the Net; the untapped potential is staggering.

Realizing that you are the only one in control of your future can be frightening; however, career transitions, while difficult, are pivotal times of tremendous opportunity: The possibilities are infinite. This is the moment to use your skills and past achievements to secure a better job and a brighter future.

In this change-driven area, according to David Beirne of Ramsey/Beirne Associates, Inc., there is one dependable constant: No matter what your background or objectives—a new job in the management information systems (MIS) area, or creation of on-line marketing for a company just breaking into the electronic free-trade zone—you must demonstrate that you thrive on change and that you are technologically savvy as well as comfortable in and aware of every significant aspect of your area of expertise. Whether you are an engineer or a software designer, intranet- or Internet-oriented, you are as good as the currency and depth of your knowledge and skills.

Companies need innovative and dedicated people to survive and grow, and the right people are not always easy to find. Few companies looking for entry-level talent (or higher) in information technology expect to attract it just through classified advertising. Some increasingly turn to operations such as Silicon Valley Career Center or Monster Board that maintain huge databases of candidates for positions and operate on-line and via e-mail. At higher levels, from the upper ranks of middle management right up to executive positions such as chief executive officer (CEO) and chief operating officer (COO), executive recruiters can be of assistance: giving you insights into your career and potential that you may not have considered, and matching you with opportunities that you may have been unaware of. Companies still want to see resumes, but they tend to pay particular attention to what comes over their human networks. (In infotech, as David Beirne puts it, "good people know other good people—and good people know about the good jobs.")

Executive recruiters, using a more organized network, help companies by examining their employment needs and then prescreening and narrowing the field of potential candidates to present only those who seem to be a good fit. This works to your advantage: A search consultant can brief you on prospective companies and what sort of employees they are looking for, give you frank advice about your interview style, and prepare you for the sort of questions to expect. You can also be reassured that because the company has gone to the expense of contacting a recruiter, there is a genuine interest in filling the position promptly. Executive recruiters can also be helpful if you *don't* get a certain job: They can tell you why another candidate was chosen, and can coach you on how to improve for your next interview. Always remember: When an executive recruiter tries to contact you, take the call. It might be a new beginning for you.

THERE ARE TWO TYPES OF EXECUTIVE RECRUITERS

Although there are a number of ways to effectively market yourself, this book deals exclusively with executive recruiters, also known as headhunters or executive search consultants. What is an executive recruiter, and what role can he or she play in your success? There are two basic types: retained and contingency. Both are paid by the companies that hire them, not by job seekers, but they differ in method, and sometimes the salary level, on which they operate.

Retained executive recruiters are headhunters who work on a contract with a client company. They are hired by companies to find a particular executive for a specific position and are subsequently paid a retainer fee (one-third at inception of the search, one-third at the halfway point, and one-third when the candidate is chosen and hired). These recruiters often handle the absolute crème de la crème. Corporate giants in information technology and related companies such as James Barksdale, CEO of Netscape; Robert Herbold, COO of Microsoft; Eric Schmidt, CEO of Novell; and William Razzouk, president and COO of America Online, for example, were all placed by headhunters in this category. The average placement, however, is most often a rung or two lower. Though retained recruiters may be hired to fill a position with compensation in the millions or as low as $50,000, the average assignment generally runs between $75,000 and $125,000.

Contingency recruiters fill the gap between entry-level placements (generally handled by employment agency professionals) and those handled by the retained recruiter. The compensation level starts at about $30,000 and peaks at about $50,000. There are, however, exceptions, as a handful of contingency recruiters will place professionals with compensation levels exceeding $100,000. Recruiters in this category handle the bulk of lower to middle management and general management assignments. They are referred to as contingency recruiters because their fee is paid at the conclusion of the assignment or "contingent upon" the successful placement.

GETTING THEIR ATTENTION

Job seekers who wish to become part of recruiters' preferred lists (meaning that they deem you a strong candidate whom they will consider for any appropriate position) should employ certain steps in order to stand out from the rest of the crowd. Firms such as Korn/Ferry International, Spencer Stuart, Heidrick & Struggles, Russell Reynolds Associates, Christian & Timbers, Ramsey/Beirne Associates, Fenwick Partners, Norm Sanders Associates, and others collectively receive in excess of one million resumes annually.

Prior to sending your resume to any executive recruiter, make certain that you contact the search firm to see if it has the specialists who speak the language of infotech and know where someone with your background is going to be just the right fit. While many large search firms are labeled as generalist firms because they place executives in most functional disciplines and industries, they often have individuals and departments specializing in infotech, so making sure that your resume is being sent to the appropriate recruiters is time well spent.

Also, don't discount numerous smaller firms, or specialty boutiques that specialize in your area, which may prove to be an even better choice for someone with your background and experience. Today the majority of specialists and generalists have Web sites. If you don't check them out (and if you don't visit the sites of companies that interest you) you aren't doing your homework. This book (which has its own Web site!—http://www.job-seekers.com) specializes in recruiters seeking to fill positions in which infotech knowledge and experience are essential. Don't hesitate to call firms and ask them about their specialties if you have any questions. Again, a little digging on your part, particularly through on-line resources, may pay off, saving you countless hours of following up with recruiters who are not able to help you.

NOW WHAT?

After you target recruiters or firms that specialize in your area of interest and experience in information technology or services, make certain that you are specific as to what you've done and what you are seeking. Don't generalize your credentials. The main question client companies have when reviewing resumes is, "What can this person do for us?" Answer that question on your resume by giving concrete examples of your accomplishments, and how your past companies have benefited from your contributions. It's impossible that you made no difference to your past company. Even if you feel your contribution was small, mention it. If you are seeking an entry-level position, are your skills and education suited to a vendor (those who make the hardware and software) or to service and support for a corporate client? Or, are you ready to help an end user, a company that needs your skills to broaden its capabilities in information/telecommunications applications to grow its core business? Think of your resume and cover letter as an outline for what you'll talk about when you meet a recruiter face-to-face.

Also use your resume, cover letter, and interview as chances to focus on what you expect to accomplish in the future. For example, if you have been involved in an MIS support function but want to expand your skills, make sure that that is clear in your cover letter and on your resume. The mistake that often plagues job seekers is trying to be everything to everyone. Also, if there are certain jobs that you are qualified for but are adamant about not doing, say so, and save your recruiter and yourself from arranging interviews for jobs that you wouldn't accept anyway. Another advantage to being specific about what you want is that if a client company calls with an opening that meets your criteria, the headhunter will be more likely to think of you.

Being realistic about your qualifications is helpful to both your headhunter and yourself. If you have 15 years of experience as a middle management expert in systems design and procurement for a corporation, it is not prudent to think that you will land a position as a vice president for marketing in an information technology company because you took a marketing course in college. Instead, suggests Charles Polachi, think through your capabilities and try to emphasize elements of your background that will make you attractive to either a vendor (of software or hardware) or a systems consultant for whom your end-user orientation will be valuable. If you've been a software designer who has collateral business and people management skills, consider management opportunities in Internet-related companies.

USE EVERY CONTACT AS AN OPPORTUNITY

One potential pitfall in the preparation of your credentials is the urge to stretch the truth. There is nothing wrong with highlighting or emphasizing various responsibilities or accomplishments. But in the desperation of trying to land a job, the temptation is strong to make certain "adjustments" to your credentials. A five-year stint at your last company may transform itself into seven years because the company you want to work for requires seven years' prior experience. Or in describing your position as director of sales and marketing for a division of a telecommunications equipment manufacturer you may state you increased your division's profit margin by 20 percent when the reality is that the increase was only 10 percent. Although you may think you're getting an edge by means of what you may perceive as inconsequential padding, the truth is that recruiters can smell these embellishments a mile away; detecting them is what they do for a living. Keep in mind that if you're caught lying, the recruiter will not deal with you again (if he or she does, perhaps you should be suspicious of the *recruiter's* integrity). Also, executive search is in many ways a close-knit community—there's a good chance that other recruiters may learn what you're up to. And, if you by some chance land the job anyway, you may find yourself in a position for which you are not qualified, which could, in an extreme case, mean lawsuits for you and possibly your headhunter.

Always return your recruiters' calls promptly and politely. Every contact is an opportunity to give them more confidence in you both as a candidate and as someone they'd like to help.

And don't overlook the possibility that you can be helpful to them, too. If a recruiter mentions an opening that's inappropriate for you but might interest someone else you know, say so. Your honesty will be appreciated and remembered. Providing a valuable contact to a recruiter is not only a nice thing for you to do for someone but it may also be rewarding to you somewhere down the line.

If you are currently employed but are always keeping your eyes open for other career opportunities, the above suggestions certainly apply to you, but we would offer a few additional tips.

You may at some point in your professional life receive a call from a recruiter. It may come during a time when you are completely content with your career and the company you work for and you may not be interested in even taking the call. We would recommend that you not ignore a call from a recruiter for two reasons: First, although you are a happy camper, a recruiter might be considering you for an even better position. In fact, the only way you might be able to enhance your career is to change over to a job that has different functions and new ways of exploiting your skills and experience, as suggested above. And, second, the job the recruiter is considering you for may in fact not suit you. But it might be ideal for a colleague or friend with a slightly different background who is unemployed or unhappy in his or her job.

Also, many employed executives are concerned about confidentiality if they decide to speak with a recruiter. Don't hesitate to mention this if it is a potential problem. Recruiters are used to these situations and know it is essential to maintain confidentiality. If your situation is highly sensitive, instruct your headhunter to leave messages on your home answering machine—just be sure to check your messages frequently during the day. If you reach the interview stage with a recruiter, the majority of meetings will naturally be held off-site, generally at the office of the recruiter or even perhaps at your residence. Discretion is the watchword for such meetings.

There is no doubt that finding a new job can be a challenging experience. Although executive search professionals should represent only a portion of your job search efforts, knowing how to utilize this valuable asset is essential. We hope that we have been able to provide you with a sense of the marketplace today, which recruiters are best for you, and how you can effectively work with them. Best of luck!

Chapter 1

Introduction to Resumes

The employment resume—its style, organization, and content—has long been a topic of considerable discussion and debate. Like religion and politics, this is a subject fraught with controversy. It is one of those topics where there are many "experts" who will provide you with considerable "professional" advice and counsel as long as you are willing to listen.

Should you wish to put this statement to the test, let me suggest that the next time you are at lunch or dinner with a group of friends or business colleagues, introduce the subject of "resume preparation" and ask a few of the following questions:

1. How long should a resume be?
2. What is the best resume format? How should it be organized?
3. Should there be a statement of job objective? If so, how should it be worded?
4. Should the resume contain personal data—age, height, weight, marital status, number of children?
5. Should hobbies and extracurricular activities be included?
6. How important is salary history? Should it be shown at all?
7. Where should education be described—near the end or the beginning of the resume?
8. What writing style is the most effective?
9. What is the best format for computer scanning and resume database search?

These, and similar questions, are guaranteed to spark a lively discussion punctuated with considerable difference of opinion. There will be those who claim that "Everyone knows that a resume should never be longer than a single page." Others will assert that "Two pages are quite acceptable." Still others will be adamant that "Two pages can never begin to do justice to 10 years of professional experience and accomplishment." All may use logical and persuasive arguments, with each sounding more convincing than the last. Who is right? Which argument should you believe? What works best?

As a consultant and executive with considerable employment experience, I can tell you that there are good answers to these questions. There is a right and a wrong way to prepare an employment resume. There are items that should definitely be included in the resume, and there are those that are best left out. There are resume formats that have consistently proven more effective than others, and there are those that should be avoided.

There are appropriate answers to these and many other questions associated with the subject of effective resume preparation. But you cannot expect to get expert advice on resume preparation over casual dinner conversation with a few friends whose expertise consists mainly of preparation of their first resume and a few articles read somewhere in a trade journal. This is hardly the type of advice that you need to prepare a resume that will be successful in launching you on a new and prosperous career track.

What I am about to share with you are the observations and advice of a human resources consultant and former personnel executive who has had considerable experience in the corporate employment function of a major Fortune 200 company. This is knowledge gleaned from years of employment experience—knowledge gained from the reading of thousands of employment resumes and the hiring of hundreds of employees at the professional, managerial, and executive level. This advice is based on firsthand observation of those resumes that resulted in job interviews and those that did not. This is advice based on "inside" knowledge of what makes professional employment managers tick—what motivates them to respond favorably to one resume and "turns them off" on the next. It will guide you in preparing a resume that will best display your qualifications and maximize your potential for landing interviews.

This chapter will provide you with an understanding of what happens in a typical company employment department. Where does your resume go? Who reads it? What is the basis for determining interest or lack of interest? What does the employment manager look for in a resume? How is the resume read? Who makes the final decision on your resume? Answers to these and similar questions should provide you with valuable insight that will enable you to design your resume to successfully compete for an employment interview. They will also serve as the basis for better understanding the recommendations made later in this chapter on such topics as resume format, content, style, appearance, and so on.

COMPETITION

In larger companies, it is not uncommon for the corporate employment department to receive as many as 40,000 to 50,000 resumes during the course of an average business year. Some receive considerably more. The annual employment volume of such firms typically runs in the range of 200 to 300 hires per year. Assuming an average of two to three interviews per hire, these firms will interview 400 to 900 employment candidates in meeting their employment requirements. This means that only 400 to 900 of the total 40,000 to 50,000 resumes received will result in an employment interview. In other words, only one or two out of every 100 resumes will result in an employment interview. Those are not very encouraging odds!

You are thus beginning your employment search at a decided statistical disadvantage. For every 100 resumes mailed to prospective employers, on the average you can expect only one or two interviews to result. These statistics alone should persuade you of the importance of a well-prepared and effective resume.

It is estimated that the average employment manager of a major corporation will read more than 20,000 resumes a year. Assuming no vacation time and 260 workdays in a year, this is equivalent to a weeknight workload of more than 75 resumes. Since employment managers must frequently travel, however, and most do take time off for holidays and vacations, it is estimated that this number is actually closer to 100. Since each resume averages 1½ pages in length, the employment manager has an average of 150 pages of reading to do each evening—a sizable chore!

Since the employment manager frequently spends the entire workday interviewing employment candidates, most resumes are normally read during the evening hours. Additionally, since evenings are often used by the manager to plan employment strategies, write recruitment advertising, and do other planning work necessary to the employment process, the amount of evening time left to read resumes may be only an hour or two.

In many cases, the employment manager is unable to read resumes until later in the evening. The early evening hours must often be used by the manager to make telephone calls to make job offers, follow up with candidates on outstanding offers, prescreen prospective candidates, and so on. These calls can usually be made only during the early part of the evening, leaving resume reading until later.

As you can well imagine, by 10 or 11 P.M. (following a full day of interviewing and several early evening phone calls) the typical employment manager is probably tired. He or she must now read an estimated 150 pages of resumes before retiring for the evening. You can well imagine how thoroughly these resumes will be read.

The technique used by most employment managers in reviewing resumes is not an in-depth, step-by-step reading process. Instead, it is a process of rapidly skimming the resume in a systematic way to determine whether or not the individual has qualifications and career interests consistent with the company's current employment requirements.

Considering all of these factors, resumes that are poorly prepared, sloppy, or in any other way difficult to read will receive very little consideration. Resumes are thought to be indicative of the overall personal style of the writer. Thus the inference that is frequently drawn from such poorly written resumes is that the applicant is likewise a sloppy, uncaring, of disorganized individual. Why then should the employment manager risk bringing this individual in for interviews? In such cases, the resume will more likely than not be stamped "no interest," and the employment manager will quickly move on to the next resume.

By now I hope that you are convinced that the general appearance of the resume is critical to its impact and effectiveness. It should be obvious that readability is likewise a major criterion for resume success. Resume organization and format are therefore extremely important factors to consider if your resume is to be successful in this difficult and competitive arena.

We now move on to a general discussion of the organization and operation of the typical company employment department. We carefully trace the steps through which your resume will likely pass, from the point of receipt by the department to final determination of application status.

RESUME PROCESSING

In the case of a company with a large employment department, the department is normally subdivided into functional specialties with each employment manager having accountability for a given area. For example, there may be an Administrative Employment Manager who has accountability for all administrative hiring: Accounting, Finance, Law, Data Processing, Human Resources, and so on. A Technical Employment Manager may also exist with accountability for all technical hiring: Research and Development, Central Engineering, Technical Services, Quality Control, and so on. Likewise, there may be an Operations Employment Manager with responsibility for all hiring related to manufacturing or plant operations. Marketing and Sales may also be represented by a separate employment manager.

As resumes are received by the employment department, there is usually one person who is designated to open and sort the mail into the appropriate categories for distribution to the individual employment managers. Once received by the employment manager's administrative assistant, the screening process will begin with the assistant "screening out" those resumes that are clearly not of interest to the employment manager. Thus if the employer is a steel company, the resumes of botanists, foresters, artists, and so forth are likely to be "screen out" at this point. Likewise, the administrative assistant may eliminate illegible, sloppy, or otherwise undesirable resumes.

The next step is for the employment manager to read the resume to determine whether there is an opening that is an appropriate match for the applicant's credentials. If not, the resume is usually marked "no interest," coded, and sent to Word Processing where an appropriate "no interest letter" is prepared and sent to the applicant. A copy of this letter along with the original resume is then returned to the employment department for filing and future reference.

At this point, "no interest" resumes are normally divided into two categories: (1) those in which the employer will probably have no future interest and (2) those having a high likelihood of interest at some future time ("future possibles"). Those in which the company is likely to have future interest are normally placed in an active file for future reference and review. In some cases, these "future interest" resumes are electronically scanned and stored on a computer resume data base. The remaining resumes are placed in a dead file with no possibility of future review.

When the employment manager determines that there is a reasonable match between the candidate's qualifications and the employment needs of a given department, the next step is a review of the resume by the hiring manager (the manager having the employment opening). Having reviewed the resume and determined that there is a probable match between the candidate's qualifications and interests and the requirements of the position, the hiring manager then notifies the employment manager of this interest and requests that the employment manager schedule the candidate for an interview. If, on the other hand, there is no interest, the hiring manager indicates this to the employment manager, and the resume is processed as described above.

In the case of the more sophisticated employers, there is usually one additional step in the process prior to extending an invitation for an interview. This step is referred to as the "telephone screen." This means that either the hiring manager or the employment manager will phone the candidate for the purpose of conducting a mini-interview. This telephone interview is intended to determine whether the candidate has sufficient qualifications and interest to warrant the time and expense of an on-site interview. Additionally, employers frequently use this preliminary interview to determine the validity of the information provided on the resume—a good reason to be factual in describing your qualifications and accomplishments!

There are three critical points in the resume-processing procedure at which your resume may be screened out and marked "no interest":

1. Administrative Assistant—screened for obvious incompatibility, incompleteness, sloppiness, or illegibility.
2. Employment Manager—screened for incompatibility with current openings and required candidate specifications.
3. Hiring Manager—screened for insufficient or inappropriate qualifications when compared with job requirements.

The highly competitive nature of the employment market, coupled with the thorough screening provided by the prospective employer, makes the preparation of a professional and effective resume an absolute must if one expects to be successful in the employment or job-hunting process! The resume cannot be left to chance. It must be carefully and deliberately designed if it is to successfully survive the rigors of the company's screening process.

Let's now take a closer look at the process used by the employment manager to screen resumes. How does he or she read a resume? What is the employment manager looking for? What will determine which resumes are screened out?

CANDIDATE SPECIFICATION

The very first step in the typical employment process is the preparation of an "employment requisition" by the hiring manager. This document is normally signed by the hiring manager's function head and human resources manager and is then forwarded to the appropriate employment manager. The purpose of the employment requisition is normally threefold:

1. Provides management authorization to hire.
2. Communicates basic data about the opening—title, level, salary range, reporting relationship, maximum starting salary, key job responsibilities, and so on.
3. Communicates basic or fundamental candidate specifications—type and level of education required, type and level of experience sought, technical and administrative skills required, and so forth.

Any good professional employment manager knows that the employment requisition seldom provides sufficient information to do a professional job of identifying and recruiting a well-qualified candidate. Considerably more information will usually be needed, and the employment manager is quick to arrange a meeting with the hiring manager to develop a more thorough and comprehensive candidate specification. The following are examples of typical "candidate specs."

Both of these candidate specs are highly detailed and very particular about the kind of qualifications that will satisfy the employment requirement. Very little has been left to chance. There is a clear understanding of both the educational and experience requirements for candidates who would receive serious consideration for employment.

Job Title: Chief Project Engineer
Job Level: 600 Points
Department: Central Engineering
Group: Mechanical
Education:
  Preferred: M.S. Mechanical Engineering
  Acceptable: B.S. Mechanical Engineering
Experience:
  Eight plus years experience in the design, development, installation, start-up, and debugging of Herrington Winders and auxiliary equipment. Demonstrated project leadership of projects in the eight to ten million range. Must have managed groups of five or more professionals.
Maximum Starting Salary: $85,000

Now let's look at another example.

Job Title: Director—Human Resources
Job Level: 1,200 Points
Department: Human Resources
Reporting Relationship: Sr. Vice President—Administration
Maximum Starting Salary: $100,000
Estimated Bonus: 20% to 30%
Education: Masters in Human Resources Management
Experience:

> Requires a minimum 15 years experience in Human Resources in a corporation of 20,000 plus employees. Experience must include a broad range of Human Resources experience to include: Employment, Compensation & Benefits, Training & Development, and Employee Relations. Must be up-to-date with modern concepts in such areas as Human Resources Planning, Organization Effectiveness, and Executive Assessment. Experience must include demonstrated management leadership in the direction and guidance of decentralized, autonomous division Personnel functions in a multidivision and highly diversified company. Must have played key role in the development and execution of corporate-wide labor relations strategy in a multiunion setting. Must have managed a staff of at least 20 mid-management and professional level Human Resource professionals.

HOW RESUMES ARE READ

The candidate specification, as shown in the examples, is the basic tool of the employment manager when it comes to reading an employment resume. Actually the term "reading" is misleading when describing the process by which most employment managers review employment resumes. More precisely, the experienced employment manager rapidly scans for basic qualification highlights. The question that is constantly being asked by the employment manager is "Does this individual meet all of the critical qualifications of the candidate spec?"

The typical employment manager does not bother to read a resume in any degree of detail unless the preliminary scan indicates that the applicant has some of the essential skills and experience sought. In such cases, as key phrases and headings begin to match the candidate spec, the manager slows down and begins to read with a more critical eye. If several key criteria appear to be met, the employment professional will usually return to the beginning of the resume and begin a more thorough, detailed reading. To the contrary, if quick scanning of the resume indicates that few, if any, of the candidate's qualifications appear to match the current requirements, no time is lost in moving on to the next resume.

QUICK "KNOCKOUT" FACTORS

In scanning the employment resume, the employment manager is looking for key "knockout" factors—factors that clearly spell no interest and signal the employment manager to stop reading and move on to the next resume. Some of these quick knockout factors are:

1. Job objective incompatible with current openings
2. Inappropriate or insufficient educational credentials
3. Incompatible salary requirements
4. Geographic restrictions incompatible with current openings
5. Lack of U.S. citizenship or permanent resident status
6. Resume poorly organized, sloppy, or hard to read
7. Too many employers in too short a period of time
8. Too many pages—a book instead of a resume

Any of these factors quickly signals the employment manager that it would be a waste of time to read any further. These are generally sure knockout factors and warrant use of the no interest stamp. These same factors should be consciously avoided when preparing your employment resume.

CRITICAL READING

Having successfully passed the quick knockout factors test and avoided the no interest stamp, your resume must now undergo a more thorough and critical scanning. Concentration is now centered on the Work Experience section of the resume as the following questions are considered:

1. Are there sufficient years and level of experience?
2. Is experience in the appropriate areas?
3. Is the candidate missing any critical experience?
4. Does the candidate have sufficient breadth and depth of technical knowledge?
5. Does the applicant have sufficient management or leadership skills?
6. Are any technical or managerial skills missing?
7. Is there a solid record of accomplishment?
8. How does this candidate compare with others currently under consideration?
9. Based on overall qualifications, what are the probabilities that an offer would be made—50%, 75%, 90% (as measured against past candidates with similar credentials)?

There is little advice that can be given to the resume writer in this area. You are what you are, and the facts cannot be changed. You either have the qualifications and experience sought, or you don't. At best, you can hope that through diligent application of professional resume preparation techniques, you have done an excellent job of clearly presenting your overall skills, knowledge, accomplishments, and other pertinent professional qualifications.

There is nothing mysterious or mystical about the resume-reading process. It is essentially logical and straightforward. It is a process whereby the employment manager or hiring manager simply compares the candidate's qualifications and interests with the candidate's hiring spec in an effort to determine the candidate's degree of qualifications and the desirability of moving to the interview (or phone screen) step. Neatness, clarity, organization, style, and format are the key ingredients; they are critical to the impact and effectiveness of the employment resume.

Chapter 2

Introduction to Cover Letters

The cover letter that accompanies your employment resume is perhaps one of the most important letters you will ever write. Other than your resume, it is the single key document that will introduce you to a prospective employer and, if well-written, pave the way to that all-important job interview. It is an integral part of your overall job hunting campaign, and it can make or break you, depending upon how well it is written. Construction of this document should therefore be given very careful attention. The care that you give to writing this letter will certainly be a major factor in getting your job search off to an excellent start. Conversely, a poorly written letter will surely scuttle your campaign before it even begins.

THE PURPOSE OF THE COVER LETTER

Before you can expect to write an effective cover letter, you must understand its purpose. Without a clear understanding of what this letter is intended to accomplish, chances are it will be poorly designed, vague, and totally ineffective. On the other hand, understanding the purpose of this letter is truly paramount to maximizing its impact and effectiveness.

What is the purpose of the cover letter? What is it intended to do?

Well, first and foremost, it is a business letter used to transmit your resume to a prospective employer. So, it is a business transmittal letter. Second, it is a letter of introduction. It is used not only to transmit your resume but also to introduce you and your background to the employer. Third, and importantly, it is a sales letter, intended to convince the prospective employer that you have something valuable to contribute and that it will be worth the employer's time to grant you an interview.

To summarize, then, the purpose of a cover letter is:

1. To serve as a business transmittal letter for your resume.
2. To introduce you and your employment credentials to the employer.
3. To generate employer interest in interviewing you.

Certainly, knowing that these are the three main objectives of a well-written cover letter will provide you with some basic starting points. For now, it is important to simply keep these objectives in mind as we further explore the topic of effective cover letters.

FROM THE EMPLOYER'S PERSPECTIVE

When contemplating good cover letter design and construction, it is important to keep one very important fact in mind: The cover letter must be written from the employer's perspective.

Stated differently, good cover letter writing must take into consideration that the end result you seek is employer action. More specifically, you want the employer to grant you an interview, so it is important to understand those factors that will motivate an employer to do so.

To understand this important phenomenon, it is necessary to realistically address the following questions:

1. How does the employer read the cover letter?
2. What are the key factors the employer is looking for (and expects to find) in the cover letter?
3. What are the motivational factors that will pique the employer's curiosity and create a desire to interview you?

I think you will agree that these are some very important questions to ask if you are to be successful in designing cover letters that will be truly helpful to your job hunting program. You must pay close attention to the needs of the prospective employer, rather than just your own, if you expect to write cover letters that will motivate him or her to take action. Cover letters must, therefore, be "employer focused" rather than "job searcher focused" if you want to really maximize their overall effectiveness.

Top sales producers have always known that the most important principle in sales success, whether selling goods or services, is selling to the needs of the buyer. What is the customer really buying? Where are the priorities? What specific needs does he or she need to satisfy? Without knowing the answers to these questions, it is easy for the salesperson to emphasize product characteristics and attributes that have absolutely no relationship to the customer's real needs, and deemphasize characteristics and attributes that are truly important. The result—no sale!

In the ideal sense, therefore, it is important to research your target companies very well to determine what it is that they are buying (i.e., looking for in a successful employment candidate). If you are conducting a general broadcast campaign covering several hundred companies, such individual company research may simply not be feasible. If, on the other hand, you are targeting a dozen or so employers for whom you would really like to work, such research is not only feasible but should be considered an "absolute must." Careful advance research, in this case, will pay huge dividends, returning your initial investment of time and effort manyfold.

Even in the case of the general broadcast campaign, where you have targeted several hundred companies, there are clearly some things that you can do to focus your cover letters on the real needs of these employers. Here are some guidelines for conducting meaningful employer needs research:

1. Divide your target list of employers into industry groupings.
2. Using industry trade publications and key newspapers (available in most libraries), thoroughly research each industry grouping for answers to the following questions:
   a. What is the general state of this industry?
   b. What are the major problems faced by companies in this industry?
   c. What are the barriers or roadblocks that stand in the way of solving these problems
   d. What knowledge, skills, and capabilities are needed to address these problems and roadblocks?
   e. What major trends and changes are being driven by companies in this industry?
   f. What new knowledge, skills, and capabilities are needed to successfully drive these changes and trends?

Having conducted this research, you are now in a position to better focus your cover letter on key needs areas of interest to the majority of companies in each of your targeted industry groupings. This provides you with the opportunity to showcase your overall knowledge, skills, and capabilities in relation to those important needs areas. Such focusing substantially increases your chances for hitting the employer's bull's-eye, which will result in job interviews.

Where you can narrow your list to a dozen or so key companies, individual company research can have even greater payoff. Here, you have the opportunity to really zero in on the specific needs of the employer, and you can bring into play a number of research techniques for doing so. The research you do here can, in fact, be tailored to each individual firm; so you can substantially increase your probability of success and up by quite a bit the number of potential interview opportunities.

In many ways, the methodology used in conducting single-firm research is similar to that already described for industry-wide research. You will note some of these similarities as you review the following guidelines for researching the single firm.

1. Determine the firms you would like to target for individual research (firms for which you would really like to work).
2. Using industry trade publications and key newspapers (available at your local library) as well as annual reports, 10K forms, and product literature (available from the target firm's public affairs and marketing departments), thoroughly research for answers to the following questions:
   a. What is the general state of the company?
   b. How does it stack up against competition?
   c. What are the key problems and issues with which it is currently wrestling?
   d. What are the key barriers that must be removed in order to resolve these problems/issues?
   e. What knowledge, skills, and capabilities are needed to remove these key barriers?
   f. What are the company's strategic goals?
   g. What are the key changes that will need to come about for realization of these goals?
   h. What new knowledge, skills, and capabilities will be needed to bring about these critical changes?

Here, as with research of industry groupings, individual company research enables you to use the cover letter to highlight your knowledge, skills, and capabilities in areas that are of importance to the firm. In the case of individual firm research, however, there is the added advantage of being able to tailor the cover letter to target your qualifications to very specific, known needs of the employer. This can provide you with a substantial competitive advantage!

Another technique that you should employ when doing individual firm research is networking. If you don't already belong, you might consider joining specific industry or professional associations to which employees of your individual target firms belong. Using your common membership in these organizations as the basis, you can call these employees for certain inside information. Here are some questions you might consider asking:

1. Is the firm hiring people in your functional specialty?
2. Are there openings in this group now?
3. Who within the company is the key line manager (i.e., outside human resources) responsible for hiring for this group?
4. What are the key things this manager tends to look for in a successful candidate (e.g., technical knowledge, skills, style)?
5. What key problems/issues is the group currently wrestling with?
6. What kinds of skills and capabilities are they looking for to address these issues?
7. What are the major strategic changes this group is attempting to bring about?
8. What qualifications and attributes is the group seeking to help them orchestrate these strategic changes?

Answers to these questions can give you a tremendous competitive advantage when designing an effective cover letter and employment resume. You will have substantial ammunition for targeting and highlighting those qualifications of greatest interest to the employer. Here, you can make the most of your opportunity for successful self-marketing by focusing on the critical needs not only of the organization but of the functional hiring group as well. Clearly, this is a technique you should employ if you want to maximize your chances of getting hired!

The underlying principle behind this needs research methodology, whether industry grouping or individual company research, is that organizations are always looking for individuals who will be "value adding"—that is, individuals who can help them solve key problems and realize their strategic goals. These are the candidates who are seen as the value-adding change agents—the leaders who will help move the company ahead rather than cause it to stand still. Employer needs research will allow you to design effective cover letters that can truly set you apart from the competition and substantially improve your chances for landing interviews.

Chapter 3

Introduction to Interviewing

INTERVIEW THEORY

By definition, the employment interview is a two-way discussion between a job applicant and a prospective employer with the objective of exploring the probable compatibility between the applicant's qualifications and the needs of the employer, for the purpose of making an employment decision. It is the intent of both parties during this discussion to gain as much relevant information as possible on which to base this decision. Further, it is their intent to use the information obtained during the interview process to predict, with some level of accuracy, the probability for a successful match.

Modern interview theory subscribes to a single, universal theory around which almost all employment selection processes are designed. This theory is as follows:

Past performance and behavior are the most reliable factors known in predicting future performance and behavior.

With this theory in mind, it is important for the interviewee to know that the employer's basic interview strategy will be to use the interview discussion to uncover past performance and behavioral evidence in those areas that the employer considers important to successful job performance. These important areas are commonly known as selection criteria. It is against these criteria that the employer will be comparing the qualifications of prospective candidates, and eventually arriving at a final employment decision.

It should be evident that, as the candidate, it will be necessary for you to get some definition of these selection criteria if you expect to be successful in developing an effective counterstrategy. The key to accomplishing this is to force yourself to think as the employer does. Specifically, the question to ask is, "How does the employer go about developing candidate selection criteria?"

DEVELOPING THE CANDIDATE SPECIFICATION

The first step used by the employer in structuring an interview strategy is usually development of what is commonly known in professional employment circles as the candidate specification. This document typically describes the candidate sought by the employer in terms of such qualifications as knowledge, skills, experience, and other dimensions thought to be necessary to successful job performance. The candidate specification is normally prepared by the hiring manager, with occasional assistance provided by other department managers and/or the human resources department.

When well-prepared and carefully thought out, this specification can be a very valuable document. It frequently serves as the focal point for the employer's entire interview strategy. Advance knowledge of the contents of the document could prove equally as valuable to the interviewee, since it could be used as the basis for formulating an effective counterstrategy. Since this is not a practical consideration, the candidate must go through the same process as the employer in attempting to construct this specification.

When preparing the candidate specification, most hiring managers will review such things as the position description, current year's objectives, business plans, and so on. In essence, the manager is reviewing the general responsibilities of the position in an effort to determine the kind of person needed to meet these requirements. Such review typically results in a candidate specification that includes the following general categories: (1) education, (2) knowledge, (3) experience, (4) skills, and (5) personal attributes.

A typical candidate specification would probably read as follows:

Education.   BS degree in mechanical engineering preferred; degree in chemical engineering acceptable.

Knowledge.   Paper machine project engineering; wet end sheet formation.

Experience.   Two plus years in design, installation, and start-up of tissue and/or towel machines; twin wire-forming machine experience helpful.

Skills.   Solid engineering skills in mechanical design; project leadership of contractor personnel.

Personal Attributes.   Intelligent, articulate; able to work effectively in fast-paced construction/start-up environment; willing to work long hours, including frequent evenings and weekends; willing to travel at least 40 percent of the time, including weekend travel.

Although admittedly a fairly abbreviated description, this candidate specification is very similar to those used by most organizations.

The employer's strategy now becomes one of interviewing to determine how well the prospective candidate meets this specification. In my example, some of the candidate's qualifications for the position will be evident from a quick review of the applicant's resume. However, such areas as "level of engineering knowledge" and "level of intelligence" cannot be measured by using the applicant's resume. These can only be ascertained through the interview process.

INTERVIEWEE STRATEGY

Considering the employer's interview strategy, as defined earlier in this chapter, how can the interviewee formulate a meaningful counterstrategy? What steps can the interviewee take to maximize the potential for a favorable interview outcome?

In my judgment, there are a number of things you can do to duplicate fairly accurately the employer's thinking process, thereby allowing yourself to plan an effective counterstrategy that will allow you to "stack the deck" in your favor. Here are some of them:

Advance Information

You will want to obtain as much information as possible about the position, prior to the actual interview. Although much of this information is readily available just for the asking, it has always amazed me how few employment candidates ever bother to request it.

Don't be shy about requesting this information since many employers are willing to provide it to you if it is available. The strategic advantage of acquiring this information in advance of the interview far outweighs the risks of an employer politely declining your request.

Where available without too much difficulty, you should request the following in advance of your visit:

1. Position job description
2. Job objectives—current year
3. Department objectives—current year
4. Departmental or functional business plan
5. Annual report

Candidate Specification

During your initial telephone conversation with the employer, you should make it a point to ask for a verbal description of the kind of person they are seeking. Ask the employer to tell you not only what qualifications they are seeking, but also which of these qualifications they consider to be the most important. If time allows, and you can avoid sounding pushy, ask why these factors are considered to be important.

If the employer begins to balk, suggest that you need this information to determine whether or not you are interested in the position and whether you feel you have sufficient qualifications to warrant investing your time in further discussions. This should seem a reasonable request at this stage of the relationship and you will usually get what you want.

It is best to request answers to these questions at the beginning of your discussions, since you will lose considerable leverage once the employer has ascertained that you are interested in the position and are prepared to go to the next step.

Position Analysis

As with the employer, one of your first steps in formulating your interview strategy is to conduct an analysis of the position for which you will be interviewing. This procedure is similar to the employers' when they form the candidate specification. You will need to review the key responsibilities of the position in an effort to translate these into probable candidate selection criteria. The advance documents that you have collected from the employer should prove very helpful at this point.

The following set of questions should help you to walk through this process in a logical and thorough fashion. Space is provided for you to fill in your answers as you go along.

1. What are the *key ongoing responsibilities* of this position? (Job description should prove helpful here.) _____

   _____

   _____

   _____

2. What are the *key technical problems* to be solved, and *challenges* to be met, in satisfying these ongoing responsibilities? _____

   _____

   _____

   _____

3. What *technical* and/or *professional knowledge* does this suggest that a person must have in order to successfully solve these problems and meet these challenges? _____

   _____

   _____

   _____

4. What are the *specific objectives* for this position for the *current year?* _____

   _____

   _____

   _____

5. What are the *key technical challenges* that must be met and *problems* that must be solved if these objectives are to be successfully achieved? _____

   _____

   _____

   _____

6. What *technical* and/or *professional knowledge* does this suggest that a person must have in order to successfully solve these problems and accomplish these objectives? _____

   _____

Combined Candidate Specification

You now have two sources from which to construct a candidate specification. The first is the initial telephone conversation with the prospective employer, and the second is the position analysis that you have just completed.

Chances are, if you have done a particularly thorough job with your position analysis, you may well have given more thought to the qualifications necessary to successful job performance than has the employer with whom you will be interviewing. This could serve to place you at a decided strategic advantage during the interview, allowing you to highlight important aspects of your background that are critical to achievement of desired organizational results.

Be careful not to get carried away with your newfound power, however, since this could serve to alienate the interviewer and cause you to be labeled as a show-off or "know-it-all."

Now, pause for a moment to review the overall candidate requirements as defined by both you and the employer. With these requirements in mind, use the following set of questions to help you to translate these overall requirements into a combined candidate specification.

1. *Formal Education:*   Considering the technical challenges of this position and the knowledge required, what formal education/training should the ideal candidate have (degree level and major)? Why? _____

_____

_____

2. *Training:*   What informal education (training courses, seminars, etc.) would likely provide the required knowledge? _____

_____

_____

3. *Experience:*   What level (number of years) and kind of experience would likely yield the depth and breadth of knowledge necessary for successful performance in this position? _____

_____

_____

4. *Related Experience:*   What related or similar kinds of experience might yield the same kind of knowledge, and would therefore be an acceptable alternative?

_____

_____

_____

5. *Skills:*   What specific skills ar required by the position, and how might these be acquired? _____

_____

_____

6. *Personal Attributes:*   What personal attributes and characteristics are probably important for successful performance of this position? _____

_____

_____

Job Seekers Guide to Silicon Valley Recruiters

Abbatiello, Christine Murphy — *Information Technology Recruiter*
Winter, Wyman & Company
1100 Circle 75 Parkway, Suite 800
Atlanta, GA 30339
Telephone: (770) 933-1525
Recruiter Classification: Contingency; **Lowest/Average Salary:** $30,000/$60,000; **Industry Concentration:** Generalist with a primary focus in High Technology, Information Technology; **Function Concentration:** Generalist

Abbott, Peter D. — *Partner*
The Abbott Group, Inc.
530 College Parkway, Suite N
Annapolis, MD 21401
Telephone: (410) 757-4100
Recruiter Classification: Retained; **Lowest/Average Salary:** $90,000/$90,000; **Industry Concentration:** Generalist with a primary focus in Electronics, High Technology, Information Technology; **Function Concentration:** Generalist with a primary focus in Administration, Engineering, Finance/Accounting, General Management, Human Resources, Marketing, Research and Development

Abell, Vincent W. — *Executive Recruiter*
MSI International
8521 Leesburg Pike, Suite 435
Vienna, VA 22182
Telephone: (703) 893-5669
Recruiter Classification: Contingency; **Lowest/Average Salary:** $30,000/$75,000; **Industry Concentration:** Generalist with a primary focus in High Technology, Information Technology; **Function Concentration:** Generalist with a primary focus in Administration, Engineering, Finance/Accounting, General Management, Marketing, Sales

Abernathy, Donald E. — *Accounting Recruiter*
Don Richard Associates of Charlotte
2650 One First Union Center
301 South College Street
Charlotte, NC 28202-6000
Telephone: (704) 377-6447
Recruiter Classification: Contingency, Executive Temporary; **Lowest/Average Salary:** $30,000/$50,000; **Industry Concentration:** Generalist with a primary focus in High Technology; **Function Concentration:** Finance/Accounting

Abramson, Roye — *Associate*
Source Services Corporation
379 Thornall Street
Edison, NJ 08837
Telephone: (908) 494-2800
Recruiter Classification: Contingency; **Lowest/Average Salary:** $30,000/$50,000; **Industry Concentration:** Information Technology; **Function Concentration:** Engineering, Finance/Accounting

Acquaviva, Jay — *Software Engineering Recruiter*
Winter, Wyman & Company
950 Winter Street, Suite 3100
Waltham, MA 02154-1294
Telephone: (617) 890-7000
Recruiter Classification: Contingency; **Lowest/Average Salary:** $40,000/$75,000; **Industry Concentration:** High Technology, Information Technology; **Function Concentration:** Engineering

Adams, Jeffrey C. — *Managing Principal*
Telford, Adams & Alexander/Jeffrey C. Adams & Co., Inc.
455 Market Street, Suite 1910
San Francisco, CA 94105
Telephone: (415) 546-4150
Recruiter Classification: Retained; **Lowest/Average Salary:** $50,000/$90,000; **Industry Concentration:** Generalist with a primary focus in High Technology, Information Technology; **Function Concentration:** Generalist

Adams, Len — *Executive Vice President*
The KPA Group
150 Broadway, Suite 1802
New York, NY 10038
Telephone: (212) 964-3640
Recruiter Classification: Contingency, Executive Temporary; **Lowest/Average Salary:** $20,000/$40,000; **Industry Concentration:** Information Technology; **Function Concentration:** Finance/Accounting, Human Resources

Adler, Louis S. — *President*
CJA - The Adler Group
17852 17th Street
Suite 209
Tustin, CA 92780
Telephone: (714) 573-1820
Recruiter Classification: Retained; **Lowest/Average Salary:** $50,000/$90,000; **Industry Concentration:** Generalist with a primary focus in Electronics, High Technology, Information Technology; **Function Concentration:** Generalist with a primary focus in Engineering, Finance/Accounting, General Management, Human Resources, Marketing, Research and Development, Sales

Ahearn, Jennifer — *Consultant*
Logix, Inc.
1601 Trapelo Road
Waltham, MA 02154
Telephone: (617) 890-0500
Recruiter Classification: Retained; **Lowest/Average Salary:** $60,000/$75,000; **Industry Concentration:** High Technology; **Function Concentration:** Engineering

Aheran, Jennifer — *Consultant*
Logix Partners
1601 Trapelo Road
Waltham, MA 02154
Telephone: (617) 890-0500
Recruiter Classification: Retained; **Lowest/Average Salary:** $60,000/$75,000; **Industry Concentration:** High Technology; **Function Concentration:** Engineering

Aiken, David — *Partner*
Commonwealth Consultants
4840 Roswell Road
Atlanta, GA 30342
Telephone: (404) 256-0000
Recruiter Classification: Contingency; **Lowest/Average Salary:** $30,000/$90,000; **Industry Concentration:** High Technology; **Function Concentration:** Sales

Ainsworth, Lawrence — *Account Executive*
Search West, Inc.
1888 Century Park East
Suite 2050
Los Angeles, CA 90067-1736
Telephone: (310) 284-8888
Recruiter Classification: Contingency; **Lowest/Average Salary:**
$40,000/$60,000; **Industry Concentration:** Electronics;
Function Concentration: Marketing, Sales

Akin, J.R. "Jack" — *President*
J.R. Akin & Company Inc.
7181 College Parkway, Suite 30
Fort Myers, FL 33907
Telephone: (941) 395-1575
Recruiter Classification: Retained; **Lowest/Average Salary:**
$90,000/$90,000; **Industry Concentration:** Generalist with a
primary focus in Electronics, High Technology, Information
Technology; **Function Concentration:** Generalist with a
primary focus in Administration, Engineering,
Finance/Accounting, General Management, Human Resources,
Marketing, Sales, Women/Minorities

Albert, Richard — *Associate*
Source Services Corporation
One CityPlace, Suite 170
St. Louis, MO 63141
Telephone: (314) 432-4500
Recruiter Classification: Contingency; **Lowest/Average Salary:**
$30,000/$50,000; **Industry Concentration:** Information
Technology; **Function Concentration:** Engineering,
Finance/Accounting

Albertini, Nancy — *President and CEO*
Taylor-Winfield, Inc.
12801 N. Central Expressway
Suite 1260
Dallas, TX 75243
Telephone: (214) 392-1400
Recruiter Classification: Retained; **Lowest/Average Salary:**
$90,000/$90,000; **Industry Concentration:** High Technology,
Information Technology; **Function Concentration:** Generalist
with a primary focus in Finance/Accounting, General
Management, Research and Development, Sales

Albright, Cindy — *Executive Recruiter*
Summerfield Associates, Inc.
6555 Quince Road, Suite 311
Memphis, TN 38119
Telephone: (901) 753-7068
Recruiter Classification: Contingency; **Lowest/Average Salary:**
$20,000/$30,000; **Industry Concentration:** Generalist with a
primary focus in Information; **Function Concentration:**
Generalist

Alexander, Karen — *Partner*
Huntington Group
6527 Main Street
Trumbull, CT 06611
Telephone: (203) 261-1166
Recruiter Classification: Retained; **Lowest/Average Salary:**
$90,000/$90,000; **Industry Concentration:** Information
Technology; **Function Concentration:** Generalist

Alford, Holly — *Associate*
Source Services Corporation
5429 LBJ Freeway, Suite 275
Dallas, TX 75240
Telephone: (214) 387-1600
Recruiter Classification: Contingency; **Lowest/Average Salary:**
$30,000/$50,000; **Industry Concentration:** Information
Technology; **Function Concentration:** Engineering,
Finance/Accounting

Allen, Don — *President*
D.S. Allen Associates, Inc.
1119 Raritan Rd., Ste. 2
Clark, NJ 07066
Telephone: (732) 574-1600
Recruiter Classification: Contingency; **Lowest/Average Salary:**
$60,000/$90,000; **Industry Concentration:** High Technology,
Information Technology; **Function Concentration:**
Finance/Accounting, General Management, Human Resources,
Marketing, Sales

Allen, Jean E. — *Principal*
Lamalie Amrop International
200 Park Avenue
New York, NY 10166-0136
Telephone: (212) 953-7900
Recruiter Classification: Retained; **Lowest/Average Salary:**
$90,000/$90,000; **Industry Concentration:** Generalist with a
primary focus in High Technology; **Function Concentration:**
Generalist

Allen, Scott — *Executive Recruiter*
Chrisman & Company, Incorporated
350 South Figueroa Street, Suite 550
Los Angeles, CA 90071
Telephone: (213) 620-1192
Recruiter Classification: Retained; **Lowest/Average Salary:**
$75,000/$90,000; **Industry Concentration:** Information
Technology; **Function Concentration:** Generalist with a
primary focus in Finance/Accounting, General Management,
Women/Minorities

Allen, Wade H. — *President*
Cendea Connection International
13740 Research Boulevard
Building 0-1
Austin, TX 78750
Telephone: (512) 219-6000
Recruiter Classification: Retained; **Lowest/Average Salary:**
$75,000/$90,000; **Industry Concentration:** Generalist with a
primary focus in Electronics, High Technology, Information
Technology; **Function Concentration:** Generalist with a
primary focus in General Management, Marketing, Sales

Allen, William L. — *Vice President*
The Hindman Company
Browenton Place, Suite 110
2000 Warrington Way
Louisville, KY 40222
Telephone: (502) 426-4040
Recruiter Classification: Retained; **Lowest/Average Salary:**
$50,000/$90,000; **Industry Concentration:** Generalist with a
primary focus in Electronics, High Technology; **Function
Concentration:** Generalist with a primary focus in Engineering,
Finance/Accounting, General Management, Human Resources,
Marketing, Sales

Allerton, Donald T. — *Partner*
Allerton Heneghan & O'Neill
70 West Madison Street, Suite 2015
Chicago, IL 60602
Telephone: (312) 263-1075
Recruiter Classification: Retained; **Lowest/Average Salary:**
$90,000/$90,000; **Industry Concentration:** Generalist with a
primary focus in Electronics, High Technology; **Function
Concentration:** Generalist with a primary focus in Engineering,
General Management, Human Resources, Marketing, Research
and Development, Women/Minorities

Allred, J. Michael — *Director*
Spencer Stuart
One Atlantic Center, Suite 3230
1201 West Peachtree Street
Atlanta, GA 30309
Telephone: (404) 892-2800
Recruiter Classification: Retained; **Lowest/Average Salary:**
$90,000/$90,000; **Industry Concentration:** Electronics, High
Technology, Information Technology; **Function Concentration:**
Generalist with a primary focus in General Management,
Marketing, Sales

Alpeyrie, Jean-Louis — *Partner*
Heidrick & Struggles, Inc.
245 Park Avenue, Suite 4300
New York, NY 10167-0152
Telephone: (212) 867-9876
Recruiter Classification: Retained; **Lowest/Average Salary:**
$75,000/$90,000; **Industry Concentration:** Generalist with a
primary focus in High Technology; **Function Concentration:**
Generalist

Alringer, Marc — *Associate*
Source Services Corporation
4510 Executive Drive, Suite 200
San Diego, CA 92121
Telephone: (619) 552-0300
Recruiter Classification: Contingency; **Lowest/Average Salary:**
$30,000/$50,000; **Industry Concentration:** Information
Technology; **Function Concentration:** Engineering,
Finance/Accounting

Altreuter, Rose — *Manager Interim Professionals*
The ALTCO Group
100 Menlo Park, Ste. 214
Edison, NJ 08837
Telephone: (732) 549-6100
Recruiter Classification: Contingency; **Lowest/Average Salary:**
$40,000/$50,000; **Industry Concentration:** Generalist with a
primary focus in Electronics, High Technology; **Function
Concentration:** Generalist with a primary focus in
Administration, Engineering, Finance/Accounting, Human
Resources, Marketing, Research and Development

Altreuter, Rose — *President Interim Professionals*
ALTCO Temporary Services
100 Menlo Park
Edison, NJ 08837
Telephone: (908) 549-6100
Recruiter Classification: Executive Temporary; **Lowest/Average
Salary:** $20,000/$30,000; **Industry Concentration:** Electronics;
Function Concentration: Finance/Accounting, Human
Resources, Marketing, Women/Minorities

Ambler, Peter W. — *President*
Peter W. Ambler Company
14651 Dallas Parkway, Suite 402
Dallas, TX 75240
Telephone: (972) 404-8712
Recruiter Classification: Retained; **Lowest/Average Salary:**
$60,000/$90,000; **Industry Concentration:** Generalist with a
primary focus in Electronics, High Technology, Information
Technology; **Function Concentration:** Generalist with a
primary focus in Engineering, Finance/Accounting, General
Management, Human Resources, Marketing, Research and
Development, Sales

Ames, George C. — *President*
Ames O'Neill Associates
330 Motor Parkway
Hauppauge, NY 11788
Telephone: (516) 582-4800
Recruiter Classification: Contingency; **Lowest/Average Salary:**
$40,000/$60,000; **Industry Concentration:** Generalist with a
primary focus in Electronics, High Technology, Information
Technology; **Function Concentration:** Generalist with a
primary focus in Engineering, Human Resources, Marketing,
Research and Development, Sales

Amico, Robert — *Associate*
Source Services Corporation
71 Spit Brook Road, Suite 305
Nashua, NH 03060
Telephone: (603) 888-7650
Recruiter Classification: Contingency; **Lowest/Average Salary:**
$30,000/$50,000; **Industry Concentration:** Information
Technology; **Function Concentration:** Engineering,
Finance/Accounting

Anderson, David C. — *Managing Partner*
Heidrick & Struggles, Inc.
2200 Ross Avenue, Suite 4700E
Dallas, TX 75201-2787
Telephone: (214) 220-2130
Recruiter Classification: Retained; **Lowest/Average Salary:**
$75,000/$90,000; **Industry Concentration:** Generalist with a
primary focus in High Technology; **Function Concentration:**
Generalist

Anderson, Dean C. — *Partner*
Corporate Resources Professional Placement
4205 Lancaster Lane, Suite 107
Plymouth, MN 55441
Telephone: (612) 550-9222
Recruiter Classification: Contingency; **Lowest/Average Salary:**
$40,000/$60,000; **Industry Concentration:** Electronics, High
Technology; **Function Concentration:** Engineering, Research
and Development

Anderson, Maria H. — *Senior Consultant*
Barton Associates, Inc.
One Riverway, Suite 2500
Houston, TX 77056
Telephone: (713) 961-9111
Recruiter Classification: Retained; **Lowest/Average Salary:**
$75,000/$90,000; **Industry Concentration:** Generalist with a
primary focus in Electronics, High Technology, Information
Technology; **Function Concentration:** Generalist with a
primary focus in Administration, Finance/Accounting, General
Management, Human Resources, Marketing, Research and
Development, Women/Minorities

Anderson, Mary — *Managing Director*
Source Services Corporation
425 California Street, Suite 1200
San Francisco, CA 94104
Telephone: (415) 434-2410
Recruiter Classification: Contingency; **Lowest/Average Salary:**
$30,000/$50,000; **Industry Concentration:** Information
Technology; **Function Concentration:** Engineering,
Finance/Accounting

Anderson, Matthew — *Associate*
Source Services Corporation
161 Ottawa NW, Suite 409D
Grand Rapids, MI 49503
Telephone: (616) 451-2400
Recruiter Classification: Contingency; **Lowest/Average Salary:**
$30,000/$50,000; **Industry Concentration:** Information
Technology; **Function Concentration:** Engineering,
Finance/Accounting

Anderson, Richard — *Vice President*
Grant Cooper and Associates
795 Office Parkway, Suite 117
St. Louis, MO 63141
Telephone: (314) 567-4690
Recruiter Classification: Retained; **Lowest/Average Salary:**
$60,000/$90,000; **Industry Concentration:** Generalist with a
primary focus in Electronics; **Function Concentration:**
Generalist with a primary focus in Administration, Engineering,
Finance/Accounting, General Management, Human Resources,
Marketing, Sales

Anderson, Steve — *Executive Recruiter*
CPS Inc.
One Westbrook Corporate Centre, Suite 600
Westchester, IL 60154
Telephone: (708) 531-8370
Recruiter Classification: Contingency; **Lowest/Average Salary:**
$30,000/$50,000; **Industry Concentration:** Generalist with a
primary focus in Electronics, High Technology, Information
Technology; **Function Concentration:** Engineering, Research
and Development, Sales, Women/Minorities

Anderson, Terry — *Executive Director*
Intech Summit Group, Inc.
5075 Shoreham Place, Suite 280
San Diego, CA 92116
Telephone: (619) 452-2100
Recruiter Classification: Retained; **Lowest/Average Salary:**
$60,000/$75,000; **Industry Concentration:** Generalist with a
primary focus in High Technology, Information Technology;
Function Concentration: Generalist with a primary focus in
Finance/Accounting, Marketing

Andrews, J. Douglas — *Partner*
Clarey & Andrews, Inc.
1200 Shermer Road, Suite 108
Northbrook, IL 60062
Telephone: (847) 498-2870
Recruiter Classification: Retained; **Lowest/Average Salary:**
$90,000/$90,000; **Industry Concentration:** Generalist with a
primary focus in Electronics, High Technology; **Function
Concentration:** Generalist with a primary focus in
Administration, Finance/Accounting, General Management,
Human Resources

Antoine, Brian — *Senior Consultant*
Paul-Tittle Associates, Inc.
1485 Chain Bridge Road, #304
McLean, VA 22101
Telephone: (703) 442-0500
Recruiter Classification: Retained; **Lowest/Average Salary:**
$60,000/$75,000; **Industry Concentration:** High Technology;
Function Concentration: Administration, Engineering,
Human Resources, Marketing, Sales

Apostle, George — *President*
Search Dynamics, Inc.
9420 West Foster Avenue, Suite 200
Chicago, IL 60656-1006
Telephone: (312) 992-3900
Recruiter Classification: Contingency; **Lowest/Average Salary:**
$40,000/$90,000; **Industry Concentration:** Electronics, High
Technology, Information Technology; **Function Concentration:**
Administration, Engineering, General Management, Research
and Development

Archer, Sandra F. — *Director*
Ryan, Miller & Associates Inc.
4601 Wilshire Boulevard, Suite 225
Los Angeles, CA 90010
Telephone: (213) 938-4768
Recruiter Classification: Contingency; **Lowest/Average Salary:**
$50,000/$60,000; **Industry Concentration:** Generalist with a
primary focus in High Technology; **Function Concentration:**
Generalist with a primary focus in Finance/Accounting

Argentin, Jo — *Consultant*
Executive Placement Consultants, Inc.
2700 River Road, Suite 107
Des Plaines, IL 60018
Telephone: (847) 298-6445
Recruiter Classification: Contingency; **Lowest/Average Salary:**
$40,000/$75,000; **Industry Concentration:** Generalist with a
primary focus in Electronics, High Technology, Information
Technology; **Function Concentration:** Finance/Accounting,
Human Resources, Marketing

Arms, Douglas — *Legal Consultant*
TOPAZ International, Inc.
383 Northfield Avenue
West Orange, NJ 07052
Telephone: (201) 669-7300
Recruiter Classification: Contingency; **Lowest/Average Salary:**
$40,000/$75,000; **Industry Concentration:** Electronics, High
Technology; **Function Concentration:** Generalist with a
primary focus in Women/Minorities

Arms, Douglas — *Legal Consultant*
TOPAZ Legal Solutions
383 Northfield Avenue
West Orange, NJ 07052
Telephone: (201) 669-7300
Recruiter Classification: Executive Temporary; **Lowest/Average
Salary:** $40,000/$75,000; **Industry Concentration:** Electronics,
High Technology; **Function Concentration:** Generalist with a
primary focus in Women/Minorities

Arnold, David W. — *Senior Vice President*
Christian & Timbers
25825 Science Park Drive, Suite 400
Cleveland, OH 44122
Telephone: (216) 765-5867
Recruiter Classification: Retained; **Lowest/Average Salary:**
$140,000/$160,000; **Industry Concentration:** Generalist with
a primary focus in High Technology, Information Technology;
Function Concentration: Generalist with a primary focus in
Engineering, Finance/Accounting, General Management,
Marketing, Research and Development, Sales,
Women/Minorities

Arnson, Craig — *Regional Manager*
Hernand & Partners
333 West Wacker Drive, Suite 700
Chicago, IL 60606
Telephone: (312) 346-5420
Recruiter Classification: Executive Temporary; **Lowest/Average
Salary:** $60,000/$90,000; **Industry Concentration:** High
Technology, Information Technology; **Function Concentration:**
Engineering

Aronin, Michael — *Senior Consultant*
Fisher-Todd Associates
535 Fifth Avenue, Suite 710
New York, NY 10017
Telephone: (212) 986-9052
Recruiter Classification: Contingency; **Lowest/Average Salary:**
$50,000/$75,000; **Industry Concentration:** Generalist with a
primary focus in Information Technology; **Function
Concentration:** Generalist with a primary focus in
Administration, General Management, Marketing, Research
and Development, Sales, Women/Minorities

Arseneault, Daniel S. — *Executive Recruiter*
MSI International
200 Galleria Parkway
Suite 1610
Atlanta, GA 30339
Telephone: (404) 951-1208
Recruiter Classification: Contingency; **Lowest/Average Salary:**
$30,000/$75,000; **Industry Concentration:** Generalist with a
primary focus in Electronics, High Technology; **Function
Concentration:** Generalist with a primary focus in
Administration, Engineering, Finance/Accounting, General
Management, Marketing, Sales

Ascher, Susan P. — *President*
The Ascher Group
25 Pompton Avenue, Suite 310
Verona, NJ 07044
Telephone: (201) 239-6116
Recruiter Classification: Retained, Executive Temporary;
Lowest/Average Salary: $50,000/$90,000; **Industry
Concentration:** Generalist with a primary focus in Information
Technology; **Function Concentration:** Generalist with a
primary focus in Administration, Finance/Accounting, General
Management, Human Resources, Marketing,
Women/Minorities

Ashton, Barbara L. — *President*
Ashton Computer Professionals Inc.
Lonsdale Quay
15-C Chesterfield Pl.
Vancouver, B.C., CANADA V7M 3K3
Telephone: (604) 904-0304
Recruiter Classification: Contingency; **Lowest/Average Salary:**
$30,000/$60,000; **Industry Concentration:** High Technology,
Information Technology; **Function Concentration:** Research
and Development

Asquith, Peter S. — *Vice President*
Ames Personnel Consultants, Inc.
P.O. Box 651
Brunswick, ME 04011
Telephone: (207) 729-5158
Recruiter Classification: Executive Temporary; **Lowest/Average
Salary:** $30,000/$60,000; **Industry Concentration:** Generalist
with a primary focus in High Technology; **Function
Concentration:** Generalist with a primary focus in Engineering,
Finance/Accounting, General Management, Human Resources,
Marketing, Research and Development, Sales

Aston, Kathy — *Director*
Marra Peters & Partners
Millburn Esplanade
Millburn, NJ 07041
Telephone: (201) 376-8999
Recruiter Classification: Retained; **Average Salary:** $90,000;
Industry Concentration: Generalist with a primary focus in
Information Technology; **Function Concentration:** Generalist
with a primary focus in Administration, Engineering,
Finance/Accounting, General Management, Human Resources,
Marketing, Research and Development, Sales

Atkins, Laurie — *Senior Associate*
Battalia Winston International
300 Park Avenue
New York, NY 10022
Telephone: (212) 308-8080
Recruiter Classification: Retained; **Lowest/Average Salary:**
$90,000/$90,000; **Industry Concentration:** Generalist with a
primary focus in Electronics, High Technology; **Function
Concentration:** Generalist with a primary focus in General
Management, Human Resources, Marketing

Atkinson, S. Graham — *Principal*
Raymond Karsan Associates
522 East Genesee Street
Fayetteville, NY 13066
Telephone: (315) 637-4600
Recruiter Classification: Retained; **Lowest/Average Salary:**
$30,000/$90,000; **Industry Concentration:** Generalist with a
primary focus in Information Technology; **Function
Concentration:** Generalist

Attell, Harold — *Vice President*
A.E. Feldman Associates
445 Northern Boulevard
Great Neck, NY 11021
Telephone: (516) 466-4708
Recruiter Classification: Contingency; **Lowest/Average Salary:**
$60,000/$90,000; **Industry Concentration:** Generalist with a
primary focus in Electronics, High Technology, Information
Technology; **Function Concentration:** Generalist with a primary
focus in Administration, General Management, Marketing, Sales

Atwood, Barrie — *Associate*
The Abbott Group, Inc.
530 College Parkway, Suite N
Annapolis, MD 21401
Telephone: (410) 757-4100
Lowest/Average Salary: $90,000/$90,000; **Industry Concentration:** Generalist with a primary focus in Electronics, High Technology, Information Technology; **Function Concentration:** Generalist with a primary focus in Administration, Engineering, Human Resources, Research and Development, Women/Minorities

Aubin, Richard E. — *Chairman*
Aubin International Inc.
281 Winter Street, #380
Waltham, MA 02154
Telephone: (617) 890-1722
Recruiter Classification: Retained; **Lowest/Average Salary:** $90,000/$90,000; **Industry Concentration:** Generalist with a primary focus in Electronics, High Technology, Information Technology; **Function Concentration:** Generalist

Austin Lockton, Kathy — *Senior Associate*
Juntunen-Combs-Poirier
600 Montgomery Street, 2nd Floor
San Francisco, CA 94111
Telephone: (415) 291-1699
Recruiter Classification: Retained; **Lowest/Average Salary:** $90,000/$90,000; **Industry Concentration:** High Technology, Information Technology; **Function Concentration:** Finance/Accounting, General Management, Marketing, Sales

Axelrod, Nancy R. — *Vice President*
A.T. Kearney, Inc.
225 Reinekers Lane
Alexandria, VA 22314
Telephone: (703) 739-4624
Recruiter Classification: Retained; **Lowest/Average Salary:** $90,000/$90,000; **Industry Concentration:** Generalist with a primary focus in High Technology, Information Technology; **Function Concentration:** Generalist with a primary focus in Engineering, Finance/Accounting, General Management

Bachmann, Jerry — *Senior Search Consultant*
Kaye-Bassman International Corp.
18333 Preston Road, Suite 500
Dallas, TX 75252
Telephone: (972) 931-5242
Recruiter Classification: Retained; **Lowest/Average Salary:** $50,000/$75,000; **Industry Concentration:** Information Technology

Bacon, Cheri — *Executive Search Consultant*
Gaffney Management Consultants
35 North Brandon Drive
Glendale Heights, IL 60139-2087
Telephone: (630) 307-3380
Recruiter Classification: Retained; **Lowest/Average Salary:** $50,000/$90,000; **Industry Concentration:** Generalist with a primary focus in Electronics, High Technology; **Function Concentration:** Generalist with a primary focus in Engineering, Finance/Accounting, General Management, Human Resources, Marketing, Research and Development, Sales

Badger, Fred H. — *President*
The Badger Group
4125 Blackhawk Plaza Circle, Suite 270
Danville, CA 94506
Telephone: (510) 736-5553
Recruiter Classification: Retained; **Lowest/Average Salary:** $90,000/$90,000; **Industry Concentration:** Generalist with a primary focus in Electronics, High Technology, Information Technology; **Function Concentration:** Generalist with a primary focus in Engineering, Finance/Accounting, General Management, Human Resources, Marketing, Research and Development, Sales

Baeder, Jeremy — *Vice President*
Executive Manning Corporation
3000 N.E. 30th Place, Suite 402/405/411
Fort Lauderdale, FL 33306
Telephone: (954) 561-5100
Recruiter Classification: Retained; **Lowest/Average Salary:** $75,000/$90,000; **Industry Concentration:** Generalist with a primary focus in Electronics, High Technology, Information Technology; **Function Concentration:** Generalist with a primary focus in Administration, Engineering, General Management, Human Resources, Research and Development, Sales, Women/Minorities

Baer, Kenneth — *Associate*
Source Services Corporation
701 West Cypress Creek Road, Suite 202
Ft. Lauderdale, FL 33309
Telephone: (954) 771-0777
Recruiter Classification: Contingency; **Lowest/Average Salary:** $30,000/$50,000; **Industry Concentration:** Information Technology; **Function Concentration:** Engineering, Finance/Accounting

Baglio, Robert — *Associate*
Source Services Corporation
8614 Westwood Center, Suite 750
Vienna, VA 22182
Telephone: (703) 790-5610
Recruiter Classification: Contingency; **Lowest/Average Salary:** $30,000/$50,000; **Industry Concentration:** Information Technology; **Function Concentration:** Engineering, Finance/Accounting

Baier, Rebecca — *Associate*
Source Services Corporation
5429 LBJ Freeway, Suite 275
Dallas, TX 75240
Telephone: (214) 387-1600
Recruiter Classification: Contingency; **Lowest/Average Salary:** $30,000/$50,000; **Industry Concentration:** Information Technology; **Function Concentration:** Engineering, Finance/Accounting

Bailey, David O. — *Consultant*
Ray & Berndtson
245 Park Avenue, 33rd Floor
New York, NY 10167
Telephone: (212) 370-1316
Recruiter Classification: Retained; **Lowest/Average Salary:** $90,000/$90,000; **Industry Concentration:** Information Technology; **Function Concentration:** Generalist

Bailey, Paul — *Vice President*
Austin-McGregor International
12005 Ford Road, Suite 720
Dallas, TX 75234-7247
Telephone: (972) 488-0500
Recruiter Classification: Retained; **Lowest/Average Salary:**
$50,000/$90,000; **Industry Concentration:** Generalist with a
primary focus in Electronics, High Technology, Information
Technology; **Function Concentration:** Generalist

Baird, John — *Contract Recruiter*
Professional Search Consultants
3050 Post Oak Boulevard, Suite 1615
Houston, TX 77056
Telephone: (713) 960-9215
Recruiter Classification: Executive Temporary; **Lowest/Average
Salary:** $50,000/$60,000; **Industry Concentration:** Generalist
with a primary focus in Information Technology; **Function
Concentration:** Engineering, Sales

Baje, Sarah — *Vice President Consulting Services*
Innovative Search Group, LLC
8097 Roswell Road
Suite C-101
Atlanta, GA 30350-3936
Telephone: (770) 399-9093
Recruiter Classification: Retained; **Lowest/Average Salary:**
$40,000/$90,000; **Industry Concentration:** Generalist with a
primary focus in Electronics, High Technology, Information
Technology; **Function Concentration:** Generalist with a
primary focus in Engineering, Finance/Accounting, General
Management, Human Resources, Marketing, Research and
Development, Sales, Women/Minorities

Baker, Bill — *Vice President Corporate
Development*
Kaye-Bassman International Corp.
18333 Preston Road, Suite 500
Dallas, TX 75252
Telephone: (972) 931-5242
Recruiter Classification: Retained; **Lowest/Average Salary:**
$75,000/$90,000; **Industry Concentration:** Information
Technology; **Function Concentration:** Marketing, Sales

Baker, Gary M. — *Vice President*
Cochran, Cochran & Yale, Inc.
955 East Henrietta Road
Rochester, NY 14623
Telephone: (716) 424-6060
Recruiter Classification: Retained; **Lowest/Average Salary:**
$40,000/$60,000; **Industry Concentration:** Generalist with a
primary focus in Electronics, High Technology, Information
Technology; **Function Concentration:** Generalist with a
primary focus in Engineering, Finance/Accounting, General
Management, Human Resources, Marketing, Sales,
Women/Minorities

Baker, Gerry — *Vice President/Managing Director*
A.T. Kearney, Inc.
130 Adelaide Street West, Suite 2710
Toronto, Ontario, CANADA M5H 3P5
Telephone: (416) 947-1990
Recruiter Classification: Retained; **Lowest/Average Salary:**
$90,000/$90,000; **Industry Concentration:** Generalist with a
primary focus in High Technology, Information Technology;
Function Concentration: Generalist with a primary focus in
Engineering, Finance/Accounting, General Management

Bakken, Mark — *Associate*
Source Services Corporation
5429 LBJ Freeway, Suite 275
Dallas, TX 75240
Telephone: (214) 387-1600
Recruiter Classification: Contingency; **Lowest/Average Salary:**
$30,000/$50,000; **Industry Concentration:** Information
Technology; **Function Concentration:** Engineering,
Finance/Accounting

Balbone, Rich — *Vice President*
Executive Manning Corporation
3000 N.E. 30th Place, Suite 402/405/411
Fort Lauderdale, FL 33306
Telephone: (954) 561-5100
Recruiter Classification: Retained; **Lowest/Average Salary:**
$75,000/$90,000; **Industry Concentration:** Generalist with a
primary focus in Electronics, High Technology, Information
Technology; **Function Concentration:** Generalist with a
primary focus in Administration, Engineering, General
Management, Human Resources, Research and Development,
Sales, Women/Minorities

Balch, Randy — *Executive Recruiter*
CPS Inc.
One Westbrook Corporate Centre, Suite 600
Westchester, IL 60154
Telephone: (708) 531-8370
Recruiter Classification: Contingency; **Lowest/Average Salary:**
$30,000/$50,000; **Industry Concentration:** Generalist with a
primary focus in Electronics, High Technology, Information
Technology; **Function Concentration:** Engineering, Research
and Development, Sales, Women/Minorities

Balchumas, Charles — *Managing Director*
Source Services Corporation
5343 North 16th Street, Suite 270
Phoenix, AZ 85016
Telephone: (602) 230-0220
Recruiter Classification: Contingency; **Lowest/Average Salary:**
$30,000/$50,000; **Industry Concentration:** Information
Technology; **Function Concentration:** Engineering,
Finance/Accounting

Baldwin, Keith R. — *Owner*
The Baldwin Group
550 West Campus Drive
Arlington Heights, IL 60004
Telephone: (847) 394-4303
Recruiter Classification: Retained; **Lowest/Average Salary:**
$75,000/$90,000; **Industry Concentration:** Generalist with a
primary focus in Electronics, Information Technology; **Function
Concentration:** Generalist with a primary focus in Engineering,
Finance/Accounting, General Management, Human Resources,
Marketing, Research and Development, Women/Minorities

Baltaglia, Michael — *Search Consultant*
Cochran, Cochran & Yale, Inc.
955 East Henrietta Road
Rochester, NY 14623
Telephone: (716) 424-6060
Recruiter Classification: Retained; **Lowest/Average Salary:**
$50,000/$75,000; **Industry Concentration:** Generalist with a
primary focus in High Technology, Information Technology;
Function Concentration: Generalist with a primary focus in
Engineering, Finance/Accounting, General Management,
Human Resources, Marketing, Sales, Women/Minorities

Balter, Sidney — *Associate*
Source Services Corporation
120 East Baltimore Street, Suite 1950
Baltimore, MD 21202
Telephone: (410) 727-4050
Recruiter Classification: Contingency; **Lowest/Average Salary:**
$30,000/$50,000; **Industry Concentration:** Information
Technology; **Function Concentration:** Engineering,
Finance/Accounting

Baltin, Carrie — *Account Executive*
Search West, Inc.
340 North Westlake Boulevard
Suite 200
Westlake Village, CA 91362-3761
Telephone: (805) 496-6811
Recruiter Classification: Contingency; **Lowest/Average Salary:**
$40,000/$60,000; **Industry Concentration:** Electronics, High
Technology; **Function Concentration:** Engineering, Marketing,
Research and Development, Sales

Banko, Scott — *Associate*
Source Services Corporation
3 Summit Park Drive, Suite 550
Independence, OH 44131
Telephone: (216) 328-5900
Recruiter Classification: Contingency; **Lowest/Average Salary:**
$30,000/$50,000; **Industry Concentration:** Information
Technology; **Function Concentration:** Engineering,
Finance/Accounting

Baranowski, Peter — *Associate*
Source Services Corporation
71 Spit Brook Road, Suite 305
Nashua, NH 03060
Telephone: (603) 888-7650
Recruiter Classification: Contingency; **Lowest/Average Salary:**
$30,000/$50,000; **Industry Concentration:** Information
Technology; **Function Concentration:** Engineering,
Finance/Accounting

Barbosa, Frank — *Senior Vice President*
Skott/Edwards Consultants, Inc.
1776 On the Green
Morristown, NJ 07006
Telephone: (973) 644-0900
Recruiter Classification: Retained; **Lowest/Average Salary:**
$90,000/$90,000; **Industry Concentration:** Electronics, High
Technology, Information Technology; **Function Concentration:**
Engineering, General Management, Marketing, Sales

Barbour, Mary Beth — *Consultant*
Tully/Woodmansee International, Inc.
524 6th Avenue, Suite 210
Seattle, WA 98119
Telephone: (206) 285-9200
Recruiter Classification: Retained; **Lowest/Average Salary:**
$60,000/$90,000; **Industry Concentration:** Generalist with a
primary focus in Electronics, High Technology, Information
Technology; **Function Concentration:** Generalist with a
primary focus in Engineering, Finance/Accounting, General
Management, Human Resources, Marketing, Research and
Development, Sales, Women/Minorities

Barger, H. Carter — *President*
Barger & Sargeant, Inc.
22 Windermere Road, Suite 500
P.O. Box 1420
Center Harbor, NH 03226-1420
Telephone: (603) 253-4700
Recruiter Classification: Retained; **Lowest/Average Salary:**
$90,000/$90,000; **Industry Concentration:** Generalist with
a primary focus in Electronics, High Technology,
Information Technology; **Function Concentration:**
Generalist with a primary focus in Engineering,
Finance/Accounting, General Management, Human
Resources, Marketing

Barlow, Ken H. — *Senior Vice President,
Southeast*
The Cherbonnier Group, Inc.
390 Towne Center Boulevard
Suite B
Ridgeland, MS 39157
Telephone: (601) 952-0020
Recruiter Classification: Retained; **Lowest/Average Salary:**
$75,000/$90,000; **Industry Concentration:** Generalist with a
primary focus in Electronics, High Technology, Information
Technology; **Function Concentration:** Generalist with a
primary focus in Administration, Engineering,
Finance/Accounting, General Management, Marketing,
Research and Development, Sales

Barnaby, Richard — *Associate*
Source Services Corporation
3 Summit Park Drive, Suite 550
Independence, OH 44131
Telephone: (216) 328-5900
Recruiter Classification: Contingency; **Lowest/Average Salary:**
$30,000/$50,000; **Industry Concentration:** Information
Technology; **Function Concentration:** Engineering,
Finance/Accounting

Barnes, Gary — *Senior Partner*
Brigade Inc.
21483 Shannon Court
P.O. Box 1974
Cupertino, CA 95015-1974
Telephone: (408) 973-0600
Recruiter Classification: Retained; **Lowest/Average Salary:**
$90,000/$90,000; **Industry Concentration:** Electronics, High
Technology, Information Technology; **Function
Concentration:** Engineering, Finance/Accounting, General
Management, Human Resources, Marketing,
Women/Minorities

Barnes, Gregory — *Vice President*
Korn/Ferry International
1100 Louisiana, Suite 3400
Houston, TX 77002
Telephone: (713) 651-1834
Recruiter Classification: Retained; **Lowest/Average Salary:**
$100,000/$150,000; **Industry Concentration:** Generalist with a
primary focus in Information Technology; **Function
Concentration:** Generalist

Barnes, Richard E. — *President*
Barnes Development Group, LLC
1017 West Glen Oaks Lane, Suite 108
Mequon, WI 53092
Telephone: (414) 241-8468
Recruiter Classification: Retained; **Lowest/Average Salary:**
$50,000/$75,000; **Industry Concentration:** Generalist with a
primary focus in Electronics, Information Technology; **Function
Concentration:** Generalist with a primary focus in
Administration, Engineering, Finance/Accounting, General
Management, Human Resources, Marketing, Research and
Development, Sales

Barnes, Roanne L. — *Executive Vice President*
Barnes Development Group, LLC
1017 West Glen Oaks Lane, Suite 108
Mequon, WI 53092
Telephone: (414) 241-8468
Recruiter Classification: Retained; **Lowest/Average Salary:**
$50,000/$75,000; **Industry Concentration:** Generalist with a
primary focus in Electronics; **Function Concentration:**
Generalist with a primary focus in Administration, Engineering,
Finance/Accounting, General Management, Human Resources,
Marketing, Research and Development, Sales

Barnett, Barbara — *Consultant Information
Systems Search and Engineering*
D. Brown and Associates, Inc.
610 S.W. Alder, Suite 1111
Portland, OR 97205
Telephone: (503) 224-6860
Recruiter Classification: Contingency; **Lowest/Average Salary:**
$40,000/$60,000; **Industry Concentration:** Electronics, High
Technology, Information Technology; **Function Concentration:**
Engineering, Finance/Accounting

Barnum, Toni M. — *Partner*
Stone Murphy & Olson
5500 Wayzata Boulevard
Suite 1020
Minneapolis, MN 55416
Telephone: (612) 591-2300
Recruiter Classification: Retained; **Lowest/Average Salary:**
$75,000/$90,000; **Industry Concentration:** Generalist with a
primary focus in High Technology, Information Technology;
Function Concentration: Generalist with a primary focus in
Finance/Accounting, General Management, Marketing

Baron, Len — *President*
Industrial Recruiters Associates, Inc.
20 Hurlbut Street, 1st Floor
West Hartford, CT 06110
Telephone: (860) 953-3643
Recruiter Classification: Contingency; **Lowest/Average Salary:**
$30,000/$90,000; **Industry Concentration:** Electronics, High
Technology, Information Technology; **Function Concentration:**
Generalist with a primary focus in Engineering, Marketing,
Research and Development

Bartels, Fredrick — *Associate*
Source Services Corporation
4510 Executive Drive, Suite 200
San Diego, CA 92121
Telephone: (619) 552-0300
Recruiter Classification: Contingency; **Lowest/Average Salary:**
$30,000/$50,000; **Industry Concentration:** Information
Technology; **Function Concentration:** Engineering,
Finance/Accounting

Bartesch, Heinz — *Director*
The Search Firm, Inc.
595 Market Street, Suite 1400
San Francisco, CA 94105
Telephone: (415) 777-3900
Recruiter Classification: Contingency; **Lowest/Average Salary:**
$40,000/$75,000; **Industry Concentration:** Electronics, High
Technology, Information Technology

Bartfield, Philip — *Associate*
Source Services Corporation
5 Independence Way
Princeton, NJ 08540
Telephone: (609) 452-7277
Recruiter Classification: Contingency; **Lowest/Average Salary:**
$30,000/$50,000; **Industry Concentration:** Information
Technology; **Function Concentration:** Engineering,
Finance/Accounting

Barthold, James A. — *Associate*
McNichol Associates
620 Chestnut Street, Suite 1031
Philadelphia, PA 19106
Telephone: (215) 922-4142
Recruiter Classification: Retained; **Lowest/Average Salary:**
$75,000/$90,000; **Industry Concentration:** High Technology;
Function Concentration: Generalist with a primary focus in
Administration, Engineering, Finance/Accounting, General
Management, Human Resources, Marketing, Research and
Development, Sales, Women/Minorities

Bartholdi, Ted — *Vice President*
Bartholdi & Company, Inc.
14 Douglass Way
Exeter, NH 03833
Telephone: (603) 772-4228
Recruiter Classification: Retained; **Lowest/Average Salary:**
$60,000/$90,000; **Industry Concentration:** High Technology,
Information Technology; **Function Concentration:** Generalist
with a primary focus in Engineering, Finance/Accounting,
General Management, Marketing, Research and Development,
Sales

Bartholdi, Theodore G. — *President*
Bartholdi & Company, Inc.
10040 E. Happy Valley Road
Suite 244
Scottsdale, AZ 85255
Telephone: (602) 596-1117
Recruiter Classification: Retained; **Lowest/Average Salary:**
$60,000/$90,000; **Industry Concentration:** High Technology,
Information Technology; **Function Concentration:** Generalist
with a primary focus in Engineering, Finance/Accounting,
General Management, Marketing, Research and Development,
Sales

Bartholomew, Katie — *Vice President Personnel
Services*
C. Berger & Company
327 E. Gundersen Drive
Carol Stream, IL 60188
Telephone: (630) 653-1115
Recruiter Classification: Retained; **Lowest/Average Salary:**
$40,000/$60,000; **Industry Concentration:** High Technology,
Information Technology; **Function Concentration:**
Administration

Barton, Gary R. — *Partner*
Barton Associates, Inc.
One Riverway, Suite 2500
Houston, TX 77056
Telephone: (713) 961-9111
Recruiter Classification: Retained; **Lowest/Average Salary:**
$75,000/$90,000; **Industry Concentration:** Generalist with a
primary focus in Electronics, High Technology, Information
Technology; **Function Concentration:** Generalist with a
primary focus in Administration, Finance/Accounting, General
Management, Human Resources, Marketing, Sales

Barton, James — *Associate*
Source Services Corporation
1 Gatehall Drive, Suite 250
Parsippany, NJ 07054
Telephone: (201) 267-3222
Recruiter Classification: Contingency; **Lowest/Average Salary:**
$30,000/$50,000; **Industry Concentration:** Information
Technology; **Function Concentration:** Engineering,
Finance/Accounting

Bason, Maurice L. — *President*
Bason Associates Inc.
11311 Cornell Park Drive
Cincinnati, OH 45242
Telephone: (513) 469-9881
Recruiter Classification: Retained; **Lowest/Average Salary:**
$60,000/$90,000; **Industry Concentration:** Generalist with a
primary focus in High Technology; **Function Concentration:**
Generalist with a primary focus in Administration, Engineering,
Finance/Accounting, General Management, Human Resources,
Marketing, Research and Development, Sales

Bass, M. Lynn — *Consultant*
Ray & Berndtson
One Allen Center
500 Dallas, Suite 3010
Houston, TX 77002
Telephone: (713) 309-1400
Recruiter Classification: Retained; **Lowest/Average Salary:**
$90,000/$90,000; **Industry Concentration:** Generalist with a
primary focus in High Technology, Information Technology;
Function Concentration: Generalist with a primary focus in
Administration, Finance/Accounting, General Management,
Human Resources, Marketing, Research and Development,
Sales, Women/Minorities

Bassett, Denise — *Recruiter*
Don Richard Associates of Charlotte
2650 One First Union Center
301 South College Street
Charlotte, NC 28202-6000
Telephone: (704) 377-6447
Recruiter Classification: Contingency; **Lowest/Average Salary:**
$30,000/$40,000; **Industry Concentration:** Information
Technology

Bassler, John — *Managing Director Eastern
Region*
Korn/Ferry International
237 Park Avenue
New York, NY 10017
Telephone: (212) 687-1834
Recruiter Classification: Retained; **Lowest/Average Salary:**
$100,000/$150,000; **Industry Concentration:** Generalist with a
primary focus in Information Technology; **Function
Concentration:** Generalist

Bassman, Robert — *Chairman and CEO*
Kaye-Bassman International Corp.
18333 Preston Road, Suite 500
Dallas, TX 75252
Telephone: (972) 931-5242
Recruiter Classification: Retained; **Lowest/Average Salary:**
$40,000/$60,000; **Industry Concentration:** High
Technology, Information Technology; **Function
Concentration:** Generalist

Bassman, Sandy — *Executive Vice President*
Kaye-Bassman International Corp.
18333 Preston Road, Suite 500
Dallas, TX 75252
Telephone: (972) 931-5242
Recruiter Classification: Executive Temporary; **Lowest/Average
Salary:** $40,000/$60,000; **Industry Concentration:** High
Technology, Information Technology; **Function Concentration:**
Generalist

Battalia, O. William — *Chairman*
Battalia Winston International
300 Park Avenue
New York, NY 10022
Telephone: (212) 308-8080
Recruiter Classification: Retained; **Lowest/Average Salary:**
$90,000/$90,000; **Industry Concentration:** Generalist with a
primary focus in Electronics, Information Technology; **Function
Concentration:** Generalist with a primary focus in
Finance/Accounting, General Management, Human Resources,
Marketing, Sales

Batte, Carol — *Associate*
Source Services Corporation
520 Post Oak Boulevard, Suite 700
Houston, TX 77027
Telephone: (713) 439-1077
Recruiter Classification: Contingency; **Lowest/Average Salary:**
$30,000/$50,000; **Industry Concentration:** Information
Technology; **Function Concentration:** Engineering,
Finance/Accounting

Battles, Jonathan — *Principal*
Korn/Ferry International
2 Logan Square, Suite 2530
Philadelphia, PA 19103
Telephone: (215) 568-9911
Recruiter Classification: Retained; **Lowest/Average Salary:**
$100,000/$150,000; **Industry Concentration:** Generalist with a
primary focus in Information Technology; **Function
Concentration:** Generalist

Beal, Richard D. — *Vice President*
A.T. Kearney, Inc.
Lincoln Plaza, Suite 4170
500 North Akard Street
Dallas, TX 75201
Telephone: (214) 969-0010
Recruiter Classification: Retained; **Lowest/Average Salary:**
$90,000/$90,000; **Industry Concentration:** Generalist with a
primary focus in High Technology; **Function Concentration:**
Generalist with a primary focus in Engineering, Research and
Development

Beall, Charles P. — *President/Managing Director*
Beall & Company, Inc.
535 Colonial Park Drive
Roswell, GA 30075
Telephone: (404) 992-0900
Recruiter Classification: Retained; **Lowest/Average Salary:**
$90,000/$90,000; **Industry Concentration:** Generalist with a
primary focus in High Technology; **Function Concentration:**
Generalist

Bearman, Linda — *Vice President*
Grant Cooper and Associates
795 Office Parkway, Suite 117
St. Louis, MO 63141
Telephone: (314) 567-4690
Recruiter Classification: Retained; **Lowest/Average Salary:**
$60,000/$90,000; **Industry Concentration:** Generalist with a
primary focus in Electronics; **Function Concentration:**
Generalist with a primary focus in Administration, Engineering,
Finance/Accounting, General Management, Human Resources,
Marketing, Sales

Beaudin, Elizabeth C. — *Partner*
Callan Associates, Ltd.
2021 Spring Road, Suite 175
Oak Brook, IL 60521
Telephone: (708) 832-7080
Recruiter Classification: Retained; **Lowest/Average Salary:**
$90,000/$90,000; **Industry Concentration:** Generalist with a
primary focus in Electronics, High Technology, Information
Technology; **Function Concentration:** Generalist with a
primary focus in Administration, Engineering,
Finance/Accounting, General Management, Human Resources,
Marketing, Research and Development, Sales,
Women/Minorities

Beaulieu, Genie A. — *Director Communications*
Romac & Associates
183 Middle Street, 3rd Floor
P.O. Box 7040
Portland, ME 04112
Telephone: (207) 773-4749
Recruiter Classification: Executive Temporary;
Lowest/Average Salary: $60,000/$60,000; **Industry
Concentration:** High Technology, Information
Technology; **Function Concentration:**
Finance/Accounting

Beaver, Bentley H. — *Managing Director*
The Onstott Group, Inc.
60 William Street
Wellesley, MA 02181
Telephone: (781) 235-3050
Recruiter Classification: Retained; **Lowest/Average Salary:**
$90,000/$90,000; **Industry Concentration:** Generalist with a
primary focus in Electronics, High Technology, Information
Technology; **Function Concentration:** Generalist with a
primary focus in Engineering, Finance/Accounting, General
Management, Human Resources, Marketing, Research and
Development, Sales

Beaver, Robert — *Associate*
Source Services Corporation
1290 Oakmead Parkway, Suite 318
Sunnyvale, CA 94086
Telephone: (408) 738-8440
Recruiter Classification: Contingency; **Lowest/Average Salary:**
$30,000/$50,000; **Industry Concentration:** Information
Technology; **Function Concentration:** Engineering,
Finance/Accounting

Beaver, Robert W. — *Vice President*
Executive Manning Corporation
3000 N.E. 30th Place, Suite 402/405/411
Fort Lauderdale, FL 33306
Telephone: (954) 561-5100
Recruiter Classification: Retained; **Lowest/Average Salary:**
$75,000/$90,000; **Industry Concentration:** Generalist with a
primary focus in Electronics, High Technology; **Function
Concentration:** Generalist

Beck, Michael — *Consultant*
Don Richard Associates of Richmond, Inc.
7275 Glen Forest Drive, Suite 200
Richmond, VA 23226
Telephone: (804) 282-6300
Recruiter Classification: Contingency; **Lowest/Average Salary:**
$30,000/$50,000; **Industry Concentration:** Information
Technology

Beckvold, John B. — *Principal*
Atlantic Search Group, Inc.
One Liberty Square
Boston, MA 02109
Telephone: (617) 426-9700
Recruiter Classification: Contingency; **Lowest/Average Salary:**
$20,000/$60,000; **Industry Concentration:** Generalist with a
primary focus in Electronics, High Technology, Information
Technology; **Function Concentration:** Finance/Accounting

Beeson, William B. — *Vice President*
Lawrence-Leiter & Co. Management Conultants
4400 Shawnee-Mission Parkway, Suite 204
Shawnee-Mission, KS 66205
Telephone: (913) 677-5500
Recruiter Classification: Retained; **Lowest/Average Salary:**
$50,000/$90,000; **Industry Concentration:** Generalist with a
primary focus in Electronics; **Function Concentration:**
Generalist

Belden, Jeannette — *Associate*
Source Services Corporation
10220 SW Greenburg Road, Suite 625
Portland, OR 97223
Telephone: (503) 768-4546
Recruiter Classification: Contingency; **Lowest/Average Salary:**
$30,000/$50,000; **Industry Concentration:** Information
Technology; **Function Concentration:** Engineering,
Finance/Accounting

Belfrey, Edward — *Aviation Specialist*
Dunhill Professional Search of Irvine, Inc.
9 Executive Circle, Suite 240
Irvine, CA 92614
Telephone: (714) 474-6666
Recruiter Classification: Contingency; **Lowest/Average Salary:**
$75,000/$90,000; **Industry Concentration:** High Technology;
Function Concentration: Generalist with a primary focus in
Engineering, Marketing, Sales

Belin, Jean — *Consultant*
Boyden
500 East Broward Boulevard
Suite 1050
Ft. Lauderdale, FL 33394
Telephone: (954) 522-8885
Recruiter Classification: Retained; **Lowest/Average Salary:**
$90,000/$90,000; **Industry Concentration:** Generalist with a
primary focus in Electronics, High Technology, Information
Technology; **Function Concentration:** Generalist with a
primary focus in Engineering, Finance/Accounting, General
Management, Human Resources, Marketing, Sales,
Women/Minorities

Bell, Lisa — *Information Technology Recruiter*
Winter, Wyman & Company
950 Winter Street, Suite 3100
Waltham, MA 02154-1294
Telephone: (617) 890-7000
Recruiter Classification: Contingency; **Lowest/Average Salary:**
$30,000/$60,000; **Industry Concentration:** Generalist with a
primary focus in Information Technology; **Function
Concentration:** Generalist

Bence, Robert J. — *Executive Vice
President/Managing Director Information
Technology*
DHR International, Inc.
8182 Maryland Avenue, Suite 200
Clayton, MO 63105
Telephone: (314) 725-1191
Recruiter Classification: Retained; **Lowest/Average Salary:**
$60,000/$90,000; **Industry Concentration:** Information
Technology; **Function Concentration:** Generalist

Bender, Alan — *President*
Bender Executive Search
45 North Station Plaza
Suite 315
Great Neck, NY 11021
Telephone: (516) 773-4300
Recruiter Classification: Retained; **Lowest/Average Salary:**
$75,000/$90,000; **Industry Concentration:** Generalist with a
primary focus in Information Technology; **Function
Concentration:** General Management, Marketing, Sales,
Women/Minorities

Benjamin, Maurita — *Associate*
Source Services Corporation
8614 Westwood Center, Suite 750
Vienna, VA 22182
Telephone: (703) 790-5610
Recruiter Classification: Contingency; **Lowest/Average Salary:**
$30,000/$50,000; **Industry Concentration:** Information
Technology; **Function Concentration:** Engineering,
Finance/Accounting

Bennett, Jo — *Vice President*
Battalia Winston International
300 Park Avenue
New York, NY 10022
Telephone: (212) 308-8080
Recruiter Classification: Retained; **Lowest/Average Salary:**
$90,000/$90,000; **Industry Concentration:** Generalist with a
primary focus in Electronics, High Technology; **Function
Concentration:** Generalist with a primary focus in Engineering,
Finance/Accounting, General Management, Human Resources,
Marketing, Sales, Women/Minorities

Bennett, Joan — *Director Research/Recruiter*
Adams & Associates International
463-D W. Russell Street
Barrington, IL 60010
Telephone: (847) 304-5300
Recruiter Classification: Retained; **Lowest/Average Salary:**
$75,000/$75,000; **Industry Concentration:** Generalist with a
primary focus in Electronics; **Function Concentration:**
Generalist with a primary focus in Engineering, General
Management, Marketing

Bennett, Ness — *Recruiter*
Technical Connections Inc.
11400 Olympic Boulevard, Suite 770
Los Angeles, CA 90064
Telephone: (310) 479-8830
Recruiter Classification: Contingency; **Lowest/Average
Salary:** $40,000/$75,000; **Industry Concentration:** High
Technology, Information Technology; **Function
Concentration:** Generalist

Benson, Edward — *Associate*
Source Services Corporation
1601 East Flamingo Road, Suite 18
Las Vegas, NV 89119
Telephone: (702) 796-9676
Recruiter Classification: Contingency; **Lowest/Average Salary:**
$30,000/$50,000; **Industry Concentration:** Information
Technology; **Function Concentration:** Engineering,
Finance/Accounting

Bentley, Mark — *Associate*
The Thomas Tucker Company
425 California Street, Suite 2502
San Francisco, CA 94104
Telephone: (415) 693-5900
Recruiter Classification: Retained; **Lowest/Average Salary:**
$60,000/$90,000; **Industry Concentration:** High Technology,
Information Technology; **Function Concentration:** Research
and Development

Beran, Helena — *Associate*
Michael J. Cavanagh and Associates
60 St. Clair Avenue East
Suite 905
Toronto, Ontario, CANADA M4T 1N5
Telephone: (416) 324-9661
Recruiter Classification: Retained; **Lowest/Average Salary:**
$80,000/$100,000; **Industry Concentration:** Generalist with a
primary focus in Electronics, Information Technology; **Function
Concentration:** Generalist with a primary focus in
Administration, Engineering, Finance/Accounting, General
Management, Human Resources, Marketing

Berger, Carol — *President*
C. Berger & Company
327 E. Gundersen Drive
Carol Stream, IL 60188
Telephone: (630) 653-1115
Recruiter Classification: Retained; **Lowest/Average Salary:**
$40,000/$60,000; **Industry Concentration:** Information
Technology; **Function Concentration:** Administration

Berger, Jeffrey — *Associate*
Source Services Corporation
10300 West 103rd Street, Suite 101
Overland Park, KS 66214
Telephone: (913) 888-8885
Recruiter Classification: Contingency; **Lowest/Average Salary:**
$30,000/$50,000; **Industry Concentration:** Information
Technology; **Function Concentration:** Engineering,
Finance/Accounting

Berkhemer-Credaire, Betsy — *President*
Berkhemer Clayton Incorporated
Union Station
800 N. Alameda Street, Suite. 200
Los Angeles, CA 90012
Telephone: (213) 621-2300
Recruiter Classification: Retained; **Lowest/Average Salary:**
$75,000/$90,000; **Industry Concentration:** Generalist with a
primary focus in High Technology, Information Technology;
Function Concentration: Generalist with a primary focus in
General Management, Marketing, Sales, Women/Minorities

Bernard, Bryan — *Associate*
Source Services Corporation
520 Post Oak Boulevard, Suite 700
Houston, TX 77027
Telephone: (713) 439-1077
Recruiter Classification: Contingency; **Lowest/Average Salary:**
$30,000/$50,000; **Industry Concentration:** Information
Technology; **Function Concentration:** Engineering,
Finance/Accounting

Bernas, Sharon — *Associate*
Source Services Corporation
3 Summit Park Drive, Suite 550
Independence, OH 44131
Telephone: (216) 328-5900
Recruiter Classification: Contingency; **Lowest/Average Salary:**
$30,000/$50,000; **Industry Concentration:** Information
Technology; **Function Concentration:** Engineering,
Finance/Accounting

Berry, Harold B. — *Vice President*
The Hindman Company
Browenton Place, Suite 110
2000 Warrington Way
Louisville, KY 40222
Telephone: (502) 426-4040
Recruiter Classification: Retained; **Lowest/Average Salary:**
$50,000/$90,000; **Industry Concentration:** Generalist with a
primary focus in Electronics, High Technology; **Function
Concentration:** Generalist with a primary focus in Engineering,
Finance/Accounting, General Management, Human Resources,
Marketing, Sales

Bettick, Michael J. — *Professional Recruiter*
A.J. Burton Group, Inc.
120 East Baltimore Street, Suite 2220
Baltimore, MD 21202
Telephone: (410) 752-5244
Recruiter Classification: Contingency; **Lowest/Average Salary:**
$40,000/$75,000; **Industry Concentration:** Generalist with a
primary focus in High Technology, Information Technology;
Function Concentration: Generalist with a primary focus in
Administration, Finance/Accounting, General Management,
Human Resources

Betts, Suzette — *Associate*
Source Services Corporation
520 Post Oak Boulevard, Suite 700
Houston, TX 77027
Telephone: (713) 439-1077
Recruiter Classification: Contingency; **Lowest/Average Salary:**
$30,000/$50,000; **Industry Concentration:** Information
Technology; **Function Concentration:** Engineering,
Finance/Accounting

Bickett, Nicole — *Associate*
Source Services Corporation
111 Monument Circle, Suite 3930
Indianapolis, IN 46204
Telephone: (317) 631-2900
Recruiter Classification: Contingency; **Lowest/Average Salary:**
$30,000/$50,000; **Industry Concentration:** Information
Technology; **Function Concentration:** Engineering,
Finance/Accounting

Bidelman, Richard — *Managing Director*
Source Services Corporation
1601 East Flamingo Road, Suite 18
Las Vegas, NV 89119
Telephone: (702) 796-9676
Recruiter Classification: Contingency; **Lowest/Average Salary:**
$30,000/$50,000; **Industry Concentration:** Information
Technology; **Function Concentration:** Engineering,
Finance/Accounting

Biestek, Paul J. — *President*
Paul J. Biestek Associates, Inc.
10600 W. Higgins Road, Suite 300
Rosemont, IL 60018
Telephone: (847) 825-5131
Recruiter Classification: Retained; **Lowest/Average Salary:**
$70,000/$90,000; **Industry Concentration:** Generalist with a
primary focus in Electronics, High Technology; **Function
Concentration:** Generalist with a primary focus in Engineering,
General Management, Human Resources, Marketing, Research
and Development, Sales

Bigelow, Dennis — *Vice President*
Marshall Consultants, Inc.
360 East 65th Street
New York, NY 10021
Telephone: (212) 628-8400
Recruiter Classification: Retained; **Lowest/Average Salary:**
$30,000/$50,000; **Industry Concentration:** Electronics, High
Technology, Information Technology; **Function Concentration:**
Marketing

Biggins, Joseph — *Information Technology
Recruiter*
Winter, Wyman & Company
950 Winter Street, Suite 3100
Waltham, MA 02154-1294
Telephone: (617) 890-7000
Recruiter Classification: Contingency; **Lowest/Average Salary:**
$30,000/$60,000; **Industry Concentration:** Generalist with a
primary focus in Information Technology; **Function
Concentration:** Generalist

Billington, William H. — *Partner*
Spriggs & Company, Inc.
1701 East Lake Avenue
Suite 265
Glenview, IL 60025
Telephone: (708) 657-7181
Recruiter Classification: Retained; **Lowest/Average Salary:**
$60,000/$90,000; **Industry Concentration:** Generalist with a
primary focus in Electronics; **Function Concentration:**
Generalist with a primary focus in General Management,
Human Resources, Marketing, Sales

Biolsi, Joseph — *Associate*
Source Services Corporation
15260 Ventura Boulevard, Suite 380
Sherman Oaks, CA 91403
Telephone: (818) 905-1500
Recruiter Classification: Contingency; **Lowest/Average Salary:**
$30,000/$50,000; **Industry Concentration:** Information
Technology; **Function Concentration:** Engineering,
Finance/Accounting

Birns, Douglas — *Associate*
Source Services Corporation
155 Federal Street, Suite 410
Boston, MA 02110
Telephone: (617) 482-8211
Recruiter Classification: Contingency; **Lowest/Average Salary:**
$30,000/$50,000; **Industry Concentration:** Information
Technology; **Function Concentration:** Engineering,
Finance/Accounting

Birt, Peter — *Administrator Recruitment Support*
Ashton Computer Professionals Inc.
Lonsdale Quay
15-C Chesterfield Pl.
Vancouver, B.C., CANADA V7M 3K3
Telephone: (604) 904-0304
Recruiter Classification: Contingency; **Lowest/Average Salary:**
$30,000/$60,000; **Industry Concentration:** High Technology,
Information Technology; **Function Concentration:** Research
and Development

Bishop, Susan — *President*
Bishop Partners
708 Third Avenue
Suite 2200
New York, NY 10017
Telephone: (212) 986-3419
Recruiter Classification: Retained; **Lowest/Average Salary:**
$90,000/$90,000; **Industry Concentration:** Information
Technology; **Function Concentration:** Generalist with a
primary focus in Finance/Accounting, General Management,
Marketing, Sales

Blackmon, Sharon — *Vice President*
The Abbott Group, Inc.
530 College Parkway, Suite N
Annapolis, MD 21401
Telephone: (410) 757-4100
Recruiter Classification: Retained; **Lowest/Average Salary:**
$90,000/$90,000; **Industry Concentration:** Generalist with a
primary focus in Electronics, High Technology, Information
Technology; **Function Concentration:** Generalist with a
primary focus in Administration, Engineering, General
Management, Human Resources, Marketing,
Women/Minorities

Blackshaw, Brian M. — *Partner*
Blackshaw, Olmstead, Lynch & Koenig
3414 Peachtree Road
Suite 1010
Atlanta, GA 30326
Telephone: (404) 261-7770
Recruiter Classification: Retained; **Lowest/Average Salary:**
$90,000/$90,000; **Industry Concentration:** Generalist with a
primary focus in Electronics, High Technology, Information
Technology; **Function Concentration:** Generalist with a
primary focus in Finance/Accounting, General Management,
Human Resources, Sales

Bladon, Andrew — *Vice President/Executive Director*
Don Richard Associates of Tampa, Inc.
100 North Tampa Street, Suite 1925
Tampa, FL 33602
Telephone: (813) 221-7930
Recruiter Classification: Contingency, Executive Temporary;
Lowest/Average Salary: $20,000/$50,000; **Industry
Concentration:** Generalist with a primary focus in High
Technology, Information Technology; **Function Concentration:**
Generalist with a primary focus in Administration,
Finance/Accounting, Research and Development

Blake, Eileen — *Senior Consultant*
Howard Fischer Associates, Inc.
1800 John F. Kennedy Boulevard, 7th Floor
Philadelphia, PA 19103
Telephone: (215) 568-8363
Recruiter Classification: Retained; **Lowest/Average Salary:**
$90,000/$90,000; **Industry Concentration:** High Technology;
Function Concentration: Generalist

Bland, Walter — *Associate*
Source Services Corporation
925 Westchester Avenue, Suite 309
White Plains, NY 10604
Telephone: (914) 428-9100
Recruiter Classification: Contingency; **Lowest/Average Salary:**
$30,000/$50,000; **Industry Concentration:** Information
Technology; **Function Concentration:** Engineering,
Finance/Accounting

Blanton, Julia — *Director - Sales and Marketing*
Blanton and Company
P.O. Box 94041
Birmingham, AL 35220-4041
Telephone: (205) 836-3063
Recruiter Classification: Contingency; **Lowest/Average Salary:**
$75,000/$75,000; **Industry Concentration:** Generalist with a
primary focus in Electronics, High Technology, Information
Technology; **Function Concentration:** Generalist with a
primary focus in Engineering, Marketing, Sales

Blanton, Thomas — *Partner*
Blanton and Company
P.O. Box 94041
Birmingham, AL 35220-4041
Telephone: (205) 836-3063
Recruiter Classification: Contingency; **Lowest/Average Salary:**
$75,000/$75,000; **Industry Concentration:** Generalist with a
primary focus in Electronics, High Technology, Information
Technology; **Function Concentration:** Generalist with a
primary focus in Engineering, General Management,
Marketing, Research and Development, Sales

Blassaras, Peggy — *Associate*
Source Services Corporation
111 Monument Circle, Suite 3930
Indianapolis, IN 46204
Telephone: (317) 631-2900
Recruiter Classification: Contingency; **Lowest/Average Salary:**
$30,000/$50,000; **Industry Concentration:** Information
Technology; **Function Concentration:** Engineering,
Finance/Accounting

Blaydes, James — *Search Consultant*
Kaye-Bassman International Corp.
18333 Preston Road, Suite 500
Dallas, TX 75252
Telephone: (972) 931-5242
Recruiter Classification: Retained; **Lowest/Average Salary:**
$60,000/$75,000; **Industry Concentration:** Information
Technology

Blecker, Jay — *Executive Recruiter*
TSS Consulting, Ltd.
2425 East Camelback Road
Suite 375
Phoenix, AZ 85016
Telephone: (602) 955-7000
Recruiter Classification: Contingency; **Lowest/Average Salary:**
$60,000/$75,000; **Industry Concentration:** Electronics, High
Technology; **Function Concentration:** Engineering, General
Management, Marketing

Blickle, Michael — *Associate*
Source Services Corporation
One South Main Street, Suite 1440
Dayton, OH 45402
Telephone: (513) 461-4660
Recruiter Classification: Contingency; **Lowest/Average Salary:**
$30,000/$50,000; **Industry Concentration:** Information
Technology; **Function Concentration:** Engineering,
Finance/Accounting

Bliley, Jerry — *Senior Director*
Spencer Stuart
One University Avenue
Suite 801
Toronto, Ontario, CANADA M5J 2P1
Telephone: (416) 361-0311
Recruiter Classification: Retained; **Lowest/Average Salary:**
$90,000/$90,000; **Industry Concentration:** Generalist with a
primary focus in Electronics, High Technology, Information
Technology; **Function Concentration:** Generalist with a
primary focus in Finance/Accounting, General Management,
Human Resources, Marketing, Sales

Blim, Barbara — *Principal*
JDG Associates, Ltd.
1700 Research Boulevard
Rockville, MD 20850
Telephone: (301) 340-2210
Recruiter Classification: Contingency; **Lowest/Average
Salary:** $50,000/$90,000; **Industry Concentration:**
Electronics, High Technology, Information Technology;
Function Concentration: Engineering, Research and
Development, Sales

Bloch, Suzanne — *Associate*
Source Services Corporation
701 West Cypress Creek Road, Suite 202
Ft. Lauderdale, FL 33309
Telephone: (954) 771-0777
Recruiter Classification: Contingency; **Lowest/Average Salary:**
$30,000/$50,000; **Industry Concentration:** Information
Technology; **Function Concentration:** Engineering,
Finance/Accounting

Bloch, Terry L. — *Technical Director*
Southern Research Services
3837 Northdale Boulevard
Suite 363
Tampa, FL 33624
Telephone: (813) 269-9595
Recruiter Classification: Retained; **Lowest/Average Salary:**
$40,000/$90,000; **Industry Concentration:** Electronics, High
Technology; **Function Concentration:** Engineering,
Finance/Accounting, General Management, Human Resources,
Marketing, Research and Development

Bloch, Thomas L. — *President*
Southern Research Services
3837 Northdale Boulevard
Suite 363
Tampa, FL 33624
Telephone: (813) 269-9595
Recruiter Classification: Retained; **Lowest/Average Salary:**
$40,000/$90,000; **Industry Concentration:** Electronics, High
Technology; **Function Concentration:** Engineering,
Finance/Accounting, General Management, Human Resources,
Marketing

Blocher, John — *Managing Director*
Source Services Corporation
10300 West 103rd Street, Suite 101
Overland Park, KS 66214
Telephone: (913) 888-8885
Recruiter Classification: Contingency; **Lowest/Average Salary:**
$30,000/$50,000; **Industry Concentration:** Information
Technology; **Function Concentration:** Engineering,
Finance/Accounting

Block, Randy — *President*
Block & Associates
20 Sunnyside Avenue, Suite A332
Mill Valley, CA 94941
Telephone: (415) 389-9710
Recruiter Classification: Retained; **Lowest/Average Salary:**
$90,000/$90,000; **Industry Concentration:** Electronics;
Function Concentration: Generalist

Bloom, Howard C. — *Principal*
Hernand & Partners
5000 Quorum Drive, Suite 160
Dallas, TX 75240
Telephone: (214) 661-1485
Recruiter Classification: Executive Temporary; **Lowest/Average
Salary:** $60,000/$90,000; **Industry Concentration:** High
Technology, Information Technology; **Function Concentration:**
Engineering

Bloom, Joyce — *Principal*
Hernand & Partners
5000 Quorum Drive, Suite 160
Dallas, TX 75240
Telephone: (214) 661-1485
Recruiter Classification: Executive Temporary; **Lowest/Average Salary:** $60,000/$90,000; **Industry Concentration:** High Technology, Information Technology; **Function Concentration:** Engineering

Bloomer, James E. — *Vice President*
L.W. Foote Company
110 110th Avenue N.E.
Suite 603
Bellevue, WA 98004-5840
Telephone: (206) 451-1660
Recruiter Classification: Retained; **Lowest/Average Salary:** $75,000/$90,000; **Industry Concentration:** Generalist with a primary focus in Electronics, High Technology, Information Technology; **Function Concentration:** Generalist with a primary focus in Administration, Engineering, General Management, Marketing, Research and Development, Sales

Bluhm, Claudia — *Executive Search Consultant*
Schweichler Associates, Inc.
200 Tamal Vista, Building 200, Suite 100
Corte Madera, CA 94925
Telephone: (415) 924-7200
Recruiter Classification: Retained; **Lowest/Average Salary:** $90,000/$90,000; **Industry Concentration:** Electronics, High Technology, Information Technology; **Function Concentration:** Administration, Engineering, Finance/Accounting, General Management, Human Resources, Marketing, Research and Development, Sales

Blumenthal, Paula — *Partner*
J.P. Canon Associates
225 Broadway, Ste. 3602, 36th Fl.
New York, NY 10007-3001
Telephone: (212) 233-3131
Recruiter Classification: Contingency; **Lowest/Average Salary:** $40,000/$75,000; **Industry Concentration:** Generalist with a primary focus in Electronics; **Function Concentration:** Engineering

Blunt, Peter — *Account Executive*
Hernand & Partners
770 Tamalpais Drive, Suite 204
Corte Madera, CA 94925
Telephone: (415) 927-7000
Recruiter Classification: Executive Temporary; **Lowest/Average Salary:** $60,000/$90,000; **Industry Concentration:** High Technology, Information Technology; **Function Concentration:** Engineering

Boag, John — *Senior Associate*
Norm Sanders Associates
2 Village Court
Hazlet, NJ 07730
Telephone: (732) 264-3700
Recruiter Classification: Retained; **Lowest/Average Salary:** $90,000/$90,000; **Industry Concentration:** Information Technology; **Function Concentration:** Generalist

Boccella, Ralph — *Senior Recruiter*
Susan C. Goldberg Associates
65 LaSalle Road
West Hartford, CT 06107
Telephone: (860) 236-4597
Recruiter Classification: Contingency; **Lowest/Average Salary:** $40,000/$75,000; **Industry Concentration:** High Technology; **Function Concentration:** Finance/Accounting

Boczany, William J. — *Director*
The Guild Corporation
8260 Greensboro Drive, Suite 460
McLean, VA 22102
Telephone: (703) 761-4023
Recruiter Classification: Contingency; **Lowest/Average Salary:** $40,000/$50,000; **Industry Concentration:** Electronics, High Technology, Information Technology; **Function Concentration:** Engineering, Finance/Accounting, General Management, Research and Development

Boehm, Robin — *Consultant Information Systems Search and Engineering*
D. Brown and Associates, Inc.
610 S.W. Alder, Suite 1111
Portland, OR 97205
Telephone: (503) 224-6860
Recruiter Classification: Contingency; **Lowest/Average Salary:** $40,000/$60,000; **Industry Concentration:** Electronics, High Technology, Information Technology; **Function Concentration:** Engineering, Finance/Accounting

Boehmer, John — *Partner*
Huntington Group
6527 Main Street
Trumbull, CT 06611
Telephone: (203) 261-1166
Recruiter Classification: Retained; **Lowest/Average Salary:** $90,000/$90,000; **Industry Concentration:** Information Technology; **Function Concentration:** Generalist

Boel, Werner — *Senior Associate*
The Dalley Hewitt Company
1401 Peachtree Street, Suite 500
Atlanta, GA 30309
Telephone: (404) 885-6642
Recruiter Classification: Retained; **Lowest/Average Salary:** $50,000/$90,000; **Industry Concentration:** Generalist with a primary focus in Information Technology; **Function Concentration:** Generalist with a primary focus in Administration, Engineering, Finance/Accounting, General Management, Human Resources, Marketing, Research and Development, Sales

Boesel, James — *Consultant*
Logix Partners
1601 Trapelo Road
Waltham, MA 02154
Telephone: (617) 890-0500
Recruiter Classification: Retained; **Lowest/Average Salary:** $60,000/$75,000; **Industry Concentration:** High Technology; **Function Concentration:** Engineering

Boesel, Jim — *Consultant*
Logix, Inc.
1601 Trapelo Road
Waltham, MA 02154
Telephone: (617) 890-0500
Recruiter Classification: Retained; **Lowest/Average Salary:**
$60,000/$75,000; **Industry Concentration:** High Technology;
Function Concentration: Engineering

Bogansky, Amy — *Vice President*
Conex Incorporated
150 East 52nd Street, 2nd Floor
New York, NY 10022
Telephone: (212) 371-3737
Recruiter Classification: Retained; **Lowest/Average Salary:**
$75,000/$75,000; **Industry Concentration:** Generalist with a
primary focus in Electronics, High Technology, Information
Technology; **Function Concentration:** Generalist with a
primary focus in Engineering, General Management,
Marketing, Research and Development, Sales

Bohle, John B. — *Partner*
Ray & Berndtson
2029 Century Park East, Suite 1000
Los Angeles, CA 90067
Telephone: (310) 557-2828
Recruiter Classification: Retained; **Lowest/Average Salary:**
$90,000/$90,000; **Industry Concentration:** High Technology;
Function Concentration: Generalist

Bohn, Steve J. — *General Manager*
MSI International
2170 West State Road 434
Suite 454
Longwood, FL 32779
Telephone: (407) 788-7700
Recruiter Classification: Contingency; **Lowest/Average Salary:**
$30,000/$60,000; **Industry Concentration:** Generalist with a
primary focus in High Technology, Information Technology;
Function Concentration: Generalist with a primary focus in
Administration, Engineering, Finance/Accounting, General
Management, Marketing, Sales

Boltrus, Dick — *Partner*
Sink, Walker, Boltrus International
60 Walnut Street
Wellesley, MA 02181
Telephone: (617) 237-1199
Recruiter Classification: Retained; **Lowest/Average Salary:**
$90,000/$90,000; **Industry Concentration:** Electronics, High
Technology, Information Technology; **Function Concentration:**
Engineering, General Management, Research and
Development, Sales

Bond, Allan — *Senior Consultant/Director*
Walden Associates
1601 Trapelo Road
Waltham, MA 02154
Telephone: (617) 890-8885
Recruiter Classification: Retained; **Lowest/Average Salary:**
$90,000/$90,000; **Industry Concentration:** High Technology,
Information Technology; **Function Concentration:** General
Management

Bond, James L. — *Vice President*
People Management Northeast Incorporated
One Darling Drive, Avon Park South
Avon, CT 06001
Telephone: (860) 678-8900
Recruiter Classification: Retained; **Lowest/Average Salary:**
$75,000/$90,000; **Industry Concentration:** Generalist with a
primary focus in Information Technology; **Function
Concentration:** Generalist

Bond, Robert J. — *Managing Partner*
Romac & Associates
125 Summer Street, Suite 1450
Boston, MA 02110
Telephone: (617) 439-4300
Recruiter Classification: Executive Temporary; **Lowest/Average
Salary:** $60,000/$60,000; **Industry Concentration:** High
Technology, Information Technology; **Function Concentration:**
Finance/Accounting

Bongiovanni, Vincent — *Senior Partner*
ESA Professional Consultants
141 Durham Road
Suite 16
Madison, CT 06443
Telephone: (203) 245-1983
Recruiter Classification: Retained; **Lowest/Average Salary:**
$50,000/$75,000; **Industry Concentration:** Electronics, High
Technology, Information Technology; **Function
Concentration:** Engineering, General Management, Human
Resources, Marketing, Research and Development,
Women/Minorities

Bonner, Lale D. — *Manager Technical
Recruitment*
Don Richard Associates of Charlotte
2650 One First Union Center
301 South College Street
Charlotte, NC 28202-6000
Telephone: (704) 377-6447
Recruiter Classification: Contingency; **Lowest/Average Salary:**
$30,000/$40,000; **Industry Concentration:** High Technology,
Information Technology

Booth, Ronald — *Associate*
Source Services Corporation
5343 North 16th Street, Suite 270
Phoenix, AZ 85016
Telephone: (602) 230-0220
Recruiter Classification: Contingency; **Lowest/Average Salary:**
$30,000/$50,000; **Industry Concentration:** Information
Technology; **Function Concentration:** Engineering,
Finance/Accounting

Bordelon, Amanda — *Director*
Paul-Tittle Associates, Inc.
1485 Chain Bridge Road, #304
McLean, VA 22101
Telephone: (703) 442-0500
Recruiter Classification: Retained; **Lowest/Average Salary:**
$60,000/$75,000; **Industry Concentration:** High Technology,
Information Technology

Borenstine, Alvin — *President*
Synergistics Associates Ltd.
400 North State Street, Suite 400
Chicago, IL 60610-
Telephone: (312) 467-5450
Recruiter Classification: Retained; **Lowest/Average Salary:**
$90,000/$90,000; **Industry Concentration:** Generalist with a
primary focus in Information Technology; **Function
Concentration:** Generalist

Borkin, Andrew — *President*
Strategic Advancement Inc.
242 Old New Brunswick Road
Suite 100
Piscataway, NJ 08854
Telephone: (908) 562-1222
Recruiter Classification: Retained; **Lowest/Average Salary:**
$50,000/$90,000; **Industry Concentration:** Electronics,
Information Technology; **Function Concentration:**
Administration, Engineering, Finance/Accounting, General
Management, Human Resources, Marketing, Research and
Development

Borland, James — *Senior Vice President*
Goodrich & Sherwood Associates, Inc.
521 Fifth Avenue
New York, NY 10175
Telephone: (212) 697-4131
Recruiter Classification: Retained; **Lowest/Average Salary:**
$60,000/$90,000; **Industry Concentration:** Generalist with a
primary focus in Information Technology; **Function
Concentration:** Generalist with a primary focus in
Administration, Finance/Accounting, General Management,
Human Resources, Marketing, Sales

Bormann, Cindy Ann — *Manager*
MSI International
5215 North O'Connor Boulevard
Suite 1875
Irving, TX 75039
Telephone: (214) 869-3939
Recruiter Classification: Contingency; **Lowest/Average
Salary:** $30,000/$60,000; **Industry Concentration:** Generalist
with a primary focus in High Technology, Information
Technology; **Function Concentration:** Generalist with a
primary focus in Administration, Engineering,
Finance/Accounting, General Management,
Marketing, Sales

Bostic, James E. — *Vice President Operations*
Phillips Resource Group
330 Pelham Road, Building A
Greenville, SC 29615
Telephone: (864) 271-6350
Recruiter Classification: Contingency; **Lowest/Average
Salary:** $40,000/$50,000; **Industry Concentration:**
Generalist with a primary focus in Electronics, High
Technology, Information Technology; **Function
Concentration:** Generalist with a primary focus in
Administration, Engineering, General Management, Human
Resources, Marketing, Research and Development, Sales,
Women/Minorities

Bosward, Allan — *Associate*
Source Services Corporation
1290 Oakmead Parkway, Suite 318
Sunnyvale, CA 94086
Telephone: (408) 738-8440
Recruiter Classification: Contingency; **Lowest/Average Salary:**
$30,000/$50,000; **Industry Concentration:** Information
Technology; **Function Concentration:** Engineering,
Finance/Accounting

Bourrie, Sharon D. — *Director*
Chartwell Partners International, Inc.
275 Battery Street, Suite 2180
San Francisco, CA 94111
Telephone: (415) 296-0600
Recruiter Classification: Retained; **Lowest/Average Salary:**
$90,000/$90,000; **Industry Concentration:** Generalist with a
primary focus in High Technology, Information Technology;
Function Concentration: Generalist with a primary focus in
Finance/Accounting, General Management, Human Resources,
Marketing, Women/Minorities

Bowden, Otis H. — *Managing Director*
BowdenGlobal, Ltd.
6450 Rockside Woods Boulevard
Suite 100
Cleveland, OH 44131
Telephone: (216) 328-2088
Recruiter Classification: Retained; **Lowest/Average Salary:**
$90,000/$90,000; **Industry Concentration:** Generalist with a
primary focus in Electronics, High Technology; **Function
Concentration:** Generalist with a primary focus in Engineering,
Finance/Accounting, General Management, Human Resources,
Marketing, Research and Development, Women/Minorities

Bowen, Tad — *Vice President*
Executive Search International
60 Walnut Street
Wellesley, MA 02181
Telephone: (617) 239-0303
Recruiter Classification: Retained; **Lowest/Average Salary:**
$75,000/$90,000; **Industry Concentration:** Generalist with a
primary focus in High Technology; **Function Concentration:**
Generalist with a primary focus in General Management

Boyd, Lew — *President*
Coastal International Inc.
28 Green Street
Newbury, MA 01951
Telephone: (508) 462-2436
Recruiter Classification: Retained; **Lowest/Average Salary:**
$75,000/$90,000; **Industry Concentration:** High Technology,
Information Technology; **Function Concentration:**
Finance/Accounting, General Management, Marketing, Sales

Boyle, Russell E. — *Consultant*
Egon Zehnder International Inc.
350 Park Avenue
New York, NY 10022
Telephone: (212) 838-9199
Recruiter Classification: Retained; **Lowest/Average Salary:**
$90,000/$90,000; **Industry Concentration:** Generalist with a
primary focus in High Technology; **Function Concentration:**
Generalist

Brackman, Janet — *Recruiter*
Dahl-Morrow International
12020 Sunrise Valley Drive
Reston, VA 20191
Telephone: (703) 860-6868
Recruiter Classification: Retained; **Lowest/Average Salary:**
$75,000/$90,000; **Industry Concentration:** Electronics, High
Technology, Information Technology; **Function
Concentration:** Generalist with a primary focus in
Engineering, Finance/Accounting, General Management,
Marketing, Sales

Bradley, Dalena — *Researcher*
Woodworth International Group
620 SW 5th Avenue, Suite 1225
Portland, OR 97204
Telephone: (503) 225-5000
Recruiter Classification: Retained; **Lowest/Average Salary:**
$60,000/$90,000; **Industry Concentration:** Generalist with a
primary focus in Electronics, High Technology, Information
Technology; **Function Concentration:** Generalist with a
primary focus in Engineering, Finance/Accounting, General
Management, Human Resources, Marketing, Research and
Development, Sales

Bradshaw, Monte — *Vice President*
Christian & Timbers
25825 Science Park Drive, Suite 400
Cleveland, OH 44122
Telephone: (216) 765-5868
Recruiter Classification: Retained; **Lowest/Average Salary:**
$100,000/$100,000; **Industry Concentration:** Generalist with a
primary focus in Electronics, High Technology, Information
Technology; **Function Concentration:** Generalist with a
primary focus in Engineering, Finance/Accounting, General
Management, Human Resources, Marketing, Research and
Development

Brady, Dick — *Associate*
William Guy & Associates
Telephone: Unpublished
Recruiter Classification: Retained; **Lowest/Average Salary:**
$50,000/$90,000; **Industry Concentration:** Generalist with
a primary focus in Electronics, High Technology,
Information Technology; **Function Concentration:**
Generalist with a primary focus in Administration,
Engineering, Finance/Accounting, General Management,
Human Resources, Research and Development,
Women/Minorities

Brady, Robert — *Executive Recruiter*
CPS Inc.
One Westbrook Corporate Centre, Suite 600
Westchester, IL 60154
Telephone: (708) 531-8370
Recruiter Classification: Contingency; **Lowest/Average
Salary:** $30,000/$50,000; **Industry Concentration:** Generalist
with a primary focus in Electronics, High Technology,
Information Technology; **Function Concentration:**
Engineering, Research and Development, Sales,
Women/Minorities

Brandeis, Richard — *Executive Recruiter*
CPS Inc.
One Westbrook Corporate Centre, Suite 600
Westchester, IL 60154
Telephone: (708) 531-8370
Recruiter Classification: Contingency; **Lowest/Average Salary:**
$30,000/$50,000; **Industry Concentration:** Generalist with a
primary focus in Electronics, High Technology, Information
Technology; **Function Concentration:** Engineering, Research
and Development, Sales, Women/Minorities

Brandenburg, David — *Staffing Consultant*
Professional Staffing Consultants
1331 Lamar, Suite 1459
Houston, TX 77010
Telephone: (713) 659-8383
Recruiter Classification: Retained; **Lowest/Average Salary:**
$50,000/$75,000; **Industry Concentration:** Generalist with a
primary focus in Information Technology; **Function
Concentration:** Generalist with a primary focus in Engineering,
Finance/Accounting, General Management, Human Resources

Brassard, Gary — *Associate*
Source Services Corporation
111 Monument Circle, Suite 3930
Indianapolis, IN 46204
Telephone: (317) 631-2900
Recruiter Classification: Contingency; **Lowest/Average Salary:**
$30,000/$50,000; **Industry Concentration:** Information
Technology; **Function Concentration:** Engineering,
Finance/Accounting

Bratches, Howard — *Senior Partner*
Thorndike Deland Associates
275 Madison Avenue, Suite 1300
New York, NY 10016
Telephone: (212) 661-6200
Recruiter Classification: Retained; **Lowest/Average Salary:**
$100,000/$125,000; **Industry Concentration:** Generalist with a
primary focus in Information Technology; **Function
Concentration:** Generalist with a primary focus in
Finance/Accounting, General Management, Human Resources,
Marketing, Sales

Bremer, Brian — *Associate*
Source Services Corporation
5 Independence Way
Princeton, NJ 08540
Telephone: (609) 452-7277
Recruiter Classification: Contingency; **Lowest/Average Salary:**
$30,000/$50,000; **Industry Concentration:** Information
Technology; **Function Concentration:** Engineering,
Finance/Accounting

Brennen, Richard J. — *Senior Director*
Spencer Stuart
401 North Michigan Avenue, Suite 3400
Chicago, IL 60611-4244
Telephone: (312) 822-0080
Recruiter Classification: Retained; **Lowest/Average Salary:**
$90,000/$90,000; **Industry Concentration:** Generalist with a
primary focus in High Technology, Information Technology;
Function Concentration: General Management, Research and
Development, Sales

Brewster, Edward — *Associate*
Source Services Corporation
9020 Capital of Texas Highway
Building I, Suite 337
Austin, TX 78759
Telephone: (512) 345-7473
Recruiter Classification: Contingency; **Lowest/Average Salary:**
$30,000/$50,000; **Industry Concentration:** Information
Technology; **Function Concentration:** Engineering,
Finance/Accounting

Brieger, Steve — *Principal*
Thorne, Brieger Associates Inc.
11 East 44th Street
New York, NY 10017
Telephone: (212) 682-5424
Recruiter Classification: Retained; **Lowest/Average Salary:**
$90,000/$90,000; **Industry Concentration:** Generalist with a
primary focus in Electronics, High Technology; **Function
Concentration:** Generalist with a primary focus in
Administration, Engineering, Finance/Accounting, General
Management, Human Resources, Marketing, Research and
Development, Sales

Brill, Pamela — *Search Consultant*
C. Berger & Company
327 E. Gundersen Drive
Carol Stream, IL 60188
Telephone: (630) 653-1115
Recruiter Classification: Retained; **Lowest/Average Salary:**
$40,000/$60,000; **Industry Concentration:** Information
Technology; **Function Concentration:** Administration

Brindise, Michael J. — *President*
Dynamic Search Systems, Inc.
3800 North Wilke Road, Suite 485
Arlington Heights, IL 60004
Telephone: (847) 259-3444
Recruiter Classification: Contingency; **Lowest/Average Salary:**
$30,000/$60,000; **Industry Concentration:** Generalist with a
primary focus in High Technology, Information Technology

Britt, Stephen — *Recruiter*
Keith Bagg & Associates Inc.
85 Richmond St., W., Ste. 700
Toronto, Ontario, CANADA M5H 2C9
Telephone: (416) 863-1800
Recruiter Classification: Contingency; **Lowest/Average Salary:**
$40,000/$60,000; **Industry Concentration:** Generalist with a
primary focus in Electronics, High Technology; **Function
Concentration:** Engineering, Research and Development

Brkovich, Deanna — *Software Engineering
Recruiter*
Corporate Recruiters Ltd.
490-1140 West Pender Street
Vancouver, British Columbia, CANADA V6E 4G1
Telephone: (604) 687-5993
Recruiter Classification: Contingency; **Lowest/Average Salary:**
$40,000/$60,000; **Industry Concentration:** High Technology;
Function Concentration: Engineering

Broadhurst, Austin — *Partner*
Lamalie Amrop International
Metro Center, One Station Place
Stamford, CT 06902-6800
Telephone: (203) 324-4445
Recruiter Classification: Retained; **Lowest/Average Salary:**
$90,000/$90,000; **Industry Concentration:** Generalist with a
primary focus in High Technology; **Function Concentration:**
Generalist

Brocaglia, Joyce — *Vice President*
Alta Associates, Inc.
8 Bartles Corner Road, Suite 021
Flemington, NJ 08822
Telephone: (908) 806-8442
Recruiter Classification: Retained; **Lowest/Average Salary:**
$50,000/$90,000; **Industry Concentration:** Generalist
with a primary focus in High Technology, Information
Technology; **Function Concentration:**
Finance/Accounting

Bronger, Patricia — *Associate*
Source Services Corporation
500 108th Avenue NE, Suite 1780
Bellevue, WA 98004
Telephone: (206) 454-6400
Recruiter Classification: Contingency; **Lowest/Average Salary:**
$30,000/$50,000; **Industry Concentration:** Information
Technology; **Function Concentration:** Engineering,
Finance/Accounting

Brooks, Bernard E. — *Partner*
Mruk & Partners/EMA Partners Int'l
675 Third Avenue, Suite 1805
New York, NY 10017
Telephone: (212) 983-7676
Recruiter Classification: Retained; **Lowest/Average Salary:**
$75,000/$90,000; **Industry Concentration:** Information
Technology; **Function Concentration:** Generalist with a
primary focus in Administration, Finance/Accounting, General
Management, Sales, Women/Minorities

Brooks, Charles — *Recruiter*
Corporate Recruiters Ltd.
490-1140 West Pender Street
Vancouver, British Columbia, CANADA V6E 4G1
Telephone: (604) 687-5993
Recruiter Classification: Contingency; **Lowest/Average
Salary:** $50,000/$60,000; **Industry Concentration:**
Electronics, High Technology; **Function Concentration:**
Engineering

Brooks, Kimberllay — *Recruiter*
Corporate Recruiters Ltd.
490-1140 West Pender Street
Vancouver, British Columbia, CANADA V6E 4G1
Telephone: (604) 687-5993
Recruiter Classification: Contingency; **Lowest/Average Salary:**
$50,000/$60,000; **Industry Concentration:** Electronics, High
Technology; **Function Concentration:** Engineering

Brophy, Melissa — *President*
Maximum Management Corp.
420 Lexington Avenue
Suite 2016
New York, NY 10170
Telephone: (212) 867-4646
Recruiter Classification: Contingency, Executive Temporary;
Lowest/Average Salary: $30,000/$75,000; **Industry
Concentration:** Generalist with a primary focus in Information
Technology; **Function Concentration:** Human Resources

Brother, Joy — *Vice President*
Charles Luntz & Associates. Inc.
14323 South Outer 40 Drive
Suite 400 South
Chesterfield, MO 63017-5734
Telephone: (314) 275-7992
Recruiter Classification: Retained; **Lowest/Average Salary:**
$40,000/$75,000; **Industry Concentration:** Electronics, High
Technology, Information Technology; **Function Concentration:**
Generalist with a primary focus in Administration, Engineering,
Finance/Accounting, General Management, Human Resources,
Marketing, Sales

Brovender, Claire — *Software Engineering
Recruiter*
Winter, Wyman & Company
950 Winter Street, Suite 3100
Waltham, MA 02154-1294
Telephone: (617) 890-7000
Recruiter Classification: Contingency; **Lowest/Average
Salary:** $40,000/$75,000; **Industry Concentration:** High
Technology, Information Technology; **Function
Concentration:** Engineering

Brown, Buzz — *President*
Brown, Bernardy, Van Remmen, Inc.
12100 Wilshire Boulevard, Suite M-40
Los Angeles, CA 90025
Telephone: (310) 826-5777
Recruiter Classification: Contingency; **Lowest/Average Salary:**
$30,000/$75,000; **Industry Concentration:** Electronics, High
Technology; **Function Concentration:** Marketing

Brown, Charlene N. — *President*
Accent on Achievement, Inc.
3190 Rochester Road, Suite 104
Troy, MI 48083
Telephone: (248) 528-1390
Recruiter Classification: Contingency, Executive Temporary;
Lowest/Average Salary: $30,000/$60,000; **Industry
Concentration:** Generalist with a primary focus in High
Technology, Information Technology; **Function Concentration:**
Finance/Accounting

Brown, Clifford — *Associate*
Source Services Corporation
111 Founders Plaza, Suite 1501E
Hartford, CT 06108
Telephone: (860) 528-0300
Recruiter Classification: Contingency; **Lowest/Average Salary:**
$30,000/$50,000; **Industry Concentration:** Information
Technology; **Function Concentration:** Engineering,
Finance/Accounting

Brown, D. Perry — *Partner*
Don Richard Associates of Washington, D.C., Inc.
5 Choke Cherry Road, Suite 378
Rockville, MD 20850
Telephone: (301) 590-9800
Recruiter Classification: Contingency, Executive Temporary;
Lowest/Average Salary: $30,000/$60,000; **Industry
Concentration:** High Technology; **Function Concentration:**
Finance/Accounting

Brown, Daniel — *Associate*
Source Services Corporation
500 108th Avenue NE, Suite 1780
Bellevue, WA 98004
Telephone: (206) 454-6400
Recruiter Classification: Contingency; **Lowest/Average Salary:**
$30,000/$50,000; **Industry Concentration:** Information
Technology; **Function Concentration:** Engineering,
Finance/Accounting

Brown, Dennis — *President*
D. Brown and Associates, Inc.
610 S.W. Alder, Suite 1111
Portland, OR 97205
Telephone: (503) 224-6860
Recruiter Classification: Contingency; **Lowest/Average Salary:**
$40,000/$60,000; **Industry Concentration:** Electronics, High
Technology, Information Technology; **Function Concentration:**
Engineering, Finance/Accounting

Brown, Gina — *Partner*
Strategic Alliance Network, Ltd.
10901 Reed Hartman Highway
Suite 217
Cincinnati, OH 45242
Telephone: (513) 792-2800
Recruiter Classification: Retained, Contingency;
Lowest/Average Salary: $30,000/$90,000; **Industry
Concentration:** High Technology, Information Technology;
Function Concentration: Finance/Accounting, Marketing, Sales

Brown, Kevin P. — *Principal*
Raymond Karsan Associates
170 So. Warner Road
Wayne, PA 19087
Telephone: (610) 971-9171
Recruiter Classification: Retained; **Lowest/Average Salary:**
$30,000/$90,000; **Industry Concentration:** Generalist with a
primary focus in Information Technology; **Function
Concentration:** Generalist

Brown, Larry C. — *Managing Director*
Horton International
10 Tower Lane
Avon, CT 06001
Telephone: (860) 674-8701
Recruiter Classification: Retained; **Lowest/Average Salary:**
$90,000/$90,000; **Industry Concentration:** Generalist with a
primary focus in Electronics, High Technology, Information
Technology; **Function Concentration:** Generalist with a
primary focus in Administration, Finance/Accounting, General
Management, Human Resources, Marketing, Sales,
Women/Minorities

Brown, S. Ross — *Managing Partner*
Egon Zehnder International Inc.
100 Spear Street, Suite 920
San Francisco, CA 94105
Telephone: (415) 904-7800
Recruiter Classification: Retained; **Lowest/Average Salary:**
$90,000/$90,000; **Industry Concentration:** Generalist with a
primary focus in High Technology; **Function Concentration:**
Generalist

Brown, Steffan — *Researcher*
Woodworth International Group
620 SW 5th Avenue, Suite 1225
Portland, OR 97204
Telephone: (503) 225-5000
Recruiter Classification: Retained; **Lowest/Average Salary:**
$60,000/$90,000; **Industry Concentration:** Generalist with a
primary focus in Electronics, High Technology, Information
Technology; **Function Concentration:** Generalist with a
primary focus in Engineering, Finance/Accounting, General
Management, Human Resources, Marketing, Research and
Development, Sales

Brown, Steven — *Associate*
Source Services Corporation
5429 LBJ Freeway, Suite 275
Dallas, TX 75240
Telephone: (214) 387-1600
Recruiter Classification: Contingency; **Lowest/Average Salary:**
$30,000/$50,000; **Industry Concentration:** Information
Technology; **Function Concentration:** Engineering,
Finance/Accounting

Browne, Michael — *Associate*
Source Services Corporation
20 Burlington Mall Road, Suite 405
Burlington, MA 01803
Telephone: (617) 272-5000
Recruiter Classification: Contingency; **Lowest/Average Salary:**
$30,000/$50,000; **Industry Concentration:** Information
Technology; **Function Concentration:** Engineering,
Finance/Accounting

Bruce, Michael C. — *Director*
Spencer Stuart
10900 Wilshire Boulevard, Suite 800
Los Angeles, CA 90024-6524
Telephone: (310) 209-0610
Recruiter Classification: Retained; **Lowest/Average Salary:**
$90,000/$90,000; **Industry Concentration:** High Technology,
Information Technology; **Function Concentration:** Generalist

Brudno, Robert J. — *Managing Director*
Savoy Partners, Ltd.
1620 L Street N.W., Suite 801
Washington, DC 20036
Telephone: (202) 887-0666
Recruiter Classification: Retained; **Lowest/Average Salary:**
$90,000/$90,000; **Industry Concentration:** Generalist with a
primary focus in Electronics, High Technology, Information
Technology; **Function Concentration:** Generalist with a
primary focus in Administration, Engineering,
Finance/Accounting, General Management, Human Resources,
Marketing, Sales, Women/Minorities

Brunner, Terry — *Associate*
Source Services Corporation
2000 Town Center, Suite 850
Southfield, MI 48075
Telephone: (810) 352-6520
Recruiter Classification: Contingency; **Lowest/Average Salary:**
$30,000/$50,000; **Industry Concentration:** Information
Technology; **Function Concentration:** Engineering,
Finance/Accounting

Bruno, Deborah F. — *Vice President*
The Hindman Company
Browenton Place, Suite 110
2000 Warrington Way
Louisville, KY 40222
Telephone: (502) 426-4040
Recruiter Classification: Retained; **Lowest/Average Salary:**
$50,000/$90,000; **Industry Concentration:** Generalist with a
primary focus in Electronics, High Technology; **Function
Concentration:** Generalist with a primary focus in Engineering,
Finance/Accounting, General Management, Human Resources,
Marketing, Sales, Women/Minorities

Brunson, Therese — *Principal*
Kors Montgomery International
1980 Post Oak Boulevard, Suite 2280
Houston, TX 77056
Telephone: (713) 840-7101
Recruiter Classification: Retained; **Lowest/Average Salary:**
$90,000/$90,000; **Industry Concentration:** High Technology,
Information Technology; **Function Concentration:** Engineering,
General Management, Marketing, Research and Development,
Sales

Bryant, Henry — *Consultant Accounting and
Finance*
D. Brown and Associates, Inc.
610 S.W. Alder, Suite 1111
Portland, OR 97205
Telephone: (503) 224-6860
Recruiter Classification: Contingency; **Lowest/Average Salary:**
$40,000/$60,000; **Industry Concentration:** Electronics, High
Technology, Information Technology; **Function Concentration:**
Engineering, Finance/Accounting

Bryant, Laura — *Senior Consultant*
Paul-Tittle Associates, Inc.
1485 Chain Bridge Road, #304
McLean, VA 22101
Telephone: (703) 442-0500
Recruiter Classification: Retained; **Lowest/Average Salary:**
$60,000/$75,000; **Industry Concentration:** Information
Technology; **Function Concentration:** Engineering

Bryant, Richard D. — *President*
Bryant Associates, Inc.
1390 The Point
Barrington, IL 60010
Telephone: (847) 382-0795
Recruiter Classification: Contingency; **Lowest/Average Salary:**
$30,000/$60,000; **Industry Concentration:** Generalist with a
primary focus in Electronics, High Technology, Information
Technology; **Function Concentration:** Generalist with a
primary focus in Engineering, Finance/Accounting, Human
Resources, Marketing, Research and Development, Sales

Bryant, Shari G. — *Consultant*
Bryant Associates, Inc.
1390 The Point
Barrington, IL 60010
Telephone: (847) 382-0795
Recruiter Classification: Contingency; **Lowest/Average Salary:**
$30,000/$60,000; **Industry Concentration:** Generalist with a
primary focus in Electronics, High Technology; **Function
Concentration:** Generalist with a primary focus in Engineering,
Finance/Accounting, General Management, Marketing,
Research and Development, Sales

Bryza, Robert M. — *Chairman and President*
Robert Lowell International
12200 Park Central Drive, Suite 120
Dallas, TX 75251
Telephone: (214) 233-2270
Recruiter Classification: Retained; **Lowest/Average Salary:**
$50,000/$60,000; **Industry Concentration:** Generalist with a
primary focus in Electronics, High Technology, Information
Technology; **Function Concentration:** Generalist with a
primary focus in Administration, Engineering,
Finance/Accounting, General Management, Human Resources,
Marketing, Research and Development, Sales,
Women/Minorities

Brzezinski, Ronald T. — *Associate*
Callan Associates, Ltd.
2021 Spring Road, Suite 175
Oak Brook, IL 60521
Telephone: (708) 832-7080
Recruiter Classification: Retained; **Lowest/Average Salary:**
$90,000/$90,000; **Industry Concentration:** Generalist with
a primary focus in Electronics, High Technology,
Information Technology; **Function Concentration:**
Generalist with a primary focus in Engineering,
Finance/Accounting, General Management, Human
Resources, Marketing, Research and Development, Sales,
Women/Minorities

Buckles, Donna — *Recruiter*
Cochran, Cochran & Yale, Inc.
955 East Henrietta Road
Rochester, NY 14623
Telephone: (716) 424-6060
Recruiter Classification: Retained; **Lowest/Average Salary:**
$50,000/$75,000; **Industry Concentration:** Generalist with a
primary focus in High Technology, Information Technology;
Function Concentration: Generalist with a primary focus in
Engineering, Finance/Accounting, General Management,
Human Resources, Sales, Women/Minorities

Budill, Edward — *Contract Recruiter*
Professional Search Consultants
3050 Post Oak Boulevard, Suite 1615
Houston, TX 77056
Telephone: (713) 960-9215
Recruiter Classification: Executive Temporary; **Lowest/Average
Salary:** $75,000/$75,000; **Industry Concentration:** Information
Technology; **Function Concentration:** Engineering, General
Management, Marketing, Sales

Bueschel, David A. — *Principal*
Shepherd Bueschel & Provus, Inc.
401 North Michigan Avenue, Suite 3020
Chicago, IL 60611-5555
Telephone: (312) 832-3020
Recruiter Classification: Retained; **Lowest/Average Salary:**
$150,000/$225,000; **Industry Concentration:** Generalist
with a primary focus in Electronics, High Technology,
Information Technology; **Function Concentration:** Generalist
with a primary focus in General Management, Marketing,
Sales

Buggy, Linda — *Senior Associate Recruiting*
Bonnell Associates Ltd.
2960 Post Road, Suite 200
Southport, CT 06490
Telephone: (203) 319-7214
Lowest/Average Salary: $90,000/$90,000; **Industry
Concentration:** Generalist with a primary focus in
Information Technology; **Function Concentration:**
Generalist with a primary focus in Finance/Accounting,
General Management, Human Resources, Sales,
Women/Minorities

Bullock, Conni — *Director Research*
Earley Kielty and Associates, Inc.
Two Pennsylvania Plaza
New York, NY 10121
Telephone: (212) 736-5626
Recruiter Classification: Retained; **Lowest/Average Salary:**
$90,000/$90,000; **Industry Concentration:** Generalist with a
primary focus in Information Technology; **Function
Concentration:** Generalist with a primary focus in
Administration, Finance/Accounting, General Management,
Human Resources, Marketing, Research and Development,
Sales, Women/Minorities

Burch, Donald — *Associate*
Source Services Corporation
925 Westchester Avenue, Suite 309
White Plains, NY 10604
Telephone: (914) 428-9100
Recruiter Classification: Contingency; **Lowest/Average Salary:**
$30,000/$50,000; **Industry Concentration:** Information
Technology; **Function Concentration:** Engineering,
Finance/Accounting

Burch, R. Stuart — *Executive Director*
Russell Reynolds Associates, Inc.
1700 Pennsylvania Avenue N.W.
Suite 850
Washington, DC 20006-4709
Telephone: (202) 628-2150
Recruiter Classification: Retained; **Lowest/Average Salary:**
$90,000/$90,000; **Industry Concentration:** Generalist with a
primary focus in High Technology; **Function Concentration:**
Generalist

Burchill, Greg — *Principal*
BGB Associates
P.O. Box 556
Itasca, IL 60143
Telephone: (630) 250-8993
Recruiter Classification: Contingency; **Lowest/Average Salary:**
$30,000/$75,000; **Industry Concentration:** Generalist with a
primary focus in Electronics, High Technology, Information
Technology; **Function Concentration:** Generalist with a
primary focus in Engineering, Finance/Accounting, General
Management, Human Resources, Marketing, Sales,
Women/Minorities

Burden, Gene — *Senior Vice President, Northwest*
The Cherbonnier Group, Inc.
1520 140th Avenue, N.E.
Suite 100
Bellevue, WA 67389
Telephone: (425) 644-9435
Recruiter Classification: Retained; **Lowest/Average Salary:**
$75,000/$90,000; **Industry Concentration:** Generalist with a
primary focus in Electronics, High Technology, Information
Technology; **Function Concentration:** Generalist with a
primary focus in Administration, Engineering,
Finance/Accounting, General Management, Marketing,
Research and Development, Sales

Burfield, Elaine — *Senior Vice President*
Skott/Edwards Consultants, Inc.
1776 On the Green
Morristown, NJ 07006
Telephone: (973) 644-0900
Recruiter Classification: Retained; **Lowest/Average Salary:**
$90,000/$90,000; **Industry Concentration:** Information
Technology; **Function Concentration:** Finance/Accounting,
General Management, Marketing, Research and Development,
Sales

Burke, John — *President*
The Experts
200 Reservoir Street
Needham, MA 02194
Telephone: (617) 449-6700
Recruiter Classification: Executive Temporary; **Lowest/Average
Salary:** $50,000/$90,000; **Industry Concentration:** Generalist
with a primary focus in High Technology, Information
Technology; **Function Concentration:** Generalist with a
primary focus in Administration, Engineering,
Finance/Accounting, General Management, Human Resources,
Marketing, Research and Development, Sales

Burke, Karen A. — *Principal*
Mazza & Riley, Inc. (a Korn/Ferry International
affiliate)
55 William Street, Suite 120
Wellesley, MA 02181-4000
Telephone: (617) 235-7724
Recruiter Classification: Retained; **Lowest/Average Salary:**
$90,000/$90,000; **Industry Concentration:** Generalist with a
primary focus in High Technology, Information Technology;
Function Concentration: Generalist with a primary focus in
Finance/Accounting, General Management, Marketing, Sales

Burkhill, John — *President*
The Talley Group
P.O. Box 2918
Stanton, VA 24402
Telephone: (540) 248-7009
Recruiter Classification: Retained; **Lowest/Average Salary:**
$30,000/$60,000; **Industry Concentration:** Generalist with a
primary focus in Electronics, Information Technology; **Function
Concentration:** Generalist with a primary focus in Engineering,
Finance/Accounting, Human Resources, Marketing, Sales

Burmaster, Holly — *Software Quality Assurance
Recruiter*
Winter, Wyman & Company
950 Winter Street, Suite 3100
Waltham, MA 02154-1294
Telephone: (617) 890-7000
Recruiter Classification: Contingency; **Lowest/Average Salary:**
$40,000/$75,000; **Industry Concentration:** Information
Technology; **Function Concentration:** Generalist

Burns, Alan — *Partner*
The Enns Partners Inc.
70 University Avenue, Suite 410, P.O. Box 14
Toronto, Ontario, CANADA M5J 2M4
Telephone: (416) 598-0012
Recruiter Classification: Retained; **Lowest/Average Salary:**
$75,000/$90,000; **Industry Concentration:** Generalist with a
primary focus in Electronics, High Technology; **Function
Concentration:** Generalist with a primary focus in
Administration, Finance/Accounting, General Management,
Human Resources, Marketing, Sales

Busch, Jack — *President*
Busch International
One First Street, Suite One
Los Altos, CA 94022-2754
Telephone: (650) 949-1115
Recruiter Classification: Retained; **Lowest/Average Salary:**
$90,000/$90,000; **Industry Concentration:** Electronics, High
Technology, Information Technology; **Function Concentration:**
Generalist with a primary focus in Engineering,
Finance/Accounting, General Management, Marketing,
Research and Development, Sales

Busterna, Charles — *Vice President*
The KPA Group
150 Broadway, Suite 1802
New York, NY 10038
Telephone: (212) 964-3640
Recruiter Classification: Contingency; **Lowest/Average Salary:**
$20,000/$40,000; **Industry Concentration:** High Technology,
Information Technology; **Function Concentration:**
Administration, Finance/Accounting, Human Resources,
Marketing

Butcher, Pascale — *Executive Recruiter*
F-O-R-T-U-N-E Personnel Consultants of Manatee
County
923 4th Street West
Palmetto, FL 34221
Telephone: (941) 729-3674
Recruiter Classification: Contingency; **Lowest/Average Salary:**
$30,000/$50,000; **Industry Concentration:** Electronics, High
Technology; **Function Concentration:** Finance/Accounting

Button, David R. — *Principal*
The Button Group
1608 Emory Circle
Plano, TX 75093
Telephone: (972) 985-0619
Recruiter Classification: Retained, Contingency;
Lowest/Average Salary: $60,000/$90,000; **Industry Concentration:** Generalist with a primary focus in High Technology, Information Technology; **Function Concentration:** Generalist with a primary focus in Engineering, General Management, Marketing, Research and Development, Sales

Buttrey, Daniel — *Managing Director*
Source Services Corporation
100 North Tryon Street, Suite 3130
Charlotte, NC 28202
Telephone: (704) 333-8311
Recruiter Classification: Contingency; **Lowest/Average Salary:** $30,000/$50,000; **Industry Concentration:** Information Technology; **Function Concentration:** Engineering, Finance/Accounting

Buzolits, Patrick — *Associate*
Source Services Corporation
2000 Town Center, Suite 850
Southfield, MI 48075
Telephone: (810) 352-6520
Recruiter Classification: Contingency; **Lowest/Average Salary:** $30,000/$50,000; **Industry Concentration:** Information Technology; **Function Concentration:** Engineering, Finance/Accounting

Bye, Randy — *Managing Partner*
Romac & Associates
3200 Beechleaf Court
Suite 409
Raleigh, NC 27625
Telephone: (919) 878-4454
Recruiter Classification: Executive Temporary; **Lowest/Average Salary:** $60,000/$60,000; **Industry Concentration:** High Technology, Information Technology; **Function Concentration:** Finance/Accounting

Cafero, Les — *Associate*
Source Services Corporation
425 California Street, Suite 1200
San Francisco, CA 94104
Telephone: (415) 434-2410
Recruiter Classification: Contingency; **Lowest/Average Salary:** $30,000/$50,000; **Industry Concentration:** Information Technology; **Function Concentration:** Engineering, Finance/Accounting

Cahill, Peter M. — *President*
Peter M. Cahill Associates, Inc.
P.O. Box 401, 100 Main Street
Southington, CT 06489
Telephone: (203) 628-3963
Recruiter Classification: Contingency; **Lowest/Average Salary:** $60,000/$50,000; **Industry Concentration:** Generalist with a primary focus in Electronics, High Technology; **Function Concentration:** Generalist with a primary focus in Engineering, General Management, Human Resources, Marketing, Research and Development, Sales

Calivas, Kay — *Professional Recruiter*
A.J. Burton Group, Inc.
120 East Baltimore Street, Suite 2220
Baltimore, MD 21202
Telephone: (410) 752-5244
Recruiter Classification: Contingency; **Lowest/Average Salary:** $40,000/$75,000; **Industry Concentration:** Generalist with a primary focus in High Technology, Information Technology; **Function Concentration:** Generalist with a primary focus in Administration, Finance/Accounting, General Management, Human Resources

Call, David — *Manager*
Cochran, Cochran & Yale, Inc.
955 East Henrietta Road
Rochester, NY 14623
Telephone: (716) 424-6060
Recruiter Classification: Retained; **Lowest/Average Salary:** $50,000/$75,000; **Industry Concentration:** Generalist with a primary focus in High Technology, Information Technology; **Function Concentration:** Generalist with a primary focus in Engineering, Finance/Accounting, General Management, Human Resources, Marketing, Sales, Women/Minorities

Callan, Robert M. — *Partner*
Callan Associates, Ltd.
2021 Spring Road, Suite 175
Oak Brook, IL 60521
Telephone: (708) 832-7080
Recruiter Classification: Retained; **Lowest/Average Salary:** $90,000/$90,000; **Industry Concentration:** Generalist with a primary focus in Electronics, High Technology, Information Technology; **Function Concentration:** Generalist with a primary focus in Administration, Engineering, Finance/Accounting, General Management, Human Resources, Marketing, Research and Development, Sales, Women/Minorities

Calogeras, Chris — *Consultant*
The Sager Company
1619 Brookpark Road
Cleveland, OH 44109-5816
Telephone: (216) 459-1300
Recruiter Classification: Retained; **Lowest/Average Salary:** $75,000/$90,000; **Industry Concentration:** Generalist with a primary focus in Electronics, High Technology; **Function Concentration:** Generalist with a primary focus in Engineering, Finance/Accounting, General Management, Human Resources, Marketing, Research and Development, Sales

Cameron, James W. — *President*
Cameron Consulting
1112 Austin Avenue
Pacific Grove, CA 93950
Telephone: (408) 646-8415
Recruiter Classification: Retained; **Lowest/Average Salary:** $60,000/$90,000; **Industry Concentration:** Generalist with a primary focus in Electronics, Information Technology; **Function Concentration:** Generalist with a primary focus in Engineering, Finance/Accounting, General Management, Human Resources, Marketing, Research and Development, Sales

Campbell, E. — *Associate*
Source Services Corporation
120 East Baltimore Street, Suite 1950
Baltimore, MD 21202
Telephone: (410) 727-4050
Recruiter Classification: Contingency; **Lowest/Average Salary:**
$30,000/$50,000; **Industry Concentration:** Information
Technology; **Function Concentration:** Engineering,
Finance/Accounting

Campbell, Gary — *Branch Manager*
Romac & Associates
Three Ravinia Drive
Suite 1460
Atlanta, GA 30346
Telephone: (404) 604-3880
Recruiter Classification: Executive Temporary; **Lowest/Average
Salary:** $60,000/$60,000; **Industry Concentration:** High
Technology, Information Technology; **Function Concentration:**
Finance/Accounting

Campbell, Jeff — *Associate*
Source Services Corporation
425 California Street, Suite 1200
San Francisco, CA 94104
Telephone: (415) 434-2410
Recruiter Classification: Contingency; **Lowest/Average Salary:**
$30,000/$50,000; **Industry Concentration:** Information
Technology; **Function Concentration:** Engineering,
Finance/Accounting

Campbell, Patricia A. — *Managing Director*
The Onstott Group, Inc.
60 William Street
Wellesley, MA 02181
Telephone: (781) 235-3050
Recruiter Classification: Retained; **Lowest/Average Salary:**
$90,000/$90,000; **Industry Concentration:** Generalist with a
primary focus in High Technology, Information Technology;
Function Concentration: Generalist with a primary focus in
General Management, Human Resources, Marketing, Sales,
Women/Minorities

Campbell, Robert Scott — *Principal*
Wellington Management Group
5201 Great America Parkway
Suite 320
Santa Clara, CA 95054
Telephone: Unpublished
Recruiter Classification: Retained; **Lowest/Average Salary:**
$90,000/$90,000; **Industry Concentration:** Generalist with a
primary focus in High Technology, Information Technology;
Function Concentration: Generalist with a primary focus in
Finance/Accounting, General Management, Marketing, Sales

Campbell, Robert Scott — *Principal*
Wellington Management Group
1601 Market Street, Suite 2902
Philadelphia, PA 19103-2499
Telephone: (215) 569-8900
Recruiter Classification: Retained; **Lowest/Average Salary:**
$90,000/$90,000; **Industry Concentration:** Generalist with a
primary focus in High Technology, Information Technology;
Function Concentration: Generalist with a primary focus in
Finance/Accounting, General Management, Marketing, Sales

Campbell, W. Ross — *Consultant*
Egon Zehnder International Inc.
1 First Canadian Place
P.O. Box 179
Toronto, Ontario, CANADA M5X 1C7
Telephone: (416) 364-0222
Recruiter Classification: Retained; **Lowest/Average Salary:**
$90,000/$90,000; **Industry Concentration:** Generalist with a
primary focus in High Technology; **Function Concentration:**
Generalist

Cannavino, Matthew J. — *Associate*
Financial Resource Associates, Inc.
105 West Orange Street
Altamonte Springs, FL 32714
Telephone: (407) 869-7000
Recruiter Classification: Contingency; **Lowest/Average Salary:**
$40,000/$60,000; **Industry Concentration:** Information
Technology; **Function Concentration:** Finance/Accounting,
Sales

Capizzi, Karen — *Search Consultant*
Cochran, Cochran & Yale, Inc.
955 East Henrietta Road
Rochester, NY 14623
Telephone: (716) 424-6060
Recruiter Classification: Retained; **Lowest/Average Salary:**
$50,000/$75,000; **Industry Concentration:** Generalist with a
primary focus in High Technology, Information Technology;
Function Concentration: Generalist with a primary focus in
Engineering, Finance/Accounting, General Management,
Human Resources, Marketing, Sales, Women/Minorities

Cappe, Richard R. — *President*
Roberts Ryan and Bentley
1107 Kenilworth Drive, Suite 208
Towson, MD 21204
Telephone: (410) 321-6600
Recruiter Classification: Retained; **Lowest/Average Salary:**
$90,000/$90,000; **Industry Concentration:** Information
Technology; **Function Concentration:** Administration, General
Management

Capra, Jamie — *Partner*
Warren, Morris & Madison
132 Chapel Street
Portsmouth, NH 03801
Telephone: (603) 431-7929
Recruiter Classification: Retained; **Lowest/Average Salary:**
$75,000/$90,000; **Industry Concentration:** High Technology;
Function Concentration: Generalist

Carideo, Joseph — *Partner*
Thorndike Deland Associates
275 Madison Avenue, Suite 1300
New York, NY 10016
Telephone: (212) 661-6200
Recruiter Classification: Retained; **Lowest/Average Salary:**
$100,000/$125,000; **Industry Concentration:** Generalist with a
primary focus in Information Technology; **Function
Concentration:** Generalist with a primary focus in
Finance/Accounting, General Management, Human Resources,
Marketing, Sales

Carlson, Eric — *Associate*
Source Services Corporation
500 108th Avenue NE, Suite 1780
Bellevue, WA 98004
Telephone: (206) 454-6400
Recruiter Classification: Contingency; **Lowest/Average Salary:**
$30,000/$50,000; **Industry Concentration:** Information
Technology; **Function Concentration:** Engineering,
Finance/Accounting

Carlton, Patricia — *Senior Associate*
JDG Associates, Ltd.
1700 Research Boulevard
Rockville, MD 20850
Telephone: (301) 340-2210
Recruiter Classification: Contingency; **Lowest/Average Salary:**
$50,000/$90,000; **Industry Concentration:** High Technology,
Information Technology; **Function Concentration:** Engineering,
Finance/Accounting, Research and Development

Carnal, Rick — *Associate*
Source Services Corporation
3 Summit Park Drive, Suite 550
Independence, OH 44131
Telephone: (216) 328-5900
Recruiter Classification: Contingency; **Lowest/Average Salary:**
$30,000/$50,000; **Industry Concentration:** Information
Technology; **Function Concentration:** Engineering,
Finance/Accounting

Carrington, Timothy — *Principal*
Korn/Ferry International
303 Peachtree Street N.E.
Suite 1600
Atlanta, GA 30308
Telephone: (404) 577-7542
Recruiter Classification: Retained; **Lowest/Average Salary:**
$100,000/$150,000; **Industry Concentration:** Generalist with a
primary focus in Information Technology; **Function
Concentration:** Generalist

Carro, Carl R. — *Managing Director*
Executive Search Consultants International, Inc.
330 Fifth Avenue
Suite 5501
New York, NY 10118
Telephone: (212) 333-1900
Recruiter Classification: Retained; **Lowest/Average Salary:**
$90,000/$90,000; **Industry Concentration:** Generalist with a
primary focus in High Technology, Information Technology;
Function Concentration: Generalist with a primary focus in
Finance/Accounting, General Management, Human Resources,
Marketing

Carrott, Gregory T. — *Managing Partner*
Egon Zehnder International Inc.
1 First Canadian Place
P.O. Box 179
Toronto, Ontario, CANADA M5X 1C7
Telephone: (416) 364-0222
Recruiter Classification: Retained; **Lowest/Average Salary:**
$90,000/$90,000; **Industry Concentration:** Generalist with a
primary focus in High Technology; **Function Concentration:**
Generalist

Carter, I. Wayne — *Partner*
Heidrick & Struggles, Inc.
300 South Grand Avenue, Suite 2400
Los Angeles, CA 90071
Telephone: (213) 625-8811
Recruiter Classification: Retained; **Lowest/Average Salary:**
$75,000/$90,000; **Industry Concentration:** Generalist with a
primary focus in High Technology; **Function Concentration:**
Generalist

Carter, Jon F. — *Consultant*
Egon Zehnder International Inc.
100 Spear Street, Suite 920
San Francisco, CA 94105
Telephone: (415) 904-7800
Recruiter Classification: Retained; **Lowest/Average Salary:**
$90,000/$90,000; **Industry Concentration:** Generalist with a
primary focus in High Technology; **Function Concentration:**
Generalist

Carter, Linda — *Associate*
Source Services Corporation
5429 LBJ Freeway, Suite 275
Dallas, TX 75240
Telephone: (214) 387-1600
Recruiter Classification: Contingency; **Lowest/Average Salary:**
$30,000/$50,000; **Industry Concentration:** Information
Technology; **Function Concentration:** Engineering,
Finance/Accounting

Caruthers, Robert D. — *Associate*
James Mead & Company
164 Kings Highway North
Westport, CT 06880
Telephone: (203) 454-5544
Recruiter Classification: Retained; **Lowest/Average Salary:**
$90,000/$90,000; **Industry Concentration:** Electronics;
Function Concentration: General Management, Marketing,
Sales

Carvalho-Esteves, Maria — *Associate*
Source Services Corporation
379 Thornall Street
Edison, NJ 08837
Telephone: (908) 494-2800
Recruiter Classification: Contingency; **Lowest/Average Salary:**
$30,000/$50,000; **Industry Concentration:** Information
Technology; **Function Concentration:** Engineering,
Finance/Accounting

Cary, Con — *President*
Cary & Associates
P.O. Box 2043
Winter Park, FL 32790-2043
Telephone: (407) 647-1145
Recruiter Classification: Retained; **Lowest/Average Salary:**
$30,000/$75,000; **Industry Concentration:** Generalist with a
primary focus in Electronics; **Function Concentration:**
Generalist with a primary focus in Administration, Engineering,
Finance/Accounting, Human Resources, Marketing, Sales

Cashman, Tracy — *Information Technology
Recruiter*
Winter, Wyman & Company
950 Winter Street, Suite 3100
Waltham, MA 02154-1294
Telephone: (617) 890-7000
Recruiter Classification: Contingency; **Lowest/Average Salary:**
$30,000/$60,000; **Industry Concentration:** Information
Technology; **Function Concentration:** Generalist

Cast, Donald — *Recruiter*
Dunhill International Search of New Haven
59 Elm Street
New Haven, CT 06510
Telephone: (203) 562-0511
Recruiter Classification: Contingency; **Lowest/Average Salary:** $30,000/$50,000; **Industry Concentration:** High Technology, Information Technology; **Function Concentration:** Marketing, Sales

Castillo, Eduardo — *Principal*
Korn/Ferry International
Daniel Zambrano 525
Col. Chepe Vera
Monterrey, N.L., MEXICO 11000
Telephone: (528) 348-4355
Recruiter Classification: Retained; **Lowest/Average Salary:** $100,000/$150,000; **Industry Concentration:** Generalist with a primary focus in Information Technology; **Function Concentration:** Generalist

Castle, Lisa — *Associate*
Source Services Corporation
379 Thornall Street
Edison, NJ 08837
Telephone: (908) 494-2800
Recruiter Classification: Contingency; **Lowest/Average Salary:** $30,000/$50,000; **Industry Concentration:** Information Technology; **Function Concentration:** Engineering, Finance/Accounting

Caudill, Nancy — *Vice President*
Bishop Partners
708 Third Avenue
Suite 2200
New York, NY 10017
Telephone: (212) 986-3419
Recruiter Classification: Retained; **Lowest/Average Salary:** $90,000/$90,000; **Industry Concentration:** High Technology, Information Technology; **Function Concentration:** Generalist with a primary focus in Sales

Caudill, Nancy — *Managing Director*
Webb, Johnson Associates, Inc.
280 Park Avenue, 43rd Floor
New York, NY 10017
Telephone: (212) 661-3700
Recruiter Classification: Retained; **Lowest/Average Salary:** $90,000/$90,000; **Industry Concentration:** Generalist with a primary focus in High Technology; **Function Concentration:** Generalist

Cavanagh, Michael J. — *President*
Michael J. Cavanagh and Associates
60 St. Clair Avenue East
Suite 905
Toronto, Ontario, CANADA M4T 1N5
Telephone: (416) 324-9661
Recruiter Classification: Retained; **Lowest/Average Salary:** $80,000/$100,000; **Industry Concentration:** Generalist with a primary focus in Electronics, Information Technology; **Function Concentration:** Generalist with a primary focus in Administration, Engineering, Finance/Accounting, General Management, Human Resources, Marketing

Cavolina, Michael — *Managing Director*
Carver Search Consultants
9303 East Bullard, Suite 1
Clovis, CA 93611-8211
Telephone: (209) 298-7791
Recruiter Classification: Contingency; **Lowest/Average Salary:** $50,000/$75,000; **Industry Concentration:** Generalist with a primary focus in High Technology; **Function Concentration:** Engineering, General Management, Human Resources, Marketing, Research and Development, Sales, Women/Minorities

Celenza, Catherine — *Executive Recruiter*
CPS Inc.
303 Congress Street, 5th Floor
Boston, MA 02210
Telephone: (617) 439-7950
Recruiter Classification: Contingency; **Lowest/Average Salary:** $30,000/$50,000; **Industry Concentration:** Generalist with a primary focus in Electronics, High Technology, Information Technology; **Function Concentration:** Engineering, Research and Development, Sales, Women/Minorities

Cersosimo, Rocco — *Associate*
Source Services Corporation
Foster Plaza VI
681 Anderson Drive, 2nd Floor
Pittsburgh, PA 15220
Telephone: (412) 928-8300
Recruiter Classification: Contingency; **Lowest/Average Salary:** $30,000/$50,000; **Industry Concentration:** Information Technology; **Function Concentration:** Engineering, Finance/Accounting

Cesafsky, Barry R. — *Partner*
Lamalie Amrop International
225 West Wacker Drive
Chicago, IL 60606-1229
Telephone: (312) 782-3113
Recruiter Classification: Retained; **Lowest/Average Salary:** $90,000/$90,000; **Industry Concentration:** Generalist with a primary focus in Information Technology; **Function Concentration:** Generalist with a primary focus in Administration

Chamberlin, Michael A. — *Executive Search Consultant*
Tower Consultants, Ltd.
4195 N.E. Hyline Drive
Jensen Beach, FL 34957
Telephone: (561) 225-5151
Recruiter Classification: Retained; **Lowest/Average Salary:** $60,000/$90,000; **Industry Concentration:** Generalist with a primary focus in High Technology, Information Technology; **Function Concentration:** Administration, Human Resources, Women/Minorities

Champion, Geoffrey — *Managing Vice President Advanced Technology*
Korn/Ferry International
2180 Sand Hill Road
Menlo Park, CA 94025
Telephone: (415) 233-2733
Recruiter Classification: Retained; **Lowest/Average Salary:** $100,000/$150,000; **Industry Concentration:** Generalist with a primary focus in Information Technology; **Function Concentration:** Generalist

Chan, Margaret — *Managing Director*
Webb, Johnson Associates, Inc.
280 Park Avenue, 43rd Floor
New York, NY 10017
Telephone: (212) 661-3700
Recruiter Classification: Retained; **Lowest/Average Salary:**
$90,000/$90,000; **Industry Concentration:** Generalist with a
primary focus in High Technology; **Function Concentration:**
Generalist

Chappell, Peter — *Managing Director*
The Bankers Group
10 South Riverside Plaza, Suite 1424
Chicago, IL 60606
Telephone: (312) 930-9456
Recruiter Classification: Contingency; **Lowest/Average Salary:**
$50,000/$75,000; **Industry Concentration:** Generalist with a
primary focus in High Technology, Information Technology;
Function Concentration: Generalist with a primary focus in
Administration, Finance/Accounting, General Management,
Human Resources, Marketing, Sales, Women/Minorities

Chase, James — *Associate*
Source Services Corporation
1500 West Park Drive, Suite 390
Westborough, MA 01581
Telephone: (508) 366-2600
Recruiter Classification: Contingency; **Lowest/Average Salary:**
$30,000/$50,000; **Industry Concentration:** Information
Technology; **Function Concentration:** Engineering,
Finance/Accounting

Chatterjie, Alok — *Executive Recruiter*
MSI International
8521 Leesburg Pike, Suite 435
Vienna, VA 22182
Telephone: (703) 893-5669
Recruiter Classification: Contingency; **Lowest/Average Salary:**
$30,000/$75,000; **Industry Concentration:** High Technology,
Information Technology; **Function Concentration:** Generalist
with a primary focus in Administration, Engineering,
Finance/Accounting, General Management, Marketing, Sales

Chavous, C. Crawford — *Consultant*
Phillips Resource Group
330 Pelham Road, Building A
Greenville, SC 29615
Telephone: (864) 271-6350
Recruiter Classification: Contingency; **Lowest/Average Salary:**
$40,000/$50,000; **Industry Concentration:** Generalist with a
primary focus in Electronics, High Technology, Information
Technology; **Function Concentration:** Generalist with a
primary focus in Administration, Engineering, General
Management, Human Resources, Marketing, Research and
Development, Sales, Women/Minorities

Cheah, Victor — *Associate*
Source Services Corporation
20 Burlington Mall Road, Suite 405
Burlington, MA 01803
Telephone: (617) 272-5000
Recruiter Classification: Contingency; **Lowest/Average Salary:**
$30,000/$50,000; **Industry Concentration:** Information
Technology; **Function Concentration:** Engineering,
Finance/Accounting

Cherbonnier, L. Michael — *President*
The Cherbonnier Group, Inc.
3050 Post Oak Boulevard, Suite 1600
Houston, TX 77056
Telephone: (713) 688-4701
Recruiter Classification: Retained; **Lowest/Average Salary:**
$75,000/$90,000; **Industry Concentration:** Generalist with
a primary focus in Electronics, High Technology,
Information Technology; **Function Concentration:**
Generalist with a primary focus in Administration,
Engineering, Finance/Accounting, General Management,
Human Resources, Marketing, Research and Development,
Sales

Cherbonnier, L. Michael — *President*
TCG International, Inc.
471 North Post Oak Lane
Houston, TX 77024
Telephone: (713) 960-9511
Recruiter Classification: Executive Temporary; **Lowest/Average
Salary:** $75,000/$90,000; **Industry Concentration:** Generalist
with a primary focus in Electronics, High Technology,
Information Technology; **Function Concentration:** Generalist
with a primary focus in Engineering, Finance/Accounting,
General Management, Marketing, Research and Development,
Sales

Chorman, Marilyn A. — *Director*
Research/Recruiter
Hite Executive Search
6515 Chase Drive
P.O. Box 43217
Cleveland, OH 44143
Telephone: (216) 461-1600
Recruiter Classification: Retained; **Lowest/Average Salary:**
$90,000/$90,000; **Industry Concentration:** Generalist with a
primary focus in Information Technology; **Function
Concentration:** Generalist with a primary focus in
Administration, General Management, Human Resources,
Women/Minorities

Christenson, H. Alan — *Managing Partner*
Christenson & Hutchison
466 Southern Boulevard
Chatham, NJ 07928-1462
Telephone: (201) 966-1600
Recruiter Classification: Retained; **Lowest/Average Salary:**
$75,000/$90,000; **Industry Concentration:** Generalist with a
primary focus in Electronics, High Technology, Information
Technology; **Function Concentration:** Generalist with a
primary focus in Finance/Accounting, General Management,
Human Resources, Marketing, Sales

Christian, Jeffrey E. — *President and CEO*
Christian & Timbers
25825 Science Park Drive, Suite 400
Cleveland, OH 44122
Telephone: (216) 765-5877
Recruiter Classification: Retained; **Lowest/Average Salary:**
$90,000/$90,000; **Industry Concentration:** Electronics, High
Technology, Information Technology; **Function
Concentration:** General Management, Marketing, Sales,
Women/Minorities

Christian, Philip — *Consultant*
Ray & Berndtson
One Allen Center
500 Dallas, Suite 3010
Houston, TX 77002
Telephone: (713) 309-1400
Recruiter Classification: Retained; **Lowest/Average Salary:**
$90,000/$90,000; **Industry Concentration:** Generalist with a
primary focus in High Technology, Information Technology;
Function Concentration: Generalist with a primary focus in
Administration, Finance/Accounting, General Management,
Human Resources, Marketing, Research and Development,
Sales, Women/Minorities

Christiansen, Amy — *Executive Recruiter*
CPS Inc.
One Westbrook Corporate Centre, Suite 600
Westchester, IL 60154
Telephone: (708) 531-8370
Recruiter Classification: Contingency; **Lowest/Average Salary:**
$30,000/$50,000; **Industry Concentration:** Generalist with a
primary focus in Electronics, High Technology, Information
Technology; **Function Concentration:** Engineering, Research
and Development, Sales, Women/Minorities

Christiansen, Doug — *Executive Recruiter*
CPS Inc.
One Westbrook Corporate Centre, Suite 600
Westchester, IL 60154
Telephone: (708) 531-8370
Recruiter Classification: Contingency; **Lowest/Average Salary:**
$30,000/$50,000; **Industry Concentration:** Generalist with a
primary focus in Electronics, High Technology, Information
Technology; **Function Concentration:** Engineering, Research
and Development, Sales, Women/Minorities

Christman, Joel — *Associate*
Source Services Corporation
525 Vine Street, Suite 2250
Cincinnati, OH 45202
Telephone: (513) 651-3303
Recruiter Classification: Contingency; **Lowest/Average Salary:**
$30,000/$50,000; **Industry Concentration:** Information
Technology; **Function Concentration:** Engineering,
Finance/Accounting

Christoff, Matthew J. — *Director*
Spencer Stuart
401 North Michigan Avenue, Suite 3400
Chicago, IL 60611-4244
Telephone: (312) 822-0080
Recruiter Classification: Retained; **Lowest/Average Salary:**
$90,000/$90,000; **Industry Concentration:** Generalist with a
primary focus in Information Technology; **Function
Concentration:** Generalist with a primary focus in General
Management, Marketing

Christy, Michael T. — *Partner*
Heidrick & Struggles, Inc.
8000 Towers Crescent Drive, Suite 555
Vienna, VA 22182-2700
Telephone: (703) 761-4830
Recruiter Classification: Retained; **Lowest/Average Salary:**
$75,000/$90,000; **Industry Concentration:** Generalist with a
primary focus in High Technology; **Function Concentration:**
Generalist

Chronopoulos, Dennis — *Associate*
Source Services Corporation
20 Burlington Mall Road, Suite 405
Burlington, MA 01803
Telephone: (617) 272-5000
Recruiter Classification: Contingency; **Lowest/Average Salary:**
$30,000/$50,000; **Industry Concentration:** Information
Technology; **Function Concentration:** Engineering,
Finance/Accounting

Cimino, James J. — *Vice President*
Executive Search, Ltd.
4830 Interstate Drive
Cincinnati, OH 45246
Telephone: (513) 874-6901
Recruiter Classification: Retained; **Lowest/Average Salary:**
$60,000/$90,000; **Industry Concentration:** Generalist with a
primary focus in High Technology; **Function Concentration:**
Engineering, General Management, Research and
Development

Cimino, Ron — *Vice President*
Paul-Tittle Associates, Inc.
1485 Chain Bridge Road, #304
McLean, VA 22101
Telephone: (703) 442-0500
Recruiter Classification: Retained; **Lowest/Average Salary:**
$60,000/$75,000; **Industry Concentration:** High Technology,
Information Technology; **Function Concentration:** Engineering,
General Management, Human Resources, Marketing, Sales

Cimino, Terry N. — *Director Technical Services*
Executive Search, Ltd.
4830 Interstate Drive
Cincinnati, OH 45246
Telephone: (513) 874-6901
Recruiter Classification: Retained; **Lowest/Average Salary:**
$50,000/$75,000; **Industry Concentration:** Generalist with a
primary focus in Electronics, High Technology; **Function
Concentration:** Engineering, General Management

Cizek, John T. — *Principal*
Cizek Associates, Inc.
2021 Midwest Road, Suite 200
Oak Brook, IL 60521
Telephone: (630) 953-8570
Recruiter Classification: Retained; **Lowest/Average Salary:**
$75,000/$90,000; **Industry Concentration:** Generalist with a
primary focus in Electronics, High Technology; **Function
Concentration:** Generalist with a primary focus in
Administration, Engineering, Finance/Accounting, General
Management, Human Resources, Marketing, Research and
Development, Sales

Cizek, Marti J. — *President*
Cizek Associates, Inc.
2390 East Camelback Road, Suite 300
Phoenix, AZ 85016
Telephone: (602) 553-1066
Recruiter Classification: Retained; **Lowest/Average Salary:**
$75,000/$90,000; **Industry Concentration:** Generalist with a
primary focus in Electronics, High Technology; **Function
Concentration:** Generalist with a primary focus in
Administration, Engineering, Finance/Accounting, General
Management, Human Resources, Marketing, Research and
Development, Sales, Women/Minorities

Cizynski, Katherine W. — *Associate*
James Mead & Company
164 Kings Highway North
Westport, CT 06880
Telephone: (203) 454-5544
Recruiter Classification: Retained; **Lowest/Average Salary:**
$90,000/$90,000; **Industry Concentration:** Electronics;
Function Concentration: General Management, Marketing,
Sales

Clarey, Jack R. — *Partner*
Clarey & Andrews, Inc.
1200 Shermer Road, Suite 108
Northbrook, IL 60062
Telephone: (847) 498-2870
Recruiter Classification: Retained; **Lowest/Average Salary:**
$90,000/$90,000; **Industry Concentration:** Generalist with a
primary focus in Electronics, High Technology; **Function
Concentration:** Generalist with a primary focus in
Administration, Finance/Accounting, General Management,
Human Resources

Clark, James — *Manager/Lab Recruiter*
CPS Inc.
363 East Lincoln Highway, Suite E
DeKalb, IL 60115
Telephone: (815) 756-1221
Recruiter Classification: Contingency; **Lowest/Average
Salary:** $30,000/$50,000; **Industry Concentration:** Generalist
with a primary focus in Electronics, High Technology,
Information Technology; **Function Concentration:**
Engineering, Research and Development, Sales,
Women/Minorities

Clark, John — *Senior Recruiter*
Tate Consulting Inc.
23257 SR 7
Suite 109
Boca Raton, FL 33428
Telephone: (516) 852-8283
Recruiter Classification: Retained; **Lowest/Average Salary:**
$60,000/$75,000; **Industry Concentration:** High Technology,
Information Technology; **Function Concentration:** Engineering,
Research and Development

Clark, Julie — *Contract Services Division
Recruiter*
Corporate Recruiters Ltd.
490-1140 West Pender Street
Vancouver, British Columbia, CANADA V6E 4G1
Telephone: (604) 687-5993
Recruiter Classification: Contingency; **Lowest/Average Salary:**
$30,000/$60,000; **Industry Concentration:** Generalist with a
primary focus in Electronics, High Technology, Information
Technology

Clasen, Ryan — *Account Director*
Warren, Morris & Madison
2190 Carmel Valley Road
Del Mar, CA 92014
Telephone: (619) 481-3388
Recruiter Classification: Retained; **Lowest/Average Salary:**
$50,000/$75,000; **Industry Concentration:** High Technology;
Function Concentration: Generalist

Clauhsen, Elizabeth A. — *Senior Vice President*
Savoy Partners, Ltd.
1620 L Street N.W., Suite 801
Washington, DC 20036
Telephone: (202) 887-0666
Recruiter Classification: Retained; **Lowest/Average Salary:**
$90,000/$90,000; **Industry Concentration:** Generalist with a
primary focus in Electronics, High Technology, Information
Technology; **Function Concentration:** Generalist with a
primary focus in Administration, Engineering,
Finance/Accounting, General Management, Human Resources,
Marketing, Sales, Women/Minorities

Clawson, Bob — *Managing Director*
Source Services Corporation
3701 West Algonquin Road, Suite 380
Rolling Meadows, IL 60008
Telephone: (847) 392-0244
Recruiter Classification: Contingency; **Lowest/Average Salary:**
$30,000/$50,000; **Industry Concentration:** Information
Technology; **Function Concentration:** Engineering,
Finance/Accounting

Clawson, Robert — *Managing Director*
Source Services Corporation
150 South Wacker Drive, Suite 400
Chicago, IL 60606
Telephone: (312) 346-7000
Recruiter Classification: Contingency; **Lowest/Average Salary:**
$30,000/$50,000; **Industry Concentration:** Information
Technology; **Function Concentration:** Engineering,
Finance/Accounting

Clayton, Fred J. — *Executive Vice President*
Berkhemer Clayton Incorporated
Union Station
800 N. Alameda Street, Suite 200
Los Angeles, CA 90012
Telephone: (213) 621-2300
Recruiter Classification: Retained; **Lowest/Average Salary:**
$75,000/$90,000; **Industry Concentration:** Generalist with a
primary focus in Electronics, High Technology, Information
Technology; **Function Concentration:** Generalist with a
primary focus in Administration, Finance/Accounting, General
Management, Human Resources, Marketing,
Women/Minorities

Clegg, Cynthia — *Managing Director*
Horton International
10 Tower Lane
Avon, CT 06001
Telephone: (860) 674-8701
Recruiter Classification: Retained; **Lowest/Average Salary:**
$90,000/$90,000; **Industry Concentration:** High Technology;
Function Concentration: Generalist

Cline, Mark — *Manager Operations*
NYCOR Search, Inc.
4930 West 77th Street, Suite 300
Minneapolis, MN 55435
Telephone: (612) 831-6444
Recruiter Classification: Contingency; **Lowest/Average Salary:**
$40,000/$75,000; **Industry Concentration:** Generalist with a
primary focus in Electronics, High Technology, Information
Technology; **Function Concentration:** Engineering, Research
and Development

Clough, Geoff — *Executive Director*
Intech Summit Group, Inc.
5075 Shoreham Place, Suite 280
San Diego, CA 92116
Telephone: (619) 452-2100
Recruiter Classification: Retained; **Lowest/Average Salary:**
$50,000/$75,000; **Industry Concentration:** High Technology,
Information Technology; **Function Concentration:** Generalist
with a primary focus in Engineering, General Management,
Marketing, Research and Development, Sales

Cloutier, Gisella — *Vice President*
Dinte Resources, Inc.
8300 Greensboro Drive
Suite 880
McLean, VA 22102
Telephone: (703) 448-3300
Recruiter Classification: Executive Temporary; **Lowest/Average
Salary:** $90,000/$90,000; **Industry Concentration:** Generalist
with a primary focus in High Technology, Information
Technology; **Function Concentration:** Generalist with a
primary focus in Finance/Accounting, General Management,
Human Resources, Marketing, Sales

Cocchiaro, Richard — *Regional President*
Romac & Associates
20 North Wacker Drive
Suite 2420
Chicago, IL 60606
Telephone: (312) 263-0902
Recruiter Classification: Executive Temporary; **Lowest/Average
Salary:** $60,000/$60,000; **Industry Concentration:** High
Technology, Information Technology; **Function Concentration:**
Finance/Accounting

Cocconi, Alan — *Associate*
Source Services Corporation
150 South Wacker Drive, Suite 400
Chicago, IL 60606
Telephone: (312) 346-7000
Recruiter Classification: Contingency; **Lowest/Average Salary:**
$30,000/$50,000; **Industry Concentration:** Information
Technology; **Function Concentration:** Engineering,
Finance/Accounting

Cochran, Hale — *Partner*
Fenwick Partners
57 Bedford Street, Suite 101
Lexington, MA 02173
Telephone: (617) 862-3370
Recruiter Classification: Retained; **Lowest/Average Salary:**
$90,000/$90,000; **Industry Concentration:** Electronics, High
Technology, Information Technology; **Function Concentration:**
Engineering, Finance/Accounting, General Management,
Marketing, Research and Development, Sales

Cochran, Scott P. — *Vice President*
The Badger Group
4125 Blackhawk Plaza Circle, Suite 270
Danville, CA 94506
Telephone: (510) 736-5553
Recruiter Classification: Retained; **Lowest/Average Salary:**
$90,000/$90,000; **Industry Concentration:** Generalist with a
primary focus in Electronics, High Technology, Information
Technology; **Function Concentration:** Generalist with a
primary focus in Engineering, Finance/Accounting, General
Management, Human Resources, Marketing, Research and
Development, Sales

Cochrun, James — *Associate*
Source Services Corporation
9020 Capital of Texas Highway
Building I, Suite 337
Austin, TX 78759
Telephone: (512) 345-7473
Recruiter Classification: Contingency; **Lowest/Average Salary:**
$30,000/$50,000; **Industry Concentration:** Information
Technology; **Function Concentration:** Engineering,
Finance/Accounting

Coe, Karen J. — *President*
Coe & Company International Inc.
1535 400-3rd Avenue SW
Center Tower
Calgary, Alberta, Canada T20 4H2
Telephone: (403) 232-8833
Recruiter Classification: Retained; **Lowest/Average Salary:**
$75,000/$90,000; **Industry Concentration:** High Technology,
Information Technology; **Function Concentration:** Generalist
with a primary focus in Engineering, Human Resources,
Marketing, Sales

Coffey, Patty — *Information Technology Recruiter*
Winter, Wyman & Company
950 Winter Street, Suite 3100
Waltham, MA 02154-1294
Telephone: (617) 890-7000
Recruiter Classification: Contingency; **Lowest/Average Salary:**
$30,000/$60,000; **Industry Concentration:** Generalist with a
primary focus in Information Technology; **Function
Concentration:** Generalist

Coffman, Brian — *Vice President*
Kossuth & Associates, Inc.
800 Bellevue Way N.E., Suite 400
Bellevue, WA 98004
Telephone: (206) 450-9050
Recruiter Classification: Retained; **Lowest/Average Salary:**
$50,000/$90,000; **Industry Concentration:** High Technology,
Information Technology; **Function Concentration:** Generalist
with a primary focus in Administration, Engineering,
Finance/Accounting, General Management, Human Resources,
Marketing, Research and Development, Sales,
Women/Minorities

Cohen, Michael R. — *Chief Executive Officer*
Intech Summit Group, Inc.
5075 Shoreham Place, Suite 280
San Diego, CA 92116
Telephone: (619) 452-2100
Recruiter Classification: Retained; **Lowest/Average Salary:**
$60,000/$90,000; **Industry Concentration:** Generalist with a
primary focus in High Technology, Information Technology;
Function Concentration: Generalist with a primary focus in
Finance/Accounting, General Management, Human Resources

Cohen, Pamela — *Legal Consultant*
TOPAZ International, Inc.
383 Northfield Avenue
West Orange, NJ 07052
Telephone: (201) 669-7300
Recruiter Classification: Contingency; **Lowest/Average Salary:**
$40,000/$75,000; **Industry Concentration:** Electronics, High
Technology; **Function Concentration:** Generalist with a
primary focus in Women/Minorities

Cohen, Pamela — *Legal Consultant*
TOPAZ Legal Solutions
383 Northfield Avenue
West Orange, NJ 07052
Telephone: (201) 669-7300
Recruiter Classification: Executive Temporary; **Lowest/Average Salary:** $40,000/$75,000; **Industry Concentration:** Electronics, High Technology; **Function Concentration:** Generalist with a primary focus in Women/Minorities

Cohen, Robert C. — *Chief Executive Officer*
Intech Summit Group, Inc.
5075 Shoreham Place, Suite 280
San Diego, CA 92116
Telephone: (619) 452-2100
Recruiter Classification: Retained; **Lowest/Average Salary:** $75,000/$90,000; **Industry Concentration:** Generalist with a primary focus in Electronics, High Technology, Information Technology; **Function Concentration:** Generalist with a primary focus in Administration, Engineering, Finance/Accounting, General Management, Human Resources, Marketing, Research and Development, Sales, Women/Minorities

Colasanto, Frank M. — *Principal*
W.R. Rosato & Associates, Inc.
61 Broadway, 26th Floor
New York, NY 10006
Telephone: (212) 509-5700
Recruiter Classification: Retained; **Lowest/Average Salary:** $90,000/$90,000; **Industry Concentration:** High Technology, Information Technology; **Function Concentration:** Administration, Marketing, Research and Development, Sales

Cole, Kevin — *Partner*
Don Richard Associates of Washington, D.C., Inc.
8180 Greensboro Drive, Suite 1020
McLean, VA 22102
Telephone: (703) 827-5990
Recruiter Classification: Contingency, Executive Temporary; **Lowest/Average Salary:** $40,000/$60,000; **Industry Concentration:** High Technology; **Function Concentration:** Finance/Accounting

Cole, Rosalie — *Associate*
Source Services Corporation
150 South Wacker Drive, Suite 400
Chicago, IL 60606
Telephone: (312) 346-7000
Recruiter Classification: Contingency; **Lowest/Average Salary:** $30,000/$50,000; **Industry Concentration:** Information Technology; **Function Concentration:** Engineering, Finance/Accounting

Coleman, J. Kevin — *President*
J. Kevin Coleman & Associates, Inc.
416 Hermosa Place
So. Pasadena, CA 91030
Telephone: (818) 403-0704
Recruiter Classification: Retained; **Lowest/Average Salary:** $60,000/$90,000; **Industry Concentration:** Generalist with a primary focus in High Technology; **Function Concentration:** Generalist with a primary focus in Engineering, Finance/Accounting, General Management, Human Resources, Marketing

Coleman, Patricia — *Principal*
Korn/Ferry International
233 South Wacker
Chicago, IL 60606
Telephone: (312) 466-1834
Recruiter Classification: Retained; **Lowest/Average Salary:** $100,000/$150,000; **Industry Concentration:** Generalist with a primary focus in Information Technology; **Function Concentration:** Generalist

Colling, Douglas — *Principal*
KPMG Management Consulting
2300 Yonge Street
Toronto, Ontario, CANADA M4P 1G2
Telephone: (416) 482-5786
Recruiter Classification: Executive Temporary; **Lowest/Average Salary:** $75,000/$90,000; **Industry Concentration:** Generalist with a primary focus in Electronics, High Technology, Information Technology; **Function Concentration:** Generalist with a primary focus in Administration, Engineering, Finance/Accounting, General Management, Human Resources, Marketing, Research and Development, Sales

Collins, Scott — *Associate*
Source Services Corporation
5343 North 16th Street, Suite 270
Phoenix, AZ 85016
Telephone: (602) 230-0220
Recruiter Classification: Contingency; **Lowest/Average Salary:** $30,000/$50,000; **Industry Concentration:** Information Technology; **Function Concentration:** Engineering, Finance/Accounting

Collins, Tom — *Vice President*
J.B. Homer Associates, Inc.
Graybar Building
420 Lexington Avenue, Suite 2328
New York, NY 10170
Telephone: (212) 697-3300
Recruiter Classification: Retained; **Lowest/Average Salary:** $90,000/$90,000; **Industry Concentration:** Generalist with a primary focus in Information Technology; **Function Concentration:** Generalist

Collis, Gerald — *Executive Recruiter*
TSS Consulting, Ltd.
2425 East Camelback Road
Suite 375
Phoenix, AZ 85016
Telephone: (602) 955-7000
Recruiter Classification: Contingency; **Lowest/Average Salary:** $60,000/$75,000; **Industry Concentration:** Electronics, High Technology; **Function Concentration:** Engineering, General Management, Marketing

Colman, Michael — *President*
Executive Placement Consultants, Inc.
2700 River Road, Suite 107
Des Plaines, IL 60018
Telephone: (847) 298-6445
Recruiter Classification: Contingency; **Lowest/Average Salary:** $40,000/$75,000; **Industry Concentration:** Generalist with a primary focus in Electronics, High Technology, Information Technology; **Function Concentration:** Finance/Accounting, Human Resources, Marketing

Colvin, Teresa A. — *Executive Recruiter*
Jonas, Walters & Assoc., Inc.
1110 North Old World Third St., Suite 510
Milwaukee, WI 53203-1102
Telephone: (414) 291-2828
Recruiter Classification: Retained; **Lowest/Average Salary:**
$50,000/$90,000; **Industry Concentration:** Information
Technology; **Function Concentration:** Generalist with a
primary focus in Engineering, General Management, Human
Resources, Marketing, Research and Development, Sales,
Women/Minorities

Comai, Christine — *Associate*
Source Services Corporation
2000 Town Center, Suite 850
Southfield, MI 48075
Telephone: (810) 352-6520
Recruiter Classification: Contingency; **Lowest/Average Salary:**
$30,000/$50,000; **Industry Concentration:** Information
Technology; **Function Concentration:** Engineering,
Finance/Accounting

Combs, Stephen L. — *Managing Director*
Juntunen-Combs-Poirier
600 Montgomery Street, 2nd Floor
San Francisco, CA 94111
Telephone: (415) 291-1699
Recruiter Classification: Retained; **Lowest/Average Salary:**
$90,000/$90,000; **Industry Concentration:** High Technology,
Information Technology; **Function Concentration:**
Finance/Accounting, Marketing, Sales

Combs, Thomas — *Associate*
Source Services Corporation
161 Ottawa NW, Suite 409D
Grand Rapids, MI 49503
Telephone: (616) 451-2400
Recruiter Classification: Contingency; **Lowest/Average Salary:**
$30,000/$50,000; **Industry Concentration:** Information
Technology; **Function Concentration:** Engineering,
Finance/Accounting

Compton, Tonya — *Recruiter/Research*
Dunhill Professional Search of Irvine, Inc.
9 Executive Circle, Suite 240
Irvine, CA 92614
Telephone: (714) 474-6666
Recruiter Classification: Contingency; **Lowest/Average
Salary:** $50,000/$75,000; **Industry Concentration:** High
Technology; **Function Concentration:** Generalist with a
primary focus in Engineering, General Management,
Marketing, Sales

Cona, Joseph A. — *President*
Cona Personnel Search
625 South Second Avenue
Springfield, IL 62704-2500
Telephone: (217) 522-3933
Recruiter Classification: Contingency; **Lowest/Average Salary:**
$20,000/$50,000; **Industry Concentration:** Generalist with a
primary focus in Information Technology; **Function
Concentration:** Generalist with a primary focus in
Administration, Engineering, Finance/Accounting, General
Management

Conard, Rodney J. — *President*
Conard Associates, Inc.
74 Northeastern Boulevard, Suite 22A
Nashua, NH 03062
Telephone: (603) 886-0600
Recruiter Classification: Retained; **Lowest/Average Salary:**
$100,000/$125,000; **Industry Concentration:** Generalist with a
primary focus in High Technology; **Function Concentration:**
Generalist with a primary focus in Finance/Accounting,
General Management, Marketing

Coneys, Bridget — *Associate*
Source Services Corporation
8614 Westwood Center, Suite 750
Vienna, VA 22182
Telephone: (703) 790-5610
Recruiter Classification: Contingency; **Lowest/Average Salary:**
$30,000/$50,000; **Industry Concentration:** Information
Technology; **Function Concentration:** Engineering,
Finance/Accounting

Conley, Kevin E. — *Partner*
Lamalie Amrop International
10 Post Office Square
Boston, MA 02109-4603
Telephone: (617) 292-6242
Recruiter Classification: Retained; **Lowest/Average Salary:**
$90,000/$90,000; **Industry Concentration:** Generalist with a
primary focus in High Technology; **Function Concentration:**
Generalist

Connelly, Scott — *Recruiter*
Technical Connections Inc.
11400 Olympic Boulevard, Suite 770
Los Angeles, CA 90064
Telephone: (310) 479-8830
Recruiter Classification: Contingency; **Lowest/Average Salary:**
$40,000/$60,000; **Industry Concentration:** High Technology,
Information Technology; **Function Concentration:** Generalist

Conners, Theresa — *Division Manager*
D. Brown and Associates, Inc.
610 S.W. Alder, Suite 1111
Portland, OR 97205
Telephone: (503) 224-6860
Recruiter Classification: Contingency; **Lowest/Average Salary:**
$40,000/$60,000; **Industry Concentration:** Electronics, High
Technology, Information Technology; **Function Concentration:**
Engineering, Finance/Accounting

Connolly, Cathryn — *Associate/Executive
Recruiter*
Strategic Associates, Inc.
13915 Burnet Road, Suite 300
Austin, TX 78728
Telephone: (512) 218-8222
Recruiter Classification: Contingency; **Lowest/Average Salary:**
$50,000/$60,000; **Industry Concentration:** Electronics, High
Technology, Information Technology; **Function Concentration:**
General Management, Women/Minorities

Connor, Michele — *Executive Recruiter*
Abraham & London, Ltd.
7 Old Sherman Turnpike, Suite 209
Danbury, CT 06810
Telephone: (203) 730-4000
Recruiter Classification: Contingency; **Lowest/Average Salary:**
$50,000/$75,000; **Industry Concentration:** Information
Technology; **Function Concentration:** Marketing

Conway, Maureen — *President*
Conway & Associates
1007 Church Street
Suite 408
Evanston, IL 60201
Telephone: (847) 866-6832
Recruiter Classification: Retained; **Lowest/Average Salary:**
$60,000/$90,000; **Industry Concentration:** Generalist with a
primary focus in Information Technology; **Function
Concentration:** Generalist with a primary focus in
Administration, Engineering, Finance/Accounting, General
Management, Human Resources, Marketing, Research and
Development, Sales

Conway, William P. — *Executive Recruiter*
Phillips Resource Group
330 Pelham Road, Building A
Greenville, SC 29615
Telephone: (864) 271-6350
Recruiter Classification: Contingency; **Lowest/Average Salary:**
$40,000/$50,000; **Industry Concentration:** Electronics, High
Technology, Information Technology; **Function Concentration:**
Generalist with a primary focus in Administration, Engineering,
General Management, Human Resources, Marketing, Research
and Development, Sales, Women/Minorities

Cook, Charlene — *Associate*
Source Services Corporation
15260 Ventura Boulevard, Suite 380
Sherman Oaks, CA 91403
Telephone: (818) 905-1500
Recruiter Classification: Contingency; **Lowest/Average Salary:**
$30,000/$50,000; **Industry Concentration:** Information
Technology; **Function Concentration:** Engineering,
Finance/Accounting

Cook, Dennis — *Vice President*
A.T. Kearney, Inc.
130 Adelaide Street West, Suite 2710
Toronto, Ontario, CANADA M5H 3P5
Telephone: (416) 947-1990
Recruiter Classification: Retained; **Lowest/Average Salary:**
$90,000/$90,000; **Industry Concentration:** Generalist with a
primary focus in High Technology, Information Technology;
Function Concentration: Generalist with a primary focus in
Engineering, Finance/Accounting, General Management

Cooke, Katherine H. — *Managing Director*
Horton International
10 Tower Lane
Avon, CT 06001
Telephone: (860) 674-8701
Recruiter Classification: Retained; **Lowest/Average Salary:**
$90,000/$90,000; **Industry Concentration:** Generalist with a
primary focus in Electronics, High Technology; **Function
Concentration:** Generalist with a primary focus in Engineering,
Finance/Accounting, General Management, Human Resources,
Marketing, Sales

Cooper, William — *Account Executive*
Search West, Inc.
750 The City Drive South
Suite 100
Orange, CA 92668-4940
Telephone: (714) 748-0400
Recruiter Classification: Contingency; **Lowest/Average Salary:**
$40,000/$60,000; **Industry Concentration:** Information
Technology; **Function Concentration:** Generalist

Cornehlsen, James H. — *Senior Vice President*
Skott/Edwards Consultants, Inc.
500 Fifth Avenue, 26th Floor
New York, NY 10110
Telephone: (212) 382-1166
Recruiter Classification: Retained; **Lowest/Average Salary:**
$90,000/$90,000; **Industry Concentration:** Information
Technology; **Function Concentration:** Administration,
Finance/Accounting, General Management, Marketing, Sales

Corrigan, Gerald F. — *Managing Partner*
The Corrigan Group
1333 Ocean Avenue
Santa Monica, CA 90401
Telephone: (310) 260-9488
Recruiter Classification: Retained; **Lowest/Average Salary:**
$90,000/$120,000; **Industry Concentration:** Generalist with a
primary focus in Information; **Function Concentration:**
Generalist with a primary focus in Administration,
Finance/Accounting, General Management, Human Resources,
Marketing, Sales

Cortina Del Valle, Pedro — *Partner*
Ray & Berndtson
Palo Santo No. 6
Colonia Lomas Altas
Mexico City, D.F., MEXICO 11950
Telephone: (525) 570-7462
Recruiter Classification: Retained; **Lowest/Average Salary:**
$90,000/$90,000; **Industry Concentration:** Generalist with a
primary focus in High Technology, Information Technology;
Function Concentration: Generalist with a primary focus in
Administration, Finance/Accounting, General Management,
Human Resources, Marketing, Research and Development,
Sales, Women/Minorities

Cossitt, Chip — *Account Director*
Warren, Morris & Madison
2190 Carmel Valley Road
Del Mar, CA 92014
Telephone: (619) 481-3388
Recruiter Classification: Retained; **Lowest/Average Salary:**
$50,000/$75,000; **Industry Concentration:** High Technology;
Function Concentration: Generalist

Costello, Lynda — *Executive Search Consultant*
Coe & Company International Inc.
1535 400-3rd Avenue SW
Center Tower
Calgary, Alberta, Canada T20 4H2
Telephone: (403) 232-8833
Recruiter Classification: Retained; **Lowest/Average Salary:**
$75,000/$90,000; **Industry Concentration:** High Technology,
Information Technology; **Function Concentration:** Generalist
with a primary focus in Administration, Engineering,
Finance/Accounting, General Management, Human Resources,
Marketing, Research and Development, Sales

Cottingham, R.L. — *Director Legal Search*
Marvin L. Silcott & Associates, Inc.
7557 Rambler Road, Suite 1336
Dallas, TX 75231
Telephone: (214) 369-7802
Recruiter Classification: Contingency; **Lowest/Average Salary:**
$60,000/$90,000; **Industry Concentration:** Generalist with a
primary focus in Electronics, High Technology; **Function
Concentration:** Generalist with a primary focus in
Administration

Cotugno, James — *Associate*
Source Services Corporation
1 Gatehall Drive, Suite 250
Parsippany, NJ 07054
Telephone: (201) 267-3222
Recruiter Classification: Contingency; **Lowest/Average Salary:**
$30,000/$50,000; **Industry Concentration:** Information
Technology; **Function Concentration:** Engineering,
Finance/Accounting

Coughlin, Stephen — *Associate*
Source Services Corporation
100 North Tryon Street, Suite 3130
Charlotte, NC 28202
Telephone: (704) 333-8311
Recruiter Classification: Contingency; **Lowest/Average Salary:**
$30,000/$50,000; **Industry Concentration:** Information
Technology; **Function Concentration:** Engineering,
Finance/Accounting

Coulman, Karen — *Executive Recruiter*
CPS Inc.
One Westbrook Corporate Centre, Suite 600
Westchester, IL 60154
Telephone: (708) 531-8370
Recruiter Classification: Contingency; **Lowest/Average Salary:**
$30,000/$50,000; **Industry Concentration:** Generalist with a
primary focus in Electronics, High Technology, Information
Technology; **Function Concentration:** Engineering, Research
and Development, Sales, Women/Minorities

Courtney, Brendan — *Vice President*
A.J. Burton Group, Inc.
120 East Baltimore Street, Suite 2220
Baltimore, MD 21202
Telephone: (410) 752-5244
Recruiter Classification: Contingency; **Lowest/Average Salary:**
$40,000/$75,000; **Industry Concentration:** Generalist with a
primary focus in High Technology, Information Technology;
Function Concentration: Generalist with a primary focus in
Administration, Finance/Accounting, General Management,
Human Resources

Cowell, Roy A. — *President*
Cowell & Associates, Ltd.
100 Forest Place
P-22
Oak Park, IL 60301
Telephone: (708) 383-6618
Recruiter Classification: Retained; **Lowest/Average Salary:**
$75,000/$90,000; **Industry Concentration:** Generalist with a
primary focus in Electronics, Information Technology; **Function
Concentration:** Generalist with a primary focus in
Finance/Accounting, General Management, Marketing

Coyle, Hugh F. — *Vice President*
A.J. Burton Group, Inc.
120 East Baltimore Street, Suite 2220
Baltimore, MD 21202
Telephone: (410) 752-5244
Recruiter Classification: Contingency, Executive Temporary;
Lowest/Average Salary: $40,000/$75,000; **Industry
Concentration:** Generalist with a primary focus in High
Technology, Information Technology; **Function Concentration:**
Generalist with a primary focus in Administration,
Finance/Accounting, General Management, Human Resources

Cram, Noel — *Vice President*
R.P. Barone Associates
57 Green Street
Woodbridge, NJ 07095
Telephone: (908) 634-4300
Recruiter Classification: Contingency; **Lowest/Average Salary:**
$30,000/$75,000; **Industry Concentration:** Electronics,
Information Technology; **Function Concentration:** Engineering,
Research and Development

Crane, Howard C. — *Director*
Chartwell Partners International, Inc.
275 Battery Street, Suite 2180
San Francisco, CA 94111
Telephone: (415) 296-0600
Recruiter Classification: Retained; **Lowest/Average Salary:**
$90,000/$90,000; **Industry Concentration:** Generalist with a
primary focus in Electronics, High Technology, Information
Technology; **Function Concentration:** Generalist with a
primary focus in Finance/Accounting, General Management,
Human Resources, Marketing, Sales

Crath, Paul F. — *Partner*
Price Waterhouse
Suite 3000, Box 82 Royal Trust Tower
Toronto Dominion Centre
Toronto, Ontario, CANADA M5K 1G8
Telephone: (416) 863-1133
Recruiter Classification: Retained; **Lowest/Average Salary:**
$75,000/$90,000; **Industry Concentration:** Generalist with a
primary focus in High Technology; **Function Concentration:**
Generalist with a primary focus in Administration, Engineering,
Finance/Accounting, General Management, Human Resources,
Marketing, Research and Development, Sales

Critchley, Walter — *President*
Cochran, Cochran & Yale, Inc.
5166 Main Street
Williamsville, NY 14221
Telephone: (716) 631-1300
Recruiter Classification: Retained; **Lowest/Average Salary:**
$50,000/$75,000; **Industry Concentration:** Generalist with a
primary focus in High Technology, Information Technology;
Function Concentration: Generalist with a primary focus in
Engineering, Finance/Accounting, General Management,
Human Resources, Marketing, Sales, Women/Minorities

Cronin, Richard J. — *President, SPHR*
Hodge-Cronin & Associates, Inc.
9575 West Higgins Road, Suite 904
Rosemont, IL 60018
Telephone: (847) 692-2041
Recruiter Classification: Retained; **Lowest/Average Salary:**
$90,000/$100,000; **Industry Concentration:** Generalist with a
primary focus in Electronics; **Function Concentration:**
Generalist

Crosler, Yvonne — *Director*
Paul-Tittle Associates, Inc.
1485 Chain Bridge Road, #304
McLean, VA 22101
Telephone: (703) 442-0500
Recruiter Classification: Retained; **Lowest/Average Salary:**
$60,000/$75,000; **Industry Concentration:** High Technology;
Function Concentration: Administration, Finance/Accounting,
Human Resources, Marketing, Sales, Women/Minorities

Crowder, Edward W. — *President*
Crowder & Company
2050 North Woodward Avenue, Suite 335
Bloomfield Hills, MI 48304
Telephone: (248) 645-0909
Recruiter Classification: Retained; **Lowest/Average Salary:**
$90,000/$90,000; **Industry Concentration:** Generalist with a
primary focus in Electronics; **Function Concentration:**
Generalist with a primary focus in Engineering,
Finance/Accounting, General Management, Human Resources,
Marketing, Sales, Women/Minorities

Crumpton, Marc — *Consultant*
Walden Associates
1601 Trapelo Road
Waltham, MA 02154
Telephone: (617) 890-8885
Recruiter Classification: Retained; **Lowest/Average Salary:**
$90,000/$90,000; **Industry Concentration:** High Technology,
Information Technology; **Function Concentration:** General
Management

Crumpton, Marc — *Consultant/Director*
Logix, Inc.
1601 Trapelo Road
Waltham, MA 02154
Telephone: (617) 890-0500
Recruiter Classification: Retained; **Lowest/Average Salary:**
$60,000/$75,000; **Industry Concentration:** High Technology,
Information Technology; **Function Concentration:**
Engineering

Crumpton, Marc — *Consultant/Director*
Logix Partners
1601 Trapelo Road
Waltham, MA 02154
Telephone: (617) 890-0500
Recruiter Classification: Retained; **Lowest/Average Salary:**
$60,000/$75,000; **Industry Concentration:** High Technology,
Information Technology; **Function Concentration:**
Engineering

Cruse, O.D. — *Senior Director*
Spencer Stuart
1717 Main Street, Suite 5300
Dallas, TX 75201-4605
Telephone: (214) 658-1777
Recruiter Classification: Retained; **Lowest/Average Salary:**
$90,000/$90,000; **Industry Concentration:** Electronics, High
Technology, Information Technology; **Function Concentration:**
Engineering, Finance/Accounting, General Management,
Marketing, Research and Development, Sales,
Women/Minorities

Cruz, Catherine — *Office Manager/Legal
Consultant*
TOPAZ International, Inc.
383 Northfield Avenue
West Orange, NJ 07052
Telephone: (201) 669-7300
Recruiter Classification: Contingency; **Lowest/Average Salary:**
$40,000/$75,000; **Industry Concentration:** Electronics, High
Technology; **Function Concentration:** Generalist with a
primary focus in Women/Minorities

Cruz, Catherine — *Office Manager/Legal
Consultant*
TOPAZ Legal Solutions
383 Northfield Avenue
West Orange, NJ 07052
Telephone: (201) 669-7300
Recruiter Classification: Executive Temporary; **Lowest/Average
Salary:** $40,000/$75,000; **Industry Concentration:** Electronics,
High Technology; **Function Concentration:** Generalist with a
primary focus in Women/Minorities

Cuddihy, Paul — *Vice President*
Dahl-Morrow International
12020 Sunrise Valley Drive
Reston, VA 20191
Telephone: (703) 860-6868
Recruiter Classification: Retained; **Lowest/Average Salary:**
$75,000/$90,000; **Industry Concentration:** Electronics, High
Technology, Information Technology; **Function Concentration:**
Generalist with a primary focus in Engineering,
Finance/Accounting, General Management, Marketing, Sales

Cuddy, Brian C. — *Managing Partner*
Romac & Associates
125 Summer Street, Suite 1450
Boston, MA 02110
Telephone: (617) 439-4300
Recruiter Classification: Executive Temporary; **Lowest/Average
Salary:** $60,000/$60,000; **Industry Concentration:** High
Technology, Information Technology; **Function Concentration:**
Finance/Accounting

Cuddy, Patricia — *Associate*
Source Services Corporation
379 Thornall Street
Edison, NJ 08837
Telephone: (908) 494-2800
Recruiter Classification: Contingency; **Lowest/Average Salary:**
$30,000/$50,000; **Industry Concentration:** Information
Technology; **Function Concentration:** Engineering,
Finance/Accounting

Cunningham, Lawrence — *Vice President,
Bio-Pharmaceutical Division*
Howard Fischer Associates, Inc.
1800 John F. Kennedy Boulevard, 7th Floor
Philadelphia, PA 19103
Telephone: (215) 568-8363
Recruiter Classification: Retained; **Lowest/Average Salary:**
$90,000/$90,000; **Industry Concentration:** Generalist with a
primary focus in High Technology; **Function Concentration:**
Generalist with a primary focus in Administration,
Finance/Accounting, General Management, Human Resources,
Marketing, Research and Development, Sales,
Women/Minorities

Cunningham, Robert Y. — *Director Consulting
Services*
Goodrich & Sherwood Associates, Inc.
521 Fifth Avenue
New York, NY 10175
Telephone: (212) 697-4131
Recruiter Classification: Retained; **Lowest/Average Salary:**
$60,000/$90,000; **Industry Concentration:** Generalist with a
primary focus in Information Technology; **Function
Concentration:** Generalist with a primary focus in
Administration, Finance/Accounting, General Management,
Human Resources, Marketing, Sales

Cunningham, Sheila — *Director/Recruiter*
Adams & Associates International
463-D W. Russell Street
Barrington, IL 60010
Telephone: (847) 304-5300
Recruiter Classification: Retained; **Lowest/Average Salary:**
$75,000/$75,000; **Industry Concentration:** Generalist with a
primary focus in High Technology, Information Technology;
Function Concentration: Generalist with a primary focus in
Engineering, General Management, Marketing

Curci, Donald L. — *President and CEO*
A.R.I. International
5199 E. Pacific Coast Highway
Long Beach, CA 90804-3304
Telephone: (562) 498-7644
Recruiter Classification: Retained; **Lowest/Average Salary:**
$90,000/$90,000; **Industry Concentration:** Generalist with a
primary focus in Electronics, High Technology, Information
Technology; **Function Concentration:** Generalist with a
primary focus in Administration, Engineering, General
Management, Human Resources, Marketing, Research and
Development, Sales

Curren, Camella — *Associate*
Source Services Corporation
4170 Ashford Dunwoody Road, Suite 285
Atlanta, GA 30319
Telephone: (404) 255-2045
Recruiter Classification: Contingency; **Lowest/Average Salary:**
$30,000/$50,000; **Industry Concentration:** Information
Technology; **Function Concentration:** Engineering,
Finance/Accounting

Curtis, Ellissa — *Search Consultant*
Cochran, Cochran & Yale, Inc.
955 East Henrietta Road
Rochester, NY 14623
Telephone: (716) 424-6060
Recruiter Classification: Retained; **Lowest/Average Salary:**
$50,000/$75,000; **Industry Concentration:** High Technology,
Information Technology; **Function Concentration:** Generalist
with a primary focus in Engineering, Finance/Accounting,
General Management, Human Resources, Marketing, Sales,
Women/Minorities

Cushman, Judith — *President*
Judith Cushman & Associates
1125 12th Avenue, NW
Suite B-1A
Issaquah, WA 98027
Telephone: (425) 392-8660
Recruiter Classification: Retained; **Lowest/Average Salary:**
$30,000/$90,000; **Industry Concentration:** Generalist with a
primary focus in Electronics, High Technology, **Function
Concentration:** Generalist

Cutka, Matthew — *Associate*
Source Services Corporation
2029 Century Park East, Suite 1350
Los Angeles, CA 90067
Telephone: (310) 277-8092
Recruiter Classification: Contingency; **Lowest/Average Salary:**
$30,000/$50,000; **Industry Concentration:** Information
Technology; **Function Concentration:** Engineering,
Finance/Accounting

Cyphers, Ralph R. — *Senior Associate/Executive
Recruiter*
Strategic Associates, Inc.
13915 Burnet Road, Suite 300
Austin, TX 78728
Telephone: (512) 218-8222
Recruiter Classification: Contingency; **Lowest/Average Salary:**
$90,000/$90,000; **Industry Concentration:** High Technology,
Information Technology; **Function Concentration:** General
Management

Czamanske, Paul W. — *President and CEO*
Compass Group Ltd.
401 South Old Woodward Avenue
Suite 460
Birmingham, MI 48009-6613
Telephone: (248) 540-9110
Recruiter Classification: Retained; **Lowest/Average Salary:**
$75,000/$90,000; **Industry Concentration:** Electronics,
Information Technology; **Function Concentration:** Engineering,
Finance/Accounting, General Management, Human Resources,
Marketing, Research and Development, Sales,
Women/Minorities

Czepiel, Susan — *Executive Recruiter*
CPS Inc.
303 Congress Street, 5th Floor
Boston, MA 02210
Telephone: (617) 439-7950
Recruiter Classification: Contingency; **Lowest/Average Salary:**
$30,000/$50,000; **Industry Concentration:** Generalist with a
primary focus in Electronics, High Technology, Information
Technology; **Function Concentration:** Engineering, Research
and Development, Sales, Women/Minorities

D'Alessio, Gary A. — *President*
Chicago Legal Search, Ltd.
33 North Dearborn Street, Suite 2302
Chicago, IL 60602-3109
Telephone: (312) 251-2580
Recruiter Classification: Contingency; **Lowest/Average Salary:**
$50,000/$90,000; **Industry Concentration:** Electronics, High
Technology, Information Technology; **Function Concentration:**
Women/Minorities

Dabich, Thomas M. — *Vice President*
Robert Harkins Associates, Inc.
P.O. Box 236
1248 West Main Street
Ephrata, PA 17522
Telephone: (717) 733-9664
Recruiter Classification: Contingency; **Lowest/Average Salary:**
$40,000/$60,000; **Industry Concentration:** Generalist with a
primary focus in Electronics; **Function Concentration:**
Generalist with a primary focus in Finance/Accounting

Daily, John C. — *Executive Vice President*
Handy HRM Corp.
250 Park Avenue
New York, NY 10177-0074
Telephone: (212) 210-5653
Recruiter Classification: Retained; **Lowest/Average Salary:**
$90,000/$90,000; **Industry Concentration:** High Technology,
Information Technology; **Function Concentration:** Engineering,
General Management, Marketing, Sales

Dalton, Bret — *Vice President*
Robert W. Dingman Company, Inc.
650 Hampshire Road
Suite 116
Westlake Village, CA 91361
Telephone: (805) 778-1777
Recruiter Classification: Retained; **Lowest/Average Salary:**
$100,000/$145,000; **Industry Concentration:** Generalist with a
primary focus in High Technology; **Function Concentration:**
Generalist with a primary focus in Administration, Engineering,
Finance/Accounting, General Management, Human Resources,
Marketing, Sales

Danforth, W. Michael — *Executive Vice President*
Hyde Danforth Wold & Co.
5950 Berkshire Lane, Suite 1600
Dallas, TX 75225
Telephone: (214) 691-5966
Recruiter Classification: Retained; **Lowest/Average Salary:**
$50,000/$75,000; **Industry Concentration:** Generalist with a
primary focus in Electronics, High Technology; **Function
Concentration:** Generalist with a primary focus in
Administration, General Management, Human Resources,
Sales

Daniel, Beverly — *Partner*
Foy, Schneid & Daniel, Inc.
555 Madison Avenue, 12th Floor
New York, NY 10022
Telephone: (212) 980-2525
Recruiter Classification: Retained; **Lowest/Average Salary:**
$60,000/$90,000; **Industry Concentration:** Generalist with a
primary focus in Information Technology; **Function
Concentration:** Generalist with a primary focus in Engineering,
Finance/Accounting, General Management, Human Resources,
Marketing

Daniels, C. Eugene — *Vice President*
Sigma Group International
6551 South Revere Parkway
Suite 125
Englewood, CO 80111-6410
Telephone: (303) 792-9881
Recruiter Classification: Retained; **Lowest/Average Salary:**
$90,000/$90,000; **Industry Concentration:** Generalist with a
primary focus in High Technology; **Function Concentration:**
Generalist with a primary focus in Administration, Engineering,
Finance/Accounting, General Management, Human Resources,
Marketing

Daniels, Donna — *Executive Recruiter*
Jonas, Walters & Assoc., Inc.
1110 North Old World Third St., Suite 510
Milwaukee, WI 53203-1102
Telephone: (414) 291-2828
Recruiter Classification: Retained; **Lowest/Average Salary:**
$60,000/$90,000; **Industry Concentration:** Generalist with a
primary focus in High Technology; **Function Concentration:**
Generalist with a primary focus in Marketing, Sales,
Women/Minorities

Dankberg, Iris — *Associate*
Source Services Corporation
4170 Ashford Dunwoody Road, Suite 285
Atlanta, GA 30319
Telephone: (404) 255-2045
Recruiter Classification: Contingency; **Lowest/Average Salary:**
$30,000/$50,000; **Industry Concentration:** Information
Technology; **Function Concentration:** Engineering,
Finance/Accounting

Danoff, Audrey — *Recruiter*
Don Richard Associates of Tidewater, Inc.
4701 Columbus Street, Suite 102
Virginia Beach, VA 23462
Telephone: (757) 518-8600
Recruiter Classification: Contingency, Executive Temporary;
Lowest/Average Salary: $20,000/$30,000; **Industry
Concentration:** Generalist with a primary focus in Information
Technology; **Function Concentration:** Marketing, Sales

Darter, Steven M. — *President*
People Management Northeast Incorporated
One Darling Drive, Avon Park South
Avon, CT 06001
Telephone: (860) 678-8900
Recruiter Classification: Retained; **Lowest/Average Salary:**
$75,000/$90,000; **Industry Concentration:** Generalist with a
primary focus in Information Technology; **Function
Concentration:** Generalist

Davis, Bert — *President*
Bert Davis Executive Search, Inc.
425 Madison Avenue
New York, NY 10017
Telephone: (212) 838-4000
Recruiter Classification: Contingency; **Lowest/Average Salary:**
$60,000/$60,000; **Industry Concentration:** Information
Technology; **Function Concentration:** Finance/Accounting,
General Management, Marketing, Research and Development,
Sales, Women/Minorities

Davis, C. Scott — *Associate*
Source Services Corporation
7730 East Bellview Avenue, Suite 302
Englewood, CO 80111
Telephone: (303) 773-3700
Recruiter Classification: Contingency; **Lowest/Average Salary:**
$30,000/$50,000; **Industry Concentration:** Information
Technology; **Function Concentration:** Engineering,
Finance/Accounting

Davis, Elease — *Associate*
Source Services Corporation
525 Vine Street, Suite 2250
Cincinnati, OH 45202
Telephone: (513) 651-3303
Recruiter Classification: Contingency; **Lowest/Average Salary:**
$30,000/$50,000; **Industry Concentration:** Information
Technology; **Function Concentration:** Engineering,
Finance/Accounting

Davis, G. Gordon — *President*
Davis & Company
3419 Via Lido, Suite 615
Newport Beach, CA 92663
Telephone: (714) 376-6995
Recruiter Classification: Retained; **Lowest/Average Salary:**
$50,000/$75,000; **Industry Concentration:** Generalist with a
primary focus in Electronics, High Technology, Information
Technology; **Function Concentration:** Generalist with a
primary focus in Administration, Engineering,
Finance/Accounting, General Management, Human Resources,
Marketing, Research and Development, Sales

Davis, John — *Consultant*
John J. Davis & Associates, Inc.
521 Fifth Avenue, Suite 1740
New York, NY 10175
Telephone: (212) 286-9489
Recruiter Classification: Retained; **Lowest/Average Salary:**
$90,000/$90,000; **Industry Concentration:** Information
Technology; **Function Concentration:** Generalist

Davis, John J. — *President*
John J. Davis & Associates, Inc.
P.O. Box G
Short Hills, NJ 07078
Telephone: (201) 467-8339
Recruiter Classification: Retained; **Lowest/Average Salary:**
$90,000/$90,000; **Industry Concentration:** Information
Technology; **Function Concentration:** Generalist

Davis, Steven M. — *Consultant*
Sullivan & Company
20 Exchange Place, 50th Floor
New York, NY 10005
Telephone: (212) 422-3000
Recruiter Classification: Retained; **Lowest/Average Salary:**
$90,000/$90,000; **Industry Concentration:** Generalist with a
primary focus in Information Technology; **Function
Concentration:** Generalist

Davison, Patricia E. — *Principal*
Lamalie Amrop International
Thanksgiving Tower
1601 Elm Street
Dallas, TX 75201-4768
Telephone: (214) 754-0019
Recruiter Classification: Retained; **Lowest/Average Salary:**
$90,000/$90,000; **Industry Concentration:** Generalist with a
primary focus in High Technology; **Function Concentration:**
Generalist with a primary focus in Finance/Accounting,
General Management, Marketing, Sales

Dawson, Joe — *Executive Recruiter*
S.C. International, Ltd.
1430 Branding Lane, Suite 119
Downers Grove, IL 60515
Telephone: (708) 963-3033
Recruiter Classification: Contingency; **Lowest/Average Salary:**
$30,000/$50,000; **Industry Concentration:** Information
Technology; **Function Concentration:** Administration, Human
Resources

Dawson, William — *Associate*
Source Services Corporation
8614 Westwood Center, Suite 750
Vienna, VA 22182
Telephone: (703) 790-5610
Recruiter Classification: Contingency; **Lowest/Average Salary:**
$30,000/$50,000; **Industry Concentration:** Information
Technology; **Function Concentration:** Engineering,
Finance/Accounting

De Brun, Thomas P. — *Partner*
Ray & Berndtson
One Park Plaza, Suite 420
Irvine, CA 92614
Telephone: (714) 476-8844
Recruiter Classification: Retained; **Lowest/Average Salary:**
$90,000/$90,000; **Industry Concentration:** Generalist with a
primary focus in High Technology, Information Technology;
Function Concentration: Generalist with a primary focus in
Administration, Finance/Accounting, General Management,
Human Resources, Marketing, Research and Development,
Sales, Women/Minorities

de Gury, Glenn — *Vice President*
Taylor-Winfield, Inc.
12801 N. Central Expressway
Suite 1260
Dallas, TX 75243
Telephone: (214) 392-1400
Recruiter Classification: Retained; **Lowest/Average Salary:**
$90,000/$90,000; **Industry Concentration:** High Technology,
Information Technology; **Function Concentration:** Generalist
with a primary focus in Finance/Accounting, General
Management, Research and Development, Sales

Dean, Mary — *Principal Advanced Technology*
Korn/Ferry International
2180 Sand Hill Road
Menlo Park, CA 94025
Telephone: (415) 233-2733
Recruiter Classification: Retained; **Lowest/Average Salary:**
$100,000/$150,000; **Industry Concentration:** Generalist with a
primary focus in Information Technology; **Function
Concentration:** Generalist

Deaver, Henry C. — *Consultant*
Ray & Berndtson
Sears Tower, 233 South Wacker Drive, Suite 4020
Chicago, IL 60606-6310
Telephone: (312) 876-0730
Recruiter Classification: Retained; **Lowest/Average Salary:**
$90,000/$90,000; **Industry Concentration:** Generalist with a
primary focus in High Technology, Information Technology;
Function Concentration: Generalist with a primary focus in
Administration, Finance/Accounting, General Management,
Human Resources, Marketing, Research and Development,
Sales, Women/Minorities

Debus, Wayne — *Associate*
Source Services Corporation
5343 North 16th Street, Suite 270
Phoenix, AZ 85016
Telephone: (602) 230-0220
Recruiter Classification: Contingency; **Lowest/Average Salary:**
$30,000/$50,000; **Industry Concentration:** Information
Technology; **Function Concentration:** Engineering,
Finance/Accounting

Deck, Jack — *Managing Director*
Source Services Corporation
One CityPlace, Suite 170
St. Louis, MO 63141
Telephone: (314) 432-4500
Recruiter Classification: Contingency; **Lowest/Average Salary:**
$30,000/$50,000; **Industry Concentration:** Information
Technology; **Function Concentration:** Engineering,
Finance/Accounting

DeCorrevont, James — *President*
DeCorrevont & Associates
1122 North Clark Street
Chicago, IL 60610
Telephone: (312) 642-9300
Recruiter Classification: Contingency; **Lowest/Average Salary:**
$40,000/$90,000; **Industry Concentration:** Generalist with a
primary focus in High Technology, Information Technology;
Function Concentration: Generalist with a primary focus in
Administration, Finance/Accounting, Human Resources,
Marketing, Sales, Women/Minorities

DeCorrevont, James — *President*
DeCorrevont & Associates
225 Country Club Drive
Largo, FL 34641
Telephone: (312) 642-9300
Recruiter Classification: Contingency; **Lowest/Average Salary:**
$40,000/$90,000; **Industry Concentration:** Generalist with a
primary focus in High Technology, Information Technology;
Function Concentration: Generalist with a primary focus in
Administration, Finance/Accounting, Human Resources,
Marketing, Sales, Women/Minorities

DeGioia, Joseph — *President*
JDG Associates, Ltd.
1700 Research Boulevard
Rockville, MD 20850
Telephone: (301) 340-2210
Recruiter Classification: Contingency; **Lowest/Average Salary:**
$50,000/$90,000; **Industry Concentration:** Electronics, High
Technology, Information Technology; **Function Concentration:**
Generalist with a primary focus in Administration, Engineering,
Finance/Accounting, Research and Development

DeHart, Donna — *Vice President*
Tower Consultants, Ltd.
771 East Lancaster Avenue
Villanova, PA 19085
Telephone: (610) 519-1700
Recruiter Classification: Retained; **Lowest/Average Salary:**
$60,000/$90,000; **Industry Concentration:** Generalist with a
primary focus in High Technology, Information Technology;
Function Concentration: Administration, Human Resources,
Women/Minorities

Del Prete, Karen — *Vice President*
Gilbert Tweed/INESA
415 Madison Avenue
New York, NY 10017
Telephone: (212) 758-3000
Recruiter Classification: Retained; **Lowest/Average Salary:**
$90,000/$90,000; **Industry Concentration:** Generalist with a
primary focus in High Technology, Information Technology;
Function Concentration: Generalist

Delaney, Patrick J. — *Principal*
Sensible Solutions, Inc.
239 West Coolidge Avenue
Barrington, IL 60010
Telephone: (847) 382-0070
Recruiter Classification: Retained, Executive Temporary;
Lowest/Average Salary: $60,000/$90,000; **Industry
Concentration:** Generalist with a primary focus in Electronics,
High Technology, Information Technology; **Function
Concentration:** Generalist with a primary focus in
Administration, Engineering, Finance/Accounting, General
Management, Human Resources, Marketing, Sales

Delmonico, Laura — *Professional Recruiter*
A.J. Burton Group, Inc.
120 East Baltimore Street, Suite 2220
Baltimore, MD 21202
Telephone: (410) 752-5244
Recruiter Classification: Contingency; **Lowest/Average Salary:**
$40,000/$75,000; **Industry Concentration:** Generalist with a
primary focus in High Technology, Information Technology;
Function Concentration: Generalist with a primary focus in
Administration, Finance/Accounting, General Management,
Human Resources

DeLong, Art — *Vice President*
Richard Kader & Associates
7850 Freeway Circle, Suite 201
Cleveland, OH 44130
Telephone: (440) 891-1700
Recruiter Classification: Contingency; **Lowest/Average Salary:**
$40,000/$50,000; **Industry Concentration:** Generalist with a
primary focus in High Technology; **Function Concentration:**
Generalist with a primary focus in General Management,
Human Resources, Marketing, Research and Development,
Sales, Women/Minorities

DeMarco, Robert — *Managing Director*
Source Services Corporation
1500 West Park Drive, Suite 390
Westborough, MA 01581
Telephone: (508) 366-2600
Recruiter Classification: Contingency; **Lowest/Average Salary:**
$30,000/$50,000; **Industry Concentration:** Information
Technology; **Function Concentration:** Engineering,
Finance/Accounting

Demchak, James P. — *Partner*
Sandhurst Associates
4851 LBJ Freeway, Suite 601
Dallas, TX 75244
Telephone: (214) 458-1212
Recruiter Classification: Retained; **Lowest/Average Salary:**
$75,000/$90,000; **Industry Concentration:** Generalist with a
primary focus in High Technology; **Function Concentration:**
Generalist with a primary focus in Finance/Accounting, Human
Resources, Marketing, Sales

Desai, Sushila — *Search Consultant*
Sink, Walker, Boltrus International
60 Walnut Street
Wellesley, MA 02181
Telephone: (617) 237-1199
Recruiter Classification: Retained; **Lowest/Average Salary:**
$90,000/$90,000; **Industry Concentration:** Electronics, High
Technology, Information Technology; **Function Concentration:**
Engineering, General Management, Research and
Development, Sales

Desgrosellier, Gary P. — *President*
Personnel Unlimited/Executive Search
25 West Nora
Spokane, WA 99205
Telephone: (509) 326-8880
Recruiter Classification: Contingency; **Lowest/Average Salary:**
$30,000/$60,000; **Industry Concentration:** Generalist with a
primary focus in High Technology; **Function Concentration:**
Generalist with a primary focus in Engineering,
Finance/Accounting, Human Resources, Marketing, Sales

Desmond, Dennis — *Executive Vice
President/Partner*
Beall & Company, Inc.
535 Colonial Park Drive
Roswell, GA 30075
Telephone: (404) 992-0900
Recruiter Classification: Retained; **Lowest/Average Salary:**
$90,000/$90,000; **Industry Concentration:** Generalist with a
primary focus in High Technology; **Function Concentration:**
Generalist with a primary focus in Administration, Engineering,
Finance/Accounting, General Management, Human Resources,
Marketing, Research and Development, Sales

Desmond, Mary — *Associate*
Source Services Corporation
150 South Wacker Drive, Suite 400
Chicago, IL 60606
Telephone: (312) 346-7000
Recruiter Classification: Contingency; **Lowest/Average Salary:**
$30,000/$50,000; **Industry Concentration:** Information
Technology; **Function Concentration:** Engineering,
Finance/Accounting

Dever, Mary — *Associate*
Source Services Corporation
505 East 200 South, Suite 300
Salt Lake City, UT 84102
Telephone: (801) 328-0011
Recruiter Classification: Contingency; **Lowest/Average Salary:**
$30,000/$50,000; **Industry Concentration:** Information
Technology; **Function Concentration:** Engineering,
Finance/Accounting

Devito, Alice — *Associate*
Source Services Corporation
925 Westchester Avenue, Suite 309
White Plains, NY 10604
Telephone: (914) 428-9100
Recruiter Classification: Contingency; **Lowest/Average Salary:**
$30,000/$50,000; **Industry Concentration:** Information
Technology; **Function Concentration:** Engineering,
Finance/Accounting

deVry, Kimberly A. — *Executive Search Recruiter*
Tower Consultants, Ltd.
771 East Lancaster Avenue
Villanova, PA 19085
Telephone: (610) 519-1700
Recruiter Classification: Retained; **Lowest/Average Salary:**
$60,000/$90,000; **Industry Concentration:** Generalist with a
primary focus in High Technology, Information Technology;
Function Concentration: Administration, Human Resources,
Women/Minorities

deWilde, David M. — *Managing Director*
Chartwell Partners International, Inc.
275 Battery Street, Suite 2180
San Francisco, CA 94111
Telephone: (415) 296-0600
Recruiter Classification: Retained; **Lowest/Average Salary:**
$90,000/$90,000; **Industry Concentration:** Generalist with a
primary focus in High Technology, Information Technology;
Function Concentration: Finance/Accounting, General
Management, Human Resources, Marketing,
Women/Minorities

Dezember, Steve — *Partner*
Ray & Berndtson
191 Peachtree Street, NE, Suite 3800
Atlanta, GA 30303-1757
Telephone: (404) 215-4600
Recruiter Classification: Retained; **Lowest/Average Salary:**
$90,000/$90,000; **Industry Concentration:** Generalist with a
primary focus in High Technology, Information Technology;
Function Concentration: Generalist with a primary focus in
Administration, Finance/Accounting, General Management,
Human Resources, Marketing, Research and Development,
Sales, Women/Minorities

Di Filippo, Thomas — *Associate*
Source Services Corporation
20 Burlington Mall Road, Suite 405
Burlington, MA 01803
Telephone: (617) 272-5000
Recruiter Classification: Contingency; **Lowest/Average Salary:**
$30,000/$50,000; **Industry Concentration:** Information
Technology; **Function Concentration:** Engineering,
Finance/Accounting

DiCioccio, Carmen — *Search Consultant*
Cochran, Cochran & Yale, Inc.
5166 Main Street
Williamsville, NY 14221
Telephone: (716) 631-1300
Recruiter Classification: Retained; **Lowest/Average Salary:**
$50,000/$75,000; **Industry Concentration:** Generalist with a
primary focus in High Technology, Information Technology;
Function Concentration: Generalist with a primary focus in
Engineering, Finance/Accounting, General Management,
Human Resources, Marketing, Sales, Women/Minorities

Dicker, Barry — *Managing Partner*
ESA Professional Consultants
141 Durham Road
Suite 16
Madison, CT 06443
Telephone: (203) 245-1983
Recruiter Classification: Retained; **Lowest/Average Salary:**
$50,000/$75,000; **Industry Concentration:** Electronics, High
Technology, Information Technology; **Function Concentration:**
Engineering, General Management, Human Resources,
Women/Minorities

Dickey, Chester W. — *President and CEO*
Bowden & Company, Inc.
5000 Rockside Road, Suite 550
Cleveland, OH 44131
Telephone: (216) 447-1800
Recruiter Classification: Retained; **Lowest/Average Salary:**
$90,000/$90,000; **Industry Concentration:** Generalist with a
primary focus in High Technology, Information Technology;
Function Concentration: Generalist

Dickey, Chester W. — *President and CEO*
Bowden & Company, Inc.
9420 Hunters Pond Drive
Tampa, FL 33647
Telephone: (813) 973-8592
Recruiter Classification: Retained; **Lowest/Average Salary:**
$90,000/$90,000; **Industry Concentration:** Generalist with a
primary focus in High Technology, Information Technology;
Function Concentration: Generalist

Dickson, Duke — *Associate*
A.D. & Associates Executive Search, Inc.
5589 Woodsong Drive, Suite 100
Atlanta, GA 30338-2933
Telephone: (770) 393-0021
Recruiter Classification: Contingency; **Lowest/Average Salary:**
$50,000/$75,000; **Industry Concentration:** Generalist with a
primary focus in High Technology, Information Technology;
Function Concentration: Generalist with a primary focus in
Engineering, Finance/Accounting, General Management,
Human Resources, Marketing, Research and Development,
Sales, Women/Minorities

Diers, Gary — *Associate*
Source Services Corporation
10220 SW Greenburg Road, Suite 625
Portland, OR 97223
Telephone: (503) 768-4546
Recruiter Classification: Contingency; **Lowest/Average Salary:**
$30,000/$50,000; **Industry Concentration:** Information
Technology; **Function Concentration:** Engineering,
Finance/Accounting

Dietz, David S. — *Manager*
MSI International
201 St. Charles Avenue
Suite 2205
New Orleans, LA 70170
Telephone: (504) 522-6700
Recruiter Classification: Contingency; **Lowest/Average Salary:**
$30,000/$60,000; **Industry Concentration:** Generalist with a
primary focus in High Technology, Information Technology;
Function Concentration: Generalist with a primary focus in
Administration, Engineering, Finance/Accounting, General
Management, Marketing, Sales

DiFilippo, James — *Vice President Retail*
Korn/Ferry International
237 Park Avenue
New York, NY 10017
Telephone: (212) 687-1834
Recruiter Classification: Retained; **Lowest/Average Salary:**
$100,000/$150,000; **Industry Concentration:** Generalist with a
primary focus in Information Technology; **Function
Concentration:** Generalist

Dillon, Larry — *Chief Executive Officer*
Predictor Systems
39350 Civic Center Drive, Suite 440
Fremont, CA 94538
Telephone: (510) 713-0840
Recruiter Classification: Retained; **Lowest/Average Salary:**
$90,000/$90,000; **Industry Concentration:** Electronics, High
Technology, Information Technology; **Function Concentration:**
Engineering, Finance/Accounting, Sales

DiMarchi, Paul — *President*
DiMarchi Partners, Inc.
1225 17th Street, Suite 1460
Denver, CO 80202
Telephone: (303) 292-9300
Recruiter Classification: Retained; **Lowest/Average Salary:**
$90,000/$90,000; **Industry Concentration:** Generalist with a
primary focus in High Technology; **Function Concentration:**
Generalist with a primary focus in Engineering,
Finance/Accounting, General Management, Marketing, Sales

DiMarchi, Paul — *President*
DiMarchi Partners, Inc.
885 Arapahoe Avenue
Boulder, CO 80302
Telephone: (303) 415-9300
Recruiter Classification: Retained; **Lowest/Average Salary:**
$90,000/$90,000; **Industry Concentration:** Generalist with a
primary focus in High Technology; **Function Concentration:**
Generalist with a primary focus in Engineering,
Finance/Accounting, General Management, Marketing, Sales

Dingeldey, Peter E. — *Vice President*
Search Advisors International Corp.
777 South Harbour Island Boulevard
Suite 925
Tampa, FL 33602
Telephone: (813) 221-7555
Recruiter Classification: Retained; **Lowest/Average Salary:**
$75,000/$90,000; **Industry Concentration:** Generalist with a
primary focus in Electronics, High Technology, Information
Technology; **Function Concentration:** Generalist with a
primary focus in Administration, Engineering,
Finance/Accounting, General Management, Human Resources,
Marketing, Research and Development, Sales,
Women/Minorities

Dingman, Bruce — *President*
Robert W. Dingman Company, Inc.
650 Hampshire Road
Suite 116
Westlake Village, CA 91361
Telephone: (805) 778-1777
Recruiter Classification: Retained; **Lowest/Average Salary:**
$100,000/$145,000; **Industry Concentration:** Generalist with a
primary focus in Electronics, High Technology; **Function
Concentration:** Generalist with a primary focus in
Administration, Engineering, Finance/Accounting, General
Management, Human Resources, Marketing, Sales

Dingman, Robert W. — *Chairman*
Robert W. Dingman Company, Inc.
650 Hampshire Road
Suite 116
Westlake Village, CA 91361
Telephone: (805) 778-1777
Recruiter Classification: Retained; **Lowest/Average Salary:**
$100,000/$145,000; **Industry Concentration:** Electronics, High
Technology; **Function Concentration:** Generalist with a
primary focus in Administration, Finance/Accounting, General
Management, Human Resources, Marketing, Sales

Dinte, Paul — *President*
Dinte Resources, Inc.
8300 Greensboro Drive
Suite 880
McLean, VA 22102
Telephone: (703) 448-3300
Recruiter Classification: Retained, Executive Temporary;
Lowest/Average Salary: $75,000/$90,000; **Industry
Concentration:** Generalist with a primary focus in High
Technology, Information Technology; **Function Concentration:**
Generalist with a primary focus in Finance/Accounting,
General Management, Human Resources, Marketing

DiSalvo, Fred — *Vice President*
The Cambridge Group Ltd
161A John Jefferson Road
Williamsburg, VA 23185
Telephone: (757) 565-1150
Recruiter Classification: Contingency; **Lowest/Average Salary:**
$60,000/$75,000; **Industry Concentration:** Generalist with a
primary focus in High Technology, Information Technology;
Function Concentration: Administration, Finance/Accounting,
General Management, Human Resources, Marketing, Research
and Development, Sales, Women/Minorities

Diskin, Rochelle — *Account Executive*
Search West, Inc.
340 North Westlake Boulevard
Suite 200
Westlake Village, CA 91362-3761
Telephone: (805) 496-6811
Recruiter Classification: Contingency; **Lowest/Average Salary:**
$40,000/$60,000; **Industry Concentration:** Electronics;
Function Concentration: Administration, Finance/Accounting,
Marketing

Dittmar, Richard — *Associate*
Source Services Corporation
4200 West Cypress Street, Suite 101
Tampa, FL 33607
Telephone: (813) 879-2221
Recruiter Classification: Contingency; **Lowest/Average Salary:**
$30,000/$50,000; **Industry Concentration:** Information
Technology; **Function Concentration:** Engineering,
Finance/Accounting

Divine, Robert S. — *Principal*
O'Shea, Divine & Company, Inc.
610 Newport Center Drive, Suite 1040
Newport Beach, CA 92660
Telephone: (714) 720-9070
Recruiter Classification: Retained; **Lowest/Average Salary:**
$75,000/$90,000; **Industry Concentration:** Generalist with a
primary focus in Electronics, High Technology, Information
Technology; **Function Concentration:** Generalist with a
primary focus in Engineering, Finance/Accounting, General
Management, Human Resources, Marketing, Research and
Development, Sales

Dixon, Aris — *Executive Recruiter*
CPS Inc.
One Westbrook Corporate Centre, Suite 600
Westchester, IL 60154
Telephone: (708) 531-8370
Recruiter Classification: Contingency; **Lowest/Average Salary:**
$30,000/$50,000; **Industry Concentration:** Generalist with a
primary focus in Electronics, High Technology, Information
Technology; **Function Concentration:** Engineering, Research
and Development, Sales, Women/Minorities

Do, Sonnie — *Executive Recruiter*
Whitney & Associates, Inc.
920 Second Avenue South, Suite 625
Minneapolis, MN 55402-4035
Telephone: (612) 338-5600
Recruiter Classification: Contingency; **Lowest/Average Salary:**
$20,000/$50,000; **Industry Concentration:** Generalist with a
primary focus in Electronics, High Technology, Information
Technology; **Function Concentration:** Finance/Accounting

Dobrow, Samuel — *Associate*
Source Services Corporation
4170 Ashford Dunwoody Road, Suite 285
Atlanta, GA 30319
Telephone: (404) 255-2045
Recruiter Classification: Contingency; **Lowest/Average Salary:**
$30,000/$50,000; **Industry Concentration:** Information
Technology; **Function Concentration:** Engineering,
Finance/Accounting

Doele, Donald C. — *Vice President*
Goodrich & Sherwood Associates, Inc.
One Independence Way
Princeton, NJ 08540
Telephone: (609) 452-0202
Recruiter Classification: Retained; **Lowest/Average Salary:**
$60,000/$90,000; **Industry Concentration:** Generalist with a
primary focus in Information Technology; **Function
Concentration:** Generalist with a primary focus in
Administration, Finance/Accounting, General Management,
Human Resources, Marketing, Sales

Doman, Matthew — *Executive Recruiter*
S.C. International, Ltd.
1430 Branding Lane, Suite 119
Downers Grove, IL 60515
Telephone: (708) 963-3033
Recruiter Classification: Contingency; **Lowest/Average Salary:**
$30,000/$50,000; **Industry Concentration:** Information
Technology; **Function Concentration:** Administration, Human
Resources

Donahue, Debora — *Associate*
Source Services Corporation
505 East 200 South, Suite 300
Salt Lake City, UT 84102
Telephone: (801) 328-0011
Recruiter Classification: Contingency; **Lowest/Average Salary:**
$30,000/$50,000; **Industry Concentration:** Information
Technology; **Function Concentration:** Engineering,
Finance/Accounting

Donath, Linda — *Dahl-Morrow International*
Dahl-Morrow International
12020 Sunrise Valley Drive
Reston, VA 20191
Telephone: (703) 860-6868
Recruiter Classification: Retained; **Lowest/Average Salary:**
$75,000/$90,000; **Industry Concentration:** Electronics, High
Technology, Information Technology; **Function Concentration:**
Generalist with a primary focus in Engineering,
Finance/Accounting, General Management, Marketing, Sales

Dong, Stephen — *Associate*
Executive Search, Ltd.
4830 Interstate Drive
Cincinnati, OH 45246
Telephone: (513) 874-6901
Recruiter Classification: Retained; **Lowest/Average Salary:**
$50,000/$75,000; **Industry Concentration:** Generalist with a
primary focus in Electronics, High Technology, Information
Technology

Donnelly, Patti — *Associate*
Source Services Corporation
150 South Warner Road, Suite 238
King of Prussia, PA 19406
Telephone: (610) 341-1960
Recruiter Classification: Contingency; **Lowest/Average Salary:**
$30,000/$50,000; **Industry Concentration:** Information
Technology; **Function Concentration:** Engineering,
Finance/Accounting

Dorfner, Martin — *Associate*
Source Services Corporation
Foster Plaza VI
681 Anderson Drive, 2nd Floor
Pittsburgh, PA 15220
Telephone: (412) 928-8300
Recruiter Classification: Contingency; **Lowest/Average Salary:**
$30,000/$50,000; **Industry Concentration:** Information
Technology; **Function Concentration:** Engineering,
Finance/Accounting

Dorsey, Jim — *Executive Recruiter*
Ryan, Miller & Associates Inc.
4601 Wilshire Boulevard, Suite 225
Los Angeles, CA 90010
Telephone: (213) 938-4768
Recruiter Classification: Contingency; **Lowest/Average Salary:**
$60,000/$75,000; **Industry Concentration:** High Technology;
Function Concentration: Generalist

Dotson, M. Ileen — *Principal*
Dotson & Associates
412 East 55th Street, Suite 8A
New York, NY 10022
Telephone: (212) 593-4274
Recruiter Classification: Contingency; **Lowest/Average Salary:**
$75,000/$90,000; **Industry Concentration:** Generalist with a
primary focus in High Technology, Information Technology;
Function Concentration: General Management, Marketing,
Sales, Women/Minorities

Dow, Lori — *Managing Partner*
Davidson, Laird & Associates, Inc.
29260 Franklin, Suite 110
Southfield, MI 48034
Telephone: (248) 358-2160
Recruiter Classification: Contingency; **Lowest/Average Salary:**
$60,000/$75,000; **Industry Concentration:** Generalist with a
primary focus in High Technology; **Function Concentration:**
Generalist with a primary focus in Administration, Engineering,
Finance/Accounting, General Management, Human Resources,
Sales, Women/Minorities

Dowdall, Jean — *Vice President*
A.T. Kearney, Inc.
225 Reinekers Lane
Alexandria, VA 22314
Telephone: (703) 739-4624
Recruiter Classification: Retained; **Lowest/Average Salary:**
$90,000/$90,000; **Industry Concentration:** Generalist with a
primary focus in High Technology, Information Technology;
Function Concentration: Generalist with a primary focus in
Engineering, Finance/Accounting, General Management

Dowell, Chris — *Senior Vice President*
The Abbott Group, Inc.
1577 Spring Hill Road
Vienna, VA 22182
Telephone: (703) 790-0314
Recruiter Classification: Retained; **Lowest/Average Salary:**
$90,000/$90,000; **Industry Concentration:** Generalist with a
primary focus in Electronics, High Technology, Information
Technology; **Function Concentration:** Generalist with a
primary focus in Administration, Engineering,
Finance/Accounting, General Management, Human Resources,
Marketing, Research and Development

Dowell, Mary K. — *Principal*
Professional Search Associates
12459 Lewis Street, Suite 102
Garden Grove, CA 92640-6606
Telephone: (714) 740-0919
Recruiter Classification: Contingency; **Lowest/Average Salary:**
$40,000/$75,000; **Industry Concentration:** Generalist with a
primary focus in Information Technology; **Function
Concentration:** Finance/Accounting, General Management,
Human Resources, Marketing, Sales

Dowlatzadch, Homayoun — *Associate*
Source Services Corporation
4510 Executive Drive, Suite 200
San Diego, CA 92121
Telephone: (619) 552-0300
Recruiter Classification: Contingency; **Lowest/Average Salary:**
$30,000/$50,000; **Industry Concentration:** Information
Technology; **Function Concentration:** Engineering,
Finance/Accounting

Downs, William — *Associate*
Source Services Corporation
4170 Ashford Dunwoody Road, Suite 285
Atlanta, GA 30319
Telephone: (404) 255-2045
Recruiter Classification: Contingency; **Lowest/Average Salary:**
$30,000/$50,000; **Industry Concentration:** Information
Technology; **Function Concentration:** Engineering,
Finance/Accounting

Doyle, Bobby — *Executive Recruiter*
Richard, Wayne and Roberts
24 Greenway Plaza, Suite 1304
Houston, TX 77046-2493
Telephone: (713) 629-6681
Recruiter Classification: Retained; **Lowest/Average Salary:**
$50,000/$90,000; **Industry Concentration:** Generalist with a
primary focus in High Technology; **Function Concentration:**
Generalist with a primary focus in Engineering

Doyle, James W. — *Managing Director*
Executive Search Consultants International, Inc.
330 Fifth Avenue
Suite 5501
New York, NY 10118
Telephone: (212) 333-1900
Recruiter Classification: Retained; **Lowest/Average Salary:**
$90,000/$90,000; **Industry Concentration:** Generalist with a
primary focus in High Technology, Information Technology;
Function Concentration: Generalist with a primary focus in
Finance/Accounting, General Management, Human Resources,
Marketing

Doyle, Marie — *Senior Consultant*
Spectra International Inc.
6991 East Camelback Road, Suite B-305
Scottsdale, AZ 85251
Telephone: (602) 481-0411
Recruiter Classification: Contingency; **Lowest/Average Salary:**
$50,000/$60,000; **Industry Concentration:** Electronics;
Function Concentration: Engineering

Dreifus, Donald — *Account Executive*
Search West, Inc.
1888 Century Park East
Suite 2050
Los Angeles, CA 90067-1736
Telephone: (310) 284-8888
Recruiter Classification: Contingency; Lowest/Average Salary: $40,000/$60,000; Industry Concentration: Generalist with a primary focus in Electronics, High Technology, Information Technology; Function Concentration: Generalist with a primary focus in Administration, Finance/Accounting, General Management, Marketing

Dressler, Ralph — *Senior Consultant*
Romac & Associates
1040 North Kings Highway
Suite 624
Cherry Hill, NJ 08034
Telephone: (609) 482-9677
Recruiter Classification: Executive Temporary; Lowest/Average Salary: $60,000/$60,000; Industry Concentration: High Technology, Information Technology; Function Concentration: Finance/Accounting

Drew, David R. — *President*
Drew & Associates
201 NE Park Plaza Drive
Suite 201
Vancouver, WA 98684
Telephone: (360) 254-2120
Recruiter Classification: Retained; Lowest/Average Salary: $75,000/$75,000; Industry Concentration: Generalist with a primary focus in Electronics, High Technology; Function Concentration: Generalist with a primary focus in Engineering, Finance/Accounting, General Management, Human Resources, Research and Development, Sales, Women/Minorities

Drexler, Robert — *President*
Robert Drexler Associates, Inc.
210 River Street
Hackensack, NJ 07601
Telephone: (201) 342-0200
Recruiter Classification: Retained; Lowest/Average Salary: $50,000/$90,000; Industry Concentration: Electronics, High Technology; Function Concentration: Engineering, General Management, Research and Development

Dromeshauser, Peter — *President*
Dromeshauser Associates
20 William Street
Wellesley, MA 02181
Telephone: (617) 239-0222
Recruiter Classification: Retained; Lowest/Average Salary: $90,000/$90,000; Industry Concentration: Electronics, High Technology, Information Technology; Function Concentration: General Management, Marketing, Sales

Drury, James J. — *Managing Director*
Spencer Stuart
401 North Michigan Avenue, Suite 3400
Chicago, IL 60611-4244
Telephone: (312) 822-0080
Recruiter Classification: Retained; Lowest/Average Salary: $90,000/$90,000; Industry Concentration: Generalist with a primary focus in Electronics, High Technology; Function Concentration: Generalist with a primary focus in Administration, Finance/Accounting, General Management, Human Resources, Marketing, Sales

Dubbs, William — *President*
Williams Executive Search, Inc.
4200 Norwest Center
90 South 7th Street
Minneapolis, MN 55402
Telephone: (612) 339-2900
Recruiter Classification: Retained; Lowest/Average Salary: $90,000/$90,000; Industry Concentration: Generalist with a primary focus in High Technology; Function Concentration: Generalist with a primary focus in Finance/Accounting, General Management, Marketing, Sales

Dubrow, Richard M. — *Executive Vice President*
R/K International, Inc.
191 Post Road West
Westport, CT 06880
Telephone: (203) 221-2747
Recruiter Classification: Retained; Lowest/Average Salary: $75,000/$90,000; Industry Concentration: Generalist with a primary focus in Electronics; Function Concentration: Generalist with a primary focus in Engineering, Finance/Accounting, General Management, Human Resources, Marketing, Research and Development, Sales

Duckworth, Donald R. — *Managing Director*
Johnson Smith & Knisely Accord
600 Peachtree Street, Suite 3860
Atlanta, GA 30308
Telephone: (404) 874-2100
Recruiter Classification: Retained; Lowest/Average Salary: $90,000/$90,000; Industry Concentration: High Technology, Information Technology; Function Concentration: General Management, Human Resources, Sales

Duelks, John — *Associate*
Source Services Corporation
4170 Ashford Dunwoody Road, Suite 285
Atlanta, GA 30319
Telephone: (404) 255-2045
Recruiter Classification: Contingency; Lowest/Average Salary: $30,000/$50,000; Industry Concentration: Information Technology; Function Concentration: Engineering, Finance/Accounting

Dugan, John H. — *President*
J.H. Dugan and Associates, Inc.
225 Crossroads Boulevard, Suite 416
Carmel, CA 93923
Telephone: (408) 625-5880
Recruiter Classification: Retained; Lowest/Average Salary: $50,000/$75,000; Industry Concentration: High Technology; Function Concentration: Engineering, General Management, Marketing, Research and Development, Sales, Women/Minorities

Duggan, James P. — *Vice President*
Slayton International, Inc./I-I-C Partners
181 West Madison Street, Suite 4510
Chicago, IL 60602
Telephone: (312) 456-0080
Recruiter Classification: Retained; Lowest/Average Salary: $90,000/$90,000; Industry Concentration: Generalist with a primary focus in High Technology, Information Technology; Function Concentration: Generalist with a primary focus in Engineering, General Management, Sales

Duley, Richard I. — *Vice President/General Manager*
ARJay & Associates
875 Walnut Street, Suite 150
Cary, NC 27511
Telephone: (919) 469-5540
Recruiter Classification: Contingency; **Lowest/Average Salary:** $40,000/$90,000; **Industry Concentration:** Generalist with a primary focus in Electronics; **Function Concentration:** Generalist with a primary focus in Engineering, Finance/Accounting, General Management, Human Resources, Marketing, Research and Development, Sales

Dunbar, Geoffrey T. — *Partner*
Heidrick & Struggles, Inc.
300 South Grand Avenue, Suite 2400
Los Angeles, CA 90071
Telephone: (213) 625-8811
Recruiter Classification: Retained; **Lowest/Average Salary:** $75,000/$90,000; **Industry Concentration:** Generalist with a primary focus in High Technology; **Function Concentration:** Generalist

Dunbar, Marilynne — *Consultant*
Ray & Berndtson/Lovas Stanley
Royal Bank Plaza, South Tower, Suite 3150
200 Bay Street, P.O. Box 125
Toronto, Ontario, CANADA M5J 2J3
Telephone: (416) 366-1990
Recruiter Classification: Retained; **Lowest/Average Salary:** $90,000/$90,000; **Industry Concentration:** Generalist with a primary focus in High Technology, Information Technology; **Function Concentration:** Generalist with a primary focus in Finance/Accounting, General Management, Human Resources, Marketing, Women/Minorities

Duncan, Dana — *Associate*
Source Services Corporation
5429 LBJ Freeway, Suite 275
Dallas, TX 75240
Telephone: (214) 387-1600
Recruiter Classification: Contingency; **Lowest/Average Salary:** $30,000/$50,000; **Industry Concentration:** Information Technology; **Function Concentration:** Engineering, Finance/Accounting

Dunkel, David L. — *Managing Partner*
Romac & Associates
120 Hyde Park Place
Suite 200
Tampa, FL 33606
Telephone: (813) 229-5575
Recruiter Classification: Executive Temporary; **Lowest/Average Salary:** $60,000/$60,000; **Industry Concentration:** High Technology, Information Technology; **Function Concentration:** Finance/Accounting

Dunlop, Eric — *Information Technology Recruiter*
Southwestern Professional Services
2451 Atrium Way
Nashville, TN 37214
Telephone: (615) 391-2722
Recruiter Classification: Contingency; **Lowest/Average Salary:** $40,000/$60,000; **Industry Concentration:** High Technology, Information Technology; **Function Concentration:** Sales

Dunlow, Aimee — *Associate*
Source Services Corporation
5429 LBJ Freeway, Suite 275
Dallas, TX 75240
Telephone: (214) 387-1600
Recruiter Classification: Contingency; **Lowest/Average Salary:** $30,000/$50,000; **Industry Concentration:** Information Technology; **Function Concentration:** Engineering, Finance/Accounting

Dunman, Betsy L. — *President*
Crawford & Crofford
15327 NW 60th Avenue, Suite 240
Miami Lakes, FL 33014
Telephone: (305) 820-0855
Recruiter Classification: Contingency, Executive Temporary; **Lowest/Average Salary:** $30,000/$60,000; **Industry Concentration:** Generalist with a primary focus in Electronics, High Technology, Information Technology; **Function Concentration:** Generalist with a primary focus in Administration, Engineering, Finance/Accounting, General Management, Marketing, Research and Development, Sales

Dupont, Rick — *Chief Financial Officer*
Source Services Corporation
5580 LBJ Freeway, Suite 300
Dallas, TX 75240
Telephone: (214) 385-3002
Recruiter Classification: Contingency; **Lowest/Average Salary:** $30,000/$50,000; **Industry Concentration:** Information Technology; **Function Concentration:** Engineering, Finance/Accounting

Durakis, Charles A. — *President*
C.A. Durakis Associates, Inc.
5550 Sterret Place, Suite 302
Columbia, MD 21044
Telephone: (410) 740-5590
Recruiter Classification: Retained; **Lowest/Average Salary:** $90,000/$90,000; **Industry Concentration:** Generalist with a primary focus in Electronics, High Technology, Information Technology; **Function Concentration:** Generalist with a primary focus in Finance/Accounting, General Management, Human Resources, Marketing

Dussick, Vince — *President*
Dussick Management Associates
149 Durham Road
Madison, CT 06443
Telephone: (203) 245-9311
Recruiter Classification: Contingency; **Lowest/Average Salary:** $50,000/$60,000; **Industry Concentration:** Generalist with a primary focus in High Technology, Information Technology; **Function Concentration:** Generalist with a primary focus in Marketing, Research and Development, Sales, Women/Minorities

Dwyer, Julie — *Executive Recruiter*
CPS Inc.
One Westbrook Corporate Centre, Suite 600
Westchester, IL 60154
Telephone: (708) 531-8370
Recruiter Classification: Contingency; **Lowest/Average Salary:** $30,000/$50,000; **Industry Concentration:** Generalist with a primary focus in Electronics, High Technology, Information Technology; **Function Concentration:** Engineering, Research and Development, Sales, Women/Minorities

Earhart, William D. — *Principal*
Sanford Rose Associates
6230 Busch Boulevard
Suite 418
Columbus, OH 43229
Telephone: (614) 436-3778
Recruiter Classification: Contingency; **Lowest/Average Salary:**
$30,000/$75,000; **Industry Concentration:** Generalist with a
primary focus in High Technology; **Function Concentration:**
Generalist

Ebeling, John A. — *Vice President*
Gilbert Tweed/INESA
155 Prospect Avenue
West Orange, NJ 07052
Telephone: (201) 731-3033
Recruiter Classification: Retained; **Lowest/Average Salary:**
$90,000/$90,000; **Industry Concentration:** Generalist with a
primary focus in Electronics, High Technology, Information
Technology; **Function Concentration:** Generalist with a
primary focus in General Management, Human Resources,
Marketing, Research and Development, Sales,
Women/Minorities

Edmond, Bruce — *Recruiter*
Corporate Recruiters Ltd.
490-1140 West Pender Street
Vancouver, British Columbia, CANADA V6E 4G1
Telephone: (604) 687-5993
Recruiter Classification: Contingency; **Lowest/Average Salary:**
$40,000/$75,000; **Industry Concentration:** Electronics, High
Technology; **Function Concentration:** General Management,
Marketing, Sales

Edwards, Dorothy — *Manager*
MSI International
800 Gessner, Suite 1220
Houston, TX 77024
Telephone: (713) 722-0050
Recruiter Classification: Contingency; **Lowest/Average Salary:**
$30,000/$75,000; **Industry Concentration:** Generalist with a
primary focus in High Technology, Information Technology;
Function Concentration: Generalist with a primary focus in
Administration, Engineering, Finance/Accounting, General
Management, Marketing, Sales

Edwards, Douglas W. — *Consultant*
Egon Zehnder International Inc.
One Atlantic Center, Suite 3000
1201 West Peachtree Street N.E.
Atlanta, GA 30309
Telephone: (404) 875-3000
Recruiter Classification: Retained; **Lowest/Average Salary:**
$90,000/$90,000; **Industry Concentration:** Generalist with a
primary focus in High Technology; **Function Concentration:**
Generalist

Edwards, John W. — *Managing Director*
The Bedford Group
154 Quicksand Pond Road
Little Compton, RI 02837
Telephone: (401) 635-4646
Recruiter Classification: Retained; **Lowest/Average Salary:**
$60,000/$90,000; **Industry Concentration:** Electronics, High
Technology, Information Technology; **Function Concentration:**
Generalist with a primary focus in Engineering, General
Management, Marketing, Research and Development

Edwards, Robert — *Recruiter*
J.P. Canon Associates
225 Broadway, Ste. 3602, 36th Fl.
New York, NY 10007-3001
Telephone: (212) 233-3131
Recruiter Classification: Contingency; **Lowest/Average Salary:**
$40,000/$75,000; **Industry Concentration:** Generalist with a
primary focus in Electronics; **Function Concentration:**
Engineering

Edwards, Verba L. — *President and CEO*
Wing Tips & Pumps, Inc.
P.O. Box 99580
Troy, MI 48099
Telephone: (810) 641-0980
Recruiter Classification: Contingency; **Lowest/Average Salary:**
$20,000/$60,000; **Industry Concentration:** Generalist with a
primary focus in Electronics, High Technology, Information
Technology; **Function Concentration:** Generalist with a primary
focus in Administration, Engineering, Finance/Accounting,
General Management, Human Resources, Marketing, Research
and Development, Sales, Women/Minorities

Eggena, Roger — *Executive Recruiter*
Phillips Resource Group
Ridgeway Business Park
3125 Ashley Phosphate Road, Suite 106
North Charleston, SC 29418
Telephone: (803) 552-8840
Recruiter Classification: Contingency; **Lowest/Average Salary:**
$40,000/$50,000; **Industry Concentration:** Electronics, High
Technology, Information Technology; **Function Concentration:**
Administration, Engineering, Finance/Accounting, General
Management, Human Resources, Marketing, Research and
Development, Sales

Eggert, Scott — *Associate*
Source Services Corporation
1105 Schrock Road, Suite 510
Columbus, OH 43229
Telephone: (614) 846-3311
Recruiter Classification: Contingency; **Lowest/Average Salary:**
$30,000/$50,000; **Industry Concentration:** Information
Technology; **Function Concentration:** Engineering,
Finance/Accounting

Ehrgott, Elizabeth — *Associate Director*
The Ascher Group
25 Pompton Avenue, Suite 310
Verona, NJ 07044
Telephone: (201) 239-6116
Recruiter Classification: Retained, Executive Temporary;
Lowest/Average Salary: $50,000/$90,000; **Industry
Concentration:** Generalist with a primary focus in Information
Technology; **Function Concentration:** Generalist with a
primary focus in Administration, Finance/Accounting, General
Management, Human Resources, Marketing,
Women/Minorities

Ehrhart, Jennifer — *Executive Recruiter/Manager*
ADOW's Executeam
10921 Reed Hartman Highway, Suite 225
Blue Ash, OH 45242-2830
Telephone: (513) 891-5335
Recruiter Classification: Executive Temporary; **Lowest/Average
Salary:** $60,000/$90,000; **Industry Concentration:** Generalist
with a primary focus in Electronics, High Technology,
Information Technology; **Function Concentration:** Generalist
with a primary focus in Administration, Engineering,
Finance/Accounting, General Management, Human Resources,
Marketing, Women/Minorities

Eiseman, Joe — *Managing Director*
Source Services Corporation
1 Gatehall Drive, Suite 250
Parsippany, NJ 07054
Telephone: (201) 267-3222
Recruiter Classification: Contingency; **Lowest/Average Salary:**
$30,000/$50,000; **Industry Concentration:** Information
Technology; **Function Concentration:** Engineering,
Finance/Accounting

Eiseman, Joe — *Managing Director*
Source Services Corporation
15 Essex Road, Suite 201
Paramus, NJ 07652
Telephone: (201) 845-3900
Recruiter Classification: Contingency; **Lowest/Average Salary:**
$30,000/$50,000; **Industry Concentration:** Information
Technology; **Function Concentration:** Engineering,
Finance/Accounting

Eiseman, Joe — *Managing Director*
Source Services Corporation
925 Westchester Avenue, Suite 309
White Plains, NY 10604
Telephone: (914) 428-9100
Recruiter Classification: Contingency; **Lowest/Average Salary:**
$30,000/$50,000; **Industry Concentration:** Information
Technology; **Function Concentration:** Engineering,
Finance/Accounting

Elder, Tom — *Associate*
Juntunen-Combs-Poirier
111 Bayhill Drive, Suite 255
San Bruno, CA 94066
Telephone: (415) 635-0184
Recruiter Classification: Retained; **Lowest/Average Salary:**
$90,000/$90,000; **Industry Concentration:** High Technology,
Information Technology; **Function Concentration:** Engineering,
Finance/Accounting, General Management, Research and
Development

Eldridge, Charles B. — *Partner*
Ray & Berndtson
191 Peachtree Street, NE, Suite 3800
Atlanta, GA 30303-1757
Telephone: (404) 215-4600
Recruiter Classification: Retained; **Lowest/Average Salary:**
$90,000/$90,000; **Industry Concentration:** Generalist with a
primary focus in High Technology, Information Technology;
Function Concentration: Generalist with a primary focus in
Administration, Finance/Accounting, General Management,
Human Resources, Marketing, Research and Development,
Sales, Women/Minorities

Elliott, A. Larry — *Partner*
Heidrick & Struggles, Inc.
8000 Towers Crescent Drive, Suite 555
Vienna, VA 22182-2700
Telephone: (703) 761-4830
Recruiter Classification: Retained; **Lowest/Average Salary:**
$75,000/$90,000; **Industry Concentration:** Generalist with a
primary focus in High Technology; **Function Concentration:**
Generalist

Ellis, Patricia — *Associate*
Source Services Corporation
7730 East Bellview Avenue, Suite 302
Englewood, CO 80111
Telephone: (303) 773-3700
Recruiter Classification: Contingency; **Lowest/Average Salary:**
$30,000/$50,000; **Industry Concentration:** Information
Technology; **Function Concentration:** Engineering,
Finance/Accounting

Ellis, Ted K. — *Vice President - Bristol/Southeast*
The Hindman Company
325 Springlake Road
Bristol, VA 24201
Telephone: (540) 669-5006
Recruiter Classification: Retained; **Lowest/Average Salary:**
$50,000/$90,000; **Industry Concentration:** Generalist with a
primary focus in Electronics, High Technology; **Function
Concentration:** Generalist with a primary focus in Engineering,
Finance/Accounting, General Management, Human Resources,
Marketing, Sales

Ellis, William — *President*
Interspace Interactive Inc.
521 Fifth Avenue
New York, NY 10017
Telephone: (212) 867-6661
Recruiter Classification: Contingency; **Lowest/Average
Salary:** $50,000/$60,000; **Industry Concentration:**
Generalist with a primary focus in Information Technology;
Function Concentration: Generalist with a primary
focus in Engineering, Finance/Accounting, General
Management, Human Resources, Marketing, Sales,
Women/Minorities

Ellison, Richard — *Principal*
Sanford Rose Associates
545 North Broad Street
Suite 2
Canfield, OH 44406-9204
Telephone: (216) 533-9270
Recruiter Classification: Contingency;
Lowest/Average Salary: $30,000/$75,000; **Industry
Concentration:** Generalist with a primary focus in
Information Technology; **Function Concentration:**
Generalist

Elnaggar, Hani — *Associate*
Juntunen-Combs-Poirier
600 Montgomery Street, 2nd Floor
San Francisco, CA 94111
Telephone: (415) 291-1699
Recruiter Classification: Retained; **Lowest/Average Salary:**
$90,000/$90,000; **Industry Concentration:** High Technology,
Information Technology; **Function Concentration:** General
Management, Marketing, Sales

Emerson, Randall — *Managing Director*
Source Services Corporation
111 Monument Circle, Suite 3930
Indianapolis, IN 46204
Telephone: (317) 631-2900
Recruiter Classification: Contingency; **Lowest/Average Salary:**
$30,000/$50,000; **Industry Concentration:** Information
Technology; **Function Concentration:** Engineering,
Finance/Accounting

Emery, Jodie A. — *Principal*
Lamalie Amrop International
Metro Center, One Station Place
Stamford, CT 06902-6800
Telephone: (203) 324-4445
Recruiter Classification: Retained; **Lowest/Average Salary:**
$90,000/$90,000; **Industry Concentration:** Generalist with a
primary focus in High Technology; **Function Concentration:**
Generalist

Enfield, Jerry J. — *Vice President*
Executive Manning Corporation
3000 N.E. 30th Place, Suite 402/405/411
Fort Lauderdale, FL 33306
Telephone: (954) 561-5100
Recruiter Classification: Retained; **Lowest/Average Salary:**
$75,000/$90,000; **Industry Concentration:** Generalist with a
primary focus in Electronics, High Technology; **Function
Concentration:** Generalist

England, Mark — *Vice President*
Austin-McGregor International
12005 Ford Road, Suite 720
Dallas, TX 75234-7247
Telephone: (972) 488-0500
Recruiter Classification: Retained; **Lowest/Average Salary:**
$50,000/$90,000; **Industry Concentration:** Generalist with a
primary focus in Electronics, High Technology; **Function
Concentration:** Generalist with a primary focus in Engineering,
Finance/Accounting, General Management, Human Resources,
Marketing, Research and Development, Sales,
Women/Minorities

Engle, Bryan — *Managing Director*
Source Services Corporation
120 East Baltimore Street, Suite 1950
Baltimore, MD 21202
Telephone: (410) 727-4050
Recruiter Classification: Contingency; **Lowest/Average Salary:**
$30,000/$50,000; **Industry Concentration:** Information
Technology; **Function Concentration:** Engineering,
Finance/Accounting

Engler, Peter G — *Partner*
Lautz Grotte Engler
One Bush Street, Suite 550
San Francisco, CA 94104
Telephone: (415) 834-3100
Recruiter Classification: Retained; **Lowest/Average Salary:**
$90,000/$90,000; **Industry Concentration:** Generalist with a
primary focus in Electronics, High Technology; **Function
Concentration:** Generalist with a primary focus in Marketing

Enns, George — *Partner*
The Enns Partners Inc.
70 University Avenue, Suite 410, P.O. Box 14
Toronto, Ontario, CANADA M5J 2M4
Telephone: (416) 598-0012
Recruiter Classification: Retained; **Lowest/Average Salary:**
$75,000/$90,000; **Industry Concentration:** Generalist with a
primary focus in Electronics, High Technology; **Function
Concentration:** Generalist with a primary focus in
Administration, Finance/Accounting, General Management,
Human Resources, Marketing, Sales

Epstein, Kathy J. — *Principal*
Lamalie Amrop International
10 Post Office Square
Boston, MA 02109-4603
Telephone: (617) 292-6242
Recruiter Classification: Retained; **Lowest/Average Salary:**
$90,000/$90,000; **Industry Concentration:** Generalist with a
primary focus in High Technology; **Function Concentration:**
Generalist

Erder, Debra — *Vice President*
Canny, Bowen Inc.
200 Park Avenue
49th Floor
New York, NY 10166
Telephone: (212) 949-6611
Recruiter Classification: Retained; **Lowest/Average Salary:**
$90,000/$120,000; **Industry Concentration:** Generalist with a
primary focus in Information Technology; **Function
Concentration:** Generalist with a primary focus in
Finance/Accounting, Human Resources, Marketing

Erikson, Theodore J. — *President*
Erikson Consulting Associates, Inc.
230 Park Avenue
Suite 1000
New York, NY 10169
Telephone: (212) 808-3053
Recruiter Classification: Retained; **Lowest/Average Salary:**
$90,000/$90,000; **Industry Concentration:** Electronics, High
Technology, Information Technology; **Function Concentration:**
General Management, Research and Development

Ervin, Darlene — *Executive Recruiter*
CPS Inc.
One Westbrook Corporate Centre, Suite 600
Westchester, IL 60154
Telephone: (708) 531-8370
Recruiter Classification: Contingency; **Lowest/Average Salary:**
$30,000/$50,000; **Industry Concentration:** Generalist with a
primary focus in Electronics, High Technology, Information
Technology; **Function Concentration:** Engineering, Research
and Development, Sales, Women/Minorities

Ervin, Russell — *Associate*
Source Services Corporation
10220 SW Greenburg Road, Suite 625
Portland, OR 97223
Telephone: (503) 768-4546
Recruiter Classification: Contingency; **Lowest/Average Salary:**
$30,000/$50,000; **Industry Concentration:** Information
Technology; **Function Concentration:** Engineering,
Finance/Accounting

Esposito, Mark — *Vice President*
Christian & Timbers
100 Park Avenue, 16th Floor
New York, NY 10017
Telephone: (212) 880-6446
Recruiter Classification: Retained; **Lowest/Average Salary:**
$90,000/$90,000; **Industry Concentration:** Generalist with a
primary focus in High Technology, Information Technology;
Function Concentration: Generalist with a primary focus in
Finance/Accounting, Marketing, Research and Development,
Sales

Estes, Susan — *Recruiter*
The Talley Group
P.O. Box 2918
Stanton, VA 24402
Telephone: (540) 248-7009
Recruiter Classification: Retained; **Lowest/Average Salary:**
$30,000/$60,000; **Industry Concentration:** Electronics,
Information Technology

Eustis, Lucy R. — *Unit Manager*
MSI International
201 St. Charles Avenue
Suite 2205
New Orleans, LA 70170
Telephone: (504) 522-6700
Recruiter Classification: Contingency; **Lowest/Average Salary:**
$30,000/$60,000; **Industry Concentration:** Generalist with a
primary focus in High Technology, Information Technology;
Function Concentration: Generalist with a primary focus in
Administration, Engineering, Finance/Accounting, General
Management, Marketing, Sales

Evans, David — *Vice President*
Executive Manning Corporation
3000 N.E. 30th Place, Suite 402/405/411
Fort Lauderdale, FL 33306
Telephone: (954) 561-5100
Recruiter Classification: Retained; **Lowest/Average Salary:**
$75,000/$90,000; **Industry Concentration:** Generalist with a
primary focus in Electronics, High Technology, Information
Technology; **Function Concentration:** Generalist with a
primary focus in Administration, Engineering, General
Management, Human Resources, Research and Development,
Sales, Women/Minorities

Evans, Timothy — *Associate*
Source Services Corporation
1500 West Park Drive, Suite 390
Westborough, MA 01581
Telephone: (508) 366-2600
Recruiter Classification: Contingency; **Lowest/Average Salary:**
$30,000/$50,000; **Industry Concentration:** Information
Technology; **Function Concentration:** Engineering,
Finance/Accounting

Fagerstrom, Jon — *Associate*
Source Services Corporation
4510 Executive Drive, Suite 200
San Diego, CA 92121
Telephone: (619) 552-0300
Recruiter Classification: Contingency; **Lowest/Average Salary:**
$30,000/$50,000; **Industry Concentration:** Information
Technology; **Function Concentration:** Engineering,
Finance/Accounting

Fahlin, Kelly — *Information Technology Recruiter*
Winter, Wyman & Company
950 Winter Street, Suite 3100
Waltham, MA 02154-1294
Telephone: (617) 890-7000
Recruiter Classification: Contingency; **Lowest/Average Salary:**
$30,000/$60,000; **Industry Concentration:** Generalist with a
primary focus in Information Technology; **Function
Concentration:** Generalist

Fairlie, Suzanne F. — *President*
ProSearch, Inc.
610 West Germantown Pike, Suite 120
Plymouth Meeting, PA 19462
Telephone: (610) 834-8260
Recruiter Classification: Contingency; **Lowest/Average Salary:**
$40,000/$60,000; **Industry Concentration:** High Technology,
Information Technology; **Function Concentration:**
Women/Minorities

Fales, Scott — *Associate*
Source Services Corporation
161 Ottawa NW, Suite 409D
Grand Rapids, MI 49503
Telephone: (616) 451-2400
Recruiter Classification: Contingency; **Lowest/Average Salary:**
$30,000/$50,000; **Industry Concentration:** Information
Technology; **Function Concentration:** Engineering,
Finance/Accounting

Falk, John — *Regional Vice President*
D.S. Allen Associates, Inc.
24200 Chagrin Blvd., Ste. 222
Beachwood, OH 44122
Telephone: (216) 831-1701
Recruiter Classification: Contingency; **Lowest/Average Salary:**
$60,000/$90,000; **Industry Concentration:** High Technology,
Information Technology; **Function Concentration:** General
Management, Marketing, Sales

Fancher, Robert L. — *Vice President*
Bason Associates Inc.
11311 Cornell Park Drive
Cincinnati, OH 45242
Telephone: (513) 469-9881
Recruiter Classification: Retained; **Lowest/Average Salary:**
$60,000/$90,000; **Industry Concentration:** Generalist with a
primary focus in High Technology; **Function Concentration:**
Generalist with a primary focus in Administration, Engineering,
Finance/Accounting, General Management, Human Resources,
Marketing, Research and Development, Sales

Fanning, Paul — *Associate*
Source Services Corporation
15260 Ventura Boulevard, Suite 380
Sherman Oaks, CA 91403
Telephone: (818) 905-1500
Recruiter Classification: Contingency; **Lowest/Average Salary:**
$30,000/$50,000; **Industry Concentration:** Information
Technology; **Function Concentration:** Engineering,
Finance/Accounting

Farler, Wiley — *Managing Director*
Source Services Corporation
Foster Plaza VI
681 Anderson Drive, 2nd Floor
Pittsburgh, PA 15220
Telephone: (412) 928-8300
Recruiter Classification: Contingency; **Lowest/Average Salary:**
$30,000/$50,000; **Industry Concentration:** Information
Technology; **Function Concentration:** Engineering,
Finance/Accounting

Farley, Leon A. — *Managing Partner*
Leon A. Farley Associates
468 Jackson Street
San Francisco, CA 94111
Telephone: (415) 989-0989
Recruiter Classification: Retained; **Lowest/Average Salary:**
$90,000/$90,000; **Industry Concentration:** Generalist with a
primary focus in Electronics, High Technology, Information
Technology; **Function Concentration:** Generalist with a
primary focus in Engineering, Finance/Accounting, General
Management, Human Resources, Marketing, Sales

Farrow, Jerry M. — *Managing Partner*
McCormack & Farrow
695 Town Center Drive
Suite 660
Costa Mesa, CA 92626
Telephone: (714) 549-7222
Recruiter Classification: Retained; **Lowest/Average Salary:**
$75,000/$90,000; **Industry Concentration:** Generalist with a
primary focus in Electronics, High Technology, Information
Technology; **Function Concentration:** Generalist with a
primary focus in Administration, Engineering,
Finance/Accounting, General Management, Human Resources,
Marketing, Sales

Farthing, Andrew R. — *Contract Manager*
Parfitt Recruiting and Consulting
1540 140th Avenue NE #201
Bellevue, WA 98005
Telephone: (206) 646-6300
Recruiter Classification: Contingency; **Lowest/Average Salary:**
$30,000/$75,000; **Industry Concentration:** Generalist with a
primary focus in Information Technology; **Function
Concentration:** Engineering

Fawkes, Elizabeth — *Director*
Paul-Tittle Associates, Inc.
1485 Chain Bridge Road, #304
McLean, VA 22101
Telephone: (703) 442-0500
Recruiter Classification: Retained; **Lowest/Average Salary:**
$60,000/$75,000; **Industry Concentration:** High Technology;
Function Concentration: Marketing, Sales

Fechheimer, Peter — *Associate*
Source Services Corporation
1290 Oakmead Parkway, Suite 318
Sunnyvale, CA 94086
Telephone: (408) 738-8440
Recruiter Classification: Contingency; **Lowest/Average Salary:**
$30,000/$50,000; **Industry Concentration:** Information
Technology; **Function Concentration:** Engineering,
Finance/Accounting

Feder, Gwen — *Consultant*
Egon Zehnder International Inc.
350 Park Avenue
New York, NY 10022
Telephone: (212) 838-9199
Recruiter Classification: Retained; **Lowest/Average Salary:**
$90,000/$90,000; **Industry Concentration:** Generalist with a
primary focus in High Technology; **Function Concentration:**
Generalist

Federman, Jack R. — *Principal*
W.R. Rosato & Associates, Inc.
61 Broadway, 26th Floor
New York, NY 10006
Telephone: (212) 509-5700
Recruiter Classification: Retained; **Lowest/Average Salary:**
$90,000/$90,000; **Industry Concentration:** High Technology,
Information Technology; **Function Concentration:**
Administration, Marketing, Research and Development, Sales

Feldman, Abe — *President*
A.E. Feldman Associates
445 Northern Boulevard
Great Neck, NY 11021
Telephone: (516) 466-4708
Recruiter Classification: Contingency, Executive Temporary;
Lowest/Average Salary: $60,000/$90,000; **Industry
Concentration:** Generalist with a primary focus in Electronics,
High Technology, Information Technology; **Function
Concentration:** Generalist with a primary focus in
Administration, General Management, Marketing, Sales

Feldman, Kimberley — *Consultant*
Atlantic Search Group, Inc.
One Liberty Square
Boston, MA 02109
Telephone: (617) 426-9700
Recruiter Classification: Contingency; **Lowest/Average Salary:**
$20,000/$60,000; **Industry Concentration:** Generalist with a
primary focus in Electronics, Information Technology; **Function
Concentration:** Finance/Accounting

Fennell, Patrick — *Managing Director*
Korn/Ferry International
Scotia Plaza
40 King Street West
Toronto, Ontario, CANADA M5H 3Y2
Telephone: (416) 366-1300
Recruiter Classification: Retained; **Lowest/Average Salary:**
$100,000/$150,000; **Industry Concentration:** Generalist with a
primary focus in Information Technology; **Function
Concentration:** Generalist

Ferguson, Kenneth — *Associate*
Source Services Corporation
4170 Ashford Dunwoody Road, Suite 285
Atlanta, GA 30319
Telephone: (404) 255-2045
Recruiter Classification: Contingency; **Lowest/Average Salary:**
$30,000/$50,000; **Industry Concentration:** Information
Technology; **Function Concentration:** Engineering,
Finance/Accounting

Ferneborg, Jay W. — *Vice President/Partner*
Ferneborg & Associates, Inc.
1450 Fashion Island Boulevard, Suite 650
San Mateo, CA 94404
Telephone: (415) 577-0100
Recruiter Classification: Retained; **Lowest/Average Salary:**
$90,000/$90,000; **Industry Concentration:** Generalist with a
primary focus in Electronics, High Technology, Information
Technology; **Function Concentration:** Generalist with a
primary focus in Administration, Finance/Accounting, General
Management, Human Resources, Marketing, Sales

Ferneborg, John R. — *President*
Ferneborg & Associates, Inc.
1450 Fashion Island Boulevard, Suite 650
San Mateo, CA 94404
Telephone: (415) 577-0100
Recruiter Classification: Retained; **Lowest/Average Salary:**
$90,000/$90,000; **Industry Concentration:** Generalist with a
primary focus in Electronics, High Technology, Information
Technology; **Function Concentration:** Generalist with a
primary focus in Administration, Finance/Accounting, General
Management, Human Resources, Marketing, Sales

Ferrara, David M. — *Senior Vice President*
Intech Summit Group, Inc.
5075 Shoreham Place, Suite 280
San Diego, CA 92116
Telephone: (619) 452-2100
Recruiter Classification: Retained; **Lowest/Average Salary:**
$90,000/$90,000; **Industry Concentration:** Information
Technology; **Function Concentration:** Research and
Development

Feyder, Michael — *Vice President*
A.T. Kearney, Inc.
Biltmore Tower
500 South Grand Avenue, Suite 1780
Los Angeles, CA 90071
Telephone: (213) 689-6800
Recruiter Classification: Retained; **Lowest/Average Salary:**
$90,000/$90,000; **Industry Concentration:** Generalist with a
primary focus in High Technology; **Function Concentration:**
Generalist with a primary focus in General Management,
Marketing, Sales

Field, Andrew — *Associate*
Source Services Corporation
7730 East Bellview Avenue, Suite 302
Englewood, CO 80111
Telephone: (303) 773-3700
Recruiter Classification: Contingency; **Lowest/Average Salary:**
$30,000/$50,000; **Industry Concentration:** Information
Technology; **Function Concentration:** Engineering,
Finance/Accounting

Fields, Fredric — *Vice President and Diretor of
Marketing*
C.A. Durakis Associates, Inc.
5550 Sterret Place, Suite 302
Columbia, MD 21044
Telephone: (410) 740-5590
Recruiter Classification: Retained; **Lowest/Average Salary:**
$90,000/$90,000; **Industry Concentration:** Generalist with a
primary focus in Electronics, High Technology, Information
Technology; **Function Concentration:** Generalist

Fienberg, Chester — *President*
Drummond Associates, Inc.
50 Broadway, Suite 1201
New York, NY 10004
Telephone: (212) 248-1120
Recruiter Classification: Contingency; **Lowest/Average
Salary:** $40,000/$75,000; **Industry Concentration:**
Information Technology; **Function Concentration:**
Finance/Accounting

Fifield, George C. — *Consultant*
Egon Zehnder International Inc.
California Plaza II, Suite 3580
300 South Grand Avenue
Los Angeles, CA 90071
Telephone: (213) 621-8900
Recruiter Classification: Retained; **Lowest/Average Salary:**
$90,000/$90,000; **Industry Concentration:** Generalist with a
primary focus in High Technology; **Function Concentration:**
Generalist

Fincher, Richard P. — *President*
Phase II Management
25 Stonybrook Road
Westport, CT 06880
Telephone: (203) 226-7252
Recruiter Classification: Retained; **Lowest/Average Salary:**
$60,000/$90,000; **Industry Concentration:** Generalist with a
primary focus in Electronics; **Function Concentration:**
Generalist with a primary focus in Engineering,
Finance/Accounting, General Management, Marketing,
Research and Development, Sales

Fingers, David — *Branch Manager*
Bradford & Galt, Inc.
8575 West 110th Street, Suite 302
Overland Park, KS 66210
Telephone: (913) 663-1264
Recruiter Classification: Contingency; **Lowest/Average Salary:**
$30,000/$30,000; **Industry Concentration:** Generalist with a
primary focus in Information Technology; **Function
Concentration:** Generalist

Fini, Ron — *Consultant*
The Sager Company
1619 Brookpark Road
Cleveland, OH 44109-5816
Telephone: (216) 459-1300
Recruiter Classification: Retained; **Lowest/Average Salary:**
$75,000/$90,000; **Industry Concentration:** Generalist with a
primary focus in Electronics, High Technology; **Function
Concentration:** Generalist with a primary focus in Engineering,
Finance/Accounting, General Management, Human Resources,
Marketing, Research and Development, Sales

Fink, Neil J. — *President*
Neil Fink Associates
900 North Point Street
Suite 401
San Francisco, CA 94109
Telephone: (415) 441-3777
Recruiter Classification: Retained; **Lowest/Average Salary:**
$75,000/$90,000; **Industry Concentration:** Electronics,
Information Technology; **Function Concentration:** Engineering,
General Management, Marketing, Sales

Finkel, Leslie — *Managing Director*
Source Services Corporation
150 South Warner Road, Suite 238
King of Prussia, PA 19406
Telephone: (610) 341-1960
Recruiter Classification: Contingency; **Lowest/Average Salary:**
$30,000/$50,000; **Industry Concentration:** Information
Technology; **Function Concentration:** Engineering,
Finance/Accounting

Finnerty, James — *Associate*
Source Services Corporation
20 Burlington Mall Road, Suite 405
Burlington, MA 01803
Telephone: (617) 272-5000
Recruiter Classification: Contingency; **Lowest/Average Salary:** $30,000/$50,000; **Industry Concentration:** Information Technology; **Function Concentration:** Engineering, Finance/Accounting

Fiorelli, Cheryl — *Recruiter/Researcher*
Tower Consultants, Ltd.
771 East Lancaster Avenue
Villanova, PA 19085
Telephone: (610) 519-1700
Recruiter Classification: Retained; **Lowest/Average Salary:** $60,000/$75,000; **Industry Concentration:** Generalist with a primary focus in High Technology, Information Technology; **Function Concentration:** Administration, Human Resources, Women/Minorities

Fischer, Adam — *Vice President, Telecommunications*
Howard Fischer Associates, Inc.
1800 John F. Kennedy Boulevard, 7th Floor
Philadelphia, PA 19103
Telephone: (215) 568-8363
Recruiter Classification: Retained; **Lowest/Average Salary:** $90,000/$90,000; **Industry Concentration:** Generalist with a primary focus in High Technology; **Function Concentration:** Generalist with a primary focus in Administration, Finance/Accounting, General Management, Human Resources, Marketing, Research and Development, Sales, Women/Minorities

Fischer, Howard M. — *President and CEO*
Howard Fischer Associates, Inc.
1800 John F. Kennedy Boulevard, 7th Floor
Philadelphia, PA 19103
Telephone: (215) 568-8363
Recruiter Classification: Retained; **Lowest/Average Salary:** $90,000/$90,000; **Industry Concentration:** Generalist with a primary focus in High Technology, Information Technology; **Function Concentration:** Generalist with a primary focus in Administration, Finance/Accounting, General Management, Human Resources, Marketing, Research and Development, Sales, Women/Minorities

Fischer, John C. — *Office Managing Director*
Horton International
10 Tower Lane
Avon, CT 06001
Telephone: (860) 674-8701
Recruiter Classification: Retained; **Lowest/Average Salary:** $90,000/$90,000; **Industry Concentration:** Generalist with a primary focus in Information Technology; **Function Concentration:** Generalist with a primary focus in Finance/Accounting, General Management, Sales

Fishback, Joren — *President*
Derek Associates, Inc.
P.O. Box 13
Mendon, MA 01756-0013
Telephone: (508) 883-2289
Recruiter Classification: Contingency; **Lowest/Average Salary:** $40,000/$60,000; **Industry Concentration:** Information Technology; **Function Concentration:** Engineering, Marketing, Sales

Fisher, Neal — *Principal*
Fisher Personnel Management Services
1219 Morningside Drive
Manhattan Beach, CA 90266
Telephone: (310) 546-7507
Recruiter Classification: Retained; **Lowest/Average Salary:** $75,000/$75,000; **Industry Concentration:** Generalist with a primary focus in Electronics, High Technology, Information Technology; **Function Concentration:** Generalist with a primary focus in Engineering, Finance/Accounting, General Management, Human Resources, Marketing, Research and Development, Sales

Fishler, Stu — *Vice President*
A.T. Kearney, Inc.
Biltmore Tower
500 South Grand Avenue, Suite 1780
Los Angeles, CA 90071
Telephone: (213) 689-6800
Recruiter Classification: Retained; **Lowest/Average Salary:** $90,000/$90,000; **Industry Concentration:** Generalist with a primary focus in High Technology, Information Technology; **Function Concentration:** Generalist with a primary focus in Engineering, Finance/Accounting, General Management

Fitzgerald, Brian — *Associate*
Source Services Corporation
5429 LBJ Freeway, Suite 275
Dallas, TX 75240
Telephone: (214) 387-1600
Recruiter Classification: Contingency; **Lowest/Average Salary:** $30,000/$50,000; **Industry Concentration:** Information Technology; **Function Concentration:** Engineering, Finance/Accounting

Fitzgerald, Diane — *Principal*
Fitzgerald Associates
21 Muzzey Street
Lexington, MA 02173
Telephone: (617) 863-1945
Recruiter Classification: Retained; **Lowest/Average Salary:** $60,000/$90,000; **Industry Concentration:** High Technology, Information Technology; **Function Concentration:** Generalist with a primary focus in Finance/Accounting, General Management, Marketing, Research and Development, Sales, Women/Minorities

Fitzgerald, Geoffrey — *Principal*
Fitzgerald Associates
21 Muzzey Street
Lexington, MA 02173
Telephone: (617) 863-1945
Recruiter Classification: Retained; **Lowest/Average Salary:** $60,000/$90,000; **Industry Concentration:** High Technology, Information Technology; **Function Concentration:** Generalist with a primary focus in Finance/Accounting, General Management, Marketing, Research and Development, Sales, Women/Minorities

Flanagan, Robert M. — *President*
Robert M. Flanagan & Associates, Ltd.
Fields Lane, JMK Building
North Salem, NY 10560-0339
Telephone: (914) 277-7210
Recruiter Classification: Retained; **Lowest/Average Salary:**
$90,000/$90,000; **Industry Concentration:** Generalist with a
primary focus in Information Technology; **Function
Concentration:** Generalist with a primary focus in
Administration, Finance/Accounting, Human Resources,
Marketing, Sales

Flanders, Karen — *Regional Manager*
Advanced Information Management
900 Wilshire Boulevard, Suite 1424
Los Angeles, CA 90017
Telephone: (213) 243-9236
Recruiter Classification: Contingency; **Lowest/Average Salary:**
$20,000/$40,000; **Industry Concentration:** Information
Technology; **Function Concentration:** Human Resources,
Research and Development, Women/Minorities

Flannery, Peter F. — *Senior Vice President
Operations*
Jonas, Walters & Assoc., Inc.
1110 North Old World Third St., Suite 510
Milwaukee, WI 53203-1102
Telephone: (414) 291-2828
Recruiter Classification: Retained; **Lowest/Average Salary:**
$60,000/$90,000; **Industry Concentration:** Generalist with a
primary focus in Electronics; **Function Concentration:**
Generalist with a primary focus in Administration, Engineering,
Finance/Accounting, General Management, Human Resources,
Marketing, Research and Development, Sales

Fletcher, David — *Professional Recruiter*
A.J. Burton Group, Inc.
120 East Baltimore Street, Suite 2220
Baltimore, MD 21202
Telephone: (410) 752-5244
Recruiter Classification: Contingency; **Lowest/Average Salary:**
$40,000/$75,000; **Industry Concentration:** Generalist with a
primary focus in High Technology, Information Technology;
Function Concentration: Generalist with a primary focus in
Administration, Finance/Accounting, General Management,
Human Resources

Flood, Michael — *Managing Director*
Norman Broadbent International, Inc.
200 Park Avenue, 20th Floor
New York, NY 10166
Telephone: (212) 953-6990
Recruiter Classification: Retained; **Lowest/Average Salary:**
$90,000/$90,000; **Industry Concentration:** High Technology,
Information Technology; **Function Concentration:**
Finance/Accounting, General Management, Human Resources,
Marketing, Sales

Flora, Dodi — *Regional Director*
Crawford & Crofford
15327 NW 60th Avenue, Suite 240
Miami Lakes, FL 33014
Telephone: (305) 820-0855
Recruiter Classification: Contingency, Executive Temporary;
Lowest/Average Salary: $30,000/$60,000; **Industry
Concentration:** Electronics, High Technology; **Function
Concentration:** Administration, Engineering,
Finance/Accounting, General Management, Human Resources,
Sales

Flores, Agustin — *Partner*
Ward Howell International, Inc.
Rexer Seleccion de Ejecutivos, S.C.
Blvd. Adolfo Lopez Mateos 20, Col. San Angel Inn
Mexico City, D.F., MEXICO 01060
Telephone: (525) 550-9180
Recruiter Classification: Retained; **Lowest/Average Salary:**
$75,000/$90,000; **Industry Concentration:** Information
Technology; **Function Concentration:** Generalist

Florio, Robert — *Associate*
Source Services Corporation
525 Vine Street, Suite 2250
Cincinnati, OH 45202
Telephone: (513) 651-3303
Recruiter Classification: Contingency; **Lowest/Average Salary:**
$30,000/$50,000; **Industry Concentration:** Information
Technology; **Function Concentration:** Engineering,
Finance/Accounting

Flowers, Hayden — *Executive Recruiter*
Southwestern Professional Services
101 West Renner Road, Suite 230
Richardson, TX 75082
Telephone: (214) 705-9500
Recruiter Classification: Contingency; **Lowest/Average Salary:**
$30,000/$75,000; **Industry Concentration:** Electronics,
Information Technology; **Function Concentration:** Engineering

Flynn, Erin — *Consultant*
Neil Fink Associates
900 North Point Street
Suite 401
San Francisco, CA 94109
Telephone: (415) 441-3777
Recruiter Classification: Retained; **Lowest/Average Salary:**
$75,000/$90,000; **Industry Concentration:** Electronics,
Information Technology; **Function Concentration:** Engineering,
General Management, Marketing, Sales

Fogarty, Michael — *Executive Recruiter*
CPS Inc.
One Westbrook Corporate Centre, Suite 600
Westchester, IL 60154
Telephone: (708) 531-8370
Recruiter Classification: Contingency; **Lowest/Average Salary:**
$30,000/$50,000; **Industry Concentration:** Generalist with a
primary focus in Electronics, High Technology, Information
Technology; **Function Concentration:** Engineering, Research
and Development, Sales, Women/Minorities

Foley, Eileen — *Information Technology Recruiter*
Winter, Wyman & Company
950 Winter Street, Suite 3100
Waltham, MA 02154-1294
Telephone: (617) 890-7000
Recruiter Classification: Contingency; **Lowest/Average Salary:**
$30,000/$60,000; **Industry Concentration:** Generalist with a
primary focus in Information Technology; **Function
Concentration:** Generalist

Folkerth, Gene — *President*
Gene Folkerth & Associates, Inc.
970 Patriot Square
Dayton, OH 45459-4042
Telephone: (513) 291-2722
Recruiter Classification: Executive Temporary; **Lowest/Average
Salary:** $40,000/$75,000; **Industry Concentration:** Generalist
with a primary focus in Electronics; **Function Concentration:**
Generalist with a primary focus in Engineering, Human
Resources, Research and Development

Fone, Carol — *Consultant/Market Research*
Walden Associates
1601 Trapelo Road
Waltham, MA 02154
Telephone: (617) 890-8885
Recruiter Classification: Retained; **Lowest/Average Salary:**
$90,000/$90,000; **Industry Concentration:** High Technology,
Information Technology; **Function Concentration:** General
Management

Fong, Robert — *Principal*
Korn/Ferry International
600 University Street, Suite 3111
Seattle, WA 98101
Telephone: (206) 447-1834
Recruiter Classification: Retained; **Lowest/Average Salary:**
$100,000/$150,000; **Industry Concentration:** Generalist with a
primary focus in Information Technology; **Function
Concentration:** Generalist

Foote, Leland W. — *President*
L.W. Foote Company
110 110th Avenue N.E.
Suite 603
Bellevue, WA 98004-5840
Telephone: (206) 451-1660
Recruiter Classification: Retained; **Lowest/Average Salary:**
$75,000/$90,000; **Industry Concentration:** Generalist with a
primary focus in Electronics, High Technology, Information
Technology; **Function Concentration:** Generalist with a
primary focus in Administration, Engineering,
Finance/Accounting, General Management, Human Resources,
Marketing, Research and Development, Sales,
Women/Minorities

Ford, Sandra D. — *Managing Director*
The Ford Group, Inc.
485 Devon Park Drive, Suite 110
Wayne, PA 19087
Telephone: (610) 975-9007
Recruiter Classification: Retained; **Lowest/Average Salary:**
$90,000/$90,000; **Industry Concentration:** High Technology,
Information Technology; **Function Concentration:**
Finance/Accounting, General Management, Human Resources,
Marketing, Women/Minorities

Foreman, David C. — *Senior Associate*
Koontz, Jeffries & Associates, Inc.
18-22 Bank Street
Summit, NJ 07901
Telephone: (908) 598-1900
Recruiter Classification: Retained; **Lowest/Average Salary:**
$60,000/$90,000; **Industry Concentration:** Generalist with a
primary focus in Electronics, High Technology; **Function
Concentration:** Generalist with a primary focus in
Administration, Engineering, Finance/Accounting, General
Management, Human Resources, Marketing, Research and
Development, Sales, Women/Minorities

Foreman, Rebecca — *Associate*
Aubin International Inc.
281 Winter Street, #380
Waltham, MA 02154
Telephone: (617) 890-1722
Recruiter Classification: Retained; **Lowest/Average Salary:**
$90,000/$90,000; **Industry Concentration:** Generalist with a
primary focus in High Technology; **Function Concentration:**
Generalist

Forestier, Lois — *Associate*
Source Services Corporation
2 Penn Plaza, Suite 1176
New York, NY 10121
Telephone: (212) 760-2200
Recruiter Classification: Contingency; **Lowest/Average Salary:**
$30,000/$50,000; **Industry Concentration:** Information
Technology; **Function Concentration:** Engineering,
Finance/Accounting

Forman, Donald R. — *Principal*
Stanton Chase International
2 Lincoln Center
5420 LBJ Freeway #780
Dallas, TX 75240
Telephone: (972) 404-8411
Recruiter Classification: Retained; **Lowest/Average Salary:**
$75,000/$90,000; **Industry Concentration:** Generalist with a
primary focus in High Technology; **Function Concentration:**
Generalist with a primary focus in Administration, Engineering,
Marketing, Sales

Foster, Bonnie — *Partner*
Kirkman & Searing, Inc.
8045 Leesburg Pike
Suite 540
Vienna, VA 22182
Telephone: (703) 761-7020
Recruiter Classification: Retained; **Lowest/Average Salary:**
$90,000/$90,000; **Industry Concentration:** High Technology,
Information Technology; **Function Concentration:** General
Management, Marketing, Sales

Foster, Bradley — *Associate*
Source Services Corporation
2000 Town Center, Suite 850
Southfield, MI 48075
Telephone: (810) 352-6520
Recruiter Classification: Contingency; **Lowest/Average Salary:**
$30,000/$50,000; **Industry Concentration:** Information
Technology; **Function Concentration:** Engineering,
Finance/Accounting

Foster, Dwight E. — *Chairman/Executive
Managing Director*
D.E. Foster Partners Inc.
570 Lexington Avenue, 14th Floor
New York, NY 10022
Telephone: (212) 872-6232
Recruiter Classification: Retained; **Lowest/Average Salary:**
$90,000/$90,000; **Industry Concentration:** Generalist with a
primary focus in Electronics; **Function Concentration:**
Finance/Accounting, General Management

Foster, John — *Associate*
Source Services Corporation
8614 Westwood Center, Suite 750
Vienna, VA 22182
Telephone: (703) 790-5610
Recruiter Classification: Contingency; **Lowest/Average Salary:**
$30,000/$50,000; **Industry Concentration:** Information
Technology; **Function Concentration:** Engineering,
Finance/Accounting

Fotia, Frank — *Principal*
JDG Associates, Ltd.
1700 Research Boulevard
Rockville, MD 20850
Telephone: (301) 340-2210
Recruiter Classification: Contingency; **Lowest/Average Salary:**
$50,000/$90,000; **Industry Concentration:** High Technology,
Information Technology; **Function Concentration:** Engineering,
Finance/Accounting, Research and Development

Fowler, Thomas A. — *Vice President -
Dallas/Southwest*
The Hindman Company
Suite 200, The Tower at Williams Square
5215 North O'Connor Road
Irving, TX 75039
Telephone: (214) 868-9122
Recruiter Classification: Retained; **Lowest/Average Salary:**
$50,000/$90,000; **Industry Concentration:** Generalist with a
primary focus in Electronics, High Technology; **Function
Concentration:** Generalist with a primary focus in Engineering,
Finance/Accounting, General Management, Human Resources,
Marketing, Sales

Francis, Brad — *Managing Director*
Source Services Corporation
7730 East Bellview Avenue, Suite 302
Englewood, CO 80111
Telephone: (303) 773-3700
Recruiter Classification: Contingency; **Lowest/Average Salary:**
$30,000/$50,000; **Industry Concentration:** Information
Technology; **Function Concentration:** Engineering,
Finance/Accounting

Francis, John — *Vice President*
Zwell International
2 Embarcadero Center, Suite 200
San Francisco, CA 94111
Telephone: (415) 835-1337
Recruiter Classification: Retained; **Lowest/Average Salary:**
$75,000/$90,000; **Industry Concentration:** Generalist with a
primary focus in Electronics, High Technology; **Function
Concentration:** Generalist with a primary focus in Engineering,
General Management, Human Resources, Marketing, Research
and Development, Sales, Women/Minorities

Frank, Valerie S. — *Executive Vice President*
Norman Roberts & Associates, Inc.
1800 Century Park East, Suite 430
Los Angeles, CA 90067
Telephone: (310) 552-1112
Recruiter Classification: Retained; **Lowest/Average Salary:**
$75,000/$90,000; **Industry Concentration:** Information
Technology; **Function Concentration:** Generalist with a
primary focus in Administration, Engineering,
Finance/Accounting, General Management, Human Resources,
Women/Minorities

Frantino, Michael — *Associate*
Source Services Corporation
379 Thornall Street
Edison, NJ 08837
Telephone: (908) 494-2800
Recruiter Classification: Contingency; **Lowest/Average Salary:**
$30,000/$50,000; **Industry Concentration:** Information
Technology; **Function Concentration:** Engineering,
Finance/Accounting

Frazier, John — *Manager*
Cochran, Cochran & Yale, Inc.
955 East Henrietta Road
Rochester, NY 14623
Telephone: (716) 424-6060
Recruiter Classification: Retained; **Lowest/Average Salary:**
$40,000/$60,000; **Industry Concentration:** Generalist with a
primary focus in High Technology, Information Technology;
Function Concentration: Generalist with a primary focus in
Engineering, Finance/Accounting, General Management,
Human Resources, Marketing, Sales, Women/Minorities

Frederick, Dianne — *Associate*
Source Services Corporation
525 Vine Street, Suite 2250
Cincinnati, OH 45202
Telephone: (513) 651-3303
Recruiter Classification: Contingency; **Lowest/Average Salary:**
$30,000/$50,000; **Industry Concentration:** Information
Technology; **Function Concentration:** Engineering,
Finance/Accounting

Fredericks, Ward A. — *Chairman*
Mixtec Group
31255 Cedar Valley Drive
Suite 300-327
Westlake Village, CA 91362
Telephone: (818) 889-8819
Recruiter Classification: Contingency; **Lowest/Average Salary:**
$60,000/$90,000; **Industry Concentration:** High Technology;
Function Concentration: Generalist with a primary focus in
Administration, General Management, Marketing, Sales

Freeh, Thomas — *Managing Director*
Source Services Corporation
4170 Ashford Dunwoody Road, Suite 285
Atlanta, GA 30319
Telephone: (404) 255-2045
Recruiter Classification: Contingency; **Lowest/Average Salary:**
$30,000/$50,000; **Industry Concentration:** Information
Technology; **Function Concentration:** Engineering,
Finance/Accounting

Freeman, Mark — *Partner*
ESA Professional Consultants
141 Durham Road
Suite 16
Madison, CT 06443
Telephone: (203) 245-1983
Recruiter Classification: Retained; **Lowest/Average Salary:**
$50,000/$75,000; **Industry Concentration:** Electronics, High
Technology, Information Technology; **Function Concentration:**
Engineering, General Management, Human Resources,
Marketing, Research and Development, Women/Minorities

French, William G. — *Partner*
Preng & Associates, Inc.
2925 Briarpark, Suite 1111
Houston, TX 77042
Telephone: (713) 266-2600
Recruiter Classification: Retained; **Lowest/Average Salary:**
$90,000/$90,000; **Industry Concentration:** High Technology,
Information Technology; **Function Concentration:** Generalist
with a primary focus in Engineering, Finance/Accounting,
General Management, Human Resources, Marketing, Research
and Development

Fribush, Richard — *Professional Recruiter*
A.J. Burton Group, Inc.
120 East Baltimore Street, Suite 2220
Baltimore, MD 21202
Telephone: (410) 752-5244
Recruiter Classification: Contingency; **Lowest/Average Salary:**
$40,000/$75,000; **Industry Concentration:** Generalist with a
primary focus in High Technology, Information Technology;
Function Concentration: Generalist with a primary focus in
Administration, Finance/Accounting, General Management,
Human Resources

Friedman, Deborah — *Associate*
Source Services Corporation
425 California Street, Suite 1200
San Francisco, CA 94104
Telephone: (415) 434-2410
Recruiter Classification: Contingency; **Lowest/Average Salary:**
$30,000/$50,000; **Industry Concentration:** Information
Technology; **Function Concentration:** Engineering,
Finance/Accounting

Friedman, Donna L. — *President*
Tower Consultants, Ltd.
4195 N.E. Hyline Drive
Jensen Beach, FL 34957
Telephone: (561) 225-5151
Recruiter Classification: Retained; **Lowest/Average Salary:**
$60,000/$90,000; **Industry Concentration:** Generalist with a
primary focus in High Technology, Information Technology;
Function Concentration: Administration, Human Resources,
Women/Minorities

Friedman, Helen E. — *Partner*
McCormack & Farrow
695 Town Center Drive
Suite 660
Costa Mesa, CA 92626
Telephone: (714) 549-7222
Recruiter Classification: Retained; **Lowest/Average Salary:**
$75,000/$90,000; **Industry Concentration:** Generalist with a
primary focus in High Technology; **Function Concentration:**
Generalist with a primary focus in Administration,
Finance/Accounting, General Management, Human Resources,
Research and Development, Women/Minorities

Friel, Thomas J. — *Partner*
Heidrick & Struggles, Inc.
2740 Sand Hill Road
Menlo Park, CA 94025
Telephone: (415) 234-1500
Recruiter Classification: Retained; **Lowest/Average Salary:**
$75,000/$90,000; **Industry Concentration:** Generalist with a
primary focus in High Technology; **Function Concentration:**
Generalist

Fuhrman, Dennis — *Managing Director*
Source Services Corporation
500 108th Avenue NE, Suite 1780
Bellevue, WA 98004
Telephone: (206) 454-6400
Recruiter Classification: Contingency; **Lowest/Average Salary:**
$30,000/$50,000; **Industry Concentration:** Information
Technology; **Function Concentration:** Engineering,
Finance/Accounting

Fujino, Rickey — *Associate*
Source Services Corporation
1290 Oakmead Parkway, Suite 318
Sunnyvale, CA 94086
Telephone: (408) 738-8440
Recruiter Classification: Contingency; **Lowest/Average Salary:**
$30,000/$50,000; **Industry Concentration:** Information
Technology; **Function Concentration:** Engineering,
Finance/Accounting

Fulger, Herbert — *Associate*
Source Services Corporation
3 Summit Park Drive, Suite 550
Independence, OH 44131
Telephone: (216) 328-5900
Recruiter Classification: Contingency; **Lowest/Average Salary:**
$30,000/$50,000; **Industry Concentration:** Information
Technology; **Function Concentration:** Engineering,
Finance/Accounting

Fulgham MacCarthy, Ann — *Managing Principal*
Columbia Consulting Group
230 Park Avenue, Suite 456
New York, NY 10169
Telephone: (212) 983-2525
Recruiter Classification: Retained; **Lowest/Average Salary:**
$75,000/$90,000; **Industry Concentration:** Generalist with a
primary focus in High Technology, Information Technology;
Function Concentration: Generalist with a primary focus in
Engineering, Finance/Accounting, Human Resources,
Marketing, Sales

Fulmer, Karen — *Consultant*
Bench International
116 N. Robertson Boulevard
Suite 503
Los Angeles, CA 90048
Telephone: (310) 854-9900
Recruiter Classification: Retained; **Lowest/Average Salary:**
$75,000/$90,000; **Industry Concentration:** High Technology;
Function Concentration: Research and Development

Furlong, James W. — *President*
Furlong Search, Inc.
634 East Main Street
Hillsboro, OR 97123
Telephone: (503) 640-3221
Recruiter Classification: Retained; **Lowest/Average Salary:**
$90,000/$90,000; **Industry Concentration:** Electronics, High
Technology; **Function Concentration:** Generalist with a
primary focus in Engineering, Finance/Accounting, General
Management, Marketing, Research and Development, Sales

Furlong, James W. — *President*
Furlong Search, Inc.
550 Tyndall Street, Suite 11
Los Altos, CA 94022
Telephone: (415) 856-8484
Recruiter Classification: Retained; **Lowest/Average Salary:**
$90,000/$90,000; **Industry Concentration:** Electronics, High
Technology; **Function Concentration:** Generalist with a
primary focus in Engineering, Finance/Accounting, General
Management, Marketing, Research and Development, Sales

Furlong, James W. — *President*
Furlong Search, Inc.
19312 Romar Street
Northridge, CA 91324
Telephone: (818) 885-7044
Recruiter Classification: Retained; **Lowest/Average Salary:**
$90,000/$90,000; **Industry Concentration:** Electronics, High
Technology; **Function Concentration:** Generalist with a
primary focus in Engineering, Finance/Accounting, General
Management, Marketing, Research and Development, Sales

Fust, Sheely F. — *Partner*
Ray & Berndtson
2029 Century Park East, Suite 1000
Los Angeles, CA 90067
Telephone: (310) 557-2828
Recruiter Classification: Retained; **Lowest/Average Salary:**
$90,000/$90,000; **Industry Concentration:** Generalist with a
primary focus in High Technology, Information Technology;
Function Concentration: Generalist with a primary focus in
Administration, Finance/Accounting, General Management,
Human Resources, Marketing, Research and Development,
Sales, Women/Minorities

Fyhrie, David — *Associate*
Source Services Corporation
3701 West Algonquin Road, Suite 380
Rolling Meadows, IL 60008
Telephone: (847) 392-0244
Recruiter Classification: Contingency; **Lowest/Average Salary:**
$30,000/$50,000; **Industry Concentration:** Information
Technology; **Function Concentration:** Engineering,
Finance/Accounting

Gabel, Gregory N. — *Vice President*
Canny, Bowen Inc.
200 Park Avenue
49th Floor
New York, NY 10166
Telephone: (212) 949-6611
Recruiter Classification: Retained; **Lowest/Average Salary:**
$90,000/$90,000; **Industry Concentration:** Generalist with a
primary focus in Electronics, High Technology, Information
Technology; **Function Concentration:** Generalist with a
primary focus in Engineering, Finance/Accounting, General
Management, Human Resources, Marketing, Research and
Development, Sales, Women/Minorities

Gabriel, David L. — *Managing Director*
The Arcus Group
100 North Central (At Main), Suite 1200
Dallas, TX 75201
Telephone: (214) 744-2100
Recruiter Classification: Retained; **Lowest/Average Salary:**
$90,000/$90,000; **Industry Concentration:** Generalist with a
primary focus in Electronics, High Technology, Information
Technology; **Function Concentration:** Generalist with a
primary focus in Administration, Engineering,
Finance/Accounting, General Management, Human Resources,
Marketing, Research and Development, Women/Minorities

Gadison, William — *Executive Recruiter*
Richard, Wayne and Roberts
24 Greenway Plaza, Suite 1304
Houston, TX 77046-2493
Telephone: (713) 629-6681
Recruiter Classification: Retained; **Lowest/Average Salary:**
$40,000/$60,000; **Industry Concentration:** Generalist with a
primary focus in Electronics, High Technology; **Function
Concentration:** Generalist

Gaffney, Keith — *Managing Director Executive
Search*
Gaffney Management Consultants
35 North Brandon Drive
Glendale Heights, IL 60139-2087
Telephone: (630) 307-3380
Recruiter Classification: Retained; **Lowest/Average Salary:**
$60,000/$90,000; **Industry Concentration:** Generalist with a
primary focus in Electronics, High Technology; **Function
Concentration:** Generalist with a primary focus in Engineering,
General Management, Research and Development,
Women/Minorities

Gaffney, Megan — *Associate*
Source Services Corporation
8614 Westwood Center, Suite 750
Vienna, VA 22182
Telephone: (703) 790-5610
Recruiter Classification: Contingency; **Lowest/Average Salary:**
$30,000/$50,000; **Industry Concentration:** Information
Technology; **Function Concentration:** Engineering,
Finance/Accounting

Gaffney, William — *President*
Gaffney Management Consultants
35 North Brandon Drive
Glendale Heights, IL 60139-2087
Telephone: (630) 307-3380
Recruiter Classification: Retained; **Lowest/Average Salary:**
$60,000/$90,000; **Industry Concentration:** Generalist with a
primary focus in Electronics, High Technology; **Function
Concentration:** Generalist with a primary focus in Engineering,
General Management, Research and Development,
Women/Minorities

Gaines, Jay — *President*
Jay Gaines & Company, Inc.
450 Park Avenue
New York, NY 10022
Telephone: (212) 308-9222
Recruiter Classification: Retained; **Lowest/Average Salary:**
$200,000/$500,000; **Industry Concentration:** Generalist with a
primary focus in Electronics, High Technology, Information
Technology; **Function Concentration:** Generalist with a
primary focus in Finance/Accounting, General Management,
Marketing, Sales

Gaines, Ronni L. — *President*
TOPAZ Legal Solutions
383 Northfield Avenue
West Orange, NJ 07052
Telephone: (201) 669-7300
Recruiter Classification: Executive Temporary; **Lowest/Average
Salary:** $40,000/$75,000; **Industry Concentration:** Electronics,
High Technology; **Function Concentration:** Generalist with a
primary focus in Women/Minorities

Gaines, Ronni L. — *Partner*
TOPAZ International, Inc.
383 Northfield Avenue
West Orange, NJ 07052
Telephone: (201) 669-7300
Recruiter Classification: Contingency; **Lowest/Average Salary:**
$40,000/$75,000; **Industry Concentration:** Electronics, High
Technology; **Function Concentration:** Generalist with a
primary focus in Women/Minorities

Galante, Suzanne M. — *Vice President*
Vlcek & Company, Inc.
620 Newport Center Drive
Suite 1100
Newport Beach, CA 92660
Telephone: (714) 752-0661
Recruiter Classification: Retained; **Lowest/Average Salary:**
$90,000/$90,000; **Industry Concentration:** Generalist with a
primary focus in High Technology, Information Technology;
Function Concentration: Generalist with a primary focus in
Engineering, Finance/Accounting, General Management,
Human Resources, Marketing, Sales, Women/Minorities

Galbraith, Deborah M. — *Senior Associate*
Stratford Group
1760 Manley Road
Maumee, OH 43537
Telephone: (419) 897-5419
Recruiter Classification: Retained; **Lowest/Average Salary:**
$75,000/$90,000; **Industry Concentration:** Generalist with a
primary focus in High Technology, Information Technology;
Function Concentration: Administration, Engineering, General
Management, Human Resources, Marketing, Research and
Development, Sales, Women/Minorities

Gale, Rhoda E. — *Senior Associate*
E.G. Jones Associates, Ltd.
1505 York Road
Lutherville, MD 21093
Telephone: (410) 337-4925
Recruiter Classification: Contingency; **Lowest/Average Salary:**
$40,000/$60,000; **Industry Concentration:** High Technology;
Function Concentration: Engineering, Marketing, Research and
Development, Sales

Gallagher, Terence M. — *Chief Operating Officer*
Battalia Winston International
120 Wood Avenue, South
Iselin, NJ 08830
Telephone: (908) 549-2002
Recruiter Classification: Retained; **Lowest/Average Salary:**
$90,000/$90,000; **Industry Concentration:** Generalist with a
primary focus in Electronics, High Technology, Information
Technology; **Function Concentration:** Generalist with a
primary focus in Administration, Finance/Accounting, General
Management, Human Resources, Marketing, Sales,
Women/Minorities

Gallin, Larry — *President*
Gallin Associates, Inc.
P.O. Box 1065
Safety Harbor, FL 34695-1065
Telephone: (813) 724-8303
Recruiter Classification: Retained; **Lowest/Average Salary:**
$50,000/$75,000; **Industry Concentration:** Electronics;
Function Concentration: Engineering, Research and
Development

Gamble, Ira — *Associate*
Source Services Corporation
1290 Oakmead Parkway, Suite 318
Sunnyvale, CA 94086
Telephone: (408) 738-8440
Recruiter Classification: Contingency; **Lowest/Average Salary:**
$30,000/$50,000; **Industry Concentration:** Information
Technology; **Function Concentration:** Engineering,
Finance/Accounting

Gantar, Donna — *Senior Consultant*
Howard Fischer Associates, Inc.
1800 John F. Kennedy Boulevard, 7th Floor
Philadelphia, PA 19103
Telephone: (215) 568-8363
Recruiter Classification: Retained; **Lowest/Average Salary:**
$90,000/$90,000; **Industry Concentration:** Generalist with a
primary focus in High Technology; **Function Concentration:**
Generalist with a primary focus in Administration,
Finance/Accounting, General Management, Human Resources,
Marketing, Research and Development, Sales,
Women/Minorities

Garcia, Samuel K. — *Technical Recruiter*
Southwestern Professional Services
2451 Atrium Way
Nashville, TN 37214
Telephone: (615) 391-2722
Recruiter Classification: Contingency; **Lowest/Average Salary:**
$30,000/$50,000; **Industry Concentration:** Information
Technology; **Function Concentration:** Engineering, Sales

Gardiner, E. Nicholas P. — *President*
Gardiner International
101 East 52nd Street
New York, NY 10022
Telephone: (212) 838-0707
Recruiter Classification: Retained; **Lowest/Average Salary:**
$90,000/$90,000; **Industry Concentration:** Generalist with a
primary focus in Information Technology; **Function
Concentration:** Generalist with a primary focus in
Finance/Accounting, General Management, Marketing

Gardner, Michael — *Associate*
Source Services Corporation
2 Penn Plaza, Suite 1176
New York, NY 10121
Telephone: (212) 760-2200
Recruiter Classification: Contingency; **Lowest/Average Salary:**
$30,000/$50,000; **Industry Concentration:** Information
Technology; **Function Concentration:** Engineering,
Finance/Accounting

Gares, Conrad — *Executive Recruiter*
TSS Consulting, Ltd.
2425 East Camelback Road
Suite 375
Phoenix, AZ 85016
Telephone: (602) 955-7000
Recruiter Classification: Contingency; **Lowest/Average Salary:**
$60,000/$75,000; **Industry Concentration:** Electronics, High
Technology; **Function Concentration:** Engineering, General
Management, Marketing

Garfinkle, Steven M. — *Managing Director*
Battalia Winston International
20 William Street
Wellesley Hills, MA 02181
Telephone: (617) 239-1400
Recruiter Classification: Retained; **Lowest/Average Salary:**
$90,000/$90,000; **Industry Concentration:** Generalist with a
primary focus in Electronics, High Technology, Information
Technology; **Function Concentration:** Generalist with a
primary focus in Engineering, Finance/Accounting, General
Management, Human Resources, Marketing, Research and
Development, Sales, Women/Minorities

Garrett, James — *Staffing Consultant*
International Staffing Consultants, Inc.
500 Newport Center Drive, Suite 300
Newport Beach, CA 92660-7003
Telephone: (714) 721-7990
Recruiter Classification: Contingency; **Lowest/Average Salary:**
$30,000/$60,000; **Industry Concentration:** Generalist with a
primary focus in High Technology; **Function Concentration:**
Engineering

Garrett, Mark — *Associate*
Source Services Corporation
One CityPlace, Suite 170
St. Louis, MO 63141
Telephone: (314) 432-4500
Recruiter Classification: Contingency; **Lowest/Average Salary:**
$30,000/$50,000; **Industry Concentration:** Information
Technology; **Function Concentration:** Engineering,
Finance/Accounting

Garzone, Dolores — *Executive Recruiter*
M.A. Churchill & Associates, Inc.
Morelyn Plaza #307
1111 Street Road
Southampton, PA 18966
Telephone: (215) 953-0300
Recruiter Classification: Retained; **Lowest/Average Salary:**
$50,000/$75,000; **Industry Concentration:** High Technology,
Information Technology; **Function Concentration:** General
Management, Marketing, Sales

Gates, Lucille C. — *Principal*
Lamalie Amrop International
Chevron Tower
1301 McKinney Street
Houston, TX 77010-3034
Telephone: (713) 739-8602
Recruiter Classification: Retained; **Lowest/Average Salary:**
$90,000/$90,000; **Industry Concentration:** Generalist with a
primary focus in High Technology; **Function Concentration:**
Generalist

Gauthier, Robert C. — *Managing Director*
Columbia Consulting Group
20 South Charles Street, 9th Floor
Baltimore, MD 21201
Telephone: (410) 385-2525
Recruiter Classification: Retained; **Lowest/Average Salary:**
$75,000/$90,000; **Industry Concentration:** Generalist with a
primary focus in High Technology, Information Technology;
Function Concentration: Generalist with a primary focus in
Finance/Accounting, General Management, Human Resources,
Marketing, Sales

Geiger, Jan — *Outplacement Manager*
Wilcox, Bertoux & Miller
100 Howe Avenue, Suite 155N
Sacramento, CA 95825
Telephone: (916) 977-3700
Recruiter Classification: Contingency; **Lowest/Average Salary:**
$40,000/$75,000; **Industry Concentration:** Information
Technology; **Function Concentration:** Administration,
Finance/Accounting, General Management

Gennawey, Robert — *Managing Director*
Source Services Corporation
One Park Plaza, Suite 560
Irvine, CA 92714
Telephone: (714) 660-1666
Recruiter Classification: Contingency; **Lowest/Average Salary:**
$30,000/$50,000; **Industry Concentration:** Information
Technology; **Function Concentration:** Engineering,
Finance/Accounting

George, Delores F. — *President and Owner*
Delores F. George Human Resource Management
& Consulting Industry
269 Hamilton Street, Suite 1
Worcester, MA 01604
Telephone: (508) 754-3451
Recruiter Classification: Contingency; **Lowest/Average Salary:**
$60,000/$60,000; **Industry Concentration:** Generalist with a
primary focus in Electronics, High Technology, Information
Technology; **Function Concentration:** Generalist with a
primary focus in Administration, Finance/Accounting, General
Management, Human Resources, Marketing, Research and
Development, Sales, Women/Minorities

Gerbasi, Michael — *Senior Partner/CEO*
The Sager Company
1619 Brookpark Road
Cleveland, OH 44109-5816
Telephone: (216) 459-1300
Recruiter Classification: Retained; **Lowest/Average Salary:**
$75,000/$90,000; **Industry Concentration:** Generalist with a
primary focus in Electronics, High Technology; **Function
Concentration:** Generalist with a primary focus in Engineering,
Finance/Accounting, General Management, Human Resources,
Marketing, Research and Development, Sales

Gerbosi, Karen — *Vice President Records
Management*
Hernand & Partners
770 Tamalpais Drive, Suite 204
Corte Madera, CA 94925
Telephone: (415) 927-7000
Recruiter Classification: Executive Temporary; **Industry
Concentration:** High Technology, Information Technology;
Function Concentration: Engineering

Germain, Valerie — *Managing Director*
Jay Gaines & Company, Inc.
450 Park Avenue
New York, NY 10022
Telephone: (212) 308-9222
Recruiter Classification: Retained; **Lowest/Average Salary:**
$200,000/$250,000; **Industry Concentration:** Generalist with a
primary focus in Information Technology; **Function
Concentration:** Generalist with a primary focus in
Administration, General Management, Marketing, Sales

Germaine, Debra — *Partner*
Fenwick Partners
57 Bedford Street, Suite 101
Lexington, MA 02173
Telephone: (617) 862-3370
Recruiter Classification: Retained; **Lowest/Average Salary:**
$90,000/$90,000; **Industry Concentration:** Electronics, High
Technology, Information Technology; **Function Concentration:**
Generalist

Gerster, J.P. — *Associate*
Juntunen-Combs-Poirier
111 Bayhill Drive, Suite 255
San Bruno, CA 94066
Telephone: (415) 635-0184
Recruiter Classification: Retained; **Lowest/Average Salary:**
$90,000/$90,000; **Industry Concentration:** High Technology,
Information Technology; **Function Concentration:** Engineering,
Finance/Accounting, General Management, Research and
Development

Gestwick, Daniel — *Search Consultant*
Cochran, Cochran & Yale, Inc.
5166 Main Street
Williamsville, NY 14221
Telephone: (716) 631-1300
Recruiter Classification: Retained; **Lowest/Average Salary:**
$50,000/$75,000; **Industry Concentration:** Generalist with a
primary focus in High Technology, Information Technology;
Function Concentration: Generalist with a primary focus in
Engineering, Finance/Accounting, General Management,
Human Resources, Marketing, Sales, Women/Minorities

Gettys, James R. — *President*
International Staffing Consultants, Inc.
500 Newport Center Drive, Suite 300
Newport Beach, CA 92660-7003
Telephone: (714) 721-7990
Recruiter Classification: Contingency, Executive Temporary;
Lowest/Average Salary: $60,000/$90,000; **Industry
Concentration:** Generalist with a primary focus in Electronics;
Function Concentration: Generalist with a primary focus in
Administration, Engineering, General Management, Human
Resources, Marketing

Ghurani, Mac — *Associate*
Gary Kaplan & Associates
201 South Lake Avenue
Suite 600
Pasadena, CA 91101
Telephone: (818) 796-8100
Recruiter Classification: Retained; **Lowest/Average Salary:**
$75,000/$90,000; **Industry Concentration:** Generalist with a
primary focus in Electronics, High Technology, Information
Technology; **Function Concentration:** Generalist with a
primary focus in Engineering, Finance/Accounting, General
Management, Human Resources, Marketing, Research and
Development

Gibbs, John S. — *Director*
Spencer Stuart
277 Park Avenue, 29th Floor
New York, NY 10172
Telephone: (212) 336-0200
Recruiter Classification: Retained; **Lowest/Average Salary:**
$90,000/$90,000; **Industry Concentration:** Generalist with a
primary focus in Electronics, High Technology; **Function
Concentration:** Generalist with a primary focus in
Administration, Finance/Accounting, General Management,
Human Resources, Marketing, Sales

Gibson, Bruce — *President*
Gibson & Company Inc.
250 North Sunnyslope Road, Suite 300
Brookfield, WI 53005
Telephone: (414) 785-8100
Recruiter Classification: Retained; **Lowest/Average Salary:**
$100,000/$100,000; **Industry Concentration:** Generalist with a
primary focus in High Technology, Information Technology;
Function Concentration: Generalist

Gideon, Mark — *Managing Director*
Eagle Search Associates
336 Bon Air Center, #295
Greenbrae, CA 94904
Telephone: (415) 398-6066
Recruiter Classification: Retained; **Lowest/Average Salary:**
$50,000/$75,000; **Industry Concentration:** High Technology,
Information Technology; **Function Concentration:** Marketing,
Sales

Giesy, John — *Associate*
Source Services Corporation
1105 Schrock Road, Suite 510
Columbus, OH 43229
Telephone: (614) 846-3311
Recruiter Classification: Contingency; **Lowest/Average Salary:**
$30,000/$50,000; **Industry Concentration:** Information
Technology; **Function Concentration:** Engineering,
Finance/Accounting

Gilbert, Jerry — *Member Advisory Board*
Gilbert & Van Campen International
Graybar Building, 420 Lexington Avenue
New York, NY 10170
Telephone: (212) 661-2122
Recruiter Classification: Retained; **Lowest/Average Salary:**
$90,000/$90,000; **Industry Concentration:** Generalist with a
primary focus in High Technology; **Function Concentration:**
Generalist with a primary focus in Finance/Accounting,
General Management, Human Resources, Marketing, Sales,
Women/Minorities

Gilchrist, Robert J. — *Managing Director*
Horton International
10 Tower Lane
Avon, CT 06001
Telephone: (860) 674-8701
Recruiter Classification: Retained; **Lowest/Average Salary:**
$90,000/$90,000; **Industry Concentration:** Electronics, High
Technology; **Function Concentration:** Generalist with a
primary focus in Engineering, Finance/Accounting, General
Management, Human Resources, Marketing

Giles, Joe L. — *President*
Joe L. Giles and Associates, Inc.
15565 Northland Drive
Suite 608 West
Southfield, MI 48075
Telephone: (248) 569-8660
Recruiter Classification: Contingency; **Lowest/Average Salary:**
$30,000/$60,000; **Industry Concentration:** Generalist with a
primary focus in Electronics, High Technology, Information
Technology; **Function Concentration:** Generalist with a
primary focus in Engineering, Finance/Accounting, Human
Resources, Research and Development, Women/Minorities

Gilinsky, David — *Associate*
Source Services Corporation
3 Summit Park Drive, Suite 550
Independence, OH 44131
Telephone: (216) 328-5900
Recruiter Classification: Contingency; **Lowest/Average Salary:**
$30,000/$50,000; **Industry Concentration:** Information
Technology; **Function Concentration:** Engineering,
Finance/Accounting

Gill, Patricia — *Managing Principal*
Columbia Consulting Group
P.O. Box 1483
Princeton, NJ 08542-1483
Telephone: (609) 466-8900
Recruiter Classification: Retained; **Lowest/Average Salary:**
$75,000/$90,000; **Industry Concentration:** Generalist with a
primary focus in Electronics, High Technology, Information
Technology; **Function Concentration:** Generalist with a
primary focus in Finance/Accounting, General Management,
Human Resources, Marketing, Sales

Gillespie, Thomas — *Contract Recruiter*
Professional Search Consultants
3050 Post Oak Boulevard, Suite 1615
Houston, TX 77056
Telephone: (713) 960-9215
Recruiter Classification: Executive Temporary; **Lowest/Average
Salary:** $50,000/$60,000; **Industry Concentration:** Generalist
with a primary focus in High Technology; **Function
Concentration:** Generalist with a primary focus in Engineering,
Human Resources, Sales

Gilmore, Connie — *Vice President*
Taylor-Winfield, Inc.
12801 N. Central Expressway
Suite 1260
Dallas, TX 75243
Telephone: (214) 392-1400
Recruiter Classification: Retained; **Lowest/Average Salary:**
$90,000/$90,000; **Industry Concentration:** High Technology,
Information Technology; **Function Concentration:** Generalist
with a primary focus in Finance/Accounting, General
Management, Research and Development, Sales

Gilreath, James M. — *President*
Gilreath Weatherby, Inc.
P.O. Box 1483 - 3 Hidden Ledge Road
Manchester-by-the-Sea, MA 01944
Telephone: (508) 526-8771
Recruiter Classification: Retained; **Lowest/Average Salary:**
$75,000/$90,000; **Industry Concentration:** Generalist with a
primary focus in High Technology; **Function Concentration:**
Generalist with a primary focus in Engineering,
Finance/Accounting, General Management, Human Resources,
Marketing

Giries, Juliet D. — *Senior Consultant*
Barton Associates, Inc.
One Riverway, Suite 2500
Houston, TX 77056
Telephone: (713) 961-9111
Recruiter Classification: Retained; **Lowest/Average Salary:**
$75,000/$90,000; **Industry Concentration:** Generalist with a
primary focus in Electronics, High Technology, Information
Technology; **Function Concentration:** Generalist with a
primary focus in Finance/Accounting, Human Resources,
Marketing, Research and Development, Sales

Girsinger, Linda — *Recruiter*
Industrial Recruiters Associates, Inc.
20 Hurlbut Street, 1st Floor
West Hartford, CT 06110
Telephone: (860) 953-3643
Recruiter Classification: Contingency; **Lowest/Average
Salary:** $30,000/$90,000; **Industry Concentration:**
Electronics, High Technology, Information Technology;
Function Concentration: Generalist with a primary
focus in Engineering, Marketing, Research and
Development

Glacy, Kurt — *Software Engineering Recruiter*
Winter, Wyman & Company
950 Winter Street, Suite 3100
Waltham, MA 02154-1294
Telephone: (617) 890-7000
Recruiter Classification: Contingency; **Lowest/Average
Salary:** $40,000/$75,000; **Industry Concentration:** High
Technology, Information Technology; **Function
Concentration:** Engineering

Gladstone, Martin J. — *Executiver Recruiter*
MSI International
229 Peachtree Street, NE
Suite 1201
Atlanta, GA 30303
Telephone: (404) 659-5050
Recruiter Classification: Contingency; **Lowest/Average Salary:**
$30,000/$75,000; **Industry Concentration:** Generalist with a
primary focus in Information Technology; **Function
Concentration:** Generalist with a primary focus in
Administration, Engineering, Finance/Accounting, General
Management, Marketing, Sales

Glass, Sharon — *Consultant/Director*
Logix Partners
1601 Trapelo Road
Waltham, MA 02154
Telephone: (617) 890-0500
Recruiter Classification: Retained; **Lowest/Average Salary:**
$60,000/$75,000; **Industry Concentration:** High Technology;
Function Concentration: Engineering

Glass, Sharon — *Director*
Logix, Inc.
1601 Trapelo Road
Waltham, MA 02154
Telephone: (617) 890-0500
Recruiter Classification: Retained; **Lowest/Average Salary:**
$60,000/$75,000; **Industry Concentration:** High Technology;
Function Concentration: Engineering

Glickman, Leenie — *Associate*
Source Services Corporation
20 Burlington Mall Road, Suite 405
Burlington, MA 01803
Telephone: (617) 272-5000
Recruiter Classification: Contingency; **Lowest/Average Salary:**
$30,000/$50,000; **Industry Concentration:** Information
Technology; **Function Concentration:** Engineering,
Finance/Accounting

Gloss, Frederick C. — *President*
F. Gloss International
1595 Spring Hill Road, Suite 350
Vienna, VA 22182
Telephone: (703) 847-0010
Recruiter Classification: Retained; **Lowest/Average Salary:**
$90,000/$90,000; **Industry Concentration:** High Technology,
Information Technology; **Function Concentration:** Engineering,
General Management, Marketing, Research and Development,
Sales

Gluzman, Arthur — *Associate*
Source Services Corporation
2000 Town Center, Suite 850
Southfield, MI 48075
Telephone: (810) 352-6520
Recruiter Classification: Contingency; **Lowest/Average Salary:**
$30,000/$50,000; **Industry Concentration:** Information
Technology; **Function Concentration:** Engineering,
Finance/Accounting

Gnatowski, Bruce — *Associate*
Source Services Corporation
8614 Westwood Center, Suite 750
Vienna, VA 22182
Telephone: (703) 790-5610
Recruiter Classification: Contingency; **Lowest/Average Salary:**
$30,000/$50,000; **Industry Concentration:** Information
Technology; **Function Concentration:** Engineering,
Finance/Accounting

Goar, Duane R. — *Partner*
Sandhurst Associates
4851 LBJ Freeway, Suite 601
Dallas, TX 75244
Telephone: (214) 458-1212
Recruiter Classification: Retained; **Lowest/Average Salary:**
$75,000/$90,000; **Industry Concentration:** Generalist with a
primary focus in High Technology; **Function Concentration:**
Generalist with a primary focus in Finance/Accounting, Human
Resources, Marketing, Sales

Gobert, Larry — *Chief Operating Officer*
Professional Search Consultants
3050 Post Oak Boulevard, Suite 1615
Houston, TX 77056
Telephone: (713) 960-9215
Recruiter Classification: Executive Temporary;
Lowest/Average Salary: $75,000/$75,000; **Industry
Concentration:** Generalist with a primary focus in Electronics,
High Technology; **Function Concentration:** Generalist with a
primary focus in Finance/Accounting, General Management,
Marketing

Goedtke, Steven — *Consultant*
Southwestern Professional Services
2451 Atrium Way
Nashville, TN 37214
Telephone: (615) 391-2722
Recruiter Classification: Contingency; **Lowest/Average Salary:**
$30,000/$50,000; **Industry Concentration:** Generalist with a
primary focus in Electronics, High Technology, Information
Technology; **Function Concentration:** Sales

Gold, Donald — *Associate*
Executive Search, Ltd.
4830 Interstate Drive
Cincinnati, OH 45246
Telephone: (513) 874-6901
Recruiter Classification: Retained; **Lowest/Average Salary:**
$50,000/$75,000; **Industry Concentration:** Generalist with a
primary focus in High Technology; **Function Concentration:**
Finance/Accounting

Gold, Stacey — *Research Associate*
Earley Kielty and Associates, Inc.
Two Pennsylvania Plaza
New York, NY 10121
Telephone: (212) 736-5626
Recruiter Classification: Retained; **Lowest/Average Salary:**
$90,000/$90,000; **Industry Concentration:** Generalist with a
primary focus in Information Technology; **Function
Concentration:** Generalist with a primary focus in
Administration, Finance/Accounting, General Management,
Human Resources, Marketing, Research and Development,
Sales, Women/Minorities

Goldberg, Susan C. — *President*
Susan C. Goldberg Associates
65 LaSalle Road
West Hartford, CT 06107
Telephone: (860) 236-4597
Recruiter Classification: Contingency; **Lowest/Average Salary:**
$40,000/$60,000; **Industry Concentration:** High Technology;
Function Concentration: Finance/Accounting

Golde, Lisa — *Consultant*
Tully/Woodmansee International, Inc.
1088 U.S. 27 North
Lake Placid, FL 33852
Telephone: (941) 465-1024
Recruiter Classification: Retained; **Lowest/Average Salary:**
$60,000/$90,000; **Industry Concentration:** Generalist with a
primary focus in Information Technology; **Function
Concentration:** Generalist with a primary focus in Engineering,
Finance/Accounting, General Management, Marketing, Sales,
Women/Minorities

Goldenberg, Susan — *Senior Associate*
Grant Cooper and Associates
795 Office Parkway, Suite 117
St. Louis, MO 63141
Telephone: (314) 567-4690
Recruiter Classification: Retained; **Lowest/Average Salary:**
$60,000/$90,000; **Industry Concentration:** Generalist with a
primary focus in Electronics, High Technology, Information
Technology; **Function Concentration:** Generalist with a
primary focus in Administration, Engineering,
Finance/Accounting, General Management, Human Resources,
Marketing, Research and Development, Sales

Goldman, Michael L. — *President/Executive
Recruiter*
Strategic Associates, Inc.
13915 Burnet Road, Suite 300
Austin, TX 78728
Telephone: (512) 218-8222
Recruiter Classification: Contingency; **Lowest/Average Salary:**
$50,000/$90,000; **Industry Concentration:** Electronics, High
Technology, Information Technology

Goldsmith, Fred J. — *President*
Fred J. Goldsmith Associates
14056 Margate Street
Sherman Oaks, CA 91401
Telephone: (818) 783-3931
Recruiter Classification: Retained; **Lowest/Average Salary:**
$60,000/$75,000; **Industry Concentration:** Generalist with a
primary focus in Electronics, High Technology; **Function
Concentration:** Generalist with a primary focus in Engineering,
Finance/Accounting, General Management, Human Resources,
Marketing, Sales

Goldstein, Steven G. — *President*
The Jonathan Stevens Group, Inc.
116 Village Boulevard
Suite 200
Princeton, NJ 08540-5799
Telephone: (609) 734-7444
Recruiter Classification: Retained; **Lowest/Average Salary:**
$40,000/$75,000; **Industry Concentration:** Generalist with a
primary focus in Electronics, Information Technology; **Function
Concentration:** Generalist with a primary focus in Engineering,
Finance/Accounting, Human Resources, Marketing

Gomez, Cristina — *Associate*
Juntunen-Combs-Poirier
600 Montgomery Street, 2nd Floor
San Francisco, CA 94111
Telephone: (415) 291-1699
Recruiter Classification: Retained; **Lowest/Average Salary:**
$90,000/$90,000; **Industry Concentration:** High Technology,
Information Technology; **Function Concentration:** General
Management, Marketing, Sales

Gonye, Peter K. — *Consultant*
Egon Zehnder International Inc.
350 Park Avenue
New York, NY 10022
Telephone: (212) 838-9199
Recruiter Classification: Retained; **Lowest/Average Salary:**
$90,000/$90,000; **Industry Concentration:** Generalist with a
primary focus in High Technology; **Function Concentration:**
Generalist

Gonzalez, Kristen — *Professional Recruiter*
A.J. Burton Group, Inc.
120 East Baltimore Street, Suite 2220
Baltimore, MD 21202
Telephone: (410) 752-5244
Recruiter Classification: Contingency; **Lowest/Average Salary:**
$40,000/$75,000; **Industry Concentration:** Generalist with a
primary focus in High Technology, Information Technology;
Function Concentration: Generalist with a primary focus in
Administration, Finance/Accounting, General Management,
Human Resources

Gonzalez, Rafael — *Principal*
Korn/Ferry International
Montes Urales 641
Lomas De Chapultepec
Mexico City, D.F., MEXICO 11000
Telephone: (525) 202-0046
Recruiter Classification: Retained; **Lowest/Average Salary:**
$100,000/$150,000; **Industry Concentration:** Generalist with a
primary focus in Information Technology; **Function
Concentration:** Generalist

Goodere, Greg — *Associate*
Splaine & Associates, Inc.
15951 Los Gatos Boulevard
Los Gatos, CA 95032
Telephone: (408) 354-3664
Recruiter Classification: Retained; **Lowest/Average Salary:**
$90,000/$90,000; **Industry Concentration:** High Technology;
Function Concentration: Generalist

Goodman, Dawn M. — *Project Associate*
Bason Associates Inc.
11311 Cornell Park Drive
Cincinnati, OH 45242
Telephone: (513) 469-9881
Recruiter Classification: Retained; **Lowest/Average Salary:**
$60,000/$90,000; **Industry Concentration:** Generalist with a
primary focus in High Technology; **Function Concentration:**
Generalist with a primary focus in Administration, Engineering,
Finance/Accounting, General Management, Human Resources,
Marketing, Research and Development, Sales

Goodman, Victor — *President*
Anderson Sterling Associates
18623 Ventura Boulevard, Suite 207
Tarzana, CA 91356
Telephone: (818) 996-0921
Recruiter Classification: Executive Temporary; **Lowest/Average
Salary:** $30,000/$60,000; **Industry Concentration:** Electronics,
High Technology, Information Technology; **Function
Concentration:** Engineering, Finance/Accounting, General
Management, Human Resources, Marketing, Research and
Development, Sales, Women/Minorities

Goodridge, Benjamin — *Executive Recruiter*
S.C. International, Ltd.
1430 Branding Lane, Suite 119
Downers Grove, IL 60515
Telephone: (708) 963-3033
Recruiter Classification: Contingency; **Lowest/Average Salary:**
$30,000/$50,000; **Industry Concentration:** Information
Technology; **Function Concentration:** Administration, Human
Resources

Goodwin, Gary — *Associate*
Source Services Corporation
2 Penn Plaza, Suite 1176
New York, NY 10121
Telephone: (212) 760-2200
Recruiter Classification: Contingency; **Lowest/Average Salary:**
$30,000/$50,000; **Industry Concentration:** Information
Technology; **Function Concentration:** Engineering,
Finance/Accounting

Goodwin, Tim — *Senior Director*
William Guy & Associates
P.O. Box 57407
Sherman Oaks, CA 91413
Telephone:Unpublished
Recruiter Classification: Retained; **Lowest/Average Salary:**
$50,000/$90,000; **Industry Concentration:** Electronics, High
Technology, Information Technology; **Function Concentration:**
Generalist with a primary focus in Administration, Engineering,
Finance/Accounting, General Management, Research and
Development, Women/Minorities

Gordon, Elliot — *Vice President*
Korn/Ferry International
1300 Dove Street
Suite 300
Newport Beach, CA 92660
Telephone: (714) 851-1834
Recruiter Classification: Retained; **Lowest/Average Salary:**
$100,000/$150,000; **Industry Concentration:** Generalist with a
primary focus in High Technology; **Function Concentration:**
Generalist

Gordon, Gerald L. — *Senior Associate*
E.G. Jones Associates, Ltd.
1505 York Road
Lutherville, MD 21093
Telephone: (410) 337-4925
Recruiter Classification: Contingency; **Lowest/Average Salary:**
$20,000/$50,000; **Industry Concentration:** Generalist with a
primary focus in Information Technology; **Function
Concentration:** Generalist with a primary focus in
Administration, Finance/Accounting, General Management,
Marketing, Sales

Gordon, Gloria — *Vice President*
A.T. Kearney, Inc.
Biltmore Tower
500 South Grand Avenue, Suite 1780
Los Angeles, CA 90071
Telephone: (213) 689-6800
Recruiter Classification: Retained; **Lowest/Average Salary:**
$90,000/$90,000; **Industry Concentration:** Generalist with a
primary focus in Information Technology; **Function
Concentration:** Generalist

Gordon, Teri — *Director*
Don Richard Associates of Washington, D.C., Inc.
8180 Greensboro Drive, Suite 1020
McLean, VA 22102
Telephone: (703) 827-5990
Recruiter Classification: Executive Temporary; **Lowest/Average
Salary:** $20,000/$30,000; **Industry Concentration:** High
Technology; **Function Concentration:** Administration,
Finance/Accounting, Human Resources

Gore, Les — *Managing Partner*
Executive Search International
60 Walnut Street
Wellesley, MA 02181
Telephone: (617) 239-0303
Recruiter Classification: Retained; **Lowest/Average Salary:**
$75,000/$90,000; **Industry Concentration:** High Technology;
Function Concentration: Generalist

Gorfinkle, Gayle — *Partner*
Executive Search International
60 Walnut Street
Wellesley, MA 02181
Telephone: (617) 239-0303
Recruiter Classification: Retained; **Lowest/Average Salary:**
$75,000/$90,000; **Industry Concentration:** Electronics, High
Technology; **Function Concentration:** Generalist

Gorman, Patrick — *Associate*
Source Services Corporation
425 California Street, Suite 1200
San Francisco, CA 94104
Telephone: (415) 434-2410
Recruiter Classification: Contingency; **Lowest/Average Salary:**
$30,000/$50,000; **Industry Concentration:** Information
Technology; **Function Concentration:** Engineering,
Finance/Accounting

Gorman, T. Patrick — *Vice President*
Techsearch Services, Inc.
6 Hachaliah Brown Drive
Somers, NY 10589
Telephone: (914) 277-2727
Recruiter Classification: Contingency; **Lowest/Average Salary:**
$50,000/$75,000; **Industry Concentration:** High Technology,
Information Technology; **Function Concentration:**
Finance/Accounting

Gostyla, Rick — *Senior Director*
Spencer Stuart
3000 Sand Hill Road
Building 2, Suite 175
Menlo Park, CA 94025
Telephone: (415) 688-1285
Recruiter Classification: Retained; **Lowest/Average Salary:**
$90,000/$90,000; **Industry Concentration:** Electronics, High
Technology, Information Technology; **Function Concentration:**
Administration, Engineering, Finance/Accounting, General
Management, Human Resources, Marketing, Research and
Development, Sales

Gottenberg, Norbert — *Director*
Spencer Stuart
277 Park Avenue, 29th Floor
New York, NY 10172
Telephone: (212) 336-0200
Recruiter Classification: Retained; **Lowest/Average Salary:**
$50,000/$75,000; **Industry Concentration:** High Technology

Gould, Adam — *Director/Multimedia*
Logix, Inc.
1601 Trapelo Road
Waltham, MA 02154
Telephone: (617) 890-0500
Recruiter Classification: Retained; **Lowest/Average Salary:**
$60,000/$75,000; **Industry Concentration:** High Technology;
Function Concentration: Engineering

Gould, Adam — *Consultant/Director*
Logix Partners
1601 Trapelo Road
Waltham, MA 02154
Telephone: (617) 890-0500
Recruiter Classification: Retained; **Lowest/Average Salary:**
$60,000/$75,000; **Industry Concentration:** High Technology;
Function Concentration: Engineering

Gould, Dana — *Senior Consultant*
Logix Partners
1601 Trapelo Road
Waltham, MA 02154
Telephone: (617) 890-0500
Recruiter Classification: Retained; **Lowest/Average Salary:**
$60,000/$75,000; **Industry Concentration:** High Technology,
Information Technology; **Function Concentration:** Engineering

Gould, Dana — *Senior Consultant*
Logix, Inc.
1601 Trapelo Road
Waltham, MA 02154
Telephone: (617) 890-0500
Recruiter Classification: Retained; **Lowest/Average Salary:**
$60,000/$75,000; **Industry Concentration:** High Technology,
Information Technology; **Function Concentration:** Engineering,
Research and Development

Gourley, Timothy — *Associate*
Source Services Corporation
155 Federal Street, Suite 410
Boston, MA 02110
Telephone: (617) 482-8211
Recruiter Classification: Contingency; **Lowest/Average Salary:**
$30,000/$50,000; **Industry Concentration:** Information
Technology; **Function Concentration:** Engineering,
Finance/Accounting

Grado, Eduardo — *Associate*
Source Services Corporation
5429 LBJ Freeway, Suite 275
Dallas, TX 75240
Telephone: (214) 387-1600
Recruiter Classification: Contingency; **Lowest/Average Salary:**
$30,000/$50,000; **Industry Concentration:** Information
Technology; **Function Concentration:** Engineering,
Finance/Accounting

Grady, James — *Account Executive*
Search West, Inc.
100 Pine Street, Suite 2500
San Francisco, CA 94111-5203
Telephone: (415) 788-1770
Recruiter Classification: Contingency; **Lowest/Average Salary:**
$40,000/$60,000; **Industry Concentration:** Electronics, High
Technology; **Function Concentration:** Administration,
Marketing, Sales

Graff, Jack — *Associate*
Source Services Corporation
5343 North 16th Street, Suite 270
Phoenix, AZ 85016
Telephone: (602) 230-0220
Recruiter Classification: Contingency; **Lowest/Average Salary:**
$30,000/$50,000; **Industry Concentration:** Information
Technology; **Function Concentration:** Engineering,
Finance/Accounting

Graham, Craig — *Partner*
Ward Howell International, Inc.
141 Adelaide Street West
Suite 1800
Toronto, Ontario, CANADA M5H 3L5
Telephone: (416) 862-1273
Recruiter Classification: Retained; **Lowest/Average Salary:**
$75,000/$90,000; **Industry Concentration:** Information
Technology; **Function Concentration:** Generalist

Graham, Dale — *Executive Recruiter*
CPS Inc.
One Westbrook Corporate Centre, Suite 600
Westchester, IL 60154
Telephone: (708) 531-8370
Recruiter Classification: Contingency; **Lowest/Average Salary:**
$30,000/$50,000; **Industry Concentration:** Generalist with a
primary focus in Electronics, High Technology, Information
Technology; **Function Concentration:** Engineering, Research
and Development, Sales, Women/Minorities

Graham, Shannon — *Associate*
Source Services Corporation
7730 East Bellview Avenue, Suite 302
Englewood, CO 80111
Telephone: (303) 773-3700
Recruiter Classification: Contingency; **Lowest/Average Salary:**
$30,000/$50,000; **Industry Concentration:** Information
Technology; **Function Concentration:** Engineering,
Finance/Accounting

Grandinetti, Suzanne — *Associate*
Source Services Corporation
1500 West Park Drive, Suite 390
Westborough, MA 01581
Telephone: (508) 366-2600
Recruiter Classification: Contingency; **Lowest/Average Salary:**
$30,000/$50,000; **Industry Concentration:** Information
Technology; **Function Concentration:** Engineering,
Finance/Accounting

Grant, Michael — *Vice President*
Zwell International
300 South Wacker Drive, Suite 650
Chicago, IL 60606
Telephone: (312) 663-3737
Recruiter Classification: Retained; **Lowest/Average Salary:**
$75,000/$90,000; **Industry Concentration:** Generalist with a
primary focus in High Technology, Information Technology;
Function Concentration: Generalist with a primary focus in
Engineering, Finance/Accounting, General Management,
Human Resources, Marketing, Research and Development,
Sales

Grantham, John — *President*
Grantham & Co., Inc.
136 Erwin Road
Chapel Hill, NC 27514
Telephone: (919) 932-5650
Recruiter Classification: Retained; **Lowest/Average Salary:**
$85,000/$90,000; **Industry Concentration:** Generalist with a
primary focus in Information Technology; **Function
Concentration:** Generalist with a primary focus in Engineering,
Finance/Accounting, General Management, Human Resources,
Marketing, Research and Development, Sales

Grantham, Philip H. — *Managing Principal*
Columbia Consulting Group
20 South Charles Street, 9th Floor
Baltimore, MD 21201
Telephone: (410) 385-2525
Recruiter Classification: Retained; **Lowest/Average Salary:**
$75,000/$90,000; **Industry Concentration:** Generalist with a
primary focus in Electronics, High Technology, Information
Technology; **Function Concentration:** Generalist with a
primary focus in Engineering, Finance/Accounting, Human
Resources, Marketing, Sales, Women/Minorities

Grasch, Jerry E. — *Vice President*
The Hindman Company
Browenton Place, Suite 110
2000 Warrington Way
Louisville, KY 40222
Telephone: (502) 426-4040
Recruiter Classification: Retained; **Lowest/Average Salary:**
$50,000/$90,000; **Industry Concentration:** Generalist with a
primary focus in Electronics, High Technology; **Function
Concentration:** Generalist with a primary focus in Engineering,
Finance/Accounting, General Management, Human Resources,
Marketing, Sales

Graves, Rosemarie — *Partner*
Don Richard Associates of Washington, D.C., Inc.
8201 Corporate Drive, Suite 620
Landover, MD 20785
Telephone: (301) 474-3900
Recruiter Classification: Contingency, Executive Temporary;
Lowest/Average Salary: $40,000/$60,000; **Industry
Concentration:** High Technology; **Function Concentration:**
Finance/Accounting

Gray, Betty — *Executive Recruiter*
Accent on Achievement, Inc.
3190 Rochester Road, Suite 104
Troy, MI 48083
Telephone: (248) 528-1390
Recruiter Classification: Contingency; **Lowest/Average Salary:** $30,000/$50,000; **Industry Concentration:** Generalist with a primary focus in High Technology, Information Technology; **Function Concentration:** Finance/Accounting

Gray, Heather — *Associate*
Source Services Corporation
520 Post Oak Boulevard, Suite 700
Houston, TX 77027
Telephone: (713) 439-1077
Recruiter Classification: Contingency; **Lowest/Average Salary:** $30,000/$50,000; **Industry Concentration:** Information Technology; **Function Concentration:** Engineering, Finance/Accounting

Gray, Russell — *Associate*
Source Services Corporation
1290 Oakmead Parkway, Suite 318
Sunnyvale, CA 94086
Telephone: (408) 738-8440
Recruiter Classification: Contingency; **Lowest/Average Salary:** $30,000/$50,000; **Industry Concentration:** Information Technology; **Function Concentration:** Engineering, Finance/Accounting

Graziano, Lisa — *Associate*
Source Services Corporation
1 Gatehall Drive, Suite 250
Parsippany, NJ 07054
Telephone: (201) 267-3222
Recruiter Classification: Contingency; **Lowest/Average Salary:** $30,000/$50,000; **Industry Concentration:** Information Technology; **Function Concentration:** Engineering, Finance/Accounting

Grebenstein, Charles R. — *Senior Vice President*
Skott/Edwards Consultants, Inc.
1776 On the Green
Morristown, NJ 07006
Telephone: (973) 644-0900
Recruiter Classification: Retained; **Lowest/Average Salary:** $90,000/$90,000; **Industry Concentration:** High Technology; **Function Concentration:** Engineering, Finance/Accounting, General Management, Marketing, Research and Development, Sales

Green, Jane — *Executive Recruiter*
Phillips Resource Group
330 Pelham Road, Building A
Greenville, SC 29615
Telephone: (864) 271-6350
Recruiter Classification: Contingency; **Lowest/Average Salary:** $40,000/$50,000; **Industry Concentration:** Electronics, High Technology, Information Technology; **Function Concentration:** Administration, Engineering, Finance/Accounting, General Management, Human Resources, Marketing, Research and Development, Sales

Green, Jean — *Vice President*
Broward-Dobbs, Inc.
1532 Dunwoody Village Parkway, Suite 200
Atlanta, GA 30338
Telephone: (770) 399-0744
Recruiter Classification: Contingency; **Lowest/Average Salary:** $40,000/$50,000; **Industry Concentration:** Generalist with a primary focus in Electronics, High Technology, Information Technology; **Function Concentration:** Engineering, Human Resources

Green, Marc — *Executive Recruiter*
TSS Consulting, Ltd.
2425 East Camelback Road
Suite 375
Phoenix, AZ 85016
Telephone: (602) 955-7000
Recruiter Classification: Contingency; **Lowest/Average Salary:** $60,000/$75,000; **Industry Concentration:** Electronics, High Technology; **Function Concentration:** Engineering, General Management, Marketing

Greene, Luke — *President*
Broward-Dobbs, Inc.
1532 Dunwoody Village Parkway, Suite 200
Atlanta, GA 30338
Telephone: (770) 399-0744
Recruiter Classification: Contingency; **Lowest/Average Salary:** $40,000/$60,000; **Industry Concentration:** Generalist with a primary focus in High Technology; **Function Concentration:** Engineering

Gregor, Joie A. — *Partner*
Heidrick & Struggles, Inc.
600 Superior Avenue East
Suite 2500
Cleveland, OH 44114-2650
Telephone: (216) 241-7410
Recruiter Classification: Retained; **Lowest/Average Salary:** $75,000/$90,000; **Industry Concentration:** Generalist with a primary focus in High Technology; **Function Concentration:** Generalist

Gregory, Gary A. — *Vice President*
John Kurosky & Associates
3 Corporate Park Drive, Suite 210
Irvine, CA 92714
Telephone: (714) 851-6370
Recruiter Classification: Retained; **Lowest/Average Salary:** $75,000/$90,000; **Industry Concentration:** Generalist with a primary focus in Electronics, High Technology; **Function Concentration:** Generalist

Gregory, Stephen — *Consultant*
Don Richard Associates of Richmond, Inc.
7275 Glen Forest Drive, Suite 200
Richmond, VA 23226
Telephone: (804) 282-6300
Recruiter Classification: Contingency; **Lowest/Average Salary:** $30,000/$50,000; **Industry Concentration:** Information Technology

Gresia, Paul — *Associate*
Source Services Corporation
8614 Westwood Center, Suite 750
Vienna, VA 22182
Telephone: (703) 790-5610
Recruiter Classification: Contingency; **Lowest/Average Salary:** $30,000/$50,000; **Industry Concentration:** Information Technology; **Function Concentration:** Engineering, Finance/Accounting

Grey, Fred — *Director/Executive Recruiter*
J.B. Homer Associates, Inc.
Graybar Building
420 Lexington Avenue, Suite 2328
New York, NY 10170
Telephone: (212) 697-3300
Recruiter Classification: Retained; **Lowest/Average Salary:** $90,000/$90,000; **Industry Concentration:** Generalist with a primary focus in Information Technology; **Function Concentration:** Generalist

Griffin, Cathy — *Vice President*
A.T. Kearney, Inc.
153 East 53rd Street
New York, NY 10022
Telephone: (212) 751-7040
Recruiter Classification: Retained; **Lowest/Average Salary:**
$90,000/$90,000; **Industry Concentration:** Generalist with a
primary focus in High Technology, Information Technology;
Function Concentration: Generalist with a primary focus in
Engineering, Finance/Accounting, General Management

Groban, Jack — *Vice President/Managing Director*
A.T. Kearney, Inc.
Biltmore Tower
500 South Grand Avenue, Suite 1780
Los Angeles, CA 90071
Telephone: (213) 689-6800
Recruiter Classification: Retained; **Lowest/Average Salary:**
$90,000/$90,000; **Industry Concentration:** Generalist with a
primary focus in Information Technology; **Function
Concentration:** Generalist with a primary focus in
Finance/Accounting

Groner, David — *Associate*
Source Services Corporation
150 South Wacker Drive, Suite 400
Chicago, IL 60606
Telephone: (312) 346-7000
Recruiter Classification: Contingency; **Lowest/Average Salary:**
$30,000/$50,000; **Industry Concentration:** Information
Technology; **Function Concentration:** Engineering,
Finance/Accounting

Groover, David — *Unit Manager*
MSI International
200 Galleria Parkway
Suite 1610
Atlanta, GA 30339
Telephone: (404) 951-1208
Recruiter Classification: Contingency; **Lowest/Average Salary:**
$30,000/$60,000; **Industry Concentration:** Generalist with a
primary focus in High Technology; **Function Concentration:**
Administration, Engineering, Finance/Accounting, General
Management, Marketing, Sales

Grossman, James — *Associate*
Source Services Corporation
10300 West 103rd Street, Suite 101
Overland Park, KS 66214
Telephone: (913) 888-8885
Recruiter Classification: Contingency; **Lowest/Average Salary:**
$30,000/$50,000; **Industry Concentration:** Information
Technology; **Function Concentration:** Engineering,
Finance/Accounting

Grossman, Martin — *Associate*
Source Services Corporation
15600 N.W. 67th Avenue, Suite 210
Miami Lakes, FL 33014
Telephone: (305) 556-8000
Recruiter Classification: Contingency; **Lowest/Average Salary:**
$30,000/$50,000; **Industry Concentration:** Information
Technology; **Function Concentration:** Engineering,
Finance/Accounting

Grotte, Lawrence C. — *Partner*
Lautz Grotte Engler
One Bush Street, Suite 550
San Francisco, CA 94104
Telephone: (415) 834-3100
Recruiter Classification: Retained; **Lowest/Average Salary:**
$90,000/$90,000; **Industry Concentration:** Generalist with a
primary focus in Electronics, High Technology, Information
Technology; **Function Concentration:** Generalist with a
primary focus in Engineering, Finance/Accounting, General
Management, Human Resources, Marketing, Sales

Grumulaitis, Leo — *Associate*
Source Services Corporation
5429 LBJ Freeway, Suite 275
Dallas, TX 75240
Telephone: (214) 387-1600
Recruiter Classification: Contingency; **Lowest/Average Salary:**
$30,000/$50,000; **Industry Concentration:** Information
Technology; **Function Concentration:** Engineering,
Finance/Accounting

Grzybowski, Jill — *Executive Recruiter*
CPS Inc.
One Westbrook Corporate Centre, Suite 600
Westchester, IL 60154
Telephone: (708) 531-8370
Recruiter Classification: Contingency; **Lowest/Average Salary:**
$30,000/$50,000; **Industry Concentration:** Generalist with a
primary focus in Electronics, High Technology, Information
Technology; **Function Concentration:** Engineering, Research
and Development, Sales, Women/Minorities

Guc, Stephen — *Associate*
Source Services Corporation
2000 Town Center, Suite 850
Southfield, MI 48075
Telephone: (810) 352-6520
Recruiter Classification: Contingency; **Lowest/Average Salary:**
$30,000/$50,000; **Industry Concentration:** Information
Technology; **Function Concentration:** Engineering,
Finance/Accounting

Gurnani, Angali — *Consultant*
Executive Placement Consultants, Inc.
2700 River Road, Suite 107
Des Plaines, IL 60018
Telephone: (847) 298-6445
Recruiter Classification: Contingency; **Lowest/Average Salary:**
$40,000/$75,000; **Industry Concentration:** Generalist with a
primary focus in Electronics, High Technology, Information
Technology; **Function Concentration:** Generalist with a
primary focus in Finance/Accounting, Human Resources,
Marketing

Guthrie, Stuart — *Associate*
Source Services Corporation
One Park Plaza, Suite 560
Irvine, CA 92714
Telephone: (714) 660-1666
Recruiter Classification: Contingency; **Lowest/Average Salary:**
$30,000/$50,000; **Industry Concentration:** Information
Technology; **Function Concentration:** Engineering,
Finance/Accounting

Gutknecht, Steven — *Executive Recruiter*
Jacobson Associates
150 North Wacker Drive
Suite 1120
Chicago, IL 60606
Telephone: (312) 726-1578
Recruiter Classification: Contingency; **Lowest/Average Salary:**
$20,000/$50,000; **Industry Concentration:** High Technology;
Function Concentration: Generalist

Guy, C. William — *Managing Director*
William Guy & Associates
P.O. Box 57407
Sherman Oaks, CA 91413
Telephone: Unpublished
Recruiter Classification: Retained; **Lowest/Average Salary:**
$50,000/$90,000; **Industry Concentration:** Generalist with a
primary focus in Electronics, High Technology, Information
Technology; **Function Concentration:** Generalist with a
primary focus in Administration, Engineering,
Finance/Accounting, General Management, Human Resources,
Marketing, Research and Development, Women/Minorities

Haas, Margaret P. — *President*
The Haas Associates, Inc.
443 West 24th Street
New York, NY 10011
Telephone: (212) 741-2457
Recruiter Classification: Retained; **Lowest/Average Salary:**
$60,000/$90,000; **Industry Concentration:** High Technology,
Information Technology; **Function Concentration:**
Administration, Finance/Accounting, General Management,
Human Resources, Marketing, Sales

Hacker-Taylor, Dianna — *Associate*
Source Services Corporation
525 Vine Street, Suite 2250
Cincinnati, OH 45202
Telephone: (513) 651-3303
Recruiter Classification: Contingency; **Lowest/Average Salary:**
$30,000/$50,000; **Industry Concentration:** Information
Technology; **Function Concentration:** Engineering,
Finance/Accounting

Haddad, Charles — *Managing Partner*
Romac & Associates
1770 Kirby Parkway
Suite 216
Memphis, TN 38138-7405
Telephone: (901) 756-6050
Recruiter Classification: Executive Temporary; **Lowest/Average
Salary:** $60,000/$60,000; **Industry Concentration:** High
Technology, Information Technology; **Function Concentration:**
Finance/Accounting

Hagerty, Kenneth — *Principal Advanced
Technology*
Korn/Ferry International
Presidential Plaza
900 19th Street, N.W.
Washington, DC 20006
Telephone: (202) 822-9444
Recruiter Classification: Retained; **Lowest/Average Salary:**
$100,000/$150,000; **Industry Concentration:** Generalist with a
primary focus in Information Technology; **Function
Concentration:** Generalist

Haider, Martin — *Associate*
Source Services Corporation
7730 East Bellview Avenue, Suite 302
Englewood, CO 80111
Telephone: (303) 773-3700
Recruiter Classification: Contingency; **Lowest/Average Salary:**
$30,000/$50,000; **Industry Concentration:** Information
Technology; **Function Concentration:** Engineering,
Finance/Accounting

Hailes, Brian — *Executive Director*
Russell Reynolds Associates, Inc.
The Hurt Building
50 Hurt Plaza, Suite 600
Atlanta, GA 30303-2914
Telephone: (404) 577-3000
Recruiter Classification: Retained; **Lowest/Average Salary:**
$90,000/$90,000; **Industry Concentration:** Generalist with a
primary focus in High Technology; **Function Concentration:**
Generalist

Hailey, H.M. — *Vice President Operations*
Damon & Associates, Inc.
7515 Greenville Avenue, Suite 900
Dallas, TX 75231
Telephone: (214) 696-6990
Recruiter Classification: Contingency; **Lowest/Average Salary:**
$30,000/$50,000; **Industry Concentration:** Generalist with a
primary focus in Electronics, High Technology, Information
Technology; **Function Concentration:** General Management,
Marketing, Sales

Halbrich, Mitch — *Professional Recruiter*
A.J. Burton Group, Inc.
120 East Baltimore Street, Suite 2220
Baltimore, MD 21202
Telephone: (410) 752-5244
Recruiter Classification: Contingency; **Lowest/Average Salary:**
$40,000/$75,000; **Industry Concentration:** Generalist with a
primary focus in High Technology, Information Technology;
Function Concentration: Generalist with a primary focus in
Administration, Finance/Accounting, General Management,
Human Resources

Hales, Daphne — *Associate*
Source Services Corporation
4170 Ashford Dunwoody Road, Suite 285
Atlanta, GA 30319
Telephone: (404) 255-2045
Recruiter Classification: Contingency; **Lowest/Average Salary:**
$30,000/$50,000; **Industry Concentration:** Information
Technology; **Function Concentration:** Engineering,
Finance/Accounting

Hall, Marty B. — *Executive Vice President*
Catlin-Wells & White
5413 Patterson Avenue
Suite 200
Richmond, VA 23226
Telephone: (804) 288-8800
Recruiter Classification: Contingency; **Lowest/Average Salary:**
$50,000/$60,000; **Industry Concentration:** High Technology,
Information Technology; **Function Concentration:** Generalist

Hall, Peter V. — *Managing Director*
Chartwell Partners International, Inc.
275 Battery Street, Suite 2180
San Francisco, CA 94111
Telephone: (415) 296-0600
Recruiter Classification: Retained; **Lowest/Average Salary:**
$90,000/$90,000; **Industry Concentration:** Generalist with a
primary focus in Information Technology; **Function
Concentration:** Generalist with a primary focus in
Finance/Accounting, General Management, Marketing, Sales,
Women/Minorities

Hall, Robert — *Partner*
Don Richard Associates of Tidewater, Inc.
4701 Columbus Street, Suite 102
Virginia Beach, VA 23462
Telephone: (757) 518-8600
Recruiter Classification: Contingency, Executive Temporary;
Lowest/Average Salary: $40,000/$60,000; **Industry
Concentration:** High Technology, Information Technology;
Function Concentration: Engineering

Halladay, Patti — *Principal*
Intersource, Ltd.
1509-A West 6th Street
Austin, TX 78703
Telephone: (512) 457-0883
Recruiter Classification: Retained; **Lowest/Average Salary:**
$40,000/$75,000; **Industry Concentration:** Generalist with a
primary focus in High Technology; **Function Concentration:**
Finance/Accounting, Human Resources

Haller, Mark — *Associate*
Source Services Corporation
525 Vine Street, Suite 2250
Cincinnati, OH 45202
Telephone: (513) 651-3303
Recruiter Classification: Contingency; **Lowest/Average Salary:**
$30,000/$50,000; **Industry Concentration:** Information
Technology; **Function Concentration:** Engineering,
Finance/Accounting

Hallock, Peter B. — *Senior Vice President*
Goodrich & Sherwood Associates, Inc.
401 Merritt Seven Corporate Park
Norwalk, CT 06851
Telephone: (203) 847-2525
Recruiter Classification: Retained; **Lowest/Average Salary:**
$60,000/$90,000; **Industry Concentration:** Generalist with a
primary focus in Information Technology; **Function
Concentration:** Generalist with a primary focus in
Administration, Finance/Accounting, General Management,
Human Resources, Marketing, Sales

Hamburg, Jennifer Power — *Senior Associate*
Ledbetter/Davidson International, Inc.
101 Park Avenue
Suite 2508
New York, NY 10178
Telephone: (212) 687-6600
Recruiter Classification: Retained; **Lowest/Average Salary:**
$90,000/$90,000; **Industry Concentration:** High Technology;
Function Concentration: Finance/Accounting, General
Management, Human Resources, Marketing, Research and
Development, Sales

Hamilton, John R. — *Partner*
Ray & Berndtson
245 Park Avenue, 33rd Floor
New York, NY 10167
Telephone: (212) 370-1316
Recruiter Classification: Retained; **Lowest/Average Salary:**
$90,000/$90,000; **Industry Concentration:** Generalist with a
primary focus in High Technology, Information Technology;
Function Concentration: Generalist with a primary focus in
Administration, Finance/Accounting, General Management,
Human Resources, Marketing, Research and Development,
Sales, Women/Minorities

Hamm, Gary — *Associate*
Source Services Corporation
5429 LBJ Freeway, Suite 275
Dallas, TX 75240
Telephone: (214) 387-1600
Recruiter Classification: Contingency; **Lowest/Average Salary:**
$30,000/$50,000; **Industry Concentration:** Information
Technology; **Function Concentration:** Engineering,
Finance/Accounting

Hamm, Mary Kay — *Managing Partner*
Romac & Associates
530 East Swedesford Road
Suite 202
Valley Forge, PA 19087
Telephone: (215) 687-6107
Recruiter Classification: Executive Temporary; **Lowest/Average
Salary:** $60,000/$60,000; **Industry Concentration:** High
Technology, Information Technology; **Function Concentration:**
Finance/Accounting

Hanes, Leah — *Partner*
Ray & Berndtson
2029 Century Park East, Suite 1000
Los Angeles, CA 90067
Telephone: (310) 557-2828
Recruiter Classification: Retained; **Lowest/Average Salary:**
$90,000/$90,000; **Industry Concentration:** Generalist with a
primary focus in High Technology, Information Technology;
Function Concentration: Generalist with a primary focus in
Administration, Finance/Accounting, General Management,
Human Resources, Marketing, Research and Development,
Sales, Women/Minorities

Hanley, Alan P. — *Partner*
Williams, Roth & Krueger Inc.
20 North Wacker Drive
Chicago, IL 60606
Telephone: (312) 977-0800
Recruiter Classification: Retained; **Lowest/Average Salary:**
$90,000/$90,000; **Industry Concentration:** Generalist with a
primary focus in High Technology; **Function Concentration:**
Generalist with a primary focus in Engineering,
Finance/Accounting, General Management, Human Resources,
Marketing, Research and Development, Sales

Hanley, J. Patrick — *Senior Vice President*
Canny, Bowen Inc.
200 Park Avenue
49th Floor
New York, NY 10166
Telephone: (212) 949-6611
Recruiter Classification: Retained; **Lowest/Average Salary:**
$120,000/$120,000; **Industry Concentration:** Generalist with a
primary focus in Electronics; **Function Concentration:**
Generalist with a primary focus in Administration,
Finance/Accounting, General Management, Human Resources

Hanley, Maureen E. — *Vice President*
Gilbert Tweed/INESA
155 Prospect Avenue
West Orange, NJ 07052
Telephone: (201) 731-3033
Recruiter Classification: Retained; **Lowest/Average Salary:**
$90,000/$90,000; **Industry Concentration:** Generalist with a
primary focus in High Technology, Information Technology;
Function Concentration: Generalist with a primary focus in
Finance/Accounting, General Management, Human Resources,
Marketing, Sales

Hanley, Steven — *Associate*
Source Services Corporation
8614 Westwood Center, Suite 750
Vienna, VA 22182
Telephone: (703) 790-5610
Recruiter Classification: Contingency; **Lowest/Average Salary:**
$30,000/$50,000; **Industry Concentration:** Information
Technology; **Function Concentration:** Engineering,
Finance/Accounting

Hanna, Dwight — *President*
Cadillac Associates
100 South Sunrise Way, Suite 353
Palm Springs, CA 92262
Telephone: (619) 327-0920
Recruiter Classification: Contingency; **Lowest/Average Salary:**
$60,000/$75,000; **Industry Concentration:** High Technology;
Function Concentration: Generalist

Hanna, Remon — *Associate*
Source Services Corporation
2029 Century Park East, Suite 1350
Los Angeles, CA 90067
Telephone: (310) 277-8092
Recruiter Classification: Contingency; **Lowest/Average Salary:**
$30,000/$50,000; **Industry Concentration:** Information
Technology; **Function Concentration:** Engineering,
Finance/Accounting

Hansen, David G. — *Executive Vice President*
Ott & Hansen, Inc.
136 South Oak Knoll, Suite 300
Pasadena, CA 91101
Telephone: (818) 578-0551
Recruiter Classification: Retained; **Lowest/Average Salary:**
$75,000/$90,000; **Industry Concentration:** Generalist with a
primary focus in Electronics, Information Technology; **Function
Concentration:** Generalist with a primary focus in
Finance/Accounting, General Management, Human Resources,
Marketing

Hanson, Grant M. — *Associate Director*
Goodrich & Sherwood Associates, Inc.
6 Century Drive
Parsippany, NJ 07054
Telephone: (201) 455-7100
Recruiter Classification: Retained; **Lowest/Average Salary:**
$60,000/$90,000; **Industry Concentration:** Generalist with a
primary focus in Information Technology; **Function
Concentration:** Generalist with a primary focus in
Administration, Finance/Accounting, General Management,
Human Resources, Marketing, Sales

Hanson, Lee — *Consultant*
Heidrick & Struggles, Inc.
Four Embarcadero Center, Suite 3570
San Francisco, CA 94111
Telephone: (415) 981-2854
Recruiter Classification: Retained; **Lowest/Average Salary:**
$75,000/$90,000; **Industry Concentration:** Generalist with a
primary focus in High Technology; **Function Concentration:**
Generalist with a primary focus in Finance/Accounting

Harbaugh, Paul J. — *Executive Vice President*
International Management Advisors, Inc.
516 Fifth Avenue
New York, NY 10036-7501
Telephone: (212) 758-7770
Recruiter Classification: Retained; **Lowest/Average Salary:**
$75,000/$90,000; **Industry Concentration:** Generalist with a
primary focus in Electronics, High Technology; **Function
Concentration:** Generalist with a primary focus in Engineering,
Finance/Accounting, General Management, Human Resources,
Marketing, Research and Development, Women/Minorities

Harbert, David O. — *Partner*
Sweeney Harbert & Mummert, Inc.
777 South Harbour Island Boulevard
Suite 130
Tampa, FL 33602
Telephone: (813) 229-5360
Recruiter Classification: Retained; **Lowest/Average Salary:**
$90,000/$90,000; **Industry Concentration:** Generalist with a
primary focus in Information Technology; **Function
Concentration:** Generalist with a primary focus in Engineering,
Finance/Accounting, General Management, Human Resources,
Marketing, Women/Minorities

Hardison, Richard L. — *President*
Hardison & Company
4975 Preston Park Boulevard, Suite 150
Plano, TX 75093
Telephone: (972) 985-6990
Recruiter Classification: Retained; **Lowest/Average Salary:**
$150,000/$180,000; **Industry Concentration:** Generalist with a
primary focus in Electronics, High Technology; **Function
Concentration:** Generalist with a primary focus in Engineering,
Finance/Accounting, General Management, Human Resources,
Marketing, Women/Minorities

Harelick, Arthur S. — *Office of the President*
Ashway, Ltd.
295 Madison Avenue
New York, NY 10017
Telephone: (212) 679-3300
Recruiter Classification: Contingency; **Lowest/Average Salary:**
$30,000/$90,000; **Industry Concentration:** High Technology;
Function Concentration: General Management

Harfenist, Harry — *President*
Parker Page Group
12550 Biscayne Boulevard
Suite 209
Miami, FL 33181
Telephone: (305) 892-2822
Recruiter Classification: Executive Temporary; **Lowest/Average
Salary:** $30,000/$75,000; **Industry Concentration:** Generalist
with a primary focus in Electronics, High Technology; **Function
Concentration:** Generalist

Hargis, N. Leann — *Senior Associate*
Montgomery Resources, Inc.
555 Montgomery Street, Suite 1650
San Francisco, CA 94111
Telephone: (415) 956-4242
Recruiter Classification: Contingency; **Lowest/Average Salary:**
$30,000/$60,000; **Industry Concentration:** High Technology;
Function Concentration: Finance/Accounting

Harkins, Robert E. — *President*
Robert Harkins Associates, Inc.
P.O. Box 236
1248 West Main Street
Ephrata, PA 17522
Telephone: (717) 733-9664
Recruiter Classification: Contingency; **Lowest/Average Salary:**
$40,000/$60,000; **Industry Concentration:** Generalist with a
primary focus in Electronics; **Function Concentration:**
Engineering, General Management, Human Resources

Harney, Elyane — *Senior Associate*
Gary Kaplan & Associates
201 South Lake Avenue
Suite 600
Pasadena, CA 91101
Telephone: (818) 796-8100
Recruiter Classification: Retained; **Lowest/Average Salary:**
$75,000/$90,000; **Industry Concentration:** Generalist with a
primary focus in Electronics, High Technology, Information
Technology; **Function Concentration:** Generalist with a
primary focus in Engineering, Finance/Accounting, General
Management, Human Resources, Marketing, Research and
Development

Harp, Kimberly — *Associate*
Source Services Corporation
7730 East Bellview Avenue, Suite 302
Englewood, CO 80111
Telephone: (303) 773-3700
Recruiter Classification: Contingency; **Lowest/Average Salary:**
$30,000/$50,000; **Industry Concentration:** Information
Technology; **Function Concentration:** Engineering,
Finance/Accounting

Harris, Jack — *Vice President*
A.T. Kearney, Inc.
130 Adelaide Street West, Suite 2710
Toronto, Ontario, CANADA M5H 3P5
Telephone: (416) 947-1990
Recruiter Classification: Retained; **Lowest/Average Salary:**
$90,000/$90,000; **Industry Concentration:** Generalist with a
primary focus in High Technology, Information Technology;
Function Concentration: Generalist with a primary focus in
Engineering, Finance/Accounting, General Management

Harris, Joe W. — *Executive Recruiter*
Cendea Connection International
13740 Research Boulevard
Building 0-1
Austin, TX 78750
Telephone: (512) 219-6000
Recruiter Classification: Retained; **Lowest/Average Salary:**
$75,000/$90,000; **Industry Concentration:** Generalist with a
primary focus in Electronics, High Technology, Information
Technology; **Function Concentration:** Generalist with a
primary focus in General Management, Marketing, Sales

Harris, Seth O. — *Vice President*
Christian & Timbers
24 New England Executive Park
Burlington, MA 01803
Telephone: (617) 229-9515
Recruiter Classification: Retained; **Lowest/Average Salary:**
$90,000/$90,000; **Industry Concentration:** Generalist with a
primary focus in Electronics, High Technology, Information
Technology; **Function Concentration:** Generalist with a
primary focus in Engineering, Finance/Accounting, General
Management, Human Resources, Marketing, Research and
Development, Sales

Harrison, Patricia — *Associate*
Source Services Corporation
5429 LBJ Freeway, Suite 275
Dallas, TX 75240
Telephone: (214) 387-1600
Recruiter Classification: Contingency; **Lowest/Average Salary:**
$30,000/$50,000; **Industry Concentration:** Information
Technology; **Function Concentration:** Engineering,
Finance/Accounting

Harrison, Priscilla — *Executive Recruiter*
Phillips Resource Group
330 Pelham Road, Building A
Greenville, SC 29615
Telephone: (864) 271-6350
Recruiter Classification: Contingency; **Lowest/Average Salary:**
$40,000/$50,000; **Industry Concentration:** Electronics, High
Technology, Information Technology; **Function Concentration:**
Administration, Engineering, Finance/Accounting, General
Management, Human Resources, Marketing, Research and
Development, Sales

Harrison, Victor — *Executive Vice President*
Intelligent Management Solutions, Inc. (IMS)
6464 South Quebec
Englewood, CO 80111
Telephone: (303) 290-9500
Recruiter Classification: Retained; **Lowest/Average Salary:**
$60,000/$75,000; **Industry Concentration:** High Technology,
Information Technology; **Function Concentration:** Generalist

Hart, Crystal — *Associate*
Source Services Corporation
One Park Plaza, Suite 560
Irvine, CA 92714
Telephone: (714) 660-1666
Recruiter Classification: Contingency; **Lowest/Average Salary:**
$30,000/$50,000; **Industry Concentration:** Information
Technology; **Function Concentration:** Engineering,
Finance/Accounting

Hart, James — *Associate*
Source Services Corporation
One CityPlace, Suite 170
St. Louis, MO 63141
Telephone: (314) 432-4500
Recruiter Classification: Contingency; **Lowest/Average Salary:**
$30,000/$50,000; **Industry Concentration:** Information
Technology; **Function Concentration:** Engineering,
Finance/Accounting

Hart, Robert T. — *Director*
D.E. Foster Partners Inc.
Stamford Square, 3001 Summer Street, 5th Floor
Stamford, CT 06905
Telephone: (203) 406-8247
Recruiter Classification: Retained; **Lowest/Average Salary:**
$90,000/$90,000; **Industry Concentration:** Generalist with a
primary focus in Information Technology; **Function
Concentration:** Generalist with a primary focus in
Administration, Finance/Accounting, General Management,
Human Resources, Marketing, Research and Development,
Sales, Women/Minorities

Hartle, Larry — *Executive Recruiter*
CPS Inc.
One Westbrook Corporate Centre, Suite 600
Westchester, IL 60154
Telephone: (708) 531-8370
Recruiter Classification: Contingency; **Lowest/Average Salary:**
$30,000/$50,000; **Industry Concentration:** Generalist with a
primary focus in Electronics, High Technology, Information
Technology; **Function Concentration:** Engineering, Research
and Development, Sales, Women/Minorities

Hartzman, Deborah — *Regional Manager*
Advanced Information Management
900 Wilshire Boulevard, Suite 1424
Los Angeles, CA 90017
Telephone: (213) 243-9236
Recruiter Classification: Contingency; **Lowest/Average Salary:**
$20,000/$40,000; **Industry Concentration:** Information
Technology; **Function Concentration:** Human Resources,
Women/Minorities

Harvey, Mike — *President*
Advanced Executive Resources
3040 Charlevoix Drive, SE
Grand Rapids, MI 49546
Telephone: (616) 942-4030
Recruiter Classification: Retained; **Lowest/Average Salary:**
$30,000/$50,000; **Industry Concentration:** Generalist with a
primary focus in Electronics, High Technology, Information
Technology; **Function Concentration:** Generalist with a
primary focus in Engineering, Finance/Accounting, General
Management, Human Resources, Marketing, Research and
Development, Sales, Women/Minorities

Harwood, Brian — *Associate*
Source Services Corporation
111 Founders Plaza, Suite 1501E
Hartford, CT 06108
Telephone: (860) 528-0300
Recruiter Classification: Contingency; **Lowest/Average Salary:**
$30,000/$50,000; **Industry Concentration:** Information
Technology; **Function Concentration:** Engineering,
Finance/Accounting

Haselby, James — *Associate*
Source Services Corporation
10300 West 103rd Street, Suite 101
Overland Park, KS 66214
Telephone: (913) 888-8885
Recruiter Classification: Contingency; **Lowest/Average Salary:**
$30,000/$50,000; **Industry Concentration:** Information
Technology; **Function Concentration:** Engineering,
Finance/Accounting

Hasten, Lawrence — *Associate*
Source Services Corporation
15260 Ventura Boulevard, Suite 380
Sherman Oaks, CA 91403
Telephone: (818) 905-1500
Recruiter Classification: Contingency; **Lowest/Average Salary:**
$30,000/$50,000; **Industry Concentration:** Information
Technology; **Function Concentration:** Engineering,
Finance/Accounting

Haughton, Michael — *Senior Vice President*
DeFrain, Mayer LLC
6900 College Boulevard
Suite 300
Overland Park, KS 66211
Telephone: (913) 345-0500
Recruiter Classification: Retained; **Lowest/Average Salary:**
$50,000/$90,000; **Industry Concentration:** Generalist with a
primary focus in Electronics, High Technology; **Function
Concentration:** Generalist with a primary focus in Engineering,
Finance/Accounting, General Management, Human Resources,
Marketing, Sales

Hauswirth, Jeffrey M. — *Director*
Spencer Stuart
One University Avenue
Suite 801
Toronto, Ontario, CANADA M5J 2P1
Telephone: (416) 361-0311
Recruiter Classification: Retained; **Lowest/Average Salary:**
$90,000/$90,000; **Industry Concentration:** Generalist with a
primary focus in High Technology, Information Technology;
Function Concentration: Generalist with a primary focus in
Engineering, General Management, Human Resources,
Marketing, Research and Development, Sales

Hauver, Scott — *Consultant*
Logix Partners
1601 Trapelo Road
Waltham, MA 02154
Telephone: (617) 890-0500
Recruiter Classification: Retained; **Lowest/Average Salary:**
$60,000/$75,000; **Industry Concentration:** High Technology;
Function Concentration: Engineering

Havener, Donald Clarke — *Partner*
The Abbott Group, Inc.
530 College Parkway, Suite N
Annapolis, MD 21401
Telephone: (410) 757-4100
Recruiter Classification: Retained; **Lowest/Average Salary:**
$90,000/$90,000; **Industry Concentration:** Generalist with a
primary focus in Electronics, High Technology, Information
Technology; **Function Concentration:** Generalist with a primary
focus in Engineering, Finance/Accounting, General Management,
Human Resources, Marketing, Research and Development

Hawksworth, A. Dwight — *President*
A.D. & Associates Executive Search, Inc.
5589 Woodsong Drive, Suite 100
Atlanta, GA 30338-2933
Telephone: (770) 393-0021
Recruiter Classification: Contingency; **Lowest/Average Salary:**
$50,000/$75,000; **Industry Concentration:** Generalist with a
primary focus in High Technology, Information Technology;
Function Concentration: Generalist with a primary focus in
Engineering, Finance/Accounting, General Management,
Human Resources, Marketing, Research and Development,
Sales, Women/Minorities

Hayes, Lee — *Associate*
Source Services Corporation
3701 West Algonquin Road, Suite 380
Rolling Meadows, IL 60008
Telephone: (847) 392-0244
Recruiter Classification: Contingency; **Lowest/Average Salary:**
$30,000/$50,000; **Industry Concentration:** Information
Technology; **Function Concentration:** Engineering,
Finance/Accounting

Hayes, Stacy — *Consultant*
The McCormick Group, Inc.
1400 Wilson Boulevard
Arlington, VA 22209
Telephone: (703) 841-1700
Recruiter Classification: Retained; **Lowest/Average Salary:**
$40,000/$60,000; **Industry Concentration:** High Technology,
Information Technology; **Function Concentration:** Engineering,
Marketing, Sales

Haystead, Steve — *Executive Recruiter*
Advanced Executive Resources
3040 Charlevoix Drive, SE
Grand Rapids, MI 49546
Telephone: (616) 942-4030
Recruiter Classification: Retained; **Lowest/Average Salary:**
$30,000/$50,000; **Industry Concentration:** Generalist with a
primary focus in Electronics, High Technology, Information
Technology; **Function Concentration:** Generalist with a
primary focus in Engineering, Finance/Accounting, General
Management, Human Resources, Marketing, Research and
Development, Sales, Women/Minorities

Hazerjian, Cynthia — *Executive Recruiter*
CPS Inc.
303 Congress Street, 5th Floor
Boston, MA 02210
Telephone: (617) 439-7950
Recruiter Classification: Contingency; **Lowest/Average Salary:**
$30,000/$50,000; **Industry Concentration:** Generalist with a
primary focus in Electronics, High Technology, Information
Technology; **Function Concentration:** Engineering, Research
and Development, Sales, Women/Minorities

Heacock, Burt E. — *Executive Vice President*
Paul-Tittle Associates, Inc.
1485 Chain Bridge Road, #304
McLean, VA 22101
Telephone: (703) 442-0500
Recruiter Classification: Retained; **Lowest/Average Salary:**
$90,000/$90,000; **Industry Concentration:** Electronics, High
Technology, Information Technology; **Function Concentration:**
Engineering, Finance/Accounting, General Management,
Marketing, Sales, Women/Minorities

Heafey, Bill — *Executive Recruiter*
CPS Inc.
One Westbrook Corporate Centre, Suite 600
Westchester, IL 60154
Telephone: (708) 531-8370
Recruiter Classification: Contingency; **Lowest/Average Salary:**
$30,000/$50,000; **Industry Concentration:** Generalist with a
primary focus in Electronics, High Technology, Information
Technology; **Function Concentration:** Engineering, Research
and Development, Sales, Women/Minorities

Heaney, Thomas — *Vice President*
Korn/Ferry International
4816 IDS Center
Minneapolis, MN 55402
Telephone: (612) 333-1834
Recruiter Classification: Retained; **Lowest/Average Salary:**
$100,000/$150,000; **Industry Concentration:** Generalist with a
primary focus in Information Technology; **Function
Concentration:** Generalist

Hechkoff, Robert B. — *President*
Quantex Associates, Inc.
444 Madison Avenue, Suite 710
New York, NY 10022
Telephone: (212) 935-2100
Recruiter Classification: Retained; **Lowest/Average Salary:**
$90,000/$90,000; **Industry Concentration:** High Technology,
Information Technology; **Function Concentration:** General
Management, Human Resources, Marketing, Sales

Hedlund, David — *President*
Hedlund Corporation
One IBM Plaza, Suite 2618
Chicago, IL 60611
Telephone: (312) 755-1400
Recruiter Classification: Contingency; **Lowest/Average Salary:**
$75,000/$90,000; **Industry Concentration:** High Technology,
Information Technology; **Function Concentration:** Engineering,
Finance/Accounting, Marketing

Heffelfinger, Thomas V. — *President*
Heffelfinger Associates, Inc.
Chestnut Green
470 Washington Street
Norwood, MA 02062
Telephone: (617) 769-6650
Recruiter Classification: Retained; **Lowest/Average Salary:**
$60,000/$90,000; **Industry Concentration:** Electronics, High
Technology, Information Technology; **Function Concentration:**
Engineering, General Management, Marketing, Sales

Heideman, Mary Marren — *Vice President*
DeFrain, Mayer LLC
6900 College Boulevard
Suite 300
Overland Park, KS 66211
Telephone: (913) 345-0500
Recruiter Classification: Retained; **Lowest/Average Salary:**
$50,000/$75,000; **Industry Concentration:** Generalist with a
primary focus in High Technology; **Function Concentration:**
Generalist with a primary focus in Engineering,
Finance/Accounting, Human Resources

Heiken, Barbara E. — *President*
Randell-Heiken, Inc.
The Lincoln Building
60 East 42nd Street, Suite 2022
New York, NY 10165
Telephone: (212) 490-1313
Recruiter Classification: Retained; **Lowest/Average Salary:**
$60,000/$90,000; **Industry Concentration:** Generalist with a
primary focus in High Technology, Information Technology;
Function Concentration: Generalist with a primary focus in
General Management, Human Resources, Marketing, Sales,
Women/Minorities

Heinrich, Scott — *Associate*
Source Services Corporation
500 108th Avenue NE, Suite 1780
Bellevue, WA 98004
Telephone: (206) 454-6400
Recruiter Classification: Contingency; **Lowest/Average Salary:**
$30,000/$50,000; **Industry Concentration:** Information
Technology; **Function Concentration:** Engineering,
Finance/Accounting

Heinze, David — *President*
Heinze & Associates, Inc.
3033 Excelsior Boulevard, Suite 300
Minneapolis, MN 55416
Telephone: (612) 924-2389
Recruiter Classification: Retained; **Lowest/Average Salary:**
$75,000/$90,000; **Industry Concentration:** Generalist with a
primary focus in Electronics, High Technology; **Function
Concentration:** Generalist with a primary focus in Engineering,
Finance/Accounting, General Management, Human Resources,
Marketing, Research and Development, Sales

Helgeson, Burton H. — *Senior Associate*
Norm Sanders Associates
2 Village Court
Hazlet, NJ 07730
Telephone: (732) 264-3700
Recruiter Classification: Retained; **Lowest/Average Salary:**
$90,000/$90,000; **Industry Concentration:** Information
Technology; **Function Concentration:** Generalist

Helminiak, Audrey — *Executive Recruiter*
Gaffney Management Consultants
35 North Brandon Drive
Glendale Heights, IL 60139-2087
Telephone: (630) 307-3380
Recruiter Classification: Retained; **Lowest/Average Salary:**
$60,000/$90,000; **Industry Concentration:** Generalist with a
primary focus in Electronics, High Technology; **Function
Concentration:** Generalist with a primary focus in Engineering,
General Management, Human Resources, Marketing, Research
and Development, Sales, Women/Minorities

Henard, John B. — *Partner*
Lamalie Amrop International
Northdale Plaza, 3903 Northdale Boulevard
Tampa, FL 33624-1864
Telephone: (813) 961-7494
Recruiter Classification: Retained; **Lowest/Average Salary:**
$90,000/$90,000; **Industry Concentration:** Generalist with a
primary focus in High Technology; **Function Concentration:**
Generalist with a primary focus in General Management,
Marketing, Sales

Hendrickson, David L. — *Partner*
Heidrick & Struggles, Inc.
51 Weaver Street
Greenwich Office Park #3
Greenwich, CT 06831-5150
Telephone: (203) 629-3200
Recruiter Classification: Retained; **Lowest/Average Salary:**
$75,000/$90,000; **Industry Concentration:** Generalist with a
primary focus in High Technology; **Function Concentration:**
Generalist

Heneghan, Donald A. — *Partner*
Allerton Heneghan & O'Neill
70 West Madison Street, Suite 2015
Chicago, IL 60602
Telephone: (312) 263-1075
Recruiter Classification: Retained; **Lowest/Average Salary:**
$90,000/$90,000; **Industry Concentration:** Generalist with a
primary focus in Electronics, High Technology, Information
Technology; **Function Concentration:** Generalist with a
primary focus in Finance/Accounting, General Management,
Human Resources, Marketing, Research and Development,
Women/Minorities

Henn, George W. — *President*
G.W. Henn & Company
42 East Gay Street, Suite 1312
Columbus, OH 43215-3119
Telephone: (614) 469-9666
Recruiter Classification: Retained; **Lowest/Average Salary:**
$90,000/$90,000; **Industry Concentration:** Generalist with a
primary focus in High Technology; **Function Concentration:**
Generalist with a primary focus in Engineering,
Finance/Accounting, Human Resources, Marketing, Research
and Development

Henneberry, Ward — *Associate*
Source Services Corporation
500 108th Avenue NE, Suite 1780
Bellevue, WA 98004
Telephone: (206) 454-6400
Recruiter Classification: Contingency; **Lowest/Average Salary:**
$30,000/$50,000; **Industry Concentration:** Information
Technology; **Function Concentration:** Engineering,
Finance/Accounting

Henry, Mary — *Vice President*
Conex Incorporated
150 East 52nd Street, 2nd Floor
New York, NY 10022
Telephone: (212) 371-3737
Recruiter Classification: Retained; **Lowest/Average Salary:**
$75,000/$75,000; **Industry Concentration:** Generalist with a
primary focus in Electronics, High Technology, Information
Technology; **Function Concentration:** Generalist with a
primary focus in Engineering, General Management,
Marketing, Research and Development, Sales

Henry, Patrick — *Executive Recruiter*
F-O-R-T-U-N-E Personnel Consultants of
Huntsville, Inc.
3311 Bob Wallace Avenue, Suite 204
Huntsville, AL 35805
Telephone: (205) 534-7282
Recruiter Classification: Contingency, Executive Temporary;
Lowest/Average Salary: $30,000/$60,000; **Industry
Concentration:** Electronics, High Technology, Information
Technology; **Function Concentration:** Engineering, Research
and Development

Henshaw, Bob — *Executive Recruiter*
F-O-R-T-U-N-E Personnel Consultants of
Huntsville, Inc.
3311 Bob Wallace Avenue, Suite 204
Huntsville, AL 35805
Telephone: (205) 534-7282
Recruiter Classification: Contingency, Executive Temporary;
Lowest/Average Salary: $30,000/$75,000; **Industry
Concentration:** High Technology; **Function Concentration:**
Engineering, General Management, Human Resources,
Research and Development, Sales

Hensley, Bert — *Managing Director*
Morgan Samuels Co., Inc.
9171 Wilshire Boulevard
Suite 428
Beverly Hills, CA 90210
Telephone: (310) 278-9660
Recruiter Classification: Retained; **Lowest/Average Salary:**
$100,000/$150,000; **Industry Concentration:** Generalist with a
primary focus in Information Technology; **Function
Concentration:** Generalist with a primary focus in
Finance/Accounting, General Management, Human Resources

Hensley, Gayla — *Principal*
Atlantic Search Group, Inc.
One Liberty Square
Boston, MA 02109
Telephone: (617) 426-9700
Recruiter Classification: Contingency; **Lowest/Average Salary:**
$20,000/$60,000; **Industry Concentration:** Generalist with a
primary focus in Electronics, High Technology, Information
Technology; **Function Concentration:** Finance/Accounting

Hergenrather, Richard A. — *President and CEO*
Hergenrather & Company
401 West Charlton Avenue
Spokane, WA 99208-7246
Telephone: (509) 466-6700
Recruiter Classification: Retained; **Lowest/Average Salary:**
$60,000/$90,000; **Industry Concentration:** Generalist with a
primary focus in Electronics, High Technology, Information
Technology; **Function Concentration:** Generalist with a
primary focus in Engineering, Finance/Accounting, General
Management, Human Resources, Marketing, Research and
Development, Sales

Herman, Eugene J. — *Executive Vice President*
Earley Kielty and Associates, Inc.
Two Pennsylvania Plaza
New York, NY 10121
Telephone: (212) 736-5626
Recruiter Classification: Retained; **Lowest/Average Salary:**
$90,000/$90,000; **Industry Concentration:** Generalist with a
primary focus in Information Technology; **Function
Concentration:** Generalist with a primary focus in
Administration, Finance/Accounting, General Management,
Human Resources, Marketing, Research and Development,
Sales, Women/Minorities

Herman, Pat — *Executive Recruiter*
Whitney & Associates, Inc.
920 Second Avenue South, Suite 625
Minneapolis, MN 55402-4035
Telephone: (612) 338-5600
Recruiter Classification: Contingency; **Lowest/Average Salary:**
$20,000/$50,000; **Industry Concentration:** Generalist with a
primary focus in Electronics, High Technology, Information
Technology; **Function Concentration:** Finance/Accounting

Herman, Shelli — *Senior Associate*
Gary Kaplan & Associates
201 South Lake Avenue
Suite 600
Pasadena, CA 91101
Telephone: (818) 796-8100
Recruiter Classification: Retained; **Lowest/Average Salary:**
$75,000/$90,000; **Industry Concentration:** Generalist with a
primary focus in Electronics, High Technology, Information
Technology; **Function Concentration:** Generalist with a primary
focus in Engineering, Finance/Accounting, General Management,
Human Resources, Marketing, Research and Development

Hernand, Warren L. — *President*
Hernand & Partners
770 Tamalpais Drive, Suite 204
Corte Madera, CA 94925
Telephone: (415) 927-7000
Recruiter Classification: Executive Temporary; **Lowest/Average
Salary:** $60,000/$90,000; **Industry Concentration:** High
Technology, Information Technology; **Function Concentration:**
Engineering

Hernandez, Ruben — *Associate*
Source Services Corporation
15600 N.W. 67th Avenue, Suite 210
Miami Lakes, FL 33014
Telephone: (305) 556-8000
Recruiter Classification: Contingency; **Lowest/Average Salary:**
$30,000/$50,000; **Industry Concentration:** Information
Technology; **Function Concentration:** Engineering,
Finance/Accounting

Heroux, David — *Associate*
Source Services Corporation
15260 Ventura Boulevard, Suite 380
Sherman Oaks, CA 91403
Telephone: (818) 905-1500
Recruiter Classification: Contingency; **Lowest/Average Salary:**
$30,000/$50,000; **Industry Concentration:** Information
Technology; **Function Concentration:** Engineering,
Finance/Accounting

Hertan, Richard L. — *President and COO*
Executive Manning Corporation
3000 N.E. 30th Place, Suite 402/405/411
Fort Lauderdale, FL 33306
Telephone: (954) 561-5100
Recruiter Classification: Retained; **Lowest/Average Salary:**
$75,000/$90,000; **Industry Concentration:** Generalist with a
primary focus in Electronics, High Technology; **Function
Concentration:** Generalist

Hertlein, James N.J. — *Consultant*
Boyden/Zay & Company
333 Clay Street
Suite 3810
Houston, TX 77002-4102
Telephone: (713) 655-0123
Recruiter Classification: Retained; **Lowest/Average Salary:**
$90,000/$90,000; **Industry Concentration:** Generalist with
a primary focus in High Technology, Information
Technology; **Function Concentration:** Generalist with a
primary focus in Engineering, General Management, Human
Resources

Herzog, Sarah — *Associate*
Source Services Corporation
One Park Plaza, Suite 560
Irvine, CA 92714
Telephone: (714) 660-1666
Recruiter Classification: Contingency; **Lowest/Average Salary:**
$30,000/$50,000; **Industry Concentration:** Information
Technology; **Function Concentration:** Engineering,
Finance/Accounting

Hewitt, Rives D. — *Principal*
The Dalley Hewitt Company
1401 Peachtree Street, Suite 500
Atlanta, GA 30309
Telephone: (404) 885-6642
Recruiter Classification: Retained; **Lowest/Average Salary:**
$50,000/$90,000; **Industry Concentration:** Generalist with a
primary focus in Information Technology; **Function
Concentration:** Generalist with a primary focus in
Administration, Engineering, Finance/Accounting, General
Management, Human Resources, Marketing, Research and
Development, Sales

Hewitt, W. Davis — *Principal*
The Dalley Hewitt Company
1401 Peachtree Street, Suite 500
Atlanta, GA 30309
Telephone: (404) 885-6642
Recruiter Classification: Retained; **Lowest/Average Salary:**
$50,000/$90,000; **Industry Concentration:** Generalist with a
primary focus in Information Technology; **Function
Concentration:** Generalist with a primary focus in
Administration, Engineering, Finance/Accounting, General
Management, Human Resources, Marketing, Research and
Development, Sales

Hicks, Albert M. — *President*
Phillips Resource Group
330 Pelham Road, Building A
Greenville, SC 29615
Telephone: (864) 271-6350
Recruiter Classification: Contingency; **Lowest/Average Salary:**
$40,000/$50,000; **Industry Concentration:** Generalist with a
primary focus in Electronics, High Technology, Information
Technology; **Function Concentration:** Generalist with a
primary focus in Administration, Engineering, General
Management, Human Resources, Marketing, Research and
Development, Sales, Women/Minorities

Hicks, Mike — *Executive Recruiter*
Damon & Associates, Inc.
7515 Greenville Avenue, Suite 900
Dallas, TX 75231
Telephone: (214) 696-6990
Recruiter Classification: Contingency; **Lowest/Average Salary:**
$30,000/$75,000; **Industry Concentration:** Electronics, High
Technology; **Function Concentration:** Generalist

Higgins, Dave — *Partner*
Warren, Morris & Madison
132 Chapel Street
Portsmouth, NH 03801
Telephone: (603) 431-7929
Recruiter Classification: Retained; **Lowest/Average Salary:**
$75,000/$90,000; **Industry Concentration:** High Technology;
Function Concentration: Generalist

Higgins, Donna — *Vice President,
Bio-Pharmaceutical Division*
Howard Fischer Associates, Inc.
1800 John F. Kennedy Boulevard, 7th Floor
Philadelphia, PA 19103
Telephone: (215) 568-8363
Recruiter Classification: Retained; **Lowest/Average Salary:**
$90,000/$90,000; **Industry Concentration:** Generalist with a
primary focus in High Technology; **Function Concentration:**
Generalist with a primary focus in Administration,
Finance/Accounting, General Management, Human Resources,
Marketing, Research and Development, Sales,
Women/Minorities

Hight, Susan — *Associate*
Source Services Corporation
150 South Warner Road, Suite 238
King of Prussia, PA 19406
Telephone: (610) 341-1960
Recruiter Classification: Contingency; **Lowest/Average Salary:**
$30,000/$50,000; **Industry Concentration:** Information
Technology; **Function Concentration:** Engineering,
Finance/Accounting

Hilbert, Laurence — *Managing Director*
Source Services Corporation
9020 Capital of Texas Highway
Building I, Suite 337
Austin, TX 78759
Telephone: (512) 345-7473
Recruiter Classification: Contingency; **Lowest/Average Salary:**
$30,000/$50,000; **Industry Concentration:** Information
Technology; **Function Concentration:** Engineering,
Finance/Accounting

Hildebrand, Thomas B. — *President*
Professional Resources Group, Inc.
1331 50th Street, Suite 102
West Des Moines, IA 50266-1602
Telephone: (515) 222-0248
Recruiter Classification: Executive Temporary; **Lowest/Average
Salary:** $60,000/$90,000; **Industry Concentration:** Generalist
with a primary focus in Information Technology; **Function
Concentration:** Generalist with a primary focus in
Administration, Finance/Accounting, General Management,
Human Resources, Marketing

Hilgenberg, Thomas — *Associate*
Source Services Corporation
1233 North Mayfair Road, Suite 300
Milwaukee, WI 53226
Telephone: (414) 774-6700
Recruiter Classification: Contingency; **Lowest/Average Salary:**
$30,000/$50,000; **Industry Concentration:** Information
Technology; **Function Concentration:** Engineering,
Finance/Accounting

Hill, Emery — *Manager*
MSI International
4801 Independence Boulevard
Suite 408
Charlotte, NC 28212
Telephone: (704) 535-6610
Recruiter Classification: Contingency; **Lowest/Average Salary:**
$30,000/$60,000; **Industry Concentration:** Generalist with a
primary focus in High Technology, Information Technology;
Function Concentration: Generalist with a primary focus in
Administration, Engineering, Finance/Accounting, General
Management, Marketing, Sales

Hillen, Skip — *Vice President*
The McCormick Group, Inc.
20 Walnut Street, Suite 308
Wellesley Hills, MA 02181
Telephone: (617) 239-1233
Recruiter Classification: Retained, Contingency;
Lowest/Average Salary: $50,000/$75,000; **Industry
Concentration:** Generalist with a primary focus in High
Technology, Information Technology; **Function Concentration:**
Generalist with a primary focus in Engineering, General
Management, Human Resources, Marketing, Sales

Hilliker, Alan D. — *Consultant*
Egon Zehnder International Inc.
350 Park Avenue
New York, NY 10022
Telephone: (212) 838-9199
Recruiter Classification: Retained; **Lowest/Average Salary:**
$90,000/$90,000; **Industry Concentration:** Generalist with a
primary focus in High Technology; **Function Concentration:**
Generalist

Hillyer, Carolyn — *Associate*
Source Services Corporation
10300 West 103rd Street, Suite 101
Overland Park, KS 66214
Telephone: (913) 888-8885
Recruiter Classification: Contingency; **Lowest/Average Salary:**
$30,000/$50,000; **Industry Concentration:** Information
Technology; **Function Concentration:** Engineering,
Finance/Accounting

Himes, Dirk — *Vice President*
A.T. Kearney, Inc.
222 West Adams Street
Chicago, IL 60606
Telephone: (312) 648-0111
Recruiter Classification: Retained; **Lowest/Average Salary:**
$90,000/$90,000; **Industry Concentration:** Generalist with a
primary focus in High Technology, Information Technology;
Function Concentration: Generalist with a primary focus in
Engineering, Finance/Accounting, General Management

Himlin, Amy — *Search Consultant*
Cochran, Cochran & Yale, Inc.
955 East Henrietta Road
Rochester, NY 14623
Telephone: (716) 424-6060
Recruiter Classification: Retained; **Lowest/Average Salary:**
$50,000/$75,000; **Industry Concentration:** High Technology,
Information Technology; **Function Concentration:** Generalist
with a primary focus in Engineering, Finance/Accounting,
General Management, Human Resources, Marketing, Sales,
Women/Minorities

Hindman, Neil C. — *President*
The Hindman Company
Browenton Place, Suite 110
2000 Warrington Way
Louisville, KY 40222
Telephone: (502) 426-4040
Recruiter Classification: Retained; **Lowest/Average Salary:**
$50,000/$90,000; **Industry Concentration:** Generalist with a
primary focus in Electronics, High Technology; **Function
Concentration:** Generalist with a primary focus in Engineering,
Finance/Accounting, General Management, Human Resources,
Marketing, Sales

Hinojosa, Oscar — *Associate*
Source Services Corporation
5429 LBJ Freeway, Suite 275
Dallas, TX 75240
Telephone: (214) 387-1600
Recruiter Classification: Contingency; **Lowest/Average Salary:**
$30,000/$50,000; **Industry Concentration:** Information
Technology; **Function Concentration:** Engineering,
Finance/Accounting

Hnatuik, Ivan — *Information Technology
Recruiter*
Corporate Recruiters Ltd.
490-1140 West Pender Street
Vancouver, British Columbia, CANADA V6E 4G1
Telephone: (604) 687-5993
Recruiter Classification: Contingency; **Lowest/Average Salary:**
$40,000/$50,000; **Industry Concentration:** Information
Technology

Hochberg, Brian — *National Accounts Manager*
M.A. Churchill & Associates, Inc.
Morelyn Plaza #307
1111 Street Road
Southampton, PA 18966
Telephone: (215) 953-0300
Recruiter Classification: Retained; **Lowest/Average Salary:**
$50,000/$75,000; **Industry Concentration:** High Technology,
Information Technology; **Function Concentration:** General
Management, Marketing, Research and Development, Sales

Hockett, William — *Principal*
Hockett Associates, Inc.
P.O. Box 1765
Los Altos, CA 94023
Telephone: (415) 941-8815
Recruiter Classification: Retained; **Lowest/Average Salary:**
$100,000/$170,000; **Industry Concentration:** Generalist with a
primary focus in High Technology; **Function Concentration:**
Generalist with a primary focus in Finance/Accounting,
General Management, Marketing, Research and Development,
Sales

Hocking, Jeffrey — *Principal*
Korn/Ferry International
The Transamerica Pyramid
600 Montgomery Street
San Francisco, CA 94111
Telephone: (415) 956-1834
Recruiter Classification: Retained; **Lowest/Average Salary:**
$100,000/$150,000; **Industry Concentration:** Generalist with a
primary focus in Information Technology; **Function
Concentration:** Generalist

Hoevel, Michael J. — *Partner*
Poirier, Hoevel & Co.
12400 Wilshire Boulevard, Suite 915
Los Angeles, CA 90025
Telephone: (310) 207-3427
Recruiter Classification: Retained; **Lowest/Average Salary:**
$75,000/$90,000; **Industry Concentration:** Generalist with a
primary focus in Electronics, High Technology, Information
Technology; **Function Concentration:** Generalist with a
primary focus in Administration, Engineering,
Finance/Accounting, Human Resources, Marketing, Sales,
Women/Minorities

Hoffman, Brian — *Information Technology
Recruiter*
Winter, Wyman & Company
950 Winter Street, Suite 3100
Waltham, MA 02154-1294
Telephone: (617) 890-7000
Recruiter Classification: Contingency; **Lowest/Average Salary:**
$30,000/$60,000; **Industry Concentration:** Generalist with a
primary focus in Information Technology; **Function
Concentration:** Generalist

Hoffman, Stephen — *Managing Director*
Source Services Corporation
1290 Oakmead Parkway, Suite 318
Sunnyvale, CA 94086
Telephone: (408) 738-8440
Recruiter Classification: Contingency; **Lowest/Average Salary:**
$30,000/$50,000; **Industry Concentration:** Information
Technology; **Function Concentration:** Engineering,
Finance/Accounting

Hofner, Andrew — *Associate*
Source Services Corporation
150 South Wacker Drive, Suite 400
Chicago, IL 60606
Telephone: (312) 346-7000
Recruiter Classification: Contingency; **Lowest/Average Salary:**
$30,000/$50,000; **Industry Concentration:** Information
Technology; **Function Concentration:** Engineering,
Finance/Accounting

Hofner, Kevin E. — *Partner*
Lamalie Amrop International
Chevron Tower
1301 McKinney Street
Houston, TX 77010-3034
Telephone: (713) 739-8602
Recruiter Classification: Retained; **Lowest/Average Salary:**
$90,000/$90,000; **Industry Concentration:** Generalist with a
primary focus in High Technology; **Function Concentration:**
Generalist

Hokanson, Mark D. — *Vice President*
Crowder & Company
2050 North Woodward Avenue, Suite 335
Bloomfield Hills, MI 48304
Telephone: (248) 645-0909
Recruiter Classification: Retained; **Lowest/Average Salary:**
$75,000/$75,000; **Industry Concentration:** Generalist with a
primary focus in Electronics; **Function Concentration:**
Generalist with a primary focus in Engineering,
Finance/Accounting, General Management, Human Resources,
Marketing, Research and Development, Sales

Holden, Richard B. — *President*
Ames Personnel Consultants, Inc.
P.O. Box 651
Brunswick, ME 04011
Telephone: (207) 729-5158
Recruiter Classification: Executive Temporary; **Lowest/Average
Salary:** $30,000/$60,000; **Industry Concentration:** Generalist
with a primary focus in High Technology; **Function
Concentration:** Generalist with a primary focus in Engineering,
Finance/Accounting, General Management, Human Resources,
Marketing, Research and Development, Sales

Holland, John A. — *Vice President*
Holland, McFadzean & Associates, Inc.
2901 Tasman Drive
Suite 204
Santa Clara, CA 95054
Telephone: (408) 496-0775
Recruiter Classification: Retained; **Lowest/Average Salary:**
$90,000/$90,000; **Industry Concentration:** Electronics, High
Technology, Information Technology; **Function Concentration:**
Generalist with a primary focus in Engineering,
Finance/Accounting, General Management, Human Resources,
Marketing, Research and Development, Sales

Holland, Kathleen — *Legal Consultant*
TOPAZ International, Inc.
383 Northfield Avenue
West Orange, NJ 07052
Telephone: (201) 669-7300
Recruiter Classification: Contingency; **Lowest/Average Salary:**
$40,000/$75,000; **Industry Concentration:** Electronics, High
Technology; **Function Concentration:** Generalist with a
primary focus in Women/Minorities

Holland, Kathleen — *Legal Consultant*
TOPAZ Legal Solutions
383 Northfield Avenue
West Orange, NJ 07052
Telephone: (201) 669-7300
Recruiter Classification: Executive Temporary; **Lowest/Average
Salary:** $40,000/$75,000; **Industry Concentration:** Electronics,
High Technology; **Function Concentration:** Generalist with a
primary focus in Women/Minorities

Holland, Rose Mary — *Consultant*
Price Waterhouse
2401 Toronto Dominion Tower
Edmonton Centre
Edmonton, Alberta, CANADA T5J 2Z1
Telephone: (403) 493-8200
Recruiter Classification: Retained; **Lowest/Average Salary:**
$75,000/$75,000; **Industry Concentration:** Generalist with a
primary focus in High Technology; **Function Concentration:**
Generalist with a primary focus in Administration, Engineering,
Finance/Accounting, General Management, Human Resources,
Marketing, Sales

Hollins, Howard D. — *Executive Recruiter*
MSI International
1900 North 18th Street
Suite 303
Monroe, LA 71201
Telephone: (318) 324-0406
Recruiter Classification: Contingency; **Lowest/Average Salary:**
$30,000/$75,000; **Industry Concentration:** Generalist with a
primary focus in High Technology; **Function Concentration:**
Generalist with a primary focus in Administration, Engineering,
Finance/Accounting, General Management, Marketing, Sales

Holmes, Lawrence J. — *Managing Director*
Columbia Consulting Group
20 South Charles Street, 9th Floor
Baltimore, MD 21201
Telephone: (410) 385-2525
Recruiter Classification: Retained; **Lowest/Average Salary:**
$75,000/$90,000; **Industry Concentration:** Generalist with a
primary focus in High Technology, Information Technology;
Function Concentration: Generalist with a primary focus in
Finance/Accounting, General Management, Human Resources,
Marketing, Research and Development, Sales

Holodnak, William A. — *President*
J. Robert Scott
27 State Street
Boston, MA 02109
Telephone: (617) 720-2770
Recruiter Classification: Retained; **Lowest/Average Salary:**
$75,000/$90,000; **Industry Concentration:** Generalist with a
primary focus in Electronics, High Technology, Information
Technology; **Function Concentration:** Generalist with a
primary focus in Finance/Accounting, General Management,
Human Resources

Holt, Carol — *Vice President*
Bartholdi & Company, Inc.
12020 Sunrise Valley Drive
Suite 160
Reston, VA 20191
Telephone: (703) 476-5519
Recruiter Classification: Retained; **Lowest/Average Salary:**
$60,000/$90,000; **Industry Concentration:** High Technology,
Information Technology; **Function Concentration:** Generalist
with a primary focus in Engineering, Finance/Accounting,
General Management, Marketing, Research and Development,
Sales

Homer, Judy B. — *President*
J.B. Homer Associates, Inc.
Graybar Building
420 Lexington Avenue, Suite 2328
New York, NY 10170
Telephone: (212) 697-3300
Recruiter Classification: Retained; **Lowest/Average Salary:**
$90,000/$90,000; **Industry Concentration:** Generalist with a
primary focus in Information Technology; **Function
Concentration:** Generalist

Hooker, Lisa — *Partner*
Ray & Berndtson
245 Park Avenue, 33rd Floor
New York, NY 10167
Telephone: (212) 370-1316
Recruiter Classification: Retained; **Lowest/Average Salary:**
$90,000/$90,000; **Industry Concentration:** Information
Technology; **Function Concentration:** Generalist

Hoover, Catherine — *Associate*
J.L. Mark Associates, Inc.
2000 Arapahoe Street, Suite 505
Denver, CO 80205
Telephone: (303) 292-0360
Recruiter Classification: Retained; **Lowest/Average Salary:**
$60,000/$90,000; **Industry Concentration:** Generalist with a
primary focus in High Technology, Information Technology;
Function Concentration: Generalist with a primary focus in
Administration, Finance/Accounting, General Management,
Human Resources, Marketing, Research and Development,
Sales

Hopgood, Earl — *Principal*
JDG Associates, Ltd.
1700 Research Boulevard
Rockville, MD 20850
Telephone: (301) 340-2210
Recruiter Classification: Contingency; **Lowest/Average Salary:**
$50,000/$90,000; **Industry Concentration:** Electronics, High
Technology, Information Technology; **Function Concentration:**
Engineering, General Management, Marketing, Research and
Development

Hopkins, Chester A. — *Senior Vice President*
Handy HRM Corp.
250 Park Avenue
New York, NY 10177-0074
Telephone: (212) 557-0400
Recruiter Classification: Retained; **Lowest/Average Salary:**
$90,000/$90,000; **Industry Concentration:** Generalist with a
primary focus in Electronics; **Function Concentration:**
Generalist with a primary focus in Administration,
Finance/Accounting, General Management, Human Resources,
Marketing, Research and Development, Sales

Hopper, John W. — *Associate*
William Guy & Associates
P.O. Box 57407
Sherman Oaks, CA 91413
Telephone: Unpublished
Recruiter Classification: Retained; **Lowest/Average Salary:**
$50,000/$90,000; **Industry Concentration:** Generalist with a
primary focus in Electronics, High Technology, Information
Technology; **Function Concentration:** Generalist with a
primary focus in Administration, Engineering, Research and
Development, Sales

Horgan, Thomas F. — *Partner*
Nadzam, Lusk, Horgan & Associates, Inc.
3211 Scott Boulevard
Suite 205
Santa Clara, CA 95054-3091
Telephone: (408) 727-6601
Recruiter Classification: Retained; **Lowest/Average Salary:**
$90,000/$90,000; **Industry Concentration:** Generalist with a
primary focus in Electronics, High Technology, Information
Technology; **Function Concentration:** Generalist

Horner, Gregory — *Sales and Marketing Recruiter*
Corporate Recruiters Ltd.
490-1140 West Pender Street
Vancouver, British Columbia, CANADA V6E 4G1
Telephone: (604) 687-5993
Recruiter Classification: Contingency; **Lowest/Average Salary:**
$50,000/$90,000; **Industry Concentration:** Electronics, High
Technology, Information Technology; **Function Concentration:**
Marketing, Sales

Horton, Robert H. — *Chairman and President*
Horton International
420 Lexington Avenue, Suite 810
New York, NY 10170
Telephone: (212) 973-3780
Recruiter Classification: Retained; **Lowest/Average Salary:**
$90,000/$90,000; **Industry Concentration:** Generalist with a
primary focus in Electronics; **Function Concentration:**
Generalist with a primary focus in General Management

Hostetter, Kristi — *Associate*
Source Services Corporation
1105 Schrock Road, Suite 510
Columbus, OH 43229
Telephone: (614) 846-3311
Recruiter Classification: Contingency; **Lowest/Average Salary:**
$30,000/$50,000; **Industry Concentration:** Information
Technology; **Function Concentration:** Engineering,
Finance/Accounting

Houchins, William M. — *Vice President*
Christian & Timbers
8840 Stanford Boulevard
Suite 25900
Columbia, MD 21045
Telephone: (410) 872-0200
Recruiter Classification: Retained; **Lowest/Average Salary:**
$90,000/$90,000; **Industry Concentration:** Electronics, High
Technology, Information Technology; **Function Concentration:**
Generalist with a primary focus in Engineering,
Finance/Accounting, General Management, Human Resources,
Marketing, Research and Development, Sales,
Women/Minorities

Houterloot, Tim — *Associate*
Source Services Corporation
111 Monument Circle, Suite 3930
Indianapolis, IN 46204
Telephone: (317) 631-2900
Recruiter Classification: Contingency; **Lowest/Average Salary:**
$30,000/$50,000; **Industry Concentration:** Information
Technology; **Function Concentration:** Engineering,
Finance/Accounting

Houver, Scott — *Consultant*
Logix, Inc.
1601 Trapelo Road
Waltham, MA 02154
Telephone: (617) 890-0500
Recruiter Classification: Retained; **Lowest/Average Salary:**
$60,000/$75,000; **Industry Concentration:** High Technology;
Function Concentration: Engineering

Howard, Lee Ann — *Principal*
Lamalie Amrop International
Metro Center, One Station Place
Stamford, CT 06902-6800
Telephone: (203) 324-4445
Recruiter Classification: Retained; **Lowest/Average Salary:**
$90,000/$90,000; **Industry Concentration:** Generalist with a
primary focus in High Technology; **Function Concentration:**
Generalist

Howe, Theodore — *General Manager*
Romac & Associates
Commerce Tower, Suite 1700
P.O. Box 13264
Kansas City, MO 64199
Telephone: (816) 221-1020
Recruiter Classification: Executive Temporary; **Lowest/Average
Salary:** $60,000/$60,000; **Industry Concentration:** High
Technology, Information Technology; **Function Concentration:**
Finance/Accounting

Howell, Robert B. — *Principal*
Atlantic Search Group, Inc.
One Liberty Square
Boston, MA 02109
Telephone: (617) 426-9700
Recruiter Classification: Contingency; **Lowest/Average Salary:**
$20,000/$60,000; **Industry Concentration:** Generalist with a
primary focus in Electronics, High Technology, Information
Technology; **Function Concentration:** Finance/Accounting

Howell, Robert B. — *Principal*
Atlantic Search Group, Inc.
One Liberty Square
Boston, MA 02109
Telephone: (617) 426-9700
Recruiter Classification: Contingency; **Lowest/Average Salary:**
$20,000/$60,000; **Industry Concentration:** Generalist with a
primary focus in Electronics, Information Technology; **Function
Concentration:** Finance/Accounting

Hoyda, Louis A. — *Partner*
Thorndike Deland Associates
275 Madison Avenue, Suite 1300
New York, NY 10016
Telephone: (212) 661-6200
Recruiter Classification: Retained; **Lowest/Average Salary:**
$100,000/$125,000; **Industry Concentration:** Generalist with a
primary focus in Information Technology; **Function
Concentration:** Generalist with a primary focus in
Finance/Accounting, General Management, Human Resources,
Marketing, Sales

Hubert, David L. — *Director Operations*
ARJay & Associates
3286 Clower Street, Suite A-202
Snellville, GA 30278
Telephone: (404) 979-3799
Recruiter Classification: Contingency; **Lowest/Average Salary:**
$40,000/$90,000; **Industry Concentration:** Generalist with a
primary focus in Electronics; **Function Concentration:**
Engineering, Finance/Accounting

Hucko, Donald S. — *Senior Vice President*
Jonas, Walters & Assoc., Inc.
1110 North Old World Third St., Suite 510
Milwaukee, WI 53203-1102
Telephone: (414) 291-2828
Recruiter Classification: Retained; **Lowest/Average Salary:**
$50,000/$90,000; **Industry Concentration:** Generalist with a
primary focus in Electronics, Information Technology; **Function
Concentration:** Generalist with a primary focus in
Administration, Engineering, Finance/Accounting, General
Management, Human Resources, Marketing, Sales

Hudson, Reginald M. — *President*
Search Bureau International
P.O. Box 377608
Chicago, IL 60637
Telephone: (708) 210-1834
Recruiter Classification: Contingency; **Lowest/Average Salary:**
$40,000/$60,000; **Industry Concentration:** Generalist with a
primary focus in High Technology, Information Technology;
Function Concentration: Generalist with a primary focus in
Engineering, Finance/Accounting, General Management,
Human Resources, Marketing, Research and Development,
Sales, Women/Minorities

Huff, William Z. — *Huff Associates*
Huff Associates
95 Reef Drive
Ocean City, NJ 08226
Telephone: (609) 399-2867
Recruiter Classification: Retained; **Lowest/Average Salary:**
$50,000/$60,000; **Industry Concentration:** Generalist with a
primary focus in Electronics, High Technology, Information
Technology; **Function Concentration:** Engineering, General
Management, Marketing, Research and Development, Sales

Hughes, Barbara — *Associate*
Source Services Corporation
1290 Oakmead Parkway, Suite 318
Sunnyvale, CA 94086
Telephone: (408) 738-8440
Recruiter Classification: Contingency; **Lowest/Average Salary:**
$30,000/$50,000; **Industry Concentration:** Information
Technology; **Function Concentration:** Engineering,
Finance/Accounting

Hughes, Cathy N. — *Recruiter*
The Ogdon Partnership
375 Park Avenue, Suite 2409
New York, NY 10152-0175
Telephone: (212) 308-1600
Recruiter Classification: Retained; **Lowest/Average Salary:**
$90,000/$90,000; **Industry Concentration:** Generalist with a
primary focus in Information Technology; **Function
Concentration:** Generalist with a primary focus in
Administration, Finance/Accounting, General Management,
Human Resources, Marketing, Sales, Women/Minorities

Hughes, Donald J. — *Managing Partner*
Hughes & Company
3682 King Street
P.O. Box 16944
Alexandria, VA 22303-0944
Telephone: (703) 379-2499
Recruiter Classification: Retained; **Lowest/Average Salary:**
$75,000/$90,000; **Industry Concentration:** Information
Technology; **Function Concentration:** General Management,
Human Resources, Marketing, Sales

Hughes, James J. — *Vice President*
R.P. Barone Associates
57 Green Street
Woodbridge, NJ 07095
Telephone: (908) 634-4300
Recruiter Classification: Contingency; **Lowest/Average Salary:**
$30,000/$75,000; **Industry Concentration:** Generalist with a
primary focus in Electronics; **Function Concentration:**
Generalist with a primary focus in Engineering, General
Management, Marketing

Hughes, Randall — *Associate*
Source Services Corporation
4200 West Cypress Street, Suite 101
Tampa, FL 33607
Telephone: (813) 879-2221
Recruiter Classification: Contingency; **Lowest/Average Salary:**
$30,000/$50,000; **Industry Concentration:** Information
Technology; **Function Concentration:** Engineering,
Finance/Accounting

Hull, Chuck — *Software Engineering Recruiter*
Winter, Wyman & Company
950 Winter Street, Suite 3100
Waltham, MA 02154-1294
Telephone: (617) 890-7000
Recruiter Classification: Contingency; **Lowest/Average Salary:**
$40,000/$75,000; **Industry Concentration:** High Technology,
Information Technology; **Function Concentration:** Engineering

Hult, Dana — *Associate*
Source Services Corporation
71 Spit Brook Road, Suite 305
Nashua, NH 03060
Telephone: (603) 888-7650
Recruiter Classification: Contingency; **Lowest/Average Salary:**
$30,000/$50,000; **Industry Concentration:** Information
Technology; **Function Concentration:** Engineering,
Finance/Accounting

Humphrey, Joan — *Executive Recruiter*
Abraham & London, Ltd.
7 Old Sherman Turnpike, Suite 209
Danbury, CT 06810
Telephone: (203) 730-4000
Recruiter Classification: Contingency; **Lowest/Average Salary:**
$40,000/$75,000; **Industry Concentration:** High Technology,
Information Technology; **Function Concentration:** Marketing,
Sales

Humphrey, Titus — *Associate*
Source Services Corporation
1290 Oakmead Parkway, Suite 318
Sunnyvale, CA 94086
Telephone: (408) 738-8440
Recruiter Classification: Contingency; **Lowest/Average Salary:**
$30,000/$50,000; **Industry Concentration:** Information
Technology; **Function Concentration:** Engineering,
Finance/Accounting

Hunsaker, Floyd — *Principal*
Woodworth International Group
620 SW 5th Avenue, Suite 1225
Portland, OR 97204
Telephone: (503) 225-5000
Recruiter Classification: Retained; **Lowest/Average Salary:**
$60,000/$90,000; **Industry Concentration:** Generalist with a
primary focus in Electronics, High Technology, Information
Technology; **Function Concentration:** Generalist with a
primary focus in Engineering, General Management, Human
Resources, Sales

Hunter, Gabe — *Executive Recruiter*
Phillips Resource Group
330 Pelham Road, Building A
Greenville, SC 29615
Telephone: (864) 271-6350
Recruiter Classification: Contingency; **Lowest/Average Salary:**
$40,000/$50,000; **Industry Concentration:** Generalist with a
primary focus in Electronics, High Technology, Information
Technology; **Function Concentration:** Generalist with a
primary focus in Administration, Engineering, General
Management, Human Resources, Marketing, Research and
Development, Sales, Women/Minorities

Hunter, Steven — *President*
Diamond Tax Recruiting
Two Pennsylvania Plaza, Suite 1985
New York, NY 10121
Telephone: (212) 695-4220
Recruiter Classification: Contingency; **Lowest/Average Salary:**
$50,000/$75,000; **Industry Concentration:** Electronics, High
Technology; **Function Concentration:** Finance/Accounting

Huntoon, Cliff — *Executive Recruiter*
Richard, Wayne and Roberts
24 Greenway Plaza, Suite 1304
Houston, TX 77046-2493
Telephone: (713) 629-6681
Recruiter Classification: Retained; **Lowest/Average Salary:**
$50,000/$90,000; **Industry Concentration:** Generalist with a
primary focus in High Technology; **Function Concentration:**
Generalist with a primary focus in Engineering

Hurley, Janeen — *Software Engineering Recruiter*
Winter, Wyman & Company
950 Winter Street, Suite 3100
Waltham, MA 02154-1294
Telephone: (617) 890-7000
Recruiter Classification: Contingency; **Lowest/Average Salary:**
$40,000/$75,000; **Industry Concentration:** High Technology,
Information Technology; **Function Concentration:** Engineering

Hurtado, Jaime — *Associate*
Source Services Corporation
879 West 190th Street, Suite 250
Los Angeles, CA 90248
Telephone: (310) 323-6633
Recruiter Classification: Contingency; **Lowest/Average Salary:**
$30,000/$50,000; **Industry Concentration:** Information
Technology; **Function Concentration:** Engineering,
Finance/Accounting

Hussey, Wayne — *Consultant Associate*
Krecklo & Associates Inc.
Scotia Plaza, Suite 4900 ·
40 King Street West
Toronto, Ontario, CANADA M5H 4A2
Telephone: (416) 777-6799
Recruiter Classification: Retained; **Lowest/Average Salary:**
$75,000/$90,000; **Industry Concentration:** Generalist with a
primary focus in Information Technology

Hutchison, Richard H. — *Executive Recruiter*
Rurak & Associates, Inc.
1350 Connecticut Avenue N.W.
Suite 801
Washington, DC 20036
Telephone: (202) 293-7603
Recruiter Classification: Retained; **Lowest/Average Salary:**
$90,000/$90,000; **Industry Concentration:** Generalist with a
primary focus in High Technology, Information Technology;
Function Concentration: Generalist with a primary focus in
Finance/Accounting, General Management, Human Resources,
Marketing, Sales

Hutchison, William K. — *Partner*
Christenson & Hutchison
466 Southern Boulevard
Chatham, NJ 07928-1462
Telephone: (201) 966-1600
Recruiter Classification: Retained; **Lowest/Average Salary:**
$75,000/$90,000; **Industry Concentration:** Generalist with a
primary focus in Electronics, High Technology, Information
Technology; **Function Concentration:** Generalist with a
primary focus in Finance/Accounting, General Management,
Human Resources, Marketing, Sales

Hutton, Thomas J. — *Vice President*
The Thomas Tucker Company
425 California Street, Suite 2502
San Francisco, CA 94104
Telephone: (415) 693-5900
Recruiter Classification: Retained; **Lowest/Average Salary:**
$90,000/$90,000; **Industry Concentration:** Generalist with a
primary focus in Electronics, High Technology, Information
Technology; **Function Concentration:** Generalist with a
primary focus in Engineering, General Management

Hybels, Cynthia — *Professional Recruiter*
A.J. Burton Group, Inc.
120 East Baltimore Street, Suite 2220
Baltimore, MD 21202
Telephone: (410) 752-5244
Recruiter Classification: Contingency; **Lowest/Average Salary:**
$40,000/$75,000; **Industry Concentration:** Generalist with a
primary focus in High Technology, Information Technology;
Function Concentration: Generalist with a primary focus in
Administration, Finance/Accounting, General Management,
Human Resources

Hyde, W. Jerry — *President*
Hyde Danforth Wold & Co.
5950 Berkshire Lane, Suite 1600
Dallas, TX 75225
Telephone: (214) 691-5966
Recruiter Classification: Retained; **Lowest/Average Salary:**
$60,000/$75,000; **Industry Concentration:** Generalist with a
primary focus in High Technology; **Function Concentration:**
Generalist with a primary focus in Administration,
Finance/Accounting, Human Resources, Sales,
Women/Minorities

Hykes, Don A. — *Vice President/Managing
Director*
A.T. Kearney, Inc.
8500 Normandale Lake Boulevard
Suite 1630
Minneapolis, MN 55437
Telephone: (612) 921-8436
Recruiter Classification: Retained; **Lowest/Average Salary:**
$90,000/$90,000; **Industry Concentration:** Generalist with a
primary focus in High Technology; **Function Concentration:**
Generalist with a primary focus in Administration, Engineering,
Finance/Accounting, General Management, Human Resources,
Marketing, Research and Development, Sales

Hylas, Lisa — *Associate*
Source Services Corporation
15600 N.W. 67th Avenue, Suite 210
Miami Lakes, FL 33014
Telephone: (305) 556-8000
Recruiter Classification: Contingency; **Lowest/Average Salary:**
$30,000/$50,000; **Industry Concentration:** Information
Technology; **Function Concentration:** Engineering,
Finance/Accounting

Hyman, Linda — *Vice President*
Korn/Ferry International
One Palmer Square
Princeton, NJ 08542
Telephone: (609) 921-8811
Recruiter Classification: Retained; **Lowest/Average Salary:**
$100,000/$150,000; **Industry Concentration:** Generalist with a
primary focus in Information Technology; **Function
Concentration:** Generalist

Iannacone, Kelly — *Executive Recruiter*
Abraham & London, Ltd.
4 Rhode Island Avenue
Cherry Hill, NJ 08002
Telephone: (609) 429-6825
Recruiter Classification: Contingency, Executive Temporary;
Lowest/Average Salary: $40,000/$75,000; **Industry
Concentration:** High Technology, Information Technology;
Function Concentration: Marketing, Sales

Ide, Ian — *Information Technology Recruiter*
Winter, Wyman & Company
950 Winter Street, Suite 3100
Waltham, MA 02154-1294
Telephone: (617) 890-7000
Recruiter Classification: Contingency; **Lowest/Average Salary:**
$30,000/$60,000; **Industry Concentration:** Generalist with a
primary focus in Information Technology; **Function
Concentration:** Generalist

Imely, Larry S. — *Vice President*
Stratford Group
6120 Parkland Boulevard
Cleveland, OH 44124
Telephone: (216) 460-3232
Recruiter Classification: Retained; **Lowest/Average Salary:**
$90,000/$90,000; **Industry Concentration:** Generalist with a
primary focus in High Technology; **Function Concentration:**
Engineering, General Management, Sales, Women/Minorities

Imhof, Kirk — *Associate*
Source Services Corporation
505 East 200 South, Suite 300
Salt Lake City, UT 84102
Telephone: (801) 328-0011
Recruiter Classification: Contingency; **Lowest/Average Salary:**
$30,000/$50,000; **Industry Concentration:** Information
Technology; **Function Concentration:** Engineering,
Finance/Accounting

Inger, Barry — *Associate*
Source Services Corporation
20 Burlington Mall Road, Suite 405
Burlington, MA 01803
Telephone: (617) 272-5000
Recruiter Classification: Contingency; **Lowest/Average Salary:**
$30,000/$50,000; **Industry Concentration:** Information
Technology; **Function Concentration:** Engineering,
Finance/Accounting

Inguagiato, Gregory — *Manager*
MSI International
6345 Balboa Boulevard
Suite 335
Encino, CA 91316
Telephone: (818) 342-0222
Recruiter Classification: Contingency; **Lowest/Average Salary:**
$30,000/$60,000; **Industry Concentration:** Generalist with a
primary focus in High Technology, Information Technology;
Function Concentration: Generalist with a primary focus in
Administration, Engineering, Finance/Accounting, General
Management, Marketing, Sales

Inskeep, Thomas — *Associate*
Source Services Corporation
150 South Warner Road, Suite 238
King of Prussia, PA 19406
Telephone: (610) 341-1960
Recruiter Classification: Contingency; **Lowest/Average Salary:**
$30,000/$50,000; **Industry Concentration:** Information
Technology; **Function Concentration:** Engineering,
Finance/Accounting

Intravaia, Salvatore — *Associate*
Source Services Corporation
2 Penn Plaza, Suite 1176
New York, NY 10121
Telephone: (212) 760-2200
Recruiter Classification: Contingency; **Lowest/Average Salary:**
$30,000/$50,000; **Industry Concentration:** Information
Technology; **Function Concentration:** Engineering,
Finance/Accounting

Inzinna, Dennis — *Executive Vice President*
AlternaStaff
1155 Avenue of the Americas, 15th Floor
New York, NY 10036
Telephone: (212) 302-1141
Recruiter Classification: Executive Temporary; **Lowest/Average
Salary:** $30,000/$60,000; **Industry Concentration:** Electronics,
High Technology; **Function Concentration:** Engineering,
General Management, Human Resources, Research and
Development

Irish, Alan — *Executive Recruiter*
CPS Inc.
One Westbrook Corporate Centre, Suite 600
Westchester, IL 60154
Telephone: (708) 531-8370
Recruiter Classification: Contingency; **Lowest/Average Salary:**
$30,000/$50,000; **Industry Concentration:** Generalist with a
primary focus in Electronics, High Technology, Information
Technology; **Function Concentration:** Engineering, Research
and Development, Sales, Women/Minorities

Irwin, Mark — *Associate*
Source Services Corporation
10220 SW Greenburg Road, Suite 625
Portland, OR 97223
Telephone: (503) 768-4546
Recruiter Classification: Contingency; **Lowest/Average Salary:**
$30,000/$50,000; **Industry Concentration:** Information
Technology; **Function Concentration:** Engineering,
Finance/Accounting

Issacs, Judith A. — *Senior Associate*
Grant Cooper and Associates
795 Office Parkway, Suite 117
St. Louis, MO 63141
Telephone: (314) 567-4690
Recruiter Classification: Retained; **Lowest/Average Salary:**
$60,000/$90,000; **Industry Concentration:** Generalist with a
primary focus in Electronics; **Function Concentration:**
Generalist with a primary focus in Administration, Engineering,
Finance/Accounting, General Management, Human Resources,
Marketing, Sales

Jackowitz, Todd — *Vice President*
J. Robert Scott
27 State Street
Boston, MA 02109
Telephone: (617) 720-2770
Recruiter Classification: Retained; **Lowest/Average Salary:**
$75,000/$90,000; **Industry Concentration:** Generalist with a
primary focus in Electronics, High Technology, Information
Technology; **Function Concentration:** Generalist

Jackson, Barry — *Recruiter*
Morgan Hunter Corp.
6800 College Boulevard, Suite 550
Overland Park, KS 66211
Telephone: (913) 491-3434
Recruiter Classification: Contingency; **Lowest/Average Salary:**
$30,000/$40,000; **Industry Concentration:** Information
Technology; **Function Concentration:** Generalist

Jackson, Joan — *Vice President*
A.T. Kearney, Inc.
225 Reinekers Lane
Alexandria, VA 22314
Telephone: (703) 739-4624
Recruiter Classification: Retained; **Lowest/Average Salary:**
$90,000/$90,000; **Industry Concentration:** Generalist with a
primary focus in High Technology, Information Technology;
Function Concentration: Generalist with a primary focus in
Engineering, Finance/Accounting, General Management

Jacobs, Martin J. — *Executive Vice President/Recruiter*
The Rubicon Group
P.O. Box 2159
Scottsdale, AZ 85252-2159
Telephone: (602) 423-9280
Recruiter Classification: Contingency; **Lowest/Average Salary:** $30,000/$60,000; **Industry Concentration:** Generalist with a primary focus in Electronics, High Technology, Information Technology; **Function Concentration:** Generalist with a primary focus in Administration, Engineering, Finance/Accounting, General Management, Marketing, Research and Development

Jacobs, Mike — *Principal*
Thorne, Brieger Associates Inc.
11 East 44th Street
New York, NY 10017
Telephone: (212) 682-5424
Recruiter Classification: Retained; **Lowest/Average Salary:** $90,000/$90,000; **Industry Concentration:** Generalist with a primary focus in Electronics; **Function Concentration:** Generalist with a primary focus in Administration, Engineering, Finance/Accounting, General Management, Human Resources, Marketing, Research and Development, Sales

Jacobson, Carolyn — *Associate*
The Abbott Group, Inc.
1577 Spring Hill Road
Vienna, VA 22182
Telephone: (410) 757-4100
Recruiter Classification: Retained; **Lowest/Average Salary:** $90,000/$90,000; **Industry Concentration:** Generalist with a primary focus in Electronics, High Technology, Information Technology; **Function Concentration:** Generalist with a primary focus in Administration, Engineering, General Management, Human Resources, Marketing, Research and Development, Women/Minorities

Jacobson, Hayley — *Associate*
Source Services Corporation
2 Penn Plaza, Suite 1176
New York, NY 10121
Telephone: (212) 760-2200
Recruiter Classification: Contingency; **Lowest/Average Salary:** $30,000/$50,000; **Industry Concentration:** Information Technology; **Function Concentration:** Engineering, Finance/Accounting

Jacobson, Rick — *President*
The Windham Group
114 Winchester Road
Fairlawn, OH 44333
Telephone: (330) 867-1075
Recruiter Classification: Retained; **Lowest/Average Salary:** $75,000/$90,000; **Industry Concentration:** Generalist with a primary focus in Electronics, Information Technology; **Function Concentration:** Generalist with a primary focus in Finance/Accounting, General Management, Human Resources, Marketing, Sales

Jadulang, Vincent — *Associate*
Source Services Corporation
One Park Plaza, Suite 560
Irvine, CA 92714
Telephone: (714) 660-1666
Recruiter Classification: Contingency; **Lowest/Average Salary:** $30,000/$50,000; **Industry Concentration:** Information Technology; **Function Concentration:** Engineering, Finance/Accounting

Jaffe, Mark — *Partner*
Wyatt & Jaffe
9900 Bren Road East, Suite 550
Minnetonka, MN 55343-9668
Telephone: (612) 945-0099
Recruiter Classification: Retained; **Lowest/Average Salary:** $90,000/$90,000; **Industry Concentration:** High Technology; **Function Concentration:** Generalist with a primary focus in Engineering, General Management, Human Resources, Marketing, Research and Development

James, Bruce — *Recruiter*
Roberson and Company
10752 North 89th Place, Suite 202
Scottsdale, AZ 85260
Telephone: (602) 391-3200
Recruiter Classification: Contingency; **Lowest/Average Salary:** $40,000/$50,000; **Industry Concentration:** Generalist with a primary focus in Electronics, High Technology, Information Technology; **Function Concentration:** Generalist with a primary focus in Administration, Engineering, General Management, Human Resources, Marketing, Sales

James, Richard — *President*
Criterion Executive Search, Inc.
5420 Bay Center Drive, Suite 101
Tampa, FL 33609-3402
Telephone: (813) 286-2000
Recruiter Classification: Contingency; **Lowest/Average Salary:** $40,000/$90,000; **Industry Concentration:** Generalist with a primary focus in Electronics, High Technology, Information Technology; **Function Concentration:** Generalist with a primary focus in Administration, Engineering, Finance/Accounting, Research and Development, Women/Minorities

Janis, Laurence — *Partner*
Integrated Search Solutions Group, LLC
33 Main Street
Port Washington, NY 11050
Telephone: (516) 767-3030
Recruiter Classification: Retained; **Lowest/Average Salary:** $90,000/$90,000; **Industry Concentration:** Generalist with a primary focus in Electronics, High Technology, Information Technology; **Function Concentration:** Generalist with a primary focus in Human Resources, Marketing, Sales

Jansen, Douglas L. — *President*
Search Northwest Associates
10117 SE Sunnyside, Suite F-727
Clackamas, OR 97015
Telephone: (503) 654-1487
Recruiter Classification: Contingency; **Lowest/Average Salary:** $40,000/$75,000; **Industry Concentration:** Electronics, High Technology; **Function Concentration:** Engineering, Research and Development

Jansen, John F. — *President*
Delta Services
11711 Memorial Drive
Suite 252
Houston, TX 77024
Telephone: (713) 975-7725
Recruiter Classification: Retained; **Lowest/Average Salary:**
$75,000/$90,000; **Industry Concentration:** Information
Technology; **Function Concentration:** Engineering,
Finance/Accounting, Human Resources, Marketing, Research
and Development, Sales

Janssen, Don — *Consultant*
Howard Fischer Associates, Inc.
1800 John F. Kennedy Boulevard, 7th Floor
Philadelphia, PA 19103
Telephone: (215) 568-8363
Recruiter Classification: Retained; **Lowest/Average Salary:**
$90,000/$90,000; **Industry Concentration:** Generalist with a
primary focus in High Technology; **Function Concentration:**
Generalist with a primary focus in Administration,
Finance/Accounting, General Management, Human Resources,
Marketing, Research and Development, Sales,
Women/Minorities

Januale, Lois — *Search Consultant*
Cochran, Cochran & Yale, Inc.
5166 Main Street
Williamsville, NY 14221
Telephone: (716) 631-1300
Recruiter Classification: Retained; **Lowest/Average Salary:**
$50,000/$75,000; **Industry Concentration:** Generalist with a
primary focus in High Technology, Information Technology;
Function Concentration: Generalist with a primary focus in
Engineering, Finance/Accounting, General Management,
Human Resources, Marketing, Sales, Women/Minorities

Januleski, Geoff — *Associate*
Source Services Corporation
150 South Warner Road, Suite 238
King of Prussia, PA 19406
Telephone: (610) 341-1960
Recruiter Classification: Contingency; **Lowest/Average Salary:**
$30,000/$50,000; **Industry Concentration:** Information
Technology; **Function Concentration:** Engineering,
Finance/Accounting

Jaworski, Mary A. — *Consultant*
Tully/Woodmansee International, Inc.
110 Genesee Street, Suite 240
Auburn, NY 13021
Telephone: (315) 252-5703
Recruiter Classification: Retained; **Lowest/Average Salary:**
$60,000/$90,000; **Industry Concentration:** Generalist with a
primary focus in Electronics, High Technology, Information
Technology; **Function Concentration:** Generalist with a
primary focus in Engineering, Finance/Accounting, General
Management, Human Resources, Marketing, Research and
Development, Sales, Women/Minorities

Jazylo, John V. — *Senior Vice President*
Skott/Edwards Consultants, Inc.
1776 On the Green
Morristown, NJ 07006
Telephone: (973) 644-0900
Recruiter Classification: Retained; **Lowest/Average Salary:**
$90,000/$90,000; **Industry Concentration:** Electronics, High
Technology, Information Technology; **Function Concentration:**
Generalist with a primary focus in Administration,
Finance/Accounting

Jazylo, John V. — *Senior Vice President*
Handy HRM Corp.
250 Park Avenue
New York, NY 10177-0074
Telephone: (212) 210-5612
Recruiter Classification: Retained; **Lowest/Average Salary:**
$90,000/$90,000; **Industry Concentration:** Generalist with
a primary focus in Electronics, High Technology,
Information Technology; **Function Concentration:**
Finance/Accounting, General Management, Marketing,
Sales, Women/Minorities

Jeffers, Richard B. — *Principal*
Dieckmann & Associates, Ltd.
180 North Stetson, Suite 5555
Two Prudential Plaza
Chicago, IL 60601
Telephone: (312) 819-5900
Recruiter Classification: Retained; **Lowest/Average Salary:**
$90,000/$90,000; **Industry Concentration:** Generalist with a
primary focus in High Technology, Information Technology;
Function Concentration: Generalist with a primary focus in
Finance/Accounting, General Management, Marketing, Sales,
Women/Minorities

Jeltema, John — *Associate*
Source Services Corporation
One Park Plaza, Suite 560
Irvine, CA 92714
Telephone: (714) 660-1666
Recruiter Classification: Contingency; **Lowest/Average Salary:**
$30,000/$50,000; **Industry Concentration:** Information
Technology; **Function Concentration:** Engineering,
Finance/Accounting

Jensen, Christine K. — *Vice President*
John Kurosky & Associates
3 Corporate Park Drive, Suite 210
Irvine, CA 92714
Telephone: (714) 851-6370
Recruiter Classification: Retained; **Lowest/Average Salary:**
$90,000/$90,000; **Industry Concentration:** High Technology,
Information Technology; **Function Concentration:** Research
and Development

Jensen, Robert — *Associate*
Source Services Corporation
3701 West Algonquin Road, Suite 380
Rolling Meadows, IL 60008
Telephone: (847) 392-0244
Recruiter Classification: Contingency; **Lowest/Average Salary:**
$30,000/$50,000; **Industry Concentration:** Information
Technology; **Function Concentration:** Engineering,
Finance/Accounting

Jerolman, Gregg — *Vice President*
Masserman & Associates, Inc.
191 Post Road West
Westport, CT 06880
Telephone: (203) 221-2870
Lowest/Average Salary: $75,000/$90,000; **Industry
Concentration:** High Technology

Joffe, Barry — *Director Executive Search Consulting*
Bason Associates Inc.
11311 Cornell Park Drive
Cincinnati, OH 45242
Telephone: (513) 469-9881
Recruiter Classification: Retained; **Lowest/Average Salary:** $60,000/$90,000; **Industry Concentration:** Generalist with a primary focus in High Technology; **Function Concentration:** Generalist with a primary focus in Administration, Engineering, Finance/Accounting, General Management, Human Resources, Marketing, Research and Development, Sales

Johnson, Brian — *Professional Recruiter*
A.J. Burton Group, Inc.
120 East Baltimore Street, Suite 2220
Baltimore, MD 21202
Telephone: (410) 752-5244
Recruiter Classification: Contingency; **Lowest/Average Salary:** $40,000/$75,000; **Industry Concentration:** Generalist with a primary focus in High Technology, Information Technology; **Function Concentration:** Generalist with a primary focus in Administration, Finance/Accounting, General Management, Human Resources

Johnson, David A. — *Executive Search Consultant*
Gaffney Management Consultants
35 North Brandon Drive
Glendale Heights, IL 60139-2087
Telephone: (630) 307-3380
Recruiter Classification: Retained; **Lowest/Average Salary:** $60,000/$90,000; **Industry Concentration:** Generalist with a primary focus in Electronics, High Technology; **Function Concentration:** Generalist with a primary focus in Engineering, Finance/Accounting, General Management, Human Resources, Marketing, Research and Development, Sales

Johnson, Douglas — *Executive Recruiter*
Quality Search
P.O. Box 752294
Dayton, OH 45475-2294
Telephone: (500) 442-1305
Recruiter Classification: Contingency; **Lowest/Average Salary:** $30,000/$50,000; **Industry Concentration:** Electronics, High Technology, Information Technology; **Function Concentration:** Engineering, General Management, Human Resources, Marketing, Research and Development, Sales, Women/Minorities

Johnson, Greg — *Managing Director*
Source Services Corporation
525 Vine Street, Suite 2250
Cincinnati, OH 45202
Telephone: (513) 651-3303
Recruiter Classification: Contingency; **Lowest/Average Salary:** $30,000/$50,000; **Industry Concentration:** Information Technology; **Function Concentration:** Engineering, Finance/Accounting

Johnson, Harold E. — *Senior Partner*
Lamalie Amrop International
200 Park Avenue
New York, NY 10166-0136
Telephone: (212) 953-7900
Recruiter Classification: Retained; **Lowest/Average Salary:** $90,000/$90,000; **Industry Concentration:** Generalist with a primary focus in High Technology; **Function Concentration:** Generalist

Johnson, John W. — *Managing Director*
Webb, Johnson Associates, Inc.
280 Park Avenue, 43rd Floor
New York, NY 10017
Telephone: (212) 661-3700
Recruiter Classification: Retained; **Lowest/Average Salary:** $90,000/$90,000; **Industry Concentration:** Generalist with a primary focus in High Technology; **Function Concentration:** Generalist with a primary focus in Administration, Engineering, Finance/Accounting, General Management, Human Resources, Marketing, Research and Development, Sales

Johnson, Julie M. — *Executive Recruiter*
International Staffing Consultants, Inc.
500 Newport Center Drive, Suite 300
Newport Beach, CA 92660-7003
Telephone: (714) 721-7990
Recruiter Classification: Contingency; **Lowest/Average Salary:** $40,000/$60,000; **Industry Concentration:** Generalist with a primary focus in Electronics, High Technology, Information Technology; **Function Concentration:** Generalist with a primary focus in Engineering, General Management, Marketing, Research and Development, Sales

Johnson, Kathleen A. — *Partner*
Barton Associates, Inc.
One Riverway, Suite 2500
Houston, TX 77056
Telephone: (713) 961-9111
Recruiter Classification: Retained; **Lowest/Average Salary:** $75,000/$90,000; **Industry Concentration:** Generalist with a primary focus in Electronics, High Technology, Information Technology; **Function Concentration:** Generalist with a primary focus in Administration, Finance/Accounting, General Management, Human Resources, Marketing, Sales

Johnson, Keith — *Managing Partner*
Romac & Associates
760 Pillsbury Center
200 South Sixth Street
Minneapolis, MN 55402
Telephone: (612) 334-5990
Recruiter Classification: Executive Temporary; **Lowest/Average Salary:** $60,000/$60,000; **Industry Concentration:** High Technology, Information Technology; **Function Concentration:** Finance/Accounting

Johnson, LaDonna — *Manager Recruting*
Gans, Gans & Associates
175 N.Franklin Street Suite 401
Chicago, IL 60606
Telephone: (312) 357-9600
Recruiter Classification: Retained; **Lowest/Average Salary:** $75,000/$90,000; **Industry Concentration:** Generalist with a primary focus in Information Technology; **Function Concentration:** Generalist with a primary focus in Finance/Accounting, General Management, Human Resources, Women/Minorities

Johnson, Pete — *Recruiter*
Morgan Hunter Corp.
6800 College Boulevard, Suite 550
Overland Park, KS 66211
Telephone: (913) 491-3434
Recruiter Classification: Contingency; **Lowest/Average Salary:** $30,000/$40,000; **Industry Concentration:** Information Technology; **Function Concentration:** Generalist

Johnson, Peter — *Software Engineering Recruiter*
Winter, Wyman & Company
950 Winter Street, Suite 3100
Waltham, MA 02154-1294
Telephone: (617) 890-7000
Recruiter Classification: Contingency; **Lowest/Average Salary:**
$40,000/$75,000; **Industry Concentration:** High Technology,
Information Technology; **Function Concentration:** Engineering

Johnson, Robert J. — *President*
Quality Search
P.O. Box 752294
Dayton, OH 45475-2294
Telephone: (500) 442-1305
Recruiter Classification: Contingency; **Lowest/Average Salary:**
$30,000/$50,000; **Industry Concentration:** Electronics, High
Technology, Information Technology; **Function Concentration:**
Engineering, General Management, Human Resources,
Marketing, Research and Development, Sales,
Women/Minorities

Johnson, Rocky — *Vice President/Managing Director*
A.T. Kearney, Inc.
Lincoln Plaza, Suite 4170
500 North Akard Street
Dallas, TX 75201
Telephone: (214) 969-0010
Recruiter Classification: Retained; **Lowest/Average Salary:**
$90,000/$90,000; **Industry Concentration:** Generalist with a
primary focus in High Technology; **Function Concentration:**
Generalist with a primary focus in General Management

Johnson, Ronald S. — *President*
Ronald S. Johnson Associates, Inc.
11661 San Vicente Boulevard, Suite 400
Los Angeles, CA 90049
Telephone: (310) 820-5855
Recruiter Classification: Retained; **Lowest/Average Salary:**
$90,000/$90,000; **Industry Concentration:** Generalist with a
primary focus in Electronics, High Technology, Information
Technology; **Function Concentration:** Generalist

Johnson, Stanley C. — *President*
Johnson & Company
11 Grumman Hill Road
Wilton, CT 06897
Telephone: (203) 761-1212
Recruiter Classification: Retained; **Lowest/Average Salary:**
$90,000/$90,000; **Industry Concentration:** Generalist with a
primary focus in Electronics, Information Technology; **Function
Concentration:** Generalist with a primary focus in Engineering,
Finance/Accounting, General Management, Human Resources,
Marketing, Sales

Johnson, Valerie — *Executive Search Consultant*
Coe & Company International Inc.
1535 400-3rd Avenue SW
Center Tower
Calgary, Alberta, Canada T20 4H2
Telephone: (403) 232-8833
Recruiter Classification: Retained; **Lowest/Average Salary:**
$75,000/$90,000; **Industry Concentration:** High Technology,
Information Technology; **Function Concentration:** Generalist
with a primary focus in Administration, Engineering,
Finance/Accounting, General Management, Human Resources,
Marketing, Research and Development, Sales

Johnston, James R. — *Principal*
The Stevenson Group of Delaware Inc.
836 Farmington Avenue, Suite 223
West Hartford, CT 06119-1544
Telephone: (860) 232-3393
Recruiter Classification: Retained; **Lowest/Average Salary:**
$75,000/$90,000; **Industry Concentration:** Electronics;
Function Concentration: Generalist

Johnston, Michael — *Partner*
Robertson-Surrette Executive Search
Barrington Tower 10th Floor
Scotia Square, P.O. Box 2166
Halifax, Nova Scotia, B3J-3C4
Telephone: (902) 425-1330
Recruiter Classification: Retained; **Lowest/Average Salary:**
$50,000/$75,000; **Industry Concentration:** Generalist with a
primary focus in High Technology, Information Technology;
Function Concentration: Generalist with a primary focus in
Engineering, Finance/Accounting, General Management,
Human Resources, Marketing, Research and Development,
Sales

Johnstone, Grant — *Associate*
Source Services Corporation
520 Post Oak Boulevard, Suite 700
Houston, TX 77027
Telephone: (713) 439-1077
Recruiter Classification: Contingency; **Lowest/Average Salary:**
$30,000/$50,000; **Industry Concentration:** Information
Technology; **Function Concentration:** Engineering,
Finance/Accounting

Jones, Amy E. — *Office Support Recruiter*
The Corporate Connection, Ltd.
7202 Glen Forest Drive
Richmond, VA 23226
Telephone: (804) 288-8844
Recruiter Classification: Contingency; **Lowest/Average Salary:**
$20,000/$30,000; **Industry Concentration:** Generalist with a
primary focus in Electronics, High Technology, Information
Technology; **Function Concentration:** Generalist with a
primary focus in Administration, Engineering,
Finance/Accounting, General Management, Human Resources,
Marketing, Sales, Women/Minorities

Jones, B.J. — *Principal*
Intersource, Ltd.
515 East Carefree Highway
P.O. Box 42033438
Phoenix, AZ 80080
Telephone: (602) 780-4540
Recruiter Classification: Retained; **Lowest/Average Salary:**
$30,000/$75,000; **Industry Concentration:** Generalist with a
primary focus in High Technology; **Function Concentration:**
Finance/Accounting

Jones, Barbara — *Senior Vice President*
Kaye-Bassman International Corp.
18333 Preston Road, Suite 500
Dallas, TX 75252
Telephone: (972) 931-5242
Recruiter Classification: Retained; **Lowest/Average Salary:**
$60,000/$90,000; **Industry Concentration:** High Technology,
Information Technology; **Function Concentration:** Generalist
with a primary focus in Human Resources, Marketing, Sales,
Women/Minorities

Jones, Barbara J. — *Senior Vice President*
Kaye-Bassman International Corp.
18333 Preston Road, Suite 500
Dallas, TX 75252
Telephone: (972) 931-5242
Recruiter Classification: Executive Temporary; **Lowest/Average Salary:** $40,000/$60,000; **Industry Concentration:** High Technology, Information Technology; **Function Concentration:** Generalist

Jones, Daniel F. — *Principal*
Atlantic Search Group, Inc.
One Liberty Square
Boston, MA 02109
Telephone: (617) 426-9700
Recruiter Classification: Contingency; **Lowest/Average Salary:** $20,000/$60,000; **Industry Concentration:** Generalist with a primary focus in Electronics, High Technology, Information Technology; **Function Concentration:** Finance/Accounting

Jones, Francis E. — *President*
Earley Kielty and Associates, Inc.
One Landmark Square
Stamford, CT 06901
Telephone: (203) 324-6723
Recruiter Classification: Retained; **Lowest/Average Salary:** $90,000/$90,000; **Industry Concentration:** Generalist with a primary focus in Information Technology; **Function Concentration:** Generalist with a primary focus in Administration, Finance/Accounting, General Management, Human Resources, Marketing, Research and Development, Sales, Women/Minorities

Jones, Gary — *Consultant/Recruiter*
BGB Associates
P.O. Box 556
Itasca, IL 60143
Telephone: (630) 250-8993
Recruiter Classification: Contingency; **Lowest/Average Salary:** $20,000/$50,000; **Industry Concentration:** Generalist with a primary focus in Information Technology; **Function Concentration:** Generalist with a primary focus in Administration, Engineering, Finance/Accounting, General Management, Human Resources, Marketing, Sales, Women/Minorities

Jones, Rodney — *Associate*
Source Services Corporation
379 Thornall Street
Edison, NJ 08837
Telephone: (908) 494-2800
Recruiter Classification: Contingency; **Lowest/Average Salary:** $30,000/$50,000; **Industry Concentration:** Information Technology; **Function Concentration:** Engineering, Finance/Accounting

Jones, Ronald T. — *President*
ARJay & Associates
3286 Clower Street, Suite A-202
Snellville, GA 30278
Telephone: (404) 979-3799
Recruiter Classification: Contingency; **Lowest/Average Salary:** $40,000/$90,000; **Industry Concentration:** Generalist with a primary focus in Electronics; **Function Concentration:** Generalist with a primary focus in Engineering, Finance/Accounting, General Management, Human Resources, Marketing, Research and Development, Sales

Jordan, Jon — *Search Consultant*
Cochran, Cochran & Yale, Inc.
955 East Henrietta Road
Rochester, NY 14623
Telephone: (716) 424-6060
Recruiter Classification: Retained; **Lowest/Average Salary:** $50,000/$75,000; **Industry Concentration:** Generalist with a primary focus in High Technology, Information Technology; **Function Concentration:** Generalist with a primary focus in Engineering, Finance/Accounting, General Management, Human Resources, Marketing, Sales, Women/Minorities

Jorgensen, Tom — *Vice President*
The Talley Group
P.O. Box 2918
Stanton, VA 24402
Telephone: (540) 248-7009
Recruiter Classification: Retained; **Lowest/Average Salary:** $30,000/$60,000; **Industry Concentration:** Generalist with a primary focus in Electronics; **Function Concentration:** Engineering, Finance/Accounting

Joyce, William J. — *Principal*
The Guild Corporation
8260 Greensboro Drive, Suite 460
McLean, VA 22102
Telephone: (703) 761-4023
Recruiter Classification: Contingency; **Lowest/Average Salary:** $40,000/$50,000; **Industry Concentration:** Electronics, High Technology, Information Technology; **Function Concentration:** Engineering, Finance/Accounting, General Management, Research and Development

Jozwik, Peter — *Managing Director*
The Search Firm, Inc.
595 Market Street, Suite 1400
San Francisco, CA 94105
Telephone: (415) 777-3900
Recruiter Classification: Contingency; **Lowest/Average Salary:** $40,000/$75,000; **Industry Concentration:** Electronics, High Technology, Information Technology

Judge, Alfred L. — *President*
The Cambridge Group Ltd
1175 Post Road East
Westport, CT 06880
Telephone: (203) 226-4243
Recruiter Classification: Contingency; **Lowest/Average Salary:** $60,000/$75,000; **Industry Concentration:** Generalist with a primary focus in High Technology, Information Technology; **Function Concentration:** Administration, Finance/Accounting, General Management, Human Resources, Marketing, Research and Development, Sales, Women/Minorities

Judy, Otto — *Executive Recruiter*
CPS Inc.
One Westbrook Corporate Centre, Suite 600
Westchester, IL 60154
Telephone: (708) 531-8370
Recruiter Classification: Contingency; **Lowest/Average Salary:** $30,000/$50,000; **Industry Concentration:** Generalist with a primary focus in Electronics, High Technology, Information Technology; **Function Concentration:** Engineering, Research and Development, Sales, Women/Minorities

Juelis, John J. — *Vice President*
Peeney Associates
141 South Avenue
Fanwood, NJ 07023
Telephone: (908) 322-2324
Recruiter Classification: Retained; **Lowest/Average Salary:**
$60,000/$90,000; **Industry Concentration:** Generalist with a
primary focus in Electronics; **Function Concentration:**
Generalist with a primary focus in Administration, Engineering,
Finance/Accounting, General Management, Human Resources,
Marketing, Research and Development, Sales,
Women/Minorities

Juratovac, Michael — *Senior Associate*
Montgomery Resources, Inc.
555 Montgomery Street, Suite 1650
San Francisco, CA 94111
Telephone: (415) 956-4242
Recruiter Classification: Contingency; **Lowest/Average Salary:**
$30,000/$60,000; **Industry Concentration:** High Technology;
Function Concentration: Finance/Accounting

Juska, Frank — *Vice President*
Rusher, Loscavio & LoPresto
180 Montgomery Street, Suite 1616
San Francisco, CA 94104-4239
Telephone: (415) 765-6600
Recruiter Classification: Retained; **Lowest/Average Salary:**
$75,000/$90,000; **Industry Concentration:** Electronics, High
Technology, Information Technology; **Function Concentration:**
Administration, Engineering, General Management

Kacyn, Louis J. — *Consultant*
Egon Zehnder International Inc.
One First National Plaza
21 South Clark Street, Suite 3300
Chicago, IL 60603-2006
Telephone: (312) 782-4500
Recruiter Classification: Retained; **Lowest/Average Salary:**
$90,000/$90,000; **Industry Concentration:** Generalist with a
primary focus in High Technology; **Function Concentration:**
Generalist

Kaiser, Donald J. — *President*
Dunhill International Search of New Haven
59 Elm Street
New Haven, CT 06510
Telephone: (203) 562-0511
Recruiter Classification: Contingency; **Lowest/Average Salary:**
$30,000/$75,000; **Industry Concentration:** Generalist with a
primary focus in Electronics, High Technology, Information
Technology; **Function Concentration:** Generalist with a
primary focus in Administration, Engineering,
Finance/Accounting, General Management, Human Resources,
Marketing, Sales

Kane, Frank — *Professional Recruiter*
A.J. Burton Group, Inc.
4550 Montgomery Avenue, Ste. 325 North
Bethesda, MD 20814
Telephone: (301) 654-0082
Recruiter Classification: Contingency, Executive Temporary;
Lowest/Average Salary: $40,000/$75,000; **Industry
Concentration:** Generalist with a primary focus in High
Technology, Information Technology; **Function Concentration:**
Generalist with a primary focus in Administration,
Finance/Accounting, General Management, Human Resources

Kane, Karen — *Consultant*
Howard Fischer Associates, Inc.
1800 John F. Kennedy Boulevard, 7th Floor
Philadelphia, PA 19103
Telephone: (215) 568-8363
Recruiter Classification: Retained; **Lowest/Average Salary:**
$90,000/$90,000; **Industry Concentration:** Generalist with a
primary focus in High Technology; **Function Concentration:**
Generalist with a primary focus in Administration,
Finance/Accounting, General Management, Human Resources,
Marketing, Research and Development, Sales,
Women/Minorities

Kanovsky, Gerald — *Chairman*
Career Consulting Group, Inc.
1100 Summer Street
Stamford, CT 06905
Telephone: (203) 975-8800
Recruiter Classification: Contingency; **Lowest/Average Salary:**
$40,000/$75,000; **Industry Concentration:** Information
Technology; **Function Concentration:** Marketing, Sales

Kanovsky, Marlene — *President*
Career Consulting Group, Inc.
1100 Summer Street
Stamford, CT 06905
Telephone: (203) 975-8800
Recruiter Classification: Contingency; **Lowest/Average Salary:**
$40,000/$50,000; **Industry Concentration:** Information
Technology; **Function Concentration:** Marketing, Sales

Kanrich, Susan Azaria — *Director*
AlternaStaff
1155 Avenue of the Americas, 15th Floor
New York, NY 10036
Telephone: (212) 302-1141
Recruiter Classification: Executive Temporary; **Lowest/Average
Salary:** $30,000/$60,000; **Industry Concentration:** Electronics,
High Technology; **Function Concentration:** Engineering,
General Management, Human Resources, Research and
Development

Kaplan, Alexandra — *Principal*
J.M. Eagle Partners Ltd.
10140 North Port Washington Rd.
Mequon, WI 53092
Telephone: (414) 241-1113
Recruiter Classification: Contingency; **Lowest/Average Salary:**
$60,000/$90,000; **Industry Concentration:** Electronics, High
Technology, Information Technology; **Function Concentration:**
Generalist

Kaplan, Gary — *President*
Gary Kaplan & Associates
201 South Lake Avenue
Suite 600
Pasadena, CA 91101
Telephone: (818) 796-8100
Recruiter Classification: Retained; **Lowest/Average Salary:**
$75,000/$90,000; **Industry Concentration:** Generalist with a
primary focus in Electronics, High Technology, Information
Technology; **Function Concentration:** Generalist with a
primary focus in Engineering, Finance/Accounting, General
Management, Human Resources, Marketing, Research and
Development, Sales

Kaplan, Traci — *Associate*
Source Services Corporation
8614 Westwood Center, Suite 750
Vienna, VA 22182
Telephone: (703) 790-5610
Recruiter Classification: Contingency; **Lowest/Average Salary:**
$30,000/$50,000; **Industry Concentration:** Information
Technology; **Function Concentration:** Engineering,
Finance/Accounting

Karalis, William — *Executive Recruiter*
CPS Inc.
One Westbrook Corporate Centre, Suite 600
Westchester, IL 60154
Telephone: (708) 531-8370
Recruiter Classification: Contingency; **Lowest/Average Salary:**
$30,000/$50,000; **Industry Concentration:** Generalist with a
primary focus in Electronics, High Technology, Information
Technology; **Function Concentration:** Engineering, Research
and Development, Sales, Women/Minorities

Kartin, Martin C. — *President*
Martin Kartin and Company, Inc.
211 East 70th Street
New York, NY 10021
Telephone: (212) 628-7676
Recruiter Classification: Retained; **Lowest/Average Salary:**
$60,000/$90,000; **Industry Concentration:** Generalist with a
primary focus in Electronics; **Function Concentration:**
Generalist with a primary focus in Finance/Accounting,
General Management, Human Resources, Marketing, Research
and Development, Sales, Women/Minorities

Kasmouski, Steve — *Software Engineering
Recruiter*
Winter, Wyman & Company
950 Winter Street, Suite 3100
Waltham, MA 02154-1294
Telephone: (617) 890-7000
Recruiter Classification: Contingency; **Lowest/Average Salary:**
$40,000/$75,000; **Industry Concentration:** High Technology,
Information Technology; **Function Concentration:** Engineering

Kasprzyk, Michael — *Associate*
Source Services Corporation
8614 Westwood Center, Suite 750
Vienna, VA 22182
Telephone: (703) 790-5610
Recruiter Classification: Contingency; **Lowest/Average Salary:**
$30,000/$50,000; **Industry Concentration:** Information
Technology; **Function Concentration:** Engineering,
Finance/Accounting

Katz, Cyndi — *Account Executive*
Search West, Inc.
1888 Century Park East
Suite 2050
Los Angeles, CA 90067-1736
Telephone: (310) 284-8888
Recruiter Classification: Contingency; **Lowest/Average Salary:**
$40,000/$60,000; **Industry Concentration:** Generalist with a
primary focus in Electronics; **Function Concentration:**
Administration

Kaye, Jeffrey — *President and COO*
Kaye-Bassman International Corp.
18333 Preston Road, Suite 500
Dallas, TX 75252
Telephone: (972) 931-5242
Recruiter Classification: Executive Temporary; **Lowest/Average
Salary:** $40,000/$60,000; **Industry Concentration:** High
Technology, Information Technology; **Function Concentration:**
Generalist

Keating, Pierson — *Partner*
Nordeman Grimm, Inc.
717 Fifth Avenue, 26th Floor
New York, NY 10022
Telephone: (212) 935-1000
Recruiter Classification: Retained; **Lowest/Average Salary:**
$90,000/$90,000; **Industry Concentration:** Generalist with a
primary focus in Information Technology; **Function
Concentration:** Generalist with a primary focus in
Finance/Accounting, General Management, Human Resources,
Marketing, Research and Development, Sales

Kehoe, Mike — *Executive Recruiter*
CPS Inc.
One Westbrook Corporate Centre, Suite 600
Westchester, IL 60154
Telephone: (708) 531-8370
Recruiter Classification: Contingency; **Lowest/Average Salary:**
$30,000/$50,000; **Industry Concentration:** Generalist with a
primary focus in Electronics, High Technology, Information
Technology; **Function Concentration:** Engineering, Research
and Development, Sales, Women/Minorities

Keitel, Robert S. — *Vice President*
A.T. Kearney, Inc.
3 Lagoon Drive, Suite 160
Redwood City, CA 94065
Telephone: (415) 637-6600
Recruiter Classification: Retained; **Lowest/Average Salary:**
$90,000/$90,000; **Industry Concentration:** Generalist with a
primary focus in High Technology; **Function Concentration:**
Generalist with a primary focus in General Management

Keith, Stephanie — *Recruiter*
Southwestern Professional Services
9485 Regency Square Boulevard, Suite 110
Jacksonville, FL 32225
Telephone: (904) 464-0400
Recruiter Classification: Contingency; **Lowest/Average Salary:**
$40,000/$60,000; **Industry Concentration:** High Technology;
Function Concentration: Finance/Accounting

Kelbell, Scott — *Senior Information Technology
Recruiter*
Comprehensive Search
RR6, Box 444
Hendersonville, NC 28792
Telephone: (704) 685-0220
Recruiter Classification: Contingency; **Lowest/Average Salary:**
$30,000/$60,000; **Industry Concentration:** Generalist with a
primary focus in Information Technology; **Function
Concentration:** Generalist

Keller, Barbara E. — *Senior Consultant*
Barton Associates, Inc.
One Riverway, Suite 2500
Houston, TX 77056
Telephone: (713) 961-9111
Recruiter Classification: Retained; **Lowest/Average Salary:**
$75,000/$90,000; **Industry Concentration:** Generalist with a
primary focus in Electronics, High Technology, Information
Technology; **Function Concentration:** Generalist with a
primary focus in Finance/Accounting, General Management,
Human Resources, Marketing, Sales

Kells, John — *President*
Heffelfinger Associates, Inc.
Chestnut Green
470 Washington Street
Norwood, MA 02062
Telephone: (617) 769-6650
Recruiter Classification: Retained; **Lowest/Average Salary:**
$60,000/$90,000; **Industry Concentration:** Electronics, High
Technology, Information Technology; **Function Concentration:**
Engineering, General Management, Marketing, Sales

Kelly, Elizabeth Ann — *Senior Associate*
Wellington Management Group
1601 Market Street, Suite 2902
Philadelphia, PA 19103-2499
Telephone: (215) 569-8900
Recruiter Classification: Retained; **Lowest/Average Salary:**
$90,000/$90,000; **Industry Concentration:** Generalist with a
primary focus in High Technology, Information Technology;
Function Concentration: Generalist with a primary focus in
General Management, Human Resources, Marketing, Sales,
Women/Minorities

Kelly, Robert — *Associate*
Source Services Corporation
100 North Tryon Street, Suite 3130
Charlotte, NC 28202
Telephone: (704) 333-8311
Recruiter Classification: Contingency; **Lowest/Average Salary:**
$30,000/$50,000; **Industry Concentration:** Information
Technology; **Function Concentration:** Engineering,
Finance/Accounting

Kelly, Sheri — *Associate/Executive Recruiter*
Strategic Associates, Inc.
13915 Burnet Road, Suite 300
Austin, TX 78728
Telephone: (512) 218-8222
Recruiter Classification: Contingency; **Lowest/Average Salary:**
$50,000/$60,000; **Industry Concentration:** Electronics, High
Technology, Information Technology; **Function Concentration:**
General Management, Women/Minorities

Kelly, Susan D. — *President*
S.D. Kelly & Associates, Inc.
990 Washington Street
Dedham, MA 02026
Telephone: (617) 326-8038
Recruiter Classification: Contingency; **Lowest/Average Salary:**
$60,000/$75,000; **Industry Concentration:** Electronics, High
Technology; **Function Concentration:** Engineering, General
Management, Marketing, Sales

Kelso, Patricia C. — *Associate Partner*
Barton Associates, Inc.
One Riverway, Suite 2500
Houston, TX 77056
Telephone: (713) 961-9111
Recruiter Classification: Retained; **Lowest/Average Salary:**
$75,000/$90,000; **Industry Concentration:** Generalist with a
primary focus in Electronics, High Technology, Information
Technology; **Function Concentration:** Generalist with a
primary focus in Administration, General Management, Human
Resources, Marketing, Sales

Kennedy, Craig — *Associate*
Source Services Corporation
10220 SW Greenburg Road, Suite 625
Portland, OR 97223
Telephone: (503) 768-4546
Recruiter Classification: Contingency; **Lowest/Average Salary:**
$30,000/$50,000; **Industry Concentration:** Information
Technology; **Function Concentration:** Engineering,
Finance/Accounting

Kennedy, Paul — *Associate*
Source Services Corporation
One Park Plaza, Suite 560
Irvine, CA 92714
Telephone: (714) 660-1666
Recruiter Classification: Contingency; **Lowest/Average Salary:**
$30,000/$50,000; **Industry Concentration:** Information
Technology; **Function Concentration:** Engineering,
Finance/Accounting

Kennedy, Walter — *Managing Director*
Source Services Corporation
80 South 8th Street
Minneapolis, MN 55402
Telephone: (612) 332-6460
Recruiter Classification: Contingency; **Lowest/Average Salary:**
$30,000/$50,000; **Industry Concentration:** Information
Technology; **Function Concentration:** Engineering,
Finance/Accounting

Kennedy, Walter — *Branch Manager*
Romac & Associates
111 North Orange Avenue
Suite 1150
Orlando, FL 32801
Telephone: (407) 843-0765
Recruiter Classification: Executive Temporary; **Lowest/Average
Salary:** $60,000/$60,000; **Industry Concentration:** High
Technology, Information Technology; **Function Concentration:**
Finance/Accounting

Kennedy, Walter — *Managing Director*
Source Services Corporation
8500 Normandale Lake, Suite 955
Bloomington, MN 55437
Telephone: (612) 835-5100
Recruiter Classification: Contingency; **Lowest/Average Salary:**
$30,000/$50,000; **Industry Concentration:** Information
Technology; **Function Concentration:** Engineering,
Finance/Accounting

Kenney, Jeanne — *Associate*
Source Services Corporation
425 California Street, Suite 1200
San Francisco, CA 94104
Telephone: (415) 434-2410
Recruiter Classification: Contingency; **Lowest/Average Salary:**
$30,000/$50,000; **Industry Concentration:** Information
Technology; **Function Concentration:** Engineering,
Finance/Accounting

Kent, Melvin — *Owner*
Melvin Kent & Associates, Inc.
6477 Quarry Lane, Suite 100
Dublin, OH 43017
Telephone: (614) 798-9501
Recruiter Classification: Retained; **Lowest/Average Salary:**
$75,000/$90,000; **Industry Concentration:** Generalist with a
primary focus in High Technology, Information Technology;
Function Concentration: Generalist with a primary focus in
Finance/Accounting, General Management, Human Resources,
Marketing, Sales

Kenzer, Robert D. — *Chairman*
Kenzer Corp.
777 Third Avenue, 26th Floor
New York, NY 10017
Telephone: (212) 308-4300
Recruiter Classification: Retained; **Lowest/Average Salary:**
$50,000/$90,000; **Industry Concentration:** Information
Technology; **Function Concentration:** Generalist with a
primary focus in Administration, Finance/Accounting, General
Management, Human Resources, Marketing

Kerester, Jonathon — *Account Executive*
Cadillac Associates
8033 Sunset Boulevard, Suite 5200
Los Angeles, CA 90046
Telephone: (213) 385-9111
Recruiter Classification: Contingency; **Lowest/Average Salary:**
$60,000/$75,000; **Industry Concentration:** Generalist with a
primary focus in High Technology; **Function Concentration:**
Generalist

Kern, Jerry L. — *Executive Vice President*
ADOW's Executeam
2734 Chancellor Drive, Suite 102
Crestview Hills, KY 41017-3443
Telephone: (606) 344-8600
Recruiter Classification: Executive Temporary; **Lowest/Average
Salary:** $60,000/$90,000; **Industry Concentration:** Generalist
with a primary focus in Electronics, High Technology,
Information Technology; **Function Concentration:** Generalist
with a primary focus in Administration, Engineering,
Finance/Accounting, General Management, Human Resources,
Marketing, Research and Development, Women/Minorities

Kern, Kathleen G. — *President*
ADOW's Executeam
36 East Fourth Street, Suite 1020
Cincinnati, OH 45202-3810
Telephone: (513) 721-2369
Recruiter Classification: Executive Temporary; **Lowest/Average
Salary:** $60,000/$90,000; **Industry Concentration:** Generalist
with a primary focus in Electronics, High Technology,
Information Technology; **Function Concentration:** Generalist
with a primary focus in Administration, Engineering,
Finance/Accounting, General Management, Human Resources,
Marketing, Women/Minorities

Kershaw, Lisa — *Consultant*
Tanton Mitchell/Paul Ray Berndtson
710-1050 West Pender Street
Vancouver, British Columbia, CANADA V6E 3S7
Telephone: (604) 685-0261
Recruiter Classification: Retained; **Lowest/Average Salary:**
$75,000/$90,000; **Industry Concentration:** Generalist with a
primary focus in High Technology; **Function Concentration:**
Generalist with a primary focus in Administration,
Finance/Accounting, General Management, Human Resources,
Marketing, Sales

Keshishian, Gregory — *Senior Vice President,*
Executive Compensation Practice
Handy HRM Corp.
250 Park Avenue
New York, NY 10177-0074
Telephone: (212) 210-5650
Recruiter Classification: Retained; **Lowest/Average Salary:**
$90,000/$90,000; **Industry Concentration:** Generalist with a
primary focus in Electronics, High Technology; **Function
Concentration:** Generalist with a primary focus in
Finance/Accounting, General Management, Human Resources

Keyser, Anne — *Vice President*
A.T. Kearney, Inc.
One Memorial Drive, 14th Floor
Cambridge, MA 02142
Telephone: (617) 374-2600
Recruiter Classification: Retained; **Lowest/Average Salary:**
$90,000/$90,000; **Industry Concentration:** Generalist with a
primary focus in High Technology, Information Technology;
Function Concentration: Generalist with a primary focus in
Engineering, Finance/Accounting, General Management

Kielty, John L. — *Chairman*
Earley Kielty and Associates, Inc.
Two Pennsylvania Plaza
New York, NY 10121
Telephone: (212) 736-5626
Recruiter Classification: Retained; **Lowest/Average Salary:**
$90,000/$90,000; **Industry Concentration:** Generalist with a
primary focus in Information Technology; **Function
Concentration:** Generalist with a primary focus in
Administration, Finance/Accounting, General Management,
Human Resources, Marketing, Research and Development,
Sales, Women/Minorities

Kilcoyne, Pat — *Executive Recruiter*
CPS Inc.
One Westbrook Corporate Centre, Suite 600
Westchester, IL 60154
Telephone: (708) 531-8370
Recruiter Classification: Contingency; **Lowest/Average Salary:**
$30,000/$50,000; **Industry Concentration:** Generalist with a
primary focus in Electronics, High Technology, Information
Technology; **Function Concentration:** Engineering, Research
and Development, Sales, Women/Minorities

King, Bill — *Vice President Administration*
The McCormick Group, Inc.
1400 Wilson Boulevard
Arlington, VA 22209
Telephone: (703) 841-1700
Recruiter Classification: Retained; **Lowest/Average Salary:**
$50,000/$90,000; **Industry Concentration:** High Technology,
Information Technology; **Function Concentration:** Engineering,
Finance/Accounting, General Management, Human Resources,
Marketing, Sales

King, Margaret — *Vice President*
Christian & Timbers
20833 Stevens Creek Boulevard, Suite 200
Cupertino, CA 95014
Telephone: (408) 446-5440
Recruiter Classification: Retained; **Lowest/Average Salary:**
$90,000/$90,000; **Industry Concentration:** Electronics, High
Technology, Information Technology; **Function Concentration:**
Generalist with a primary focus in Engineering,
Finance/Accounting, General Management, Human Resources,
Marketing, Research and Development, Sales

King, Shannon — *Associate*
Source Services Corporation
4510 Executive Drive, Suite 200
San Diego, CA 92121
Telephone: (619) 552-0300
Recruiter Classification: Contingency; **Lowest/Average Salary:**
$30,000/$50,000; **Industry Concentration:** Information
Technology; **Function Concentration:** Engineering,
Finance/Accounting

King, Steven — *Office of the President*
Ashway, Ltd.
295 Madison Avenue
New York, NY 10017
Telephone: (212) 679-3300
Recruiter Classification: Contingency; **Lowest/Average Salary:**
$30,000/$90,000; **Industry Concentration:** High Technology;
Function Concentration: General Management

Kinney, Carol — *Associate*
Dussick Management Associates
149 Durham Road
Madison, CT 06443
Telephone: (203) 245-9311
Recruiter Classification: Contingency; **Lowest/Average Salary:**
$50,000/$60,000; **Industry Concentration:** Generalist with a
primary focus in High Technology, Information Technology;
Function Concentration: Generalist with a primary focus in
Marketing, Research and Development, Sales,
Women/Minorities

Kinser, Richard E. — *President*
Richard Kinser & Associates
919 Third Avenue, 10th Floor
New York, NY 10022
Telephone: (212) 593-5429
Recruiter Classification: Retained; **Lowest/Average Salary:**
$90,000/$90,000; **Industry Concentration:** Generalist with a
primary focus in Electronics, High Technology; **Function
Concentration:** Generalist with a primary focus in Engineering,
Finance/Accounting, General Management, Human Resources,
Marketing, Research and Development

Kinsey, Joanne — *Recruiter*
Eastridge InfoTech
2355 Northside Drive, Suite 180
San Diego, CA 92108
Telephone: (619) 260-2048
Recruiter Classification: Contingency; **Lowest/Average Salary:**
$40,000/$60,000; **Industry Concentration:** High Technology,
Information Technology

Kip, Luanne S. — *President*
Kip Williams, Inc.
355 Lexington Avenue, 11th Floor
New York, NY 10017-6603
Telephone: (212) 661-1225
Recruiter Classification: Retained; **Lowest/Average Salary:**
$75,000/$90,000; **Industry Concentration:** Generalist with a
primary focus in Information Technology; **Function
Concentration:** Generalist with a primary focus in General
Management, Human Resources, Marketing, Sales,
Women/Minorities

Kirkman, J. Michael — *Partner*
Kirkman & Searing, Inc.
8045 Leesburg Pike
Suite 540
Vienna, VA 22182
Telephone: (703) 761-7020
Recruiter Classification: Retained; **Lowest/Average Salary:**
$90,000/$90,000; **Industry Concentration:** High Technology,
Information Technology; **Function Concentration:** General
Management, Marketing, Sales

Kirschner, Alan — *Associate*
Source Services Corporation
2 Penn Plaza, Suite 1176
New York, NY 10121
Telephone: (212) 760-2200
Recruiter Classification: Contingency; **Lowest/Average Salary:**
$30,000/$50,000; **Industry Concentration:** Information
Technology; **Function Concentration:** Engineering,
Finance/Accounting

Kishbaugh, Herbert S. — *President*
Kishbaugh Associates International
2 Elm Square
Andover, MA 01810
Telephone: (508) 475-7224
Recruiter Classification: Retained; **Lowest/Average Salary:**
$75,000/$90,000; **Industry Concentration:** Generalist with a
primary focus in High Technology, Information Technology;
Function Concentration: Generalist with a primary focus in
Administration, Finance/Accounting, General Management,
Human Resources, Marketing, Research and Development,
Sales

Kixmiller, David B. — *Managing Partner*
Heidrick & Struggles, Inc.
2740 Sand Hill Road
Menlo Park, CA 94025
Telephone: (415) 234-1500
Recruiter Classification: Retained; **Lowest/Average Salary:**
$75,000/$90,000; **Industry Concentration:** Generalist with a
primary focus in High Technology; **Function Concentration:**
Generalist

Kkorzyniewski, Nicole — *Executive Recruiter*
CPS Inc.
One Westbrook Corporate Centre, Suite 600
Westchester, IL 60154
Telephone: (708) 531-8370
Recruiter Classification: Contingency; **Lowest/Average Salary:**
$30,000/$50,000; **Industry Concentration:** Generalist with a
primary focus in Electronics, High Technology, Information
Technology; **Function Concentration:** Engineering, Research
and Development, Sales, Women/Minorities

Klages, Constance W. — *President*
International Management Advisors, Inc.
516 Fifth Avenue
New York, NY 10036-7501
Telephone: (212) 758-7770
Recruiter Classification: Retained; **Lowest/Average Salary:**
$75,000/$90,000; **Industry Concentration:** Generalist with a
primary focus in Electronics, High Technology; **Function
Concentration:** Generalist with a primary focus in Engineering,
Finance/Accounting, General Management, Human Resources,
Marketing, Research and Development, Women/Minorities

Klauck, James J. — *Managing Director*
Horton International
10 Tower Lane
Avon, CT 06001
Telephone: (860) 674-8701
Recruiter Classification: Retained; **Lowest/Average Salary:**
$90,000/$90,000; **Industry Concentration:** Generalist with a
primary focus in Electronics; **Function Concentration:**
Generalist with a primary focus in Administration, Engineering,
Finance/Accounting, General Management, Human Resources,
Marketing, Research and Development, Sales

Klavens, Cecile J. — *President*
The Pickwick Group, Inc.
One Washington Street, Suite 111
Wellesley, MA 02181
Telephone: (617) 235-6222
Recruiter Classification: Executive Temporary; **Lowest/Average
Salary:** $40,000/$60,000; **Industry Concentration:** Generalist
with a primary focus in Electronics, High Technology,
Information Technology; **Function Concentration:** Generalist
with a primary focus in Finance/Accounting, General
Management, Human Resources, Marketing,
Women/Minorities

Klein, Brandon — *Professional Recruiter*
A.J. Burton Group, Inc.
120 East Baltimore Street, Suite 2220
Baltimore, MD 21202
Telephone: (410) 752-5244
Recruiter Classification: Contingency; **Lowest/Average Salary:**
$40,000/$75,000; **Industry Concentration:** Generalist with a
primary focus in High Technology, Information Technology;
Function Concentration: Generalist with a primary focus in
Administration, Finance/Accounting, General Management,
Human Resources

Klein, Gary — *Vice President*
A.T. Kearney, Inc.
153 East 53rd Street
New York, NY 10022
Telephone: (212) 751-7040
Recruiter Classification: Retained; **Lowest/Average Salary:**
$90,000/$90,000; **Industry Concentration:** Generalist with a
primary focus in High Technology, Information Technology;
Function Concentration: Generalist with a primary focus in
Engineering, Finance/Accounting, General Management

Klein, Mary Jo — *Search Consultant*
Cochran, Cochran & Yale, Inc.
955 East Henrietta Road
Rochester, NY 14623
Telephone: (716) 424-6060
Recruiter Classification: Retained; **Lowest/Average Salary:**
$50,000/$75,000; **Industry Concentration:** Generalist with a
primary focus in High Technology, Information Technology;
Function Concentration: Generalist with a primary focus in
Engineering, Finance/Accounting, General Management,
Human Resources, Marketing, Sales, Women/Minorities

Klein, Mel — *President*
Stewart/Laurence Associates
P.O. Box 1156
Atrium Executive Park
Englishtown, NJ 07726
Telephone: (732) 972-8000
Recruiter Classification: Retained; **Lowest/Average Salary:**
$75,000/$90,000; **Industry Concentration:** Electronics, High
Technology, Information Technology; **Function Concentration:**
General Management, Marketing, Sales

Kleinstein, Jonah A. — *President*
The Kleinstein Group
33 Wood Avenue South
Metro Park Plaza
Iselin, NJ 08830
Telephone: (908) 494-7500
Recruiter Classification: Retained; **Lowest/Average Salary:**
$60,000/$90,000; **Industry Concentration:** Generalist with a
primary focus in Electronics; **Function Concentration:**
Generalist

Kleinstein, Scott — *Associate*
Source Services Corporation
150 South Wacker Drive, Suite 400
Chicago, IL 60606
Telephone: (312) 346-7000
Recruiter Classification: Contingency; **Lowest/Average Salary:**
$30,000/$50,000; **Industry Concentration:** Information
Technology; **Function Concentration:** Engineering,
Finance/Accounting

Klopfenstein, Edward L. — *Vice President*
Crowder & Company
2050 North Woodward Avenue, Suite 335
Bloomfield Hills, MI 48304
Telephone: (248) 645-0909
Recruiter Classification: Retained; **Lowest/Average Salary:**
$75,000/$75,000; **Industry Concentration:** Generalist with a
primary focus in Electronics; **Function Concentration:**
Generalist with a primary focus in Engineering,
Finance/Accounting, General Management, Human Resources,
Marketing, Sales, Women/Minorities

Klusman, Edwin — *Associate*
Source Services Corporation
2000 Town Center, Suite 850
Southfield, MI 48075
Telephone: (810) 352-6520
Recruiter Classification: Contingency; **Lowest/Average Salary:**
$30,000/$50,000; **Industry Concentration:** Information
Technology; **Function Concentration:** Engineering,
Finance/Accounting

Knapp, Ronald A. — *President*
Knapp Consultants
184 Old Ridgefield Road
Wilton, CT 06897
Telephone: (203) 762-0790
Recruiter Classification: Retained; **Lowest/Average Salary:**
$90,000/$90,000; **Industry Concentration:** Generalist with a
primary focus in Electronics, High Technology, Information
Technology; **Function Concentration:** Generalist

Knoll, Robert — *Associate*
Source Services Corporation
One CityPlace, Suite 170
St. Louis, MO 63141
Telephone: (314) 432-4500
Recruiter Classification: Contingency; **Lowest/Average Salary:**
$30,000/$50,000; **Industry Concentration:** Information
Technology; **Function Concentration:** Engineering,
Finance/Accounting

Knotts, Jerry — *Senior Principal*
Mixtec Group
31255 Cedar Valley Drive
Suite 300-327
Westlake Village, CA 91362
Telephone: (818) 889-8819
Recruiter Classification: Contingency; **Lowest/Average Salary:**
$60,000/$90,000; **Industry Concentration:** High Technology;
Function Concentration: Generalist with a primary focus in
Administration, Engineering, Finance/Accounting, General
Management, Research and Development

Kobayashi, Rika — *Staffing Consultant*
International Staffing Consultants, Inc.
500 Newport Center Drive, Suite 300
Newport Beach, CA 92660-7003
Telephone: (714) 721-7990
Recruiter Classification: Contingency; **Lowest/Average Salary:**
$30,000/$75,000; **Industry Concentration:** Generalist with a
primary focus in Electronics, High Technology, Information
Technology; **Function Concentration:** Human Resources

Koblentz, Joel M. — *Managing Partner*
Egon Zehnder International Inc.
One Atlantic Center, Suite 3000
1201 West Peachtree Street N.E.
Atlanta, GA 30309
Telephone: (404) 875-3000
Recruiter Classification: Retained; **Lowest/Average Salary:**
$90,000/$90,000; **Industry Concentration:** Generalist with a
primary focus in High Technology; **Function Concentration:**
Generalist

Koczak, John — *Associate*
Source Services Corporation
525 Vine Street, Suite 2250
Cincinnati, OH 45202
Telephone: (513) 651-3303
Recruiter Classification: Contingency; **Lowest/Average Salary:**
$30,000/$50,000; **Industry Concentration:** Information
Technology; **Function Concentration:** Engineering,
Finance/Accounting

Koehler, Frank R. — *Principal*
The Koehler Group
P.O. Box 18156
Philadelphia, PA 19116
Telephone: (215) 673-8315
Recruiter Classification: Contingency; **Lowest/Average
Salary:** $60,000/$75,000; **Industry Concentration:** Generalist
with a primary focus in Electronics, High Technology,
Information Technology; **Function Concentration:** Human
Resources

Koenig, Joel S. — *Partner*
Blackshaw, Olmstead, Lynch & Koenig
3414 Peachtree Road
Suite 1010
Atlanta, GA 30326
Telephone: (404) 261-7770
Lowest/Average Salary: $90,000/$90,000; **Industry
Concentration:** Generalist with a primary focus in Electronics,
High Technology, Information Technology; **Function
Concentration:** Generalist with a primary focus in
Finance/Accounting, General Management, Human Resources,
Marketing, Sales

Koenig, Joel S. — *Partner*
Blackshaw, Olmstead, Lynch & Koenig
10390 Santa Monica Boulevard
Suite 270
Los Angeles, CA 90025
Telephone: (310) 785-9123
Recruiter Classification: Retained; **Lowest/Average Salary:**
$90,000/$90,000; **Industry Concentration:** Generalist
with a primary focus in Electronics, High Technology,
Information Technology; **Function Concentration:**
Generalist with a primary focus in Finance/Accounting,
General Management, Human Resources, Marketing,
Sales

Kohn, Adam P. — *Vice President/Principle*
Christian & Timbers
25825 Science Park Drive, Suite 400
Cleveland, OH 44122
Telephone: (216) 765-5869
Recruiter Classification: Retained; **Lowest/Average Salary:**
$90,000/$90,000; **Industry Concentration:** Generalist with
a primary focus in Information Technology; **Function
Concentration:** Generalist with a primary focus
in Engineering, Finance/Accounting, General
Management, Human Resources, Marketing, Sales,
Women/Minorities

Kohonoski, Michael M. — *Principal*
The Guild Corporation
8260 Greensboro Drive, Suite 460
McLean, VA 22102
Telephone: (703) 761-4023
Recruiter Classification: Contingency; **Lowest/Average Salary:**
$40,000/$50,000; **Industry Concentration:** Electronics, High
Technology, Information Technology; **Function Concentration:**
Engineering, Finance/Accounting, General Management,
Research and Development

Kondra, Vernon J. — *Director Operations*
The Douglas Reiter Company, Inc.
1221 S.W. Yamhill, Suite 301A
Portland, OR 97205
Telephone: (503) 228-6916
Recruiter Classification: Executive Temporary;
Lowest/Average Salary: $75,000/$90,000; **Industry
Concentration:** Generalist with a primary focus in High
Technology; **Function Concentration:** Generalist with a
primary focus in Administration, Engineering,
Finance/Accounting, General Management, Human
Resources, Marketing

Koontz, Donald N. — *President*
Koontz, Jeffries & Associates, Inc.
18-22 Bank Street
Summit, NJ 07901
Telephone: (908) 598-1900
Recruiter Classification: Retained; **Lowest/Average Salary:**
$75,000/$90,000; **Industry Concentration:** Generalist with a
primary focus in Electronics, High Technology; **Function
Concentration:** Generalist with a primary focus in
Administration, Engineering, Finance/Accounting, General
Management, Human Resources, Marketing, Research and
Development, Sales, Women/Minorities

Kopec, Tom — *Consultant Information Systems
Search and Engineering*
D. Brown and Associates, Inc.
610 S.W. Alder, Suite 1111
Portland, OR 97205
Telephone: (503) 224-6860
Recruiter Classification: Contingency; **Lowest/Average Salary:**
$40,000/$60,000; **Industry Concentration:** Electronics, High
Technology, Information Technology; **Function Concentration:**
Engineering, Finance/Accounting

Kors, R. Paul — *President*
Kors Montgomery International
1980 Post Oak Boulevard, Suite 2280
Houston, TX 77056
Telephone: (713) 840-7101
Recruiter Classification: Retained; **Lowest/Average Salary:**
$90,000/$90,000; **Industry Concentration:** High Technology,
Information Technology; **Function Concentration:** Engineering,
General Management, Marketing, Research and Development,
Sales

Kossuth, David — *Vice President International*
Kossuth & Associates, Inc.
800 Bellevue Way N.E., Suite 400
Bellevue, WA 98004
Telephone: (206) 450-9050
Recruiter Classification: Retained; **Lowest/Average Salary:**
$50,000/$90,000; **Industry Concentration:** Electronics, High
Technology, Information Technology; **Function Concentration:**
Generalist with a primary focus in Engineering,
Finance/Accounting, General Management, Human Resources,
Marketing, Research and Development, Sales

Kossuth, Jane — *President*
Kossuth & Associates, Inc.
800 Bellevue Way N.E., Suite 400
Bellevue, WA 98004
Telephone: (206) 450-9050
Recruiter Classification: Retained; **Lowest/Average Salary:**
$75,000/$90,000; **Industry Concentration:** Electronics, High
Technology, Information Technology; **Function Concentration:**
Generalist with a primary focus in Engineering,
Finance/Accounting, General Management, Human Resources,
Marketing, Research and Development, Sales,
Women/Minorities

Kotick, Maddy — *Consultant*
The Stevenson Group of New Jersey
560 Sylvan Avenue
Englewood Cliffs, NJ 07632
Telephone: (201) 568-1900
Recruiter Classification: Retained; **Lowest/Average Salary:**
$75,000/$90,000; **Industry Concentration:** Generalist with a
primary focus in Information Technology; **Function
Concentration:** Generalist with a primary focus in
Finance/Accounting, General Management, Human Resources,
Marketing, Sales

Kouble, Tim — *Consultant*
Logix, Inc.
1601 Trapelo Road
Waltham, MA 02154
Telephone: (617) 890-0500
Recruiter Classification: Retained; **Lowest/Average Salary:**
$60,000/$75,000; **Industry Concentration:** High Technology,
Information Technology; **Function Concentration:** Engineering

Kouble, Tim — *Consultant*
Logix Partners
1601 Trapelo Road
Waltham, MA 02154
Telephone: (617) 890-0500
Recruiter Classification: Retained; **Lowest/Average Salary:**
$60,000/$75,000; **Industry Concentration:** High Technology,
Information Technology; **Function Concentration:** Engineering

Krecklo, Brian Douglas — *President*
Krecklo & Associates Inc.
Le Cartier, 1115 Sherbrooke Street West
Suite 2401
Montreal, Quebec, CANADA H3A 1H3
Telephone: (514) 281-9999
Recruiter Classification: Retained; **Lowest/Average Salary:**
$60,000/$75,000; **Industry Concentration:** Generalist with a
primary focus in Information Technology

Krejci, Stanley L. — *Managing Director and
Partner*
Boyden Washington, D.C.
2445 M Street N.W., Suite 250
Washington, DC 20037-1435
Telephone: (202) 342-7200
Recruiter Classification: Retained; **Lowest/Average Salary:**
$75,000/$90,000; **Industry Concentration:** Generalist with a
primary focus in Electronics, High Technology, Information
Technology; **Function Concentration:** Generalist with a
primary focus in Engineering, Finance/Accounting, General
Management, Human Resources, Marketing, Research and
Development, Sales, Women/Minorities

Kreutz, Gary L. — *President*
Kreutz Consulting Group, Inc.
585 North Bank Lane, Suite 2000
Lake Forest, IL 60045
Telephone: (847) 234-9115
Recruiter Classification: Retained; **Lowest/Average Salary:**
$75,000/$150,000; **Industry Concentration:** Generalist with a
primary focus in High Technology, Information Technology;
Function Concentration: Finance/Accounting, General
Management, Marketing, Research and Development,
Women/Minorities

Krieger, Dennis F. — *Managing Director*
Seiden Krieger Associates, Inc.
375 Park Avenue
New York, NY 10152
Telephone: (212) 688-8383
Recruiter Classification: Retained; **Lowest/Average Salary:**
$90,000/$90,000; **Industry Concentration:** Generalist with a
primary focus in Electronics, High Technology, Information
Technology; **Function Concentration:** Generalist with a
primary focus in Engineering, Finance/Accounting, General
Management, Human Resources, Marketing, Research and
Development, Sales, Women/Minorities

Krueger, Kurt — *President*
Krueger Associates
100 Skokie Boulevard
Wilmette, IL 60091
Telephone: (847) 853-0550
Recruiter Classification: Retained; **Lowest/Average Salary:**
$90,000/$90,000; **Industry Concentration:** Generalist with a
primary focus in Electronics, High Technology; **Function
Concentration:** Generalist with a primary focus in Engineering,
Finance/Accounting, General Management, Human Resources,
Marketing, Research and Development

Kuhl, Teresa — *Executive Recruiter*
Don Richard Associates of Tampa, Inc.
100 North Tampa Street, Suite 1925
Tampa, FL 33602
Telephone: (813) 221-7930
Recruiter Classification: Contingency, Executive Temporary;
Lowest/Average Salary: $20,000/$50,000; **Industry
Concentration:** Generalist with a primary focus in High
Technology; **Function Concentration:** Generalist with a
primary focus in Administration, Finance/Accounting, Human
Resources, Research and Development

Kunzer, William J. — *President*
Kunzer Associates, Ltd.
1415 West 22nd Street
Oak Brook, IL 60521
Telephone: (630) 574-0010
Recruiter Classification: Retained; **Lowest/Average Salary:**
$50,000/$90,000; **Industry Concentration:** Generalist with a
primary focus in Electronics, High Technology, Information
Technology; **Function Concentration:** Generalist with a
primary focus in Engineering, Finance/Accounting, General
Management, Human Resources, Marketing, Research and
Development, Sales

Kuo, Linda — *Senior Associate*
Montgomery Resources, Inc.
555 Montgomery Street, Suite 1650
San Francisco, CA 94111
Telephone: (415) 956-4242
Recruiter Classification: Contingency; **Lowest/Average Salary:**
$30,000/$60,000; **Industry Concentration:** High Technology;
Function Concentration: Finance/Accounting

Kurrigan, Geoffrey — *Partner*
ESA Professional Consultants
141 Durham Road
Suite 16
Madison, CT 06443
Telephone: (203) 245-1983
Recruiter Classification: Retained; **Lowest/Average Salary:**
$50,000/$75,000; **Industry Concentration:** Electronics, High
Technology, Information Technology; **Function Concentration:**
Engineering, General Management, Human Resources,
Marketing, Research and Development, Women/Minorities

Kussner, Janice N. — *Partner*
Herman Smith Executive Initiatives Inc.
161 Bay Street, Suite 3600
Box 629
Toronto, Ontario, CANADA M5J 2S1
Telephone: (416) 862-8830
Recruiter Classification: Retained; **Lowest/Average Salary:**
$60,000/$75,000; **Industry Concentration:** Generalist with a
primary focus in High Technology, Information Technology;
Function Concentration: Generalist with a primary focus in
Engineering, Finance/Accounting, General Management,
Human Resources, Marketing, Sales

La Chance, Ronald — *Associate*
Source Services Corporation
15600 N.W. 67th Avenue, Suite 210
Miami Lakes, FL 33014
Telephone: (305) 556-8000
Recruiter Classification: Contingency; **Lowest/Average Salary:**
$30,000/$50,000; **Industry Concentration:** Information
Technology; **Function Concentration:** Engineering,
Finance/Accounting

Laba, Marvin — *President*
Marvin Laba & Associates
6255 Sunset Boulevard, Suite 617
Los Angeles, CA 90028
Telephone: (213) 464-1355
Recruiter Classification: Retained; **Lowest/Average Salary:**
$50,000/$75,000; **Industry Concentration:** Generalist with a
primary focus in Information Technology; **Function
Concentration:** Generalist with a primary focus in
Finance/Accounting, General Management, Human Resources,
Marketing, Sales

Laba, Stuart M. — *Senior Vice President*
Marvin Laba & Associates
250 Ridgedale Avenue, Suite #A-1
Florham Park, NJ 07932
Telephone: (201) 966-2888
Recruiter Classification: Retained; **Lowest/Average Salary:**
$50,000/$90,000; **Industry Concentration:** Generalist with a
primary focus in Information Technology; **Function
Concentration:** Generalist with a primary focus in
Finance/Accounting, General Management, Human Resources,
Sales

Labrecque, Bernard F. — *Managing Partner*
Laurendeau Labrecque/Ray & Berndtson, Inc.
1250 West Rene-Levesque Boulevard
Suite 3925
Montreal, Quebec, CANADA H3B 4W8
Telephone: (514) 937-1000
Recruiter Classification: Retained; **Lowest/Average Salary:**
$75,000/$90,000; **Industry Concentration:** Generalist with a
primary focus in Electronics, High Technology, Information
Technology; **Function Concentration:** Finance/Accounting,
General Management, Human Resources, Marketing, Research
and Development, Sales

LaCharite, Danielle — *Office Manager*
The Guild Corporation
8260 Greensboro Drive, Suite 460
McLean, VA 22102
Telephone: (703) 761-4023
Recruiter Classification: Contingency; **Lowest/Average Salary:**
$40,000/$50,000; **Industry Concentration:** Electronics, High
Technology, Information Technology; **Function Concentration:**
Engineering, Finance/Accounting, General Management,
Research and Development

Lache, Shawn E. — *Associate*
The Arcus Group
100 North Central (At Main), Suite 1200
Dallas, TX 75201
Telephone: (214) 744-2100
Recruiter Classification: Retained; **Lowest/Average Salary:**
$90,000/$90,000; **Industry Concentration:** Generalist with a
primary focus in High Technology, Information Technology;
Function Concentration: Generalist with a primary focus in
Engineering, Finance/Accounting, General Management,
Marketing, Research and Development, Sales

Laderman, David — *Manager*
Romac & Associates
530 East Swedesford Road
Suite 202
Wayne, PA 19087
Telephone: (215) 687-6107
Recruiter Classification: Executive Temporary; **Lowest/Average Salary:** $60,000/$60,000; **Industry Concentration:** High Technology, Information Technology; **Function Concentration:** Finance/Accounting

Laird, Cheryl — *Executive Recruiter*
CPS Inc.
One Westbrook Corporate Centre, Suite 600
Westchester, IL 60154
Telephone: (708) 531-8370
Recruiter Classification: Contingency; **Lowest/Average Salary:** $30,000/$50,000; **Industry Concentration:** Generalist with a primary focus in Electronics, High Technology, Information Technology; **Function Concentration:** Engineering, Research and Development, Sales, Women/Minorities

Lamb, Angus K. — *Principal*
Raymond Karsan Associates
18 Commerce Way
Woburn, MA 01801
Telephone: (617) 932-0400
Recruiter Classification: Retained; **Lowest/Average Salary:** $30,000/$90,000; **Industry Concentration:** Generalist with a primary focus in Information Technology; **Function Concentration:** Generalist

Lamb, Lynn M. — *Executive Recruiter*
F-O-R-T-U-N-E Personnel Consultants of Huntsville, Inc.
3311 Bob Wallace Avenue, Suite 204
Huntsville, AL 35805
Telephone: (205) 534-7282
Recruiter Classification: Contingency, Executive Temporary; **Lowest/Average Salary:** $30,000/$75,000; **Industry Concentration:** Electronics, High Technology

Lambert, William — *Associate*
Source Services Corporation
525 Vine Street, Suite 2250
Cincinnati, OH 45202
Telephone: (513) 651-3303
Recruiter Classification: Contingency; **Lowest/Average Salary:** $30,000/$50,000; **Industry Concentration:** Information Technology; **Function Concentration:** Engineering, Finance/Accounting

Lamia, Michael — *Associate*
Source Services Corporation
15600 N.W. 67th Avenue, Suite 210
Miami Lakes, FL 33014
Telephone: (305) 556-8000
Recruiter Classification: Contingency; **Lowest/Average Salary:** $30,000/$50,000; **Industry Concentration:** Information Technology; **Function Concentration:** Engineering, Finance/Accounting

Lanctot, William D. — *Partner*
Corporate Resources Professional Placement
4205 Lancaster Lane, Suite 107
Plymouth, MN 55441
Telephone: (612) 550-9222
Recruiter Classification: Contingency; **Lowest/Average Salary:** $40,000/$60,000; **Industry Concentration:** Electronics, High Technology; **Function Concentration:** Engineering, Research and Development

Lang, Sharon A. — *Consultant*
Ray & Berndtson
Sears Tower, 233 South Wacker Drive, Suite 4020
Chicago, IL 60606-6310
Telephone: (312) 876-0730
Recruiter Classification: Retained; **Lowest/Average Salary:** $90,000/$90,000; **Industry Concentration:** Generalist with a primary focus in High Technology, Information Technology; **Function Concentration:** Generalist with a primary focus in Administration, Finance/Accounting, General Management, Human Resources, Marketing, Research and Development, Sales, Women/Minorities

Langan, Marion — *Consultant*
Logix, Inc.
1601 Trapelo Road
Waltham, MA 02154
Telephone: (617) 890-0500
Recruiter Classification: Retained; **Lowest/Average Salary:** $60,000/$75,000; **Industry Concentration:** High Technology, Information Technology; **Function Concentration:** Research and Development

Langan, Marion — *Consultant*
Logix Partners
1601 Trapelo Road
Waltham, MA 02154
Telephone: (617) 890-0500
Recruiter Classification: Retained; **Lowest/Average Salary:** $60,000/$75,000; **Industry Concentration:** High Technology, Information Technology; **Function Concentration:** Engineering

Langford, Matt — *Executive Recruiter*
F-O-R-T-U-N-E Personnel Consultants of Huntsville, Inc.
3311 Bob Wallace Avenue, Suite 204
Huntsville, AL 35805
Telephone: (205) 534-7282
Recruiter Classification: Contingency; **Lowest/Average Salary:** $30,000/$60,000; **Industry Concentration:** Electronics, High Technology; **Function Concentration:** Engineering, Finance/Accounting

Langford, Robert W. — *President*
F-O-R-T-U-N-E Personnel Consultants of Huntsville, Inc.
3311 Bob Wallace Avenue, Suite 204
Huntsville, AL 35805
Telephone: (205) 534-7282
Recruiter Classification: Contingency, Executive Temporary; **Lowest/Average Salary:** $30,000/$75,000; **Industry Concentration:** Electronics, High Technology; **Function Concentration:** Engineering, General Management, Marketing, Sales

Lapat, Aaron D. — *Associate*
J. Robert Scott
27 State Street
Boston, MA 02109
Telephone: (617) 720-2770
Recruiter Classification: Retained; **Lowest/Average Salary:** $75,000/$90,000; **Industry Concentration:** Generalist with a primary focus in Electronics, High Technology, Information Technology; **Function Concentration:** Generalist

LaPierre, Louis — *Managing Partner*
Romac & Associates
183 Middle Street, 3rd Floor
P.O. Box 7040
Portland, ME 04112
Telephone: (207) 773-4749
Recruiter Classification: Executive Temporary; **Lowest/Average Salary:** $60,000/$60,000; **Industry Concentration:** High Technology, Information Technology; **Function Concentration:** Finance/Accounting

Lapointe, Fabien — *Associate*
Source Services Corporation
1500 West Park Drive, Suite 390
Westborough, MA 01581
Telephone: (508) 366-2600
Recruiter Classification: Contingency; **Lowest/Average Salary:** $30,000/$50,000; **Industry Concentration:** Information Technology; **Function Concentration:** Engineering, Finance/Accounting

Lardner, Lucy D. — *Consultant*
Tully/Woodmansee International, Inc.
9 Woody Lane
Sparta, NJ 07871
Telephone: (201) 726-8645
Recruiter Classification: Retained; **Lowest/Average Salary:** $60,000/$90,000; **Industry Concentration:** Generalist with a primary focus in Electronics, Information Technology; **Function Concentration:** Generalist with a primary focus in Engineering, Finance/Accounting, General Management, Human Resources, Marketing, Research and Development, Sales

Larsen, Jack B. — *President*
Jack B. Larsen & Associates
334 West Eighth Street
Erie, PA 16502
Telephone: (814) 459-3725
Recruiter Classification: Executive Temporary; **Lowest/Average Salary:** $30,000/$50,000; **Industry Concentration:** Generalist with a primary focus in Electronics, High Technology; **Function Concentration:** Generalist with a primary focus in Engineering, Finance/Accounting, General Management, Human Resources, Sales

Lasher, Charles M. — *President*
Lasher Associates
1200 South Pine Island Road, Suite 370
Fort Lauderdale, FL 33324-4402
Telephone: (305) 472-5658
Recruiter Classification: Retained; **Lowest/Average Salary:** $75,000/$90,000; **Industry Concentration:** Generalist with a primary focus in Electronics, High Technology, Information Technology; **Function Concentration:** Generalist with a primary focus in Engineering, Finance/Accounting, General Management, Human Resources, Marketing, Research and Development, Sales

Laskin, Sandy — *Associate*
Source Services Corporation
925 Westchester Avenue, Suite 309
White Plains, NY 10604
Telephone: (914) 428-9100
Recruiter Classification: Contingency; **Lowest/Average Salary:** $30,000/$50,000; **Industry Concentration:** Information Technology; **Function Concentration:** Engineering, Finance/Accounting

Laub, Stuart R. — *President*
Abraham & London, Ltd.
7 Old Sherman Turnpike, Suite 209
Danbury, CT 06810
Telephone: (203) 730-4000
Recruiter Classification: Contingency, Executive Temporary; **Lowest/Average Salary:** $40,000/$75,000; **Industry Concentration:** High Technology, Information Technology; **Function Concentration:** Marketing, Sales

Lauderback, David R. — *Vice President*
A.T. Kearney, Inc.
1200 Bank One Center
600 Superior Avenue, East
Cleveland, OH 44114-2650
Telephone: (216) 241-6880
Recruiter Classification: Retained; **Lowest/Average Salary:** $90,000/$90,000; **Industry Concentration:** Generalist with a primary focus in High Technology; **Function Concentration:** Generalist with a primary focus in Finance/Accounting, General Management, Marketing, Sales

Lautz, Lindsay A. — *Partner*
Lautz Grotte Engler
One Bush Street, Suite 550
San Francisco, CA 94104
Telephone: (415) 834-3100
Recruiter Classification: Retained; **Lowest/Average Salary:** $90,000/$90,000; **Industry Concentration:** Generalist with a primary focus in Electronics, High Technology, Information Technology; **Function Concentration:** Generalist with a primary focus in Administration, Engineering, Finance/Accounting, General Management, Human Resources, Marketing, Sales, Women/Minorities

LaValle, Michael — *Managing Partner*
Romac & Associates
Two Piedmont Plaza, Suite 701
2000 West First Street
Winston-Salem, NC 27104-4206
Telephone: (919) 725-1933
Recruiter Classification: Executive Temporary; **Lowest/Average Salary:** $60,000/$60,000; **Industry Concentration:** High Technology, Information Technology; **Function Concentration:** Finance/Accounting

Laverty, William — *Associate*
Source Services Corporation
525 Vine Street, Suite 2250
Cincinnati, OH 45202
Telephone: (513) 651-3303
Recruiter Classification: Contingency; **Lowest/Average Salary:** $30,000/$50,000; **Industry Concentration:** Information Technology; **Function Concentration:** Engineering, Finance/Accounting

Lawner, Harvey — *President*
Walden Associates
1601 Trapelo Road
Waltham, MA 02154
Telephone: (617) 890-8885
Recruiter Classification: Retained; **Lowest/Average Salary:** $90,000/$90,000; **Industry Concentration:** High Technology, Information Technology; **Function Concentration:** General Management

Lazar, Miriam — *Associate*
Source Services Corporation
120 East Baltimore Street, Suite 1950
Baltimore, MD 21202
Telephone: (410) 727-4050
Recruiter Classification: Contingency; **Lowest/Average Salary:**
$30,000/$50,000; **Industry Concentration:** Information
Technology; **Function Concentration:** Engineering,
Finance/Accounting

Leahy, Jan — *Executive Recruiter*
CPS Inc.
One Westbrook Corporate Centre, Suite 600
Westchester, IL 60154
Telephone: (708) 531-8370
Recruiter Classification: Contingency; **Lowest/Average Salary:**
$30,000/$50,000; **Industry Concentration:** Generalist with a
primary focus in Electronics, High Technology, Information
Technology; **Function Concentration:** Engineering, Research
and Development, Sales, Women/Minorities

Leblanc, Danny — *Associate*
Source Services Corporation
5429 LBJ Freeway, Suite 275
Dallas, TX 75240
Telephone: (214) 387-1600
Recruiter Classification: Contingency; **Lowest/Average Salary:**
$30,000/$50,000; **Industry Concentration:** Information
Technology; **Function Concentration:** Engineering,
Finance/Accounting

LeComte, Andre — *Consultant*
Egon Zehnder International Inc.
1 Place Ville-Marie, Suite 3310
Montreal, Quebec, CANADA H3B 3N2
Telephone: (514) 876-4249
Recruiter Classification: Retained; **Lowest/Average Salary:**
$90,000/$90,000; **Industry Concentration:** Generalist with a
primary focus in High Technology; **Function Concentration:**
Generalist

Ledbetter, Charlene — *Managing Director*
Ledbetter/Davidson International, Inc.
101 Park Avenue
Suite 2508
New York, NY 10178
Telephone: (212) 687-6600
Recruiter Classification: Retained; **Lowest/Average Salary:**
$90,000/$90,000; **Industry Concentration:** High Technology;
Function Concentration: Finance/Accounting, General
Management, Human Resources, Marketing, Research and
Development, Sales

Ledbetter, Steven G. — *Executive Recruiter*
Cendea Connection International
13740 Research Boulevard
Building 0-1
Austin, TX 78750
Telephone: (512) 219-6000
Recruiter Classification: Retained; **Lowest/Average Salary:**
$75,000/$90,000; **Industry Concentration:** Generalist with a
primary focus in Electronics, High Technology, Information
Technology; **Function Concentration:** Generalist with a
primary focus in General Management, Marketing, Sales

Lee, Everett — *Associate*
Source Services Corporation
5429 LBJ Freeway, Suite 275
Dallas, TX 75240
Telephone: (214) 387-1600
Recruiter Classification: Contingency; **Lowest/Average Salary:**
$30,000/$50,000; **Industry Concentration:** Information
Technology; **Function Concentration:** Engineering,
Finance/Accounting

Lee, Janice — *Executive Recruiter*
Summerfield Associates, Inc.
6555 Quince Road, Suite 311
Memphis, TN 38119
Telephone: (901) 753-7068
Recruiter Classification: Contingency; **Lowest/Average Salary:**
$30,000/$40,000; **Industry Concentration:** Generalist with a
primary focus in Information Technology; **Function
Concentration:** Human Resources

Lee, Roger — *Partner*
Montgomery Resources, Inc.
555 Montgomery Street, Suite 1650
San Francisco, CA 94111
Telephone: (415) 956-4242
Recruiter Classification: Contingency, Executive Temporary;
Lowest/Average Salary: $30,000/$60,000; **Industry
Concentration:** Generalist with a primary focus in
High Technology; **Function Concentration:**
Finance/Accounting

Leff, Lisa A. — *President*
Berger and Leff
One Sansome Street, Ste. 2100
San Francisco, CA 94104
Telephone: (415) 951-4750
Recruiter Classification: Contingency; **Lowest/Average Salary:**
$40,000/$75,000; **Industry Concentration:** Generalist with a
primary focus in High Technology; **Function Concentration:**
Finance/Accounting

Leigh, Rebecca — *Associate*
Source Services Corporation
9020 Capital of Texas Highway
Building I, Suite 337
Austin, TX 78759
Telephone: (512) 345-7473
Recruiter Classification: Contingency; **Lowest/Average Salary:**
$30,000/$50,000; **Industry Concentration:** Information
Technology; **Function Concentration:** Engineering,
Finance/Accounting

Leighton, Mark — *Associate*
Source Services Corporation
1500 West Park Drive, Suite 390
Westborough, MA 01581
Telephone: (508) 366-2600
Recruiter Classification: Contingency; **Lowest/Average Salary:**
$30,000/$50,000; **Industry Concentration:** Information
Technology; **Function Concentration:** Engineering,
Finance/Accounting

Leininger, Dennis — *Executive Vice President/General Manager*
Key Employment Services
1001 Office Park Road, Suite 320
West Des Moines, IA 50265-2567
Telephone: (515) 224-0446
Recruiter Classification: Contingency; **Lowest/Average Salary:** $30,000/$75,000; **Industry Concentration:** Information Technology; **Function Concentration:** Engineering, Finance/Accounting, General Management, Human Resources, Marketing, Research and Development, Sales, Women/Minorities

Leland, Paul — *Vice President*
McInturff & Associates, Inc.
209 West Central Street
Natick, MA 01760
Telephone: (617) 237-0220
Recruiter Classification: Contingency; **Lowest/Average Salary:** $50,000/$50,000; **Industry Concentration:** Electronics, High Technology, Information Technology; **Function Concentration:** General Management

Lence, Julie Anne — *Unit Manager*
MSI International
201 St. Charles Avenue
Suite 2205
New Orleans, LA 70170
Telephone: (504) 522-6700
Recruiter Classification: Contingency; **Lowest/Average Salary:** $30,000/$60,000; **Industry Concentration:** Generalist with a primary focus in High Technology, Information Technology; **Function Concentration:** Generalist with a primary focus in Administration, Engineering, Finance/Accounting, General Management, Marketing, Sales

Lenkaitis, Lewis F. — *Vice President/Managing Director*
A.T. Kearney, Inc.
1200 Bank One Center
600 Superior Avenue, East
Cleveland, OH 44114-2650
Telephone: (216) 241-6880
Recruiter Classification: Retained; **Lowest/Average Salary:** $90,000/$90,000; **Industry Concentration:** Generalist with a primary focus in High Technology; **Function Concentration:** Generalist with a primary focus in Administration, Engineering, General Management, Human Resources, Marketing, Research and Development, Sales

Lennox, Charles — *Director*
Price Waterhouse
Suite 3000, Box 82 Royal Trust Tower
Toronto Dominion Centre
Toronto, Ontario, CANADA M5K 1G8
Telephone: (416) 863-1133
Recruiter Classification: Retained; **Lowest/Average Salary:** $60,000/$90,000; **Industry Concentration:** Generalist with a primary focus in High Technology, Information Technology; **Function Concentration:** Generalist

Leon, Jeffrey J. — *Managing Director*
Russell Reynolds Associates, Inc.
200 Park Avenue
New York, NY 10166-0002
Telephone: (212) 351-2000
Recruiter Classification: Retained; **Lowest/Average Salary:** $90,000/$90,000; **Industry Concentration:** Generalist with a primary focus in Information Technology; **Function Concentration:** Generalist

Letcher, Harvey D. — *Partner*
Sandhurst Associates
4851 LBJ Freeway, Suite 601
Dallas, TX 75244
Telephone: (214) 458-1212
Recruiter Classification: Retained; **Lowest/Average Salary:** $75,000/$90,000; **Industry Concentration:** Generalist with a primary focus in High Technology; **Function Concentration:** Generalist with a primary focus in Finance/Accounting, Human Resources, Marketing, Sales

Levenson, Laurel — *Managing Director*
Source Services Corporation
4510 Executive Drive, Suite 200
San Diego, CA 92121
Telephone: (619) 552-0300
Recruiter Classification: Contingency; **Lowest/Average Salary:** $30,000/$50,000; **Industry Concentration:** Information Technology; **Function Concentration:** Engineering, Finance/Accounting

Levine, Irwin — *Associate*
Source Services Corporation
2 Penn Plaza, Suite 1176
New York, NY 10121
Telephone: (212) 760-2200
Recruiter Classification: Contingency; **Lowest/Average Salary:** $30,000/$50,000; **Industry Concentration:** Information Technology; **Function Concentration:** Engineering, Finance/Accounting

Levitt, Muriel A. — *Regional Vice President*
D.S. Allen Associates, Inc.
28188 Moulton Pkwy., Ste. 820
Laguna Niguel, CA 92677
Telephone: (714) 360-4449
Recruiter Classification: Contingency; **Lowest/Average Salary:** $60,000/$90,000; **Industry Concentration:** High Technology, Information Technology; **Function Concentration:** Finance/Accounting, General Management, Marketing, Sales

Lewicki, Christopher — *Manager*
MSI International
8521 Leesburg Pike, Suite 435
Vienna, VA 22182
Telephone: (703) 893-5669
Recruiter Classification: Contingency; **Lowest/Average Salary:** $30,000/$60,000; **Industry Concentration:** Generalist with a primary focus in High Technology, Information Technology; **Function Concentration:** Administration, Engineering, Finance/Accounting, General Management, Marketing, Sales

Lewis, Daniel — *Associate*
Source Services Corporation
2000 Town Center, Suite 850
Southfield, MI 48075
Telephone: (810) 352-6520
Recruiter Classification: Contingency; **Lowest/Average Salary:** $30,000/$50,000; **Industry Concentration:** Information Technology; **Function Concentration:** Engineering, Finance/Accounting

Lewis, Gretchen S. — *Partner*
Heidrick & Struggles, Inc.
2740 Sand Hill Road
Menlo Park, CA 94025
Telephone: (415) 234-1500
Recruiter Classification: Retained; **Lowest/Average Salary:** $75,000/$90,000; **Industry Concentration:** Generalist with a primary focus in High Technology; **Function Concentration:** Generalist

Lewis, Jon A. — *Associate*
Sandhurst Associates
4851 LBJ Freeway, Suite 601
Dallas, TX 75244
Telephone: (212) 458-1212
Recruiter Classification: Retained; **Lowest/Average Salary:** $75,000/$90,000; **Industry Concentration:** Generalist with a primary focus in High Technology, Information Technology; **Function Concentration:** Generalist with a primary focus in Administration, Finance/Accounting, General Management, Human Resources, Marketing, Sales

Lewis, Marc D. — *Senior Vice President*
Handy HRM Corp.
250 Park Avenue
New York, NY 10177-0074
Telephone: (212) 557-0400
Recruiter Classification: Retained; **Lowest/Average Salary:** $90,000/$90,000; **Industry Concentration:** Generalist with a primary focus in High Technology; **Function Concentration:** Finance/Accounting, Women/Minorities

Lewis, Susan — *Consultant*
Logix Partners
1601 Trapelo Road
Waltham, MA 02154
Telephone: (617) 890-0500
Recruiter Classification: Retained; **Lowest/Average Salary:** $60,000/$75,000; **Industry Concentration:** High Technology; **Function Concentration:** Engineering

Lewis, Susan — *Consultant*
Logix, Inc.
1601 Trapelo Road
Waltham, MA 02154
Telephone: (617) 890-0500
Recruiter Classification: Retained; **Lowest/Average Salary:** $60,000/$75,000; **Industry Concentration:** High Technology; **Function Concentration:** Engineering

Lezama Cohen, Luis — *Partner*
Ray & Berndtson
Palo Santo No. 6
Colonia Lomas Altas
Mexico City, D.F., MEXICO 11950
Telephone: (525) 570-7462
Recruiter Classification: Retained; **Lowest/Average Salary:** $90,000/$90,000; **Industry Concentration:** Generalist with a primary focus in High Technology, Information Technology; **Function Concentration:** Generalist with a primary focus in Administration, Finance/Accounting, General Management, Human Resources, Marketing, Research and Development, Sales, Women/Minorities

Lichtenauer, Eric W. — *Counselor*
Britt Associates, Inc.
2709 Black Road
Joliet, IL 60435
Telephone: (815) 744-7200
Recruiter Classification: Contingency; **Lowest/Average Salary:** $40,000/$75,000; **Industry Concentration:** Electronics, High Technology, Information Technology

Lichtenauer, William E. — *President*
Britt Associates, Inc.
2709 Black Road
Joliet, IL 60435
Telephone: (815) 744-7200
Recruiter Classification: Contingency; **Lowest/Average Salary:** $40,000/$75,000; **Industry Concentration:** Electronics, High Technology, Information Technology

Lieberman, Beverly — *President*
Halbrecht Lieberman Associates, Inc.
1200 Summer Street
Stamford, CT 06905
Telephone: (203) 327-5630
Recruiter Classification: Retained; **Lowest/Average Salary:** $90,000/$90,000; **Industry Concentration:** High Technology, Information Technology; **Function Concentration:** Generalist

Liebross, Eric — *Associate*
Source Services Corporation
1 Gatehall Drive, Suite 250
Parsippany, NJ 07054
Telephone: (201) 267-3222
Recruiter Classification: Contingency; **Lowest/Average Salary:** $30,000/$50,000; **Industry Concentration:** Information Technology; **Function Concentration:** Engineering, Finance/Accounting

Lin, Felix — *Associate*
Source Services Corporation
879 West 190th Street, Suite 250
Los Angeles, CA 90248
Telephone: (310) 323-6633
Recruiter Classification: Contingency; **Lowest/Average Salary:** $30,000/$50,000; **Industry Concentration:** Information Technology; **Function Concentration:** Engineering, Finance/Accounting

Lindberg, Eric J. — *President and CEO*
MSI International
2500 Marquis One Tower
245 Peachtree Center Ave.
Atlanta, GA 30303
Telephone: (404) 659-5236
Recruiter Classification: Contingency; **Lowest/Average Salary:** $30,000/$60,000; **Industry Concentration:** Generalist with a primary focus in High Technology, Information Technology; **Function Concentration:** Generalist with a primary focus in Administration, Engineering, Finance/Accounting, General Management, Marketing, Sales

Lindenmuth, Mary — *Account Executive*
Search West, Inc.
750 The City Drive South
Suite 100
Orange, CA 92668-4940
Telephone: (714) 748-0400
Recruiter Classification: Contingency; **Lowest/Average Salary:** $40,000/$60,000; **Industry Concentration:** Electronics, High Technology; **Function Concentration:** Administration, Finance/Accounting, General Management

Lindholst, Kai — *Managing Partner*
Egon Zehnder International Inc.
One First National Plaza
21 South Clark Street, Suite 3300
Chicago, IL 60603-2006
Telephone: (312) 782-4500
Recruiter Classification: Retained; **Lowest/Average Salary:**
$90,000/$90,000; **Industry Concentration:** Generalist with a
primary focus in High Technology; **Function Concentration:**
Generalist

Lindsay, Mary — *Senior Associate*
Norm Sanders Associates
2 Village Court
Hazlet, NJ 07730
Telephone: (732) 264-3700
Recruiter Classification: Retained; **Lowest/Average Salary:**
$90,000/$90,000; **Industry Concentration:** Information
Technology; **Function Concentration:** Generalist

Line, Joseph T. — *Vice President*
Sharrow & Associates
24735 Van Dyke
Center Line, MI 48015
Telephone: (810) 759-6910
Recruiter Classification: Contingency; **Lowest/Average Salary:**
$30,000/$50,000; **Industry Concentration:** Electronics, High
Technology

Linton, Leonard M. — *President*
Byron Leonard International, Inc.
2659 Townsgate Road, Suite 100
Westlake Village, CA 91361
Telephone: (805) 373-7500
Recruiter Classification: Retained; **Lowest/Average Salary:**
$60,000/$90,000; **Industry Concentration:** Generalist with a
primary focus in Electronics, High Technology, Information
Technology; **Function Concentration:** Generalist with a
primary focus in Administration, Engineering,
Finance/Accounting, General Management, Human Resources,
Marketing, Research and Development, Sales

Lipe, Jerold L. — *Vice President*
Compass Group Ltd.
Two Mid-America Plaza, Suite 800 South
Oakbrook Terrace, IL 60181
Telephone: (630) 954-2255
Recruiter Classification: Retained; **Lowest/Average Salary:**
$75,000/$90,000; **Industry Concentration:** Electronics,
Information Technology; **Function Concentration:** Engineering,
General Management, Human Resources, Sales,
Women/Minorities

Lipson, Harriet — *Vice President*
Lipson & Co.
1900 Avenue of the Stars
Suite 2810
Los Angeles, CA 90067
Telephone: (310) 277-4646
Recruiter Classification: Retained; **Lowest/Average Salary:**
$75,000/$90,000; **Industry Concentration:** High Technology,
Information Technology; **Function Concentration:** General
Management, Marketing

Lipson, Harriet — *Senior Search Consultant*
First Interactive Recruiting Specialists
1900 Avenue of the Stars
Suite 2810
Los Angeles, CA 90067
Telephone: (310) 277-4646
Recruiter Classification: Retained; **Lowest/Average Salary:**
$90,000/$90,000; **Industry Concentration:** Electronics, High
Technology, Information Technology; **Function Concentration:**
Generalist with a primary focus in Engineering, General
Management, Marketing, Research and Development, Sales

Lipson, Howard K. — *Principal*
First Interactive Recruiting Specialists
1900 Avenue of the Stars
Suite 2810
Los Angeles, CA 90067
Telephone: (310) 277-4646
Recruiter Classification: Retained; **Lowest/Average Salary:**
$90,000/$90,000; **Industry Concentration:** High Technology,
Information Technology; **Function Concentration:** Generalist
with a primary focus in Engineering, General Management,
Marketing, Research and Development, Sales

Lipson, Howard R. — *President*
Lipson & Co.
1900 Avenue of the Stars
Suite 2810
Los Angeles, CA 90067
Telephone: (310) 277-4646
Recruiter Classification: Retained; **Lowest/Average Salary:**
$75,000/$90,000; **Industry Concentration:** High Technology,
Information Technology; **Function Concentration:** Generalist
with a primary focus in General Management, Marketing

Lipuma, Thomas — *Associate*
Source Services Corporation
1 Gatehall Drive, Suite 250
Parsippany, NJ 07054
Telephone: (201) 267-3222
Recruiter Classification: Contingency; **Lowest/Average Salary:**
$30,000/$50,000; **Industry Concentration:** Information
Technology; **Function Concentration:** Engineering,
Finance/Accounting

Little, Elizabeth A. — *Associate*
Financial Resource Associates, Inc.
105 West Orange Street
Altamonte Springs, FL 32714
Telephone: (407) 869-7000
Recruiter Classification: Contingency; **Lowest/Average Salary:**
$40,000/$60,000; **Industry Concentration:** Information
Technology; **Function Concentration:** Finance/Accounting,
Sales

Little, Suzaane — *Executive Recruiter*
Don Richard Associates of Tampa, Inc.
100 North Tampa Street, Suite 1925
Tampa, FL 33602
Telephone: (813) 221-7930
Recruiter Classification: Contingency, Executive Temporary;
Lowest/Average Salary: $20,000/$50,000; **Industry
Concentration:** Generalist with a primary focus in Information
Technology; **Function Concentration:** Generalist with a
primary focus in Administration, Finance/Accounting

Livingston, Peter R. — *President*
Livingston, Robert and Company Inc.
Two Greenwich Plaza
Greenwich, CT 06830
Telephone: (203) 622-4901
Recruiter Classification: Retained; **Lowest/Average Salary:**
$90,000/$90,000; **Industry Concentration:** Generalist with a
primary focus in High Technology; **Function Concentration:**
Generalist

Loeb, Stephen H. — *President*
Grant Cooper and Associates
795 Office Parkway, Suite 117
St. Louis, MO 63141
Telephone: (314) 567-4690
Recruiter Classification: Retained; **Lowest/Average Salary:**
$60,000/$90,000; **Industry Concentration:** Generalist with a
primary focus in Electronics; **Function Concentration:**
Generalist with a primary focus in Administration, Engineering,
Finance/Accounting, General Management, Human Resources,
Marketing, Sales

Loewenstein, Victor H. — *Managing Partner*
Egon Zehnder International Inc.
350 Park Avenue
New York, NY 10022
Telephone: (212) 838-9199
Recruiter Classification: Retained; **Lowest/Average Salary:**
$90,000/$90,000; **Industry Concentration:** Generalist with a
primary focus in High Technology; **Function Concentration:**
Generalist

Lofthouse, Cindy — *Executive Recruiter*
CPS Inc.
One Westbrook Corporate Centre, Suite 600
Westchester, IL 60154
Telephone: (708) 531-8370
Recruiter Classification: Contingency; **Lowest/Average Salary:**
$30,000/$50,000; **Industry Concentration:** Generalist with a
primary focus in Electronics, High Technology, Information
Technology; **Function Concentration:** Engineering, Research
and Development, Sales, Women/Minorities

Lokken, Karen — *Technical Recruiter*
A.E. Feldman Associates
445 Northern Boulevard
Great Neck, NY 11021
Telephone: (516) 466-4708
Recruiter Classification: Contingency; **Lowest/Average Salary:**
$60,000/$90,000; **Industry Concentration:** Generalist with a
primary focus in Electronics, High Technology, Information
Technology; **Function Concentration:** Generalist with a
primary focus in Administration, General Management,
Marketing, Sales

Lonergan, Mark W. — *Partner*
Heidrick & Struggles, Inc.
2740 Sand Hill Road
Menlo Park, CA 94025
Telephone: (415) 234-1500
Recruiter Classification: Retained; **Lowest/Average Salary:**
$75,000/$90,000; **Industry Concentration:** Generalist with a
primary focus in High Technology; **Function Concentration:**
Generalist

Long, Helga — *Partner and Managing Director -
Global Markets*
Horton International
420 Lexington Avenue, Suite 810
New York, NY 10170
Telephone: (212) 973-3780
Recruiter Classification: Retained; **Lowest/Average Salary:**
$90,000/$90,000; **Industry Concentration:** Generalist with a
primary focus in High Technology; **Function Concentration:**
Generalist with a primary focus in Finance/Accounting,
General Management, Human Resources, Marketing, Research
and Development, Sales, Women/Minorities

Long, John — *Associate*
Source Services Corporation
4200 West Cypress Street, Suite 101
Tampa, FL 33607
Telephone: (813) 879-2221
Recruiter Classification: Contingency; **Lowest/Average Salary:**
$30,000/$50,000; **Industry Concentration:** Information
Technology; **Function Concentration:** Engineering,
Finance/Accounting

Long, John P. — *Managing Director*
John J. Davis & Associates, Inc.
521 Fifth Avenue, Suite 1740
New York, NY 10175
Telephone: (212) 286-9489
Recruiter Classification: Retained; **Lowest/Average Salary:**
$90,000/$90,000; **Industry Concentration:** Information
Technology; **Function Concentration:** Generalist with a
primary focus in General Management

Long, Mark — *Associate*
Source Services Corporation
111 Monument Circle, Suite 3930
Indianapolis, IN 46204
Telephone: (317) 631-2900
Recruiter Classification: Contingency; **Lowest/Average Salary:**
$30,000/$50,000; **Industry Concentration:** Information
Technology; **Function Concentration:** Engineering,
Finance/Accounting

Long, Milt — *Associate*
William Guy & Associates
P.O. Box 57407
Sherman Oaks, CA 91413
Telephone: Unpublished
Recruiter Classification: Retained; **Lowest/Average Salary:**
$50,000/$90,000; **Industry Concentration:** Generalist with a
primary focus in Electronics, High Technology, Information
Technology; **Function Concentration:** Generalist with a
primary focus in Administration, Engineering, General
Management, Human Resources, Women/Minorities

Long, Thomas — *Consultant*
Egon Zehnder International Inc.
1 First Canadian Place
P.O. Box 179
Toronto, Ontario, CANADA M5X 1C7
Telephone: (416) 364-0222
Recruiter Classification: Retained; **Lowest/Average Salary:**
$90,000/$90,000; **Industry Concentration:** Generalist with a
primary focus in High Technology; **Function Concentration:**
Generalist

Long, William G. — *President*
McDonald, Long & Associates, Inc.
670 White Plains Road
Scarsdale, NY 10583
Telephone: (914) 723-5400
Recruiter Classification: Retained, Executive Temporary;
Lowest/Average Salary: $75,000/$90,000; **Industry
Concentration:** Generalist with a primary focus in Electronics,
High Technology, Information Technology; **Function
Concentration:** Generalist with a primary focus in
Administration, Engineering, Finance/Accounting, General
Management, Human Resources, Marketing, Sales,
Women/Minorities

Looney, Scott — *Managing Director*
A.E. Feldman Associates
445 Northern Boulevard
Great Neck, NY 11021
Telephone: (516) 466-4708
Recruiter Classification: Contingency; **Lowest/Average Salary:**
$60,000/$90,000; **Industry Concentration:** Generalist with a
primary focus in Electronics, High Technology, Information
Technology; **Function Concentration:** Generalist with a
primary focus in Administration, General Management,
Marketing, Sales

LoPresto, Robert L. — *President - High
Technology*
Rusher, Loscavio & LoPresto
2479 Bayshore Road, Suite 700
Palo Alto, CA 94303
Telephone: (415) 494-0883
Recruiter Classification: Retained; **Lowest/Average Salary:**
$90,000/$90,000; **Industry Concentration:** Electronics, High
Technology, Information Technology; **Function Concentration:**
Administration, Engineering, General Management, Marketing,
Research and Development, Sales

LoRusso, Steve — *Account Director*
Warren, Morris & Madison
2190 Carmel Valley Road
Del Mar, CA 92014
Telephone: (619) 481-3388
Recruiter Classification: Retained; **Lowest/Average Salary:**
$50,000/$75,000; **Industry Concentration:** High Technology;
Function Concentration: Generalist

Lotufo, Donald A. — *Managing Partner*
D.A.L. Associates, Inc.
2777 Summer Street
Stamford, CT 06905
Telephone: (203) 961-8777
Recruiter Classification: Retained; **Lowest/Average Salary:**
$75,000/$90,000; **Industry Concentration:** Generalist with a
primary focus in Electronics, High Technology, Information
Technology; **Function Concentration:** Generalist with a
primary focus in Administration, Engineering,
Finance/Accounting, General Management, Human Resources,
Marketing, Research and Development, Sales

Lotz, R. James — *Chairman*
International Management Advisors, Inc.
516 Fifth Avenue
New York, NY 10036-7501
Telephone: (212) 758-7770
Recruiter Classification: Retained; **Lowest/Average Salary:**
$75,000/$90,000; **Industry Concentration:** Generalist with a
primary focus in Electronics, High Technology; **Function
Concentration:** Generalist with a primary focus in Engineering,
Finance/Accounting, General Management, Human Resources,
Marketing, Research and Development, Women/Minorities

Louden, Leo — *Software Quality Assurance
Recruiter*
Winter, Wyman & Company
950 Winter Street, Suite 3100
Waltham, MA 02154-1294
Telephone: (617) 890-7000
Recruiter Classification: Contingency; **Lowest/Average Salary:**
$40,000/$75,000; **Industry Concentration:** Information
Technology; **Function Concentration:** Generalist

Lovas, W. Carl — *Managing Partner*
Ray & Berndtson/Lovas Stanley
Royal Bank Plaza, South Tower, Suite 3150
200 Bay Street, P.O. Box 125
Toronto, Ontario, CANADA M5J 2J3
Telephone: (416) 366-1990
Recruiter Classification: Retained; **Lowest/Average Salary:**
$90,000/$90,000; **Industry Concentration:** Generalist with a
primary focus in High Technology; **Function Concentration:**
Generalist with a primary focus in Finance/Accounting,
General Management

Love, David M. — *Partner*
Ray & Berndtson
Texas Commerce Tower
2200 Ross Avenue, Suite 4500W
Dallas, TX 75201
Telephone: (214) 969-7620
Recruiter Classification: Retained; **Lowest/Average Salary:**
$90,000/$90,000; **Industry Concentration:** High Technology;
Function Concentration: Generalist

Lovely, Edward — *Senior Vice President*
The Stevenson Group of New Jersey
560 Sylvan Avenue
Englewood Cliffs, NJ 07632
Telephone: (201) 568-1900
Recruiter Classification: Retained; **Lowest/Average Salary:**
$75,000/$90,000; **Industry Concentration:** Generalist with a
primary focus in Information Technology; **Function
Concentration:** Generalist with a primary focus in
Finance/Accounting, General Management, Human Resources,
Marketing, Sales

Loving, Vikki — *President*
Intersource, Ltd.
72 Sloan Street
Roswell, GA 30075
Telephone: (770) 645-0015
Recruiter Classification: Retained; **Lowest/Average Salary:**
$90,000/$90,000; **Industry Concentration:** Generalist with a
primary focus in Electronics, High Technology, Information
Technology; **Function Concentration:** Finance/Accounting,
Human Resources, Women/Minorities

Lucarelli, Joan — *Vice President and Principal*
The Onstott Group, Inc.
60 William Street
Wellesley, MA 02181
Telephone: (781) 235-3050
Recruiter Classification: Retained; **Lowest/Average Salary:**
$90,000/$90,000; **Industry Concentration:** Generalist with a
primary focus in High Technology, Information Technology;
Function Concentration: Generalist with a primary focus in
Engineering, Finance/Accounting, General Management,
Human Resources, Marketing, Research and Development,
Sales, Women/Minorities

Lucas, Ronnie L. — *Manager*
MSI International
5215 North O'Connor Boulevard
Suite 1875
Irving, TX 75039
Telephone: (214) 869-3939
Recruiter Classification: Contingency; **Lowest/Average Salary:**
$30,000/$75,000; **Industry Concentration:** Generalist with a
primary focus in High Technology, Information Technology;
Function Concentration: Generalist with a primary focus in
Administration, Engineering, Finance/Accounting, General
Management, Marketing, Sales

Luce, Daniel — *Managing Director*
Source Services Corporation
520 Post Oak Boulevard, Suite 700
Houston, TX 77027
Telephone: (713) 439-1077
Recruiter Classification: Contingency; **Lowest/Average Salary:**
$30,000/$50,000; **Industry Concentration:** Information
Technology; **Function Concentration:** Engineering,
Finance/Accounting

Lucht, John — *President*
The John Lucht Consultancy Inc.
The Olympic Tower
641 Fifth Avenue
New York, NY 10022
Telephone: (212) 935-4660
Recruiter Classification: Retained; **Lowest/Average Salary:**
$150,000/$150,000; **Industry Concentration:** Generalist with a
primary focus in Electronics, High Technology, Information
Technology; **Function Concentration:** Generalist with a
primary focus in Administration, Engineering,
Finance/Accounting, General Management, Human Resources,
Marketing, Research and Development, Sales,
Women/Minorities

Ludder, Mark — *Associate*
Source Services Corporation
8614 Westwood Center, Suite 750
Vienna, VA 22182
Telephone: (703) 790-5610
Recruiter Classification: Contingency; **Lowest/Average Salary:**
$30,000/$50,000; **Industry Concentration:** Information
Technology; **Function Concentration:** Engineering,
Finance/Accounting

Ludlow, Michael — *Associate*
Source Services Corporation
One Park Plaza, Suite 560
Irvine, CA 92714
Telephone: (714) 660-1666
Recruiter Classification: Contingency; **Lowest/Average Salary:**
$30,000/$50,000; **Industry Concentration:** Information
Technology; **Function Concentration:** Engineering,
Finance/Accounting

Luke, A. Wayne — *Managing Partner*
Heidrick & Struggles, Inc.
One Peachtree Center
303 Peachtree Street, NE, Suite 3100
Atlanta, GA 30308
Telephone: (404) 577-2410
Recruiter Classification: Retained; **Lowest/Average Salary:**
$75,000/$90,000; **Industry Concentration:** Generalist with a
primary focus in High Technology; **Function Concentration:**
Generalist

Lumsby, George N. — *Senior Consultant*
International Management Advisors, Inc.
516 Fifth Avenue
New York, NY 10036-7501
Telephone: (212) 758-7770
Recruiter Classification: Retained; **Lowest/Average Salary:**
$75,000/$90,000; **Industry Concentration:** Generalist with a
primary focus in Electronics, High Technology; **Function
Concentration:** Generalist with a primary focus in
Engineering, Finance/Accounting, General Management,
Human Resources, Marketing, Research and Development,
Women/Minorities

Lundy, Martin — *Associate*
Source Services Corporation
20 Burlington Mall Road, Suite 405
Burlington, MA 01803
Telephone: (617) 272-5000
Recruiter Classification: Contingency; **Lowest/Average Salary:**
$30,000/$50,000; **Industry Concentration:** Information
Technology; **Function Concentration:** Engineering,
Finance/Accounting

Luntz, Charles E. — *President*
Charles Luntz & Associates. Inc.
14323 South Outer 40 Drive
Suite 400 South
Chesterfield, MO 63017-5734
Telephone: (314) 275-7992
Recruiter Classification: Retained; **Lowest/Average Salary:**
$40,000/$75,000; **Industry Concentration:** Generalist with a
primary focus in High Technology; **Function Concentration:**
Generalist with a primary focus in Administration, Engineering,
Finance/Accounting, General Management, Human Resources,
Marketing, Research and Development, Sales,
Women/Minorities

Lupica, Anthony — *Search Consultant*
Cochran, Cochran & Yale, Inc.
1333 W. 120th Avenue, Suite 311
Westminster, CO 80234
Telephone: (303) 252-4600
Recruiter Classification: Retained; **Lowest/Average Salary:**
$50,000/$75,000; **Industry Concentration:** Generalist with
a primary focus in High Technology, Information
Technology; **Function Concentration:** Generalist with a
primary focus in Engineering, Finance/Accounting, General
Management, Human Resources, Marketing, Sales,
Women/Minorities

Lyon, Jenny — *Vice President*
Marra Peters & Partners
10612 Providence Road, Suite 305
Charlotte, NC 28277
Telephone: (704) 841-8000
Recruiter Classification: Retained; **Average Salary:** $90,000;
Industry Concentration: Generalist with a primary focus
in Information Technology; **Function Concentration:**
Generalist with a primary focus in Administration,
Engineering, Finance/Accounting, General Management,
Human Resources, Marketing, Research and Development,
Sales

Lyons, J. David — *Managing Director*
Aubin International Inc.
281 Winter Street, #380
Waltham, MA 02154
Telephone: (617) 890-1722
Recruiter Classification: Retained; **Lowest/Average Salary:**
$90,000/$90,000; **Industry Concentration:** Generalist with a
primary focus in High Technology, Information Technology;
Function Concentration: Generalist with a primary focus in
Engineering, Finance/Accounting, General Management,
Human Resources, Marketing, Research and Development,
Sales

Lyons, Michael — *Associate*
Source Services Corporation
4510 Executive Drive, Suite 200
San Diego, CA 92121
Telephone: (619) 552-0300
Recruiter Classification: Contingency; **Lowest/Average Salary:**
$30,000/$50,000; **Industry Concentration:** Information
Technology; **Function Concentration:** Engineering,
Finance/Accounting

Macdonald, G. William — *President*
The Macdonald Group, Inc.
301 Route 17, Suite 800
Rutherford, NJ 07070
Telephone: (201) 939-2312
Recruiter Classification: Retained; **Lowest/Average Salary:**
$75,000/$90,000; **Industry Concentration:** Generalist with a
primary focus in High Technology, Information Technology;
Function Concentration: Generalist with a primary focus in
General Management, Human Resources, Research and
Development

MacDougall, Andrew J. — *Managing Director*
Spencer Stuart
One University Avenue
Suite 801
Toronto, Ontario, CANADA M5J 2P1
Telephone: (416) 361-0311
Recruiter Classification: Retained; **Lowest/Average Salary:**
$90,000/$90,000; **Industry Concentration:** High Technology,
Information Technology; **Function Concentration:** Generalist

MacEachern, David — *Director*
Spencer Stuart
One University Avenue
Suite 801
Toronto, Ontario, CANADA M5J 2P1
Telephone: (416) 361-0311
Recruiter Classification: Retained; **Lowest/Average Salary:**
$60,000/$75,000; **Industry Concentration:** Generalist with a
primary focus in Information Technology; **Function
Concentration:** Generalist with a primary focus in Engineering,
General Management, Human Resources

Mackenna, Kathy — *Consultant*
Plummer & Associates, Inc.
65 Rowayton Avenue
Rowayton, CT 06853
Telephone: (203) 899-1233
Recruiter Classification: Retained; **Lowest/Average Salary:**
$90,000/$90,000; **Industry Concentration:** Generalist with a
primary focus in Electronics; **Function Concentration:**
Generalist with a primary focus in Administration,
Finance/Accounting, General Management, Human Resources,
Marketing

MacKinnon, Helen — *President*
Technical Connections Inc.
11400 Olympic Boulevard, Suite 770
Los Angeles, CA 90064
Telephone: (310) 479-8830
Recruiter Classification: Contingency; **Lowest/Average Salary:**
$40,000/$60,000; **Industry Concentration:** High Technology,
Information Technology

MacMillan, James — *Associate*
Source Services Corporation
100 North Tryon Street, Suite 3130
Charlotte, NC 28202
Telephone: (704) 333-8311
Recruiter Classification: Contingency; **Lowest/Average Salary:**
$30,000/$50,000; **Industry Concentration:** Information
Technology; **Function Concentration:** Engineering,
Finance/Accounting

MacNaughton, Sperry — *President and Principal*
McNaughton Associates
3600 Lime Street, Suite 323
Riverside, CA 92501
Telephone: (909) 788-4951
Recruiter Classification: Retained; **Lowest/Average Salary:**
$60,000/$90,000; **Industry Concentration:** Generalist with a
primary focus in Electronics, High Technology, Information
Technology; **Function Concentration:** Generalist with a
primary focus in Administration, Engineering,
Finance/Accounting, Human Resources, Marketing, Sales,
Women/Minorities

MacPherson, Holly — *Associate*
Source Services Corporation
425 California Street, Suite 1200
San Francisco, CA 94104
Telephone: (415) 434-2410
Recruiter Classification: Contingency; **Lowest/Average Salary:**
$30,000/$50,000; **Industry Concentration:** Information
Technology; **Function Concentration:** Engineering,
Finance/Accounting

Macrides, Michael — *Associate*
Source Services Corporation
20 Burlington Mall Road, Suite 405
Burlington, MA 01803
Telephone: (617) 272-5000
Recruiter Classification: Contingency; **Lowest/Average Salary:**
$30,000/$50,000; **Industry Concentration:** Information
Technology; **Function Concentration:** Engineering,
Finance/Accounting

Mader, Stephen P. — *Vice President*
Christian & Timbers
24 New England Executive Park
Burlington, MA 01803
Telephone: (617) 229-9515
Recruiter Classification: Retained; **Lowest/Average Salary:**
$90,000/$90,000; **Industry Concentration:** Electronics, High
Technology, Information Technology; **Function Concentration:**
Generalist with a primary focus in Engineering,
Finance/Accounting, General Management, Marketing,
Research and Development, Sales

Magee, Harrison R. — *Vice President*
Bowden & Company, Inc.
5000 Rockside Road, Suite 550
Cleveland, OH 44131
Telephone: (216) 447-1800
Recruiter Classification: Retained; **Lowest/Average Salary:**
$90,000/$90,000; **Industry Concentration:** Generalist with a
primary focus in High Technology, Information Technology;
Function Concentration: Generalist

Maggio, Mary — *Associate*
Source Services Corporation
925 Westchester Avenue, Suite 309
White Plains, NY 10604
Telephone: (914) 428-9100
Recruiter Classification: Contingency; **Lowest/Average Salary:**
$30,000/$50,000; **Industry Concentration:** Information
Technology; **Function Concentration:** Engineering,
Finance/Accounting

Maglio, Charles J. — *President*
Maglio and Company, Inc.
450 N. Sunny Slope Road
Brookfield, WI 53005
Telephone: (414) 784-6020
Recruiter Classification: Retained; **Lowest/Average Salary:**
$50,000/$90,000; **Industry Concentration:** Generalist with a
primary focus in Electronics, High Technology, Information
Technology; **Function Concentration:** Generalist with a
primary focus in Engineering, Finance/Accounting, General
Management, Human Resources, Marketing, Research and
Development, Sales

Mahaney, Joann — *Consultant*
Heidrick & Struggles, Inc.
2740 Sand Hill Road
Menlo Park, CA 94025
Telephone: (415) 234-1500
Recruiter Classification: Retained; **Lowest/Average Salary:**
$75,000/$90,000; **Industry Concentration:** Generalist with a
primary focus in High Technology; **Function Concentration:**
Generalist

Mahmoud, Sophia — *Associate*
Source Services Corporation
425 California Street, Suite 1200
San Francisco, CA 94104
Telephone: (415) 434-2410
Recruiter Classification: Contingency; **Lowest/Average Salary:**
$30,000/$50,000; **Industry Concentration:** Information
Technology; **Function Concentration:** Engineering,
Finance/Accounting

Mairn, Todd — *Associate*
Source Services Corporation
161 Ottawa NW, Suite 409D
Grand Rapids, MI 49503
Telephone: (616) 451-2400
Recruiter Classification: Contingency; **Lowest/Average Salary:**
$30,000/$50,000; **Industry Concentration:** Information
Technology; **Function Concentration:** Engineering,
Finance/Accounting

Major, Susan — *Vice President*
A.T. Kearney, Inc.
222 West Adams Street
Chicago, IL 60606
Telephone: (312) 648-0111
Recruiter Classification: Retained; **Lowest/Average Salary:**
$90,000/$90,000; **Industry Concentration:** Generalist with a
primary focus in High Technology, Information Technology;
Function Concentration: Generalist with a primary focus in
Engineering, Finance/Accounting, General Management

Makrianes, James K. — *Managing Director*
Webb, Johnson Associates, Inc.
280 Park Avenue, 43rd Floor
New York, NY 10017
Telephone: (212) 661-3700
Recruiter Classification: Retained; **Lowest/Average Salary:**
$90,000/$90,000; **Industry Concentration:** Generalist with a
primary focus in High Technology; **Function Concentration:**
Generalist

Malcolm, Rod — *Vice President*
Korn/Ferry International
Scotia Plaza
40 King Street West
Toronto, Ontario, CANADA M5H 3Y2
Telephone: (416) 366-1300
Recruiter Classification: Retained; **Lowest/Average Salary:**
$100,000/$150,000; **Industry Concentration:** Generalist with a
primary focus in Information Technology; **Function
Concentration:** Generalist

Mallin, Ellen — *Vice President*
Howard Fischer Associates, Inc.
1800 John F. Kennedy Boulevard, 7th Floor
Philadelphia, PA 19103
Telephone: (215) 568-8363
Recruiter Classification: Retained; **Lowest/Average Salary:**
$90,000/$90,000; **Industry Concentration:** Generalist with a
primary focus in High Technology; **Function Concentration:**
Generalist with a primary focus in Administration,
Finance/Accounting, General Management, Human Resources,
Marketing, Research and Development, Sales,
Women/Minorities

Manassero, Henri J.P. — *Partner Hospitality*
International Management Advisors, Inc.
516 Fifth Avenue
New York, NY 10036-7501
Telephone: (212) 758-7770
Recruiter Classification: Retained; **Lowest/Average Salary:**
$75,000/$90,000; **Industry Concentration:** Generalist with a
primary focus in Electronics, High Technology; **Function
Concentration:** Generalist with a primary focus in Engineering,
Finance/Accounting, General Management, Human Resources,
Marketing, Research and Development, Women/Minorities

Mangum, Maria — *Vice President*
Thomas Mangum Company
1655 Hastings Ranch Drive
Pasadena, CA 91107
Telephone: (818) 351-0866
Recruiter Classification: Retained; **Lowest/Average Salary:**
$75,000/$100,000; **Industry Concentration:** Generalist with a
primary focus in Electronics, High Technology, Information
Technology; **Function Concentration:** Generalist with a
primary focus in Administration, Engineering,
Finance/Accounting, General Management, Human Resources,
Marketing, Research and Development

Mangum, William T. — *President*
Thomas Mangum Company
1655 Hastings Ranch Drive
Pasadena, CA 91107
Telephone: (818) 351-0866
Recruiter Classification: Retained; **Lowest/Average Salary:**
$75,000/$100,000; **Industry Concentration:** Generalist with a
primary focus in Electronics, High Technology, Information
Technology; **Function Concentration:** Generalist with a
primary focus in Administration, Engineering,
Finance/Accounting, General Management, Human Resources,
Marketing, Research and Development

Manns, Alex — *Executive Recruiter*
Crawford & Crofford
15327 NW 60th Avenue, Suite 240
Miami Lakes, FL 33014
Telephone: (305) 820-0855
Recruiter Classification: Contingency; **Lowest/Average Salary:**
$20,000/$50,000; **Industry Concentration:** Generalist with a
primary focus in Electronics, High Technology, Information
Technology; **Function Concentration:** Generalist with a
primary focus in Administration, Engineering,
Finance/Accounting, General Management, Human Resources,
Marketing, Sales

Mansford, Keith — *Chairman Bio-Pharmaceutical
Division*
Howard Fischer Associates, Inc.
1800 John F. Kennedy Boulevard, 7th Floor
Philadelphia, PA 19103
Telephone: (215) 568-8363
Recruiter Classification: Retained; **Lowest/Average Salary:**
$90,000/$90,000; **Industry Concentration:** High
Technology, Information Technology; **Function
Concentration:** Generalist with a primary focus in
Administration, Finance/Accounting, General Management,
Human Resources, Marketing, Research and Development,
Sales, Women/Minorities

Manzo, Renee — *Consultant*
Atlantic Search Group, Inc.
One Liberty Square
Boston, MA 02109
Telephone: (617) 426-9700
Recruiter Classification: Contingency; **Lowest/Average Salary:**
$20,000/$60,000; **Industry Concentration:** Generalist with a
primary focus in Electronics, Information Technology; **Function
Concentration:** Finance/Accounting

Maphet, Harriet — *Vice President*
The Stevenson Group of New Jersey
560 Sylvan Avenue
Englewood Cliffs, NJ 07632
Telephone: (201) 568-1900
Recruiter Classification: Retained; **Lowest/Average Salary:**
$75,000/$90,000; **Industry Concentration:** Generalist with a
primary focus in Information Technology; **Function
Concentration:** Generalist with a primary focus in
Finance/Accounting, General Management, Human Resources,
Marketing, Sales

Marcine, John W. — *Recruiter*
Keith Bagg & Associates Inc.
85 Richmond St., W., Ste. 700
Toronto, Ontario, CANADA M5H 2C9
Telephone: (416) 863-1800
Recruiter Classification: Contingency; **Lowest/Average Salary:**
$30,000/$75,000; **Industry Concentration:** Electronics, High
Technology, Information Technology; **Function Concentration:**
General Management, Marketing, Sales

Marino, Chester — *Manager*
Cochran, Cochran & Yale, Inc.
1333 W. 120th Avenue, Suite 311
Westminster, CO 80234
Telephone: (303) 252-4600
Recruiter Classification: Retained; **Lowest/Average Salary:**
$50,000/$75,000; **Industry Concentration:** Generalist with a
primary focus in High Technology, Information Technology;
Function Concentration: Generalist with a primary focus in
Engineering, Finance/Accounting, General Management,
Human Resources, Marketing, Sales, Women/Minorities

Marino, Jory J. — *Managing Director*
Sullivan & Company
20 Exchange Place, 50th Floor
New York, NY 10005
Telephone: (212) 422-3000
Recruiter Classification: Retained; **Lowest/Average Salary:**
$90,000/$90,000; **Industry Concentration:** Generalist with a
primary focus in Information Technology; **Function
Concentration:** Generalist

Marion, Michael — *Recruiter*
S.D. Kelly & Associates, Inc.
990 Washington Street
Dedham, MA 02026
Telephone: (617) 326-8038
Recruiter Classification: Contingency; **Lowest/Average Salary:**
$50,000/$60,000; **Industry Concentration:** Electronics, High
Technology; **Function Concentration:** Engineering, General
Management, Marketing, Sales

Mark, John L. — *Principal*
J.L. Mark Associates, Inc.
2000 Arapahoe Street, Suite 505
Denver, CO 80205
Telephone: (303) 292-0360
Recruiter Classification: Retained; **Lowest/Average Salary:**
$60,000/$90,000; **Industry Concentration:** Generalist with a
primary focus in High Technology, Information Technology;
Function Concentration: Generalist with a primary focus in
Administration, Finance/Accounting, General Management,
Human Resources, Marketing, Research and Development,
Sales, Women/Minorities

Mark, Lynne — *Partner*
J.L. Mark Associates, Inc.
2000 Arapahoe Street, Suite 505
Denver, CO 80205
Telephone: (303) 292-0360
Recruiter Classification: Retained; **Lowest/Average Salary:**
$60,000/$90,000; **Industry Concentration:** Generalist with a
primary focus in High Technology, Information Technology;
Function Concentration: Generalist with a primary focus in
Administration, Finance/Accounting, General Management,
Human Resources, Marketing, Research and Development,
Sales, Women/Minorities

Marks, Ira — *Principal*
Strategic Alternatives
3 Portola Road
Portola Valley, CA 94028
Telephone: (415) 851-2211
Recruiter Classification: Retained; **Lowest/Average Salary:**
$75,000/$90,000; **Industry Concentration:** Generalist with a
primary focus in Electronics, High Technology, Information
Technology; **Function Concentration:** Generalist with a
primary focus in Engineering, General Management,
Marketing, Research and Development, Sales,
Women/Minorities

Marks, Russell E. — *Managing Director*
Webb, Johnson Associates, Inc.
280 Park Avenue, 43rd Floor
New York, NY 10017
Telephone: (212) 661-3700
Recruiter Classification: Retained; **Lowest/Average Salary:**
$90,000/$90,000; **Industry Concentration:** Generalist with a
primary focus in High Technology; **Function Concentration:**
Generalist with a primary focus in Administration, Engineering,
Finance/Accounting, General Management, Human Resources,
Marketing, Research and Development, Sales

Marlow, William — *Vice President Technology*
Straube Associates
Willows Professional Park
855 Turnpike Street
North Andover, MA 01845-6105
Telephone: (508) 687-1993
Recruiter Classification: Retained; **Lowest/Average Salary:**
$60,000/$90,000; **Industry Concentration:** Generalist with a
primary focus in Electronics, High Technology; **Function
Concentration:** Generalist with a primary focus in Engineering,
Finance/Accounting, General Management, Human Resources,
Marketing, Women/Minorities

Marra, John — *Partner*
Marra Peters & Partners
Millburn Esplanade
Millburn, NJ 07041
Telephone: (201) 376-8999
Recruiter Classification: Retained; **Average Salary:** $90,000;
Industry Concentration: Generalist with a primary focus in
Information Technology; **Function Concentration:** Generalist
with a primary focus in Administration, Engineering,
Finance/Accounting, General Management, Human Resources,
Marketing, Research and Development, Sales

Marra, John — *Partner*
Marra Peters & Partners
7040 West Palmetto Park Road, Suite 145
Boca Raton, FL 33433
Telephone: (407) 347-7778
Recruiter Classification: Retained; **Average Salary:** $90,000;
Industry Concentration: Generalist with a primary focus in
Information Technology; **Function Concentration:** Generalist
with a primary focus in Administration, Engineering,
Finance/Accounting, General Management, Human Resources,
Marketing, Research and Development, Sales

Martin, David — *Associate*
The Guild Corporation
8260 Greensboro Drive, Suite 460
McLean, VA 22102
Telephone: (703) 761-4023
Recruiter Classification: Contingency; **Lowest/Average Salary:**
$40,000/$50,000; **Industry Concentration:** Electronics, High
Technology, Information Technology; **Function Concentration:**
Generalist with a primary focus in Engineering,
Finance/Accounting, General Management, Research and
Development

Martin, Jon — *Consultant*
Egon Zehnder International Inc.
1 First Canadian Place
P.O. Box 179
Toronto, Ontario, CANADA M5X 1C7
Telephone: (416) 364-0222
Recruiter Classification: Retained; **Lowest/Average Salary:**
$90,000/$90,000; **Industry Concentration:** Generalist with a
primary focus in High Technology; **Function Concentration:**
Generalist

Martin, Lois G. — *President*
The Martin Group
508 Bridle Court
Walnut Creek, CA 94596
Telephone: (510) 942-2550
Recruiter Classification: Retained; **Lowest/Average Salary:**
$75,000/$90,000; **Industry Concentration:** Information
Technology; **Function Concentration:** Finance/Accounting,
General Management, Human Resources

Martin, Malcolm — *Senior Consultant*
Paul-Tittle Associates, Inc.
1485 Chain Bridge Road, #304
McLean, VA 22101
Telephone: (703) 442-0500
Recruiter Classification: Retained; **Lowest/Average Salary:**
$60,000/$75,000; **Industry Concentration:** Information
Technology; **Function Concentration:** Engineering

Martin, Timothy P. — *Chief Executive Officer*
The Martin Group
508 Bridle Court
Walnut Creek, CA 94596
Telephone: (510) 942-2550
Recruiter Classification: Retained; **Lowest/Average Salary:**
$75,000/$90,000; **Industry Concentration:** Information
Technology; **Function Concentration:** Finance/Accounting,
General Management, Human Resources

Marumoto, William H. — *Managing Director and
Partner*
Boyden Washington, D.C.
2445 M Street N.W., Suite 250
Washington, DC 20037-1435
Telephone: (202) 342-7200
Recruiter Classification: Retained; **Lowest/Average Salary:**
$75,000/$90,000; **Industry Concentration:** Generalist with a
primary focus in Electronics, High Technology, Information
Technology; **Function Concentration:** Generalist with a
primary focus in Engineering, Finance/Accounting, General
Management, Human Resources, Marketing, Research and
Development, Sales, Women/Minorities

Marwil, Jennifer — *Associate*
Source Services Corporation
One South Main Street, Suite 1440
Dayton, OH 45402
Telephone: (513) 461-4660
Recruiter Classification: Contingency; **Lowest/Average Salary:**
$30,000/$50,000; **Industry Concentration:** Information
Technology; **Function Concentration:** Engineering,
Finance/Accounting

Marye, George — *Executive Recruiter*
Damon & Associates, Inc.
7515 Greenville Avenue, Suite 900
Dallas, TX 75231
Telephone: (214) 696-6990
Recruiter Classification: Contingency; **Lowest/Average Salary:**
$40,000/$60,000; **Industry Concentration:** Generalist with a
primary focus in High Technology, Information Technology;
Function Concentration: Sales

Mashakas, Elizabeth — *Legal Consultant*
TOPAZ International, Inc.
383 Northfield Avenue
West Orange, NJ 07052
Telephone: (201) 669-7300
Recruiter Classification: Contingency; **Lowest/Average Salary:**
$40,000/$75,000; **Industry Concentration:** Electronics, High
Technology; **Function Concentration:** Generalist with a
primary focus in Women/Minorities

Mashakas, Elizabeth — *Legal Consultant*
TOPAZ Legal Solutions
383 Northfield Avenue
West Orange, NJ 07052
Telephone: (201) 669-7300
Recruiter Classification: Executive Temporary; **Lowest/Average
Salary:** $40,000/$75,000; **Industry Concentration:** Electronics,
High Technology; **Function Concentration:** Generalist with a
primary focus in Women/Minorities

Masserman, Bruce — *President*
Masserman & Associates, Inc.
191 Post Road West
Westport, CT 06880
Telephone: (203) 221-2870
Recruiter Classification: Retained; **Lowest/Average Salary:**
$60,000/$75,000; **Industry Concentration:** Generalist with
a primary focus in High Technology, Information
Technology

Massey, R. Bruce — *Managing Director*
Horton International
330 Bay Street, Suite 1104
Toronto, Ontario, CANADA M5H 2S8
Telephone: (416) 861-0077
Recruiter Classification: Retained; **Lowest/Average Salary:**
$90,000/$90,000; **Industry Concentration:** Generalist with a
primary focus in Electronics, High Technology, Information
Technology; **Function Concentration:** Generalist with a
primary focus in Finance/Accounting, General Management,
Human Resources, Marketing, Research and Development,
Sales

Mather, David R. — *Vice President*
Christian & Timbers
20833 Stevens Creek Boulevard, Suite 200
Cupertino, CA 95014
Telephone: (408) 446-5440
Recruiter Classification: Retained; **Lowest/Average Salary:**
$90,000/$90,000; **Industry Concentration:** Generalist with a
primary focus in Electronics, High Technology, Information
Technology; **Function Concentration:** Generalist with a
primary focus in Engineering, Finance/Accounting, General
Management, Human Resources, Marketing, Research and
Development, Sales

Mathias, Douglas — *Managing Director*
Source Services Corporation
10220 SW Greenburg Road, Suite 625
Portland, OR 97223
Telephone: (503) 768-4546
Recruiter Classification: Contingency; **Lowest/Average Salary:**
$30,000/$50,000; **Industry Concentration:** Information
Technology; **Function Concentration:** Engineering,
Finance/Accounting

Mathias, Kathy — *Managing Director*
Stone Murphy & Olson
5500 Wayzata Boulevard
Suite 1020
Minneapolis, MN 55416
Telephone: (612) 591-2300
Recruiter Classification: Retained; **Lowest/Average Salary:**
$75,000/$90,000; **Industry Concentration:** Generalist with a
primary focus in High Technology; **Function Concentration:**
Generalist with a primary focus in Engineering,
Finance/Accounting, General Management, Human Resources,
Marketing, Sales, Women/Minorities

Mathis, Carrie — *Associate*
Source Services Corporation
5429 LBJ Freeway, Suite 275
Dallas, TX 75240
Telephone: (214) 387-1600
Recruiter Classification: Contingency; **Lowest/Average Salary:**
$30,000/$50,000; **Industry Concentration:** Information
Technology; **Function Concentration:** Engineering,
Finance/Accounting

Matthews, Corwin — *Associate*
Woodworth International Group
620 SW 5th Avenue, Suite 1225
Portland, OR 97204
Telephone: (503) 225-5000
Recruiter Classification: Retained; **Lowest/Average Salary:**
$60,000/$90,000; **Industry Concentration:** Generalist with a
primary focus in Electronics, High Technology, Information
Technology; **Function Concentration:** Generalist with a
primary focus in Engineering, Finance/Accounting, General
Management, Human Resources, Marketing, Research and
Development, Sales

Matthews, Mary — *Principal*
Korn/Ferry International
237 Park Avenue
New York, NY 10017
Telephone: (212) 687-1834
Recruiter Classification: Retained; **Lowest/Average Salary:**
$100,000/$150,000; **Industry Concentration:** Generalist with a
primary focus in Information Technology; **Function
Concentration:** Generalist

Matti, Suzy — *Recruiter*
Southwestern Professional Services
9485 Regency Square Boulevard, Suite 110
Jacksonville, FL 32225
Telephone: (904) 464-0400
Recruiter Classification: Contingency; **Lowest/Average Salary:** $30,000/$60,000; **Industry Concentration:** Generalist with a primary focus in Information Technology; **Function Concentration:** Marketing, Sales

Mattingly, Kathleen — *Managing Director*
Source Services Corporation
2850 National City Tower
Louisville, KY 40202
Telephone: (502) 581-9900
Recruiter Classification: Contingency; **Lowest/Average Salary:** $30,000/$50,000; **Industry Concentration:** Information Technology; **Function Concentration:** Engineering, Finance/Accounting

Matueny, Robert — *Executive Recruiter*
Ryan, Miller & Associates Inc.
4601 Wilshire Boulevard, Suite 225
Los Angeles, CA 90010
Telephone: (213) 938-4768
Recruiter Classification: Contingency; **Lowest/Average Salary:** $40,000/$50,000; **Industry Concentration:** Electronics; **Function Concentration:** Finance/Accounting

Mauer, Kristin — *Senior Associate*
Montgomery Resources, Inc.
555 Montgomery Street, Suite 1650
San Francisco, CA 94111
Telephone: (415) 956-4242
Recruiter Classification: Contingency; **Lowest/Average Salary:** $30,000/$60,000; **Industry Concentration:** High Technology; **Function Concentration:** Finance/Accounting

Maxwell, John — *Associate*
Source Services Corporation
1500 West Park Drive, Suite 390
Westborough, MA 01581
Telephone: (508) 366-2600
Recruiter Classification: Contingency; **Lowest/Average Salary:** $30,000/$50,000; **Industry Concentration:** Information Technology; **Function Concentration:** Engineering, Finance/Accounting

May, Peter — *Senior Principal*
Mixtec Group
31255 Cedar Valley Drive
Suite 300-327
Westlake Village, CA 91362
Telephone: (818) 889-8819
Recruiter Classification: Contingency; **Lowest/Average Salary:** $60,000/$90,000; **Industry Concentration:** Electronics, High Technology; **Function Concentration:** Generalist with a primary focus in Administration, Engineering, Finance/Accounting, General Management, Marketing, Research and Development, Sales

Mayer, Thomas — *Associate*
Source Services Corporation
3 Summit Park Drive, Suite 550
Independence, OH 44131
Telephone: (216) 328-5900
Recruiter Classification: Contingency; **Lowest/Average Salary:** $30,000/$50,000; **Industry Concentration:** Information Technology; **Function Concentration:** Engineering, Finance/Accounting

Mayes, Kay H. — *Director*
John Shell Associates, Inc.
115 Atrium Way, Suite 122
Columbia, SC 29223
Telephone: (803) 788-6619
Recruiter Classification: Contingency, Executive Temporary; **Lowest/Average Salary:** $20,000/$40,000; **Industry Concentration:** Generalist with a primary focus in High Technology, Information Technology; **Function Concentration:** Finance/Accounting

Mayland, Tina — *Executive Director*
Russell Reynolds Associates, Inc.
The Hurt Building
50 Hurt Plaza, Suite 600
Atlanta, GA 30303-2914
Telephone: (404) 577-3000
Recruiter Classification: Retained; **Lowest/Average Salary:** $90,000/$90,000; **Industry Concentration:** Generalist with a primary focus in High Technology; **Function Concentration:** Generalist

Maynard Taylor, Susan — *Executive Recruiter*
Chrisman & Company, Incorporated
350 South Figueroa Street, Suite 550
Los Angeles, CA 90071
Telephone: (213) 620-1192
Recruiter Classification: Retained; **Lowest/Average Salary:** $75,000/$90,000; **Industry Concentration:** Generalist with a primary focus in High Technology; **Function Concentration:** Generalist with a primary focus in Finance/Accounting, General Management, Human Resources, Marketing, Women/Minorities

Mazor, Elly — *Consultant*
Howard Fischer Associates, Inc.
1800 John F. Kennedy Boulevard, 7th Floor
Philadelphia, PA 19103
Telephone: (215) 568-8363
Recruiter Classification: Retained; **Lowest/Average Salary:** $90,000/$90,000; **Industry Concentration:** Generalist with a primary focus in High Technology; **Function Concentration:** Generalist with a primary focus in Administration, Finance/Accounting, General Management, Human Resources, Marketing, Research and Development, Sales, Women/Minorities

Mazza, David B. — *Partner*
Mazza & Riley, Inc. (a Korn/Ferry International affiliate)
55 William Street, Suite 120
Wellesley, MA 02181-4000
Telephone: (617) 235-7724
Recruiter Classification: Retained; **Lowest/Average Salary:** $90,000/$90,000; **Industry Concentration:** Generalist with a primary focus in High Technology, Information Technology; **Function Concentration:** Generalist with a primary focus in Finance/Accounting, General Management, Marketing, Sales

McAndrews, Kathy — *Executive Recruiter*
CPS Inc.
One Westbrook Corporate Centre, Suite 600
Westchester, IL 60154
Telephone: (708) 531-8370
Recruiter Classification: Contingency; **Lowest/Average Salary:**
$30,000/$50,000; **Industry Concentration:** Generalist with a
primary focus in Electronics, High Technology, Information
Technology; **Function Concentration:** Engineering, Research
and Development, Sales, Women/Minorities

McAteer, Thomas — *Partner*
Montgomery Resources, Inc.
555 Montgomery Street, Suite 1650
San Francisco, CA 94111
Telephone: (415) 956-4242
Recruiter Classification: Contingency, Executive Temporary;
Lowest/Average Salary: $30,000/$60,000; **Industry
Concentration:** Generalist with a primary focus in High
Technology; **Function Concentration:** Finance/Accounting

McBride, Dee — *President*
Deeco International
P.O. Box 57033
Salt Lake City, UT 84157
Telephone: (801) 261-3326
Recruiter Classification: Retained; **Lowest/Average Salary:**
$40,000/$60,000; **Industry Concentration:** High Technology;
Function Concentration: Engineering, General Management,
Marketing, Research and Development, Sales

McBride, Jonathan E. — *President*
McBride Associates, Inc.
1511 K Street N.W., Suite 819
Washington, DC 20005
Telephone: (202) 638-1150
Recruiter Classification: Retained; **Lowest/Average Salary:**
$150,000/$150,000; **Industry Concentration:** Generalist with a
primary focus in Electronics, High Technology; **Function
Concentration:** Generalist with a primary focus in
Administration, Finance/Accounting, General Management,
Human Resources, Marketing, Research and Development,
Sales, Women/Minorities

McCabe, Christopher — *Consultant*
Raymond Karsan Associates
2001 Westside Drive, Suite 130
Alpharetta, GA 30201
Telephone: (770) 442-8771
Recruiter Classification: Retained; **Lowest/Average Salary:**
$30,000/$90,000; **Industry Concentration:** Generalist with a
primary focus in Information Technology; **Function
Concentration:** Generalist

McCann, Cornelia B. — *Director*
Spencer Stuart
2005 Market Street, Suite 2350
Philadelphia, PA 19103
Telephone: (215) 851-6200
Recruiter Classification: Retained; **Lowest/Average Salary:**
$90,000/$90,000; **Industry Concentration:** Information
Technology; **Function Concentration:** Generalist

McCarthy, Laura — *Associate*
Source Services Corporation
8614 Westwood Center, Suite 750
Vienna, VA 22182
Telephone: (703) 790-5610
Recruiter Classification: Contingency; **Lowest/Average Salary:**
$30,000/$50,000; **Industry Concentration:** Information
Technology; **Function Concentration:** Engineering,
Finance/Accounting

McCloskey, Frank D. — *Managing Director*
Johnson Smith & Knisely Accord
181 West Madison Street, Suite 4850
Chicago, IL 60602
Telephone: (312) 920-9400
Recruiter Classification: Retained; **Lowest/Average Salary:**
$90,000/$90,000; **Industry Concentration:** High Technology,
Information Technology; **Function Concentration:** Engineering,
Finance/Accounting, General Management, Human Resources,
Marketing, Sales

McClure, James K. — *Vice President*
Korn/Ferry International
One International Place
Boston, MA 02110-1800
Telephone: (617) 345-0200
Recruiter Classification: Retained; **Lowest/Average Salary:**
$100,000/$150,000; **Industry Concentration:** Generalist with a
primary focus in High Technology; **Function Concentration:**
Generalist

McComas, Kelly E. — *Director*
The Guild Corporation
8260 Greensboro Drive, Suite 460
McLean, VA 22102
Telephone: (703) 761-4023
Recruiter Classification: Contingency; **Lowest/Average Salary:**
$40,000/$50,000; **Industry Concentration:** Electronics, High
Technology, Information Technology; **Function Concentration:**
Engineering, Finance/Accounting, General Management,
Research and Development

McConnell, Greg — *Branch Manager/Information
Technology Recruiter*
Winter, Wyman & Company
1100 Circle 75 Parkway, Suite 800
Atlanta, GA 30339
Telephone: (770) 933-1525
Recruiter Classification: Contingency; **Lowest/Average Salary:**
$30,000/$60,000; **Industry Concentration:** Generalist with a
primary focus in High Technology, Information Technology;
Function Concentration: Generalist

McCormick, Brian — *Executive Vice President*
The McCormick Group, Inc.
1400 Wilson Boulevard
Arlington, VA 22209
Telephone: (703) 841-1700
Recruiter Classification: Retained; **Lowest/Average Salary:**
$50,000/$90,000; **Industry Concentration:** High Technology,
Information Technology; **Function Concentration:** Engineering,
Finance/Accounting, General Management, Human Resources,
Marketing, Sales

McCormick, Joseph — *Associate*
Source Services Corporation
111 Founders Plaza, Suite 1501E
Hartford, CT 06108
Telephone: (860) 528-0300
Recruiter Classification: Contingency; **Lowest/Average Salary:**
$30,000/$50,000; **Industry Concentration:** Information
Technology; **Function Concentration:** Engineering,
Finance/Accounting

McCormick, William J. — *Chief Executive Officer*
The McCormick Group, Inc.
4024 Plank Road
Fredericksburg, VA 22407
Telephone: (703) 786-9777
Recruiter Classification: Retained, Contingency;
Lowest/Average Salary: $60,000/$90,000; **Industry
Concentration:** Generalist with a primary focus in High
Technology, Information Technology; **Function Concentration:**
Generalist with a primary focus in Engineering,
Finance/Accounting, General Management, Marketing,
Research and Development, Sales

McCreary, Charles "Chip" — *President*
Austin-McGregor International
12005 Ford Road, Suite 720
Dallas, TX 75234-7247
Telephone: (972) 488-0500
Recruiter Classification: Retained; **Lowest/Average Salary:**
$50,000/$90,000; **Industry Concentration:** Generalist with a
primary focus in Electronics, High Technology; **Function
Concentration:** Generalist with a primary focus in Engineering,
Finance/Accounting, General Management, Human Resources,
Marketing, Research and Development, Sales,
Women/Minorities

McCurdy, Mark — *Research Consultant*
Summerfield Associates, Inc.
6555 Quince Road, Suite 311
Memphis, TN 38119
Telephone: (901) 753-7068
Recruiter Classification: Contingency; **Lowest/Average Salary:**
$30,000/$50,000; **Industry Concentration:** Generalist with a
primary focus in Information Technology; **Function
Concentration:** Generalist

McDermott, Jeffrey T. — *Consultant*
Vlcek & Company, Inc.
620 Newport Center Drive
Suite 1100
Newport Beach, CA 92660
Telephone: (714) 752-0661
Recruiter Classification: Retained; **Lowest/Average Salary:**
$90,000/$90,000; **Industry Concentration:** Generalist with a
primary focus in High Technology, Information Technology;
Function Concentration: Generalist with a primary focus in
Engineering, Finance/Accounting, General Management,
Human Resources, Marketing, Sales, Women/Minorities

McDonald, John R. — *President*
TSS Consulting, Ltd.
2425 East Camelback Road
Suite 375
Phoenix, AZ 85016
Telephone: (602) 955-7000
Recruiter Classification: Contingency; **Lowest/Average Salary:**
$60,000/$75,000; **Industry Concentration:** Electronics, High
Technology; **Function Concentration:** Engineering, General
Management, Marketing

McDonald, Scott A. — *Partner*
McDonald Associates International
234 Washington Road
Rye, NH 03870
Telephone: (603) 433-6295
Recruiter Classification: Retained; **Lowest/Average Salary:**
$60,000/$90,000; **Industry Concentration:** Generalist with a
primary focus in Electronics, High Technology, Information
Technology; **Function Concentration:** Generalist with a
primary focus in Administration, Engineering,
Finance/Accounting, General Management, Marketing, Sales,
Women/Minorities

McDonald, Stanleigh B. — *Partner*
McDonald Associates International
1290 N. Western Avenue
Suite 209
Lake Forest, IL 60045
Telephone: (708) 234-6889
Recruiter Classification: Retained; **Lowest/Average Salary:**
$60,000/$90,000; **Industry Concentration:** Generalist with a
primary focus in Electronics, High Technology, Information
Technology; **Function Concentration:** Generalist with a
primary focus in Administration, Engineering,
Finance/Accounting, General Management, Human Resources,
Marketing, Sales, Women/Minorities

McDonnell, Julie — *Owner*
Technical Personnel of Minnesota
5354 Parkdale Drive, Suite 104
Minneapolis, MN 55416
Telephone: (612) 544-8550
Recruiter Classification: Contingency; **Lowest/Average Salary:**
$20,000/$50,000; **Industry Concentration:** Generalist with a
primary focus in Electronics, High Technology, Information
Technology; **Function Concentration:** Generalist with a
primary focus in Administration, Engineering,
Finance/Accounting, General Management, Human Resources,
Marketing, Research and Development, Sales

McDowell, Robert N. — *Partner*
Christenson & Hutchison
466 Southern Boulevard
Chatham, NJ 07928-1462
Telephone: (201) 966-1600
Recruiter Classification: Retained; **Lowest/Average Salary:**
$75,000/$90,000; **Industry Concentration:** Generalist with a
primary focus in Electronics, Information Technology; **Function
Concentration:** Generalist with a primary focus in
Finance/Accounting, General Management, Human Resources,
Marketing, Sales

McFadden, Ashton S. — *Partner*
Johnson Smith & Knisely Accord
100 Park Avenue, 15th Floor
New York, NY 10017
Telephone: (212) 885-9100
Recruiter Classification: Retained; **Lowest/Average Salary:**
$90,000/$90,000; **Industry Concentration:** Information
Technology; **Function Concentration:** Generalist with a
primary focus in Administration, Finance/Accounting, General
Management, Human Resources, Marketing, Research and
Development, Sales

McFadzen, Donna — *Principal*
Holland, McFadzean & Associates, Inc.
2901 Tasman Drive
Suite 204
Santa Clara, CA 95054
Telephone: (408) 496-0775
Recruiter Classification: Retained; **Lowest/Average Salary:**
$90,000/$90,000; **Industry Concentration:** Electronics, High
Technology, Information Technology; **Function Concentration:**
Generalist with a primary focus in Engineering,
Finance/Accounting, General Management, Human Resources,
Marketing, Research and Development, Sales

McFadzen,, James A. — *President*
Holland, McFadzean & Associates, Inc.
2901 Tasman Drive
Suite 204
Santa Clara, CA 95054
Telephone: (408) 496-0775
Recruiter Classification: Retained; **Lowest/Average Salary:**
$90,000/$90,000; **Industry Concentration:** Electronics, High
Technology, Information Technology; **Function Concentration:**
Generalist with a primary focus in Engineering,
Finance/Accounting, General Management, Human Resources,
Marketing, Research and Development, Sales

McGinnis, Rita — *Associate*
Source Services Corporation
5429 LBJ Freeway, Suite 275
Dallas, TX 75240
Telephone: (214) 387-1600
Recruiter Classification: Contingency; **Lowest/Average Salary:**
$30,000/$50,000; **Industry Concentration:** Information
Technology; **Function Concentration:** Engineering,
Finance/Accounting

McGoldrick, Terrence — *Associate*
Source Services Corporation
One South Main Street, Suite 1440
Dayton, OH 45402
Telephone: (513) 461-4660
Recruiter Classification: Contingency; **Lowest/Average Salary:**
$30,000/$50,000; **Industry Concentration:** Information
Technology; **Function Concentration:** Engineering,
Finance/Accounting

McGregor, James D. — *Vice President*
John Kurosky & Associates
3 Corporate Park Drive, Suite 210
Irvine, CA 92714
Telephone: (714) 851-6370
Recruiter Classification: Retained; **Lowest/Average Salary:**
$90,000/$90,000; **Industry Concentration:** Generalist with a
primary focus in High Technology, Information Technology;
Function Concentration: Generalist with a primary focus in
Engineering, Marketing, Sales

McGuigan, Walter J. — *Senior Associate*
Norm Sanders Associates
2 Village Court
Hazlet, NJ 07730
Telephone: (732) 264-3700
Recruiter Classification: Retained; **Lowest/Average Salary:**
$90,000/$90,000; **Industry Concentration:** Information
Technology; **Function Concentration:** Generalist

McGuire, J. Corey — *Associate*
Peter W. Ambler Company
14651 Dallas Parkway, Suite 402
Dallas, TX 75240
Telephone: (214) 404-8712
Recruiter Classification: Retained; **Lowest/Average Salary:**
$50,000/$90,000; **Industry Concentration:** Generalist with a
primary focus in Electronics; **Function Concentration:**
Generalist with a primary focus in Engineering, General
Management, Human Resources, Marketing, Sales

McGuire, Pat — *Professional Recruiter*
A.J. Burton Group, Inc.
4550 Montgomery Avenue, Ste. 325 North
Bethesda, MD 20814
Telephone: (301) 654-0082
Recruiter Classification: Contingency; **Lowest/Average Salary:**
$40,000/$75,000; **Industry Concentration:** Generalist with a
primary focus in High Technology, Information Technology;
Function Concentration: Generalist with a primary focus in
Administration, Finance/Accounting, General Management,
Human Resources

McHale, Rob — *Director*
Paul-Tittle Associates, Inc.
1485 Chain Bridge Road, #304
McLean, VA 22101
Telephone: (703) 442-0500
Recruiter Classification: Retained; **Lowest/Average Salary:**
$60,000/$75,000; **Industry Concentration:** High Technology,
Information Technology; **Function Concentration:** Engineering,
Marketing, Sales

McHugh, Keith — *Associate*
Source Services Corporation
879 West 190th Street, Suite 250
Los Angeles, CA 90248
Telephone: (310) 323-6633
Recruiter Classification: Contingency; **Lowest/Average Salary:**
$30,000/$50,000; **Industry Concentration:** Information
Technology; **Function Concentration:** Engineering,
Finance/Accounting

McIntosh, Arthur — *Associate*
Source Services Corporation
5429 LBJ Freeway, Suite 275
Dallas, TX 75240
Telephone: (214) 387-1600
Recruiter Classification: Contingency; **Lowest/Average Salary:**
$30,000/$50,000; **Industry Concentration:** Information
Technology; **Function Concentration:** Engineering,
Finance/Accounting

McIntosh, Tad — *Associate*
Source Services Corporation
5429 LBJ Freeway, Suite 275
Dallas, TX 75240
Telephone: (214) 387-1600
Recruiter Classification: Contingency; **Lowest/Average Salary:**
$30,000/$50,000; **Industry Concentration:** Information
Technology; **Function Concentration:** Engineering,
Finance/Accounting

McInturff, Robert — *President*
McInturff & Associates, Inc.
209 West Central Street
Natick, MA 01760
Telephone: (617) 237-0220
Recruiter Classification: Contingency; **Lowest/Average Salary:**
$50,000/$50,000; **Industry Concentration:** Electronics, High
Technology, Information Technology; **Function Concentration:**
General Management

McIntyre, Joel — *Regional Manager*
Phillips Resource Group
2031-A Carolina Place
P.O. Box 609
Fort Mill, SC 29715
Telephone: (803) 548-6918
Recruiter Classification: Contingency; **Lowest/Average Salary:**
$40,000/$50,000; **Industry Concentration:** Generalist with a
primary focus in Electronics, High Technology, Information
Technology; **Function Concentration:** Generalist with a
primary focus in Administration, Engineering, General
Management, Human Resources, Marketing, Research and
Development, Sales, Women/Minorities

McKell, Linda — *President*
Advanced Information Management
444 Castro Street, Suite 320
Mountain View, CA 94041
Telephone: (415) 965-7799
Recruiter Classification: Contingency; **Lowest/Average Salary:**
$20,000/$40,000; **Industry Concentration:** Information
Technology; **Function Concentration:** Human Resources,
Women/Minorities

McKeown, Morgan J. — *Vice President*
Christian & Timbers
100 Park Avenue, 16th Floor
New York, NY 10017
Telephone: (212) 880-6446
Recruiter Classification: Retained; **Lowest/Average Salary:**
$90,000/$90,000; **Industry Concentration:** High Technology,
Information Technology; **Function Concentration:** Generalist
with a primary focus in Engineering, Finance/Accounting,
General Management, Human Resources, Marketing, Sales

McKeown, Patricia A. — *Partner*
DiMarchi Partners, Inc.
1225 17th Street, Suite 1460
Denver, CO 80202
Telephone: (303) 292-9300
Recruiter Classification: Retained; **Lowest/Average Salary:**
$90,000/$90,000; **Industry Concentration:** Generalist with a
primary focus in Electronics, High Technology; **Function
Concentration:** Generalist with a primary focus in
Finance/Accounting, General Management, Human Resources,
Marketing, Sales, Women/Minorities

McKinney, Julia — *Associate*
Source Services Corporation
100 North Tryon Street, Suite 3130
Charlotte, NC 28202
Telephone: (704) 333-8311
Recruiter Classification: Contingency; **Lowest/Average Salary:**
$30,000/$50,000; **Industry Concentration:** Information
Technology; **Function Concentration:** Engineering,
Finance/Accounting

McKnight, Amy E. — *Director*
Chartwell Partners International, Inc.
275 Battery Street, Suite 2180
San Francisco, CA 94111
Telephone: (415) 296-0600
Recruiter Classification: Retained; **Lowest/Average Salary:**
$90,000/$90,000; **Industry Concentration:** Generalist with a
primary focus in High Technology; **Function Concentration:**
Generalist with a primary focus in Finance/Accounting,
Marketing, Sales, Women/Minorities

McLaughlin, John — *Managing Partner*
Romac & Associates
180 Montgomery Street
Suite 1860
San Francisco, CA 94104
Telephone: (415) 788-2815
Recruiter Classification: Executive Temporary; **Lowest/Average
Salary:** $60,000/$60,000; **Industry Concentration:** High
Technology, Information Technology; **Function Concentration:**
Finance/Accounting

McMahan, Stephen — *Managing Director*
Source Services Corporation
155 Federal Street, Suite 410
Boston, MA 02110
Telephone: (617) 482-8211
Recruiter Classification: Contingency; **Lowest/Average Salary:**
$30,000/$50,000; **Industry Concentration:** Information
Technology; **Function Concentration:** Engineering,
Finance/Accounting

McMahan, Stephen — *Managing Director*
Source Services Corporation
71 Spit Brook Road, Suite 305
Nashua, NH 03060
Telephone: (603) 888-7650
Recruiter Classification: Contingency; **Lowest/Average Salary:**
$30,000/$50,000; **Industry Concentration:** Information
Technology; **Function Concentration:** Engineering,
Finance/Accounting

McMahon, Mark J. — *Vice President/Managing
Director*
A.T. Kearney, Inc.
One Landmark Square, Suite 426
Stamford, CT 06901
Telephone: (203) 969-2222
Recruiter Classification: Retained; **Lowest/Average Salary:**
$90,000/$90,000; **Industry Concentration:** Generalist with a
primary focus in High Technology; **Function Concentration:**
Generalist

McManners, Donald E. — *President*
McManners Associates, Inc.
2525 Ontario Drive
San Jose, CA 95124
Telephone: (408) 559-9232
Recruiter Classification: Retained; **Lowest/Average Salary:**
$90,000/$90,000; **Industry Concentration:** Generalist with a
primary focus in Electronics, High Technology, Information
Technology; **Function Concentration:** Generalist with a
primary focus in Administration, Engineering, General
Management, Human Resources, Marketing, Research and
Development, Women/Minorities

McManus, Paul — *Principal*
Aubin International Inc.
281 Winter Street, #380
Waltham, MA 02154
Telephone: (617) 890-1722
Recruiter Classification: Retained; **Lowest/Average Salary:**
$90,000/$90,000; **Industry Concentration:** Generalist with a
primary focus in High Technology; **Function Concentration:**
Generalist

McMillin, Bob — *Director*
Price Waterhouse
601 West Hastings Street
Suite 1400
Vancouver, British Columbia, CANADA V6B 5A5
Telephone: (604) 682-4711
Recruiter Classification: Retained; **Lowest/Average Salary:**
$75,000/$75,000; **Industry Concentration:** Generalist with a
primary focus in High Technology; **Function Concentration:**
Generalist with a primary focus in Administration, Engineering,
Finance/Accounting, General Management, Human Resources,
Marketing, Sales

McNamara, Catherine — *Consultant*
Ray & Berndtson
Texas Commerce Tower
2200 Ross Avenue, Suite 4500W
Dallas, TX 75201
Telephone: (214) 969-7620
Recruiter Classification: Retained; **Lowest/Average Salary:**
$90,000/$90,000; **Industry Concentration:** Generalist with a
primary focus in High Technology, Information Technology;
Function Concentration: Generalist with a primary focus in
Administration, Finance/Accounting, General Management,
Human Resources, Marketing, Research and Development,
Sales, Women/Minorities

McNamara, Timothy C. — *Managing Director*
Columbia Consulting Group
20 South Charles Street, 9th Floor
Baltimore, MD 21201
Telephone: (410) 385-2525
Recruiter Classification: Retained; **Lowest/Average Salary:**
$75,000/$90,000; **Industry Concentration:** Generalist with a
primary focus in High Technology, Information Technology;
Function Concentration: Generalist with a primary focus in
Engineering, Finance/Accounting, Human Resources,
Marketing, Research and Development

McNamee, Erin — *Recruiter*
Technical Connections Inc.
11400 Olympic Boulevard, Suite 770
Los Angeles, CA 90064
Telephone: (310) 479-8830
Recruiter Classification: Contingency; **Lowest/Average Salary:**
$40,000/$60,000; **Industry Concentration:** High Technology,
Information Technology; **Function Concentration:** Generalist

McNear, Jeffrey E. — *Operations
Manager/Barrettemps Search Division*
Barrett Partners
100 North LaSalle Street, Suite 1420
Chicago, IL 60602
Telephone: (312) 443-8877
Recruiter Classification: Contingency; **Lowest/Average Salary:**
$30,000/$50,000; **Industry Concentration:** Information
Technology; **Function Concentration:** Engineering,
Finance/Accounting

McNerney, Kevin A. — *Managing Partner*
Heidrick & Struggles, Inc.
8000 Towers Crescent Drive, Suite 555
Vienna, VA 22182-2700
Telephone: (703) 761-4830
Recruiter Classification: Retained; **Lowest/Average Salary:**
$75,000/$90,000; **Industry Concentration:** Generalist with a
primary focus in High Technology; **Function Concentration:**
Generalist

McNichol, John — *President*
McNichol Associates
620 Chestnut Street, Suite 1031
Philadelphia, PA 19106
Telephone: (215) 922-4142
Recruiter Classification: Retained; **Lowest/Average Salary:**
$75,000/$90,000; **Industry Concentration:** High Technology;
Function Concentration: Generalist with a primary focus in
Administration, Engineering, Finance/Accounting, General
Management, Human Resources, Marketing, Research and
Development, Sales, Women/Minorities

McNichols, Walter B. — *Vice President*
Gary Kaplan & Associates
201 South Lake Avenue
Suite 600
Pasadena, CA 91101
Telephone: (818) 796-8100
Recruiter Classification: Retained; **Lowest/Average Salary:**
$75,000/$90,000; **Industry Concentration:** Generalist with a
primary focus in Electronics, High Technology, Information
Technology; **Function Concentration:** Generalist with a
primary focus in Engineering, Finance/Accounting, General
Management, Human Resources, Marketing, Research and
Development

McPoyle, Thomas C. — *Principal*
Sanford Rose Associates
57 West Timonium Road
Suite 310
Timonium, MD 21093
Telephone: (410) 561-5244
Recruiter Classification: Contingency; **Lowest/Average Salary:**
$30,000/$75,000; **Industry Concentration:** Generalist with a
primary focus in Electronics; **Function Concentration:**
Generalist

McSherry, James F. — *Senior Vice President
Midwest Region*
Battalia Winston International
180 North Wacker Drive, Suite 600
Chicago, IL 60606
Telephone: (312) 704-0050
Recruiter Classification: Retained; **Lowest/Average Salary:**
$90,000/$90,000; **Industry Concentration:** Generalist with a
primary focus in High Technology, Information Technology;
Function Concentration: Generalist with a primary focus in
General Management, Human Resources, Sales,
Women/Minorities

McThrall, David — *Executive Recruiter*
TSS Consulting, Ltd.
2425 East Camelback Road
Suite 375
Phoenix, AZ 85016
Telephone: (602) 955-7000
Recruiter Classification: Contingency; **Lowest/Average Salary:**
$60,000/$75,000; **Industry Concentration:** Electronics, High
Technology; **Function Concentration:** Engineering, General
Management, Marketing

Mead, James D. — *President*
James Mead & Company
164 Kings Highway North
Westport, CT 06880
Telephone: (203) 454-5544
Recruiter Classification: Retained; **Lowest/Average Salary:**
$90,000/$90,000; **Industry Concentration:** Electronics;
Function Concentration: General Management, Marketing,
Sales

Mead-Fox, David — *Vice President Healthcare*
Korn/Ferry International
One International Place
Boston, MA 02110-1800
Telephone: (617) 345-0200
Recruiter Classification: Retained; **Lowest/Average Salary:**
$100,000/$150,000; **Industry Concentration:** Generalist with a
primary focus in Information Technology; **Function
Concentration:** Generalist

Meadows, C. David — *Managing Director*
Professional Staffing Consultants
1331 Lamar, Suite 1459
Houston, TX 77010
Telephone: (713) 659-8383
Recruiter Classification: Retained; **Lowest/Average Salary:**
$50,000/$75,000; **Industry Concentration:** Generalist with a
primary focus in Information Technology; **Function
Concentration:** Generalist with a primary focus in
Engineering, Finance/Accounting, General Management,
Human Resources

Meara, Helen — *Associate*
Source Services Corporation
5 Independence Way
Princeton, NJ 08540
Telephone: (609) 452-7277
Recruiter Classification: Contingency; **Lowest/Average Salary:**
$30,000/$50,000; **Industry Concentration:** Information
Technology; **Function Concentration:** Engineering,
Finance/Accounting

Medina-Haro, Adolfo — *Managing Partner*
Heidrick & Struggles, Inc.
Torre Chapultepec, Ruben Dario No. 281 Ofna.
1403
Col. Bosque de Chapultepec
Mexico City, D.F., MEXICO 11580
Telephone: (525) 280-5200
Recruiter Classification: Retained; **Lowest/Average Salary:**
$75,000/$90,000; **Industry Concentration:** Generalist with a
primary focus in High Technology; **Function Concentration:**
Generalist

Meehan, John — *Associate*
Source Services Corporation
8614 Westwood Center, Suite 750
Vienna, VA 22182
Telephone: (703) 790-5610
Recruiter Classification: Contingency; **Lowest/Average Salary:**
$30,000/$50,000; **Industry Concentration:** Information
Technology; **Function Concentration:** Engineering,
Finance/Accounting

Mefford, Bob — *Vice President*
Executive Manning Corporation
3000 N.E. 30th Place, Suite 402/405/411
Fort Lauderdale, FL 33306
Telephone: (954) 561-5100
Recruiter Classification: Retained; **Lowest/Average Salary:**
$75,000/$90,000; **Industry Concentration:** Generalist with a
primary focus in Electronics, High Technology; **Function
Concentration:** Generalist

Meiland, A. Daniel — *Consultant*
Egon Zehnder International Inc.
350 Park Avenue
New York, NY 10022
Telephone: (212) 838-9199
Recruiter Classification: Retained; **Lowest/Average Salary:**
$90,000/$90,000; **Industry Concentration:** Generalist with a
primary focus in High Technology; **Function Concentration:**
Generalist

Mendelson, Jeffrey — *Associate*
Source Services Corporation
2 Penn Plaza, Suite 1176
New York, NY 10121
Telephone: (212) 760-2200
Recruiter Classification: Contingency; **Lowest/Average Salary:**
$30,000/$50,000; **Industry Concentration:** Information
Technology; **Function Concentration:** Engineering,
Finance/Accounting

Mendoza-Green, Robin — *Associate*
Source Services Corporation
1 Gatehall Drive, Suite 250
Parsippany, NJ 07054
Telephone: (201) 267-3222
Recruiter Classification: Contingency; **Lowest/Average Salary:**
$30,000/$50,000; **Industry Concentration:** Information
Technology; **Function Concentration:** Engineering,
Finance/Accounting

Menendez, Todd — *Executive Recruiter*
Don Richard Associates of Tampa, Inc.
100 North Tampa Street, Suite 1925
Tampa, FL 33602
Telephone: (813) 221-7930
Recruiter Classification: Contingency, Executive Temporary;
Lowest/Average Salary: $20,000/$50,000; **Industry
Concentration:** Generalist with a primary focus in
Information Technology; **Function Concentration:** Generalist
with a primary focus in Finance/Accounting, Human
Resources

Mercer, Julie — *Managing Principal*
Columbia Consulting Group
20 South Charles Street, 9th Floor
Baltimore, MD 21201
Telephone: (410) 385-2525
Recruiter Classification: Retained; **Lowest/Average Salary:**
$75,000/$90,000; **Industry Concentration:** Generalist with a
primary focus in High Technology, Information Technology;
Function Concentration: Generalist with a primary focus in
Finance/Accounting, Human Resources, Marketing,
Sales, Women/Minorities

Mertensotto, Chuck H. — *Executive Recruiter*
Whitney & Associates, Inc.
920 Second Avenue South, Suite 625
Minneapolis, MN 55402-4035
Telephone: (612) 338-5600
Recruiter Classification: Contingency, Executive Temporary;
Lowest/Average Salary: $20,000/$50,000; **Industry
Concentration:** Generalist with a primary focus in Electronics,
High Technology, Information Technology; **Function
Concentration:** Finance/Accounting

Messina, Marco — *Associate*
Source Services Corporation
500 108th Avenue NE, Suite 1780
Bellevue, WA 98004
Telephone: (206) 454-6400
Recruiter Classification: Contingency; **Lowest/Average Salary:**
$30,000/$50,000; **Industry Concentration:** Information
Technology; **Function Concentration:** Engineering,
Finance/Accounting

Metz, Alex — *President*
Hunt Advisory Services
1050 Wall Street West, Suite 330
Lyndhurst, NJ 07071
Telephone: (201) 438-8200
Recruiter Classification: Retained; **Lowest/Average Salary:**
$50,000/$75,000; **Industry Concentration:** Electronics

Metz, Dan K. — *Managing Director*
Russell Reynolds Associates, Inc.
101 California Street
Suite 3140
San Francisco, CA 94111-5829
Telephone: (415) 352-3300
Recruiter Classification: Retained; **Lowest/Average Salary:**
$90,000/$90,000; **Industry Concentration:** Generalist with a
primary focus in High Technology; **Function Concentration:**
Generalist

Meyer, Stacey — *Senior Associate*
Gary Kaplan & Associates
201 South Lake Avenue
Suite 600
Pasadena, CA 91101
Telephone: (818) 796-8100
Recruiter Classification: Retained; **Lowest/Average Salary:**
$75,000/$90,000; **Industry Concentration:** Generalist with a
primary focus in Electronics, High Technology, Information
Technology; **Function Concentration:** Generalist with a
primary focus in Engineering, Finance/Accounting, General
Management, Human Resources, Marketing, Research and
Development

Meyers, Steven — *Senior Associate*
Montgomery Resources, Inc.
555 Montgomery Street, Suite 1650
San Francisco, CA 94111
Telephone: (415) 956-4242
Recruiter Classification: Contingency, Executive Temporary;
Lowest/Average Salary: $30,000/$60,000; **Industry
Concentration:** Generalist with a primary focus in High
Technology; **Function Concentration:** Finance/Accounting

Michaels, Joseph — *Executive Recruiter*
CPS Inc.
One Westbrook Corporate Centre, Suite 600
Westchester, IL 60154
Telephone: (708) 531-8370
Recruiter Classification: Contingency; **Lowest/Average Salary:**
$30,000/$50,000; **Industry Concentration:** Generalist with a
primary focus in Electronics, High Technology, Information
Technology; **Function Concentration:** Engineering, Research
and Development, Sales, Women/Minorities

Michaels, Stewart — *Partner*
TOPAZ Legal Solutions
383 Northfield Avenue
West Orange, NJ 07052
Telephone: (201) 669-7300
Recruiter Classification: Executive Temporary; **Lowest/Average
Salary:** $40,000/$75,000; **Industry Concentration:** Electronics,
High Technology; **Function Concentration:** Generalist with a
primary focus in Women/Minorities

Michaels, Stewart — *Partner*
TOPAZ International, Inc.
383 Northfield Avenue
West Orange, NJ 07052
Telephone: (201) 669-7300
Recruiter Classification: Contingency; **Lowest/Average Salary:**
$40,000/$75,000; **Industry Concentration:** Electronics, High
Technology; **Function Concentration:** Generalist with a
primary focus in Women/Minorities

Mierzwinski, John — *Director Sales*
Industrial Recruiters Associates, Inc.
20 Hurlbut Street, 1st Floor
West Hartford, CT 06110
Telephone: (860) 953-3643
Recruiter Classification: Contingency; **Lowest/Average Salary:**
$30,000/$90,000; **Industry Concentration:** Electronics, High
Technology, Information Technology; **Function Concentration:**
Generalist with a primary focus in Engineering, Marketing,
Research and Development

Mikula, Linda — *Vice President*
Schweichler Associates, Inc.
200 Tamal Vista, Building 200, Suite 100
Corte Madera, CA 94925
Telephone: (415) 924-7200
Recruiter Classification: Retained; **Lowest/Average Salary:**
$90,000/$90,000; **Industry Concentration:** High Technology;
Function Concentration: General Management, Marketing,
Research and Development, Sales

Miles, Kenneth T. — *Executive Recruiter*
MSI International
6151 Powers Ferry Road, Suite 540
Atlanta, GA 30339
Telephone: (404) 850-6465
Recruiter Classification: Contingency; **Lowest/Average Salary:**
$30,000/$75,000; **Industry Concentration:** Generalist with a
primary focus in Electronics, High Technology; **Function
Concentration:** Generalist with a primary focus in
Administration, Engineering, Finance/Accounting, General
Management, Marketing, Sales

Miles, Marybeth — *Information Technology Recruiter*
Winter, Wyman & Company
950 Winter Street, Suite 3100
Waltham, MA 02154-1294
Telephone: (617) 890-7000
Recruiter Classification: Contingency; **Lowest/Average Salary:** $30,000/$60,000; **Industry Concentration:** Information Technology; **Function Concentration:** Generalist

Miller, Brett — *Consultant*
The McCormick Group, Inc.
1400 Wilson Boulevard
Arlington, VA 22209
Telephone: (703) 841-1700
Recruiter Classification: Retained; **Lowest/Average Salary:** $40,000/$60,000; **Industry Concentration:** High Technology, Information Technology; **Function Concentration:** Marketing, Sales

Miller, David — *Search Consultant*
Cochran, Cochran & Yale, Inc.
955 East Henrietta Road
Rochester, NY 14623
Telephone: (716) 424-6060
Recruiter Classification: Retained; **Lowest/Average Salary:** $50,000/$75,000; **Industry Concentration:** Generalist with a primary focus in High Technology, Information Technology; **Function Concentration:** Generalist with a primary focus in Engineering, Finance/Accounting, General Management, Human Resources, Marketing, Sales, Women/Minorities

Miller, George N. — *Senior Associate*
Hite Executive Search
6515 Chase Drive
P.O. Box 43217
Cleveland, OH 44143
Telephone: (216) 461-1600
Recruiter Classification: Retained; **Lowest/Average Salary:** $90,000/$90,000; **Industry Concentration:** Generalist with a primary focus in Information Technology; **Function Concentration:** Generalist with a primary focus in Administration, Human Resources, Women/Minorities

Miller, Kenneth A. — *President*
Computer Network Resources, Inc.
28231 Tinajo
Mission Viejo, CA 92692
Telephone: (714) 951-5929
Recruiter Classification: Contingency; **Lowest/Average Salary:** $60,000/$75,000; **Industry Concentration:** High Technology, Information Technology; **Function Concentration:** Sales

Miller, Larry — *Associate*
Source Services Corporation
4200 West Cypress Street, Suite 101
Tampa, FL 33607
Telephone: (813) 879-2221
Recruiter Classification: Contingency; **Lowest/Average Salary:** $30,000/$50,000; **Industry Concentration:** Information Technology; **Function Concentration:** Engineering, Finance/Accounting

Miller, Roy — *Partner*
The Enns Partners Inc.
70 University Avenue, Suite 410, P.O. Box 14
Toronto, Ontario, CANADA M5J 2M4
Telephone: (416) 598-0012
Recruiter Classification: Retained; **Lowest/Average Salary:** $75,000/$90,000; **Industry Concentration:** Generalist with a primary focus in Electronics, High Technology; **Function Concentration:** Generalist with a primary focus in Administration, Finance/Accounting, General Management, Human Resources, Marketing, Sales

Miller, Russel E. — *Executive Vice President*
ARJay & Associates
875 Walnut Street, Suite 150
Cary, NC 27511
Telephone: (919) 469-5540
Recruiter Classification: Contingency; **Lowest/Average Salary:** $40,000/$90,000; **Industry Concentration:** Generalist with a primary focus in Electronics; **Function Concentration:** Generalist with a primary focus in Engineering, Finance/Accounting, General Management, Human Resources, Marketing, Research and Development, Sales

Miller, Timothy — *Associate*
Source Services Corporation
3 Summit Park Drive, Suite 550
Independence, OH 44131
Telephone: (216) 328-5900
Recruiter Classification: Contingency; **Lowest/Average Salary:** $30,000/$50,000; **Industry Concentration:** Information Technology; **Function Concentration:** Engineering, Finance/Accounting

Milligan, Dale — *Associate*
Source Services Corporation
4170 Ashford Dunwoody Road, Suite 285
Atlanta, GA 30319
Telephone: (404) 255-2045
Recruiter Classification: Contingency; **Lowest/Average Salary:** $30,000/$50,000; **Industry Concentration:** Information Technology; **Function Concentration:** Engineering, Finance/Accounting

Mills, John — *Associate*
Source Services Corporation
1105 Schrock Road, Suite 510
Columbus, OH 43229
Telephone: (614) 846-3311
Recruiter Classification: Contingency; **Lowest/Average Salary:** $30,000/$50,000; **Industry Concentration:** Information Technology; **Function Concentration:** Engineering, Finance/Accounting

Milner, Carol — *Associate*
Source Services Corporation
One CityPlace, Suite 170
St. Louis, MO 63141
Telephone: (314) 432-4500
Recruiter Classification: Contingency; **Lowest/Average Salary:** $30,000/$50,000; **Industry Concentration:** Information Technology; **Function Concentration:** Engineering, Finance/Accounting

Milstein, Bonnie — *Executive Vice President*
Marvin Laba & Associates
6255 Sunset Boulevard, Suite 617
Los Angeles, CA 90028
Telephone: (213) 464-1355
Recruiter Classification: Retained; **Lowest/Average Salary:**
$50,000/$90,000; **Industry Concentration:** Information
Technology; **Function Concentration:** Generalist with a
primary focus in Finance/Accounting, General Management,
Human Resources, Marketing, Sales

Mingle, Larry D. — *Managing Principal*
Columbia Consulting Group
185 Helios Drive
Jupiter, FL 33477
Telephone: (561) 748-0232
Recruiter Classification: Retained; **Lowest/Average Salary:**
$75,000/$90,000; **Industry Concentration:** Generalist with a
primary focus in High Technology, Information Technology;
Function Concentration: Generalist with a primary focus in
Finance/Accounting, Human Resources, Marketing,
Sales

Miras, Cliff — *Managing Director*
Source Services Corporation
379 Thornall Street
Edison, NJ 08837
Telephone: (908) 494-2800
Recruiter Classification: Contingency; **Lowest/Average Salary:**
$30,000/$50,000; **Industry Concentration:** Information
Technology; **Function Concentration:** Engineering,
Finance/Accounting

Miras, Cliff — *Managing Director*
Source Services Corporation
5 Independence Way
Princeton, NJ 08540
Telephone: (609) 452-7277
Recruiter Classification: Contingency; **Lowest/Average Salary:**
$30,000/$50,000; **Industry Concentration:** Information
Technology; **Function Concentration:** Engineering,
Finance/Accounting

Mirtz, P. John — *Partner*
Mirtz Morice, Inc.
One Dock Street
Stamford, CT 06902
Telephone: (203) 964-9266
Recruiter Classification: Retained; **Lowest/Average Salary:**
$90,000/$90,000; **Industry Concentration:** Generalist with a
primary focus in Electronics; **Function Concentration:**
Generalist

Misiurewicz, Marc — *Search Consultant*
Cochran, Cochran & Yale, Inc.
955 East Henrietta Road
Rochester, NY 14623
Telephone: (716) 424-6060
Recruiter Classification: Retained; **Lowest/Average Salary:**
$50,000/$75,000; **Industry Concentration:** Generalist with a
primary focus in High Technology, Information Technology;
Function Concentration: Generalist with a primary focus in
Engineering, Finance/Accounting, General Management,
Human Resources, Marketing, Sales, Women/Minorities

Mitchell, F. Wayne — *Vice President*
Korn/Ferry International
3950 Lincoln Plaza
500 North Akard Street
Dallas, TX 75201
Telephone: (214) 954-1834
Recruiter Classification: Retained; **Lowest/Average Salary:**
$100,000/$150,000; **Industry Concentration:** Generalist with a
primary focus in High Technology; **Function Concentration:**
Generalist

Mitchell, Jeff — *Professional Recruiter*
A.J. Burton Group, Inc.
4550 Montgomery Avenue, Ste. 325 North
Bethesda, MD 20814
Telephone: (301) 654-0082
Recruiter Classification: Contingency; **Lowest/Average Salary:**
$40,000/$75,000; **Industry Concentration:** Generalist with a
primary focus in High Technology, Information Technology;
Function Concentration: Generalist with a primary focus in
Administration, Finance/Accounting, General Management,
Human Resources

Mitchell, John — *Managing Partner*
Romac & Associates
Plaza of the Americas
700 North Pear St. #940
Dallas, TX 75201
Telephone: (214) 720-0050
Recruiter Classification: Executive Temporary; **Lowest/Average
Salary:** $60,000/$60,000; **Industry Concentration:** High
Technology, Information Technology; **Function Concentration:**
Finance/Accounting

Mitton, Bill — *Executive Vice President*
Executive Resource, Inc.
553 South Industrial Drive
P.O. Box 356
Hartland, WI 53029-0356
Telephone: (414) 369-2540
Recruiter Classification: Contingency; **Lowest/Average Salary:**
$30,000/$50,000; **Industry Concentration:** Generalist with a
primary focus in Electronics, High Technology; **Function
Concentration:** Finance/Accounting, Human Resources

Mittwol, Myles — *Associate*
Source Services Corporation
1 Gatehall Drive, Suite 250
Parsippany, NJ 07054
Telephone: (201) 267-3222
Recruiter Classification: Contingency; **Lowest/Average Salary:**
$30,000/$50,000; **Industry Concentration:** Information
Technology; **Function Concentration:** Engineering,
Finance/Accounting

Mochwart, Donald — *Vice President*
Drummond Associates, Inc.
50 Broadway, Suite 1201
New York, NY 10004
Telephone: (212) 248-1120
Recruiter Classification: Contingency; **Lowest/Average Salary:**
$40,000/$75,000; **Industry Concentration:** Information
Technology; **Function Concentration:** Finance/Accounting

Moerbe, Ed H. — *Managing Director*
Stanton Chase International
2 Lincoln Center
5420 LBJ Freeway #780
Dallas, TX 75240
Telephone: (972) 404-8411
Recruiter Classification: Retained; **Lowest/Average Salary:**
$75,000/$90,000; **Industry Concentration:** Generalist with a
primary focus in High Technology; **Function Concentration:**
Generalist with a primary focus in Administration, Engineering,
Marketing, Sales

Mogul, Gene — *President*
Mogul Consultants, Inc.
380 North Broadway, Suite 208
Jericho, NY 11753-2109
Telephone: (516) 822-4363
Recruiter Classification: Contingency; **Lowest/Average Salary:**
$40,000/$75,000; **Industry Concentration:** Electronics, High
Technology, Information Technology; **Function Concentration:**
Generalist with a primary focus in Engineering, General
Management, Marketing, Research and Development, Sales

Mohr, Brian — *Executive Recruiter*
CPS Inc.
One Westbrook Corporate Centre, Suite 600
Westchester, IL 60154
Telephone: (708) 531-8370
Recruiter Classification: Contingency; **Lowest/Average Salary:**
$30,000/$50,000; **Industry Concentration:** Generalist with a
primary focus in Electronics, High Technology, Information
Technology; **Function Concentration:** Engineering, Research
and Development, Sales, Women/Minorities

Molitor, John L. — *Manager Accounting/Financial
Search Division*
Barrett Partners
100 North LaSalle Street, Suite 1420
Chicago, IL 60602
Telephone: (312) 443-8877
Recruiter Classification: Contingency; **Lowest/Average Salary:**
$30,000/$50,000; **Industry Concentration:** Information
Technology; **Function Concentration:** Engineering,
Finance/Accounting

Mollichelli, David — *Associate*
Source Services Corporation
One Park Plaza, Suite 560
Irvine, CA 92714
Telephone: (714) 660-1666
Recruiter Classification: Contingency; **Lowest/Average Salary:**
$30,000/$50,000; **Industry Concentration:** Information
Technology; **Function Concentration:** Engineering,
Finance/Accounting

Molnar, Robert A. — *Partner*
Johnson Smith & Knisely Accord
100 Park Avenue, 15th Floor
New York, NY 10017
Telephone: (212) 885-9100
Recruiter Classification: Retained; **Lowest/Average Salary:**
$90,000/$90,000; **Industry Concentration:** Electronics, High
Technology, Information Technology; **Function Concentration:**
Generalist

Mondragon, Philip — *Vice President*
A.T. Kearney, Inc.
Ruben Dario 281-Piso 15
Col. Bosques de Chapultepec
Mexico City D.F., MEXICO 11580
Telephone: (525) 282-0050
Recruiter Classification: Retained; **Lowest/Average Salary:**
$90,000/$90,000; **Industry Concentration:** Generalist with a
primary focus in High Technology, Information Technology;
Function Concentration: Generalist with a primary focus in
Engineering, Finance/Accounting, General Management

Montgomery, James M. — *President*
Houze, Shourds & Montgomery, Inc.
Greater L.A. World Trade Center, Suite 800
Long Beach, CA 90831-0800
Telephone: (562) 495-6495
Recruiter Classification: Retained; **Lowest/Average Salary:**
$90,000/$90,000; **Industry Concentration:** Generalist with a
primary focus in Electronics, High Technology; **Function
Concentration:** Generalist with a primary focus in
Finance/Accounting, General Management, Human Resources,
Marketing, Women/Minorities

Moodley, Logan — *Vice President*
Austin-McGregor International
12005 Ford Road, Suite 720
Dallas, TX 75234-7247
Telephone: (972) 488-0500
Recruiter Classification: Retained; **Lowest/Average Salary:**
$50,000/$90,000; **Industry Concentration:** Generalist with a
primary focus in Electronics, High Technology, Information
Technology; **Function Concentration:** Generalist

Moore, Craig — *Associate*
Source Services Corporation
20 Burlington Mall Road, Suite 405
Burlington, MA 01803
Telephone: (617) 272-5000
Recruiter Classification: Contingency; **Lowest/Average Salary:**
$30,000/$50,000; **Industry Concentration:** Information
Technology; **Function Concentration:** Engineering,
Finance/Accounting

Moore, David S. — *Managing Director*
Lynch Miller Moore, Inc.
10 South Wacker Drive, Suite 2935
Chicago, IL 60606
Telephone: (312) 876-1505
Recruiter Classification: Retained; **Lowest/Average Salary:**
$75,000/$90,000; **Industry Concentration:** Generalist with a
primary focus in Electronics, High Technology, Information
Technology; **Function Concentration:** Generalist with a
primary focus in Finance/Accounting, General Management,
Marketing

Moore, Dianna — *Associate*
Source Services Corporation
2850 National City Tower
Louisville, KY 40202
Telephone: (502) 581-9900
Recruiter Classification: Contingency; **Lowest/Average Salary:**
$30,000/$50,000; **Industry Concentration:** Information
Technology; **Function Concentration:** Engineering,
Finance/Accounting

Moore, Lemuel R. — *Executive Recruiter*
MSI International
6151 Powers Ferry Road, Suite 540
Atlanta, GA 30339
Telephone: (404) 850-6465
Recruiter Classification: Contingency; **Lowest/Average Salary:**
$30,000/$75,000; **Industry Concentration:** Generalist with a
primary focus in Electronics, High Technology; **Function
Concentration:** Generalist with a primary focus in
Administration, Engineering, Finance/Accounting, General
Management, Marketing, Sales

Moore, Mark — *Chairman and CEO*
Wheeler, Moore & Elam Co.
14800 Quorum Drive, Suite 200
Dallas, TX 75240
Telephone: (214) 386-8806
Recruiter Classification: Retained; **Lowest/Average Salary:**
$50,000/$75,000; **Industry Concentration:** Generalist with a
primary focus in Electronics, High Technology, Information
Technology; **Function Concentration:** Generalist with a
primary focus in Administration, Engineering,
Finance/Accounting, General Management, Human Resources,
Marketing, Research and Development, Sales

Moore, Suzanne — *Associate*
Source Services Corporation
8614 Westwood Center, Suite 750
Vienna, VA 22182
Telephone: (703) 790-5610
Recruiter Classification: Contingency; **Lowest/Average Salary:**
$30,000/$50,000; **Industry Concentration:** Information
Technology; **Function Concentration:** Engineering,
Finance/Accounting

Moore, T. Wills — *Consultant*
Ray & Berndtson
191 Peachtree Street, NE, Suite 3800
Atlanta, GA 30303-1757
Telephone: (404) 215-4600
Recruiter Classification: Retained; **Lowest/Average Salary:**
$90,000/$90,000; **Industry Concentration:** Generalist with a
primary focus in High Technology, Information Technology;
Function Concentration: Generalist with a primary focus in
Administration, Finance/Accounting, General Management,
Human Resources, Marketing, Research and Development,
Sales, Women/Minorities

Moore, Thomas — *Technical Recruiter*
Aureus Group
8744 Frederick Street
Omaha, NE 68124-3068
Telephone: (402) 397-2980
Recruiter Classification: Contingency; **Lowest/Average Salary:**
$30,000/$60,000; **Industry Concentration:** Electronics;
Function Concentration: Engineering

Moran, Douglas — *Associate*
Source Services Corporation
10220 SW Greenburg Road, Suite 625
Portland, OR 97223
Telephone: (503) 768-4546
Recruiter Classification: Contingency; **Lowest/Average Salary:**
$30,000/$50,000; **Industry Concentration:** Information
Technology; **Function Concentration:** Engineering,
Finance/Accounting

Moran, Gayle — *Associate*
Dussick Management Associates
149 Durham Road
Madison, CT 06443
Telephone: (203) 245-9311
Recruiter Classification: Contingency; **Lowest/Average Salary:**
$50,000/$60,000; **Industry Concentration:** Generalist with a
primary focus in High Technology, Information Technology;
Function Concentration: Generalist with a primary focus in
Marketing, Research and Development, Sales,
Women/Minorities

Morato, Rene — *Associate*
Source Services Corporation
15600 N.W. 67th Avenue, Suite 210
Miami Lakes, FL 33014
Telephone: (305) 556-8000
Recruiter Classification: Contingency; **Lowest/Average Salary:**
$30,000/$50,000; **Industry Concentration:** Information
Technology; **Function Concentration:** Engineering,
Finance/Accounting

Moretti, Denise — *Associate*
Source Services Corporation
150 South Warner Road, Suite 238
King of Prussia, PA 19406
Telephone: (610) 341-1960
Recruiter Classification: Contingency; **Lowest/Average Salary:**
$30,000/$50,000; **Industry Concentration:** Information
Technology; **Function Concentration:** Engineering,
Finance/Accounting

Morgan, Richard S. — *Partner*
Ray & Berndtson/Lovas Stanley
155 Queen Street, Suite 900
Ottawa, Ontario, CANADA K1P 6L1
Telephone: (613) 786-3191
Recruiter Classification: Retained; **Lowest/Average Salary:**
$50,000/$75,000; **Industry Concentration:** Generalist with a
primary focus in High Technology, Information Technology;
Function Concentration: Generalist with a primary focus in
General Management, Human Resources, Marketing, Research
and Development, Sales

Morgan-Christopher, Jeanie — *Director*
Information Technology Search
Kaye-Bassman International Corp.
18333 Preston Road, Suite 500
Dallas, TX 75252
Telephone: (972) 931-5242
Recruiter Classification: Retained; **Lowest/Average Salary:**
$75,000/$90,000; **Industry Concentration:** Information
Technology; **Function Concentration:** Finance/Accounting,
Research and Development, Women/Minorities

Moriarty, Mike — *Associate*
Source Services Corporation
2850 National City Tower
Louisville, KY 40202
Telephone: (502) 581-9900
Recruiter Classification: Contingency; **Lowest/Average Salary:**
$30,000/$50,000; **Industry Concentration:** Information
Technology; **Function Concentration:** Engineering,
Finance/Accounting

Morice, James L. — *Partner*
Mirtz Morice, Inc.
One Dock Street
Stamford, CT 06902
Telephone: (203) 964-9266
Recruiter Classification: Retained; **Lowest/Average Salary:**
$90,000/$90,000; **Industry Concentration:** Generalist with a
primary focus in Electronics; **Function Concentration:**
Generalist

Morrill, Nancy — *Information Technology
Recruiter*
Winter, Wyman & Company
950 Winter Street, Suite 3100
Waltham, MA 02154-1294
Telephone: (617) 890-7000
Recruiter Classification: Contingency; **Lowest/Average Salary:**
$30,000/$60,000; **Industry Concentration:** Generalist with a
primary focus in Information Technology; **Function
Concentration:** Generalist

Morris, Chuck — *Senior Managing Partner*
Warren, Morris & Madison
2190 Carmel Valley Road
Del Mar, CA 92014
Telephone: (619) 481-3388
Recruiter Classification: Retained; **Lowest/Average Salary:**
$75,000/$90,000; **Industry Concentration:** High Technology;
Function Concentration: Generalist

Morris, Scott — *Associate*
Source Services Corporation
1105 Schrock Road, Suite 510
Columbus, OH 43229
Telephone: (614) 846-3311
Recruiter Classification: Contingency; **Lowest/Average Salary:**
$30,000/$50,000; **Industry Concentration:** Information
Technology; **Function Concentration:** Engineering,
Finance/Accounting

Morrow, Melanie — *Associate*
Source Services Corporation
3 Summit Park Drive, Suite 550
Independence, OH 44131
Telephone: (216) 328-5900
Recruiter Classification: Contingency; **Lowest/Average Salary:**
$30,000/$50,000; **Industry Concentration:** Information
Technology; **Function Concentration:** Engineering,
Finance/Accounting

Mortansen, Patricia — *Vice President*
Norman Broadbent International, Inc.
Sears Tower, Suite 9850
233 South Wacker Drive
Chicago, IL 60606
Telephone: (312) 876-3300
Recruiter Classification: Retained; **Lowest/Average Salary:**
$90,000/$90,000; **Industry Concentration:** Generalist with a
primary focus in Electronics, High Technology, Information
Technology; **Function Concentration:** Generalist with a
primary focus in Finance/Accounting, General Management,
Human Resources, Marketing, Sales

Moses, Jerry — *President*
J.M. Eagle Partners Ltd.
10140 North Port Washington Rd.
Mequon, WI 53092
Telephone: (414) 241-1113
Recruiter Classification: Contingency; **Lowest/Average Salary:**
$60,000/$90,000; **Industry Concentration:** Electronics, High
Technology, Information Technology; **Function Concentration:**
Generalist

Mott, Greg — *Associate*
Source Services Corporation
5429 LBJ Freeway, Suite 275
Dallas, TX 75240
Telephone: (214) 387-1600
Recruiter Classification: Contingency; **Lowest/Average Salary:**
$30,000/$50,000; **Industry Concentration:** Information
Technology; **Function Concentration:** Engineering,
Finance/Accounting

Mouchet, Marcus — *Partner*
Commonwealth Consultants
4840 Roswell Road
Atlanta, GA 30342
Telephone: (404) 256-0000
Recruiter Classification: Contingency; **Lowest/Average Salary:**
$30,000/$90,000; **Industry Concentration:** High Technology;
Function Concentration: Sales

Moyse, Richard G. — *Principal*
Thorndike Deland Associates
275 Madison Avenue, Suite 1300
New York, NY 10016
Telephone: (212) 661-6200
Recruiter Classification: Retained; **Lowest/Average Salary:**
$100,000/$125,000; **Industry Concentration:** Generalist with a
primary focus in Information Technology; **Function
Concentration:** Generalist with a primary focus in Sales

Msidment, Roger — *Associate*
Source Services Corporation
10300 West 103rd Street, Suite 101
Overland Park, KS 66214
Telephone: (913) 888-8885
Recruiter Classification: Contingency; **Lowest/Average Salary:**
$30,000/$50,000; **Industry Concentration:** Information
Technology; **Function Concentration:** Engineering,
Finance/Accounting

Mueller, Colleen — *Associate*
Source Services Corporation
5429 LBJ Freeway, Suite 275
Dallas, TX 75240
Telephone: (214) 387-1600
Recruiter Classification: Contingency; **Lowest/Average Salary:**
$30,000/$50,000; **Industry Concentration:** Information
Technology; **Function Concentration:** Engineering,
Finance/Accounting

Mueller-Maerki, Fortunat F. — *Consultant*
Egon Zehnder International Inc.
350 Park Avenue
New York, NY 10022
Telephone: (212) 838-9199
Recruiter Classification: Retained; **Lowest/Average Salary:**
$90,000/$90,000; **Industry Concentration:** Generalist with a
primary focus in High Technology; **Function Concentration:**
Generalist

Muendel, H. Edward — *Managing Director*
Stanton Chase International
100 East Pratt Street
Suite 2530
Baltimore, MD 21202
Telephone: (410) 528-8400
Recruiter Classification: Retained; **Lowest/Average Salary:**
$75,000/$90,000; **Industry Concentration:** Generalist with a
primary focus in Electronics, High Technology; **Function
Concentration:** Generalist with a primary focus in
Administration, Engineering, Finance/Accounting, General
Management, Human Resources, Marketing, Research and
Development, Sales

Muller, Susan — *Recruiter*
Corporate Recruiters Ltd.
490-1140 West Pender Street
Vancouver, British Columbia, CANADA V6E 4G1
Telephone: (604) 687-5993
Recruiter Classification: Contingency; **Lowest/Average Salary:**
$30,000/$60,000; **Industry Concentration:** Electronics, High
Technology, Information Technology

Murphy, Corinne — *Associate*
Source Services Corporation
100 North Tryon Street, Suite 3130
Charlotte, NC 28202
Telephone: (704) 333-8311
Recruiter Classification: Contingency; **Lowest/Average Salary:**
$30,000/$50,000; **Industry Concentration:** Information
Technology; **Function Concentration:** Engineering,
Finance/Accounting

Murphy, Cornelius J. — *Senior Vice President*
Goodrich & Sherwood Associates, Inc.
250 Mill Street
Rochester, NY 14614
Telephone: (716) 777-4060
Recruiter Classification: Retained; **Lowest/Average Salary:**
$60,000/$90,000; **Industry Concentration:** Generalist with a
primary focus in Information Technology; **Function
Concentration:** Generalist with a primary focus in
Administration, Finance/Accounting, General Management,
Human Resources, Marketing, Sales

Murphy, Erin — *Executive Recruiter*
CPS Inc.
One Westbrook Corporate Centre, Suite 600
Westchester, IL 60154
Telephone: (708) 531-8370
Recruiter Classification: Contingency; **Lowest/Average Salary:**
$30,000/$50,000; **Industry Concentration:** Generalist with a
primary focus in Electronics, High Technology, Information
Technology; **Function Concentration:** Engineering, Research
and Development, Sales, Women/Minorities

Murphy, Gary J. — *Partner*
Stone Murphy & Olson
5500 Wayzata Boulevard
Suite 1020
Minneapolis, MN 55416
Telephone: (612) 591-2300
Recruiter Classification: Retained; **Lowest/Average Salary:**
$75,000/$90,000; **Industry Concentration:** Generalist with a
primary focus in Electronics, High Technology; **Function
Concentration:** Human Resources

Murphy, James — *Associate*
Source Services Corporation
4170 Ashford Dunwoody Road, Suite 285
Atlanta, GA 30319
Telephone: (404) 255-2045
Recruiter Classification: Contingency; **Lowest/Average Salary:**
$30,000/$50,000; **Industry Concentration:** Information
Technology; **Function Concentration:** Engineering,
Finance/Accounting

Murphy, Patrick J. — *President*
P.J. Murphy & Associates, Inc.
735 North Water Street
Milwaukee, WI 53202
Telephone: (414) 277-9777
Recruiter Classification: Retained; **Lowest/Average Salary:**
$60,000/$90,000; **Industry Concentration:** Generalist with a
primary focus in Information Technology; **Function
Concentration:** Generalist with a primary focus in
Administration, Finance/Accounting, General Management,
Human Resources, Marketing, Sales

Murphy, Peter — *Principal*
Korn/Ferry International
One Landmark Square
Stamford, CT 06901
Telephone: (203) 359-3350
Recruiter Classification: Retained; **Lowest/Average Salary:**
$100,000/$150,000; **Industry Concentration:** Generalist with a
primary focus in Information Technology; **Function
Concentration:** Generalist

Murphy, Timothy D. — *Executive Recruiter*
MSI International
200 Galleria Parkway
Suite 1610
Atlanta, GA 30339
Telephone: (404) 951-1208
Recruiter Classification: Contingency; **Lowest/Average Salary:**
$30,000/$60,000; **Industry Concentration:** Generalist with a
primary focus in High Technology; **Function Concentration:**
Administration, Engineering, Finance/Accounting, General
Management, Marketing, Sales

Murray, Virginia — *Vice President*
A.T. Kearney, Inc.
130 Adelaide Street West, Suite 2710
Toronto, Ontario, CANADA M5H 3P5
Telephone: (416) 947-1990
Recruiter Classification: Retained; **Lowest/Average Salary:**
$90,000/$90,000; **Industry Concentration:** Generalist with a
primary focus in High Technology, Information Technology;
Function Concentration: Generalist with a primary focus in
Engineering, Finance/Accounting, General Management

Murry, John — *Associate*
Source Services Corporation
20 Burlington Mall Road, Suite 405
Burlington, MA 01803
Telephone: (617) 272-5000
Recruiter Classification: Contingency; **Lowest/Average Salary:**
$30,000/$50,000; **Industry Concentration:** Information
Technology; **Function Concentration:** Engineering,
Finance/Accounting

Mursuli, Meredith — *Consultant*
Lasher Associates
1200 South Pine Island Road, Suite 370
Fort Lauderdale, FL 33324-4402
Telephone: (305) 472-5658
Recruiter Classification: Retained; **Lowest/Average Salary:**
$75,000/$90,000; **Industry Concentration:** Generalist with a
primary focus in Electronics, High Technology, Information
Technology; **Function Concentration:** Generalist with a
primary focus in Engineering, Finance/Accounting, General
Management, Human Resources, Marketing, Research and
Development, Sales

Myatt, James S. — *Principal*
Sanford Rose Associates
101 East Victoria Street
Suite 22
Santa Barbara, CA 93101
Telephone: (805) 966-1846
Recruiter Classification: Contingency; **Lowest/Average Salary:**
$30,000/$75,000; **Industry Concentration:** Generalist with a
primary focus in Electronics, High Technology; **Function
Concentration:** Generalist

Mydlach, Renee — *Senior Division Manager*
CPS Inc.
One Westbrook Corporate Centre, Suite 600
Westchester, IL 60154
Telephone: (708) 531-8370
Recruiter Classification: Contingency; **Lowest/Average Salary:**
$30,000/$50,000; **Industry Concentration:** Generalist with a
primary focus in Electronics, High Technology, Information
Technology; **Function Concentration:** Engineering, Research
and Development, Sales, Women/Minorities

Myers, Kay — *Recruiter*
Signature Staffing
6800 College Boulevard, Suite 550
Overland Park, KS 66211
Telephone: (913) 338-2020
Recruiter Classification: Executive Temporary; **Lowest/Average
Salary:** $30,000/$40,000; **Industry Concentration:** Generalist
with a primary focus in Electronics; **Function Concentration:**
Generalist with a primary focus in Finance/Accounting,
Marketing

Myers, Thomas — *Chief Executive Officer*
Careers Plus
29350 Pacific Coast Highway #1
Malibu, CA 90265
Telephone: (310) 589-2437
Recruiter Classification: Retained; **Lowest/Average Salary:**
$75,000/$90,000; **Industry Concentration:** Electronics;
Function Concentration: Sales

Nabers, Karen — *Associate*
Source Services Corporation
9020 Capital of Texas Highway
Building I, Suite 337
Austin, TX 78759
Telephone: (512) 345-7473
Recruiter Classification: Contingency; **Lowest/Average Salary:**
$30,000/$50,000; **Industry Concentration:** Information
Technology; **Function Concentration:** Engineering,
Finance/Accounting

Nadherny, Christopher C. — *Senior Director*
Spencer Stuart
401 North Michigan Avenue, Suite 3400
Chicago, IL 60611-4244
Telephone: (312) 822-0080
Recruiter Classification: Retained; **Lowest/Average Salary:**
$90,000/$90,000; **Industry Concentration:** Generalist with a
primary focus in High Technology; **Function Concentration:**
Generalist with a primary focus in Finance/Accounting,
General Management, Human Resources, Marketing, Sales

Nadzam, Richard I. — *Partner*
Nadzam, Lusk, Horgan & Associates, Inc.
3211 Scott Boulevard
Suite 205
Santa Clara, CA 95054-3091
Telephone: (408) 727-6601
Recruiter Classification: Retained; **Lowest/Average Salary:**
$90,000/$90,000; **Industry Concentration:** Generalist with a
primary focus in Electronics, High Technology, Information
Technology; **Function Concentration:** Generalist

Nagler, Leon G. — *Managing Director*
Nagler, Robins & Poe, Inc.
65 William Street
Wellesley Hills, MA 02181
Telephone: (617) 431-1330
Recruiter Classification: Retained; **Lowest/Average Salary:**
$90,000/$90,000; **Industry Concentration:** Generalist with a
primary focus in Electronics, High Technology, Information
Technology; **Function Concentration:** Generalist with a
primary focus in Engineering, Finance/Accounting, General
Management, Human Resources, Marketing, Research and
Development, Sales

Nagy, Les — *Managing Director*
Source Services Corporation
255 Consumers Road, Suite 404
North York, Ontario, CANADA M2J 1R1
Telephone: (416) 495-1551
Recruiter Classification: Contingency; **Lowest/Average Salary:**
$30,000/$50,000; **Industry Concentration:** Information
Technology; **Function Concentration:** Engineering,
Finance/Accounting

Naidicz, Maria — *Consultant*
Ray & Berndtson
Sears Tower, 233 South Wacker Drive, Suite 4020
Chicago, IL 60606-6310
Telephone: (312) 876-0730
Recruiter Classification: Retained; **Lowest/Average Salary:**
$90,000/$90,000; **Industry Concentration:** Generalist with a
primary focus in High Technology, Information Technology;
Function Concentration: Generalist with a primary focus in
Administration, Finance/Accounting, General Management,
Human Resources, Marketing, Research and Development,
Sales, Women/Minorities

Necessary, Rick — *Associate*
Source Services Corporation
111 Monument Circle, Suite 3930
Indianapolis, IN 46204
Telephone: (317) 631-2900
Recruiter Classification: Contingency; **Lowest/Average Salary:**
$30,000/$50,000; **Industry Concentration:** Information
Technology; **Function Concentration:** Engineering,
Finance/Accounting

Needham, Karen — *Associate*
Source Services Corporation
111 Founders Plaza, Suite 1501E
Hartford, CT 06108
Telephone: (860) 528-0300
Recruiter Classification: Contingency; **Lowest/Average Salary:**
$30,000/$50,000; **Industry Concentration:** Information
Technology; **Function Concentration:** Engineering,
Finance/Accounting

Neelin, Sharon — *Consultant*
The Caldwell Partners Amrop International
Sixty-Four Prince Arthur Avenue
Toronto, Ontario, CANADA M5R 1B4
Telephone: (416) 920-7702
Recruiter Classification: Retained; **Lowest/Average Salary:**
$60,000/$90,000; **Industry Concentration:** Generalist with a
primary focus in Electronics, High Technology, Information
Technology; **Function Concentration:** Generalist

Neely, Alan S. — *Managing Director*
Korn/Ferry International
303 Peachtree Street N.E.
Suite 1600
Atlanta, GA 30308
Telephone: (404) 577-7542
Recruiter Classification: Retained; **Lowest/Average Salary:**
$100,000/$150,000; **Industry Concentration:** Generalist with a
primary focus in High Technology; **Function Concentration:**
Generalist

Nees, Eugene C. — *Partner*
Ray & Berndtson
245 Park Avenue, 33rd Floor
New York, NY 10167
Telephone: (212) 370-1316
Recruiter Classification: Retained; **Lowest/Average Salary:**
$90,000/$90,000; **Industry Concentration:** Generalist with a
primary focus in High Technology, Information Technology;
Function Concentration: Generalist with a primary focus in
Administration, Finance/Accounting, General Management,
Human Resources, Marketing, Research and Development,
Sales, Women/Minorities

Neff, Herbert — *Associate*
Source Services Corporation
15600 N.W. 67th Avenue, Suite 210
Miami Lakes, FL 33014
Telephone: (305) 556-8000
Recruiter Classification: Contingency; **Lowest/Average Salary:**
$30,000/$50,000; **Industry Concentration:** Information
Technology; **Function Concentration:** Engineering,
Finance/Accounting

Neff, Thomas J. — *President*
Spencer Stuart
277 Park Avenue, 29th Floor
New York, NY 10172
Telephone: (212) 336-0200
Recruiter Classification: Retained; **Lowest/Average Salary:**
$90,000/$90,000; **Industry Concentration:** Generalist with a
primary focus in High Technology; **Function Concentration:**
Generalist with a primary focus in General Management

Neher, Robert L. — *Senior Executive Vice
President*
Intech Summit Group, Inc.
5075 Shoreham Place, Suite 280
San Diego, CA 92116
Telephone: (619) 452-2100
Recruiter Classification: Retained; **Lowest/Average Salary:**
$75,000/$90,000; **Industry Concentration:** Generalist with a
primary focus in Electronics, High Technology, Information
Technology; **Function Concentration:** Generalist with a
primary focus in Administration, Engineering,
Finance/Accounting, General Management, Human Resources,
Marketing, Research and Development, Sales,
Women/Minorities

Nehring, Keith — *Consultant*
Howard Fischer Associates, Inc.
1800 John F. Kennedy Boulevard, 7th Floor
Philadelphia, PA 19103
Telephone: (215) 568-8363
Recruiter Classification: Retained; **Lowest/Average Salary:**
$90,000/$90,000; **Industry Concentration:** Generalist with a
primary focus in High Technology; **Function Concentration:**
Generalist with a primary focus in Administration,
Finance/Accounting, General Management, Human Resources,
Marketing, Research and Development, Sales,
Women/Minorities

Neidhart, Craig C. — *Partner*
TNS Partners, Inc.
8140 Walnut Hill Lane
Suite 301
Dallas, TX 75231
Telephone: (214) 369-3565
Recruiter Classification: Retained; **Lowest/Average Salary:**
$90,000/$90,000; **Industry Concentration:** Generalist with a
primary focus in Electronics, High Technology; **Function
Concentration:** Generalist with a primary focus in Engineering,
Finance/Accounting, General Management, Human Resources,
Marketing, Research and Development, Sales

Nelson, Barbara — *Partner*
Herman Smith Executive Initiatives Inc.
161 Bay Street, Suite 3600
Box 629
Toronto, Ontario, CANADA M5J 2S1
Telephone: (416) 862-8830
Recruiter Classification: Retained; **Lowest/Average Salary:**
$75,000/$90,000; **Industry Concentration:** Generalist with a
primary focus in High Technology, Information Technology;
Function Concentration: Generalist with a primary focus in
General Management, Human Resources, Marketing, Sales,
Women/Minorities

Nelson, Hitch — *Associate*
Source Services Corporation
1290 Oakmead Parkway, Suite 318
Sunnyvale, CA 94086
Telephone: (408) 738-8440
Recruiter Classification: Contingency; **Lowest/Average Salary:**
$30,000/$50,000; **Industry Concentration:** Information
Technology; **Function Concentration:** Engineering,
Finance/Accounting

Nelson, Mary — *Associate*
Source Services Corporation
8614 Westwood Center, Suite 750
Vienna, VA 22182
Telephone: (703) 790-5610
Recruiter Classification: Contingency; **Lowest/Average Salary:**
$30,000/$50,000; **Industry Concentration:** Information
Technology; **Function Concentration:** Engineering,
Finance/Accounting

Nelson-Folkersen, Jeffrey — *Associate*
Source Services Corporation
4200 West Cypress Street, Suite 101
Tampa, FL 33607
Telephone: (813) 879-2221
Recruiter Classification: Contingency; **Lowest/Average Salary:**
$30,000/$50,000; **Industry Concentration:** Information
Technology; **Function Concentration:** Engineering,
Finance/Accounting

Nemec, Phillip — *Vice President Southeast Asia
Recruitment*
Dunhill International Search of New Haven
59 Elm Street
New Haven, CT 06510
Telephone: (203) 562-0511
Recruiter Classification: Contingency; **Lowest/Average Salary:**
$30,000/$60,000; **Industry Concentration:** Generalist with a
primary focus in High Technology, Information Technology;
Function Concentration: Generalist with a primary focus in
Engineering, Finance/Accounting, General Management,
Human Resources, Marketing, Sales

Nephew, Robert — *Vice President*
Christian & Timbers
24 New England Executive Park
Burlington, MA 01803
Telephone: (617) 229-9515
Recruiter Classification: Retained; **Lowest/Average Salary:**
$90,000/$90,000; **Industry Concentration:** High Technology,
Information Technology; **Function Concentration:** Generalist
with a primary focus in Engineering, Finance/Accounting,
General Management, Human Resources, Marketing, Research
and Development, Sales

Neri, Gene — *Executive Recruiter*
S.C. International, Ltd.
1430 Branding Lane, Suite 119
Downers Grove, IL 60515
Telephone: (708) 963-3033
Recruiter Classification: Contingency; **Lowest/Average Salary:**
$30,000/$50,000; **Industry Concentration:** Information
Technology; **Function Concentration:** Administration, Human
Resources

Neuberth, Jeffrey G. — *Senior Vice
President/Director*
Canny, Bowen Inc.
200 Park Avenue
49th Floor
New York, NY 10166
Telephone: (212) 949-6611
Recruiter Classification: Retained; **Lowest/Average Salary:**
$120,000/$201,000; **Industry Concentration:** Generalist with a
primary focus in High Technology, Information Technology;
Function Concentration: Generalist with a primary focus in
Engineering, Finance/Accounting, General Management,
Human Resources, Marketing, Women/Minorities

Neuwald, Debrah — *Associate*
Source Services Corporation
1233 North Mayfair Road, Suite 300
Milwaukee, WI 53226
Telephone: (414) 774-6700
Recruiter Classification: Contingency; **Lowest/Average Salary:**
$30,000/$50,000; **Industry Concentration:** Information
Technology; **Function Concentration:** Engineering,
Finance/Accounting

Newlon, Jay — *Senior Consultant*
Logix, Inc.
1601 Trapelo Road
Waltham, MA 02154
Telephone: (617) 890-0500
Recruiter Classification: Retained; **Lowest/Average Salary:**
$60,000/$75,000; **Industry Concentration:** Information
Technology; **Function Concentration:** Engineering

Newman, Lynn — *Associate*
Kishbaugh Associates International
2 Elm Square
Andover, MA 01810
Telephone: (508) 475-7224
Recruiter Classification: Retained; **Lowest/Average Salary:**
$75,000/$90,000; **Industry Concentration:** Generalist with a
primary focus in High Technology, Information Technology;
Function Concentration: Generalist with a primary focus in
Finance/Accounting, General Management, Marketing,
Research and Development, Sales

Newton, Jay — *Senior Consultant*
Logix Partners
1601 Trapelo Road
Waltham, MA 02154
Telephone: (617) 890-0500
Recruiter Classification: Retained; **Lowest/Average Salary:**
$60,000/$75,000; **Industry Concentration:** Information
Technology; **Function Concentration:** Engineering

Nguyen, John — *Staffing Consultant*
International Staffing Consultants, Inc.
500 Newport Center Drive, Suite 300
Newport Beach, CA 92660-7003
Telephone: (714) 721-7990
Recruiter Classification: Contingency; **Lowest/Average Salary:**
$40,000/$75,000; **Industry Concentration:** High Technology;
Function Concentration: Engineering

Nichols, Gary — *Senior Associate*
Koontz, Jeffries & Associates, Inc.
18-22 Bank Street
Summit, NJ 07901
Telephone: (908) 598-1900
Recruiter Classification: Retained; **Lowest/Average Salary:**
$60,000/$90,000; **Industry Concentration:** Generalist with a
primary focus in Electronics, High Technology; **Function
Concentration:** Generalist with a primary focus in
Administration, Engineering, Finance/Accounting, General
Management, Human Resources, Marketing, Research and
Development, Sales, Women/Minorities

Niejet, Michael C. — *Vice President*
O'Brien & Bell
812 Huron Road, Suite 535
Cleveland, OH 44115
Telephone: (216) 575-1212
Recruiter Classification: Retained; **Lowest/Average Salary:**
$75,000/$90,000; **Industry Concentration:** High Technology,
Information Technology; **Function Concentration:** Generalist
with a primary focus in General Management, Marketing, Sales

Noebel, Todd R. — *President*
The Noebel Search Group, Inc.
14902 Preston Road, Suite 404-102
Dallas, TX 75240
Telephone: (972) 458-7788
Recruiter Classification: Retained; **Lowest/Average Salary:**
$60,000/$90,000; **Industry Concentration:** Generalist with a
primary focus in Information Technology; **Function
Concentration:** Finance/Accounting, General Management,
Human Resources, Women/Minorities

Noguchi, Yoshi — *Industry Leader - Technology*
Ray & Berndtson
One Park Plaza, Suite 420
Irvine, CA 92614
Telephone: (714) 476-8844
Recruiter Classification: Retained; **Lowest/Average Salary:**
$90,000/$90,000; **Industry Concentration:** High Technology;
Function Concentration: Generalist

Nolan, Jean M. — *Recruiter*
S.D. Kelly & Associates, Inc.
990 Washington Street
Dedham, MA 02026
Telephone: (617) 326-8038
Recruiter Classification: Contingency; **Lowest/Average Salary:**
$50,000/$60,000; **Industry Concentration:** Electronics, High
Technology; **Function Concentration:** Engineering, Marketing,
Sales

Nolan, Robert — *Associate*
Source Services Corporation
150 South Warner Road, Suite 238
King of Prussia, PA 19406
Telephone: (610) 341-1960
Recruiter Classification: Contingency; **Lowest/Average Salary:**
$30,000/$50,000; **Industry Concentration:** Information
Technology; **Function Concentration:** Engineering,
Finance/Accounting

Nold, Robert — *Recruiter*
Roberson and Company
10752 North 89th Place, Suite 202
Scottsdale, AZ 85260
Telephone: (602) 391-3200
Recruiter Classification: Contingency; **Lowest/Average Salary:**
$40,000/$50,000; **Industry Concentration:** Generalist with a
primary focus in High Technology; **Function Concentration:**
Generalist with a primary focus in Administration, Engineering,
Human Resources, Marketing, Sales

Nolen, Shannon — *Associate*
Source Services Corporation
2029 Century Park East, Suite 1350
Los Angeles, CA 90067
Telephone: (310) 277-8092
Recruiter Classification: Contingency; **Lowest/Average Salary:**
$30,000/$50,000; **Industry Concentration:** Information
Technology; **Function Concentration:** Engineering,
Finance/Accounting

Nolte, William D. — *Principal*
W.D. Nolte & Company
6 Middlesex Road
Darien, CT 06820
Telephone: (203) 323-5858
Recruiter Classification: Retained; **Lowest/Average Salary:**
$75,000/$90,000; **Industry Concentration:** Generalist with a
primary focus in Electronics, High Technology, Information
Technology; **Function Concentration:** Generalist with a
primary focus in Engineering, Finance/Accounting, General
Management, Human Resources, Marketing, Sales

Nolton, Becky — *Vice President*
Paul-Tittle Associates, Inc.
1485 Chain Bridge Road, #304
McLean, VA 22101
Telephone: (703) 442-0500
Recruiter Classification: Retained; **Lowest/Average Salary:**
$60,000/$75,000; **Industry Concentration:** High Technology,
Information Technology; **Function Concentration:** Engineering,
Sales

Norman, Randy — *Vice President*
Austin-McGregor International
12005 Ford Road, Suite 720
Dallas, TX 75234-7247
Telephone: (972) 488-0500
Recruiter Classification: Retained; **Lowest/Average Salary:**
$50,000/$90,000; **Industry Concentration:** Generalist with a
primary focus in Electronics, High Technology; **Function
Concentration:** Generalist with a primary focus in Engineering,
Finance/Accounting, General Management, Human Resources,
Marketing, Research and Development, Sales,
Women/Minorities

Normann, Amy — *Research Associate*
Robert M. Flanagan & Associates, Ltd.
Fields Lane, JMK Building
North Salem, NY 10560-0339
Telephone: (914) 277-7210
Recruiter Classification: Retained; **Lowest/Average Salary:**
$90,000/$90,000; **Industry Concentration:** Generalist with a
primary focus in Information Technology; **Function
Concentration:** Generalist with a primary focus in
Administration, Finance/Accounting, Human Resources,
Marketing, Sales

Norris, Ken — *Vice President*
A.T. Kearney, Inc.
222 West Adams Street
Chicago, IL 60606
Telephone: (312) 648-0111
Recruiter Classification: Retained; **Lowest/Average Salary:**
$90,000/$90,000; **Industry Concentration:** Generalist with a
primary focus in High Technology, Information Technology;
Function Concentration: Generalist with a primary focus in
Engineering, Finance/Accounting, General Management

Norsell, Paul E. — *President*
Paul Norsell & Associates, Inc.
P.O. Box 6686
Auburn, CA 95604-6686
Telephone: (916) 269-0121
Recruiter Classification: Retained; **Lowest/Average Salary:**
$125,000/$135,000; **Industry Concentration:** Generalist with a
primary focus in Electronics, High Technology; **Function
Concentration:** Generalist with a primary focus in
Administration, Engineering, Finance/Accounting, General
Management, Human Resources, Marketing, Research and
Development, Sales

Norton, James B. — *Partner*
Lamalie Amrop International
191 Peachtree Street N.E.
Atlanta, GA 30303-1747
Telephone: (404) 688-0800
Recruiter Classification: Retained; **Lowest/Average Salary:**
$90,000/$90,000; **Industry Concentration:** Generalist with a
primary focus in High Technology; **Function Concentration:**
Generalist

Nosky, Richard E. — *Managing Director*
Ward Howell International, Inc.
2525 E. Arizona Biltmore Circle
Suite 124
Phoenix, AZ 85016
Telephone: (602) 955-3800
Recruiter Classification: Retained; **Lowest/Average Salary:**
$75,000/$90,000; **Industry Concentration:** Information
Technology; **Function Concentration:** Generalist

Nunziata, Peter — *Consultant*
Atlantic Search Group, Inc.
One Liberty Square
Boston, MA 02109
Telephone: (617) 426-9700
Recruiter Classification: Contingency; **Lowest/Average Salary:**
$20,000/$60,000; **Industry Concentration:** Generalist with a
primary focus in Electronics, Information Technology; **Function
Concentration:** Finance/Accounting

Nutter, Roger — *Principal*
Raymond Karsan Associates
100 Merchant Street, Suite 220
Cincinnati, OH 45246
Telephone: (513) 771-7979
Recruiter Classification: Retained; **Lowest/Average Salary:**
$30,000/$90,000; **Industry Concentration:** Generalist with a
primary focus in Information Technology; **Function
Concentration:** Generalist

Nye, David S. — *President*
Blake, Hansen & Nye, Limited
1155 Connecticut Avenue N.W.
Suite 300
Washington, DC 20036
Telephone: (202) 429-6611
Recruiter Classification: Retained; **Lowest/Average Salary:**
$75,000/$90,000; **Industry Concentration:** Generalist with a
primary focus in Electronics; **Function Concentration:**
Generalist with a primary focus in Administration,
Finance/Accounting, General Management, Human Resources

Nymark, John — *Vice President*
NYCOR Search, Inc.
4930 West 77th Street, Suite 300
Minneapolis, MN 55435
Telephone: (612) 831-6444
Recruiter Classification: Contingency; **Lowest/Average Salary:**
$40,000/$75,000; **Industry Concentration:** Generalist with a
primary focus in Electronics, High Technology, Information
Technology; **Function Concentration:** Engineering, Research
and Development

Nymark, Paul — *President*
NYCOR Search, Inc.
4930 West 77th Street, Suite 300
Minneapolis, MN 55435
Telephone: (612) 831-6444
Recruiter Classification: Contingency; **Lowest/Average Salary:**
$40,000/$75,000; **Industry Concentration:** Generalist with a
primary focus in Electronics, High Technology, Information
Technology; **Function Concentration:** Engineering, Research
and Development

O'Brien, Maggie — *Regional Manager*
Advanced Information Management
900 Wilshire Boulevard, Suite 1424
Los Angeles, CA 90017
Telephone: (213) 243-9236
Recruiter Classification: Contingency; **Lowest/Average Salary:**
$20,000/$40,000; **Industry Concentration:** Information
Technology; **Function Concentration:** Human Resources,
Research and Development, Women/Minorities

O'Brien, Susan — *Associate*
Source Services Corporation
1105 Schrock Road, Suite 510
Columbus, OH 43229
Telephone: (614) 846-3311
Recruiter Classification: Contingency; **Lowest/Average Salary:**
$30,000/$50,000; **Industry Concentration:** Information
Technology; **Function Concentration:** Engineering,
Finance/Accounting

O'Connell, Mary — *Executive Recruiter*
CPS Inc.
303 Congress Street, 5th Floor
Boston, MA 02210
Telephone: (617) 439-7950
Recruiter Classification: Contingency; **Lowest/Average Salary:**
$30,000/$50,000; **Industry Concentration:** Generalist with a
primary focus in Electronics, High Technology, Information
Technology; **Function Concentration:** Engineering, Research
and Development, Sales, Women/Minorities

O'Hara, Daniel M. — *Managing Director*
Lynch Miller Moore, Inc.
10 South Wacker Drive, Suite 2935
Chicago, IL 60606
Telephone: (312) 876-1505
Recruiter Classification: Retained; **Lowest/Average Salary:**
$75,000/$90,000; **Industry Concentration:** Generalist with a
primary focus in High Technology, Information Technology;
Function Concentration: Generalist with a primary focus in
Administration, Finance/Accounting, General Management,
Human Resources, Marketing, Research and Development,
Sales

O'Maley, Kimberlee — *Director*
Spencer Stuart
525 Market Street, Suite 3700
San Francisco, CA 94105
Telephone: (415) 495-4141
Recruiter Classification: Retained; **Lowest/Average Salary:**
$90,000/$90,000; **Industry Concentration:** Generalist with a
primary focus in High Technology; **Function Concentration:**
Generalist with a primary focus in Finance/Accounting,
General Management, Marketing, Sales

O'Neill, Kevin G. — *Senior Consultants*
HRS, Inc.
P.O. Box 4499
Pittsburgh, PA 15205
Telephone: (412) 331-4700
Recruiter Classification: Retained; **Lowest/Average Salary:**
$75,000/$75,000; **Industry Concentration:** Generalist with a
primary focus in High Technology, Information Technology

O'Reilly, John — *Director*
Stratford Group
445 Byers Road
Miamisburg, OH 45342
Telephone: (937) 859-6797
Recruiter Classification: Retained; **Lowest/Average Salary:**
$75,000/$90,000; **Industry Concentration:** Generalist with a
primary focus in High Technology, Information Technology;
Function Concentration: Generalist with a primary focus in
Finance/Accounting, General Management

Occhiboi, Emil — *Associate*
Source Services Corporation
925 Westchester Avenue, Suite 309
White Plains, NY 10604
Telephone: (914) 428-9100
Recruiter Classification: Contingency; **Lowest/Average Salary:**
$30,000/$50,000; **Industry Concentration:** Information
Technology; **Function Concentration:** Engineering,
Finance/Accounting

Ocon, Olga — *Principal*
Busch International
One First Street, Suite One
Los Altos, CA 94022-2754
Telephone: (650) 949-1115
Recruiter Classification: Retained; **Lowest/Average Salary:**
$90,000/$90,000; **Industry Concentration:** Electronics, High
Technology, Information Technology; **Function Concentration:**
Generalist with a primary focus in Engineering,
Finance/Accounting, General Management, Marketing,
Research and Development, Sales

Odom, Philip — *Executive Recruiter*
Richard, Wayne and Roberts
24 Greenway Plaza, Suite 1304
Houston, TX 77046-2493
Telephone: (713) 629-6681
Recruiter Classification: Retained; **Lowest/Average Salary:**
$50,000/$90,000; **Industry Concentration:** Generalist with a
primary focus in Information Technology; **Function
Concentration:** Generalist

Ogdon, Thomas H. — *President*
The Ogdon Partnership
375 Park Avenue, Suite 2409
New York, NY 10152-0175
Telephone: (212) 308-1600
Recruiter Classification: Retained; **Lowest/Average Salary:**
$90,000/$90,000; **Industry Concentration:** Generalist with a
primary focus in Information Technology; **Function
Concentration:** Generalist with a primary focus in
Administration, Finance/Accounting, General Management,
Human Resources, Marketing, Research and Development,
Sales

Ogilvie, Kit — *Vice President Bio-Pharmaceutical
Division*
Howard Fischer Associates, Inc.
1800 John F. Kennedy Boulevard, 7th Floor
Philadelphia, PA 19103
Telephone: (215) 568-8363
Recruiter Classification: Retained; **Lowest/Average Salary:**
$90,000/$90,000; **Industry Concentration:** High Technology;
Function Concentration: Generalist with a primary focus in
Administration, Finance/Accounting, General Management,
Human Resources, Marketing, Research and Development,
Sales, Women/Minorities

Oldfield, Theresa — *Partner*
Strategic Alliance Network, Ltd.
10901 Reed Hartman Highway
Suite 217
Cincinnati, OH 45242
Telephone: (513) 792-2800
Recruiter Classification: Retained; **Lowest/Average Salary:**
$30,000/$90,000; **Industry Concentration:** High Technology,
Information Technology; **Function Concentration:**
Finance/Accounting, Marketing, Sales

Olmstead, George T. — *Partner*
Blackshaw, Olmstead, Lynch & Koenig
3414 Peachtree Road
Suite 1010
Atlanta, GA 30326
Telephone: (404) 261-7770
Recruiter Classification: Retained; **Lowest/Average Salary:**
$90,000/$90,000; **Industry Concentration:** Generalist with a
primary focus in High Technology, Information Technology;
Function Concentration: Generalist with a primary focus in
Finance/Accounting, General Management, Human Resources,
Marketing, Sales

Olsen, Carl — *Vice President/Managing Director*
A.T. Kearney, Inc.
3 Lagoon Drive, Suite 160
Redwood City, CA 94065
Telephone: (415) 637-6600
Recruiter Classification: Retained; **Lowest/Average Salary:**
$90,000/$90,000; **Industry Concentration:** Generalist with a
primary focus in High Technology; **Function Concentration:**
Generalist with a primary focus in Engineering, General
Management, Marketing, Research and Development, Sales

Olsen, David G. — *Senior Vice President*
Handy HRM Corp.
250 Park Avenue
New York, NY 10177-0074
Telephone: (212) 210-9605
Recruiter Classification: Retained; **Lowest/Average Salary:**
$90,000/$90,000; **Industry Concentration:** Information
Technology; **Function Concentration:** Administration,
Finance/Accounting, General Management, Marketing, Sales

Olsen, Kristine — *Research Associate*
Williams Executive Search, Inc.
4200 Norwest Center
90 South 7th Street
Minneapolis, MN 55402
Telephone: (612) 339-2900
Recruiter Classification: Retained; **Lowest/Average Salary:**
$75,000/$75,000; **Industry Concentration:** Generalist with a
primary focus in High Technology; **Function Concentration:**
Generalist

Olsen, Robert — *Associate*
Source Services Corporation
150 South Wacker Drive, Suite 400
Chicago, IL 60606
Telephone: (312) 346-7000
Recruiter Classification: Contingency; **Lowest/Average Salary:**
$30,000/$50,000; **Industry Concentration:** Information
Technology; **Function Concentration:** Engineering,
Finance/Accounting

Onstott, Joseph — *Managing Director*
The Onstott Group, Inc.
430 Cowper Street
Palo Alto, CA 94301
Telephone: (415) 617-4500
Recruiter Classification: Retained; **Lowest/Average Salary:**
$90,000/$90,000; **Industry Concentration:** High Technology,
Information Technology; **Function Concentration:** Generalist
with a primary focus in Administration, Finance/Accounting,
General Management, Human Resources, Marketing, Sales

Onstott, Joseph E. — *Managing Director*
The Onstott Group, Inc.
60 William Street
Wellesley, MA 02181
Telephone: (781) 235-3050
Recruiter Classification: Retained; **Lowest/Average Salary:**
$90,000/$90,000; **Industry Concentration:** Generalist with
a primary focus in High Technology, Information
Technology; **Function Concentration:** Generalist with a
primary focus in Finance/Accounting, General Management,
Marketing, Sales

Orkin, Ralph — *Principal*
Sanford Rose Associates
26250 Euclid Avenue, Suite 629
Euclid, OH 44132
Telephone: (216) 731-0005
Recruiter Classification: Contingency; **Lowest/Average Salary:**
$30,000/$75,000; **Industry Concentration:** Generalist with a
primary focus in High Technology; **Function Concentration:**
Generalist

Orkin, Sheilah — *Principal*
Sanford Rose Associates
26250 Euclid Avenue, Suite 629
Euclid, OH 44132
Telephone: (216) 731-0005
Recruiter Classification: Contingency; **Lowest/Average Salary:**
$30,000/$75,000; **Industry Concentration:** Generalist with a
primary focus in High Technology; **Function Concentration:**
Generalist

Orr, Stacie — *Associate*
Source Services Corporation
155 Federal Street, Suite 410
Boston, MA 02110
Telephone: (617) 482-8211
Recruiter Classification: Contingency; **Lowest/Average Salary:**
$30,000/$50,000; **Industry Concentration:** Information
Technology; **Function Concentration:** Engineering,
Finance/Accounting

Osborn, Jim — *Consultant*
Southwestern Professional Services
2451 Atrium Way
Nashville, TN 37214
Telephone: (615) 391-2722
Recruiter Classification: Contingency; **Lowest/Average Salary:**
$30,000/$30,000; **Industry Concentration:** Generalist with a
primary focus in Information Technology; **Function
Concentration:** General Management

Ott, George W. — *President and CEO*
Ott & Hansen, Inc.
136 South Oak Knoll, Suite 300
Pasadena, CA 91101
Telephone: (818) 578-0551
Recruiter Classification: Retained; **Lowest/Average Salary:**
$75,000/$90,000; **Industry Concentration:** Generalist with a
primary focus in Electronics, High Technology, Information
Technology; **Function Concentration:** Generalist with a
primary focus in Finance/Accounting, General Management,
Human Resources, Marketing, Sales

Ottenritter, Chris — *Executive Recruiter*
CPS Inc.
One Westbrook Corporate Centre, Suite 600
Westchester, IL 60154
Telephone: (708) 531-8370
Recruiter Classification: Contingency; **Lowest/Average Salary:**
$30,000/$50,000; **Industry Concentration:** Generalist with a
primary focus in Electronics, High Technology, Information
Technology; **Function Concentration:** Engineering, Research
and Development, Sales, Women/Minorities

Ouellette, Christopher — *Associate*
Source Services Corporation
155 Federal Street, Suite 410
Boston, MA 02110
Telephone: (617) 482-8211
Recruiter Classification: Contingency; **Lowest/Average Salary:**
$30,000/$50,000; **Industry Concentration:** Information
Technology; **Function Concentration:** Engineering,
Finance/Accounting

Overlock, Craig — *Consultant*
Ray & Berndtson
Sears Tower, 233 South Wacker Drive, Suite 4020
Chicago, IL 60606-6310
Telephone: (312) 876-0730
Recruiter Classification: Retained; **Lowest/Average Salary:**
$90,000/$90,000; **Industry Concentration:** Generalist with a
primary focus in High Technology, Information Technology;
Function Concentration: Generalist with a primary focus in
Administration, Finance/Accounting, General Management,
Human Resources, Marketing, Research and Development,
Sales, Women/Minorities

Owen, Christopher — *Associate*
Source Services Corporation
8614 Westwood Center, Suite 750
Vienna, VA 22182
Telephone: (703) 790-5610
Recruiter Classification: Contingency; **Lowest/Average Salary:**
$30,000/$50,000; **Industry Concentration:** Information
Technology; **Function Concentration:** Engineering,
Finance/Accounting

Pace, Susan A. — *Managing Director*
Horton International
10 Tower Lane
Avon, CT 06001
Telephone: (860) 674-8701
Recruiter Classification: Retained; **Lowest/Average Salary:**
$90,000/$90,000; **Industry Concentration:** Generalist with a
primary focus in Information Technology; **Function
Concentration:** Generalist with a primary focus in Engineering,
Finance/Accounting, General Management, Human Resources,
Marketing, Sales

Pachowitz, John — *Associate*
Source Services Corporation
1233 North Mayfair Road, Suite 300
Milwaukee, WI 53226
Telephone: (414) 774-6700
Recruiter Classification: Contingency; **Lowest/Average Salary:**
$30,000/$50,000; **Industry Concentration:** Information
Technology; **Function Concentration:** Engineering,
Finance/Accounting

Pacini, Lauren R. — *Vice President*
Hite Executive Search
6515 Chase Drive
P.O. Box 43217
Cleveland, OH 44143
Telephone: (216) 461-1600
Recruiter Classification: Retained; **Lowest/Average Salary:**
$90,000/$90,000; **Industry Concentration:** Generalist with a
primary focus in Electronics, High Technology, Information
Technology; **Function Concentration:** Generalist with a
primary focus in Administration, Engineering, General
Management, Marketing, Sales

Padilla, Jose Sanchez — *Consultant*
Egon Zehnder International Inc.
Paseo de las Palmas No. 405-703
Co. Lomas de Chapultepec
Mexico City, D.F., MEXICO 11000
Telephone: (525) 540-7635
Recruiter Classification: Retained; **Lowest/Average Salary:**
$90,000/$90,000; **Industry Concentration:** Generalist with a
primary focus in High Technology; **Function Concentration:**
Generalist

Page, G. Schuyler — *Vice President*
A.T. Kearney, Inc.
Lincoln Plaza, Suite 4170
500 North Akard Street
Dallas, TX 75201
Telephone: (214) 969-0010
Recruiter Classification: Retained; **Lowest/Average Salary:**
$90,000/$90,000; **Industry Concentration:** Generalist with a
primary focus in High Technology; **Function Concentration:**
Generalist with a primary focus in Finance/Accounting

Paliwoda, William — *Associate*
Source Services Corporation
925 Westchester Avenue, Suite 309
White Plains, NY 10604
Telephone: (914) 428-9100
Recruiter Classification: Contingency; **Lowest/Average Salary:**
$30,000/$50,000; **Industry Concentration:** Information
Technology; **Function Concentration:** Engineering,
Finance/Accounting

Palma, Frank R. — *Executive Vice President*
Goodrich & Sherwood Associates, Inc.
6 Century Drive
Parsippany, NJ 07054
Telephone: (201) 455-7100
Recruiter Classification: Retained; **Lowest/Average Salary:**
$60,000/$90,000; **Industry Concentration:** Generalist with a
primary focus in Information Technology; **Function
Concentration:** Generalist with a primary focus in
Administration, Finance/Accounting, General Management,
Human Resources, Marketing, Sales

Palmer, Carlton A. — *Senior Vice
President/Partner*
Beall & Company, Inc.
535 Colonial Park Drive
Roswell, GA 30075
Telephone: (404) 992-0900
Recruiter Classification: Retained; **Lowest/Average Salary:**
$90,000/$90,000; **Industry Concentration:** Generalist with a
primary focus in High Technology; **Function Concentration:**
Generalist with a primary focus in Administration, Engineering,
Finance/Accounting, General Management, Human Resources,
Marketing, Research and Development, Sales

Palmer, James H. — *Vice President*
The Hindman Company
Browenton Place, Suite 110
2000 Warrington Way
Louisville, KY 40222
Telephone: (502) 426-4040
Recruiter Classification: Retained; **Lowest/Average Salary:**
$50,000/$90,000; **Industry Concentration:** Generalist with a
primary focus in Electronics, High Technology; **Function
Concentration:** Generalist with a primary focus in Engineering,
Finance/Accounting, General Management, Human Resources,
Marketing, Sales

Palmer, Melissa — *Executive Recruiter*
Don Richard Associates of Tampa, Inc.
100 North Tampa Street, Suite 1925
Tampa, FL 33602
Telephone: (813) 221-7930
Recruiter Classification: Contingency, Executive Temporary;
Lowest/Average Salary: $20,000/$50,000; **Industry
Concentration:** Generalist with a primary focus in High
Technology; **Function Concentration:** Generalist with a
primary focus in Administration, Finance/Accounting

Panarese, Pam — *Consultant*
Howard Fischer Associates, Inc.
1800 John F. Kennedy Boulevard, 7th Floor
Philadelphia, PA 19103
Telephone: (215) 568-8363
Recruiter Classification: Retained; **Lowest/Average Salary:**
$90,000/$90,000; **Industry Concentration:** Generalist with a
primary focus in High Technology; **Function Concentration:**
Generalist with a primary focus in Administration,
Finance/Accounting, General Management, Human Resources,
Marketing, Research and Development, Sales,
Women/Minorities

Panetta, Timothy — *Partner*
Commonwealth Consultants
4840 Roswell Road
Atlanta, GA 30342
Telephone: (404) 256-0000
Recruiter Classification: Contingency; **Lowest/Average Salary:** $30,000/$90,000; **Industry Concentration:** High Technology; **Function Concentration:** Sales

Papasadero, Kathleen — *Associate*
Woodworth International Group
620 SW 5th Avenue, Suite 1225
Portland, OR 97204
Telephone: (503) 225-5000
Recruiter Classification: Retained; **Lowest/Average Salary:** $60,000/$90,000; **Industry Concentration:** Generalist with a primary focus in Electronics, High Technology, Information Technology; **Function Concentration:** Generalist with a primary focus in Engineering, Finance/Accounting, General Management, Human Resources, Marketing, Research and Development, Sales

Papciak, Dennis J. — *President*
Temporary Accounting Personnel
2100 Wharton Street
Suite 710
Pittsburgh, PA 15203-1942
Telephone: (412) 488-9155
Recruiter Classification: Executive Temporary; **Lowest/Average Salary:** $60,000/$90,000; **Industry Concentration:** Generalist with a primary focus in High Technology; **Function Concentration:** Administration, Finance/Accounting

Papciak, Dennis J. — *President*
Accounting Personnel Associates, Inc.
2100 Wharton Street, Suite 710
Pittsburgh, PA 15203-1942
Telephone: (412) 481-6015
Recruiter Classification: Contingency; **Lowest/Average Salary:** $20,000/$50,000; **Industry Concentration:** High Technology, Information Technology; **Function Concentration:** Administration, Finance/Accounting, Women/Minorities

Papoulias, Cathy — *Vice President*
Pendleton James and Associates, Inc.
One International Place
Suite 2350
Boston, MA 02110
Telephone: (617) 261-9696
Recruiter Classification: Retained; **Lowest/Average Salary:** $90,000/$90,000; **Industry Concentration:** High Technology, Information Technology; **Function Concentration:** General Management, Marketing, Sales, Women/Minorities

Pappalardo, Charles A. — *Vice President*
Christian & Timbers
25825 Science Park Drive, Suite 400
Cleveland, OH 44122
Telephone: (216) 765-5892
Recruiter Classification: Retained; **Lowest/Average Salary:** $90,000/$90,000; **Industry Concentration:** Generalist with a primary focus in High Technology, Information Technology; **Function Concentration:** Generalist with a primary focus in General Management

Pappas, Christina E. — *Executive Search Consultant*
Williams Executive Search, Inc.
4200 Norwest Center
90 South 7th Street
Minneapolis, MN 55402
Telephone: (612) 339-2900
Recruiter Classification: Retained; **Lowest/Average Salary:** $75,000/$90,000; **Industry Concentration:** Generalist with a primary focus in High Technology; **Function Concentration:** Generalist with a primary focus in Finance/Accounting

Pappas, Jim — *Manager*
Search Dynamics, Inc.
9420 West Foster Avenue, Suite 200
Chicago, IL 60656-1006
Telephone: (312) 992-3900
Recruiter Classification: Contingency; **Lowest/Average Salary:** $40,000/$50,000; **Industry Concentration:** Electronics, High Technology, Information Technology; **Function Concentration:** Administration, Engineering, General Management, Marketing, Research and Development, Sales

Pappas, Timothy C. — *Executive Vice President*
Jonas, Walters & Assoc., Inc.
1110 North Old World Third St., Suite 510
Milwaukee, WI 53203-1102
Telephone: (414) 291-2828
Recruiter Classification: Retained; **Lowest/Average Salary:** $75,000/$90,000; **Industry Concentration:** Generalist with a primary focus in Electronics; **Function Concentration:** Generalist with a primary focus in General Management, Human Resources, Women/Minorities

Paradise, Malcolm — *Associate*
Source Services Corporation
71 Spit Brook Road, Suite 305
Nashua, NH 03060
Telephone: (603) 888-7650
Recruiter Classification: Contingency; **Lowest/Average Salary:** $30,000/$50,000; **Industry Concentration:** Information Technology; **Function Concentration:** Engineering, Finance/Accounting

Pardo, Maria Elena — *Consultant*
Smith Search, S.C.
Barranca del Muerto No. 472, Col. Alpes
Mexico City, D.F., MEXICO 01010
Telephone: (525) 593-8766
Recruiter Classification: Retained; **Lowest/Average Salary:** $60,000/$90,000; **Industry Concentration:** Generalist with a primary focus in Electronics, High Technology, Information Technology; **Function Concentration:** Generalist with a primary focus in Administration, Engineering, Finance/Accounting, General Management, Human Resources, Marketing, Sales

Parente, James — *Associate*
Source Services Corporation
925 Westchester Avenue, Suite 309
White Plains, NY 10604
Telephone: (914) 428-9100
Recruiter Classification: Contingency; **Lowest/Average Salary:** $30,000/$50,000; **Industry Concentration:** Information Technology; **Function Concentration:** Engineering, Finance/Accounting

Parfitt, William C. — *President*
Parfitt Recruiting and Consulting
1540 140th Avenue NE #201
Bellevue, WA 98005
Telephone: (206) 646-6300
Recruiter Classification: Contingency; **Lowest/Average Salary:**
$30,000/$75,000; **Industry Concentration:** Generalist with a
primary focus in Information Technology; **Function
Concentration:** Generalist

Paris, Stephen — *Executive Recruiter*
Richard, Wayne and Roberts
24 Greenway Plaza, Suite 1304
Houston, TX 77046-2493
Telephone: (713) 629-6681
Recruiter Classification: Retained; **Lowest/Average Salary:**
$40,000/$60,000; **Industry Concentration:** Generalist with a
primary focus in Information Technology; **Function
Concentration:** Generalist

Park, Dabney G. — *Senior Partner*
Mark Stanley/EMA Partners International
2121 Ponce de Leon Boulevard #630
P.O. Box 149071
Coral Gables, FL 33114
Telephone: (305) 444-1612
Recruiter Classification: Retained; **Lowest/Average Salary:**
$75,000/$90,000; **Industry Concentration:** Generalist with a
primary focus in High Technology; **Function Concentration:**
Generalist with a primary focus in Finance/Accounting,
General Management, Human Resources, Sales

Parkin, Myrna — *Recruiter*
S.D. Kelly & Associates, Inc.
990 Washington Street
Dedham, MA 02026
Telephone: (617) 326-8038
Recruiter Classification: Contingency; **Lowest/Average Salary:**
$60,000/$75,000; **Industry Concentration:** Electronics, High
Technology; **Function Concentration:** Engineering, General
Management, Marketing, Sales

Parr, James A. — *Partner*
KPMG Management Consulting
2300 Yonge Street
Toronto, Ontario, CANADA M4P 1G2
Telephone: (416) 482-5786
Recruiter Classification: Executive Temporary; **Lowest/Average
Salary:** $75,000/$90,000; **Industry Concentration:** Generalist
with a primary focus in Electronics, High Technology,
Information Technology; **Function Concentration:** Generalist
with a primary focus in Administration, Engineering,
Finance/Accounting, General Management, Human Resources,
Marketing, Research and Development, Sales

Parroco, Jason — *Associate*
Source Services Corporation
2850 National City Tower
Louisville, KY 40202
Telephone: (502) 581-9900
Recruiter Classification: Contingency; **Lowest/Average Salary:**
$30,000/$50,000; **Industry Concentration:** Information
Technology; **Function Concentration:** Engineering,
Finance/Accounting

Parry, Heather — *Executive Recruiter*
Richard, Wayne and Roberts
24 Greenway Plaza, Suite 1304
Houston, TX 77046-2493
Telephone: (713) 629-6681
Recruiter Classification: Retained; **Lowest/Average Salary:**
$40,000/$60,000; **Industry Concentration:** Generalist with a
primary focus in Information Technology; **Function
Concentration:** Generalist

Parry, William H. — *Vice President*
Horton International
24405 Chestnut Street, Suite 107
Santa Clarita, CA 91321
Telephone: (805) 222-2272
Recruiter Classification: Retained; **Lowest/Average Salary:**
$90,000/$90,000; **Industry Concentration:** Generalist with a
primary focus in Electronics; **Function Concentration:**
Generalist with a primary focus in General Management,
Human Resources, Marketing, Research and Development,
Sales

Parsons, Allison D. — *Senior Consultant*
Barton Associates, Inc.
One Riverway, Suite 2500
Houston, TX 77056
Telephone: (713) 961-9111
Recruiter Classification: Retained; **Lowest/Average Salary:**
$75,000/$90,000; **Industry Concentration:** Generalist with a
primary focus in Electronics, High Technology, Information
Technology; **Function Concentration:** Generalist with a
primary focus in Administration, General Management, Human
Resources, Marketing

Pastrana, Dario — *Managing Partner*
Egon Zehnder International Inc.
Paseo de las Palmas No. 405-703
Co. Lomas de Chapultepec
Mexico City, D.F., MEXICO 11000
Telephone: (525) 540-7635
Recruiter Classification: Retained; **Lowest/Average Salary:**
$90,000/$90,000; **Industry Concentration:** Generalist with a
primary focus in High Technology; **Function Concentration:**
Generalist

Patel, Shailesh — *Associate*
Source Services Corporation
925 Westchester Avenue, Suite 309
White Plains, NY 10604
Telephone: (914) 428-9100
Recruiter Classification: Contingency; **Lowest/Average Salary:**
$30,000/$50,000; **Industry Concentration:** Information
Technology; **Function Concentration:** Engineering,
Finance/Accounting

Paternie, Patrick — *Associate*
Source Services Corporation
One Park Plaza, Suite 560
Irvine, CA 92714
Telephone: (714) 660-1666
Recruiter Classification: Contingency; **Lowest/Average Salary:**
$30,000/$50,000; **Industry Concentration:** Information
Technology; **Function Concentration:** Engineering,
Finance/Accounting

Patrick, Donald R. — *Principal*
Sanford Rose Associates
3525 Holcomb Bridge Road
Suite 2B
Norcross, GA 30092
Telephone: (404) 449-7200
Recruiter Classification: Contingency; **Lowest/Average Salary:** $30,000/$75,000; **Industry Concentration:** Generalist with a primary focus in High Technology; **Function Concentration:** Generalist

Paul, Kathleen — *Associate*
Source Services Corporation
One CityPlace, Suite 170
St. Louis, MO 63141
Telephone: (314) 432-4500
Recruiter Classification: Contingency; **Lowest/Average Salary:** $30,000/$50,000; **Industry Concentration:** Information Technology; **Function Concentration:** Engineering, Finance/Accounting

Paul, Lisa D. — *Resource Manager*
Merit Resource Group, Inc.
7950 Dublin Boulevard, Suite 205
Dublin, CA 94568
Telephone: (510) 828-4700
Recruiter Classification: Executive Temporary; **Lowest/Average Salary:** $75,000/$90,000; **Industry Concentration:** Generalist with a primary focus in Electronics; **Function Concentration:** Generalist with a primary focus in Human Resources

Payette, Pierre — *Consultant*
Egon Zehnder International Inc.
1 Place Ville-Marie, Suite 3310
Montreal, Quebec, CANADA H3B 3N2
Telephone: (514) 876-4249
Recruiter Classification: Retained; **Lowest/Average Salary:** $90,000/$90,000; **Industry Concentration:** Generalist with a primary focus in High Technology; **Function Concentration:** Generalist

Peal, Matthew — *Associate*
Source Services Corporation
161 Ottawa NW, Suite 409D
Grand Rapids, MI 49503
Telephone: (616) 451-2400
Recruiter Classification: Contingency; **Lowest/Average Salary:** $30,000/$50,000; **Industry Concentration:** Information Technology; **Function Concentration:** Engineering, Finance/Accounting

Pearson, Robert L. — *President and CEO*
Lamalie Amrop International
Thanksgiving Tower
1601 Elm Street
Dallas, TX 75201-4768
Telephone: (214) 754-0019
Recruiter Classification: Retained; **Lowest/Average Salary:** $90,000/$90,000; **Industry Concentration:** Generalist with a primary focus in High Technology; **Function Concentration:** Generalist with a primary focus in Finance/Accounting, General Management, Human Resources, Marketing, Sales

Peasback, David R. — *Vice Chairman and CEO*
Canny, Bowen Inc.
200 Park Avenue
49th Floor
New York, NY 10166
Telephone: (212) 949-6611
Recruiter Classification: Retained; **Lowest/Average Salary:** $90,000/$90,000; **Industry Concentration:** Generalist with a primary focus in Electronics; **Function Concentration:** Generalist with a primary focus in Administration, Finance/Accounting, General Management, Human Resources, Marketing, Research and Development, Sales, Women/Minorities

Peckenpaugh, Ann D. — *Vice President*
Schweichler Associates, Inc.
200 Tamal Vista, Building 200, Suite 100
Corte Madera, CA 94925
Telephone: (415) 924-7200
Recruiter Classification: Retained; **Lowest/Average Salary:** $90,000/$90,000; **Industry Concentration:** Electronics, High Technology, Information Technology; **Function Concentration:** Engineering, Finance/Accounting, General Management, Marketing, Research and Development, Sales, Women/Minorities

Pederson, Terre — *Executive Recruiter*
Richard, Wayne and Roberts
24 Greenway Plaza, Suite 1304
Houston, TX 77046-2493
Telephone: (713) 629-6681
Recruiter Classification: Retained; **Lowest/Average Salary:** $50,000/$90,000; **Industry Concentration:** Generalist with a primary focus in Information Technology; **Function Concentration:** Generalist

Pedley, Jill — *Executive Recruiter*
CPS Inc.
One Westbrook Corporate Centre, Suite 600
Westchester, IL 60154
Telephone: (708) 531-8370
Recruiter Classification: Contingency; **Lowest/Average Salary:** $30,000/$50,000; **Industry Concentration:** Generalist with a primary focus in Electronics, High Technology, Information Technology; **Function Concentration:** Engineering, Research and Development, Sales, Women/Minorities

Peeney, James D. — *President*
Peeney Associates
141 South Avenue
Fanwood, NJ 07023
Telephone: (908) 322-2324
Recruiter Classification: Retained; **Lowest/Average Salary:** $60,000/$90,000; **Industry Concentration:** Generalist with a primary focus in Electronics; **Function Concentration:** Generalist with a primary focus in Administration, Engineering, Finance/Accounting, General Management, Human Resources, Marketing, Research and Development, Sales, Women/Minorities

Pelisson, Charles — *Vice President*
Marra Peters & Partners
Millburn Esplanade
Millburn, NJ 07041
Telephone: (201) 376-8999
Recruiter Classification: Retained; **Average Salary:** $90,000; **Industry Concentration:** Generalist with a primary focus in Information Technology; **Function Concentration:** Generalist with a primary focus in Administration, Engineering, Finance/Accounting, General Management, Human Resources, Marketing, Research and Development, Sales

Pelkey, Chris — *Consultant*
The McCormick Group, Inc.
1400 Wilson Boulevard
Arlington, VA 22209
Telephone: (703) 841-1700
Recruiter Classification: Retained; **Lowest/Average Salary:**
$40,000/$60,000; **Industry Concentration:** High Technology,
Information Technology; **Function Concentration:** Engineering,
Marketing, Sales

Percival, Chris — *Senior Legal Search Consultant*
Chicago Legal Search, Ltd.
33 North Dearborn Street, Suite 2302
Chicago, IL 60602-3109
Telephone: (312) 251-2580
Recruiter Classification: Contingency; **Lowest/Average Salary:**
$50,000/$90,000; **Industry Concentration:** Electronics, High
Technology, Information Technology; **Function Concentration:**
Women/Minorities

Peretz, Jamie — *Principal Global Financial Services*
Korn/Ferry International
237 Park Avenue
New York, NY 10017
Telephone: (212) 687-1834
Recruiter Classification: Retained; **Lowest/Average Salary:**
$100,000/$150,000; **Industry Concentration:** Generalist with a
primary focus in Information Technology; **Function
Concentration:** Generalist

Pernell, Jeanette — *Vice President*
Norman Broadbent International, Inc.
Sears Tower, Suite 9850
233 South Wacker Drive
Chicago, IL 60606
Telephone: (312) 876-3300
Recruiter Classification: Retained; **Lowest/Average Salary:**
$90,000/$90,000; **Industry Concentration:** Generalist with a
primary focus in High Technology, Information Technology;
Function Concentration: Generalist with a primary focus in
Finance/Accounting, General Management, Human Resources,
Marketing, Sales, Women/Minorities

Perry, Carolyn — *Associate*
Source Services Corporation
1 Gatehall Drive, Suite 250
Parsippany, NJ 07054
Telephone: (201) 267-3222
Recruiter Classification: Contingency; **Lowest/Average Salary:**
$30,000/$50,000; **Industry Concentration:** Information
Technology; **Function Concentration:** Engineering,
Finance/Accounting

Perry, Glen — *Recruiter*
Keith Bagg & Associates Inc.
85 Richmond St., W., Ste. 700
Toronto, Ontario, CANADA M5H 2C9
Telephone: (416) 863-1800
Recruiter Classification: Contingency; **Lowest/Average Salary:**
$30,000/$60,000; **Industry Concentration:** Electronics, High
Technology, Information Technology; **Function Concentration:**
General Management, Marketing, Sales

Persky, Barry — *President*
Barry Persky & Company, Inc.
256 Post Road East
Westport, CT 06880
Telephone: (203) 454-4500
Recruiter Classification: Retained; **Lowest/Average Salary:**
$75,000/$90,000; **Industry Concentration:** Generalist with a
primary focus in Electronics, High Technology; **Function
Concentration:** Generalist

Peternell, Melanie — *Division Supervisor*
Signature Staffing
6800 College Boulevard, Suite 550
Overland Park, KS 66211
Telephone: (913) 338-2020
Recruiter Classification: Executive Temporary; **Lowest/Average
Salary:** $30,000/$40,000; **Industry Concentration:** Generalist
with a primary focus in Electronics; **Function Concentration:**
Generalist with a primary focus in Finance/Accounting,
Marketing

Peters, James N. — *Vice President*
TNS Partners, Inc.
8140 Walnut Hill Lane
Suite 301
Dallas, TX 75231
Telephone: (214) 991-3555
Recruiter Classification: Retained; **Lowest/Average Salary:**
$90,000/$90,000; **Industry Concentration:** Generalist with a
primary focus in Electronics, High Technology, Information
Technology; **Function Concentration:** Generalist with a
primary focus in Engineering, General Management,
Marketing, Research and Development, Sales

Peters, Kevin — *Associate*
Source Services Corporation
879 West 190th Street, Suite 250
Los Angeles, CA 90248
Telephone: (310) 323-6633
Recruiter Classification: Contingency; **Lowest/Average Salary:**
$30,000/$50,000; **Industry Concentration:** Information
Technology; **Function Concentration:** Engineering,
Finance/Accounting

Petersen, Richard — *Associate*
Source Services Corporation
5343 North 16th Street, Suite 270
Phoenix, AZ 85016
Telephone: (602) 230-0220
Recruiter Classification: Contingency; **Lowest/Average Salary:**
$30,000/$50,000; **Industry Concentration:** Information
Technology; **Function Concentration:** Engineering,
Finance/Accounting

Peterson, John — *Executive Recruiter*
CPS Inc.
One Westbrook Corporate Centre, Suite 600
Westchester, IL 60154
Telephone: (708) 531-8370
Recruiter Classification: Contingency; **Lowest/Average Salary:**
$30,000/$50,000; **Industry Concentration:** Generalist with a
primary focus in Electronics, High Technology, Information
Technology; **Function Concentration:** Engineering, Research
and Development, Sales, Women/Minorities

Petty, J. Scott — *Associate*
The Arcus Group
15915 Katy Freeway, Suite 635
Houston, TX 77094
Telephone: (281) 578-3100
Recruiter Classification: Retained; **Lowest/Average Salary:** $90,000/$90,000; **Industry Concentration:** Generalist with a primary focus in High Technology, Information Technology; **Function Concentration:** Generalist with a primary focus in Administration, Engineering, Finance/Accounting, Human Resources, Marketing, Sales

Pfannkuche, Anthony V. — *Senior Director*
Spencer Stuart
10900 Wilshire Boulevard, Suite 800
Los Angeles, CA 90024-6524
Telephone: (310) 209-0610
Recruiter Classification: Retained; **Lowest/Average Salary:** $40,000/$60,000; **Industry Concentration:** Information Technology; **Function Concentration:** Generalist with a primary focus in Finance/Accounting, General Management

Pfau, Madelaine — *Partner*
Heidrick & Struggles, Inc.
2200 Ross Avenue, Suite 4700E
Dallas, TX 75201-2787
Telephone: (214) 220-2130
Recruiter Classification: Retained; **Lowest/Average Salary:** $75,000/$90,000; **Industry Concentration:** Generalist with a primary focus in High Technology; **Function Concentration:** Generalist

Pfeiffer, Irene — *Director*
Price Waterhouse
Esso Plaza - East Tower
1200 425 First Street S.W.
Calgary, Alberta, CANADA T2P 3V7
Telephone: (403) 267-1200
Recruiter Classification: Retained; **Lowest/Average Salary:** $75,000/$75,000; **Industry Concentration:** Generalist with a primary focus in High Technology; **Function Concentration:** Generalist with a primary focus in Administration, Engineering, Finance/Accounting, General Management, Human Resources, Marketing, Sales

Pfister, Shelli — *Manager Temporary Personnel Division*
Jack B. Larsen & Associates
334 West Eighth Street
Erie, PA 16502
Telephone: (814) 459-3725
Recruiter Classification: Executive Temporary; **Lowest/Average Salary:** $30,000/$50,000; **Industry Concentration:** Generalist with a primary focus in Electronics, High Technology; **Function Concentration:** Generalist with a primary focus in Engineering, Finance/Accounting, General Management, Human Resources, Sales

Phelps, Gene L. — *Partner*
McCormack & Farrow
695 Town Center Drive
Suite 660
Costa Mesa, CA 92626
Telephone: (714) 549-7222
Recruiter Classification: Retained; **Lowest/Average Salary:** $75,000/$90,000; **Industry Concentration:** Generalist with a primary focus in High Technology; **Function Concentration:** Generalist with a primary focus in Administration, Finance/Accounting, General Management, Human Resources, Marketing, Sales

Phillips, Donald L. — *Principal*
O'Shea, Divine & Company, Inc.
610 Newport Center Drive, Suite 1040
Newport Beach, CA 92660
Telephone: (714) 720-9070
Recruiter Classification: Retained; **Lowest/Average Salary:** $75,000/$90,000; **Industry Concentration:** Generalist with a primary focus in Electronics, High Technology, Information Technology; **Function Concentration:** Generalist with a primary focus in Administration, Engineering, Finance/Accounting, General Management, Human Resources, Marketing, Sales, Women/Minorities

Phillips, Richard K. — *Executive Vice President, Financial Services*
Handy HRM Corp.
250 Park Avenue
New York, NY 10177-0074
Telephone: (212) 210-5636
Recruiter Classification: Retained; **Lowest/Average Salary:** $90,000/$90,000; **Industry Concentration:** High Technology, Information Technology; **Function Concentration:** Finance/Accounting, Human Resources, Research and Development

Phinney, Bruce — *Vice President*
Paul-Tittle Associates, Inc.
1485 Chain Bridge Road, #304
McLean, VA 22101
Telephone: (703) 442-0500
Recruiter Classification: Retained; **Lowest/Average Salary:** $90,000/$90,000; **Industry Concentration:** High Technology; **Function Concentration:** Engineering, Finance/Accounting, General Management, Marketing, Research and Development

Phipps, Peggy — *Researcher*
Woodworth International Group
620 SW 5th Avenue, Suite 1225
Portland, OR 97204
Telephone: (503) 225-5000
Recruiter Classification: Retained; **Lowest/Average Salary:** $60,000/$90,000; **Industry Concentration:** Generalist with a primary focus in Electronics, High Technology, Information Technology; **Function Concentration:** Generalist with a primary focus in Engineering, Finance/Accounting, General Management, Human Resources, Marketing, Research and Development, Sales

Pickering, Dale — *President*
Agri-Tech Personnel, Inc.
3113 N.E. 69th Street
Kansas City, MO 64119
Telephone: (816) 453-7200
Recruiter Classification: Contingency; **Lowest/Average Salary:** $30,000/$75,000; **Industry Concentration:** Electronics; **Function Concentration:** Engineering, Finance/Accounting, General Management, Human Resources, Marketing, Research and Development, Sales

Pickering, Rita — *Vice President*
Agri-Tech Personnel, Inc.
3113 N.E. 69th Street
Kansas City, MO 64119
Telephone: (816) 453-7200
Recruiter Classification: Contingency; **Lowest/Average Salary:** $30,000/$75,000; **Industry Concentration:** Electronics; **Function Concentration:** Engineering, Finance/Accounting, General Management, Human Resources, Marketing, Research and Development, Sales

Pickford, Stephen T. — *President*
The Corporate Staff, Inc.
177 Bovet Road, Suite 600
San Mateo, CA 94402
Telephone: (415) 344-2613
Recruiter Classification: Executive Temporary; **Lowest/Average Salary:** $40,000/$75,000; **Industry Concentration:** Generalist with a primary focus in High Technology, Information Technology; **Function Concentration:** Generalist with a primary focus in Administration, Finance/Accounting, General Management, Human Resources, Marketing, Sales

Pierce, Mark — *Principal*
Korn/Ferry International
233 South Wacker
Chicago, IL 60606
Telephone: (312) 466-1834
Recruiter Classification: Retained; **Lowest/Average Salary:** $100,000/$150,000; **Industry Concentration:** Generalist with a primary focus in Information Technology; **Function Concentration:** Generalist

Pierce, Matthew — *Associate*
Source Services Corporation
One Park Plaza, Suite 560
Irvine, CA 92714
Telephone: (714) 660-1666
Recruiter Classification: Contingency; **Lowest/Average Salary:** $30,000/$50,000; **Industry Concentration:** Information Technology; **Function Concentration:** Engineering, Finance/Accounting

Pierotazio, John — *Executive Recruiter*
CPS Inc.
One Westbrook Corporate Centre, Suite 600
Westchester, IL 60154
Telephone: (708) 531-8370
Recruiter Classification: Contingency; **Lowest/Average Salary:** $30,000/$50,000; **Industry Concentration:** Generalist with a primary focus in Electronics, High Technology, Information Technology; **Function Concentration:** Engineering, Research and Development, Sales, Women/Minorities

Pigott, Daniel — *Senior Partner*
ESA Professional Consultants
141 Durham Road
Suite 16
Madison, CT 06443
Telephone: (203) 245-1983
Recruiter Classification: Retained; **Lowest/Average Salary:** $50,000/$75,000; **Industry Concentration:** Electronics, High Technology, Information Technology; **Function Concentration:** Engineering, General Management, Human Resources, Marketing, Research and Development, Women/Minorities

Pillow, Charles — *Associate*
Source Services Corporation
5429 LBJ Freeway, Suite 275
Dallas, TX 75240
Telephone: (214) 387-1600
Recruiter Classification: Contingency; **Lowest/Average Salary:** $30,000/$50,000; **Industry Concentration:** Information Technology; **Function Concentration:** Engineering, Finance/Accounting

Pineda, Rosanna — *Associate*
Source Services Corporation
2 Penn Plaza, Suite 1176
New York, NY 10121
Telephone: (212) 760-2200
Recruiter Classification: Contingency; **Lowest/Average Salary:** $30,000/$50,000; **Industry Concentration:** Information Technology; **Function Concentration:** Engineering, Finance/Accounting

Pinson, Stephanie L. — *President*
Gilbert Tweed/INESA
155 Prospect Avenue
West Orange, NJ 07052
Telephone: (201) 731-3033
Recruiter Classification: Retained; **Lowest/Average Salary:** $90,000/$90,000; **Industry Concentration:** Generalist with a primary focus in High Technology, Information Technology; **Function Concentration:** Generalist

Pirro, Sheri — *Associate*
Source Services Corporation
1105 Schrock Road, Suite 510
Columbus, OH 43229
Telephone: (614) 846-3311
Recruiter Classification: Contingency; **Lowest/Average Salary:** $30,000/$50,000; **Industry Concentration:** Information Technology; **Function Concentration:** Engineering, Finance/Accounting

Pitts, Charles — *President*
Contemporary Management Services, Inc.
P.O. Box 24131
Greenville, SC 29616
Telephone: (864) 244-7070
Recruiter Classification: Contingency; **Lowest/Average Salary:** $40,000/$60,000; **Industry Concentration:** Generalist with a primary focus in Electronics, Information Technology; **Function Concentration:** Generalist with a primary focus in Engineering

Plant, Jerry — *Associate*
Source Services Corporation
1 Gatehall Drive, Suite 250
Parsippany, NJ 07054
Telephone: (201) 267-3222
Recruiter Classification: Contingency; **Lowest/Average Salary:** $30,000/$50,000; **Industry Concentration:** Information Technology; **Function Concentration:** Engineering, Finance/Accounting

Plimpton, Ralph L. — *President*
R L Plimpton Associates
5655 South Yosemite Street, Suite 410
Greenwood Village, CO 80111
Telephone: (303) 771-1311
Recruiter Classification: Retained; **Lowest/Average Salary:** $40,000/$75,000; **Industry Concentration:** Generalist with a primary focus in Electronics, High Technology, Information Technology; **Function Concentration:** Finance/Accounting, General Management, Human Resources, Research and Development

Plummer, John — *President*
Plummer & Associates, Inc.
65 Rowayton Avenue
Rowayton, CT 06853
Telephone: (203) 899-1233
Recruiter Classification: Retained, Executive Temporary;
Lowest/Average Salary: $90,000/$90,000; **Industry Concentration:** Electronics, Information Technology; **Function Concentration:** Generalist with a primary focus in Finance/Accounting, General Management, Human Resources, Marketing

Poe, James B. — *Managing Director*
Nagler, Robins & Poe, Inc.
65 William Street
Wellesley Hills, MA 02181
Telephone: (617) 431-1330
Recruiter Classification: Retained; **Lowest/Average Salary:** $90,000/$90,000; **Industry Concentration:** Electronics, High Technology, Information Technology; **Function Concentration:** Generalist with a primary focus in General Management

Poirier, Frank — *Principal*
Juntunen-Combs-Poirier
111 Bayhill Drive, Suite 255
San Bruno, CA 94066
Telephone: (415) 635-0180
Recruiter Classification: Retained; **Lowest/Average Salary:** $90,000/$90,000; **Industry Concentration:** High Technology, Information Technology; **Function Concentration:** Engineering, Finance/Accounting, General Management, Research and Development

Poirier, Roland L. — *Partner*
Poirier, Hoevel & Co.
12400 Wilshire Boulevard, Suite 915
Los Angeles, CA 90025
Telephone: (310) 207-3427
Recruiter Classification: Retained; **Lowest/Average Salary:** $75,000/$90,000; **Industry Concentration:** Generalist with a primary focus in Electronics, High Technology, Information Technology; **Function Concentration:** Generalist with a primary focus in Administration, Engineering, Finance/Accounting, General Management, Human Resources, Marketing, Sales, Women/Minorities

Polachi, Charles A. — *Partner*
Fenwick Partners
57 Bedford Street, Suite 101
Lexington, MA 02173
Telephone: (617) 862-3370
Recruiter Classification: Retained; **Lowest/Average Salary:** $90,000/$90,000; **Industry Concentration:** Electronics, High Technology, Information Technology; **Function Concentration:** Generalist

Polachi, Peter V. — *Partner*
Fenwick Partners
57 Bedford Street, Suite 101
Lexington, MA 02173
Telephone: (617) 862-3370
Recruiter Classification: Retained; **Lowest/Average Salary:** $90,000/$90,000; **Industry Concentration:** Electronics, High Technology, Information Technology; **Function Concentration:** Generalist

Polansky, Mark — *Vice President Advanced Technology*
Korn/Ferry International
237 Park Avenue
New York, NY 10017
Telephone: (212) 687-1834
Recruiter Classification: Retained; **Lowest/Average Salary:** $100,000/$150,000; **Industry Concentration:** Generalist with a primary focus in Information Technology; **Function Concentration:** Generalist

Pomerance, Mark — *Executive Recruiter*
CPS Inc.
One Westbrook Corporate Centre, Suite 600
Westchester, IL 60154
Telephone: (708) 531-8370
Recruiter Classification: Contingency; **Lowest/Average Salary:** $30,000/$50,000; **Industry Concentration:** Generalist with a primary focus in Electronics, High Technology, Information Technology; **Function Concentration:** Engineering, Research and Development, Sales, Women/Minorities

Pomeroy, T. Lee — *Consultant*
Egon Zehnder International Inc.
350 Park Avenue
New York, NY 10022
Telephone: (212) 838-9199
Recruiter Classification: Retained; **Lowest/Average Salary:** $90,000/$90,000; **Industry Concentration:** Generalist with a primary focus in High Technology; **Function Concentration:** Generalist

Pompeo, Paul — *Account Executive*
Search West, Inc.
100 Pine Street, Suite 2500
San Francisco, CA 94111-5203
Telephone: (415) 788-1770
Recruiter Classification: Contingency; **Lowest/Average Salary:** $40,000/$60,000; **Industry Concentration:** Electronics; **Function Concentration:** Engineering, Marketing, Sales

Poore, Larry D. — *Managing Director*
Ward Howell International, Inc.
300 South Wacker Drive
Suite 2940
Chicago, IL 60606
Telephone: (312) 236-2211
Recruiter Classification: Retained; **Lowest/Average Salary:** $75,000/$90,000; **Industry Concentration:** Generalist with a primary focus in Information Technology; **Function Concentration:** Generalist with a primary focus in Human Resources, Women/Minorities

Poracky, John W. — *Partner*
M. Wood Company
10 North Dearborn Street, Suite 700
Chicago, IL 60602
Telephone: (312) 368-0633
Recruiter Classification: Retained; **Lowest/Average Salary:** $60,000/$90,000; **Industry Concentration:** Generalist with a primary focus in Information Technology; **Function Concentration:** Generalist with a primary focus in Finance/Accounting, General Management, Sales

Porada, Stephen D. — *President*
CAP Inc.
P.O. Box 82
Tennent, NJ 07763
Telephone: (908) 446-0383
Recruiter Classification: Contingency; **Lowest/Average Salary:**
$30,000/$50,000; **Industry Concentration:** Electronics;
Function Concentration: Engineering, General Management,
Marketing

Poremski, Paul — *Professional Recruiter*
A.J. Burton Group, Inc.
120 East Baltimore Street, Suite 2220
Baltimore, MD 21202
Telephone: (410) 752-5244
Recruiter Classification: Contingency; **Lowest/Average Salary:**
$40,000/$75,000; **Industry Concentration:** Generalist with a
primary focus in High Technology, Information Technology;
Function Concentration: Generalist with a primary focus in
Administration, Finance/Accounting, General Management,
Human Resources

Portanova, Peter M. — *Partner*
R.O.I. Associates, Inc.
401 Franklin Avenue
Garden City, NY 11530
Telephone: (516) 746-4842
Recruiter Classification: Retained; **Lowest/Average Salary:**
$60,000/$90,000; **Industry Concentration:** Electronics;
Function Concentration: General Management

Porter, Albert — *Vice President*
The Experts
200 Reservoir Street
Needham, MA 02194
Telephone: (617) 449-6700
Recruiter Classification: Executive Temporary; **Lowest/Average
Salary:** $50,000/$90,000; **Industry Concentration:** Generalist
with a primary focus in High Technology, Information
Technology; **Function Concentration:** Generalist with a
primary focus in Administration, Engineering,
Finance/Accounting, General Management, Human Resources,
Marketing, Research and Development, Sales

Poster, Lawrence D. — *Managing Director*
Catalyx Group
One Harkness Plaza, Suite 300
61 West 62nd Street
New York, NY 10023
Telephone: (212) 956-3525
Recruiter Classification: Retained; **Lowest/Average Salary:**
$90,000/$90,000; **Industry Concentration:** Electronics, High
Technology, Information Technology; **Function Concentration:**
Generalist with a primary focus in General Management,
Research and Development

Pototo, Brian — *Associate*
Source Services Corporation
1500 West Park Drive, Suite 390
Westborough, MA 01581
Telephone: (508) 366-2600
Recruiter Classification: Contingency; **Lowest/Average Salary:**
$30,000/$50,000; **Industry Concentration:** Information
Technology; **Function Concentration:** Engineering,
Finance/Accounting

Potter, Douglas C. — *Principal*
Stanton Chase International
2 Lincoln Center
5420 LBJ Freeway #780
Dallas, TX 75240
Telephone: (972) 404-8411
Recruiter Classification: Retained; **Lowest/Average Salary:**
$75,000/$90,000; **Industry Concentration:** Generalist with a
primary focus in High Technology; **Function Concentration:**
Generalist with a primary focus in Administration, Engineering,
Marketing, Sales

Powell, Danny — *Associate*
Source Services Corporation
520 Post Oak Boulevard, Suite 700
Houston, TX 77027
Telephone: (713) 439-1077
Recruiter Classification: Contingency; **Lowest/Average Salary:**
$30,000/$50,000; **Industry Concentration:** Information
Technology; **Function Concentration:** Engineering,
Finance/Accounting

Powell, Gregory — *Associate*
Source Services Corporation
8614 Westwood Center, Suite 750
Vienna, VA 22182
Telephone: (703) 790-5610
Recruiter Classification: Contingency; **Lowest/Average Salary:**
$30,000/$50,000; **Industry Concentration:** Information
Technology; **Function Concentration:** Engineering,
Finance/Accounting

Power, Michael — *Associate*
Source Services Corporation
3701 West Algonquin Road, Suite 380
Rolling Meadows, IL 60008
Telephone: (847) 392-0244
Recruiter Classification: Contingency; **Lowest/Average Salary:**
$30,000/$50,000; **Industry Concentration:** Information
Technology; **Function Concentration:** Engineering,
Finance/Accounting

Pregeant, David — *Associate*
Source Services Corporation
1290 Oakmead Parkway, Suite 318
Sunnyvale, CA 94086
Telephone: (408) 738-8440
Recruiter Classification: Contingency; **Lowest/Average Salary:**
$30,000/$50,000; **Industry Concentration:** Information
Technology; **Function Concentration:** Engineering,
Finance/Accounting

Prencipe, V. Michael — *Principal*
Raymond Karsan Associates
1500 North Beauregard Street, Suite 110
Alexandria, VA 22311
Telephone: (703) 845-1114
Recruiter Classification: Retained; **Lowest/Average Salary:**
$30,000/$90,000; **Industry Concentration:** Information
Technology; **Function Concentration:** Generalist

Press, Fred — *President*
Adept Tech Recruiting
219 Glendale Road
Scarsdale, NY 10583
Telephone: (914) 725-8583
Recruiter Classification: Contingency; **Lowest/Average Salary:**
$30,000/$75,000; **Industry Concentration:** High Technology,
Information Technology; **Function Concentration:**
Administration, Finance/Accounting

Preusse, Eric — *Associate*
Source Services Corporation
1500 West Park Drive, Suite 390
Westborough, MA 01581
Telephone: (508) 366-2600
Recruiter Classification: Contingency; **Lowest/Average Salary:**
$30,000/$50,000; **Industry Concentration:** Information
Technology; **Function Concentration:** Engineering,
Finance/Accounting

Price, Andrew G. — *Associate*
The Thomas Tucker Company
425 California Street, Suite 2502
San Francisco, CA 94104
Telephone: (415) 693-5900
Recruiter Classification: Retained; **Lowest/Average Salary:**
$90,000/$90,000; **Industry Concentration:** Generalist with a
primary focus in Electronics, High Technology, Information
Technology; **Function Concentration:** Generalist with a
primary focus in Engineering, Finance/Accounting, General
Management, Human Resources, Marketing, Research and
Development

Price, Carl — *Associate*
Source Services Corporation
3701 West Algonquin Road, Suite 380
Rolling Meadows, IL 60008
Telephone: (847) 392-0244
Recruiter Classification: Contingency; **Lowest/Average Salary:**
$30,000/$50,000; **Industry Concentration:** Information
Technology; **Function Concentration:** Engineering,
Finance/Accounting

Price, P. Anthony — *Managing Director/Area
Manager*
Russell Reynolds Associates, Inc.
101 California Street
Suite 3140
San Francisco, CA 94111-5829
Telephone: (415) 352-3300
Recruiter Classification: Retained; **Lowest/Average Salary:**
$90,000/$90,000; **Industry Concentration:** Generalist with a
primary focus in High Technology; **Function Concentration:**
Generalist

Prior, Donald — *Consultant*
The Caldwell Partners Amrop International
999 West Hastings Street
Suite 750
Vancouver, British Columbia, CANADA V6C 2W2
Telephone: (604) 669-3550
Recruiter Classification: Retained; **Lowest/Average Salary:**
$60,000/$90,000; **Industry Concentration:** Generalist with a
primary focus in High Technology, Information Technology;
Function Concentration: Generalist

Provus, Barbara L. — *Principal*
Shepherd Bueschel & Provus, Inc.
401 North Michigan Avenue, Suite 3020
Chicago, IL 60611-5555
Telephone: (312) 832-3020
Recruiter Classification: Retained; **Lowest/Average Salary:**
$150,000/$225,000; **Industry Concentration:** Generalist with a
primary focus in Information Technology; **Function
Concentration:** Generalist with a primary focus in Sales

Prumatico, John — *Vice President*
Intelligent Management Solutions, Inc. (IMS)
31B Gulf Breeze Parkway
Gulf Breeze, FL 32561
Telephone: (850) 934-4880
Recruiter Classification: Retained; **Lowest/Average Salary:**
$60,000/$75,000; **Industry Concentration:** High Technology,
Information Technology; **Function Concentration:** Generalist

Prusak, Conrad E. — *President*
Ethos Consulting Inc.
100 Pine Street
Suite 750
San Francisco, CA 94111
Telephone: (415) 397-2211
Recruiter Classification: Retained; **Lowest/Average Salary:**
$90,000/$90,000; **Industry Concentration:** Generalist with a
primary focus in High Technology, Information Technology;
Function Concentration: Generalist with a primary focus in
General Management

Prusak, Julie J. — *Partner*
Ethos Consulting Inc.
100 Pine Street
Suite 750
San Francisco, CA 94111
Telephone: (415) 397-2211
Recruiter Classification: Retained; **Lowest/Average Salary:**
$90,000/$90,000; **Industry Concentration:** Generalist with a
primary focus in High Technology, Information Technology;
Function Concentration: Generalist with a primary focus in
General Management

Pryde, Marcia P. — *Vice President/Managing
Director*
A.T. Kearney, Inc.
One Tabor Center, Suite 950
1200 Seventeenth Street
Denver, CO 80202
Telephone: (303) 626-7300
Recruiter Classification: Retained; **Lowest/Average Salary:**
$90,000/$90,000; **Industry Concentration:** Generalist with a
primary focus in High Technology; **Function Concentration:**
Generalist with a primary focus in Finance/Accounting,
General Management, Marketing, Sales

Pryor, Bill — *Executive Recruiter*
Cendea Connection International
13740 Research Boulevard
Building 0-1
Austin, TX 78750
Telephone: (512) 219-6000
Recruiter Classification: Retained; **Lowest/Average Salary:**
$75,000/$90,000; **Industry Concentration:** Generalist with a
primary focus in Electronics, High Technology, Information
Technology; **Function Concentration:** Generalist with a
primary focus in General Management, Marketing, Sales

Pugh, Judith — *Senior Vice President*
Intelligent Management Solutions, Inc. (IMS)
6464 South Quebec
Englewood, CO 80111
Telephone: (303) 290-9500
Recruiter Classification: Retained; **Lowest/Average Salary:**
$60,000/$75,000; **Industry Concentration:** High Technology,
Information Technology; **Function Concentration:** Generalist

Pugh, Judith Geist — *Senior Vice President*
InterimManagement Solutions, Inc.
6464 South Quebec Street
Englewood, CO 80111
Telephone: (303) 290-9500
Recruiter Classification: Executive Temporary; **Lowest/Average Salary:** $50,000/$90,000; **Industry Concentration:** Information Technology; **Function Concentration:** Generalist with a primary focus in Administration, Finance,/Accounting, Marketing

Pugrant, Mark A. — *Managing Director*
Grant/Morgan Associates, Inc.
7500 Old Georgetown Road
Suite 710
Bethesda, MD 20814
Telephone: (301) 718-8888
Recruiter Classification: Contingency; **Lowest/Average Salary:** $30,000/$50,000; **Industry Concentration:** High Technology; **Function Concentration:** Administration, Finance/Accounting

Quinlan, Lynne — *Software Engineering Recruiter*
Winter, Wyman & Company
950 Winter Street, Suite 3100
Waltham, MA 02154-1294
Telephone: (617) 890-7000
Recruiter Classification: Contingency; **Lowest/Average Salary:** $40,000/$75,000; **Industry Concentration:** High Technology, Information Technology; **Function Concentration:** Engineering

Quinn, Nola — *Recruiter*
Technical Connections Inc.
11400 Olympic Boulevard, Suite 770
Los Angeles, CA 90064
Telephone: (310) 479-8830
Recruiter Classification: Contingency; **Lowest/Average Salary:** $40,000/$60,000; **Industry Concentration:** High Technology, Information Technology; **Function Concentration:** Generalist

Raab, Julie — *Director National Accounts*
Dunhill Professional Search of Irvine, Inc.
9 Executive Circle, Suite 240
Irvine, CA 92614
Telephone: (714) 474-6666
Recruiter Classification: Contingency; **Lowest/Average Salary:** $50,000/$75,000; **Industry Concentration:** Electronics, High Technology; **Function Concentration:** Generalist with a primary focus in Engineering, Marketing, Sales

Rabe, William — *Executive Vice President*
Sales Executives Inc.
755 West Big Beaver Road, Suite 2107
Troy, MI 48084
Telephone: (810) 362-1900
Recruiter Classification: Contingency; **Lowest/Average Salary:** $50,000/$90,000; **Industry Concentration:** Electronics; **Function Concentration:** General Management, Marketing, Sales

Rabinowitz, Peter A. — *President*
P.A.R. Associates Inc.
60 State Street, Suite 1040
Boston, MA 02109-2706
Telephone: (617) 367-0320
Recruiter Classification: Retained; **Lowest/Average Salary:** $100,000/$125,000; **Industry Concentration:** Generalist with a primary focus in High Technology, Information Technology; **Function Concentration:** Generalist with a primary focus in Administration, Finance/Accounting, General Management, Marketing, Women/Minorities

Rachels, John W. — *Senior Consultant*
Southwestern Professional Services
2451 Atrium Way
Nashville, TN 37214
Telephone: (615) 391-2722
Recruiter Classification: Contingency; **Lowest/Average Salary:** $50,000/$50,000; **Industry Concentration:** Generalist with a primary focus in Information Technology; **Function Concentration:** Sales

Racht, Janet G. — *President*
Crowe, Chizek and Company, LLP
330 East Jefferson Boulevard
P.O. Box 7
South Bend, IN 46624
Telephone: (219) 232-3992
Recruiter Classification: Retained; **Lowest/Average Salary:** $30,000/$50,000; **Industry Concentration:** Information Technology; **Function Concentration:** Finance/Accounting, General Management, Human Resources

Radden, David B. — *Partner*
Ray & Berndtson
2029 Century Park East, Suite 1000
Los Angeles, CA 90067
Telephone: (310) 557-2828
Recruiter Classification: Retained; **Lowest/Average Salary:** $90,000/$90,000; **Industry Concentration:** High Technology; **Function Concentration:** Generalist

Raiber, Laurie Altman — *Director Interactive Media Practice*
The IMC Group of Companies Ltd.
14 East 60th Street, Suite 1200
New York, NY 10022
Telephone: (212) 838-9535
Recruiter Classification: Retained; **Lowest/Average Salary:** $75,000/$90,000; **Industry Concentration:** Information Technology; **Function Concentration:** Generalist with a primary focus in General Management, Marketing, Research and Development, Sales

Railsback, Richard — *Principal*
Korn/Ferry International
237 Park Avenue
New York, NY 10017
Telephone: (212) 687-1834
Recruiter Classification: Retained; **Lowest/Average Salary:** $100,000/$150,000; **Industry Concentration:** Generalist with a primary focus in Information Technology; **Function Concentration:** Generalist

Raines, Bruce R. — *President*
Raines International Inc.
1120 Avenue of the Americas
21st Floor
New York, NY 10036
Telephone: (212) 997-1100
Recruiter Classification: Retained; **Lowest/Average Salary:** $90,000/$90,000; **Industry Concentration:** Generalist with a primary focus in High Technology, Information Technology; **Function Concentration:** Generalist with a primary focus in Administration, Finance/Accounting, General Management, Human Resources, Marketing, Research and Development, Sales, Women/Minorities

Ramler, Carolyn S. — *Vice President*
The Corporate Connection, Ltd.
7202 Glen Forest Drive
Richmond, VA 23226
Telephone: (804) 288-8844
Recruiter Classification: Contingency; **Lowest/Average Salary:**
$20,000/$50,000; **Industry Concentration:** Generalist with a
primary focus in High Technology, Information Technology;
Function Concentration: Generalist with a primary focus in
Administration, Engineering, Finance/Accounting, General
Management, Human Resources, Marketing, Sales,
Women/Minorities

Ramsey, John H. — *President*
Mark Stanley/EMA Partners International
2121 Ponce de Leon Boulevard #630
P.O. Box 149071
Coral Gables, FL 33114
Telephone: (305) 444-1612
Recruiter Classification: Retained; **Lowest/Average Salary:**
$75,000/$90,000; **Industry Concentration:** Generalist with a
primary focus in High Technology; **Function Concentration:**
Generalist with a primary focus in Finance/Accounting,
General Management, Human Resources, Sales

Randell, James E. — *Chief Executive Officer*
Randell-Heiken, Inc.
The Lincoln Building
60 East 42nd Street, Suite 2022
New York, NY 10165
Telephone: (212) 490-1313
Recruiter Classification: Retained; **Lowest/Average Salary:**
$60,000/$90,000; **Industry Concentration:** Generalist with a
primary focus in High Technology, Information Technology;
Function Concentration: Generalist with a primary focus in
General Management, Human Resources, Marketing, Sales,
Women/Minorities

Range, Mary Jane — *Partner*
Ingram & Aydelotte Inc./I-I-C Partners
430 Park Avenue, Suite 700
New York, NY 10022
Telephone: (212) 319-7777
Recruiter Classification: Retained; **Lowest/Average Salary:**
$150,000/$150,000; **Industry Concentration:** Information
Technology

Rasmussen, Timothy — *Associate*
Source Services Corporation
1233 North Mayfair Road, Suite 300
Milwaukee, WI 53226
Telephone: (414) 774-6700
Recruiter Classification: Contingency; **Lowest/Average Salary:**
$30,000/$50,000; **Industry Concentration:** Information
Technology; **Function Concentration:** Engineering,
Finance/Accounting

Ratajczak, Paul — *Managing Director*
Source Services Corporation
15260 Ventura Boulevard, Suite 380
Sherman Oaks, CA 91403
Telephone: (818) 905-1500
Recruiter Classification: Contingency; **Lowest/Average Salary:**
$30,000/$50,000; **Industry Concentration:** Information
Technology; **Function Concentration:** Engineering,
Finance/Accounting

Ray, Marianne C. — *Partner*
Callan Associates, Ltd.
2021 Spring Road, Suite 175
Oak Brook, IL 60521
Telephone: (708) 832-7080
Recruiter Classification: Retained; **Lowest/Average Salary:**
$90,000/$90,000; **Industry Concentration:** Generalist with a
primary focus in Electronics, High Technology, Information
Technology; **Function Concentration:** Generalist with a
primary focus in Administration, Engineering,
Finance/Accounting, General Management, Human Resources,
Marketing, Research and Development, Sales,
Women/Minorities

Raymond, Anne — *Recruiter*
Anderson Sterling Associates
18623 Ventura Boulevard, Suite 207
Tarzana, CA 91356
Telephone: (818) 996-0921
Recruiter Classification: Executive Temporary; **Lowest/Average
Salary:** $30,000/$60,000; **Industry Concentration:** Electronics,
High Technology, Information Technology; **Function
Concentration:** Engineering, Finance/Accounting, General
Management, Human Resources, Marketing, Research and
Development, Sales, Women/Minorities

Reardon, Joseph — *Associate*
Source Services Corporation
155 Federal Street, Suite 410
Boston, MA 02110
Telephone: (617) 482-8211
Recruiter Classification: Contingency; **Lowest/Average Salary:**
$30,000/$50,000; **Industry Concentration:** Information
Technology; **Function Concentration:** Engineering,
Finance/Accounting

Reddick, David C. — *Managing Director*
Horton International
33 Sloan Street
Roswell, GA 30075
Telephone: (770) 640-1533
Recruiter Classification: Retained; **Lowest/Average Salary:**
$90,000/$90,000; **Industry Concentration:** Generalist with a
primary focus in High Technology, Information Technology;
Function Concentration: Generalist with a primary focus in
Engineering, Finance/Accounting, General Management,
Human Resources, Marketing, Sales, Women/Minorities

Redding, Denise — *Administrative Assistant*
The Douglas Reiter Company, Inc.
1221 S.W. Yamhill, Suite 301A
Portland, OR 97205
Telephone: (503) 228-6916
Recruiter Classification: Executive Temporary; **Lowest/Average
Salary:** $75,000/$90,000; **Industry Concentration:** Generalist
with a primary focus in High Technology; **Function
Concentration:** Generalist with a primary focus in
Administration, Engineering, Finance/Accounting, General
Management, Human Resources, Marketing

Reece, Christopher S. — *Managing Partner*
Reece & Mruk Partners
75 Second Avenue
Needham, MA 02194-2800
Telephone: (617) 449-3603
Recruiter Classification: Retained; **Lowest/Average Salary:**
$75,000/$90,000; **Industry Concentration:** Generalist with a
primary focus in High Technology, Information Technology;
Function Concentration: Generalist with a primary focus in
Engineering, Finance/Accounting, General Management,
Marketing, Women/Minorities

Reed, Brenda — *Staffing Consultant*
International Staffing Consultants, Inc.
500 Newport Center Drive, Suite 300
Newport Beach, CA 92660-7003
Telephone: (714) 721-7990
Recruiter Classification: Contingency; **Lowest/Average Salary:**
$30,000/$75,000; **Industry Concentration:** Generalist with a
primary focus in Electronics; **Function Concentration:**
Generalist with a primary focus in Administration, Engineering

Reed, Ruthann — *Technical Recruiter*
Spectra International Inc.
6991 East Camelback Road, Suite B-305
Scottsdale, AZ 85251
Telephone: (602) 481-0411
Recruiter Classification: Contingency; **Lowest/Average Salary:**
$40,000/$60,000; **Industry Concentration:** Generalist with a
primary focus in High Technology, Information Technology;
Function Concentration: Generalist with a primary focus in
Engineering, Marketing, Research and Development

Reed, Susan — *Associate*
Source Services Corporation
379 Thornall Street
Edison, NJ 08837
Telephone: (908) 494-2800
Recruiter Classification: Contingency; **Lowest/Average Salary:**
$30,000/$50,000; **Industry Concentration:** Information
Technology; **Function Concentration:** Engineering,
Finance/Accounting

Referente, Gwen — *Executive Recruiter*
Richard, Wayne and Roberts
24 Greenway Plaza, Suite 1304
Houston, TX 77046-2493
Telephone: (713) 629-6681
Recruiter Classification: Retained; **Lowest/Average Salary:**
$40,000/$60,000; **Industry Concentration:** Generalist with a
primary focus in Information Technology; **Function
Concentration:** Generalist

Regan, Thomas J. — *Vice President and CFO*
Tower Consultants, Ltd.
4195 N.E. Hyline Drive
Jensen Beach, FL 34957
Telephone: (561) 225-5151
Recruiter Classification: Retained; **Lowest/Average Salary:**
$60,000/$90,000; **Industry Concentration:** Generalist with a
primary focus in High Technology, Information Technology;
Function Concentration: Administration, Human Resources,
Women/Minorities

Reid, Katherine — *Associate*
Source Services Corporation
150 South Warner Road, Suite 238
King of Prussia, PA 19406
Telephone: (610) 341-1960
Recruiter Classification: Contingency; **Lowest/Average Salary:**
$30,000/$50,000; **Industry Concentration:** Information
Technology; **Function Concentration:** Engineering,
Finance/Accounting

Reid, Scott — *Associate*
Source Services Corporation
Foster Plaza VI
681 Anderson Drive, 2nd Floor
Pittsburgh, PA 15220
Telephone: (412) 928-8300
Recruiter Classification: Contingency; **Lowest/Average Salary:**
$30,000/$50,000; **Industry Concentration:** Information
Technology; **Function Concentration:** Engineering,
Finance/Accounting

Reifel, Laurie — *President*
Reifel & Assocaites
617 Railford Road
Glen Ellyn, IL 60137
Telephone: (630) 469-6651
Recruiter Classification: Retained; **Lowest/Average Salary:**
$75,000/$90,000; **Industry Concentration:** Generalist with a
primary focus in Electronics; **Function Concentration:**
Generalist with a primary focus in Engineering,
Finance/Accounting, General Management, Marketing,
Women/Minorities

Reifersen, Ruth F. — *Vice President*
The Jonathan Stevens Group, Inc.
116 Village Boulevard
Suite 200
Princeton, NJ 08540-5799
Telephone: (609) 734-7444
Recruiter Classification: Retained; **Lowest/Average Salary:**
$40,000/$75,000; **Industry Concentration:** Generalist with a
primary focus in Electronics, Information Technology;
Function Concentration: Generalist with a primary focus in
Engineering, Finance/Accounting, Human Resources,
Marketing

Reiser, Ellen — *Principal*
Thorndike Deland Associates
275 Madison Avenue, Suite 1300
New York, NY 10016
Telephone: (212) 661-6200
Recruiter Classification: Retained; **Lowest/Average Salary:**
$100,000/$125,000; **Industry Concentration:** Generalist with a
primary focus in Information Technology; **Function
Concentration:** Generalist with a primary focus in
Finance/Accounting, General Management, Human Resources,
Marketing, Sales

Reisinger, George L. — *President*
Sigma Group International
6551 South Revere Parkway
Suite 125
Englewood, CO 80111-6410
Telephone: (303) 792-9881
Recruiter Classification: Retained; **Lowest/Average Salary:**
$90,000/$90,000; **Industry Concentration:** Generalist with a
primary focus in High Technology; **Function Concentration:**
Generalist with a primary focus in Administration, Engineering,
Finance/Accounting, General Management, Human Resources,
Marketing

Reiter, Douglas — *President*
The Douglas Reiter Company, Inc.
1221 S.W. Yamhill, Suite 301A
Portland, OR 97205
Telephone: (503) 228-6916
Recruiter Classification: Executive Temporary; **Lowest/Average Salary:** $75,000/$90,000; **Industry Concentration:** Generalist with a primary focus in High Technology; **Function Concentration:** Generalist with a primary focus in Administration, Engineering, Finance/Accounting, General Management, Human Resources, Marketing

Remillard, Brad M. — *Vice President*
CJA - The Adler Group
17852 17th Street
Suite 209
Tustin, CA 92780
Telephone: (714) 573-1820
Recruiter Classification: Retained; **Lowest/Average Salary:** $50,000/$90,000; **Industry Concentration:** Generalist with a primary focus in Electronics, High Technology, Information Technology; **Function Concentration:** Generalist with a primary focus in Engineering, Finance/Accounting, General Management, Human Resources, Marketing, Research and Development, Sales

Renfroe, Ann-Marie — *Associate*
Source Services Corporation
1 Gatehall Drive, Suite 250
Parsippany, NJ 07054
Telephone: (201) 267-3222
Recruiter Classification: Contingency; **Lowest/Average Salary:** $30,000/$50,000; **Industry Concentration:** Information Technology; **Function Concentration:** Engineering, Finance/Accounting

Rennell, Thomas — *Associate*
Source Services Corporation
1500 West Park Drive, Suite 390
Westborough, MA 01581
Telephone: (508) 366-2600
Recruiter Classification: Contingency; **Lowest/Average Salary:** $30,000/$50,000; **Industry Concentration:** Information Technology; **Function Concentration:** Engineering, Finance/Accounting

Renner, Sandra L. — *Senior Consultant*
Spectra International Inc.
6991 East Camelback Road, Suite B-305
Scottsdale, AZ 85251
Telephone: (602) 481-0411
Recruiter Classification: Contingency; **Lowest/Average Salary:** $20,000/$50,000; **Industry Concentration:** Generalist with a primary focus in Electronics, High Technology; **Function Concentration:** Finance/Accounting

Renteria, Elizabeth — *Associate*
Source Services Corporation
15260 Ventura Boulevard, Suite 380
Sherman Oaks, CA 91403
Telephone: (818) 905-1500
Recruiter Classification: Contingency; **Lowest/Average Salary:** $30,000/$50,000; **Industry Concentration:** Information Technology; **Function Concentration:** Engineering, Finance/Accounting

Renwick, David — *Vice President*
John Kurosky & Associates
3 Corporate Park Drive, Suite 210
Irvine, CA 92714
Telephone: (714) 851-6370
Recruiter Classification: Retained; **Lowest/Average Salary:** $90,000/$90,000; **Industry Concentration:** Electronics, High Technology; **Function Concentration:** Engineering, Marketing, Sales

Resnic, Alan — *Associate*
Source Services Corporation
155 Federal Street, Suite 410
Boston, MA 02110
Telephone: (617) 482-8211
Recruiter Classification: Contingency; **Lowest/Average Salary:** $30,000/$50,000; **Industry Concentration:** Information Technology; **Function Concentration:** Engineering, Finance/Accounting

Reuter, Tandom — *Executive Recruiter*
CPS Inc.
One Westbrook Corporate Centre, Suite 600
Westchester, IL 60154
Telephone: (708) 531-8370
Recruiter Classification: Contingency; **Lowest/Average Salary:** $30,000/$50,000; **Industry Concentration:** Generalist with a primary focus in Electronics, High Technology, Information Technology; **Function Concentration:** Engineering, Research and Development, Sales, Women/Minorities

Reyman, Susan — *President*
S. Reyman & Associates Ltd.
20 North Michigan Avenue, Suite 520
Chicago, IL 60602
Telephone: (312) 580-0808
Recruiter Classification: Retained; **Lowest/Average Salary:** $75,000/$90,000; **Industry Concentration:** Generalist with a primary focus in Electronics; **Function Concentration:** Generalist with a primary focus in Administration, Engineering, Finance/Accounting, General Management, Human Resources, Marketing, Sales

Reynes, Tony — *Partner*
Tesar-Reynes, Inc.
500 North Michigan Avenue
Chicago, IL 60611
Telephone: (312) 661-0700
Recruiter Classification: Retained; **Lowest/Average Salary:** $50,000/$75,000; **Industry Concentration:** High Technology; **Function Concentration:** Marketing

Reynolds, Catherine — *Information Technology Recruiter*
Winter, Wyman & Company
101 Federal Street, 27th Floor
Boston, MA 02110-1800
Telephone: (617) 951-2700
Recruiter Classification: Contingency; **Lowest/Average Salary:** $30,000/$60,000; **Industry Concentration:** Generalist with a primary focus in Information Technology; **Function Concentration:** Generalist

Reynolds, Gregory P. — *Vice President - Account Executive*
Roberts Ryan and Bentley
7315 Wisconsin Avenue, Suite 333E
Bethesda, MD 20814
Telephone: (301) 469-3150
Recruiter Classification: Retained; **Lowest/Average Salary:** $90,000/$90,000; **Industry Concentration:** Generalist with a primary focus in Information Technology; **Function Concentration:** Generalist with a primary focus in Administration, Engineering, General Management, Marketing, Women/Minorities

Reynolds, Laura — *Associate*
Source Services Corporation
7730 East Bellview Avenue, Suite 302
Englewood, CO 80111
Telephone: (303) 773-3700
Recruiter Classification: Contingency; **Lowest/Average Salary:** $30,000/$50,000; **Industry Concentration:** Information Technology; **Function Concentration:** Engineering, Finance/Accounting

Rhoades, Michael — *Associate*
Source Services Corporation
One South Main Street, Suite 1440
Dayton, OH 45402
Telephone: (513) 461-4660
Recruiter Classification: Contingency; **Lowest/Average Salary:** $30,000/$50,000; **Industry Concentration:** Information Technology; **Function Concentration:** Engineering, Finance/Accounting

Rhodes, Bill — *Vice President*
Bench International
116 N. Robertson Boulevard
Suite 503
Los Angeles, CA 90048
Telephone: (310) 854-9900
Recruiter Classification: Retained; **Lowest/Average Salary:** $75,000/$90,000; **Industry Concentration:** Generalist with a primary focus in Electronics; **Function Concentration:** Generalist with a primary focus in Engineering, General Management, Human Resources, Marketing, Research and Development, Women/Minorities

Ribeiro, Claudia — *Associate*
Ledbetter/Davidson International, Inc.
101 Park Avenue
Suite 2508
New York, NY 10178
Telephone: (212) 687-6600
Recruiter Classification: Retained; **Lowest/Average Salary:** $90,000/$90,000; **Industry Concentration:** High Technology; **Function Concentration:** Finance/Accounting, General Management, Human Resources, Marketing, Research and Development, Sales

Rice, Marie — *Senior Consultant*
Jay Gaines & Company, Inc.
450 Park Avenue
New York, NY 10022
Telephone: (212) 308-9222
Recruiter Classification: Retained; **Lowest/Average Salary:** $200,000/$300,000; **Industry Concentration:** Generalist with a primary focus in High Technology, Information Technology; **Function Concentration:** Generalist with a primary focus in General Management, Human Resources, Marketing, Sales

Rice, Raymond D. — *President*
Logue & Rice Inc.
8000 Towers Crescent Drive
Suite 650
Vienna, VA 22182-2700
Telephone: (703) 761-4261
Recruiter Classification: Contingency; **Lowest/Average Salary:** $40,000/$90,000; **Industry Concentration:** Generalist with a primary focus in High Technology, Information Technology; **Function Concentration:** Generalist with a primary focus in Administration, Finance/Accounting, General Management, Human Resources, Women/Minorities

Richard, Albert L. — *President*
The Search Alliance, Inc.
311 Centre Street, Suite 206
Fernandina Beach, FL 32034
Telephone: (904) 277-2535
Recruiter Classification: Retained; **Lowest/Average Salary:** $90,000/$90,000; **Industry Concentration:** High Technology, Information Technology; **Function Concentration:** Generalist

Richard, Ryan — *Consultant*
Logix Partners
1601 Trapelo Road
Waltham, MA 02154
Telephone: (617) 890-0500
Recruiter Classification: Retained; **Lowest/Average Salary:** $60,000/$75,000; **Industry Concentration:** Information Technology; **Function Concentration:** Engineering

Richard, Ryan — *Consultant*
Logix, Inc.
1601 Trapelo Road
Waltham, MA 02154
Telephone: (617) 890-0500
Recruiter Classification: Retained; **Lowest/Average Salary:** $60,000/$75,000; **Industry Concentration:** Information Technology; **Function Concentration:** Engineering

Richards, Paul E. — *President*
Executive Directions
4919 Spruce Hill Drive NW
Canton, OH 44718
Telephone: (330) 499-1001
Recruiter Classification: Retained; **Lowest/Average Salary:** $75,000/$90,000; **Industry Concentration:** Electronics; **Function Concentration:** Generalist with a primary focus in Engineering, Finance/Accounting, General Management, Human Resources, Marketing, Sales

Richards, R. Glenn — *Vice President*
Executive Directions
4919 Spruce Hill Drive NW
Canton, OH 44718
Telephone: (330) 499-1001
Recruiter Classification: Retained; **Lowest/Average Salary:** $75,000/$90,000; **Industry Concentration:** Electronics; **Function Concentration:** Generalist with a primary focus in Engineering, Finance/Accounting, General Management, Human Resources, Marketing, Sales

Ridenour, Suzanne S. — *President*
Ridenour & Associates, Ltd.
One East Wacker Drive #3500
Chicago, IL 60601
Telephone: (312) 644-7888
Recruiter Classification: Retained; **Lowest/Average Salary:**
$75,000/$90,000; **Industry Concentration:** High Technology,
Information Technology; **Function Concentration:** Marketing,
Sales

Riederer, Larry — *Executive Recruiter*
CPS Inc.
One Westbrook Corporate Centre, Suite 600
Westchester, IL 60154
Telephone: (708) 531-8370
Recruiter Classification: Contingency; **Lowest/Average Salary:**
$30,000/$50,000; **Industry Concentration:** Generalist with a
primary focus in Electronics, High Technology, Information
Technology; **Function Concentration:** Engineering, Research
and Development, Sales, Women/Minorities

Rieger, Louis J. — *Managing Director*
Spencer Stuart
1111 Bagby, Suite 1616
Houston, TX 77002-2594
Telephone: (713) 225-1621
Recruiter Classification: Retained; **Lowest/Average Salary:**
$90,000/$90,000; **Industry Concentration:** Generalist with a
primary focus in Information Technology; **Function
Concentration:** Generalist with a primary focus in
Administration, Finance/Accounting, General Management,
Human Resources, Marketing, Women/Minorities

Rimmel, James E. — *Vice President -
Cleveland/Northeast*
The Hindman Company
123 Lakhani Lane
Canfield, OH 44406
Telephone: (330) 533-5450
Recruiter Classification: Retained; **Lowest/Average Salary:**
$50,000/$90,000; **Industry Concentration:** Generalist with a
primary focus in Electronics, High Technology; **Function
Concentration:** Generalist with a primary focus in
Administration, Engineering, Finance/Accounting, General
Management, Human Resources, Marketing, Sales

Rimmele, Michael — *Vice President*
The Bankers Group
10 South Riverside Plaza, Suite 1424
Chicago, IL 60606
Telephone: (312) 930-9456
Recruiter Classification: Contingency; **Lowest/Average Salary:**
$50,000/$75,000; **Industry Concentration:** Generalist with a
primary focus in High Technology, Information Technology;
Function Concentration: Generalist with a primary focus in
Administration, Finance/Accounting, General Management,
Human Resources, Marketing, Sales, Women/Minorities

Rios, Vince — *Managing Director*
Source Services Corporation
1 Corporate Drive, Suite 215
Shelton, CT 06484
Telephone: (203) 944-9001
Recruiter Classification: Contingency; **Lowest/Average Salary:**
$30,000/$50,000; **Industry Concentration:** Information
Technology; **Function Concentration:** Engineering,
Finance/Accounting

Rios, Vincent — *Managing Director*
Source Services Corporation
2 Penn Plaza, Suite 1176
New York, NY 10121
Telephone: (212) 760-2200
Recruiter Classification: Contingency; **Lowest/Average Salary:**
$30,000/$50,000; **Industry Concentration:** Information
Technology; **Function Concentration:** Engineering,
Finance/Accounting

Rippey, George E. — *Partner*
Heidrick & Struggles, Inc.
51 Weaver Street
Greenwich Office Park #3
Greenwich, CT 06831-5150
Telephone: (203) 629-3200
Recruiter Classification: Retained; **Lowest/Average Salary:**
$75,000/$90,000; **Industry Concentration:** Generalist with a
primary focus in High Technology; **Function Concentration:**
Generalist

Rizzo, L. Donald — *President*
R.P. Barone Associates
57 Green Street
Woodbridge, NJ 07095
Telephone: (908) 634-4300
Recruiter Classification: Contingency; **Lowest/Average Salary:**
$30,000/$75,000; **Industry Concentration:** Generalist with a
primary focus in Electronics, Information Technology; **Function
Concentration:** Generalist with a primary focus in Engineering,
General Management, Marketing, Research and Development,
Sales

Robb, Tammy — *Associate*
Source Services Corporation
10300 West 103rd Street, Suite 101
Overland Park, KS 66214
Telephone: (913) 888-8885
Recruiter Classification: Contingency; **Lowest/Average Salary:**
$30,000/$50,000; **Industry Concentration:** Information
Technology; **Function Concentration:** Engineering,
Finance/Accounting

Roberts, Carl R. — *Vice President/Director*
Southwestern Professional Services
2451 Atrium Way
Nashville, TN 37214
Telephone: (615) 391-2722
Recruiter Classification: Contingency; **Lowest/Average Salary:**
$20,000/$40,000; **Industry Concentration:** Generalist with a
primary focus in Information Technology; **Function
Concentration:** Generalist with a primary focus in
Finance/Accounting, Sales

Roberts, Marc — *Vice President*
The Stevenson Group of New Jersey
560 Sylvan Avenue
Englewood Cliffs, NJ 07632
Telephone: (201) 568-1900
Recruiter Classification: Retained; **Lowest/Average Salary:**
$75,000/$90,000; **Industry Concentration:** Information
Technology; **Function Concentration:** Generalist

Roberts, Mitch — *Senior Vice President*
A.E. Feldman Associates
445 Northern Boulevard
Great Neck, NY 11021
Telephone: (516) 466-4708
Recruiter Classification: Contingency, Executive Temporary;
Lowest/Average Salary: $60,000/$90,000; **Industry Concentration:** Generalist with a primary focus in Electronics, High Technology, Information Technology; **Function Concentration:** Generalist with a primary focus in Administration, General Management, Marketing, Sales

Roberts, Nick P. — *President*
Spectrum Search Associates, Inc.
1888 Century Park East, Suite 320
Los Angeles, CA 90067
Telephone: (310) 286-6921
Recruiter Classification: Contingency; **Lowest/Average Salary:** $40,000/$60,000; **Industry Concentration:** Generalist with a primary focus in Electronics, High Technology, Information Technology; **Function Concentration:** Generalist with a primary focus in Administration, Finance/Accounting, General Management, Human Resources

Roberts, Norman C. — *President*
Norman Roberts & Associates, Inc.
1800 Century Park East, Suite 430
Los Angeles, CA 90067
Telephone: (310) 552-1112
Recruiter Classification: Retained; **Lowest/Average Salary:** $75,000/$90,000; **Industry Concentration:** Information Technology; **Function Concentration:** Generalist with a primary focus in Administration, Engineering, Finance/Accounting, General Management, Human Resources, Women/Minorities

Roberts, Scott — *Vice President*
Jonas, Walters & Assoc., Inc.
1110 North Old World Third St., Suite 510
Milwaukee, WI 53203-1102
Telephone: (414) 291-2828
Recruiter Classification: Retained; **Lowest/Average Salary:** $60,000/$90,000; **Industry Concentration:** Generalist with a primary focus in Electronics, High Technology, Information Technology; **Function Concentration:** Generalist with a primary focus in Administration, Engineering, Finance/Accounting, General Management, Human Resources, Marketing, Sales

Robertson, Bruce J. — *Partner*
Lamalie Amrop International
200 Park Avenue
New York, NY 10166-0136
Telephone: (212) 953-7900
Recruiter Classification: Retained; **Lowest/Average Salary:** $90,000/$90,000; **Industry Concentration:** Generalist with a primary focus in High Technology; **Function Concentration:** Generalist

Robertson, John A. — *Search Consultant*
Kaye-Bassman International Corp.
18333 Preston Road, Suite 500
Dallas, TX 75252
Telephone: (972) 931-5242
Recruiter Classification: Retained; **Lowest/Average Salary:** $50,000/$60,000; **Industry Concentration:** Electronics, High Technology, Information Technology; **Function Concentration:** Generalist with a primary focus in Engineering, General Management, Marketing, Research and Development, Sales

Robertson, Ronald — *Chairman*
Robertson-Surrette Executive Search
Barrington Tower 10th Floor
Scotia Square, P.O. Box 2166
Halifax, Nova Scotia, B3J-3C4
Telephone: (902) 425-1330
Recruiter Classification: Retained; **Lowest/Average Salary:** $50,000/$75,000; **Industry Concentration:** Generalist with a primary focus in High Technology, Information Technology; **Function Concentration:** Generalist with a primary focus in Engineering, Finance/Accounting, General Management, Human Resources, Marketing, Research and Development, Sales

Robertson, Sherry — *Associate*
Source Services Corporation
5343 North 16th Street, Suite 270
Phoenix, AZ 85016
Telephone: (602) 230-0220
Recruiter Classification: Contingency; **Lowest/Average Salary:** $30,000/$50,000; **Industry Concentration:** Information Technology; **Function Concentration:** Engineering, Finance/Accounting

Robinette, Paul — *Account Executive*
Hernand & Partners
3949 Freshwind Circle
Westlake Village, CA 91361
Telephone: (310) 203-0149
Recruiter Classification: Executive Temporary; **Lowest/Average Salary:** $60,000/$90,000; **Industry Concentration:** High Technology, Information Technology; **Function Concentration:** Engineering

Robins, Jeri N. — *Managing Director*
Nagler, Robins & Poe, Inc.
65 William Street
Wellesley Hills, MA 02181
Telephone: (617) 431-1330
Recruiter Classification: Retained; **Lowest/Average Salary:** $90,000/$90,000; **Industry Concentration:** Generalist with a primary focus in High Technology, Information Technology; **Function Concentration:** Generalist with a primary focus in Finance/Accounting, General Management, Marketing, Sales

Robinson, Bruce — *President*
Bruce Robinson Associates
Harmon Cove Towers
Suite 8, A/L Level
Secaucus, NJ 07094
Telephone: (201) 617-9595
Recruiter Classification: Retained; **Lowest/Average Salary:** $90,000/$90,000; **Industry Concentration:** Generalist with a primary focus in High Technology, Information Technology; **Function Concentration:** Generalist with a primary focus in Administration, Engineering, Finance/Accounting, General Management, Human Resources, Marketing, Research and Development, Sales, Women/Minorities

Robinson, Eric B. — *Vice President/Partner*
Bruce Robinson Associates
Harmon Cove Towers
Suite 8, A/L Level
Secaucus, NJ 07094
Telephone: (201) 617-9595
Recruiter Classification: Retained; **Lowest/Average Salary:** $75,000/$90,000; **Industry Concentration:** Generalist with a primary focus in Information Technology; **Function Concentration:** Generalist with a primary focus in Women/Minorities

Robinson, Tonya — *Associate*
Source Services Corporation
2850 National City Tower
Louisville, KY 40202
Telephone: (502) 581-9900
Recruiter Classification: Contingency; **Lowest/Average Salary:** $30,000/$50,000; **Industry Concentration:** Information Technology; **Function Concentration:** Engineering, Finance/Accounting

Robles Cuellar, Paulina — *Partner*
Ray & Berndtson
Palo Santo No. 6
Colonia Lomas Altas
Mexico City, D.F., MEXICO 11950
Telephone: (525) 570-7462
Recruiter Classification: Retained; **Lowest/Average Salary:** $90,000/$90,000; **Industry Concentration:** Generalist with a primary focus in High Technology, Information Technology; **Function Concentration:** Generalist with a primary focus in Administration, Finance/Accounting, General Management, Human Resources, Marketing, Research and Development, Sales, Women/Minorities

Roblin, Nancy R. — *Vice President*
Paul-Tittle Associates, Inc.
1485 Chain Bridge Road, #304
McLean, VA 22101
Telephone: (703) 442-0500
Recruiter Classification: Retained; **Lowest/Average Salary:** $90,000/$90,000; **Industry Concentration:** Electronics, High Technology, Information Technology; **Function Concentration:** Engineering, Finance/Accounting, General Management, Marketing, Sales, Women/Minorities

Rockwell, Bruce — *Managing Director*
Source Services Corporation
One South Main Street, Suite 1440
Dayton, OH 45402
Telephone: (513) 461-4660
Recruiter Classification: Contingency; **Lowest/Average Salary:** $30,000/$50,000; **Industry Concentration:** Information Technology; **Function Concentration:** Engineering, Finance/Accounting

Rodriguez, Manuel — *Associate*
Source Services Corporation
15600 N.W. 67th Avenue, Suite 210
Miami Lakes, FL 33014
Telephone: (305) 556-8000
Recruiter Classification: Contingency; **Lowest/Average Salary:** $30,000/$50,000; **Industry Concentration:** Information Technology; **Function Concentration:** Engineering, Finance/Accounting

Rogers, Leah — *Vice President*
Dinte Resources, Inc.
8300 Greensboro Drive
Suite 880
McLean, VA 22102
Telephone: (703) 448-3300
Recruiter Classification: Retained, Executive Temporary; **Lowest/Average Salary:** $75,000/$90,000; **Industry Concentration:** Generalist with a primary focus in High Technology, Information Technology; **Function Concentration:** Generalist with a primary focus in Finance/Accounting, General Management, Human Resources, Marketing

Rohan, James E. — *Senior Partner*
J.P. Canon Associates
225 Broadway, Ste. 3602, 36th Fl.
New York, NY 10007-3001
Telephone: (212) 233-3131
Recruiter Classification: Contingency; **Lowest/Average Salary:** $40,000/$75,000; **Industry Concentration:** Generalist with a primary focus in Electronics; **Function Concentration:** Engineering

Rohan, Kevin A. — *Recruiter*
J.P. Canon Associates
225 Broadway, Ste. 3602, 36th Fl.
New York, NY 10007-3001
Telephone: (212) 233-3131
Recruiter Classification: Contingency; **Lowest/Average Salary:** $40,000/$75,000; **Industry Concentration:** Generalist with a primary focus in Electronics; **Function Concentration:** Engineering

Rojo, Rafael — *Vice President*
A.T. Kearney, Inc.
Ruben Dario 281-Piso 15
Col. Bosques de Chapultepec
Mexico City D.F., MEXICO 11580
Telephone: (525) 282-0050
Recruiter Classification: Retained; **Lowest/Average Salary:** $90,000/$90,000; **Industry Concentration:** Generalist with a primary focus in High Technology, Information Technology; **Function Concentration:** Generalist with a primary focus in Engineering, Finance/Accounting, General Management

Rollins, Scott — *President*
S.C. International, Ltd.
1430 Branding Lane, Suite 119
Downers Grove, IL 60515
Telephone: (708) 963-3033
Recruiter Classification: Contingency; **Lowest/Average Salary:** $30,000/$50,000; **Industry Concentration:** Information Technology; **Function Concentration:** Administration, Human Resources

Romanello, Daniel P. — *Senior Director*
Spencer Stuart
Financial Centre
695 East Main Street
Stamford, CT 06901
Telephone: (203) 324-6333
Recruiter Classification: Retained; **Lowest/Average Salary:** $90,000/$90,000; **Industry Concentration:** Electronics, High Technology, Information Technology; **Function Concentration:** Generalist with a primary focus in Engineering, Finance/Accounting, General Management, Human Resources, Marketing, Research and Development, Sales

Romang, Paula — *Account Executive*
Agri-Tech Personnel, Inc.
3113 N.E. 69th Street
Kansas City, MO 64119
Telephone: (816) 453-7200
Recruiter Classification: Contingency; **Lowest/Average Salary:** $20,000/$50,000; **Industry Concentration:** Electronics; **Function Concentration:** Engineering, Finance/Accounting, General Management, Human Resources, Marketing, Research and Development, Sales

Rorech, Maureen — *Division Vice President*
Romac & Associates
120 Hyde Park Place
Suite 200
Tampa, FL 33606
Telephone: (813) 229-5575
Recruiter Classification: Executive Temporary; **Lowest/Average Salary:** $60,000/$60,000; **Industry Concentration:** High Technology, Information Technology; **Function Concentration:** Finance/Accounting

Rosato, William R. — *President*
W.R. Rosato & Associates, Inc.
61 Broadway, 26th Floor
New York, NY 10006
Telephone: (212) 509-5700
Recruiter Classification: Retained; **Lowest/Average Salary:** $90,000/$90,000; **Industry Concentration:** High Technology, Information Technology; **Function Concentration:** Administration, Marketing, Research and Development, Sales

Rose, Robert — *Partner*
ESA Professional Consultants
141 Durham Road
Suite 16
Madison, CT 06443
Telephone: (203) 245-1983
Recruiter Classification: Retained; **Lowest/Average Salary:** $50,000/$75,000; **Industry Concentration:** Electronics, High Technology, Information Technology; **Function Concentration:** Engineering, General Management, Human Resources, Marketing, Research and Development, Women/Minorities

Rosen, Mitchell — *Associate*
Source Services Corporation
1290 Oakmead Parkway, Suite 318
Sunnyvale, CA 94086
Telephone: (408) 738-8440
Recruiter Classification: Contingency; **Lowest/Average Salary:** $30,000/$50,000; **Industry Concentration:** Information Technology; **Function Concentration:** Engineering, Finance/Accounting

Rosenstein, Michele — *Associate*
Source Services Corporation
120 East Baltimore Street, Suite 1950
Baltimore, MD 21202
Telephone: (410) 727-4050
Recruiter Classification: Contingency; **Lowest/Average Salary:** $30,000/$50,000; **Industry Concentration:** Information Technology; **Function Concentration:** Engineering, Finance/Accounting

Rosin, Jeffrey — *Principal*
Korn/Ferry International
Scotia Plaza
40 King Street West
Toronto, Ontario, CANADA M5H 3Y2
Telephone: (416) 366-1300
Recruiter Classification: Retained; **Lowest/Average Salary:** $100,000/$150,000; **Industry Concentration:** Generalist with a primary focus in Information Technology; **Function Concentration:** Generalist

Ross, Curt A. — *Consultant*
Ray & Berndtson
One Allen Center
500 Dallas, Suite 3010
Houston, TX 77002
Telephone: (713) 309-1400
Recruiter Classification: Retained; **Lowest/Average Salary:** $90,000/$90,000; **Industry Concentration:** Generalist with a primary focus in High Technology, Information Technology; **Function Concentration:** Generalist with a primary focus in Administration, Finance/Accounting, General Management, Human Resources, Marketing, Research and Development, Sales, Women/Minorities

Ross, H. Lawrence — *Managing Partner*
Ross & Company
One Gorham Island
Westport, CT 06880
Telephone: (203) 221-8200
Recruiter Classification: Retained; **Lowest/Average Salary:** $90,000/$90,000; **Industry Concentration:** High Technology, Information Technology; **Function Concentration:** Generalist with a primary focus in General Management, Marketing, Sales

Ross, Lawrence — *Consultant*
Ray & Berndtson/Lovas Stanley
Royal Bank Plaza, South Tower, Suite 3150
200 Bay Street, P.O. Box 125
Toronto, Ontario, CANADA M5J 2J3
Telephone: (416) 366-1990
Recruiter Classification: Retained; **Lowest/Average Salary:** $75,000/$90,000; **Industry Concentration:** Generalist with a primary focus in High Technology, Information Technology; **Function Concentration:** Generalist with a primary focus in Finance/Accounting, General Management, Human Resources, Marketing, Sales

Ross, Mark — *Consultant*
Ray & Berndtson/Lovas Stanley
Royal Bank Plaza, South Tower, Suite 3150
200 Bay Street, P.O. Box 125
Toronto, Ontario, CANADA M5J 2J3
Telephone: (416) 366-1990
Recruiter Classification: Retained; **Lowest/Average Salary:** $90,000/$90,000; **Industry Concentration:** High Technology, Information Technology; **Function Concentration:** Generalist with a primary focus in Finance/Accounting, General Management, Human Resources, Marketing

Ross, William J. — *President*
Flowers & Associates
1446 South Reynolds, Suite 112
P.O. Box 538
Maumee, OH 43537
Telephone: (419) 893-4816
Recruiter Classification: Contingency; **Lowest/Average Salary:** $30,000/$50,000; **Industry Concentration:** Generalist with a primary focus in High Technology; **Function Concentration:** Generalist with a primary focus in Administration, Engineering, Finance/Accounting, General Management, Human Resources, Marketing, Sales

Rossi, George A. — *Managing Partner*
Heidrick & Struggles, Inc.
One Post Office Square
Suite 3570
Boston, MA 02109-0199
Telephone: (617) 423-1140
Recruiter Classification: Retained; **Lowest/Average Salary:**
$75,000/$90,000; **Industry Concentration:** Generalist with a
primary focus in High Technology; **Function Concentration:**
Generalist

Rossi, Thomas — *Manager*
Southwestern Professional Services
2451 Atrium Way
Nashville, TN 37214
Telephone: (615) 391-2722
Recruiter Classification: Contingency; **Lowest/Average Salary:**
$40,000/$75,000; **Industry Concentration:** High Technology,
Information Technology; **Function Concentration:**
Finance/Accounting, Sales

Rotella, Marshall W. — *President*
The Corporate Connection, Ltd.
7202 Glen Forest Drive
Richmond, VA 23226
Telephone: (804) 288-8844
Recruiter Classification: Contingency; **Lowest/Average Salary:**
$20,000/$50,000; **Industry Concentration:** Generalist with a
primary focus in High Technology, Information Technology;
Function Concentration: Generalist with a primary focus in
Administration, Engineering, Finance/Accounting, General
Management, Human Resources, Marketing, Sales,
Women/Minorities

Roth, Robert J. — *Partner*
Williams, Roth & Krueger Inc.
20 North Wacker Drive
Chicago, IL 60606
Telephone: (312) 977-0800
Recruiter Classification: Retained; **Lowest/Average Salary:**
$90,000/$90,000; **Industry Concentration:** Generalist with a
primary focus in Electronics, High Technology; **Function
Concentration:** Generalist with a primary focus in Engineering,
Finance/Accounting, General Management, Human Resources,
Marketing, Research and Development, Sales

Rothenbush, Clayton — *Managing Director*
Source Services Corporation
1105 Schrock Road, Suite 510
Columbus, OH 43229
Telephone: (614) 846-3311
Recruiter Classification: Contingency; **Lowest/Average Salary:**
$30,000/$50,000; **Industry Concentration:** Information
Technology; **Function Concentration:** Engineering,
Finance/Accounting

Rothschild, John S. — *Managing Partner*
Lamalie Amrop International
225 West Wacker Drive
Chicago, IL 60606-1229
Telephone: (312) 782-3113
Recruiter Classification: Retained; **Lowest/Average Salary:**
$90,000/$90,000; **Industry Concentration:** Generalist with a
primary focus in High Technology; **Function Concentration:**
Generalist

Rottblatt, Michael — *Vice President*
Korn/Ferry International
One Landmark Square
Stamford, CT 06901
Telephone: (203) 359-3350
Recruiter Classification: Retained; **Lowest/Average Salary:**
$100,000/$150,000; **Industry Concentration:** Generalist with a
primary focus in High Technology; **Function Concentration:**
Generalist

Roussel, Vicki — *Consultant*
Logix Partners
1601 Trapelo Road
Waltham, MA 02154
Telephone: (617) 890-0500
Recruiter Classification: Retained; **Lowest/Average Salary:**
$60,000/$75,000; **Industry Concentration:** High Technology;
Function Concentration: Engineering

Roussel, Vicki J. — *Consultant*
Logix, Inc.
1601 Trapelo Road
Waltham, MA 02154
Telephone: (617) 890-0500
Recruiter Classification: Retained; **Lowest/Average Salary:**
$60,000/$75,000; **Industry Concentration:** High Technology;
Function Concentration: Engineering

Rowe, William D. — *Vice Chairman/Executive
Managing Director*
D.E. Foster Partners Inc.
200 Crescent Court, Suite 300
Dallas, TX 75201-1885
Telephone: (214) 754-2241
Recruiter Classification: Retained; **Lowest/Average Salary:**
$90,000/$90,000; **Industry Concentration:** High Technology;
Function Concentration: Generalist with a primary focus in
Finance/Accounting, General Management, Human Resources

Rowell, Roger — *Vice President*
Halbrecht Lieberman Associates, Inc.
1200 Summer Street
Stamford, CT 06905
Telephone: (203) 327-5630
Recruiter Classification: Retained; **Lowest/Average Salary:**
$90,000/$90,000; **Industry Concentration:** High Technology,
Information Technology; **Function Concentration:** Generalist

Rowland, James — *Associate*
Source Services Corporation
10300 West 103rd Street, Suite 101
Overland Park, KS 66214
Telephone: (913) 888-8885
Recruiter Classification: Contingency; **Lowest/Average Salary:**
$30,000/$50,000; **Industry Concentration:** Information
Technology; **Function Concentration:** Engineering,
Finance/Accounting

Rozentsvayg, Michael — *Consultant*
Logix Partners
1601 Trapelo Road
Waltham, MA 02154
Telephone: (617) 890-0500
Recruiter Classification: Retained; **Lowest/Average Salary:**
$60,000/$75,000; **Industry Concentration:** High Technology,
Information Technology; **Function Concentration:** Engineering

Rozentsvayg, Michael — *Consultant*
Logix, Inc.
1601 Trapelo Road
Waltham, MA 02154
Telephone: (617) 890-0500
Recruiter Classification: Retained; **Lowest/Average Salary:**
$60,000/$75,000; **Industry Concentration:** High Technology,
Information Technology; **Function Concentration:**
Engineering

Rozner, Burton L. — *President*
Oliver & Rozner Associates, Inc.
823 Walton Avenue
Mamaroneck, NY 10543
Telephone: (212) 381-6242
Recruiter Classification: Retained; **Lowest/Average Salary:**
$100,000/$175,000; **Industry Concentration:** Generalist with a
primary focus in Electronics, High Technology; **Function
Concentration:** Generalist

Rubenstein, Alan J. — *Legal Search Consultant*
Chicago Legal Search, Ltd.
33 North Dearborn Street, Suite 2302
Chicago, IL 60602-3109
Telephone: (312) 251-2580
Recruiter Classification: Contingency; **Lowest/Average Salary:**
$50,000/$90,000; **Industry Concentration:** Electronics, High
Technology, Information Technology; **Function Concentration:**
Women/Minorities

Rubinstein, Walter — *Recruiter*
Technical Connections Inc.
11400 Olympic Boulevard, Suite 770
Los Angeles, CA 90064
Telephone: (310) 479-8830
Recruiter Classification: Contingency; **Lowest/Average Salary:**
$40,000/$60,000; **Industry Concentration:** High Technology,
Information Technology; **Function Concentration:** Generalist

Rudolph, Kenneth — *Associate*
Kossuth & Associates, Inc.
800 Bellevue Way N.E., Suite 400
Bellevue, WA 98004
Telephone: (206) 450-9050
Recruiter Classification: Retained; **Lowest/Average Salary:**
$50,000/$90,000; **Industry Concentration:** High Technology,
Information Technology; **Function Concentration:** Generalist
with a primary focus in Administration, Engineering,
Finance/Accounting, General Management, Human Resources,
Marketing, Research and Development, Sales,
Women/Minorities

Rudzinsky, Howard — *Vice President/Senior
Recruiter*
Louis Rudzinsky Associates
394 Lowell Street, P.O. Box 640
Lexington, MA 02173
Telephone: (617) 862-6727
Recruiter Classification: Contingency; **Lowest/Average Salary:**
$20,000/$50,000; **Industry Concentration:** Electronics, High
Technology; **Function Concentration:** Generalist with a
primary focus in Engineering, General Management,
Marketing, Research and Development, Sales

Rudzinsky, Jeffrey — *Vice President/Senior
Recruiter*
Louis Rudzinsky Associates
394 Lowell Street, P.O. Box 640
Lexington, MA 02173
Telephone: (617) 862-6727
Recruiter Classification: Contingency; **Lowest/Average Salary:**
$30,000/$60,000; **Industry Concentration:** Electronics, High
Technology, Information Technology; **Function Concentration:**
Generalist with a primary focus in Engineering, Research and
Development

Ruge, Merrill — *Associate*
William Guy & Associates
P.O. Box 57407
Sherman Oaks, CA 91413
Telephone: Unpublished
Recruiter Classification: Retained; **Lowest/Average Salary:**
$50,000/$90,000; **Industry Concentration:** Generalist with a
primary focus in Electronics, High Technology, Information
Technology; **Function Concentration:** Generalist with a
primary focus in Administration, Engineering,
Finance/Accounting, Human Resources, Research and
Development, Sales, Women/Minorities

Runquist, U.W. — *Managing Director*
Webb, Johnson Associates, Inc.
280 Park Avenue, 43rd Floor
New York, NY 10017
Telephone: (212) 661-3700
Recruiter Classification: Retained; **Lowest/Average Salary:**
$90,000/$90,000; **Industry Concentration:** Generalist with a
primary focus in High Technology; **Function Concentration:**
Generalist

Rurak, Zbigniew T. — *President*
Rurak & Associates, Inc.
1350 Connecticut Avenue N.W.
Suite 801
Washington, DC 20036
Telephone: (202) 293-7603
Recruiter Classification: Retained; **Lowest/Average Salary:**
$90,000/$90,000; **Industry Concentration:** Generalist with a
primary focus in Electronics, High Technology; **Function
Concentration:** Generalist with a primary focus in
Finance/Accounting, General Management, Human Resources,
Marketing, Research and Development, Sales

Rush, Michael E. — *Partner*
D.A.L. Associates, Inc.
2777 Summer Street
Stamford, CT 06905
Telephone: (203) 961-8777
Recruiter Classification: Retained; **Lowest/Average Salary:**
$75,000/$90,000; **Industry Concentration:** Generalist with a
primary focus in Electronics, High Technology, Information
Technology; **Function Concentration:** Generalist with a
primary focus in Engineering, Finance/Accounting, General
Management, Marketing, Sales

Russell, Sam — *Associate Director*
The Guild Corporation
8260 Greensboro Drive, Suite 460
McLean, VA 22102
Telephone: (703) 761-4023
Recruiter Classification: Contingency; **Lowest/Average Salary:**
$40,000/$50,000; **Industry Concentration:** Electronics, High
Technology, Information Technology; **Function Concentration:**
Generalist with a primary focus in Engineering,
Finance/Accounting, General Management, Research and
Development

Russo, Karen — *Executive Recruiter*
Maximum Management Corp.
420 Lexington Avenue
Suite 2016
New York, NY 10170
Telephone: (212) 867-4646
Recruiter Classification: Contingency, Executive Temporary;
Lowest/Average Salary: $30,000/$75,000; **Industry
Concentration:** Generalist with a primary focus in Information
Technology; **Function Concentration:** Human Resources

Ryan, Annette — *Staffing Specialist*
Don Richard Associates of Tidewater, Inc.
4701 Columbus Street, Suite 102
Virginia Beach, VA 23462
Telephone: (757) 518-8600
Recruiter Classification: Contingency; **Lowest/Average Salary:**
$20,000/$40,000; **Industry Concentration:** Generalist with a
primary focus in Electronics, High Technology, Information
Technology; **Function Concentration:** Engineering, Research
and Development

Ryan, David — *Associate*
Source Services Corporation
150 South Wacker Drive, Suite 400
Chicago, IL 60606
Telephone: (312) 346-7000
Recruiter Classification: Contingency; **Lowest/Average Salary:**
$30,000/$50,000; **Industry Concentration:** Information
Technology; **Function Concentration:** Engineering,
Finance/Accounting

Ryan, Kathleen — *Associate*
Source Services Corporation
10300 West 103rd Street, Suite 101
Overland Park, KS 66214
Telephone: (913) 888-8885
Recruiter Classification: Contingency; **Lowest/Average Salary:**
$30,000/$50,000; **Industry Concentration:** Information
Technology; **Function Concentration:** Engineering,
Finance/Accounting

Ryan, Lee — *President*
Ryan, Miller & Associates Inc.
4601 Wilshire Boulevard, Suite 225
Los Angeles, CA 90010
Telephone: (213) 938-4768
Recruiter Classification: Contingency; **Lowest/Average Salary:**
$40,000/$75,000; **Industry Concentration:** High Technology,
Information Technology; **Function Concentration:**
Administration, Finance/Accounting, Human Resources

Ryan, Mark — *Associate*
Source Services Corporation
One CityPlace, Suite 170
St. Louis, MO 63141
Telephone: (314) 432-4500
Recruiter Classification: Contingency; **Lowest/Average Salary:**
$30,000/$50,000; **Industry Concentration:** Information
Technology; **Function Concentration:** Engineering,
Finance/Accounting

Ryan, Mary L. — *Manager Recruitment*
Summerfield Associates, Inc.
6555 Quince Road, Suite 311
Memphis, TN 38119
Telephone: (901) 753-7068
Recruiter Classification: Contingency; **Lowest/Average Salary:**
$30,000/$40,000; **Industry Concentration:** Generalist with a
primary focus in Information Technology; **Function
Concentration:** Generalist

Sabat, Lori S. — *President*
Alta Associates, Inc.
8 Bartles Corner Road, Suite 021
Flemington, NJ 08822
Telephone: (908) 806-8442
Recruiter Classification: Retained; **Lowest/Average Salary:**
$50,000/$90,000; **Industry Concentration:** Generalist with a
primary focus in High Technology, Information Technology;
Function Concentration: Finance/Accounting

Sacerdote, John — *Principal*
Raymond Karsan Associates
18 Commerce Way
Woburn, MA 01801
Telephone: (617) 932-0400
Recruiter Classification: Retained; **Lowest/Average Salary:**
$30,000/$90,000; **Industry Concentration:** Generalist with a
primary focus in Information Technology; **Function
Concentration:** Generalist with a primary focus in
Administration, Engineering, Finance/Accounting, General
Management, Human Resources, Marketing, Research and
Development, Sales, Women/Minorities

Sadaj, Michael — *Managing Director*
Source Services Corporation
505 East 200 South, Suite 300
Salt Lake City, UT 84102
Telephone: (801) 328-0011
Recruiter Classification: Contingency; **Lowest/Average Salary:**
$30,000/$50,000; **Industry Concentration:** Information
Technology; **Function Concentration:** Engineering,
Finance/Accounting

Safnuk, Donald — *President*
Corporate Recruiters Ltd.
490-1140 West Pender Street
Vancouver, British Columbia, CANADA V6E 4G1
Telephone: (604) 687-5993
Recruiter Classification: Contingency; **Lowest/Average Salary:**
$90,000/$90,000; **Industry Concentration:** High Technology;
Function Concentration: General Management

Sahagian, John — *Associate*
The Search Alliance, Inc.
148 East Avenue, Suite 2L
Norwalk, CT 06851
Telephone: (401) 861-2550
Recruiter Classification: Retained; **Lowest/Average Salary:**
$90,000/$90,000; **Industry Concentration:** High Technology,
Information Technology; **Function Concentration:** Generalist

Salet, Michael — *Associate*
Source Services Corporation
4170 Ashford Dunwoody Road, Suite 285
Atlanta, GA 30319
Telephone: (404) 255-2045
Recruiter Classification: Contingency; **Lowest/Average Salary:**
$30,000/$50,000; **Industry Concentration:** Information
Technology; **Function Concentration:** Engineering,
Finance/Accounting

Saletra, Andrew — *Executive Recruiter*
CPS Inc.
One Westbrook Corporate Centre, Suite 600
Westchester, IL 60154
Telephone: (708) 531-8370
Recruiter Classification: Contingency; **Lowest/Average Salary:**
$30,000/$50,000; **Industry Concentration:** Generalist with a
primary focus in Electronics, High Technology, Information
Technology; **Function Concentration:** Engineering, Research
and Development, Sales, Women/Minorities

Sallows, Jill S. — *Manager*
Crowe, Chizek and Company, LLP
330 East Jefferson Boulevard
P.O. Box 7
South Bend, IN 46624
Telephone: (219) 232-3992
Recruiter Classification: Retained; **Lowest/Average Salary:**
$30,000/$50,000; **Industry Concentration:** Information
Technology; **Function Concentration:** Finance/Accounting,
General Management, Human Resources

Salottolo, Al — *Principal*
Tactical Alternatives
2819 Crown Canyon Road, Suite 210
San Ramon, CA 94583
Telephone: (510) 831-3800
Recruiter Classification: Retained; **Lowest/Average Salary:**
$75,000/$90,000; **Industry Concentration:** High Technology,
Information Technology; **Function Concentration:** Engineering,
General Management, Marketing, Sales

Salvagno, Michael J. — *Executive Vice President*
The Cambridge Group Ltd
1175 Post Road East
Westport, CT 06880
Telephone: (203) 226-4243
Recruiter Classification: Contingency; **Lowest/Average Salary:**
$60,000/$75,000; **Industry Concentration:** Generalist with a
primary focus in High Technology, Information Technology;
Function Concentration: Administration, Finance/Accounting,
General Management, Human Resources, Marketing, Research
and Development, Sales, Women/Minorities

Samsel, Randy — *Managing Director*
Source Services Corporation
3 Summit Park Drive, Suite 550
Independence, OH 44131
Telephone: (216) 328-5900
Recruiter Classification: Contingency; **Lowest/Average Salary:**
$30,000/$50,000; **Industry Concentration:** Information
Technology; **Function Concentration:** Engineering,
Finance/Accounting

Samuelson, Robert — *Associate*
Source Services Corporation
520 Post Oak Boulevard, Suite 700
Houston, TX 77027
Telephone: (713) 439-1077
Recruiter Classification: Contingency; **Lowest/Average Salary:**
$30,000/$50,000; **Industry Concentration:** Information
Technology; **Function Concentration:** Engineering,
Finance/Accounting

Sanchez, William — *Associate*
Source Services Corporation
425 California Street, Suite 1200
San Francisco, CA 94104
Telephone: (415) 434-2410
Recruiter Classification: Contingency; **Lowest/Average Salary:**
$30,000/$50,000; **Industry Concentration:** Information
Technology; **Function Concentration:** Engineering,
Finance/Accounting

Sanders, Jason — *Managing Director*
Sanders Management Associates, Inc.
300 Lanidex Plaza
Parsippany, NJ 07054
Telephone: (201) 887-3232
Recruiter Classification: Retained; **Lowest/Average Salary:**
$90,000/$90,000; **Industry Concentration:** High Technology,
Information Technology

Sanders, Natalie — *Executive Recruiter*
CPS Inc.
One Westbrook Corporate Centre, Suite 600
Westchester, IL 60154
Telephone: (708) 531-8370
Recruiter Classification: Contingency; **Lowest/Average Salary:**
$30,000/$50,000; **Industry Concentration:** Generalist with a
primary focus in Electronics, High Technology, Information
Technology; **Function Concentration:** Engineering, Research
and Development, Sales, Women/Minorities

Sanders, Norman D. — *Managing Director*
Norm Sanders Associates
2 Village Court
Hazlet, NJ 07730
Telephone: (732) 264-3700
Recruiter Classification: Retained; **Lowest/Average Salary:**
$90,000/$90,000; **Industry Concentration:** Information
Technology; **Function Concentration:** Generalist

Saner, Harold — *Branch Manager*
Romac & Associates
1060 North Kings Highway
Suite 653
Cherry Hill, NJ 08034
Telephone: (609) 779-9077
Recruiter Classification: Executive Temporary; **Lowest/Average
Salary:** $60,000/$60,000; **Industry Concentration:** High
Technology, Information Technology; **Function Concentration:**
Finance/Accounting

Sangster, Jeffrey — *President*
F-O-R-T-U-N-E Personnel Consultants of Manatee
County
923 4th Street West
Palmetto, FL 34221
Telephone: (941) 729-3674
Recruiter Classification: Contingency; **Lowest/Average Salary:**
$30,000/$60,000; **Industry Concentration:** Electronics, High
Technology; **Function Concentration:** Engineering, General
Management, Research and Development

Sanitago, Anthony — *President*
TaxSearch, Inc.
6102 So. Memorial Drive
Tulsa, OK 74133
Telephone: (918) 252-3100
Recruiter Classification: Retained; **Lowest/Average Salary:**
$60,000/$90,000; **Industry Concentration:** Generalist with a
primary focus in Electronics, High Technology, Information
Technology; **Function Concentration:** Generalist with a
primary focus in Finance/Accounting

Sanow, Robert — *Search Consultant*
Cochran, Cochran & Yale, Inc.
955 East Henrietta Road
Rochester, NY 14623
Telephone: (716) 424-6060
Recruiter Classification: Retained; **Lowest/Average Salary:**
$50,000/$75,000; **Industry Concentration:** Generalist with a
primary focus in High Technology, Information Technology;
Function Concentration: Generalist with a primary focus in
Engineering, Finance/Accounting, General Management,
Human Resources, Marketing, Sales, Women/Minorities

Santiago, Benefrido — *Associate*
Source Services Corporation
879 West 190th Street, Suite 250
Los Angeles, CA 90248
Telephone: (310) 323-6633
Recruiter Classification: Contingency; **Lowest/Average Salary:**
$30,000/$50,000; **Industry Concentration:** Information
Technology; **Function Concentration:** Engineering,
Finance/Accounting

Santimauro, Edward — *Vice President*
Korn/Ferry International
233 South Wacker
Chicago, IL 60606
Telephone: (312) 466-1834
Recruiter Classification: Retained; **Lowest/Average Salary:**
$100,000/$150,000; **Industry Concentration:** Generalist with a
primary focus in Information Technology; **Function
Concentration:** Generalist

Sapers, Mark — *Associate*
Source Services Corporation
71 Spit Brook Road, Suite 305
Nashua, NH 03060
Telephone: (603) 888-7650
Recruiter Classification: Contingency; **Lowest/Average Salary:**
$30,000/$50,000; **Industry Concentration:** Information
Technology; **Function Concentration:** Engineering,
Finance/Accounting

Saposhnik, Doron — *Associate*
Source Services Corporation
2029 Century Park East, Suite 1350
Los Angeles, CA 90067
Telephone: (310) 277-8092
Recruiter Classification: Contingency; **Lowest/Average Salary:**
$30,000/$50,000; **Industry Concentration:** Information
Technology; **Function Concentration:** Engineering,
Finance/Accounting

Sardella, Sharon — *Associate*
Source Services Corporation
1500 West Park Drive, Suite 390
Westborough, MA 01581
Telephone: (508) 366-2600
Recruiter Classification: Contingency; **Lowest/Average Salary:**
$30,000/$50,000; **Industry Concentration:** Information
Technology; **Function Concentration:** Engineering,
Finance/Accounting

Sarn, Allan G. — *Managing Director*
Allan Sarn Associates Inc.
230 Park Avenue, Suite 1522
New York, NY 10169
Telephone: (212) 687-0600
Recruiter Classification: Retained; **Lowest/Average Salary:**
$75,000/$90,000; **Industry Concentration:** Generalist with a
primary focus in High Technology, Information Technology;
Function Concentration: Human Resources

Sarna, Edmund A. — *Executive Recruiter*
Jonas, Walters & Assoc., Inc.
1110 North Old World Third St., Suite 510
Milwaukee, WI 53203-1102
Telephone: (414) 291-2828
Recruiter Classification: Retained; **Lowest/Average Salary:**
$60,000/$60,000; **Industry Concentration:** Electronics,
Information Technology; **Function Concentration:** Generalist
with a primary focus in Administration, Engineering,
Finance/Accounting, General Management, Human Resources,
Marketing, Research and Development, Sales

Sauer, Harry J. — *Managing Partner*
Romac & Associates
1700 Market Street
Suite 2702
Philadelphia, PA 19103
Telephone: (215) 568-6810
Recruiter Classification: Executive Temporary; **Lowest/Average
Salary:** $60,000/$60,000; **Industry Concentration:** High
Technology, Information Technology; **Function Concentration:**
Finance/Accounting

Sauer, Robert C. — *Partner*
Heidrick & Struggles, Inc.
600 Superior Avenue East
Suite 2500
Cleveland, OH 44114-2650
Telephone: (216) 241-7410
Recruiter Classification: Retained; **Lowest/Average Salary:**
$75,000/$90,000; **Industry Concentration:** Generalist with a
primary focus in High Technology; **Function Concentration:**
Generalist

Sausto, Lynne — *Executive Recruiter*
Abraham & London, Ltd.
7 Old Sherman Turnpike, Suite 209
Danbury, CT 06810
Telephone: (203) 730-4000
Recruiter Classification: Contingency; **Lowest/Average Salary:**
$40,000/$75,000; **Industry Concentration:** High Technology,
Information Technology; **Function Concentration:** Marketing,
Sales

Savela, Edward — *Associate*
Source Services Corporation
4170 Ashford Dunwoody Road, Suite 285
Atlanta, GA 30319
Telephone: (404) 255-2045
Recruiter Classification: Contingency; **Lowest/Average Salary:**
$30,000/$50,000; **Industry Concentration:** Information
Technology; **Function Concentration:** Engineering,
Finance/Accounting

Savvas, Carol Diane — *Managing Director*
Ledbetter/Davidson International, Inc.
101 Park Avenue
Suite 2508
New York, NY 10178
Telephone: (212) 687-6600
Recruiter Classification: Retained; **Lowest/Average Salary:**
$90,000/$90,000; **Industry Concentration:** High Technology;
Function Concentration: Finance/Accounting, General
Management, Human Resources, Marketing, Research and
Development, Sales

Sawyer, Deborah — *Principal*
Korn/Ferry International
303 Peachtree Street N.E.
Suite 1600
Atlanta, GA 30308
Telephone: (404) 577-7542
Recruiter Classification: Retained; **Lowest/Average Salary:**
$100,000/$150,000; **Industry Concentration:** Generalist with a
primary focus in Information Technology; **Function
Concentration:** Generalist

Sawyer, Patricia L. — *Partner*
Smith & Sawyer Inc.
230 Park Avenue, 33rd Floor
New York, NY 10169
Telephone: (212) 490-4390
Recruiter Classification: Retained; **Lowest/Average Salary:**
$90,000/$90,000; **Industry Concentration:** Generalist with a
primary focus in High Technology, Information Technology;
Function Concentration: Generalist with a primary focus in
General Management, Marketing, Women/Minorities

Saxon, Alexa — *Associate*
Woodworth International Group
2591 White Owl Drive
Encinitas, CA 92024
Telephone: (760) 634-6893
Recruiter Classification: Retained; **Lowest/Average Salary:**
$60,000/$60,000; **Industry Concentration:** Generalist with a
primary focus in Electronics, High Technology, Information
Technology; **Function Concentration:** Generalist with a
primary focus in Engineering, Finance/Accounting, General
Management, Human Resources, Marketing, Sales

Scalamera, Tom — *Executive Recruiter*
CPS Inc.
One Westbrook Corporate Centre, Suite 600
Westchester, IL 60154
Telephone: (708) 531-8370
Recruiter Classification: Contingency; **Lowest/Average Salary:**
$30,000/$50,000; **Industry Concentration:** Generalist with a
primary focus in Electronics, High Technology, Information
Technology; **Function Concentration:** Engineering, Research
and Development, Sales, Women/Minorities

Schaad, Carl A. — *Partner*
Heidrick & Struggles, Inc.
One Post Office Square
Suite 3570
Boston, MA 02109-0199
Telephone: (617) 423-1140
Recruiter Classification: Retained; **Lowest/Average Salary:**
$75,000/$90,000; **Industry Concentration:** Generalist with a
primary focus in High Technology; **Function Concentration:**
Generalist

Schaefer, Frederic M. — *Vice President*
A.T. Kearney, Inc.
One Tabor Center, Suite 950
1200 Seventeenth Street
Denver, CO 80202
Telephone: (303) 626-7300
Recruiter Classification: Retained; **Lowest/Average Salary:**
$90,000/$90,000; **Industry Concentration:** Generalist with a
primary focus in High Technology; **Function Concentration:**
Generalist with a primary focus in General Management,
Marketing, Sales

Schall, William A. — *Vice President and Principal*
The Stevenson Group of New Jersey
560 Sylvan Avenue
Englewood Cliffs, NJ 07632
Telephone: (201) 568-1900
Recruiter Classification: Retained; **Lowest/Average Salary:**
$75,000/$90,000; **Industry Concentration:** High Technology,
Information Technology; **Function Concentration:** Generalist

Schappell, Marc P. — *Consultant*
Egon Zehnder International Inc.
350 Park Avenue
New York, NY 10022
Telephone: (212) 838-9199
Recruiter Classification: Retained; **Lowest/Average Salary:**
$90,000/$90,000; **Industry Concentration:** Generalist with a
primary focus in High Technology; **Function Concentration:**
Generalist

Schedra, Sharon — *Research Associate*
Earley Kielty and Associates, Inc.
Two Pennsylvania Plaza
New York, NY 10121
Telephone: (212) 736-5626
Recruiter Classification: Retained; **Lowest/Average Salary:**
$90,000/$90,000; **Industry Concentration:** Generalist with a
primary focus in Information Technology; **Function
Concentration:** Generalist with a primary focus in
Administration, Finance/Accounting, General Management,
Human Resources, Marketing, Research and Development,
Sales, Women/Minorities

Schene, Philip — *Technical Recruiter*
A.E. Feldman Associates
445 Northern Boulevard
Great Neck, NY 11021
Telephone: (516) 466-4708
Recruiter Classification: Contingency; **Lowest/Average Salary:**
$60,000/$90,000; **Industry Concentration:** Generalist with a
primary focus in Electronics, High Technology, Information
Technology; **Function Concentration:** Generalist with a
primary focus in Administration, General Management,
Marketing, Sales

Schiavone, Mary Rose — *Vice President*
Canny, Bowen Inc.
200 Park Avenue
49th Floor
New York, NY 10166
Telephone: (212) 949-6611
Recruiter Classification: Retained; **Lowest/Average Salary:**
$90,000/$90,000; **Industry Concentration:** Generalist with a
primary focus in Electronics, High Technology, Information
Technology; **Function Concentration:** Generalist with a
primary focus in Engineering, Finance/Accounting, General
Management, Human Resources, Marketing, Research and
Development, Sales

Schlpma, Christine — *Executive Recruiter*
Advanced Executive Resources
3040 Charlevoix Drive, SE
Grand Rapids, MI 49546
Telephone: (616) 942-4030
Recruiter Classification: Retained; **Lowest/Average Salary:**
$30,000/$50,000; **Industry Concentration:** Generalist with a
primary focus in Electronics, High Technology; **Function
Concentration:** Generalist with a primary focus in Engineering,
Finance/Accounting, General Management, Human Resources,
Marketing, Research and Development, Sales,
Women/Minorities

Schmidt, Frank B. — *President*
F.B. Schmidt International
30423 Canwood Place, Suite 239
Agoura Hills, CA 91301
Telephone: (818) 706-0500
Recruiter Classification: Retained; **Lowest/Average Salary:**
$60,000/$90,000; **Industry Concentration:** Information
Technology; **Function Concentration:** Marketing

Schmidt, Peter R. — *President Boyden Consulting Corp.*
Boyden
375 Park Avenue, Suite 1509
New York, NY 10152
Telephone: (212) 980-6480
Recruiter Classification: Retained; **Lowest/Average Salary:**
$75,000/$90,000; **Industry Concentration:** High Technology;
Function Concentration: Generalist with a primary focus in
Engineering, Finance/Accounting, General Management,
Human Resources, Marketing, Research and Development,
Sales, Women/Minorities

Schmidt, Peter R. — *Managing Director*
Boyden
55 Madison Avenue
Suite 400
Morristown, NJ 07960
Telephone: (201) 267-0980
Recruiter Classification: Retained; **Lowest/Average Salary:**
$90,000/$90,000; **Industry Concentration:** Generalist with a
primary focus in High Technology; **Function Concentration:**
Generalist

Schmidt, William C. — *Senior Vice President*
Christian & Timbers
25825 Science Park Drive, Suite 400
Cleveland, OH 44122
Telephone: (216) 765-5866
Recruiter Classification: Retained; **Lowest/Average Salary:**
$90,000/$90,000; **Industry Concentration:** Generalist with a
primary focus in Electronics, Information Technology; **Function
Concentration:** Generalist with a primary focus in Engineering,
General Management, Marketing, Sales

Schneider, James — *Managing Director*
The Search Firm, Inc.
595 Market Street, Suite 1400
San Francisco, CA 94105
Telephone: (415) 777-3900
Recruiter Classification: Contingency; **Lowest/Average Salary:**
$40,000/$75,000; **Industry Concentration:** Electronics, High
Technology, Information Technology

Schneiderman, Gerald — *President*
Management Resource Associates, Inc.
P.O. Box 3266
Boca Raton, FL 33427
Telephone: (561) 852-5650
Recruiter Classification: Contingency; **Lowest/Average Salary:**
$50,000/$90,000; **Industry Concentration:** Generalist with a
primary focus in Electronics, High Technology, Information
Technology; **Function Concentration:** Generalist with a
primary focus in Engineering, Finance/Accounting, General
Management, Human Resources, Marketing, Research and
Development, Sales

Schnierow, Beryl — *Associate*
Tesar-Reynes, Inc.
500 North Michigan Avenue
Chicago, IL 60611
Telephone: (312) 661-0700
Recruiter Classification: Retained; **Lowest/Average Salary:**
$50,000/$75,000; **Industry Concentration:** High Technology;
Function Concentration: Marketing

Schnit, David — *Account Director*
Warren, Morris & Madison
2190 Carmel Valley Road
Del Mar, CA 92014
Telephone: (619) 481-3388
Recruiter Classification: Retained; **Lowest/Average Salary:**
$50,000/$75,000; **Industry Concentration:** High Technology;
Function Concentration: Generalist

Schoettle, Michael B. — *Partner*
Heidrick & Struggles, Inc.
300 South Grand Avenue, Suite 2400
Los Angeles, CA 90071
Telephone: (213) 625-8811
Recruiter Classification: Retained; **Lowest/Average Salary:**
$75,000/$90,000; **Industry Concentration:** Generalist with a
primary focus in High Technology; **Function Concentration:**
Generalist

Schrenzel, Benjamin — *Consultant*
Parfitt Recruiting and Consulting
1540 140th Avenue NE #201
Bellevue, WA 98005
Telephone: (206) 646-6300
Recruiter Classification: Contingency; **Lowest/Average Salary:**
$30,000/$75,000; **Industry Concentration:** Generalist with a
primary focus in Information Technology; **Function
Concentration:** Engineering

Schroeder, James — *Associate*
Source Services Corporation
One South Main Street, Suite 1440
Dayton, OH 45402
Telephone: (513) 461-4660
Recruiter Classification: Contingency; **Lowest/Average Salary:**
$30,000/$50,000; **Industry Concentration:** Information
Technology; **Function Concentration:** Engineering,
Finance/Accounting

Schueneman, David — *Executive Recruiter*
CPS Inc.
One Westbrook Corporate Centre, Suite 600
Westchester, IL 60154
Telephone: (708) 531-8370
Recruiter Classification: Contingency; **Lowest/Average Salary:**
$30,000/$50,000; **Industry Concentration:** Generalist with a
primary focus in Electronics, High Technology, Information
Technology; **Function Concentration:** Engineering, Research
and Development, Sales, Women/Minorities

Schultz, Helen — *President*
Predictor Systems
39350 Civic Center Drive, Suite 440
Fremont, CA 94538
Telephone: (510) 713-0840
Recruiter Classification: Retained; **Lowest/Average Salary:**
$90,000/$90,000; **Industry Concentration:** Electronics, High
Technology, Information Technology; **Function Concentration:**
Engineering, Finance/Accounting, Sales

Schultz, Randy — *Associate*
Source Services Corporation
1233 North Mayfair Road, Suite 300
Milwaukee, WI 53226
Telephone: (414) 774-6700
Recruiter Classification: Contingency; **Lowest/Average Salary:**
$30,000/$50,000; **Industry Concentration:** Information
Technology; **Function Concentration:** Engineering,
Finance/Accounting

Schwalbach, Robert — *Associate*
Source Services Corporation
1290 Oakmead Parkway, Suite 318
Sunnyvale, CA 94086
Telephone: (408) 738-8440
Recruiter Classification: Contingency; **Lowest/Average Salary:**
$30,000/$50,000; **Industry Concentration:** Information
Technology; **Function Concentration:** Engineering,
Finance/Accounting

Schwam, Carol — *Vice President*
A.E. Feldman Associates
445 Northern Boulevard
Great Neck, NY 11021
Telephone: (516) 466-4708
Recruiter Classification: Contingency; **Lowest/Average Salary:**
$60,000/$90,000; **Industry Concentration:** Generalist with a
primary focus in Electronics, High Technology, Information
Technology; **Function Concentration:** Generalist with a
primary focus in Administration, General Management,
Marketing, Sales

Schwartz, Vincent P. — *Vice President*
Slayton International, Inc./I-I-C Partners
181 West Madison Street, Suite 4510
Chicago, IL 60602
Telephone: (312) 456-0080
Recruiter Classification: Retained; **Lowest/Average Salary:**
$90,000/$90,000; **Industry Concentration:** Electronics, High
Technology, Information Technology; **Function Concentration:**
Generalist

Schweichler, Lee J. — *President*
Schweichler Associates, Inc.
200 Tamal Vista, Building 200, Suite 100
Corte Madera, CA 94925
Telephone: (415) 924-7200
Recruiter Classification: Retained; **Lowest/Average Salary:**
$90,000/$90,000; **Industry Concentration:** Electronics, High
Technology, Information Technology; **Function Concentration:**
Engineering, Finance/Accounting, General Management,
Human Resources, Marketing, Research and Development,
Sales

Schwinden, William — *Associate*
Source Services Corporation
500 108th Avenue NE, Suite 1780
Bellevue, WA 98004
Telephone: (206) 454-6400
Recruiter Classification: Contingency; **Lowest/Average Salary:**
$30,000/$50,000; **Industry Concentration:** Information
Technology; **Function Concentration:** Engineering,
Finance/Accounting

Scimone, James — *Managing Director*
Source Services Corporation
15600 N.W. 67th Avenue, Suite 210
Miami Lakes, FL 33014
Telephone: (305) 556-8000
Recruiter Classification: Contingency; **Lowest/Average Salary:**
$30,000/$50,000; **Industry Concentration:** Information
Technology; **Function Concentration:** Engineering,
Finance/Accounting

Scimone, Jim — *Managing Director*
Source Services Corporation
701 West Cypress Creek Road, Suite 202
Ft. Lauderdale, FL 33309
Telephone: (954) 771-0777
Recruiter Classification: Contingency; **Lowest/Average Salary:**
$30,000/$50,000; **Industry Concentration:** Information
Technology; **Function Concentration:** Engineering,
Finance/Accounting

Scoff, Barry — *Associate*
Source Services Corporation
379 Thornall Street
Edison, NJ 08837
Telephone: (908) 494-2800
Recruiter Classification: Contingency; **Lowest/Average Salary:**
$30,000/$50,000; **Industry Concentration:** Information
Technology; **Function Concentration:** Engineering,
Finance/Accounting

Scothon, Alan — *Managing Partner*
Romac & Associates
6130 Westford Road
Dayton, OH 45426
Telephone: (513) 854-5719
Recruiter Classification: Executive Temporary; **Lowest/Average
Salary:** $60,000/$60,000; **Industry Concentration:** High
Technology, Information Technology; **Function Concentration:**
Finance/Accounting

Scott, Cory — *Partner*
Warren, Morris & Madison
132 Chapel Street
Portsmouth, NH 03801
Telephone: (603) 431-7929
Recruiter Classification: Retained; **Lowest/Average Salary:**
$75,000/$90,000; **Industry Concentration:** High Technology;
Function Concentration: Generalist

Scott, Evan — *Executive Vice President/Partner*
Howard Fischer Associates, Inc.
1800 John F. Kennedy Boulevard, 7th Floor
Philadelphia, PA 19103
Telephone: (215) 568-8363
Recruiter Classification: Retained; **Lowest/Average Salary:**
$90,000/$90,000; **Industry Concentration:** Generalist with a
primary focus in High Technology, Information Technology;
Function Concentration: Generalist with a primary focus in
Administration, Finance/Accounting, General Management,
Human Resources, Marketing, Research and Development,
Sales, Women/Minorities

Scott, Gordon S. — *Vice President*
Search Advisors International Corp.
777 South Harbour Island Boulevard
Suite 925
Tampa, FL 33602
Telephone: (813) 221-7555
Recruiter Classification: Retained; **Lowest/Average Salary:**
$75,000/$90,000; **Industry Concentration:** Generalist with a
primary focus in Electronics, High Technology, Information
Technology; **Function Concentration:** Generalist with a
primary focus in Administration, Engineering,
Finance/Accounting, General Management, Human Resources,
Marketing, Research and Development, Sales,
Women/Minorities

Scranton, Lisa — *Professional Recruiter*
A.J. Burton Group, Inc.
120 East Baltimore Street, Suite 2220
Baltimore, MD 21202
Telephone: (410) 752-5244
Recruiter Classification: Contingency; **Lowest/Average Salary:** $40,000/$75,000; **Industry Concentration:** Generalist with a primary focus in High Technology, Information Technology; **Function Concentration:** Generalist with a primary focus in Administration, Finance/Accounting, General Management, Human Resources

Seamon, Kenneth — *Associate*
Source Services Corporation
3 Summit Park Drive, Suite 550
Independence, OH 44131
Telephone: (216) 328-5900
Recruiter Classification: Contingency; **Lowest/Average Salary:** $30,000/$50,000; **Industry Concentration:** Information Technology; **Function Concentration:** Engineering, Finance/Accounting

Searing, James M. — *Partner*
Kirkman & Searing, Inc.
8045 Leesburg Pike
Suite 540
Vienna, VA 22182
Telephone: (703) 761-7020
Recruiter Classification: Retained; **Lowest/Average Salary:** $90,000/$90,000; **Industry Concentration:** High Technology, Information Technology; **Function Concentration:** General Management, Marketing, Sales

Seco, William — *Managing Partner*
Seco & Zetto Associates, Inc.
P.O. Box 225
Harrington Park, NJ 07640
Telephone: (201) 784-0674
Recruiter Classification: Contingency; **Lowest/Average Salary:** $60,000/$75,000; **Industry Concentration:** Generalist with a primary focus in High Technology, Information Technology; **Function Concentration:** Generalist with a primary focus in Marketing, Sales, Women/Minorities

Seiden, Steven A. — *President*
Seiden Krieger Associates, Inc.
375 Park Avenue
New York, NY 10152
Telephone: (212) 688-8383
Recruiter Classification: Retained; **Lowest/Average Salary:** $90,000/$90,000; **Industry Concentration:** Generalist with a primary focus in Electronics, High Technology, Information Technology; **Function Concentration:** Generalist with a primary focus in Finance/Accounting, General Management, Human Resources, Marketing, Sales, Women/Minorities

Selker, Gregory L. — *Vice President*
Christian & Timbers
25825 Science Park Drive, Suite 400
Cleveland, OH 44122
Telephone: (216) 765-5870
Recruiter Classification: Retained; **Lowest/Average Salary:** $90,000/$90,000; **Industry Concentration:** Generalist with a primary focus in High Technology, Information Technology; **Function Concentration:** Generalist

Sell, David — *Associate*
Source Services Corporation
7730 East Bellview Avenue, Suite 302
Englewood, CO 80111
Telephone: (303) 773-3700
Recruiter Classification: Contingency; **Lowest/Average Salary:** $30,000/$50,000; **Industry Concentration:** Information Technology; **Function Concentration:** Engineering, Finance/Accounting

Selvaggi, Esther — *Associate*
Source Services Corporation
150 South Warner Road, Suite 238
King of Prussia, PA 19406
Telephone: (610) 341-1960
Recruiter Classification: Contingency; **Lowest/Average Salary:** $30,000/$50,000; **Industry Concentration:** Information Technology; **Function Concentration:** Engineering, Finance/Accounting

Semple, David — *Associate*
Source Services Corporation
4170 Ashford Dunwoody Road, Suite 285
Atlanta, GA 30319
Telephone: (404) 255-2045
Recruiter Classification: Contingency; **Lowest/Average Salary:** $30,000/$50,000; **Industry Concentration:** Information Technology; **Function Concentration:** Engineering, Finance/Accounting

Semyan, John K. — *Partner*
TNS Partners, Inc.
8140 Walnut Hill Lane
Suite 301
Dallas, TX 75231
Telephone: (214) 369-3565
Recruiter Classification: Retained; **Lowest/Average Salary:** $90,000/$150,000; **Industry Concentration:** Generalist with a primary focus in Electronics, High Technology, Information Technology; **Function Concentration:** Generalist with a primary focus in Finance/Accounting, General Management, Marketing, Sales

Serba, Kerri — *Associate*
Source Services Corporation
155 Federal Street, Suite 410
Boston, MA 02110
Telephone: (617) 482-8211
Recruiter Classification: Contingency; **Lowest/Average Salary:** $30,000/$50,000; **Industry Concentration:** Information Technology; **Function Concentration:** Engineering, Finance/Accounting

Sessa, Vincent J. — *Partner*
Integrated Search Solutions Group, LLC
33 Main Street
Port Washington, NY 11050
Telephone: (516) 767-3030
Recruiter Classification: Retained; **Lowest/Average Salary:** $90,000/$90,000; **Industry Concentration:** Generalist with a primary focus in Electronics, Information Technology; **Function Concentration:** Generalist

Sevilla, Claudio A. — *General Manager*
Crawford & Crofford
15327 NW 60th Avenue, Suite 240
Miami Lakes, FL 33014
Telephone: (305) 820-0855
Recruiter Classification: Contingency; **Lowest/Average Salary:**
$30,000/$50,000; **Industry Concentration:** Generalist with a
primary focus in Electronics, Information Technology; **Function
Concentration:** Generalist with a primary focus in
Administration, Engineering, Finance/Accounting, General
Management, Marketing, Research and Development, Sales

Shackleford, David — *Associate*
Source Services Corporation
150 South Warner Road, Suite 238
King of Prussia, PA 19406
Telephone: (610) 341-1960
Recruiter Classification: Contingency; **Lowest/Average Salary:**
$30,000/$50,000; **Industry Concentration:** Information
Technology; **Function Concentration:** Engineering,
Finance/Accounting

Shamir, Ben — *Recruiter*
S.D. Kelly & Associates, Inc.
990 Washington Street
Dedham, MA 02026
Telephone: (617) 326-8038
Recruiter Classification: Contingency; **Lowest/Average Salary:**
$50,000/$60,000; **Industry Concentration:** Electronics, High
Technology; **Function Concentration:** Engineering, General
Management, Marketing, Sales

Shanks, Jennifer — *Associate*
Source Services Corporation
2029 Century Park East, Suite 1350
Los Angeles, CA 90067
Telephone: (310) 277-8092
Recruiter Classification: Contingency; **Lowest/Average Salary:**
$30,000/$50,000; **Industry Concentration:** Information
Technology; **Function Concentration:** Engineering,
Finance/Accounting

Shapanka, Samuel — *Associate*
Source Services Corporation
2 Penn Plaza, Suite 1176
New York, NY 10121
Telephone: (212) 760-2200
Recruiter Classification: Contingency; **Lowest/Average Salary:**
$30,000/$50,000; **Industry Concentration:** Information
Technology; **Function Concentration:** Engineering,
Finance/Accounting

Shapiro, Beth — *Consultant*
Howard Fischer Associates, Inc.
13750 San Pedro Avenue
Suite 810
San Antonio, TX 78232
Telephone: (210) 491-0844
Recruiter Classification: Retained; **Lowest/Average Salary:**
$90,000/$90,000; **Industry Concentration:** Generalist with a
primary focus in High Technology; **Function Concentration:**
Generalist

Shapiro, Elaine — *Executive Recruiter*
CPS Inc.
303 Congress Street, 5th Floor
Boston, MA 02210
Telephone: (617) 439-7950
Recruiter Classification: Contingency; **Lowest/Average Salary:**
$30,000/$50,000; **Industry Concentration:** Generalist with a
primary focus in Electronics, High Technology, Information
Technology; **Function Concentration:** Engineering, Research
and Development, Sales, Women/Minorities

Shattuck, Merrill B. — *President*
M.B. Shattuck and Associates, Inc.
100 Bush Street, Suite 1675
San Francisco, CA 94104
Telephone: (415) 421-6264
Recruiter Classification: Retained; **Lowest/Average Salary:**
$80,000/$100,000; **Industry Concentration:** Generalist with a
primary focus in Electronics, High Technology, Information
Technology; **Function Concentration:** Generalist with a
primary focus in Administration, Engineering, Human
Resources, Marketing, Research and Development, Sales

Shawhan, Heather — *Associate*
Source Services Corporation
879 West 190th Street, Suite 250
Los Angeles, CA 90248
Telephone: (310) 323-6633
Recruiter Classification: Contingency; **Lowest/Average Salary:**
$30,000/$50,000; **Industry Concentration:** Information
Technology; **Function Concentration:** Engineering,
Finance/Accounting

Shea, Christopher J. — *Partner*
Ingram & Aydelotte Inc./I-I-C Partners
430 Park Avenue, Suite 700
New York, NY 10022
Telephone: (212) 319-7777
Recruiter Classification: Retained; **Lowest/Average Salary:**
$150,000/$150,000; **Industry Concentration:** Information
Technology; **Function Concentration:** Finance/Accounting

Shea, Kathleen M. — *President*
The Penn Partners, Incorporated
117 South 17th Street, Suite 400
Philadelphia, PA 19103
Telephone: (215) 568-9285
Recruiter Classification: Retained; **Lowest/Average Salary:**
$60,000/$90,000; **Industry Concentration:** Generalist with a
primary focus in Electronics, High Technology; **Function
Concentration:** Generalist

Sheedy, Edward J. — *Principal*
Dieckmann & Associates, Ltd.
180 North Stetson, Suite 5555
Two Prudential Plaza
Chicago, IL 60601
Telephone: (312) 819-5900
Recruiter Classification: Retained; **Lowest/Average Salary:**
$90,000/$90,000; **Industry Concentration:** Generalist with a
primary focus in High Technology, Information Technology;
Function Concentration: Generalist with a primary focus in
Finance/Accounting, General Management, Human Resources,
Marketing, Research and Development

Shell, John C. — *President*
John Shell Associates, Inc.
115 Atrium Way, Suite 122
Columbia, SC 29223
Telephone: (803) 788-6619
Recruiter Classification: Contingency, Executive Temporary; **Lowest/Average Salary:** $20,000/$40,000; **Industry Concentration:** Generalist with a primary focus in High Technology, Information Technology; **Function Concentration:** Finance/Accounting

Shelton, Jonathan — *Associate*
Source Services Corporation
1105 Schrock Road, Suite 510
Columbus, OH 43229
Telephone: (614) 846-3311
Recruiter Classification: Contingency; **Lowest/Average Salary:** $30,000/$50,000; **Industry Concentration:** Information Technology; **Function Concentration:** Engineering, Finance/Accounting

Shemin, Grace — *Executive Recruiter*
Maximum Management Corp.
420 Lexington Avenue
Suite 2016
New York, NY 10170
Telephone: (212) 867-4646
Recruiter Classification: Contingency, Executive Temporary; **Lowest/Average Salary:** $30,000/$75,000; **Industry Concentration:** Generalist with a primary focus in Information Technology; **Function Concentration:** Human Resources

Shenfield, Peter — *Vice President*
A.T. Kearney, Inc.
130 Adelaide Street West, Suite 2710
Toronto, Ontario, CANADA M5H 3P5
Telephone: (416) 947-1990
Recruiter Classification: Retained; **Lowest/Average Salary:** $90,000/$90,000; **Industry Concentration:** Generalist with a primary focus in High Technology, Information Technology; **Function Concentration:** Generalist with a primary focus in Engineering, Finance/Accounting, General Management

Shepard, Michael J. — *Group Vice President*
MSI International
2500 Marquis One Tower
245 Peachtree Center Ave.
Atlanta, GA 30303
Telephone: (404) 659-5236
Recruiter Classification: Contingency; **Lowest/Average Salary:** $30,000/$60,000; **Industry Concentration:** Generalist with a primary focus in High Technology, Information Technology; **Function Concentration:** Generalist with a primary focus in Administration, Engineering, Finance/Accounting, General Management, Marketing, Sales

Shepherd, Daniel M. — *Principal*
Shepherd Bueschel & Provus, Inc.
401 North Michigan Avenue, Suite 3020
Chicago, IL 60611-5555
Telephone: (312) 832-3020
Recruiter Classification: Retained; **Lowest/Average Salary:** $90,000/$90,000; **Industry Concentration:** Generalist with a primary focus in High Technology; **Function Concentration:** Generalist with a primary focus in Finance/Accounting, General Management, Marketing, Sales

Sherwood, Andrew — *Chairman*
Goodrich & Sherwood Associates, Inc.
521 Fifth Avenue
New York, NY 10175
Telephone: (212) 697-4131
Recruiter Classification: Retained; **Lowest/Average Salary:** $60,000/$90,000; **Industry Concentration:** Generalist with a primary focus in Information Technology; **Function Concentration:** Generalist with a primary focus in Administration, Finance/Accounting, General Management, Human Resources, Marketing, Sales

Shield, Nancy — *Vice President*
Maximum Management Corp.
420 Lexington Avenue
Suite 2016
New York, NY 10170
Telephone: (212) 867-4646
Recruiter Classification: Contingency, Executive Temporary; **Lowest/Average Salary:** $30,000/$75,000; **Industry Concentration:** Generalist with a primary focus in Information Technology; **Function Concentration:** Human Resources

Shimp, David J. — *Partner*
Lamalie Amrop International
225 West Wacker Drive
Chicago, IL 60606-1229
Telephone: (312) 782-3113
Recruiter Classification: Retained; **Lowest/Average Salary:** $90,000/$90,000; **Industry Concentration:** Generalist with a primary focus in High Technology, Information Technology; **Function Concentration:** Generalist with a primary focus in General Management, Marketing, Sales

Shirilla, Robert M. — *Senior Vice President*
F.B. Schmidt International
30423 Canwood Place, Suite 239
Agoura Hills, CA 91301
Telephone: (818) 706-0500
Recruiter Classification: Retained; **Lowest/Average Salary:** $60,000/$90,000; **Industry Concentration:** Information Technology; **Function Concentration:** Marketing

Shontell, William — *Senior Director*
Don Richard Associates of Washington, D.C., Inc.
8180 Greensboro Drive, Suite 1020
McLean, VA 22102
Telephone: (703) 827-5990
Recruiter Classification: Contingency; **Lowest/Average Salary:** $50,000/$60,000; **Industry Concentration:** High Technology; **Function Concentration:** Finance/Accounting

Shore, Earl L. — *President*
E.L. Shore & Associates Ltd.
1201-2 St. Clair Avenue E.
Toronto, Ontario, CANADA M4T 2T5
Telephone: (416) 928-9399
Recruiter Classification: Retained; **Lowest/Average Salary:** $90,000/$90,000; **Industry Concentration:** Generalist with a primary focus in High Technology, Information Technology; **Function Concentration:** Generalist with a primary focus in Finance/Accounting, General Management, Human Resources, Marketing

Shourds, Mary E. — *Executive Vice President*
Houze, Shourds & Montgomery, Inc.
Greater L.A. World Trade Center, Suite 800
Long Beach, CA 90831-0800
Telephone: (562) 495-6495
Recruiter Classification: Retained; **Lowest/Average Salary:**
$90,000/$90,000; **Industry Concentration:** Generalist with
a primary focus in Electronics, High Technology,
Information Technology; **Function Concentration:**
Generalist

Shufelt, Doug — *Search Consultant*
Sink, Walker, Boltrus International
60 Walnut Street
Wellesley, MA 02181
Telephone: (617) 237-1199
Recruiter Classification: Retained; **Lowest/Average Salary:**
$90,000/$90,000; **Industry Concentration:** Electronics, High
Technology, Information Technology; **Function Concentration:**
Engineering, General Management, Research and
Development, Sales

Shulman, Barry — *Principal*
Shulman Associates
796 Elizabeth Street
San Francisco, CA 94114
Telephone: (415) 648-1790
Recruiter Classification: Retained; **Lowest/Average Salary:**
$60,000/$90,000; **Industry Concentration:** Electronics, High
Technology, Information Technology; **Function Concentration:**
Marketing

Sibul, Shelly Remen — *Legal Search Consultant*
Chicago Legal Search, Ltd.
33 North Dearborn Street, Suite 2302
Chicago, IL 60602-3109
Telephone: (312) 251-2580
Recruiter Classification: Contingency; **Lowest/Average Salary:**
$50,000/$90,000; **Industry Concentration:** Electronics, High
Technology, Information Technology; **Function Concentration:**
Women/Minorities

Siciliano, Gene — *President*
Western Management Associates
8351 Vicksburg Avenue
Los Angeles, CA 90045-3924
Telephone: (310) 645-1091
Recruiter Classification: Retained; **Lowest/Average Salary:**
$75,000/$90,000; **Industry Concentration:** Generalist with a
primary focus in Electronics, High Technology, Information
Technology; **Function Concentration:** Finance/Accounting,
General Management

Sickles, Robert — *Recruiter*
Dunhill Professional Search of Irvine, Inc.
9 Executive Circle, Suite 240
Irvine, CA 92614
Telephone: (714) 474-6666
Recruiter Classification: Contingency; **Lowest/Average
Salary:** $50,000/$75,000; **Industry Concentration:**
Electronics, High Technology; **Function Concentration:**
Generalist with a primary focus in Engineering, Marketing,
Sales

Siegler, Jody Cukiir — *Vice President*
A.T. Kearney, Inc.
Biltmore Tower
500 South Grand Avenue, Suite 1780
Los Angeles, CA 90071
Telephone: (213) 689-6800
Recruiter Classification: Retained; **Lowest/Average Salary:**
$90,000/$90,000; **Industry Concentration:** Generalist with a
primary focus in High Technology, Information Technology;
Function Concentration: Generalist with a primary focus in
Engineering, Finance/Accounting, General Management

Siegrist, Jeffrey M. — *Managing Director*
D.E. Foster Partners Inc.
2800 Two First Union Center
Charlotte, NC 28282
Telephone: (704) 335-5511
Recruiter Classification: Retained; **Lowest/Average Salary:**
$90,000/$90,000; **Industry Concentration:** Generalist with a
primary focus in Information Technology; **Function
Concentration:** Generalist with a primary focus in
Finance/Accounting, General Management, Human Resources,
Marketing, Research and Development

Signer, Julie — *Executive Recruiter*
CPS Inc.
One Westbrook Corporate Centre, Suite 600
Westchester, IL 60154
Telephone: (708) 531-8370
Recruiter Classification: Contingency; **Lowest/Average Salary:**
$30,000/$50,000; **Industry Concentration:** Generalist with a
primary focus in Electronics, High Technology, Information
Technology; **Function Concentration:** Engineering, Research
and Development, Sales, Women/Minorities

Siker, Paul W. — *Principal*
The Guild Corporation
8260 Greensboro Drive, Suite 460
McLean, VA 22102
Telephone: (703) 761-4023
Recruiter Classification: Contingency; **Lowest/Average Salary:**
$40,000/$50,000; **Industry Concentration:** Electronics, High
Technology, Information Technology; **Function Concentration:**
Engineering, Finance/Accounting, General Management,
Research and Development

Silcott, Marvin L. — *President/Executive Recruiter*
Marvin L. Silcott & Associates, Inc.
7557 Rambler Road, Suite 1336
Dallas, TX 75231
Telephone: (214) 369-7802
Recruiter Classification: Contingency; **Lowest/Average Salary:**
$60,000/$90,000; **Industry Concentration:** Generalist with a
primary focus in Electronics; **Function Concentration:**
Engineering, Human Resources, Research and Development,
Women/Minorities

Silcott, Marvin L. — *President*
Marvin L. Silcott & Associates, Inc.
7557 Rambler Road
Suite 1336
Dallas, TX 75231
Telephone: (214) 369-7802
Recruiter Classification: Retained; **Lowest/Average Salary:**
$75,000/$90,000; **Industry Concentration:** Generalist with a
primary focus in Electronics, High Technology; **Function
Concentration:** Generalist with a primary focus in Engineering,
Finance/Accounting, General Management, Human Resources,
Research and Development, Women/Minorities

Silkiner, David S. — *Consultant*
Ray & Berndtson
191 Peachtree Street, NE, Suite 3800
Atlanta, GA 30303-1757
Telephone: (404) 215-4600
Recruiter Classification: Retained; **Lowest/Average Salary:**
$90,000/$90,000; **Industry Concentration:** High Technology;
Function Concentration: Generalist

Sill, Igor M. — *Managing Partner*
Geneva Group International
Four Embarcadero Center, Suite 1400
San Francisco, CA 94111
Telephone: (415) 433-4646
Recruiter Classification: Retained; **Lowest/Average Salary:**
$100,000/$100,000; **Industry Concentration:** High
Technology; **Function Concentration:** Engineering, General
Management, Marketing, Research and Development, Sales

Silvas, Stephen D. — *President*
Roberson and Company
10752 North 89th Place, Suite 202
Scottsdale, AZ 85260
Telephone: (602) 391-3200
Recruiter Classification: Contingency; **Lowest/Average Salary:**
$40,000/$60,000; **Industry Concentration:** Generalist with a
primary focus in Electronics, High Technology, Information
Technology; **Function Concentration:** Generalist with a
primary focus in Engineering, Finance/Accounting, General
Management, Human Resources, Sales

Silver, Kit — *Associate*
Source Services Corporation
1290 Oakmead Parkway, Suite 318
Sunnyvale, CA 94086
Telephone: (408) 738-8440
Recruiter Classification: Contingency; **Lowest/Average Salary:**
$30,000/$50,000; **Industry Concentration:** Information
Technology; **Function Concentration:** Engineering,
Finance/Accounting

Silver, Lee — *President*
L. A. Silver Associates, Inc.
463 Worcester Road
Farmingham, MA 01701
Telephone: (508) 879-2603
Recruiter Classification: Retained; **Lowest/Average Salary:**
$90,000/$90,000; **Industry Concentration:** Generalist with a
primary focus in Electronics, High Technology, Information
Technology; **Function Concentration:** Generalist with a
primary focus in Engineering, Finance/Accounting, General
Management, Human Resources, Marketing, Research and
Development, Sales

Silverman, Paul M. — *President*
The Marshall Group
1900 East Golf Road, Suite M100
Schaumburg, IL 60173
Telephone: (708) 330-0009
Recruiter Classification: Executive Temporary; **Lowest/Average
Salary:** $50,000/$90,000; **Industry Concentration:** Generalist
with a primary focus in Electronics; **Function Concentration:**
Generalist

Simankov, Dmitry — *Consultant*
Logix, Inc.
1601 Trapelo Road
Waltham, MA 02154
Telephone: (617) 890-0500
Recruiter Classification: Retained; **Lowest/Average Salary:**
$60,000/$75,000; **Industry Concentration:** High Technology,
Information Technology; **Function Concentration:**
Engineering

Simmons, Anneta — *Executive Recruiter*
F-O-R-T-U-N-E Personnel Consultants of
Huntsville, Inc.
3311 Bob Wallace Avenue, Suite 204
Huntsville, AL 35805
Telephone: (205) 534-7282
Recruiter Classification: Contingency; **Lowest/Average Salary:**
$30,000/$60,000; **Industry Concentration:** Electronics, High
Technology; **Function Concentration:** Engineering, Marketing,
Sales

Simmons, Deborah — *Associate*
Source Services Corporation
10220 SW Greenburg Road, Suite 625
Portland, OR 97223
Telephone: (503) 768-4546
Recruiter Classification: Contingency; **Lowest/Average Salary:**
$30,000/$50,000; **Industry Concentration:** Information
Technology; **Function Concentration:** Engineering,
Finance/Accounting

Simmons, Gerald J. — *Vice Chairman, Emiritus*
Handy HRM Corp.
250 Park Avenue
New York, NY 10177-0074
Telephone: (212) 557-0400
Recruiter Classification: Retained; **Lowest/Average Salary:**
$90,000/$90,000; **Industry Concentration:** Generalist with a
primary focus in High Technology, Information Technology;
Function Concentration: Generalist with a primary focus in
Finance/Accounting, General Management

Simmons, Sandra K. — *Department Manager*
MSI International
229 Peachtree Street, NE
Suite 1201
Atlanta, GA 30303
Telephone: (404) 659-5050
Recruiter Classification: Contingency; **Lowest/Average Salary:**
$30,000/$60,000; **Industry Concentration:** Generalist with a
primary focus in High Technology; **Function Concentration:**
Administration, Engineering, Finance/Accounting, General
Management, Marketing, Sales

Simon, John — *Vice President*
John J. Davis & Associates, Inc.
521 Fifth Avenue, Suite 1740
New York, NY 10175
Telephone: (212) 286-9489
Recruiter Classification: Retained; **Lowest/Average Salary:**
$90,000/$90,000; **Industry Concentration:** Information
Technology; **Function Concentration:** Generalist

Simpson, Scott — *Executive Recruiter*
Cendea Connection International
13740 Research Boulevard
Building O-1
Austin, TX 78750
Telephone: (512) 219-6000
Recruiter Classification: Retained; **Lowest/Average Salary:** $75,000/$90,000; **Industry Concentration:** Generalist with a primary focus in Electronics, High Technology, Information Technology; **Function Concentration:** Generalist with a primary focus in General Management, Marketing, Sales

Sindler, Jay — *Professional Recruiter*
A.J. Burton Group, Inc.
120 East Baltimore Street, Suite 2220
Baltimore, MD 21202
Telephone: (410) 752-5244
Recruiter Classification: Contingency; **Lowest/Average Salary:** $40,000/$75,000; **Industry Concentration:** Generalist with a primary focus in High Technology, Information Technology; **Function Concentration:** Generalist with a primary focus in Administration, Finance/Accounting, General Management, Human Resources

Sink, Cliff — *Partner*
Sink, Walker, Boltrus International
60 Walnut Street
Wellesley, MA 02181
Telephone: (617) 237-1199
Recruiter Classification: Retained; **Lowest/Average Salary:** $90,000/$90,000; **Industry Concentration:** Electronics, High Technology, Information Technology; **Function Concentration:** Engineering, General Management, Research and Development, Sales

Sirena, Evelyn — *Associate*
Source Services Corporation
925 Westchester Avenue, Suite 309
White Plains, NY 10604
Telephone: (914) 428-9100
Recruiter Classification: Contingency; **Lowest/Average Salary:** $30,000/$50,000; **Industry Concentration:** Information Technology; **Function Concentration:** Engineering, Finance/Accounting

Sitarski, Stan — *Vice President*
Howard Fischer Associates, Inc.
1800 John F. Kennedy Boulevard, 7th Floor
Philadelphia, PA 19103
Telephone: (215) 568-8363
Recruiter Classification: Retained; **Lowest/Average Salary:** $90,000/$90,000; **Industry Concentration:** Generalist with a primary focus in High Technology; **Function Concentration:** Generalist with a primary focus in Administration, Finance/Accounting, General Management, Human Resources, Marketing, Research and Development, Sales, Women/Minorities

Skalet, Ira — *Vice President*
A.E. Feldman Associates
445 Northern Boulevard
Great Neck, NY 11021
Telephone: (516) 466-4708
Recruiter Classification: Contingency; **Lowest/Average Salary:** $60,000/$90,000; **Industry Concentration:** Generalist with a primary focus in Electronics, High Technology, Information Technology; **Function Concentration:** Generalist with a primary focus in Administration, General Management, Marketing, Sales

Skunda, Donna M. — *Vice President*
Allerton Heneghan & O'Neill
70 West Madison Street, Suite 2015
Chicago, IL 60602
Telephone: (312) 263-1075
Recruiter Classification: Retained; **Lowest/Average Salary:** $75,000/$90,000; **Industry Concentration:** Generalist with a primary focus in Electronics, High Technology; **Function Concentration:** Generalist with a primary focus in Engineering, Finance/Accounting, General Management, Marketing, Research and Development, Women/Minorities

Slayton, Richard C. — *President*
Slayton International, Inc./I-I-C Partners
181 West Madison Street, Suite 4510
Chicago, IL 60602
Telephone: (312) 456-0080
Recruiter Classification: Retained; **Lowest/Average Salary:** $90,000/$90,000; **Industry Concentration:** Electronics, Information Technology; **Function Concentration:** Engineering, Finance/Accounting, General Management, Human Resources, Marketing, Research and Development

Slayton, Richard S. — *Vice President*
Slayton International, Inc./I-I-C Partners
181 West Madison Street, Suite 4510
Chicago, IL 60602
Telephone: (312) 456-0080
Recruiter Classification: Retained; **Lowest/Average Salary:** $90,000/$90,000; **Industry Concentration:** Information Technology; **Function Concentration:** Generalist

Sloan, Scott — *Associate*
Source Services Corporation
150 South Wacker Drive, Suite 400
Chicago, IL 60606
Telephone: (312) 346-7000
Recruiter Classification: Contingency; **Lowest/Average Salary:** $30,000/$50,000; **Industry Concentration:** Information Technology; **Function Concentration:** Engineering, Finance/Accounting

Slosar, John — *Managing Director*
Boyden
375 Park Avenue, Suite 1509
New York, NY 10152
Telephone: (810) 647-4201
Recruiter Classification: Retained; **Lowest/Average Salary:** $90,000/$90,000; **Industry Concentration:** Generalist with a primary focus in Electronics, High Technology, Information Technology; **Function Concentration:** Generalist with a primary focus in Engineering, Finance/Accounting, General Management, Human Resources, Marketing, Research and Development, Sales, Women/Minorities

Smead, Michelle M. — *Vice President*
A.T. Kearney, Inc.
222 West Adams Street
Chicago, IL 60606
Telephone: (312) 648-0111
Recruiter Classification: Retained; **Lowest/Average Salary:** $90,000/$90,000; **Industry Concentration:** Generalist with a primary focus in High Technology; **Function Concentration:** Generalist with a primary focus in Administration, Finance/Accounting, General Management, Human Resources, Marketing, Sales

Smirnov, Tatiana — *Vice President*
Allan Sarn Associates Inc.
230 Park Avenue, Suite 1522
New York, NY 10169
Telephone: (212) 687-0600
Recruiter Classification: Retained; **Lowest/Average Salary:** $75,000/$90,000; **Industry Concentration:** Generalist with a primary focus in High Technology, Information Technology; **Function Concentration:** Human Resources

Smith, Ana Luz — *Consultant*
Smith Search, S.C.
Barranca del Muerto No. 472, Col. Alpes
Mexico City, D.F., MEXICO 01010
Telephone: (525) 593-8766
Recruiter Classification: Retained; **Lowest/Average Salary:** $60,000/$90,000; **Industry Concentration:** Generalist with a primary focus in Electronics, High Technology, Information Technology; **Function Concentration:** Generalist with a primary focus in Administration, Engineering, Finance/Accounting, General Management, Human Resources, Marketing, Sales

Smith, David P. — *President*
HRS, Inc.
P.O. Box 4499
Pittsburgh, PA 15205
Telephone: (412) 331-4700
Recruiter Classification: Retained; **Lowest/Average Salary:** $90,000/$90,000; **Industry Concentration:** Generalist with a primary focus in Electronics, High Technology, Information Technology; **Function Concentration:** Engineering, Finance/Accounting, General Management, Marketing, Research and Development, Sales, Women/Minorities

Smith, Grant — *Director*
Price Waterhouse
601 West Hastings Street
Suite 1400
Vancouver, British Columbia, CANADA V6B 5A5
Telephone: (604) 682-4711
Recruiter Classification: Retained; **Lowest/Average Salary:** $75,000/$75,000; **Industry Concentration:** Generalist with a primary focus in High Technology; **Function Concentration:** Generalist with a primary focus in Administration, Engineering, Finance/Accounting, General Management, Human Resources, Marketing, Sales

Smith, Herman M. — *President*
Herman Smith Executive Initiatives Inc.
161 Bay Street, Suite 3600
Box 629
Toronto, Ontario, CANADA M5J 2S1
Telephone: (416) 862-8830
Recruiter Classification: Retained; **Lowest/Average Salary:** $75,000/$90,000; **Industry Concentration:** Generalist with a primary focus in High Technology, Information Technology; **Function Concentration:** Generalist with a primary focus in Finance/Accounting, General Management, Marketing, Sales

Smith, Ian — *Staffing Consultant*
International Staffing Consultants, Inc.
500 Newport Center Drive, Suite 300
Newport Beach, CA 92660-7003
Telephone: (714) 721-7990
Recruiter Classification: Contingency; **Lowest/Average Salary:** $30,000/$75,000; **Industry Concentration:** High Technology, Information Technology; **Function Concentration:** Engineering, General Management, Marketing, Sales

Smith, John E. — *President*
Smith Search, S.C.
Barranca del Muerto No. 472, Col. Alpes
Mexico City, D.F., MEXICO 01010
Telephone: (525) 593-8766
Recruiter Classification: Retained; **Lowest/Average Salary:** $75,000/$90,000; **Industry Concentration:** Generalist with a primary focus in Electronics, High Technology; **Function Concentration:** Generalist with a primary focus in Administration, Engineering, Finance/Accounting, General Management, Human Resources, Marketing, Sales

Smith, John F. — *Vice President*
The Penn Partners, Incorporated
117 South 17th Street, Suite 400
Philadelphia, PA 19103
Telephone: (215) 568-9285
Recruiter Classification: Retained; **Lowest/Average Salary:** $60,000/$90,000; **Industry Concentration:** Generalist with a primary focus in Electronics, High Technology; **Function Concentration:** Generalist

Smith, Kevin — *Executive Recruiter*
F-O-R-T-U-N-E Personnel Consultants of Manatee County
923 4th Street West
Palmetto, FL 34221
Telephone: (941) 729-3674
Recruiter Classification: Contingency; **Lowest/Average Salary:** $30,000/$50,000; **Industry Concentration:** Electronics, High Technology; **Function Concentration:** Engineering

Smith, Lawrence — *Associate*
Source Services Corporation
One South Main Street, Suite 1440
Dayton, OH 45402
Telephone: (513) 461-4660
Recruiter Classification: Contingency; **Lowest/Average Salary:** $30,000/$50,000; **Industry Concentration:** Information Technology; **Function Concentration:** Engineering, Finance/Accounting

Smith, Lydia — *Sales Recruiter*
The Corporate Connection, Ltd.
7202 Glen Forest Drive
Richmond, VA 23226
Telephone: (804) 288-8844
Recruiter Classification: Contingency; **Lowest/Average Salary:** $20,000/$30,000; **Industry Concentration:** Generalist with a primary focus in Information Technology; **Function Concentration:** Generalist with a primary focus in Administration, Engineering, Finance/Accounting, General Management, Human Resources, Marketing, Sales, Women/Minorities

Smith, Matt D. — *Partner*
Ray & Berndtson
Sears Tower, 233 South Wacker Drive, Suite 4020
Chicago, IL 60606-6310
Telephone: (312) 876-0730
Recruiter Classification: Retained; **Lowest/Average Salary:** $90,000/$90,000; **Industry Concentration:** Generalist with a primary focus in High Technology, Information Technology; **Function Concentration:** Generalist with a primary focus in Administration, Finance/Accounting, General Management, Human Resources, Marketing, Research and Development, Sales, Women/Minorities

Smith, R. Michael — *Senior Partner*
Smith James Group, Inc.
11660 Alpharetta Highway, Suite 515
Roswell, GA 30076
Telephone: (770) 667-0212
Recruiter Classification: Retained; **Lowest/Average Salary:**
$40,000/$75,000; **Industry Concentration:** Generalist with a
primary focus in Electronics, High Technology; **Function**
Concentration: Generalist

Smith, Richard — *Executive Recruiter*
S.C. International, Ltd.
1430 Branding Lane, Suite 119
Downers Grove, IL 60515
Telephone: (708) 963-3033
Recruiter Classification: Contingency; **Lowest/Average Salary:**
$30,000/$50,000; **Industry Concentration:** Information
Technology; **Function Concentration:** Administration, Human
Resources

Smith, Robert L. — *Partner*
Smith & Sawyer Inc.
230 Park Avenue, 33rd Floor
New York, NY 10169
Telephone: (212) 490-4390
Recruiter Classification: Retained; **Lowest/Average Salary:**
$90,000/$90,000; **Industry Concentration:** Generalist with a
primary focus in Electronics, High Technology, Information
Technology; **Function Concentration:** Generalist with a
primary focus in Finance/Accounting, General Management,
Human Resources, Marketing

Smith, Ronald V. — *Executive Search Consultant*
Coe & Company International Inc.
1535 400-3rd Avenue SW
Center Tower
Calgary, Alberta, Canada T20 4H2
Telephone: (403) 232-8833
Recruiter Classification: Retained; **Lowest/Average Salary:**
$75,000/$90,000; **Industry Concentration:** High Technology,
Information Technology; **Function Concentration:** Generalist
with a primary focus in Administration, Engineering,
Finance/Accounting, General Management, Human Resources,
Marketing, Research and Development, Sales

Smith, Timothy — *Associate*
Source Services Corporation
155 Federal Street, Suite 410
Boston, MA 02110
Telephone: (617) 482-8211
Recruiter Classification: Contingency; **Lowest/Average Salary:**
$30,000/$50,000; **Industry Concentration:** Information
Technology; **Function Concentration:** Engineering,
Finance/Accounting

Smith, Timothy C. — *Consultant*
Christian & Timbers
25825 Science Park Drive, Suite 400
Cleveland, OH 44122
Telephone: (216) 514-4874
Recruiter Classification: Retained; **Lowest/Average Salary:**
$90,000/$90,000; **Industry Concentration:** Generalist with a
primary focus in Electronics, Information Technology; **Function**
Concentration: Generalist with a primary focus in
Finance/Accounting, General Management

Smock, Cynthia — *Associate*
Source Services Corporation
Foster Plaza VI
681 Anderson Drive, 2nd Floor
Pittsburgh, PA 15220
Telephone: (412) 928-8300
Recruiter Classification: Contingency; **Lowest/Average Salary:**
$30,000/$50,000; **Industry Concentration:** Information
Technology; **Function Concentration:** Engineering,
Finance/Accounting

Smoller, Howard — *Associate*
Source Services Corporation
2 Penn Plaza, Suite 1176
New York, NY 10121
Telephone: (212) 760-2200
Recruiter Classification: Contingency; **Lowest/Average Salary:**
$30,000/$50,000; **Industry Concentration:** Information
Technology; **Function Concentration:** Engineering,
Finance/Accounting

Snowden, Charles — *Associate*
Source Services Corporation
8614 Westwood Center, Suite 750
Vienna, VA 22182
Telephone: (703) 790-5610
Recruiter Classification: Contingency; **Lowest/Average Salary:**
$30,000/$50,000; **Industry Concentration:** Information
Technology; **Function Concentration:** Engineering,
Finance/Accounting

Snowhite, Rebecca — *Associate*
Source Services Corporation
525 Vine Street, Suite 2250
Cincinnati, OH 45202
Telephone: (513) 651-3303
Recruiter Classification: Contingency; **Lowest/Average Salary:**
$30,000/$50,000; **Industry Concentration:** Information
Technology; **Function Concentration:** Engineering,
Finance/Accounting

Snyder, C. Edward — *Managing Director*
Horton International
10 Tower Lane
Avon, CT 06001
Telephone: (860) 674-8701
Recruiter Classification: Retained; **Lowest/Average Salary:**
$90,000/$90,000; **Industry Concentration:** Generalist with a
primary focus in Electronics, Information Technology; **Function**
Concentration: Generalist with a primary focus in
Administration, Engineering, Finance/Accounting, General
Management, Human Resources, Marketing, Research and
Development, Sales, Women/Minorities

Snyder, James F. — *President*
Snyder & Company
35 Old Avon Village, Suite 185
Avon, CT 06001-3822
Telephone: (860) 521-9760
Recruiter Classification: Retained; **Lowest/Average Salary:**
$90,000/$90,000; **Industry Concentration:** Generalist with a
primary focus in Electronics, High Technology, Information
Technology; **Function Concentration:** Generalist with a
primary focus in Administration, Engineering,
Finance/Accounting, General Management, Human Resources,
Marketing, Research and Development, Sales

Sochacki, Michael — *Associate*
Source Services Corporation
161 Ottawa NW, Suite 409D
Grand Rapids, MI 49503
Telephone: (616) 451-2400
Recruiter Classification: Contingency; **Lowest/Average Salary:**
$30,000/$50,000; **Industry Concentration:** Information
Technology; **Function Concentration:** Engineering,
Finance/Accounting

Sola, George L. — *Vice President*
A.T. Kearney, Inc.
222 West Adams Street
Chicago, IL 60606
Telephone: (312) 648-0111
Recruiter Classification: Retained; **Lowest/Average Salary:**
$90,000/$90,000; **Industry Concentration:** Generalist with
a primary focus in High Technology; **Function
Concentration:** Generalist with a primary focus in
Engineering, General Management, Marketing, Research
and Development, Sales

Solomon, Christina — *Executive Recruiter*
Richard, Wayne and Roberts
24 Greenway Plaza, Suite 1304
Houston, TX 77046-2493
Telephone: (713) 629-6681
Recruiter Classification: Retained; **Lowest/Average Salary:**
$40,000/$60,000; **Industry Concentration:** Generalist with a
primary focus in Electronics, High Technology; **Function
Concentration:** Generalist

Solters, Jeanne — *Associate*
The Guild Corporation
8260 Greensboro Drive, Suite 460
McLean, VA 22102
Telephone: (703) 761-4023
Recruiter Classification: Contingency; **Lowest/Average Salary:**
$40,000/$50,000; **Industry Concentration:** Electronics, High
Technology, Information Technology; **Function Concentration:**
Generalist with a primary focus in Engineering,
Finance/Accounting, General Management, Research and
Development

Song, Louis — *Associate*
Source Services Corporation
4510 Executive Drive, Suite 200
San Diego, CA 92121
Telephone: (619) 552-0300
Recruiter Classification: Contingency; **Lowest/Average Salary:**
$30,000/$50,000; **Industry Concentration:** Information
Technology; **Function Concentration:** Engineering,
Finance/Accounting

Sorgen, Jay — *Associate*
Source Services Corporation
2 Penn Plaza, Suite 1176
New York, NY 10121
Telephone: (212) 760-2200
Recruiter Classification: Contingency; **Lowest/Average Salary:**
$30,000/$50,000; **Industry Concentration:** Information
Technology; **Function Concentration:** Engineering,
Finance/Accounting

Sostilio, Louis — *Associate*
Source Services Corporation
155 Federal Street, Suite 410
Boston, MA 02110
Telephone: (617) 482-8211
Recruiter Classification: Contingency; **Lowest/Average Salary:**
$30,000/$50,000; **Industry Concentration:** Information
Technology; **Function Concentration:** Engineering,
Finance/Accounting

Souder, E.G. — *President*
Souder & Associates
P.O. Box 71
Bridgewater, VA 22812
Telephone: (540) 828-2365
Recruiter Classification: Retained; **Lowest/Average Salary:**
$40,000/$75,000; **Industry Concentration:** Generalist with a
primary focus in Electronics, High Technology, Information
Technology; **Function Concentration:** Engineering, General
Management, Human Resources, Marketing, Research and
Development, Sales

Soutouras, James — *Senior Partner*
Smith James Group, Inc.
11660 Alpharetta Highway, Suite 515
Roswell, GA 30076
Telephone: (770) 667-0212
Recruiter Classification: Retained; **Lowest/Average Salary:**
$40,000/$75,000; **Industry Concentration:** Generalist with a
primary focus in Electronics, High Technology; **Function
Concentration:** Generalist

Sowerbutt, Richard S. — *Vice President*
Hite Executive Search
6515 Chase Drive
P.O. Box 43217
Cleveland, OH 44143
Telephone: (216) 461-1600
Recruiter Classification: Retained; **Lowest/Average Salary:**
$90,000/$90,000; **Industry Concentration:** Generalist with a
primary focus in High Technology; **Function Concentration:**
Generalist with a primary focus in Engineering, General
Management, Marketing, Research and Development, Sales

Spadavecchia, Jennifer — *Associate*
Alta Associates, Inc.
8 Bartles Corner Road, Suite 021
Flemington, NJ 08822
Telephone: (908) 806-8442
Recruiter Classification: Retained; **Lowest/Average Salary:**
$40,000/$75,000; **Industry Concentration:** Generalist with a
primary focus in High Technology, Information Technology;
Function Concentration: Finance/Accounting

Spann, Richard E. — *Managing Principal*
Goodrich & Sherwood Associates, Inc.
401 Merritt Seven Corporate Park
Norwalk, CT 06851
Telephone: (203) 847-2525
Recruiter Classification: Retained; **Lowest/Average Salary:**
$60,000/$90,000; **Industry Concentration:** Generalist with a
primary focus in Information Technology; **Function
Concentration:** Generalist with a primary focus in
Administration, Finance/Accounting, General Management,
Human Resources, Marketing, Sales

Spanninger, Mark J. — *Director*
The Guild Corporation
8260 Greensboro Drive, Suite 460
McLean, VA 22102
Telephone: (703) 761-4023
Recruiter Classification: Contingency; **Lowest/Average Salary:**
$40,000/$50,000; **Industry Concentration:** Electronics, High
Technology, Information Technology; **Function Concentration:**
Engineering, Finance/Accounting, General Management,
Research and Development

Spector, Michael — *Associate*
Source Services Corporation
5343 North 16th Street, Suite 270
Phoenix, AZ 85016
Telephone: (602) 230-0220
Recruiter Classification: Contingency; **Lowest/Average Salary:**
$30,000/$50,000; **Industry Concentration:** Information
Technology; **Function Concentration:** Engineering,
Finance/Accounting

Spence, Gene L. — *Partner*
Heidrick & Struggles, Inc.
245 Park Avenue, Suite 4300
New York, NY 10167-0152
Telephone: (212) 867-9876
Recruiter Classification: Retained; **Lowest/Average Salary:**
$75,000/$90,000; **Industry Concentration:** Generalist with a
primary focus in High Technology; **Function Concentration:**
Generalist

Spencer, John — *Managing Director*
Source Services Corporation
2029 Century Park East, Suite 1350
Los Angeles, CA 90067
Telephone: (310) 277-8092
Recruiter Classification: Contingency; **Lowest/Average Salary:**
$30,000/$50,000; **Industry Concentration:** Information
Technology; **Function Concentration:** Engineering,
Finance/Accounting

Spencer, John — *Managing Director*
Source Services Corporation
879 West 190th Street, Suite 250
Los Angeles, CA 90248
Telephone: (310) 323-6633
Recruiter Classification: Contingency; **Lowest/Average Salary:**
$30,000/$50,000; **Industry Concentration:** Information
Technology; **Function Concentration:** Engineering,
Finance/Accounting

Spera, Stefanie — *Vice President*
A.T. Kearney, Inc.
153 East 53rd Street
New York, NY 10022
Telephone: (212) 751-7040
Recruiter Classification: Retained; **Lowest/Average Salary:**
$90,000/$90,000; **Industry Concentration:** Generalist with
a primary focus in High Technology, Information
Technology; **Function Concentration:** Generalist with a
primary focus in Engineering, Finance/Accounting, General
Management

Spiegel, Gayle — *Senior Vice President*
L. A. Silver Associates, Inc.
463 Worcester Road
Framingham, MA 01701
Telephone: (508) 879-2603
Recruiter Classification: Retained; **Lowest/Average Salary:**
$90,000/$90,000; **Industry Concentration:** Generalist with a
primary focus in Electronics, High Technology, Information
Technology; **Function Concentration:** Generalist with a
primary focus in Engineering, Finance/Accounting, General
Management, Human Resources, Marketing, Research and
Development, Sales

Spitz, Grant — *Partner*
The Caldwell Partners Amrop International
999 West Hastings Street
Suite 750
Vancouver, British Columbia, CANADA V6C 2W2
Telephone: (604) 669-3550
Recruiter Classification: Retained; **Lowest/Average Salary:**
$60,000/$90,000; **Industry Concentration:** Generalist with a
primary focus in High Technology; **Function Concentration:**
Generalist

Splaine, Charles — *President*
Splaine & Associates, Inc.
15951 Los Gatos Boulevard
Los Gatos, CA 95032
Telephone: (408) 354-3664
Recruiter Classification: Retained; **Lowest/Average Salary:**
$90,000/$90,000; **Industry Concentration:** Electronics, High
Technology; **Function Concentration:** Generalist

Spoutz, Paul — *Associate*
Source Services Corporation
7730 East Bellview Avenue, Suite 302
Englewood, CO 80111
Telephone: (303) 773-3700
Recruiter Classification: Contingency; **Lowest/Average Salary:**
$30,000/$50,000; **Industry Concentration:** Information
Technology; **Function Concentration:** Engineering,
Finance/Accounting

Sprau, Collin L. — *Partner*
Ray & Berndtson
Sears Tower, 233 South Wacker Drive, Suite 4020
Chicago, IL 60606-6310
Telephone: (312) 876-0730
Recruiter Classification: Retained; **Lowest/Average Salary:**
$90,000/$90,000; **Industry Concentration:** Generalist with a
primary focus in Information Technology; **Function
Concentration:** Generalist with a primary focus in
Finance/Accounting, Marketing, Sales

Spriggs, Robert D. — *Partner*
Spriggs & Company, Inc.
1701 East Lake Avenue
Suite 265
Glenview, IL 60025
Telephone: (708) 657-7181
Recruiter Classification: Retained; **Lowest/Average Salary:**
$90,000/$90,000; **Industry Concentration:** Generalist with a
primary focus in Electronics, High Technology, Information
Technology; **Function Concentration:** Generalist with a
primary focus in Administration, Engineering,
Finance/Accounting, General Management, Human Resources,
Marketing, Research and Development, Sales

St. Clair, Alan — *Vice President*
TNS Partners, Inc.
8140 Walnut Hill Lane
Suite 301
Dallas, TX 75231
Telephone: (214) 369-3565
Recruiter Classification: Retained; **Lowest/Average Salary:**
$90,000/$90,000; **Industry Concentration:** Generalist with a
primary focus in Information Technology; **Function
Concentration:** Generalist with a primary focus in
Administration, Finance/Accounting, General Management,
Human Resources, Marketing, Sales

St. Martin, Peter — *Associate*
Source Services Corporation
4170 Ashford Dunwoody Road, Suite 285
Atlanta, GA 30319
Telephone: (404) 255-2045
Recruiter Classification: Contingency; **Lowest/Average Salary:**
$30,000/$50,000; **Industry Concentration:** Information
Technology; **Function Concentration:** Engineering,
Finance/Accounting

Staats, Dave — *Technical Recruiting Manager*
Southwestern Professional Services
2451 Atrium Way
Nashville, TN 37214
Telephone: (615) 391-2722
Recruiter Classification: Contingency; **Lowest/Average Salary:**
$40,000/$60,000; **Industry Concentration:** High Technology,
Information Technology; **Function Concentration:** Engineering,
Research and Development

Stack, Richard — *Associate*
Source Services Corporation
2 Penn Plaza, Suite 1176
New York, NY 10121
Telephone: (212) 760-2200
Recruiter Classification: Contingency; **Lowest/Average Salary:**
$30,000/$50,000; **Industry Concentration:** Information
Technology; **Function Concentration:** Engineering,
Finance/Accounting

Stackhouse, P. John — *Consultant*
Heidrick & Struggles, Inc.
BCE Place, 161 Bay Street, Suite 2310
P.O. Box 601
Toronto, Ontario, CANADA M5J 2S1
Telephone: (416) 361-4700
Recruiter Classification: Retained; **Lowest/Average Salary:**
$75,000/$90,000; **Industry Concentration:** Generalist with a
primary focus in High Technology; **Function Concentration:**
Generalist

Staehely, Janna — *Recruiter*
Southwestern Professional Services
2451 Atrium Way
Nashville, TN 37214
Telephone: (615) 391-2722
Recruiter Classification: Contingency; **Lowest/Average Salary:**
$50,000/$75,000; **Industry Concentration:** Information
Technology; **Function Concentration:** Engineering

Stanley, Paul R.A. — *Partner*
Ray & Berndtson/Lovas Stanley
Royal Bank Plaza, South Tower, Suite 3150
200 Bay Street, P.O. Box 125
Toronto, Ontario, CANADA M5J 2J3
Telephone: (416) 366-1990
Recruiter Classification: Retained; **Lowest/Average Salary:**
$75,000/$90,000; **Industry Concentration:** Generalist with a
primary focus in High Technology; **Function Concentration:**
Generalist with a primary focus in Finance/Accounting,
General Management, Human Resources, Research and
Development

Stanton, John — *Vice President/Managing
Director*
A.T. Kearney, Inc.
3050 Post Oak Boulevard, Suite 570
Houston, TX 77056
Telephone: (713) 621-9967
Recruiter Classification: Retained; **Lowest/Average Salary:**
$90,000/$90,000; **Industry Concentration:** Generalist with a
primary focus in High Technology, Information Technology;
Function Concentration: Generalist with a primary focus in
Engineering, Finance/Accounting, General Management

Stark, Jeff — *Principal*
Thorne, Brieger Associates Inc.
11 East 44th Street
New York, NY 10017
Telephone: (212) 682-5424
Recruiter Classification: Retained; **Lowest/Average Salary:**
$90,000/$90,000; **Industry Concentration:** Generalist with a
primary focus in Electronics; **Function Concentration:**
Generalist with a primary focus in Administration, Engineering,
Finance/Accounting, General Management, Human Resources,
Marketing, Research and Development, Sales

Starner, William S. — *Partner*
Fenwick Partners
57 Bedford Street, Suite 101
Lexington, MA 02173
Telephone: (617) 862-3370
Recruiter Classification: Retained; **Lowest/Average Salary:**
$90,000/$90,000; **Industry Concentration:** Electronics, High
Technology, Information Technology; **Function Concentration:**
Generalist

Statson, Dale E. — *President*
Sales Executives Inc.
755 West Big Beaver Road, Suite 2107
Troy, MI 48084
Telephone: (810) 362-1900
Recruiter Classification: Contingency; **Lowest/Average Salary:**
$50,000/$90,000; **Industry Concentration:** Electronics;
Function Concentration: General Management, Marketing,
Sales

Steele, Daniel — *Search Consultant*
Cochran, Cochran & Yale, Inc.
1333 W. 120th Avenue, Suite 311
Westminster, CO 80234
Telephone: (303) 252-4600
Recruiter Classification: Retained; **Lowest/Average Salary:**
$50,000/$75,000; **Industry Concentration:** Generalist with a
primary focus in High Technology, Information Technology;
Function Concentration: Generalist with a primary focus in
Engineering, Finance/Accounting, General Management,
Human Resources, Marketing, Sales, Women/Minorities

Steele, Kevin — *President*
Winter, Wyman & Company
950 Winter Street, Suite 3100
Waltham, MA 02154-1294
Telephone: (617) 890-7000
Recruiter Classification: Contingency; **Lowest/Average Salary:**
$40,000/$75,000; **Industry Concentration:** Generalist with a
primary focus in Information Technology; **Function
Concentration:** Generalist

Steer, Joe — *Executive Recruiter*
CPS Inc.
One Westbrook Corporate Centre, Suite 600
Westchester, IL 60154
Telephone: (708) 531-8370
Recruiter Classification: Contingency; **Lowest/Average Salary:**
$30,000/$50,000; **Industry Concentration:** Generalist with a
primary focus in Electronics, High Technology, Information
Technology; **Function Concentration:** Engineering, Research
and Development, Sales, Women/Minorities

Stefunek, Paul C. — *Director and Principal*
Stratford Group
6120 Parkland Boulevard
Cleveland, OH 44124
Telephone: (216) 460-3232
Recruiter Classification: Retained; **Lowest/Average Salary:**
$90,000/$90,000; **Industry Concentration:** Generalist with a
primary focus in Information Technology; **Function
Concentration:** Generalist

Stein, Terry W. — *Partner*
Stewart, Stein and Scott, Ltd.
1000 Shelard Parkway, Suite 606
Minneapolis, MN 55426
Telephone: (612) 595-4456
Recruiter Classification: Retained; **Lowest/Average Salary:**
$75,000/$90,000; **Industry Concentration:** Generalist with a
primary focus in Electronics, High Technology; **Function
Concentration:** Generalist with a primary focus in Engineering,
Finance/Accounting, General Management, Human Resources,
Marketing, Research and Development, Sales

Steinem, Andy — *Principal*
Dahl-Morrow International
12110 Sunset Hills Road
Suite 450
Reston, VA 22090
Telephone: (703) 648-1594
Recruiter Classification: Executive Temporary; **Lowest/Average
Salary:** $75,000/$90,000; **Industry Concentration:** Generalist
with a primary focus in Electronics, High Technology,
Information Technology; **Function Concentration:** Generalist

Steinem, Andy — *Principal*
Dahl-Morrow International
12020 Sunrise Valley Drive
Reston, VA 20191
Telephone: (703) 860-6868
Recruiter Classification: Retained; **Lowest/Average Salary:**
$75,000/$90,000; **Industry Concentration:** Electronics, High
Technology, Information Technology; **Function
Concentration:** Generalist with a primary focus in
Engineering, Finance/Accounting, General Management,
Marketing, Sales

Steinem, Barbara — *President*
Dahl-Morrow International
12110 Sunset Hills Road
Suite 450
Reston, VA 22090
Telephone: (703) 648-1594
Recruiter Classification: Executive Temporary; **Lowest/Average
Salary:** $75,000/$90,000; **Industry Concentration:** Generalist
with a primary focus in Electronics, High Technology,
Information Technology; **Function Concentration:** Generalist

Steinem, Barbra — *Principal*
Dahl-Morrow International
12020 Sunrise Valley Drive
Reston, VA 20191
Telephone: (703) 860-6868
Recruiter Classification: Retained; **Lowest/Average Salary:**
$75,000/$90,000; **Industry Concentration:** Electronics, High
Technology, Information Technology; **Function Concentration:**
Generalist with a primary focus in Engineering,
Finance/Accounting, General Management, Marketing, Sales

Steinman, Stephen M. — *President and CEO*
The Stevenson Group of New Jersey
560 Sylvan Avenue
Englewood Cliffs, NJ 07632
Telephone: (201) 568-1900
Recruiter Classification: Retained; **Lowest/Average Salary:**
$75,000/$90,000; **Industry Concentration:** Generalist with a
primary focus in Information Technology; **Function
Concentration:** Generalist with a primary focus in
Finance/Accounting, General Management, Human Resources,
Marketing, Sales

Stenberg, Edward — *Materials Management and
Manufacturing Recruiter*
Winter, Wyman & Company
950 Winter Street, Suite 3100
Waltham, MA 02154-1294
Telephone: (617) 890-7000
Recruiter Classification: Contingency; **Lowest/Average Salary:**
$30,000/$50,000; **Industry Concentration:** Electronics, High
Technology, Information Technology; **Function Concentration:**
Generalist

Stephens, Andrew — *Associate*
Source Services Corporation
8614 Westwood Center, Suite 750
Vienna, VA 22182
Telephone: (703) 790-5610
Recruiter Classification: Contingency; **Lowest/Average Salary:**
$30,000/$50,000; **Industry Concentration:** Information
Technology; **Function Concentration:** Engineering,
Finance/Accounting

Stephens, John — *Associate*
Source Services Corporation
15600 N.W. 67th Avenue, Suite 210
Miami Lakes, FL 33014
Telephone: (305) 556-8000
Recruiter Classification: Contingency; **Lowest/Average Salary:**
$30,000/$50,000; **Industry Concentration:** Information
Technology; **Function Concentration:** Engineering,
Finance/Accounting

Stephenson, Don L. — *President*
Ells Personnel System Inc.
9900 Bren Road East, Suite 105 Opus Center
Minnetonka, MN 55343
Telephone: (612) 932-9933
Recruiter Classification: Contingency; **Lowest/Average Salary:**
$20,000/$40,000; **Industry Concentration:** Generalist with a
primary focus in Electronics, High Technology, Information
Technology; **Function Concentration:** Generalist with a
primary focus in Administration, Engineering, Research and
Development

Sterling, Jay — *Senior Vice President*
Earley Kielty and Associates, Inc.
Two Pennsylvania Plaza
New York, NY 10121
Telephone: (212) 736-5626
Recruiter Classification: Retained; **Lowest/Average Salary:**
$90,000/$90,000; **Industry Concentration:** Generalist with a
primary focus in Information Technology; **Function
Concentration:** Generalist with a primary focus in
Administration, Finance/Accounting, General Management,
Human Resources, Marketing, Research and Development,
Sales, Women/Minorities

Stern, Stephen — *Executive Recruiter*
CPS Inc.
One Westbrook Corporate Centre, Suite 600
Westchester, IL 60154
Telephone: (708) 531-8370
Recruiter Classification: Contingency; **Lowest/Average Salary:**
$30,000/$50,000; **Industry Concentration:** Generalist with a
primary focus in Electronics, High Technology, Information
Technology; **Function Concentration:** Engineering, Research
and Development, Sales, Women/Minorities

Sterner, Doug — *Executive Recruiter*
CPS Inc.
One Westbrook Corporate Centre, Suite 600
Westchester, IL 60154
Telephone: (708) 531-8370
Recruiter Classification: Contingency; **Lowest/Average Salary:**
$30,000/$50,000; **Industry Concentration:** Generalist with a
primary focus in Electronics, High Technology, Information
Technology; **Function Concentration:** Engineering, Research
and Development, Sales, Women/Minorities

Stevens, Craig M. — *Partner*
Kirkman & Searing, Inc.
8045 Leesburg Pike
Suite 540
Vienna, VA 22182
Telephone: (703) 761-7020
Recruiter Classification: Retained; **Lowest/Average Salary:**
$90,000/$90,000; **Industry Concentration:** High Technology;
Function Concentration: Finance/Accounting, General
Management, Marketing, Sales

Stevens, Ken — *President*
The Stevens Group
P.O. Box 171079
Arlington, TX 76003-1079
Telephone: (817) 483-2700
Recruiter Classification: Retained; **Lowest/Average Salary:**
$50,000/$80,000; **Industry Concentration:** Generalist with a
primary focus in Electronics, High Technology, Information
Technology; **Function Concentration:** Generalist with a
primary focus in Administration, Engineering,
Finance/Accounting, General Management, Human Resources,
Marketing, Research and Development, Sales

Stevenson, Jane — *President, Southwest*
Howard Fischer Associates, Inc.
13750 San Pedro Avenue
Suite 810
San Antonio, TX 78232
Telephone: (210) 491-0844
Recruiter Classification: Retained; **Lowest/Average Salary:**
$90,000/$90,000; **Industry Concentration:** Generalist with a
primary focus in High Technology; **Function Concentration:**
Generalist

Stevenson, Jane — *Executive Vice
President/Partner*
Howard Fischer Associates, Inc.
1800 John F. Kennedy Boulevard, 7th Floor
Philadelphia, PA 19103
Telephone: (215) 568-8363
Recruiter Classification: Retained; **Lowest/Average Salary:**
$90,000/$90,000; **Industry Concentration:** Generalist with a
primary focus in High Technology; **Function Concentration:**
Generalist with a primary focus in Administration,
Finance/Accounting, General Management, Human Resources,
Marketing, Research and Development, Sales,
Women/Minorities

Stevenson, Terry — *Vice President*
Bartholdi & Company, Inc.
P.O. Box 947
Leadville, CO 80461
Telephone: (719) 486-2918
Recruiter Classification: Retained; **Lowest/Average Salary:**
$60,000/$90,000; **Industry Concentration:** High Technology,
Information Technology; **Function Concentration:** Generalist
with a primary focus in Engineering, Finance/Accounting,
General Management, Marketing, Research and Development,
Sales

Stewart, Jan J. — *Consultant*
Egon Zehnder International Inc.
1 First Canadian Place
P.O. Box 179
Toronto, Ontario, CANADA M5X 1C7
Telephone: (416) 364-0222
Recruiter Classification: Retained; **Lowest/Average Salary:**
$90,000/$90,000; **Industry Concentration:** Generalist with a
primary focus in High Technology; **Function Concentration:**
Generalist

Stewart, Jeffrey O. — *Partner*
Stewart, Stein and Scott, Ltd.
1000 Shelard Parkway, Suite 606
Minneapolis, MN 55426
Telephone: (612) 595-4455
Recruiter Classification: Retained; **Lowest/Average Salary:**
$75,000/$90,000; **Industry Concentration:** Generalist with a
primary focus in Electronics, High Technology; **Function
Concentration:** Generalist with a primary focus in
Engineering, Finance/Accounting, General Management,
Human Resources, Marketing, Research and Development,
Sales

Stewart, Ross M. — *Managing Director*
Human Resources Network Partners Inc.
Two Galleria Tower
13455 Noel Road, 10th Floor
Dallas, TX 75240
Telephone: (214) 702-7932
Recruiter Classification: Retained; **Lowest/Average Salary:**
$60,000/$90,000; **Industry Concentration:** Generalist with a
primary focus in Electronics, High Technology, Information
Technology; **Function Concentration:** Generalist with a
primary focus in Administration, Engineering,
Finance/Accounting, General Management, Human Resources,
Marketing, Research and Development, Sales,
Women/Minorities

Stiles, Jack D. — *Principal*
Sanford Rose Associates
10200 SW Eastridge, Suite 200
Portland, OR 97225
Telephone: (503) 297-9191
Recruiter Classification: Contingency; **Lowest/Average Salary:**
$30,000/$75,000; **Industry Concentration:** Generalist with a
primary focus in High Technology; **Function Concentration:**
Generalist

Stiles, Judy — *Director/Recruiter*
MedQuest Associates
9250 East Costilla Avenue, Suite 600
Englewood, CO 80112
Telephone: (303) 790-2009
Recruiter Classification: Contingency; **Lowest/Average Salary:**
$30,000/$75,000; **Industry Concentration:** Electronics, High
Technology; **Function Concentration:** Engineering, General
Management, Marketing, Research and Development, Sales

Stiles, Timothy — *Senior Associate*
Sanford Rose Associates
10200 SW Eastridge, Suite 200
Portland, OR 97225
Telephone: (503) 297-9191
Recruiter Classification: Contingency; **Lowest/Average Salary:**
$30,000/$75,000; **Industry Concentration:** Generalist with a
primary focus in High Technology; **Function Concentration:**
Generalist

Stirn, Bradley A. — *Managing Director*
Spencer Stuart
3000 Sand Hill Road
Building 2, Suite 175
Menlo Park, CA 94025
Telephone: (415) 688-1285
Recruiter Classification: Retained; **Lowest/Average Salary:**
$90,000/$90,000; **Industry Concentration:** High Technology,
Information Technology; **Function Concentration:** Generalist

Stokes, John — *Consultant*
Nordeman Grimm, Inc.
717 Fifth Avenue, 26th Floor
New York, NY 10022
Telephone: (212) 702-9312
Recruiter Classification: Retained; **Lowest/Average Salary:**
$150,000/$150,000; **Industry Concentration:** Generalist with a
primary focus in High Technology, Information Technology;
Function Concentration: Generalist with a primary focus in
General Management, Marketing

Stone, Robert Ryder — *Partner*
Lamalie Amrop International
Metro Center, One Station Place
Stamford, CT 06902-6800
Telephone: (203) 324-4445
Recruiter Classification: Retained; **Lowest/Average Salary:**
$90,000/$90,000; **Industry Concentration:** Generalist with a
primary focus in High Technology; **Function Concentration:**
Generalist

Stone, Susan L. — *President*
Stone Enterprises Ltd.
645 North Michigan Avenue, Suite 800
Chicago, IL 60611
Telephone: (312) 404-9300
Recruiter Classification: Contingency; **Lowest/Average Salary:**
$30,000/$90,000; **Industry Concentration:** Generalist with a
primary focus in Electronics, High Technology, Information
Technology; **Function Concentration:** Generalist with a
primary focus in Engineering, Finance/Accounting, Marketing,
Research and Development, Sales

Storm, Deborah — *Associate*
Source Services Corporation
150 South Warner Road, Suite 238
King of Prussia, PA 19406
Telephone: (610) 341-1960
Recruiter Classification: Contingency; **Lowest/Average Salary:**
$30,000/$50,000; **Industry Concentration:** Information
Technology; **Function Concentration:** Engineering,
Finance/Accounting

Stovall, Randal — *Consultant Information Systems
Search and Engineering*
D. Brown and Associates, Inc.
610 S.W. Alder, Suite 1111
Portland, OR 97205
Telephone: (503) 224-6860
Recruiter Classification: Contingency; **Lowest/Average Salary:**
$40,000/$60,000; **Industry Concentration:** Electronics, High
Technology, Information Technology; **Function Concentration:**
Engineering, Finance/Accounting

Strain, Stephen R. — *Senior Director*
Spencer Stuart
3000 Sand Hill Road
Building 2, Suite 175
Menlo Park, CA 94025
Telephone: (415) 688-1285
Recruiter Classification: Retained; **Lowest/Average Salary:**
$90,000/$90,000; **Industry Concentration:** Electronics, High
Technology, Information Technology; **Function Concentration:**
Generalist

Stranberg, James R. — *Associate*
Callan Associates, Ltd.
2021 Spring Road, Suite 175
Oak Brook, IL 60521
Telephone: (708) 832-7080
Recruiter Classification: Retained; **Lowest/Average Salary:**
$90,000/$90,000; **Industry Concentration:** Generalist with a
primary focus in Electronics, High Technology, Information
Technology; **Function Concentration:** Generalist with a
primary focus in Engineering, Finance/Accounting, General
Management, Human Resources, Marketing, Research and
Development, Sales, Women/Minorities

Strander, Dervin — *Associate*
Source Services Corporation
5429 LBJ Freeway, Suite 275
Dallas, TX 75240
Telephone: (214) 387-1600
Recruiter Classification: Contingency; **Lowest/Average Salary:** $30,000/$50,000; **Industry Concentration:** Information Technology; **Function Concentration:** Engineering, Finance/Accounting

Strassman, Mark — *Managing Partner*
Don Richard Associates of Washington, D.C., Inc.
1020 19th Street, NW, Suite 650
Washington, DC 20036
Telephone: (202) 463-7210
Recruiter Classification: Contingency, Executive Temporary; **Lowest/Average Salary:** $60,000/$75,000; **Industry Concentration:** High Technology, Information Technology; **Function Concentration:** Finance/Accounting

Stratmeyer, Karin Bergwall — *President*
Princeton Entrepreneurial Resources
600 Alexander Road, P.O. Box 2051
Princeton, NJ 08543
Telephone: (609) 243-0010
Recruiter Classification: Executive Temporary; **Lowest/Average Salary:** $75,000/$90,000; **Industry Concentration:** Generalist with a primary focus in Electronics, Information Technology; **Function Concentration:** Generalist with a primary focus in Finance/Accounting, General Management, Human Resources, Marketing

Stratton, Cary — *Vice President*
Coastal International Inc.
28 Green Street
Newbury, MA 01951
Telephone: (508) 462-2436
Recruiter Classification: Retained; **Lowest/Average Salary:** $75,000/$90,000; **Industry Concentration:** High Technology, Information Technology; **Function Concentration:** Finance/Accounting, General Management, Marketing, Sales

Strickland, Katie — *Vice President*
Grantham & Co., Inc.
136 Erwin Road
Chapel Hill, NC 27514
Telephone: (919) 932-5650
Recruiter Classification: Retained; **Lowest/Average Salary:** $85,000/$90,000; **Industry Concentration:** Generalist with a primary focus in Information Technology; **Function Concentration:** Generalist with a primary focus in Engineering, Finance/Accounting, General Management, Human Resources, Marketing, Research and Development, Sales

Stringer, Dann P. — *Senior Managing Director*
D.E. Foster Partners Inc.
2001 M Street N.W.
Washington, DC 20036
Telephone: (202) 739-8749
Recruiter Classification: Retained; **Lowest/Average Salary:** $90,000/$90,000; **Industry Concentration:** Generalist with a primary focus in Electronics, High Technology, Information Technology; **Function Concentration:** Generalist with a primary focus in Administration, Finance/Accounting, General Management, Marketing, Women/Minorities

Strom, Mark N. — *President*
Search Advisors International Corp.
777 South Harbour Island Boulevard
Suite 925
Tampa, FL 33602
Telephone: (813) 221-7555
Recruiter Classification: Retained; **Lowest/Average Salary:** $75,000/$90,000; **Industry Concentration:** Generalist with a primary focus in Electronics, High Technology, Information Technology; **Function Concentration:** Generalist with a primary focus in Administration, Engineering, Finance/Accounting, General Management, Human Resources, Marketing, Research and Development, Sales, Women/Minorities

Struzziero, Ralph E. — *President*
Romac & Associates
183 Middle Street, 3rd Floor
P.O. Box 7040
Portland, ME 04112
Telephone: (207) 773-4749
Recruiter Classification: Executive Temporary; **Lowest/Average Salary:** $60,000/$60,000; **Industry Concentration:** High Technology, Information Technology; **Function Concentration:** Finance/Accounting

Sturtz, James W. — *Vice President*
Compass Group Ltd.
401 South Old Woodward Avenue
Suite 460
Birmingham, MI 48009-6613
Telephone: (248) 540-9110
Recruiter Classification: Retained; **Lowest/Average Salary:** $75,000/$90,000; **Industry Concentration:** Electronics, Information Technology; **Function Concentration:** Engineering, General Management, Human Resources, Marketing, Research and Development, Sales, Women/Minorities

Sucato, Carolyn — *Consultant*
Jay Gaines & Company, Inc.
450 Park Avenue
New York, NY 10022
Telephone: (212) 308-9222
Recruiter Classification: Retained; **Lowest/Average Salary:** $200,000/$300,000; **Industry Concentration:** Electronics, Information Technology; **Function Concentration:** Finance/Accounting

Sullivan, Kay — *Principal*
Rusher, Loscavio & LoPresto
2479 Bayshore Road, Suite 700
Palo Alto, CA 94303
Telephone: (415) 494-0883
Recruiter Classification: Retained; **Lowest/Average Salary:** $75,000/$90,000; **Industry Concentration:** Electronics, High Technology; **Function Concentration:** General Management, Human Resources, Marketing, Research and Development, Sales, Women/Minorities

Summerfield-Beall, Dotty — *President*
Summerfield Associates, Inc.
6555 Quince Road, Suite 311
Memphis, TN 38119
Telephone: (901) 753-7068
Recruiter Classification: Contingency; **Lowest/Average Salary:** $40,000/$50,000; **Industry Concentration:** Generalist with a primary focus in Information Technology; **Function Concentration:** General Management, Human Resources, Women/Minorities

Sur, William K. — *Senior Vice President/Director*
Canny, Bowen Inc.
200 Park Avenue
49th Floor
New York, NY 10166
Telephone: (212) 949-6611
Recruiter Classification: Retained; **Lowest/Average Salary:**
$90,000/$90,000; **Industry Concentration:** Generalist with a
primary focus in Electronics, High Technology, Information
Technology; **Function Concentration:** Generalist with a
primary focus in Engineering, Finance/Accounting, General
Management, Human Resources, Marketing, Research and
Development, Sales, Women/Minorities

Surrette, Mark — *President*
Robertson-Surrette Executive Search
Barrington Tower 10th Floor
Scotia Square, P.O. Box 2166
Halifax, Nova Scotia, B3J-3C4
Telephone: (902) 425-1330
Recruiter Classification: Retained; **Lowest/Average Salary:**
$50,000/$75,000; **Industry Concentration:** Generalist with a
primary focus in High Technology, Information Technology;
Function Concentration: Generalist with a primary focus in
Engineering, Finance/Accounting, General Management,
Human Resources, Marketing, Research and Development,
Sales

Susoreny, Samali — *Associate*
Source Services Corporation
5429 LBJ Freeway, Suite 275
Dallas, TX 75240
Telephone: (214) 387-1600
Recruiter Classification: Contingency; **Lowest/Average Salary:**
$30,000/$50,000; **Industry Concentration:** Information
Technology; **Function Concentration:** Engineering,
Finance/Accounting

Sussman, Lynda — *Vice President*
Gilbert Tweed/INESA
415 Madison Avenue
New York, NY 10017
Telephone: (212) 758-3000
Recruiter Classification: Retained; **Lowest/Average Salary:**
$90,000/$90,000; **Industry Concentration:** Generalist with a
primary focus in Electronics, High Technology; **Function
Concentration:** Generalist with a primary focus in Engineering,
Finance/Accounting, General Management, Human Resources,
Women/Minorities

Sutter, Howard — *Managing Partner*
Romac & Associates
5900 North Andrews Avenue
Suite 900
Fort Lauderdale, FL 33309
Telephone: (305) 928-0811
Recruiter Classification: Executive Temporary; **Lowest/Average
Salary:** $60,000/$60,000; **Industry Concentration:** High
Technology, Information Technology; **Function Concentration:**
Finance/Accounting

Sutton, Robert J. — *Partner*
The Caldwell Partners Amrop International
400 Third Avenue S.W.
Suite 3450
Calgary, Alberta, CANADA T2P 4H2
Telephone: (403) 265-8780
Recruiter Classification: Retained; **Lowest/Average Salary:**
$60,000/$90,000; **Industry Concentration:** Generalist with a
primary focus in High Technology; **Function Concentration:**
Generalist

Swanner, William — *Managing Director*
Source Services Corporation
2000 Town Center, Suite 850
Southfield, MI 48075
Telephone: (810) 352-6520
Recruiter Classification: Contingency; **Lowest/Average Salary:**
$30,000/$50,000; **Industry Concentration:** Information
Technology; **Function Concentration:** Engineering,
Finance/Accounting

Swanson, Dick — *Principal*
Raymond Karsan Associates
18 Commerce Way
Woburn, MA 01801
Telephone: (617) 932-0400
Recruiter Classification: Retained; **Lowest/Average Salary:**
$30,000/$90,000; **Industry Concentration:** Generalist with a
primary focus in Information Technology; **Function
Concentration:** Generalist with a primary focus in
Administration, Engineering, Finance/Accounting, General
Management, Human Resources, Marketing, Research and
Development, Sales, Women/Minorities

Swartz, William K. — *President*
Swartz Executive Search
P.O. Box 14167
Scottsdale, AZ 85267
Telephone: (602) 998-0363
Recruiter Classification: Retained; **Lowest/Average Salary:**
$90,000/$90,000; **Industry Concentration:** High Technology,
Information Technology; **Function Concentration:** Generalist with
a primary focus in Engineering, Finance/Accounting, General
Management, Marketing, Research and Development, Sales

Sweeney, Anne — *Associate*
Source Services Corporation
525 Vine Street, Suite 2250
Cincinnati, OH 45202
Telephone: (513) 651-3303
Recruiter Classification: Contingency; **Lowest/Average Salary:**
$30,000/$50,000; **Industry Concentration:** Information
Technology; **Function Concentration:** Engineering,
Finance/Accounting

Sweeney, James W. — *Partner*
Sweeney Harbert & Mummert, Inc.
777 South Harbour Island Boulevard
Suite 130
Tampa, FL 33602
Telephone: (813) 229-5360
Recruiter Classification: Retained; **Lowest/Average Salary:**
$90,000/$90,000; **Industry Concentration:** Generalist with a
primary focus in Electronics, High Technology, Information
Technology; **Function Concentration:** Generalist with a
primary focus in Administration, Engineering,
Finance/Accounting, General Management, Marketing,
Research and Development

Sweet, Randall — *Associate*
Source Services Corporation
150 South Wacker Drive, Suite 400
Chicago, IL 60606
Telephone: (312) 346-7000
Recruiter Classification: Contingency; **Lowest/Average Salary:**
$30,000/$50,000; **Industry Concentration:** Information
Technology; **Function Concentration:** Engineering,
Finance/Accounting

Sweetser, Rob — *Account Director*
Warren, Morris & Madison
2190 Carmel Valley Road
Del Mar, CA 92014
Telephone: (619) 481-3388
Recruiter Classification: Retained; **Lowest/Average Salary:**
$50,000/$75,000; **Industry Concentration:** High Technology;
Function Concentration: Generalist

Swick, Jan — *Executive Recruiter*
TSS Consulting, Ltd.
2425 East Camelback Road
Suite 375
Phoenix, AZ 85016
Telephone: (602) 955-7000
Recruiter Classification: Contingency; **Lowest/Average Salary:**
$60,000/$75,000; **Industry Concentration:** Electronics, High
Technology; **Function Concentration:** Engineering, General
Management, Marketing

Swidler, J. Robert — *Managing Partner*
Egon Zehnder International Inc.
1 Place Ville-Marie, Suite 3310
Montreal, Quebec, CANADA H3B 3N2
Telephone: (514) 876-4249
Recruiter Classification: Retained; **Lowest/Average Salary:**
$90,000/$90,000; **Industry Concentration:** Generalist with a
primary focus in High Technology; **Function Concentration:**
Generalist

Swoboda, Lawrence — *Professional Recruiter*
A.J. Burton Group, Inc.
120 East Baltimore Street, Suite 2220
Baltimore, MD 21202
Telephone: (410) 752-5244
Recruiter Classification: Contingency; **Lowest/Average Salary:**
$40,000/$75,000; **Industry Concentration:** Generalist with a
primary focus in High Technology, Information Technology;
Function Concentration: Generalist with a primary focus in
Administration, Finance/Accounting, General Management,
Human Resources

Taft, David G. — *President*
Techsearch Services, Inc.
6 Hachaliah Brown Drive
Somers, NY 10589
Telephone: (914) 277-2727
Recruiter Classification: Contingency; **Lowest/Average Salary:**
$50,000/$75,000; **Industry Concentration:** High Technology,
Information Technology; **Function Concentration:**
Finance/Accounting

Taft, Steven D. — *Associate*
The Guild Corporation
8260 Greensboro Drive, Suite 460
McLean, VA 22102
Telephone: (703) 761-4023
Recruiter Classification: Contingency; **Lowest/Average Salary:**
$40,000/$50,000; **Industry Concentration:** Electronics, High
Technology, Information Technology; **Function Concentration:**
Engineering, Finance/Accounting, General Management,
Research and Development

Tankson, Dawn — *Associate*
Source Services Corporation
1 Gatehall Drive, Suite 250
Parsippany, NJ 07054
Telephone: (201) 267-3222
Recruiter Classification: Contingency; **Lowest/Average Salary:**
$30,000/$50,000; **Industry Concentration:** Information
Technology; **Function Concentration:** Engineering,
Finance/Accounting

Tanner, Frank — *Associate*
Source Services Corporation
520 Post Oak Boulevard, Suite 700
Houston, TX 77027
Telephone: (713) 439-1077
Recruiter Classification: Contingency; **Lowest/Average Salary:**
$30,000/$50,000; **Industry Concentration:** Information
Technology; **Function Concentration:** Engineering,
Finance/Accounting

Tanner, Gary — *Associate*
Source Services Corporation
505 East 200 South, Suite 300
Salt Lake City, UT 84102
Telephone: (801) 328-0011
Recruiter Classification: Contingency; **Lowest/Average Salary:**
$30,000/$50,000; **Industry Concentration:** Information
Technology; **Function Concentration:** Engineering,
Finance/Accounting

Tanton, John E. — *Partner*
Tanton Mitchell/Paul Ray Berndtson
710-1050 West Pender Street
Vancouver, British Columbia, CANADA V6E 3S7
Telephone: (604) 685-0261
Recruiter Classification: Retained; **Lowest/Average Salary:**
$75,000/$90,000; **Industry Concentration:** Generalist with a
primary focus in High Technology; **Function Concentration:**
Generalist

Tappan, Michael A. — *Managing Director*
Ward Howell International, Inc.
99 Park Avenue, Suite 2000
New York, NY 10016-1699
Telephone: (212) 697-3730
Recruiter Classification: Retained; **Lowest/Average Salary:**
$75,000/$90,000; **Industry Concentration:** Electronics;
Function Concentration: Generalist

Taylor, Charles E. — *Partner*
Lamalie Amrop International
191 Peachtree Street N.E.
Atlanta, GA 30303-1747
Telephone: (404) 688-0800
Recruiter Classification: Retained; **Lowest/Average Salary:**
$90,000/$90,000; **Industry Concentration:** Generalist with a
primary focus in High Technology; **Function Concentration:**
Generalist

Taylor, Conrad G. — *Manager*
MSI International
6151 Powers Ferry Road, Suite 540
Atlanta, GA 30339
Telephone: (404) 850-6465
Recruiter Classification: Contingency; **Lowest/Average Salary:**
$30,000/$75,000; **Industry Concentration:** Generalist with a
primary focus in High Technology, Information Technology;
Function Concentration: Generalist with a primary focus in
Administration, Engineering, Finance/Accounting, General
Management, Marketing, Sales

Taylor, James M. — *Chief Executive Officer*
The HRM Group, Inc.
321 Lorna Square
Birmingham, AL 35216
Telephone: (205) 978-7181
Recruiter Classification: Retained; **Lowest/Average Salary:**
$30,000/$50,000; **Industry Concentration:** Generalist with a
primary focus in Information Technology; **Function
Concentration:** Generalist with a primary focus in
Finance/Accounting, General Management, Human Resources,
Marketing, Sales

Taylor, Kenneth W. — *Consultant*
Egon Zehnder International Inc.
One First National Plaza
21 South Clark Street, Suite 3300
Chicago, IL 60603-2006
Telephone: (312) 782-4500
Recruiter Classification: Retained; **Lowest/Average Salary:**
$90,000/$90,000; **Industry Concentration:** Generalist with a
primary focus in High Technology; **Function Concentration:**
Generalist

Taylor, R.L. (Larry) — *Partner*
Ray & Berndtson
Sears Tower, 233 South Wacker Drive, Suite 4020
Chicago, IL 60606-6310
Telephone: (312) 876-0730
Recruiter Classification: Retained; **Lowest/Average Salary:**
$90,000/$90,000; **Industry Concentration:** Generalist with a
primary focus in High Technology, Information Technology;
Function Concentration: Generalist with a primary focus in
Administration, Finance/Accounting, General Management,
Human Resources, Marketing, Research and Development,
Sales, Women/Minorities

Teger, Stella — *Associate*
Source Services Corporation
2 Penn Plaza, Suite 1176
New York, NY 10121
Telephone: (212) 760-2200
Recruiter Classification: Contingency; **Lowest/Average Salary:**
$30,000/$50,000; **Industry Concentration:** Information
Technology; **Function Concentration:** Engineering,
Finance/Accounting

Telford, John H. — *Managing Principal*
Telford, Adams & Alexander/Telford & Co., Inc.
650 Town Center Drive, Suite 850A
Costa Mesa, CA 92626
Telephone: (714) 850-4354
Recruiter Classification: Retained; **Lowest/Average Salary:**
$90,000/$90,000; **Industry Concentration:** Generalist with a
primary focus in Electronics, High Technology, Information
Technology; **Function Concentration:** Generalist with a
primary focus in Administration, Finance/Accounting, General
Management, Human Resources, Marketing, Sales

ten Cate, Herman H. — *President*
Stoneham Associates Corp.
Royal Bank Plaza
200 Bay Street, P.O. Box 105
Toronto, Ontario, CANADA M5J 2J3
Telephone: (416) 362-0852
Recruiter Classification: Retained; **Lowest/Average Salary:**
$90,000/$90,000; **Industry Concentration:** Generalist with a
primary focus in High Technology, Information Technology;
Function Concentration: Generalist with a primary focus in
Administration, Engineering, Finance/Accounting, General
Management, Marketing

Tenero, Kymberly — *Associate*
Source Services Corporation
111 Founders Plaza, Suite 1501E
Hartford, CT 06108
Telephone: (860) 528-0300
Recruiter Classification: Contingency; **Lowest/Average Salary:**
$30,000/$50,000; **Industry Concentration:** Information
Technology; **Function Concentration:** Engineering,
Finance/Accounting

Tesar, Bob — *Partner*
Tesar-Reynes, Inc.
500 North Michigan Avenue
Chicago, IL 60611
Telephone: (312) 661-0700
Recruiter Classification: Retained; **Lowest/Average Salary:**
$50,000/$75,000; **Industry Concentration:** High Technology;
Function Concentration: Marketing

Tetrick, Tim — *Senior Consultant*
O'Connor, O'Connor, Lordi, Ltd.
Gulf Tower Suite 2727
707 Grant Street
Pittsburgh, PA 15219
Telephone: (412) 261-4020
Recruiter Classification: Retained; **Lowest/Average Salary:**
$90,000/$90,000; **Industry Concentration:** Generalist with a
primary focus in High Technology, Information Technology;
Function Concentration: Generalist with a primary focus in
Finance/Accounting, General Management, Human Resources,
Marketing, Research and Development, Sales

Theard, Susan — *Branch Manager*
Romac & Associates
650 Poydras Street, Suite 2523
New Orleans, LA 70130
Telephone: (504) 522-6611
Recruiter Classification: Executive Temporary; **Lowest/Average
Salary:** $60,000/$60,000; **Industry Concentration:** High
Technology, Information Technology; **Function Concentration:**
Finance/Accounting

Theobald, David B. — *President*
Theobald & Associates
1750 Montgomery Street
San Francisco, CA 94111
Telephone: (415) 883-6007
Recruiter Classification: Retained; **Lowest/Average Salary:**
$90,000/$90,000; **Industry Concentration:** Generalist with a
primary focus in Electronics, High Technology, Information
Technology; **Function Concentration:** Generalist with a
primary focus in Engineering, Finance/Accounting, General
Management, Human Resources, Marketing, Sales

Thielman, Joseph — *President*
Barrett Partners
100 North LaSalle Street, Suite 1420
Chicago, IL 60602
Telephone: (312) 443-8877
Recruiter Classification: Contingency; **Lowest/Average Salary:**
$30,000/$50,000; **Industry Concentration:** Information
Technology; **Function Concentration:** Engineering,
Finance/Accounting

Thies, Gary — *Recruiter*
S.D. Kelly & Associates, Inc.
990 Washington Street
Dedham, MA 02026
Telephone: (617) 326-8038
Recruiter Classification: Contingency; **Lowest/Average Salary:**
$50,000/$60,000; **Industry Concentration:** Electronics, High
Technology; **Function Concentration:** Engineering, General
Management, Marketing, Sales

Thomas, Cheryl M. — *Executive Recruiter*
CPS Inc.
One Westbrook Corporate Centre, Suite 600
Westchester, IL 60154
Telephone: (708) 531-8370
Recruiter Classification: Contingency; **Lowest/Average Salary:**
$30,000/$50,000; **Industry Concentration:** Generalist with a
primary focus in Electronics, High Technology, Information
Technology; **Function Concentration:** Engineering, Research
and Development, Sales, Women/Minorities

Thomas, Donald — *Principal*
Mixtec Group
75-355 St. Andrews
Indian Wells, CA 92210
Telephone: (619) 773-0717
Recruiter Classification: Contingency; **Lowest/Average Salary:**
$60,000/$90,000; **Industry Concentration:** Electronics, High
Technology, Information Technology; **Function Concentration:**
Generalist with a primary focus in Administration, Engineering,
General Management, Research and Development

Thomas, Ian A. — *Vice President*
International Staffing Consultants, Inc.
500 Newport Center Drive, Suite 300
Newport Beach, CA 92660-7003
Telephone: (714) 721-7990
Recruiter Classification: Contingency, Executive Temporary;
Lowest/Average Salary: $50,000/$75,000; **Industry
Concentration:** Generalist with a primary focus in Electronics,
High Technology, Information Technology; **Function
Concentration:** Generalist with a primary focus in Engineering,
General Management

Thomas, Kim — *Executive Recruiter*
CPS Inc.
One Westbrook Corporate Centre, Suite 600
Westchester, IL 60154
Telephone: (708) 531-8370
Recruiter Classification: Contingency; **Lowest/Average Salary:**
$30,000/$50,000; **Industry Concentration:** Generalist with a
primary focus in Electronics, High Technology, Information
Technology; **Function Concentration:** Engineering, Research
and Development, Sales, Women/Minorities

Thomas, Kurt J. — *Vice President*
P.J. Murphy & Associates, Inc.
735 North Water Street
Milwaukee, WI 53202
Telephone: (414) 277-9777
Recruiter Classification: Retained; **Lowest/Average Salary:**
$60,000/$90,000; **Industry Concentration:** Generalist with a
primary focus in Information Technology; **Function
Concentration:** Generalist with a primary focus in
Administration, Finance/Accounting, General Management,
Human Resources, Marketing, Sales

Thomas, Terry — *President*
The Thomas Resource Group
1630 Tiburon Boulevard
Tiburon, CA 94920
Telephone: (415) 435-5123
Recruiter Classification: Retained; **Lowest/Average Salary:**
$90,000/$90,000; **Industry Concentration:** High Technology;
Function Concentration: Generalist with a primary focus in
Finance/Accounting, General Management, Marketing

Thomas, William — *Senior Principal*
Mixtec Group
31255 Cedar Valley Drive
Suite 300-327
Westlake Village, CA 91362
Telephone: (818) 889-8819
Recruiter Classification: Contingency; **Lowest/Average Salary:**
$60,000/$90,000; **Industry Concentration:** High Technology;
Function Concentration: Generalist with a primary focus in
Administration, General Management

Thompson, Dave — *Director West Coast
Operations*
Battalia Winston International
One Sansome Street, Suite 2100
Citicorp Center
San Francisco, CA 94104
Telephone: (415) 984-3180
Recruiter Classification: Retained; **Lowest/Average Salary:**
$90,000/$90,000; **Industry Concentration:** Information
Technology; **Function Concentration:** Generalist with a
primary focus in General Management, Human Resources,
Marketing, Sales

Thompson, Kenneth L. — *Partner*
McCormack & Farrow
695 Town Center Drive
Suite 660
Costa Mesa, CA 92626
Telephone: (714) 549-7222
Recruiter Classification: Retained; **Lowest/Average Salary:**
$75,000/$90,000; **Industry Concentration:** Generalist with a
primary focus in Electronics, High Technology; **Function
Concentration:** Generalist with a primary focus in
Administration, Engineering, Finance/Accounting, General
Management, Human Resources, Marketing, Research and
Development

Thompson, Leslie — *Associate*
Source Services Corporation
879 West 190th Street, Suite 250
Los Angeles, CA 90248
Telephone: (310) 323-6633
Recruiter Classification: Contingency; **Lowest/Average Salary:**
$30,000/$50,000; **Industry Concentration:** Information
Technology; **Function Concentration:** Engineering,
Finance/Accounting

Thornton, John — *Director/Principal*
Stratford Group
6120 Parkland Boulevard
Cleveland, OH 44124
Telephone: (216) 460-3232
Recruiter Classification: Retained; **Lowest/Average Salary:**
$90,000/$90,000; **Industry Concentration:** Generalist with a
primary focus in High Technology; **Function Concentration:**
Generalist with a primary focus in Sales

Thrapp, Mark C. — *Managing Director*
Executive Search Consultants International, Inc.
330 Fifth Avenue
Suite 5501
New York, NY 10118
Telephone: (212) 333-1900
Recruiter Classification: Retained; **Lowest/Average Salary:**
$90,000/$90,000; **Industry Concentration:** Generalist with a
primary focus in High Technology, Information Technology;
Function Concentration: Generalist with a primary focus in
Finance/Accounting, General Management, Human Resources,
Marketing

Thrower, Troy — *Associate*
Source Services Corporation
2029 Century Park East, Suite 1350
Los Angeles, CA 90067
Telephone: (310) 277-8092
Recruiter Classification: Contingency; **Lowest/Average Salary:**
$30,000/$50,000; **Industry Concentration:** Information
Technology; **Function Concentration:** Engineering,
Finance/Accounting

Tilley, Kyle — *Associate*
Source Services Corporation
10300 West 103rd Street, Suite 101
Overland Park, KS 66214
Telephone: (913) 888-8885
Recruiter Classification: Contingency; **Lowest/Average Salary:**
$30,000/$50,000; **Industry Concentration:** Information
Technology; **Function Concentration:** Engineering,
Finance/Accounting

Timoney, Laura — *Vice President*
Bishop Partners
708 Third Avenue
Suite 2200
New York, NY 10017
Telephone: (212) 986-3419
Recruiter Classification: Retained; **Lowest/Average Salary:**
$90,000/$90,000; **Industry Concentration:** Information
Technology; **Function Concentration:** Generalist with a
primary focus in General Management, Marketing, Sales

Tincu, John C. — *Executive Consultant*
Ferneborg & Associates, Inc.
1450 Fashion Island Boulevard, Suite 650
San Mateo, CA 94404
Telephone: (415) 577-0100
Recruiter Classification: Retained; **Lowest/Average Salary:**
$90,000/$90,000; **Industry Concentration:** Generalist with a
primary focus in Electronics, High Technology; **Function
Concentration:** Generalist with a primary focus in
Administration, Engineering, Finance/Accounting, General
Management, Human Resources, Marketing, Sales

Tipp, George D. — *Vice President*
Intech Summit Group, Inc.
5075 Shoreham Place, Suite 280
San Diego, CA 92116
Telephone: (619) 452-2100
Recruiter Classification: Retained; **Lowest/Average Salary:**
$60,000/$75,000; **Industry Concentration:** Information
Technology; **Function Concentration:** Administration, General
Management, Research and Development, Sales

Tittle, David M. — *President*
Paul-Tittle Associates, Inc.
1485 Chain Bridge Road, #304
McLean, VA 22101
Telephone: (703) 442-0500
Recruiter Classification: Retained; **Lowest/Average Salary:**
$90,000/$90,000; **Industry Concentration:** Electronics, High
Technology, Information Technology; **Function Concentration:**
Engineering, Finance/Accounting, General Management,
Marketing, Sales, Women/Minorities

To, Raymond — *Manager Software Division*
Corporate Recruiters Ltd.
490-1140 West Pender Street
Vancouver, British Columbia, CANADA V6E 4G1
Telephone: (604) 687-5993
Recruiter Classification: Contingency; **Lowest/Average Salary:**
$30,000/$60,000; **Industry Concentration:** Information
Technology; **Function Concentration:** Engineering, Research
and Development

Tobin, Christopher — *Associate*
Source Services Corporation
One South Main Street, Suite 1440
Dayton, OH 45402
Telephone: (513) 461-4660
Recruiter Classification: Contingency; **Lowest/Average Salary:**
$30,000/$50,000; **Industry Concentration:** Information
Technology; **Function Concentration:** Engineering,
Finance/Accounting

Tolette, Skip — *President*
The Schmitt Tolette Group
577 West Saddle River Road
Upper Saddle River, NJ 07458
Telephone: (201) 327-8214
Recruiter Classification: Retained; **Lowest/Average Salary:**
$90,000/$90,000; **Industry Concentration:** Information
Technology; **Function Concentration:** Generalist

Tomasco, Ray — *Partner*
Huntington Group
6527 Main Street
Trumbull, CT 06611
Telephone: (203) 261-1166
Recruiter Classification: Retained; **Lowest/Average Salary:**
$90,000/$90,000; **Industry Concentration:** Information
Technology; **Function Concentration:** Generalist

Tootsey, Mark A. — *Vice President*
A.J. Burton Group, Inc.
4550 Montgomery Avenue, Ste. 325 North
Bethesda, MD 20814
Telephone: (301) 654-0082
Recruiter Classification: Contingency, Executive Temporary;
Lowest/Average Salary: $40,000/$75,000; **Industry
Concentration:** Generalist with a primary focus in High
Technology, Information Technology; **Function
Concentration:** Generalist with a primary focus in
Administration, Finance/Accounting, General Management,
Human Resources

Topliff, Marla — *Executive Search Consultant*
Gaffney Management Consultants
35 North Brandon Drive
Glendale Heights, IL 60139-2087
Telephone: (630) 307-3380
Recruiter Classification: Retained; **Lowest/Average Salary:**
$50,000/$90,000; **Industry Concentration:** Generalist with a
primary focus in Electronics, High Technology; **Function
Concentration:** Generalist with a primary focus in Engineering,
Finance/Accounting, General Management, Human Resources,
Marketing, Research and Development, Sales

Tovrog, Dan — *Executive Recruiter*
CPS Inc.
One Westbrook Corporate Centre, Suite 600
Westchester, IL 60154
Telephone: (708) 531-8370
Recruiter Classification: Contingency; **Lowest/Average Salary:** $30,000/$50,000; **Industry Concentration:** Generalist with a primary focus in Electronics, High Technology, Information Technology; **Function Concentration:** Engineering, Research and Development, Sales, Women/Minorities

Tracy, Ronald O. — *Consultant*
Egon Zehnder International Inc.
One First National Plaza
21 South Clark Street, Suite 3300
Chicago, IL 60603-2006
Telephone: (312) 782-4500
Recruiter Classification: Retained; **Lowest/Average Salary:** $90,000/$90,000; **Industry Concentration:** Generalist with a primary focus in High Technology; **Function Concentration:** Generalist

Travis, Michael — *Vice President*
Travis & Company
325 Boston Post Road
Sudbury, MA 01776
Telephone: (508) 443-4000
Recruiter Classification: Retained; **Lowest/Average Salary:** $90,000/$90,000; **Industry Concentration:** Electronics, High Technology, Information Technology; **Function Concentration:** Generalist

Trefzer, Kristie — *Associate*
Source Services Corporation
150 South Wacker Drive, Suite 400
Chicago, IL 60606
Telephone: (312) 346-7000
Recruiter Classification: Contingency; **Lowest/Average Salary:** $30,000/$50,000; **Industry Concentration:** Information Technology; **Function Concentration:** Engineering, Finance/Accounting

Trewhella, Michael — *Managing Director*
Source Services Corporation
161 Ottawa NW, Suite 409D
Grand Rapids, MI 49503
Telephone: (616) 451-2400
Recruiter Classification: Contingency; **Lowest/Average Salary:** $30,000/$50,000; **Industry Concentration:** Information Technology; **Function Concentration:** Engineering, Finance/Accounting

Trice, Renee — *Associate*
Source Services Corporation
Foster Plaza VI
681 Anderson Drive, 2nd Floor
Pittsburgh, PA 15220
Telephone: (412) 928-8300
Recruiter Classification: Contingency; **Lowest/Average Salary:** $30,000/$50,000; **Industry Concentration:** Information Technology; **Function Concentration:** Engineering, Finance/Accounting

Trieschmann, Daniel — *Associate*
Source Services Corporation
One CityPlace, Suite 170
St. Louis, MO 63141
Telephone: (314) 432-4500
Recruiter Classification: Contingency; **Lowest/Average Salary:** $30,000/$50,000; **Industry Concentration:** Information Technology; **Function Concentration:** Engineering, Finance/Accounting

Trieweiler, Bob — *Consultant*
Executive Placement Consultants, Inc.
2700 River Road, Suite 107
Des Plaines, IL 60018
Telephone: (847) 298-6445
Recruiter Classification: Contingency; **Lowest/Average Salary:** $40,000/$75,000; **Industry Concentration:** Generalist with a primary focus in Electronics, High Technology, Information Technology; **Function Concentration:** Generalist with a primary focus in Finance/Accounting, Human Resources, Marketing

Trimble, Patricia — *Associate*
Source Services Corporation
15260 Ventura Boulevard, Suite 380
Sherman Oaks, CA 91403
Telephone: (818) 905-1500
Recruiter Classification: Contingency; **Lowest/Average Salary:** $30,000/$50,000; **Industry Concentration:** Information Technology; **Function Concentration:** Engineering, Finance/Accounting

Trimble, Rhonda — *Associate*
Source Services Corporation
7730 East Bellview Avenue, Suite 302
Englewood, CO 80111
Telephone: (303) 773-3700
Recruiter Classification: Contingency; **Lowest/Average Salary:** $30,000/$50,000; **Industry Concentration:** Information Technology; **Function Concentration:** Engineering, Finance/Accounting

Truemper, Dean — *Executive Recruiter*
CPS Inc.
One Westbrook Corporate Centre, Suite 600
Westchester, IL 60154
Telephone: (708) 531-8370
Recruiter Classification: Contingency; **Lowest/Average Salary:** $30,000/$50,000; **Industry Concentration:** Generalist with a primary focus in Electronics, High Technology, Information Technology; **Function Concentration:** Engineering, Research and Development, Sales, Women/Minorities

Truitt, Thomas B. — *Senior Manager*
Southwestern Professional Services
2451 Atrium Way
Nashville, TN 37214
Telephone: (615) 391-2722
Recruiter Classification: Contingency; **Lowest/Average Salary:** $60,000/$90,000; **Industry Concentration:** Electronics, High Technology, Information Technology; **Function Concentration:** Engineering, Finance/Accounting, General Management

Tryon, Katey — *Senior Vice President - Managing Principal*
DeFrain, Mayer LLC
6900 College Boulevard
Suite 300
Overland Park, KS 66211
Telephone: (913) 345-0500
Recruiter Classification: Retained; **Lowest/Average Salary:** $50,000/$90,000; **Industry Concentration:** Generalist with a primary focus in Electronics; **Function Concentration:** Generalist with a primary focus in Administration, Engineering, Finance/Accounting, General Management, Human Resources, Marketing

Tscelli, Maureen — *Associate*
Source Services Corporation
155 Federal Street, Suite 410
Boston, MA 02110
Telephone: (617) 482-8211
Recruiter Classification: Contingency; **Lowest/Average Salary:** $30,000/$50,000; **Industry Concentration:** Information Technology; **Function Concentration:** Engineering, Finance/Accounting

Tschan, Stephen — *Associate*
Source Services Corporation
3 Summit Park Drive, Suite 550
Independence, OH 44131
Telephone: (216) 328-5900
Recruiter Classification: Contingency; **Lowest/Average Salary:** $30,000/$50,000; **Industry Concentration:** Information Technology; **Function Concentration:** Engineering, Finance/Accounting

Tucker, Thomas A. — *Principal*
The Thomas Tucker Company
425 California Street, Suite 2502
San Francisco, CA 94104
Telephone: (415) 693-5900
Recruiter Classification: Retained; **Lowest/Average Salary:** $90,000/$90,000; **Industry Concentration:** Generalist with a primary focus in Electronics, High Technology, Information Technology; **Function Concentration:** Generalist with a primary focus in Engineering, Finance/Accounting, General Management, Human Resources, Marketing, Research and Development

Tullberg, Tina — *Executive Recruiter*
CPS Inc.
One Westbrook Corporate Centre, Suite 600
Westchester, IL 60154
Telephone: (708) 531-8370
Recruiter Classification: Contingency; **Lowest/Average Salary:** $30,000/$50,000; **Industry Concentration:** Generalist with a primary focus in Electronics, High Technology, Information Technology; **Function Concentration:** Engineering, Research and Development, Sales, Women/Minorities

Tully, Margo L. — *Partner*
Tully/Woodmansee International, Inc.
1088 U.S. 27 North
Lake Placid, FL 33852
Telephone: (941) 465-1024
Recruiter Classification: Retained; **Lowest/Average Salary:** $60,000/$90,000; **Industry Concentration:** Generalist with a primary focus in Electronics, High Technology; **Function Concentration:** Generalist with a primary focus in Finance/Accounting, General Management, Human Resources, Marketing, Sales, Women/Minorities

Tunney, William — *Vice President*
Grant Cooper and Associates
795 Office Parkway, Suite 117
St. Louis, MO 63141
Telephone: (314) 567-4690
Recruiter Classification: Retained; **Lowest/Average Salary:** $60,000/$90,000; **Industry Concentration:** Generalist with a primary focus in Electronics; **Function Concentration:** Generalist with a primary focus in Administration, Engineering, Finance/Accounting, General Management, Human Resources, Marketing, Sales

Turner, Edward K. — *President*
Don Richard Associates of Charlotte
2650 One First Union Center
301 South College Street
Charlotte, NC 28202-6000
Telephone: (704) 377-6447
Recruiter Classification: Contingency, Executive Temporary; **Lowest/Average Salary:** $40,000/$50,000; **Industry Concentration:** Generalist with a primary focus in High Technology, Information Technology; **Function Concentration:** Administration, Finance/Accounting, General Management

Turner, Kimberly — *Senior Consultant*
Barton Associates, Inc.
One Riverway, Suite 2500
Houston, TX 77056
Telephone: (713) 961-9111
Recruiter Classification: Retained; **Lowest/Average Salary:** $75,000/$90,000; **Industry Concentration:** Generalist with a primary focus in Electronics, High Technology, Information Technology; **Function Concentration:** Generalist with a primary focus in Administration, Finance/Accounting, General Management, Human Resources, Marketing

Turner, Raymond — *Managing Director*
Source Services Corporation
111 Founders Plaza, Suite 1501E
Hartford, CT 06108
Telephone: (860) 528-0300
Recruiter Classification: Contingency; **Lowest/Average Salary:** $30,000/$50,000; **Industry Concentration:** Information Technology; **Function Concentration:** Engineering, Finance/Accounting

Tursi, Deborah J. — *Sales Recruiter*
The Corporate Connection, Ltd.
7202 Glen Forest Drive
Richmond, VA 23226
Telephone: (804) 288-8844
Recruiter Classification: Contingency; **Lowest/Average Salary:** $20,000/$30,000; **Industry Concentration:** Information Technology; **Function Concentration:** Generalist with a primary focus in Administration, Engineering, Finance/Accounting, General Management, Human Resources, Marketing, Sales, Women/Minorities

Tuttle, Donald E. — *President and CEO*
Tuttle Venture Group, Inc.
5151 Beltline Road, Suite 1018
Dallas, TX 75240
Telephone: (972) 980-1688
Recruiter Classification: Retained; **Lowest/Average Salary:** $90,000/$90,000; **Industry Concentration:** Electronics, High Technology, Information Technology; **Function Concentration:** Generalist

Tweed, Janet — *Chief Executive Officer*
Gilbert Tweed/INESA
415 Madison Avenue
New York, NY 10017
Telephone: (212) 758-3000
Recruiter Classification: Retained; **Lowest/Average Salary:**
$90,000/$90,000; **Industry Concentration:** Generalist with a
primary focus in High Technology; **Function Concentration:**
Generalist with a primary focus in Engineering,
Finance/Accounting, General Management, Human Resources,
Marketing, Research and Development, Sales

Twiste, Craig — *Senior Consultant*
Raymond Karsan Associates
3725 National Drive, Suite 115
Raleigh, NC 27612
Telephone: (919) 571-1690
Recruiter Classification: Retained; **Lowest/Average Salary:**
$30,000/$90,000; **Industry Concentration:** Generalist with a
primary focus in Information Technology; **Function
Concentration:** Generalist

Twomey, James — *Managing Director*
Source Services Corporation
20 Burlington Mall Road, Suite 405
Burlington, MA 01803
Telephone: (617) 272-5000
Recruiter Classification: Contingency; **Lowest/Average Salary:**
$30,000/$50,000; **Industry Concentration:** Information
Technology; **Function Concentration:** Engineering,
Finance/Accounting

Ulbert, Nancy — *Director Data Processing/MIS*
Aureus Group
8744 Frederick Street
Omaha, NE 68124-3068
Telephone: (402) 397-2980
Recruiter Classification: Contingency; **Lowest/Average Salary:**
$30,000/$50,000; **Industry Concentration:** Electronics, High
Technology, Information Technology; **Function Concentration:**
Administration, Engineering, Finance/Accounting, General
Management, Human Resources

Ulrich, Mary Ann — *Partner*
D.S. Allen Associates, Inc.
1119 Raritan Rd., Ste. 2
Clark, NJ 07066
Telephone: (732) 574-1600
Recruiter Classification: Contingency; **Lowest/Average Salary:**
$60,000/$90,000; **Industry Concentration:** High Technology,
Information Technology; **Function Concentration:**
Finance/Accounting, General Management, Human Resources,
Marketing, Sales

Unger, Paul T. — *Vice President*
A.T. Kearney, Inc.
225 Reinekers Lane
Alexandria, VA 22314
Telephone: (703) 739-4624
Recruiter Classification: Retained; **Lowest/Average Salary:**
$90,000/$90,000; **Industry Concentration:** Generalist with a
primary focus in Information Technology; **Function
Concentration:** Generalist with a primary focus in
Administration, Engineering, Human Resources, Marketing,
Research and Development, Sales

Unterberg, Edward L. — *Managing Director*
Russell Reynolds Associates, Inc.
200 South Wacker Drive
Suite 3600
Chicago, IL 60606-5823
Telephone: (312) 993-9696
Recruiter Classification: Retained; **Lowest/Average Salary:**
$90,000/$90,000; **Industry Concentration:** High Technology;
Function Concentration: Generalist

Utroska, Donald R. — *Partner (Practice Leader -
Europe)*
Lamalie Amrop International
225 West Wacker Drive
Chicago, IL 60606-1229
Telephone: (312) 782-3113
Recruiter Classification: Retained; **Lowest/Average Salary:**
$90,000/$90,000; **Industry Concentration:** Generalist with a
primary focus in High Technology; **Function Concentration:**
Generalist with a primary focus in General Management,
Marketing

Uzzel, Linda — *Associate*
Source Services Corporation
One South Main Street, Suite 1440
Dayton, OH 45402
Telephone: (513) 461-4660
Recruiter Classification: Contingency; **Lowest/Average Salary:**
$30,000/$50,000; **Industry Concentration:** Information
Technology; **Function Concentration:** Engineering,
Finance/Accounting

Vacca, Domenic — *Managing Partner*
Romac & Associates
1300 North Market Street
Suite 501
Wilmington, DE 19801
Telephone: (302) 658-6181
Recruiter Classification: Executive Temporary; **Lowest/Average
Salary:** $60,000/$60,000; **Industry Concentration:** High
Technology, Information Technology; **Function Concentration:**
Finance/Accounting

Vachon, David A. — *Associate*
McNichol Associates
620 Chestnut Street, Suite 1031
Philadelphia, PA 19106
Telephone: (215) 922-4142
Recruiter Classification: Retained; **Lowest/Average Salary:**
$75,000/$90,000; **Industry Concentration:** High Technology;
Function Concentration: Generalist with a primary focus in
Administration, Engineering, Finance/Accounting, General
Management, Human Resources, Marketing, Research and
Development, Sales, Women/Minorities

Vairo, Leonard A. — *Vice President*
Christian & Timbers
24 New England Executive Park
Burlington, MA 01803
Telephone: (617) 229-9515
Recruiter Classification: Retained; **Lowest/Average Salary:**
$90,000/$90,000; **Industry Concentration:** Generalist with a
primary focus in Electronics, High Technology, Information
Technology; **Function Concentration:** Generalist with a
primary focus in Engineering, Finance/Accounting, General
Management, Human Resources, Marketing, Research and
Development, Sales

Valenta, Joseph — *Director*
Princeton Entrepreneurial Resources
600 Alexander Road, P.O. Box 2051
Princeton, NJ 08543
Telephone: (609) 243-0010
Recruiter Classification: Executive Temporary; **Lowest/Average Salary:** $75,000/$90,000; **Industry Concentration:** Generalist with a primary focus in Electronics, Information Technology; **Function Concentration:** Generalist with a primary focus in Finance/Accounting, General Management, Human Resources, Marketing

Van Biesen, Jacques A.H. — *President*
Search Group Inc.
950 505 Third Street SW
Calgary, Alberta, CANADA, T2P 3E6
Telephone: (403) 292-0959
Recruiter Classification: Retained; **Lowest/Average Salary:** $75,000/$90,000; **Industry Concentration:** Generalist with a primary focus in Electronics, High Technology; **Function Concentration:** Generalist with a primary focus in Engineering, Finance/Accounting, General Management, Marketing, Research and Development

Van Campen, Jerry — *Vice President Research and Internal Services*
Gilbert & Van Campen International
Graybar Building, 420 Lexington Avenue
New York, NY 10170
Telephone: (212) 661-2122
Recruiter Classification: Retained; **Lowest/Average Salary:** $90,000/$90,000; **Industry Concentration:** Generalist with a primary focus in High Technology; **Function Concentration:** Generalist with a primary focus in Finance/Accounting, General Management, Human Resources, Marketing, Sales, Women/Minorities

Van Clieaf, Mark — *Managing Director*
MVC Associates International
36 Toronto Street, Suite 850
Toronto, Ontario, CANADA M5C 2C5
Telephone: (416) 489-1917
Recruiter Classification: Retained; **Lowest/Average Salary:** $50,000/$90,000; **Industry Concentration:** Generalist with a primary focus in High Technology, Information Technology; **Function Concentration:** Generalist with a primary focus in General Management, Human Resources, Marketing

Van Norman, Ben — *Associate*
Source Services Corporation
425 California Street, Suite 1200
San Francisco, CA 94104
Telephone: (415) 434-2410
Recruiter Classification: Contingency; **Lowest/Average Salary:** $30,000/$50,000; **Industry Concentration:** Information Technology; **Function Concentration:** Engineering, Finance/Accounting

Van Nostrand, Mara J. — *Senior Consultant*
Barton Associates, Inc.
One Riverway, Suite 2500
Houston, TX 77056
Telephone: (713) 961-9111
Recruiter Classification: Retained; **Lowest/Average Salary:** $75,000/$90,000; **Industry Concentration:** Generalist with a primary focus in Electronics, High Technology, Information Technology; **Function Concentration:** Generalist with a primary focus in General Management, Marketing

Van Remmen, Roger — *Partner*
Brown, Bernardy, Van Remmen, Inc.
12100 Wilshire Boulevard, Suite M-40
Los Angeles, CA 90025
Telephone: (310) 826-5777
Recruiter Classification: Contingency; **Lowest/Average Salary:** $30,000/$75,000; **Industry Concentration:** Electronics, High Technology; **Function Concentration:** Marketing

Van Steenkiste, Julie — *Recruiter*
Davidson, Laird & Associates, Inc.
29260 Franklin, Suite 110
Southfield, MI 48034
Telephone: (248) 358-2160
Recruiter Classification: Contingency; **Lowest/Average Salary:** $30,000/$50,000; **Industry Concentration:** Generalist with a primary focus in Electronics; **Function Concentration:** Generalist with a primary focus in Engineering, Finance/Accounting, Research and Development

Vande-Water, Katie — *Vice President*
J. Robert Scott
27 State Street
Boston, MA 02109
Telephone: (617) 720-2770
Recruiter Classification: Retained; **Lowest/Average Salary:** $75,000/$90,000; **Industry Concentration:** Generalist with a primary focus in Electronics, High Technology, Information Technology; **Function Concentration:** Generalist

Vandenbulcke, Cynthia — *Associate*
Source Services Corporation
2029 Century Park East, Suite 1350
Los Angeles, CA 90067
Telephone: (310) 277-8092
Recruiter Classification: Contingency; **Lowest/Average Salary:** $30,000/$50,000; **Industry Concentration:** Information Technology; **Function Concentration:** Engineering, Finance/Accounting

Vann, Dianne — *Principal*
The Button Group
1608 Emory Circle
Plano, TX 75093
Telephone: (972) 985-0619
Recruiter Classification: Retained, Contingency; **Lowest/Average Salary:** $60,000/$90,000; **Industry Concentration:** Generalist with a primary focus in High Technology, Information Technology; **Function Concentration:** Generalist with a primary focus in Engineering, General Management, Marketing, Research and Development, Sales

Varney, Monique — *Associate*
Source Services Corporation
500 108th Avenue NE, Suite 1780
Bellevue, WA 98004
Telephone: (206) 454-6400
Recruiter Classification: Contingency; **Lowest/Average Salary:** $30,000/$50,000; **Industry Concentration:** Information Technology; **Function Concentration:** Engineering, Finance/Accounting

Varrichio, Michael — *Managing Director*
Source Services Corporation
5429 LBJ Freeway, Suite 275
Dallas, TX 75240
Telephone: (214) 387-1600
Recruiter Classification: Contingency; **Lowest/Average Salary:** $30,000/$50,000; **Industry Concentration:** Information Technology; **Function Concentration:** Engineering, Finance/Accounting

Vaughan, David B. — *President*
Dunhill Professional Search of Irvine, Inc.
9 Executive Circle, Suite 240
Irvine, CA 92614
Telephone: (714) 474-6666
Recruiter Classification: Contingency; **Lowest/Average Salary:**
$50,000/$75,000; **Industry Concentration:** High Technology;
Function Concentration: Generalist with a primary focus in
General Management, Marketing, Sales

Velez, Hector — *Associate*
Source Services Corporation
8614 Westwood Center, Suite 750
Vienna, VA 22182
Telephone: (703) 790-5610
Recruiter Classification: Contingency; **Lowest/Average Salary:**
$30,000/$50,000; **Industry Concentration:** Information
Technology; **Function Concentration:** Engineering,
Finance/Accounting

Velten, Mark T. — *Vice President*
Boyden
55 Madison Avenue
Suite 400
Morristown, NJ 07960
Telephone: (201) 267-0980
Recruiter Classification: Retained; **Lowest/Average Salary:**
$90,000/$90,000; **Industry Concentration:** Generalist with a
primary focus in Electronics, High Technology, Information
Technology; **Function Concentration:** Generalist with a
primary focus in Engineering, Finance/Accounting, General
Management, Human Resources, Marketing, Research and
Development, Sales, Women/Minorities

Venable, William W. — *Vice President*
Thorndike Deland Associates
275 Madison Avenue, Suite 1300
New York, NY 10016
Telephone: (212) 661-6200
Recruiter Classification: Retained; **Lowest/Average Salary:**
$100,000/$125,000; **Industry Concentration:** Generalist with a
primary focus in Information Technology; **Function
Concentration:** Generalist with a primary focus in
Finance/Accounting, General Management, Human Resources,
Marketing, Sales

Vennat, Manon — *Managing Director*
Spencer Stuart
1981 Avenue McGill College
Montreal, Quebec, CANADA H3A 2Y1
Telephone: (514) 288-3377
Recruiter Classification: Retained; **Lowest/Average Salary:**
$90,000/$90,000; **Industry Concentration:** Generalist with a
primary focus in Electronics, High Technology, Information
Technology; **Function Concentration:** Generalist with a
primary focus in Administration, Finance/Accounting, General
Management, Human Resources, Marketing,
Women/Minorities

Vernon, Peter C. — *Managing Director*
Horton International
330 Bay Street, Suite 1104
Toronto, Ontario, CANADA M5H 2S8
Telephone: (416) 861-0077
Recruiter Classification: Retained; **Lowest/Average Salary:**
$90,000/$90,000; **Industry Concentration:** Generalist with a
primary focus in Electronics, High Technology, Information
Technology; **Function Concentration:** Generalist with a
primary focus in Finance/Accounting, General Management,
Human Resources, Marketing, Research and Development,
Sales

Vilella, Paul — *Managing Director*
Source Services Corporation
1111 19th Street NW, Suite 620
Washington, DC 20036
Telephone: (202) 822-0100
Recruiter Classification: Contingency; **Lowest/Average Salary:**
$30,000/$50,000; **Industry Concentration:** Information
Technology; **Function Concentration:** Engineering,
Finance/Accounting

Villella, Paul — *Managing Director*
Source Services Corporation
8614 Westwood Center, Suite 750
Vienna, VA 22182
Telephone: (703) 790-5610
Recruiter Classification: Contingency; **Lowest/Average Salary:**
$30,000/$50,000; **Industry Concentration:** Information
Technology; **Function Concentration:** Engineering,
Finance/Accounting

Vinett-Hessel, Deidre — *Associate*
Source Services Corporation
9020 Capital of Texas Highway
Building I, Suite 337
Austin, TX 78759
Telephone: (512) 345-7473
Recruiter Classification: Contingency; **Lowest/Average Salary:**
$30,000/$50,000; **Industry Concentration:** Information
Technology; **Function Concentration:** Engineering,
Finance/Accounting

Visnich, L. Christine — *Director Executive Search
Consulting*
Bason Associates Inc.
11311 Cornell Park Drive
Cincinnati, OH 45242
Telephone: (513) 469-9881
Recruiter Classification: Retained; **Lowest/Average Salary:**
$60,000/$90,000; **Industry Concentration:** Generalist with a
primary focus in High Technology; **Function Concentration:**
Generalist with a primary focus in Administration, Engineering,
Finance/Accounting, General Management, Human Resources,
Marketing, Research and Development, Sales

Viviano, Cathleen — *Associate*
Source Services Corporation
10300 West 103rd Street, Suite 101
Overland Park, KS 66214
Telephone: (913) 888-8885
Recruiter Classification: Contingency; **Lowest/Average Salary:**
$30,000/$50,000; **Industry Concentration:** Information
Technology; **Function Concentration:** Engineering,
Finance/Accounting

Vlcek, Thomas J. — *President*
Vlcek & Company, Inc.
620 Newport Center Drive
Suite 1100
Newport Beach, CA 92660
Telephone: (714) 752-0661
Recruiter Classification: Retained; **Lowest/Average Salary:**
$90,000/$90,000; **Industry Concentration:** Generalist with a
primary focus in Information Technology; **Function
Concentration:** Generalist with a primary focus in Engineering,
Finance/Accounting, General Management, Human Resources,
Marketing, Sales, Women/Minorities

Vogel, Michael S. — *President*
Vogel Associates
P.O. Box 269X
Huntingdon Valley, PA 19006-0269
Telephone: (215) 938-1700
Recruiter Classification: Contingency; **Lowest/Average Salary:** $40,000/$60,000; **Industry Concentration:** Generalist with a primary focus in High Technology; **Function Concentration:** Human Resources

Voigt, John A. — *Managing Partner*
Romac & Associates
4350 North Fairfax Drive
Suite 400
Arlington, VA 22203
Telephone: (703) 351-7600
Recruiter Classification: Executive Temporary; **Lowest/Average Salary:** $60,000/$60,000; **Industry Concentration:** High Technology, Information Technology; **Function Concentration:** Finance/Accounting

Volkman, Arthur — *Search Consultant*
Cochran, Cochran & Yale, Inc.
1333 W. 120th Avenue, Suite 311
Westminster, CO 80234
Telephone: (303) 252-4600
Recruiter Classification: Retained; **Lowest/Average Salary:** $50,000/$75,000; **Industry Concentration:** Generalist with a primary focus in High Technology, Information Technology; **Function Concentration:** Generalist with a primary focus in Engineering, Finance/Accounting, General Management, Human Resources, Marketing, Sales, Women/Minorities

von Baillou, Astrid — *Principal Managing Director*
Richard Kinser & Associates
919 Third Avenue, 10th Floor
New York, NY 10022
Telephone: (212) 593-5429
Recruiter Classification: Retained; **Lowest/Average Salary:** $90,000/$90,000; **Industry Concentration:** Generalist with a primary focus in High Technology, Information Technology; **Function Concentration:** Generalist with a primary focus in General Management, Marketing, Women/Minorities

Von Karl, Thomas — *Senior Associate*
Juntunen-Combs-Poirier
600 Montgomery Street, 2nd Floor
San Francisco, CA 94111
Telephone: (415) 291-1699
Recruiter Classification: Retained; **Lowest/Average Salary:** $90,000/$90,000; **Industry Concentration:** Information Technology; **Function Concentration:** Marketing, Sales

Vossler, James — *Professional Recruiter*
A.J. Burton Group, Inc.
4550 Montgomery Avenue, Ste. 325 North
Bethesda, MD 20814
Telephone: (301) 654-0082
Recruiter Classification: Contingency; **Lowest/Average Salary:** $40,000/$75,000; **Industry Concentration:** Generalist with a primary focus in High Technology, Information Technology; **Function Concentration:** Generalist with a primary focus in Administration, Finance/Accounting, General Management, Human Resources

Vourakis, Zan — *President*
ZanExec LLC
2063 Madrillon Road
Vienna, VA 22182
Telephone: (703) 734-9440
Recruiter Classification: Retained; **Lowest/Average Salary:** $90,000/$90,000; **Industry Concentration:** High Technology; **Function Concentration:** Engineering, Finance/Accounting, General Management, Marketing, Research and Development, Sales

Vroom, Cynthia D. — *President*
Cyntal International Ltd
310 Madison Avenue
Suite 1212
New York, NY 10017
Telephone: (212) 661-1271
Recruiter Classification: Retained; **Lowest/Average Salary:** $30,000/$50,000; **Industry Concentration:** Generalist with a primary focus in High Technology; **Function Concentration:** Generalist with a primary focus in Finance/Accounting, General Management, Human Resources, Marketing, Sales, Women/Minorities

Vujcec, John — *Associate*
Executive Search, Ltd.
4830 Interstate Drive
Cincinnati, OH 45246
Telephone: (513) 874-6901
Recruiter Classification: Retained; **Lowest/Average Salary:** $50,000/$75,000; **Industry Concentration:** Generalist with a primary focus in Electronics, Information Technology; **Function Concentration:** Human Resources

Wacholz, Rick — *Vice President*
A.T. Kearney, Inc.
One Memorial Drive, 14th Floor
Cambridge, MA 02142
Telephone: (617) 374-2600
Recruiter Classification: Retained; **Lowest/Average Salary:** $90,000/$90,000; **Industry Concentration:** Generalist with a primary focus in High Technology, Information Technology; **Function Concentration:** Generalist with a primary focus in Engineering, Finance/Accounting, General Management

Wade, Christy — *Associate*
Source Services Corporation
520 Post Oak Boulevard, Suite 700
Houston, TX 77027
Telephone: (713) 439-1077
Recruiter Classification: Contingency; **Lowest/Average Salary:** $30,000/$50,000; **Industry Concentration:** Information Technology; **Function Concentration:** Engineering, Finance/Accounting

Waldoch, D. Mark — *Consultant*
Barnes Development Group, LLC
1017 West Glen Oaks Lane, Suite 108
Mequon, WI 53092
Telephone: (414) 241-8468
Recruiter Classification: Retained; **Lowest/Average Salary:** $50,000/$75,000; **Industry Concentration:** Electronics, Information Technology; **Function Concentration:** Generalist with a primary focus in Administration, Engineering, Finance/Accounting, General Management, Human Resources, Marketing, Research and Development, Sales

Waldrop, Gary R. — *Manager*
MSI International
230 Peachtree Street, N.E.
Suite 1550
Atlanta, GA 30303
Telephone: (404) 653-7360
Recruiter Classification: Contingency; **Lowest/Average Salary:** $30,000/$60,000; **Industry Concentration:** Generalist with a primary focus in High Technology, Information Technology; **Function Concentration:** Generalist with a primary focus in Administration, Engineering, Finance/Accounting, General Management, Marketing, Sales

Walker, Ann — *Associate*
Source Services Corporation
111 Monument Circle, Suite 3930
Indianapolis, IN 46204
Telephone: (317) 631-2900
Recruiter Classification: Contingency; **Lowest/Average Salary:** $30,000/$50,000; **Industry Concentration:** Information Technology; **Function Concentration:** Engineering, Finance/Accounting

Walker, Craig H. — *Professional Recruiter*
A.J. Burton Group, Inc.
120 East Baltimore Street, Suite 2220
Baltimore, MD 21202
Telephone: (410) 752-5244
Recruiter Classification: Contingency; **Lowest/Average Salary:** $40,000/$75,000; **Industry Concentration:** Generalist with a primary focus in High Technology, Information Technology; **Function Concentration:** Generalist with a primary focus in Administration, Finance/Accounting, General Management, Human Resources

Walker, Douglas G. — *Managing Director*
Sink, Walker, Boltrus International
60 Walnut Street
Wellesley, MA 02181
Telephone: (617) 237-1199
Recruiter Classification: Retained; **Lowest/Average Salary:** $90,000/$90,000; **Industry Concentration:** Electronics, High Technology, Information Technology; **Function Concentration:** Engineering, General Management, Research and Development, Sales

Walker, Ewing J. — *Managing Director*
Ward Howell International, Inc.
1000 Louisiana Street
Suite 3150
Houston, TX 77002
Telephone: (713) 655-7155
Recruiter Classification: Retained; **Lowest/Average Salary:** $90,000/$90,000; **Industry Concentration:** High Technology; **Function Concentration:** Administration, Engineering, Finance/Accounting, General Management, Human Resources, Marketing, Women/Minorities

Walker, Richard — *Staff Manager*
Bradford & Galt, Inc.
1211 West 22nd Street, Suite 417
Oak Brook, IL 60521
Telephone: (708) 990-4644
Recruiter Classification: Contingency; **Lowest/Average Salary:** $30,000/$30,000; **Industry Concentration:** Generalist with a primary focus in Information Technology; **Function Concentration:** Generalist

Walker, Rose — *Associate*
Source Services Corporation
One Park Plaza, Suite 560
Irvine, CA 92714
Telephone: (714) 660-1666
Recruiter Classification: Contingency; **Lowest/Average Salary:** $30,000/$50,000; **Industry Concentration:** Information Technology; **Function Concentration:** Engineering, Finance/Accounting

Wallace, Toby — *Associate*
Source Services Corporation
5429 LBJ Freeway, Suite 275
Dallas, TX 75240
Telephone: (214) 387-1600
Recruiter Classification: Contingency; **Lowest/Average Salary:** $30,000/$50,000; **Industry Concentration:** Information Technology; **Function Concentration:** Engineering, Finance/Accounting

Walsh, Denis — *Senior Staffing Consultant*
Professional Staffing Consultants
1331 Lamar, Suite 1459
Houston, TX 77010
Telephone: (713) 659-8383
Recruiter Classification: Retained; **Lowest/Average Salary:** $50,000/$75,000; **Industry Concentration:** Generalist with a primary focus in Information Technology; **Function Concentration:** Generalist with a primary focus in Engineering, Finance/Accounting, General Management, Human Resources

Walsh, Kenneth A. — *President*
R/K International, Inc.
191 Post Road West
Westport, CT 06880
Telephone: (203) 221-2747
Recruiter Classification: Retained; **Lowest/Average Salary:** $75,000/$90,000; **Industry Concentration:** Generalist with a primary focus in Electronics; **Function Concentration:** Generalist with a primary focus in Engineering, Finance/Accounting, General Management, Human Resources, Marketing, Research and Development, Sales

Walsh, Patty — *Executive Recruiter*
Abraham & London, Ltd.
237 Danbury Road
Wilton, CT 06897
Telephone: (203) 834-2500
Recruiter Classification: Contingency, Executive Temporary; **Lowest/Average Salary:** $40,000/$75,000; **Industry Concentration:** High Technology, Information Technology; **Function Concentration:** Marketing, Sales

Walters, Scott — *Director*
Paul-Tittle Associates, Inc.
1485 Chain Bridge Road, #304
McLean, VA 22101
Telephone: (703) 442-0500
Recruiter Classification: Retained; **Lowest/Average Salary:** $60,000/$75,000; **Industry Concentration:** Electronics, High Technology, Information Technology; **Function Concentration:** Engineering, Marketing, Research and Development

Walters, William F. — *President*
Jonas, Walters & Assoc., Inc.
1110 North Old World Third St., Suite 510
Milwaukee, WI 53203-1102
Telephone: (414) 291-2828
Recruiter Classification: Retained; **Lowest/Average Salary:**
$75,000/$90,000; **Industry Concentration:** Generalist with a
primary focus in Electronics, High Technology; **Function
Concentration:** Generalist with a primary focus in
Administration, Engineering, Finance/Accounting, General
Management, Human Resources, Marketing, Research and
Development, Sales

Walton, Bruce H. — *Partner*
Heidrick & Struggles, Inc.
One Post Office Square
Suite 3570
Boston, MA 02109-0199
Telephone: (617) 423-1140
Recruiter Classification: Retained; **Lowest/Average Salary:**
$75,000/$90,000; **Industry Concentration:** Generalist with a
primary focus in High Technology; **Function Concentration:**
Generalist

Ward, Jim — *Executive Recruiter*
F-O-R-T-U-N-E Personnel Consultants of
Huntsville, Inc.
3311 Bob Wallace Avenue, Suite 204
Huntsville, AL 35805
Telephone: (205) 534-7282
Recruiter Classification: Contingency; **Lowest/Average Salary:**
$30,000/$75,000; **Industry Concentration:** Electronics, High
Technology, Information Technology

Ward, Les — *President*
Source Services Corporation
5580 LBJ Freeway, Suite 300
Dallas, TX 75240
Telephone: (214) 385-3002
Recruiter Classification: Contingency; **Lowest/Average Salary:**
$30,000/$50,000; **Industry Concentration:** Information
Technology; **Function Concentration:** Engineering,
Finance/Accounting

Ward, Madeleine — *Principal*
LTM Associates
1112 Elizabeth
Naperville, IL 60540
Telephone: (708) 961-3331
Recruiter Classification: Contingency; **Lowest/Average Salary:**
$50,000/$90,000; **Industry Concentration:** High Technology,
Information Technology; **Function Concentration:**
Finance/Accounting, General Management, Sales

Ward, Robert — *Associate*
Source Services Corporation
One Park Plaza, Suite 560
Irvine, CA 92714
Telephone: (714) 660-1666
Recruiter Classification: Contingency; **Lowest/Average Salary:**
$30,000/$50,000; **Industry Concentration:** Information
Technology; **Function Concentration:** Engineering,
Finance/Accounting

Ware, John C. — *Senior Director*
Spencer Stuart
3000 Sand Hill Road
Building 2, Suite 175
Menlo Park, CA 94025
Telephone: (415) 688-1285
Recruiter Classification: Retained; **Lowest/Average Salary:**
$90,000/$90,000; **Industry Concentration:** High Technology,
Information Technology; **Function Concentration:** Generalist
with a primary focus in General Management, Marketing,
Research and Development

Warnock, Phyl — *Associate*
Source Services Corporation
505 East 200 South, Suite 300
Salt Lake City, UT 84102
Telephone: (801) 328-0011
Recruiter Classification: Contingency; **Lowest/Average Salary:**
$30,000/$50,000; **Industry Concentration:** Information
Technology; **Function Concentration:** Engineering,
Finance/Accounting

Warren, Scott — *Partner*
Warren, Morris & Madison
132 Chapel Street
Portsmouth, NH 03801
Telephone: (603) 431-7929
Recruiter Classification: Retained; **Lowest/Average Salary:**
$75,000/$90,000; **Industry Concentration:** High Technology;
Function Concentration: Generalist

Warter, Mark — *Senior Recruiter*
Isaacson, Miller
334 Boylston Street, Suite 500
Boston, MA 02111
Telephone: (617) 262-6500
Recruiter Classification: Retained; **Lowest/Average Salary:**
$75,000/$90,000; **Industry Concentration:** Generalist with a
primary focus in Information Technology; **Function
Concentration:** Administration, Finance/Accounting, General
Management, Human Resources, Women/Minorities

Wasserman, Harvey — *President*
Churchill and Affiliates, Inc.
1200 Bustleton Pike, Suite 3
Feasterville, PA 19053
Telephone: (215) 364-8070
Recruiter Classification: Retained; **Lowest/Average Salary:**
$75,000/$90,000; **Industry Concentration:** Information
Technology; **Function Concentration:** Engineering, General
Management, Marketing, Sales

Wasson, Thomas W. — *Senior Director*
Spencer Stuart
Financial Centre
695 East Main Street
Stamford, CT 06901
Telephone: (203) 324-6333
Recruiter Classification: Retained; **Lowest/Average Salary:**
$90,000/$90,000; **Industry Concentration:** High Technology,
Information Technology; **Function Concentration:** Generalist

Watkins, Jeffrey P. — *Partner*
Lamalie Amrop International
191 Peachtree Street N.E.
Atlanta, GA 30303-1747
Telephone: (404) 688-0800
Recruiter Classification: Retained; **Lowest/Average Salary:**
$90,000/$90,000; **Industry Concentration:** Generalist with a
primary focus in High Technology; **Function Concentration:**
Generalist

Watkinson, Jim W. — *Vice President*
The Badger Group
4125 Blackhawk Plaza Circle, Suite 270
Danville, CA 94506
Telephone: (510) 736-5553
Recruiter Classification: Retained; **Lowest/Average Salary:**
$90,000/$90,000; **Industry Concentration:** Generalist with a
primary focus in Electronics, High Technology, Information
Technology; **Function Concentration:** Generalist with a
primary focus in Engineering, Finance/Accounting, General
Management, Human Resources, Marketing, Research and
Development, Sales

Watson, James — *Vice President*
MSI International
1050 Crown Pointe Parkway
Suite 1000
Atlanta, GA 30338
Telephone: (404) 394-2494
Recruiter Classification: Contingency; **Lowest/Average Salary:**
$30,000/$60,000; **Industry Concentration:** Generalist with a
primary focus in High Technology, Information Technology;
Function Concentration: Administration, Engineering,
Finance/Accounting, General Management, Marketing, Sales

Watson, Peggy — *Regional Manager*
Advanced Information Management
444 Castro Street, Suite 320
Mountain View, CA 94041
Telephone: (415) 965-7799
Recruiter Classification: Contingency; **Lowest/Average Salary:**
$20,000/$40,000; **Industry Concentration:** Information
Technology; **Function Concentration:** Human Resources,
Women/Minorities

Watson, Stephen — *Partner*
Ray & Berndtson
Texas Commerce Tower
2200 Ross Avenue, Suite 4500W
Dallas, TX 75201
Telephone: (214) 969-7620
Recruiter Classification: Retained; **Lowest/Average Salary:**
$90,000/$90,000; **Industry Concentration:** High Technology;
Function Concentration: Generalist

Waymire, Pamela — *Associate*
Source Services Corporation
One South Main Street, Suite 1440
Dayton, OH 45402
Telephone: (513) 461-4660
Recruiter Classification: Contingency; **Lowest/Average Salary:**
$30,000/$50,000; **Industry Concentration:** Information
Technology; **Function Concentration:** Engineering,
Finance/Accounting

Wayne, Cary S. — *President*
ProSearch Inc.
2550 SOM Center Road
Suite 320
Willoughby Hills, OH 44094
Telephone: (216) 585-9099
Recruiter Classification: Contingency; **Lowest/Average Salary:**
$40,000/$75,000; **Industry Concentration:** High Technology,
Information Technology; **Function Concentration:**
Administration, Engineering, Finance/Accounting, General
Management, Human Resources, Marketing, Research and
Development, Sales

Webb, George H. — *Managing Director*
Webb, Johnson Associates, Inc.
280 Park Avenue, 43rd Floor
New York, NY 10017
Telephone: (212) 661-3700
Recruiter Classification: Retained; **Lowest/Average Salary:**
$90,000/$90,000; **Industry Concentration:** Generalist with a
primary focus in High Technology; **Function Concentration:**
Generalist with a primary focus in Administration, Engineering,
Finance/Accounting, General Management, Human Resources,
Marketing, Research and Development, Sales

Webber, Edward — *Associate*
Source Services Corporation
155 Federal Street, Suite 410
Boston, MA 02110
Telephone: (617) 482-8211
Recruiter Classification: Contingency; **Lowest/Average Salary:**
$30,000/$50,000; **Industry Concentration:** Information
Technology; **Function Concentration:** Engineering,
Finance/Accounting

Weber, Fred — *Managing Director*
J.B. Homer Associates, Inc.
Graybar Building
420 Lexington Avenue, Suite 2328
New York, NY 10170
Telephone: (212) 697-3300
Recruiter Classification: Retained; **Lowest/Average Salary:**
$90,000/$90,000; **Industry Concentration:** Generalist with a
primary focus in Information Technology; **Function
Concentration:** Generalist

Weeks, Glenn — *Associate*
Source Services Corporation
5343 North 16th Street, Suite 270
Phoenix, AZ 85016
Telephone: (602) 230-0220
Recruiter Classification: Contingency; **Lowest/Average Salary:**
$30,000/$50,000; **Industry Concentration:** Information
Technology; **Function Concentration:** Engineering,
Finance/Accounting

Wein, Michael S. — *Chairman*
InterimManagement Solutions, Inc.
6464 South Quebec Street
Englewood, CO 80111
Telephone: (303) 290-9500
Recruiter Classification: Executive Temporary; **Lowest/Average
Salary:** $50,000/$90,000; **Industry Concentration:** Electronics,
High Technology, Information Technology; **Function
Concentration:** Generalist with a primary focus in
Administration, Engineering, Finance/Accounting, General
Management, Marketing, Research and Development, Sales

Wein, Michael S. — *President*
Media Management Resources, Inc.
6464 South Quebec Street
Englewood, CO 80111
Telephone: (303) 290-9800
Recruiter Classification: Contingency; **Lowest/Average Salary:**
$50,000/$75,000; **Industry Concentration:** High Technology,
Information Technology; **Function Concentration:**
Administration, Engineering, General Management, Marketing,
Research and Development, Sales, Women/Minorities

Wein, William — *Vice President*
Media Management Resources, Inc.
6464 South Quebec Street
Englewood, CO 80111
Telephone: (303) 290-9800
Recruiter Classification: Contingency; **Lowest/Average Salary:** $50,000/$75,000; **Industry Concentration:** High Technology, Information Technology; **Function Concentration:** Administration, Engineering, General Management, Marketing, Research and Development, Sales, Women/Minorities

Wein, William — *Associate*
InterimManagement Solutions, Inc.
6464 South Quebec Street
Englewood, CO 80111
Telephone: (303) 290-9500
Recruiter Classification: Executive Temporary; **Lowest/Average Salary:** $50,000/$90,000; **Industry Concentration:** High Technology, Information Technology; **Function Concentration:** Generalist with a primary focus in Administration, Engineering, General Management, Marketing, Sales

Weinberg, Melvin — *Managing Partner*
Romac & Associates
1001 Craig Road, Suite 260
St. Louis, MO 63146
Telephone: (314) 569-9898
Recruiter Classification: Executive Temporary; **Lowest/Average Salary:** $60,000/$60,000; **Industry Concentration:** High Technology, Information Technology; **Function Concentration:** Finance/Accounting

Weis, Theodore — *Associate*
Source Services Corporation
5343 North 16th Street, Suite 270
Phoenix, AZ 85016
Telephone: (602) 230-0220
Recruiter Classification: Contingency; **Lowest/Average Salary:** $30,000/$50,000; **Industry Concentration:** Information Technology; **Function Concentration:** Engineering, Finance/Accounting

Weiss, Elizabeth — *Associate*
Source Services Corporation
5429 LBJ Freeway, Suite 275
Dallas, TX 75240
Telephone: (214) 387-1600
Recruiter Classification: Contingency; **Lowest/Average Salary:** $30,000/$50,000; **Industry Concentration:** Information Technology; **Function Concentration:** Engineering, Finance/Accounting

Weissman-Rosenthal, Abbe —
President/Consultant
ALW Research International
60 Canterbury Road
Chatham, NJ 07928
Telephone: (201) 701-9700
Recruiter Classification: Retained; **Lowest/Average Salary:** $60,000/$75,000; **Industry Concentration:** Generalist with a primary focus in Electronics, High Technology; **Function Concentration:** Generalist with a primary focus in Engineering, Finance/Accounting, General Management, Human Resources, Marketing, Research and Development, Sales, Women/Minorities

Weisz, Laura — *Recruiter*
Anderson Sterling Associates
18623 Ventura Boulevard, Suite 207
Tarzana, CA 91356
Telephone: (818) 996-0921
Recruiter Classification: Executive Temporary; **Lowest/Average Salary:** $30,000/$60,000; **Industry Concentration:** Electronics, High Technology, Information Technology; **Function Concentration:** Engineering, Finance/Accounting, General Management, Human Resources, Marketing, Research and Development, Sales, Women/Minorities

Welch, Dale — *Software Engineering Recruiter*
Winter, Wyman & Company
950 Winter Street, Suite 3100
Waltham, MA 02154-1294
Telephone: (617) 890-7000
Recruiter Classification: Contingency; **Lowest/Average Salary:** $40,000/$75,000; **Industry Concentration:** High Technology, Information Technology; **Function Concentration:** Engineering

Welch, Robert — *Consultant*
Ray & Berndtson
2029 Century Park East, Suite 1000
Los Angeles, CA 90067
Telephone: (310) 557-2828
Recruiter Classification: Retained; **Lowest/Average Salary:** $90,000/$90,000; **Industry Concentration:** Generalist with a primary focus in High Technology, Information Technology; **Function Concentration:** Generalist with a primary focus in Administration, Finance/Accounting, General Management, Human Resources, Marketing, Research and Development, Sales, Women/Minorities

Weller, Paul S. — *Senior Partner*
Mark Stanley/EMA Partners International
1629 K Street N.W.
Suite 1100
Washington, DC 20006-1602
Telephone: (202) 785-6711
Recruiter Classification: Retained; **Lowest/Average Salary:** $75,000/$90,000; **Industry Concentration:** Generalist with a primary focus in High Technology; **Function Concentration:** Generalist with a primary focus in Finance/Accounting, General Management, Human Resources, Sales

Wenz, Alexander — *Associate*
Source Services Corporation
4510 Executive Drive, Suite 200
San Diego, CA 92121
Telephone: (619) 552-0300
Recruiter Classification: Contingency; **Lowest/Average Salary:** $30,000/$50,000; **Industry Concentration:** Information Technology; **Function Concentration:** Engineering, Finance/Accounting

Wert, Marty — *Consultant*
Parfitt Recruiting and Consulting
1540 140th Avenue NE #201
Bellevue, WA 98005
Telephone: (206) 646-6300
Recruiter Classification: Contingency; **Lowest/Average Salary:** $30,000/$75,000; **Industry Concentration:** Generalist with a primary focus in Information Technology; **Function Concentration:** Generalist

Wertheim, Denise — *Senior Consultant*
Paul-Tittle Associates, Inc.
1485 Chain Bridge Road, #304
McLean, VA 22101
Telephone: (703) 442-0500
Recruiter Classification: Retained; **Lowest/Average Salary:**
$60,000/$75,000; **Industry Concentration:** High Technology,
Information Technology; **Function Concentration:** Engineering,
Marketing, Sales

Wessling, Jerry — *Associate*
Source Services Corporation
One South Main Street, Suite 1440
Dayton, OH 45402
Telephone: (513) 461-4660
Recruiter Classification: Contingency; **Lowest/Average Salary:**
$30,000/$50,000; **Industry Concentration:** Information
Technology; **Function Concentration:** Engineering,
Finance/Accounting

Westfall, Ed — *Vice President*
Zwell International
300 South Wacker Drive, Suite 650
Chicago, IL 60606
Telephone: (312) 663-3737
Recruiter Classification: Retained; **Lowest/Average Salary:**
$75,000/$90,000; **Industry Concentration:** Generalist with a
primary focus in Electronics, High Technology; **Function
Concentration:** Generalist with a primary focus in Engineering,
Finance/Accounting, General Management, Human Resources,
Marketing, Sales

Wheatley, William — *Senior Recruiter*
Drummond Associates, Inc.
50 Broadway, Suite 1201
New York, NY 10004
Telephone: (212) 248-1120
Recruiter Classification: Contingency; **Lowest/Average Salary:**
$40,000/$75,000; **Industry Concentration:** Information
Technology; **Function Concentration:** Finance/Accounting

Wheeler, Gerard H. — *Executive Vice President*
A.J. Burton Group, Inc.
120 East Baltimore Street, Suite 2220
Baltimore, MD 21202
Telephone: (410) 752-5244
Recruiter Classification: Contingency; **Lowest/Average Salary:**
$40,000/$75,000; **Industry Concentration:** Generalist with a
primary focus in High Technology, Information Technology;
Function Concentration: Generalist with a primary focus in
Administration, Finance/Accounting, General Management,
Human Resources

Whelan, David — *Principal*
Ethos Consulting Inc.
100 Pine Street
Suite 750
San Francisco, CA 94111
Telephone: (415) 397-2211
Recruiter Classification: Retained; **Lowest/Average Salary:**
$90,000/$90,000; **Industry Concentration:** Generalist with a
primary focus in High Technology, Information Technology;
Function Concentration: Generalist with a primary focus in
General Management

White, William C. — *President*
Venture Resources Inc.
2659 Townsgate Road, Suite 119
Westlake Village, CA 91361
Telephone: (805) 371-3600
Recruiter Classification: Retained; **Lowest/Average Salary:**
$90,000/$90,000; **Industry Concentration:** Electronics, High
Technology, Information Technology; **Function Concentration:**
Generalist with a primary focus in Engineering,
Finance/Accounting, General Management, Marketing,
Research and Development, Sales

Whitfield, Jack — *Associate*
Source Services Corporation
1233 North Mayfair Road, Suite 300
Milwaukee, WI 53226
Telephone: (414) 774-6700
Recruiter Classification: Contingency; **Lowest/Average Salary:**
$30,000/$50,000; **Industry Concentration:** Information
Technology; **Function Concentration:** Engineering,
Finance/Accounting

Whitney, David L. — *President*
Whitney & Associates, Inc.
920 Second Avenue South, Suite 625
Minneapolis, MN 55402-4035
Telephone: (612) 338-5600
Recruiter Classification: Contingency, Executive Temporary;
Lowest/Average Salary: $20,000/$50,000; **Industry
Concentration:** Generalist with a primary focus in Electronics,
High Technology, Information Technology; **Function
Concentration:** Finance/Accounting

Whitt, Mimi — *Executive Recruiter*
F-O-R-T-U-N-E Personnel Consultants of
Huntsville, Inc.
3311 Bob Wallace Avenue, Suite 204
Huntsville, AL 35805
Telephone: (205) 534-7282
Recruiter Classification: Contingency; **Lowest/Average Salary:**
$30,000/$60,000; **Industry Concentration:** Electronics, High
Technology; **Function Concentration:** Engineering

Whyte, Roger J. — *President*
The Whyte Group, Inc.
4800 Montgomery Lane, Suite 600
Bethesda, MD 20814
Telephone: (301) 215-5931
Recruiter Classification: Retained; **Lowest/Average Salary:**
$75,000/$75,000; **Industry Concentration:** Information
Technology; **Function Concentration:** Generalist with a
primary focus in General Management, Human Resources,
Marketing, Sales

Wichansky, Mark — *Executive Recruiter*
TSS Consulting, Ltd.
2425 East Camelback Road
Suite 375
Phoenix, AZ 85016
Telephone: (602) 955-7000
Recruiter Classification: Contingency; **Lowest/Average Salary:**
$60,000/$75,000; **Industry Concentration:** Electronics, High
Technology; **Function Concentration:** Engineering, General
Management, Marketing

Wilburn, Dan — *Search Consultant*
Kaye-Bassman International Corp.
18333 Preston Road, Suite 500
Dallas, TX 75252
Telephone: (972) 931-5242
Recruiter Classification: Retained; **Lowest/Average Salary:**
$60,000/$60,000; **Industry Concentration:** High Technology,
Information Technology; **Function Concentration:** Engineering,
Human Resources, Marketing, Research and Development,
Sales

Wilcox, Fred T. — *President*
Wilcox, Bertoux & Miller
100 Howe Avenue, Suite 155N
Sacramento, CA 95825
Telephone: (916) 977-3700
Recruiter Classification: Contingency; **Lowest/Average Salary:**
$50,000/$90,000; **Industry Concentration:** Information
Technology; **Function Concentration:** Administration,
Finance/Accounting, General Management

Wilder, Richard B. — *Managing Principal*
Columbia Consulting Group
10725 East Cholla Lane
Scottsdale, AZ 85259
Telephone: (602) 451-1180
Recruiter Classification: Retained; **Lowest/Average Salary:**
$75,000/$90,000; **Industry Concentration:** Generalist with a
primary focus in Electronics, High Technology, Information
Technology; **Function Concentration:** Generalist with a
primary focus in Finance/Accounting, General Management,
Human Resources, Marketing, Sales

Wilkinson, Barbara — *Associate*
Beall & Company, Inc.
535 Colonial Park Drive
Roswell, GA 30075
Telephone: (404) 992-0900
Recruiter Classification: Retained; **Lowest/Average Salary:**
$90,000/$90,000; **Industry Concentration:** Generalist with a
primary focus in High Technology; **Function Concentration:**
Generalist with a primary focus in Administration, Engineering,
Finance/Accounting, General Management, Human Resources,
Marketing, Research and Development, Sales

Wilkinson, Jr. SPHR
The HRM Group, Inc.
321 Lorna Square
Birmingham, AL 35216
Telephone: (205) 978-7181
Recruiter Classification: Retained; **Lowest/Average Salary:**
$30,000/$50,000; **Industry Concentration:** Generalist with a
primary focus in Information Technology; **Function
Concentration:** Generalist with a primary focus in
Finance/Accounting, General Management, Human Resources,
Marketing, Sales

Willbrandt, Curt — *Associate*
Source Services Corporation
161 Ottawa NW, Suite 409D
Grand Rapids, MI 49503
Telephone: (616) 451-2400
Recruiter Classification: Contingency; **Lowest/Average Salary:**
$30,000/$50,000; **Industry Concentration:** Information
Technology; **Function Concentration:** Engineering,
Finance/Accounting

Williams, Angie — *Executive Recruiter*
Whitney & Associates, Inc.
920 Second Avenue South, Suite 625
Minneapolis, MN 55402-4035
Telephone: (612) 338-5600
Recruiter Classification: Contingency, Executive Temporary;
Lowest/Average Salary: $20,000/$50,000; **Industry
Concentration:** Generalist with a primary focus in Electronics,
High Technology, Information Technology; **Function
Concentration:** Finance/Accounting

Williams, Brad — *Information Technology
Recruiter*
Winter, Wyman & Company
950 Winter Street, Suite 3100
Waltham, MA 02154-1294
Telephone: (617) 890-7000
Recruiter Classification: Contingency; **Lowest/Average Salary:**
$30,000/$60,000; **Industry Concentration:** Generalist with a
primary focus in Information Technology; **Function
Concentration:** Generalist

Williams, Dave — *Consultant*
The McCormick Group, Inc.
1400 Wilson Boulevard
Arlington, VA 22209
Telephone: (703) 841-1700
Recruiter Classification: Retained; **Lowest/Average Salary:**
$40,000/$60,000; **Industry Concentration:** Generalist with a
primary focus in High Technology, Information Technology;
Function Concentration: Engineering, Marketing, Sales

Williams, Gary L. — *Consultant*
Barnes Development Group, LLC
1017 West Glen Oaks Lane, Suite 108
Mequon, WI 53092
Telephone: (414) 241-8468
Recruiter Classification: Retained; **Lowest/Average Salary:**
$50,000/$75,000; **Industry Concentration:** Generalist with a
primary focus in Electronics, Information Technology; **Function
Concentration:** Generalist with a primary focus in
Administration, Engineering, Finance/Accounting, General
Management, Human Resources, Marketing, Research and
Development, Sales

Williams, Jack — *Vice President*
A.T. Kearney, Inc.
Lincoln Plaza, Suite 4170
500 North Akard Street
Dallas, TX 75201
Telephone: (214) 969-0010
Recruiter Classification: Retained; **Lowest/Average Salary:**
$90,000/$90,000; **Industry Concentration:** Generalist with a
primary focus in High Technology, Information Technology;
Function Concentration: Generalist with a primary focus in
Engineering, Finance/Accounting, General Management

Williams, John — *Associate*
Source Services Corporation
2850 National City Tower
Louisville, KY 40202
Telephone: (502) 581-9900
Recruiter Classification: Contingency; **Lowest/Average Salary:**
$30,000/$50,000; **Industry Concentration:** Information
Technology; **Function Concentration:** Engineering,
Finance/Accounting

Williams, Roger K. — *Partner*
Williams, Roth & Krueger Inc.
20 North Wacker Drive
Chicago, IL 60606
Telephone: (312) 977-0800
Recruiter Classification: Retained; **Lowest/Average Salary:**
$90,000/$90,000; **Industry Concentration:** Generalist with a
primary focus in Electronics, High Technology, Information
Technology; **Function Concentration:** Generalist with a
primary focus in Administration, Engineering,
Finance/Accounting, General Management, Human Resources,
Marketing, Sales

Williams, Scott D. — *Partner*
Heidrick & Struggles, Inc.
2200 Ross Avenue, Suite 4700E
Dallas, TX 75201-2787
Telephone: (214) 220-2130
Recruiter Classification: Retained; **Lowest/Average Salary:**
$75,000/$90,000; **Industry Concentration:** Generalist with a
primary focus in High Technology; **Function Concentration:**
Generalist

Williams, Stephen E. — *Senior Consultant*
Barton Associates, Inc.
One Riverway, Suite 2500
Houston, TX 77056
Telephone: (713) 961-9111
Recruiter Classification: Retained; **Lowest/Average Salary:**
$75,000/$90,000; **Industry Concentration:** Generalist with a
primary focus in Electronics, High Technology, Information
Technology; **Function Concentration:** Generalist with a
primary focus in Finance/Accounting, General Management,
Human Resources, Marketing, Sales

Williams, Walter E. — *Partner*
Lamalie Amrop International
10 Post Office Square
Boston, MA 02109-4603
Telephone: (617) 292-6242
Recruiter Classification: Retained; **Lowest/Average Salary:**
$90,000/$90,000; **Industry Concentration:** Generalist with a
primary focus in High Technology; **Function Concentration:**
Generalist

Willner, Leo — *Associate*
William Guy & Associates
P.O. Box 57407
Sherman Oaks, CA 91413
Telephone:Unpublished
Recruiter Classification: Retained; **Lowest/Average Salary:**
$50,000/$90,000; **Industry Concentration:** Generalist with a
primary focus in Electronics, High Technology, Information
Technology; **Function Concentration:** Generalist with a
primary focus in Administration, Engineering, General
Management, Marketing, Research and Development, Sales,
Women/Minorities

Wilson, Don — *Partner*
Allerton Heneghan & O'Neill
70 West Madison Street, Suite 2015
Chicago, IL 60602
Telephone: (312) 263-1075
Recruiter Classification: Retained; **Lowest/Average Salary:**
$75,000/$90,000; **Industry Concentration:** Generalist with a
primary focus in Electronics; **Function Concentration:**
Generalist with a primary focus in Engineering,
Finance/Accounting, General Management, Human Resources

Wilson, John — *Vice President*
Korn/Ferry International
The Transamerica Pyramid
600 Montgomery Street
San Francisco, CA 94111
Telephone: (415) 956-1834
Recruiter Classification: Retained; **Lowest/Average Salary:**
$100,000/$150,000; **Industry Concentration:** Generalist with a
primary focus in Information Technology; **Function
Concentration:** Generalist

Wilson, Joyce — *Associate*
Source Services Corporation
One Park Plaza, Suite 560
Irvine, CA 92714
Telephone: (714) 660-1666
Recruiter Classification: Contingency; **Lowest/Average Salary:**
$30,000/$50,000; **Industry Concentration:** Information
Technology; **Function Concentration:** Engineering,
Finance/Accounting

Wilson, Patricia L. — *Partner*
Leon A. Farley Associates
468 Jackson Street
San Francisco, CA 94111
Telephone: (415) 989-0989
Recruiter Classification: Retained; **Lowest/Average Salary:**
$90,000/$90,000; **Industry Concentration:** Generalist with a
primary focus in Electronics, High Technology, Information
Technology; **Function Concentration:** Generalist with a
primary focus in Administration, Finance/Accounting, General
Management, Human Resources, Marketing, Sales,
Women/Minorities

Wilson, Steven J. — *Partner*
Herman Smith Executive Initiatives Inc.
161 Bay Street, Suite 3600
Box 629
Toronto, Ontario, CANADA M5J 2S1
Telephone: (416) 862-8830
Recruiter Classification: Retained; **Lowest/Average Salary:**
$60,000/$90,000; **Industry Concentration:** Generalist with a
primary focus in Electronics, High Technology; **Function
Concentration:** Generalist with a primary focus in Engineering,
Finance/Accounting, General Management, Human Resources,
Marketing

Wingate, Mary — *Associate*
Source Services Corporation
5429 LBJ Freeway, Suite 275
Dallas, TX 75240
Telephone: (214) 387-1600
Recruiter Classification: Contingency; **Lowest/Average Salary:**
$30,000/$50,000; **Industry Concentration:** Information
Technology; **Function Concentration:** Engineering,
Finance/Accounting

Winitz, Joel — *President*
GSW Consulting Group, Inc.
401 B Street
Suite 340
San Diego, CA 92101
Telephone: (619) 696-7900
Recruiter Classification: Retained; **Lowest/Average Salary:**
$60,000/$90,000; **Industry Concentration:** Generalist with a
primary focus in Electronics, High Technology, Information
Technology; **Function Concentration:** Generalist with a
primary focus in Engineering, Finance/Accounting, General
Management, Marketing, Research and Development, Sales

Winitz, Marla — *Vice President*
GSW Consulting Group, Inc.
401 B Street
Suite 340
San Diego, CA 92101
Telephone: (619) 696-7900
Recruiter Classification: Retained; **Lowest/Average Salary:**
$60,000/$90,000; **Industry Concentration:** Generalist with a
primary focus in Electronics, High Technology, Information
Technology; **Function Concentration:** Generalist with a
primary focus in Engineering, Finance/Accounting, General
Management, Marketing, Research and Development, Sales

Winkowski, Stephen — *Associate*
Source Services Corporation
20 Burlington Mall Road, Suite 405
Burlington, MA 01803
Telephone: (617) 272-5000
Recruiter Classification: Contingency; **Lowest/Average Salary:**
$30,000/$50,000; **Industry Concentration:** Information
Technology; **Function Concentration:** Engineering,
Finance/Accounting

Winnicki, Kimberly — *Associate*
Source Services Corporation
120 East Baltimore Street, Suite 1950
Baltimore, MD 21202
Telephone: (410) 727-4050
Recruiter Classification: Contingency; **Lowest/Average Salary:**
$30,000/$50,000; **Industry Concentration:** Information
Technology; **Function Concentration:** Engineering,
Finance/Accounting

Winograd, Glenn — *Vice President/Division
Manager*
Criterion Executive Search, Inc.
5420 Bay Center Drive, Suite 101
Tampa, FL 33609-3402
Telephone: (813) 286-2000
Recruiter Classification: Contingency; **Lowest/Average Salary:**
$40,000/$90,000; **Industry Concentration:** Generalist with a
primary focus in Electronics, High Technology, Information
Technology; **Function Concentration:** Generalist with a
primary focus in Engineering, Finance/Accounting, General
Management, Research and Development, Women/Minorities

Winston, Dale — *President*
Battalia Winston International
300 Park Avenue
New York, NY 10022
Telephone: (212) 308-8080
Recruiter Classification: Retained; **Lowest/Average Salary:**
$90,000/$90,000; **Industry Concentration:** Generalist with a
primary focus in Electronics, Information Technology; **Function
Concentration:** Generalist with a primary focus in Engineering,
Finance/Accounting, General Management, Human Resources,
Marketing, Research and Development, Sales,
Women/Minorities

Wirtshafter, Linda — *Senior Associate*
Grant Cooper and Associates
795 Office Parkway, Suite 117
St. Louis, MO 63141
Telephone: (314) 567-4690
Recruiter Classification: Retained; **Lowest/Average Salary:**
$60,000/$90,000; **Industry Concentration:** Generalist with a
primary focus in Electronics; **Function Concentration:**
Generalist

Wise, J. Herbert — *Partner*
Sandhurst Associates
4851 LBJ Freeway, Suite 601
Dallas, TX 75244
Telephone: (212) 458-1212
Recruiter Classification: Retained; **Lowest/Average Salary:**
$75,000/$90,000; **Industry Concentration:** Generalist with a
primary focus in High Technology; **Function Concentration:**
Generalist with a primary focus in Finance/Accounting, Human
Resources, Marketing, Sales

Witt, Clayton — *Director*
Paul-Tittle Associates, Inc.
1485 Chain Bridge Road, #304
McLean, VA 22101
Telephone: (703) 442-0500
Recruiter Classification: Retained; **Lowest/Average Salary:**
$60,000/$75,000; **Industry Concentration:** Electronics, High
Technology; **Function Concentration:** Engineering, Marketing,
Sales

Witte, David L. — *Chief Executive Officer*
Ward Howell International, Inc.
99 Park Avenue, Suite 2000
New York, NY 10016-1699
Telephone: (212) 697-3730
Recruiter Classification: Retained; **Lowest/Average Salary:**
$90,000/$90,000; **Industry Concentration:** Information
Technology; **Function Concentration:** Generalist with a
primary focus in Administration, Engineering, General
Management

Witzgall, William — *Associate*
Source Services Corporation
525 Vine Street, Suite 2250
Cincinnati, OH 45202
Telephone: (513) 651-3303
Recruiter Classification: Contingency; **Lowest/Average Salary:**
$30,000/$50,000; **Industry Concentration:** Information
Technology; **Function Concentration:** Engineering,
Finance/Accounting

Wold, Ted W. — *Secretary*
Hyde Danforth Wold & Co.
5950 Berkshire Lane, Suite 1600
Dallas, TX 75225
Telephone: (214) 691-5966
Recruiter Classification: Retained; **Lowest/Average Salary:**
$50,000/$75,000; **Industry Concentration:** Generalist with a
primary focus in Electronics, High Technology; **Function
Concentration:** Generalist with a primary focus in
Administration, Finance/Accounting, Human Resources,
Marketing, Research and Development

Wolf, Donald — *Associate*
Source Services Corporation
111 Founders Plaza, Suite 1501E
Hartford, CT 06108
Telephone: (860) 528-0300
Recruiter Classification: Contingency; **Lowest/Average Salary:**
$30,000/$50,000; **Industry Concentration:** Information
Technology; **Function Concentration:** Engineering,
Finance/Accounting

Wolf, Stephen M. — *Principal*
Byron Leonard International, Inc.
2659 Townsgate Road, Suite 100
Westlake Village, CA 91361
Telephone: (805) 373-7500
Recruiter Classification: Retained; **Lowest/Average Salary:**
$60,000/$90,000; **Industry Concentration:** Generalist with a
primary focus in Electronics, High Technology, Information
Technology; **Function Concentration:** Generalist with a
primary focus in Administration, Finance/Accounting, General
Management, Human Resources, Marketing, Research and
Development, Sales

Wolfe, Peter — *Managing Director*
Source Services Corporation
4200 West Cypress Street, Suite 101
Tampa, FL 33607
Telephone: (813) 879-2221
Recruiter Classification: Contingency; **Lowest/Average Salary:**
$30,000/$50,000; **Industry Concentration:** Information
Technology; **Function Concentration:** Engineering,
Finance/Accounting

Womack, Joseph — *Vice President*
The Bankers Group
10 South Riverside Plaza, Suite 1424
Chicago, IL 60606
Telephone: (312) 930-9456
Recruiter Classification: Contingency; **Lowest/Average Salary:**
$50,000/$75,000; **Industry Concentration:** Generalist with a
primary focus in High Technology, Information Technology;
Function Concentration: Generalist with a primary focus in
Administration, Finance/Accounting, General Management,
Human Resources, Marketing, Sales, Women/Minorities

Wood, Gary — *Associate*
Source Services Corporation
3 Summit Park Drive, Suite 550
Independence, OH 44131
Telephone: (216) 328-5900
Recruiter Classification: Contingency; **Lowest/Average Salary:**
$30,000/$50,000; **Industry Concentration:** Information
Technology; **Function Concentration:** Engineering,
Finance/Accounting

Wood, John S. — *Consultant*
Egon Zehnder International Inc.
350 Park Avenue
New York, NY 10022
Telephone: (212) 838-9199
Recruiter Classification: Retained; **Lowest/Average Salary:**
$90,000/$90,000; **Industry Concentration:** Generalist with a
primary focus in High Technology; **Function Concentration:**
Generalist

Wood, Milton M. — *President*
M. Wood Company
10 North Dearborn Street, Suite 700
Chicago, IL 60602
Telephone: (312) 368-0633
Recruiter Classification: Retained; **Lowest/Average Salary:**
$60,000/$90,000; **Industry Concentration:** Generalist with a
primary focus in Information Technology; **Function
Concentration:** Generalist with a primary focus in General
Management, Human Resources, Marketing, Sales

Woodhouse, Michael — *Recruitment Support*
Ashton Computer Professionals Inc.
Lonsdale Quay
15-C Chesterfield Pl.
Vancouver, B.C., CANADA V7M 3K3
Telephone: (604) 904-0304
Recruiter Classification: Contingency; **Lowest/Average Salary:**
$30,000/$60,000; **Industry Concentration:** High Technology,
Information Technology; **Function Concentration:** Research
and Development

Woodmansee, Bruce J. — *Partner*
Tully/Woodmansee International, Inc.
7720 Rivers Edge Drive, Suite 101
Columbus, OH 43235
Telephone: (614) 844-5480
Recruiter Classification: Retained; **Lowest/Average Salary:**
$60,000/$90,000; **Industry Concentration:** Generalist with a
primary focus in Electronics, High Technology; **Function
Concentration:** Generalist with a primary focus in Engineering,
Finance/Accounting, General Management, Human Resources,
Marketing, Sales

Woods, Craig — *Associate*
Source Services Corporation
One Park Plaza, Suite 560
Irvine, CA 92714
Telephone: (714) 660-1666
Recruiter Classification: Contingency; **Lowest/Average Salary:**
$30,000/$50,000; **Industry Concentration:** Information
Technology; **Function Concentration:** Engineering,
Finance/Accounting

Woodward, Lee — *Co-President*
Search Associates, Inc.
5900 Sepulveda Boulevard, Suite 104
Van Nuys, CA 91411
Telephone: (818) 989-2200
Recruiter Classification: Contingency; **Lowest/Average Salary:**
$30,000/$50,000; **Industry Concentration:** Electronics, High
Technology; **Function Concentration:** Research and
Development, Women/Minorities

Woodworth, Gail — *President*
Woodworth International Group
620 SW 5th Avenue, Suite 1225
Portland, OR 97204
Telephone: (503) 225-5000
Recruiter Classification: Retained; **Lowest/Average Salary:**
$60,000/$90,000; **Industry Concentration:** Generalist with a
primary focus in Electronics, High Technology, Information
Technology; **Function Concentration:** Generalist with a
primary focus in Engineering, Finance/Accounting, General
Management, Human Resources, Marketing, Research and
Development, Sales

Wooldridge, Jeff — *Consultant*
Ray & Berndtson
Texas Commerce Tower
2200 Ross Avenue, Suite 4500W
Dallas, TX 75201
Telephone: (214) 969-7620
Recruiter Classification: Retained; **Lowest/Average Salary:**
$90,000/$90,000; **Industry Concentration:** Generalist with a
primary focus in High Technology, Information Technology;
Function Concentration: Generalist with a primary focus in
Administration, Finance/Accounting, General Management,
Human Resources, Marketing, Research and Development,
Sales, Women/Minorities

Woollett, James — *Vice President*
Rusher, Loscavio & LoPresto
2479 Bayshore Road, Suite 700
Palo Alto, CA 94303
Telephone: (415) 494-0883
Recruiter Classification: Retained; **Lowest/Average Salary:**
$75,000/$75,000; **Industry Concentration:** Electronics, High
Technology, Information Technology; **Function Concentration:**
Generalist with a primary focus in Administration, Engineering,
General Management, Marketing, Research and Development,
Sales

Woomer, Jerome — *Associate*
Source Services Corporation
7730 East Bellview Avenue, Suite 302
Englewood, CO 80111
Telephone: (303) 773-3700
Recruiter Classification: Contingency; **Lowest/Average Salary:**
$30,000/$50,000; **Industry Concentration:** Information
Technology; **Function Concentration:** Engineering,
Finance/Accounting

Work, Alan — *Executive Vice President*
Quantex Associates, Inc.
444 Madison Avenue, Suite 710
New York, NY 10022
Telephone: (212) 935-2100
Recruiter Classification: Retained; **Lowest/Average Salary:**
$90,000/$90,000; **Industry Concentration:** Electronics, High
Technology, Information Technology; **Function Concentration:**
General Management, Human Resources, Marketing, Sales

Workman, David — *Associate*
Source Services Corporation
2850 National City Tower
Louisville, KY 40202
Telephone: (502) 581-9900
Recruiter Classification: Contingency; **Lowest/Average Salary:**
$30,000/$50,000; **Industry Concentration:** Information
Technology; **Function Concentration:** Engineering,
Finance/Accounting

Wren, Jay — *President*
Jay Wren & Associates
6355 Riverside Boulevard, Suite P
Sacramento, CA 95831
Telephone: (916) 394-2920
Recruiter Classification: Contingency; **Lowest/Average Salary:**
$30,000/$90,000; **Industry Concentration:** Information
Technology; **Function Concentration:** Marketing, Sales

Wright, A. Leo — *Vice President - Owensboro*
The Hindman Company
Corporate Center
Fourth and Frederica
Owensboro, KY 42301
Telephone: (502) 688-0010
Recruiter Classification: Retained; **Lowest/Average Salary:**
$50,000/$90,000; **Industry Concentration:** Generalist with a
primary focus in High Technology; **Function Concentration:**
Generalist with a primary focus in Administration, Engineering,
Finance/Accounting, General Management, Human Resources,
Marketing, Sales

Wright, Carl A.J. — *President*
A.J. Burton Group, Inc.
120 East Baltimore Street, Suite 2220
Baltimore, MD 21202
Telephone: (410) 752-5244
Recruiter Classification: Contingency, Executive Temporary;
Lowest/Average Salary: $40,000/$75,000; **Industry
Concentration:** Generalist with a primary focus in High
Technology, Information Technology; **Function Concentration:**
Generalist with a primary focus in Administration,
Finance/Accounting, General Management, Human Resources

Wright, Charles D. — *Senior Vice President*
Goodrich & Sherwood Associates, Inc.
401 Merritt Seven Corporate Park
Norwalk, CT 06851
Telephone: (203) 847-2525
Recruiter Classification: Retained; **Lowest/Average Salary:**
$60,000/$90,000; **Industry Concentration:** Generalist with a
primary focus in Information Technology; **Function
Concentration:** Generalist with a primary focus in
Administration, Finance/Accounting, General Management,
Human Resources, Marketing, Sales

Wright, Leslie — *Vice President and Director of
Research*
The Stevenson Group of New Jersey
560 Sylvan Avenue
Englewood Cliffs, NJ 07632
Telephone: (201) 568-1900
Recruiter Classification: Retained; **Lowest/Average Salary:**
$75,000/$90,000; **Industry Concentration:** Generalist with a
primary focus in Information Technology; **Function
Concentration:** Generalist with a primary focus in
Finance/Accounting, General Management, Human Resources,
Marketing, Sales

Wyatt, James — *President*
Wyatt & Jaffe
9900 Bren Road East, Suite 550
Minnetonka, MN 55343-9668
Telephone: (612) 945-0099
Recruiter Classification: Retained; **Lowest/Average Salary:**
$90,000/$90,000; **Industry Concentration:** High Technology;
Function Concentration: Generalist with a primary focus in
Engineering, General Management, Human Resources,
Marketing, Research and Development, Sales

Wycoff-Viola, Amy — *Associate*
Source Services Corporation
150 South Wacker Drive, Suite 400
Chicago, IL 60606
Telephone: (312) 346-7000
Recruiter Classification: Contingency; **Lowest/Average Salary:**
$30,000/$50,000; **Industry Concentration:** Information
Technology; **Function Concentration:** Engineering,
Finance/Accounting

Yaekle, Gary — *Consultant*
Tully/Woodmansee International, Inc.
7720 Rivers Edge Drive, Suite 101
Columbus, OH 43235
Telephone: (614) 587-7366
Recruiter Classification: Retained; **Lowest/Average Salary:**
$60,000/$90,000; **Industry Concentration:** Generalist with a
primary focus in Electronics, High Technology; **Function
Concentration:** Generalist with a primary focus in Engineering,
Finance/Accounting, General Management, Human Resources,
Marketing, Sales

Yang, George — *Recruiter*
Technical Connections Inc.
11400 Olympic Boulevard, Suite 770
Los Angeles, CA 90064
Telephone: (310) 479-8830
Recruiter Classification: Contingency; **Lowest/Average Salary:** $40,000/$60,000; **Industry Concentration:** High Technology, Information Technology; **Function Concentration:** Generalist

Yeaton, Robert — *Associate*
Source Services Corporation
1500 West Park Drive, Suite 390
Westborough, MA 01581
Telephone: (508) 366-2600
Recruiter Classification: Contingency; **Lowest/Average Salary:** $30,000/$50,000; **Industry Concentration:** Information Technology; **Function Concentration:** Engineering, Finance/Accounting

Yen, Maggie Yeh Ching — *Consultant*
Ray & Berndtson
One Park Plaza, Suite 420
Irvine, CA 92614
Telephone: (714) 476-8844
Recruiter Classification: Retained; **Lowest/Average Salary:** $90,000/$90,000; **Industry Concentration:** Generalist with a primary focus in High Technology, Information Technology; **Function Concentration:** Generalist with a primary focus in Administration, Finance/Accounting, General Management, Human Resources, Marketing, Research and Development, Sales, Women/Minorities

Yossem, Sheila — *Associate*
Bishop Partners
708 Third Avenue
Suite 2200
New York, NY 10017
Telephone: (212) 986-3419
Lowest/Average Salary: $90,000/$90,000; **Industry Concentration:** High Technology, Information Technology; **Function Concentration:** Generalist

Young, Heather — *Director*
The Guild Corporation
8260 Greensboro Drive, Suite 460
McLean, VA 22102
Telephone: (703) 761-4023
Recruiter Classification: Contingency; **Lowest/Average Salary:** $40,000/$50,000; **Industry Concentration:** Electronics, High Technology, Information Technology; **Function Concentration:** Engineering, Finance/Accounting, General Management, Research and Development

Young, Lesley — *Account Executive*
Search West, Inc.
340 North Westlake Boulevard
Suite 200
Westlake Village, CA 91362-3761
Telephone: (805) 496-6811
Recruiter Classification: Contingency; **Lowest/Average Salary:** $40,000/$60,000; **Industry Concentration:** Information Technology; **Function Concentration:** Marketing, Sales

Youngberg, David — *Managing Director*
Source Services Corporation
1233 North Mayfair Road, Suite 300
Milwaukee, WI 53226
Telephone: (414) 774-6700
Recruiter Classification: Contingency; **Lowest/Average Salary:** $30,000/$50,000; **Industry Concentration:** Information Technology; **Function Concentration:** Engineering, Finance/Accounting

Yungerberg, Steven — *President*
Steven Yungerberg Associates Inc.
P.O. Box 458
Minneapolis, MN 55331-0458
Telephone: (612) 470-2288
Recruiter Classification: Retained; **Lowest/Average Salary:** $75,000/$90,000; **Industry Concentration:** Generalist with a primary focus in Information Technology; **Function Concentration:** Generalist with a primary focus in Finance/Accounting, General Management, Human Resources, Marketing, Sales, Women/Minorities

Zaccaria, Jack — *President*
The Zaccaria Group, Inc.
25 E. Spring Valley Avenue
Maywood, NJ 07607
Telephone: Unpublished
Recruiter Classification: Retained; **Lowest/Average Salary:** $60,000/$90,000; **Industry Concentration:** Information Technology; **Function Concentration:** Human Resources, Marketing

Zadfar, Maryanne — *Vice President*
The Thomas Tucker Company
425 California Street, Suite 2502
San Francisco, CA 94104
Telephone: (415) 693-5900
Recruiter Classification: Retained; **Lowest/Average Salary:** $90,000/$90,000; **Industry Concentration:** Generalist with a primary focus in Electronics, High Technology, Information Technology; **Function Concentration:** Engineering, Human Resources, Research and Development

Zaffrann, Craig S. — *Vice President*
P.J. Murphy & Associates, Inc.
735 North Water Street
Milwaukee, WI 53202
Telephone: (414) 277-9777
Recruiter Classification: Retained; **Lowest/Average Salary:** $60,000/$90,000; **Industry Concentration:** Generalist with a primary focus in Information Technology; **Function Concentration:** Generalist with a primary focus in Administration, Finance/Accounting, General Management, Human Resources, Marketing, Sales

Zahradka, James F. — *Vice President*
P.J. Murphy & Associates, Inc.
735 North Water Street
Milwaukee, WI 53202
Telephone: (414) 277-9777
Recruiter Classification: Retained; **Lowest/Average Salary:** $60,000/$90,000; **Industry Concentration:** Generalist with a primary focus in Information Technology; **Function Concentration:** Generalist with a primary focus in Administration, Finance/Accounting, General Management, Human Resources, Marketing, Sales

Zaleta, Andy R. — *Vice President/Managing Director*
A.T. Kearney, Inc.
One Memorial Drive, 14th Floor
Cambridge, MA 02142
Telephone: (617) 374-2600
Recruiter Classification: Retained; **Lowest/Average Salary:** $90,000/$90,000; **Industry Concentration:** Generalist with a primary focus in High Technology, Information Technology; **Function Concentration:** Generalist with a primary focus in Engineering, Finance/Accounting, General Management

Zamborsky, George — *Managing Partner*
Boyden
12444 Powerscourt Drive
Suite 301
St. Louis, MO 63131
Telephone: (314) 984-2590
Recruiter Classification: Retained; **Lowest/Average Salary:** $90,000/$90,000; **Industry Concentration:** Generalist with a primary focus in Electronics, High Technology, Information Technology; **Function Concentration:** Generalist with a primary focus in Engineering, Finance/Accounting, General Management, Human Resources, Marketing, Research and Development, Sales, Women/Minorities

Zarnoski, Henry — *Vice President Technical Recruitment*
Dunhill International Search of New Haven
59 Elm Street
New Haven, CT 06510
Telephone: (203) 562-0511
Recruiter Classification: Contingency; **Lowest/Average Salary:** $30,000/$60,000; **Industry Concentration:** Electronics, High Technology, Information Technology; **Function Concentration:** Engineering

Zaslav, Debra M. — *Principal*
Telford, Adams & Alexander/Telford & Co., Inc.
650 Town Center Drive, Suite 850A
Costa Mesa, CA 92626
Telephone: (714) 850-4354
Recruiter Classification: Retained; **Lowest/Average Salary:** $90,000/$90,000; **Industry Concentration:** Generalist with a primary focus in Electronics, High Technology, Information Technology; **Function Concentration:** Generalist with a primary focus in Administration, Finance/Accounting, General Management, Human Resources, Marketing, Sales

Zatzick, Michael — *Account Executive*
Search West, Inc.
1888 Century Park East
Suite 2050
Los Angeles, CA 90067-1736
Telephone: (310) 284-8888
Recruiter Classification: Contingency; **Lowest/Average Salary:** $40,000/$60,000; **Industry Concentration:** Electronics, High Technology; **Function Concentration:** Engineering, Research and Development, Sales

Zavrel, Mark — *Associate*
Source Services Corporation
8614 Westwood Center, Suite 750
Vienna, VA 22182
Telephone: (703) 790-5610
Recruiter Classification: Contingency; **Lowest/Average Salary:** $30,000/$50,000; **Industry Concentration:** Information Technology; **Function Concentration:** Engineering, Finance/Accounting

Zee, Wanda — *Vice President*
Tesar-Reynes, Inc.
500 North Michigan Avenue
Chicago, IL 60611
Telephone: (312) 661-0700
Recruiter Classification: Retained; **Lowest/Average Salary:** $50,000/$75,000; **Industry Concentration:** High Technology; **Function Concentration:** Marketing

Zegel, Gary — *Associate*
Source Services Corporation
155 Federal Street, Suite 410
Boston, MA 02110
Telephone: (617) 482-8211
Recruiter Classification: Contingency; **Lowest/Average Salary:** $30,000/$50,000; **Industry Concentration:** Information Technology; **Function Concentration:** Engineering, Finance/Accounting

Zell, David M. — *President and CEO*
Logix Partners
1601 Trapelo Road
Waltham, MA 02154
Telephone: (617) 890-0500
Recruiter Classification: Retained; **Lowest/Average Salary:** $60,000/$75,000; **Industry Concentration:** High Technology, Information Technology; **Function Concentration:** Engineering

Zetter, Roger — *Director Logistic Division*
Hunt Ltd.
1050 Wall Street West
Lybdhurst, NJ 07071
Telephone: (201) 438-8200
Recruiter Classification: Contingency; **Lowest/Average Salary:** $50,000/$60,000; **Industry Concentration:** Electronics; **Function Concentration:** Generalist

Zetto, Kathryn — *Vice President/Partner*
Seco & Zetto Associates, Inc.
P.O. Box 225
Harrington Park, NJ 07640
Telephone: (201) 784-0674
Recruiter Classification: Contingency; **Lowest/Average Salary:** $60,000/$60,000; **Industry Concentration:** Generalist with a primary focus in High Technology, Information Technology; **Function Concentration:** Generalist with a primary focus in Marketing, Sales, Women/Minorities

Zila, Laurie M. — *Manager Client Services*
Princeton Entrepreneurial Resources
600 Alexander Road, P.O. Box 2051
Princeton, NJ 08543
Telephone: (609) 243-0010
Recruiter Classification: Executive Temporary; **Lowest/Average Salary:** $75,000/$90,000; **Industry Concentration:** Generalist with a primary focus in Electronics, Information Technology; **Function Concentration:** Generalist with a primary focus in Finance/Accounting, General Management, Human Resources, Marketing

Zilliacus, Patrick W. — *Secretary and Treasurer*
Larsen, Whitney, Blecksmith & Zilliacus
888 West 6th Street, Suite 500
Los Angeles, CA 90017
Telephone: (213) 243-0033
Recruiter Classification: Retained; **Lowest/Average Salary:** $75,000/$90,000; **Industry Concentration:** Electronics, High Technology, Information Technology; **Function Concentration:** Generalist

Zimbal, Mark — *Associate*
Source Services Corporation
1233 North Mayfair Road, Suite 300
Milwaukee, WI 53226
Telephone: (414) 774-6700
Recruiter Classification: Contingency; **Lowest/Average Salary:**
$30,000/$50,000; **Industry Concentration:** Information
Technology; **Function Concentration:** Engineering,
Finance/Accounting

Zimont, Scott — *Associate*
Source Services Corporation
520 Post Oak Boulevard, Suite 700
Houston, TX 77027
Telephone: (713) 439-1077
Recruiter Classification: Contingency; **Lowest/Average Salary:**
$30,000/$50,000; **Industry Concentration:** Information
Technology; **Function Concentration:** Engineering,
Finance/Accounting

Zinn, Don — *Vice President*
Quantex Associates, Inc.
444 Madison Avenue, Suite 710
New York, NY 10022
Telephone: (212) 935-2100
Recruiter Classification: Retained; **Lowest/Average Salary:**
$90,000/$90,000; **Industry Concentration:** Electronics, High
Technology, Information Technology; **Function Concentration:**
General Management, Human Resources, Marketing, Sales

Zucker, Nancy — *Executive Recruiter*
Maximum Management Corp.
420 Lexington Avenue
Suite 2016
New York, NY 10170
Telephone: (212) 867-4646
Recruiter Classification: Contingency, Executive Temporary;
Lowest/Average Salary: $30,000/$75,000; **Industry
Concentration:** Generalist with a primary focus in Information
Technology; **Function Concentration:** Human Resources

Zwell, Michael — *President and CEO*
Zwell International
300 South Wacker Drive, Suite 650
Chicago, IL 60606
Telephone: (312) 663-3737
Recruiter Classification: Retained; **Lowest/Average Salary:**
$75,000/$90,000; **Industry Concentration:** Generalist with a
primary focus in Electronics; **Function Concentration:**
Generalist with a primary focus in Engineering,
Finance/Accounting, General Management, Human Resources,
Marketing, Sales

Industry Specialization Index by Recruiter

Industry Specialization Index by Recruiter

This index is arranged into four business sectors, including the generalist category, and provides a breakdown of the primary and secondary lines of industry specializations of each executive recruiter. Many recruiters have multiple listings in this index depending on the various specializations in which they are engaged. *Recruiters listed in the generalist category serve all industry specializations.*

1. Generalist
2. Electronics

3. High Technology
4. Information Technology

1. Generalist

Abbatiello, Christine Murphy — *Winter, Wyman & Company*
Abbott, Peter D. — *The Abbott Group, Inc.*
Abell, Vincent W. — *MSI International*
Abernathy, Donald E. — *Don Richard Associates of Charlotte*
Adams, Jeffrey C. — *Telford, Adams & Alexander/Jeffrey C. Adams & Co., Inc.*
Adler, Louis S. — *CJA - The Adler Group*
Akin, J.R. "Jack" — *J.R. Akin & Company Inc.*
Albright, Cindy — *Summerfield Associates, Inc.*
Allen, Jean E. — *Lamalie Amrop International*
Allen, Wade H. — *Cendea Connection International*
Allen, William L. — *The Hindman Company*
Allerton, Donald T. — *Allerton Heneghan & O'Neill*
Alpeyrie, Jean-Louis — *Heidrick & Struggles, Inc.*
Altreuter, Rose — *The ALTCO Group*
Ambler, Peter W. — *Peter W. Ambler Company*
Ames, George C. — *Ames O'Neill Associates*
Anderson, David C. — *Heidrick & Struggles, Inc.*
Anderson, Maria H. — *Barton Associates, Inc.*
Anderson, Richard — *Grant Cooper and Associates*
Anderson, Steve — *CPS Inc.*
Anderson, Terry — *Intech Summit Group, Inc.*
Andrews, J. Douglas — *Clarey & Andrews, Inc.*
Archer, Sandra F. — *Ryan, Miller & Associates Inc.*
Argentin, Jo — *Executive Placement Consultants, Inc.*
Arnold, David W. — *Christian & Timbers*
Aronin, Michael — *Fisher-Todd Associates*
Arseneault, Daniel S. — *MSI International*
Ascher, Susan P. — *The Ascher Group*
Asquith, Peter S. — *Ames Personnel Consultants, Inc.*
Aston, Kathy — *Marra Peters & Partners*
Atkins, Laurie — *Battalia Winston International*
Atkinson, S. Graham — *Raymond Karsan Associates*
Attell, Harold — *A.E. Feldman Associates*
Atwood, Barrie — *The Abbott Group, Inc.*
Aubin, Richard E. — *Aubin International Inc.*
Axelrod, Nancy R. — *A.T. Kearney, Inc.*
Bacon, Cheri — *Gaffney Management Consultants*
Badger, Fred H. — *The Badger Group*
Baeder, Jeremy — *Executive Manning Corporation*
Bailey, Paul — *Austin-McGregor International*
Baird, John — *Professional Search Consultants*
Baje, Sarah — *Innovative Search Group, LLC*
Baker, Gary M. — *Cochran, Cochran & Yale, Inc.*
Baker, Gerry — *A.T. Kearney, Inc.*
Balbone, Rich — *Executive Manning Corporation*
Balch, Randy — *CPS Inc.*
Baldwin, Keith R. — *The Baldwin Group*
Baltaglia, Michael — *Cochran, Cochran & Yale, Inc.*
Barbour, Mary Beth — *Tully/Woodmansee International, Inc.*
Barger, H. Carter — *Barger & Sargeant, Inc.*
Barlow, Ken H. — *The Cherbonnier Group, Inc.*
Barnes, Gregory — *Korn/Ferry International*
Barnes, Richard E. — *Barnes Development Group, LLC*

Barnes, Roanne L. — *Barnes Development Group, LLC*
Barnum, Toni M. — *Stone Murphy & Olson*
Barton, Gary R. — *Barton Associates, Inc.*
Bason, Maurice L. — *Bason Associates Inc.*
Bass, M. Lynn — *Ray & Berndtson*
Bassler, John — *Korn/Ferry International*
Battalia, O. William — *Battalia Winston International*
Battles, Jonathan — *Korn/Ferry International*
Beal, Richard D. — *A.T. Kearney, Inc.*
Beall, Charles P. — *Beall & Company, Inc.*
Bearman, Linda — *Grant Cooper and Associates*
Beaudin, Elizabeth C. — *Callan Associates, Ltd.*
Beaver, Bentley H. — *The Onstott Group, Inc.*
Beaver, Robert W. — *Executive Manning Corporation*
Beckvold, John B. — *Atlantic Search Group, Inc.*
Beeson, William B. — *Lawrence-Leiter & Co. Management Conultants*
Belin, Jean — *Boyden*
Bell, Lisa — *Winter, Wyman & Company*
Bender, Alan — *Bender Executive Search*
Bennett, Jo — *Battalia Winston International*
Bennett, Joan — *Adams & Associates International*
Beran, Helena — *Michael J. Cavanagh and Associates*
Berkhemer-Credaire, Betsy — *Berkhemer Clayton Incorporated*
Berry, Harold B. — *The Hindman Company*
Bettick, Michael J. — *A.J. Burton Group, Inc.*
Biestek, Paul J. — *Paul J. Biestek Associates, Inc.*
Biggins, Joseph — *Winter, Wyman & Company*
Billington, William H. — *Spriggs & Company, Inc.*
Blackmon, Sharon — *The Abbott Group, Inc.*
Blackshaw, Brian M. — *Blackshaw, Olmstead, Lynch & Koenig*
Bladon, Andrew — *Don Richard Associates of Tampa, Inc.*
Blanton, Julia — *Blanton and Company*
Blanton, Thomas — *Blanton and Company*
Bliley, Jerry — *Spencer Stuart*
Bloomer, James E. — *L.W. Foote Company*
Blumenthal, Paula — *J.P. Canon Associates*
Boel, Werner — *The Dalley Hewitt Company*
Bogansky, Amy — *Conex Incorporated*
Bohn, Steve J. — *MSI International*
Bond, James L. — *People Management Northeast Incorporated*
Borenstine, Alvin — *Synergistics Associates Ltd.*
Borland, James — *Goodrich & Sherwood Associates, Inc.*
Bormann, Cindy Ann — *MSI International*
Bostic, James E. — *Phillips Resource Group*
Bourrie, Sharon D. — *Chartwell Partners International, Inc.*
Bowden, Otis H. — *BowdenGlobal, Ltd.*
Bowen, Tad — *Executive Search International*
Boyle, Russell E. — *Egon Zehnder International Inc.*
Bradley, Dalena — *Woodworth International Group*
Bradshaw, Monte — *Christian & Timbers*
Brady, Dick — *William Guy & Associates*
Brady, Robert — *CPS Inc.*
Brandeis, Richard — *CPS Inc.*

Brandenburg, David — *Professional Staffing Consultants*
Bratches, Howard — *Thorndike Deland Associates*
Brennen, Richard J. — *Spencer Stuart*
Brieger, Steve — *Thorne, Brieger Associates Inc.*
Brindise, Michael J. — *Dynamic Search Systems, Inc.*
Britt, Stephen — *Keith Bagg & Associates Inc.*
Broadhurst, Austin — *Lamalie Amrop International*
Brocaglia, Joyce — *Alta Associates, Inc.*
Brophy, Melissa — *Maximum Management Corp.*
Brown, Charlene N. — *Accent on Achievement, Inc.*
Brown, Kevin P. — *Raymond Karsan Associates*
Brown, Larry C. — *Horton International*
Brown, S. Ross — *Egon Zehnder International Inc.*
Brown, Steffan — *Woodworth International Group*
Brudno, Robert J. — *Savoy Partners, Ltd.*
Bruno, Deborah F. — *The Hindman Company*
Bryant, Richard D. — *Bryant Associates, Inc.*
Bryant, Shari G. — *Bryant Associates, Inc.*
Bryza, Robert M. — *Robert Lowell International*
Brzezinski, Ronald T. — *Callan Associates, Ltd.*
Buckles, Donna — *Cochran, Cochran & Yale, Inc.*
Bueschel, David A. — *Shepherd Bueschel & Provus, Inc.*
Buggy, Linda — *Bonnell Associates Ltd.*
Bullock, Conni — *Earley Kielty and Associates, Inc.*
Burch, R. Stuart — *Russell Reynolds Associates, Inc.*
Burchill, Greg — *BGB Associates*
Burden, Gene — *The Cherbonnier Group, Inc.*
Burke, John — *The Experts*
Burke, Karen A. — *Mazza & Riley, Inc. (a Korn/Ferry International affiliate)*
Burkhill, John — *The Talley Group*
Burns, Alan — *The Enns Partners Inc.*
Button, David R. — *The Button Group*
Cahill, Peter M. — *Peter M. Cahill Associates, Inc.*
Calivas, Kay — *A.J. Burton Group, Inc.*
Call, David — *Cochran, Cochran & Yale, Inc.*
Callan, Robert M. — *Callan Associates, Ltd.*
Calogeras, Chris — *The Sager Company*
Cameron, James W. — *Cameron Consulting*
Campbell, Patricia A. — *The Onstott Group, Inc.*
Campbell, Robert Scott — *Wellington Management Group*
Campbell, Robert Scott — *Wellington Management Group*
Campbell, W. Ross — *Egon Zehnder International Inc.*
Capizzi, Karen — *Cochran, Cochran & Yale, Inc.*
Carideo, Joseph — *Thorndike Deland Associates*
Carrington, Timothy — *Korn/Ferry International*
Carro, Carl R. — *Executive Search Consultants International, Inc.*
Carrott, Gregory T. — *Egon Zehnder International Inc.*
Carter, I. Wayne — *Heidrick & Struggles, Inc.*
Carter, Jon F. — *Egon Zehnder International Inc.*
Cary, Con — *Cary & Associates*
Castillo, Eduardo — *Korn/Ferry International*
Caudill, Nancy — *Webb, Johnson Associates, Inc.*

Cavanagh, Michael J. — *Michael J. Cavanagh and Associates*
Cavolina, Michael — *Carver Search Consultants*
Celenza, Catherine — *CPS Inc.*
Cesafsky, Barry R. — *Lamalie Amrop International*
Chamberlin, Michael A. — *Tower Consultants, Ltd.*
Champion, Geoffrey — *Korn/Ferry International*
Chan, Margaret — *Webb, Johnson Associates, Inc.*
Chappell, Peter — *The Bankers Group*
Chavous, C. Crawford — *Phillips Resource Group*
Cherbonnier, L. Michael — *TCG International, Inc.*
Cherbonnier, L. Michael — *The Cherbonnier Group, Inc.*
Chorman, Marilyn A. — *Hite Executive Search*
Christenson, H. Alan — *Christenson & Hutchison*
Christian, Philip — *Ray & Berndtson*
Christiansen, Amy — *CPS Inc.*
Christiansen, Doug — *CPS Inc.*
Christoff, Matthew J. — *Spencer Stuart*
Christy, Michael T. — *Heidrick & Struggles, Inc.*
Cimino, James J. — *Executive Search, Ltd.*
Cimino, Terry N. — *Executive Search, Ltd.*
Cizek, John T. — *Cizek Associates, Inc.*
Cizek, Marti J. — *Cizek Associates, Inc.*
Clarey, Jack R. — *Clarey & Andrews, Inc.*
Clark, James — *CPS Inc.*
Clark, Julie — *Corporate Recruiters Ltd.*
Clauhsen, Elizabeth A. — *Savoy Partners, Ltd.*
Clayton, Fred J. — *Berkhemer Clayton Incorporated*
Cline, Mark — *NYCOR Search, Inc.*
Cloutier, Gisella — *Dinte Resources, Inc.*
Cochran, Scott P. — *The Badger Group*
Coffey, Patty — *Winter, Wyman & Company*
Cohen, Michael R. — *Intech Summit Group, Inc.*
Cohen, Robert C. — *Intech Summit Group, Inc.*
Coleman, J. Kevin — *J. Kevin Coleman & Associates, Inc.*
Coleman, Patricia — *Korn/Ferry International*
Colling, Douglas — *KPMG Management Consulting*
Collins, Tom — *J.B. Homer Associates, Inc.*
Colman, Michael — *Executive Placement Consultants, Inc.*
Cona, Joseph A. — *Cona Personnel Search*
Conard, Rodney J. — *Conard Associates, Inc.*
Conley, Kevin E. — *Lamalie Amrop International*
Conway, Maureen — *Conway & Associates*
Cook, Dennis — *A.T. Kearney, Inc.*
Cooke, Katherine H. — *Horton International*
Corrigan, Gerald F. — *The Corrigan Group*
Cortina Del Valle, Pedro — *Ray & Berndtson*
Cottingham, R.L. — *Marvin L. Silcott & Associates, Inc.*
Coulman, Karen — *CPS Inc.*
Courtney, Brendan — *A.J. Burton Group, Inc.*
Cowell, Roy A. — *Cowell & Associates, Ltd.*
Coyle, Hugh F. — *A.J. Burton Group, Inc.*
Crane, Howard C. — *Chartwell Partners International, Inc.*
Crath, Paul F. — *Price Waterhouse*
Critchley, Walter — *Cochran, Cochran & Yale, Inc.*
Cronin, Richard J. — *Hodge-Cronin & Associates, Inc.*

Fifield, George C. — *Egon Zehnder International Inc.*
Fincher, Richard P. — *Phase II Management*
Fingers, David — *Bradford & Galt, Inc.*
Fini, Ron — *The Sager Company*
Fiorelli, Cheryl — *Tower Consultants, Ltd.*
Fischer, Adam — *Howard Fischer Associates, Inc.*
Fischer, Howard M. — *Howard Fischer Associates, Inc.*
Fischer, John C. — *Horton International*
Fisher, Neal — *Fisher Personnel Management Services*
Fishler, Stu — *A.T. Kearney, Inc.*
Flanagan, Robert M. — *Robert M. Flanagan & Associates, Ltd.*
Flannery, Peter F. — *Jonas, Walters & Assoc., Inc.*
Fletcher, David — *A.J. Burton Group, Inc.*
Fogarty, Michael — *CPS Inc.*
Foley, Eileen — *Winter, Wyman & Company*
Folkerth, Gene — *Gene Folkerth & Associates, Inc.*
Fong, Robert — *Korn/Ferry International*
Foote, Leland W. — *L.W. Foote Company*
Foreman, David C. — *Koontz, Jeffries & Associates, Inc.*
Foreman, Rebecca — *Aubin International Inc.*
Forman, Donald R. — *Stanton Chase International*
Foster, Dwight E. — *D.E. Foster Partners Inc.*
Fowler, Thomas A. — *The Hindman Company*
Francis, John — *Zwell International*
Frazier, John — *Cochran, Cochran & Yale, Inc.*
Fribush, Richard — *A.J. Burton Group, Inc.*
Friedman, Donna L. — *Tower Consultants, Ltd.*
Friedman, Helen E. — *McCormack & Farrow*
Friel, Thomas J. — *Heidrick & Struggles, Inc.*
Fulgham MacCarthy, Ann — *Columbia Consulting Group*
Fust, Sheely F. — *Ray & Berndtson*
Gabel, Gregory N. — *Canny, Bowen Inc.*
Gabriel, David L. — *The Arcus Group*
Gadison, William — *Richard, Wayne and Roberts*
Gaffney, Keith — *Gaffney Management Consultants*
Gaffney, William — *Gaffney Management Consultants*
Gaines, Jay — *Jay Gaines & Company, Inc.*
Galante, Suzanne M. — *Vlcek & Company, Inc.*
Galbraith, Deborah M. — *Stratford Group*
Gallagher, Terence M. — *Battalia Winston International*
Gantar, Donna — *Howard Fischer Associates, Inc.*
Gardiner, E. Nicholas P. — *Gardiner International*
Garfinkle, Steven M. — *Battalia Winston International*
Garrett, James — *International Staffing Consultants, Inc.*
Gates, Lucille C. — *Lamalie Amrop International*
Gauthier, Robert C. — *Columbia Consulting Group*
George, Delores F. — *Delores F. George Human Resource Management & Consulting Industry*
Gerbasi, Michael — *The Sager Company*
Germain, Valerie — *Jay Gaines & Company, Inc.*
Gestwick, Daniel — *Cochran, Cochran & Yale, Inc.*
Gettys, James R. — *International Staffing Consultants, Inc.*

Ghurani, Mac — *Gary Kaplan & Associates*
Gibbs, John S. — *Spencer Stuart*
Gibson, Bruce — *Gibson & Company Inc.*
Gilbert, Jerry — *Gilbert & Van Campen International*
Giles, Joe L. — *Joe L. Giles and Associates, Inc.*
Gill, Patricia — *Columbia Consulting Group*
Gillespie, Thomas — *Professional Search Consultants*
Gilreath, James M. — *Gilreath Weatherby, Inc.*
Giries, Juliet D. — *Barton Associates, Inc.*
Gladstone, Martin J. — *MSI International*
Goar, Duane R. — *Sandhurst Associates*
Gobert, Larry — *Professional Search Consultants*
Goedtke, Steven — *Southwestern Professional Services*
Gold, Donald — *Executive Search, Ltd.*
Gold, Stacey — *Earley Kielty and Associates, Inc.*
Golde, Lisa — *Tully/Woodmansee International, Inc.*
Goldenberg, Susan — *Grant Cooper and Associates*
Goldsmith, Fred J. — *Fred J. Goldsmith Associates*
Goldstein, Steven G. — *The Jonathan Stevens Group, Inc.*
Gonye, Peter K. — *Egon Zehnder International Inc.*
Gonzalez, Kristen — *A.J. Burton Group, Inc.*
Gonzalez, Rafael — *Korn/Ferry International*
Goodman, Dawn M. — *Bason Associates Inc.*
Gordon, Elliot — *Korn/Ferry International*
Gordon, Gerald L. — *E.G. Jones Associates, Ltd.*
Gordon, Gloria — *A.T. Kearney, Inc.*
Graham, Dale — *CPS Inc.*
Grant, Michael — *Zwell International*
Grantham, John — *Grantham & Co., Inc.*
Grantham, Philip H. — *Columbia Consulting Group*
Grasch, Jerry E. — *The Hindman Company*
Gray, Betty — *Accent on Achievement, Inc.*
Green, Jean — *Broward-Dobbs, Inc.*
Greene, Luke — *Broward-Dobbs, Inc.*
Gregor, Joie A. — *Heidrick & Struggles, Inc.*
Gregory, Gary A. — *John Kurosky & Associates*
Grey, Fred — *J.B. Homer Associates, Inc.*
Griffin, Cathy — *A.T. Kearney, Inc.*
Groban, Jack — *A.T. Kearney, Inc.*
Groover, David — *MSI International*
Grotte, Lawrence C. — *Lautz Grotte Engler*
Grzybowski, Jill — *CPS Inc.*
Gurnani, Angali — *Executive Placement Consultants, Inc.*
Guy, C. William — *William Guy & Associates*
Hagerty, Kenneth — *Korn/Ferry International*
Hailes, Brian — *Russell Reynolds Associates, Inc.*
Hailey, H.M. — *Damon & Associates, Inc.*
Halbrich, Mitch — *A.J. Burton Group, Inc.*
Hall, Peter V. — *Chartwell Partners International, Inc.*
Halladay, Patti — *Intersource, Ltd.*
Hallock, Peter B. — *Goodrich & Sherwood Associates, Inc.*
Hamilton, John R. — *Ray & Berndtson*
Hanes, Leah — *Ray & Berndtson*
Hanley, Alan P. — *Williams, Roth & Krueger Inc.*
Hanley, J. Patrick — *Canny, Bowen Inc.*
Hanley, Maureen E. — *Gilbert Tweed/INESA*

Johnson, Brian — *A.J. Burton Group, Inc.*
Johnson, David A. — *Gaffney Management Consultants*
Johnson, Harold E. — *Lamalie Amrop International*
Johnson, John W. — *Webb, Johnson Associates, Inc.*
Johnson, Julie M. — *International Staffing Consultants, Inc.*
Johnson, Kathleen A. — *Barton Associates, Inc.*
Johnson, LaDonna — *Gans, Gans & Associates*
Johnson, Rocky — *A.T. Kearney, Inc.*
Johnson, Ronald S. — *Ronald S. Johnson Associates, Inc.*
Johnson, Stanley C. — *Johnson & Company*
Johnston, Michael — *Robertson-Surrette Executive Search*
Jones, Amy E. — *The Corporate Connection, Ltd.*
Jones, B.J. — *Intersource, Ltd.*
Jones, Daniel F. — *Atlantic Search Group, Inc.*
Jones, Francis E. — *Earley Kielty and Associates, Inc.*
Jones, Gary — *BGB Associates*
Jones, Ronald T. — *ARJay & Associates*
Jordan, Jon — *Cochran, Cochran & Yale, Inc.*
Jorgensen, Tom — *The Talley Group*
Judge, Alfred L. — *The Cambridge Group Ltd*
Judy, Otto — *CPS Inc.*
Juelis, John J. — *Peeney Associates*
Kacyn, Louis J. — *Egon Zehnder International Inc.*
Kaiser, Donald J. — *Dunhill International Search of New Haven*
Kane, Frank — *A.J. Burton Group, Inc.*
Kane, Karen — *Howard Fischer Associates, Inc.*
Kaplan, Gary — *Gary Kaplan & Associates*
Karalis, William — *CPS Inc.*
Kartin, Martin C. — *Martin Kartin and Company, Inc.*
Katz, Cyndi — *Search West, Inc.*
Keating, Pierson — *Nordeman Grimm, Inc.*
Kehoe, Mike — *CPS Inc.*
Keitel, Robert S. — *A.T. Kearney, Inc.*
Kelbell, Scott — *Comprehensive Search*
Keller, Barbara E. — *Barton Associates, Inc.*
Kelly, Elizabeth Ann — *Wellington Management Group*
Kelso, Patricia C. — *Barton Associates, Inc.*
Kent, Melvin — *Melvin Kent & Associates, Inc.*
Kerester, Jonathon — *Cadillac Associates*
Kern, Jerry L. — *ADOW's Executeam*
Kern, Kathleen G. — *ADOW's Executeam*
Kershaw, Lisa — *Tanton Mitchell/Paul Ray Berndtson*
Keshishian, Gregory — *Handy HRM Corp.*
Keyser, Anne — *A.T. Kearney, Inc.*
Kielty, John L. — *Earley Kielty and Associates, Inc.*
Kilcoyne, Pat — *CPS Inc.*
Kinney, Carol — *Dussick Management Associates*
Kinser, Richard E. — *Richard Kinser & Associates*
Kip, Luanne S. — *Kip Williams, Inc.*
Kishbaugh, Herbert S. — *Kishbaugh Associates International*
Kixmiller, David B. — *Heidrick & Struggles, Inc.*
Kkorzyniewski, Nicole — *CPS Inc.*
Klages, Constance W. — *International Management Advisors, Inc.*
Klauck, James J. — *Horton International*

Klavens, Cecile J. — *The Pickwick Group, Inc.*
Klein, Brandon — *A.J. Burton Group, Inc.*
Klein, Gary — *A.T. Kearney, Inc.*
Klein, Mary Jo — *Cochran, Cochran & Yale, Inc.*
Kleinstein, Jonah A. — *The Kleinstein Group*
Klopfenstein, Edward L. — *Crowder & Company*
Knapp, Ronald A. — *Knapp Consultants*
Kobayashi, Rika — *International Staffing Consultants, Inc.*
Koblentz, Joel M. — *Egon Zehnder International Inc.*
Koehler, Frank R. — *The Koehler Group*
Koenig, Joel S. — *Blackshaw, Olmstead, Lynch & Koenig*
Koenig, Joel S. — *Blackshaw, Olmstead, Lynch & Koenig*
Kohn, Adam P. — *Christian & Timbers*
Kondra, Vernon J. — *The Douglas Reiter Company, Inc.*
Koontz, Donald N. — *Koontz, Jeffries & Associates, Inc.*
Kotick, Maddy — *The Stevenson Group of New Jersey*
Krecklo, Brian Douglas — *Krecklo & Associates Inc.*
Krejci, Stanley L. — *Boyden Washington, D.C.*
Kreutz, Gary L. — *Kreutz Consulting Group, Inc.*
Krieger, Dennis F. — *Seiden Krieger Associates, Inc.*
Krueger, Kurt — *Krueger Associates*
Kuhl, Teresa — *Don Richard Associates of Tampa, Inc.*
Kunzer, William J. — *Kunzer Associates, Ltd.*
Kussner, Janice N. — *Herman Smith Executive Initiatives Inc.*
Laba, Marvin — *Marvin Laba & Associates*
Laba, Stuart M. — *Marvin Laba & Associates*
Labrecque, Bernard F. — *Laurendeau Labrecque/Ray & Berndtson, Inc.*
Lache, Shawn E. — *The Arcus Group*
Laird, Cheryl — *CPS Inc.*
Lamb, Angus K. — *Raymond Karsan Associates*
Lang, Sharon A. — *Ray & Berndtson*
Lapat, Aaron D. — *J. Robert Scott*
Lardner, Lucy D. — *Tully/Woodmansee International, Inc.*
Larsen, Jack B. — *Jack B. Larsen & Associates*
Lasher, Charles M. — *Lasher Associates*
Lauderback, David R. — *A.T. Kearney, Inc.*
Lautz, Lindsay A. — *Lautz Grotte Engler*
Leahy, Jan — *CPS Inc.*
LeComte, Andre — *Egon Zehnder International Inc.*
Ledbetter, Steven G. — *Cendea Connection International*
Lee, Janice — *Summerfield Associates, Inc.*
Lee, Roger — *Montgomery Resources, Inc.*
Leff, Lisa A. — *Berger and Leff*
Lence, Julie Anne — *MSI International*
Lenkaitis, Lewis F. — *A.T. Kearney, Inc.*
Lennox, Charles — *Price Waterhouse*
Leon, Jeffrey J. — *Russell Reynolds Associates, Inc.*
Letcher, Harvey D. — *Sandhurst Associates*
Lewicki, Christopher — *MSI International*
Lewis, Gretchen S. — *Heidrick & Struggles, Inc.*
Lewis, Jon A. — *Sandhurst Associates*

McSherry, James F. — *Battalia Winston International*
Mead-Fox, David — *Korn/Ferry International*
Meadows, C. David — *Professional Staffing Consultants*
Medina-Haro, Adolfo — *Heidrick & Struggles, Inc.*
Mefford, Bob — *Executive Manning Corporation*
Meiland, A. Daniel — *Egon Zehnder International Inc.*
Menendez, Todd — *Don Richard Associates of Tampa, Inc.*
Mercer, Julie — *Columbia Consulting Group*
Mertensotto, Chuck H. — *Whitney & Associates, Inc.*
Metz, Dan K. — *Russell Reynolds Associates, Inc.*
Meyer, Stacey — *Gary Kaplan & Associates*
Meyers, Steven — *Montgomery Resources, Inc.*
Michaels, Joseph — *CPS Inc.*
Miles, Kenneth T. — *MSI International*
Miller, David — *Cochran, Cochran & Yale, Inc.*
Miller, George N. — *Hite Executive Search*
Miller, Roy — *The Enns Partners Inc.*
Miller, Russel E. — *ARJay & Associates*
Mingle, Larry D. — *Columbia Consulting Group*
Mirtz, P. John — *Mirtz Morice, Inc.*
Misiurewicz, Marc — *Cochran, Cochran & Yale, Inc.*
Mitchell, F. Wayne — *Korn/Ferry International*
Mitchell, Jeff — *A.J. Burton Group, Inc.*
Mitton, Bill — *Executive Resource, Inc.*
Moerbe, Ed H. — *Stanton Chase International*
Mohr, Brian — *CPS Inc.*
Mondragon, Philip — *A.T. Kearney, Inc.*
Montgomery, James M. — *Houze, Shourds & Montgomery, Inc.*
Moodley, Logan — *Austin-McGregor International*
Moore, David S. — *Lynch Miller Moore, Inc.*
Moore, Lemuel R. — *MSI International*
Moore, Mark — *Wheeler, Moore & Elam Co.*
Moore, T. Wills — *Ray & Berndtson*
Moran, Gayle — *Dussick Management Associates*
Morgan, Richard S. — *Ray & Berndtson/Lovas Stanley*
Morice, James L. — *Mirtz Morice, Inc.*
Morrill, Nancy — *Winter, Wyman & Company*
Mortansen, Patricia — *Norman Broadbent International, Inc.*
Moyse, Richard G. — *Thorndike Deland Associates*
Mueller-Maerki, Fortunat F. — *Egon Zehnder International Inc.*
Muendel, H. Edward — *Stanton Chase International*
Murphy, Cornelius J. — *Goodrich & Sherwood Associates, Inc.*
Murphy, Erin — *CPS Inc.*
Murphy, Gary J. — *Stone Murphy & Olson*
Murphy, Patrick J. — *P.J. Murphy & Associates, Inc.*
Murphy, Peter — *Korn/Ferry International*
Murphy, Timothy D. — *MSI International*
Murray, Virginia — *A.T. Kearney, Inc.*
Mursuli, Meredith — *Lasher Associates*
Myatt, James S. — *Sanford Rose Associates*
Mydlach, Renee — *CPS Inc.*
Myers, Kay — *Signature Staffing*

Nadherny, Christopher C. — *Spencer Stuart*
Nadzam, Richard I. — *Nadzam, Lusk, Horgan & Associates, Inc.*
Nagler, Leon G. — *Nagler, Robins & Poe, Inc.*
Naidicz, Maria — *Ray & Berndtson*
Neelin, Sharon — *The Caldwell Partners Amrop International*
Neely, Alan S. — *Korn/Ferry International*
Nees, Eugene C. — *Ray & Berndtson*
Neff, Thomas J. — *Spencer Stuart*
Neher, Robert L. — *Intech Summit Group, Inc.*
Nehring, Keith — *Howard Fischer Associates, Inc.*
Neidhart, Craig C. — *TNS Partners, Inc.*
Nelson, Barbara — *Herman Smith Executive Initiatives Inc.*
Nemec, Phillip — *Dunhill International Search of New Haven*
Neuberth, Jeffrey G. — *Canny, Bowen Inc.*
Newman, Lynn — *Kishbaugh Associates International*
Nichols, Gary — *Koontz, Jeffries & Associates, Inc.*
Noebel, Todd R. — *The Noebel Search Group, Inc.*
Nold, Robert — *Roberson and Company*
Nolte, William D. — *W.D. Nolte & Company*
Norman, Randy — *Austin-McGregor International*
Normann, Amy — *Robert M. Flanagan & Associates, Ltd.*
Norris, Ken — *A.T. Kearney, Inc.*
Norsell, Paul E. — *Paul Norsell & Associates, Inc.*
Norton, James B. — *Lamalie Amrop International*
Nunziata, Peter — *Atlantic Search Group, Inc.*
Nutter, Roger — *Raymond Karsan Associates*
Nye, David S. — *Blake, Hansen & Nye, Limited*
Nymark, John — *NYCOR Search, Inc.*
Nymark, Paul — *NYCOR Search, Inc.*
O'Connell, Mary — *CPS Inc.*
O'Hara, Daniel M. — *Lynch Miller Moore, Inc.*
O'Maley, Kimberlee — *Spencer Stuart*
O'Neill, Kevin G. — *HRS, Inc.*
O'Reilly, John — *Stratford Group*
Odom, Philip — *Richard, Wayne and Roberts*
Ogdon, Thomas H. — *The Ogdon Partnership*
Olmstead, George T. — *Blackshaw, Olmstead, Lynch & Koenig*
Olsen, Carl — *A.T. Kearney, Inc.*
Olsen, Kristine — *Williams Executive Search, Inc.*
Onstott, Joseph E. — *The Onstott Group, Inc.*
Orkin, Ralph — *Sanford Rose Associates*
Orkin, Sheilah — *Sanford Rose Associates*
Osborn, Jim — *Southwestern Professional Services*
Ott, George W. — *Ott & Hansen, Inc.*
Ottenritter, Chris — *CPS Inc.*
Overlock, Craig — *Ray & Berndtson*
Pace, Susan A. — *Horton International*
Pacini, Lauren R. — *Hite Executive Search*
Padilla, Jose Sanchez — *Egon Zehnder International Inc.*
Page, G. Schuyler — *A.T. Kearney, Inc.*
Palma, Frank R. — *Goodrich & Sherwood Associates, Inc.*
Palmer, Carlton A. — *Beall & Company, Inc.*
Palmer, James H. — *The Hindman Company*
Palmer, Melissa — *Don Richard Associates of Tampa, Inc.*
Panarese, Pam — *Howard Fischer Associates, Inc.*

Papasadero, Kathleen — *Woodworth International Group*
Papciak, Dennis J. — *Temporary Accounting Personnel*
Pappalardo, Charles A. — *Christian & Timbers*
Pappas, Christina E. — *Williams Executive Search, Inc.*
Pappas, Timothy C. — *Jonas, Walters & Assoc., Inc.*
Pardo, Maria Elena — *Smith Search, S.C.*
Parfitt, William C. — *Parfitt Recruiting and Consulting*
Paris, Stephen — *Richard, Wayne and Roberts*
Park, Dabney G. — *Mark Stanley/EMA Partners International*
Parr, James A. — *KPMG Management Consulting*
Parry, Heather — *Richard, Wayne and Roberts*
Parry, William H. — *Horton International*
Parsons, Allison D. — *Barton Associates, Inc.*
Pastrana, Dario — *Egon Zehnder International Inc.*
Patrick, Donald R. — *Sanford Rose Associates*
Paul, Lisa D. — *Merit Resource Group, Inc.*
Payette, Pierre — *Egon Zehnder International Inc.*
Pearson, Robert L. — *Lamalie Amrop International*
Peasback, David R. — *Canny, Bowen Inc.*
Pederson, Terre — *Richard, Wayne and Roberts*
Pedley, Jill — *CPS Inc.*
Peeney, James D. — *Peeney Associates*
Pelisson, Charles — *Marra Peters & Partners*
Peretz, Jamie — *Korn/Ferry International*
Pernell, Jeanette — *Norman Broadbent International, Inc.*
Persky, Barry — *Barry Persky & Company, Inc.*
Peternell, Melanie — *Signature Staffing*
Peters, James N. — *TNS Partners, Inc.*
Peterson, John — *CPS Inc.*
Petty, J. Scott — *The Arcus Group*
Pfau, Madelaine — *Heidrick & Struggles, Inc.*
Pfeiffer, Irene — *Price Waterhouse*
Pfister, Shelli — *Jack B. Larsen & Associates*
Phelps, Gene L. — *McCormack & Farrow*
Phillips, Donald L. — *O'Shea, Divine & Company, Inc.*
Phipps, Peggy — *Woodworth International Group*
Pickford, Stephen T. — *The Corporate Staff, Inc.*
Pierce, Mark — *Korn/Ferry International*
Pierotazio, John — *CPS Inc.*
Pinson, Stephanie L. — *Gilbert Tweed/INESA*
Pitts, Charles — *Contemporary Management Services, Inc.*
Plimpton, Ralph L. — *R L Plimpton Associates*
Poirier, Roland L. — *Poirier, Hoevel & Co.*
Polansky, Mark — *Korn/Ferry International*
Pomerance, Mark — *CPS Inc.*
Pomeroy, T. Lee — *Egon Zehnder International Inc.*
Poore, Larry D. — *Ward Howell International, Inc.*
Poracky, John W. — *M. Wood Company*
Poremski, Paul — *A.J. Burton Group, Inc.*
Porter, Albert — *The Experts*
Potter, Douglas C. — *Stanton Chase International*
Price, Andrew G. — *The Thomas Tucker Company*
Price, P. Anthony — *Russell Reynolds Associates, Inc.*

Prior, Donald — *The Caldwell Partners Amrop International*
Provus, Barbara L. — *Shepherd Bueschel & Provus, Inc.*
Prusak, Conrad E. — *Ethos Consulting Inc.*
Prusak, Julie J. — *Ethos Consulting Inc.*
Pryde, Marcia P. — *A.T. Kearney, Inc.*
Pryor, Bill — *Cendea Connection International*
Rabinowitz, Peter A. — *P.A.R. Associates Inc.*
Rachels, John W. — *Southwestern Professional Services*
Railsback, Richard — *Korn/Ferry International*
Raines, Bruce R. — *Raines International Inc.*
Ramler, Carolyn S. — *The Corporate Connection, Ltd.*
Ramsey, John H. — *Mark Stanley/EMA Partners International*
Randell, James E. — *Randell-Heiken, Inc.*
Ray, Marianne C. — *Callan Associates, Ltd.*
Reddick, David C. — *Horton International*
Redding, Denise — *The Douglas Reiter Company, Inc.*
Reece, Christopher S. — *Reece & Mruk Partners*
Reed, Brenda — *International Staffing Consultants, Inc.*
Reed, Ruthann — *Spectra International Inc.*
Referente, Gwen — *Richard, Wayne and Roberts*
Regan, Thomas J. — *Tower Consultants, Ltd.*
Reifel, Laurie — *Reifel & Assocaites*
Reifersen, Ruth F. — *The Jonathan Stevens Group, Inc.*
Reiser, Ellen — *Thorndike Deland Associates*
Reisinger, George L. — *Sigma Group International*
Reiter, Douglas — *The Douglas Reiter Company, Inc.*
Remillard, Brad M. — *CJA - The Adler Group*
Renner, Sandra L. — *Spectra International Inc.*
Reuter, Tandom — *CPS Inc.*
Reyman, Susan — *S. Reyman & Associates Ltd.*
Reynolds, Catherine — *Winter, Wyman & Company*
Reynolds, Gregory P. — *Roberts Ryan and Bentley*
Rhodes, Bill — *Bench International*
Rice, Marie — *Jay Gaines & Company, Inc.*
Rice, Raymond D. — *Logue & Rice Inc.*
Riederer, Larry — *CPS Inc.*
Rieger, Louis J. — *Spencer Stuart*
Rimmel, James E. — *The Hindman Company*
Rimmele, Michael — *The Bankers Group*
Rippey, George E. — *Heidrick & Struggles, Inc.*
Rizzo, L. Donald — *R.P. Barone Associates*
Roberts, Carl R. — *Southwestern Professional Services*
Roberts, Mitch — *A.E. Feldman Associates*
Roberts, Nick P. — *Spectrum Search Associates, Inc.*
Roberts, Scott — *Jonas, Walters & Assoc., Inc.*
Robertson, Bruce J. — *Lamalie Amrop International*
Robertson, Ronald — *Robertson-Surrette Executive Search*
Robins, Jeri N. — *Nagler, Robins & Poe, Inc.*
Robinson, Bruce — *Bruce Robinson Associates*
Robinson, Eric B. — *Bruce Robinson Associates*
Robles Cuellar, Paulina — *Ray & Berndtson*
Rogers, Leah — *Dinte Resources, Inc.*
Rohan, James E. — *J.P. Canon Associates*

Rohan, Kevin A. — *J.P. Canon Associates*
Rojo, Rafael — *A.T. Kearney, Inc.*
Rosin, Jeffrey — *Korn/Ferry International*
Ross, Curt A. — *Ray & Berndtson*
Ross, Lawrence — *Ray & Berndtson/Lovas Stanley*
Ross, William J. — *Flowers & Associates*
Rossi, George A. — *Heidrick & Struggles, Inc.*
Rotella, Marshall W. — *The Corporate Connection, Ltd.*
Roth, Robert J. — *Williams, Roth & Krueger Inc.*
Rothschild, John S. — *Lamalie Amrop International*
Rottblatt, Michael — *Korn/Ferry International*
Rozner, Burton L. — *Oliver & Rozner Associates, Inc.*
Ruge, Merrill — *William Guy & Associates*
Runquist, U.W. — *Webb, Johnson Associates, Inc.*
Rurak, Zbigniew T. — *Rurak & Associates, Inc.*
Rush, Michael E. — *D.A.L. Associates, Inc.*
Russo, Karen — *Maximum Management Corp.*
Ryan, Annette — *Don Richard Associates of Tidewater, Inc.*
Ryan, Mary L. — *Summerfield Associates, Inc.*
Sabat, Lori S. — *Alta Associates, Inc.*
Sacerdote, John — *Raymond Karsan Associates*
Saletra, Andrew — *CPS Inc.*
Salvagno, Michael J. — *The Cambridge Group Ltd*
Sanders, Natalie — *CPS Inc.*
Sanitago, Anthony — *TaxSearch, Inc.*
Sanow, Robert — *Cochran, Cochran & Yale, Inc.*
Santimauro, Edward — *Korn/Ferry International*
Sarn, Allan G. — *Allan Sarn Associates Inc.*
Sauer, Robert C. — *Heidrick & Struggles, Inc.*
Sawyer, Deborah — *Korn/Ferry International*
Sawyer, Patricia L. — *Smith & Sawyer Inc.*
Saxon, Alexa — *Woodworth International Group*
Scalamera, Tom — *CPS Inc.*
Schaad, Carl A. — *Heidrick & Struggles, Inc.*
Schaefer, Frederic M. — *A.T. Kearney, Inc.*
Schappell, Marc P. — *Egon Zehnder International Inc.*
Schedra, Sharon — *Earley Kielty and Associates, Inc.*
Schene, Philip — *A.E. Feldman Associates*
Schiavone, Mary Rose — *Canny, Bowen Inc.*
Schlpma, Christine — *Advanced Executive Resources*
Schmidt, Peter R. — *Boyden*
Schmidt, William C. — *Christian & Timbers*
Schneiderman, Gerald — *Management Resource Associates, Inc.*
Schoettle, Michael B. — *Heidrick & Struggles, Inc.*
Schrenzel, Benjamin — *Parfitt Recruiting and Consulting*
Schueneman, David — *CPS Inc.*
Schwam, Carol — *A.E. Feldman Associates*
Scott, Evan — *Howard Fischer Associates, Inc.*
Scott, Gordon S. — *Search Advisors International Corp.*
Scranton, Lisa — *A.J. Burton Group, Inc.*
Seco, William — *Seco & Zetto Associates, Inc.*
Seiden, Steven A. — *Seiden Krieger Associates, Inc.*
Selker, Gregory L. — *Christian & Timbers*
Semyan, John K. — *TNS Partners, Inc.*
Sessa, Vincent J. — *Integrated Search Solutions Group, LLC*

Sevilla, Claudio A. — *Crawford & Crofford*
Shapiro, Beth — *Howard Fischer Associates, Inc.*
Shapiro, Elaine — *CPS Inc.*
Shattuck, Merrill B. — *M.B. Shattuck and Associates, Inc.*
Shea, Kathleen M. — *The Penn Partners, Incorporated*
Sheedy, Edward J. — *Dieckmann & Associates, Ltd.*
Shell, John C. — *John Shell Associates, Inc.*
Shemin, Grace — *Maximum Management Corp.*
Shenfield, Peter — *A.T. Kearney, Inc.*
Shepard, Michael J. — *MSI International*
Shepherd, Daniel M. — *Shepherd Bueschel & Provus, Inc.*
Sherwood, Andrew — *Goodrich & Sherwood Associates, Inc.*
Shield, Nancy — *Maximum Management Corp.*
Shimp, David J. — *Lamalie Amrop International*
Shore, Earl L. — *E.L. Shore & Associates Ltd.*
Shourds, Mary E. — *Houze, Shourds & Montgomery, Inc.*
Siciliano, Gene — *Western Management Associates*
Siegler, Jody Cukiir — *A.T. Kearney, Inc.*
Siegrist, Jeffrey M. — *D.E. Foster Partners Inc.*
Signer, Julie — *CPS Inc.*
Silcott, Marvin L. — *Marvin L. Silcott & Associates, Inc.*
Silcott, Marvin L. — *Marvin L. Silcott & Associates, Inc.*
Silvas, Stephen D. — *Roberson and Company*
Silver, Lee — *L. A. Silver Associates, Inc.*
Silverman, Paul M. — *The Marshall Group*
Simmons, Gerald J. — *Handy HRM Corp.*
Simmons, Sandra K. — *MSI International*
Simpson, Scott — *Cendea Connection International*
Sindler, Jay — *A.J. Burton Group, Inc.*
Sitarski, Stan — *Howard Fischer Associates, Inc.*
Skalet, Ira — *A.E. Feldman Associates*
Skunda, Donna M. — *Allerton Heneghan & O'Neill*
Slosar, John — *Boyden*
Smead, Michelle M. — *A.T. Kearney, Inc.*
Smirnov, Tatiana — *Allan Sarn Associates Inc.*
Smith, Ana Luz — *Smith Search, S.C.*
Smith, David P. — *HRS, Inc.*
Smith, Grant — *Price Waterhouse*
Smith, Herman M. — *Herman Smith Executive Initiatives Inc.*
Smith, John E. — *Smith Search, S.C.*
Smith, John F. — *The Penn Partners, Incorporated*
Smith, Lydia — *The Corporate Connection, Ltd.*
Smith, Matt D. — *Ray & Berndtson*
Smith, R. Michael — *Smith James Group, Inc.*
Smith, Robert L. — *Smith & Sawyer Inc.*
Smith, Timothy C. — *Christian & Timbers*
Snyder, C. Edward — *Horton International*
Snyder, James F. — *Snyder & Company*
Sola, George L. — *A.T. Kearney, Inc.*
Solomon, Christina — *Richard, Wayne and Roberts*
Souder, E.G. — *Souder & Associates*
Soutouras, James — *Smith James Group, Inc.*
Sowerbutt, Richard S. — *Hite Executive Search*
Spadavecchia, Jennifer — *Alta Associates, Inc.*

von Baillou, Astrid — *Richard Kinser & Associates*
Vossler, James — *A.J. Burton Group, Inc.*
Vroom, Cynthia D. — *Cyntal International Ltd*
Vujcec, John — *Executive Search, Ltd.*
Wacholz, Rick — *A.T. Kearney, Inc.*
Waldrop, Gary R. — *MSI International*
Walker, Craig H. — *A.J. Burton Group, Inc.*
Walker, Richard — *Bradford & Galt, Inc.*
Walsh, Denis — *Professional Staffing Consultants*
Walsh, Kenneth A. — *R/K International, Inc.*
Walters, William F. — *Jonas, Walters & Assoc., Inc.*
Walton, Bruce H. — *Heidrick & Struggles, Inc.*
Warter, Mark — *Isaacson, Miller*
Watkins, Jeffrey P. — *Lamalie Amrop International*
Watkinson, Jim W. — *The Badger Group*
Watson, James — *MSI International*
Webb, George H. — *Webb, Johnson Associates, Inc.*
Weber, Fred — *J.B. Homer Associates, Inc.*
Weissman-Rosenthal, Abbe — *ALW Research International*
Welch, Robert — *Ray & Berndtson*
Weller, Paul S. — *Mark Stanley/EMA Partners International*
Wert, Marty — *Parfitt Recruiting and Consulting*
Westfall, Ed — *Zwell International*
Wheeler, Gerard H. — *A.J. Burton Group, Inc.*
Whelan, David — *Ethos Consulting Inc.*
Whitney, David L. — *Whitney & Associates, Inc.*
Wilder, Richard B. — *Columbia Consulting Group*
Wilkinson, Barbara — *Beall & Company, Inc.*
Wilkinson, Jr. SPHR
Wilkinson, Charles E. — *The HRM Group, Inc.*
Williams, Angie — *Whitney & Associates, Inc.*
Williams, Brad — *Winter, Wyman & Company*
Williams, Dave — *The McCormick Group, Inc.*
Williams, Gary L. — *Barnes Development Group, LLC*
Williams, Jack — *A.T. Kearney, Inc.*
Williams, Roger K. — *Williams, Roth & Krueger Inc.*
Williams, Scott D. — *Heidrick & Struggles, Inc.*
Williams, Stephen E. — *Barton Associates, Inc.*
Williams, Walter E. — *Lamalie Amrop International*
Willner, Leo — *William Guy & Associates*
Wilson, Don — *Allerton Heneghan & O'Neill*
Wilson, John — *Korn/Ferry International*
Wilson, Patricia L. — *Leon A. Farley Associates*
Wilson, Steven J. — *Herman Smith Executive Initiatives Inc.*
Winitz, Joel — *GSW Consulting Group, Inc.*
Winitz, Marla — *GSW Consulting Group, Inc.*
Winograd, Glenn — *Criterion Executive Search, Inc.*
Winston, Dale — *Battalia Winston International*
Wirtshafter, Linda — *Grant Cooper and Associates*
Wise, J. Herbert — *Sandhurst Associates*
Wold, Ted W. — *Hyde Danforth Wold & Co.*
Wolf, Stephen M. — *Byron Leonard International, Inc.*
Womack, Joseph — *The Bankers Group*
Wood, John S. — *Egon Zehnder International Inc.*
Wood, Milton M. — *M. Wood Company*
Woodmansee, Bruce J. — *Tully/Woodmansee International, Inc.*

Woodworth, Gail — *Woodworth International Group*
Wooldridge, Jeff — *Ray & Berndtson*
Wright, A. Leo — *The Hindman Company*
Wright, Carl A.J. — *A.J. Burton Group, Inc.*
Wright, Charles D. — *Goodrich & Sherwood Associates, Inc.*
Wright, Leslie — *The Stevenson Group of New Jersey*
Yaekle, Gary — *Tully/Woodmansee International, Inc.*
Yen, Maggie Yeh Ching — *Ray & Berndtson*
Yungerberg, Steven — *Steven Yungerberg Associates Inc.*
Zadfar, Maryanne — *The Thomas Tucker Company*
Zaffrann, Craig S. — *P.J. Murphy & Associates, Inc.*
Zahradka, James F. — *P.J. Murphy & Associates, Inc.*
Zaleta, Andy R. — *A.T. Kearney, Inc.*
Zamborsky, George — *Boyden*
Zaslav, Debra M. — *Telford, Adams & Alexander/Telford & Co., Inc.*
Zetto, Kathryn — *Seco & Zetto Associates, Inc.*
Zila, Laurie M. — *Princeton Entrepreneurial Resources*
Zucker, Nancy — *Maximum Management Corp.*
Zwell, Michael — *Zwell International*

2. Electronics

Abbott, Peter D. — *The Abbott Group, Inc.*
Adler, Louis S. — *CJA - The Adler Group*
Ainsworth, Lawrence — *Search West, Inc.*
Akin, J.R. "Jack" — *J.R. Akin & Company Inc.*
Allen, Wade H. — *Cendea Connection International*
Allen, William L. — *The Hindman Company*
Allerton, Donald T. — *Allerton Heneghan & O'Neill*
Allred, J. Michael — *Spencer Stuart*
Altreuter, Rose — *ALTCO Temporary Services*
Altreuter, Rose — *The ALTCO Group*
Ambler, Peter W. — *Peter W. Ambler Company*
Ames, George C. — *Ames O'Neill Associates*
Anderson, Dean C. — *Corporate Resources Professional Placement*
Anderson, Maria H. — *Barton Associates, Inc.*
Anderson, Richard — *Grant Cooper and Associates*
Anderson, Steve — *CPS Inc.*
Andrews, J. Douglas — *Clarey & Andrews, Inc.*
Apostle, George — *Search Dynamics, Inc.*
Argentin, Jo — *Executive Placement Consultants, Inc.*
Arms, Douglas — *TOPAZ International, Inc.*
Arms, Douglas — *TOPAZ Legal Solutions*
Arseneault, Daniel S. — *MSI International*
Atkins, Laurie — *Battalia Winston International*
Attell, Harold — *A.E. Feldman Associates*
Atwood, Barrie — *The Abbott Group, Inc.*
Aubin, Richard E. — *Aubin International Inc.*
Bacon, Cheri — *Gaffney Management Consultants*
Badger, Fred H. — *The Badger Group*
Baeder, Jeremy — *Executive Manning Corporation*
Bailey, Paul — *Austin-McGregor International*
Baje, Sarah — *Innovative Search Group, LLC*

Baker, Gary M. — *Cochran, Cochran & Yale, Inc.*
Balbone, Rich — *Executive Manning Corporation*
Balch, Randy — *CPS Inc.*
Baldwin, Keith R. — *The Baldwin Group*
Baltin, Carrie — *Search West, Inc.*
Barbosa, Frank — *Skott/Edwards Consultants, Inc.*
Barbour, Mary Beth — *Tully/Woodmansee International, Inc.*
Barger, H. Carter — *Barger & Sargeant, Inc.*
Barlow, Ken H. — *The Cherbonnier Group, Inc.*
Barnes, Gary — *Brigade Inc.*
Barnes, Richard E. — *Barnes Development Group, LLC*
Barnes, Roanne L. — *Barnes Development Group, LLC*
Barnett, Barbara — *D. Brown and Associates, Inc.*
Baron, Len — *Industrial Recruiters Associates, Inc.*
Bartesch, Heinz — *The Search Firm, Inc.*
Barton, Gary R. — *Barton Associates, Inc.*
Battalia, O. William — *Battalia Winston International*
Bearman, Linda — *Grant Cooper and Associates*
Beaudin, Elizabeth C. — *Callan Associates, Ltd.*
Beaver, Bentley H. — *The Onstott Group, Inc.*
Beaver, Robert W. — *Executive Manning Corporation*
Beckvold, John B. — *Atlantic Search Group, Inc.*
Beeson, William B. — *Lawrence-Leiter & Co. Management Conultants*
Belin, Jean — *Boyden*
Bennett, Jo — *Battalia Winston International*
Bennett, Joan — *Adams & Associates International*
Beran, Helena — *Michael J. Cavanagh and Associates*
Berry, Harold B. — *The Hindman Company*
Biestek, Paul J. — *Paul J. Biestek Associates, Inc.*
Bigelow, Dennis — *Marshall Consultants, Inc.*
Billington, William H. — *Spriggs & Company, Inc.*
Blackmon, Sharon — *The Abbott Group, Inc.*
Blackshaw, Brian M. — *Blackshaw, Olmstead, Lynch & Koenig*
Blanton, Julia — *Blanton and Company*
Blanton, Thomas — *Blanton and Company*
Blecker, Jay — *TSS Consulting, Ltd.*
Bliley, Jerry — *Spencer Stuart*
Blim, Barbara — *JDG Associates, Ltd.*
Bloch, Terry L. — *Southern Research Services*
Bloch, Thomas L. — *Southern Research Services*
Block, Randy — *Block & Associates*
Bloomer, James E. — *L.W. Foote Company*
Bluhm, Claudia — *Schweichler Associates, Inc.*
Blumenthal, Paula — *J.P. Canon Associates*
Boczany, William J. — *The Guild Corporation*
Boehm, Robin — *D. Brown and Associates, Inc.*
Bogansky, Amy — *Conex Incorporated*
Boltrus, Dick — *Sink, Walker, Boltrus International*
Bongiovanni, Vincent — *ESA Professional Consultants*
Borkin, Andrew — *Strategic Advancement Inc.*
Bostic, James E. — *Phillips Resource Group*
Bowden, Otis H. — *BowdenGlobal, Ltd.*
Brackman, Janet — *Dahl-Morrow International*
Bradley, Dalena — *Woodworth International Group*
Bradshaw, Monte — *Christian & Timbers*
Brady, Dick — *William Guy & Associates*

Brady, Robert — *CPS Inc.*
Brandeis, Richard — *CPS Inc.*
Brieger, Steve — *Thorne, Brieger Associates Inc.*
Britt, Stephen — *Keith Bagg & Associates Inc.*
Brooks, Charles — *Corporate Recruiters Ltd.*
Brooks, Kimberllay — *Corporate Recruiters Ltd.*
Brother, Joy — *Charles Luntz & Associates. Inc.*
Brown, Buzz — *Brown, Bernardy, Van Remmen, Inc.*
Brown, Dennis — *D. Brown and Associates, Inc.*
Brown, Larry C. — *Horton International*
Brown, Steffan — *Woodworth International Group*
Brudno, Robert J. — *Savoy Partners, Ltd.*
Bruno, Deborah F. — *The Hindman Company*
Bryant, Henry — *D. Brown and Associates, Inc.*
Bryant, Richard D. — *Bryant Associates, Inc.*
Bryant, Shari G. — *Bryant Associates, Inc.*
Bryza, Robert M. — *Robert Lowell International*
Brzezinski, Ronald T. — *Callan Associates, Ltd.*
Bueschel, David A. — *Shepherd Bueschel & Provus, Inc.*
Burchill, Greg — *BGB Associates*
Burden, Gene — *The Cherbonnier Group, Inc.*
Burkhill, John — *The Talley Group*
Burns, Alan — *The Enns Partners Inc.*
Busch, Jack — *Busch International*
Butcher, Pascale — *F-O-R-T-U-N-E Personnel Consultants of Manatee County*
Cahill, Peter M. — *Peter M. Cahill Associates, Inc.*
Callan, Robert M. — *Callan Associates, Ltd.*
Calogeras, Chris — *The Sager Company*
Cameron, James W. — *Cameron Consulting*
Caruthers, Robert D. — *James Mead & Company*
Cary, Con — *Cary & Associates*
Cavanagh, Michael J. — *Michael J. Cavanagh and Associates*
Celenza, Catherine — *CPS Inc.*
Chavous, C. Crawford — *Phillips Resource Group*
Cherbonnier, L. Michael — *TCG International, Inc.*
Cherbonnier, L. Michael — *The Cherbonnier Group, Inc.*
Christenson, H. Alan — *Christenson & Hutchison*
Christian, Jeffrey E. — *Christian & Timbers*
Christiansen, Amy — *CPS Inc.*
Christiansen, Doug — *CPS Inc.*
Cimino, Terry N. — *Executive Search, Ltd.*
Cizek, John T. — *Cizek Associates, Inc.*
Cizek, Marti J. — *Cizek Associates, Inc.*
Cizynski, Katherine W. — *James Mead & Company*
Clarey, Jack R. — *Clarey & Andrews, Inc.*
Clark, James — *CPS Inc.*
Clark, Julie — *Corporate Recruiters Ltd.*
Clauhsen, Elizabeth A. — *Savoy Partners, Ltd.*
Clayton, Fred J. — *Berkhemer Clayton Incorporated*
Cline, Mark — *NYCOR Search, Inc.*
Cochran, Hale — *Fenwick Partners*
Cochran, Scott P. — *The Badger Group*
Cohen, Pamela — *TOPAZ International, Inc.*
Cohen, Pamela — *TOPAZ Legal Solutions*
Cohen, Robert C. — *Intech Summit Group, Inc.*
Colling, Douglas — *KPMG Management Consulting*
Collis, Gerald — *TSS Consulting, Ltd.*

Colman, Michael — *Executive Placement Consultants, Inc.*
Conners, Theresa — *D. Brown and Associates, Inc.*
Connolly, Cathryn — *Strategic Associates, Inc.*
Conway, William P. — *Phillips Resource Group*
Cooke, Katherine H. — *Horton International*
Cottingham, R.L. — *Marvin L. Silcott & Associates, Inc.*
Coulman, Karen — *CPS Inc.*
Cowell, Roy A. — *Cowell & Associates, Ltd.*
Cram, Noel — *R.P. Barone Associates*
Crane, Howard C. — *Chartwell Partners International, Inc.*
Cronin, Richard J. — *Hodge-Cronin & Associates, Inc.*
Crowder, Edward W. — *Crowder & Company*
Cruse, O.D. — *Spencer Stuart*
Cruz, Catherine — *TOPAZ International, Inc.*
Cruz, Catherine — *TOPAZ Legal Solutions*
Cuddihy, Paul — *Dahl-Morrow International*
Curci, Donald L. — *A.R.I. International*
Cushman, Judith — *Judith Cushman & Associates*
Czamanske, Paul W. — *Compass Group Ltd.*
Czepiel, Susan — *CPS Inc.*
D'Alessio, Gary A. — *Chicago Legal Search, Ltd.*
Dabich, Thomas M. — *Robert Harkins Associates, Inc.*
Danforth, W. Michael — *Hyde Danforth Wold & Co.*
Davis, G. Gordon — *Davis & Company*
DeGioia, Joseph — *JDG Associates, Ltd.*
Delaney, Patrick J. — *Sensible Solutions, Inc.*
Desai, Sushila — *Sink, Walker, Boltrus International*
Dicker, Barry — *ESA Professional Consultants*
Dillon, Larry — *Predictor Systems*
Dingeldey, Peter E. — *Search Advisors International Corp.*
Dingman, Bruce — *Robert W. Dingman Company, Inc.*
Dingman, Robert W. — *Robert W. Dingman Company, Inc.*
Diskin, Rochelle — *Search West, Inc.*
Divine, Robert S. — *O'Shea, Divine & Company, Inc.*
Dixon, Aris — *CPS Inc.*
Do, Sonnie — *Whitney & Associates, Inc.*
Donath, Linda — *Dahl-Morrow International*
Dong, Stephen — *Executive Search, Ltd.*
Dowell, Chris — *The Abbott Group, Inc.*
Doyle, Marie — *Spectra International Inc.*
Dreifus, Donald — *Search West, Inc.*
Drew, David R. — *Drew & Associates*
Drexler, Robert — *Robert Drexler Associates, Inc.*
Dromeshauser, Peter — *Dromeshauser Associates*
Drury, James J. — *Spencer Stuart*
Dubrow, Richard M. — *R/K International, Inc.*
Duley, Richard I. — *ARJay & Associates*
Dunman, Betsy L. — *Crawford & Crofford*
Durakis, Charles A. — *C.A. Durakis Associates, Inc.*
Dwyer, Julie — *CPS Inc.*
Ebeling, John A. — *Gilbert Tweed/INESA*
Edmond, Bruce — *Corporate Recruiters Ltd.*
Edwards, John W. — *The Bedford Group*
Edwards, Robert — *J.P. Canon Associates*

Edwards, Verba L. — *Wing Tips & Pumps, Inc.*
Eggena, Roger — *Phillips Resource Group*
Ehrhart, Jennifer — *ADOW's Executeam*
Ellis, Ted K. — *The Hindman Company*
Enfield, Jerry J. — *Executive Manning Corporation*
England, Mark — *Austin-McGregor International*
Engler, Peter G — *Lautz Grotte Engler*
Enns, George — *The Enns Partners Inc.*
Erikson, Theodore J. — *Erikson Consulting Associates, Inc.*
Ervin, Darlene — *CPS Inc.*
Estes, Susan — *The Talley Group*
Evans, David — *Executive Manning Corporation*
Farley, Leon A. — *Leon A. Farley Associates*
Farrow, Jerry M. — *McCormack & Farrow*
Feldman, Abe — *A.E. Feldman Associates*
Feldman, Kimberley — *Atlantic Search Group, Inc.*
Ferneborg, Jay W. — *Ferneborg & Associates, Inc.*
Ferneborg, John R. — *Ferneborg & Associates, Inc.*
Fields, Fredric — *C.A. Durakis Associates, Inc.*
Fincher, Richard P. — *Phase II Management*
Fini, Ron — *The Sager Company*
Fink, Neil J. — *Neil Fink Associates*
Fisher, Neal — *Fisher Personnel Management Services*
Flannery, Peter F. — *Jonas, Walters & Assoc., Inc.*
Flora, Dodi — *Crawford & Crofford*
Flowers, Hayden — *Southwestern Professional Services*
Flynn, Erin — *Neil Fink Associates*
Fogarty, Michael — *CPS Inc.*
Folkerth, Gene — *Gene Folkerth & Associates, Inc.*
Foote, Leland W. — *L.W. Foote Company*
Foreman, David C. — *Koontz, Jeffries & Associates, Inc.*
Foster, Dwight E. — *D.E. Foster Partners Inc.*
Fowler, Thomas A. — *The Hindman Company*
Francis, John — *Zwell International*
Freeman, Mark — *ESA Professional Consultants*
Furlong, James W. — *Furlong Search, Inc.*
Furlong, James W. — *Furlong Search, Inc.*
Furlong, James W. — *Furlong Search, Inc.*
Gabel, Gregory N. — *Canny, Bowen Inc.*
Gabriel, David L. — *The Arcus Group*
Gadison, William — *Richard, Wayne and Roberts*
Gaffney, Keith — *Gaffney Management Consultants*
Gaffney, William — *Gaffney Management Consultants*
Gaines, Jay — *Jay Gaines & Company, Inc.*
Gaines, Ronni L. — *TOPAZ International, Inc.*
Gaines, Ronni L. — *TOPAZ Legal Solutions*
Gallagher, Terence M. — *Battalia Winston International*
Gallin, Larry — *Gallin Associates, Inc.*
Gares, Conrad — *TSS Consulting, Ltd.*
Garfinkle, Steven M. — *Battalia Winston International*
George, Delores F. — *Delores F. George Human Resource Management & Consulting Industry*
Gerbasi, Michael — *The Sager Company*
Germaine, Debra — *Fenwick Partners*
Gettys, James R. — *International Staffing Consultants, Inc.*
Ghurani, Mac — *Gary Kaplan & Associates*

Johnston, James R. — *The Stevenson Group of Delaware Inc.*
Jones, Amy E. — *The Corporate Connection, Ltd.*
Jones, Daniel F. — *Atlantic Search Group, Inc.*
Jones, Ronald T. — *ARJay & Associates*
Jorgensen, Tom — *The Talley Group*
Joyce, William J. — *The Guild Corporation*
Jozwik, Peter — *The Search Firm, Inc.*
Judy, Otto — *CPS Inc.*
Juelis, John J. — *Peeney Associates*
Juska, Frank — *Rusher, Loscavio & LoPresto*
Kaiser, Donald J. — *Dunhill International Search of New Haven*
Kanrich, Susan Azaria — *AlternaStaff*
Kaplan, Alexandra — *J.M. Eagle Partners Ltd.*
Kaplan, Gary — *Gary Kaplan & Associates*
Karalis, William — *CPS Inc.*
Kartin, Martin C. — *Martin Kartin and Company, Inc.*
Katz, Cyndi — *Search West, Inc.*
Kehoe, Mike — *CPS Inc.*
Keller, Barbara E. — *Barton Associates, Inc.*
Kells, John — *Heffelfinger Associates, Inc.*
Kelly, Sheri — *Strategic Associates, Inc.*
Kelly, Susan D. — *S.D. Kelly & Associates, Inc.*
Kelso, Patricia C. — *Barton Associates, Inc.*
Kern, Jerry L. — *ADOW's Executeam*
Kern, Kathleen G. — *ADOW's Executeam*
Keshishian, Gregory — *Handy HRM Corp.*
Kilcoyne, Pat — *CPS Inc.*
King, Margaret — *Christian & Timbers*
Kinser, Richard E. — *Richard Kinser & Associates*
Kkorzyniewski, Nicole — *CPS Inc.*
Klages, Constance W. — *International Management Advisors, Inc.*
Klauck, James J. — *Horton International*
Klavens, Cecile J. — *The Pickwick Group, Inc.*
Klein, Mel — *Stewart/Laurence Associates*
Kleinstein, Jonah A. — *The Kleinstein Group*
Klopfenstein, Edward L. — *Crowder & Company*
Knapp, Ronald A. — *Knapp Consultants*
Kobayashi, Rika — *International Staffing Consultants, Inc.*
Koehler, Frank R. — *The Koehler Group*
Koenig, Joel S. — *Blackshaw, Olmstead, Lynch & Koenig*
Koenig, Joel S. — *Blackshaw, Olmstead, Lynch & Koenig*
Kohonoski, Michael M. — *The Guild Corporation*
Koontz, Donald N. — *Koontz, Jeffries & Associates, Inc.*
Kopec, Tom — *D. Brown and Associates, Inc.*
Kossuth, David — *Kossuth & Associates, Inc.*
Kossuth, Jane — *Kossuth & Associates, Inc.*
Krejci, Stanley L. — *Boyden Washington, D.C.*
Krieger, Dennis F. — *Seiden Krieger Associates, Inc.*
Krueger, Kurt — *Krueger Associates*
Kunzer, William J. — *Kunzer Associates, Ltd.*
Kurrigan, Geoffrey — *ESA Professional Consultants*
Labrecque, Bernard F. — *Laurendeau Labrecque/Ray & Berndtson, Inc.*
LaCharite, Danielle — *The Guild Corporation*
Laird, Cheryl — *CPS Inc.*
Lamb, Lynn M. — *F-O-R-T-U-N-E Personnel Consultants of Huntsville, Inc.*

Lanctot, William D. — *Corporate Resources Professional Placement*
Langford, Matt — *F-O-R-T-U-N-E Personnel Consultants of Huntsville, Inc.*
Langford, Robert W. — *F-O-R-T-U-N-E Personnel Consultants of Huntsville, Inc.*
Lapat, Aaron D. — *J. Robert Scott*
Lardner, Lucy D. — *Tully/Woodmansee International, Inc.*
Larsen, Jack B. — *Jack B. Larsen & Associates*
Lasher, Charles M. — *Lasher Associates*
Lautz, Lindsay A. — *Lautz Grotte Engler*
Leahy, Jan — *CPS Inc.*
Ledbetter, Steven G. — *Cendea Connection International*
Leland, Paul — *McInturff & Associates, Inc.*
Lichtenauer, Eric W. — *Britt Associates, Inc.*
Lichtenauer, William E. — *Britt Associates, Inc.*
Lindenmuth, Mary — *Search West, Inc.*
Line, Joseph T. — *Sharrow & Associates*
Linton, Leonard M. — *Byron Leonard International, Inc.*
Lipe, Jerold L. — *Compass Group Ltd.*
Lipson, Harriet — *First Interactive Recruiting Specialists*
Loeb, Stephen H. — *Grant Cooper and Associates*
Lofthouse, Cindy — *CPS Inc.*
Lokken, Karen — *A.E. Feldman Associates*
Long, Milt — *William Guy & Associates*
Long, William G. — *McDonald, Long & Associates, Inc.*
Looney, Scott — *A.E. Feldman Associates*
LoPresto, Robert L. — *Rusher, Loscavio & LoPresto*
Lotufo, Donald A. — *D.A.L. Associates, Inc.*
Lotz, R. James — *International Management Advisors, Inc.*
Loving, Vikki — *Intersource, Ltd.*
Lucht, John — *The John Lucht Consultancy Inc.*
Lumsby, George N. — *International Management Advisors, Inc.*
Mackenna, Kathy — *Plummer & Associates, Inc.*
MacNaughton, Sperry — *McNaughton Associates*
Mader, Stephen P. — *Christian & Timbers*
Maglio, Charles J. — *Maglio and Company, Inc.*
Manassero, Henri J.P. — *International Management Advisors, Inc.*
Mangum, Maria — *Thomas Mangum Company*
Mangum, William T. — *Thomas Mangum Company*
Manns, Alex — *Crawford & Crofford*
Manzo, Renee — *Atlantic Search Group, Inc.*
Marcine, John W. — *Keith Bagg & Associates Inc.*
Marion, Michael — *S.D. Kelly & Associates, Inc.*
Marks, Ira — *Strategic Alternatives*
Marlow, William — *Straube Associates*
Martin, David — *The Guild Corporation*
Marumoto, William H. — *Boyden Washington, D.C.*
Mashakas, Elizabeth — *TOPAZ International, Inc.*
Mashakas, Elizabeth — *TOPAZ Legal Solutions*
Massey, R. Bruce — *Horton International*
Mather, David R. — *Christian & Timbers*
Matthews, Corwin — *Woodworth International Group*
Matueny, Robert — *Ryan, Miller & Associates Inc.*
May, Peter — *Mixtec Group*

McAndrews, Kathy — *CPS Inc.*
McBride, Jonathan E. — *McBride Associates, Inc.*
McComas, Kelly E. — *The Guild Corporation*
McCreary, Charles "Chip" — *Austin-McGregor International*
McDonald, John R. — *TSS Consulting, Ltd.*
McDonald, Scott A. — *McDonald Associates International*
McDonald, Stanleigh B. — *McDonald Associates International*
McDonnell, Julie — *Technical Personnel of Minnesota*
McDowell, Robert N. — *Christenson & Hutchison*
McFadzen, Donna — *Holland, McFadzean & Associates, Inc.*
McFadzen, James A. — *Holland, McFadzean & Associates, Inc.*
McGuire, J. Corey — *Peter W. Ambler Company*
McInturff, Robert — *McInturff & Associates, Inc.*
McIntyre, Joel — *Phillips Resource Group*
McKeown, Patricia A. — *DiMarchi Partners, Inc.*
McManners, Donald E. — *McManners Associates, Inc.*
McNichols, Walter B. — *Gary Kaplan & Associates*
McPoyle, Thomas C. — *Sanford Rose Associates*
McThrall, David — *TSS Consulting, Ltd.*
Mead, James D. — *James Mead & Company*
Mefford, Bob — *Executive Manning Corporation*
Mertensotto, Chuck H. — *Whitney & Associates, Inc.*
Metz, Alex — *Hunt Advisory Services*
Meyer, Stacey — *Gary Kaplan & Associates*
Michaels, Joseph — *CPS Inc.*
Michaels, Stewart — *TOPAZ International, Inc.*
Michaels, Stewart — *TOPAZ Legal Solutions*
Mierzwinski, John — *Industrial Recruiters Associates, Inc.*
Miles, Kenneth T. — *MSI International*
Miller, Roy — *The Enns Partners Inc.*
Miller, Russel E. — *ARJay & Associates*
Mirtz, P. John — *Mirtz Morice, Inc.*
Mitton, Bill — *Executive Resource, Inc.*
Mogul, Gene — *Mogul Consultants, Inc.*
Mohr, Brian — *CPS Inc.*
Molnar, Robert A. — *Johnson Smith & Knisely Accord*
Montgomery, James M. — *Houze, Shourds & Montgomery, Inc.*
Moodley, Logan — *Austin-McGregor International*
Moore, David S. — *Lynch Miller Moore, Inc.*
Moore, Lemuel R. — *MSI International*
Moore, Mark — *Wheeler, Moore & Elam Co.*
Moore, Thomas — *Aureus Group*
Morice, James L. — *Mirtz Morice, Inc.*
Mortansen, Patricia — *Norman Broadbent International, Inc.*
Moses, Jerry — *J.M. Eagle Partners Ltd.*
Muendel, H. Edward — *Stanton Chase International*
Muller, Susan — *Corporate Recruiters Ltd.*
Murphy, Erin — *CPS Inc.*
Murphy, Gary J. — *Stone Murphy & Olson*
Mursuli, Meredith — *Lasher Associates*
Myatt, James S. — *Sanford Rose Associates*
Mydlach, Renee — *CPS Inc.*
Myers, Kay — *Signature Staffing*

Myers, Thomas — *Careers Plus*
Nadzam, Richard I. — *Nadzam, Lusk, Horgan & Associates, Inc.*
Nagler, Leon G. — *Nagler, Robins & Poe, Inc.*
Neelin, Sharon — *The Caldwell Partners Amrop International*
Neher, Robert L. — *Intech Summit Group, Inc.*
Neidhart, Craig C. — *TNS Partners, Inc.*
Nichols, Gary — *Koontz, Jeffries & Associates, Inc.*
Nolan, Jean M. — *S.D. Kelly & Associates, Inc.*
Nolte, William D. — *W.D. Nolte & Company*
Norman, Randy — *Austin-McGregor International*
Norsell, Paul E. — *Paul Norsell & Associates, Inc.*
Nunziata, Peter — *Atlantic Search Group, Inc.*
Nye, David S. — *Blake, Hansen & Nye, Limited*
Nymark, John — *NYCOR Search, Inc.*
Nymark, Paul — *NYCOR Search, Inc.*
O'Connell, Mary — *CPS Inc.*
Ocon, Olga — *Busch International*
Ott, George W. — *Ott & Hansen, Inc.*
Ottenritter, Chris — *CPS Inc.*
Pacini, Lauren R. — *Hite Executive Search*
Palmer, James H. — *The Hindman Company*
Papasadero, Kathleen — *Woodworth International Group*
Pappas, Jim — *Search Dynamics, Inc.*
Pappas, Timothy C. — *Jonas, Walters & Assoc., Inc.*
Pardo, Maria Elena — *Smith Search, S.C.*
Parkin, Myrna — *S.D. Kelly & Associates, Inc.*
Parr, James A. — *KPMG Management Consulting*
Parry, William H. — *Horton International*
Parsons, Allison D. — *Barton Associates, Inc.*
Paul, Lisa D. — *Merit Resource Group, Inc.*
Peasback, David R. — *Canny, Bowen Inc.*
Peckenpaugh, Ann D. — *Schweichler Associates, Inc.*
Pedley, Jill — *CPS Inc.*
Peeney, James D. — *Peeney Associates*
Percival, Chris — *Chicago Legal Search, Ltd.*
Perry, Glen — *Keith Bagg & Associates Inc.*
Persky, Barry — *Barry Persky & Company, Inc.*
Peternell, Melanie — *Signature Staffing*
Peters, James N. — *TNS Partners, Inc.*
Peterson, John — *CPS Inc.*
Pfister, Shelli — *Jack B. Larsen & Associates*
Phelps, Gene L. — *McCormack & Farrow*
Phillips, Donald L. — *O'Shea, Divine & Company, Inc.*
Phipps, Peggy — *Woodworth International Group*
Pickering, Dale — *Agri-Tech Personnel, Inc.*
Pickering, Rita — *Agri-Tech Personnel, Inc.*
Pierotazio, John — *CPS Inc.*
Pigott, Daniel — *ESA Professional Consultants*
Pitts, Charles — *Contemporary Management Services, Inc.*
Plimpton, Ralph L. — *R L Plimpton Associates*
Plummer, John — *Plummer & Associates, Inc.*
Poe, James B. — *Nagler, Robins & Poe, Inc.*
Poirier, Roland L. — *Poirier, Hoevel & Co.*
Polachi, Charles A. — *Fenwick Partners*
Polachi, Peter V. — *Fenwick Partners*
Pomerance, Mark — *CPS Inc.*
Pompeo, Paul — *Search West, Inc.*
Porada, Stephen D. — *CAP Inc.*
Portanova, Peter M. — *R.O.I. Associates, Inc.*

Poster, Lawrence D. — *Catalyx Group*
Price, Andrew G. — *The Thomas Tucker Company*
Pryor, Bill — *Cendea Connection International*
Raab, Julie — *Dunhill Professional Search of Irvine, Inc.*
Rabe, William — *Sales Executives Inc.*
Ray, Marianne C. — *Callan Associates, Ltd.*
Raymond, Anne — *Anderson Sterling Associates*
Reed, Brenda — *International Staffing Consultants, Inc.*
Reifel, Laurie — *Reifel & Assocaites*
Reifersen, Ruth F. — *The Jonathan Stevens Group, Inc.*
Remillard, Brad M. — *CJA - The Adler Group*
Renner, Sandra L. — *Spectra International Inc.*
Renwick, David — *John Kurosky & Associates*
Reuter, Tandom — *CPS Inc.*
Reyman, Susan — *S. Reyman & Associates Ltd.*
Rhodes, Bill — *Bench International*
Richards, Paul E. — *Executive Directions*
Richards, R. Glenn — *Executive Directions*
Riederer, Larry — *CPS Inc.*
Rimmel, James E. — *The Hindman Company*
Rizzo, L. Donald — *R.P. Barone Associates*
Roberts, Mitch — *A.E. Feldman Associates*
Roberts, Nick P. — *Spectrum Search Associates, Inc.*
Roberts, Scott — *Jonas, Walters & Assoc., Inc.*
Robertson, John A. — *Kaye-Bassman International Corp.*
Roblin, Nancy R. — *Paul-Tittle Associates, Inc.*
Rohan, James E. — *J.P. Canon Associates*
Rohan, Kevin A. — *J.P. Canon Associates*
Romanello, Daniel P. — *Spencer Stuart*
Romang, Paula — *Agri-Tech Personnel, Inc.*
Rose, Robert — *ESA Professional Consultants*
Roth, Robert J. — *Williams, Roth & Krueger Inc.*
Rozner, Burton L. — *Oliver & Rozner Associates, Inc.*
Rubenstein, Alan J. — *Chicago Legal Search, Ltd.*
Rudzinsky, Howard — *Louis Rudzinsky Associates*
Rudzinsky, Jeffrey — *Louis Rudzinsky Associates*
Ruge, Merrill — *William Guy & Associates*
Rurak, Zbigniew T. — *Rurak & Associates, Inc.*
Rush, Michael E. — *D.A.L. Associates, Inc.*
Russell, Sam — *The Guild Corporation*
Ryan, Annette — *Don Richard Associates of Tidewater, Inc.*
Saletra, Andrew — *CPS Inc.*
Sanders, Natalie — *CPS Inc.*
Sangster, Jeffrey — *F-O-R-T-U-N-E Personnel Consultants of Manatee County*
Sanitago, Anthony — *TaxSearch, Inc.*
Sarna, Edmund A. — *Jonas, Walters & Assoc., Inc.*
Saxon, Alexa — *Woodworth International Group*
Scalamera, Tom — *CPS Inc.*
Schene, Philip — *A.E. Feldman Associates*
Schiavone, Mary Rose — *Canny, Bowen Inc.*
Schlpma, Christine — *Advanced Executive Resources*
Schmidt, William C. — *Christian & Timbers*
Schneider, James — *The Search Firm, Inc.*
Schneiderman, Gerald — *Management Resource Associates, Inc.*
Schueneman, David — *CPS Inc.*
Schultz, Helen — *Predictor Systems*

Schwam, Carol — *A.E. Feldman Associates*
Schwartz, Vincent P. — *Slayton International, Inc./I-I-C Partners*
Schweichler, Lee J. — *Schweichler Associates, Inc.*
Scott, Gordon S. — *Search Advisors International Corp.*
Seiden, Steven A. — *Seiden Krieger Associates, Inc.*
Semyan, John K. — *TNS Partners, Inc.*
Sessa, Vincent J. — *Integrated Search Solutions Group, LLC*
Sevilla, Claudio A. — *Crawford & Crofford*
Shamir, Ben — *S.D. Kelly & Associates, Inc.*
Shapiro, Elaine — *CPS Inc.*
Shattuck, Merrill B. — *M.B. Shattuck and Associates, Inc.*
Shea, Kathleen M. — *The Penn Partners, Incorporated*
Shourds, Mary E. — *Houze, Shourds & Montgomery, Inc.*
Shufelt, Doug — *Sink, Walker, Boltrus International*
Shulman, Barry — *Shulman Associates*
Sibul, Shelly Remen — *Chicago Legal Search, Ltd.*
Siciliano, Gene — *Western Management Associates*
Sickles, Robert — *Dunhill Professional Search of Irvine, Inc.*
Signer, Julie — *CPS Inc.*
Siker, Paul W. — *The Guild Corporation*
Silcott, Marvin L. — *Marvin L. Silcott & Associates, Inc.*
Silcott, Marvin L. — *Marvin L. Silcott & Associates, Inc.*
Silvas, Stephen D. — *Roberson and Company*
Silver, Lee — *L. A. Silver Associates, Inc.*
Silverman, Paul M. — *The Marshall Group*
Simmons, Anneta — *F-O-R-T-U-N-E Personnel Consultants of Huntsville, Inc.*
Simpson, Scott — *Cendea Connection International*
Sink, Cliff — *Sink, Walker, Boltrus International*
Skalet, Ira — *A.E. Feldman Associates*
Skunda, Donna M. — *Allerton Heneghan & O'Neill*
Slayton, Richard C. — *Slayton International, Inc./I-I-C Partners*
Slosar, John — *Boyden*
Smith, Ana Luz — *Smith Search, S.C.*
Smith, David P. — *HRS, Inc.*
Smith, John E. — *Smith Search, S.C.*
Smith, John F. — *The Penn Partners, Incorporated*
Smith, Kevin — *F-O-R-T-U-N-E Personnel Consultants of Manatee County*
Smith, R. Michael — *Smith James Group, Inc.*
Smith, Robert L. — *Smith & Sawyer Inc.*
Smith, Timothy C. — *Christian & Timbers*
Snyder, C. Edward — *Horton International*
Snyder, James F. — *Snyder & Company*
Solomon, Christina — *Richard, Wayne and Roberts*
Solters, Jeanne — *The Guild Corporation*
Souder, E.G. — *Souder & Associates*
Soutouras, James — *Smith James Group, Inc.*
Spanninger, Mark J. — *The Guild Corporation*
Spiegel, Gayle — *L. A. Silver Associates, Inc.*

Woodworth, Gail — *Woodworth International Group*
Woollett, James — *Rusher, Loscavio & LoPresto*
Work, Alan — *Quantex Associates, Inc.*
Yaekle, Gary — *Tully/Woodmansee International, Inc.*
Young, Heather — *The Guild Corporation*
Zadfar, Maryanne — *The Thomas Tucker Company*
Zamborsky, George — *Boyden*
Zarnoski, Henry — *Dunhill International Search of New Haven*
Zaslav, Debra M. — *Telford, Adams & Alexander/Telford & Co., Inc.*
Zatzick, Michael — *Search West, Inc.*
Zetter, Roger — *Hunt Ltd.*
Zila, Laurie M. — *Princeton Entrepreneurial Resources*
Zilliacus, Patrick W. — *Larsen, Whitney, Blecksmith & Zilliacus*
Zinn, Don — *Quantex Associates, Inc.*
Zwell, Michael — *Zwell International*

3. High Technology

Abbatiello, Christine Murphy — *Winter, Wyman & Company*
Abbott, Peter D. — *The Abbott Group, Inc.*
Abell, Vincent W. — *MSI International*
Abernathy, Donald E. — *Don Richard Associates of Charlotte*
Acquaviva, Jay — *Winter, Wyman & Company*
Adams, Jeffrey C. — *Telford, Adams & Alexander/Jeffrey C. Adams & Co., Inc.*
Adler, Louis S. — *CJA - The Adler Group*
Ahearn, Jennifer — *Logix, Inc.*
Aheran, Jennifer — *Logix Partners*
Aiken, David — *Commonwealth Consultants*
Akin, J.R. "Jack" — *J.R. Akin & Company Inc.*
Albertini, Nancy — *Taylor-Winfield, Inc.*
Allen, Don — *D.S. Allen Associates, Inc.*
Allen, Jean E. — *Lamalie Amrop International*
Allen, Wade H. — *Cendea Connection International*
Allen, William L. — *The Hindman Company*
Allerton, Donald T. — *Allerton Heneghan & O'Neill*
Allred, J. Michael — *Spencer Stuart*
Alpeyrie, Jean-Louis — *Heidrick & Struggles, Inc.*
Altreuter, Rose — *The ALTCO Group*
Ambler, Peter W. — *Peter W. Ambler Company*
Ames, George C. — *Ames O'Neill Associates*
Anderson, David C. — *Heidrick & Struggles, Inc.*
Anderson, Dean C. — *Corporate Resources Professional Placement*
Anderson, Maria H. — *Barton Associates, Inc.*
Anderson, Steve — *CPS Inc.*
Anderson, Terry — *Intech Summit Group, Inc.*
Andrews, J. Douglas — *Clarey & Andrews, Inc.*
Antoine, Brian — *Paul-Tittle Associates, Inc.*
Apostle, George — *Search Dynamics, Inc.*
Archer, Sandra F. — *Ryan, Miller & Associates Inc.*
Argentin, Jo — *Executive Placement Consultants, Inc.*
Arms, Douglas — *TOPAZ International, Inc.*
Arms, Douglas — *TOPAZ Legal Solutions*
Arnold, David W. — *Christian & Timbers*
Arnson, Craig — *Hernand & Partners*

Arseneault, Daniel S. — *MSI International*
Ashton, Barbara L. — *Ashton Computer Professionals Inc.*
Asquith, Peter S. — *Ames Personnel Consultants, Inc.*
Atkins, Laurie — *Battalia Winston International*
Attell, Harold — *A.E. Feldman Associates*
Atwood, Barrie — *The Abbott Group, Inc.*
Aubin, Richard E. — *Aubin International Inc.*
Austin Lockton, Kathy — *Juntunen-Combs-Poirier*
Axelrod, Nancy R. — *A.T. Kearney, Inc.*
Bacon, Cheri — *Gaffney Management Consultants*
Badger, Fred H. — *The Badger Group*
Baeder, Jeremy — *Executive Manning Corporation*
Bailey, Paul — *Austin-McGregor International*
Baje, Sarah — *Innovative Search Group, LLC*
Baker, Gary M. — *Cochran, Cochran & Yale, Inc.*
Baker, Gerry — *A.T. Kearney, Inc.*
Balbone, Rich — *Executive Manning Corporation*
Balch, Randy — *CPS Inc.*
Baltaglia, Michael — *Cochran, Cochran & Yale, Inc.*
Baltin, Carrie — *Search West, Inc.*
Barbosa, Frank — *Skott/Edwards Consultants, Inc.*
Barbour, Mary Beth — *Tully/Woodmansee International, Inc.*
Barger, H. Carter — *Barger & Sargeant, Inc.*
Barlow, Ken H. — *The Cherbonnier Group, Inc.*
Barnes, Gary — *Brigade Inc.*
Barnett, Barbara — *D. Brown and Associates, Inc.*
Barnum, Toni M. — *Stone Murphy & Olson*
Baron, Len — *Industrial Recruiters Associates, Inc.*
Bartesch, Heinz — *The Search Firm, Inc.*
Barthold, James A. — *McNichol Associates*
Bartholdi, Ted — *Bartholdi & Company, Inc.*
Bartholdi, Theodore G. — *Bartholdi & Company, Inc.*
Bartholomew, Katie — *C. Berger & Company*
Barton, Gary R. — *Barton Associates, Inc.*
Bason, Maurice L. — *Bason Associates Inc.*
Bass, M. Lynn — *Ray & Berndtson*
Bassman, Robert — *Kaye-Bassman International Corp.*
Bassman, Sandy — *Kaye-Bassman International Corp.*
Beal, Richard D. — *A.T. Kearney, Inc.*
Beall, Charles P. — *Beall & Company, Inc.*
Beaudin, Elizabeth C. — *Callan Associates, Ltd.*
Beaulieu, Genie A. — *Romac & Associates*
Beaver, Bentley H. — *The Onstott Group, Inc.*
Beaver, Robert W. — *Executive Manning Corporation*
Beckvold, John B. — *Atlantic Search Group, Inc.*
Belfrey, Edward — *Dunhill Professional Search of Irvine, Inc.*
Belin, Jean — *Boyden*
Bennett, Jo — *Battalia Winston International*
Bennett, Ness — *Technical Connections Inc.*
Bentley, Mark — *The Thomas Tucker Company*
Berkhemer-Credaire, Betsy — *Berkhemer Clayton Incorporated*
Berry, Harold B. — *The Hindman Company*
Bettick, Michael J. — *A.J. Burton Group, Inc.*
Biestek, Paul J. — *Paul J. Biestek Associates, Inc.*
Bigelow, Dennis — *Marshall Consultants, Inc.*
Birt, Peter — *Ashton Computer Professionals Inc.*
Blackmon, Sharon — *The Abbott Group, Inc.*

Blackshaw, Brian M. — *Blackshaw, Olmstead, Lynch & Koenig*
Bladon, Andrew — *Don Richard Associates of Tampa, Inc.*
Blake, Eileen — *Howard Fischer Associates, Inc.*
Blanton, Julia — *Blanton and Company*
Blanton, Thomas — *Blanton and Company*
Blecker, Jay — *TSS Consulting, Ltd.*
Bliley, Jerry — *Spencer Stuart*
Blim, Barbara — *JDG Associates, Ltd.*
Bloch, Terry L. — *Southern Research Services*
Bloch, Thomas L. — *Southern Research Services*
Bloom, Howard C. — *Hernand & Partners*
Bloom, Joyce — *Hernand & Partners*
Bloomer, James E. — *L.W. Foote Company*
Bluhm, Claudia — *Schweichler Associates, Inc.*
Blunt, Peter — *Hernand & Partners*
Boccella, Ralph — *Susan C. Goldberg Associates*
Boczany, William J. — *The Guild Corporation*
Boehm, Robin — *D. Brown and Associates, Inc.*
Boesel, James — *Logix Partners*
Boesel, Jim — *Logix, Inc.*
Bogansky, Amy — *Conex Incorporated*
Bohle, John B. — *Ray & Berndtson*
Bohn, Steve J. — *MSI International*
Boltrus, Dick — *Sink, Walker, Boltrus International*
Bond, Allan — *Walden Associates*
Bond, Robert J. — *Romac & Associates*
Bongiovanni, Vincent — *ESA Professional Consultants*
Bonner, Lale D. — *Don Richard Associates of Charlotte*
Bordelon, Amanda — *Paul-Tittle Associates, Inc.*
Bormann, Cindy Ann — *MSI International*
Bostic, James E. — *Phillips Resource Group*
Bourrie, Sharon D. — *Chartwell Partners International, Inc.*
Bowden, Otis H. — *BowdenGlobal, Ltd.*
Bowen, Tad — *Executive Search International*
Boyd, Lew — *Coastal International Inc.*
Boyle, Russell E. — *Egon Zehnder International Inc.*
Brackman, Janet — *Dahl-Morrow International*
Bradley, Dalena — *Woodworth International Group*
Bradshaw, Monte — *Christian & Timbers*
Brady, Dick — *William Guy & Associates*
Brady, Robert — *CPS Inc.*
Brandeis, Richard — *CPS Inc.*
Brennen, Richard J. — *Spencer Stuart*
Brieger, Steve — *Thorne, Brieger Associates Inc.*
Brindise, Michael J. — *Dynamic Search Systems, Inc.*
Britt, Stephen — *Keith Bagg & Associates Inc.*
Brkovich, Deanna — *Corporate Recruiters Ltd.*
Broadhurst, Austin — *Lamalie Amrop International*
Brocaglia, Joyce — *Alta Associates, Inc.*
Brooks, Charles — *Corporate Recruiters Ltd.*
Brooks, Kimberllay — *Corporate Recruiters Ltd.*
Brother, Joy — *Charles Luntz & Associates. Inc.*
Brovender, Claire — *Winter, Wyman & Company*
Brown, Buzz — *Brown, Bernardy, Van Remmen, Inc.*
Brown, Charlene N. — *Accent on Achievement, Inc.*

Brown, D. Perry — *Don Richard Associates of Washington, D.C., Inc.*
Brown, Dennis — *D. Brown and Associates, Inc.*
Brown, Gina — *Strategic Alliance Network, Ltd.*
Brown, Larry C. — *Horton International*
Brown, S. Ross — *Egon Zehnder International Inc.*
Brown, Steffan — *Woodworth International Group*
Bruce, Michael C. — *Spencer Stuart*
Brudno, Robert J. — *Savoy Partners, Ltd.*
Bruno, Deborah F. — *The Hindman Company*
Brunson, Therese — *Kors Montgomery International*
Bryant, Henry — *D. Brown and Associates, Inc.*
Bryant, Richard D. — *Bryant Associates, Inc.*
Bryant, Shari G. — *Bryant Associates, Inc.*
Bryza, Robert M. — *Robert Lowell International*
Brzezinski, Ronald T. — *Callan Associates, Ltd.*
Buckles, Donna — *Cochran, Cochran & Yale, Inc.*
Bueschel, David A. — *Shepherd Bueschel & Provus, Inc.*
Burch, R. Stuart — *Russell Reynolds Associates, Inc.*
Burchill, Greg — *BGB Associates*
Burden, Gene — *The Cherbonnier Group, Inc.*
Burke, John — *The Experts*
Burke, Karen A. — *Mazza & Riley, Inc. (a Korn/Ferry International affiliate)*
Burns, Alan — *The Enns Partners Inc.*
Busch, Jack — *Busch International*
Busterna, Charles — *The KPA Group*
Butcher, Pascale — *F-O-R-T-U-N-E Personnel Consultants of Manatee County*
Button, David R. — *The Button Group*
Bye, Randy — *Romac & Associates*
Cahill, Peter M. — *Peter M. Cahill Associates, Inc.*
Calivas, Kay — *A.J. Burton Group, Inc.*
Call, David — *Cochran, Cochran & Yale, Inc.*
Callan, Robert M. — *Callan Associates, Ltd.*
Calogeras, Chris — *The Sager Company*
Campbell, Gary — *Romac & Associates*
Campbell, Patricia A. — *The Onstott Group, Inc.*
Campbell, Robert Scott — *Wellington Management Group*
Campbell, Robert Scott — *Wellington Management Group*
Campbell, W. Ross — *Egon Zehnder International Inc.*
Capizzi, Karen — *Cochran, Cochran & Yale, Inc.*
Capra, Jamie — *Warren, Morris & Madison*
Carlton, Patricia — *JDG Associates, Ltd.*
Carro, Carl R. — *Executive Search Consultants International, Inc.*
Carrott, Gregory T. — *Egon Zehnder International Inc.*
Carter, I. Wayne — *Heidrick & Struggles, Inc.*
Carter, Jon F. — *Egon Zehnder International Inc.*
Cast, Donald — *Dunhill International Search of New Haven*
Caudill, Nancy — *Bishop Partners*
Caudill, Nancy — *Webb, Johnson Associates, Inc.*
Cavolina, Michael — *Carver Search Consultants*
Celenza, Catherine — *CPS Inc.*
Chamberlin, Michael A. — *Tower Consultants, Ltd.*
Chan, Margaret — *Webb, Johnson Associates, Inc.*
Chappell, Peter — *The Bankers Group*
Chatterjie, Alok — *MSI International*

Chavous, C. Crawford — *Phillips Resource Group*
Cherbonnier, L. Michael — *TCG International, Inc.*
Cherbonnier, L. Michael — *The Cherbonnier Group, Inc.*
Christenson, H. Alan — *Christenson & Hutchison*
Christian, Jeffrey E. — *Christian & Timbers*
Christian, Philip — *Ray & Berndtson*
Christiansen, Amy — *CPS Inc.*
Christiansen, Doug — *CPS Inc.*
Christy, Michael T. — *Heidrick & Struggles, Inc.*
Cimino, James J. — *Executive Search, Ltd.*
Cimino, Ron — *Paul-Tittle Associates, Inc.*
Cimino, Terry N. — *Executive Search, Ltd.*
Cizek, John T. — *Cizek Associates, Inc.*
Cizek, Marti J. — *Cizek Associates, Inc.*
Clarey, Jack R. — *Clarey & Andrews, Inc.*
Clark, James — *CPS Inc.*
Clark, John — *Tate Consulting Inc.*
Clark, Julie — *Corporate Recruiters Ltd.*
Clasen, Ryan — *Warren, Morris & Madison*
Clauhsen, Elizabeth A. — *Savoy Partners, Ltd.*
Clayton, Fred J. — *Berkhemer Clayton Incorporated*
Clegg, Cynthia — *Horton International*
Cline, Mark — *NYCOR Search, Inc.*
Clough, Geoff — *Intech Summit Group, Inc.*
Cloutier, Gisella — *Dinte Resources, Inc.*
Cocchiaro, Richard — *Romac & Associates*
Cochran, Hale — *Fenwick Partners*
Cochran, Scott P. — *The Badger Group*
Coe, Karen J. — *Coe & Company International Inc.*
Coffman, Brian — *Kossuth & Associates, Inc.*
Cohen, Michael R. — *Intech Summit Group, Inc.*
Cohen, Pamela — *TOPAZ International, Inc.*
Cohen, Pamela — *TOPAZ Legal Solutions*
Cohen, Robert C. — *Intech Summit Group, Inc.*
Colasanto, Frank M. — *W.R. Rosato & Associates, Inc.*
Cole, Kevin — *Don Richard Associates of Washington, D.C., Inc.*
Coleman, J. Kevin — *J. Kevin Coleman & Associates, Inc.*
Colling, Douglas — *KPMG Management Consulting*
Collis, Gerald — *TSS Consulting, Ltd.*
Colman, Michael — *Executive Placement Consultants, Inc.*
Combs, Stephen L. — *Juntunen-Combs-Poirier*
Compton, Tonya — *Dunhill Professional Search of Irvine, Inc.*
Conard, Rodney J. — *Conard Associates, Inc.*
Conley, Kevin E. — *Lamalie Amrop International*
Connelly, Scott — *Technical Connections Inc.*
Conners, Theresa — *D. Brown and Associates, Inc.*
Connolly, Cathryn — *Strategic Associates, Inc.*
Conway, William P. — *Phillips Resource Group*
Cook, Dennis — *A.T. Kearney, Inc.*
Cooke, Katherine H. — *Horton International*
Cortina Del Valle, Pedro — *Ray & Berndtson*
Cossitt, Chip — *Warren, Morris & Madison*
Costello, Lynda — *Coe & Company International Inc.*
Cottingham, R.L. — *Marvin L. Silcott & Associates, Inc.*

Coulman, Karen — *CPS Inc.*
Courtney, Brendan — *A.J. Burton Group, Inc.*
Coyle, Hugh F. — *A.J. Burton Group, Inc.*
Crane, Howard C. — *Chartwell Partners International, Inc.*
Crath, Paul F. — *Price Waterhouse*
Critchley, Walter — *Cochran, Cochran & Yale, Inc.*
Crosler, Yvonne — *Paul-Tittle Associates, Inc.*
Crumpton, Marc — *Logix Partners*
Crumpton, Marc — *Logix, Inc.*
Crumpton, Marc — *Walden Associates*
Cruse, O.D. — *Spencer Stuart*
Cruz, Catherine — *TOPAZ International, Inc.*
Cruz, Catherine — *TOPAZ Legal Solutions*
Cuddihy, Paul — *Dahl-Morrow International*
Cuddy, Brian C. — *Romac & Associates*
Cunningham, Lawrence — *Howard Fischer Associates, Inc.*
Cunningham, Sheila — *Adams & Associates International*
Curci, Donald L. — *A.R.I. International*
Curtis, Ellissa — *Cochran, Cochran & Yale, Inc.*
Cushman, Judith — *Judith Cushman & Associates*
Cyphers, Ralph R. — *Strategic Associates, Inc.*
Czepiel, Susan — *CPS Inc.*
D'Alessio, Gary A. — *Chicago Legal Search, Ltd.*
Daily, John C. — *Handy HRM Corp.*
Dalton, Bret — *Robert W. Dingman Company, Inc.*
Danforth, W. Michael — *Hyde Danforth Wold & Co.*
Daniels, C. Eugene — *Sigma Group International*
Daniels, Donna — *Jonas, Walters & Assoc., Inc.*
Davis, G. Gordon — *Davis & Company*
Davison, Patricia E. — *Lamalie Amrop International*
De Brun, Thomas P. — *Ray & Berndtson*
de Gury, Glenn — *Taylor-Winfield, Inc.*
Deaver, Henry C. — *Ray & Berndtson*
DeCorrevont, James — *DeCorrevont & Associates*
DeCorrevont, James — *DeCorrevont & Associates*
DeGioia, Joseph — *JDG Associates, Ltd.*
DeHart, Donna — *Tower Consultants, Ltd.*
Del Prete, Karen — *Gilbert Tweed/INESA*
Delaney, Patrick J. — *Sensible Solutions, Inc.*
Delmonico, Laura — *A.J. Burton Group, Inc.*
DeLong, Art — *Richard Kader & Associates*
Demchak, James P. — *Sandhurst Associates*
Desai, Sushila — *Sink, Walker, Boltrus International*
Desgrosellier, Gary P. — *Personnel Unlimited/Executive Search*
Desmond, Dennis — *Beall & Company, Inc.*
deVry, Kimberly A. — *Tower Consultants, Ltd.*
deWilde, David M. — *Chartwell Partners International, Inc.*
Dezember, Steve — *Ray & Berndtson*
DiCioccio, Carmen — *Cochran, Cochran & Yale, Inc.*
Dicker, Barry — *ESA Professional Consultants*
Dickey, Chester W. — *Bowden & Company, Inc.*
Dickey, Chester W. — *Bowden & Company, Inc.*
Dickson, Duke — *A.D. & Associates Executive Search, Inc.*
Dietz, David S. — *MSI International*
Dillon, Larry — *Predictor Systems*

DiMarchi, Paul — *DiMarchi Partners, Inc.*
DiMarchi, Paul — *DiMarchi Partners, Inc.*
Dingeldey, Peter E. — *Search Advisors International Corp.*
Dingman, Bruce — *Robert W. Dingman Company, Inc.*
Dingman, Robert W. — *Robert W. Dingman Company, Inc.*
Dinte, Paul — *Dinte Resources, Inc.*
DiSalvo, Fred — *The Cambridge Group Ltd*
Divine, Robert S. — *O'Shea, Divine & Company, Inc.*
Dixon, Aris — *CPS Inc.*
Do, Sonnie — *Whitney & Associates, Inc.*
Donath, Linda — *Dahl-Morrow International*
Dong, Stephen — *Executive Search, Ltd.*
Dorsey, Jim — *Ryan, Miller & Associates Inc.*
Dotson, M. Ileen — *Dotson & Associates*
Dow, Lori — *Davidson, Laird & Associates, Inc.*
Dowdall, Jean — *A.T. Kearney, Inc.*
Dowell, Chris — *The Abbott Group, Inc.*
Doyle, Bobby — *Richard, Wayne and Roberts*
Doyle, James W. — *Executive Search Consultants International, Inc.*
Dreifus, Donald — *Search West, Inc.*
Dressler, Ralph — *Romac & Associates*
Drew, David R. — *Drew & Associates*
Drexler, Robert — *Robert Drexler Associates, Inc.*
Dromeshauser, Peter — *Dromeshauser Associates*
Drury, James J. — *Spencer Stuart*
Dubbs, William — *Williams Executive Search, Inc.*
Duckworth, Donald R. — *Johnson Smith & Knisely Accord*
Dugan, John H. — *J.H. Dugan and Associates, Inc.*
Duggan, James P. — *Slayton International, Inc./ I-I-C Partners*
Dunbar, Geoffrey T. — *Heidrick & Struggles, Inc.*
Dunbar, Marilynne — *Ray & Berndtson/Lovas Stanley*
Dunkel, David L. — *Romac & Associates*
Dunlop, Eric — *Southwestern Professional Services*
Dunman, Betsy L. — *Crawford & Crofford*
Durakis, Charles A. — *C.A. Durakis Associates, Inc.*
Dussick, Vince — *Dussick Management Associates*
Dwyer, Julie — *CPS Inc.*
Earhart, William D. — *Sanford Rose Associates*
Ebeling, John A. — *Gilbert Tweed/INESA*
Edmond, Bruce — *Corporate Recruiters Ltd.*
Edwards, Dorothy — *MSI International*
Edwards, Douglas W. — *Egon Zehnder International Inc.*
Edwards, John W. — *The Bedford Group*
Edwards, Verba L. — *Wing Tips & Pumps, Inc.*
Eggena, Roger — *Phillips Resource Group*
Ehrhart, Jennifer — *ADOW's Executeam*
Elder, Tom — *Juntunen-Combs-Poirier*
Eldridge, Charles B. — *Ray & Berndtson*
Elliott, A. Larry — *Heidrick & Struggles, Inc.*
Ellis, Ted K. — *The Hindman Company*
Elnaggar, Hani — *Juntunen-Combs-Poirier*
Emery, Jodie A. — *Lamalie Amrop International*
Enfield, Jerry J. — *Executive Manning Corporation*

England, Mark — *Austin-McGregor International*
Engler, Peter G — *Lautz Grotte Engler*
Enns, George — *The Enns Partners Inc.*
Epstein, Kathy J. — *Lamalie Amrop International*
Erikson, Theodore J. — *Erikson Consulting Associates, Inc.*
Ervin, Darlene — *CPS Inc.*
Esposito, Mark — *Christian & Timbers*
Eustis, Lucy R. — *MSI International*
Evans, David — *Executive Manning Corporation*
Fairlie, Suzanne F. — *ProSearch, Inc.*
Falk, John — *D.S. Allen Associates, Inc.*
Fancher, Robert L. — *Bason Associates Inc.*
Farley, Leon A. — *Leon A. Farley Associates*
Farrow, Jerry M. — *McCormack & Farrow*
Fawkes, Elizabeth — *Paul-Tittle Associates, Inc.*
Feder, Gwen — *Egon Zehnder International Inc.*
Federman, Jack R. — *W.R. Rosato & Associates, Inc.*
Feldman, Abe — *A.E. Feldman Associates*
Ferneborg, Jay W. — *Ferneborg & Associates, Inc.*
Ferneborg, John R. — *Ferneborg & Associates, Inc.*
Feyder, Michael — *A.T. Kearney, Inc.*
Fields, Fredric — *C.A. Durakis Associates, Inc.*
Fifield, George C. — *Egon Zehnder International Inc.*
Fini, Ron — *The Sager Company*
Fiorelli, Cheryl — *Tower Consultants, Ltd.*
Fischer, Adam — *Howard Fischer Associates, Inc.*
Fischer, Howard M. — *Howard Fischer Associates, Inc.*
Fisher, Neal — *Fisher Personnel Management Services*
Fishler, Stu — *A.T. Kearney, Inc.*
Fitzgerald, Diane — *Fitzgerald Associates*
Fitzgerald, Geoffrey — *Fitzgerald Associates*
Fletcher, David — *A.J. Burton Group, Inc.*
Flood, Michael — *Norman Broadbent International, Inc.*
Flora, Dodi — *Crawford & Crofford*
Fogarty, Michael — *CPS Inc.*
Fone, Carol — *Walden Associates*
Foote, Leland W. — *L.W. Foote Company*
Ford, Sandra D. — *The Ford Group, Inc.*
Foreman, David C. — *Koontz, Jeffries & Associates, Inc.*
Foreman, Rebecca — *Aubin International Inc.*
Forman, Donald R. — *Stanton Chase International*
Foster, Bonnie — *Kirkman & Searing, Inc.*
Fotia, Frank — *JDG Associates, Ltd.*
Fowler, Thomas A. — *The Hindman Company*
Francis, John — *Zwell International*
Frazier, John — *Cochran, Cochran & Yale, Inc.*
Fredericks, Ward A. — *Mixtec Group*
Freeman, Mark — *ESA Professional Consultants*
French, William G. — *Preng & Associates, Inc.*
Fribush, Richard — *A.J. Burton Group, Inc.*
Friedman, Donna L. — *Tower Consultants, Ltd.*
Friedman, Helen E. — *McCormack & Farrow*
Friel, Thomas J. — *Heidrick & Struggles, Inc.*
Fulgham MacCarthy, Ann — *Columbia Consulting Group*
Fulmer, Karen — *Bench International*
Furlong, James W. — *Furlong Search, Inc.*
Furlong, James W. — *Furlong Search, Inc.*
Furlong, James W. — *Furlong Search, Inc.*
Fust, Sheely F. — *Ray & Berndtson*

Gabel, Gregory N. — *Canny, Bowen Inc.*
Gabriel, David L. — *The Arcus Group*
Gadison, William — *Richard, Wayne and Roberts*
Gaffney, Keith — *Gaffney Management Consultants*
Gaffney, William — *Gaffney Management Consultants*
Gaines, Jay — *Jay Gaines & Company, Inc.*
Gaines, Ronni L. — *TOPAZ International, Inc.*
Gaines, Ronni L. — *TOPAZ Legal Solutions*
Galante, Suzanne M. — *Vlcek & Company, Inc.*
Galbraith, Deborah M. — *Stratford Group*
Gale, Rhoda E. — *E.G. Jones Associates, Ltd.*
Gallagher, Terence M. — *Battalia Winston International*
Gantar, Donna — *Howard Fischer Associates, Inc.*
Gares, Conrad — *TSS Consulting, Ltd.*
Garfinkle, Steven M. — *Battalia Winston International*
Garrett, James — *International Staffing Consultants, Inc.*
Garzone, Dolores — *M.A. Churchill & Associates, Inc.*
Gates, Lucille C. — *Lamalie Amrop International*
Gauthier, Robert C. — *Columbia Consulting Group*
George, Delores F. — *Delores F. George Human Resource Management & Consulting Industry*
Gerbasi, Michael — *The Sager Company*
Gerbosi, Karen — *Hernand & Partners*
Germaine, Debra — *Fenwick Partners*
Gerster, J.P. — *Juntunen-Combs-Poirier*
Gestwick, Daniel — *Cochran, Cochran & Yale, Inc.*
Ghurani, Mac — *Gary Kaplan & Associates*
Gibbs, John S. — *Spencer Stuart*
Gibson, Bruce — *Gibson & Company Inc.*
Gideon, Mark — *Eagle Search Associates*
Gilbert, Jerry — *Gilbert & Van Campen International*
Gilchrist, Robert J. — *Horton International*
Giles, Joe L. — *Joe L. Giles and Associates, Inc.*
Gill, Patricia — *Columbia Consulting Group*
Gillespie, Thomas — *Professional Search Consultants*
Gilmore, Connie — *Taylor-Winfield, Inc.*
Gilreath, James M. — *Gilreath Weatherby, Inc.*
Giries, Juliet D. — *Barton Associates, Inc.*
Girsinger, Linda — *Industrial Recruiters Associates, Inc.*
Glacy, Kurt — *Winter, Wyman & Company*
Glass, Sharon — *Logix Partners*
Glass, Sharon — *Logix, Inc.*
Gloss, Frederick C. — *F. Gloss International*
Goar, Duane R. — *Sandhurst Associates*
Gobert, Larry — *Professional Search Consultants*
Goedtke, Steven — *Southwestern Professional Services*
Gold, Donald — *Executive Search, Ltd.*
Goldberg, Susan C. — *Susan C. Goldberg Associates*
Goldenberg, Susan — *Grant Cooper and Associates*
Goldman, Michael L. — *Strategic Associates, Inc.*
Goldsmith, Fred J. — *Fred J. Goldsmith Associates*
Gomez, Cristina — *Juntunen-Combs-Poirier*

Gonye, Peter K. — *Egon Zehnder International Inc.*
Gonzalez, Kristen — *A.J. Burton Group, Inc.*
Goodere, Greg — *Splaine & Associates, Inc.*
Goodman, Dawn M. — *Bason Associates Inc.*
Goodman, Victor — *Anderson Sterling Associates*
Goodwin, Tim — *William Guy & Associates*
Gordon, Elliot — *Korn/Ferry International*
Gordon, Teri — *Don Richard Associates of Washington, D.C., Inc.*
Gore, Les — *Executive Search International*
Gorfinkle, Gayle — *Executive Search International*
Gorman, T. Patrick — *Techsearch Services, Inc.*
Gostyla, Rick — *Spencer Stuart*
Gottenberg, Norbert — *Spencer Stuart*
Gould, Adam — *Logix Partners*
Gould, Adam — *Logix, Inc.*
Gould, Dana — *Logix Partners*
Gould, Dana — *Logix, Inc.*
Grady, James — *Search West, Inc.*
Graham, Dale — *CPS Inc.*
Grant, Michael — *Zwell International*
Grantham, Philip H. — *Columbia Consulting Group*
Grasch, Jerry E. — *The Hindman Company*
Graves, Rosemarie — *Don Richard Associates of Washington, D.C., Inc.*
Gray, Betty — *Accent on Achievement, Inc.*
Grebenstein, Charles R. — *Skott/Edwards Consultants, Inc.*
Green, Jane — *Phillips Resource Group*
Green, Jean — *Broward-Dobbs, Inc.*
Green, Marc — *TSS Consulting, Ltd.*
Greene, Luke — *Broward-Dobbs, Inc.*
Gregor, Joie A. — *Heidrick & Struggles, Inc.*
Gregory, Gary A. — *John Kurosky & Associates*
Griffin, Cathy — *A.T. Kearney, Inc.*
Groover, David — *MSI International*
Grotte, Lawrence C. — *Lautz Grotte Engler*
Grzybowski, Jill — *CPS Inc.*
Gurnani, Angali — *Executive Placement Consultants, Inc.*
Gutknecht, Steven — *Jacobson Associates*
Guy, C. William — *William Guy & Associates*
Haas, Margaret P. — *The Haas Associates, Inc.*
Haddad, Charles — *Romac & Associates*
Hailes, Brian — *Russell Reynolds Associates, Inc.*
Hailey, H.M. — *Damon & Associates, Inc.*
Halbrich, Mitch — *A.J. Burton Group, Inc.*
Hall, Marty B. — *Catlin-Wells & White*
Hall, Robert — *Don Richard Associates of Tidewater, Inc.*
Halladay, Patti — *Intersource, Ltd.*
Hamburg, Jennifer Power — *Ledbetter/Davidson International, Inc.*
Hamilton, John R. — *Ray & Berndtson*
Hamm, Mary Kay — *Romac & Associates*
Hanes, Leah — *Ray & Berndtson*
Hanley, Alan P. — *Williams, Roth & Krueger Inc.*
Hanley, Maureen E. — *Gilbert Tweed/INESA*
Hanna, Dwight — *Cadillac Associates*
Hanson, Lee — *Heidrick & Struggles, Inc.*
Harbaugh, Paul J. — *International Management Advisors, Inc.*
Hardison, Richard L. — *Hardison & Company*
Harelick, Arthur S. — *Ashway, Ltd.*
Harfenist, Harry — *Parker Page Group*

Jeffers, Richard B. — *Dieckmann & Associates, Ltd.*
Jensen, Christine K. — *John Kurosky & Associates*
Jerolman, Gregg — *Masserman & Associates, Inc.*
Joffe, Barry — *Bason Associates Inc.*
Johnson, Brian — *A.J. Burton Group, Inc.*
Johnson, David A. — *Gaffney Management Consultants*
Johnson, Douglas — *Quality Search*
Johnson, Harold E. — *Lamalie Amrop International*
Johnson, John W. — *Webb, Johnson Associates, Inc.*
Johnson, Julie M. — *International Staffing Consultants, Inc.*
Johnson, Kathleen A. — *Barton Associates, Inc.*
Johnson, Keith — *Romac & Associates*
Johnson, Peter — *Winter, Wyman & Company*
Johnson, Robert J. — *Quality Search*
Johnson, Rocky — *A.T. Kearney, Inc.*
Johnson, Ronald S. — *Ronald S. Johnson Associates, Inc.*
Johnson, Valerie — *Coe & Company International Inc.*
Johnston, Michael — *Robertson-Surrette Executive Search*
Jones, Amy E. — *The Corporate Connection, Ltd.*
Jones, B.J. — *Intersource, Ltd.*
Jones, Barbara — *Kaye-Bassman International Corp.*
Jones, Barbara J. — *Kaye-Bassman International Corp.*
Jones, Daniel F. — *Atlantic Search Group, Inc.*
Jordan, Jon — *Cochran, Cochran & Yale, Inc.*
Joyce, William J. — *The Guild Corporation*
Jozwik, Peter — *The Search Firm, Inc.*
Judge, Alfred L. — *The Cambridge Group Ltd*
Judy, Otto — *CPS Inc.*
Juratovac, Michael — *Montgomery Resources, Inc.*
Juska, Frank — *Rusher, Loscavio & LoPresto*
Kacyn, Louis J. — *Egon Zehnder International Inc.*
Kaiser, Donald J. — *Dunhill International Search of New Haven*
Kane, Frank — *A.J. Burton Group, Inc.*
Kane, Karen — *Howard Fischer Associates, Inc.*
Kanrich, Susan Azaria — *AlternaStaff*
Kaplan, Alexandra — *J.M. Eagle Partners Ltd.*
Kaplan, Gary — *Gary Kaplan & Associates*
Karalis, William — *CPS Inc.*
Kasmouski, Steve — *Winter, Wyman & Company*
Kaye, Jeffrey — *Kaye-Bassman International Corp.*
Kehoe, Mike — *CPS Inc.*
Keitel, Robert S. — *A.T. Kearney, Inc.*
Keith, Stephanie — *Southwestern Professional Services*
Keller, Barbara E. — *Barton Associates, Inc.*
Kells, John — *Heffelfinger Associates, Inc.*
Kelly, Elizabeth Ann — *Wellington Management Group*
Kelly, Sheri — *Strategic Associates, Inc.*
Kelly, Susan D. — *S.D. Kelly & Associates, Inc.*
Kelso, Patricia C. — *Barton Associates, Inc.*
Kennedy, Walter — *Romac & Associates*
Kent, Melvin — *Melvin Kent & Associates, Inc.*
Kerester, Jonathon — *Cadillac Associates*
Kern, Jerry L. — *ADOW's Executeam*

Kern, Kathleen G. — *ADOW's Executeam*
Kershaw, Lisa — *Tanton Mitchell/Paul Ray Berndtson*
Keshishian, Gregory — *Handy HRM Corp.*
Keyser, Anne — *A.T. Kearney, Inc.*
Kilcoyne, Pat — *CPS Inc.*
King, Bill — *The McCormick Group, Inc.*
King, Margaret — *Christian & Timbers*
King, Steven — *Ashway, Ltd.*
Kinney, Carol — *Dussick Management Associates*
Kinser, Richard E. — *Richard Kinser & Associates*
Kinsey, Joanne — *Eastridge InfoTech*
Kirkman, J. Michael — *Kirkman & Searing, Inc.*
Kishbaugh, Herbert S. — *Kishbaugh Associates International*
Kixmiller, David B. — *Heidrick & Struggles, Inc.*
Kkorzyniewski, Nicole — *CPS Inc.*
Klages, Constance W. — *International Management Advisors, Inc.*
Klavens, Cecile J. — *The Pickwick Group, Inc.*
Klein, Brandon — *A.J. Burton Group, Inc.*
Klein, Gary — *A.T. Kearney, Inc.*
Klein, Mary Jo — *Cochran, Cochran & Yale, Inc.*
Klein, Mel — *Stewart/Laurence Associates*
Knapp, Ronald A. — *Knapp Consultants*
Knotts, Jerry — *Mixtec Group*
Kobayashi, Rika — *International Staffing Consultants, Inc.*
Koblentz, Joel M. — *Egon Zehnder International Inc.*
Koehler, Frank R. — *The Koehler Group*
Koenig, Joel S. — *Blackshaw, Olmstead, Lynch & Koenig*
Koenig, Joel S. — *Blackshaw, Olmstead, Lynch & Koenig*
Kohonoski, Michael M. — *The Guild Corporation*
Kondra, Vernon J. — *The Douglas Reiter Company, Inc.*
Koontz, Donald N. — *Koontz, Jeffries & Associates, Inc.*
Kopec, Tom — *D. Brown and Associates, Inc.*
Kors, R. Paul — *Kors Montgomery International*
Kossuth, David — *Kossuth & Associates, Inc.*
Kossuth, Jane — *Kossuth & Associates, Inc.*
Kouble, Tim — *Logix Partners*
Kouble, Tim — *Logix, Inc.*
Krejci, Stanley L. — *Boyden Washington, D.C.*
Kreutz, Gary L. — *Kreutz Consulting Group, Inc.*
Krieger, Dennis F. — *Seiden Krieger Associates, Inc.*
Krueger, Kurt — *Krueger Associates*
Kuhl, Teresa — *Don Richard Associates of Tampa, Inc.*
Kunzer, William J. — *Kunzer Associates, Ltd.*
Kuo, Linda — *Montgomery Resources, Inc.*
Kurrigan, Geoffrey — *ESA Professional Consultants*
Kussner, Janice N. — *Herman Smith Executive Initiatives Inc.*
Labrecque, Bernard F. — *Laurendeau Labrecque/Ray & Berndtson, Inc.*
LaCharite, Danielle — *The Guild Corporation*
Lache, Shawn E. — *The Arcus Group*
Laderman, David — *Romac & Associates*
Laird, Cheryl — *CPS Inc.*
Lamb, Lynn M. — *F-O-R-T-U-N-E Personnel Consultants of Huntsville, Inc.*

Lanctot, William D. — *Corporate Resources Professional Placement*
Lang, Sharon A. — *Ray & Berndtson*
Langan, Marion — *Logix Partners*
Langan, Marion — *Logix, Inc.*
Langford, Matt — *F-O-R-T-U-N-E Personnel Consultants of Huntsville, Inc.*
Langford, Robert W. — *F-O-R-T-U-N-E Personnel Consultants of Huntsville, Inc.*
Lapat, Aaron D. — *J. Robert Scott*
LaPierre, Louis — *Romac & Associates*
Larsen, Jack B. — *Jack B. Larsen & Associates*
Lasher, Charles M. — *Lasher Associates*
Laub, Stuart R. — *Abraham & London, Ltd.*
Lauderback, David R. — *A.T. Kearney, Inc.*
Lautz, Lindsay A. — *Lautz Grotte Engler*
LaValle, Michael — *Romac & Associates*
Lawner, Harvey — *Walden Associates*
Leahy, Jan — *CPS Inc.*
LeComte, Andre — *Egon Zehnder International Inc.*
Ledbetter, Charlene — *Ledbetter/Davidson International, Inc.*
Ledbetter, Steven G. — *Cendea Connection International*
Lee, Roger — *Montgomery Resources, Inc.*
Leff, Lisa A. — *Berger and Leff*
Leland, Paul — *McInturff & Associates, Inc.*
Lence, Julie Anne — *MSI International*
Lenkaitis, Lewis F. — *A.T. Kearney, Inc.*
Lennox, Charles — *Price Waterhouse*
Letcher, Harvey D. — *Sandhurst Associates*
Levitt, Muriel A. — *D.S. Allen Associates, Inc.*
Lewicki, Christopher — *MSI International*
Lewis, Gretchen S. — *Heidrick & Struggles, Inc.*
Lewis, Jon A. — *Sandhurst Associates*
Lewis, Marc D. — *Handy HRM Corp.*
Lewis, Susan — *Logix Partners*
Lewis, Susan — *Logix, Inc.*
Lezama Cohen, Luis — *Ray & Berndtson*
Lichtenauer, Eric W. — *Britt Associates, Inc.*
Lichtenauer, William E. — *Britt Associates, Inc.*
Lieberman, Beverly — *Halbrecht Lieberman Associates, Inc.*
Lindberg, Eric J. — *MSI International*
Lindenmuth, Mary — *Search West, Inc.*
Lindholst, Kai — *Egon Zehnder International Inc.*
Line, Joseph T. — *Sharrow & Associates*
Linton, Leonard M. — *Byron Leonard International, Inc.*
Lipson, Harriet — *First Interactive Recruiting Specialists*
Lipson, Harriet — *Lipson & Co.*
Lipson, Howard K. — *First Interactive Recruiting Specialists*
Lipson, Howard R. — *Lipson & Co.*
Livingston, Peter R. — *Livingston, Robert and Company Inc.*
Loewenstein, Victor H. — *Egon Zehnder International Inc.*
Lofthouse, Cindy — *CPS Inc.*
Lokken, Karen — *A.E. Feldman Associates*
Lonergan, Mark W. — *Heidrick & Struggles, Inc.*
Long, Helga — *Horton International*
Long, Milt — *William Guy & Associates*
Long, Thomas — *Egon Zehnder International Inc.*

Long, William G. — *McDonald, Long & Associates, Inc.*
Looney, Scott — *A.E. Feldman Associates*
LoPresto, Robert L. — *Rusher, Loscavio & LoPresto*
LoRusso, Steve — *Warren, Morris & Madison*
Lotufo, Donald A. — *D.A.L. Associates, Inc.*
Lotz, R. James — *International Management Advisors, Inc.*
Lovas, W. Carl — *Ray & Berndtson/Lovas Stanley*
Love, David M. — *Ray & Berndtson*
Loving, Vikki — *Intersource, Ltd.*
Lucarelli, Joan — *The Onstott Group, Inc.*
Lucas, Ronnie L. — *MSI International*
Lucht, John — *The John Lucht Consultancy Inc.*
Luke, A. Wayne — *Heidrick & Struggles, Inc.*
Lumsby, George N. — *International Management Advisors, Inc.*
Luntz, Charles E. — *Charles Luntz & Associates. Inc.*
Lupica, Anthony — *Cochran, Cochran & Yale, Inc.*
Lyons, J. David — *Aubin International Inc.*
Macdonald, G. William — *The Macdonald Group, Inc.*
MacDougall, Andrew J. — *Spencer Stuart*
MacKinnon, Helen — *Technical Connections Inc.*
MacNaughton, Sperry — *McNaughton Associates*
Mader, Stephen P. — *Christian & Timbers*
Magee, Harrison R. — *Bowden & Company, Inc.*
Maglio, Charles J. — *Maglio and Company, Inc.*
Mahaney, Joann — *Heidrick & Struggles, Inc.*
Major, Susan — *A.T. Kearney, Inc.*
Makrianes, James K. — *Webb, Johnson Associates, Inc.*
Mallin, Ellen — *Howard Fischer Associates, Inc.*
Manassero, Henri J.P. — *International Management Advisors, Inc.*
Mangum, Maria — *Thomas Mangum Company*
Mangum, William T. — *Thomas Mangum Company*
Manns, Alex — *Crawford & Crofford*
Mansford, Keith — *Howard Fischer Associates, Inc.*
Marcine, John W. — *Keith Bagg & Associates Inc.*
Marino, Chester — *Cochran, Cochran & Yale, Inc.*
Marion, Michael — *S.D. Kelly & Associates, Inc.*
Mark, John L. — *J.L. Mark Associates, Inc.*
Mark, Lynne — *J.L. Mark Associates, Inc.*
Marks, Ira — *Strategic Alternatives*
Marks, Russell E. — *Webb, Johnson Associates, Inc.*
Marlow, William — *Straube Associates*
Martin, David — *The Guild Corporation*
Martin, Jon — *Egon Zehnder International Inc.*
Marumoto, William H. — *Boyden Washington, D.C.*
Marye, George — *Damon & Associates, Inc.*
Mashakas, Elizabeth — *TOPAZ International, Inc.*
Mashakas, Elizabeth — *TOPAZ Legal Solutions*
Masserman, Bruce — *Masserman & Associates, Inc.*
Massey, R. Bruce — *Horton International*
Mather, David R. — *Christian & Timbers*
Mathias, Kathy — *Stone Murphy & Olson*
Matthews, Corwin — *Woodworth International Group*

Mauer, Kristin — *Montgomery Resources, Inc.*
May, Peter — *Mixtec Group*
Mayes, Kay H. — *John Shell Associates, Inc.*
Mayland, Tina — *Russell Reynolds Associates, Inc.*
Maynard Taylor, Susan — *Chrisman & Company, Incorporated*
Mazor, Elly — *Howard Fischer Associates, Inc.*
Mazza, David B. — *Mazza & Riley, Inc. (a Korn/Ferry International affiliate)*
McAndrews, Kathy — *CPS Inc.*
McAteer, Thomas — *Montgomery Resources, Inc.*
McBride, Dee — *Deeco International*
McBride, Jonathan E. — *McBride Associates, Inc.*
McCloskey, Frank D. — *Johnson Smith & Knisely Accord*
McClure, James K. — *Korn/Ferry International*
McComas, Kelly E. — *The Guild Corporation*
McConnell, Greg — *Winter, Wyman & Company*
McCormick, Brian — *The McCormick Group, Inc.*
McCormick, William J. — *The McCormick Group, Inc.*
McCreary, Charles "Chip" — *Austin-McGregor International*
McDermott, Jeffrey T. — *Vlcek & Company, Inc.*
McDonald, John R. — *TSS Consulting, Ltd.*
McDonald, Scott A. — *McDonald Associates International*
McDonald, Stanleigh B. — *McDonald Associates International*
McDonnell, Julie — *Technical Personnel of Minnesota*
McFadzen, Donna — *Holland, McFadzean & Associates, Inc.*
McFadzen, James A. — *Holland, McFadzean & Associates, Inc.*
McGregor, James D. — *John Kurosky & Associates*
McGuire, Pat — *A.J. Burton Group, Inc.*
McHale, Rob — *Paul-Tittle Associates, Inc.*
McInturff, Robert — *McInturff & Associates, Inc.*
McIntyre, Joel — *Phillips Resource Group*
McKeown, Morgan J. — *Christian & Timbers*
McKeown, Patricia A. — *DiMarchi Partners, Inc.*
McKnight, Amy E. — *Chartwell Partners International, Inc.*
McLaughlin, John — *Romac & Associates*
McMahon, Mark J. — *A.T. Kearney, Inc.*
McManners, Donald E. — *McManners Associates, Inc.*
McManus, Paul — *Aubin International Inc.*
McMillin, Bob — *Price Waterhouse*
McNamara, Catherine — *Ray & Berndtson*
McNamara, Timothy C. — *Columbia Consulting Group*
McNamee, Erin — *Technical Connections Inc.*
McNerney, Kevin A. — *Heidrick & Struggles, Inc.*
McNichol, John — *McNichol Associates*
McNichols, Walter B. — *Gary Kaplan & Associates*
McSherry, James F. — *Battalia Winston International*
McThrall, David — *TSS Consulting, Ltd.*
Medina-Haro, Adolfo — *Heidrick & Struggles, Inc.*
Mefford, Bob — *Executive Manning Corporation*
Meiland, A. Daniel — *Egon Zehnder International Inc.*

Mercer, Julie — *Columbia Consulting Group*
Mertensotto, Chuck H. — *Whitney & Associates, Inc.*
Metz, Dan K. — *Russell Reynolds Associates, Inc.*
Meyer, Stacey — *Gary Kaplan & Associates*
Meyers, Steven — *Montgomery Resources, Inc.*
Michaels, Joseph — *CPS Inc.*
Michaels, Stewart — *TOPAZ International, Inc.*
Michaels, Stewart — *TOPAZ Legal Solutions*
Mierzwinski, John — *Industrial Recruiters Associates, Inc.*
Mikula, Linda — *Schweichler Associates, Inc.*
Miles, Kenneth T. — *MSI International*
Miller, Brett — *The McCormick Group, Inc.*
Miller, David — *Cochran, Cochran & Yale, Inc.*
Miller, Kenneth A. — *Computer Network Resources, Inc.*
Miller, Roy — *The Enns Partners Inc.*
Mingle, Larry D. — *Columbia Consulting Group*
Misiurewicz, Marc — *Cochran, Cochran & Yale, Inc.*
Mitchell, F. Wayne — *Korn/Ferry International*
Mitchell, Jeff — *A.J. Burton Group, Inc.*
Mitchell, John — *Romac & Associates*
Mitton, Bill — *Executive Resource, Inc.*
Moerbe, Ed H. — *Stanton Chase International*
Mogul, Gene — *Mogul Consultants, Inc.*
Mohr, Brian — *CPS Inc.*
Molnar, Robert A. — *Johnson Smith & Knisely Accord*
Mondragon, Philip — *A.T. Kearney, Inc.*
Montgomery, James M. — *Houze, Shourds & Montgomery, Inc.*
Moodley, Logan — *Austin-McGregor International*
Moore, David S. — *Lynch Miller Moore, Inc.*
Moore, Lemuel R. — *MSI International*
Moore, Mark — *Wheeler, Moore & Elam Co.*
Moore, T. Wills — *Ray & Berndtson*
Moran, Gayle — *Dussick Management Associates*
Morgan, Richard S. — *Ray & Berndtson/Lovas Stanley*
Morris, Chuck — *Warren, Morris & Madison*
Mortansen, Patricia — *Norman Broadbent International, Inc.*
Moses, Jerry — *J.M. Eagle Partners Ltd.*
Mouchet, Marcus — *Commonwealth Consultants*
Mueller-Maerki, Fortunat F. — *Egon Zehnder International Inc.*
Muendel, H. Edward — *Stanton Chase International*
Muller, Susan — *Corporate Recruiters Ltd.*
Murphy, Erin — *CPS Inc.*
Murphy, Gary J. — *Stone Murphy & Olson*
Murphy, Timothy D. — *MSI International*
Murray, Virginia — *A.T. Kearney, Inc.*
Mursuli, Meredith — *Lasher Associates*
Myatt, James S. — *Sanford Rose Associates*
Mydlach, Renee — *CPS Inc.*
Nadherny, Christopher C. — *Spencer Stuart*
Nadzam, Richard I. — *Nadzam, Lusk, Horgan & Associates, Inc.*
Nagler, Leon G. — *Nagler, Robins & Poe, Inc.*
Naidicz, Maria — *Ray & Berndtson*
Neelin, Sharon — *The Caldwell Partners Amrop International*
Neely, Alan S. — *Korn/Ferry International*
Nees, Eugene C. — *Ray & Berndtson*

Neff, Thomas J. — *Spencer Stuart*
Neher, Robert L. — *Intech Summit Group, Inc.*
Nehring, Keith — *Howard Fischer Associates, Inc.*
Neidhart, Craig C. — *TNS Partners, Inc.*
Nelson, Barbara — *Herman Smith Executive Initiatives Inc.*
Nemec, Phillip — *Dunhill International Search of New Haven*
Nephew, Robert — *Christian & Timbers*
Neuberth, Jeffrey G. — *Canny, Bowen Inc.*
Newman, Lynn — *Kishbaugh Associates International*
Nguyen, John — *International Staffing Consultants, Inc.*
Nichols, Gary — *Koontz, Jeffries & Associates, Inc.*
Niejet, Michael C. — *O'Brien & Bell*
Noguchi, Yoshi — *Ray & Berndtson*
Nolan, Jean M. — *S.D. Kelly & Associates, Inc.*
Nold, Robert — *Roberson and Company*
Nolte, William D. — *W.D. Nolte & Company*
Nolton, Becky — *Paul-Tittle Associates, Inc.*
Norman, Randy — *Austin-McGregor International*
Norris, Ken — *A.T. Kearney, Inc.*
Norsell, Paul E. — *Paul Norsell & Associates, Inc.*
Norton, James B. — *Lamalie Amrop International*
Nymark, John — *NYCOR Search, Inc.*
Nymark, Paul — *NYCOR Search, Inc.*
O'Connell, Mary — *CPS Inc.*
O'Hara, Daniel M. — *Lynch Miller Moore, Inc.*
O'Maley, Kimberlee — *Spencer Stuart*
O'Neill, Kevin G. — *HRS, Inc.*
O'Reilly, John — *Stratford Group*
Ocon, Olga — *Busch International*
Ogilvie, Kit — *Howard Fischer Associates, Inc.*
Oldfield, Theresa — *Strategic Alliance Network, Ltd.*
Olmstead, George T. — *Blackshaw, Olmstead, Lynch & Koenig*
Olsen, Carl — *A.T. Kearney, Inc.*
Olsen, Kristine — *Williams Executive Search, Inc.*
Onstott, Joseph — *The Onstott Group, Inc.*
Onstott, Joseph E. — *The Onstott Group, Inc.*
Orkin, Ralph — *Sanford Rose Associates*
Orkin, Sheilah — *Sanford Rose Associates*
Ott, George W. — *Ott & Hansen, Inc.*
Ottenritter, Chris — *CPS Inc.*
Overlock, Craig — *Ray & Berndtson*
Pacini, Lauren R. — *Hite Executive Search*
Padilla, Jose Sanchez — *Egon Zehnder International Inc.*
Page, G. Schuyler — *A.T. Kearney, Inc.*
Palmer, Carlton A. — *Beall & Company, Inc.*
Palmer, James H. — *The Hindman Company*
Palmer, Melissa — *Don Richard Associates of Tampa, Inc.*
Panarese, Pam — *Howard Fischer Associates, Inc.*
Panetta, Timothy — *Commonwealth Consultants*
Papasadero, Kathleen — *Woodworth International Group*
Papciak, Dennis J. — *Accounting Personnel Associates, Inc.*
Papciak, Dennis J. — *Temporary Accounting Personnel*
Papoulias, Cathy — *Pendleton James and Associates, Inc.*
Pappalardo, Charles A. — *Christian & Timbers*

Pappas, Christina E. — *Williams Executive Search, Inc.*
Pappas, Jim — *Search Dynamics, Inc.*
Pardo, Maria Elena — *Smith Search, S.C.*
Park, Dabney G. — *Mark Stanley/EMA Partners International*
Parkin, Myrna — *S.D. Kelly & Associates, Inc.*
Parr, James A. — *KPMG Management Consulting*
Parsons, Allison D. — *Barton Associates, Inc.*
Pastrana, Dario — *Egon Zehnder International Inc.*
Patrick, Donald R. — *Sanford Rose Associates*
Payette, Pierre — *Egon Zehnder International Inc.*
Pearson, Robert L. — *Lamalie Amrop International*
Peckenpaugh, Ann D. — *Schweichler Associates, Inc.*
Pedley, Jill — *CPS Inc.*
Pelkey, Chris — *The McCormick Group, Inc.*
Percival, Chris — *Chicago Legal Search, Ltd.*
Pernell, Jeanette — *Norman Broadbent International, Inc.*
Perry, Glen — *Keith Bagg & Associates Inc.*
Persky, Barry — *Barry Persky & Company, Inc.*
Peters, James N. — *TNS Partners, Inc.*
Peterson, John — *CPS Inc.*
Petty, J. Scott — *The Arcus Group*
Pfau, Madelaine — *Heidrick & Struggles, Inc.*
Pfeiffer, Irene — *Price Waterhouse*
Pfister, Shelli — *Jack B. Larsen & Associates*
Phelps, Gene L. — *McCormack & Farrow*
Phillips, Donald L. — *O'Shea, Divine & Company, Inc.*
Phillips, Richard K. — *Handy HRM Corp.*
Phinney, Bruce — *Paul-Tittle Associates, Inc.*
Phipps, Peggy — *Woodworth International Group*
Pickford, Stephen T. — *The Corporate Staff, Inc.*
Pierotazio, John — *CPS Inc.*
Pigott, Daniel — *ESA Professional Consultants*
Pinson, Stephanie L. — *Gilbert Tweed/INESA*
Plimpton, Ralph L. — *R L Plimpton Associates*
Poe, James B. — *Nagler, Robins & Poe, Inc.*
Poirier, Frank — *Juntunen-Combs-Poirier*
Poirier, Roland L. — *Poirier, Hoevel & Co.*
Polachi, Charles A. — *Fenwick Partners*
Polachi, Peter V. — *Fenwick Partners*
Pomerance, Mark — *CPS Inc.*
Pomeroy, T. Lee — *Egon Zehnder International Inc.*
Poremski, Paul — *A.J. Burton Group, Inc.*
Porter, Albert — *The Experts*
Poster, Lawrence D. — *Catalyx Group*
Potter, Douglas C. — *Stanton Chase International*
Press, Fred — *Adept Tech Recruiting*
Price, Andrew G. — *The Thomas Tucker Company*
Price, P. Anthony — *Russell Reynolds Associates, Inc.*
Prior, Donald — *The Caldwell Partners Amrop International*
Prumatico, John — *Intelligent Management Solutions, Inc. (IMS)*
Prusak, Conrad E. — *Ethos Consulting Inc.*
Prusak, Julie J. — *Ethos Consulting Inc.*
Pryde, Marcia P. — *A.T. Kearney, Inc.*
Pryor, Bill — *Cendea Connection International*
Pugh, Judith — *Intelligent Management Solutions, Inc. (IMS)*

Pugrant, Mark A. — *Grant/Morgan Associates, Inc.*
Quinlan, Lynne — *Winter, Wyman & Company*
Quinn, Nola — *Technical Connections Inc.*
Raab, Julie — *Dunhill Professional Search of Irvine, Inc.*
Rabinowitz, Peter A. — *P.A.R. Associates Inc.*
Radden, David B. — *Ray & Berndtson*
Raines, Bruce R. — *Raines International Inc.*
Ramler, Carolyn S. — *The Corporate Connection, Ltd.*
Ramsey, John H. — *Mark Stanley/EMA Partners International*
Randell, James E. — *Randell-Heiken, Inc.*
Ray, Marianne C. — *Callan Associates, Ltd.*
Raymond, Anne — *Anderson Sterling Associates*
Reddick, David C. — *Horton International*
Redding, Denise — *The Douglas Reiter Company, Inc.*
Reece, Christopher S. — *Reece & Mruk Partners*
Reed, Ruthann — *Spectra International Inc.*
Regan, Thomas J. — *Tower Consultants, Ltd.*
Reisinger, George L. — *Sigma Group International*
Reiter, Douglas — *The Douglas Reiter Company, Inc.*
Remillard, Brad M. — *CJA - The Adler Group*
Renner, Sandra L. — *Spectra International Inc.*
Renwick, David — *John Kurosky & Associates*
Reuter, Tandom — *CPS Inc.*
Reynes, Tony — *Tesar-Reynes, Inc.*
Ribeiro, Claudia — *Ledbetter/Davidson International, Inc.*
Rice, Marie — *Jay Gaines & Company, Inc.*
Rice, Raymond D. — *Logue & Rice Inc.*
Richard, Albert L. — *The Search Alliance, Inc.*
Ridenour, Suzanne S. — *Ridenour & Associates, Ltd.*
Riederer, Larry — *CPS Inc.*
Rimmel, James E. — *The Hindman Company*
Rimmele, Michael — *The Bankers Group*
Rippey, George E. — *Heidrick & Struggles, Inc.*
Roberts, Mitch — *A.E. Feldman Associates*
Roberts, Nick P. — *Spectrum Search Associates, Inc.*
Roberts, Scott — *Jonas, Walters & Assoc., Inc.*
Robertson, Bruce J. — *Lamalie Amrop International*
Robertson, John A. — *Kaye-Bassman International Corp.*
Robertson, Ronald — *Robertson-Surrette Executive Search*
Robinette, Paul — *Hernand & Partners*
Robins, Jeri N. — *Nagler, Robins & Poe, Inc.*
Robinson, Bruce — *Bruce Robinson Associates*
Robles Cuellar, Paulina — *Ray & Berndtson*
Roblin, Nancy R. — *Paul-Tittle Associates, Inc.*
Rogers, Leah — *Dinte Resources, Inc.*
Rojo, Rafael — *A.T. Kearney, Inc.*
Romanello, Daniel P. — *Spencer Stuart*
Rorech, Maureen — *Romac & Associates*
Rosato, William R. — *W.R. Rosato & Associates, Inc.*
Rose, Robert — *ESA Professional Consultants*
Ross, Curt A. — *Ray & Berndtson*
Ross, H. Lawrence — *Ross & Company*
Ross, Lawrence — *Ray & Berndtson/Lovas Stanley*
Ross, Mark — *Ray & Berndtson/Lovas Stanley*
Ross, William J. — *Flowers & Associates*

Rossi, George A. — *Heidrick & Struggles, Inc.*
Rossi, Thomas — *Southwestern Professional Services*
Rotella, Marshall W. — *The Corporate Connection, Ltd.*
Roth, Robert J. — *Williams, Roth & Krueger Inc.*
Rothschild, John S. — *Lamalie Amrop International*
Rottblatt, Michael — *Korn/Ferry International*
Roussel, Vicki — *Logix Partners*
Roussel, Vicki J. — *Logix, Inc.*
Rowe, William D. — *D.E. Foster Partners Inc.*
Rowell, Roger — *Halbrecht Lieberman Associates, Inc.*
Rozentsvayg, Michael — *Logix Partners*
Rozentsvayg, Michael — *Logix, Inc.*
Rozner, Burton L. — *Oliver & Rozner Associates, Inc.*
Rubenstein, Alan J. — *Chicago Legal Search, Ltd.*
Rubinstein, Walter — *Technical Connections Inc.*
Rudolph, Kenneth — *Kossuth & Associates, Inc.*
Rudzinsky, Howard — *Louis Rudzinsky Associates*
Rudzinsky, Jeffrey — *Louis Rudzinsky Associates*
Ruge, Merrill — *William Guy & Associates*
Runquist, U.W. — *Webb, Johnson Associates, Inc.*
Rurak, Zbigniew T. — *Rurak & Associates, Inc.*
Rush, Michael E. — *D.A.L. Associates, Inc.*
Russell, Sam — *The Guild Corporation*
Ryan, Annette — *Don Richard Associates of Tidewater, Inc.*
Ryan, Lee — *Ryan, Miller & Associates Inc.*
Sabat, Lori S. — *Alta Associates, Inc.*
Safnuk, Donald — *Corporate Recruiters Ltd.*
Sahagian, John — *The Search Alliance, Inc.*
Saletra, Andrew — *CPS Inc.*
Salottolo, Al — *Tactical Alternatives*
Salvagno, Michael J. — *The Cambridge Group Ltd*
Sanders, Jason — *Sanders Management Associates, Inc.*
Sanders, Natalie — *CPS Inc.*
Saner, Harold — *Romac & Associates*
Sangster, Jeffrey — *F-O-R-T-U-N-E Personnel Consultants of Manatee County*
Sanitago, Anthony — *TaxSearch, Inc.*
Sanow, Robert — *Cochran, Cochran & Yale, Inc.*
Sarn, Allan G. — *Allan Sarn Associates Inc.*
Sauer, Harry J. — *Romac & Associates*
Sauer, Robert C. — *Heidrick & Struggles, Inc.*
Sausto, Lynne — *Abraham & London, Ltd.*
Savvas, Carol Diane — *Ledbetter/Davidson International, Inc.*
Sawyer, Patricia L. — *Smith & Sawyer Inc.*
Saxon, Alexa — *Woodworth International Group*
Scalamera, Tom — *CPS Inc.*
Schaad, Carl A. — *Heidrick & Struggles, Inc.*
Schaefer, Frederic M. — *A.T. Kearney, Inc.*
Schall, William A. — *The Stevenson Group of New Jersey*
Schappell, Marc P. — *Egon Zehnder International Inc.*
Schene, Philip — *A.E. Feldman Associates*
Schiavone, Mary Rose — *Canny, Bowen Inc.*
Schlpma, Christine — *Advanced Executive Resources*
Schmidt, Peter R. — *Boyden*
Schmidt, Peter R. — *Boyden*
Schneider, James — *The Search Firm, Inc.*

Stevenson, Jane — *Howard Fischer Associates, Inc.*
Stevenson, Terry — *Bartholdi & Company, Inc.*
Stewart, Jan J. — *Egon Zehnder International Inc.*
Stewart, Jeffrey O. — *Stewart, Stein and Scott, Ltd.*
Stewart, Ross M. — *Human Resources Network Partners Inc.*
Stiles, Jack D. — *Sanford Rose Associates*
Stiles, Judy — *MedQuest Associates*
Stiles, Timothy — *Sanford Rose Associates*
Stirn, Bradley A. — *Spencer Stuart*
Stokes, John — *Nordeman Grimm, Inc.*
Stone, Robert Ryder — *Lamalie Amrop International*
Stone, Susan L. — *Stone Enterprises Ltd.*
Stovall, Randal — *D. Brown and Associates, Inc.*
Strain, Stephen R. — *Spencer Stuart*
Stranberg, James R. — *Callan Associates, Ltd.*
Strassman, Mark — *Don Richard Associates of Washington, D.C., Inc.*
Stratton, Cary — *Coastal International Inc.*
Stringer, Dann P. — *D.E. Foster Partners Inc.*
Strom, Mark N. — *Search Advisors International Corp.*
Struzziero, Ralph E. — *Romac & Associates*
Sullivan, Kay — *Rusher, Loscavio & LoPresto*
Sur, William K. — *Canny, Bowen Inc.*
Surrette, Mark — *Robertson-Surrette Executive Search*
Sussman, Lynda — *Gilbert Tweed/INESA*
Sutter, Howard — *Romac & Associates*
Sutton, Robert J. — *The Caldwell Partners Amrop International*
Swartz, William K. — *Swartz Executive Search*
Sweeney, James W. — *Sweeney Harbert & Mummert, Inc.*
Sweetser, Rob — *Warren, Morris & Madison*
Swick, Jan — *TSS Consulting, Ltd.*
Swidler, J. Robert — *Egon Zehnder International Inc.*
Swoboda, Lawrence — *A.J. Burton Group, Inc.*
Taft, David G. — *Techsearch Services, Inc.*
Taft, Steven D. — *The Guild Corporation*
Tanton, John E. — *Tanton Mitchell/Paul Ray Berndtson*
Taylor, Charles E. — *Lamalie Amrop International*
Taylor, Conrad G. — *MSI International*
Taylor, Kenneth W. — *Egon Zehnder International Inc.*
Taylor, R.L. (Larry) — *Ray & Berndtson*
Telford, John H. — *Telford, Adams & Alexander/Telford & Co., Inc.*
ten Cate, Herman H. — *Stoneham Associates Corp.*
Tesar, Bob — *Tesar-Reynes, Inc.*
Tetrick, Tim — *O'Connor, O'Connor, Lordi, Ltd.*
Theard, Susan — *Romac & Associates*
Theobald, David B. — *Theobald & Associates*
Thies, Gary — *S.D. Kelly & Associates, Inc.*
Thomas, Cheryl M. — *CPS Inc.*
Thomas, Donald — *Mixtec Group*
Thomas, Ian A. — *International Staffing Consultants, Inc.*
Thomas, Kim — *CPS Inc.*
Thomas, Terry — *The Thomas Resource Group*
Thomas, William — *Mixtec Group*
Thompson, Kenneth L. — *McCormack & Farrow*

Thornton, John — *Stratford Group*
Thrapp, Mark C. — *Executive Search Consultants International, Inc.*
Tincu, John C. — *Ferneborg & Associates, Inc.*
Tittle, David M. — *Paul-Tittle Associates, Inc.*
Tootsey, Mark A. — *A.J. Burton Group, Inc.*
Topliff, Marla — *Gaffney Management Consultants*
Tovrog, Dan — *CPS Inc.*
Tracy, Ronald O. — *Egon Zehnder International Inc.*
Travis, Michael — *Travis & Company*
Trieweiler, Bob — *Executive Placement Consultants, Inc.*
Truemper, Dean — *CPS Inc.*
Truitt, Thomas B. — *Southwestern Professional Services*
Tucker, Thomas A. — *The Thomas Tucker Company*
Tullberg, Tina — *CPS Inc.*
Tully, Margo L. — *Tully/Woodmansee International, Inc.*
Turner, Edward K. — *Don Richard Associates of Charlotte*
Turner, Kimberly — *Barton Associates, Inc.*
Tuttle, Donald E. — *Tuttle Venture Group, Inc.*
Tweed, Janet — *Gilbert Tweed/INESA*
Ulbert, Nancy — *Aureus Group*
Ulrich, Mary Ann — *D.S. Allen Associates, Inc.*
Unterberg, Edward L. — *Russell Reynolds Associates, Inc.*
Utroska, Donald R. — *Lamalie Amrop International*
Vacca, Domenic — *Romac & Associates*
Vachon, David A. — *McNichol Associates*
Vairo, Leonard A. — *Christian & Timbers*
Van Biesen, Jacques A.H. — *Search Group Inc.*
Van Campen, Jerry — *Gilbert & Van Campen International*
Van Clieaf, Mark — *MVC Associates International*
Van Nostrand, Mara J. — *Barton Associates, Inc.*
Van Remmen, Roger — *Brown, Bernardy, Van Remmen, Inc.*
Vande-Water, Katie — *J. Robert Scott*
Vann, Dianne — *The Button Group*
Vaughan, David B. — *Dunhill Professional Search of Irvine, Inc.*
Velten, Mark T. — *Boyden*
Vennat, Manon — *Spencer Stuart*
Vernon, Peter C. — *Horton International*
Visnich, L. Christine — *Bason Associates Inc.*
Vogel, Michael S. — *Vogel Associates*
Voigt, John A. — *Romac & Associates*
Volkman, Arthur — *Cochran, Cochran & Yale, Inc.*
von Baillou, Astrid — *Richard Kinser & Associates*
Vossler, James — *A.J. Burton Group, Inc.*
Vourakis, Zan — *ZanExec LLC*
Vroom, Cynthia D. — *Cyntal International Ltd*
Wacholz, Rick — *A.T. Kearney, Inc.*
Waldrop, Gary R. — *MSI International*
Walker, Craig H. — *A.J. Burton Group, Inc.*
Walker, Douglas G. — *Sink, Walker, Boltrus International*
Walker, Ewing J. — *Ward Howell International, Inc.*
Walsh, Patty — *Abraham & London, Ltd.*

Walters, Scott — *Paul-Tittle Associates, Inc.*
Walters, William F. — *Jonas, Walters & Assoc., Inc.*
Walton, Bruce H. — *Heidrick & Struggles, Inc.*
Ward, Jim — *F-O-R-T-U-N-E Personnel Consultants of Huntsville, Inc.*
Ward, Madeleine — *LTM Associates*
Ware, John C. — *Spencer Stuart*
Warren, Scott — *Warren, Morris & Madison*
Wasson, Thomas W. — *Spencer Stuart*
Watkins, Jeffrey P. — *Lamalie Amrop International*
Watkinson, Jim W. — *The Badger Group*
Watson, James — *MSI International*
Watson, Stephen — *Ray & Berndtson*
Wayne, Cary S. — *ProSearch Inc.*
Webb, George H. — *Webb, Johnson Associates, Inc.*
Wein, Michael S. — *InterimManagement Solutions, Inc.*
Wein, Michael S. — *Media Management Resources, Inc.*
Wein, William — *InterimManagement Solutions, Inc.*
Wein, William — *Media Management Resources, Inc.*
Weinberg, Melvin — *Romac & Associates*
Weissman-Rosenthal, Abbe — *ALW Research International*
Weisz, Laura — *Anderson Sterling Associates*
Welch, Dale — *Winter, Wyman & Company*
Welch, Robert — *Ray & Berndtson*
Weller, Paul S. — *Mark Stanley/EMA Partners International*
Wertheim, Denise — *Paul-Tittle Associates, Inc.*
Westfall, Ed — *Zwell International*
Wheeler, Gerard H. — *A.J. Burton Group, Inc.*
Whelan, David — *Ethos Consulting Inc.*
White, William C. — *Venture Resources Inc.*
Whitney, David L. — *Whitney & Associates, Inc.*
Whitt, Mimi — *F-O-R-T-U-N-E Personnel Consultants of Huntsville, Inc.*
Wichansky, Mark — *TSS Consulting, Ltd.*
Wilburn, Dan — *Kaye-Bassman International Corp.*
Wilder, Richard B. — *Columbia Consulting Group*
Wilkinson, Barbara — *Beall & Company, Inc.*
Williams, Angie — *Whitney & Associates, Inc.*
Williams, Dave — *The McCormick Group, Inc.*
Williams, Jack — *A.T. Kearney, Inc.*
Williams, Roger K. — *Williams, Roth & Krueger Inc.*
Williams, Scott D. — *Heidrick & Struggles, Inc.*
Williams, Stephen E. — *Barton Associates, Inc.*
Williams, Walter E. — *Lamalie Amrop International*
Willner, Leo — *William Guy & Associates*
Wilson, Patricia L. — *Leon A. Farley Associates*
Wilson, Steven J. — *Herman Smith Executive Initiatives Inc.*
Winitz, Joel — *GSW Consulting Group, Inc.*
Winitz, Marla — *GSW Consulting Group, Inc.*
Winograd, Glenn — *Criterion Executive Search, Inc.*
Wise, J. Herbert — *Sandhurst Associates*
Witt, Clayton — *Paul-Tittle Associates, Inc.*
Wold, Ted W. — *Hyde Danforth Wold & Co.*

Wolf, Stephen M. — *Byron Leonard International, Inc.*
Womack, Joseph — *The Bankers Group*
Wood, John S. — *Egon Zehnder International Inc.*
Woodhouse, Michael — *Ashton Computer Professionals Inc.*
Woodmansee, Bruce J. — *Tully/Woodmansee International, Inc.*
Woodward, Lee — *Search Associates, Inc.*
Woodworth, Gail — *Woodworth International Group*
Wooldridge, Jeff — *Ray & Berndtson*
Woollett, James — *Rusher, Loscavio & LoPresto*
Work, Alan — *Quantex Associates, Inc.*
Wright, A. Leo — *The Hindman Company*
Wright, Carl A.J. — *A.J. Burton Group, Inc.*
Wyatt, James — *Wyatt & Jaffe*
Yaekle, Gary — *Tully/Woodmansee International, Inc.*
Yang, George — *Technical Connections Inc.*
Yen, Maggie Yeh Ching — *Ray & Berndtson*
Yossem, Sheila — *Bishop Partners*
Young, Heather — *The Guild Corporation*
Zadfar, Maryanne — *The Thomas Tucker Company*
Zaleta, Andy R. — *A.T. Kearney, Inc.*
Zamborsky, George — *Boyden*
Zarnoski, Henry — *Dunhill International Search of New Haven*
Zaslav, Debra M. — *Telford, Adams & Alexander/Telford & Co., Inc.*
Zatzick, Michael — *Search West, Inc.*
Zee, Wanda — *Tesar-Reynes, Inc.*
Zell, David M. — *Logix Partners*
Zetto, Kathryn — *Seco & Zetto Associates, Inc.*
Zilliacus, Patrick W. — *Larsen, Whitney, Blecksmith & Zilliacus*
Zinn, Don — *Quantex Associates, Inc.*

4. Information Technology

Abbatiello, Christine Murphy — *Winter, Wyman & Company*
Abbott, Peter D. — *The Abbott Group, Inc.*
Abell, Vincent W. — *MSI International*
Abramson, Roye — *Source Services Corporation*
Acquaviva, Jay — *Winter, Wyman & Company*
Adams, Jeffrey C. — *Telford, Adams & Alexander/Jeffrey C. Adams & Co., Inc.*
Adams, Len — *The KPA Group*
Adler, Louis S. — *CJA - The Adler Group*
Akin, J.R. "Jack" — *J.R. Akin & Company Inc.*
Albert, Richard — *Source Services Corporation*
Albertini, Nancy — *Taylor-Winfield, Inc.*
Albright, Cindy — *Summerfield Associates, Inc.*
Alexander, Karen — *Huntington Group*
Alford, Holly — *Source Services Corporation*
Allen, Don — *D.S. Allen Associates, Inc.*
Allen, Scott — *Chrisman & Company, Incorporated*
Allen, Wade H. — *Cendea Connection International*
Allred, J. Michael — *Spencer Stuart*
Alringer, Marc — *Source Services Corporation*
Ambler, Peter W. — *Peter W. Ambler Company*
Ames, George C. — *Ames O'Neill Associates*
Amico, Robert — *Source Services Corporation*
Anderson, Maria H. — *Barton Associates, Inc.*

Anderson, Mary — *Source Services Corporation*
Anderson, Matthew — *Source Services Corporation*
Anderson, Steve — *CPS Inc.*
Anderson, Terry — *Intech Summit Group, Inc.*
Apostle, George — *Search Dynamics, Inc.*
Argentin, Jo — *Executive Placement Consultants, Inc.*
Arnold, David W. — *Christian & Timbers*
Arnson, Craig — *Hernand & Partners*
Aronin, Michael — *Fisher-Todd Associates*
Ascher, Susan P. — *The Ascher Group*
Ashton, Barbara L. — *Ashton Computer Professionals Inc.*
Aston, Kathy — *Marra Peters & Partners*
Atkinson, S. Graham — *Raymond Karsan Associates*
Attell, Harold — *A.E. Feldman Associates*
Atwood, Barrie — *The Abbott Group, Inc.*
Aubin, Richard E. — *Aubin International Inc.*
Austin Lockton, Kathy — *Juntunen-Combs-Poirier*
Axelrod, Nancy R. — *A.T. Kearney, Inc.*
Bachmann, Jerry — *Kaye-Bassman International Corp.*
Badger, Fred H. — *The Badger Group*
Baeder, Jeremy — *Executive Manning Corporation*
Baer, Kenneth — *Source Services Corporation*
Baglio, Robert — *Source Services Corporation*
Baier, Rebecca — *Source Services Corporation*
Bailey, David O. — *Ray & Berndtson*
Bailey, Paul — *Austin-McGregor International*
Baird, John — *Professional Search Consultants*
Baje, Sarah — *Innovative Search Group, LLC*
Baker, Bill — *Kaye-Bassman International Corp.*
Baker, Gary M. — *Cochran, Cochran & Yale, Inc.*
Baker, Gerry — *A.T. Kearney, Inc.*
Bakken, Mark — *Source Services Corporation*
Balbone, Rich — *Executive Manning Corporation*
Balch, Randy — *CPS Inc.*
Balchumas, Charles — *Source Services Corporation*
Baldwin, Keith R. — *The Baldwin Group*
Baltaglia, Michael — *Cochran, Cochran & Yale, Inc.*
Balter, Sidney — *Source Services Corporation*
Banko, Scott — *Source Services Corporation*
Baranowski, Peter — *Source Services Corporation*
Barbosa, Frank — *Skott/Edwards Consultants, Inc.*
Barbour, Mary Beth — *Tully/Woodmansee International, Inc.*
Barger, H. Carter — *Barger & Sargeant, Inc.*
Barlow, Ken H. — *The Cherbonnier Group, Inc.*
Barnaby, Richard — *Source Services Corporation*
Barnes, Gary — *Brigade Inc.*
Barnes, Gregory — *Korn/Ferry International*
Barnes, Richard E. — *Barnes Development Group, LLC*
Barnett, Barbara — *D. Brown and Associates, Inc.*
Barnum, Toni M. — *Stone Murphy & Olson*
Baron, Len — *Industrial Recruiters Associates, Inc.*
Bartels, Fredrick — *Source Services Corporation*
Bartesch, Heinz — *The Search Firm, Inc.*
Bartfield, Philip — *Source Services Corporation*
Bartholdi, Ted — *Bartholdi & Company, Inc.*
Bartholdi, Theodore G. — *Bartholdi & Company, Inc.*
Bartholomew, Katie — *C. Berger & Company*

Barton, Gary R. — *Barton Associates, Inc.*
Barton, James — *Source Services Corporation*
Bass, M. Lynn — *Ray & Berndtson*
Bassett, Denise — *Don Richard Associates of Charlotte*
Bassler, John — *Korn/Ferry International*
Bassman, Robert — *Kaye-Bassman International Corp.*
Bassman, Sandy — *Kaye-Bassman International Corp.*
Battalia, O. William — *Battalia Winston International*
Batte, Carol — *Source Services Corporation*
Battles, Jonathan — *Korn/Ferry International*
Beaudin, Elizabeth C. — *Callan Associates, Ltd.*
Beaulieu, Genie A. — *Romac & Associates*
Beaver, Bentley H. — *The Onstott Group, Inc.*
Beaver, Robert — *Source Services Corporation*
Beck, Michael — *Don Richard Associates of Richmond, Inc.*
Beckvold, John B. — *Atlantic Search Group, Inc.*
Belden, Jeannette — *Source Services Corporation*
Belin, Jean — *Boyden*
Bell, Lisa — *Winter, Wyman & Company*
Bence, Robert J. — *DHR International, Inc.*
Bender, Alan — *Bender Executive Search*
Benjamin, Maurita — *Source Services Corporation*
Bennett, Ness — *Technical Connections Inc.*
Benson, Edward — *Source Services Corporation*
Bentley, Mark — *The Thomas Tucker Company*
Beran, Helena — *Michael J. Cavanagh and Associates*
Berger, Carol — *C. Berger & Company*
Berger, Jeffrey — *Source Services Corporation*
Berkhemer-Credaire, Betsy — *Berkhemer Clayton Incorporated*
Bernard, Bryan — *Source Services Corporation*
Bernas, Sharon — *Source Services Corporation*
Bettick, Michael J. — *A.J. Burton Group, Inc.*
Betts, Suzette — *Source Services Corporation*
Bickett, Nicole — *Source Services Corporation*
Bidelman, Richard — *Source Services Corporation*
Bigelow, Dennis — *Marshall Consultants, Inc.*
Biggins, Joseph — *Winter, Wyman & Company*
Biolsi, Joseph — *Source Services Corporation*
Birns, Douglas — *Source Services Corporation*
Birt, Peter — *Ashton Computer Professionals Inc.*
Bishop, Susan — *Bishop Partners*
Blackmon, Sharon — *The Abbott Group, Inc.*
Blackshaw, Brian M. — *Blackshaw, Olmstead, Lynch & Koenig*
Bladon, Andrew — *Don Richard Associates of Tampa, Inc.*
Bland, Walter — *Source Services Corporation*
Blanton, Julia — *Blanton and Company*
Blanton, Thomas — *Blanton and Company*
Blassaras, Peggy — *Source Services Corporation*
Blaydes, James — *Kaye-Bassman International Corp.*
Blickle, Michael — *Source Services Corporation*
Bliley, Jerry — *Spencer Stuart*
Blim, Barbara — *JDG Associates, Ltd.*
Bloch, Suzanne — *Source Services Corporation*
Blocher, John — *Source Services Corporation*
Bloom, Howard C. — *Hernand & Partners*
Bloom, Joyce — *Hernand & Partners*
Bloomer, James E. — *L.W. Foote Company*

Bluhm, Claudia — *Schweichler Associates, Inc.*
Blunt, Peter — *Hernand & Partners*
Boag, John — *Norm Sanders Associates*
Boczany, William J. — *The Guild Corporation*
Boehm, Robin — *D. Brown and Associates, Inc.*
Boehmer, John — *Huntington Group*
Boel, Werner — *The Dalley Hewitt Company*
Bogansky, Amy — *Conex Incorporated*
Bohn, Steve J. — *MSI International*
Boltrus, Dick — *Sink, Walker, Boltrus International*
Bond, Allan — *Walden Associates*
Bond, James L. — *People Management Northeast Incorporated*
Bond, Robert J. — *Romac & Associates*
Bongiovanni, Vincent — *ESA Professional Consultants*
Bonner, Lale D. — *Don Richard Associates of Charlotte*
Booth, Ronald — *Source Services Corporation*
Bordelon, Amanda — *Paul-Tittle Associates, Inc.*
Borenstine, Alvin — *Synergistics Associates Ltd.*
Borkin, Andrew — *Strategic Advancement Inc.*
Borland, James — *Goodrich & Sherwood Associates, Inc.*
Bormann, Cindy Ann — *MSI International*
Bostic, James E. — *Phillips Resource Group*
Bosward, Allan — *Source Services Corporation*
Bourrie, Sharon D. — *Chartwell Partners International, Inc.*
Boyd, Lew — *Coastal International Inc.*
Brackman, Janet — *Dahl-Morrow International*
Bradley, Dalena — *Woodworth International Group*
Bradshaw, Monte — *Christian & Timbers*
Brady, Dick — *William Guy & Associates*
Brady, Robert — *CPS Inc.*
Brandeis, Richard — *CPS Inc.*
Brandenburg, David — *Professional Staffing Consultants*
Brassard, Gary — *Source Services Corporation*
Bratches, Howard — *Thorndike Deland Associates*
Bremer, Brian — *Source Services Corporation*
Brennen, Richard J. — *Spencer Stuart*
Brewster, Edward — *Source Services Corporation*
Brill, Pamela — *C. Berger & Company*
Brindise, Michael J. — *Dynamic Search Systems, Inc.*
Brocaglia, Joyce — *Alta Associates, Inc.*
Bronger, Patricia — *Source Services Corporation*
Brooks, Bernard E. — *Mruk & Partners/EMA Partners Int'l*
Brophy, Melissa — *Maximum Management Corp.*
Brother, Joy — *Charles Luntz & Associates. Inc.*
Brovender, Claire — *Winter, Wyman & Company*
Brown, Charlene N. — *Accent on Achievement, Inc.*
Brown, Clifford — *Source Services Corporation*
Brown, Daniel — *Source Services Corporation*
Brown, Dennis — *D. Brown and Associates, Inc.*
Brown, Gina — *Strategic Alliance Network, Ltd.*
Brown, Kevin P. — *Raymond Karsan Associates*
Brown, Larry C. — *Horton International*
Brown, Steffan — *Woodworth International Group*
Brown, Steven — *Source Services Corporation*
Browne, Michael — *Source Services Corporation*

Bruce, Michael C. — *Spencer Stuart*
Brudno, Robert J. — *Savoy Partners, Ltd.*
Brunner, Terry — *Source Services Corporation*
Brunson, Therese — *Kors Montgomery International*
Bryant, Henry — *D. Brown and Associates, Inc.*
Bryant, Laura — *Paul-Tittle Associates, Inc.*
Bryant, Richard D. — *Bryant Associates, Inc.*
Bryza, Robert M. — *Robert Lowell International*
Brzezinski, Ronald T. — *Callan Associates, Ltd.*
Buckles, Donna — *Cochran, Cochran & Yale, Inc.*
Budill, Edward — *Professional Search Consultants*
Bueschel, David A. — *Shepherd Bueschel & Provus, Inc.*
Buggy, Linda — *Bonnell Associates Ltd.*
Bullock, Conni — *Earley Kielty and Associates, Inc.*
Burch, Donald — *Source Services Corporation*
Burchill, Greg — *BGB Associates*
Burden, Gene — *The Cherbonnier Group, Inc.*
Burfield, Elaine — *Skott/Edwards Consultants, Inc.*
Burke, John — *The Experts*
Burke, Karen A. — *Mazza & Riley, Inc. (a Korn/Ferry International affiliate)*
Burkhill, John — *The Talley Group*
Burmaster, Holly — *Winter, Wyman & Company*
Busch, Jack — *Busch International*
Busterna, Charles — *The KPA Group*
Button, David R. — *The Button Group*
Buttrey, Daniel — *Source Services Corporation*
Buzolits, Patrick — *Source Services Corporation*
Bye, Randy — *Romac & Associates*
Cafero, Les — *Source Services Corporation*
Calivas, Kay — *A.J. Burton Group, Inc.*
Call, David — *Cochran, Cochran & Yale, Inc.*
Callan, Robert M. — *Callan Associates, Ltd.*
Cameron, James W. — *Cameron Consulting*
Campbell, E. — *Source Services Corporation*
Campbell, Gary — *Romac & Associates*
Campbell, Jeff — *Source Services Corporation*
Campbell, Patricia A. — *The Onstott Group, Inc.*
Campbell, Robert Scott — *Wellington Management Group*
Campbell, Robert Scott — *Wellington Management Group*
Cannavino, Matthew J. — *Financial Resource Associates, Inc.*
Capizzi, Karen — *Cochran, Cochran & Yale, Inc.*
Cappe, Richard R. — *Roberts Ryan and Bentley*
Carideo, Joseph — *Thorndike Deland Associates*
Carlson, Eric — *Source Services Corporation*
Carlton, Patricia — *JDG Associates, Ltd.*
Carnal, Rick — *Source Services Corporation*
Carrington, Timothy — *Korn/Ferry International*
Carro, Carl R. — *Executive Search Consultants International, Inc.*
Carter, Linda — *Source Services Corporation*
Carvalho-Esteves, Maria — *Source Services Corporation*
Cashman, Tracy — *Winter, Wyman & Company*
Cast, Donald — *Dunhill International Search of New Haven*
Castillo, Eduardo — *Korn/Ferry International*
Castle, Lisa — *Source Services Corporation*
Caudill, Nancy — *Bishop Partners*
Cavanagh, Michael J. — *Michael J. Cavanagh and Associates*

Celenza, Catherine — *CPS Inc.*
Cersosimo, Rocco — *Source Services Corporation*
Cesafsky, Barry R. — *Lamalie Amrop International*
Chamberlin, Michael A. — *Tower Consultants, Ltd.*
Champion, Geoffrey — *Korn/Ferry International*
Chappell, Peter — *The Bankers Group*
Chase, James — *Source Services Corporation*
Chatterjie, Alok — *MSI International*
Chavous, C. Crawford — *Phillips Resource Group*
Cheah, Victor — *Source Services Corporation*
Cherbonnier, L. Michael — *TCG International, Inc.*
Cherbonnier, L. Michael — *The Cherbonnier Group, Inc.*
Chorman, Marilyn A. — *Hite Executive Search*
Christenson, H. Alan — *Christenson & Hutchison*
Christian, Jeffrey E. — *Christian & Timbers*
Christian, Philip — *Ray & Berndtson*
Christiansen, Amy — *CPS Inc.*
Christiansen, Doug — *CPS Inc.*
Christman, Joel — *Source Services Corporation*
Christoff, Matthew J. — *Spencer Stuart*
Chronopoulos, Dennis — *Source Services Corporation*
Cimino, Ron — *Paul-Tittle Associates, Inc.*
Clark, James — *CPS Inc.*
Clark, John — *Tate Consulting Inc.*
Clark, Julie — *Corporate Recruiters Ltd.*
Clauhsen, Elizabeth A. — *Savoy Partners, Ltd.*
Clawson, Bob — *Source Services Corporation*
Clawson, Robert — *Source Services Corporation*
Clayton, Fred J. — *Berkhemer Clayton Incorporated*
Cline, Mark — *NYCOR Search, Inc.*
Clough, Geoff — *Intech Summit Group, Inc.*
Cloutier, Gisella — *Dinte Resources, Inc.*
Cocchiaro, Richard — *Romac & Associates*
Cocconi, Alan — *Source Services Corporation*
Cochran, Hale — *Fenwick Partners*
Cochran, Scott P. — *The Badger Group*
Cochrun, James — *Source Services Corporation*
Coe, Karen J. — *Coe & Company International Inc.*
Coffey, Patty — *Winter, Wyman & Company*
Coffman, Brian — *Kossuth & Associates, Inc.*
Cohen, Michael R. — *Intech Summit Group, Inc.*
Cohen, Robert C. — *Intech Summit Group, Inc.*
Colasanto, Frank M. — *W.R. Rosato & Associates, Inc.*
Cole, Rosalie — *Source Services Corporation*
Coleman, Patricia — *Korn/Ferry International*
Colling, Douglas — *KPMG Management Consulting*
Collins, Scott — *Source Services Corporation*
Collins, Tom — *J.B. Homer Associates, Inc.*
Colman, Michael — *Executive Placement Consultants, Inc.*
Colvin, Teresa A. — *Jonas, Walters & Assoc., Inc.*
Comai, Christine — *Source Services Corporation*
Combs, Stephen L. — *Juntunen-Combs-Poirier*
Combs, Thomas — *Source Services Corporation*
Cona, Joseph A. — *Cona Personnel Search*
Coneys, Bridget — *Source Services Corporation*
Connelly, Scott — *Technical Connections Inc.*
Conners, Theresa — *D. Brown and Associates, Inc.*

Connolly, Cathryn — *Strategic Associates, Inc.*
Connor, Michele — *Abraham & London, Ltd.*
Conway, Maureen — *Conway & Associates*
Conway, William P. — *Phillips Resource Group*
Cook, Charlene — *Source Services Corporation*
Cook, Dennis — *A.T. Kearney, Inc.*
Cooper, William — *Search West, Inc.*
Cornehlsen, James H. — *Skott/Edwards Consultants, Inc.*
Corrigan, Gerald F. — *The Corrigan Group*
Cortina Del Valle, Pedro — *Ray & Berndtson*
Costello, Lynda — *Coe & Company International Inc.*
Cotugno, James — *Source Services Corporation*
Coughlin, Stephen — *Source Services Corporation*
Coulman, Karen — *CPS Inc.*
Courtney, Brendan — *A.J. Burton Group, Inc.*
Cowell, Roy A. — *Cowell & Associates, Ltd.*
Coyle, Hugh F. — *A.J. Burton Group, Inc.*
Cram, Noel — *R.P. Barone Associates*
Crane, Howard C. — *Chartwell Partners International, Inc.*
Critchley, Walter — *Cochran, Cochran & Yale, Inc.*
Crumpton, Marc — *Logix Partners*
Crumpton, Marc — *Logix, Inc.*
Crumpton, Marc — *Walden Associates*
Cruse, O.D. — *Spencer Stuart*
Cuddihy, Paul — *Dahl-Morrow International*
Cuddy, Brian C. — *Romac & Associates*
Cuddy, Patricia — *Source Services Corporation*
Cunningham, Robert Y. — *Goodrich & Sherwood Associates, Inc.*
Cunningham, Sheila — *Adams & Associates International*
Curci, Donald L. — *A.R.I. International*
Curren, Camella — *Source Services Corporation*
Curtis, Ellissa — *Cochran, Cochran & Yale, Inc.*
Cutka, Matthew — *Source Services Corporation*
Cyphers, Ralph R. — *Strategic Associates, Inc.*
Czamanske, Paul W. — *Compass Group Ltd.*
Czepiel, Susan — *CPS Inc.*
D'Alessio, Gary A. — *Chicago Legal Search, Ltd.*
Daily, John C. — *Handy HRM Corp.*
Daniel, Beverly — *Foy, Schneid & Daniel, Inc.*
Dankberg, Iris — *Source Services Corporation*
Danoff, Audrey — *Don Richard Associates of Tidewater, Inc.*
Darter, Steven M. — *People Management Northeast Incorporated*
Davis, Bert — *Bert Davis Executive Search, Inc.*
Davis, C. Scott — *Source Services Corporation*
Davis, Elease — *Source Services Corporation*
Davis, G. Gordon — *Davis & Company*
Davis, John — *John J. Davis & Associates, Inc.*
Davis, John J. — *John J. Davis & Associates, Inc.*
Davis, Steven M. — *Sullivan & Company*
Dawson, Joe — *S.C. International, Ltd.*
Dawson, William — *Source Services Corporation*
De Brun, Thomas P. — *Ray & Berndtson*
de Gury, Glenn — *Taylor-Winfield, Inc.*
Dean, Mary — *Korn/Ferry International*
Deaver, Henry C. — *Ray & Berndtson*
Debus, Wayne — *Source Services Corporation*
Deck, Jack — *Source Services Corporation*
DeCorrevont, James — *DeCorrevont & Associates*
DeCorrevont, James — *DeCorrevont & Associates*

Finnerty, James — *Source Services Corporation*
Fiorelli, Cheryl — *Tower Consultants, Ltd.*
Fischer, Howard M. — *Howard Fischer Associates, Inc.*
Fischer, John C. — *Horton International*
Fishback, Joren — *Derek Associates, Inc.*
Fisher, Neal — *Fisher Personnel Management Services*
Fishler, Stu — *A.T. Kearney, Inc.*
Fitzgerald, Brian — *Source Services Corporation*
Fitzgerald, Diane — *Fitzgerald Associates*
Fitzgerald, Geoffrey — *Fitzgerald Associates*
Flanagan, Robert M. — *Robert M. Flanagan & Associates, Ltd.*
Flanders, Karen — *Advanced Information Management*
Fletcher, David — *A.J. Burton Group, Inc.*
Flood, Michael — *Norman Broadbent International, Inc.*
Flores, Agustin — *Ward Howell International, Inc.*
Florio, Robert — *Source Services Corporation*
Flowers, Hayden — *Southwestern Professional Services*
Flynn, Erin — *Neil Fink Associates*
Fogarty, Michael — *CPS Inc.*
Foley, Eileen — *Winter, Wyman & Company*
Fone, Carol — *Walden Associates*
Fong, Robert — *Korn/Ferry International*
Foote, Leland W. — *L.W. Foote Company*
Ford, Sandra D. — *The Ford Group, Inc.*
Forestier, Lois — *Source Services Corporation*
Foster, Bonnie — *Kirkman & Searing, Inc.*
Foster, Bradley — *Source Services Corporation*
Foster, John — *Source Services Corporation*
Fotia, Frank — *JDG Associates, Ltd.*
Francis, Brad — *Source Services Corporation*
Frank, Valerie S. — *Norman Roberts & Associates, Inc.*
Frantino, Michael — *Source Services Corporation*
Frazier, John — *Cochran, Cochran & Yale, Inc.*
Frederick, Dianne — *Source Services Corporation*
Freeh, Thomas — *Source Services Corporation*
Freeman, Mark — *ESA Professional Consultants*
French, William G. — *Preng & Associates, Inc.*
Fribush, Richard — *A.J. Burton Group, Inc.*
Friedman, Deborah — *Source Services Corporation*
Friedman, Donna L. — *Tower Consultants, Ltd.*
Fuhrman, Dennis — *Source Services Corporation*
Fujino, Rickey — *Source Services Corporation*
Fulger, Herbert — *Source Services Corporation*
Fulgham MacCarthy, Ann — *Columbia Consulting Group*
Fust, Sheely F. — *Ray & Berndtson*
Fyhrie, David — *Source Services Corporation*
Gabel, Gregory N. — *Canny, Bowen Inc.*
Gabriel, David L. — *The Arcus Group*
Gaffney, Megan — *Source Services Corporation*
Gaines, Jay — *Jay Gaines & Company, Inc.*
Galante, Suzanne M. — *Vlcek & Company, Inc.*
Galbraith, Deborah M. — *Stratford Group*
Gallagher, Terence M. — *Battalia Winston International*
Gamble, Ira — *Source Services Corporation*
Garcia, Samuel K. — *Southwestern Professional Services*
Gardiner, E. Nicholas P. — *Gardiner International*

Gardner, Michael — *Source Services Corporation*
Garfinkle, Steven M. — *Battalia Winston International*
Garrett, Mark — *Source Services Corporation*
Garzone, Dolores — *M.A. Churchill & Associates, Inc.*
Gauthier, Robert C. — *Columbia Consulting Group*
Geiger, Jan — *Wilcox, Bertoux & Miller*
Gennawey, Robert — *Source Services Corporation*
George, Delores F. — *Delores F. George Human Resource Management & Consulting Industry*
Gerbosi, Karen — *Hernand & Partners*
Germain, Valerie — *Jay Gaines & Company, Inc.*
Germaine, Debra — *Fenwick Partners*
Gerster, J.P. — *Juntunen-Combs-Poirier*
Gestwick, Daniel — *Cochran, Cochran & Yale, Inc.*
Ghurani, Mac — *Gary Kaplan & Associates*
Gibson, Bruce — *Gibson & Company Inc.*
Gideon, Mark — *Eagle Search Associates*
Giesy, John — *Source Services Corporation*
Giles, Joe L. — *Joe L. Giles and Associates, Inc.*
Gilinsky, David — *Source Services Corporation*
Gill, Patricia — *Columbia Consulting Group*
Gilmore, Connie — *Taylor-Winfield, Inc.*
Giries, Juliet D. — *Barton Associates, Inc.*
Girsinger, Linda —. *Industrial Recruiters Associates, Inc.*
Glacy, Kurt — *Winter, Wyman & Company*
Gladstone, Martin J. — *MSI International*
Glickman, Leenie — *Source Services Corporation*
Gloss, Frederick C. — *F. Gloss International*
Gluzman, Arthur — *Source Services Corporation*
Gnatowski, Bruce — *Source Services Corporation*
Goedtke, Steven — *Southwestern Professional Services*
Gold, Stacey — *Earley Kielty and Associates, Inc.*
Golde, Lisa — *Tully/Woodmansee International, Inc.*
Goldenberg, Susan — *Grant Cooper and Associates*
Goldman, Michael L. — *Strategic Associates, Inc.*
Goldstein, Steven G. — *The Jonathan Stevens Group, Inc.*
Gomez, Cristina — *Juntunen-Combs-Poirier*
Gonzalez, Kristen — *A.J. Burton Group, Inc.*
Gonzalez, Rafael — *Korn/Ferry International*
Goodman, Victor — *Anderson Sterling Associates*
Goodridge, Benjamin — *S.C. International, Ltd.*
Goodwin, Gary — *Source Services Corporation*
Goodwin, Tim — *William Guy & Associates*
Gordon, Gerald L. — *E.G. Jones Associates, Ltd.*
Gordon, Gloria — *A.T. Kearney, Inc.*
Gorman, Patrick — *Source Services Corporation*
Gorman, T. Patrick — *Techsearch Services, Inc.*
Gostyla, Rick — *Spencer Stuart*
Gould, Dana — *Logix Partners*
Gould, Dana — *Logix, Inc.*
Gourley, Timothy — *Source Services Corporation*
Grado, Eduardo — *Source Services Corporation*
Graff, Jack — *Source Services Corporation*
Graham, Craig — *Ward Howell International, Inc.*
Graham, Dale — *CPS Inc.*
Graham, Shannon — *Source Services Corporation*
Grandinetti, Suzanne — *Source Services Corporation*

Grant, Michael — *Zwell International*
Grantham, John — *Grantham & Co., Inc.*
Grantham, Philip H. — *Columbia Consulting Group*
Gray, Betty — *Accent on Achievement, Inc.*
Gray, Heather — *Source Services Corporation*
Gray, Russell — *Source Services Corporation*
Graziano, Lisa — *Source Services Corporation*
Green, Jane — *Phillips Resource Group*
Green, Jean — *Broward-Dobbs, Inc.*
Gregory, Stephen — *Don Richard Associates of Richmond, Inc.*
Gresia, Paul — *Source Services Corporation*
Grey, Fred — *J.B. Homer Associates, Inc.*
Griffin, Cathy — *A.T. Kearney, Inc.*
Groban, Jack — *A.T. Kearney, Inc.*
Groner, David — *Source Services Corporation*
Grossman, James — *Source Services Corporation*
Grossman, Martin — *Source Services Corporation*
Grotte, Lawrence C. — *Lautz Grotte Engler*
Grumulaitis, Leo — *Source Services Corporation*
Grzybowski, Jill — *CPS Inc.*
Guc, Stephen — *Source Services Corporation*
Gurnani, Angali — *Executive Placement Consultants, Inc.*
Guthrie, Stuart — *Source Services Corporation*
Guy, C. William — *William Guy & Associates*
Haas, Margaret P. — *The Haas Associates, Inc.*
Hacker-Taylor, Dianna — *Source Services Corporation*
Haddad, Charles — *Romac & Associates*
Hagerty, Kenneth — *Korn/Ferry International*
Haider, Martin — *Source Services Corporation*
Hailey, H.M. — *Damon & Associates, Inc.*
Halbrich, Mitch — *A.J. Burton Group, Inc.*
Hales, Daphne — *Source Services Corporation*
Hall, Marty B. — *Catlin-Wells & White*
Hall, Peter V. — *Chartwell Partners International, Inc.*
Hall, Robert — *Don Richard Associates of Tidewater, Inc.*
Haller, Mark — *Source Services Corporation*
Hallock, Peter B. — *Goodrich & Sherwood Associates, Inc.*
Hamilton, John R. — *Ray & Berndtson*
Hamm, Gary — *Source Services Corporation*
Hamm, Mary Kay — *Romac & Associates*
Hanes, Leah — *Ray & Berndtson*
Hanley, Maureen E. — *Gilbert Tweed/INESA*
Hanley, Steven — *Source Services Corporation*
Hanna, Remon — *Source Services Corporation*
Hansen, David G. — *Ott & Hansen, Inc.*
Hanson, Grant M. — *Goodrich & Sherwood Associates, Inc.*
Harbert, David O. — *Sweeney Harbert & Mummert, Inc.*
Harney, Elyane — *Gary Kaplan & Associates*
Harp, Kimberly — *Source Services Corporation*
Harris, Jack — *A.T. Kearney, Inc.*
Harris, Joe W. — *Cendea Connection International*
Harris, Seth O. — *Christian & Timbers*
Harrison, Patricia — *Source Services Corporation*
Harrison, Priscilla — *Phillips Resource Group*
Harrison, Victor — *Intelligent Management Solutions, Inc. (IMS)*
Hart, Crystal — *Source Services Corporation*

Hart, James — *Source Services Corporation*
Hart, Robert T. — *D.E. Foster Partners Inc.*
Hartle, Larry — *CPS Inc.*
Hartzman, Deborah — *Advanced Information Management*
Harvey, Mike — *Advanced Executive Resources*
Harwood, Brian — *Source Services Corporation*
Haselby, James — *Source Services Corporation*
Hasten, Lawrence — *Source Services Corporation*
Hauswirth, Jeffrey M. — *Spencer Stuart*
Havener, Donald Clarke — *The Abbott Group, Inc.*
Hawksworth, A. Dwight — *A.D. & Associates Executive Search, Inc.*
Hayes, Lee — *Source Services Corporation*
Hayes, Stacy — *The McCormick Group, Inc.*
Haystead, Steve — *Advanced Executive Resources*
Hazerjian, Cynthia — *CPS Inc.*
Heacock, Burt E. — *Paul-Tittle Associates, Inc.*
Heafey, Bill — *CPS Inc.*
Heaney, Thomas — *Korn/Ferry International*
Hechkoff, Robert B. — *Quantex Associates, Inc.*
Hedlund, David — *Hedlund Corporation*
Heffelfinger, Thomas V. — *Heffelfinger Associates, Inc.*
Heiken, Barbara E. — *Randell-Heiken, Inc.*
Heinrich, Scott — *Source Services Corporation*
Helgeson, Burton H. — *Norm Sanders Associates*
Heneghan, Donald A. — *Allerton Heneghan & O'Neill*
Henneberry, Ward — *Source Services Corporation*
Henry, Mary — *Conex Incorporated*
Henry, Patrick — *F-O-R-T-U-N-E Personnel Consultants of Huntsville, Inc.*
Hensley, Bert — *Morgan Samuels Co., Inc.*
Hensley, Gayla — *Atlantic Search Group, Inc.*
Hergenrather, Richard A. — *Hergenrather & Company*
Herman, Eugene J. — *Earley Kielty and Associates, Inc.*
Herman, Pat — *Whitney & Associates, Inc.*
Herman, Shelli — *Gary Kaplan & Associates*
Hernand, Warren L. — *Hernand & Partners*
Hernandez, Ruben — *Source Services Corporation*
Heroux, David — *Source Services Corporation*
Hertlein, James N.J. — *Boyden/Zay & Company*
Herzog, Sarah — *Source Services Corporation*
Hewitt, Rives D. — *The Dalley Hewitt Company*
Hewitt, W. Davis — *The Dalley Hewitt Company*
Hicks, Albert M. — *Phillips Resource Group*
Hight, Susan — *Source Services Corporation*
Hilbert, Laurence — *Source Services Corporation*
Hildebrand, Thomas B. — *Professional Resources Group, Inc.*
Hilgenberg, Thomas — *Source Services Corporation*
Hill, Emery — *MSI International*
Hillen, Skip — *The McCormick Group, Inc.*
Hillyer, Carolyn — *Source Services Corporation*
Himes, Dirk — *A.T. Kearney, Inc.*
Himlin, Amy — *Cochran, Cochran & Yale, Inc.*
Hinojosa, Oscar — *Source Services Corporation*
Hnatuik, Ivan — *Corporate Recruiters Ltd.*
Hochberg, Brian — *M.A. Churchill & Associates, Inc.*
Hocking, Jeffrey — *Korn/Ferry International*

Hoevel, Michael J. — *Poirier, Hoevel & Co.*
Hoffman, Brian — *Winter, Wyman & Company*
Hoffman, Stephen — *Source Services Corporation*
Hofner, Andrew — *Source Services Corporation*
Holland, John A. — *Holland, McFadzean & Associates, Inc.*
Holmes, Lawrence J. — *Columbia Consulting Group*
Holodnak, William A. — *J. Robert Scott*
Holt, Carol — *Bartholdi & Company, Inc.*
Homer, Judy B. — *J.B. Homer Associates, Inc.*
Hooker, Lisa — *Ray & Berndtson*
Hoover, Catherine — *J.L. Mark Associates, Inc.*
Hopgood, Earl — *JDG Associates, Ltd.*
Hopper, John W. — *William Guy & Associates*
Horgan, Thomas F. — *Nadzam, Lusk, Horgan & Associates, Inc.*
Horner, Gregory — *Corporate Recruiters Ltd.*
Hostetter, Kristi — *Source Services Corporation*
Houchins, William M. — *Christian & Timbers*
Houterloot, Tim — *Source Services Corporation*
Howe, Theodore — *Romac & Associates*
Howell, Robert B. — *Atlantic Search Group, Inc.*
Howell, Robert B. — *Atlantic Search Group, Inc.*
Hoyda, Louis A. — *Thorndike Deland Associates*
Hucko, Donald S. — *Jonas, Walters & Assoc., Inc.*
Hudson, Reginald M. — *Search Bureau International*
Huff, William Z. — *Huff Associates*
Hughes, Barbara — *Source Services Corporation*
Hughes, Cathy N. — *The Ogdon Partnership*
Hughes, Donald J. — *Hughes & Company*
Hughes, Randall — *Source Services Corporation*
Hull, Chuck — *Winter, Wyman & Company*
Hult, Dana — *Source Services Corporation*
Humphrey, Joan — *Abraham & London, Ltd.*
Humphrey, Titus — *Source Services Corporation*
Hunsaker, Floyd — *Woodworth International Group*
Hunter, Gabe — *Phillips Resource Group*
Hurley, Janeen — *Winter, Wyman & Company*
Hurtado, Jaime — *Source Services Corporation*
Hussey, Wayne — *Krecklo & Associates Inc.*
Hutchison, Richard H. — *Rurak & Associates, Inc.*
Hutchison, William K. — *Christenson & Hutchison*
Hutton, Thomas J. — *The Thomas Tucker Company*
Hybels, Cynthia — *A.J. Burton Group, Inc.*
Hylas, Lisa — *Source Services Corporation*
Hyman, Linda — *Korn/Ferry International*
Iannacone, Kelly — *Abraham & London, Ltd.*
Ide, Ian — *Winter, Wyman & Company*
Imhof, Kirk — *Source Services Corporation*
Inger, Barry — *Source Services Corporation*
Inguagiato, Gregory — *MSI International*
Inskeep, Thomas — *Source Services Corporation*
Intravaia, Salvatore — *Source Services Corporation*
Irish, Alan — *CPS Inc.*
Irwin, Mark — *Source Services Corporation*
Jackowitz, Todd — *J. Robert Scott*
Jackson, Barry — *Morgan Hunter Corp.*
Jackson, Joan — *A.T. Kearney, Inc.*
Jacobs, Martin J. — *The Rubicon Group*
Jacobson, Carolyn — *The Abbott Group, Inc.*
Jacobson, Hayley — *Source Services Corporation*

Jacobson, Rick — *The Windham Group*
Jadulang, Vincent — *Source Services Corporation*
James, Bruce — *Roberson and Company*
James, Richard — *Criterion Executive Search, Inc.*
Janis, Laurence — *Integrated Search Solutions Group, LLC*
Jansen, John F. — *Delta Services*
Januale, Lois — *Cochran, Cochran & Yale, Inc.*
Januleski, Geoff — *Source Services Corporation*
Jaworski, Mary A. — *Tully/Woodmansee International, Inc.*
Jazylo, John V. — *Handy HRM Corp.*
Jazylo, John V. — *Skott/Edwards Consultants, Inc.*
Jeffers, Richard B. — *Dieckmann & Associates, Ltd.*
Jeltema, John — *Source Services Corporation*
Jensen, Christine K. — *John Kurosky & Associates*
Jensen, Robert — *Source Services Corporation*
Johnson, Brian — *A.J. Burton Group, Inc.*
Johnson, Douglas — *Quality Search*
Johnson, Greg — *Source Services Corporation*
Johnson, Julie M. — *International Staffing Consultants, Inc.*
Johnson, Kathleen A. — *Barton Associates, Inc.*
Johnson, Keith — *Romac & Associates*
Johnson, LaDonna — *Gans, Gans & Associates*
Johnson, Pete — *Morgan Hunter Corp.*
Johnson, Peter — *Winter, Wyman & Company*
Johnson, Robert J. — *Quality Search*
Johnson, Ronald S. — *Ronald S. Johnson Associates, Inc.*
Johnson, Stanley C. — *Johnson & Company*
Johnson, Valerie — *Coe & Company International Inc.*
Johnston, Michael — *Robertson-Surrette Executive Search*
Johnstone, Grant — *Source Services Corporation*
Jones, Amy E. — *The Corporate Connection, Ltd.*
Jones, Barbara — *Kaye-Bassman International Corp.*
Jones, Barbara J. — *Kaye-Bassman International Corp.*
Jones, Daniel F. — *Atlantic Search Group, Inc.*
Jones, Francis E. — *Earley Kielty and Associates, Inc.*
Jones, Gary — *BGB Associates*
Jones, Rodney — *Source Services Corporation*
Jordan, Jon — *Cochran, Cochran & Yale, Inc.*
Joyce, William J. — *The Guild Corporation*
Jozwik, Peter — *The Search Firm, Inc.*
Judge, Alfred L. — *The Cambridge Group Ltd*
Judy, Otto — *CPS Inc.*
Juska, Frank — *Rusher, Loscavio & LoPresto*
Kaiser, Donald J. — *Dunhill International Search of New Haven*
Kane, Frank — *A.J. Burton Group, Inc.*
Kanovsky, Gerald — *Career Consulting Group, Inc.*
Kanovsky, Marlene — *Career Consulting Group, Inc.*
Kaplan, Alexandra — *J.M. Eagle Partners Ltd.*
Kaplan, Gary — *Gary Kaplan & Associates*
Kaplan, Traci — *Source Services Corporation*
Karalis, William — *CPS Inc.*
Kasmouski, Steve — *Winter, Wyman & Company*
Kasprzyk, Michael — *Source Services Corporation*
Kaye, Jeffrey — *Kaye-Bassman International Corp.*

Keating, Pierson — *Nordeman Grimm, Inc.*
Kehoe, Mike — *CPS Inc.*
Kelbell, Scott — *Comprehensive Search*
Keller, Barbara E. — *Barton Associates, Inc.*
Kells, John — *Heffelfinger Associates, Inc.*
Kelly, Elizabeth Ann — *Wellington Management Group*
Kelly, Robert — *Source Services Corporation*
Kelly, Sheri — *Strategic Associates, Inc.*
Kelso, Patricia C. — *Barton Associates, Inc.*
Kennedy, Craig — *Source Services Corporation*
Kennedy, Paul — *Source Services Corporation*
Kennedy, Walter — *Romac & Associates*
Kennedy, Walter — *Source Services Corporation*
Kennedy, Walter — *Source Services Corporation*
Kenney, Jeanne — *Source Services Corporation*
Kent, Melvin — *Melvin Kent & Associates, Inc.*
Kenzer, Robert D. — *Kenzer Corp.*
Kern, Jerry L. — *ADOW's Executeam*
Kern, Kathleen G. — *ADOW's Executeam*
Keyser, Anne — *A.T. Kearney, Inc.*
Kielty, John L. — *Earley Kielty and Associates, Inc.*
Kilcoyne, Pat — *CPS Inc.*
King, Bill — *The McCormick Group, Inc.*
King, Margaret — *Christian & Timbers*
King, Shannon — *Source Services Corporation*
Kinney, Carol — *Dussick Management Associates*
Kinsey, Joanne — *Eastridge InfoTech*
Kip, Luanne S. — *Kip Williams, Inc.*
Kirkman, J. Michael — *Kirkman & Searing, Inc.*
Kirschner, Alan — *Source Services Corporation*
Kishbaugh, Herbert S. — *Kishbaugh Associates International*
Kkorzyniewski, Nicole — *CPS Inc.*
Klavens, Cecile J. — *The Pickwick Group, Inc.*
Klein, Brandon — *A.J. Burton Group, Inc.*
Klein, Gary — *A.T. Kearney, Inc.*
Klein, Mary Jo — *Cochran, Cochran & Yale, Inc.*
Klein, Mel — *Stewart/Laurence Associates*
Kleinstein, Scott — *Source Services Corporation*
Klusman, Edwin — *Source Services Corporation*
Knapp, Ronald A. — *Knapp Consultants*
Knoll, Robert — *Source Services Corporation*
Kobayashi, Rika — *International Staffing Consultants, Inc.*
Koczak, John — *Source Services Corporation*
Koehler, Frank R. — *The Koehler Group*
Koenig, Joel S. — *Blackshaw, Olmstead, Lynch & Koenig*
Koenig, Joel S. — *Blackshaw, Olmstead, Lynch & Koenig*
Kohn, Adam P. — *Christian & Timbers*
Kohonoski, Michael M. — *The Guild Corporation*
Kopec, Tom — *D. Brown and Associates, Inc.*
Kors, R. Paul — *Kors Montgomery International*
Kossuth, David — *Kossuth & Associates, Inc.*
Kossuth, Jane — *Kossuth & Associates, Inc.*
Kotick, Maddy — *The Stevenson Group of New Jersey*
Kouble, Tim — *Logix Partners*
Kouble, Tim — *Logix, Inc.*
Krecklo, Brian Douglas — *Krecklo & Associates Inc.*
Krejci, Stanley L. — *Boyden Washington, D.C.*
Kreutz, Gary L. — *Kreutz Consulting Group, Inc.*
Krieger, Dennis F. — *Seiden Krieger Associates, Inc.*

Kunzer, William J. — *Kunzer Associates, Ltd.*
Kurrigan, Geoffrey — *ESA Professional Consultants*
Kussner, Janice N. — *Herman Smith Executive Initiatives Inc.*
La Chance, Ronald — *Source Services Corporation*
Laba, Marvin — *Marvin Laba & Associates*
Laba, Stuart M. — *Marvin Laba & Associates*
Labrecque, Bernard F. — *Laurendeau Labrecque/Ray & Berndtson, Inc.*
LaCharite, Danielle — *The Guild Corporation*
Lache, Shawn E. — *The Arcus Group*
Laderman, David — *Romac & Associates*
Laird, Cheryl — *CPS Inc.*
Lamb, Angus K. — *Raymond Karsan Associates*
Lambert, William — *Source Services Corporation*
Lamia, Michael — *Source Services Corporation*
Lang, Sharon A. — *Ray & Berndtson*
Langan, Marion — *Logix Partners*
Langan, Marion — *Logix, Inc.*
Lapat, Aaron D. — *J. Robert Scott*
LaPierre, Louis — *Romac & Associates*
Lapointe, Fabien — *Source Services Corporation*
Lardner, Lucy D. — *Tully/Woodmansee International, Inc.*
Lasher, Charles M. — *Lasher Associates*
Laskin, Sandy — *Source Services Corporation*
Laub, Stuart R. — *Abraham & London, Ltd.*
Lautz, Lindsay A. — *Lautz Grotte Engler*
LaValle, Michael — *Romac & Associates*
Laverty, William — *Source Services Corporation*
Lawner, Harvey — *Walden Associates*
Lazar, Miriam — *Source Services Corporation*
Leahy, Jan — *CPS Inc.*
Leblanc, Danny — *Source Services Corporation*
Ledbetter, Steven G. — *Cendea Connection International*
Lee, Everett — *Source Services Corporation*
Lee, Janice — *Summerfield Associates, Inc.*
Leigh, Rebecca — *Source Services Corporation*
Leighton, Mark — *Source Services Corporation*
Leininger, Dennis — *Key Employment Services*
Leland, Paul — *McInturff & Associates, Inc.*
Lence, Julie Anne — *MSI International*
Lennox, Charles — *Price Waterhouse*
Leon, Jeffrey J. — *Russell Reynolds Associates, Inc.*
Levenson, Laurel — *Source Services Corporation*
Levine, Irwin — *Source Services Corporation*
Levitt, Muriel A. — *D.S. Allen Associates, Inc.*
Lewicki, Christopher — *MSI International*
Lewis, Daniel — *Source Services Corporation*
Lewis, Jon A. — *Sandhurst Associates*
Lezama Cohen, Luis — *Ray & Berndtson*
Lichtenauer, Eric W. — *Britt Associates, Inc.*
Lichtenauer, William E. — *Britt Associates, Inc.*
Lieberman, Beverly — *Halbrecht Lieberman Associates, Inc.*
Liebross, Eric — *Source Services Corporation*
Lin, Felix — *Source Services Corporation*
Lindberg, Eric J. — *MSI International*
Lindsay, Mary — *Norm Sanders Associates*
Linton, Leonard M. — *Byron Leonard International, Inc.*
Lipe, Jerold L. — *Compass Group Ltd.*

Lipson, Harriet — *First Interactive Recruiting Specialists*
Lipson, Harriet — *Lipson & Co.*
Lipson, Howard K. — *First Interactive Recruiting Specialists*
Lipson, Howard R. — *Lipson & Co.*
Lipuma, Thomas — *Source Services Corporation*
Little, Elizabeth A. — *Financial Resource Associates, Inc.*
Little, Suzaane — *Don Richard Associates of Tampa, Inc.*
Lofthouse, Cindy — *CPS Inc.*
Lokken, Karen — *A.E. Feldman Associates*
Long, John — *Source Services Corporation*
Long, John P. — *John J. Davis & Associates, Inc.*
Long, Mark — *Source Services Corporation*
Long, Milt — *William Guy & Associates*
Long, William G. — *McDonald, Long & Associates, Inc.*
Looney, Scott — *A.E. Feldman Associates*
LoPresto, Robert L. — *Rusher, Loscavio & LoPresto*
Lotufo, Donald A. — *D.A.L. Associates, Inc.*
Louden, Leo — *Winter, Wyman & Company*
Lovely, Edward — *The Stevenson Group of New Jersey*
Loving, Vikki — *Intersource, Ltd.*
Lucarelli, Joan — *The Onstott Group, Inc.*
Lucas, Ronnie L. — *MSI International*
Luce, Daniel — *Source Services Corporation*
Lucht, John — *The John Lucht Consultancy Inc.*
Ludder, Mark — *Source Services Corporation*
Ludlow, Michael — *Source Services Corporation*
Lundy, Martin — *Source Services Corporation*
Lupica, Anthony — *Cochran, Cochran & Yale, Inc.*
Lyon, Jenny — *Marra Peters & Partners*
Lyons, J. David — *Aubin International Inc.*
Lyons, Michael — *Source Services Corporation*
Macdonald, G. William — *The Macdonald Group, Inc.*
MacDougall, Andrew J. — *Spencer Stuart*
MacEachern, David — *Spencer Stuart*
MacKinnon, Helen — *Technical Connections Inc.*
MacMillan, James — *Source Services Corporation*
MacNaughton, Sperry — *McNaughton Associates*
MacPherson, Holly — *Source Services Corporation*
Macrides, Michael — *Source Services Corporation*
Mader, Stephen P. — *Christian & Timbers*
Magee, Harrison R. — *Bowden & Company, Inc.*
Maggio, Mary — *Source Services Corporation*
Maglio, Charles J. — *Maglio and Company, Inc.*
Mahmoud, Sophia — *Source Services Corporation*
Mairn, Todd — *Source Services Corporation*
Major, Susan — *A.T. Kearney, Inc.*
Malcolm, Rod — *Korn/Ferry International*
Mangum, Maria — *Thomas Mangum Company*
Mangum, William T. — *Thomas Mangum Company*
Manns, Alex — *Crawford & Crofford*
Mansford, Keith — *Howard Fischer Associates, Inc.*
Manzo, Renee — *Atlantic Search Group, Inc.*
Maphet, Harriet — *The Stevenson Group of New Jersey*
Marcine, John W. — *Keith Bagg & Associates Inc.*

Marino, Chester — *Cochran, Cochran & Yale, Inc.*
Marino, Jory J. — *Sullivan & Company*
Mark, John L. — *J.L. Mark Associates, Inc.*
Mark, Lynne — *J.L. Mark Associates, Inc.*
Marks, Ira — *Strategic Alternatives*
Marra, John — *Marra Peters & Partners*
Marra, John — *Marra Peters & Partners*
Martin, David — *The Guild Corporation*
Martin, Lois G. — *The Martin Group*
Martin, Malcolm — *Paul-Tittle Associates, Inc.*
Martin, Timothy P. — *The Martin Group*
Marumoto, William H. — *Boyden Washington, D.C.*
Marwil, Jennifer — *Source Services Corporation*
Marye, George — *Damon & Associates, Inc.*
Masserman, Bruce — *Masserman & Associates, Inc.*
Massey, R. Bruce — *Horton International*
Mather, David R. — *Christian & Timbers*
Mathias, Douglas — *Source Services Corporation*
Mathis, Carrie — *Source Services Corporation*
Matthews, Corwin — *Woodworth International Group*
Matthews, Mary — *Korn/Ferry International*
Matti, Suzy — *Southwestern Professional Services*
Mattingly, Kathleen — *Source Services Corporation*
Maxwell, John — *Source Services Corporation*
Mayer, Thomas — *Source Services Corporation*
Mayes, Kay H. — *John Shell Associates, Inc.*
Mazza, David B. — *Mazza & Riley, Inc. (a Korn/Ferry International affiliate)*
McAndrews, Kathy — *CPS Inc.*
McCabe, Christopher — *Raymond Karsan Associates*
McCann, Cornelia B. — *Spencer Stuart*
McCarthy, Laura — *Source Services Corporation*
McCloskey, Frank D. — *Johnson Smith & Knisely Accord*
McComas, Kelly E. — *The Guild Corporation*
McConnell, Greg — *Winter, Wyman & Company*
McCormick, Brian — *The McCormick Group, Inc.*
McCormick, Joseph — *Source Services Corporation*
McCormick, William J. — *The McCormick Group, Inc.*
McCurdy, Mark — *Summerfield Associates, Inc.*
McDermott, Jeffrey T. — *Vlcek & Company, Inc.*
McDonald, Scott A. — *McDonald Associates International*
McDonald, Stanleigh B. — *McDonald Associates International*
McDonnell, Julie — *Technical Personnel of Minnesota*
McDowell, Robert N. — *Christenson & Hutchison*
McFadden, Ashton S. — *Johnson Smith & Knisely Accord*
McFadzen, Donna — *Holland, McFadzean & Associates, Inc.*
McFadzen, James A. — *Holland, McFadzean & Associates, Inc.*
McGinnis, Rita — *Source Services Corporation*
McGoldrick, Terrence — *Source Services Corporation*
McGregor, James D. — *John Kurosky & Associates*
McGuigan, Walter J. — *Norm Sanders Associates*
McGuire, Pat — *A.J. Burton Group, Inc.*

McHale, Rob — *Paul-Tittle Associates, Inc.*
McHugh, Keith — *Source Services Corporation*
McIntosh, Arthur — *Source Services Corporation*
McIntosh, Tad — *Source Services Corporation*
McInturff, Robert — *McInturff & Associates, Inc.*
McIntyre, Joel — *Phillips Resource Group*
McKell, Linda — *Advanced Information Management*
McKeown, Morgan J. — *Christian & Timbers*
McKinney, Julia — *Source Services Corporation*
McLaughlin, John — *Romac & Associates*
McMahan, Stephen — *Source Services Corporation*
McMahan, Stephen — *Source Services Corporation*
McManners, Donald E. — *McManners Associates, Inc.*
McNamara, Catherine — *Ray & Berndtson*
McNamara, Timothy C. — *Columbia Consulting Group*
McNamee, Erin — *Technical Connections Inc.*
McNear, Jeffrey E. — *Barrett Partners*
McNichols, Walter B. — *Gary Kaplan & Associates*
McSherry, James F. — *Battalia Winston International*
Mead-Fox, David — *Korn/Ferry International*
Meadows, C. David — *Professional Staffing Consultants*
Meara, Helen — *Source Services Corporation*
Meehan, John — *Source Services Corporation*
Mendelson, Jeffrey — *Source Services Corporation*
Mendoza-Green, Robin — *Source Services Corporation*
Menendez, Todd — *Don Richard Associates of Tampa, Inc.*
Mercer, Julie — *Columbia Consulting Group*
Mertensotto, Chuck H. — *Whitney & Associates, Inc.*
Messina, Marco — *Source Services Corporation*
Meyer, Stacey — *Gary Kaplan & Associates*
Michaels, Joseph — *CPS Inc.*
Mierzwinski, John — *Industrial Recruiters Associates, Inc.*
Miles, Marybeth — *Winter, Wyman & Company*
Miller, Brett — *The McCormick Group, Inc.*
Miller, David — *Cochran, Cochran & Yale, Inc.*
Miller, George N. — *Hite Executive Search*
Miller, Kenneth A. — *Computer Network Resources, Inc.*
Miller, Larry — *Source Services Corporation*
Miller, Timothy — *Source Services Corporation*
Milligan, Dale — *Source Services Corporation*
Mills, John — *Source Services Corporation*
Milner, Carol — *Source Services Corporation*
Milstein, Bonnie — *Marvin Laba & Associates*
Mingle, Larry D. — *Columbia Consulting Group*
Miras, Cliff — *Source Services Corporation*
Miras, Cliff — *Source Services Corporation*
Misiurewicz, Marc — *Cochran, Cochran & Yale, Inc.*
Mitchell, Jeff — *A.J. Burton Group, Inc.*
Mitchell, John — *Romac & Associates*
Mittwol, Myles — *Source Services Corporation*
Mochwart, Donald — *Drummond Associates, Inc.*
Mogul, Gene — *Mogul Consultants, Inc.*
Mohr, Brian — *CPS Inc.*

Molitor, John L. — *Barrett Partners*
Mollichelli, David — *Source Services Corporation*
Molnar, Robert A. — *Johnson Smith & Knisely Accord*
Mondragon, Philip — *A.T. Kearney, Inc.*
Moodley, Logan — *Austin-McGregor International*
Moore, Craig — *Source Services Corporation*
Moore, David S. — *Lynch Miller Moore, Inc.*
Moore, Dianna — *Source Services Corporation*
Moore, Mark — *Wheeler, Moore & Elam Co.*
Moore, Suzanne — *Source Services Corporation*
Moore, T. Wills — *Ray & Berndtson*
Moran, Douglas — *Source Services Corporation*
Moran, Gayle — *Dussick Management Associates*
Morato, Rene — *Source Services Corporation*
Moretti, Denise — *Source Services Corporation*
Morgan, Richard S. — *Ray & Berndtson/Lovas Stanley*
Morgan-Christopher, Jeanie — *Kaye-Bassman International Corp.*
Moriarty, Mike — *Source Services Corporation*
Morrill, Nancy — *Winter, Wyman & Company*
Morris, Scott — *Source Services Corporation*
Morrow, Melanie — *Source Services Corporation*
Mortansen, Patricia — *Norman Broadbent International, Inc.*
Moses, Jerry — *J.M. Eagle Partners Ltd.*
Mott, Greg — *Source Services Corporation*
Moyse, Richard G. — *Thorndike Deland Associates*
Msidment, Roger — *Source Services Corporation*
Mueller, Colleen — *Source Services Corporation*
Muller, Susan — *Corporate Recruiters Ltd.*
Murphy, Corinne — *Source Services Corporation*
Murphy, Cornelius J. — *Goodrich & Sherwood Associates, Inc.*
Murphy, Erin — *CPS Inc.*
Murphy, James — *Source Services Corporation*
Murphy, Patrick J. — *P.J. Murphy & Associates, Inc.*
Murphy, Peter — *Korn/Ferry International*
Murray, Virginia — *A.T. Kearney, Inc.*
Murry, John — *Source Services Corporation*
Mursuli, Meredith — *Lasher Associates*
Mydlach, Renee — *CPS Inc.*
Nabers, Karen — *Source Services Corporation*
Nadzam, Richard I. — *Nadzam, Lusk, Horgan & Associates, Inc.*
Nagler, Leon G. — *Nagler, Robins & Poe, Inc.*
Nagy, Les — *Source Services Corporation*
Naidicz, Maria — *Ray & Berndtson*
Necessary, Rick — *Source Services Corporation*
Needham, Karen — *Source Services Corporation*
Neelin, Sharon — *The Caldwell Partners Amrop International*
Nees, Eugene C. — *Ray & Berndtson*
Neff, Herbert — *Source Services Corporation*
Neher, Robert L. — *Intech Summit Group, Inc.*
Nelson, Barbara — *Herman Smith Executive Initiatives Inc.*
Nelson, Hitch — *Source Services Corporation*
Nelson, Mary — *Source Services Corporation*
Nelson-Folkersen, Jeffrey — *Source Services Corporation*
Nemec, Phillip — *Dunhill International Search of New Haven*
Nephew, Robert — *Christian & Timbers*

Neri, Gene — *S.C. International, Ltd.*
Neuberth, Jeffrey G. — *Canny, Bowen Inc.*
Neuwald, Debrah — *Source Services Corporation*
Newlon, Jay — *Logix, Inc.*
Newman, Lynn — *Kishbaugh Associates International*
Newton, Jay — *Logix Partners*
Niejet, Michael C. — *O'Brien & Bell*
Noebel, Todd R. — *The Noebel Search Group, Inc.*
Nolan, Robert — *Source Services Corporation*
Nolen, Shannon — *Source Services Corporation*
Nolte, William D. — *W.D. Nolte & Company*
Nolton, Becky — *Paul-Tittle Associates, Inc.*
Normann, Amy — *Robert M. Flanagan & Associates, Ltd.*
Norris, Ken — *A.T. Kearney, Inc.*
Nosky, Richard E. — *Ward Howell International, Inc.*
Nunziata, Peter — *Atlantic Search Group, Inc.*
Nutter, Roger — *Raymond Karsan Associates*
Nymark, John — *NYCOR Search, Inc.*
Nymark, Paul — *NYCOR Search, Inc.*
O'Brien, Maggie — *Advanced Information Management*
O'Brien, Susan — *Source Services Corporation*
O'Connell, Mary — *CPS Inc.*
O'Hara, Daniel M. — *Lynch Miller Moore, Inc.*
O'Neill, Kevin G. — *HRS, Inc.*
O'Reilly, John — *Stratford Group*
Occhiboi, Emil — *Source Services Corporation*
Ocon, Olga — *Busch International*
Odom, Philip — *Richard, Wayne and Roberts*
Ogdon, Thomas H. — *The Ogdon Partnership*
Oldfield, Theresa — *Strategic Alliance Network, Ltd.*
Olmstead, George T. — *Blackshaw, Olmstead, Lynch & Koenig*
Olsen, David G. — *Handy HRM Corp.*
Olsen, Robert — *Source Services Corporation*
Onstott, Joseph — *The Onstott Group, Inc.*
Onstott, Joseph E. — *The Onstott Group, Inc.*
Orr, Stacie — *Source Services Corporation*
Osborn, Jim — *Southwestern Professional Services*
Ott, George W. — *Ott & Hansen, Inc.*
Ottenritter, Chris — *CPS Inc.*
Ouellette, Christopher — *Source Services Corporation*
Overlock, Craig — *Ray & Berndtson*
Owen, Christopher — *Source Services Corporation*
Pace, Susan A. — *Horton International*
Pachowitz, John — *Source Services Corporation*
Pacini, Lauren R. — *Hite Executive Search*
Paliwoda, William — *Source Services Corporation*
Palma, Frank R. — *Goodrich & Sherwood Associates, Inc.*
Papasadero, Kathleen — *Woodworth International Group*
Papciak, Dennis J. — *Accounting Personnel Associates, Inc.*
Papoulias, Cathy — *Pendleton James and Associates, Inc.*
Pappalardo, Charles A. — *Christian & Timbers*
Pappas, Jim — *Search Dynamics, Inc.*
Paradise, Malcolm — *Source Services Corporation*
Pardo, Maria Elena — *Smith Search, S.C.*

Parente, James — *Source Services Corporation*
Parfitt, William C. — *Parfitt Recruiting and Consulting*
Paris, Stephen — *Richard, Wayne and Roberts*
Parr, James A. — *KPMG Management Consulting*
Parroco, Jason — *Source Services Corporation*
Parry, Heather — *Richard, Wayne and Roberts*
Parsons, Allison D. — *Barton Associates, Inc.*
Patel, Shailesh — *Source Services Corporation*
Paternie, Patrick — *Source Services Corporation*
Paul, Kathleen — *Source Services Corporation*
Peal, Matthew — *Source Services Corporation*
Peckenpaugh, Ann D. — *Schweichler Associates, Inc.*
Pederson, Terre — *Richard, Wayne and Roberts*
Pedley, Jill — *CPS Inc.*
Pelisson, Charles — *Marra Peters & Partners*
Pelkey, Chris — *The McCormick Group, Inc.*
Percival, Chris — *Chicago Legal Search, Ltd.*
Peretz, Jamie — *Korn/Ferry International*
Pernell, Jeanette — *Norman Broadbent International, Inc.*
Perry, Carolyn — *Source Services Corporation*
Perry, Glen — *Keith Bagg & Associates Inc.*
Peters, James N. — *TNS Partners, Inc.*
Peters, Kevin — *Source Services Corporation*
Petersen, Richard — *Source Services Corporation*
Peterson, John — *CPS Inc.*
Petty, J. Scott — *The Arcus Group*
Pfannkuche, Anthony V. — *Spencer Stuart*
Phillips, Donald L. — *O'Shea, Divine & Company, Inc.*
Phillips, Richard K. — *Handy HRM Corp.*
Phipps, Peggy — *Woodworth International Group*
Pickford, Stephen T. — *The Corporate Staff, Inc.*
Pierce, Mark — *Korn/Ferry International*
Pierce, Matthew — *Source Services Corporation*
Pierotazio, John — *CPS Inc.*
Pigott, Daniel — *ESA Professional Consultants*
Pillow, Charles — *Source Services Corporation*
Pineda, Rosanna — *Source Services Corporation*
Pinson, Stephanie L. — *Gilbert Tweed/INESA*
Pirro, Sheri — *Source Services Corporation*
Pitts, Charles — *Contemporary Management Services, Inc.*
Plant, Jerry — *Source Services Corporation*
Plimpton, Ralph L. — *R L Plimpton Associates*
Plummer, John — *Plummer & Associates, Inc.*
Poe, James B. — *Nagler, Robins & Poe, Inc.*
Poirier, Frank — *Juntunen-Combs-Poirier*
Poirier, Roland L. — *Poirier, Hoevel & Co.*
Polachi, Charles A. — *Fenwick Partners*
Polachi, Peter V. — *Fenwick Partners*
Polansky, Mark — *Korn/Ferry International*
Pomerance, Mark — *CPS Inc.*
Poore, Larry D. — *Ward Howell International, Inc.*
Poracky, John W. — *M. Wood Company*
Poremski, Paul — *A.J. Burton Group, Inc.*
Porter, Albert — *The Experts*
Poster, Lawrence D. — *Catalyx Group*
Pototo, Brian — *Source Services Corporation*
Powell, Danny — *Source Services Corporation*
Powell, Gregory — *Source Services Corporation*
Power, Michael — *Source Services Corporation*
Pregeant, David — *Source Services Corporation*

Rudolph, Kenneth — *Kossuth & Associates, Inc.*
Rudzinsky, Jeffrey — *Louis Rudzinsky Associates*
Ruge, Merrill — *William Guy & Associates*
Rush, Michael E. — *D.A.L. Associates, Inc.*
Russell, Sam — *The Guild Corporation*
Russo, Karen — *Maximum Management Corp.*
Ryan, Annette — *Don Richard Associates of Tidewater, Inc.*
Ryan, David — *Source Services Corporation*
Ryan, Kathleen — *Source Services Corporation*
Ryan, Lee — *Ryan, Miller & Associates Inc.*
Ryan, Mark — *Source Services Corporation*
Ryan, Mary L. — *Summerfield Associates, Inc.*
Sabat, Lori S. — *Alta Associates, Inc.*
Sacerdote, John — *Raymond Karsan Associates*
Sadaj, Michael — *Source Services Corporation*
Sahagian, John — *The Search Alliance, Inc.*
Salet, Michael — *Source Services Corporation*
Saletra, Andrew — *CPS Inc.*
Sallows, Jill S. — *Crowe, Chizek and Company, LLP*
Salottolo, Al — *Tactical Alternatives*
Salvagno, Michael J. — *The Cambridge Group Ltd*
Samsel, Randy — *Source Services Corporation*
Samuelson, Robert — *Source Services Corporation*
Sanchez, William — *Source Services Corporation*
Sanders, Jason — *Sanders Management Associates, Inc.*
Sanders, Natalie — *CPS Inc.*
Sanders, Norman D. — *Norm Sanders Associates*
Saner, Harold — *Romac & Associates*
Sanitago, Anthony — *TaxSearch, Inc.*
Sanow, Robert — *Cochran, Cochran & Yale, Inc.*
Santiago, Benefrido — *Source Services Corporation*
Santimauro, Edward — *Korn/Ferry International*
Sapers, Mark — *Source Services Corporation*
Saposhnik, Doron — *Source Services Corporation*
Sardella, Sharon — *Source Services Corporation*
Sarn, Allan G. — *Allan Sarn Associates Inc.*
Sarna, Edmund A. — *Jonas, Walters & Assoc., Inc.*
Sauer, Harry J. — *Romac & Associates*
Sausto, Lynne — *Abraham & London, Ltd.*
Savela, Edward — *Source Services Corporation*
Sawyer, Deborah — *Korn/Ferry International*
Sawyer, Patricia L. — *Smith & Sawyer Inc.*
Saxon, Alexa — *Woodworth International Group*
Scalamera, Tom — *CPS Inc.*
Schall, William A. — *The Stevenson Group of New Jersey*
Schedra, Sharon — *Earley Kielty and Associates, Inc.*
Schene, Philip — *A.E. Feldman Associates*
Schiavone, Mary Rose — *Canny, Bowen Inc.*
Schmidt, Frank B. — *F.B. Schmidt International*
Schmidt, William C. — *Christian & Timbers*
Schneider, James — *The Search Firm, Inc.*
Schneiderman, Gerald — *Management Resource Associates, Inc.*
Schrenzel, Benjamin — *Parfitt Recruiting and Consulting*
Schroeder, James — *Source Services Corporation*
Schueneman, David — *CPS Inc.*
Schultz, Helen — *Predictor Systems*
Schultz, Randy — *Source Services Corporation*

Schwalbach, Robert — *Source Services Corporation*
Schwam, Carol — *A.E. Feldman Associates*
Schwartz, Vincent P. — *Slayton International, Inc./I-I-C Partners*
Schweichler, Lee J. — *Schweichler Associates, Inc.*
Schwinden, William — *Source Services Corporation*
Scimone, James — *Source Services Corporation*
Scimone, Jim — *Source Services Corporation*
Scoff, Barry — *Source Services Corporation*
Scothon, Alan — *Romac & Associates*
Scott, Evan — *Howard Fischer Associates, Inc.*
Scott, Gordon S. — *Search Advisors International Corp.*
Scranton, Lisa — *A.J. Burton Group, Inc.*
Seamon, Kenneth — *Source Services Corporation*
Searing, James M. — *Kirkman & Searing, Inc.*
Seco, William — *Seco & Zetto Associates, Inc.*
Seiden, Steven A. — *Seiden Krieger Associates, Inc.*
Selker, Gregory L. — *Christian & Timbers*
Sell, David — *Source Services Corporation*
Selvaggi, Esther — *Source Services Corporation*
Semple, David — *Source Services Corporation*
Semyan, John K. — *TNS Partners, Inc.*
Serba, Kerri — *Source Services Corporation*
Sessa, Vincent J. — *Integrated Search Solutions Group, LLC*
Sevilla, Claudio A. — *Crawford & Crofford*
Shackleford, David — *Source Services Corporation*
Shanks, Jennifer — *Source Services Corporation*
Shapanka, Samuel — *Source Services Corporation*
Shapiro, Elaine — *CPS Inc.*
Shattuck, Merrill B. — *M.B. Shattuck and Associates, Inc.*
Shawhan, Heather — *Source Services Corporation*
Shea, Christopher J. — *Ingram & Aydelotte Inc./I-I-C Partners*
Sheedy, Edward J. — *Dieckmann & Associates, Ltd.*
Shell, John C. — *John Shell Associates, Inc.*
Shelton, Jonathan — *Source Services Corporation*
Shemin, Grace — *Maximum Management Corp.*
Shenfield, Peter — *A.T. Kearney, Inc.*
Shepard, Michael J. — *MSI International*
Sherwood, Andrew — *Goodrich & Sherwood Associates, Inc.*
Shield, Nancy — *Maximum Management Corp.*
Shimp, David J. — *Lamalie Amrop International*
Shirilla, Robert M. — *F.B. Schmidt International*
Shore, Earl L. — *E.L. Shore & Associates Ltd.*
Shourds, Mary E. — *Houze, Shourds & Montgomery, Inc.*
Shufelt, Doug — *Sink, Walker, Boltrus International*
Shulman, Barry — *Shulman Associates*
Sibul, Shelly Remen — *Chicago Legal Search, Ltd.*
Siciliano, Gene — *Western Management Associates*
Siegler, Jody Cukiir — *A.T. Kearney, Inc.*
Siegrist, Jeffrey M. — *D.E. Foster Partners Inc.*
Signer, Julie — *CPS Inc.*
Siker, Paul W. — *The Guild Corporation*
Silvas, Stephen D. — *Roberson and Company*

Silver, Kit — *Source Services Corporation*
Silver, Lee — *L. A. Silver Associates, Inc.*
Simankov, Dmitry — *Logix, Inc.*
Simmons, Deborah — *Source Services Corporation*
Simmons, Gerald J. — *Handy HRM Corp.*
Simon, John — *John J. Davis & Associates, Inc.*
Simpson, Scott — *Cendea Connection International*
Sindler, Jay — *A.J. Burton Group, Inc.*
Sink, Cliff — *Sink, Walker, Boltrus International*
Sirena, Evelyn — *Source Services Corporation*
Skalet, Ira — *A.E. Feldman Associates*
Slayton, Richard C. — *Slayton International, Inc./I-I-C Partners*
Slayton, Richard S. — *Slayton International, Inc./I-I-C Partners*
Sloan, Scott — *Source Services Corporation*
Slosar, John — *Boyden*
Smirnov, Tatiana — *Allan Sarn Associates Inc.*
Smith, Ana Luz — *Smith Search, S.C.*
Smith, David P. — *HRS, Inc.*
Smith, Herman M. — *Herman Smith Executive Initiatives Inc.*
Smith, Ian — *International Staffing Consultants, Inc.*
Smith, Lawrence — *Source Services Corporation*
Smith, Lydia — *The Corporate Connection, Ltd.*
Smith, Matt D. — *Ray & Berndtson*
Smith, Richard — *S.C. International, Ltd.*
Smith, Robert L. — *Smith & Sawyer Inc.*
Smith, Ronald V. — *Coe & Company International Inc.*
Smith, Timothy — *Source Services Corporation*
Smith, Timothy C. — *Christian & Timbers*
Smock, Cynthia — *Source Services Corporation*
Smoller, Howard — *Source Services Corporation*
Snowden, Charles — *Source Services Corporation*
Snowhite, Rebecca — *Source Services Corporation*
Snyder, C. Edward — *Horton International*
Snyder, James F. — *Snyder & Company*
Sochacki, Michael — *Source Services Corporation*
Solters, Jeanne — *The Guild Corporation*
Song, Louis — *Source Services Corporation*
Sorgen, Jay — *Source Services Corporation*
Sostilio, Louis — *Source Services Corporation*
Souder, E.G. — *Souder & Associates*
Spadavecchia, Jennifer — *Alta Associates, Inc.*
Spann, Richard E. — *Goodrich & Sherwood Associates, Inc.*
Spanninger, Mark J. — *The Guild Corporation*
Spector, Michael — *Source Services Corporation*
Spencer, John — *Source Services Corporation*
Spencer, John — *Source Services Corporation*
Spera, Stefanie — *A.T. Kearney, Inc.*
Spiegel, Gayle — *L. A. Silver Associates, Inc.*
Spoutz, Paul — *Source Services Corporation*
Sprau, Collin L. — *Ray & Berndtson*
Spriggs, Robert D. — *Spriggs & Company, Inc.*
St. Clair, Alan — *TNS Partners, Inc.*
St. Martin, Peter — *Source Services Corporation*
Staats, Dave — *Southwestern Professional Services*
Stack, Richard — *Source Services Corporation*
Staehely, Janna — *Southwestern Professional Services*

Stanton, John — *A.T. Kearney, Inc.*
Starner, William S. — *Fenwick Partners*
Steele, Daniel — *Cochran, Cochran & Yale, Inc.*
Steele, Kevin — *Winter, Wyman & Company*
Steer, Joe — *CPS Inc.*
Stefunek, Paul C. — *Stratford Group*
Steinem, Andy — *Dahl-Morrow International*
Steinem, Andy — *Dahl-Morrow International*
Steinem, Barbara — *Dahl-Morrow International*
Steinem, Barbra — *Dahl-Morrow International*
Steinman, Stephen M. — *The Stevenson Group of New Jersey*
Stenberg, Edward — *Winter, Wyman & Company*
Stephens, Andrew — *Source Services Corporation*
Stephens, John — *Source Services Corporation*
Stephenson, Don L. — *Ells Personnel System Inc.*
Sterling, Jay — *Earley Kielty and Associates, Inc.*
Stern, Stephen — *CPS Inc.*
Sterner, Doug — *CPS Inc.*
Stevens, Ken — *The Stevens Group*
Stevenson, Terry — *Bartholdi & Company, Inc.*
Stewart, Ross M. — *Human Resources Network Partners Inc.*
Stirn, Bradley A. — *Spencer Stuart*
Stokes, John — *Nordeman Grimm, Inc.*
Stone, Susan L. — *Stone Enterprises Ltd.*
Storm, Deborah — *Source Services Corporation*
Stovall, Randal — *D. Brown and Associates, Inc.*
Strain, Stephen R. — *Spencer Stuart*
Stranberg, James R. — *Callan Associates, Ltd.*
Strander, Dervin — *Source Services Corporation*
Strassman, Mark — *Don Richard Associates of Washington, D.C., Inc.*
Stratmeyer, Karin Bergwall — *Princeton Entrepreneurial Resources*
Stratton, Cary — *Coastal International Inc.*
Strickland, Katie — *Grantham & Co., Inc.*
Stringer, Dann P. — *D.E. Foster Partners Inc.*
Strom, Mark N. — *Search Advisors International Corp.*
Struzziero, Ralph E. — *Romac & Associates*
Sturtz, James W. — *Compass Group Ltd.*
Sucato, Carolyn — *Jay Gaines & Company, Inc.*
Summerfield-Beall, Dotty — *Summerfield Associates, Inc.*
Sur, William K. — *Canny, Bowen Inc.*
Surrette, Mark — *Robertson-Surrette Executive Search*
Susoreny, Samali — *Source Services Corporation*
Sutter, Howard — *Romac & Associates*
Swanner, William — *Source Services Corporation*
Swanson, Dick — *Raymond Karsan Associates*
Swartz, William K. — *Swartz Executive Search*
Sweeney, Anne — *Source Services Corporation*
Sweeney, James W. — *Sweeney Harbert & Mummert, Inc.*
Sweet, Randall — *Source Services Corporation*
Swoboda, Lawrence — *A.J. Burton Group, Inc.*
Taft, David G. — *Techsearch Services, Inc.*
Taft, Steven D. — *The Guild Corporation*
Tankson, Dawn — *Source Services Corporation*
Tanner, Frank — *Source Services Corporation*
Tanner, Gary — *Source Services Corporation*
Taylor, Conrad G. — *MSI International*
Taylor, James M. — *The HRM Group, Inc.*
Taylor, R.L. (Larry) — *Ray & Berndtson*
Teger, Stella — *Source Services Corporation*

Telford, John H. — *Telford, Adams & Alexander/Telford & Co., Inc.*
ten Cate, Herman H. — *Stoneham Associates Corp.*
Tenero, Kymberly — *Source Services Corporation*
Tetrick, Tim — *O'Connor, O'Connor, Lordi, Ltd.*
Theard, Susan — *Romac & Associates*
Theobald, David B. — *Theobald & Associates*
Thielman, Joseph — *Barrett Partners*
Thomas, Cheryl M. — *CPS Inc.*
Thomas, Donald — *Mixtec Group*
Thomas, Ian A. — *International Staffing Consultants, Inc.*
Thomas, Kim — *CPS Inc.*
Thomas, Kurt J. — *P.J. Murphy & Associates, Inc.*
Thompson, Dave — *Battalia Winston International*
Thompson, Leslie — *Source Services Corporation*
Thrapp, Mark C. — *Executive Search Consultants International, Inc.*
Thrower, Troy — *Source Services Corporation*
Tilley, Kyle — *Source Services Corporation*
Timoney, Laura — *Bishop Partners*
Tipp, George D. — *Intech Summit Group, Inc.*
Tittle, David M. — *Paul-Tittle Associates, Inc.*
To, Raymond — *Corporate Recruiters Ltd.*
Tobin, Christopher — *Source Services Corporation*
Tolette, Skip — *The Schmitt Tolette Group*
Tomasco, Ray — *Huntington Group*
Tootsey, Mark A. — *A.J. Burton Group, Inc.*
Tovrog, Dan — *CPS Inc.*
Travis, Michael — *Travis & Company*
Trefzer, Kristie — *Source Services Corporation*
Trewhella, Michael — *Source Services Corporation*
Trice, Renee — *Source Services Corporation*
Trieschmann, Daniel — *Source Services Corporation*
Trieweiler, Bob — *Executive Placement Consultants, Inc.*
Trimble, Patricia — *Source Services Corporation*
Trimble, Rhonda — *Source Services Corporation*
Truemper, Dean — *CPS Inc.*
Truitt, Thomas B. — *Southwestern Professional Services*
Tscelli, Maureen — *Source Services Corporation*
Tschan, Stephen — *Source Services Corporation*
Tucker, Thomas A. — *The Thomas Tucker Company*
Tullberg, Tina — *CPS Inc.*
Turner, Edward K. — *Don Richard Associates of Charlotte*
Turner, Kimberly — *Barton Associates, Inc.*
Turner, Raymond — *Source Services Corporation*
Tursi, Deborah J. — *The Corporate Connection, Ltd.*
Tuttle, Donald E. — *Tuttle Venture Group, Inc.*
Twiste, Craig — *Raymond Karsan Associates*
Twomey, James — *Source Services Corporation*
Ulbert, Nancy — *Aureus Group*
Ulrich, Mary Ann — *D.S. Allen Associates, Inc.*
Unger, Paul T. — *A.T. Kearney, Inc.*
Uzzel, Linda — *Source Services Corporation*
Vacca, Domenic — *Romac & Associates*
Vairo, Leonard A. — *Christian & Timbers*
Valenta, Joseph — *Princeton Entrepreneurial Resources*
Van Clieaf, Mark — *MVC Associates International*

Van Norman, Ben — *Source Services Corporation*
Van Nostrand, Mara J. — *Barton Associates, Inc.*
Vande-Water, Katie — *J. Robert Scott*
Vandenbulcke, Cynthia — *Source Services Corporation*
Vann, Dianne — *The Button Group*
Varney, Monique — *Source Services Corporation*
Varrichio, Michael — *Source Services Corporation*
Velez, Hector — *Source Services Corporation*
Velten, Mark T. — *Boyden*
Venable, William W. — *Thorndike Deland Associates*
Vennat, Manon — *Spencer Stuart*
Vernon, Peter C. — *Horton International*
Vilella, Paul — *Source Services Corporation*
Villella, Paul — *Source Services Corporation*
Vinett-Hessel, Deidre — *Source Services Corporation*
Viviano, Cathleen — *Source Services Corporation*
Vlcek, Thomas J. — *Vlcek & Company, Inc.*
Voigt, John A. — *Romac & Associates*
Volkman, Arthur — *Cochran, Cochran & Yale, Inc.*
von Baillou, Astrid — *Richard Kinser & Associates*
Von Karl, Thomas — *Juntunen-Combs-Poirier*
Vossler, James — *A.J. Burton Group, Inc.*
Vujcec, John — *Executive Search, Ltd.*
Wacholz, Rick — *A.T. Kearney, Inc.*
Wade, Christy — *Source Services Corporation*
Waldoch, D. Mark — *Barnes Development Group, LLC*
Waldrop, Gary R. — *MSI International*
Walker, Ann — *Source Services Corporation*
Walker, Craig H. — *A.J. Burton Group, Inc.*
Walker, Douglas G. — *Sink, Walker, Boltrus International*
Walker, Richard — *Bradford & Galt, Inc.*
Walker, Rose — *Source Services Corporation*
Wallace, Toby — *Source Services Corporation*
Walsh, Denis — *Professional Staffing Consultants*
Walsh, Patty — *Abraham & London, Ltd.*
Walters, Scott — *Paul-Tittle Associates, Inc.*
Ward, Jim — *F-O-R-T-U-N-E Personnel Consultants of Huntsville, Inc.*
Ward, Les — *Source Services Corporation*
Ward, Madeleine — *LTM Associates*
Ward, Robert — *Source Services Corporation*
Ware, John C. — *Spencer Stuart*
Warnock, Phyl — *Source Services Corporation*
Warter, Mark — *Isaacson, Miller*
Wasserman, Harvey — *Churchill and Affiliates, Inc.*
Wasson, Thomas W. — *Spencer Stuart*
Watkinson, Jim W. — *The Badger Group*
Watson, James — *MSI International*
Watson, Peggy — *Advanced Information Management*
Waymire, Pamela — *Source Services Corporation*
Wayne, Cary S. — *ProSearch Inc.*
Webber, Edward — *Source Services Corporation*
Weber, Fred — *J.B. Homer Associates, Inc.*
Weeks, Glenn — *Source Services Corporation*
Wein, Michael S. — *InterimManagement Solutions, Inc.*
Wein, Michael S. — *Media Management Resources, Inc.*

Wein, William — *InterimManagement Solutions, Inc.*

Wein, William — *Media Management Resources, Inc.*

Weinberg, Melvin — *Romac & Associates*

Weis, Theodore — *Source Services Corporation*

Weiss, Elizabeth — *Source Services Corporation*

Weisz, Laura — *Anderson Sterling Associates*

Welch, Dale — *Winter, Wyman & Company*

Welch, Robert — *Ray & Berndtson*

Wenz, Alexander — *Source Services Corporation*

Wert, Marty — *Parfitt Recruiting and Consulting*

Wertheim, Denise — *Paul-Tittle Associates, Inc.*

Wessling, Jerry — *Source Services Corporation*

Wheatley, William — *Drummond Associates, Inc.*

Wheeler, Gerard H. — *A.J. Burton Group, Inc.*

Whelan, David — *Ethos Consulting Inc.*

White, William C. — *Venture Resources Inc.*

Whitfield, Jack — *Source Services Corporation*

Whitney, David L. — *Whitney & Associates, Inc.*

Whyte, Roger J. — *The Whyte Group, Inc.*

Wilburn, Dan — *Kaye-Bassman International Corp.*

Wilcox, Fred T. — *Wilcox, Bertoux & Miller*

Wilder, Richard B. — *Columbia Consulting Group*

Wilkinson, Jr. SPHR

Wilkinson, Charles E. — *The HRM Group, Inc.*

Willbrandt, Curt — *Source Services Corporation*

Williams, Angie — *Whitney & Associates, Inc.*

Williams, Brad — *Winter, Wyman & Company*

Williams, Dave — *The McCormick Group, Inc.*

Williams, Gary L. — *Barnes Development Group, LLC*

Williams, Jack — *A.T. Kearney, Inc.*

Williams, John — *Source Services Corporation*

Williams, Roger K. — *Williams, Roth & Krueger Inc.*

Williams, Stephen E. — *Barton Associates, Inc.*

Willner, Leo — *William Guy & Associates*

Wilson, John — *Korn/Ferry International*

Wilson, Joyce — *Source Services Corporation*

Wilson, Patricia L. — *Leon A. Farley Associates*

Wingate, Mary — *Source Services Corporation*

Winitz, Joel — *GSW Consulting Group, Inc.*

Winitz, Marla — *GSW Consulting Group, Inc.*

Winkowski, Stephen — *Source Services Corporation*

Winnicki, Kimberly — *Source Services Corporation*

Winograd, Glenn — *Criterion Executive Search, Inc.*

Winston, Dale — *Battalia Winston International*

Witte, David L. — *Ward Howell International, Inc.*

Witzgall, William — *Source Services Corporation*

Wolf, Donald — *Source Services Corporation*

Wolf, Stephen M. — *Byron Leonard International, Inc.*

Wolfe, Peter — *Source Services Corporation*

Womack, Joseph — *The Bankers Group*

Wood, Gary — *Source Services Corporation*

Wood, Milton M. — *M. Wood Company*

Woodhouse, Michael — *Ashton Computer Professionals Inc.*

Woods, Craig — *Source Services Corporation*

Woodworth, Gail — *Woodworth International Group*

Wooldridge, Jeff — *Ray & Berndtson*

Woollett, James — *Rusher, Loscavio & LoPresto*

Woomer, Jerome — *Source Services Corporation*

Work, Alan — *Quantex Associates, Inc.*

Workman, David — *Source Services Corporation*

Wren, Jay — *Jay Wren & Associates*

Wright, Carl A.J. — *A.J. Burton Group, Inc.*

Wright, Charles D. — *Goodrich & Sherwood Associates, Inc.*

Wright, Leslie — *The Stevenson Group of New Jersey*

Wycoff-Viola, Amy — *Source Services Corporation*

Yang, George — *Technical Connections Inc.*

Yeaton, Robert — *Source Services Corporation*

Yen, Maggie Yeh Ching — *Ray & Berndtson*

Yossem, Sheila — *Bishop Partners*

Young, Heather — *The Guild Corporation*

Young, Lesley — *Search West, Inc.*

Youngberg, David — *Source Services Corporation*

Yungerberg, Steven — *Steven Yungerberg Associates Inc.*

Zaccaria, Jack — *The Zaccaria Group, Inc.*

Zadfar, Maryanne — *The Thomas Tucker Company*

Zaffrann, Craig S. — *P.J. Murphy & Associates, Inc.*

Zahradka, James F. — *P.J. Murphy & Associates, Inc.*

Zaleta, Andy R. — *A.T. Kearney, Inc.*

Zamborsky, George — *Boyden*

Zarnoski, Henry — *Dunhill International Search of New Haven*

Zaslav, Debra M. — *Telford, Adams & Alexander/Telford & Co., Inc.*

Zavrel, Mark — *Source Services Corporation*

Zegel, Gary — *Source Services Corporation*

Zell, David M. — *Logix Partners*

Zetto, Kathryn — *Seco & Zetto Associates, Inc.*

Zila, Laurie M. — *Princeton Entrepreneurial Resources*

Zilliacus, Patrick W. — *Larsen, Whitney, Blecksmith & Zilliacus*

Zimbal, Mark — *Source Services Corporation*

Zimont, Scott — *Source Services Corporation*

Zinn, Don — *Quantex Associates, Inc.*

Zucker, Nancy — *Maximum Management Corp.*

Function Specialization Index by Recruiter

Function Specialization Index by Recruiter

This index is arranged into 10 selected business functions, including the generalist category, and provides a breakdown of the primary and secondary lines of function specializations of each executive recruiter. Many recruiters have multiple listings in this index depending on the various specializations in which they are engaged. *Recruiters listed in the generalist category serve all function specializations.*

1. Generalist
2. Administration
3. Engineering
4. Finance/Accounting
5. General Management

6. Human Resources
7. Marketing
8. Research/Development
9. Sales
10. Women/Minorities

1. Generalist

Abbatiello, Christine Murphy — *Winter, Wyman & Company*
Abbott, Peter D. — *The Abbott Group, Inc.*
Abell, Vincent W. — *MSI International*
Adams, Jeffrey C. — *Telford, Adams & Alexander/Jeffrey C. Adams & Co., Inc.*
Adler, Louis S. — *CJA - The Adler Group*
Akin, J.R. "Jack" — *J.R. Akin & Company Inc.*
Albertini, Nancy — *Taylor-Winfield, Inc.*
Albright, Cindy — *Summerfield Associates, Inc.*
Alexander, Karen — *Huntington Group*
Allen, Jean E. — *Lamalie Amrop International*
Allen, Scott — *Chrisman & Company, Incorporated*
Allen, Wade H. — *Cendea Connection International*
Allen, William L. — *The Hindman Company*
Allerton, Donald T. — *Allerton Heneghan & O'Neill*
Allred, J. Michael — *Spencer Stuart*
Alpeyrie, Jean-Louis — *Heidrick & Struggles, Inc.*
Altreuter, Rose — *The ALTCO Group*
Ambler, Peter W. — *Peter W. Ambler Company*
Ames, George C. — *Ames O'Neill Associates*
Anderson, David C. — *Heidrick & Struggles, Inc.*
Anderson, Maria H. — *Barton Associates, Inc.*
Anderson, Richard — *Grant Cooper and Associates*
Anderson, Terry — *Intech Summit Group, Inc.*
Andrews, J. Douglas — *Clarey & Andrews, Inc.*
Archer, Sandra F. — *Ryan, Miller & Associates Inc.*
Arms, Douglas — *TOPAZ International, Inc.*
Arms, Douglas — *TOPAZ Legal Solutions*
Arnold, David W. — *Christian & Timbers*
Aronin, Michael — *Fisher-Todd Associates*
Arseneault, Daniel S. — *MSI International*
Ascher, Susan P. — *The Ascher Group*
Asquith, Peter S. — *Ames Personnel Consultants, Inc.*
Aston, Kathy — *Marra Peters & Partners*
Atkins, Laurie — *Battalia Winston International*
Atkinson, S. Graham — *Raymond Karsan Associates*
Attell, Harold — *A.E. Feldman Associates*
Atwood, Barrie — *The Abbott Group, Inc.*
Aubin, Richard E. — *Aubin International Inc.*
Axelrod, Nancy R. — *A.T. Kearney, Inc.*
Bacon, Cheri — *Gaffney Management Consultants*
Badger, Fred H. — *The Badger Group*
Baeder, Jeremy — *Executive Manning Corporation*
Bailey, David O. — *Ray & Berndtson*
Bailey, Paul — *Austin-McGregor International*
Baje, Sarah — *Innovative Search Group, LLC*
Baker, Gary M. — *Cochran, Cochran & Yale, Inc.*
Baker, Gerry — *A.T. Kearney, Inc.*
Balbone, Rich — *Executive Manning Corporation*
Baldwin, Keith R. — *The Baldwin Group*
Baltaglia, Michael — *Cochran, Cochran & Yale, Inc.*
Barbour, Mary Beth — *Tully/Woodmansee International, Inc.*
Barger, H. Carter — *Barger & Sargeant, Inc.*
Barlow, Ken H. — *The Cherbonnier Group, Inc.*
Barnes, Gregory — *Korn/Ferry International*
Barnes, Richard E. — *Barnes Development Group, LLC*

Barnes, Roanne L. — *Barnes Development Group, LLC*
Barnum, Toni M. — *Stone Murphy & Olson*
Baron, Len — *Industrial Recruiters Associates, Inc.*
Barthold, James A. — *McNichol Associates*
Bartholdi, Ted — *Bartholdi & Company, Inc.*
Bartholdi, Theodore G. — *Bartholdi & Company, Inc.*
Barton, Gary R. — *Barton Associates, Inc.*
Bason, Maurice L. — *Bason Associates Inc.*
Bass, M. Lynn — *Ray & Berndtson*
Bassler, John — *Korn/Ferry International*
Bassman, Robert — *Kaye-Bassman International Corp.*
Bassman, Sandy — *Kaye-Bassman International Corp.*
Battalia, O. William — *Battalia Winston International*
Battles, Jonathan — *Korn/Ferry International*
Beal, Richard D. — *A.T. Kearney, Inc.*
Beall, Charles P. — *Beall & Company, Inc.*
Bearman, Linda — *Grant Cooper and Associates*
Beaudin, Elizabeth C. — *Callan Associates, Ltd.*
Beaver, Bentley H. — *The Onstott Group, Inc.*
Beaver, Robert W. — *Executive Manning Corporation*
Beeson, William B. — *Lawrence-Leiter & Co. Management Conultants*
Belfrey, Edward — *Dunhill Professional Search of Irvine, Inc.*
Belin, Jean — *Boyden*
Bell, Lisa — *Winter, Wyman & Company*
Bence, Robert J. — *DHR International, Inc.*
Bennett, Jo — *Battalia Winston International*
Bennett, Joan — *Adams & Associates International*
Bennett, Ness — *Technical Connections Inc.*
Beran, Helena — *Michael J. Cavanagh and Associates*
Berkhemer-Credaire, Betsy — *Berkhemer Clayton Incorporated*
Berry, Harold B. — *The Hindman Company*
Bettick, Michael J. — *A.J. Burton Group, Inc.*
Biestek, Paul J. — *Paul J. Biestek Associates, Inc.*
Biggins, Joseph — *Winter, Wyman & Company*
Billington, William H. — *Spriggs & Company, Inc.*
Bishop, Susan — *Bishop Partners*
Blackmon, Sharon — *The Abbott Group, Inc.*
Blackshaw, Brian M. — *Blackshaw, Olmstead, Lynch & Koenig*
Bladon, Andrew — *Don Richard Associates of Tampa, Inc.*
Blake, Eileen — *Howard Fischer Associates, Inc.*
Blanton, Julia — *Blanton and Company*
Blanton, Thomas — *Blanton and Company*
Bliley, Jerry — *Spencer Stuart*
Block, Randy — *Block & Associates*
Bloomer, James E. — *L.W. Foote Company*
Boag, John — *Norm Sanders Associates*
Boehmer, John — *Huntington Group*
Boel, Werner — *The Dalley Hewitt Company*
Bogansky, Amy — *Conex Incorporated*
Bohle, John B. — *Ray & Berndtson*
Bohn, Steve J. — *MSI International*
Bond, James L. — *People Management Northeast Incorporated*
Borenstine, Alvin — *Synergistics Associates Ltd.*

Borland, James — *Goodrich & Sherwood Associates, Inc.*
Bormann, Cindy Ann — *MSI International*
Bostic, James E. — *Phillips Resource Group*
Bourrie, Sharon D. — *Chartwell Partners International, Inc.*
Bowden, Otis H. — *BowdenGlobal, Ltd.*
Bowen, Tad — *Executive Search International*
Boyle, Russell E. — *Egon Zehnder International Inc.*
Brackman, Janet — *Dahl-Morrow International*
Bradley, Dalena — *Woodworth International Group*
Bradshaw, Monte — *Christian & Timbers*
Brady, Dick — *William Guy & Associates*
Brandenburg, David — *Professional Staffing Consultants*
Bratches, Howard — *Thorndike Deland Associates*
Brieger, Steve — *Thorne, Brieger Associates Inc.*
Broadhurst, Austin — *Lamalie Amrop International*
Brooks, Bernard E. — *Mruk & Partners/EMA Partners Int'l*
Brother, Joy — *Charles Luntz & Associates. Inc.*
Brown, Kevin P. — *Raymond Karsan Associates*
Brown, Larry C. — *Horton International*
Brown, S. Ross — *Egon Zehnder International Inc.*
Brown, Steffan — *Woodworth International Group*
Bruce, Michael C. — *Spencer Stuart*
Brudno, Robert J. — *Savoy Partners, Ltd.*
Bruno, Deborah F. — *The Hindman Company*
Bryant, Richard D. — *Bryant Associates, Inc.*
Bryant, Shari G. — *Bryant Associates, Inc.*
Bryza, Robert M. — *Robert Lowell International*
Brzezinski, Ronald T. — *Callan Associates, Ltd.*
Buckles, Donna — *Cochran, Cochran & Yale, Inc.*
Bueschel, David A. — *Shepherd Bueschel & Provus, Inc.*
Buggy, Linda — *Bonnell Associates Ltd.*
Bullock, Conni — *Earley Kielty and Associates, Inc.*
Burch, R. Stuart — *Russell Reynolds Associates, Inc.*
Burchill, Greg — *BGB Associates*
Burden, Gene — *The Cherbonnier Group, Inc.*
Burke, John — *The Experts*
Burke, Karen A. — *Mazza & Riley, Inc. (a Korn/Ferry International affiliate)*
Burkhill, John — *The Talley Group*
Burmaster, Holly — *Winter, Wyman & Company*
Burns, Alan — *The Enns Partners Inc.*
Busch, Jack — *Busch International*
Button, David R. — *The Button Group*
Cahill, Peter M. — *Peter M. Cahill Associates, Inc.*
Calivas, Kay — *A.J. Burton Group, Inc.*
Call, David — *Cochran, Cochran & Yale, Inc.*
Callan, Robert M. — *Callan Associates, Ltd.*
Calogeras, Chris — *The Sager Company*
Cameron, James W. — *Cameron Consulting*
Campbell, Patricia A. — *The Onstott Group, Inc.*
Campbell, Robert Scott — *Wellington Management Group*
Campbell, Robert Scott — *Wellington Management Group*
Campbell, W. Ross — *Egon Zehnder International Inc.*

Capizzi, Karen — *Cochran, Cochran & Yale, Inc.*
Capra, Jamie — *Warren, Morris & Madison*
Carideo, Joseph — *Thorndike Deland Associates*
Carrington, Timothy — *Korn/Ferry International*
Carro, Carl R. — *Executive Search Consultants International, Inc.*
Carrott, Gregory T. — *Egon Zehnder International Inc.*
Carter, I. Wayne — *Heidrick & Struggles, Inc.*
Carter, Jon F. — *Egon Zehnder International Inc.*
Cary, Con — *Cary & Associates*
Cashman, Tracy — *Winter, Wyman & Company*
Castillo, Eduardo — *Korn/Ferry International*
Caudill, Nancy — *Bishop Partners*
Caudill, Nancy — *Webb, Johnson Associates, Inc.*
Cavanagh, Michael J. — *Michael J. Cavanagh and Associates*
Cesafsky, Barry R. — *Lamalie Amrop International*
Champion, Geoffrey — *Korn/Ferry International*
Chan, Margaret — *Webb, Johnson Associates, Inc.*
Chappell, Peter — *The Bankers Group*
Chatterjie, Alok — *MSI International*
Chavous, C. Crawford — *Phillips Resource Group*
Cherbonnier, L. Michael — *TCG International, Inc.*
Cherbonnier, L. Michael — *The Cherbonnier Group, Inc.*
Chorman, Marilyn A. — *Hite Executive Search*
Christenson, H. Alan — *Christenson & Hutchison*
Christian, Philip — *Ray & Berndtson*
Christoff, Matthew J. — *Spencer Stuart*
Christy, Michael T. — *Heidrick & Struggles, Inc.*
Cizek, John T. — *Cizek Associates, Inc.*
Cizek, Marti J. — *Cizek Associates, Inc.*
Clarey, Jack R. — *Clarey & Andrews, Inc.*
Clasen, Ryan — *Warren, Morris & Madison*
Clauhsen, Elizabeth A. — *Savoy Partners, Ltd.*
Clayton, Fred J. — *Berkhemer Clayton Incorporated*
Clegg, Cynthia — *Horton International*
Clough, Geoff — *Intech Summit Group, Inc.*
Cloutier, Gisella — *Dinte Resources, Inc.*
Cochran, Scott P. — *The Badger Group*
Coe, Karen J. — *Coe & Company International Inc.*
Coffey, Patty — *Winter, Wyman & Company*
Coffman, Brian — *Kossuth & Associates, Inc.*
Cohen, Michael R. — *Intech Summit Group, Inc.*
Cohen, Pamela — *TOPAZ International, Inc.*
Cohen, Pamela — *TOPAZ Legal Solutions*
Cohen, Robert C. — *Intech Summit Group, Inc.*
Coleman, J. Kevin — *J. Kevin Coleman & Associates, Inc.*
Coleman, Patricia — *Korn/Ferry International*
Colling, Douglas — *KPMG Management Consulting*
Collins, Tom — *J.B. Homer Associates, Inc.*
Colvin, Teresa A. — *Jonas, Walters & Assoc., Inc.*
Compton, Tonya — *Dunhill Professional Search of Irvine, Inc.*
Cona, Joseph A. — *Cona Personnel Search*
Conard, Rodney J. — *Conard Associates, Inc.*
Conley, Kevin E. — *Lamalie Amrop International*
Connelly, Scott — *Technical Connections Inc.*
Conway, Maureen — *Conway & Associates*
Conway, William P. — *Phillips Resource Group*
Cook, Dennis — *A.T. Kearney, Inc.*

Evans, David — *Executive Manning Corporation*
Fahlin, Kelly — *Winter, Wyman & Company*
Fancher, Robert L. — *Bason Associates Inc.*
Farley, Leon A. — *Leon A. Farley Associates*
Farrow, Jerry M. — *McCormack & Farrow*
Feder, Gwen — *Egon Zehnder International Inc.*
Feldman, Abe — *A.E. Feldman Associates*
Fennell, Patrick — *Korn/Ferry International*
Ferneborg, Jay W. — *Ferneborg & Associates, Inc.*
Ferneborg, John R. — *Ferneborg & Associates, Inc.*
Feyder, Michael — *A.T. Kearney, Inc.*
Fields, Fredric — *C.A. Durakis Associates, Inc.*
Fifield, George C. — *Egon Zehnder International Inc.*
Fincher, Richard P. — *Phase II Management*
Fingers, David — *Bradford & Galt, Inc.*
Fini, Ron — *The Sager Company*
Fischer, Adam — *Howard Fischer Associates, Inc.*
Fischer, Howard M. — *Howard Fischer Associates, Inc.*
Fischer, John C. — *Horton International*
Fisher, Neal — *Fisher Personnel Management Services*
Fishler, Stu — *A.T. Kearney, Inc.*
Fitzgerald, Diane — *Fitzgerald Associates*
Fitzgerald, Geoffrey — *Fitzgerald Associates*
Flanagan, Robert M. — *Robert M. Flanagan & Associates, Ltd.*
Flannery, Peter F. — *Jonas, Walters & Assoc., Inc.*
Fletcher, David — *A.J. Burton Group, Inc.*
Flores, Agustin — *Ward Howell International, Inc.*
Foley, Eileen — *Winter, Wyman & Company*
Folkerth, Gene — *Gene Folkerth & Associates, Inc.*
Fong, Robert — *Korn/Ferry International*
Foote, Leland W. — *L.W. Foote Company*
Foreman, David C. — *Koontz, Jeffries & Associates, Inc.*
Foreman, Rebecca — *Aubin International Inc.*
Forman, Donald R. — *Stanton Chase International*
Fowler, Thomas A. — *The Hindman Company*
Francis, John — *Zwell International*
Frank, Valerie S. — *Norman Roberts & Associates, Inc.*
Frazier, John — *Cochran, Cochran & Yale, Inc.*
Fredericks, Ward A. — *Mixtec Group*
French, William G. — *Preng & Associates, Inc.*
Fribush, Richard — *A.J. Burton Group, Inc.*
Friedman, Helen E. — *McCormack & Farrow*
Friel, Thomas J. — *Heidrick & Struggles, Inc.*
Fulgham MacCarthy, Ann — *Columbia Consulting Group*
Furlong, James W. — *Furlong Search, Inc.*
Furlong, James W. — *Furlong Search, Inc.*
Furlong, James W. — *Furlong Search, Inc.*
Fust, Sheely F. — *Ray & Berndtson*
Gabel, Gregory N. — *Canny, Bowen Inc.*
Gabriel, David L. — *The Arcus Group*
Gadison, William — *Richard, Wayne and Roberts*
Gaffney, Keith — *Gaffney Management Consultants*
Gaffney, William — *Gaffney Management Consultants*
Gaines, Jay — *Jay Gaines & Company, Inc.*
Gaines, Ronni L. — *TOPAZ International, Inc.*
Gaines, Ronni L. — *TOPAZ Legal Solutions*
Galante, Suzanne M. — *Vlcek & Company, Inc.*

Gallagher, Terence M. — *Battalia Winston International*
Gantar, Donna — *Howard Fischer Associates, Inc.*
Gardiner, E. Nicholas P. — *Gardiner International*
Garfinkle, Steven M. — *Battalia Winston International*
Gates, Lucille C. — *Lamalie Amrop International*
Gauthier, Robert C. — *Columbia Consulting Group*
George, Delores F. — *Delores F. George Human Resource Management & Consulting Industry*
Gerbasi, Michael — *The Sager Company*
Germain, Valerie — *Jay Gaines & Company, Inc.*
Germaine, Debra — *Fenwick Partners*
Gestwick, Daniel — *Cochran, Cochran & Yale, Inc.*
Gettys, James R. — *International Staffing Consultants, Inc.*
Ghurani, Mac — *Gary Kaplan & Associates*
Gibbs, John S. — *Spencer Stuart*
Gibson, Bruce — *Gibson & Company Inc.*
Gilbert, Jerry — *Gilbert & Van Campen International*
Gilchrist, Robert J. — *Horton International*
Giles, Joe L. — *Joe L. Giles and Associates, Inc.*
Gill, Patricia — *Columbia Consulting Group*
Gillespie, Thomas — *Professional Search Consultants*
Gilmore, Connie — *Taylor-Winfield, Inc.*
Gilreath, James M. — *Gilreath Weatherby, Inc.*
Giries, Juliet D. — *Barton Associates, Inc.*
Girsinger, Linda — *Industrial Recruiters Associates, Inc.*
Gladstone, Martin J. — *MSI International*
Goar, Duane R. — *Sandhurst Associates*
Gobert, Larry — *Professional Search Consultants*
Gold, Stacey — *Earley Kielty and Associates, Inc.*
Golde, Lisa — *Tully/Woodmansee International, Inc.*
Goldenberg, Susan — *Grant Cooper and Associates*
Goldsmith, Fred J. — *Fred J. Goldsmith Associates*
Goldstein, Steven G. — *The Jonathan Stevens Group, Inc.*
Gonye, Peter K. — *Egon Zehnder International Inc.*
Gonzalez, Kristen — *A.J. Burton Group, Inc.*
Gonzalez, Rafael — *Korn/Ferry International*
Goodere, Greg — *Splaine & Associates, Inc.*
Goodman, Dawn M. — *Bason Associates Inc.*
Goodwin, Tim — *William Guy & Associates*
Gordon, Elliot — *Korn/Ferry International*
Gordon, Gerald L. — *E.G. Jones Associates, Ltd.*
Gordon, Gloria — *A.T. Kearney, Inc.*
Gore, Les — *Executive Search International*
Gorfinkle, Gayle — *Executive Search International*
Graham, Craig — *Ward Howell International, Inc.*
Grant, Michael — *Zwell International*
Grantham, John — *Grantham & Co., Inc.*
Grantham, Philip H. — *Columbia Consulting Group*
Grasch, Jerry E. — *The Hindman Company*
Gregor, Joie A. — *Heidrick & Struggles, Inc.*
Gregory, Gary A. — *John Kurosky & Associates*
Grey, Fred — *J.B. Homer Associates, Inc.*
Griffin, Cathy — *A.T. Kearney, Inc.*
Groban, Jack — *A.T. Kearney, Inc.*

Grotte, Lawrence C. — *Lautz Grotte Engler*
Gurnani, Angali — *Executive Placement Consultants, Inc.*
Gutknecht, Steven — *Jacobson Associates*
Guy, C. William — *William Guy & Associates*
Hagerty, Kenneth — *Korn/Ferry International*
Hailes, Brian — *Russell Reynolds Associates, Inc.*
Halbrich, Mitch — *A.J. Burton Group, Inc.*
Hall, Marty B. — *Catlin-Wells & White*
Hall, Peter V. — *Chartwell Partners International, Inc.*
Hallock, Peter B. — *Goodrich & Sherwood Associates, Inc.*
Hamilton, John R. — *Ray & Berndtson*
Hanes, Leah — *Ray & Berndtson*
Hanley, Alan P. — *Williams, Roth & Krueger Inc.*
Hanley, J. Patrick — *Canny, Bowen Inc.*
Hanley, Maureen E. — *Gilbert Tweed/INESA*
Hanna, Dwight — *Cadillac Associates*
Hansen, David G. — *Ott & Hansen, Inc.*
Hanson, Grant M. — *Goodrich & Sherwood Associates, Inc.*
Hanson, Lee — *Heidrick & Struggles, Inc.*
Harbaugh, Paul J. — *International Management Advisors, Inc.*
Harbert, David O. — *Sweeney Harbert & Mummert, Inc.*
Hardison, Richard L. — *Hardison & Company*
Harfenist, Harry — *Parker Page Group*
Harney, Elyane — *Gary Kaplan & Associates*
Harris, Jack — *A.T. Kearney, Inc.*
Harris, Joe W. — *Cendea Connection International*
Harris, Seth O. — *Christian & Timbers*
Harrison, Victor — *Intelligent Management Solutions, Inc. (IMS)*
Hart, Robert T. — *D.E. Foster Partners Inc.*
Harvey, Mike — *Advanced Executive Resources*
Haughton, Michael — *DeFrain, Mayer LLC*
Hauswirth, Jeffrey M. — *Spencer Stuart*
Havener, Donald Clarke — *The Abbott Group, Inc.*
Hawksworth, A. Dwight — *A.D. & Associates Executive Search, Inc.*
Haystead, Steve — *Advanced Executive Resources*
Heaney, Thomas — *Korn/Ferry International*
Heideman, Mary Marren — *DeFrain, Mayer LLC*
Heiken, Barbara E. — *Randell-Heiken, Inc.*
Heinze, David — *Heinze & Associates, Inc.*
Helgeson, Burton H. — *Norm Sanders Associates*
Helminiak, Audrey — *Gaffney Management Consultants*
Henard, John B. — *Lamalie Amrop International*
Hendrickson, David L. — *Heidrick & Struggles, Inc.*
Heneghan, Donald A. — *Allerton Heneghan & O'Neill*
Henn, George W. — *G.W. Henn & Company*
Henry, Mary — *Conex Incorporated*
Hensley, Bert — *Morgan Samuels Co., Inc.*
Hergenrather, Richard A. — *Hergenrather & Company*
Herman, Eugene J. — *Earley Kielty and Associates, Inc.*
Herman, Shelli — *Gary Kaplan & Associates*
Hertan, Richard L. — *Executive Manning Corporation*

Hertlein, James N.J. — *Boyden/Zay & Company*
Hewitt, Rives D. — *The Dalley Hewitt Company*
Hewitt, W. Davis — *The Dalley Hewitt Company*
Hicks, Albert M. — *Phillips Resource Group*
Hicks, Mike — *Damon & Associates, Inc.*
Higgins, Dave — *Warren, Morris & Madison*
Higgins, Donna — *Howard Fischer Associates, Inc.*
Hildebrand, Thomas B. — *Professional Resources Group, Inc.*
Hill, Emery — *MSI International*
Hillen, Skip — *The McCormick Group, Inc.*
Hilliker, Alan D. — *Egon Zehnder International Inc.*
Himes, Dirk — *A.T. Kearney, Inc.*
Himlin, Amy — *Cochran, Cochran & Yale, Inc.*
Hindman, Neil C. — *The Hindman Company*
Hockett, William — *Hockett Associates, Inc.*
Hocking, Jeffrey — *Korn/Ferry International*
Hoevel, Michael J. — *Poirier, Hoevel & Co.*
Hoffman, Brian — *Winter, Wyman & Company*
Hofner, Kevin E. — *Lamalie Amrop International*
Hokanson, Mark D. — *Crowder & Company*
Holden, Richard B. — *Ames Personnel Consultants, Inc.*
Holland, John A. — *Holland, McFadzean & Associates, Inc.*
Holland, Kathleen — *TOPAZ International, Inc.*
Holland, Kathleen — *TOPAZ Legal Solutions*
Holland, Rose Mary — *Price Waterhouse*
Hollins, Howard D. — *MSI International*
Holmes, Lawrence J. — *Columbia Consulting Group*
Holodnak, William A. — *J. Robert Scott*
Holt, Carol — *Bartholdi & Company, Inc.*
Homer, Judy B. — *J.B. Homer Associates, Inc.*
Hooker, Lisa — *Ray & Berndtson*
Hoover, Catherine — *J.L. Mark Associates, Inc.*
Hopkins, Chester A. — *Handy HRM Corp.*
Hopper, John W. — *William Guy & Associates*
Horgan, Thomas F. — *Nadzam, Lusk, Horgan & Associates, Inc.*
Horton, Robert H. — *Horton International*
Houchins, William M. — *Christian & Timbers*
Howard, Lee Ann — *Lamalie Amrop International*
Hoyda, Louis A. — *Thorndike Deland Associates*
Hucko, Donald S. — *Jonas, Walters & Assoc., Inc.*
Hudson, Reginald M. — *Search Bureau International*
Hughes, Cathy N. — *The Ogdon Partnership*
Hughes, James J. — *R.P. Barone Associates*
Hunsaker, Floyd — *Woodworth International Group*
Hunter, Gabe — *Phillips Resource Group*
Huntoon, Cliff — *Richard, Wayne and Roberts*
Hutchison, Richard H. — *Rurak & Associates, Inc.*
Hutchison, William K. — *Christenson & Hutchison*
Hutton, Thomas J. — *The Thomas Tucker Company*
Hybels, Cynthia — *A.J. Burton Group, Inc.*
Hyde, W. Jerry — *Hyde Danforth Wold & Co.*
Hykes, Don A. — *A.T. Kearney, Inc.*
Hyman, Linda — *Korn/Ferry International*
Ide, Ian — *Winter, Wyman & Company*
Inguagiato, Gregory — *MSI International*
Issacs, Judith A. — *Grant Cooper and Associates*

Jackowitz, Todd — *J. Robert Scott*
Jackson, Barry — *Morgan Hunter Corp.*
Jackson, Joan — *A.T. Kearney, Inc.*
Jacobs, Martin J. — *The Rubicon Group*
Jacobs, Mike — *Thorne, Brieger Associates Inc.*
Jacobson, Carolyn — *The Abbott Group, Inc.*
Jacobson, Rick — *The Windham Group*
Jaffe, Mark — *Wyatt & Jaffe*
James, Bruce — *Roberson and Company*
James, Richard — *Criterion Executive Search, Inc.*
Janis, Laurence — *Integrated Search Solutions Group, LLC*
Janssen, Don — *Howard Fischer Associates, Inc.*
Januale, Lois — *Cochran, Cochran & Yale, Inc.*
Jaworski, Mary A. — *Tully/Woodmansee International, Inc.*
Jazylo, John V. — *Skott/Edwards Consultants, Inc.*
Jeffers, Richard B. — *Dieckmann & Associates, Ltd.*
Joffe, Barry — *Bason Associates Inc.*
Johnson, Brian — *A.J. Burton Group, Inc.*
Johnson, David A. — *Gaffney Management Consultants*
Johnson, Harold E. — *Lamalie Amrop International*
Johnson, John W. — *Webb, Johnson Associates, Inc.*
Johnson, Julie M. — *International Staffing Consultants, Inc.*
Johnson, Kathleen A. — *Barton Associates, Inc.*
Johnson, LaDonna — *Gans, Gans & Associates*
Johnson, Pete — *Morgan Hunter Corp.*
Johnson, Rocky — *A.T. Kearney, Inc.*
Johnson, Ronald S. — *Ronald S. Johnson Associates, Inc.*
Johnson, Stanley C. — *Johnson & Company*
Johnson, Valerie — *Coe & Company International Inc.*
Johnston, James R. — *The Stevenson Group of Delaware Inc.*
Johnston, Michael — *Robertson-Surrette Executive Search*
Jones, Amy E. — *The Corporate Connection, Ltd.*
Jones, Barbara — *Kaye-Bassman International Corp.*
Jones, Barbara J. — *Kaye-Bassman International Corp.*
Jones, Francis E. — *Earley Kielty and Associates, Inc.*
Jones, Gary — *BGB Associates*
Jones, Ronald T. — *ARJay & Associates*
Jordan, Jon — *Cochran, Cochran & Yale, Inc.*
Juelis, John J. — *Peeney Associates*
Kacyn, Louis J. — *Egon Zehnder International Inc.*
Kaiser, Donald J. — *Dunhill International Search of New Haven*
Kane, Frank — *A.J. Burton Group, Inc.*
Kane, Karen — *Howard Fischer Associates, Inc.*
Kaplan, Alexandra — *J.M. Eagle Partners Ltd.*
Kaplan, Gary — *Gary Kaplan & Associates*
Kartin, Martin C. — *Martin Kartin and Company, Inc.*
Kaye, Jeffrey — *Kaye-Bassman International Corp.*
Keating, Pierson — *Nordeman Grimm, Inc.*
Keitel, Robert S. — *A.T. Kearney, Inc.*
Kelbell, Scott — *Comprehensive Search*
Keller, Barbara E. — *Barton Associates, Inc.*

Kelly, Elizabeth Ann — *Wellington Management Group*
Kelso, Patricia C. — *Barton Associates, Inc.*
Kent, Melvin — *Melvin Kent & Associates, Inc.*
Kenzer, Robert D. — *Kenzer Corp.*
Kerester, Jonathon — *Cadillac Associates*
Kern, Jerry L. — *ADOW's Executeam*
Kern, Kathleen G. — *ADOW's Executeam*
Kershaw, Lisa — *Tanton Mitchell/Paul Ray Berndtson*
Keshishian, Gregory — *Handy HRM Corp.*
Keyser, Anne — *A.T. Kearney, Inc.*
Kielty, John L. — *Earley Kielty and Associates, Inc.*
King, Margaret — *Christian & Timbers*
Kinney, Carol — *Dussick Management Associates*
Kinser, Richard E. — *Richard Kinser & Associates*
Kip, Luanne S. — *Kip Williams, Inc.*
Kishbaugh, Herbert S. — *Kishbaugh Associates International*
Kixmiller, David B. — *Heidrick & Struggles, Inc.*
Klages, Constance W. — *International Management Advisors, Inc.*
Klauck, James J. — *Horton International*
Klavens, Cecile J. — *The Pickwick Group, Inc.*
Klein, Brandon — *A.J. Burton Group, Inc.*
Klein, Gary — *A.T. Kearney, Inc.*
Klein, Mary Jo — *Cochran, Cochran & Yale, Inc.*
Kleinstein, Jonah A. — *The Kleinstein Group*
Klopfenstein, Edward L. — *Crowder & Company*
Knapp, Ronald A. — *Knapp Consultants*
Knotts, Jerry — *Mixtec Group*
Koblentz, Joel M. — *Egon Zehnder International Inc.*
Koenig, Joel S. — *Blackshaw, Olmstead, Lynch & Koenig*
Koenig, Joel S. — *Blackshaw, Olmstead, Lynch & Koenig*
Kohn, Adam P. — *Christian & Timbers*
Kondra, Vernon J. — *The Douglas Reiter Company, Inc.*
Koontz, Donald N. — *Koontz, Jeffries & Associates, Inc.*
Kossuth, David — *Kossuth & Associates, Inc.*
Kossuth, Jane — *Kossuth & Associates, Inc.*
Kotick, Maddy — *The Stevenson Group of New Jersey*
Krejci, Stanley L. — *Boyden Washington, D.C.*
Krieger, Dennis F. — *Seiden Krieger Associates, Inc.*
Krueger, Kurt — *Krueger Associates*
Kuhl, Teresa — *Don Richard Associates of Tampa, Inc.*
Kunzer, William J. — *Kunzer Associates, Ltd.*
Kussner, Janice N. — *Herman Smith Executive Initiatives Inc.*
Laba, Marvin — *Marvin Laba & Associates*
Laba, Stuart M. — *Marvin Laba & Associates*
Lache, Shawn E. — *The Arcus Group*
Lamb, Angus K. — *Raymond Karsan Associates*
Lang, Sharon A. — *Ray & Berndtson*
Lapat, Aaron D. — *J. Robert Scott*
Lardner, Lucy D. — *Tully/Woodmansee International, Inc.*
Larsen, Jack B. — *Jack B. Larsen & Associates*
Lasher, Charles M. — *Lasher Associates*
Lauderback, David R. — *A.T. Kearney, Inc.*
Lautz, Lindsay A. — *Lautz Grotte Engler*

LeComte, Andre — *Egon Zehnder International Inc.*
Ledbetter, Steven G. — *Cendea Connection International*
Lence, Julie Anne — *MSI International*
Lenkaitis, Lewis F. — *A.T. Kearney, Inc.*
Lennox, Charles — *Price Waterhouse*
Leon, Jeffrey J. — *Russell Reynolds Associates, Inc.*
Letcher, Harvey D. — *Sandhurst Associates*
Lewis, Gretchen S. — *Heidrick & Struggles, Inc.*
Lewis, Jon A. — *Sandhurst Associates*
Lezama Cohen, Luis — *Ray & Berndtson*
Lieberman, Beverly — *Halbrecht Lieberman Associates, Inc.*
Lindberg, Eric J. — *MSI International*
Lindholst, Kai — *Egon Zehnder International Inc.*
Lindsay, Mary — *Norm Sanders Associates*
Linton, Leonard M. — *Byron Leonard International, Inc.*
Lipson, Harriet — *First Interactive Recruiting Specialists*
Lipson, Howard K. — *First Interactive Recruiting Specialists*
Lipson, Howard R. — *Lipson & Co.*
Little, Suzaane — *Don Richard Associates of Tampa, Inc.*
Livingston, Peter R. — *Livingston, Robert and Company Inc.*
Loeb, Stephen H. — *Grant Cooper and Associates*
Loewenstein, Victor H. — *Egon Zehnder International Inc.*
Lokken, Karen — *A.E. Feldman Associates*
Lonergan, Mark W. — *Heidrick & Struggles, Inc.*
Long, Helga — *Horton International*
Long, John P. — *John J. Davis & Associates, Inc.*
Long, Milt — *William Guy & Associates*
Long, Thomas — *Egon Zehnder International Inc.*
Long, William G. — *McDonald, Long & Associates, Inc.*
Looney, Scott — *A.E. Feldman Associates*
LoRusso, Steve — *Warren, Morris & Madison*
Lotufo, David A. — *D.A.L. Associates, Inc.*
Lotz, R. James — *International Management Advisors, Inc.*
Louden, Leo — *Winter, Wyman & Company*
Lovas, W. Carl — *Ray & Berndtson/Lovas Stanley*
Love, David M. — *Ray & Berndtson*
Lovely, Edward — *The Stevenson Group of New Jersey*
Lucarelli, Joan — *The Onstott Group, Inc.*
Lucas, Ronnie L. — *MSI International*
Lucht, John — *The John Lucht Consultancy Inc.*
Luke, A. Wayne — *Heidrick & Struggles, Inc.*
Lumsby, George N. — *International Management Advisors, Inc.*
Luntz, Charles E. — *Charles Luntz & Associates. Inc.*
Lupica, Anthony — *Cochran, Cochran & Yale, Inc.*
Lyon, Jenny — *Marra Peters & Partners*
Lyons, J. David — *Aubin International Inc.*
Macdonald, G. William — *The Macdonald Group, Inc.*
MacDougall, Andrew J. — *Spencer Stuart*
MacEachern, David — *Spencer Stuart*
Mackenna, Kathy — *Plummer & Associates, Inc.*

MacNaughton, Sperry — *McNaughton Associates*
Mader, Stephen P. — *Christian & Timbers*
Magee, Harrison R. — *Bowden & Company, Inc.*
Maglio, Charles J. — *Maglio and Company, Inc.*
Mahaney, Joann — *Heidrick & Struggles, Inc.*
Major, Susan — *A.T. Kearney, Inc.*
Makrianes, James K. — *Webb, Johnson Associates, Inc.*
Malcolm, Rod — *Korn/Ferry International*
Mallin, Ellen — *Howard Fischer Associates, Inc.*
Manassero, Henri J.P. — *International Management Advisors, Inc.*
Mangum, Maria — *Thomas Mangum Company*
Mangum, William T. — *Thomas Mangum Company*
Manns, Alex — *Crawford & Crofford*
Mansford, Keith — *Howard Fischer Associates, Inc.*
Maphet, Harriet — *The Stevenson Group of New Jersey*
Marino, Chester — *Cochran, Cochran & Yale, Inc.*
Marino, Jory J. — *Sullivan & Company*
Mark, John L. — *J.L. Mark Associates, Inc.*
Mark, Lynne — *J.L. Mark Associates, Inc.*
Marks, Ira — *Strategic Alternatives*
Marks, Russell E. — *Webb, Johnson Associates, Inc.*
Marlow, William — *Straube Associates*
Marra, John — *Marra Peters & Partners*
Marra, John — *Marra Peters & Partners*
Martin, David — *The Guild Corporation*
Martin, Jon — *Egon Zehnder International Inc.*
Marumoto, William H. — *Boyden Washington, D.C.*
Mashakas, Elizabeth — *TOPAZ International, Inc.*
Mashakas, Elizabeth — *TOPAZ Legal Solutions*
Massey, R. Bruce — *Horton International*
Mather, David R. — *Christian & Timbers*
Mathias, Kathy — *Stone Murphy & Olson*
Matthews, Corwin — *Woodworth International Group*
Matthews, Mary — *Korn/Ferry International*
May, Peter — *Mixtec Group*
Mayland, Tina — *Russell Reynolds Associates, Inc.*
Maynard Taylor, Susan — *Chrisman & Company, Incorporated*
Mazor, Elly — *Howard Fischer Associates, Inc.*
Mazza, David B. — *Mazza & Riley, Inc. (a Korn/Ferry International affiliate)*
McBride, Jonathan E. — *McBride Associates, Inc.*
McCabe, Christopher — *Raymond Karsan Associates*
McCann, Cornelia B. — *Spencer Stuart*
McClure, James K. — *Korn/Ferry International*
McConnell, Greg — *Winter, Wyman & Company*
McCormick, William J. — *The McCormick Group, Inc.*
McCreary, Charles "Chip" — *Austin-McGregor International*
McCurdy, Mark — *Summerfield Associates, Inc.*
McDermott, Jeffrey T. — *Vlcek & Company, Inc.*
McDonald, Scott A. — *McDonald Associates International*
McDonald, Stanleigh B. — *McDonald Associates International*

McDonnell, Julie — *Technical Personnel of Minnesota*
McDowell, Robert N. — *Christenson & Hutchison*
McFadden, Ashton S. — *Johnson Smith & Knisely Accord*
McFadzen, Donna — *Holland, McFadzean & Associates, Inc.*
McFadzen, James A. — *Holland, McFadzean & Associates, Inc.*
McGregor, James D. — *John Kurosky & Associates*
McGuigan, Walter J. — *Norm Sanders Associates*
McGuire, J. Corey — *Peter W. Ambler Company*
McGuire, Pat — *A.J. Burton Group, Inc.*
McIntyre, Joel — *Phillips Resource Group*
McKeown, Morgan J. — *Christian & Timbers*
McKeown, Patricia A. — *DiMarchi Partners, Inc.*
McKnight, Amy E. — *Chartwell Partners International, Inc.*
McMahon, Mark J. — *A.T. Kearney, Inc.*
McManners, Donald E. — *McManners Associates, Inc.*
McManus, Paul — *Aubin International Inc.*
McMillin, Bob — *Price Waterhouse*
McNamara, Catherine — *Ray & Berndtson*
McNamara, Timothy C. — *Columbia Consulting Group*
McNamee, Erin — *Technical Connections Inc.*
McNerney, Kevin A. — *Heidrick & Struggles, Inc.*
McNichol, John — *McNichol Associates*
McNichols, Walter B. — *Gary Kaplan & Associates*
McPoyle, Thomas C. — *Sanford Rose Associates*
McSherry, James F. — *Battalia Winston International*
Mead-Fox, David — *Korn/Ferry International*
Meadows, C. David — *Professional Staffing Consultants*
Medina-Haro, Adolfo — *Heidrick & Struggles, Inc.*
Mefford, Bob — *Executive Manning Corporation*
Meiland, A. Daniel — *Egon Zehnder International Inc.*
Menendez, Todd — *Don Richard Associates of Tampa, Inc.*
Mercer, Julie — *Columbia Consulting Group*
Metz, Dan K. — *Russell Reynolds Associates, Inc.*
Meyer, Stacey — *Gary Kaplan & Associates*
Michaels, Stewart — *TOPAZ International, Inc.*
Michaels, Stewart — *TOPAZ Legal Solutions*
Mierzwinski, John — *Industrial Recruiters Associates, Inc.*
Miles, Kenneth T. — *MSI International*
Miles, Marybeth — *Winter, Wyman & Company*
Miller, David — *Cochran, Cochran & Yale, Inc.*
Miller, George N. — *Hite Executive Search*
Miller, Roy — *The Enns Partners Inc.*
Miller, Russel E. — *ARJay & Associates*
Milstein, Bonnie — *Marvin Laba & Associates*
Mingle, Larry D. — *Columbia Consulting Group*
Mirtz, P. John — *Mirtz Morice, Inc.*
Misiurewicz, Marc — *Cochran, Cochran & Yale, Inc.*
Mitchell, F. Wayne — *Korn/Ferry International*
Mitchell, Jeff — *A.J. Burton Group, Inc.*
Moerbe, Ed H. — *Stanton Chase International*
Mogul, Gene — *Mogul Consultants, Inc.*

Molnar, Robert A. — *Johnson Smith & Knisely Accord*
Mondragon, Philip — *A.T. Kearney, Inc.*
Montgomery, James M. — *Houze, Shourds & Montgomery, Inc.*
Moodley, Logan — *Austin-McGregor International*
Moore, David S. — *Lynch Miller Moore, Inc.*
Moore, Lemuel R. — *MSI International*
Moore, Mark — *Wheeler, Moore & Elam Co.*
Moore, T. Wills — *Ray & Berndtson*
Moran, Gayle — *Dussick Management Associates*
Morgan, Richard S. — *Ray & Berndtson/Lovas Stanley*
Morice, James L. — *Mirtz Morice, Inc.*
Morrill, Nancy — *Winter, Wyman & Company*
Morris, Chuck — *Warren, Morris & Madison*
Mortansen, Patricia — *Norman Broadbent International, Inc.*
Moses, Jerry — *J.M. Eagle Partners Ltd.*
Moyse, Richard G. — *Thorndike Deland Associates*
Mueller-Maerki, Fortunat F. — *Egon Zehnder International Inc.*
Muendel, H. Edward — *Stanton Chase International*
Murphy, Cornelius J. — *Goodrich & Sherwood Associates, Inc.*
Murphy, Patrick J. — *P.J. Murphy & Associates, Inc.*
Murphy, Peter — *Korn/Ferry International*
Murray, Virginia — *A.T. Kearney, Inc.*
Mursuli, Meredith — *Lasher Associates*
Myatt, James S. — *Sanford Rose Associates*
Myers, Kay — *Signature Staffing*
Nadherny, Christopher C. — *Spencer Stuart*
Nadzam, Richard I. — *Nadzam, Lusk, Horgan & Associates, Inc.*
Nagler, Leon G. — *Nagler, Robins & Poe, Inc.*
Naidicz, Maria — *Ray & Berndtson*
Neelin, Sharon — *The Caldwell Partners Amrop International*
Neely, Alan S. — *Korn/Ferry International*
Nees, Eugene C. — *Ray & Berndtson*
Neff, Thomas J. — *Spencer Stuart*
Neher, Robert L. — *Intech Summit Group, Inc.*
Nehring, Keith — *Howard Fischer Associates, Inc.*
Neidhart, Craig C. — *TNS Partners, Inc.*
Nelson, Barbara — *Herman Smith Executive Initiatives Inc.*
Nemec, Phillip — *Dunhill International Search of New Haven*
Nephew, Robert — *Christian & Timbers*
Neuberth, Jeffrey G. — *Canny, Bowen Inc.*
Newman, Lynn — *Kishbaugh Associates International*
Nichols, Gary — *Koontz, Jeffries & Associates, Inc.*
Niejet, Michael C. — *O'Brien & Bell*
Noguchi, Yoshi — *Ray & Berndtson*
Nold, Robert — *Roberson and Company*
Nolte, William D. — *W.D. Nolte & Company*
Norman, Randy — *Austin-McGregor International*
Normann, Amy — *Robert M. Flanagan & Associates, Ltd.*
Norris, Ken — *A.T. Kearney, Inc.*
Norsell, Paul E. — *Paul Norsell & Associates, Inc.*
Norton, James B. — *Lamalie Amrop International*

Reed, Brenda — *International Staffing Consultants, Inc.*
Reed, Ruthann — *Spectra International Inc.*
Referente, Gwen — *Richard, Wayne and Roberts*
Reifel, Laurie — *Reifel & Assocaites*
Reifersen, Ruth F. — *The Jonathan Stevens Group, Inc.*
Reiser, Ellen — *Thorndike Deland Associates*
Reisinger, George L. — *Sigma Group International*
Reiter, Douglas — *The Douglas Reiter Company, Inc.*
Remillard, Brad M. — *CJA - The Adler Group*
Reyman, Susan — *S. Reyman & Associates Ltd.*
Reynolds, Catherine — *Winter, Wyman & Company*
Reynolds, Gregory P. — *Roberts Ryan and Bentley*
Rhodes, Bill — *Bench International*
Rice, Marie — *Jay Gaines & Company, Inc.*
Rice, Raymond D. — *Logue & Rice Inc.*
Richard, Albert L. — *The Search Alliance, Inc.*
Richards, Paul E. — *Executive Directions*
Richards, R. Glenn — *Executive Directions*
Rieger, Louis J. — *Spencer Stuart*
Rimmel, James E. — *The Hindman Company*
Rimmele, Michael — *The Bankers Group*
Rippey, George E. — *Heidrick & Struggles, Inc.*
Rizzo, L. Donald — *R.P. Barone Associates*
Roberts, Carl R. — *Southwestern Professional Services*
Roberts, Marc — *The Stevenson Group of New Jersey*
Roberts, Mitch — *A.E. Feldman Associates*
Roberts, Nick P. — *Spectrum Search Associates, Inc.*
Roberts, Norman C. — *Norman Roberts & Associates, Inc.*
Roberts, Scott — *Jonas, Walters & Assoc., Inc.*
Robertson, Bruce J. — *Lamalie Amrop International*
Robertson, John A. — *Kaye-Bassman International Corp.*
Robertson, Ronald — *Robertson-Surrette Executive Search*
Robins, Jeri N. — *Nagler, Robins & Poe, Inc.*
Robinson, Bruce — *Bruce Robinson Associates*
Robinson, Eric B. — *Bruce Robinson Associates*
Robles Cuellar, Paulina — *Ray & Berndtson*
Rogers, Leah — *Dinte Resources, Inc.*
Rojo, Rafael — *A.T. Kearney, Inc.*
Romanello, Daniel P. — *Spencer Stuart*
Rosin, Jeffrey — *Korn/Ferry International*
Ross, Curt A. — *Ray & Berndtson*
Ross, H. Lawrence — *Ross & Company*
Ross, Lawrence — *Ray & Berndtson/Lovas Stanley*
Ross, Mark — *Ray & Berndtson/Lovas Stanley*
Ross, William J. — *Flowers & Associates*
Rossi, George A. — *Heidrick & Struggles, Inc.*
Rotella, Marshall W. — *The Corporate Connection, Ltd.*
Roth, Robert J. — *Williams, Roth & Krueger Inc.*
Rothschild, John S. — *Lamalie Amrop International*
Rottblatt, Michael — *Korn/Ferry International*
Rowe, William D. — *D.E. Foster Partners Inc.*
Rowell, Roger — *Halbrecht Lieberman Associates, Inc.*

Rozner, Burton L. — *Oliver & Rozner Associates, Inc.*
Rubinstein, Walter — *Technical Connections Inc.*
Rudolph, Kenneth — *Kossuth & Associates, Inc.*
Rudzinsky, Howard — *Louis Rudzinsky Associates*
Rudzinsky, Jeffrey — *Louis Rudzinsky Associates*
Ruge, Merrill — *William Guy & Associates*
Runquist, U.W. — *Webb, Johnson Associates, Inc.*
Rurak, Zbigniew T. — *Rurak & Associates, Inc.*
Rush, Michael E. — *D.A.L. Associates, Inc.*
Russell, Sam — *The Guild Corporation*
Ryan, Mary L. — *Summerfield Associates, Inc.*
Sacerdote, John — *Raymond Karsan Associates*
Sahagian, John — *The Search Alliance, Inc.*
Sanders, Norman D. — *Norm Sanders Associates*
Sanitago, Anthony — *TaxSearch, Inc.*
Sanow, Robert — *Cochran, Cochran & Yale, Inc.*
Santimauro, Edward — *Korn/Ferry International*
Sarna, Edmund A. — *Jonas, Walters & Assoc., Inc.*
Sauer, Robert C. — *Heidrick & Struggles, Inc.*
Sawyer, Deborah — *Korn/Ferry International*
Sawyer, Patricia L. — *Smith & Sawyer Inc.*
Saxon, Alexa — *Woodworth International Group*
Schaad, Carl A. — *Heidrick & Struggles, Inc.*
Schaefer, Frederic M. — *A.T. Kearney, Inc.*
Schall, William A. — *The Stevenson Group of New Jersey*
Schappell, Marc P. — *Egon Zehnder International Inc.*
Schedra, Sharon — *Earley Kielty and Associates, Inc.*
Schene, Philip — *A.E. Feldman Associates*
Schiavone, Mary Rose — *Canny, Bowen Inc.*
Schlpma, Christine — *Advanced Executive Resources*
Schmidt, Peter R. — *Boyden*
Schmidt, Peter R. — *Boyden*
Schmidt, William C. — *Christian & Timbers*
Schneiderman, Gerald — *Management Resource Associates, Inc.*
Schnit, David — *Warren, Morris & Madison*
Schoettle, Michael B. — *Heidrick & Struggles, Inc.*
Schwam, Carol — *A.E. Feldman Associates*
Schwartz, Vincent P. — *Slayton International, Inc./I-I-C Partners*
Scott, Cory — *Warren, Morris & Madison*
Scott, Evan — *Howard Fischer Associates, Inc.*
Scott, Gordon S. — *Search Advisors International Corp.*
Scranton, Lisa — *A.J. Burton Group, Inc.*
Seco, William — *Seco & Zetto Associates, Inc.*
Seiden, Steven A. — *Seiden Krieger Associates, Inc.*
Selker, Gregory L. — *Christian & Timbers*
Semyan, John K. — *TNS Partners, Inc.*
Sessa, Vincent J. — *Integrated Search Solutions Group, LLC*
Sevilla, Claudio A. — *Crawford & Crofford*
Shapiro, Beth — *Howard Fischer Associates, Inc.*
Shattuck, Merrill B. — *M.B. Shattuck and Associates, Inc.*
Shea, Kathleen M. — *The Penn Partners, Incorporated*
Sheedy, Edward J. — *Dieckmann & Associates, Ltd.*
Shenfield, Peter — *A.T. Kearney, Inc.*
Shepard, Michael J. — *MSI International*

ten Cate, Herman H. — *Stoneham Associates Corp.*
Tetrick, Tim — *O'Connor, O'Connor, Lordi, Ltd.*
Theobald, David B. — *Theobald & Associates*
Thomas, Donald — *Mixtec Group*
Thomas, Ian A. — *International Staffing Consultants, Inc.*
Thomas, Kurt J. — *P.J. Murphy & Associates, Inc.*
Thomas, Terry — *The Thomas Resource Group*
Thomas, William — *Mixtec Group*
Thompson, Dave — *Battalia Winston International*
Thompson, Kenneth L. — *McCormack & Farrow*
Thornton, John — *Stratford Group*
Thrapp, Mark C. — *Executive Search Consultants International, Inc.*
Timoney, Laura — *Bishop Partners*
Tincu, John C. — *Ferneborg & Associates, Inc.*
Tolette, Skip — *The Schmitt Tolette Group*
Tomasco, Ray — *Huntington Group*
Tootsey, Mark A. — *A.J. Burton Group, Inc.*
Topliff, Marla — *Gaffney Management Consultants*
Tracy, Ronald O. — *Egon Zehnder International Inc.*
Travis, Michael — *Travis & Company*
Trieweiler, Bob — *Executive Placement Consultants, Inc.*
Tryon, Katey — *DeFrain, Mayer LLC*
Tucker, Thomas A. — *The Thomas Tucker Company*
Tully, Margo L. — *Tully/Woodmansee International, Inc.*
Tunney, William — *Grant Cooper and Associates*
Turner, Kimberly — *Barton Associates, Inc.*
Tursi, Deborah J. — *The Corporate Connection, Ltd.*
Tuttle, Donald E. — *Tuttle Venture Group, Inc.*
Tweed, Janet — *Gilbert Tweed/INESA*
Twiste, Craig — *Raymond Karsan Associates*
Unger, Paul T. — *A.T. Kearney, Inc.*
Unterberg, Edward L. — *Russell Reynolds Associates, Inc.*
Utroska, Donald R. — *Lamalie Amrop International*
Vachon, David A. — *McNichol Associates*
Vairo, Leonard A. — *Christian & Timbers*
Valenta, Joseph — *Princeton Entrepreneurial Resources*
Van Biesen, Jacques A.H. — *Search Group Inc.*
Van Campen, Jerry — *Gilbert & Van Campen International*
Van Clieaf, Mark — *MVC Associates International*
Van Nostrand, Mara J. — *Barton Associates, Inc.*
Van Steenkiste, Julie — *Davidson, Laird & Associates, Inc.*
Vande-Water, Katie — *J. Robert Scott*
Vann, Dianne — *The Button Group*
Vaughan, David B. — *Dunhill Professional Search of Irvine, Inc.*
Velten, Mark T. — *Boyden*
Venable, William W. — *Thorndike Deland Associates*
Vennat, Manon — *Spencer Stuart*
Vernon, Peter C. — *Horton International*
Visnich, L. Christine — *Bason Associates Inc.*
Vlcek, Thomas J. — *Vlcek & Company, Inc.*

Volkman, Arthur — *Cochran, Cochran & Yale, Inc.*
von Baillou, Astrid — *Richard Kinser & Associates*
Vossler, James — *A.J. Burton Group, Inc.*
Vroom, Cynthia D. — *Cyntal International Ltd*
Wacholz, Rick — *A.T. Kearney, Inc.*
Waldoch, D. Mark — *Barnes Development Group, LLC*
Waldrop, Gary R. — *MSI International*
Walker, Craig H. — *A.J. Burton Group, Inc.*
Walker, Richard — *Bradford & Galt, Inc.*
Walsh, Denis — *Professional Staffing Consultants*
Walsh, Kenneth A. — *R/K International, Inc.*
Walters, William F. — *Jonas, Walters & Assoc., Inc.*
Walton, Bruce H. — *Heidrick & Struggles, Inc.*
Ware, John C. — *Spencer Stuart*
Warren, Scott — *Warren, Morris & Madison*
Wasson, Thomas W. — *Spencer Stuart*
Watkins, Jeffrey P. — *Lamalie Amrop International*
Watkinson, Jim W. — *The Badger Group*
Watson, Stephen — *Ray & Berndtson*
Webb, George H. — *Webb, Johnson Associates, Inc.*
Weber, Fred — *J.B. Homer Associates, Inc.*
Wein, Michael S. — *InterimManagement Solutions, Inc.*
Wein, William — *InterimManagement Solutions, Inc.*
Weissman-Rosenthal, Abbe — *ALW Research International*
Welch, Robert — *Ray & Berndtson*
Weller, Paul S. — *Mark Stanley/EMA Partners International*
Wert, Marty — *Parfitt Recruiting and Consulting*
Westfall, Ed — *Zwell International*
Wheeler, Gerard H. — *A.J. Burton Group, Inc.*
Whelan, David — *Ethos Consulting Inc.*
White, William C. — *Venture Resources Inc.*
Whyte, Roger J. — *The Whyte Group, Inc.*
Wilder, Richard B. — *Columbia Consulting Group*
Wilkinson, Barbara — *Beall & Company, Inc.*
Wilkinson, Jr. SPHR
Wilkinson, Charles E. — *The HRM Group, Inc.*
Williams, Brad — *Winter, Wyman & Company*
Williams, Gary L. — *Barnes Development Group, LLC*
Williams, Jack — *A.T. Kearney, Inc.*
Williams, Roger K. — *Williams, Roth & Krueger Inc.*
Williams, Scott D. — *Heidrick & Struggles, Inc.*
Williams, Stephen E. — *Barton Associates, Inc.*
Williams, Walter E. — *Lamalie Amrop International*
Willner, Leo — *William Guy & Associates*
Wilson, Don — *Allerton Heneghan & O'Neill*
Wilson, John — *Korn/Ferry International*
Wilson, Patricia L. — *Leon A. Farley Associates*
Wilson, Steven J. — *Herman Smith Executive Initiatives Inc.*
Winitz, Joel — *GSW Consulting Group, Inc.*
Winitz, Marla — *GSW Consulting Group, Inc.*
Winograd, Glenn — *Criterion Executive Search, Inc.*
Winston, Dale — *Battalia Winston International*
Wirtshafter, Linda — *Grant Cooper and Associates*
Wise, J. Herbert — *Sandhurst Associates*

Witte, David L. — *Ward Howell International, Inc.*
Wold, Ted W. — *Hyde Danforth Wold & Co.*
Wolf, Stephen M. — *Byron Leonard International, Inc.*
Womack, Joseph — *The Bankers Group*
Wood, John S. — *Egon Zehnder International Inc.*
Wood, Milton M. — *M. Wood Company*
Woodmansee, Bruce J. — *Tully/Woodmansee International, Inc.*
Woodworth, Gail — *Woodworth International Group*
Wooldridge, Jeff — *Ray & Berndtson*
Woollett, James — *Rusher, Loscavio & LoPresto*
Wright, A. Leo — *The Hindman Company*
Wright, Carl A.J. — *A.J. Burton Group, Inc.*
Wright, Charles D. — *Goodrich & Sherwood Associates, Inc.*
Wright, Leslie — *The Stevenson Group of New Jersey*
Wyatt, James — *Wyatt & Jaffe*
Yaekle, Gary — *Tully/Woodmansee International, Inc.*
Yang, George —- *Technical Connections Inc.*
Yen, Maggie Yeh Ching — *Ray & Berndtson*
Yossem, Sheila — *Bishop Partners*
Yungerberg, Steven — *Steven Yungerberg Associates Inc.*
Zaffrann, Craig S. — *P.J. Murphy & Associates, Inc.*
Zahradka, James F. — *P.J. Murphy & Associates, Inc.*
Zaleta, Andy R. — *A.T. Kearney, Inc.*
Zamborsky, George — *Boyden*
Zaslav, Debra M. — *Telford, Adams & Alexander/Telford & Co., Inc.*
Zetter, Roger — *Hunt Ltd.*
Zetto, Kathryn — *Seco & Zetto Associates, Inc.*
Zila, Laurie M. — *Princeton Entrepreneurial Resources*
Zilliacus, Patrick W. — *Larsen, Whitney, Blecksmith & Zilliacus*
Zwell, Michael — *Zwell International*

2. Administration

Abbott, Peter D. — *The Abbott Group, Inc.*
Abell, Vincent W. — *MSI International*
Akin, J.R. "Jack" — *J.R. Akin & Company Inc.*
Altreuter, Rose — *The ALTCO Group*
Anderson, Maria H. — *Barton Associates, Inc.*
Anderson, Richard — *Grant Cooper and Associates*
Andrews, J. Douglas — *Clarey & Andrews, Inc.*
Antoine, Brian — *Paul-Tittle Associates, Inc.*
Apostle, George — *Search Dynamics, Inc.*
Aronin, Michael — *Fisher-Todd Associates*
Arseneault, Daniel S. — *MSI International*
Ascher, Susan P. — *The Ascher Group*
Aston, Kathy — *Marra Peters & Partners*
Attell, Harold — *A.E. Feldman Associates*
Atwood, Barrie — *The Abbott Group, Inc.*
Baeder, Jeremy — *Executive Manning Corporation*
Balbone, Rich — *Executive Manning Corporation*
Barlow, Ken H. — *The Cherbonnier Group, Inc.*
Barnes, Richard E. — *Barnes Development Group, LLC*
Barnes, Roanne L. — *Barnes Development Group, LLC*

Barthold, James A. — *McNichol Associates*
Bartholomew, Katie — *C. Berger & Company*
Barton, Gary R. — *Barton Associates, Inc.*
Bason, Maurice L. — *Bason Associates Inc.*
Bass, M. Lynn — *Ray & Berndtson*
Bearman, Linda — *Grant Cooper and Associates*
Beaudin, Elizabeth C. — *Callan Associates, Ltd.*
Beran, Helena — *Michael J. Cavanagh and Associates*
Berger, Carol — *C. Berger & Company*
Bettick, Michael J. — *A.J. Burton Group, Inc.*
Blackmon, Sharon — *The Abbott Group, Inc.*
Bladon, Andrew — *Don Richard Associates of Tampa, Inc.*
Bloomer, James E. — *L.W. Foote Company*
Bluhm, Claudia — *Schweichler Associates, Inc.*
Boel, Werner — *The Dalley Hewitt Company*
Bohn, Steve J. — *MSI International*
Borkin, Andrew — *Strategic Advancement Inc.*
Borland, James — *Goodrich & Sherwood Associates, Inc.*
Bormann, Cindy Ann — *MSI International*
Bostic, James E. — *Phillips Resource Group*
Brady, Dick — *William Guy & Associates*
Brieger, Steve — *Thorne, Brieger Associates Inc.*
Brill, Pamela — *C. Berger & Company*
Brooks, Bernard E. — *Mruk & Partners/EMA Partners Int'l*
Brother, Joy — *Charles Luntz & Associates. Inc.*
Brown, Larry C. — *Horton International*
Brudno, Robert J. — *Savoy Partners, Ltd.*
Bryza, Robert M. — *Robert Lowell International*
Bullock, Conni — *Earley Kielty and Associates, Inc.*
Burden, Gene — *The Cherbonnier Group, Inc.*
Burke, John — *The Experts*
Burns, Alan — *The Enns Partners Inc.*
Busterna, Charles — *The KPA Group*
Calivas, Kay — *A.J. Burton Group, Inc.*
Callan, Robert M. — *Callan Associates, Ltd.*
Cappe, Richard R. — *Roberts Ryan and Bentley*
Cary, Con — *Cary & Associates*
Cavanagh, Michael J. — *Michael J. Cavanagh and Associates*
Cesafsky, Barry R. — *Lamalie Amrop International*
Chamberlin, Michael A. — *Tower Consultants, Ltd.*
Chappell, Peter — *The Bankers Group*
Chatterjie, Alok — *MSI International*
Chavous, C. Crawford — *Phillips Resource Group*
Cherbonnier, L. Michael — *The Cherbonnier Group, Inc.*
Chorman, Marilyn A. — *Hite Executive Search*
Christian, Philip — *Ray & Berndtson*
Cizek, John T. — *Cizek Associates, Inc.*
Cizek, Marti J. — *Cizek Associates, Inc.*
Clarey, Jack R. — *Clarey & Andrews, Inc.*
Clauhsen, Elizabeth A. — *Savoy Partners, Ltd.*
Clayton, Fred J. — *Berkhemer Clayton Incorporated*
Coffman, Brian — *Kossuth & Associates, Inc.*
Cohen, Robert C. — *Intech Summit Group, Inc.*
Colasanto, Frank M. — *W.R. Rosato & Associates, Inc.*
Colling, Douglas — *KPMG Management Consulting*
Cona, Joseph A. — *Cona Personnel Search*

Conway, Maureen — *Conway & Associates*
Conway, William P. — *Phillips Resource Group*
Cornehlsen, James H. — *Skott/Edwards Consultants, Inc.*
Corrigan, Gerald F. — *The Corrigan Group*
Cortina Del Valle, Pedro — *Ray & Berndtson*
Costello, Lynda — *Coe & Company International Inc.*
Cottingham, R.L. — *Marvin L. Silcott & Associates, Inc.*
Courtney, Brendan — *A.J. Burton Group, Inc.*
Coyle, Hugh F. — *A.J. Burton Group, Inc.*
Crath, Paul F. — *Price Waterhouse*
Crosler, Yvonne — *Paul-Tittle Associates, Inc.*
Cunningham, Lawrence — *Howard Fischer Associates, Inc.*
Cunningham, Robert Y. — *Goodrich & Sherwood Associates, Inc.*
Curci, Donald L. — *A.R.I. International*
Dalton, Bret — *Robert W. Dingman Company, Inc.*
Danforth, W. Michael — *Hyde Danforth Wold & Co.*
Daniels, C. Eugene — *Sigma Group International*
Davis, G. Gordon — *Davis & Company*
Dawson, Joe — *S.C. International, Ltd.*
De Brun, Thomas P. — *Ray & Berndtson*
Deaver, Henry C. — *Ray & Berndtson*
DeCorrevont, James — *DeCorrevont & Associates*
DeCorrevont, James — *DeCorrevont & Associates*
DeGioia, Joseph — *JDG Associates, Ltd.*
DeHart, Donna — *Tower Consultants, Ltd.*
Delaney, Patrick J. — *Sensible Solutions, Inc.*
Delmonico, Laura — *A.J. Burton Group, Inc.*
Desmond, Dennis — *Beall & Company, Inc.*
deVry, Kimberly A. — *Tower Consultants, Ltd.*
Dezember, Steve — *Ray & Berndtson*
Dietz, David S. — *MSI International*
Dingeldey, Peter E. — *Search Advisors International Corp.*
Dingman, Bruce — *Robert W. Dingman Company, Inc.*
Dingman, Robert W. — *Robert W. Dingman Company, Inc.*
DiSalvo, Fred — *The Cambridge Group Ltd*
Diskin, Rochelle — *Search West, Inc.*
Doele, Donald C. — *Goodrich & Sherwood Associates, Inc.*
Doman, Matthew — *S.C. International, Ltd.*
Dow, Lori — *Davidson, Laird & Associates, Inc.*
Dowell, Chris — *The Abbott Group, Inc.*
Dreifus, Donald — *Search West, Inc.*
Drury, James J. — *Spencer Stuart*
Dunman, Betsy L. — *Crawford & Crofford*
Edwards, Dorothy — *MSI International*
Edwards, Verba L. — *Wing Tips & Pumps, Inc.*
Eggena, Roger — *Phillips Resource Group*
Ehrgott, Elizabeth — *The Ascher Group*
Ehrhart, Jennifer — *ADOW's Executeam*
Eldridge, Charles B. — *Ray & Berndtson*
Enns, George — *The Enns Partners Inc.*
Eustis, Lucy R. — *MSI International*
Evans, David — *Executive Manning Corporation*
Fancher, Robert L. — *Bason Associates Inc.*
Farrow, Jerry M. — *McCormack & Farrow*
Federman, Jack R. — *W.R. Rosato & Associates, Inc.*

Feldman, Abe — *A.E. Feldman Associates*
Ferneborg, Jay W. — *Ferneborg & Associates, Inc.*
Ferneborg, John R. — *Ferneborg & Associates, Inc.*
Fiorelli, Cheryl — *Tower Consultants, Ltd.*
Fischer, Adam — *Howard Fischer Associates, Inc.*
Fischer, Howard M. — *Howard Fischer Associates, Inc.*
Flanagan, Robert M. — *Robert M. Flanagan & Associates, Ltd.*
Flannery, Peter F. — *Jonas, Walters & Assoc., Inc.*
Fletcher, David — *A.J. Burton Group, Inc.*
Flora, Dodi — *Crawford & Crofford*
Foote, Leland W. — *L.W. Foote Company*
Foreman, David C. — *Koontz, Jeffries & Associates, Inc.*
Forman, Donald R. — *Stanton Chase International*
Frank, Valerie S. — *Norman Roberts & Associates, Inc.*
Fredericks, Ward A. — *Mixtec Group*
Fribush, Richard — *A.J. Burton Group, Inc.*
Friedman, Donna L. — *Tower Consultants, Ltd.*
Friedman, Helen E. — *McCormack & Farrow*
Fust, Sheely F. — *Ray & Berndtson*
Gabriel, David L. — *The Arcus Group*
Galbraith, Deborah M. — *Stratford Group*
Gallagher, Terence M. — *Battalia Winston International*
Gantar, Donna — *Howard Fischer Associates, Inc.*
Geiger, Jan — *Wilcox, Bertoux & Miller*
George, Delores F. — *Delores F. George Human Resource Management & Consulting Industry*
Germain, Valerie — *Jay Gaines & Company, Inc.*
Gettys, James R. — *International Staffing Consultants, Inc.*
Gibbs, John S. — *Spencer Stuart*
Gladstone, Martin J. — *MSI International*
Gold, Stacey — *Earley Kielty and Associates, Inc.*
Goldenberg, Susan — *Grant Cooper and Associates*
Gonzalez, Kristen — *A.J. Burton Group, Inc.*
Goodman, Dawn M. — *Bason Associates Inc.*
Goodridge, Benjamin — *S.C. International, Ltd.*
Goodwin, Tim — *William Guy & Associates*
Gordon, Gerald L. — *E.G. Jones Associates, Ltd.*
Gordon, Teri — *Don Richard Associates of Washington, D.C., Inc.*
Gostyla, Rick — *Spencer Stuart*
Grady, James — *Search West, Inc.*
Green, Jane — *Phillips Resource Group*
Groover, David — *MSI International*
Guy, C. William — *William Guy & Associates*
Haas, Margaret P. — *The Haas Associates, Inc.*
Halbrich, Mitch — *A.J. Burton Group, Inc.*
Hallock, Peter B. — *Goodrich & Sherwood Associates, Inc.*
Hamilton, John R. — *Ray & Berndtson*
Hanes, Leah — *Ray & Berndtson*
Hanley, J. Patrick — *Canny, Bowen Inc.*
Hanson, Grant M. — *Goodrich & Sherwood Associates, Inc.*
Harrison, Priscilla — *Phillips Resource Group*
Hart, Robert T. — *D.E. Foster Partners Inc.*
Herman, Eugene J. — *Earley Kielty and Associates, Inc.*
Hewitt, Rives D. — *The Dalley Hewitt Company*
Hewitt, W. Davis — *The Dalley Hewitt Company*
Hicks, Albert M. — *Phillips Resource Group*

Murphy, Cornelius J. — *Goodrich & Sherwood Associates, Inc.*
Murphy, Patrick J. — *P.J. Murphy & Associates, Inc.*
Murphy, Timothy D. — *MSI International*
Naidicz, Maria — *Ray & Berndtson*
Nees, Eugene C. — *Ray & Berndtson*
Neher, Robert L. — *Intech Summit Group, Inc.*
Nehring, Keith — *Howard Fischer Associates, Inc.*
Neri, Gene — *S.C. International, Ltd.*
Nichols, Gary — *Koontz, Jeffries & Associates, Inc.*
Nold, Robert — *Roberson and Company*
Normann, Amy — *Robert M. Flanagan & Associates, Ltd.*
Norsell, Paul E. — *Paul Norsell & Associates, Inc.*
Nye, David S. — *Blake, Hansen & Nye, Limited*
O'Hara, Daniel M. — *Lynch Miller Moore, Inc.*
Ogdon, Thomas H. — *The Ogdon Partnership*
Ogilvie, Kit — *Howard Fischer Associates, Inc.*
Olsen, David G. — *Handy HRM Corp.*
Onstott, Joseph — *The Onstott Group, Inc.*
Overlock, Craig — *Ray & Berndtson*
Pacini, Lauren R. — *Hite Executive Search*
Palma, Frank R. — *Goodrich & Sherwood Associates, Inc.*
Palmer, Carlton A. — *Beall & Company, Inc.*
Palmer, Melissa — *Don Richard Associates of Tampa, Inc.*
Panarese, Pam — *Howard Fischer Associates, Inc.*
Papciak, Dennis J. — *Accounting Personnel Associates, Inc.*
Papciak, Dennis J. — *Temporary Accounting Personnel*
Pappas, Jim — *Search Dynamics, Inc.*
Pardo, Maria Elena — *Smith Search, S.C.*
Parr, James A. — *KPMG Management Consulting*
Parsons, Allison D. — *Barton Associates, Inc.*
Peasback, David R. — *Canny, Bowen Inc.*
Peeney, James D. — *Peeney Associates*
Pelisson, Charles — *Marra Peters & Partners*
Petty, J. Scott — *The Arcus Group*
Pfeiffer, Irene — *Price Waterhouse*
Phelps, Gene L. — *McCormack & Farrow*
Phillips, Donald L. — *O'Shea, Divine & Company, Inc.*
Pickford, Stephen T. — *The Corporate Staff, Inc.*
Poirier, Roland L. — *Poirier, Hoevel & Co.*
Poremski, Paul — *A.J. Burton Group, Inc.*
Porter, Albert — *The Experts*
Potter, Douglas C. — *Stanton Chase International*
Press, Fred — *Adept Tech Recruiting*
Pugh, Judith Geist — *InterimManagement Solutions, Inc.*
Pugrant, Mark A. — *Grant/Morgan Associates, Inc.*
Rabinowitz, Peter A. — *P.A.R. Associates Inc.*
Raines, Bruce R. — *Raines International Inc.*
Ramler, Carolyn S. — *The Corporate Connection, Ltd.*
Ray, Marianne C. — *Callan Associates, Ltd.*
Redding, Denise — *The Douglas Reiter Company, Inc.*
Reed, Brenda — *International Staffing Consultants, Inc.*
Regan, Thomas J. — *Tower Consultants, Ltd.*
Reisinger, George L. — *Sigma Group International*

Reiter, Douglas — *The Douglas Reiter Company, Inc.*
Reyman, Susan — *S. Reyman & Associates Ltd.*
Reynolds, Gregory P. — *Roberts Ryan and Bentley*
Rice, Raymond D. — *Logue & Rice Inc.*
Rieger, Louis J. — *Spencer Stuart*
Rimmel, James E. — *The Hindman Company*
Rimmele, Michael — *The Bankers Group*
Roberts, Mitch — *A.E. Feldman Associates*
Roberts, Nick P. — *Spectrum Search Associates, Inc.*
Roberts, Norman C. — *Norman Roberts & Associates, Inc.*
Roberts, Scott — *Jonas, Walters & Assoc., Inc.*
Robinson, Bruce — *Bruce Robinson Associates*
Robles Cuellar, Paulina — *Ray & Berndtson*
Rollins, Scott — *S.C. International, Ltd.*
Rosato, William R. — *W.R. Rosato & Associates, Inc.*
Ross, Curt A. — *Ray & Berndtson*
Ross, William J. — *Flowers & Associates*
Rotella, Marshall W. — *The Corporate Connection, Ltd.*
Rudolph, Kenneth — *Kossuth & Associates, Inc.*
Ruge, Merrill — *William Guy & Associates*
Ryan, Lee — *Ryan, Miller & Associates Inc.*
Sacerdote, John — *Raymond Karsan Associates*
Salvagno, Michael J. — *The Cambridge Group Ltd*
Sarna, Edmund A. — *Jonas, Walters & Assoc., Inc.*
Schedra, Sharon — *Earley Kiely and Associates, Inc.*
Schene, Philip — *A.E. Feldman Associates*
Schwam, Carol — *A.E. Feldman Associates*
Scott, Evan — *Howard Fischer Associates, Inc.*
Scott, Gordon S. — *Search Advisors International Corp.*
Scranton, Lisa — *A.J. Burton Group, Inc.*
Sevilla, Claudio A. — *Crawford & Crofford*
Shattuck, Merrill B. — *M.B. Shattuck and Associates, Inc.*
Shepard, Michael J. — *MSI International*
Sherwood, Andrew — *Goodrich & Sherwood Associates, Inc.*
Simmons, Sandra K. — *MSI International*
Sindler, Jay — *A.J. Burton Group, Inc.*
Sitarski, Stan — *Howard Fischer Associates, Inc.*
Skalet, Ira — *A.E. Feldman Associates*
Smead, Michelle M. — *A.T. Kearney, Inc.*
Smith, Ana Luz — *Smith Search, S.C.*
Smith, Grant — *Price Waterhouse*
Smith, John E. — *Smith Search, S.C.*
Smith, Lydia — *The Corporate Connection, Ltd.*
Smith, Matt D. — *Ray & Berndtson*
Smith, Richard — *S.C. International, Ltd.*
Smith, Ronald V. — *Coe & Company International Inc.*
Snyder, C. Edward — *Horton International*
Snyder, James F. — *Snyder & Company*
Spann, Richard E. — *Goodrich & Sherwood Associates, Inc.*
Spriggs, Robert D. — *Spriggs & Company, Inc.*
St. Clair, Alan — *TNS Partners, Inc.*
Stark, Jeff — *Thorne, Brieger Associates Inc.*
Stephenson, Don L. — *Ells Personnel System Inc.*
Sterling, Jay — *Earley Kiety and Associates, Inc.*
Stevens, Ken — *The Stevens Group*

Stevenson, Jane — *Howard Fischer Associates, Inc.*
Stewart, Ross M. — *Human Resources Network Partners Inc.*
Stringer, Dann P. — *D.E. Foster Partners Inc.*
Strom, Mark N. — *Search Advisors International Corp.*
Swanson, Dick — *Raymond Karsan Associates*
Sweeney, James W. — *Sweeney Harbert & Mummert, Inc.*
Swoboda, Lawrence — *A.J. Burton Group, Inc.*
Taylor, Conrad G. — *MSI International*
Taylor, R.L. (Larry) — *Ray & Berndtson*
Telford, John H. — *Telford, Adams & Alexander/Telford & Co., Inc.*
ten Cate, Herman H. — *Stoneham Associates Corp.*
Thomas, Donald — *Mixtec Group*
Thomas, Kurt J. — *P.J. Murphy & Associates, Inc.*
Thomas, William — *Mixtec Group*
Thompson, Kenneth L. — *McCormack & Farrow*
Tincu, John C. — *Ferneborg & Associates, Inc.*
Tipp, George D. — *Intech Summit Group, Inc.*
Tootsey, Mark A. — *A.J. Burton Group, Inc.*
Tryon, Katey — *DeFrain, Mayer LLC*
Tunney, William — *Grant Cooper and Associates*
Turner, Edward K. — *Don Richard Associates of Charlotte*
Turner, Kimberly — *Barton Associates, Inc.*
Tursi, Deborah J. — *The Corporate Connection, Ltd.*
Ulbert, Nancy — *Aureus Group*
Unger, Paul T. — *A.T. Kearney, Inc.*
Vachon, David A. — *McNichol Associates*
Vennat, Manon — *Spencer Stuart*
Visnich, L. Christine — *Bason Associates Inc.*
Vossler, James — *A.J. Burton Group, Inc.*
Waldoch, D. Mark — *Barnes Development Group, LLC*
Waldrop, Gary R. — *MSI International*
Walker, Craig H. — *A.J. Burton Group, Inc.*
Walker, Ewing J. — *Ward Howell International, Inc.*
Walters, William F. — *Jonas, Walters & Assoc., Inc.*
Warter, Mark — *Isaacson, Miller*
Watson, James — *MSI International*
Wayne, Cary S. — *ProSearch Inc.*
Webb, George H. — *Webb, Johnson Associates, Inc.*
Wein, Michael S. — *InterimManagement Solutions, Inc.*
Wein, Michael S. — *Media Management Resources, Inc.*
Wein, William — *InterimManagement Solutions, Inc.*
Wein, William — *Media Management Resources, Inc.*
Welch, Robert — *Ray & Berndtson*
Wheeler, Gerard H. — *A.J. Burton Group, Inc.*
Wilcox, Fred T. — *Wilcox, Bertoux & Miller*
Wilkinson, Barbara — *Beall & Company, Inc.*
Williams, Gary L. — *Barnes Development Group, LLC*
Williams, Roger K. — *Williams, Roth & Krueger Inc.*
Willner, Leo — *William Guy & Associates*

Wilson, Patricia L. — *Leon A. Farley Associates*
Witte, David L. — *Ward Howell International, Inc.*
Wold, Ted W. — *Hyde Danforth Wold & Co.*
Wolf, Stephen M. — *Byron Leonard International, Inc.*
Womack, Joseph — *The Bankers Group*
Wooldridge, Jeff — *Ray & Berndtson*
Woollett, James — *Rusher, Loscavio & LoPresto*
Wright, A. Leo — *The Hindman Company*
Wright, Carl A.J. — *A.J. Burton Group, Inc.*
Wright, Charles D. — *Goodrich & Sherwood Associates, Inc.*
Yen, Maggie Yeh Ching — *Ray & Berndtson*
Zaffrann, Craig S. — *P.J. Murphy & Associates, Inc.*
Zahradka, James F. — *P.J. Murphy & Associates, Inc.*
Zaslav, Debra M. — *Telford, Adams & Alexander/Telford & Co., Inc.*

3. Engineering

Abbott, Peter D. — *The Abbott Group, Inc.*
Abell, Vincent W. — *MSI International*
Abramson, Roye — *Source Services Corporation*
Acquaviva, Jay — *Winter, Wyman & Company*
Adler, Louis S. — *CJA - The Adler Group*
Ahearn, Jennifer — *Logix, Inc.*
Aheran, Jennifer — *Logix Partners*
Akin, J.R. "Jack" — *J.R. Akin & Company Inc.*
Albert, Richard — *Source Services Corporation*
Alford, Holly — *Source Services Corporation*
Allen, William L. — *The Hindman Company*
Allerton, Donald T. — *Allerton Heneghan & O'Neill*
Alringer, Marc — *Source Services Corporation*
Altreuter, Rose — *The ALTCO Group*
Ambler, Peter W. — *Peter W. Ambler Company*
Ames, George C. — *Ames O'Neill Associates*
Amico, Robert — *Source Services Corporation*
Anderson, Dean C. — *Corporate Resources Professional Placement*
Anderson, Mary — *Source Services Corporation*
Anderson, Matthew — *Source Services Corporation*
Anderson, Richard — *Grant Cooper and Associates*
Anderson, Steve — *CPS Inc.*
Antoine, Brian — *Paul-Tittle Associates, Inc.*
Apostle, George — *Search Dynamics, Inc.*
Arnold, David W. — *Christian & Timbers*
Arnson, Craig — *Hernand & Partners*
Arseneault, Daniel S. — *MSI International*
Asquith, Peter S. — *Ames Personnel Consultants, Inc.*
Aston, Kathy — *Marra Peters & Partners*
Atwood, Barrie — *The Abbott Group, Inc.*
Axelrod, Nancy R. — *A.T. Kearney, Inc.*
Bacon, Cheri — *Gaffney Management Consultants*
Badger, Fred H. — *The Badger Group*
Baeder, Jeremy — *Executive Manning Corporation*
Baer, Kenneth — *Source Services Corporation*
Baglio, Robert — *Source Services Corporation*
Baier, Rebecca — *Source Services Corporation*
Baird, John — *Professional Search Consultants*
Baje, Sarah — *Innovative Search Group, LLC*
Baker, Gary M. — *Cochran, Cochran & Yale, Inc.*
Baker, Gerry — *A.T. Kearney, Inc.*

Bakken, Mark — *Source Services Corporation*
Balbone, Rich — *Executive Manning Corporation*
Balch, Randy — *CPS Inc.*
Balchumas, Charles — *Source Services Corporation*
Baldwin, Keith R. — *The Baldwin Group*
Baltaglia, Michael — *Cochran, Cochran & Yale, Inc.*
Balter, Sidney — *Source Services Corporation*
Baltin, Carrie — *Search West, Inc.*
Banko, Scott — *Source Services Corporation*
Baranowski, Peter — *Source Services Corporation*
Barbosa, Frank — *Skott/Edwards Consultants, Inc.*
Barbour, Mary Beth — *Tully/Woodmansee International, Inc.*
Barger, H. Carter — *Barger & Sargeant, Inc.*
Barlow, Ken H. — *The Cherbonnier Group, Inc.*
Barnaby, Richard — *Source Services Corporation*
Barnes, Gary — *Brigade Inc.*
Barnes, Richard E. — *Barnes Development Group, LLC*
Barnes, Roanne L. — *Barnes Development Group, LLC*
Barnett, Barbara — *D. Brown and Associates, Inc.*
Baron, Len — *Industrial Recruiters Associates, Inc.*
Bartels, Fredrick — *Source Services Corporation*
Bartfield, Philip — *Source Services Corporation*
Barthold, James A. — *McNichol Associates*
Bartholdi, Ted — *Bartholdi & Company, Inc.*
Bartholdi, Theodore G. — *Bartholdi & Company, Inc.*
Barton, James — *Source Services Corporation*
Bason, Maurice L. — *Bason Associates Inc.*
Batte, Carol — *Source Services Corporation*
Beal, Richard D. — *A.T. Kearney, Inc.*
Bearman, Linda — *Grant Cooper and Associates*
Beaudin, Elizabeth C. — *Callan Associates, Ltd.*
Beaver, Bentley H. — *The Onstott Group, Inc.*
Beaver, Robert — *Source Services Corporation*
Belden, Jeannette — *Source Services Corporation*
Belfrey, Edward — *Dunhill Professional Search of Irvine, Inc.*
Belin, Jean — *Boyden*
Benjamin, Maurita — *Source Services Corporation*
Bennett, Jo — *Battalia Winston International*
Bennett, Joan — *Adams & Associates International*
Benson, Edward — *Source Services Corporation*
Beran, Helena — *Michael J. Cavanagh and Associates*
Berger, Jeffrey — *Source Services Corporation*
Bernard, Bryan — *Source Services Corporation*
Bernas, Sharon — *Source Services Corporation*
Berry, Harold B. — *The Hindman Company*
Betts, Suzette — *Source Services Corporation*
Bickett, Nicole — *Source Services Corporation*
Bidelman, Richard — *Source Services Corporation*
Biestek, Paul J. — *Paul J. Biestek Associates, Inc.*
Biolsi, Joseph — *Source Services Corporation*
Birns, Douglas — *Source Services Corporation*
Blackmon, Sharon — *The Abbott Group, Inc.*
Bland, Walter — *Source Services Corporation*
Blanton, Julia — *Blanton and Company*
Blanton, Thomas — *Blanton and Company*
Blassaras, Peggy — *Source Services Corporation*
Blecker, Jay — *TSS Consulting, Ltd.*
Blickle, Michael — *Source Services Corporation*
Blim, Barbara — *JDG Associates, Ltd.*

Bloch, Suzanne — *Source Services Corporation*
Bloch, Terry L. — *Southern Research Services*
Bloch, Thomas L. — *Southern Research Services*
Blocher, John — *Source Services Corporation*
Bloom, Howard C. — *Hernand & Partners*
Bloom, Joyce — *Hernand & Partners*
Bloomer, James E. — *L.W. Foote Company*
Bluhm, Claudia — *Schweichler Associates, Inc.*
Blumenthal, Paula — *J.P. Canon Associates*
Blunt, Peter — *Hernand & Partners*
Boczany, William J. — *The Guild Corporation*
Boehm, Robin — *D. Brown and Associates, Inc.*
Boel, Werner — *The Dalley Hewitt Company*
Boesel, James — *Logix Partners*
Boesel, Jim — *Logix, Inc.*
Bogansky, Amy — *Conex Incorporated*
Bohn, Steve J. — *MSI International*
Boltrus, Dick — *Sink, Walker, Boltrus International*
Bongiovanni, Vincent — *ESA Professional Consultants*
Booth, Ronald — *Source Services Corporation*
Borkin, Andrew — *Strategic Advancement Inc.*
Bormann, Cindy Ann — *MSI International*
Bostic, James E. — *Phillips Resource Group*
Bosward, Allan — *Source Services Corporation*
Bowden, Otis H. — *BowdenGlobal, Ltd.*
Brackman, Janet — *Dahl-Morrow International*
Bradley, Dalena — *Woodworth International Group*
Bradshaw, Monte — *Christian & Timbers*
Brady, Dick — *William Guy & Associates*
Brady, Robert — *CPS Inc.*
Brandeis, Richard — *CPS Inc.*
Brandenburg, David — *Professional Staffing Consultants*
Brassard, Gary — *Source Services Corporation*
Bremer, Brian — *Source Services Corporation*
Brewster, Edward — *Source Services Corporation*
Brieger, Steve — *Thorne, Brieger Associates Inc.*
Britt, Stephen — *Keith Bagg & Associates Inc.*
Brkovich, Deanna — *Corporate Recruiters Ltd.*
Bronger, Patricia — *Source Services Corporation*
Brooks, Charles — *Corporate Recruiters Ltd.*
Brooks, Kimberllay — *Corporate Recruiters Ltd.*
Brother, Joy — *Charles Luntz & Associates. Inc.*
Brovender, Claire — *Winter, Wyman & Company*
Brown, Clifford — *Source Services Corporation*
Brown, Daniel — *Source Services Corporation*
Brown, Dennis — *D. Brown and Associates, Inc.*
Brown, Steffan — *Woodworth International Group*
Brown, Steven — *Source Services Corporation*
Browne, Michael — *Source Services Corporation*
Brudno, Robert J. — *Savoy Partners, Ltd.*
Brunner, Terry — *Source Services Corporation*
Bruno, Deborah F. — *The Hindman Company*
Brunson, Therese — *Kors Montgomery International*
Bryant, Henry — *D. Brown and Associates, Inc.*
Bryant, Laura — *Paul-Tittle Associates, Inc.*
Bryant, Richard D. — *Bryant Associates, Inc.*
Bryant, Shari G. — *Bryant Associates, Inc.*
Bryza, Robert M. — *Robert Lowell International*
Brzezinski, Ronald T. — *Callan Associates, Ltd.*
Buckles, Donna — *Cochran, Cochran & Yale, Inc.*
Budill, Edward — *Professional Search Consultants*
Burch, Donald — *Source Services Corporation*

Burchill, Greg — *BGB Associates*
Burden, Gene — *The Cherbonnier Group, Inc.*
Burke, John — *The Experts*
Burkhill, John — *The Talley Group*
Busch, Jack — *Busch International*
Button, David R. — *The Button Group*
Buttrey, Daniel — *Source Services Corporation*
Buzolits, Patrick — *Source Services Corporation*
Cafero, Les — *Source Services Corporation*
Cahill, Peter M. — *Peter M. Cahill Associates, Inc.*
Call, David — *Cochran, Cochran & Yale, Inc.*
Callan, Robert M. — *Callan Associates, Ltd.*
Calogeras, Chris — *The Sager Company*
Cameron, James W. — *Cameron Consulting*
Campbell, E. — *Source Services Corporation*
Campbell, Jeff — *Source Services Corporation*
Capizzi, Karen — *Cochran, Cochran & Yale, Inc.*
Carlson, Eric — *Source Services Corporation*
Carlton, Patricia — *JDG Associates, Ltd.*
Carnal, Rick — *Source Services Corporation*
Carter, Linda — *Source Services Corporation*
Carvalho-Esteves, Maria — *Source Services Corporation*
Cary, Con — *Cary & Associates*
Castle, Lisa — *Source Services Corporation*
Cavanagh, Michael J. — *Michael J. Cavanagh and Associates*
Cavolina, Michael — *Carver Search Consultants*
Celenza, Catherine — *CPS Inc.*
Cersosimo, Rocco — *Source Services Corporation*
Chase, James — *Source Services Corporation*
Chatterjie, Alok — *MSI International*
Chavous, C. Crawford — *Phillips Resource Group*
Cheah, Victor — *Source Services Corporation*
Cherbonnier, L. Michael — *TCG International, Inc.*
Cherbonnier, L. Michael — *The Cherbonnier Group, Inc.*
Christiansen, Amy — *CPS Inc.*
Christiansen, Doug — *CPS Inc.*
Christman, Joel — *Source Services Corporation*
Chronopoulos, Dennis — *Source Services Corporation*
Cimino, James J. — *Executive Search, Ltd.*
Cimino, Ron — *Paul-Tittle Associates, Inc.*
Cimino, Terry N. — *Executive Search, Ltd.*
Cizek, John T. — *Cizek Associates, Inc.*
Cizek, Marti J. — *Cizek Associates, Inc.*
Clark, James — *CPS Inc.*
Clark, John — *Tate Consulting Inc.*
Clauhsen, Elizabeth A. — *Savoy Partners, Ltd.*
Clawson, Bob — *Source Services Corporation*
Clawson, Robert — *Source Services Corporation*
Cline, Mark — *NYCOR Search, Inc.*
Clough, Geoff — *Intech Summit Group, Inc.*
Cocconi, Alan — *Source Services Corporation*
Cochran, Hale — *Fenwick Partners*
Cochran, Scott P. — *The Badger Group*
Cochrun, James — *Source Services Corporation*
Coe, Karen J. — *Coe & Company International Inc.*
Coffman, Brian — *Kossuth & Associates, Inc.*
Cohen, Robert C. — *Intech Summit Group, Inc.*
Cole, Rosalie — *Source Services Corporation*
Coleman, J. Kevin — *J. Kevin Coleman & Associates, Inc.*

Colling, Douglas — *KPMG Management Consulting*
Collins, Scott — *Source Services Corporation*
Collis, Gerald — *TSS Consulting, Ltd.*
Colvin, Teresa A. — *Jonas, Walters & Assoc., Inc.*
Comai, Christine — *Source Services Corporation*
Combs, Thomas — *Source Services Corporation*
Compton, Tonya — *Dunhill Professional Search of Irvine, Inc.*
Cona, Joseph A. — *Cona Personnel Search*
Coneys, Bridget — *Source Services Corporation*
Conners, Theresa — *D. Brown and Associates, Inc.*
Conway, Maureen — *Conway & Associates*
Conway, William P. — *Phillips Resource Group*
Cook, Charlene — *Source Services Corporation*
Cook, Dennis — *A.T. Kearney, Inc.*
Cooke, Katherine H. — *Horton International*
Costello, Lynda — *Coe & Company International Inc.*
Cotugno, James — *Source Services Corporation*
Coughlin, Stephen — *Source Services Corporation*
Coulman, Karen — *CPS Inc.*
Cram, Noel — *R.P. Barone Associates*
Crath, Paul F. — *Price Waterhouse*
Critchley, Walter — *Cochran, Cochran & Yale, Inc.*
Crowder, Edward W. — *Crowder & Company*
Crumpton, Marc — *Logix Partners*
Crumpton, Marc — *Logix, Inc.*
Cruse, O.D. — *Spencer Stuart*
Cuddihy, Paul — *Dahl-Morrow International*
Cuddy, Patricia — *Source Services Corporation*
Cunningham, Sheila — *Adams & Associates International*
Curci, Donald L. — *A.R.I. International*
Curren, Camella — *Source Services Corporation*
Curtis, Ellissa — *Cochran, Cochran & Yale, Inc.*
Cutka, Matthew — *Source Services Corporation*
Czamanske, Paul W. — *Compass Group Ltd.*
Czepiel, Susan — *CPS Inc.*
Daily, John C. — *Handy HRM Corp.*
Dalton, Bret — *Robert W. Dingman Company, Inc.*
Daniel, Beverly — *Foy, Schneid & Daniel, Inc.*
Daniels, C. Eugene — *Sigma Group International*
Dankberg, Iris — *Source Services Corporation*
Davis, C. Scott — *Source Services Corporation*
Davis, Elease — *Source Services Corporation*
Davis, G. Gordon — *Davis & Company*
Dawson, William — *Source Services Corporation*
Debus, Wayne — *Source Services Corporation*
Deck, Jack — *Source Services Corporation*
DeGioia, Joseph — *JDG Associates, Ltd.*
Delaney, Patrick J. — *Sensible Solutions, Inc.*
DeMarco, Robert — *Source Services Corporation*
Desai, Sushila — *Sink, Walker, Boltrus International*
Desgrosellier, Gary P. — *Personnel Unlimited/Executive Search*
Desmond, Dennis — *Beall & Company, Inc.*
Desmond, Mary — *Source Services Corporation*
Dever, Mary — *Source Services Corporation*
Devito, Alice — *Source Services Corporation*
Di Filippo, Thomas — *Source Services Corporation*

DiCioccio, Carmen — *Cochran, Cochran & Yale, Inc.*
Dicker, Barry — *ESA Professional Consultants*
Dickson, Duke — *A.D. & Associates Executive Search, Inc.*
Diers, Gary — *Source Services Corporation*
Dietz, David S. — *MSI International*
Dillon, Larry — *Predictor Systems*
DiMarchi, Paul — *DiMarchi Partners, Inc.*
DiMarchi, Paul — *DiMarchi Partners, Inc.*
Dingeldey, Peter E. — *Search Advisors International Corp.*
Dingman, Bruce — *Robert W. Dingman Company, Inc.*
Dittmar, Richard — *Source Services Corporation*
Divine, Robert S. — *O'Shea, Divine & Company, Inc.*
Dixon, Aris — *CPS Inc.*
Dobrow, Samuel — *Source Services Corporation*
Donahue, Debora — *Source Services Corporation*
Donath, Linda — *Dahl-Morrow International*
Donnelly, Patti — *Source Services Corporation*
Dorfner, Martin — *Source Services Corporation*
Dow, Lori — *Davidson, Laird & Associates, Inc.*
Dowdall, Jean — *A.T. Kearney, Inc.*
Dowell, Chris — *The Abbott Group, Inc.*
Dowlatzadch, Homayoun — *Source Services Corporation*
Downs, William — *Source Services Corporation*
Doyle, Bobby — *Richard, Wayne and Roberts*
Doyle, Marie — *Spectra International Inc.*
Drew, David R. — *Drew & Associates*
Drexler, Robert — *Robert Drexler Associates, Inc.*
Dubrow, Richard M. — *R/K International, Inc.*
Duelks, John — *Source Services Corporation*
Dugan, John H. — *J.H. Dugan and Associates, Inc.*
Duggan, James P. — *Slayton International, Inc./ I-I-C Partners*
Duley, Richard I. — *ARJay & Associates*
Duncan, Dana — *Source Services Corporation*
Dunlow, Aimee — *Source Services Corporation*
Dunman, Betsy L. — *Crawford & Crofford*
Dupont, Rick — *Source Services Corporation*
Dwyer, Julie — *CPS Inc.*
Edwards, Dorothy — *MSI International*
Edwards, John W. — *The Bedford Group*
Edwards, Robert — *J.P. Canon Associates*
Edwards, Verba L. — *Wing Tips & Pumps, Inc.*
Eggena, Roger — *Phillips Resource Group*
Eggert, Scott — *Source Services Corporation*
Ehrhart, Jennifer — *ADOW's Executeam*
Eiseman, Joe — *Source Services Corporation*
Eiseman, Joe — *Source Services Corporation*
Eiseman, Joe — *Source Services Corporation*
Elder, Tom — *Juntunen-Combs-Poirier*
Ellis, Patricia — *Source Services Corporation*
Ellis, Ted K. — *The Hindman Company*
Ellis, William — *Interspace Interactive Inc.*
Emerson, Randall — *Source Services Corporation*
England, Mark — *Austin-McGregor International*
Engle, Bryan — *Source Services Corporation*
Ervin, Darlene — *CPS Inc.*
Ervin, Russell — *Source Services Corporation*
Eustis, Lucy R. — *MSI International*
Evans, David — *Executive Manning Corporation*
Evans, Timothy — *Source Services Corporation*

Fagerstrom, Jon — *Source Services Corporation*
Fales, Scott — *Source Services Corporation*
Fancher, Robert L. — *Bason Associates Inc.*
Fanning, Paul — *Source Services Corporation*
Farler, Wiley — *Source Services Corporation*
Farley, Leon A. — *Leon A. Farley Associates*
Farrow, Jerry M. — *McCormack & Farrow*
Farthing, Andrew R. — *Parfitt Recruiting and Consulting*
Fechheimer, Peter — *Source Services Corporation*
Ferguson, Kenneth — *Source Services Corporation*
Field, Andrew — *Source Services Corporation*
Fincher, Richard P. — *Phase II Management*
Fini, Ron — *The Sager Company*
Fink, Neil J. — *Neil Fink Associates*
Finkel, Leslie — *Source Services Corporation*
Finnerty, James — *Source Services Corporation*
Fishback, Joren — *Derek Associates, Inc.*
Fisher, Neal — *Fisher Personnel Management Services*
Fishler, Stu — *A.T. Kearney, Inc.*
Fitzgerald, Brian — *Source Services Corporation*
Flannery, Peter F. — *Jonas, Walters & Assoc., Inc.*
Flora, Dodi — *Crawford & Crofford*
Florio, Robert — *Source Services Corporation*
Flowers, Hayden — *Southwestern Professional Services*
Flynn, Erin — *Neil Fink Associates*
Fogarty, Michael — *CPS Inc.*
Folkerth, Gene — *Gene Folkerth & Associates, Inc.*
Foote, Leland W. — *L.W. Foote Company*
Foreman, David C. — *Koontz, Jeffries & Associates, Inc.*
Forestier, Lois — *Source Services Corporation*
Forman, Donald R. — *Stanton Chase International*
Foster, Bradley — *Source Services Corporation*
Foster, John — *Source Services Corporation*
Fotia, Frank — *JDG Associates, Ltd.*
Fowler, Thomas A. — *The Hindman Company*
Francis, Brad — *Source Services Corporation*
Francis, John — *Zwell International*
Frank, Valerie S. — *Norman Roberts & Associates, Inc.*
Frantino, Michael — *Source Services Corporation*
Frazier, John — *Cochran, Cochran & Yale, Inc.*
Frederick, Dianne — *Source Services Corporation*
Freeh, Thomas — *Source Services Corporation*
Freeman, Mark — *ESA Professional Consultants*
French, William G. — *Preng & Associates, Inc.*
Friedman, Deborah — *Source Services Corporation*
Fuhrman, Dennis — *Source Services Corporation*
Fujino, Rickey — *Source Services Corporation*
Fulger, Herbert — *Source Services Corporation*
Fulgham MacCarthy, Ann — *Columbia Consulting Group*
Furlong, James W. — *Furlong Search, Inc.*
Furlong, James W. — *Furlong Search, Inc.*
Furlong, James W. — *Furlong Search, Inc.*
Fyhrie, David — *Source Services Corporation*
Gabel, Gregory N. — *Canny, Bowen Inc.*
Gabriel, David L. — *The Arcus Group*
Gaffney, Keith — *Gaffney Management Consultants*
Gaffney, Megan — *Source Services Corporation*

Heacock, Burt E. — *Paul-Tittle Associates, Inc.*
Heafey, Bill — *CPS Inc.*
Hedlund, David — *Hedlund Corporation*
Heffelfinger, Thomas V. — *Heffelfinger Associates, Inc.*
Heideman, Mary Marren — *DeFrain, Mayer LLC*
Heinrich, Scott — *Source Services Corporation*
Heinze, David — *Heinze & Associates, Inc.*
Helminiak, Audrey — *Gaffney Management Consultants*
Henn, George W. — *G.W. Henn & Company*
Henneberry, Ward — *Source Services Corporation*
Henry, Mary — *Conex Incorporated*
Henry, Patrick — *F-O-R-T-U-N-E Personnel Consultants of Huntsville, Inc.*
Henshaw, Bob — *F-O-R-T-U-N-E Personnel Consultants of Huntsville, Inc.*
Hergenrather, Richard A. — *Hergenrather & Company*
Herman, Shelli — *Gary Kaplan & Associates*
Hernand, Warren L. — *Hernand & Partners*
Hernandez, Ruben — *Source Services Corporation*
Heroux, David — *Source Services Corporation*
Hertlein, James N.J. — *Boyden/Zay & Company*
Herzog, Sarah — *Source Services Corporation*
Hewitt, Rives D. — *The Dalley Hewitt Company*
Hewitt, W. Davis — *The Dalley Hewitt Company*
Hicks, Albert M. — *Phillips Resource Group*
Hight, Susan — *Source Services Corporation*
Hilbert, Laurence — *Source Services Corporation*
Hilgenberg, Thomas — *Source Services Corporation*
Hill, Emery — *MSI International*
Hillen, Skip — *The McCormick Group, Inc.*
Hillyer, Carolyn — *Source Services Corporation*
Himes, Dirk — *A.T. Kearney, Inc.*
Himlin, Amy — *Cochran, Cochran & Yale, Inc.*
Hindman, Neil C. — *The Hindman Company*
Hinojosa, Oscar — *Source Services Corporation*
Hoevel, Michael J. — *Poirier, Hoevel & Co.*
Hoffman, Stephen — *Source Services Corporation*
Hofner, Andrew — *Source Services Corporation*
Hokanson, Mark D. — *Crowder & Company*
Holden, Richard B. — *Ames Personnel Consultants, Inc.*
Holland, John A. — *Holland, McFadzean & Associates, Inc.*
Holland, Rose Mary — *Price Waterhouse*
Hollins, Howard D. — *MSI International*
Holt, Carol — *Bartholdi & Company, Inc.*
Hopgood, Earl — *JDG Associates, Ltd.*
Hopper, John W. — *William Guy & Associates*
Hostetter, Kristi — *Source Services Corporation*
Houchins, William M. — *Christian & Timbers*
Houterloot, Tim — *Source Services Corporation*
Houver, Scott — *Logix, Inc.*
Hubert, David L. — *ARlay & Associates*
Hucko, Donald S. — *Jonas, Walters & Assoc., Inc.*
Hudson, Reginald M. — *Search Bureau International*
Huff, William Z. — *Huff Associates*
Hughes, Barbara — *Source Services Corporation*
Hughes, James J. — *R.P. Barone Associates*
Hughes, Randall — *Source Services Corporation*
Hull, Chuck — *Winter, Wyman & Company*
Hult, Dana — *Source Services Corporation*

Humphrey, Titus — *Source Services Corporation*
Hunsaker, Floyd — *Woodworth International Group*
Hunter, Gabe — *Phillips Resource Group*
Huntoon, Cliff — *Richard, Wayne and Roberts*
Hurley, Janeen — *Winter, Wyman & Company*
Hurtado, Jaime — *Source Services Corporation*
Hutton, Thomas J. — *The Thomas Tucker Company*
Hykes, Don A. — *A.T. Kearney, Inc.*
Hylas, Lisa — *Source Services Corporation*
Imely, Larry S. — *Stratford Group*
Imhof, Kirk — *Source Services Corporation*
Inger, Barry — *Source Services Corporation*
Inguagiato, Gregory — *MSI International*
Inskeep, Thomas — *Source Services Corporation*
Intravaia, Salvatore — *Source Services Corporation*
Inzinna, Dennis — *AlternaStaff*
Irish, Alan — *CPS Inc.*
Irwin, Mark — *Source Services Corporation*
Issacs, Judith A. — *Grant Cooper and Associates*
Jackson, Joan — *A.T. Kearney, Inc.*
Jacobs, Martin J. — *The Rubicon Group*
Jacobs, Mike — *Thorne, Brieger Associates Inc.*
Jacobson, Carolyn — *The Abbott Group, Inc.*
Jacobson, Hayley — *Source Services Corporation*
Jadulang, Vincent — *Source Services Corporation*
Jaffe, Mark — *Wyatt & Jaffe*
James, Bruce — *Roberson and Company*
James, Richard — *Criterion Executive Search, Inc.*
Jansen, Douglas L. — *Search Northwest Associates*
Jansen, John F. — *Delta Services*
Januale, Lois — *Cochran, Cochran & Yale, Inc.*
Januleski, Geoff — *Source Services Corporation*
Jaworski, Mary A. — *Tully/Woodmansee International, Inc.*
Jeltema, John — *Source Services Corporation*
Jensen, Robert — *Source Services Corporation*
Joffe, Barry — *Bason Associates Inc.*
Johnson, David A. — *Gaffney Management Consultants*
Johnson, Douglas — *Quality Search*
Johnson, Greg — *Source Services Corporation*
Johnson, John W. — *Webb, Johnson Associates, Inc.*
Johnson, Julie M. — *International Staffing Consultants, Inc.*
Johnson, Peter — *Winter, Wyman & Company*
Johnson, Robert J. — *Quality Search*
Johnson, Stanley C. — *Johnson & Company*
Johnson, Valerie — *Coe & Company International Inc.*
Johnston, Michael — *Robertson-Surrette Executive Search*
Johnstone, Grant — *Source Services Corporation*
Jones, Amy E. — *The Corporate Connection, Ltd.*
Jones, Gary — *BGB Associates*
Jones, Rodney — *Source Services Corporation*
Jones, Ronald T. — *ARlay & Associates*
Jordan, Jon — *Cochran, Cochran & Yale, Inc.*
Jorgensen, Tom — *The Talley Group*
Joyce, William J. — *The Guild Corporation*
Judy, Otto — *CPS Inc.*
Juelis, John J. — *Peeney Associates*
Juska, Frank — *Rusher, Loscavio & LoPresto*

Lyon, Jenny — *Marra Peters & Partners*
Lyons, J. David — *Aubin International Inc.*
Lyons, Michael — *Source Services Corporation*
MacEachern, David — *Spencer Stuart*
MacMillan, James — *Source Services Corporation*
MacNaughton, Sperry — *McNaughton Associates*
MacPherson, Holly — *Source Services Corporation*
Macrides, Michael — *Source Services Corporation*
Mader, Stephen P. — *Christian & Timbers*
Maggio, Mary — *Source Services Corporation*
Maglio, Charles J. — *Maglio and Company, Inc.*
Mahmoud, Sophia — *Source Services Corporation*
Mairn, Todd — *Source Services Corporation*
Major, Susan — *A.T. Kearney, Inc.*
Manassero, Henri J.P. — *International Management Advisors, Inc.*
Mangum, Maria — *Thomas Mangum Company*
Mangum, William T. — *Thomas Mangum Company*
Manns, Alex — *Crawford & Crofford*
Marino, Chester — *Cochran, Cochran & Yale, Inc.*
Marion, Michael — *S.D. Kelly & Associates, Inc.*
Marks, Ira — *Strategic Alternatives*
Marks, Russell E. — *Webb, Johnson Associates, Inc.*
Marlow, William — *Straube Associates*
Marra, John — *Marra Peters & Partners*
Marra, John — *Marra Peters & Partners*
Martin, David — *The Guild Corporation*
Martin, Malcolm — *Paul-Tittle Associates, Inc.*
Marumoto, William H. — *Boyden Washington, D.C.*
Marwil, Jennifer — *Source Services Corporation*
Mather, David R. — *Christian & Timbers*
Mathias, Douglas — *Source Services Corporation*
Mathias, Kathy — *Stone Murphy & Olson*
Mathis, Carrie — *Source Services Corporation*
Matthews, Corwin — *Woodworth International Group*
Mattingly, Kathleen — *Source Services Corporation*
Maxwell, John — *Source Services Corporation*
May, Peter — *Mixtec Group*
Mayer, Thomas — *Source Services Corporation*
McAndrews, Kathy — *CPS Inc.*
McBride, Dee — *Deeco International*
McCarthy, Laura — *Source Services Corporation*
McCloskey, Frank D. — *Johnson Smith & Knisely Accord*
McComas, Kelly E. — *The Guild Corporation*
McCormick, Brian — *The McCormick Group, Inc.*
McCormick, Joseph — *Source Services Corporation*
McCormick, William J. — *The McCormick Group, Inc.*
McCreary, Charles "Chip" — *Austin-McGregor International*
McDermott, Jeffrey T. — *Vlcek & Company, Inc.*
McDonald, John R. — *TSS Consulting, Ltd.*
McDonald, Scott A. — *McDonald Associates International*
McDonald, Stanleigh B. — *McDonald Associates International*
McDonnell, Julie — *Technical Personnel of Minnesota*

McFadzen, Donna — *Holland, McFadzean & Associates, Inc.*
McFadzen, James A. — *Holland, McFadzean & Associates, Inc.*
McGinnis, Rita — *Source Services Corporation*
McGoldrick, Terrence — *Source Services Corporation*
McGregor, James D. — *John Kurosky & Associates*
McGuire, J. Corey — *Peter W. Ambler Company*
McHale, Rob — *Paul-Tittle Associates, Inc.*
McHugh, Keith — *Source Services Corporation*
McIntosh, Arthur — *Source Services Corporation*
McIntosh, Tad — *Source Services Corporation*
McIntyre, Joel — *Phillips Resource Group*
McKeown, Morgan J. — *Christian & Timbers*
McKinney, Julia — *Source Services Corporation*
McMahan, Stephen — *Source Services Corporation*
McMahan, Stephen — *Source Services Corporation*
McManners, Donald E. — *McManners Associates, Inc.*
McMillin, Bob — *Price Waterhouse*
McNamara, Timothy C. — *Columbia Consulting Group*
McNear, Jeffrey E. — *Barrett Partners*
McNichol, John — *McNichol Associates*
McNichols, Walter B. — *Gary Kaplan & Associates*
McThrall, David — *TSS Consulting, Ltd.*
Meadows, C. David — *Professional Staffing Consultants*
Meara, Helen — *Source Services Corporation*
Meehan, John — *Source Services Corporation*
Mendelson, Jeffrey — *Source Services Corporation*
Mendoza-Green, Robin — *Source Services Corporation*
Messina, Marco — *Source Services Corporation*
Meyer, Stacey — *Gary Kaplan & Associates*
Michaels, Joseph — *CPS Inc.*
Mierzwinski, John — *Industrial Recruiters Associates, Inc.*
Miles, Kenneth T. — *MSI International*
Miller, David — *Cochran, Cochran & Yale, Inc.*
Miller, Larry — *Source Services Corporation*
Miller, Russel E. — *ARJay & Associates*
Miller, Timothy — *Source Services Corporation*
Milligan, Dale — *Source Services Corporation*
Mills, John — *Source Services Corporation*
Milner, Carol — *Source Services Corporation*
Miras, Cliff — *Source Services Corporation*
Miras, Cliff — *Source Services Corporation*
Misiurewicz, Marc — *Cochran, Cochran & Yale, Inc.*
Mittwol, Myles — *Source Services Corporation*
Moerbe, Ed H. — *Stanton Chase International*
Mogul, Gene — *Mogul Consultants, Inc.*
Mohr, Brian — *CPS Inc.*
Molitor, John L. — *Barrett Partners*
Mollichelli, David — *Source Services Corporation*
Mondragon, Philip — *A.T. Kearney, Inc.*
Moore, Craig — *Source Services Corporation*
Moore, Dianna — *Source Services Corporation*
Moore, Lemuel R. — *MSI International*
Moore, Mark — *Wheeler, Moore & Elam Co.*
Moore, Suzanne — *Source Services Corporation*
Moore, Thomas — *Aureus Group*

Moran, Douglas — *Source Services Corporation*
Morato, Rene — *Source Services Corporation*
Moretti, Denise — *Source Services Corporation*
Moriarty, Mike — *Source Services Corporation*
Morris, Scott — *Source Services Corporation*
Morrow, Melanie — *Source Services Corporation*
Mott, Greg — *Source Services Corporation*
Msidment, Roger — *Source Services Corporation*
Mueller, Colleen — *Source Services Corporation*
Muendel, H. Edward — *Stanton Chase International*
Murphy, Corinne — *Source Services Corporation*
Murphy, Erin — *CPS Inc.*
Murphy, James — *Source Services Corporation*
Murphy, Timothy D. — *MSI International*
Murray, Virginia — *A.T. Kearney, Inc.*
Murry, John — *Source Services Corporation*
Mursuli, Meredith — *Lasher Associates*
Mydlach, Renee — *CPS Inc.*
Nabers, Karen — *Source Services Corporation*
Nagler, Leon G. — *Nagler, Robins & Poe, Inc.*
Nagy, Les — *Source Services Corporation*
Necessary, Rick — *Source Services Corporation*
Needham, Karen — *Source Services Corporation*
Neff, Herbert — *Source Services Corporation*
Neher, Robert L. — *Intech Summit Group, Inc.*
Neidhart, Craig C. — *TNS Partners, Inc.*
Nelson, Hitch — *Source Services Corporation*
Nelson, Mary — *Source Services Corporation*
Nelson-Folkersen, Jeffrey — *Source Services Corporation*
Nemec, Phillip — *Dunhill International Search of New Haven*
Nephew, Robert — *Christian & Timbers*
Neuberth, Jeffrey G. — *Canny, Bowen Inc.*
Neuwald, Debrah — *Source Services Corporation*
Newlon, Jay — *Logix, Inc.*
Newton, Jay — *Logix Partners*
Nguyen, John — *International Staffing Consultants, Inc.*
Nichols, Gary — *Koontz, Jeffries & Associates, Inc.*
Nolan, Jean M. — *S.D. Kelly & Associates, Inc.*
Nolan, Robert — *Source Services Corporation*
Nold, Robert — *Roberson and Company*
Nolen, Shannon — *Source Services Corporation*
Nolte, William D. — *W.D. Nolte & Company*
Nolton, Becky — *Paul-Tittle Associates, Inc.*
Norman, Randy — *Austin-McGregor International*
Norris, Ken — *A.T. Kearney, Inc.*
Norsell, Paul E. — *Paul Norsell & Associates, Inc.*
Nymark, John — *NYCOR Search, Inc.*
Nymark, Paul — *NYCOR Search, Inc.*
O'Brien, Susan — *Source Services Corporation*
O'Connell, Mary — *CPS Inc.*
Occhiboi, Emil — *Source Services Corporation*
Ocon, Olga — *Busch International*
Olsen, Carl — *A.T. Kearney, Inc.*
Olsen, Robert — *Source Services Corporation*
Orr, Stacie — *Source Services Corporation*
Ottenritter, Chris — *CPS Inc.*
Ouellette, Christopher — *Source Services Corporation*
Owen, Christopher — *Source Services Corporation*
Pace, Susan A. — *Horton International*
Pachowitz, John — *Source Services Corporation*

Pacini, Lauren R. — *Hite Executive Search*
Paliwoda, William — *Source Services Corporation*
Palmer, Carlton A. — *Beall & Company, Inc.*
Palmer, James H. — *The Hindman Company*
Papasadero, Kathleen — *Woodworth International Group*
Pappas, Jim — *Search Dynamics, Inc.*
Paradise, Malcolm — *Source Services Corporation*
Pardo, Maria Elena — *Smith Search, S.C.*
Parente, James — *Source Services Corporation*
Parkin, Myrna — *S.D. Kelly & Associates, Inc.*
Parr, James A. — *KPMG Management Consulting*
Parroco, Jason — *Source Services Corporation*
Patel, Shailesh — *Source Services Corporation*
Paternie, Patrick — *Source Services Corporation*
Paul, Kathleen — *Source Services Corporation*
Peal, Matthew — *Source Services Corporation*
Peckenpaugh, Ann D. — *Schweichler Associates, Inc.*
Pedley, Jill — *CPS Inc.*
Peeney, James D. — *Peeney Associates*
Pelisson, Charles — *Marra Peters & Partners*
Pelkey, Chris — *The McCormick Group, Inc.*
Perry, Carolyn — *Source Services Corporation*
Peters, James N. — *TNS Partners, Inc.*
Peters, Kevin — *Source Services Corporation*
Petersen, Richard — *Source Services Corporation*
Peterson, John — *CPS Inc.*
Petty, J. Scott — *The Arcus Group*
Pfeiffer, Irene — *Price Waterhouse*
Pfister, Shelli — *Jack B. Larsen & Associates*
Phillips, Donald L. — *O'Shea, Divine & Company, Inc.*
Phinney, Bruce — *Paul-Tittle Associates, Inc.*
Phipps, Peggy — *Woodworth International Group*
Pickering, Dale — *Agri-Tech Personnel, Inc.*
Pickering, Rita — *Agri-Tech Personnel, Inc.*
Pierce, Matthew — *Source Services Corporation*
Pierotazio, John — *CPS Inc.*
Pigott, Daniel — *ESA Professional Consultants*
Pillow, Charles — *Source Services Corporation*
Pineda, Rosanna — *Source Services Corporation*
Pirro, Sheri — *Source Services Corporation*
Pitts, Charles — *Contemporary Management Services, Inc.*
Plant, Jerry — *Source Services Corporation*
Poirier, Frank — *Juntunen-Combs-Poirier*
Poirier, Roland L. — *Poirier, Hoevel & Co.*
Pomerance, Mark — *CPS Inc.*
Pompeo, Paul — *Search West, Inc.*
Porada, Stephen D. — *CAP Inc.*
Porter, Albert — *The Experts*
Pototo, Brian — *Source Services Corporation*
Potter, Douglas C. — *Stanton Chase International*
Powell, Danny — *Source Services Corporation*
Powell, Gregory — *Source Services Corporation*
Power, Michael — *Source Services Corporation*
Pregeant, David — *Source Services Corporation*
Preusse, Eric — *Source Services Corporation*
Price, Andrew G. — *The Thomas Tucker Company*
Price, Carl — *Source Services Corporation*
Quinlan, Lynne — *Winter, Wyman & Company*
Raab, Julie — *Dunhill Professional Search of Irvine, Inc.*
Ramler, Carolyn S. — *The Corporate Connection, Ltd.*

Rasmussen, Timothy — *Source Services Corporation*
Ratajczak, Paul — *Source Services Corporation*
Ray, Marianne C. — *Callan Associates, Ltd.*
Raymond, Anne — *Anderson Sterling Associates*
Reardon, Joseph — *Source Services Corporation*
Reddick, David C. — *Horton International*
Redding, Denise — *The Douglas Reiter Company, Inc.*
Reece, Christopher S. — *Reece & Mruk Partners*
Reed, Brenda — *International Staffing Consultants, Inc.*
Reed, Ruthann — *Spectra International Inc.*
Reed, Susan — *Source Services Corporation*
Reid, Katherine — *Source Services Corporation*
Reid, Scott — *Source Services Corporation*
Reifel, Laurie — *Reifel & Assocaites*
Reifersen, Ruth F. — *The Jonathan Stevens Group, Inc.*
Reisinger, George L. — *Sigma Group International*
Reiter, Douglas — *The Douglas Reiter Company, Inc.*
Remillard, Brad M. — *CJA - The Adler Group*
Renfroe, Ann-Marie — *Source Services Corporation*
Rennell, Thomas — *Source Services Corporation*
Renteria, Elizabeth — *Source Services Corporation*
Renwick, David — *John Kurosky & Associates*
Resnic, Alan — *Source Services Corporation*
Reuter, Tandom — *CPS Inc.*
Reyman, Susan — *S. Reyman & Associates Ltd.*
Reynolds, Gregory P. — *Roberts Ryan and Bentley*
Reynolds, Laura — *Source Services Corporation*
Rhoades, Michael — *Source Services Corporation*
Rhodes, Bill — *Bench International*
Richard, Ryan — *Logix Partners*
Richard, Ryan — *Logix, Inc.*
Richards, Paul E. — *Executive Directions*
Richards, R. Glenn — *Executive Directions*
Riederer, Larry — *CPS Inc.*
Rimmel, James E. — *The Hindman Company*
Rios, Vince — *Source Services Corporation*
Rios, Vincent — *Source Services Corporation*
Rizzo, L. Donald — *R.P. Barone Associates*
Robb, Tammy — *Source Services Corporation*
Roberts, Norman C. — *Norman Roberts & Associates, Inc.*
Roberts, Scott — *Jonas, Walters & Assoc., Inc.*
Robertson, John A. — *Kaye-Bassman International Corp.*
Robertson, Ronald — *Robertson-Surrette Executive Search*
Robertson, Sherry — *Source Services Corporation*
Robinette, Paul — *Hernand & Partners*
Robinson, Bruce — *Bruce Robinson Associates*
Robinson, Tonya — *Source Services Corporation*
Roblin, Nancy R. — *Paul-Tittle Associates, Inc.*
Rockwell, Bruce — *Source Services Corporation*
Rodriguez, Manuel — *Source Services Corporation*
Rohan, James E. — *J.P. Canon Associates*
Rohan, Kevin A. — *J.P. Canon Associates*
Rojo, Rafael — *A.T. Kearney, Inc.*
Romanello, Daniel P. — *Spencer Stuart*
Romang, Paula — *Agri-Tech Personnel, Inc.*
Rose, Robert — *ESA Professional Consultants*

Rosen, Mitchell — *Source Services Corporation*
Rosenstein, Michele — *Source Services Corporation*
Ross, William J. — *Flowers & Associates*
Rotella, Marshall W. — *The Corporate Connection, Ltd.*
Roth, Robert J. — *Williams, Roth & Krueger Inc.*
Rothenbush, Clayton — *Source Services Corporation*
Roussel, Vicki — *Logix Partners*
Roussel, Vicki J. — *Logix, Inc.*
Rowland, James — *Source Services Corporation*
Rozentsvayg, Michael — *Logix Partners*
Rozentsvayg, Michael — *Logix, Inc.*
Rudolph, Kenneth — *Kossuth & Associates, Inc.*
Rudzinsky, Howard — *Louis Rudzinsky Associates*
Rudzinsky, Jeffrey — *Louis Rudzinsky Associates*
Ruge, Merrill — *William Guy & Associates*
Rush, Michael E. — *D.A.L. Associates, Inc.*
Russell, Sam — *The Guild Corporation*
Ryan, Annette — *Don Richard Associates of Tidewater, Inc.*
Ryan, David — *Source Services Corporation*
Ryan, Kathleen — *Source Services Corporation*
Ryan, Mark — *Source Services Corporation*
Sacerdote, John — *Raymond Karsan Associates*
Sadaj, Michael — *Source Services Corporation*
Salet, Michael — *Source Services Corporation*
Saletra, Andrew — *CPS Inc.*
Salottolo, Al — *Tactical Alternatives*
Samsel, Randy — *Source Services Corporation*
Samuelson, Robert — *Source Services Corporation*
Sanchez, William — *Source Services Corporation*
Sanders, Natalie — *CPS Inc.*
Sangster, Jeffrey — *F-O-R-T-U-N-E Personnel Consultants of Manatee County*
Sanow, Robert — *Cochran, Cochran & Yale, Inc.*
Santiago, Benefrido — *Source Services Corporation*
Sapers, Mark — *Source Services Corporation*
Saposhnik, Doron — *Source Services Corporation*
Sardella, Sharon — *Source Services Corporation*
Sarna, Edmund A. — *Jonas, Walters & Assoc., Inc.*
Savela, Edward — *Source Services Corporation*
Saxon, Alexa — *Woodworth International Group*
Scalamera, Tom — *CPS Inc.*
Schiavone, Mary Rose — *Canny, Bowen Inc.*
Schlpma, Christine — *Advanced Executive Resources*
Schmidt, Peter R. — *Boyden*
Schmidt, William C. — *Christian & Timbers*
Schneiderman, Gerald — *Management Resource Associates, Inc.*
Schrenzel, Benjamin — *Parfitt Recruiting and Consulting*
Schroeder, James — *Source Services Corporation*
Schueneman, David — *CPS Inc.*
Schultz, Helen — *Predictor Systems*
Schultz, Randy — *Source Services Corporation*
Schwalbach, Robert — *Source Services Corporation*
Schweichler, Lee J. — *Schweichler Associates, Inc.*
Schwinden, William — *Source Services Corporation*
Scimone, James — *Source Services Corporation*

Scimone, Jim — *Source Services Corporation*
Scoff, Barry — *Source Services Corporation*
Scott, Gordon S. — *Search Advisors International Corp.*
Seamon, Kenneth — *Source Services Corporation*
Sell, David — *Source Services Corporation*
Selvaggi, Esther — *Source Services Corporation*
Semple, David — *Source Services Corporation*
Serba, Kerri — *Source Services Corporation*
Sevilla, Claudio A. — *Crawford & Crofford*
Shackleford, David — *Source Services Corporation*
Shamir, Ben — *S.D. Kelly & Associates, Inc.*
Shanks, Jennifer — *Source Services Corporation*
Shapanka, Samuel — *Source Services Corporation*
Shapiro, Elaine — *CPS Inc.*
Shattuck, Merrill B. — *M.B. Shattuck and Associates, Inc.*
Shawhan, Heather — *Source Services Corporation*
Shelton, Jonathan — *Source Services Corporation*
Shenfield, Peter — *A.T. Kearney, Inc.*
Shepard, Michael J. — *MSI International*
Shufelt, Doug — *Sink, Walker, Boltrus International*
Sickles, Robert — *Dunhill Professional Search of Irvine, Inc.*
Siegler, Jody Cukiir — *A.T. Kearney, Inc.*
Signer, Julie — *CPS Inc.*
Siker, Paul W. — *The Guild Corporation*
Silcott, Marvin L. — *Marvin L. Silcott & Associates, Inc.*
Silcott, Marvin L. — *Marvin L. Silcott & Associates, Inc.*
Sill, Igor M. — *Geneva Group International*
Silvas, Stephen D. — *Roberson and Company*
Silver, Kit — *Source Services Corporation*
Silver, Lee — *L. A. Silver Associates, Inc.*
Simankov, Dmitry — *Logix, Inc.*
Simmons, Anneta — *F-O-R-T-U-N-E Personnel Consultants of Huntsville, Inc.*
Simmons, Deborah — *Source Services Corporation*
Simmons, Sandra K. — *MSI International*
Sink, Cliff — *Sink, Walker, Boltrus International*
Sirena, Evelyn — *Source Services Corporation*
Skunda, Donna M. — *Allerton Heneghan & O'Neill*
Slayton, Richard C. — *Slayton International, Inc./I-I-C Partners*
Sloan, Scott — *Source Services Corporation*
Slosar, John — *Boyden*
Smith, Ana Luz — *Smith Search, S.C.*
Smith, David P. — *HRS, Inc.*
Smith, Grant — *Price Waterhouse*
Smith, Ian — *International Staffing Consultants, Inc.*
Smith, John E. — *Smith Search, S.C.*
Smith, Kevin — *F-O-R-T-U-N-E Personnel Consultants of Manatee County*
Smith, Lawrence — *Source Services Corporation*
Smith, Lydia — *The Corporate Connection, Ltd.*
Smith, Ronald V. — *Coe & Company International Inc.*
Smith, Timothy — *Source Services Corporation*
Smock, Cynthia — *Source Services Corporation*
Smoller, Howard — *Source Services Corporation*
Snowden, Charles — *Source Services Corporation*

Snowhite, Rebecca — *Source Services Corporation*
Snyder, C. Edward — *Horton International*
Snyder, James F. — *Snyder & Company*
Sochacki, Michael — *Source Services Corporation*
Sola, George L. — *A.T. Kearney, Inc.*
Solters, Jeanne — *The Guild Corporation*
Song, Louis — *Source Services Corporation*
Sorgen, Jay — *Source Services Corporation*
Sostilio, Louis — *Source Services Corporation*
Souder, E.G. — *Souder & Associates*
Sowerbutt, Richard S. — *Hite Executive Search*
Spanninger, Mark J. — *The Guild Corporation*
Spector, Michael — *Source Services Corporation*
Spencer, John — *Source Services Corporation*
Spencer, John — *Source Services Corporation*
Spera, Stefanie — *A.T. Kearney, Inc.*
Spiegel, Gayle — *L. A. Silver Associates, Inc.*
Spoutz, Paul — *Source Services Corporation*
Spriggs, Robert D. — *Spriggs & Company, Inc.*
St. Martin, Peter — *Source Services Corporation*
Staats, Dave — *Southwestern Professional Services*
Stack, Richard — *Source Services Corporation*
Staehely, Janna — *Southwestern Professional Services*
Stanton, John — *A.T. Kearney, Inc.*
Stark, Jeff — *Thorne, Brieger Associates Inc.*
Steele, Daniel — *Cochran, Cochran & Yale, Inc.*
Steer, Joe — *CPS Inc.*
Stein, Terry W. — *Stewart, Stein and Scott, Ltd.*
Steinem, Andy — *Dahl-Morrow International*
Steinem, Barbra — *Dahl-Morrow International*
Stephens, Andrew — *Source Services Corporation*
Stephens, John — *Source Services Corporation*
Stephenson, Don L. — *Ells Personnel System Inc.*
Stern, Stephen — *CPS Inc.*
Sterner, Doug — *CPS Inc.*
Stevens, Ken — *The Stevens Group*
Stevenson, Terry — *Bartholdi & Company, Inc.*
Stewart, Jeffrey O. — *Stewart, Stein and Scott, Ltd.*
Stewart, Ross M. — *Human Resources Network Partners Inc.*
Stiles, Judy — *MedQuest Associates*
Stone, Susan L. — *Stone Enterprises Ltd.*
Storm, Deborah — *Source Services Corporation*
Stovall, Randal — *D. Brown and Associates, Inc.*
Stranberg, James R. — *Callan Associates, Ltd.*
Strander, Dervin — *Source Services Corporation*
Strickland, Katie — *Grantham & Co., Inc.*
Strom, Mark N. — *Search Advisors International Corp.*
Sturtz, James W. — *Compass Group Ltd.*
Sur, William K. — *Canny, Bowen Inc.*
Surrette, Mark — *Robertson-Surrette Executive Search*
Susoreny, Samali — *Source Services Corporation*
Sussman, Lynda — *Gilbert Tweed/INESA*
Swanner, William — *Source Services Corporation*
Swanson, Dick — *Raymond Karsan Associates*
Swartz, William K. — *Swartz Executive Search*
Sweeney, Anne — *Source Services Corporation*
Sweeney, James W. — *Sweeney Harbert & Mummert, Inc.*
Sweet, Randall — *Source Services Corporation*
Swick, Jan — *TSS Consulting, Ltd.*
Taft, Steven D. — *The Guild Corporation*

Tankson, Dawn — *Source Services Corporation*
Tanner, Frank — *Source Services Corporation*
Tanner, Gary — *Source Services Corporation*
Taylor, Conrad G. — *MSI International*
Teger, Stella — *Source Services Corporation*
ten Cate, Herman H. — *Stoneham Associates Corp.*
Tenero, Kymberly — *Source Services Corporation*
Theobald, David B. — *Theobald & Associates*
Thielman, Joseph — *Barrett Partners*
Thies, Gary — *S.D. Kelly & Associates, Inc.*
Thomas, Cheryl M. — *CPS Inc.*
Thomas, Donald — *Mixtec Group*
Thomas, Ian A. — *International Staffing Consultants, Inc.*
Thomas, Kim — *CPS Inc.*
Thompson, Kenneth L. — *McCormack & Farrow*
Thompson, Leslie — *Source Services Corporation*
Thrower, Troy — *Source Services Corporation*
Tilley, Kyle — *Source Services Corporation*
Tincu, John C. — *Ferneborg & Associates, Inc.*
Tittle, David M. — *Paul-Tittle Associates, Inc.*
To, Raymond — *Corporate Recruiters Ltd.*
Tobin, Christopher — *Source Services Corporation*
Topliff, Marla — *Gaffney Management Consultants*
Tovrog, Dan — *CPS Inc.*
Trefzer, Kristie — *Source Services Corporation*
Trewhella, Michael — *Source Services Corporation*
Trice, Renee — *Source Services Corporation*
Trieschmann, Daniel — *Source Services Corporation*
Trimble, Patricia — *Source Services Corporation*
Trimble, Rhonda — *Source Services Corporation*
Truemper, Dean — *CPS Inc.*
Truitt, Thomas B. — *Southwestern Professional Services*
Tryon, Katey — *DeFrain, Mayer LLC*
Tscelli, Maureen — *Source Services Corporation*
Tschan, Stephen — *Source Services Corporation*
Tucker, Thomas A. — *The Thomas Tucker Company*
Tullberg, Tina — *CPS Inc.*
Tunney, William — *Grant Cooper and Associates*
Turner, Raymond — *Source Services Corporation*
Tursi, Deborah J. — *The Corporate Connection, Ltd.*
Tweed, Janet — *Gilbert Tweed/INESA*
Twomey, James — *Source Services Corporation*
Ulbert, Nancy — *Aureus Group*
Unger, John T. — *A.T. Kearney, Inc.*
Uzzel, Linda — *Source Services Corporation*
Vachon, David A. — *McNichol Associates*
Vairo, Leonard A. — *Christian & Timbers*
Van Biesen, Jacques A.H. — *Search Group Inc.*
Van Norman, Ben — *Source Services Corporation*
Van Steenkiste, Julie — *Davidson, Laird & Associates, Inc.*
Vandenbulcke, Cynthia — *Source Services Corporation*
Vann, Dianne — *The Button Group*
Varney, Monique — *Source Services Corporation*
Varrichio, Michael — *Source Services Corporation*
Velez, Hector — *Source Services Corporation*
Velten, Mark T. — *Boyden*
Vilella, Paul — *Source Services Corporation*

Villella, Paul — *Source Services Corporation*
Vinett-Hessel, Deidre — *Source Services Corporation*
Visnich, L. Christine — *Bason Associates Inc.*
Viviano, Cathleen — *Source Services Corporation*
Vlcek, Thomas J. — *Vlcek & Company, Inc.*
Volkman, Arthur — *Cochran, Cochran & Yale, Inc.*
Vourakis, Zan — *ZanExec LLC*
Wacholz, Rick — *A.T. Kearney, Inc.*
Wade, Christy — *Source Services Corporation*
Waldoch, D. Mark — *Barnes Development Group, LLC*
Waldrop, Gary R. — *MSI International*
Walker, Ann — *Source Services Corporation*
Walker, Douglas G. — *Sink, Walker, Boltrus International*
Walker, Ewing J. — *Ward Howell International, Inc.*
Walker, Rose — *Source Services Corporation*
Wallace, Toby — *Source Services Corporation*
Walsh, Denis — *Professional Staffing Consultants*
Walsh, Kenneth A. — *R/K International, Inc.*
Walters, Scott — *Paul-Tittle Associates, Inc.*
Walters, William F. — *Jonas, Walters & Assoc., Inc.*
Ward, Les — *Source Services Corporation*
Ward, Robert — *Source Services Corporation*
Warnock, Phyl — *Source Services Corporation*
Wasserman, Harvey — *Churchill and Affiliates, Inc.*
Watkinson, Jim W. — *The Badger Group*
Watson, James — *MSI International*
Waymire, Pamela — *Source Services Corporation*
Wayne, Cary S. — *ProSearch Inc.*
Webb, George H. — *Webb, Johnson Associates, Inc.*
Webber, Edward — *Source Services Corporation*
Weeks, Glenn — *Source Services Corporation*
Wein, Michael S. — *InterimManagement Solutions, Inc.*
Wein, Michael S. — *Media Management Resources, Inc.*
Wein, William — *InterimManagement Solutions, Inc.*
Wein, William — *Media Management Resources, Inc.*
Weis, Theodore — *Source Services Corporation*
Weiss, Elizabeth — *Source Services Corporation*
Weissman-Rosenthal, Abbe — *ALW Research International*
Weisz, Laura — *Anderson Sterling Associates*
Welch, Dale — *Winter, Wyman & Company*
Wenz, Alexander — *Source Services Corporation*
Wertheim, Denise — *Paul-Tittle Associates, Inc.*
Wessling, Jerry — *Source Services Corporation*
Westfall, Ed — *Zwell International*
White, William C. — *Venture Resources Inc.*
Whitfield, Jack — *Source Services Corporation*
Whitt, Mimi — *F-O-R-T-U-N-E Personnel Consultants of Huntsville, Inc.*
Wichansky, Mark — *TSS Consulting, Ltd.*
Wilburn, Dan — *Kaye-Bassman International Corp.*
Wilkinson, Barbara — *Beall & Company, Inc.*
Willbrandt, Curt — *Source Services Corporation*
Williams, Dave — *The McCormick Group, Inc.*

Williams, Gary L. — *Barnes Development Group, LLC*
Williams, Jack — *A.T. Kearney, Inc.*
Williams, John — *Source Services Corporation*
Williams, Roger K. — *Williams, Roth & Krueger Inc.*
Willner, Leo — *William Guy & Associates*
Wilson, Don — *Allerton Heneghan & O'Neill*
Wilson, Joyce — *Source Services Corporation*
Wilson, Steven J. — *Herman Smith Executive Initiatives Inc.*
Wingate, Mary — *Source Services Corporation*
Winitz, Joel — *GSW Consulting Group, Inc.*
Winitz, Marla — *GSW Consulting Group, Inc.*
Winkowski, Stephen — *Source Services Corporation*
Winnicki, Kimberly — *Source Services Corporation*
Winograd, Glenn — *Criterion Executive Search, Inc.*
Winston, Dale — *Battalia Winston International*
Witt, Clayton — *Paul-Tittle Associates, Inc.*
Witte, David L. — *Ward Howell International, Inc.*
Witzgall, William — *Source Services Corporation*
Wolf, Donald — *Source Services Corporation*
Wolfe, Peter — *Source Services Corporation*
Wood, Gary — *Source Services Corporation*
Woodmansee, Bruce J. — *Tully/Woodmansee International, Inc.*
Woods, Craig — *Source Services Corporation*
Woodworth, Gail — *Woodworth International Group*
Woollett, James — *Rusher, Loscavio & LoPresto*
Woomer, Jerome — *Source Services Corporation*
Workman, David — *Source Services Corporation*
Wright, A. Leo — *The Hindman Company*
Wyatt, James — *Wyatt & Jaffe*
Wycoff-Viola, Amy — *Source Services Corporation*
Yaekle, Gary — *Tully/Woodmansee International, Inc.*
Yeaton, Robert — *Source Services Corporation*
Young, Heather — *The Guild Corporation*
Youngberg, David — *Source Services Corporation*
Zadfar, Maryanne — *The Thomas Tucker Company*
Zaleta, Andy R. — *A.T. Kearney, Inc.*
Zamborsky, George — *Boyden*
Zarnoski, Henry — *Dunhill International Search of New Haven*
Zatzick, Michael — *Search West, Inc.*
Zavrel, Mark — *Source Services Corporation*
Zegel, Gary — *Source Services Corporation*
Zell, David M. — *Logix Partners*
Zimbal, Mark — *Source Services Corporation*
Zimont, Scott — *Source Services Corporation*
Zwell, Michael — *Zwell International*

4. Finance/Accounting

Abbott, Peter D. — *The Abbott Group, Inc.*
Abell, Vincent W. — *MSI International*
Abernathy, Donald E. — *Don Richard Associates of Charlotte*
Abramson, Roye — *Source Services Corporation*
Adams, Len — *The KPA Group*
Adler, Louis S. — *CJA - The Adler Group*
Akin, J.R. "Jack" — *J.R. Akin & Company Inc.*

Albert, Richard — *Source Services Corporation*
Albertini, Nancy — *Taylor-Winfield, Inc.*
Alford, Holly — *Source Services Corporation*
Allen, Don — *D.S. Allen Associates, Inc.*
Allen, Scott — *Chrisman & Company, Incorporated*
Allen, William L. — *The Hindman Company*
Alringer, Marc — *Source Services Corporation*
Altreuter, Rose — *ALTCO Temporary Services*
Altreuter, Rose — *The ALTCO Group*
Ambler, Peter W. — *Peter W. Ambler Company*
Amico, Robert — *Source Services Corporation*
Anderson, Maria H. — *Barton Associates, Inc.*
Anderson, Mary — *Source Services Corporation*
Anderson, Matthew — *Source Services Corporation*
Anderson, Richard — *Grant Cooper and Associates*
Anderson, Terry — *Intech Summit Group, Inc.*
Andrews, J. Douglas — *Clarey & Andrews, Inc.*
Archer, Sandra F. — *Ryan, Miller & Associates Inc.*
Argentin, Jo — *Executive Placement Consultants, Inc.*
Arnold, David W. — *Christian & Timbers*
Arseneault, Daniel S. — *MSI International*
Ascher, Susan P. — *The Ascher Group*
Asquith, Peter S. — *Ames Personnel Consultants, Inc.*
Aston, Kathy — *Marra Peters & Partners*
Austin Lockton, Kathy — *Juntunen-Combs-Poirier*
Axelrod, Nancy R. — *A.T. Kearney, Inc.*
Bacon, Cheri — *Gaffney Management Consultants*
Badger, Fred H. — *The Badger Group*
Baer, Kenneth — *Source Services Corporation*
Baglio, Robert — *Source Services Corporation*
Baier, Rebecca — *Source Services Corporation*
Baje, Sarah — *Innovative Search Group, LLC*
Baker, Gary M. — *Cochran, Cochran & Yale, Inc.*
Baker, Gerry — *A.T. Kearney, Inc.*
Bakken, Mark — *Source Services Corporation*
Balchumas, Charles — *Source Services Corporation*
Baldwin, Keith R. — *The Baldwin Group*
Baltaglia, Michael — *Cochran, Cochran & Yale, Inc.*
Balter, Sidney — *Source Services Corporation*
Banko, Scott — *Source Services Corporation*
Baranowski, Peter — *Source Services Corporation*
Barbour, Mary Beth — *Tully/Woodmansee International, Inc.*
Barger, H. Carter — *Barger & Sargeant, Inc.*
Barlow, Ken H. — *The Cherbonnier Group, Inc.*
Barnaby, Richard — *Source Services Corporation*
Barnes, Gary — *Brigade Inc.*
Barnes, Richard E. — *Barnes Development Group, LLC*
Barnes, Roanne L. — *Barnes Development Group, LLC*
Barnett, Barbara — *D. Brown and Associates, Inc.*
Barnum, Toni M. — *Stone Murphy & Olson*
Bartels, Fredrick — *Source Services Corporation*
Bartfield, Philip — *Source Services Corporation*
Barthold, James A. — *McNichol Associates*
Bartholdi, Ted — *Bartholdi & Company, Inc.*
Bartholdi, Theodore G. — *Bartholdi & Company, Inc.*
Barton, Gary R. — *Barton Associates, Inc.*

Barton, James — *Source Services Corporation*
Bason, Maurice L. — *Bason Associates Inc.*
Bass, M. Lynn — *Ray & Berndtson*
Battalia, O. William — *Battalia Winston International*
Batte, Carol — *Source Services Corporation*
Bearman, Linda — *Grant Cooper and Associates*
Beaudin, Elizabeth C. — *Callan Associates, Ltd.*
Beaulieu, Genie A. — *Romac & Associates*
Beaver, Bentley H. — *The Onstott Group, Inc.*
Beaver, Robert — *Source Services Corporation*
Beckvold, John B. — *Atlantic Search Group, Inc.*
Belden, Jeannette — *Source Services Corporation*
Belin, Jean — *Boyden*
Benjamin, Maurita — *Source Services Corporation*
Bennett, Jo — *Battalia Winston International*
Benson, Edward — *Source Services Corporation*
Beran, Helena — *Michael J. Cavanagh and Associates*
Berger, Jeffrey — *Source Services Corporation*
Bernard, Bryan — *Source Services Corporation*
Bernas, Sharon — *Source Services Corporation*
Berry, Harold B. — *The Hindman Company*
Bettick, Michael J. — *A.J. Burton Group, Inc.*
Betts, Suzette — *Source Services Corporation*
Bickett, Nicole — *Source Services Corporation*
Bidelman, Richard — *Source Services Corporation*
Biolsi, Joseph — *Source Services Corporation*
Birns, Douglas — *Source Services Corporation*
Bishop, Susan — *Bishop Partners*
Blackshaw, Brian M. — *Blackshaw, Olmstead, Lynch & Koenig*
Bladon, Andrew — *Don Richard Associates of Tampa, Inc.*
Bland, Walter — *Source Services Corporation*
Blassaras, Peggy — *Source Services Corporation*
Blickle, Michael — *Source Services Corporation*
Bliley, Jerry — *Spencer Stuart*
Bloch, Suzanne — *Source Services Corporation*
Bloch, Terry L. — *Southern Research Services*
Bloch, Thomas L. — *Southern Research Services*
Blocher, John — *Source Services Corporation*
Bluhm, Claudia — *Schweichler Associates, Inc.*
Boccella, Ralph — *Susan C. Goldberg Associates*
Boczany, William J. — *The Guild Corporation*
Boehm, Robin — *D. Brown and Associates, Inc.*
Boel, Werner — *The Dalley Hewitt Company*
Bohn, Steve J. — *MSI International*
Bond, Robert J. — *Romac & Associates*
Booth, Ronald — *Source Services Corporation*
Borkin, Andrew — *Strategic Advancement Inc.*
Borland, James — *Goodrich & Sherwood Associates, Inc.*
Bormann, Cindy Ann — *MSI International*
Bosward, Allan — *Source Services Corporation*
Bourrie, Sharon D. — *Chartwell Partners International, Inc.*
Bowden, Otis H. — *BowdenGlobal, Ltd.*
Boyd, Lew — *Coastal International Inc.*
Brackman, Janet — *Dahl-Morrow International*
Bradley, Dalena — *Woodworth International Group*
Bradshaw, Monte — *Christian & Timbers*
Brady, Dick — *William Guy & Associates*
Brandenburg, David — *Professional Staffing Consultants*
Brassard, Gary — *Source Services Corporation*

Bratches, Howard — *Thorndike Deland Associates*
Bremer, Brian — *Source Services Corporation*
Brewster, Edward — *Source Services Corporation*
Brieger, Steve — *Thorne, Brieger Associates Inc.*
Brocaglia, Joyce — *Alta Associates, Inc.*
Bronger, Patricia — *Source Services Corporation*
Brooks, Bernard E. — *Mruk & Partners/EMA Partners Int'l*
Brother, Joy — *Charles Luntz & Associates. Inc.*
Brown, Charlene N. — *Accent on Achievement, Inc.*
Brown, Clifford — *Source Services Corporation*
Brown, D. Perry — *Don Richard Associates of Washington, D.C., Inc.*
Brown, Daniel — *Source Services Corporation*
Brown, Dennis — *D. Brown and Associates, Inc.*
Brown, Gina — *Strategic Alliance Network, Ltd.*
Brown, Larry C. — *Horton International*
Brown, Steffan — *Woodworth International Group*
Brown, Steven — *Source Services Corporation*
Browne, Michael — *Source Services Corporation*
Brudno, Robert J. — *Savoy Partners, Ltd.*
Brunner, Terry — *Source Services Corporation*
Bruno, Deborah F. — *The Hindman Company*
Bryant, Henry — *D. Brown and Associates, Inc.*
Bryant, Richard D. — *Bryant Associates, Inc.*
Bryant, Shari G. — *Bryant Associates, Inc.*
Bryza, Robert M. — *Robert Lowell International*
Brzezinski, Ronald T. — *Callan Associates, Ltd.*
Buckles, Donna — *Cochran, Cochran & Yale, Inc.*
Buggy, Linda — *Bonnell Associates Ltd.*
Bullock, Conni — *Earley Kielty and Associates, Inc.*
Burch, Donald — *Source Services Corporation*
Burchill, Greg — *BGB Associates*
Burden, Gene — *The Cherbonnier Group, Inc.*
Burfield, Elaine — *Skott/Edwards Consultants, Inc.*
Burke, John — *The Experts*
Burke, Karen A. — *Mazza & Riley, Inc. (a Korn/Ferry International affiliate)*
Burkhill, John — *The Talley Group*
Burns, Alan — *The Enns Partners Inc.*
Busch, Jack — *Busch International*
Busterna, Charles — *The KPA Group*
Butcher, Pascale — *F-O-R-T-U-N-E Personnel Consultants of Manatee County*
Buttrey, Daniel — *Source Services Corporation*
Buzolits, Patrick — *Source Services Corporation*
Bye, Randy — *Romac & Associates*
Cafero, Les — *Source Services Corporation*
Calivas, Kay — *A.J. Burton Group, Inc.*
Call, David — *Cochran, Cochran & Yale, Inc.*
Callan, Robert M. — *Callan Associates, Ltd.*
Calogeras, Chris — *The Sager Company*
Cameron, James W. — *Cameron Consulting*
Campbell, E. — *Source Services Corporation*
Campbell, Gary — *Romac & Associates*
Campbell, Jeff — *Source Services Corporation*
Campbell, Robert Scott — *Wellington Management Group*
Campbell, Robert Scott — *Wellington Management Group*
Cannavino, Matthew J. — *Financial Resource Associates, Inc.*
Capizzi, Karen — *Cochran, Cochran & Yale, Inc.*
Carideo, Joseph — *Thorndike Deland Associates*

Dickson, Duke — *A.D. & Associates Executive Search, Inc.*
Diers, Gary — *Source Services Corporation*
Dietz, David S. — *MSI International*
Dillon, Larry — *Predictor Systems*
DiMarchi, Paul — *DiMarchi Partners, Inc.*
DiMarchi, Paul — *DiMarchi Partners, Inc.*
Dingeldey, Peter E. — *Search Advisors International Corp.*
Dingman, Bruce — *Robert W. Dingman Company, Inc.*
Dingman, Robert W. — *Robert W. Dingman Company, Inc.*
Dinte, Paul — *Dinte Resources, Inc.*
DiSalvo, Fred — *The Cambridge Group Ltd*
Diskin, Rochelle — *Search West, Inc.*
Dittmar, Richard — *Source Services Corporation*
Divine, Robert S. — *O'Shea, Divine & Company, Inc.*
Do, Sonnie — *Whitney & Associates, Inc.*
Dobrow, Samuel — *Source Services Corporation*
Doele, Donald C. — *Goodrich & Sherwood Associates, Inc.*
Donahue, Debora — *Source Services Corporation*
Donath, Linda — *Dahl-Morrow International*
Donnelly, Patti — *Source Services Corporation*
Dorfner, Martin — *Source Services Corporation*
Dow, Lori — *Davidson, Laird & Associates, Inc.*
Dowdall, Jean — *A.T. Kearney, Inc.*
Dowell, Chris — *The Abbott Group, Inc.*
Dowell, Mary K. — *Professional Search Associates*
Dowlatzadch, Homayoun — *Source Services Corporation*
Downs, William — *Source Services Corporation*
Doyle, James W. — *Executive Search Consultants International, Inc.*
Dreifus, Donald — *Search West, Inc.*
Dressler, Ralph — *Romac & Associates*
Drew, David R. — *Drew & Associates*
Drury, James J. — *Spencer Stuart*
Dubbs, William — *Williams Executive Search, Inc.*
Dubrow, Richard M. — *R/K International, Inc.*
Duelks, John — *Source Services Corporation*
Duley, Richard I. — *ARJay & Associates*
Dunbar, Marilynne — *Ray & Berndtson/Lovas Stanley*
Duncan, Dana — *Source Services Corporation*
Dunkel, David L. — *Romac & Associates*
Dunlow, Aimee — *Source Services Corporation*
Dunman, Betsy L. — *Crawford & Crofford*
Dupont, Rick — *Source Services Corporation*
Durakis, Charles A. — *C.A. Durakis Associates, Inc.*
Edwards, Dorothy — *MSI International*
Edwards, Verba L. — *Wing Tips & Pumps, Inc.*
Eggena, Roger — *Phillips Resource Group*
Eggert, Scott — *Source Services Corporation*
Ehrgott, Elizabeth — *The Ascher Group*
Ehrhart, Jennifer — *ADOW's Executeam*
Eiseman, Joe — *Source Services Corporation*
Eiseman, Joe — *Source Services Corporation*
Eiseman, Joe — *Source Services Corporation*
Elder, Tom — *Juntunen-Combs-Poirier*
Eldridge, Charles B. — *Ray & Berndtson*
Ellis, Patricia — *Source Services Corporation*
Ellis, Ted K. — *The Hindman Company*

Ellis, William — *Interspace Interactive Inc.*
Emerson, Randall — *Source Services Corporation*
England, Mark — *Austin-McGregor International*
Engle, Bryan — *Source Services Corporation*
Enns, George — *The Enns Partners Inc.*
Erder, Debra — *Canny, Bowen Inc.*
Ervin, Russell — *Source Services Corporation*
Esposito, Mark — *Christian & Timbers*
Eustis, Lucy R. — *MSI International*
Evans, Timothy — *Source Services Corporation*
Fagerstrom, Jon — *Source Services Corporation*
Fales, Scott — *Source Services Corporation*
Fancher, Robert L. — *Bason Associates Inc.*
Fanning, Paul — *Source Services Corporation*
Farler, Wiley — *Source Services Corporation*
Farley, Leon A. — *Leon A. Farley Associates*
Farrow, Jerry M. — *McCormack & Farrow*
Fechheimer, Peter — *Source Services Corporation*
Feldman, Kimberley — *Atlantic Search Group, Inc.*
Ferguson, Kenneth — *Source Services Corporation*
Ferneborg, Jay W. — *Ferneborg & Associates, Inc.*
Ferneborg, John R. — *Ferneborg & Associates, Inc.*
Field, Andrew — *Source Services Corporation*
Fienberg, Chester — *Drummond Associates, Inc.*
Fincher, Richard P. — *Phase II Management*
Fini, Ron — *The Sager Company*
Finkel, Leslie — *Source Services Corporation*
Finnerty, James — *Source Services Corporation*
Fischer, Adam — *Howard Fischer Associates, Inc.*
Fischer, Howard M. — *Howard Fischer Associates, Inc.*
Fischer, John C. — *Horton International*
Fisher, Neal — *Fisher Personnel Management Services*
Fishler, Stu — *A.T. Kearney, Inc.*
Fitzgerald, Brian — *Source Services Corporation*
Fitzgerald, Diane — *Fitzgerald Associates*
Fitzgerald, Geoffrey — *Fitzgerald Associates*
Flanagan, Robert M. — *Robert M. Flanagan & Associates, Ltd.*
Flannery, Peter F. — *Jonas, Walters & Assoc., Inc.*
Fletcher, David — *A.J. Burton Group, Inc.*
Flood, Michael — *Norman Broadbent International, Inc.*
Flora, Dodi — *Crawford & Crofford*
Florio, Robert — *Source Services Corporation*
Foote, Leland W. — *L.W. Foote Company*
Ford, Sandra D. — *The Ford Group, Inc.*
Foreman, David C. — *Koontz, Jeffries & Associates, Inc.*
Forestier, Lois — *Source Services Corporation*
Foster, Bradley — *Source Services Corporation*
Foster, Dwight E. — *D.E. Foster Partners Inc.*
Foster, John — *Source Services Corporation*
Fotia, Frank — *JDG Associates, Ltd.*
Fowler, Thomas A. — *The Hindman Company*
Francis, Brad — *Source Services Corporation*
Frank, Valerie S. — *Norman Roberts & Associates, Inc.*
Frantino, Michael — *Source Services Corporation*
Frazier, John — *Cochran, Cochran & Yale, Inc.*
Frederick, Dianne — *Source Services Corporation*
Freeh, Thomas — *Source Services Corporation*
French, William G. — *Preng & Associates, Inc.*
Fribush, Richard — *A.J. Burton Group, Inc.*

Friedman, Deborah — *Source Services Corporation*
Friedman, Helen E. — *McCormack & Farrow*
Fuhrman, Dennis — *Source Services Corporation*
Fujino, Rickey — *Source Services Corporation*
Fulger, Herbert — *Source Services Corporation*
Fulgham MacCarthy, Ann — *Columbia Consulting Group*
Furlong, James W. — *Furlong Search, Inc.*
Furlong, James W. — *Furlong Search, Inc.*
Furlong, James W. — *Furlong Search, Inc.*
Fust, Sheely F. — *Ray & Berndtson*
Fyhrie, David — *Source Services Corporation*
Gabel, Gregory N. — *Canny, Bowen Inc.*
Gabriel, David L. — *The Arcus Group*
Gaffney, Megan — *Source Services Corporation*
Gaines, Jay — *Jay Gaines & Company, Inc.*
Galante, Suzanne M. — *Vlcek & Company, Inc.*
Gallagher, Terence M. — *Battalia Winston International*
Gamble, Ira — *Source Services Corporation*
Gantar, Donna — *Howard Fischer Associates, Inc.*
Gardiner, E. Nicholas P. — *Gardiner International*
Gardner, Michael — *Source Services Corporation*
Garfinkle, Steven M. — *Battalia Winston International*
Garrett, Mark — *Source Services Corporation*
Gauthier, Robert C. — *Columbia Consulting Group*
Geiger, Jan — *Wilcox, Bertoux & Miller*
Gennawey, Robert — *Source Services Corporation*
George, Delores F. — *Delores F. George Human Resource Management & Consulting Industry*
Gerbasi, Michael — *The Sager Company*
Gerster, J.P. — *Juntunen-Combs-Poirier*
Gestwick, Daniel — *Cochran, Cochran & Yale, Inc.*
Ghurani, Mac — *Gary Kaplan & Associates*
Gibbs, John S. — *Spencer Stuart*
Giesy, John — *Source Services Corporation*
Gilbert, Jerry — *Gilbert & Van Campen International*
Gilchrist, Robert J. — *Horton International*
Giles, Joe L. — *Joe L. Giles and Associates, Inc.*
Gilinsky, David — *Source Services Corporation*
Gill, Patricia — *Columbia Consulting Group*
Gilmore, Connie — *Taylor-Winfield, Inc.*
Gilreath, James M. — *Gilreath Weatherby, Inc.*
Giries, Juliet D. — *Barton Associates, Inc.*
Gladstone, Martin J. — *MSI International*
Glickman, Leenie — *Source Services Corporation*
Gluzman, Arthur — *Source Services Corporation*
Gnatowski, Bruce — *Source Services Corporation*
Goar, Duane R. — *Sandhurst Associates*
Gobert, Larry — *Professional Search Consultants*
Gold, Donald — *Executive Search, Ltd.*
Gold, Stacey — *Earley Kielty and Associates, Inc.*
Goldberg, Susan C. — *Susan C. Goldberg Associates*
Golde, Lisa — *Tully/Woodmansee International, Inc.*
Goldenberg, Susan — *Grant Cooper and Associates*
Goldsmith, Fred J. — *Fred J. Goldsmith Associates*
Goldstein, Steven G. — *The Jonathan Stevens Group, Inc.*
Gonzalez, Kristen — *A.J. Burton Group, Inc.*

Goodman, Dawn M. — *Bason Associates Inc.*
Goodman, Victor — *Anderson Sterling Associates*
Goodwin, Gary — *Source Services Corporation*
Goodwin, Tim — *William Guy & Associates*
Gordon, Gerald L. — *E.G. Jones Associates, Ltd.*
Gordon, Teri — *Don Richard Associates of Washington, D.C., Inc.*
Gorman, Patrick — *Source Services Corporation*
Gorman, T. Patrick — *Techsearch Services, Inc.*
Gostyla, Rick — *Spencer Stuart*
Gourley, Timothy — *Source Services Corporation*
Grado, Eduardo — *Source Services Corporation*
Graff, Jack — *Source Services Corporation*
Graham, Shannon — *Source Services Corporation*
Grandinetti, Suzanne — *Source Services Corporation*
Grant, Michael — *Zwell International*
Grantham, John — *Grantham & Co., Inc.*
Grantham, Philip H. — *Columbia Consulting Group*
Grasch, Jerry E. — *The Hindman Company*
Graves, Rosemarie — *Don Richard Associates of Washington, D.C., Inc.*
Gray, Betty — *Accent on Achievement, Inc.*
Gray, Heather — *Source Services Corporation*
Gray, Russell — *Source Services Corporation*
Graziano, Lisa — *Source Services Corporation*
Grebenstein, Charles R. — *Skott/Edwards Consultants, Inc.*
Green, Jane — *Phillips Resource Group*
Gresia, Paul — *Source Services Corporation*
Griffin, Cathy — *A.T. Kearney, Inc.*
Groban, Jack — *A.T. Kearney, Inc.*
Groner, David — *Source Services Corporation*
Groover, David — *MSI International*
Grossman, James — *Source Services Corporation*
Grossman, Martin — *Source Services Corporation*
Grotte, Lawrence C. — *Lautz Grotte Engler*
Grumulaitis, Leo — *Source Services Corporation*
Guc, Stephen — *Source Services Corporation*
Gurnani, Angali — *Executive Placement Consultants, Inc.*
Guthrie, Stuart — *Source Services Corporation*
Guy, C. William — *William Guy & Associates*
Haas, Margaret P. — *The Haas Associates, Inc.*
Hacker-Taylor, Dianna — *Source Services Corporation*
Haddad, Charles — *Romac & Associates*
Haider, Martin — *Source Services Corporation*
Halbrich, Mitch — *A.J. Burton Group, Inc.*
Hales, Daphne — *Source Services Corporation*
Hall, Peter V. — *Chartwell Partners International, Inc.*
Halladay, Patti — *Intersource, Ltd.*
Haller, Mark — *Source Services Corporation*
Hallock, Peter B. — *Goodrich & Sherwood Associates, Inc.*
Hamburg, Jennifer Power — *Ledbetter/Davidson International, Inc.*
Hamilton, John R. — *Ray & Berndtson*
Hamm, Gary — *Source Services Corporation*
Hamm, Mary Kay — *Romac & Associates*
Hanes, Leah — *Ray & Berndtson*
Hanley, Alan P. — *Williams, Roth & Krueger Inc.*
Hanley, J. Patrick — *Canny, Bowen Inc.*
Hanley, Maureen E. — *Gilbert Tweed/INESA*
Hanley, Steven — *Source Services Corporation*

Hanna, Remon — *Source Services Corporation*
Hansen, David G. — *Ott & Hansen, Inc.*
Hanson, Grant M. — *Goodrich & Sherwood Associates, Inc.*
Hanson, Lee — *Heidrick & Struggles, Inc.*
Harbaugh, Paul J. — *International Management Advisors, Inc.*
Harbert, David O. — *Sweeney Harbert & Mummert, Inc.*
Hardison, Richard L. — *Hardison & Company*
Hargis, N. Leann — *Montgomery Resources, Inc.*
Harney, Elyane — *Gary Kaplan & Associates*
Harp, Kimberly — *Source Services Corporation*
Harris, Jack — *A.T. Kearney, Inc.*
Harris, Seth O. — *Christian & Timbers*
Harrison, Patricia — *Source Services Corporation*
Harrison, Priscilla — *Phillips Resource Group*
Hart, Crystal — *Source Services Corporation*
Hart, James — *Source Services Corporation*
Hart, Robert T. — *D.E. Foster Partners Inc.*
Harvey, Mike — *Advanced Executive Resources*
Harwood, Brian — *Source Services Corporation*
Haselby, James — *Source Services Corporation*
Hasten, Lawrence — *Source Services Corporation*
Haughton, Michael — *DeFrain, Mayer LLC*
Havener, Donald Clarke — *The Abbott Group, Inc.*
Hawksworth, A. Dwight — *A.D. & Associates Executive Search, Inc.*
Hayes, Lee — *Source Services Corporation*
Haystead, Steve — *Advanced Executive Resources*
Heacock, Burt E. — *Paul-Tittle Associates, Inc.*
Hedlund, David — *Hedlund Corporation*
Heideman, Mary Marren — *DeFrain, Mayer LLC*
Heinrich, Scott — *Source Services Corporation*
Heinze, David — *Heinze & Associates, Inc.*
Heneghan, Donald A. — *Allerton Heneghan & O'Neill*
Henn, George W. — *G.W. Henn & Company*
Henneberry, Ward — *Source Services Corporation*
Hensley, Bert — *Morgan Samuels Co., Inc.*
Hensley, Gayla — *Atlantic Search Group, Inc.*
Hergenrather, Richard A. — *Hergenrather & Company*
Herman, Eugene J. — *Earley Kielty and Associates, Inc.*
Herman, Pat — *Whitney & Associates, Inc.*
Herman, Shelli — *Gary Kaplan & Associates*
Hernandez, Ruben — *Source Services Corporation*
Heroux, David — *Source Services Corporation*
Herzog, Sarah — *Source Services Corporation*
Hewitt, Rives D. — *The Dalley Hewitt Company*
Hewitt, W. Davis — *The Dalley Hewitt Company*
Higgins, Donna — *Howard Fischer Associates, Inc.*
Hight, Susan — *Source Services Corporation*
Hilbert, Laurence — *Source Services Corporation*
Hildebrand, Thomas B. — *Professional Resources Group, Inc.*
Hilgenberg, Thomas — *Source Services Corporation*
Hill, Emery — *MSI International*
Hillyer, Carolyn — *Source Services Corporation*
Himes, Dirk — *A.T. Kearney, Inc.*
Himlin, Amy — *Cochran, Cochran & Yale, Inc.*
Hindman, Neil C. — *The Hindman Company*

Hinojosa, Oscar — *Source Services Corporation*
Hockett, William — *Hockett Associates, Inc.*
Hoevel, Michael J. — *Poirier, Hoevel & Co.*
Hoffman, Stephen — *Source Services Corporation*
Hofner, Andrew — *Source Services Corporation*
Hokanson, Mark D. — *Crowder & Company*
Holden, Richard B. — *Ames Personnel Consultants, Inc.*
Holland, John A. — *Holland, McFadzean & Associates, Inc.*
Holland, Rose Mary — *Price Waterhouse*
Hollins, Howard D. — *MSI International*
Holmes, Lawrence J. — *Columbia Consulting Group*
Holodnak, William A. — *J. Robert Scott*
Holt, Carol — *Bartholdi & Company, Inc.*
Hoover, Catherine — *J.L. Mark Associates, Inc.*
Hopkins, Chester A. — *Handy HRM Corp.*
Hostetter, Kristi — *Source Services Corporation*
Houchins, William M. — *Christian & Timbers*
Houterloot, Tim — *Source Services Corporation*
Howe, Theodore — *Romac & Associates*
Howell, Robert B. — *Atlantic Search Group, Inc.*
Howell, Robert B. — *Atlantic Search Group, Inc.*
Hoyda, Louis A. — *Thorndike Deland Associates*
Hubert, David L. — *ARJay & Associates*
Hucko, Donald S. — *Jonas, Walters & Assoc., Inc.*
Hudson, Reginald M. — *Search Bureau International*
Hughes, Barbara — *Source Services Corporation*
Hughes, Cathy N. — *The Ogdon Partnership*
Hughes, Randall — *Source Services Corporation*
Hult, Dana — *Source Services Corporation*
Humphrey, Titus — *Source Services Corporation*
Hunter, Steven — *Diamond Tax Recruiting*
Hurtado, Jaime — *Source Services Corporation*
Hutchison, Richard H. — *Rurak & Associates, Inc.*
Hutchison, William K. — *Christenson & Hutchison*
Hybels, Cynthia — *A.J. Burton Group, Inc.*
Hyde, W. Jerry — *Hyde Danforth Wold & Co.*
Hykes, Don A. — *A.T. Kearney, Inc.*
Hylas, Lisa — *Source Services Corporation*
Imhof, Kirk — *Source Services Corporation*
Inger, Barry — *Source Services Corporation*
Inguagiato, Gregory — *MSI International*
Inskeep, Thomas — *Source Services Corporation*
Intravaia, Salvatore — *Source Services Corporation*
Irwin, Mark — *Source Services Corporation*
Issacs, Judith A. — *Grant Cooper and Associates*
Jackson, Joan — *A.T. Kearney, Inc.*
Jacobs, Martin J. — *The Rubicon Group*
Jacobs, Mike — *Thorne, Brieger Associates Inc.*
Jacobson, Hayley — *Source Services Corporation*
Jacobson, Rick — *The Windham Group*
Jadulang, Vincent — *Source Services Corporation*
James, Richard — *Criterion Executive Search, Inc.*
Jansen, John F. — *Delta Services*
Janssen, Don — *Howard Fischer Associates, Inc.*
Januale, Lois — *Cochran, Cochran & Yale, Inc.*
Januleski, Geoff — *Source Services Corporation*
Jaworski, Mary A. — *Tully/Woodmansee International, Inc.*
Jazylo, John V. — *Handy HRM Corp.*
Jazylo, John V. — *Skott/Edwards Consultants, Inc.*

Laverty, William — *Source Services Corporation*
Lazar, Miriam — *Source Services Corporation*
Leblanc, Danny — *Source Services Corporation*
Ledbetter, Charlene — *Ledbetter/Davidson International, Inc.*
Lee, Everett — *Source Services Corporation*
Lee, Roger — *Montgomery Resources, Inc.*
Leff, Lisa A. — *Berger and Leff*
Leigh, Rebecca — *Source Services Corporation*
Leighton, Mark — *Source Services Corporation*
Leininger, Dennis — *Key Employment Services*
Lence, Julie Anne — *MSI International*
Letcher, Harvey D. — *Sandhurst Associates*
Levenson, Laurel — *Source Services Corporation*
Levine, Irwin — *Source Services Corporation*
Levitt, Muriel A. — *D.S. Allen Associates, Inc.*
Lewicki, Christopher — *MSI International*
Lewis, Daniel — *Source Services Corporation*
Lewis, Jon A. — *Sandhurst Associates*
Lewis, Marc D. — *Handy HRM Corp.*
Lezama Cohen, Luis — *Ray & Berndtson*
Liebross, Eric — *Source Services Corporation*
Lin, Felix — *Source Services Corporation*
Lindberg, Eric J. — *MSI International*
Lindenmuth, Mary — *Search West, Inc.*
Linton, Leonard M. — *Byron Leonard International, Inc.*
Lipuma, Thomas — *Source Services Corporation*
Little, Elizabeth A. — *Financial Resource Associates, Inc.*
Little, Suzaane — *Don Richard Associates of Tampa, Inc.*
Loeb, Stephen H. — *Grant Cooper and Associates*
Long, Helga — *Horton International*
Long, John — *Source Services Corporation*
Long, Mark — *Source Services Corporation*
Long, William G. — *McDonald, Long & Associates, Inc.*
Lotufo, Donald A. — *D.A.L. Associates, Inc.*
Lotz, R. James — *International Management Advisors, Inc.*
Lovas, W. Carl — *Ray & Berndtson/Lovas Stanley*
Lovely, Edward — *The Stevenson Group of New Jersey*
Loving, Vikki — *Intersource, Ltd.*
Lucarelli, Joan — *The Onstott Group, Inc.*
Lucas, Ronnie L. — *MSI International*
Luce, Daniel — *Source Services Corporation*
Lucht, John — *The John Lucht Consultancy Inc.*
Ludder, Mark — *Source Services Corporation*
Ludlow, Michael — *Source Services Corporation*
Lumsby, George N. — *International Management Advisors, Inc.*
Lundy, Martin — *Source Services Corporation*
Luntz, Charles E. — *Charles Luntz & Associates. Inc.*
Lupica, Anthony — *Cochran, Cochran & Yale, Inc.*
Lyon, Jenny — *Marra Peters & Partners*
Lyons, J. David — *Aubin International Inc.*
Lyons, Michael — *Source Services Corporation*
Mackenna, Kathy — *Plummer & Associates, Inc.*
MacMillan, James — *Source Services Corporation*
MacNaughton, Sperry — *McNaughton Associates*
MacPherson, Holly — *Source Services Corporation*
Macrides, Michael — *Source Services Corporation*

Mader, Stephen P. — *Christian & Timbers*
Maggio, Mary — *Source Services Corporation*
Maglio, Charles J. — *Maglio and Company, Inc.*
Mahmoud, Sophia — *Source Services Corporation*
Mairn, Todd — *Source Services Corporation*
Major, Susan — *A.T. Kearney, Inc.*
Mallin, Ellen — *Howard Fischer Associates, Inc.*
Manassero, Henri J.P. — *International Management Advisors, Inc.*
Mangum, Maria — *Thomas Mangum Company*
Mangum, William T. — *Thomas Mangum Company*
Manns, Alex — *Crawford & Crofford*
Mansford, Keith — *Howard Fischer Associates, Inc.*
Manzo, Renee — *Atlantic Search Group, Inc.*
Maphet, Harriet — *The Stevenson Group of New Jersey*
Marino, Chester — *Cochran, Cochran & Yale, Inc.*
Mark, John L. — *J.L. Mark Associates, Inc.*
Mark, Lynne — *J.L. Mark Associates, Inc.*
Marks, Russell E. — *Webb, Johnson Associates, Inc.*
Marlow, William — *Straube Associates*
Marra, John — *Marra Peters & Partners*
Marra, John — *Marra Peters & Partners*
Martin, David — *The Guild Corporation*
Martin, Lois G. — *The Martin Group*
Martin, Timothy P. — *The Martin Group*
Marumoto, William H. — *Boyden Washington, D.C.*
Marwil, Jennifer — *Source Services Corporation*
Massey, R. Bruce — *Horton International*
Mather, David R. — *Christian & Timbers*
Mathias, Douglas — *Source Services Corporation*
Mathias, Kathy — *Stone Murphy & Olson*
Mathis, Carrie — *Source Services Corporation*
Matthews, Corwin — *Woodworth International Group*
Mattingly, Kathleen — *Source Services Corporation*
Matueny, Robert — *Ryan, Miller & Associates Inc.*
Mauer, Kristin — *Montgomery Resources, Inc.*
Maxwell, John — *Source Services Corporation*
May, Peter — *Mixtec Group*
Mayer, Thomas — *Source Services Corporation*
Mayes, Kay H. — *John Shell Associates, Inc.*
Maynard Taylor, Susan — *Chrisman & Company, Incorporated*
Mazor, Elly — *Howard Fischer Associates, Inc.*
Mazza, David B. — *Mazza & Riley, Inc. (a Korn/Ferry International affiliate)*
McAteer, Thomas — *Montgomery Resources, Inc.*
McBride, Jonathan E. — *McBride Associates, Inc.*
McCarthy, Laura — *Source Services Corporation*
McCloskey, Frank D. — *Johnson Smith & Knisely Accord*
McComas, Kelly E. — *The Guild Corporation*
McCormick, Brian — *The McCormick Group, Inc.*
McCormick, Joseph — *Source Services Corporation*
McCormick, William J. — *The McCormick Group, Inc.*
McCreary, Charles "Chip" — *Austin-McGregor International*
McDermott, Jeffrey T. — *Vlcek & Company, Inc.*

McDonald, Scott A. — *McDonald Associates International*
McDonald, Stanleigh B. — *McDonald Associates International*
McDonnell, Julie — *Technical Personnel of Minnesota*
McDowell, Robert N. — *Christenson & Hutchison*
McFadden, Ashton S. — *Johnson Smith & Knisely Accord*
McFadzen, Donna — *Holland, McFadzean & Associates, Inc.*
McFadzen, James A. — *Holland, McFadzean & Associates, Inc.*
McGinnis, Rita — *Source Services Corporation*
McGoldrick, Terrence — *Source Services Corporation*
McGuire, Pat — *A.J. Burton Group, Inc.*
McHugh, Keith — *Source Services Corporation*
McIntosh, Arthur — *Source Services Corporation*
McIntosh, Tad — *Source Services Corporation*
McKeown, Morgan J. — *Christian & Timbers*
McKeown, Patricia A. — *DiMarchi Partners, Inc.*
McKinney, Julia — *Source Services Corporation*
McKnight, Amy E. — *Chartwell Partners International, Inc.*
McLaughlin, John — *Romac & Associates*
McMahan, Stephen — *Source Services Corporation*
McMahan, Stephen — *Source Services Corporation*
McMillin, Bob — *Price Waterhouse*
McNamara, Catherine — *Ray & Berndtson*
McNamara, Timothy C. — *Columbia Consulting Group*
McNear, Jeffrey E. — *Barrett Partners*
McNichol, John — *McNichol Associates*
McNichols, Walter B. — *Gary Kaplan & Associates*
Meadows, C. David — *Professional Staffing Consultants*
Meara, Helen — *Source Services Corporation*
Meehan, John — *Source Services Corporation*
Mendelson, Jeffrey — *Source Services Corporation*
Mendoza-Green, Robin — *Source Services Corporation*
Menendez, Todd — *Don Richard Associates of Tampa, Inc.*
Mercer, Julie — *Columbia Consulting Group*
Mertensotto, Chuck H. — *Whitney & Associates, Inc.*
Messina, Marco — *Source Services Corporation*
Meyer, Stacey — *Gary Kaplan & Associates*
Meyers, Steven — *Montgomery Resources, Inc.*
Miles, Kenneth T. — *MSI International*
Miller, David — *Cochran, Cochran & Yale, Inc.*
Miller, Larry — *Source Services Corporation*
Miller, Roy — *The Enns Partners Inc.*
Miller, Russel E. — *ARJay & Associates*
Miller, Timothy — *Source Services Corporation*
Milligan, Dale — *Source Services Corporation*
Mills, John — *Source Services Corporation*
Milner, Carol — *Source Services Corporation*
Milstein, Bonnie — *Marvin Laba & Associates*
Mingle, Larry D. — *Columbia Consulting Group*
Miras, Cliff — *Source Services Corporation*
Miras, Cliff — *Source Services Corporation*

Misiurewicz, Marc — *Cochran, Cochran & Yale, Inc.*
Mitchell, Jeff — *A.J. Burton Group, Inc.*
Mitchell, John — *Romac & Associates*
Mitton, Bill — *Executive Resource, Inc.*
Mittwol, Myles — *Source Services Corporation*
Mochwart, Donald — *Drummond Associates, Inc.*
Molitor, John L. — *Barrett Partners*
Mollichelli, David — *Source Services Corporation*
Mondragon, Philip — *A.T. Kearney, Inc.*
Montgomery, James M. — *Houze, Shourds & Montgomery, Inc.*
Moore, Craig — *Source Services Corporation*
Moore, David S. — *Lynch Miller Moore, Inc.*
Moore, Dianna — *Source Services Corporation*
Moore, Lemuel R. — *MSI International*
Moore, Mark — *Wheeler, Moore & Elam Co.*
Moore, Suzanne — *Source Services Corporation*
Moore, T. Wills — *Ray & Berndtson*
Moran, Douglas — *Source Services Corporation*
Morato, Rene — *Source Services Corporation*
Moretti, Denise — *Source Services Corporation*
Morgan-Christopher, Jeanie — *Kaye-Bassman International Corp.*
Moriarty, Mike — *Source Services Corporation*
Morris, Scott — *Source Services Corporation*
Morrow, Melanie — *Source Services Corporation*
Mortansen, Patricia — *Norman Broadbent International, Inc.*
Mott, Greg — *Source Services Corporation*
Msidment, Roger — *Source Services Corporation*
Mueller, Colleen — *Source Services Corporation*
Muendel, H. Edward — *Stanton Chase International*
Murphy, Corinne — *Source Services Corporation*
Murphy, Cornelius J. — *Goodrich & Sherwood Associates, Inc.*
Murphy, James — *Source Services Corporation*
Murphy, Patrick J. — *P.J. Murphy & Associates, Inc.*
Murphy, Timothy D. — *MSI International*
Murray, Virginia — *A.T. Kearney, Inc.*
Murry, John — *Source Services Corporation*
Mursuli, Meredith — *Lasher Associates*
Myers, Kay — *Signature Staffing*
Nabers, Karen — *Source Services Corporation*
Nadherny, Christopher C. — *Spencer Stuart*
Nagler, Leon G. — *Nagler, Robins & Poe, Inc.*
Nagy, Les — *Source Services Corporation*
Naidicz, Maria — *Ray & Berndtson*
Necessary, Rick — *Source Services Corporation*
Needham, Karen — *Source Services Corporation*
Nees, Eugene C. — *Ray & Berndtson*
Neff, Herbert — *Source Services Corporation*
Neher, Robert L. — *Intech Summit Group, Inc.*
Nehring, Keith — *Howard Fischer Associates, Inc.*
Neidhart, Craig C. — *TNS Partners, Inc.*
Nelson, Hitch — *Source Services Corporation*
Nelson, Mary — *Source Services Corporation*
Nelson-Folkersen, Jeffrey — *Source Services Corporation*
Nemec, Phillip — *Dunhill International Search of New Haven*
Nephew, Robert — *Christian & Timbers*
Neuberth, Jeffrey G. — *Canny, Bowen Inc.*
Neuwald, Debrah — *Source Services Corporation*

Newman, Lynn — *Kishbaugh Associates International*
Nichols, Gary — *Koontz, Jeffries & Associates, Inc.*
Noebel, Todd R. — *The Noebel Search Group, Inc.*
Nolan, Robert — *Source Services Corporation*
Nolen, Shannon — *Source Services Corporation*
Nolte, William D. — *W.D. Nolte & Company*
Norman, Randy — *Austin-McGregor International*
Normann, Amy — *Robert M. Flanagan & Associates, Ltd.*
Norris, Ken — *A.T. Kearney, Inc.*
Norsell, Paul E. — *Paul Norsell & Associates, Inc.*
Nunziata, Peter — *Atlantic Search Group, Inc.*
Nye, David S. — *Blake, Hansen & Nye, Limited*
O'Brien, Susan — *Source Services Corporation*
O'Hara, Daniel M. — *Lynch Miller Moore, Inc.*
O'Maley, Kimberlee — *Spencer Stuart*
O'Reilly, John — *Stratford Group*
Occhiboi, Emil — *Source Services Corporation*
Ocon, Olga — *Busch International*
Ogdon, Thomas H. — *The Ogdon Partnership*
Ogilvie, Kit — *Howard Fischer Associates, Inc.*
Oldfield, Theresa — *Strategic Alliance Network, Ltd.*
Olmstead, George T. — *Blackshaw, Olmstead, Lynch & Koenig*
Olsen, David G. — *Handy HRM Corp.*
Olsen, Robert — *Source Services Corporation*
Onstott, Joseph — *The Onstott Group, Inc.*
Onstott, Joseph E. — *The Onstott Group, Inc.*
Orr, Stacie — *Source Services Corporation*
Ott, George W. — *Ott & Hansen, Inc.*
Ouellette, Christopher — *Source Services Corporation*
Overlock, Craig — *Ray & Berndtson*
Owen, Christopher — *Source Services Corporation*
Pace, Susan A. — *Horton International*
Pachowitz, John — *Source Services Corporation*
Page, G. Schuyler — *A.T. Kearney, Inc.*
Paliwoda, William — *Source Services Corporation*
Palma, Frank R. — *Goodrich & Sherwood Associates, Inc.*
Palmer, Carlton A. — *Beall & Company, Inc.*
Palmer, James H. — *The Hindman Company*
Palmer, Melissa — *Don Richard Associates of Tampa, Inc.*
Panarese, Pam — *Howard Fischer Associates, Inc.*
Papasadero, Kathleen — *Woodworth International Group*
Papciak, Dennis J. — *Accounting Personnel Associates, Inc.*
Papciak, Dennis J. — *Temporary Accounting Personnel*
Pappas, Christina E. — *Williams Executive Search, Inc.*
Paradise, Malcolm — *Source Services Corporation*
Pardo, Maria Elena — *Smith Search, S.C.*
Parente, James — *Source Services Corporation*
Park, Dabney G. — *Mark Stanley/EMA Partners International*
Parr, James A. — *KPMG Management Consulting*
Parroco, Jason — *Source Services Corporation*
Patel, Shailesh — *Source Services Corporation*
Paternie, Patrick — *Source Services Corporation*

Paul, Kathleen — *Source Services Corporation*
Peal, Matthew — *Source Services Corporation*
Pearson, Robert L. — *Lamalie Amrop International*
Peasback, David R. — *Canny, Bowen Inc.*
Peckenpaugh, Ann D. — *Schweichler Associates, Inc.*
Peeney, James D. — *Peeney Associates*
Pelisson, Charles — *Marra Peters & Partners*
Pernell, Jeanette — *Norman Broadbent International, Inc.*
Perry, Carolyn — *Source Services Corporation*
Peternell, Melanie — *Signature Staffing*
Peters, Kevin — *Source Services Corporation*
Petersen, Richard — *Source Services Corporation*
Petty, J. Scott — *The Arcus Group*
Pfannkuche, Anthony V. — *Spencer Stuart*
Pfeiffer, Irene — *Price Waterhouse*
Pfister, Shelli — *Jack B. Larsen & Associates*
Phelps, Gene L. — *McCormack & Farrow*
Phillips, Donald L. — *O'Shea, Divine & Company, Inc.*
Phillips, Richard K. — *Handy HRM Corp.*
Phinney, Bruce — *Paul-Tittle Associates, Inc.*
Phipps, Peggy — *Woodworth International Group*
Pickering, Dale — *Agri-Tech Personnel, Inc.*
Pickering, Rita — *Agri-Tech Personnel, Inc.*
Pickford, Stephen T. — *The Corporate Staff, Inc.*
Pierce, Matthew — *Source Services Corporation*
Pillow, Charles — *Source Services Corporation*
Pineda, Rosanna — *Source Services Corporation*
Pirro, Sheri — *Source Services Corporation*
Plant, Jerry — *Source Services Corporation*
Plimpton, Ralph L. — *R L Plimpton Associates*
Plummer, John — *Plummer & Associates, Inc.*
Poirier, Frank — *Juntunen-Combs-Poirier*
Poirier, Roland L. — *Poirier, Hoevel & Co.*
Poracky, John W. — *M. Wood Company*
Poremski, Paul — *A.J. Burton Group, Inc.*
Porter, Albert — *The Experts*
Pototo, Brian — *Source Services Corporation*
Powell, Danny — *Source Services Corporation*
Powell, Gregory — *Source Services Corporation*
Power, Michael — *Source Services Corporation*
Pregeant, David — *Source Services Corporation*
Press, Fred — *Adept Tech Recruiting*
Preusse, Eric — *Source Services Corporation*
Price, Andrew G. — *The Thomas Tucker Company*
Price, Carl — *Source Services Corporation*
Pryde, Marcia P. — *A.T. Kearney, Inc.*
Pugh, Judith Geist — *InterimManagement Solutions, Inc.*
Pugrant, Mark A. — *Grant/Morgan Associates, Inc.*
Rabinowitz, Peter A. — *P.A.R. Associates Inc.*
Racht, Janet G. — *Crowe, Chizek and Company, LLP*
Raines, Bruce R. — *Raines International Inc.*
Ramler, Carolyn S. — *The Corporate Connection, Ltd.*
Ramsey, John H. — *Mark Stanley/EMA Partners International*
Rasmussen, Timothy — *Source Services Corporation*
Ratajczak, Paul — *Source Services Corporation*
Ray, Marianne C. — *Callan Associates, Ltd.*
Raymond, Anne — *Anderson Sterling Associates*
Reardon, Joseph — *Source Services Corporation*

Reddick, David C. — *Horton International*
Redding, Denise — *The Douglas Reiter Company, Inc.*
Reece, Christopher S. — *Reece & Mruk Partners*
Reed, Susan — *Source Services Corporation*
Reid, Katherine — *Source Services Corporation*
Reid, Scott — *Source Services Corporation*
Reifel, Laurie — *Reifel & Assocaites*
Reifersen, Ruth F. — *The Jonathan Stevens Group, Inc.*
Reiser, Ellen — *Thorndike Deland Associates*
Reisinger, George L. — *Sigma Group International*
Reiter, Douglas — *The Douglas Reiter Company, Inc.*
Remillard, Brad M. — *CJA - The Adler Group*
Renfroe, Ann-Marie — *Source Services Corporation*
Rennell, Thomas — *Source Services Corporation*
Renner, Sandra L. — *Spectra International Inc.*
Renteria, Elizabeth — *Source Services Corporation*
Resnic, Alan — *Source Services Corporation*
Reyman, Susan — *S. Reyman & Associates Ltd.*
Reynolds, Laura — *Source Services Corporation*
Rhoades, Michael — *Source Services Corporation*
Ribeiro, Claudia — *Ledbetter/Davidson International, Inc.*
Rice, Raymond D. — *Logue & Rice Inc.*
Richards, Paul E. — *Executive Directions*
Richards, R. Glenn — *Executive Directions*
Rieger, Louis J. — *Spencer Stuart*
Rimmel, James E. — *The Hindman Company*
Rimmele, Michael — *The Bankers Group*
Rios, Vince — *Source Services Corporation*
Rios, Vincent — *Source Services Corporation*
Robb, Tammy — *Source Services Corporation*
Roberts, Carl R. — *Southwestern Professional Services*
Roberts, Nick P. — *Spectrum Search Associates, Inc.*
Roberts, Norman C. — *Norman Roberts & Associates, Inc.*
Roberts, Scott — *Jonas, Walters & Assoc., Inc.*
Robertson, Ronald — *Robertson-Surrette Executive Search*
Robertson, Sherry — *Source Services Corporation*
Robins, Jeri N. — *Nagler, Robins & Poe, Inc.*
Robinson, Bruce — *Bruce Robinson Associates*
Robinson, Tonya — *Source Services Corporation*
Robles Cuellar, Paulina — *Ray & Berndtson*
Roblin, Nancy R. — *Paul-Tittle Associates, Inc.*
Rockwell, Bruce — *Source Services Corporation*
Rodriguez, Manuel — *Source Services Corporation*
Rogers, Leah — *Dinte Resources, Inc.*
Rojo, Rafael — *A.T. Kearney, Inc.*
Romanello, Daniel P. — *Spencer Stuart*
Romang, Paula — *Agri-Tech Personnel, Inc.*
Rorech, Maureen — *Romac & Associates*
Rosen, Mitchell — *Source Services Corporation*
Rosenstein, Michele — *Source Services Corporation*
Ross, Curt A. — *Ray & Berndtson*
Ross, Lawrence — *Ray & Berndtson/Lovas Stanley*
Ross, Mark — *Ray & Berndtson/Lovas Stanley*
Ross, William J. — *Flowers & Associates*

Rossi, Thomas — *Southwestern Professional Services*
Rotella, Marshall W. — *The Corporate Connection, Ltd.*
Roth, Robert J. — *Williams, Roth & Krueger Inc.*
Rothenbush, Clayton — *Source Services Corporation*
Rowe, William D. — *D.E. Foster Partners Inc.*
Rowland, James — *Source Services Corporation*
Rudolph, Kenneth — *Kossuth & Associates, Inc.*
Ruge, Merrill — *William Guy & Associates*
Rurak, Zbigniew T. — *Rurak & Associates, Inc.*
Rush, Michael E. — *D.A.L. Associates, Inc.*
Russell, Sam — *The Guild Corporation*
Ryan, David — *Source Services Corporation*
Ryan, Kathleen — *Source Services Corporation*
Ryan, Lee — *Ryan, Miller & Associates Inc.*
Ryan, Mark — *Source Services Corporation*
Sabat, Lori S. — *Alta Associates, Inc.*
Sacerdote, John — *Raymond Karsan Associates*
Sadaj, Michael — *Source Services Corporation*
Salet, Michael — *Source Services Corporation*
Sallows, Jill S. — *Crowe, Chizek and Company, LLP*
Salvagno, Michael J. — *The Cambridge Group Ltd*
Samsel, Randy — *Source Services Corporation*
Samuelson, Robert — *Source Services Corporation*
Sanchez, William — *Source Services Corporation*
Saner, Harold — *Romac & Associates*
Sanitago, Anthony — *TaxSearch, Inc.*
Sanow, Robert — *Cochran, Cochran & Yale, Inc.*
Santiago, Benefrido — *Source Services Corporation*
Sapers, Mark — *Source Services Corporation*
Saposhnik, Doron — *Source Services Corporation*
Sardella, Sharon — *Source Services Corporation*
Sarna, Edmund A. — *Jonas, Walters & Assoc., Inc.*
Sauer, Harry J. — *Romac & Associates*
Savela, Edward — *Source Services Corporation*
Savvas, Carol Diane — *Ledbetter/Davidson International, Inc.*
Saxon, Alexa — *Woodworth International Group*
Schedra, Sharon — *Earley Kielty and Associates, Inc.*
Schiavone, Mary Rose — *Canny, Bowen Inc.*
Schlpma, Christine — *Advanced Executive Resources*
Schmidt, Peter R. — *Boyden*
Schneiderman, Gerald — *Management Resource Associates, Inc.*
Schroeder, James — *Source Services Corporation*
Schultz, Helen — *Predictor Systems*
Schultz, Randy — *Source Services Corporation*
Schwalbach, Robert — *Source Services Corporation*
Schweichler, Lee J. — *Schweichler Associates, Inc.*
Schwinden, William — *Source Services Corporation*
Scimone, James — *Source Services Corporation*
Scimone, Jim — *Source Services Corporation*
Scoff, Barry — *Source Services Corporation*
Scothon, Alan — *Romac & Associates*
Scott, Evan — *Howard Fischer Associates, Inc.*
Scott, Gordon S. — *Search Advisors International Corp.*

Scranton, Lisa — *A.J. Burton Group, Inc.*
Seamon, Kenneth — *Source Services Corporation*
Seiden, Steven A. — *Seiden Krieger Associates, Inc.*
Sell, David — *Source Services Corporation*
Selvaggi, Esther — *Source Services Corporation*
Semple, David — *Source Services Corporation*
Semyan, John K. — *TNS Partners, Inc.*
Serba, Kerri — *Source Services Corporation*
Sevilla, Claudio A. — *Crawford & Crofford*
Shackleford, David — *Source Services Corporation*
Shanks, Jennifer — *Source Services Corporation*
Shapanka, Samuel — *Source Services Corporation*
Shawhan, Heather — *Source Services Corporation*
Shea, Christopher J. — *Ingram & Aydelotte Inc./ I-I-C Partners*
Sheedy, Edward J. — *Dieckmann & Associates, Ltd.*
Shell, John C. — *John Shell Associates, Inc.*
Shelton, Jonathan — *Source Services Corporation*
Shenfield, Peter — *A.T. Kearney, Inc.*
Shepard, Michael J. — *MSI International*
Shepherd, Daniel M. — *Shepherd Bueschel & Provus, Inc.*
Sherwood, Andrew — *Goodrich & Sherwood Associates, Inc.*
Shontell, William — *Don Richard Associates of Washington, D.C., Inc.*
Shore, Earl L. — *E.L. Shore & Associates Ltd.*
Siciliano, Gene — *Western Management Associates*
Siegler, Jody Cukiir — *A.T. Kearney, Inc.*
Siegrist, Jeffrey M. — *D.E. Foster Partners Inc.*
Siker, Paul W. — *The Guild Corporation*
Silcott, Marvin L. — *Marvin L. Silcott & Associates, Inc.*
Silvas, Stephen D. — *Roberson and Company*
Silver, Kit — *Source Services Corporation*
Silver, Lee — *L. A. Silver Associates, Inc.*
Simmons, Deborah — *Source Services Corporation*
Simmons, Gerald J. — *Handy HRM Corp.*
Simmons, Sandra K. — *MSI International*
Sindler, Jay — *A.J. Burton Group, Inc.*
Sirena, Evelyn — *Source Services Corporation*
Sitarski, Stan — *Howard Fischer Associates, Inc.*
Skunda, Donna M. — *Allerton Heneghan & O'Neill*
Slayton, Richard C. — *Slayton International, Inc./I-I-C Partners*
Sloan, Scott — *Source Services Corporation*
Slosar, John — *Boyden*
Smead, Michelle M. — *A.T. Kearney, Inc.*
Smith, Ana Luz — *Smith Search, S.C.*
Smith, David P. — *HRS, Inc.*
Smith, Grant — *Price Waterhouse*
Smith, Herman M. — *Herman Smith Executive Initiatives Inc.*
Smith, John E. — *Smith Search, S.C.*
Smith, Lawrence — *Source Services Corporation*
Smith, Lydia — *The Corporate Connection, Ltd.*
Smith, Matt D. — *Ray & Berndtson*
Smith, Robert L. — *Smith & Sawyer Inc.*
Smith, Ronald V. — *Coe & Company International Inc.*
Smith, Timothy — *Source Services Corporation*

Smith, Timothy C. — *Christian & Timbers*
Smock, Cynthia — *Source Services Corporation*
Smoller, Howard — *Source Services Corporation*
Snowden, Charles — *Source Services Corporation*
Snowhite, Rebecca — *Source Services Corporation*
Snyder, C. Edward — *Horton International*
Snyder, James F. — *Snyder & Company*
Sochacki, Michael — *Source Services Corporation*
Solters, Jeanne — *The Guild Corporation*
Song, Louis — *Source Services Corporation*
Sorgen, Jay — *Source Services Corporation*
Sostilio, Louis — *Source Services Corporation*
Spadavecchia, Jennifer — *Alta Associates, Inc.*
Spann, Richard E. — *Goodrich & Sherwood Associates, Inc.*
Spanninger, Mark J. — *The Guild Corporation*
Spector, Michael — *Source Services Corporation*
Spencer, John — *Source Services Corporation*
Spencer, John — *Source Services Corporation*
Spera, Stefanie — *A.T. Kearney, Inc.*
Spiegel, Gayle — *L. A. Silver Associates, Inc.*
Spoutz, Paul — *Source Services Corporation*
Sprau, Collin L. — *Ray & Berndtson*
Spriggs, Robert D. — *Spriggs & Company, Inc.*
St. Clair, Alan — *TNS Partners, Inc.*
St. Martin, Peter — *Source Services Corporation*
Stack, Richard — *Source Services Corporation*
Stanley, Paul R.A. — *Ray & Berndtson/Lovas Stanley*
Stanton, John — *A.T. Kearney, Inc.*
Stark, Jeff — *Thorne, Brieger Associates Inc.*
Steele, Daniel — *Cochran, Cochran & Yale, Inc.*
Stein, Terry W. — *Stewart, Stein and Scott, Ltd.*
Steinem, Andy — *Dahl-Morrow International*
Steinem, Barbra — *Dahl-Morrow International*
Steinman, Stephen M. — *The Stevenson Group of New Jersey*
Stephens, Andrew — *Source Services Corporation*
Stephens, John — *Source Services Corporation*
Sterling, Jay — *Earley Kielty and Associates, Inc.*
Stevens, Craig M. — *Kirkman & Searing, Inc.*
Stevens, Ken — *The Stevens Group*
Stevenson, Jane — *Howard Fischer Associates, Inc.*
Stevenson, Terry — *Bartholdi & Company, Inc.*
Stewart, Jeffrey O. — *Stewart, Stein and Scott, Ltd.*
Stewart, Ross M. — *Human Resources Network Partners Inc.*
Stone, Susan L. — *Stone Enterprises Ltd.*
Storm, Deborah — *Source Services Corporation*
Stovall, Randal — *D. Brown and Associates, Inc.*
Stranberg, James R. — *Callan Associates, Ltd.*
Strander, Dervin — *Source Services Corporation*
Strassman, Mark — *Don Richard Associates of Washington, D.C., Inc.*
Stratmeyer, Karin Bergwall — *Princeton Entrepreneurial Resources*
Stratton, Cary — *Coastal International Inc.*
Strickland, Katie — *Grantham & Co., Inc.*
Stringer, Dann P. — *D.E. Foster Partners Inc.*
Strom, Mark N. — *Search Advisors International Corp.*
Struzziero, Ralph E. — *Romac & Associates*
Sucato, Carolyn — *Jay Gaines & Company, Inc.*
Sur, William K. — *Canny, Bowen Inc.*

Surrette, Mark — *Robertson-Surrette Executive Search*
Susoreny, Samali — *Source Services Corporation*
Sussman, Lynda — *Gilbert Tweed/INESA*
Sutter, Howard — *Romac & Associates*
Swanner, William — *Source Services Corporation*
Swanson, Dick — *Raymond Karsan Associates*
Swartz, William K. — *Swartz Executive Search*
Sweeney, Anne — *Source Services Corporation*
Sweeney, James W. — *Sweeney Harbert & Mummert, Inc.*
Sweet, Randall — *Source Services Corporation*
Swoboda, Lawrence — *A.J. Burton Group, Inc.*
Taft, David G. — *Techsearch Services, Inc.*
Taft, Steven D. — *The Guild Corporation*
Tankson, Dawn — *Source Services Corporation*
Tanner, Frank — *Source Services Corporation*
Tanner, Gary — *Source Services Corporation*
Taylor, Conrad G. — *MSI International*
Taylor, James M. — *The HRM Group, Inc.*
Taylor, R.L. (Larry) — *Ray & Berndtson*
Teger, Stella — *Source Services Corporation*
Telford, John H. — *Telford, Adams & Alexander/Telford & Co., Inc.*
ten Cate, Herman H. — *Stoneham Associates Corp.*
Tenero, Kymberly — *Source Services Corporation*
Tetrick, Tim — *O'Connor, O'Connor, Lordi, Ltd.*
Theard, Susan — *Romac & Associates*
Theobald, David B. — *Theobald & Associates*
Thielman, Joseph — *Barrett Partners*
Thomas, Kurt J. — *P.J. Murphy & Associates, Inc.*
Thomas, Terry — *The Thomas Resource Group*
Thompson, Kenneth L. — *McCormack & Farrow*
Thompson, Leslie — *Source Services Corporation*
Thrapp, Mark C. — *Executive Search Consultants International, Inc.*
Thrower, Troy — *Source Services Corporation*
Tilley, Kyle — *Source Services Corporation*
Tincu, John C. — *Ferneborg & Associates, Inc.*
Tittle, David M. — *Paul-Tittle Associates, Inc.*
Tobin, Christopher — *Source Services Corporation*
Tootsey, Mark A. — *A.J. Burton Group, Inc.*
Topliff, Marla — *Gaffney Management Consultants*
Trefzer, Kristie — *Source Services Corporation*
Trewhella, Michael — *Source Services Corporation*
Trice, Renee — *Source Services Corporation*
Trieschmann, Daniel — *Source Services Corporation*
Trieweiler, Bob — *Executive Placement Consultants, Inc.*
Trimble, Patricia — *Source Services Corporation*
Trimble, Rhonda — *Source Services Corporation*
Truitt, Thomas B. — *Southwestern Professional Services*
Tryon, Katey — *DeFrain, Mayer LLC*
Tscelli, Maureen — *Source Services Corporation*
Tschan, Stephen — *Source Services Corporation*
Tucker, Thomas A. — *The Thomas Tucker Company*
Tully, Margo L. — *Tully/Woodmansee International, Inc.*
Tunney, William — *Grant Cooper and Associates*
Turner, Edward K. — *Don Richard Associates of Charlotte*

Turner, Kimberly — *Barton Associates, Inc.*
Turner, Raymond — *Source Services Corporation*
Tursi, Deborah J. — *The Corporate Connection, Ltd.*
Tweed, Janet — *Gilbert Tweed/INESA*
Twomey, James — *Source Services Corporation*
Ulbert, Nancy — *Aureus Group*
Ulrich, Mary Ann — *D.S. Allen Associates, Inc.*
Uzzel, Linda — *Source Services Corporation*
Vacca, Domenic — *Romac & Associates*
Vachon, David A. — *McNichol Associates*
Vairo, Leonard A. — *Christian & Timbers*
Valenta, Joseph — *Princeton Entrepreneurial Resources*
Van Biesen, Jacques A.H. — *Search Group Inc.*
Van Campen, Jerry — *Gilbert & Van Campen International*
Van Norman, Ben — *Source Services Corporation*
Van Steenkiste, Julie — *Davidson, Laird & Associates, Inc.*
Vandenbulcke, Cynthia — *Source Services Corporation*
Varney, Monique — *Source Services Corporation*
Varrichio, Michael — *Source Services Corporation*
Velez, Hector — *Source Services Corporation*
Velten, Mark T. — *Boyden*
Venable, William W. — *Thorndike Deland Associates*
Vennat, Manon — *Spencer Stuart*
Vernon, Peter C. — *Horton International*
Vilella, Paul — *Source Services Corporation*
Villella, Paul — *Source Services Corporation*
Vinett-Hessel, Deidre — *Source Services Corporation*
Visnich, L. Christine — *Bason Associates Inc.*
Viviano, Cathleen — *Source Services Corporation*
Vlcek, Thomas J. — *Vlcek & Company, Inc.*
Voigt, John A. — *Romac & Associates*
Volkman, Arthur — *Cochran, Cochran & Yale, Inc.*
Vossler, James — *A.J. Burton Group, Inc.*
Vourakis, Zan — *ZanExec LLC*
Vroom, Cynthia D. — *Cyntal International Ltd*
Wacholz, Rick — *A.T. Kearney, Inc.*
Wade, Christy — *Source Services Corporation*
Waldoch, D. Mark — *Barnes Development Group, LLC*
Waldrop, Gary R. — *MSI International*
Walker, Ann — *Source Services Corporation*
Walker, Craig H. — *A.J. Burton Group, Inc.*
Walker, Ewing J. — *Ward Howell International, Inc.*
Walker, Rose — *Source Services Corporation*
Wallace, Toby — *Source Services Corporation*
Walsh, Denis — *Professional Staffing Consultants*
Walsh, Kenneth A. — *R/K International, Inc.*
Walters, William F. — *Jonas, Walters & Assoc., Inc.*
Ward, Les — *Source Services Corporation*
Ward, Madeleine — *LTM Associates*
Ward, Robert — *Source Services Corporation*
Warnock, Phyl — *Source Services Corporation*
Warter, Mark — *Isaacson, Miller*
Watkinson, Jim W. — *The Badger Group*
Watson, James — *MSI International*
Waymire, Pamela — *Source Services Corporation*
Wayne, Cary S. — *ProSearch Inc.*

Webb, George H. — *Webb, Johnson Associates, Inc.*
Webber, Edward — *Source Services Corporation*
Weeks, Glenn — *Source Services Corporation*
Wein, Michael S. — *InterimManagement Solutions, Inc.*
Weinberg, Melvin — *Romac & Associates*
Weis, Theodore — *Source Services Corporation*
Weiss, Elizabeth — *Source Services Corporation*
Weissman-Rosenthal, Abbe — *ALW Research International*
Weisz, Laura — *Anderson Sterling Associates*
Welch, Robert — *Ray & Berndtson*
Weller, Paul S. — *Mark Stanley/EMA Partners International*
Wenz, Alexander — *Source Services Corporation*
Wessling, Jerry — *Source Services Corporation*
Westfall, Ed — *Zwell International*
Wheatley, William — *Drummond Associates, Inc.*
Wheeler, Gerard H. — *A.J. Burton Group, Inc.*
White, William C. — *Venture Resources Inc.*
Whitfield, Jack — *Source Services Corporation*
Whitney, David L. — *Whitney & Associates, Inc.*
Wilcox, Fred T. — *Wilcox, Bertoux & Miller*
Wilder, Richard B. — *Columbia Consulting Group*
Wilkinson, Barbara — *Beall & Company, Inc.*
Wilkinson, Jr. SPHR
Wilkinson, Charles E. — *The HRM Group, Inc.*
Willbrandt, Curt — *Source Services Corporation*
Williams, Angie — *Whitney & Associates, Inc.*
Williams, Gary L. — *Barnes Development Group, LLC*
Williams, Jack — *A.T. Kearney, Inc.*
Williams, John — *Source Services Corporation*
Williams, Roger K. — *Williams, Roth & Krueger Inc.*
Williams, Stephen E. — *Barton Associates, Inc.*
Wilson, Don — *Allerton Heneghan & O'Neill*
Wilson, Joyce — *Source Services Corporation*
Wilson, Patricia L. — *Leon A. Farley Associates*
Wilson, Steven J. — *Herman Smith Executive Initiatives Inc.*
Wingate, Mary — *Source Services Corporation*
Winitz, Joel — *GSW Consulting Group, Inc.*
Winitz, Marla — *GSW Consulting Group, Inc.*
Winkowski, Stephen — *Source Services Corporation*
Winnicki, Kimberly — *Source Services Corporation*
Winograd, Glenn — *Criterion Executive Search, Inc.*
Winston, Dale — *Battalia Winston International*
Wise, J. Herbert — *Sandhurst Associates*
Witzgall, William — *Source Services Corporation*
Wold, Ted W. — *Hyde Danforth Wold & Co.*
Wolf, Donald — *Source Services Corporation*
Wolf, Stephen M. — *Byron Leonard International, Inc.*
Wolfe, Peter — *Source Services Corporation*
Womack, Joseph — *The Bankers Group*
Wood, Gary — *Source Services Corporation*
Woodmansee, Bruce J. — *Tully/Woodmansee International, Inc.*
Woods, Craig — *Source Services Corporation*
Woodworth, Gail — *Woodworth International Group*
Wooldridge, Jeff — *Ray & Berndtson*

Woomer, Jerome — *Source Services Corporation*
Workman, David — *Source Services Corporation*
Wright, A. Leo — *The Hindman Company*
Wright, Carl A.J. — *A.J. Burton Group, Inc.*
Wright, Charles D. — *Goodrich & Sherwood Associates, Inc.*
Wright, Leslie — *The Stevenson Group of New Jersey*
Wycoff-Viola, Amy — *Source Services Corporation*
Yaekle, Gary — *Tully/Woodmansee International, Inc.*
Yeaton, Robert — *Source Services Corporation*
Yen, Maggie Yeh Ching — *Ray & Berndtson*
Young, Heather — *The Guild Corporation*
Youngberg, David — *Source Services Corporation*
Yungerberg, Steven — *Steven Yungerberg Associates Inc.*
Zaffrann, Craig S. — *P.J. Murphy & Associates, Inc.*
Zahradka, James F. — *P.J. Murphy & Associates, Inc.*
Zaleta, Andy R. — *A.T. Kearney, Inc.*
Zamborsky, George — *Boyden*
Zaslav, Debra M. — *Telford, Adams & Alexander/Telford & Co., Inc.*
Zavrel, Mark — *Source Services Corporation*
Zegel, Gary — *Source Services Corporation*
Zila, Laurie M. — *Princeton Entrepreneurial Resources*
Zimbal, Mark — *Source Services Corporation*
Zimont, Scott — *Source Services Corporation*
Zwell, Michael — *Zwell International*

5. General Management

Abbott, Peter D. — *The Abbott Group, Inc.*
Abell, Vincent W. — *MSI International*
Adler, Louis S. — *CJA - The Adler Group*
Akin, J.R. "Jack" — *J.R. Akin & Company Inc.*
Albertini, Nancy — *Taylor-Winfield, Inc.*
Allen, Don — *D.S. Allen Associates, Inc.*
Allen, Scott — *Chrisman & Company, Incorporated*
Allen, Wade H. — *Cendea Connection International*
Allen, William L. — *The Hindman Company*
Allerton, Donald T. — *Allerton Heneghan & O'Neill*
Allred, J. Michael — *Spencer Stuart*
Ambler, Peter W. — *Peter W. Ambler Company*
Anderson, Maria H. — *Barton Associates, Inc.*
Anderson, Richard — *Grant Cooper and Associates*
Andrews, J. Douglas — *Clarey & Andrews, Inc.*
Apostle, George — *Search Dynamics, Inc.*
Arnold, David W. — *Christian & Timbers*
Aronin, Michael — *Fisher-Todd Associates*
Arseneault, Daniel S. — *MSI International*
Ascher, Susan P. — *The Ascher Group*
Asquith, Peter S. — *Ames Personnel Consultants, Inc.*
Aston, Kathy — *Marra Peters & Partners*
Atkins, Laurie — *Battalia Winston International*
Attell, Harold — *A.E. Feldman Associates*
Austin Lockton, Kathy — *Juntunen-Combs-Poirier*
Axelrod, Nancy R. — *A.T. Kearney, Inc.*

Bacon, Cheri — *Gaffney Management Consultants*
Badger, Fred H. — *The Badger Group*
Baeder, Jeremy — *Executive Manning Corporation*
Baje, Sarah — *Innovative Search Group, LLC*
Baker, Gary M. — *Cochran, Cochran & Yale, Inc.*
Baker, Gerry — *A.T. Kearney, Inc.*
Balbone, Rich — *Executive Manning Corporation*
Baldwin, Keith R. — *The Baldwin Group*
Baltaglia, Michael — *Cochran, Cochran & Yale, Inc.*
Barbosa, Frank — *Skott/Edwards Consultants, Inc.*
Barbour, Mary Beth — *Tully/Woodmansee International, Inc.*
Barger, H. Carter — *Barger & Sargeant, Inc.*
Barlow, Ken H. — *The Cherbonnier Group, Inc.*
Barnes, Gary — *Brigade Inc.*
Barnes, Richard E. — *Barnes Development Group, LLC*
Barnes, Roanne L. — *Barnes Development Group, LLC*
Barnum, Toni M. — *Stone Murphy & Olson*
Barthold, James A. — *McNichol Associates*
Bartholdi, Ted — *Bartholdi & Company, Inc.*
Bartholdi, Theodore G. — *Bartholdi & Company, Inc.*
Barton, Gary R. — *Barton Associates, Inc.*
Bason, Maurice L. — *Bason Associates Inc.*
Bass, M. Lynn — *Ray & Berndtson*
Battalia, O. William — *Battalia Winston International*
Bearman, Linda — *Grant Cooper and Associates*
Beaudin, Elizabeth C. — *Callan Associates, Ltd.*
Beaver, Bentley H. — *The Onstott Group, Inc.*
Belin, Jean — *Boyden*
Bender, Alan — *Bender Executive Search*
Bennett, Jo — *Battalia Winston International*
Bennett, Joan — *Adams & Associates International*
Beran, Helena — *Michael J. Cavanagh and Associates*
Berkhemer-Credaire, Betsy — *Berkhemer Clayton Incorporated*
Berry, Harold B. — *The Hindman Company*
Bettick, Michael J. — *A.J. Burton Group, Inc.*
Biestek, Paul J. — *Paul J. Biestek Associates, Inc.*
Billington, William H. — *Spriggs & Company, Inc.*
Bishop, Susan — *Bishop Partners*
Blackmon, Sharon — *The Abbott Group, Inc.*
Blackshaw, Brian M. — *Blackshaw, Olmstead, Lynch & Koenig*
Blanton, Thomas — *Blanton and Company*
Blecker, Jay — *TSS Consulting, Ltd.*
Bliley, Jerry — *Spencer Stuart*
Bloch, Terry L. — *Southern Research Services*
Bloch, Thomas L. — *Southern Research Services*
Bloomer, James E. — *L.W. Foote Company*
Bluhm, Claudia — *Schweichler Associates, Inc.*
Boczany, William J. — *The Guild Corporation*
Boel, Werner — *The Dalley Hewitt Company*
Bogansky, Amy — *Conex Incorporated*
Bohn, Steve J. — *MSI International*
Boltrus, Dick — *Sink, Walker, Boltrus International*
Bond, Allan — *Walden Associates*
Bongiovanni, Vincent — *ESA Professional Consultants*
Borkin, Andrew — *Strategic Advancement Inc.*

Borland, James — *Goodrich & Sherwood Associates, Inc.*
Bormann, Cindy Ann — *MSI International*
Bostic, James E. — *Phillips Resource Group*
Bourrie, Sharon D. — *Chartwell Partners International, Inc.*
Bowden, Otis H. — *BowdenGlobal, Ltd.*
Bowen, Tad — *Executive Search International*
Boyd, Lew — *Coastal International Inc.*
Brackman, Janet — *Dahl-Morrow International*
Bradley, Dalena — *Woodworth International Group*
Bradshaw, Monte — *Christian & Timbers*
Brady, Dick — *William Guy & Associates*
Brandenburg, David — *Professional Staffing Consultants*
Bratches, Howard — *Thorndike Deland Associates*
Brennen, Richard J. — *Spencer Stuart*
Brieger, Steve — *Thorne, Brieger Associates Inc.*
Brooks, Bernard E. — *Mruk & Partners/EMA Partners Int'l*
Brother, Joy — *Charles Luntz & Associates. Inc.*
Brown, Larry C. — *Horton International*
Brown, Steffan — *Woodworth International Group*
Brudno, Robert J. — *Savoy Partners, Ltd.*
Bruno, Deborah F. — *The Hindman Company*
Brunson, Therese — *Kors Montgomery International*
Bryant, Shari G. — *Bryant Associates, Inc.*
Bryza, Robert M. — *Robert Lowell International*
Brzezinski, Ronald T. — *Callan Associates, Ltd.*
Buckles, Donna — *Cochran, Cochran & Yale, Inc.*
Budill, Edward — *Professional Search Consultants*
Bueschel, David A. — *Shepherd Bueschel & Provus, Inc.*
Buggy, Linda — *Bonnell Associates Ltd.*
Bullock, Conni — *Earley Kielty and Associates, Inc.*
Burchill, Greg — *BGB Associates*
Burden, Gene — *The Cherbonnier Group, Inc.*
Burfield, Elaine — *Skott/Edwards Consultants, Inc.*
Burke, John — *The Experts*
Burke, Karen A. — *Mazza & Riley, Inc. (a Korn/Ferry International affiliate)*
Burns, Alan — *The Enns Partners Inc.*
Busch, Jack — *Busch International*
Button, David R. — *The Button Group*
Cahill, Peter M. — *Peter M. Cahill Associates, Inc.*
Calivas, Kay — *A.J. Burton Group, Inc.*
Call, David — *Cochran, Cochran & Yale, Inc.*
Callan, Robert M. — *Callan Associates, Ltd.*
Calogeras, Chris — *The Sager Company*
Cameron, James W. — *Cameron Consulting*
Campbell, Patricia A. — *The Onstott Group, Inc.*
Campbell, Robert Scott — *Wellington Management Group*
Campbell, Robert Scott — *Wellington Management Group*
Capizzi, Karen — *Cochran, Cochran & Yale, Inc.*
Cappe, Richard R. — *Roberts Ryan and Bentley*
Carideo, Joseph — *Thorndike Deland Associates*
Carro, Carl R. — *Executive Search Consultants International, Inc.*
Caruthers, Robert D. — *James Mead & Company*
Cavanagh, Michael J. — *Michael J. Cavanagh and Associates*

Cavolina, Michael — *Carver Search Consultants*
Chappell, Peter — *The Bankers Group*
Chatterjie, Alok — *MSI International*
Chavous, C. Crawford — *Phillips Resource Group*
Cherbonnier, L. Michael — *TCG International, Inc.*
Cherbonnier, L. Michael — *The Cherbonnier Group, Inc.*
Chorman, Marilyn A. — *Hite Executive Search*
Christenson, H. Alan — *Christenson & Hutchison*
Christian, Jeffrey E. — *Christian & Timbers*
Christian, Philip — *Ray & Berndtson*
Christoff, Matthew J. — *Spencer Stuart*
Cimino, James J. — *Executive Search, Ltd.*
Cimino, Ron — *Paul-Tittle Associates, Inc.*
Cimino, Terry N. — *Executive Search, Ltd.*
Cizek, John T. — *Cizek Associates, Inc.*
Cizek, Marti J. — *Cizek Associates, Inc.*
Cizynski, Katherine W. — *James Mead & Company*
Clarey, Jack R. — *Clarey & Andrews, Inc.*
Clauhsen, Elizabeth A. — *Savoy Partners, Ltd.*
Clayton, Fred J. — *Berkhemer Clayton Incorporated*
Clough, Geoff — *Intech Summit Group, Inc.*
Cloutier, Gisella — *Dinte Resources, Inc.*
Cochran, Hale — *Fenwick Partners*
Cochran, Scott P. — *The Badger Group*
Coffman, Brian — *Kossuth & Associates, Inc.*
Cohen, Michael R. — *Intech Summit Group, Inc.*
Cohen, Robert C. — *Intech Summit Group, Inc.*
Coleman, J. Kevin — *J. Kevin Coleman & Associates, Inc.*
Colling, Douglas — *KPMG Management Consulting*
Collis, Gerald — *TSS Consulting, Ltd.*
Colvin, Teresa A. — *Jonas, Walters & Assoc., Inc.*
Compton, Tonya — *Dunhill Professional Search of Irvine, Inc.*
Cona, Joseph A. — *Cona Personnel Search*
Conard, Rodney J. — *Conard Associates, Inc.*
Connolly, Cathryn — *Strategic Associates, Inc.*
Conway, Maureen — *Conway & Associates*
Conway, William P. — *Phillips Resource Group*
Cook, Dennis — *A.T. Kearney, Inc.*
Cooke, Katherine H. — *Horton International*
Cornehlsen, James H. — *Skott/Edwards Consultants, Inc.*
Corrigan, Gerald F. — *The Corrigan Group*
Cortina Del Valle, Pedro — *Ray & Berndtson*
Costello, Lynda — *Coe & Company International Inc.*
Courtney, Brendan — *A.J. Burton Group, Inc.*
Cowell, Roy A. — *Cowell & Associates, Ltd.*
Coyle, Hugh F. — *A.J. Burton Group, Inc.*
Crane, Howard C. — *Chartwell Partners International, Inc.*
Crath, Paul F. — *Price Waterhouse*
Critchley, Walter — *Cochran, Cochran & Yale, Inc.*
Crowder, Edward W. — *Crowder & Company*
Crumpton, Marc — *Walden Associates*
Cruse, O.D. — *Spencer Stuart*
Cuddihy, Paul — *Dahl-Morrow International*
Cunningham, Lawrence — *Howard Fischer Associates, Inc.*

Cunningham, Robert Y. — *Goodrich & Sherwood Associates, Inc.*
Cunningham, Sheila — *Adams & Associates International*
Curci, Donald L. — *A.R.I. International*
Curtis, Ellissa — *Cochran, Cochran & Yale, Inc.*
Cyphers, Ralph R. — *Strategic Associates, Inc.*
Czamanske, Paul W. — *Compass Group Ltd.*
Daily, John C. — *Handy HRM Corp.*
Dalton, Bret — *Robert W. Dingman Company, Inc.*
Danforth, W. Michael — *Hyde Danforth Wold & Co.*
Daniel, Beverly — *Foy, Schneid & Daniel, Inc.*
Daniels, C. Eugene — *Sigma Group International*
Davis, Bert — *Bert Davis Executive Search, Inc.*
Davis, G. Gordon — *Davis & Company*
Davison, Patricia E. — *Lamalie Amrop International*
De Brun, Thomas P. — *Ray & Berndtson*
de Gury, Glenn — *Taylor-Winfield, Inc.*
Deaver, Henry C. — *Ray & Berndtson*
Delaney, Patrick J. — *Sensible Solutions, Inc.*
Delmonico, Laura — *A.J. Burton Group, Inc.*
DeLong, Art — *Richard Kader & Associates*
Desai, Sushila — *Sink, Walker, Boltrus International*
Desmond, Dennis — *Beall & Company, Inc.*
deWilde, David M. — *Chartwell Partners International, Inc.*
Dezember, Steve — *Ray & Berndtson*
DiCioccio, Carmen — *Cochran, Cochran & Yale, Inc.*
Dicker, Barry — *ESA Professional Consultants*
Dickson, Duke — *A.D. & Associates Executive Search, Inc.*
Dietz, David S. — *MSI International*
DiMarchi, Paul — *DiMarchi Partners, Inc.*
DiMarchi, Paul — *DiMarchi Partners, Inc.*
Dingeldey, Peter E. — *Search Advisors International Corp.*
Dingman, Bruce — *Robert W. Dingman Company, Inc.*
Dingman, Robert W. — *Robert W. Dingman Company, Inc.*
Dinte, Paul — *Dinte Resources, Inc.*
DiSalvo, Fred — *The Cambridge Group Ltd*
Divine, Robert S. — *O'Shea, Divine & Company, Inc.*
Doele, Donald C. — *Goodrich & Sherwood Associates, Inc.*
Donath, Linda — *Dahl-Morrow International*
Dotson, M. Ileen — *Dotson & Associates*
Dow, Lori — *Davidson, Laird & Associates, Inc.*
Dowdall, Jean — *A.T. Kearney, Inc.*
Dowell, Chris — *The Abbott Group, Inc.*
Dowell, Mary K. — *Professional Search Associates*
Doyle, James W. — *Executive Search Consultants International, Inc.*
Dreifus, Donald — *Search West, Inc.*
Drew, David R. — *Drew & Associates*
Drexler, Robert — *Robert Drexler Associates, Inc.*
Dromeshauser, Peter — *Dromeshauser Associates*
Drury, James J. — *Spencer Stuart*
Dubbs, William — *Williams Executive Search, Inc.*
Dubrow, Richard M. — *R/K International, Inc.*

Duckworth, Donald R. — *Johnson Smith & Knisely Accord*
Dugan, John H. — *J.H. Dugan and Associates, Inc.*
Duggan, James P. — *Slayton International, Inc./I-I-C Partners*
Duley, Richard I. — *ARJay & Associates*
Dunbar, Marilynne — *Ray & Berndtson/Lovas Stanley*
Dunman, Betsy L. — *Crawford & Crofford*
Durakis, Charles A. — *C.A. Durakis Associates, Inc.*
Ebeling, John A. — *Gilbert Tweed/INESA*
Edmond, Bruce — *Corporate Recruiters Ltd.*
Edwards, Dorothy — *MSI International*
Edwards, John W. — *The Bedford Group*
Edwards, Verba L. — *Wing Tips & Pumps, Inc.*
Eggena, Roger — *Phillips Resource Group*
Ehrgott, Elizabeth — *The Ascher Group*
Ehrhart, Jennifer — *ADOW's Executeam*
Elder, Tom — *Juntunen-Combs-Poirier*
Eldridge, Charles B. — *Ray & Berndtson*
Ellis, Ted K. — *The Hindman Company*
Ellis, William — *Interspace Interactive Inc.*
Elnaggar, Hani — *Juntunen-Combs-Poirier*
England, Mark — *Austin-McGregor International*
Enns, George — *The Enns Partners Inc.*
Erikson, Theodore J. — *Erikson Consulting Associates, Inc.*
Eustis, Lucy R. — *MSI International*
Evans, David — *Executive Manning Corporation*
Falk, John — *D.S. Allen Associates, Inc.*
Fancher, Robert L. — *Bason Associates Inc.*
Farley, Leon A. — *Leon A. Farley Associates*
Farrow, Jerry M. — *McCormack & Farrow*
Feldman, Abe — *A.E. Feldman Associates*
Ferneborg, Jay W. — *Ferneborg & Associates, Inc.*
Ferneborg, John R. — *Ferneborg & Associates, Inc.*
Feyder, Michael — *A.T. Kearney, Inc.*
Fincher, Richard P. — *Phase II Management*
Fini, Ron — *The Sager Company*
Fink, Neil J. — *Neil Fink Associates*
Fischer, Adam — *Howard Fischer Associates, Inc.*
Fischer, Howard M. — *Howard Fischer Associates, Inc.*
Fischer, John C. — *Horton International*
Fisher, Neal — *Fisher Personnel Management Services*
Fishler, Stu — *A.T. Kearney, Inc.*
Fitzgerald, Diane — *Fitzgerald Associates*
Fitzgerald, Geoffrey — *Fitzgerald Associates*
Flannery, Peter F. — *Jonas, Walters & Assoc., Inc.*
Fletcher, David — *A.J. Burton Group, Inc.*
Flood, Michael — *Norman Broadbent International, Inc.*
Flora, Dodi — *Crawford & Crofford*
Flynn, Erin — *Neil Fink Associates*
Fone, Carol — *Walden Associates*
Foote, Leland W. — *L.W. Foote Company*
Ford, Sandra D. — *The Ford Group, Inc.*
Foreman, David C. — *Koontz, Jeffries & Associates, Inc.*
Foster, Bonnie — *Kirkman & Searing, Inc.*
Foster, Dwight E. — *D.E. Foster Partners Inc.*
Fowler, Thomas A. — *The Hindman Company*
Francis, John — *Zwell International*

Frank, Valerie S. — *Norman Roberts & Associates, Inc.*
Frazier, John — *Cochran, Cochran & Yale, Inc.*
Fredericks, Ward A. — *Mixtec Group*
Freeman, Mark — *ESA Professional Consultants*
French, William G. — *Preng & Associates, Inc.*
Fribush, Richard — *A.J. Burton Group, Inc.*
Friedman, Helen E. — *McCormack & Farrow*
Furlong, James W. — *Furlong Search, Inc.*
Furlong, James W. — *Furlong Search, Inc.*
Furlong, James W. — *Furlong Search, Inc.*
Fust, Sheely F. — *Ray & Berndtson*
Gabel, Gregory N. — *Canny, Bowen Inc.*
Gabriel, David L. — *The Arcus Group*
Gaffney, Keith — *Gaffney Management Consultants*
Gaffney, William — *Gaffney Management Consultants*
Gaines, Jay — *Jay Gaines & Company, Inc.*
Galante, Suzanne M. — *Vlcek & Company, Inc.*
Galbraith, Deborah M. — *Stratford Group*
Gallagher, Terence M. — *Battalia Winston International*
Gantar, Donna — *Howard Fischer Associates, Inc.*
Gardiner, E. Nicholas P. — *Gardiner International*
Gares, Conrad — *TSS Consulting, Ltd.*
Garfinkle, Steven M. — *Battalia Winston International*
Garzone, Dolores — *M.A. Churchill & Associates, Inc.*
Gauthier, Robert C. — *Columbia Consulting Group*
Geiger, Jan — *Wilcox, Bertoux & Miller*
George, Delores F. — *Delores F. George Human Resource Management & Consulting Industry*
Gerbasi, Michael — *The Sager Company*
Germain, Valerie — *Jay Gaines & Company, Inc.*
Gerster, J.P. — *Juntunen-Combs-Poirier*
Gestwick, Daniel — *Cochran, Cochran & Yale, Inc.*
Gettys, James R. — *International Staffing Consultants, Inc.*
Ghurani, Mac — *Gary Kaplan & Associates*
Gibbs, John S. — *Spencer Stuart*
Gilbert, Jerry — *Gilbert & Van Campen International*
Gilchrist, Robert J. — *Horton International*
Gill, Patricia — *Columbia Consulting Group*
Gilmore, Connie — *Taylor-Winfield, Inc.*
Gilreath, James M. — *Gilreath Weatherby, Inc.*
Gladstone, Martin J. — *MSI International*
Gloss, Frederick C. — *F. Gloss International*
Gobert, Larry — *Professional Search Consultants*
Gold, Stacey — *Earley Kielty and Associates, Inc.*
Golde, Lisa — *Tully/Woodmansee International, Inc.*
Goldenberg, Susan — *Grant Cooper and Associates*
Goldsmith, Fred J. — *Fred J. Goldsmith Associates*
Gomez, Cristina — *Juntunen-Combs-Poirier*
Gonzalez, Kristen — *A.J. Burton Group, Inc.*
Goodman, Dawn M. — *Bason Associates Inc.*
Goodman, Victor — *Anderson Sterling Associates*
Goodwin, Tim — *William Guy & Associates*
Gordon, Gerald L. — *E.G. Jones Associates, Ltd.*
Gostyla, Rick — *Spencer Stuart*
Grant, Michael — *Zwell International*

Grantham, John — *Grantham & Co., Inc.*
Grasch, Jerry E. — *The Hindman Company*
Grebenstein, Charles R. — *Skott/Edwards Consultants, Inc.*
Green, Jane — *Phillips Resource Group*
Green, Marc — *TSS Consulting, Ltd.*
Griffin, Cathy — *A.T. Kearney, Inc.*
Groover, David — *MSI International*
Grotte, Lawrence C. — *Lautz Grotte Engler*
Guy, C. William — *William Guy & Associates*
Haas, Margaret P. — *The Haas Associates, Inc.*
Hailey, H.M. — *Damon & Associates, Inc.*
Halbrich, Mitch — *A.J. Burton Group, Inc.*
Hall, Peter V. — *Chartwell Partners International, Inc.*
Hallock, Peter B. — *Goodrich & Sherwood Associates, Inc.*
Hamburg, Jennifer Power — *Ledbetter/Davidson International, Inc.*
Hamilton, John R. — *Ray & Berndtson*
Hanes, Leah — *Ray & Berndtson*
Hanley, Alan P. — *Williams, Roth & Krueger Inc.*
Hanley, J. Patrick — *Canny, Bowen Inc.*
Hanley, Maureen E. — *Gilbert Tweed/INESA*
Hansen, David G. — *Ott & Hansen, Inc.*
Hanson, Grant M. — *Goodrich & Sherwood Associates, Inc.*
Harbaugh, Paul J. — *International Management Advisors, Inc.*
Harbert, David O. — *Sweeney Harbert & Mummert, Inc.*
Hardison, Richard L. — *Hardison & Company*
Harelick, Arthur S. — *Ashway, Ltd.*
Harkins, Robert E. — *Robert Harkins Associates, Inc.*
Harney, Elyane — *Gary Kaplan & Associates*
Harris, Jack — *A.T. Kearney, Inc.*
Harris, Joe W. — *Cendea Connection International*
Harris, Seth O. — *Christian & Timbers*
Harrison, Priscilla — *Phillips Resource Group*
Hart, Robert T. — *D.E. Foster Partners Inc.*
Harvey, Mike — *Advanced Executive Resources*
Haughton, Michael — *DeFrain, Mayer LLC*
Hauswirth, Jeffrey M. — *Spencer Stuart*
Havener, Donald Clarke — *The Abbott Group, Inc.*
Hawksworth, A. Dwight — *A.D. & Associates Executive Search, Inc.*
Haystead, Steve — *Advanced Executive Resources*
Heacock, Burt E. — *Paul-Tittle Associates, Inc.*
Hechkoff, Robert B. — *Quantex Associates, Inc.*
Heffelfinger, Thomas V. — *Heffelfinger Associates, Inc.*
Heiken, Barbara E. — *Randell-Heiken, Inc.*
Heinze, David — *Heinze & Associates, Inc.*
Helminiak, Audrey — *Gaffney Management Consultants*
Henard, John B. — *Lamalie Amrop International*
Heneghan, Donald A. — *Allerton Heneghan & O'Neill*
Henry, Mary — *Conex Incorporated*
Henshaw, Bob — *F-O-R-T-U-N-E Personnel Consultants of Huntsville, Inc.*
Hensley, Bert — *Morgan Samuels Co., Inc.*
Hergenrather, Richard A. — *Hergenrather & Company*

Herman, Eugene J. — *Earley Kielty and Associates, Inc.*
Herman, Shelli — *Gary Kaplan & Associates*
Hertlein, James N.J. — *Boyden/Zay & Company*
Hewitt, Rives D. — *The Dalley Hewitt Company*
Hewitt, W. Davis — *The Dalley Hewitt Company*
Hicks, Albert M. — *Phillips Resource Group*
Higgins, Donna — *Howard Fischer Associates, Inc.*
Hildebrand, Thomas B. — *Professional Resources Group, Inc.*
Hill, Emery — *MSI International*
Hillen, Skip — *The McCormick Group, Inc.*
Himes, Dirk — *A.T. Kearney, Inc.*
Himlin, Amy — *Cochran, Cochran & Yale, Inc.*
Hindman, Neil C. — *The Hindman Company*
Hochberg, Brian — *M.A. Churchill & Associates, Inc.*
Hockett, William — *Hockett Associates, Inc.*
Hokanson, Mark D. — *Crowder & Company*
Holden, Richard B. — *Ames Personnel Consultants, Inc.*
Holland, John A. — *Holland, McFadzean & Associates, Inc.*
Holland, Rose Mary — *Price Waterhouse*
Hollins, Howard D. — *MSI International*
Holmes, Lawrence J. — *Columbia Consulting Group*
Holodnak, William A. — *J. Robert Scott*
Holt, Carol — *Bartholdi & Company, Inc.*
Hoover, Catherine — *J.L. Mark Associates, Inc.*
Hopgood, Earl — *JDG Associates, Ltd.*
Hopkins, Chester A. — *Handy HRM Corp.*
Horton, Robert H. — *Horton International*
Houchins, William M. — *Christian & Timbers*
Hoyda, Louis A. — *Thorndike Deland Associates*
Hucko, Donald S. — *Jonas, Walters & Assoc., Inc.*
Hudson, Reginald M. — *Search Bureau International*
Huff, William Z. — *Huff Associates*
Hughes, Cathy N. — *The Ogdon Partnership*
Hughes, Donald J. — *Hughes & Company*
Hughes, James J. — *R.P. Barone Associates*
Hunsaker, Floyd — *Woodworth International Group*
Hunter, Gabe — *Phillips Resource Group*
Hutchison, Richard H. — *Rurak & Associates, Inc.*
Hutchison, William K. — *Christenson & Hutchison*
Hutton, Thomas J. — *The Thomas Tucker Company*
Hybels, Cynthia — *A.J. Burton Group, Inc.*
Hykes, Don A. — *A.T. Kearney, Inc.*
Imely, Larry S. — *Stratford Group*
Inguagiato, Gregory — *MSI International*
Inzinna, Dennis — *AlternaStaff*
Issacs, Judith A. — *Grant Cooper and Associates*
Jackson, Joan — *A.T. Kearney, Inc.*
Jacobs, Martin J. — *The Rubicon Group*
Jacobs, Mike — *Thorne, Brieger Associates Inc.*
Jacobson, Carolyn — *The Abbott Group, Inc.*
Jacobson, Rick — *The Windham Group*
Jaffe, Mark — *Wyatt & Jaffe*
James, Bruce — *Roberson and Company*
Janssen, Don — *Howard Fischer Associates, Inc.*
Januale, Lois — *Cochran, Cochran & Yale, Inc.*

Jaworski, Mary A. — *Tully/Woodmansee International, Inc.*
Jazylo, John V. — *Handy HRM Corp.*
Jeffers, Richard B. — *Dieckmann & Associates, Ltd.*
Joffe, Barry — *Bason Associates Inc.*
Johnson, Brian — *A.J. Burton Group, Inc.*
Johnson, David A. — *Gaffney Management Consultants*
Johnson, Douglas — *Quality Search*
Johnson, John W. — *Webb, Johnson Associates, Inc.*
Johnson, Julie M. — *International Staffing Consultants, Inc.*
Johnson, Kathleen A. — *Barton Associates, Inc.*
Johnson, LaDonna — *Gans, Gans & Associates*
Johnson, Robert J. — *Quality Search*
Johnson, Rocky — *A.T. Kearney, Inc.*
Johnson, Stanley C. — *Johnson & Company*
Johnson, Valerie — *Coe & Company International Inc.*
Johnston, Michael — *Robertson-Surrette Executive Search*
Jones, Amy E. — *The Corporate Connection, Ltd.*
Jones, Francis E. — *Earley Kielty and Associates, Inc.*
Jones, Gary — *BGB Associates*
Jones, Ronald T. — *ARJay & Associates*
Jordan, Jon — *Cochran, Cochran & Yale, Inc.*
Joyce, William J. — *The Guild Corporation*
Judge, Alfred L. — *The Cambridge Group Ltd*
Juelis, John J. — *Peeney Associates*
Juska, Frank — *Rusher, Loscavio & LoPresto*
Kaiser, Donald J. — *Dunhill International Search of New Haven*
Kane, Frank — *A.J. Burton Group, Inc.*
Kane, Karen — *Howard Fischer Associates, Inc.*
Kanrich, Susan Azaria — *AlternaStaff*
Kaplan, Gary — *Gary Kaplan & Associates*
Kartin, Martin C. — *Martin Kartin and Company, Inc.*
Keating, Pierson — *Nordeman Grimm, Inc.*
Keitel, Robert S. — *A.T. Kearney, Inc.*
Keller, Barbara E. — *Barton Associates, Inc.*
Kells, John — *Heffelfinger Associates, Inc.*
Kelly, Elizabeth Ann — *Wellington Management Group*
Kelly, Sheri — *Strategic Associates, Inc.*
Kelly, Susan D. — *S.D. Kelly & Associates, Inc.*
Kelso, Patricia C. — *Barton Associates, Inc.*
Kent, Melvin — *Melvin Kent & Associates, Inc.*
Kenzer, Robert D. — *Kenzer Corp.*
Kern, Jerry L. — *ADOW's Executeam*
Kern, Kathleen G. — *ADOW's Executeam*
Kershaw, Lisa — *Tanton Mitchell/Paul Ray Berndtson*
Keshishian, Gregory — *Handy HRM Corp.*
Keyser, Anne — *A.T. Kearney, Inc.*
Kielty, John L. — *Earley Kielty and Associates, Inc.*
King, Bill — *The McCormick Group, Inc.*
King, Margaret — *Christian & Timbers*
King, Steven — *Ashway, Ltd.*
Kinser, Richard E. — *Richard Kinser & Associates*
Kip, Luanne S. — *Kip Williams, Inc.*
Kirkman, J. Michael — *Kirkman & Searing, Inc.*
Kishbaugh, Herbert S. — *Kishbaugh Associates International*

Klages, Constance W. — *International Management Advisors, Inc.*
Klauck, James J. — *Horton International*
Klavens, Cecile J. — *The Pickwick Group, Inc.*
Klein, Brandon — *A.J. Burton Group, Inc.*
Klein, Gary — *A.T. Kearney, Inc.*
Klein, Mary Jo — *Cochran, Cochran & Yale, Inc.*
Klein, Mel — *Stewart/Laurence Associates*
Klopfenstein, Edward L. — *Crowder & Company*
Knotts, Jerry — *Mixtec Group*
Koenig, Joel S. — *Blackshaw, Olmstead, Lynch & Koenig*
Koenig, Joel S. — *Blackshaw, Olmstead, Lynch & Koenig*
Kohn, Adam P. — *Christian & Timbers*
Kohonoski, Michael M. — *The Guild Corporation*
Kondra, Vernon J. — *The Douglas Reiter Company, Inc.*
Koontz, Donald N. — *Koontz, Jeffries & Associates, Inc.*
Kors, R. Paul — *Kors Montgomery International*
Kossuth, David — *Kossuth & Associates, Inc.*
Kossuth, Jane — *Kossuth & Associates, Inc.*
Kotick, Maddy — *The Stevenson Group of New Jersey*
Krejci, Stanley L. — *Boyden Washington, D.C.*
Kreutz, Gary L. — *Kreutz Consulting Group, Inc.*
Krieger, Dennis F. — *Seiden Krieger Associates, Inc.*
Krueger, Kurt — *Krueger Associates*
Kunzer, William J. — *Kunzer Associates, Ltd.*
Kurrigan, Geoffrey — *ESA Professional Consultants*
Kussner, Janice N. — *Herman Smith Executive Initiatives Inc.*
Laba, Marvin — *Marvin Laba & Associates*
Laba, Stuart M. — *Marvin Laba & Associates*
Labrecque, Bernard F. — *Laurendeau Labrecque/Ray & Berndtson, Inc.*
LaCharite, Danielle — *The Guild Corporation*
Lache, Shawn E. — *The Arcus Group*
Lang, Sharon A. — *Ray & Berndtson*
Langford, Robert W. — *F-O-R-T-U-N-E Personnel Consultants of Huntsville, Inc.*
Lardner, Lucy D. — *Tully/Woodmansee International, Inc.*
Larsen, Jack B. — *Jack B. Larsen & Associates*
Lasher, Charles M. — *Lasher Associates*
Lauderback, David R. — *A.T. Kearney, Inc.*
Lautz, Lindsay A. — *Lautz Grotte Engler*
Lawner, Harvey — *Walden Associates*
Ledbetter, Charlene — *Ledbetter/Davidson International, Inc.*
Ledbetter, Steven G. — *Cendea Connection International*
Leininger, Dennis — *Key Employment Services*
Leland, Paul — *McInturff & Associates, Inc.*
Lence, Julie Anne — *MSI International*
Lenkaitis, Lewis F. — *A.T. Kearney, Inc.*
Levitt, Muriel A. — *D.S. Allen Associates, Inc.*
Lewicki, Christopher — *MSI International*
Lewis, Jon A. — *Sandhurst Associates*
Lezama Cohen, Luis — *Ray & Berndtson*
Lindberg, Eric J. — *MSI International*
Lindenmuth, Mary — *Search West, Inc.*
Linton, Leonard M. — *Byron Leonard International, Inc.*

Lipe, Jerold L. — *Compass Group Ltd.*
Lipson, Harriet — *First Interactive Recruiting Specialists*
Lipson, Harriet — *Lipson & Co.*
Lipson, Howard K. — *First Interactive Recruiting Specialists*
Lipson, Howard R. — *Lipson & Co.*
Loeb, Stephen H. — *Grant Cooper and Associates*
Lokken, Karen — *A.E. Feldman Associates*
Long, Helga — *Horton International*
Long, John P. — *John J. Davis & Associates, Inc.*
Long, Milt — *William Guy & Associates*
Long, William G. — *McDonald, Long & Associates, Inc.*
Looney, Scott — *A.E. Feldman Associates*
LoPresto, Robert L. — *Rusher, Loscavio & LoPresto*
Lotufo, Donald A. — *D.A.L. Associates, Inc.*
Lotz, R. James — *International Management Advisors, Inc.*
Lovas, W. Carl — *Ray & Berndtson/Lovas Stanley*
Lovely, Edward — *The Stevenson Group of New Jersey*
Lucarelli, Joan — *The Onstott Group, Inc.*
Lucas, Ronnie L. — *MSI International*
Lucht, John — *The John Lucht Consultancy Inc.*
Lumsby, George N. — *International Management Advisors, Inc.*
Luntz, Charles E. — *Charles Luntz & Associates. Inc.*
Lupica, Anthony — *Cochran, Cochran & Yale, Inc.*
Lyon, Jenny — *Marra Peters & Partners*
Lyons, J. David — *Aubin International Inc.*
Macdonald, G. William — *The Macdonald Group, Inc.*
MacEachern, David — *Spencer Stuart*
Mackenna, Kathy — *Plummer & Associates, Inc.*
Mader, Stephen P. — *Christian & Timbers*
Maglio, Charles J. — *Maglio and Company, Inc.*
Major, Susan — *A.T. Kearney, Inc.*
Mallin, Ellen — *Howard Fischer Associates, Inc.*
Manassero, Henri J.P. — *International Management Advisors, Inc.*
Mangum, Maria — *Thomas Mangum Company*
Mangum, William T. — *Thomas Mangum Company*
Manns, Alex — *Crawford & Crofford*
Mansford, Keith — *Howard Fischer Associates, Inc.*
Maphet, Harriet — *The Stevenson Group of New Jersey*
Marcine, John W. — *Keith Bagg & Associates Inc.*
Marino, Chester — *Cochran, Cochran & Yale, Inc.*
Marion, Michael — *S.D. Kelly & Associates, Inc.*
Mark, John L. — *J.L. Mark Associates, Inc.*
Mark, Lynne — *J.L. Mark Associates, Inc.*
Marks, Ira — *Strategic Alternatives*
Marks, Russell E. — *Webb, Johnson Associates, Inc.*
Marlow, William — *Straube Associates*
Marra, John — *Marra Peters & Partners*
Marra, John — *Marra Peters & Partners*
Martin, David — *The Guild Corporation*
Martin, Lois G. — *The Martin Group*
Martin, Timothy P. — *The Martin Group*

Marumoto, William H. — *Boyden Washington, D.C.*
Massey, R. Bruce — *Horton International*
Mather, David R. — *Christian & Timbers*
Mathias, Kathy — *Stone Murphy & Olson*
Matthews, Corwin — *Woodworth International Group*
May, Peter — *Mixtec Group*
Maynard Taylor, Susan — *Chrisman & Company, Incorporated*
Mazor, Elly — *Howard Fischer Associates, Inc.*
Mazza, David B. — *Mazza & Riley, Inc. (a Korn/Ferry International affiliate)*
McBride, Dee — *Deeco International*
McBride, Jonathan E. — *McBride Associates, Inc.*
McCloskey, Frank D. — *Johnson Smith & Knisely Accord*
McComas, Kelly E. — *The Guild Corporation*
McCormick, Brian — *The McCormick Group, Inc.*
McCormick, William J. — *The McCormick Group, Inc.*
McCreary, Charles "Chip" — *Austin-McGregor International*
McDermott, Jeffrey T. — *Vlcek & Company, Inc.*
McDonald, John R. — *TSS Consulting, Ltd.*
McDonald, Scott A. — *McDonald Associates International*
McDonald, Stanleigh B. — *McDonald Associates International*
McDonnell, Julie — *Technical Personnel of Minnesota*
McDowell, Robert N. — *Christenson & Hutchison*
McFadden, Ashton S. — *Johnson Smith & Knisely Accord*
McFadzen, Donna — *Holland, McFadzean & Associates, Inc.*
McFadzen, James A. — *Holland, McFadzean & Associates, Inc.*
McGuire, J. Corey — *Peter W. Ambler Company*
McGuire, Pat — *A.J. Burton Group, Inc.*
McInturff, Robert — *McInturff & Associates, Inc.*
McIntyre, Joel — *Phillips Resource Group*
McKeown, Morgan J. — *Christian & Timbers*
McKeown, Patricia A. — *DiMarchi Partners, Inc.*
McManners, Donald E. — *McManners Associates, Inc.*
McMillin, Bob — *Price Waterhouse*
McNamara, Catherine — *Ray & Berndtson*
McNichol, John — *McNichol Associates*
McNichols, Walter B. — *Gary Kaplan & Associates*
McSherry, James F. — *Battalia Winston International*
McThrall, David — *TSS Consulting, Ltd.*
Mead, James D. — *James Mead & Company*
Meadows, C. David — *Professional Staffing Consultants*
Meyer, Stacey — *Gary Kaplan & Associates*
Mikula, Linda — *Schweichler Associates, Inc.*
Miles, Kenneth T. — *MSI International*
Miller, David — *Cochran, Cochran & Yale, Inc.*
Miller, Roy — *The Enns Partners Inc.*
Miller, Russel E. — *ARJay & Associates*
Milstein, Bonnie — *Marvin Laba & Associates*
Misiurewicz, Marc — *Cochran, Cochran & Yale, Inc.*
Mitchell, Jeff — *A.J. Burton Group, Inc.*

Randell, James E. — *Randell-Heiken, Inc.*
Ray, Marianne C. — *Callan Associates, Ltd.*
Raymond, Anne — *Anderson Sterling Associates*
Reddick, David C. — *Horton International*
Redding, Denise — *The Douglas Reiter Company, Inc.*
Reece, Christopher S. — *Reece & Mruk Partners*
Reifel, Laurie — *Reifel & Assocaites*
Reiser, Ellen — *Thorndike Deland Associates*
Reisinger, George L. — *Sigma Group International*
Reiter, Douglas — *The Douglas Reiter Company, Inc.*
Remillard, Brad M. — *CJA - The Adler Group*
Reyman, Susan — *S. Reyman & Associates Ltd.*
Reynolds, Gregory P. — *Roberts Ryan and Bentley*
Rhodes, Bill — *Bench International*
Ribeiro, Claudia — *Ledbetter/Davidson International, Inc.*
Rice, Marie — *Jay Gaines & Company, Inc.*
Rice, Raymond D. — *Logue & Rice Inc.*
Richards, Paul E. — *Executive Directions*
Richards, R. Glenn — *Executive Directions*
Rieger, Louis J. — *Spencer Stuart*
Rimmel, James E. — *The Hindman Company*
Rimmele, Michael — *The Bankers Group*
Rizzo, L. Donald — *R.P. Barone Associates*
Roberts, Mitch — *A.E. Feldman Associates*
Roberts, Nick P. — *Spectrum Search Associates, Inc.*
Roberts, Norman C. — *Norman Roberts & Associates, Inc.*
Roberts, Scott — *Jonas, Walters & Assoc., Inc.*
Robertson, John A. — *Kaye-Bassman International Corp.*
Robertson, Ronald — *Robertson-Surrette Executive Search*
Robins, Jeri N. — *Nagler, Robins & Poe, Inc.*
Robinson, Bruce — *Bruce Robinson Associates*
Robles Cuellar, Paulina — *Ray & Berndtson*
Roblin, Nancy R. — *Paul-Tittle Associates, Inc.*
Rogers, Leah — *Dinte Resources, Inc.*
Rojo, Rafael — *A.T. Kearney, Inc.*
Romanello, Daniel P. — *Spencer Stuart*
Romang, Paula — *Agri-Tech Personnel, Inc.*
Rose, Robert — *ESA Professional Consultants*
Ross, Curt A. — *Ray & Berndtson*
Ross, H. Lawrence — *Ross & Company*
Ross, Lawrence — *Ray & Berndtson/Lovas Stanley*
Ross, Mark — *Ray & Berndtson/Lovas Stanley*
Ross, William J. — *Flowers & Associates*
Rotella, Marshall W. — *The Corporate Connection, Ltd.*
Roth, Robert J. — *Williams, Roth & Krueger Inc.*
Rowe, William D. — *D.E. Foster Partners Inc.*
Rudolph, Kenneth — *Kossuth & Associates, Inc.*
Rudzinsky, Howard — *Louis Rudzinsky Associates*
Rurak, Zbigniew T. — *Rurak & Associates, Inc.*
Rush, Michael E. — *D.A.L. Associates, Inc.*
Russell, Sam — *The Guild Corporation*
Sacerdote, John — *Raymond Karsan Associates*
Safnuk, Donald — *Corporate Recruiters Ltd.*
Sallows, Jill S. — *Crowe, Chizek and Company, LLP*
Salottolo, Al — *Tactical Alternatives*
Salvagno, Michael J. — *The Cambridge Group Ltd*
Sangster, Jeffrey — *F-O-R-T-U-N-E Personnel Consultants of Manatee County*

Sanow, Robert — *Cochran, Cochran & Yale, Inc.*
Sarna, Edmund A. — *Jonas, Walters & Assoc., Inc.*
Savvas, Carol Diane — *Ledbetter/Davidson International, Inc.*
Sawyer, Patricia L. — *Smith & Sawyer Inc.*
Saxon, Alexa — *Woodworth International Group*
Schaefer, Frederic M. — *A.T. Kearney, Inc.*
Schedra, Sharon — *Earley Kielty and Associates, Inc.*
Schene, Philip — *A.E. Feldman Associates*
Schiavone, Mary Rose — *Canny, Bowen Inc.*
Schlpma, Christine — *Advanced Executive Resources*
Schmidt, Peter R. — *Boyden*
Schmidt, William C. — *Christian & Timbers*
Schneiderman, Gerald — *Management Resource Associates, Inc.*
Schwam, Carol — *A.E. Feldman Associates*
Schweichler, Lee J. — *Schweichler Associates, Inc.*
Scott, Evan — *Howard Fischer Associates, Inc.*
Scott, Gordon S. — *Search Advisors International Corp.*
Scranton, Lisa — *A.J. Burton Group, Inc.*
Searing, James M. — *Kirkman & Searing, Inc.*
Seiden, Steven A. — *Seiden Krieger Associates, Inc.*
Semyan, John K. — *TNS Partners, Inc.*
Sevilla, Claudio A. — *Crawford & Crofford*
Shamir, Ben — *S.D. Kelly & Associates, Inc.*
Sheedy, Edward J. — *Dieckmann & Associates, Ltd.*
Shenfield, Peter — *A.T. Kearney, Inc.*
Shepard, Michael J. — *MSI International*
Shepherd, Daniel M. — *Shepherd Bueschel & Provus, Inc.*
Sherwood, Andrew — *Goodrich & Sherwood Associates, Inc.*
Shimp, David J. — *Lamalie Amrop International*
Shore, Earl L. — *E.L. Shore & Associates Ltd.*
Shufelt, Doug — *Sink, Walker, Boltrus International*
Siciliano, Gene — *Western Management Associates*
Siegler, Jody Cukiir — *A.T. Kearney, Inc.*
Siegrist, Jeffrey M. — *D.E. Foster Partners Inc.*
Siker, Paul W. — *The Guild Corporation*
Silcott, Marvin L. — *Marvin L. Silcott & Associates, Inc.*
Sill, Igor M. — *Geneva Group International*
Silvas, Stephen D. — *Roberson and Company*
Silver, Lee — *L. A. Silver Associates, Inc.*
Simmons, Gerald J. — *Handy HRM Corp.*
Simmons, Sandra K. — *MSI International*
Simpson, Scott — *Cendea Connection International*
Sindler, Jay — *A.J. Burton Group, Inc.*
Sink, Cliff — *Sink, Walker, Boltrus International*
Sitarski, Stan — *Howard Fischer Associates, Inc.*
Skalet, Ira — *A.E. Feldman Associates*
Skunda, Donna M. — *Allerton Heneghan & O'Neill*
Slayton, Richard C. — *Slayton International, Inc./I-I-C Partners*
Slosar, John — *Boyden*
Smead, Michelle M. — *A.T. Kearney, Inc.*
Smith, Ana Luz — *Smith Search, S.C.*

Smith, David P. — *HRS, Inc.*
Smith, Grant — *Price Waterhouse*
Smith, Herman M. — *Herman Smith Executive Initiatives Inc.*
Smith, Ian — *International Staffing Consultants, Inc.*
Smith, John E. — *Smith Search, S.C.*
Smith, Lydia — *The Corporate Connection, Ltd.*
Smith, Matt D. — *Ray & Berndtson*
Smith, Robert L. — *Smith & Sawyer Inc.*
Smith, Ronald V. — *Coe & Company International Inc.*
Smith, Timothy C. — *Christian & Timbers*
Snyder, C. Edward — *Horton International*
Snyder, James F. — *Snyder & Company*
Sola, George L. — *A.T. Kearney, Inc.*
Solters, Jeanne — *The Guild Corporation*
Souder, E.G. — *Souder & Associates*
Sowerbutt, Richard S. — *Hite Executive Search*
Spann, Richard E. — *Goodrich & Sherwood Associates, Inc.*
Spanninger, Mark J. — *The Guild Corporation*
Spera, Stefanie — *A.T. Kearney, Inc.*
Spiegel, Gayle — *L. A. Silver Associates, Inc.*
Spriggs, Robert D. — *Spriggs & Company, Inc.*
St. Clair, Alan — *TNS Partners, Inc.*
Stanley, Paul R.A. — *Ray & Berndtson/Lovas Stanley*
Stanton, John — *A.T. Kearney, Inc.*
Stark, Jeff — *Thorne, Brieger Associates Inc.*
Statson, Dale E. — *Sales Executives Inc.*
Steele, Daniel — *Cochran, Cochran & Yale, Inc.*
Stein, Terry W. — *Stewart, Stein and Scott, Ltd.*
Steinem, Andy — *Dahl-Morrow International*
Steinem, Barbra — *Dahl-Morrow International*
Steinman, Stephen M. — *The Stevenson Group of New Jersey*
Sterling, Jay — *Earley Kielty and Associates, Inc.*
Stevens, Craig M. — *Kirkman & Searing, Inc.*
Stevens, Ken — *The Stevens Group*
Stevenson, Jane — *Howard Fischer Associates, Inc.*
Stevenson, Terry — *Bartholdi & Company, Inc.*
Stewart, Jeffrey O. — *Stewart, Stein and Scott, Ltd.*
Stewart, Ross M. — *Human Resources Network Partners Inc.*
Stiles, Judy — *MedQuest Associates*
Stokes, John — *Nordeman Grimm, Inc.*
Stranberg, James R. — *Callan Associates, Ltd.*
Stratmeyer, Karin Bergwall — *Princeton Entrepreneurial Resources*
Stratton, Cary — *Coastal International Inc.*
Strickland, Katie — *Grantham & Co., Inc.*
Stringer, Dann P. — *D.E. Foster Partners Inc.*
Strom, Mark N. — *Search Advisors International Corp.*
Sturtz, James W. — *Compass Group Ltd.*
Sullivan, Kay — *Rusher, Loscavio & LoPresto*
Summerfield-Beall, Dotty — *Summerfield Associates, Inc.*
Sur, William K. — *Canny, Bowen Inc.*
Surrette, Mark — *Robertson-Surrette Executive Search*
Sussman, Lynda — *Gilbert Tweed/INESA*
Swanson, Dick — *Raymond Karsan Associates*
Swartz, William K. — *Swartz Executive Search*

Sweeney, James W. — *Sweeney Harbert & Mummert, Inc.*
Swick, Jan — *TSS Consulting, Ltd.*
Swoboda, Lawrence — *A.J. Burton Group, Inc.*
Taft, Steven D. — *The Guild Corporation*
Taylor, Conrad G. — *MSI International*
Taylor, James M. — *The HRM Group, Inc.*
Taylor, R.L. (Larry) — *Ray & Berndtson*
Telford, John H. — *Telford, Adams & Alexander/Telford & Co., Inc.*
ten Cate, Herman H. — *Stoneham Associates Corp.*
Tetrick, Tim — *O'Connor, O'Connor, Lordi, Ltd.*
Theobald, David B. — *Theobald & Associates*
Thies, Gary — *S.D. Kelly & Associates, Inc.*
Thomas, Donald — *Mixtec Group*
Thomas, Ian A. — *International Staffing Consultants, Inc.*
Thomas, Kurt J. — *P.J. Murphy & Associates, Inc.*
Thomas, Terry — *The Thomas Resource Group*
Thomas, William — *Mixtec Group*
Thompson, Dave — *Battalia Winston International*
Thompson, Kenneth L. — *McCormack & Farrow*
Thrapp, Mark C. — *Executive Search Consultants International, Inc.*
Timoney, Laura — *Bishop Partners*
Tincu, John C. — *Ferneborg & Associates, Inc.*
Tipp, George D. — *Intech Summit Group, Inc.*
Tittle, David M. — *Paul-Tittle Associates, Inc.*
Tootsey, Mark A. — *A.J. Burton Group, Inc.*
Topliff, Marla — *Gaffney Management Consultants*
Truitt, Thomas B. — *Southwestern Professional Services*
Tryon, Katey — *DeFrain, Mayer LLC*
Tucker, Thomas A. — *The Thomas Tucker Company*
Tully, Margo L. — *Tully/Woodmansee International, Inc.*
Tunney, William — *Grant Cooper and Associates*
Turner, Edward K. — *Don Richard Associates of Charlotte*
Turner, Kimberly — *Barton Associates, Inc.*
Tursi, Deborah J. — *The Corporate Connection, Ltd.*
Tweed, Janet — *Gilbert Tweed/INESA*
Ulbert, Nancy — *Aureus Group*
Ulrich, Mary Ann — *D.S. Allen Associates, Inc.*
Utroska, Donald R. — *Lamalie Amrop International*
Vachon, David A. — *McNichol Associates*
Vairo, Leonard A. — *Christian & Timbers*
Valenta, Joseph — *Princeton Entrepreneurial Resources*
Van Biesen, Jacques A.H. — *Search Group Inc.*
Van Campen, Jerry — *Gilbert & Van Campen International*
Van Clieaf, Mark — *MVC Associates International*
Van Nostrand, Mara J. — *Barton Associates, Inc.*
Vann, Dianne — *The Button Group*
Vaughan, David B. — *Dunhill Professional Search of Irvine, Inc.*
Velten, Mark T. — *Boyden*
Venable, William W. — *Thorndike Deland Associates*
Vennat, Manon — *Spencer Stuart*
Vernon, Peter C. — *Horton International*

Visnich, L. Christine — *Bason Associates Inc.*
Vlcek, Thomas J. — *Vlcek & Company, Inc.*
Volkman, Arthur — *Cochran, Cochran & Yale, Inc.*
von Baillou, Astrid — *Richard Kinser & Associates*
Vossler, James — *A.J. Burton Group, Inc.*
Vourakis, Zan — *ZanExec LLC*
Vroom, Cynthia D. — *Cyntal International Ltd*
Wacholz, Rick — *A.T. Kearney, Inc.*
Waldoch, D. Mark — *Barnes Development Group, LLC*
Waldrop, Gary R. — *MSI International*
Walker, Craig H. — *A.J. Burton Group, Inc.*
Walker, Douglas G. — *Sink, Walker, Boltrus International*
Walker, Ewing J. — *Ward Howell International, Inc.*
Walsh, Denis — *Professional Staffing Consultants*
Walsh, Kenneth A. — *R/K International, Inc.*
Walters, William F. — *Jonas, Walters & Assoc., Inc.*
Ward, Madeleine — *LTM Associates*
Ware, John C. — *Spencer Stuart*
Warter, Mark — *Isaacson, Miller*
Wasserman, Harvey — *Churchill and Affiliates, Inc.*
Watkinson, Jim W. — *The Badger Group*
Watson, James — *MSI International*
Wayne, Cary S. — *ProSearch Inc.*
Webb, George H. — *Webb, Johnson Associates, Inc.*
Wein, Michael S. — *InterimManagement Solutions, Inc.*
Wein, Michael S. — *Media Management Resources, Inc.*
Wein, William — *InterimManagement Solutions, Inc.*
Wein, William — *Media Management Resources, Inc.*
Weissman-Rosenthal, Abbe — *ALW Research International*
Weisz, Laura — *Anderson Sterling Associates*
Welch, Robert — *Ray & Berndtson*
Weller, Paul S. — *Mark Stanley/EMA Partners International*
Westfall, Ed — *Zwell International*
Wheeler, Gerard H. — *A.J. Burton Group, Inc.*
Whelan, David — *Ethos Consulting Inc.*
White, William C. — *Venture Resources Inc.*
Whyte, Roger J. — *The Whyte Group, Inc.*
Wichansky, Mark — *TSS Consulting, Ltd.*
Wilcox, Fred T. — *Wilcox, Bertoux & Miller*
Wilder, Richard B. — *Columbia Consulting Group*
Wilkinson, Barbara — *Beall & Company, Inc.*
Wilkinson, Jr. SPHR
Wilkinson, Charles E. — *The HRM Group, Inc.*
Williams, Gary L. — *Barnes Development Group, LLC*
Williams, Jack — *A.T. Kearney, Inc.*
Williams, Roger K. — *Williams, Roth & Krueger Inc.*
Williams, Stephen E. — *Barton Associates, Inc.*
Willner, Leo — *William Guy & Associates*
Wilson, Don — *Allerton Heneghan & O'Neill*
Wilson, Patricia L. — *Leon A. Farley Associates*
Wilson, Steven J. — *Herman Smith Executive Initiatives Inc.*

Winitz, Joel — *GSW Consulting Group, Inc.*
Winitz, Marla — *GSW Consulting Group, Inc.*
Winograd, Glenn — *Criterion Executive Search, Inc.*
Winston, Dale — *Battalia Winston International*
Witte, David L. — *Ward Howell International, Inc.*
Wolf, Stephen M. — *Byron Leonard International, Inc.*
Womack, Joseph — *The Bankers Group*
Wood, Milton M. — *M. Wood Company*
Woodmansee, Bruce J. — *Tully/Woodmansee International, Inc.*
Woodworth, Gail — *Woodworth International Group*
Wooldridge, Jeff — *Ray & Berndtson*
Woollett, James — *Rusher, Loscavio & LoPresto*
Work, Alan — *Quantex Associates, Inc.*
Wright, A. Leo — *The Hindman Company*
Wright, Carl A.J. — *A.J. Burton Group, Inc.*
Wright, Charles D. — *Goodrich & Sherwood Associates, Inc.*
Wright, Leslie — *The Stevenson Group of New Jersey*
Wyatt, James — *Wyatt & Jaffe*
Yaekle, Gary — *Tully/Woodmansee International, Inc.*
Yen, Maggie Yeh Ching — *Ray & Berndtson*
Young, Heather — *The Guild Corporation*
Yungerberg, Steven — *Steven Yungerberg Associates Inc.*
Zaffrann, Craig S. — *P.J. Murphy & Associates, Inc.*
Zahradka, James F. — *P.J. Murphy & Associates, Inc.*
Zaleta, Andy R. — *A.T. Kearney, Inc.*
Zamborsky, George — *Boyden*
Zaslav, Debra M. — *Telford, Adams & Alexander/Telford & Co., Inc.*
Zila, Laurie M. — *Princeton Entrepreneurial Resources*
Zinn, Don — *Quantex Associates, Inc.*
Zwell, Michael — *Zwell International*

6. Human Resources

Abbott, Peter D. — *The Abbott Group, Inc.*
Adams, Len — *The KPA Group*
Adler, Louis S. — *CJA - The Adler Group*
Akin, J.R. "Jack" — *J.R. Akin & Company Inc.*
Allen, Don — *D.S. Allen Associates, Inc.*
Allen, William L. — *The Hindman Company*
Allerton, Donald T. — *Allerton Heneghan & O'Neill*
Altreuter, Rose — *ALTCO Temporary Services*
Altreuter, Rose — *The ALTCO Group*
Ambler, Peter W. — *Peter W. Ambler Company*
Ames, George C. — *Ames O'Neill Associates*
Anderson, Maria H. — *Barton Associates, Inc.*
Anderson, Richard — *Grant Cooper and Associates*
Andrews, J. Douglas — *Clarey & Andrews, Inc.*
Antoine, Brian — *Paul-Tittle Associates, Inc.*
Argentin, Jo — *Executive Placement Consultants, Inc.*
Ascher, Susan P. — *The Ascher Group*
Asquith, Peter S. — *Ames Personnel Consultants, Inc.*
Aston, Kathy — *Marra Peters & Partners*

Atkins, Laurie — *Battalia Winston International*
Atwood, Barrie — *The Abbott Group, Inc.*
Bacon, Cheri — *Gaffney Management Consultants*
Badger, Fred H. — *The Badger Group*
Baeder, Jeremy — *Executive Manning Corporation*
Baje, Sarah — *Innovative Search Group, LLC*
Baker, Gary M. — *Cochran, Cochran & Yale, Inc.*
Balbone, Rich — *Executive Manning Corporation*
Baldwin, Keith R. — *The Baldwin Group*
Baltaglia, Michael — *Cochran, Cochran & Yale, Inc.*
Barbour, Mary Beth — *Tully/Woodmansee International, Inc.*
Barger, H. Carter — *Barger & Sargeant, Inc.*
Barnes, Gary — *Brigade Inc.*
Barnes, Richard E. — *Barnes Development Group, LLC*
Barnes, Roanne L. — *Barnes Development Group, LLC*
Barthold, James A. — *McNichol Associates*
Barton, Gary R. — *Barton Associates, Inc.*
Bason, Maurice L. — *Bason Associates Inc.*
Bass, M. Lynn — *Ray & Berndtson*
Battalia, O. William — *Battalia Winston International*
Bearman, Linda — *Grant Cooper and Associates*
Beaudin, Elizabeth C. — *Callan Associates, Ltd.*
Beaver, Bentley H. — *The Onstott Group, Inc.*
Belin, Jean — *Boyden*
Bennett, Jo — *Battalia Winston International*
Beran, Helena — *Michael J. Cavanagh and Associates*
Berry, Harold B. — *The Hindman Company*
Bettick, Michael J. — *A.J. Burton Group, Inc.*
Biestek, Paul J. — *Paul J. Biestek Associates, Inc.*
Billington, William H. — *Spriggs & Company, Inc.*
Blackmon, Sharon — *The Abbott Group, Inc.*
Blackshaw, Brian M. — *Blackshaw, Olmstead, Lynch & Koenig*
Bliley, Jerry — *Spencer Stuart*
Bloch, Terry L. — *Southern Research Services*
Bloch, Thomas L. — *Southern Research Services*
Bluhm, Claudia — *Schweichler Associates, Inc.*
Boel, Werner — *The Dalley Hewitt Company*
Bongiovanni, Vincent — *ESA Professional Consultants*
Borkin, Andrew — *Strategic Advancement Inc.*
Borland, James — *Goodrich & Sherwood Associates, Inc.*
Bostic, James E. — *Phillips Resource Group*
Bourrie, Sharon D. — *Chartwell Partners International, Inc.*
Bowden, Otis H. — *BowdenGlobal, Ltd.*
Bradley, Dalena — *Woodworth International Group*
Bradshaw, Monte — *Christian & Timbers*
Brady, Dick — *William Guy & Associates*
Brandenburg, David — *Professional Staffing Consultants*
Bratches, Howard — *Thorndike Deland Associates*
Brieger, Steve — *Thorne, Brieger Associates Inc.*
Brophy, Melissa — *Maximum Management Corp.*
Brother, Joy — *Charles Luntz & Associates. Inc.*
Brown, Larry C. — *Horton International*
Brown, Steffan — *Woodworth International Group*
Brudno, Robert J. — *Savoy Partners, Ltd.*

Bruno, Deborah F. — *The Hindman Company*
Bryant, Richard D. — *Bryant Associates, Inc.*
Bryza, Robert M. — *Robert Lowell International*
Brzezinski, Ronald T. — *Callan Associates, Ltd.*
Buckles, Donna — *Cochran, Cochran & Yale, Inc.*
Buggy, Linda — *Bonnell Associates Ltd.*
Bullock, Conni — *Earley Kielty and Associates, Inc.*
Burchill, Greg — *BGB Associates*
Burke, John — *The Experts*
Burkhill, John — *The Talley Group*
Burns, Alan — *The Enns Partners Inc.*
Busterna, Charles — *The KPA Group*
Cahill, Peter M. — *Peter M. Cahill Associates, Inc.*
Calivas, Kay — *A.J. Burton Group, Inc.*
Call, David — *Cochran, Cochran & Yale, Inc.*
Callan, Robert M. — *Callan Associates, Ltd.*
Calogeras, Chris — *The Sager Company*
Cameron, James W. — *Cameron Consulting*
Campbell, Patricia A. — *The Onstott Group, Inc.*
Capizzi, Karen — *Cochran, Cochran & Yale, Inc.*
Carideo, Joseph — *Thorndike Deland Associates*
Carro, Carl R. — *Executive Search Consultants International, Inc.*
Cary, Con — *Cary & Associates*
Cavanagh, Michael J. — *Michael J. Cavanagh and Associates*
Cavolina, Michael — *Carver Search Consultants*
Chamberlin, Michael A. — *Tower Consultants, Ltd.*
Chappell, Peter — *The Bankers Group*
Chavous, C. Crawford — *Phillips Resource Group*
Cherbonnier, L. Michael — *The Cherbonnier Group, Inc.*
Chorman, Marilyn A. — *Hite Executive Search*
Christenson, H. Alan — *Christenson & Hutchison*
Christian, Philip — *Ray & Berndtson*
Cimino, Ron — *Paul-Tittle Associates, Inc.*
Cizek, John T. — *Cizek Associates, Inc.*
Cizek, Marti J. — *Cizek Associates, Inc.*
Clarey, Jack R. — *Clarey & Andrews, Inc.*
Clauhsen, Elizabeth A. — *Savoy Partners, Ltd.*
Clayton, Fred J. — *Berkhemer Clayton Incorporated*
Cloutier, Gisella — *Dinte Resources, Inc.*
Cochran, Scott P. — *The Badger Group*
Coe, Karen J. — *Coe & Company International Inc.*
Coffman, Brian — *Kossuth & Associates, Inc.*
Cohen, Michael R. — *Intech Summit Group, Inc.*
Cohen, Robert C. — *Intech Summit Group, Inc.*
Coleman, J. Kevin — *J. Kevin Coleman & Associates, Inc.*
Colling, Douglas — *KPMG Management Consulting*
Colman, Michael — *Executive Placement Consultants, Inc.*
Colvin, Teresa A. — *Jonas, Walters & Assoc., Inc.*
Conway, Maureen — *Conway & Associates*
Conway, William P. — *Phillips Resource Group*
Cooke, Katherine H. — *Horton International*
Corrigan, Gerald F. — *The Corrigan Group*
Cortina Del Valle, Pedro — *Ray & Berndtson*
Costello, Lynda — *Coe & Company International Inc.*
Courtney, Brendan — *A.J. Burton Group, Inc.*
Coyle, Hugh F. — *A.J. Burton Group, Inc.*

Crane, Howard C. — *Chartwell Partners International, Inc.*
Crath, Paul F. — *Price Waterhouse*
Critchley, Walter — *Cochran, Cochran & Yale, Inc.*
Crosler, Yvonne — *Paul-Tittle Associates, Inc.*
Crowder, Edward W. — *Crowder & Company*
Cunningham, Lawrence — *Howard Fischer Associates, Inc.*
Cunningham, Robert Y. — *Goodrich & Sherwood Associates, Inc.*
Curci, Donald L. — *A.R.I. International*
Curtis, Ellissa — *Cochran, Cochran & Yale, Inc.*
Czamanske, Paul W. — *Compass Group Ltd.*
Dalton, Bret — *Robert W. Dingman Company, Inc.*
Danforth, W. Michael — *Hyde Danforth Wold & Co.*
Daniel, Beverly — *Foy, Schneid & Daniel, Inc.*
Daniels, C. Eugene — *Sigma Group International*
Davis, G. Gordon — *Davis & Company*
Dawson, Joe — *S.C. International, Ltd.*
De Brun, Thomas P. — *Ray & Berndtson*
Deaver, Henry C. — *Ray & Berndtson*
DeCorrevont, James — *DeCorrevont & Associates*
DeCorrevont, James — *DeCorrevont & Associates*
DeHart, Donna — *Tower Consultants, Ltd.*
Delaney, Patrick J. — *Sensible Solutions, Inc.*
Delmonico, Laura — *A.J. Burton Group, Inc.*
DeLong, Art — *Richard Kader & Associates*
Demchak, James P. — *Sandhurst Associates*
Desgrosellier, Gary P. — *Personnel Unlimited/Executive Search*
Desmond, Dennis — *Beall & Company, Inc.*
deVry, Kimberly A. — *Tower Consultants, Ltd.*
deWilde, David M. — *Chartwell Partners International, Inc.*
Dezember, Steve — *Ray & Berndtson*
DiCioccio, Carmen — *Cochran, Cochran & Yale, Inc.*
Dicker, Barry — *ESA Professional Consultants*
Dickson, Duke — *A.D. & Associates Executive Search, Inc.*
Dingeldey, Peter E. — *Search Advisors International Corp.*
Dingman, Bruce — *Robert W. Dingman Company, Inc.*
Dingman, Robert W. — *Robert W. Dingman Company, Inc.*
Dinte, Paul — *Dinte Resources, Inc.*
DiSalvo, Fred — *The Cambridge Group Ltd*
Divine, Robert S. — *O'Shea, Divine & Company, Inc.*
Doele, Donald C. — *Goodrich & Sherwood Associates, Inc.*
Doman, Matthew — *S.C. International, Ltd.*
Dow, Lori — *Davidson, Laird & Associates, Inc.*
Dowell, Chris — *The Abbott Group, Inc.*
Dowell, Mary K. — *Professional Search Associates*
Doyle, James W. — *Executive Search Consultants International, Inc.*
Drew, David R. — *Drew & Associates*
Drury, James J. — *Spencer Stuart*
Dubrow, Richard M. — *R/K International, Inc.*
Duckworth, Donald R. — *Johnson Smith & Knisely Accord*
Duley, Richard I. — *ARJay & Associates*

Dunbar, Marilynne — *Ray & Berndtson/Lovas Stanley*
Durakis, Charles A. — *C.A. Durakis Associates, Inc.*
Ebeling, John A. — *Gilbert Tweed/INESA*
Edwards, Verba L. — *Wing Tips & Pumps, Inc.*
Eggena, Roger — *Phillips Resource Group*
Ehrgott, Elizabeth — *The Ascher Group*
Ehrhart, Jennifer — *ADOW's Executeam*
Eldridge, Charles B. — *Ray & Berndtson*
Ellis, Ted K. — *The Hindman Company*
Ellis, William — *Interspace Interactive Inc.*
England, Mark — *Austin-McGregor International*
Enns, George — *The Enns Partners Inc.*
Erder, Debra — *Canny, Bowen Inc.*
Evans, David — *Executive Manning Corporation*
Fancher, Robert L. — *Bason Associates Inc.*
Farley, Leon A. — *Leon A. Farley Associates*
Farrow, Jerry M. — *McCormack & Farrow*
Ferneborg, Jay W. — *Ferneborg & Associates, Inc.*
Ferneborg, John R. — *Ferneborg & Associates, Inc.*
Fini, Ron — *The Sager Company*
Fiorelli, Cheryl — *Tower Consultants, Ltd.*
Fischer, Adam — *Howard Fischer Associates, Inc.*
Fischer, Howard M. — *Howard Fischer Associates, Inc.*
Fisher, Neal — *Fisher Personnel Management Services*
Flanagan, Robert M. — *Robert M. Flanagan & Associates, Ltd.*
Flanders, Karen — *Advanced Information Management*
Flannery, Peter F. — *Jonas, Walters & Assoc., Inc.*
Fletcher, David — *A.J. Burton Group, Inc.*
Flood, Michael — *Norman Broadbent International, Inc.*
Flora, Dodi — *Crawford & Crofford*
Folkerth, Gene — *Gene Folkerth & Associates, Inc.*
Foote, Leland W. — *L.W. Foote Company*
Ford, Sandra D. — *The Ford Group, Inc.*
Foreman, David C. — *Koontz, Jeffries & Associates, Inc.*
Fowler, Thomas A. — *The Hindman Company*
Francis, John — *Zwell International*
Frank, Valerie S. — *Norman Roberts & Associates, Inc.*
Frazier, John — *Cochran, Cochran & Yale, Inc.*
Freeman, Mark — *ESA Professional Consultants*
French, William G. — *Preng & Associates, Inc.*
Fribush, Richard — *A.J. Burton Group, Inc.*
Friedman, Donna L. — *Tower Consultants, Ltd.*
Friedman, Helen E. — *McCormack & Farrow*
Fulgham MacCarthy, Ann — *Columbia Consulting Group*
Fust, Sheely F. — *Ray & Berndtson*
Gabel, Gregory N. — *Canny, Bowen Inc.*
Gabriel, David L. — *The Arcus Group*
Galante, Suzanne M. — *Vlcek & Company, Inc.*
Galbraith, Deborah M. — *Stratford Group*
Gallagher, Terence M. — *Battalia Winston International*
Gantar, Donna — *Howard Fischer Associates, Inc.*
Garfinkle, Steven M. — *Battalia Winston International*
Gauthier, Robert C. — *Columbia Consulting Group*

Hykes, Don A. — *A.T. Kearney, Inc.*
Inzinna, Dennis — *AlternaStaff*
Issacs, Judith A. — *Grant Cooper and Associates*
Jacobs, Mike — *Thorne, Brieger Associates Inc.*
Jacobson, Carolyn — *The Abbott Group, Inc.*
Jacobson, Rick — *The Windham Group*
Jaffe, Mark — *Wyatt & Jaffe*
James, Bruce — *Roberson and Company*
Janis, Laurence — *Integrated Search Solutions Group, LLC*
Jansen, John F. — *Delta Services*
Janssen, Don — *Howard Fischer Associates, Inc.*
Januale, Lois — *Cochran, Cochran & Yale, Inc.*
Jaworski, Mary A. — *Tully/Woodmansee International, Inc.*
Joffe, Barry — *Bason Associates Inc.*
Johnson, Brian — *A.J. Burton Group, Inc.*
Johnson, David A. — *Gaffney Management Consultants*
Johnson, Douglas — *Quality Search*
Johnson, John W. — *Webb, Johnson Associates, Inc.*
Johnson, Kathleen A. — *Barton Associates, Inc.*
Johnson, LaDonna — *Gans, Gans & Associates*
Johnson, Robert J. — *Quality Search*
Johnson, Stanley C. — *Johnson & Company*
Johnson, Valerie — *Coe & Company International Inc.*
Johnston, Michael — *Robertson-Surrette Executive Search*
Jones, Amy E. — *The Corporate Connection, Ltd.*
Jones, Barbara — *Kaye-Bassman International Corp.*
Jones, Francis E. — *Earley Kielty and Associates, Inc.*
Jones, Gary — *BGB Associates*
Jones, Ronald T. — *ARJay & Associates*
Jordan, Jon — *Cochran, Cochran & Yale, Inc.*
Judge, Alfred L. — *The Cambridge Group Ltd*
Juelis, John J. — *Peeney Associates*
Kaiser, Donald J. — *Dunhill International Search of New Haven*
Kane, Frank — *A.J. Burton Group, Inc.*
Kane, Karen — *Howard Fischer Associates, Inc.*
Kanrich, Susan Azaria — *AlternaStaff*
Kaplan, Gary — *Gary Kaplan & Associates*
Kartin, Martin C. — *Martin Kartin and Company, Inc.*
Keating, Pierson — *Nordeman Grimm, Inc.*
Keller, Barbara E. — *Barton Associates, Inc.*
Kelly, Elizabeth Ann — *Wellington Management Group*
Kelso, Patricia C. — *Barton Associates, Inc.*
Kent, Melvin — *Melvin Kent & Associates, Inc.*
Kenzer, Robert D. — *Kenzer Corp.*
Kern, Jerry L. — *ADOW's Executeam*
Kern, Kathleen G. — *ADOW's Executeam*
Kershaw, Lisa — *Tanton Mitchell/Paul Ray Berndtson*
Keshishian, Gregory — *Handy HRM Corp.*
Kielty, John L. — *Earley Kielty and Associates, Inc.*
King, Bill — *The McCormick Group, Inc.*
King, Margaret — *Christian & Timbers*
Kinser, Richard E. — *Richard Kinser & Associates*
Kip, Luanne S. — *Kip Williams, Inc.*
Kishbaugh, Herbert S. — *Kishbaugh Associates International*

Klages, Constance W. — *International Management Advisors, Inc.*
Klauck, James J. — *Horton International*
Klavens, Cecile J. — *The Pickwick Group, Inc.*
Klein, Brandon — *A.J. Burton Group, Inc.*
Klein, Mary Jo — *Cochran, Cochran & Yale, Inc.*
Klopfenstein, Edward L. — *Crowder & Company*
Kobayashi, Rika — *International Staffing Consultants, Inc.*
Koehler, Frank R. — *The Koehler Group*
Koenig, Joel S. — *Blackshaw, Olmstead, Lynch & Koenig*
Koenig, Joel S. — *Blackshaw, Olmstead, Lynch & Koenig*
Kohn, Adam P. — *Christian & Timbers*
Kondra, Vernon J. — *The Douglas Reiter Company, Inc.*
Koontz, Donald N. — *Koontz, Jeffries & Associates, Inc.*
Kossuth, David — *Kossuth & Associates, Inc.*
Kossuth, Jane — *Kossuth & Associates, Inc.*
Kotick, Maddy — *The Stevenson Group of New Jersey*
Krejci, Stanley L. — *Boyden Washington, D.C.*
Krieger, Dennis F. — *Seiden Krieger Associates, Inc.*
Krueger, Kurt — *Krueger Associates*
Kuhl, Teresa — *Don Richard Associates of Tampa, Inc.*
Kunzer, William J. — *Kunzer Associates, Ltd.*
Kurrigan, Geoffrey — *ESA Professional Consultants*
Kussner, Janice N. — *Herman Smith Executive Initiatives Inc.*
Laba, Marvin — *Marvin Laba & Associates*
Laba, Stuart M. — *Marvin Laba & Associates*
Labrecque, Bernard F. — *Laurendeau Labrecque/Ray & Berndtson, Inc.*
Lang, Sharon A. — *Ray & Berndtson*
Lardner, Lucy D. — *Tully/Woodmansee International, Inc.*
Larsen, Jack B. — *Jack B. Larsen & Associates*
Lasher, Charles M. — *Lasher Associates*
Lautz, Lindsay A. — *Lautz Grotte Engler*
Ledbetter, Charlene — *Ledbetter/Davidson International, Inc.*
Lee, Janice — *Summerfield Associates, Inc.*
Leininger, Dennis — *Key Employment Services*
Lenkaitis, Lewis F. — *A.T. Kearney, Inc.*
Letcher, Harvey D. — *Sandhurst Associates*
Lewis, Jon A. — *Sandhurst Associates*
Lezama Cohen, Luis — *Ray & Berndtson*
Linton, Leonard M. — *Byron Leonard International, Inc.*
Lipe, Jerold L. — *Compass Group Ltd.*
Loeb, Stephen H. — *Grant Cooper and Associates*
Long, Helga — *Horton International*
Long, Milt — *William Guy & Associates*
Long, William G. — *McDonald, Long & Associates, Inc.*
Lotufo, Donald A. — *D.A.L. Associates, Inc.*
Lotz, R. James — *International Management Advisors, Inc.*
Lovely, Edward — *The Stevenson Group of New Jersey*
Loving, Vikki — *Intersource, Ltd.*
Lucarelli, Joan — *The Onstott Group, Inc.*

Lucht, John — *The John Lucht Consultancy Inc.*

Lumsby, George N. — *International Management Advisors, Inc.*

Luntz, Charles E. — *Charles Luntz & Associates. Inc.*

Lupica, Anthony — *Cochran, Cochran & Yale, Inc.*

Lyon, Jenny — *Marra Peters & Partners*

Lyons, J. David — *Aubin International Inc.*

Macdonald, G. William — *The Macdonald Group, Inc.*

MacEachern, David — *Spencer Stuart*

Mackenna, Kathy — *Plummer & Associates, Inc.*

MacNaughton, Sperry — *McNaughton Associates*

Maglio, Charles J. — *Maglio and Company, Inc.*

Mallin, Ellen — *Howard Fischer Associates, Inc.*

Manassero, Henri J.P. — *International Management Advisors, Inc.*

Mangum, Maria — *Thomas Mangum Company*

Mangum, William T. — *Thomas Mangum Company*

Manns, Alex — *Crawford & Crofford*

Mansfield, Keith — *Howard Fischer Associates, Inc.*

Maphet, Harriet — *The Stevenson Group of New Jersey*

Marino, Chester — *Cochran, Cochran & Yale, Inc.*

Mark, John L. — *J.L. Mark Associates, Inc.*

Mark, Lynne — *J.L. Mark Associates, Inc.*

Marks, Russell E. — *Webb, Johnson Associates, Inc.*

Marlow, William — *Straube Associates*

Marra, John — *Marra Peters & Partners*

Marra, John — *Marra Peters & Partners*

Martin, Lois G. — *The Martin Group*

Martin, Timothy P. — *The Martin Group*

Marumoto, William H. — *Boyden Washington, D.C.*

Massey, R. Bruce — *Horton International*

Mather, David R. — *Christian & Timbers*

Mathias, Kathy — *Stone Murphy & Olson*

Matthews, Corwin — *Woodworth International Group*

Maynard Taylor, Susan — *Chrisman & Company, Incorporated*

Mazor, Elly — *Howard Fischer Associates, Inc.*

McBride, Jonathan E. — *McBride Associates, Inc.*

McCloskey, Frank D. — *Johnson Smith & Knisely Accord*

McCormick, Brian — *The McCormick Group, Inc.*

McCreary, Charles "Chip" — *Austin-McGregor International*

McDermott, Jeffrey T. — *Vlcek & Company, Inc.*

McDonald, Stanleigh B. — *McDonald Associates International*

McDonnell, Julie — *Technical Personnel of Minnesota*

McDowell, Robert N. — *Christenson & Hutchison*

McFadden, Ashton S. — *Johnson Smith & Knisely Accord*

McFadzen, Donna — *Holland, McFadzean & Associates, Inc.*

McFadzen, James A. — *Holland, McFadzean & Associates, Inc.*

McGuire, J. Corey — *Peter W. Ambler Company*

McGuire, Pat — *A.J. Burton Group, Inc.*

McIntyre, Joel — *Phillips Resource Group*

McKell, Linda — *Advanced Information Management*

McKeown, Morgan J. — *Christian & Timbers*

McKeown, Patricia A. — *DiMarchi Partners, Inc.*

McManners, Donald E. — *McManners Associates, Inc.*

McMillin, Bob — *Price Waterhouse*

McNamara, Catherine — *Ray & Berndtson*

McNamara, Timothy C. — *Columbia Consulting Group*

McNichol, John — *McNichol Associates*

McNichols, Walter B. — *Gary Kaplan & Associates*

McSherry, James F. — *Battalia Winston International*

Meadows, C. David — *Professional Staffing Consultants*

Menendez, Todd — *Don Richard Associates of Tampa, Inc.*

Mercer, Julie — *Columbia Consulting Group*

Meyer, Stacey — *Gary Kaplan & Associates*

Miller, David — *Cochran, Cochran & Yale, Inc.*

Miller, George N. — *Hite Executive Search*

Miller, Roy — *The Enns Partners Inc.*

Miller, Russel E. — *ARJay & Associates*

Milstein, Bonnie — *Marvin Laba & Associates*

Mingle, Larry D. — *Columbia Consulting Group*

Misiurewicz, Marc — *Cochran, Cochran & Yale, Inc.*

Mitchell, Jeff — *A.J. Burton Group, Inc.*

Mitton, Bill — *Executive Resource, Inc.*

Montgomery, James M. — *Houze, Shourds & Montgomery, Inc.*

Moore, Mark — *Wheeler, Moore & Elam Co.*

Moore, T. Wills — *Ray & Berndtson*

Morgan, Richard S. — *Ray & Berndtson/Lovas Stanley*

Mortansen, Patricia — *Norman Broadbent International, Inc.*

Muendel, H. Edward — *Stanton Chase International*

Murphy, Cornelius J. — *Goodrich & Sherwood Associates, Inc.*

Murphy, Gary J. — *Stone Murphy & Olson*

Murphy, Patrick J. — *P.J. Murphy & Associates, Inc.*

Mursuli, Meredith — *Lasher Associates*

Nadherny, Christopher C. — *Spencer Stuart*

Nagler, Leon G. — *Nagler, Robins & Poe, Inc.*

Naidicz, Maria — *Ray & Berndtson*

Nees, Eugene C. — *Ray & Berndtson*

Neher, Robert L. — *Intech Summit Group, Inc.*

Nehring, Keith — *Howard Fischer Associates, Inc.*

Neidhart, Craig C. — *TNS Partners, Inc.*

Nelson, Barbara — *Herman Smith Executive Initiatives Inc.*

Nemec, Phillip — *Dunhill International Search of New Haven*

Nephew, Robert — *Christian & Timbers*

Neri, Gene — *S.C. International, Ltd.*

Neuberth, Jeffrey G. — *Canny, Bowen Inc.*

Nichols, Gary — *Koontz, Jeffries & Associates, Inc.*

Noebel, Todd R. — *The Noebel Search Group, Inc.*

Nold, Robert — *Roberson and Company*

Nolte, William D. — *W.D. Nolte & Company*

Norman, Randy — *Austin-McGregor International*
Normann, Amy — *Robert M. Flanagan & Associates, Ltd.*
Norsell, Paul E. — *Paul Norsell & Associates, Inc.*
Nye, David S. — *Blake, Hansen & Nye, Limited*
O'Brien, Maggie — *Advanced Information Management*
O'Hara, Daniel M. — *Lynch Miller Moore, Inc.*
Ogdon, Thomas H. — *The Ogdon Partnership*
Ogilvie, Kit — *Howard Fischer Associates, Inc.*
Olmstead, George T. — *Blackshaw, Olmstead, Lynch & Koenig*
Onstott, Joseph — *The Onstott Group, Inc.*
Ott, George W. — *Ott & Hansen, Inc.*
Overlock, Craig — *Ray & Berndtson*
Pace, Susan A. — *Horton International*
Palma, Frank R. — *Goodrich & Sherwood Associates, Inc.*
Palmer, Carlton A. — *Beall & Company, Inc.*
Palmer, James H. — *The Hindman Company*
Panarese, Pam — *Howard Fischer Associates, Inc.*
Papasadero, Kathleen — *Woodworth International Group*
Pappas, Timothy C. — *Jonas, Walters & Assoc., Inc.*
Pardo, Maria Elena — *Smith Search, S.C.*
Park, Dabney G. — *Mark Stanley/EMA Partners International*
Parr, James A. — *KPMG Management Consulting*
Parry, William H. — *Horton International*
Parsons, Allison D. — *Barton Associates, Inc.*
Paul, Lisa D. — *Merit Resource Group, Inc.*
Pearson, Robert L. — *Lamalie Amrop International*
Peasback, David R. — *Canny, Bowen Inc.*
Peeney, James D. — *Peeney Associates*
Pelisson, Charles — *Marra Peters & Partners*
Pernell, Jeanette — *Norman Broadbent International, Inc.*
Petty, J. Scott — *The Arcus Group*
Pfeiffer, Irene — *Price Waterhouse*
Pfister, Shelli — *Jack B. Larsen & Associates*
Phelps, Gene L. — *McCormack & Farrow*
Phillips, Donald L. — *O'Shea, Divine & Company, Inc.*
Phillips, Richard K. — *Handy HRM Corp.*
Phipps, Peggy — *Woodworth International Group*
Pickering, Dale — *Agri-Tech Personnel, Inc.*
Pickering, Rita — *Agri-Tech Personnel, Inc.*
Pickford, Stephen T. — *The Corporate Staff, Inc.*
Pigott, Daniel — *ESA Professional Consultants*
Plimpton, Ralph L. — *R L Plimpton Associates*
Plummer, John — *Plummer & Associates, Inc.*
Poirier, Roland L. — *Poirier, Hoevel & Co.*
Poore, Larry D. — *Ward Howell International, Inc.*
Poremski, Paul — *A.J. Burton Group, Inc.*
Porter, Albert — *The Experts*
Price, Andrew G. — *The Thomas Tucker Company*
Racht, Janet G. — *Crowe, Chizek and Company, LLP*
Raines, Bruce R. — *Raines International Inc.*
Ramler, Carolyn S. — *The Corporate Connection, Ltd.*
Ramsey, John H. — *Mark Stanley/EMA Partners International*
Randell, James E. — *Randell-Heiken, Inc.*

Ray, Marianne C. — *Callan Associates, Ltd.*
Raymond, Anne — *Anderson Sterling Associates*
Reddick, David C. — *Horton International*
Redding, Denise — *The Douglas Reiter Company, Inc.*
Regan, Thomas J. — *Tower Consultants, Ltd.*
Reifersen, Ruth F. — *The Jonathan Stevens Group, Inc.*
Reiser, Ellen — *Thorndike Deland Associates*
Reisinger, George L. — *Sigma Group International*
Reiter, Douglas — *The Douglas Reiter Company, Inc.*
Remillard, Brad M. — *CJA - The Adler Group*
Reyman, Susan — *S. Reyman & Associates Ltd.*
Rhodes, Bill — *Bench International*
Ribeiro, Claudia — *Ledbetter/Davidson International, Inc.*
Rice, Marie — *Jay Gaines & Company, Inc.*
Rice, Raymond D. — *Logue & Rice Inc.*
Richards, Paul E. — *Executive Directions*
Richards, R. Glenn — *Executive Directions*
Rieger, Louis J. — *Spencer Stuart*
Rimmel, James E. — *The Hindman Company*
Rimmele, Michael — *The Bankers Group*
Roberts, Nick P. — *Spectrum Search Associates, Inc.*
Roberts, Norman C. — *Norman Roberts & Associates, Inc.*
Roberts, Scott — *Jonas, Walters & Assoc., Inc.*
Robertson, Ronald — *Robertson-Surrette Executive Search*
Robinson, Bruce — *Bruce Robinson Associates*
Robles Cuellar, Paulina — *Ray & Berndtson*
Rogers, Leah — *Dinte Resources, Inc.*
Rollins, Scott — *S.C. International, Ltd.*
Romanello, Daniel P. — *Spencer Stuart*
Romang, Paula — *Agri-Tech Personnel, Inc.*
Rose, Robert — *ESA Professional Consultants*
Ross, Curt A. — *Ray & Berndtson*
Ross, Lawrence — *Ray & Berndtson/Lovas Stanley*
Ross, Mark — *Ray & Berndtson/Lovas Stanley*
Ross, William J. — *Flowers & Associates*
Rotella, Marshall W. — *The Corporate Connection, Ltd.*
Roth, Robert J. — *Williams, Roth & Krueger Inc.*
Rowe, William D. — *D.E. Foster Partners Inc.*
Rudolph, Kenneth — *Kossuth & Associates, Inc.*
Ruge, Merrill — *William Guy & Associates*
Rurak, Zbigniew T. — *Rurak & Associates, Inc.*
Russo, Karen — *Maximum Management Corp.*
Ryan, Lee — *Ryan, Miller & Associates Inc.*
Sacerdote, John — *Raymond Karsan Associates*
Sallows, Jill S. — *Crowe, Chizek and Company, LLP*
Salvagno, Michael J. — *The Cambridge Group Ltd*
Sanow, Robert — *Cochran, Cochran & Yale, Inc.*
Sarn, Allan G. — *Allan Sarn Associates Inc.*
Sarna, Edmund A. — *Jonas, Walters & Assoc., Inc.*
Savvas, Carol Diane — *Ledbetter/Davidson International, Inc.*
Saxon, Alexa — *Woodworth International Group*
Schedra, Sharon — *Earley Kielty and Associates, Inc.*
Schiavone, Mary Rose — *Canny, Bowen Inc.*
Schlpma, Christine — *Advanced Executive Resources*
Schmidt, Peter R. — *Boyden*

Walker, Ewing J. — *Ward Howell International, Inc.*

Walsh, Denis — *Professional Staffing Consultants*

Walsh, Kenneth A. — *R/K International, Inc.*

Walters, William F. — *Jonas, Walters & Assoc., Inc.*

Warter, Mark — *Isaacson, Miller*

Watkinson, Jim W. — *The Badger Group*

Watson, Peggy — *Advanced Information Management*

Wayne, Cary S. — *ProSearch Inc.*

Webb, George H. — *Webb, Johnson Associates, Inc.*

Weissman-Rosenthal, Abbe — *ALW Research International*

Weisz, Laura — *Anderson Sterling Associates*

Welch, Robert — *Ray & Berndtson*

Weller, Paul S. — *Mark Stanley/EMA Partners International*

Westfall, Ed — *Zwell International*

Wheeler, Gerard H. — *A.J. Burton Group, Inc.*

Whyte, Roger J. — *The Whyte Group, Inc.*

Wilburn, Dan — *Kaye-Bassman International Corp.*

Wilder, Richard B. — *Columbia Consulting Group*

Wilkinson, Barbara — *Beall & Company, Inc.*

Wilkinson, Jr. SPHR

Wilkinson, Charles E. — *The HRM Group, Inc.*

Williams, Gary L. — *Barnes Development Group, LLC*

Williams, Roger K. — *Williams, Roth & Krueger Inc.*

Williams, Stephen E. — *Barton Associates, Inc.*

Wilson, Don — *Allerton Heneghan & O'Neill*

Wilson, Patricia L. — *Leon A. Farley Associates*

Wilson, Steven J. — *Herman Smith Executive Initiatives Inc.*

Winston, Dale — *Battalia Winston International*

Wise, J. Herbert — *Sandhurst Associates*

Wold, Ted W. — *Hyde Danforth Wold & Co.*

Wolf, Stephen M. — *Byron Leonard International, Inc.*

Womack, Joseph — *The Bankers Group*

Wood, Milton M. — *M. Wood Company*

Woodmansee, Bruce J. — *Tully/Woodmansee International, Inc.*

Woodworth, Gail — *Woodworth International Group*

Wooldridge, Jeff — *Ray & Berndtson*

Work, Alan — *Quantex Associates, Inc.*

Wright, A. Leo — *The Hindman Company*

Wright, Carl A.J. — *A.J. Burton Group, Inc.*

Wright, Charles D. — *Goodrich & Sherwood Associates, Inc.*

Wright, Leslie — *The Stevenson Group of New Jersey*

Wyatt, James — *Wyatt & Jaffe*

Yaekle, Gary — *Tully/Woodmansee International, Inc.*

Yen, Maggie Yeh Ching — *Ray & Berndtson*

Yungerberg, Steven — *Steven Yungerberg Associates Inc.*

Zaccaria, Jack — *The Zaccaria Group, Inc.*

Zadfar, Maryanne — *The Thomas Tucker Company*

Zaffrann, Craig S. — *P.J. Murphy & Associates, Inc.*

Zahradka, James F. — *P.J. Murphy & Associates, Inc.*

Zamborsky, George — *Boyden*

Zaslav, Debra M. — *Telford, Adams & Alexander/Telford & Co., Inc.*

Zila, Laurie M. — *Princeton Entrepreneurial Resources*

Zinn, Don — *Quantex Associates, Inc.*

Zucker, Nancy — *Maximum Management Corp.*

Zwell, Michael — *Zwell International*

7. Marketing

Abbott, Peter D. — *The Abbott Group, Inc.*

Abell, Vincent W. — *MSI International*

Adler, Louis S. — *CJA - The Adler Group*

Ainsworth, Lawrence — *Search West, Inc.*

Akin, J.R. "Jack" — *J.R. Akin & Company Inc.*

Allen, Don — *D.S. Allen Associates, Inc.*

Allen, Wade H. — *Cendea Connection International*

Allen, William L. — *The Hindman Company*

Allerton, Donald T. — *Allerton Heneghan & O'Neill*

Allred, J. Michael — *Spencer Stuart*

Altreuter, Rose — *ALTCO Temporary Services*

Altreuter, Rose — *The ALTCO Group*

Ambler, Peter W. — *Peter W. Ambler Company*

Ames, George C. — *Ames O'Neill Associates*

Anderson, Maria H. — *Barton Associates, Inc.*

Anderson, Richard — *Grant Cooper and Associates*

Anderson, Terry — *Intech Summit Group, Inc.*

Antoine, Brian — *Paul-Tittle Associates, Inc.*

Argentin, Jo — *Executive Placement Consultants, Inc.*

Arnold, David W. — *Christian & Timbers*

Aronin, Michael — *Fisher-Todd Associates*

Arseneault, Daniel S. — *MSI International*

Ascher, Susan P. — *The Ascher Group*

Asquith, Peter S. — *Ames Personnel Consultants, Inc.*

Aston, Kathy — *Marra Peters & Partners*

Atkins, Laurie — *Battalia Winston International*

Attell, Harold — *A.E. Feldman Associates*

Austin Lockton, Kathy — *Juntunen-Combs-Poirier*

Bacon, Cheri — *Gaffney Management Consultants*

Badger, Fred H. — *The Badger Group*

Baje, Sarah — *Innovative Search Group, LLC*

Baker, Bill — *Kaye-Bassman International Corp.*

Baker, Gary M. — *Cochran, Cochran & Yale, Inc.*

Baldwin, Keith R. — *The Baldwin Group*

Baltaglia, Michael — *Cochran, Cochran & Yale, Inc.*

Baltin, Carrie — *Search West, Inc.*

Barbosa, Frank — *Skott/Edwards Consultants, Inc.*

Barbour, Mary Beth — *Tully/Woodmansee International, Inc.*

Barger, H. Carter — *Barger & Sargeant, Inc.*

Barlow, Ken H. — *The Cherbonnier Group, Inc.*

Barnes, Gary — *Brigade Inc.*

Barnes, Richard E. — *Barnes Development Group, LLC*

Barnes, Roanne L. — *Barnes Development Group, LLC*

Barnum, Toni M. — *Stone Murphy & Olson*

Baron, Len — *Industrial Recruiters Associates, Inc.*

Barthold, James A. — *McNichol Associates*

Colasanto, Frank M. — *W.R. Rosato & Associates, Inc.*

Coleman, J. Kevin — *J. Kevin Coleman & Associates, Inc.*

Colling, Douglas — *KPMG Management Consulting*

Collis, Gerald — *TSS Consulting, Ltd.*

Colman, Michael — *Executive Placement Consultants, Inc.*

Colvin, Teresa A. — *Jonas, Walters & Assoc., Inc.*

Combs, Stephen L. — *Juntunen-Combs-Poirier*

Compton, Tonya — *Dunhill Professional Search of Irvine, Inc.*

Conard, Rodney J. — *Conard Associates, Inc.*

Connor, Michele — *Abraham & London, Ltd.*

Conway, Maureen — *Conway & Associates*

Conway, William P. — *Phillips Resource Group*

Cooke, Katherine H. — *Horton International*

Cornehlsen, James H. — *Skott/Edwards Consultants, Inc.*

Corrigan, Gerald F. — *The Corrigan Group*

Cortina Del Valle, Pedro — *Ray & Berndtson*

Costello, Lynda — *Coe & Company International Inc.*

Cowell, Roy A. — *Cowell & Associates, Ltd.*

Crane, Howard C. — *Chartwell Partners International, Inc.*

Crath, Paul F. — *Price Waterhouse*

Critchley, Walter — *Cochran, Cochran & Yale, Inc.*

Crosler, Yvonne — *Paul-Tittle Associates, Inc.*

Crowder, Edward W. — *Crowder & Company*

Cruse, O.D. — *Spencer Stuart*

Cuddihy, Paul — *Dahl-Morrow International*

Cunningham, Lawrence — *Howard Fischer Associates, Inc.*

Cunningham, Robert Y. — *Goodrich & Sherwood Associates, Inc.*

Cunningham, Sheila — *Adams & Associates International*

Curci, Donald L. — *A.R.I. International*

Curtis, Ellissa — *Cochran, Cochran & Yale, Inc.*

Czamanske, Paul W. — *Compass Group Ltd.*

Daily, John C. — *Handy HRM Corp.*

Dalton, Bret — *Robert W. Dingman Company, Inc.*

Daniel, Beverly — *Foy, Schneid & Daniel, Inc.*

Daniels, C. Eugene — *Sigma Group International*

Daniels, Donna — *Jonas, Walters & Assoc., Inc.*

Danoff, Audrey — *Don Richard Associates of Tidewater, Inc.*

Davis, Bert — *Bert Davis Executive Search, Inc.*

Davis, G. Gordon — *Davis & Company*

Davison, Patricia E. — *Lamalie Amrop International*

De Brun, Thomas P. — *Ray & Berndtson*

Deaver, Henry C. — *Ray & Berndtson*

DeCorrevont, James — *DeCorrevont & Associates*

DeCorrevont, James — *DeCorrevont & Associates*

Delaney, Patrick J. — *Sensible Solutions, Inc.*

DeLong, Art — *Richard Kader & Associates*

Demchak, James P. — *Sandhurst Associates*

Desgrosellier, Gary P. — *Personnel Unlimited/Executive Search*

Desmond, Dennis — *Beall & Company, Inc.*

deWilde, David M. — *Chartwell Partners International, Inc.*

Dezember, Steve — *Ray & Berndtson*

DiCioccio, Carmen — *Cochran, Cochran & Yale, Inc.*

Dickson, Duke — *A.D. & Associates Executive Search, Inc.*

Dietz, David S. — *MSI International*

DiMarchi, Paul — *DiMarchi Partners, Inc.*

DiMarchi, Paul — *DiMarchi Partners, Inc.*

Dingeldey, Peter E. — *Search Advisors International Corp.*

Dingman, Bruce — *Robert W. Dingman Company, Inc.*

Dingman, Robert W. — *Robert W. Dingman Company, Inc.*

Dinte, Paul — *Dinte Resources, Inc.*

DiSalvo, Fred — *The Cambridge Group Ltd*

Diskin, Rochelle — *Search West, Inc.*

Divine, Robert S. — *O'Shea, Divine & Company, Inc.*

Doele, Donald C. — *Goodrich & Sherwood Associates, Inc.*

Donath, Linda — *Dahl-Morrow International*

Dotson, M. Ileen — *Dotson & Associates*

Dowell, Chris — *The Abbott Group, Inc.*

Dowell, Mary K. — *Professional Search Associates*

Doyle, James W. — *Executive Search Consultants International, Inc.*

Dreifus, Donald — *Search West, Inc.*

Dromeshauser, Peter — *Dromeshauser Associates*

Drury, James J. — *Spencer Stuart*

Dubbs, William — *Williams Executive Search, Inc.*

Dubrow, Richard M. — *R/K International, Inc.*

Dugan, John H. — *J.H. Dugan and Associates, Inc.*

Duley, Richard I. — *ARJay & Associates*

Dunbar, Marilynne — *Ray & Berndtson/Lovas Stanley*

Dunman, Betsy L. — *Crawford & Crofford*

Durakis, Charles A. — *C.A. Durakis Associates, Inc.*

Dussick, Vince — *Dussick Management Associates*

Ebeling, John A. — *Gilbert Tweed/INESA*

Edmond, Bruce — *Corporate Recruiters Ltd.*

Edwards, Dorothy — *MSI International*

Edwards, John W. — *The Bedford Group*

Edwards, Verba L. — *Wing Tips & Pumps, Inc.*

Eggena, Roger — *Phillips Resource Group*

Ehrgott, Elizabeth — *The Ascher Group*

Ehrhart, Jennifer — *ADOW's Executeam*

Eldridge, Charles B. — *Ray & Berndtson*

Ellis, Ted K. — *The Hindman Company*

Ellis, William — *Interspace Interactive Inc.*

Elnaggar, Hani — *Juntunen-Combs-Poirier*

England, Mark — *Austin-McGregor International*

Engler, Peter G — *Lautz Grotte Engler*

Enns, George — *The Enns Partners Inc.*

Erder, Debra — *Canny, Bowen Inc.*

Esposito, Mark — *Christian & Timbers*

Eustis, Lucy R. — *MSI International*

Falk, John — *D.S. Allen Associates, Inc.*

Fancher, Robert L. — *Bason Associates Inc.*

Farley, Leon A. — *Leon A. Farley Associates*

Farrow, Jerry M. — *McCormack & Farrow*

Fawkes, Elizabeth — *Paul-Tittle Associates, Inc.*

Hart, Robert T. — *D.E. Foster Partners Inc.*
Harvey, Mike — *Advanced Executive Resources*
Haughton, Michael — *DeFrain, Mayer LLC*
Hauswirth, Jeffrey M. — *Spencer Stuart*
Havener, Donald Clarke — *The Abbott Group, Inc.*
Hawksworth, A. Dwight — *A.D. & Associates Executive Search, Inc.*
Hayes, Stacy — *The McCormick Group, Inc.*
Haystead, Steve — *Advanced Executive Resources*
Heacock, Burt E. — *Paul-Tittle Associates, Inc.*
Hechkoff, Robert B. — *Quantex Associates, Inc.*
Hedlund, David — *Hedlund Corporation*
Heffelfinger, Thomas V. — *Heffelfinger Associates, Inc.*
Heiken, Barbara E. — *Randell-Heiken, Inc.*
Heinze, David — *Heinze & Associates, Inc.*
Helminiak, Audrey — *Gaffney Management Consultants*
Henard, John B. — *Lamalie Amrop International*
Heneghan, Donald A. — *Allerton Heneghan & O'Neill*
Henn, George W. — *G.W. Henn & Company*
Henry, Mary — *Conex Incorporated*
Hergenrather, Richard A. — *Hergenrather & Company*
Herman, Eugene J. — *Earley Kielty and Associates, Inc.*
Herman, Shelli — *Gary Kaplan & Associates*
Hewitt, Rives D. — *The Dalley Hewitt Company*
Hewitt, W. Davis — *The Dalley Hewitt Company*
Hicks, Albert M. — *Phillips Resource Group*
Higgins, Donna — *Howard Fischer Associates, Inc.*
Hildebrand, Thomas B. — *Professional Resources Group, Inc.*
Hill, Emery — *MSI International*
Hillen, Skip — *The McCormick Group, Inc.*
Himlin, Amy — *Cochran, Cochran & Yale, Inc.*
Hindman, Neil C. — *The Hindman Company*
Hochberg, Brian — *M.A. Churchill & Associates, Inc.*
Hockett, William — *Hockett Associates, Inc.*
Hoevel, Michael J. — *Poirier, Hoevel & Co.*
Hokanson, Mark D. — *Crowder & Company*
Holden, Richard B. — *Ames Personnel Consultants, Inc.*
Holland, John A. — *Holland, McFadzean & Associates, Inc.*
Holland, Rose Mary — *Price Waterhouse*
Hollins, Howard D. — *MSI International*
Holmes, Lawrence J. — *Columbia Consulting Group*
Holt, Carol — *Bartholdi & Company, Inc.*
Hoover, Catherine — *J.L. Mark Associates, Inc.*
Hopgood, Earl — *JDG Associates, Ltd.*
Hopkins, Chester A. — *Handy HRM Corp.*
Horner, Gregory — *Corporate Recruiters Ltd.*
Houchins, William M. — *Christian & Timbers*
Hoyda, Louis A. — *Thorndike Deland Associates*
Hucko, Donald S. — *Jonas, Walters & Assoc., Inc.*
Hudson, Reginald M. — *Search Bureau International*
Huff, William Z. — *Huff Associates*
Hughes, Cathy N. — *The Ogdon Partnership*
Hughes, Donald J. — *Hughes & Company*
Hughes, James J. — *R.P. Barone Associates*

Humphrey, Joan — *Abraham & London, Ltd.*
Hunter, Gabe — *Phillips Resource Group*
Hutchison, Richard H. — *Rurak & Associates, Inc.*
Hutchison, William K. — *Christenson & Hutchison*
Hykes, Don A. — *A.T. Kearney, Inc.*
Iannacone, Kelly — *Abraham & London, Ltd.*
Inguagiato, Gregory — *MSI International*
Issacs, Judith A. — *Grant Cooper and Associates*
Jacobs, Martin J. — *The Rubicon Group*
Jacobs, Mike — *Thorne, Brieger Associates Inc.*
Jacobson, Carolyn — *The Abbott Group, Inc.*
Jacobson, Rick — *The Windham Group*
Jaffe, Mark — *Wyatt & Jaffe*
James, Bruce — *Roberson and Company*
Janis, Laurence — *Integrated Search Solutions Group, LLC*
Jansen, John F. — *Delta Services*
Janssen, Don — *Howard Fischer Associates, Inc.*
Januale, Lois — *Cochran, Cochran & Yale, Inc.*
Jaworski, Mary A. — *Tully/Woodmansee International, Inc.*
Jazylo, John V. — *Handy HRM Corp.*
Jeffers, Richard B. — *Dieckmann & Associates, Ltd.*
Joffe, Barry — *Bason Associates Inc.*
Johnson, David A. — *Gaffney Management Consultants*
Johnson, Douglas — *Quality Search*
Johnson, John W. — *Webb, Johnson Associates, Inc.*
Johnson, Julie M. — *International Staffing Consultants, Inc.*
Johnson, Kathleen A. — *Barton Associates, Inc.*
Johnson, Robert J. — *Quality Search*
Johnson, Stanley C. — *Johnson & Company*
Johnson, Valerie — *Coe & Company International Inc.*
Johnston, Michael — *Robertson-Surrette Executive Search*
Jones, Amy E. — *The Corporate Connection, Ltd.*
Jones, Barbara — *Kaye-Bassman International Corp.*
Jones, Francis E. — *Earley Kielty and Associates, Inc.*
Jones, Gary — *BGB Associates*
Jones, Ronald T. — *ARJay & Associates*
Jordan, Jon — *Cochran, Cochran & Yale, Inc.*
Judge, Alfred L. — *The Cambridge Group Ltd*
Juelis, John J. — *Peeney Associates*
Kaiser, Donald J. — *Dunhill International Search of New Haven*
Kane, Karen — *Howard Fischer Associates, Inc.*
Kanovsky, Gerald — *Career Consulting Group, Inc.*
Kanovsky, Marlene — *Career Consulting Group, Inc.*
Kaplan, Gary — *Gary Kaplan & Associates*
Kartin, Martin C. — *Martin Kartin and Company, Inc.*
Keating, Pierson — *Nordeman Grimm, Inc.*
Keller, Barbara E. — *Barton Associates, Inc.*
Kells, John — *Heffelfinger Associates, Inc.*
Kelly, Elizabeth Ann — *Wellington Management Group*
Kelly, Susan D. — *S.D. Kelly & Associates, Inc.*
Kelso, Patricia C. — *Barton Associates, Inc.*

Mathias, Kathy — *Stone Murphy & Olson*
Matthews, Corwin — *Woodworth International Group*
Matti, Suzy — *Southwestern Professional Services*
May, Peter — *Mixtec Group*
Maynard Taylor, Susan — *Chrisman & Company, Incorporated*
Mazor, Elly — *Howard Fischer Associates, Inc.*
Mazza, David B. — *Mazza & Riley, Inc. (a Korn/Ferry International affiliate)*
McBride, Dee — *Deeco International*
McBride, Jonathan E. — *McBride Associates, Inc.*
McCloskey, Frank D. — *Johnson Smith & Knisely Accord*
McCormick, Brian — *The McCormick Group, Inc.*
McCormick, William J. — *The McCormick Group, Inc.*
McCreary, Charles "Chip" — *Austin-McGregor International*
McDermott, Jeffrey T. — *Vlcek & Company, Inc.*
McDonald, John R. — *TSS Consulting, Ltd.*
McDonald, Scott A. — *McDonald Associates International*
McDonald, Stanleigh B. — *McDonald Associates International*
McDonnell, Julie — *Technical Personnel of Minnesota*
McDowell, Robert N. — *Christenson & Hutchison*
McFadden, Ashton S. — *Johnson Smith & Knisely Accord*
McFadzen, Donna — *Holland, McFadzean & Associates, Inc.*
McFadzen, James A. — *Holland, McFadzean & Associates, Inc.*
McGregor, James D. — *John Kurosky & Associates*
McGuire, J. Corey — *Peter W. Ambler Company*
McHale, Rob — *Paul-Tittle Associates, Inc.*
McIntyre, Joel — *Phillips Resource Group*
McKeown, Morgan J. — *Christian & Timbers*
McKeown, Patricia A. — *DiMarchi Partners, Inc.*
McKnight, Amy E. — *Chartwell Partners International, Inc.*
McManners, Donald E. — *McManners Associates, Inc.*
McMillin, Bob — *Price Waterhouse*
McNamara, Catherine — *Ray & Berndtson*
McNamara, Timothy C. — *Columbia Consulting Group*
McNichol, John — *McNichol Associates*
McNichols, Walter B. — *Gary Kaplan & Associates*
McThrall, David — *TSS Consulting, Ltd.*
Mead, James D. — *James Mead & Company*
Mercer, Julie — *Columbia Consulting Group*
Meyer, Stacey — *Gary Kaplan & Associates*
Mierzwinski, John — *Industrial Recruiters Associates, Inc.*
Mikula, Linda — *Schweichler Associates, Inc.*
Miles, Kenneth T. — *MSI International*
Miller, Brett — *The McCormick Group, Inc.*
Miller, David — *Cochran, Cochran & Yale, Inc.*
Miller, Roy — *The Enns Partners Inc.*
Miller, Russel E. — *ARJay & Associates*
Milstein, Bonnie — *Marvin Laba & Associates*
Mingle, Larry D. — *Columbia Consulting Group*
Misiurewicz, Marc — *Cochran, Cochran & Yale, Inc.*

Moerbe, Ed H. — *Stanton Chase International*
Mogul, Gene — *Mogul Consultants, Inc.*
Montgomery, James M. — *Houze, Shourds & Montgomery, Inc.*
Moore, David S. — *Lynch Miller Moore, Inc.*
Moore, Lemuel R. — *MSI International*
Moore, Mark — *Wheeler, Moore & Elam Co.*
Moore, T. Wills — *Ray & Berndtson*
Moran, Gayle — *Dussick Management Associates*
Morgan, Richard S. — *Ray & Berndtson/Lovas Stanley*
Mortansen, Patricia — *Norman Broadbent International, Inc.*
Muendel, H. Edward — *Stanton Chase International*
Murphy, Cornelius J. — *Goodrich & Sherwood Associates, Inc.*
Murphy, Patrick J. — *P.J. Murphy & Associates, Inc.*
Murphy, Timothy D. — *MSI International*
Mursuli, Meredith — *Lasher Associates*
Myers, Kay — *Signature Staffing*
Nadherny, Christopher C. — *Spencer Stuart*
Nagler, Leon G. — *Nagler, Robins & Poe, Inc.*
Naidicz, Maria — *Ray & Berndtson*
Nees, Eugene C. — *Ray & Berndtson*
Neher, Robert L. — *Intech Summit Group, Inc.*
Nehring, Keith — *Howard Fischer Associates, Inc.*
Neidhart, Craig C. — *TNS Partners, Inc.*
Nelson, Barbara — *Herman Smith Executive Initiatives Inc.*
Nemec, Phillip — *Dunhill International Search of New Haven*
Nephew, Robert — *Christian & Timbers*
Neuberth, Jeffrey G. — *Canny, Bowen Inc.*
Newman, Lynn — *Kishbaugh Associates International*
Nichols, Gary — *Koontz, Jeffries & Associates, Inc.*
Niejet, Michael C. — *O'Brien & Bell*
Nolan, Jean M. — *S.D. Kelly & Associates, Inc.*
Nold, Robert — *Roberson and Company*
Nolte, William D. — *W.D. Nolte & Company*
Norman, Randy — *Austin-McGregor International*
Normann, Amy — *Robert M. Flanagan & Associates, Ltd.*
Norsell, Paul E. — *Paul Norsell & Associates, Inc.*
O'Hara, Daniel M. — *Lynch Miller Moore, Inc.*
O'Maley, Kimberlee — *Spencer Stuart*
Ocon, Olga — *Busch International*
Ogdon, Thomas H. — *The Ogdon Partnership*
Ogilvie, Kit — *Howard Fischer Associates, Inc.*
Oldfield, Theresa — *Strategic Alliance Network, Ltd.*
Olmstead, George T. — *Blackshaw, Olmstead, Lynch & Koenig*
Olsen, Carl — *A.T. Kearney, Inc.*
Olsen, David G. — *Handy HRM Corp.*
Onstott, Joseph — *The Onstott Group, Inc.*
Onstott, Joseph E. — *The Onstott Group, Inc.*
Ott, George W. — *Ott & Hansen, Inc.*
Overlock, Craig — *Ray & Berndtson*
Pace, Susan A. — *Horton International*
Pacini, Lauren R. — *Hite Executive Search*
Palma, Frank R. — *Goodrich & Sherwood Associates, Inc.*
Palmer, Carlton A. — *Beall & Company, Inc.*

Palmer, James H. — *The Hindman Company*
Panarese, Pam — *Howard Fischer Associates, Inc.*
Papasadero, Kathleen — *Woodworth International Group*
Papoulias, Cathy — *Pendleton James and Associates, Inc.*
Pappas, Jim — *Search Dynamics, Inc.*
Pardo, Maria Elena — *Smith Search, S.C.*
Parkin, Myrna — *S.D. Kelly & Associates, Inc.*
Parr, James A. — *KPMG Management Consulting*
Parry, William H. — *Horton International*
Parsons, Allison D. — *Barton Associates, Inc.*
Pearson, Robert L. — *Lamalie Amrop International*
Peasback, David R. — *Canny, Bowen Inc.*
Peckenpaugh, Ann D. — *Schweichler Associates, Inc.*
Peeney, James D. — *Peeney Associates*
Pelisson, Charles — *Marra Peters & Partners*
Pelkey, Chris — *The McCormick Group, Inc.*
Pernell, Jeanette — *Norman Broadbent International, Inc.*
Perry, Glen — *Keith Bagg & Associates Inc.*
Peternell, Melanie — *Signature Staffing*
Peters, James N. — *TNS Partners, Inc.*
Petty, J. Scott — *The Arcus Group*
Pfeiffer, Irene — *Price Waterhouse*
Phelps, Gene L. — *McCormack & Farrow*
Phillips, Donald L. — *O'Shea, Divine & Company, Inc.*
Phinney, Bruce — *Paul-Tittle Associates, Inc.*
Phipps, Peggy — *Woodworth International Group*
Pickering, Dale — *Agri-Tech Personnel, Inc.*
Pickering, Rita — *Agri-Tech Personnel, Inc.*
Pickford, Stephen T. — *The Corporate Staff, Inc.*
Pigott, Daniel — *ESA Professional Consultants*
Plummer, John — *Plummer & Associates, Inc.*
Poirier, Roland L. — *Poirier, Hoevel & Co.*
Pompeo, Paul — *Search West, Inc.*
Porada, Stephen D. — *CAP Inc.*
Porter, Albert — *The Experts*
Potter, Douglas C. — *Stanton Chase International*
Price, Andrew G. — *The Thomas Tucker Company*
Pryde, Marcia P. — *A.T. Kearney, Inc.*
Pryor, Bill — *Cendea Connection International*
Pugh, Judith Geist — *InterimManagement Solutions, Inc.*
Raab, Julie — *Dunhill Professional Search of Irvine, Inc.*
Rabe, William — *Sales Executives Inc.*
Rabinowitz, Peter A. — *P.A.R. Associates Inc.*
Raiber, Laurie Altman — *The IMC Group of Companies Ltd.*
Raines, Bruce R. — *Raines International Inc.*
Ramler, Carolyn S. — *The Corporate Connection, Ltd.*
Randell, James E. — *Randell-Heiken, Inc.*
Ray, Marianne C. — *Callan Associates, Ltd.*
Raymond, Anne — *Anderson Sterling Associates*
Reddick, David C. — *Horton International*
Redding, Denise — *The Douglas Reiter Company, Inc.*
Reece, Christopher S. — *Reece & Mruk Partners*
Reed, Ruthann — *Spectra International Inc.*
Reifel, Laurie — *Reifel & Assocaites*
Reifersen, Ruth F. — *The Jonathan Stevens Group, Inc.*

Reiser, Ellen — *Thorndike Deland Associates*
Reisinger, George L. — *Sigma Group International*
Reiter, Douglas — *The Douglas Reiter Company, Inc.*
Remillard, Brad M. — *CJA - The Adler Group*
Renwick, David — *John Kurosky & Associates*
Reyman, Susan — *S. Reyman & Associates Ltd.*
Reynes, Tony — *Tesar-Reynes, Inc.*
Reynolds, Gregory P. — *Roberts Ryan and Bentley*
Rhodes, Bill — *Bench International*
Ribeiro, Claudia — *Ledbetter/Davidson International, Inc.*
Rice, Marie — *Jay Gaines & Company, Inc.*
Richards, Paul E. — *Executive Directions*
Richards, R. Glenn — *Executive Directions*
Ridenour, Suzanne S. — *Ridenour & Associates, Ltd.*
Rieger, Louis J. — *Spencer Stuart*
Rimmel, James E. — *The Hindman Company*
Rimmele, Michael — *The Bankers Group*
Rizzo, L. Donald — *R.P. Barone Associates*
Roberts, Mitch — *A.E. Feldman Associates*
Roberts, Scott — *Jonas, Walters & Assoc., Inc.*
Robertson, John A. — *Kaye-Bassman International Corp.*
Robertson, Ronald — *Robertson-Surrette Executive Search*
Robins, Jeri N. — *Nagler, Robins & Poe, Inc.*
Robinson, Bruce — *Bruce Robinson Associates*
Robles Cuellar, Paulina — *Ray & Berndtson*
Roblin, Nancy R. — *Paul-Tittle Associates, Inc.*
Rogers, Leah — *Dinte Resources, Inc.*
Romanello, Daniel P. — *Spencer Stuart*
Romang, Paula — *Agri-Tech Personnel, Inc.*
Rosato, William R. — *W.R. Rosato & Associates, Inc.*
Rose, Robert — *ESA Professional Consultants*
Ross, Curt A. — *Ray & Berndtson*
Ross, H. Lawrence — *Ross & Company*
Ross, Lawrence — *Ray & Berndtson/Lovas Stanley*
Ross, Mark — *Ray & Berndtson/Lovas Stanley*
Ross, William J. — *Flowers & Associates*
Rotella, Marshall W. — *The Corporate Connection, Ltd.*
Roth, Robert J. — *Williams, Roth & Krueger Inc.*
Rudolph, Kenneth — *Kossuth & Associates, Inc.*
Rudzinsky, Howard — *Louis Rudzinsky Associates*
Rurak, Zbigniew T. — *Rurak & Associates, Inc.*
Rush, Michael E. — *D.A.L. Associates, Inc.*
Sacerdote, John — *Raymond Karsan Associates*
Salottolo, Al — *Tactical Alternatives*
Salvagno, Michael J. — *The Cambridge Group Ltd*
Sanow, Robert — *Cochran, Cochran & Yale, Inc.*
Sarna, Edmund A. — *Jonas, Walters & Assoc., Inc.*
Sausto, Lynne — *Abraham & London, Ltd.*
Savvas, Carol Diane — *Ledbetter/Davidson International, Inc.*
Sawyer, Patricia L. — *Smith & Sawyer Inc.*
Saxon, Alexa — *Woodworth International Group*
Schaefer, Frederic M. — *A.T. Kearney, Inc.*
Schedra, Sharon — *Earley Kielty and Associates, Inc.*
Schene, Philip — *A.E. Feldman Associates*
Schiavone, Mary Rose — *Canny, Bowen Inc.*
Schlpma, Christine — *Advanced Executive Resources*
Schmidt, Frank B. — *F.B. Schmidt International*

Schmidt, Peter R. — *Boyden*
Schmidt, William C. — *Christian & Timbers*
Schneiderman, Gerald — *Management Resource Associates, Inc.*
Schnierow, Beryl — *Tesar-Reynes, Inc.*
Schwam, Carol — *A.E. Feldman Associates*
Schweichler, Lee J. — *Schweichler Associates, Inc.*
Scott, Evan — *Howard Fischer Associates, Inc.*
Scott, Gordon S. — *Search Advisors International Corp.*
Searing, James M. — *Kirkman & Searing, Inc.*
Seco, William — *Seco & Zetto Associates, Inc.*
Seiden, Steven A. — *Seiden Krieger Associates, Inc.*
Semyan, John K. — *TNS Partners, Inc.*
Sevilla, Claudio A. — *Crawford & Crofford*
Shamir, Ben — *S.D. Kelly & Associates, Inc.*
Shattuck, Merrill B. — *M.B. Shattuck and Associates, Inc.*
Sheedy, Edward J. — *Dieckmann & Associates, Ltd.*
Shepard, Michael J. — *MSI International*
Shepherd, Daniel M. — *Shepherd Bueschel & Provus, Inc.*
Sherwood, Andrew — *Goodrich & Sherwood Associates, Inc.*
Shimp, David J. — *Lamalie Amrop International*
Shirilla, Robert M. — *F.B. Schmidt International*
Shore, Earl L. — *E.L. Shore & Associates Ltd.*
Shulman, Barry — *Shulman Associates*
Sickles, Robert — *Dunhill Professional Search of Irvine, Inc.*
Siegrist, Jeffrey M. — *D.E. Foster Partners Inc.*
Sill, Igor N. — *Geneva Group International*
Silver, Lee — *L. A. Silver Associates, Inc.*
Simmons, Anneta — *F-O-R-T-U-N-E Personnel Consultants of Huntsville, Inc.*
Simmons, Sandra K. — *MSI International*
Simpson, Scott — *Cendea Connection International*
Sitarski, Stan — *Howard Fischer Associates, Inc.*
Skalet, Ira — *A.E. Feldman Associates*
Skunda, Donna M. — *Allerton Heneghan & O'Neill*
Slayton, Richard C. — *Slayton International, Inc./I-I-C Partners*
Slosar, John — *Boyden*
Smead, Michelle M. — *A.T. Kearney, Inc.*
Smith, Ana Luz — *Smith Search, S.C.*
Smith, David P. — *HRS, Inc.*
Smith, Grant — *Price Waterhouse*
Smith, Herman M. — *Herman Smith Executive Initiatives Inc.*
Smith, Ian — *International Staffing Consultants, Inc.*
Smith, John E. — *Smith Search, S.C.*
Smith, Lydia — *The Corporate Connection, Ltd.*
Smith, Matt D. — *Ray & Berndtson*
Smith, Robert L. — *Smith & Sawyer Inc.*
Smith, Ronald V. — *Coe & Company International Inc.*
Snyder, C. Edward — *Horton International*
Snyder, James F. — *Snyder & Company*
Sola, George L. — *A.T. Kearney, Inc.*
Souder, E.G. — *Souder & Associates*
Sowerbutt, Richard S. — *Hite Executive Search*

Spann, Richard E. — *Goodrich & Sherwood Associates, Inc.*
Spiegel, Gayle — *L. A. Silver Associates, Inc.*
Sprau, Collin L. — *Ray & Berndtson*
Spriggs, Robert D. — *Spriggs & Company, Inc.*
St. Clair, Alan — *TNS Partners, Inc.*
Stark, Jeff — *Thorne, Brieger Associates Inc.*
Statson, Dale E. — *Sales Executives Inc.*
Steele, Daniel — *Cochran, Cochran & Yale, Inc.*
Stein, Terry W. — *Stewart, Stein and Scott, Ltd.*
Steinem, Andy — *Dahl-Morrow International*
Steinem, Barbra — *Dahl-Morrow International*
Steinman, Stephen M. — *The Stevenson Group of New Jersey*
Sterling, Jay — *Earley Kielty and Associates, Inc.*
Stevens, Craig M. — *Kirkman & Searing, Inc.*
Stevens, Ken — *The Stevens Group*
Stevenson, Jane — *Howard Fischer Associates, Inc.*
Stevenson, Terry — *Bartholdi & Company, Inc.*
Stewart, Jeffrey O. — *Stewart, Stein and Scott, Ltd.*
Stewart, Ross M. — *Human Resources Network Partners Inc.*
Stiles, Judy — *MedQuest Associates*
Stokes, John — *Nordeman Grimm, Inc.*
Stone, Susan L. — *Stone Enterprises Ltd.*
Stranberg, James R. — *Callan Associates, Ltd.*
Stratmeyer, Karin Bergwall — *Princeton Entrepreneurial Resources*
Stratton, Cary — *Coastal International Inc.*
Strickland, Katie — *Grantham & Co., Inc.*
Stringer, Dann P. — *D.E. Foster Partners Inc.*
Strom, Mark N. — *Search Advisors International Corp.*
Sturtz, James W. — *Compass Group Ltd.*
Sullivan, Kay — *Rusher, Loscavio & LoPresto*
Sur, William K. — *Canny, Bowen Inc.*
Surrette, Mark — *Robertson-Surrette Executive Search*
Swanson, Dick — *Raymond Karsan Associates*
Swartz, William K. — *Swartz Executive Search*
Sweeney, James W. — *Sweeney Harbert & Mummert, Inc.*
Swick, Jan — *TSS Consulting, Ltd.*
Taylor, Conrad G. — *MSI International*
Taylor, James M. — *The HRM Group, Inc.*
Taylor, R.L. (Larry) — *Ray & Berndtson*
Telford, John H. — *Telford, Adams & Alexander/Telford & Co., Inc.*
ten Cate, Herman H. — *Stoneham Associates Corp.*
Tesar, Bob — *Tesar-Reynes, Inc.*
Tetrick, Tim — *O'Connor, O'Connor, Lordi, Ltd.*
Theobald, David B. — *Theobald & Associates*
Thies, Gary — *S.D. Kelly & Associates, Inc.*
Thomas, Kurt J. — *P.J. Murphy & Associates, Inc.*
Thomas, Terry — *The Thomas Resource Group*
Thompson, Dave — *Battalia Winston International*
Thompson, Kenneth L. — *McCormack & Farrow*
Thrapp, Mark C. — *Executive Search Consultants International, Inc.*
Timoney, Laura — *Bishop Partners*
Tincu, John C. — *Ferneborg & Associates, Inc.*
Tittle, David M. — *Paul-Tittle Associates, Inc.*
Topliff, Marla — *Gaffney Management Consultants*

Zila, Laurie M. — *Princeton Entrepreneurial Resources*
Zinn, Don — *Quantex Associates, Inc.*
Zwell, Michael — *Zwell International*

8. Research/Development

Abbott, Peter D. — *The Abbott Group, Inc.*
Adler, Louis S. — *CJA - The Adler Group*
Albertini, Nancy — *Taylor-Winfield, Inc.*
Allerton, Donald T. — *Allerton Heneghan & O'Neill*
Altreuter, Rose — *The ALTCO Group*
Ambler, Peter W. — *Peter W. Ambler Company*
Ames, George C. — *Ames O'Neill Associates*
Anderson, Dean C. — *Corporate Resources Professional Placement*
Anderson, Maria H. — *Barton Associates, Inc.*
Anderson, Steve — *CPS Inc.*
Apostle, George — *Search Dynamics, Inc.*
Arnold, David W. — *Christian & Timbers*
Aronin, Michael — *Fisher-Todd Associates*
Ashton, Barbara L. — *Ashton Computer Professionals Inc.*
Asquith, Peter S. — *Ames Personnel Consultants, Inc.*
Aston, Kathy — *Marra Peters & Partners*
Atwood, Barrie — *The Abbott Group, Inc.*
Bacon, Cheri — *Gaffney Management Consultants*
Badger, Fred H. — *The Badger Group*
Baeder, Jeremy — *Executive Manning Corporation*
Baje, Sarah — *Innovative Search Group, LLC*
Balbone, Rich — *Executive Manning Corporation*
Balch, Randy — *CPS Inc.*
Baldwin, Keith R. — *The Baldwin Group*
Baltin, Carrie — *Search West, Inc.*
Barbour, Mary Beth — *Tully/Woodmansee International, Inc.*
Barlow, Ken H. — *The Cherbonnier Group, Inc.*
Barnes, Richard E. — *Barnes Development Group, LLC*
Barnes, Roanne L. — *Barnes Development Group, LLC*
Baron, Len — *Industrial Recruiters Associates, Inc.*
Barthold, James A. — *McNichol Associates*
Bartholdi, Ted — *Bartholdi & Company, Inc.*
Bartholdi, Theodore G. — *Bartholdi & Company, Inc.*
Bason, Maurice L. — *Bason Associates Inc.*
Bass, M. Lynn — *Ray & Berndtson*
Beal, Richard D. — *A.T. Kearney, Inc.*
Beaudin, Elizabeth C. — *Callan Associates, Ltd.*
Beaver, Bentley H. — *The Onstott Group, Inc.*
Bentley, Mark — *The Thomas Tucker Company*
Biestek, Paul J. — *Paul J. Biestek Associates, Inc.*
Birt, Peter — *Ashton Computer Professionals Inc.*
Bladon, Andrew — *Don Richard Associates of Tampa, Inc.*
Blanton, Thomas — *Blanton and Company*
Blim, Barbara — *JDG Associates, Ltd.*
Bloch, Terry L. — *Southern Research Services*
Bloomer, James E. — *L.W. Foote Company*
Bluhm, Claudia — *Schweichler Associates, Inc.*
Boczany, William J. — *The Guild Corporation*
Boel, Werner — *The Dalley Hewitt Company*
Bogansky, Amy — *Conex Incorporated*
Boltrus, Dick — *Sink, Walker, Boltrus International*

Bongiovanni, Vincent — *ESA Professional Consultants*
Borkin, Andrew — *Strategic Advancement Inc.*
Bostic, James E. — *Phillips Resource Group*
Bowden, Otis H. — *BowdenGlobal, Ltd.*
Bradley, Dalena — *Woodworth International Group*
Bradshaw, Monte — *Christian & Timbers*
Brady, Dick — *William Guy & Associates*
Brady, Robert — *CPS Inc.*
Brandeis, Richard — *CPS Inc.*
Brennen, Richard J. — *Spencer Stuart*
Brieger, Steve — *Thorne, Brieger Associates Inc.*
Britt, Stephen — *Keith Bagg & Associates Inc.*
Brown, Steffan — *Woodworth International Group*
Brunson, Therese — *Kors Montgomery International*
Bryant, Richard D. — *Bryant Associates, Inc.*
Bryant, Shari G. — *Bryant Associates, Inc.*
Bryza, Robert M. — *Robert Lowell International*
Brzezinski, Ronald T. — *Callan Associates, Ltd.*
Bullock, Conni — *Earley Kielty and Associates, Inc.*
Burden, Gene — *The Cherbonnier Group, Inc.*
Burfield, Elaine — *Skott/Edwards Consultants, Inc.*
Burke, John — *The Experts*
Busch, Jack — *Busch International*
Button, David R. — *The Button Group*
Cahill, Peter M. — *Peter M. Cahill Associates, Inc.*
Callan, Robert M. — *Callan Associates, Ltd.*
Calogeras, Chris — *The Sager Company*
Cameron, James W. — *Cameron Consulting*
Carlton, Patricia — *JDG Associates, Ltd.*
Cavolina, Michael — *Carver Search Consultants*
Celenza, Catherine — *CPS Inc.*
Chavous, C. Crawford — *Phillips Resource Group*
Cherbonnier, L. Michael — *TCG International, Inc.*
Cherbonnier, L. Michael — *The Cherbonnier Group, Inc.*
Christian, Philip — *Ray & Berndtson*
Christiansen, Amy — *CPS Inc.*
Christiansen, Doug — *CPS Inc.*
Cimino, James J. — *Executive Search, Ltd.*
Cizek, John T. — *Cizek Associates, Inc.*
Cizek, Marti J. — *Cizek Associates, Inc.*
Clark, James — *CPS Inc.*
Clark, John — *Tate Consulting Inc.*
Cline, Mark — *NYCOR Search, Inc.*
Clough, Geoff — *Intech Summit Group, Inc.*
Cochran, Hale — *Fenwick Partners*
Cochran, Scott P. — *The Badger Group*
Coffman, Brian — *Kossuth & Associates, Inc.*
Cohen, Robert C. — *Intech Summit Group, Inc.*
Colasanto, Frank M. — *W.R. Rosato & Associates, Inc.*
Colling, Douglas — *KPMG Management Consulting*
Colvin, Teresa A. — *Jonas, Walters & Assoc., Inc.*
Conway, Maureen — *Conway & Associates*
Conway, William P. — *Phillips Resource Group*
Cortina Del Valle, Pedro — *Ray & Berndtson*
Costello, Lynda — *Coe & Company International Inc.*
Coulman, Karen — *CPS Inc.*
Cram, Noel — *R.P. Barone Associates*
Crath, Paul F. — *Price Waterhouse*

Cruse, O.D. — *Spencer Stuart*
Cunningham, Lawrence — *Howard Fischer Associates, Inc.*
Curci, Donald L. — *A.R.I. International*
Czamanske, Paul W. — *Compass Group Ltd.*
Czepiel, Susan — *CPS Inc.*
Davis, Bert — *Bert Davis Executive Search, Inc.*
Davis, G. Gordon — *Davis & Company*
De Brun, Thomas P. — *Ray & Berndtson*
de Gury, Glenn — *Taylor-Winfield, Inc.*
Deaver, Henry C. — *Ray & Berndtson*
DeGioia, Joseph — *JDG Associates, Ltd.*
DeLong, Art — *Richard Kader & Associates*
Desai, Sushila — *Sink, Walker, Boltrus International*
Desmond, Dennis — *Beall & Company, Inc.*
Dezember, Steve — *Ray & Berndtson*
Dickson, Duke — *A.D. & Associates Executive Search, Inc.*
Dingeldey, Peter E. — *Search Advisors International Corp.*
DiSalvo, Fred — *The Cambridge Group Ltd*
Divine, Robert S. — *O'Shea, Divine & Company, Inc.*
Dixon, Aris — *CPS Inc.*
Dowell, Chris — *The Abbott Group, Inc.*
Drew, David R. — *Drew & Associates*
Drexler, Robert — *Robert Drexler Associates, Inc.*
Dubrow, Richard M. — *R/K International, Inc.*
Dugan, John H. — *J.H. Dugan and Associates, Inc.*
Duley, Richard I. — *ARJay & Associates*
Dunman, Betsy L. — *Crawford & Crofford*
Dussick, Vince — *Dussick Management Associates*
Dwyer, Julie — *CPS Inc.*
Ebeling, John A. — *Gilbert Tweed/INESA*
Edwards, John W. — *The Bedford Group*
Edwards, Verba L. — *Wing Tips & Pumps, Inc.*
Eggena, Roger — *Phillips Resource Group*
Elder, Tom — *Juntunen-Combs-Poirier*
Eldridge, Charles B. — *Ray & Berndtson*
England, Mark — *Austin-McGregor International*
Erikson, Theodore J. — *Erikson Consulting Associates, Inc.*
Ervin, Darlene — *CPS Inc.*
Esposito, Mark — *Christian & Timbers*
Evans, David — *Executive Manning Corporation*
Fancher, Robert L. — *Bason Associates Inc.*
Federman, Jack R. — *W.R. Rosato & Associates, Inc.*
Ferrara, David M. — *Intech Summit Group, Inc.*
Fincher, Richard P. — *Phase II Management*
Fini, Ron — *The Sager Company*
Fischer, Adam — *Howard Fischer Associates, Inc.*
Fischer, Howard M. — *Howard Fischer Associates, Inc.*
Fisher, Neal — *Fisher Personnel Management Services*
Fitzgerald, Diane — *Fitzgerald Associates*
Fitzgerald, Geoffrey — *Fitzgerald Associates*
Flanders, Karen — *Advanced Information Management*
Flannery, Peter F. — *Jonas, Walters & Assoc., Inc.*
Fogarty, Michael — *CPS Inc.*
Folkerth, Gene — *Gene Folkerth & Associates, Inc.*

Foote, Leland W. — *L.W. Foote Company*
Foreman, David C. — *Koontz, Jeffries & Associates, Inc.*
Fotia, Frank — *JDG Associates, Ltd.*
Francis, John — *Zwell International*
Freeman, Mark — *ESA Professional Consultants*
French, William G. — *Preng & Associates, Inc.*
Friedman, Helen E. — *McCormack & Farrow*
Fulmer, Karen — *Bench International*
Furlong, James W. — *Furlong Search, Inc.*
Furlong, James W. — *Furlong Search, Inc.*
Furlong, James W. — *Furlong Search, Inc.*
Fust, Sheely F. — *Ray & Berndtson*
Gabel, Gregory N. — *Canny, Bowen Inc.*
Gabriel, David L. — *The Arcus Group*
Gaffney, Keith — *Gaffney Management Consultants*
Gaffney, William — *Gaffney Management Consultants*
Galbraith, Deborah M. — *Stratford Group*
Gale, Rhoda E. — *E.G. Jones Associates, Ltd.*
Gallin, Larry — *Gallin Associates, Inc.*
Gantar, Donna — *Howard Fischer Associates, Inc.*
Garfinkle, Steven M. — *Battalia Winston International*
George, Delores F. — *Delores F. George Human Resource Management & Consulting Industry*
Gerbasi, Michael — *The Sager Company*
Gerster, J.P. — *Juntunen-Combs-Poirier*
Ghurani, Mac — *Gary Kaplan & Associates*
Giles, Joe L. — *Joe L. Giles and Associates, Inc.*
Gilmore, Connie — *Taylor-Winfield, Inc.*
Giries, Juliet D. — *Barton Associates, Inc.*
Girsinger, Linda — *Industrial Recruiters Associates, Inc.*
Gloss, Frederick C. — *F. Gloss International*
Gold, Stacey — *Earley Kielty and Associates, Inc.*
Goldenberg, Susan — *Grant Cooper and Associates*
Goodman, Dawn M. — *Bason Associates Inc.*
Goodman, Victor — *Anderson Sterling Associates*
Goodwin, Tim — *William Guy & Associates*
Gostyla, Rick — *Spencer Stuart*
Gould, Dana — *Logix, Inc.*
Graham, Dale — *CPS Inc.*
Grant, Michael — *Zwell International*
Grantham, John — *Grantham & Co., Inc.*
Grebenstein, Charles R. — *Skott/Edwards Consultants, Inc.*
Green, Jane — *Phillips Resource Group*
Grzybowski, Jill — *CPS Inc.*
Guy, C. William — *William Guy & Associates*
Hamburg, Jennifer Power — *Ledbetter/Davidson International, Inc.*
Hamilton, John R. — *Ray & Berndtson*
Hanes, Leah — *Ray & Berndtson*
Hanley, Alan P. — *Williams, Roth & Krueger Inc.*
Harbaugh, Paul J. — *International Management Advisors, Inc.*
Harney, Elyane — *Gary Kaplan & Associates*
Harris, Seth O. — *Christian & Timbers*
Harrison, Priscilla — *Phillips Resource Group*
Hart, Robert T. — *D.E. Foster Partners Inc.*
Hartle, Larry — *CPS Inc.*
Harvey, Mike — *Advanced Executive Resources*
Hauswirth, Jeffrey M. — *Spencer Stuart*

Havener, Donald Clarke — *The Abbott Group, Inc.*

Hawksworth, A. Dwight — *A.D. & Associates Executive Search, Inc.*

Haystead, Steve — *Advanced Executive Resources*

Hazerjian, Cynthia — *CPS Inc.*

Heafey, Bill — *CPS Inc.*

Heinze, David — *Heinze & Associates, Inc.*

Helminiak, Audrey — *Gaffney Management Consultants*

Heneghan, Donald A. — *Allerton Heneghan & O'Neill*

Henn, George W. — *G.W. Henn & Company*

Henry, Mary — *Conex Incorporated*

Henry, Patrick — *F-O-R-T-U-N-E Personnel Consultants of Huntsville, Inc.*

Henshaw, Bob — *F-O-R-T-U-N-E Personnel Consultants of Huntsville, Inc.*

Hergenrather, Richard A. — *Hergenrather & Company*

Herman, Eugene J. — *Earley Kielty and Associates, Inc.*

Herman, Shelli — *Gary Kaplan & Associates*

Hewitt, Rives D. — *The Dalley Hewitt Company*

Hewitt, W. Davis — *The Dalley Hewitt Company*

Hicks, Albert M. — *Phillips Resource Group*

Higgins, Donna — *Howard Fischer Associates, Inc.*

Hochberg, Brian — *M.A. Churchill & Associates, Inc.*

Hockett, William — *Hockett Associates, Inc.*

Hokanson, Mark D. — *Crowder & Company*

Holden, Richard B. — *Ames Personnel Consultants, Inc.*

Holland, John A. — *Holland, McFadzean & Associates, Inc.*

Holmes, Lawrence J. — *Columbia Consulting Group*

Holt, Carol — *Bartholdi & Company, Inc.*

Hoover, Catherine — *J.L. Mark Associates, Inc.*

Hopgood, Earl — *JDG Associates, Ltd.*

Hopkins, Chester A. — *Handy HRM Corp.*

Hopper, John W. — *William Guy & Associates*

Houchins, William M. — *Christian & Timbers*

Hudson, Reginald M. — *Search Bureau International*

Huff, William Z. — *Huff Associates*

Hunter, Gabe — *Phillips Resource Group*

Hykes, Don A. — *A.T. Kearney, Inc.*

Inzinna, Dennis — *AlternaStaff*

Irish, Alan — *CPS Inc.*

Jacobs, Martin J. — *The Rubicon Group*

Jacobs, Mike — *Thorne, Brieger Associates Inc.*

Jacobson, Carolyn — *The Abbott Group, Inc.*

Jaffe, Mark — *Wyatt & Jaffe*

James, Richard — *Criterion Executive Search, Inc.*

Jansen, Douglas L. — *Search Northwest Associates*

Jansen, John F. — *Delta Services*

Janssen, Don — *Howard Fischer Associates, Inc.*

Jaworski, Mary A. — *Tully/Woodmansee International, Inc.*

Jensen, Christine K. — *John Kurosky & Associates*

Joffe, Barry — *Bason Associates Inc.*

Johnson, David A. — *Gaffney Management Consultants*

Johnson, Douglas — *Quality Search*

Johnson, John W. — *Webb, Johnson Associates, Inc.*

Johnson, Julie M. — *International Staffing Consultants, Inc.*

Johnson, Robert J. — *Quality Search*

Johnson, Valerie — *Coe & Company International Inc.*

Johnston, Michael — *Robertson-Surrette Executive Search*

Jones, Francis E. — *Earley Kielty and Associates, Inc.*

Jones, Ronald T. — *ARJay & Associates*

Joyce, William J. — *The Guild Corporation*

Judge, Alfred L. — *The Cambridge Group Ltd*

Judy, Otto — *CPS Inc.*

Juelis, John J. — *Peeney Associates*

Kane, Karen — *Howard Fischer Associates, Inc.*

Kanrich, Susan Azaria — *AlternaStaff*

Kaplan, Gary — *Gary Kaplan & Associates*

Karalis, William — *CPS Inc.*

Kartin, Martin C. — *Martin Kartin and Company, Inc.*

Keating, Pierson — *Nordeman Grimm, Inc.*

Kehoe, Mike — *CPS Inc.*

Kern, Jerry L. — *ADOW's Executeam*

Kielty, John L. — *Earley Kielty and Associates, Inc.*

Kilcoyne, Pat — *CPS Inc.*

King, Margaret — *Christian & Timbers*

Kinney, Carol — *Dussick Management Associates*

Kinser, Richard E. — *Richard Kinser & Associates*

Kishbaugh, Herbert S. — *Kishbaugh Associates International*

Kkorzyniewski, Nicole — *CPS Inc.*

Klages, Constance W. — *International Management Advisors, Inc.*

Klauck, James J. — *Horton International*

Knotts, Jerry — *Mixtec Group*

Kohonoski, Michael M. — *The Guild Corporation*

Koontz, Donald N. — *Koontz, Jeffries & Associates, Inc.*

Kors, R. Paul — *Kors Montgomery International*

Kossuth, David — *Kossuth & Associates, Inc.*

Kossuth, Jane — *Kossuth & Associates, Inc.*

Krejci, Stanley L. — *Boyden Washington, D.C.*

Kreutz, Gary L. — *Kreutz Consulting Group, Inc.*

Krieger, Dennis F. — *Seiden Krieger Associates, Inc.*

Krueger, Kurt — *Krueger Associates*

Kuhl, Teresa — *Don Richard Associates of Tampa, Inc.*

Kunzer, William J. — *Kunzer Associates, Ltd.*

Kurrigan, Geoffrey — *ESA Professional Consultants*

Labrecque, Bernard F. — *Laurendeau Labrecque/Ray & Berndtson, Inc.*

LaCharite, Danielle — *The Guild Corporation*

Lache, Shawn E. — *The Arcus Group*

Laird, Cheryl — *CPS Inc.*

Lanctot, William D. — *Corporate Resources Professional Placement*

Lang, Sharon A. — *Ray & Berndtson*

Langan, Marion — *Logix, Inc.*

Lardner, Lucy D. — *Tully/Woodmansee International, Inc.*

Lasher, Charles M. — *Lasher Associates*

Leahy, Jan — *CPS Inc.*

Peckenpaugh, Ann D. — *Schweichler Associates, Inc.*
Pedley, Jill — *CPS Inc.*
Peeney, James D. — *Peeney Associates*
Pelisson, Charles — *Marra Peters & Partners*
Peters, James N. — *TNS Partners, Inc.*
Peterson, John — *CPS Inc.*
Phillips, Richard K. — *Handy HRM Corp.*
Phinney, Bruce — *Paul-Tittle Associates, Inc.*
Phipps, Peggy — *Woodworth International Group*
Pickering, Dale — *Agri-Tech Personnel, Inc.*
Pickering, Rita — *Agri-Tech Personnel, Inc.*
Pierotazio, John — *CPS Inc.*
Pigott, Daniel — *ESA Professional Consultants*
Plimpton, Ralph L. — *R L Plimpton Associates*
Poirier, Frank — *Juntunen-Combs-Poirier*
Pomerance, Mark — *CPS Inc.*
Porter, Albert — *The Experts*
Poster, Lawrence D. — *Catalyx Group*
Price, Andrew G. — *The Thomas Tucker Company*
Raiber, Laurie Altman — *The IMC Group of Companies Ltd.*
Raines, Bruce R. — *Raines International Inc.*
Ray, Marianne C. — *Callan Associates, Ltd.*
Raymond, Anne — *Anderson Sterling Associates*
Reed, Ruthann — *Spectra International Inc.*
Remillard, Brad M. — *CJA - The Adler Group*
Reuter, Tandom — *CPS Inc.*
Rhodes, Bill — *Bench International*
Ribeiro, Claudia — *Ledbetter/Davidson International, Inc.*
Riederer, Larry — *CPS Inc.*
Rizzo, L. Donald — *R.P. Barone Associates*
Robertson, John A. — *Kaye-Bassman International Corp.*
Robertson, Ronald — *Robertson-Surrette Executive Search*
Robinson, Bruce — *Bruce Robinson Associates*
Robles Cuellar, Paulina — *Ray & Berndtson*
Romanello, Daniel P. — *Spencer Stuart*
Romang, Paula — *Agri-Tech Personnel, Inc.*
Rosato, William R. — *W.R. Rosato & Associates, Inc.*
Rose, Robert — *ESA Professional Consultants*
Ross, Curt A. — *Ray & Berndtson*
Roth, Robert J. — *Williams, Roth & Krueger Inc.*
Rudolph, Kenneth — *Kossuth & Associates, Inc.*
Rudzinsky, Howard — *Louis Rudzinsky Associates*
Rudzinsky, Jeffrey — *Louis Rudzinsky Associates*
Ruge, Merrill — *William Guy & Associates*
Rurak, Zbigniew T. — *Rurak & Associates, Inc.*
Russell, Sam — *The Guild Corporation*
Ryan, Annette — *Don Richard Associates of Tidewater, Inc.*
Sacerdote, John — *Raymond Karsan Associates*
Saletra, Andrew — *CPS Inc.*
Salvagno, Michael J. — *The Cambridge Group Ltd*
Sanders, Natalie — *CPS Inc.*
Sangster, Jeffrey — *F-O-R-T-U-N-E Personnel Consultants of Manatee County*
Sarna, Edmund A. — *Jonas, Walters & Assoc., Inc.*
Savvas, Carol Diane — *Ledbetter/Davidson International, Inc.*
Scalamera, Tom — *CPS Inc.*
Schedra, Sharon — *Earley Kielty and Associates, Inc.*

Schiavone, Mary Rose — *Canny, Bowen Inc.*
Schlpma, Christine — *Advanced Executive Resources*
Schmidt, Peter R. — *Boyden*
Schneiderman, Gerald — *Management Resource Associates, Inc.*
Schueneman, David — *CPS Inc.*
Schweichler, Lee J. — *Schweichler Associates, Inc.*
Scott, Evan — *Howard Fischer Associates, Inc.*
Scott, Gordon S. — *Search Advisors International Corp.*
Sevilla, Claudio A. — *Crawford & Crofford*
Shapiro, Elaine — *CPS Inc.*
Shattuck, Merrill B. — *M.B. Shattuck and Associates, Inc.*
Sheedy, Edward J. — *Dieckmann & Associates, Ltd.*
Shufelt, Doug — *Sink, Walker, Boltrus International*
Siegrist, Jeffrey M. — *D.E. Foster Partners Inc.*
Signer, Julie — *CPS Inc.*
Siker, Paul W. — *The Guild Corporation*
Silcott, Marvin L. — *Marvin L. Silcott & Associates, Inc.*
Silcott, Marvin L. — *Marvin L. Silcott & Associates, Inc.*
Sill, Igor M. — *Geneva Group International*
Silver, Lee — *L. A. Silver Associates, Inc.*
Sink, Cliff — *Sink, Walker, Boltrus International*
Sitarski, Stan — *Howard Fischer Associates, Inc.*
Skunda, Donna M. — *Allerton Heneghan & O'Neill*
Slayton, Richard C. — *Slayton International, Inc./I-I-C Partners*
Slosar, John — *Boyden*
Smith, David P. — *HRS, Inc.*
Smith, Matt D. — *Ray & Berndtson*
Smith, Ronald V. — *Coe & Company International Inc.*
Snyder, C. Edward — *Horton International*
Snyder, James F. — *Snyder & Company*
Sola, George L. — *A.T. Kearney, Inc.*
Solters, Jeanne — *The Guild Corporation*
Souder, E.G. — *Souder & Associates*
Sowerbutt, Richard S. — *Hite Executive Search*
Spanninger, Mark J. — *The Guild Corporation*
Spiegel, Gayle — *L. A. Silver Associates, Inc.*
Spriggs, Robert D. — *Spriggs & Company, Inc.*
Staats, Dave — *Southwestern Professional Services*
Stanley, Paul R.A. — *Ray & Berndtson/Lovas Stanley*
Stark, Jeff — *Thorne, Brieger Associates Inc.*
Steer, Joe — *CPS Inc.*
Stein, Terry W. — *Stewart, Stein and Scott, Ltd.*
Stephenson, Don L. — *Ells Personnel System Inc.*
Sterling, Jay — *Earley Kielty and Associates, Inc.*
Stern, Stephen — *CPS Inc.*
Sterner, Doug — *CPS Inc.*
Stevens, Ken — *The Stevens Group*
Stevenson, Jane — *Howard Fischer Associates, Inc.*
Stevenson, Terry — *Bartholdi & Company, Inc.*
Stewart, Jeffrey O. — *Stewart, Stein and Scott, Ltd.*
Stewart, Ross M. — *Human Resources Network Partners Inc.*

Stiles, Judy — *MedQuest Associates*
Stone, Susan L. — *Stone Enterprises Ltd.*
Stranberg, James R. — *Callan Associates, Ltd.*
Strickland, Katie — *Grantham & Co., Inc.*
Strom, Mark N. — *Search Advisors International Corp.*
Sturtz, James W. — *Compass Group Ltd.*
Sullivan, Kay — *Rusher, Loscavio & LoPresto*
Sur, William K. — *Canny, Bowen Inc.*
Surrette, Mark — *Robertson-Surrette Executive Search*
Swanson, Dick — *Raymond Karsan Associates*
Swartz, William K. — *Swartz Executive Search*
Sweeney, James W. — *Sweeney Harbert & Mummert, Inc.*
Taft, Steven D. — *The Guild Corporation*
Taylor, R.L. (Larry) — *Ray & Berndtson*
Tetrick, Tim — *O'Connor, O'Connor, Lordi, Ltd.*
Thomas, Cheryl M. — *CPS Inc.*
Thomas, Donald — *Mixtec Group*
Thomas, Kim — *CPS Inc.*
Thompson, Kenneth L. — *McCormack & Farrow*
Tipp, George D. — *Intech Summit Group, Inc.*
To, Raymond — *Corporate Recruiters Ltd.*
Topliff, Marla — *Gaffney Management Consultants*
Tovrog, Dan — *CPS Inc.*
Truemper, Dean — *CPS Inc.*
Tucker, Thomas A. — *The Thomas Tucker Company*
Tullberg, Tina — *CPS Inc.*
Tweed, Janet — *Gilbert Tweed/INESA*
Unger, Paul T. — *A.T. Kearney, Inc.*
Vachon, David A. — *McNichol Associates*
Vairo, Leonard A. — *Christian & Timbers*
Van Biesen, Jacques A.H. — *Search Group Inc.*
Van Steenkiste, Julie — *Davidson, Laird & Associates, Inc.*
Vann, Dianne — *The Button Group*
Velten, Mark T. — *Boyden*
Vernon, Peter C. — *Horton International*
Visnich, L. Christine — *Bason Associates Inc.*
Vourakis, Zan — *ZanExec LLC*
Waldoch, D. Mark — *Barnes Development Group, LLC*
Walker, Douglas G. — *Sink, Walker, Boltrus International*
Walsh, Kenneth A. — *R/K International, Inc.*
Walters, Scott — *Paul-Tittle Associates, Inc.*
Walters, William F. — *Jonas, Walters & Assoc., Inc.*
Ware, John C. — *Spencer Stuart*
Watkinson, Jim W. — *The Badger Group*
Wayne, Cary S. — *ProSearch Inc.*
Webb, George H. — *Webb, Johnson Associates, Inc.*
Wein, Michael S. — *InterimManagement Solutions, Inc.*
Wein, Michael S. — *Media Management Resources, Inc.*
Wein, William — *Media Management Resources, Inc.*
Weissman-Rosenthal, Abbe — *ALW Research International*
Weisz, Laura — *Anderson Sterling Associates*
Welch, Robert — *Ray & Berndtson*
White, William C. — *Venture Resources Inc.*

Wilburn, Dan — *Kaye-Bassman International Corp.*
Wilkinson, Barbara — *Beall & Company, Inc.*
Williams, Gary L. — *Barnes Development Group, LLC*
Willner, Leo — *William Guy & Associates*
Winitz, Joel — *GSW Consulting Group, Inc.*
Winitz, Marla — *GSW Consulting Group, Inc.*
Winograd, Glenn — *Criterion Executive Search, Inc.*
Winston, Dale — *Battalia Winston International*
Wold, Ted W. — *Hyde Danforth Wold & Co.*
Wolf, Stephen M. — *Byron Leonard International, Inc.*
Woodhouse, Michael — *Ashton Computer Professionals Inc.*
Woodward, Lee — *Search Associates, Inc.*
Woodworth, Gail — *Woodworth International Group*
Wooldridge, Jeff — *Ray & Berndtson*
Woollett, James — *Rusher, Loscavio & LoPresto*
Wyatt, James — *Wyatt & Jaffe*
Yen, Maggie Yeh Ching — *Ray & Berndtson*
Young, Heather — *The Guild Corporation*
Zadfar, Maryanne — *The Thomas Tucker Company*
Zamborsky, George — *Boyden*
Zatzick, Michael — *Search West, Inc.*

9. Sales

Abell, Vincent W. — *MSI International*
Adler, Louis S. — *CJA - The Adler Group*
Aiken, David — *Commonwealth Consultants*
Ainsworth, Lawrence — *Search West, Inc.*
Akin, J.R. "Jack" — *J.R. Akin & Company Inc.*
Albertini, Nancy — *Taylor-Winfield, Inc.*
Allen, Don — *D.S. Allen Associates, Inc.*
Allen, Wade H. — *Cendea Connection International*
Allen, William L. — *The Hindman Company*
Allred, J. Michael — *Spencer Stuart*
Ambler, Peter W. — *Peter W. Ambler Company*
Ames, George C. — *Ames O'Neill Associates*
Anderson, Richard — *Grant Cooper and Associates*
Anderson, Steve — *CPS Inc.*
Antoine, Brian — *Paul-Tittle Associates, Inc.*
Arnold, David W. — *Christian & Timbers*
Aronin, Michael — *Fisher-Todd Associates*
Arseneault, Daniel S. — *MSI International*
Asquith, Peter S. — *Ames Personnel Consultants, Inc.*
Aston, Kathy — *Marra Peters & Partners*
Attell, Harold — *A.E. Feldman Associates*
Austin Lockton, Kathy — *Juntunen-Combs-Poirier*
Bacon, Cheri — *Gaffney Management Consultants*
Badger, Fred H. — *The Badger Group*
Baeder, Jeremy — *Executive Manning Corporation*
Baird, John — *Professional Search Consultants*
Baje, Sarah — *Innovative Search Group, LLC*
Baker, Bill — *Kaye-Bassman International Corp.*
Baker, Gary M. — *Cochran, Cochran & Yale, Inc.*
Balbone, Rich — *Executive Manning Corporation*
Balch, Randy — *CPS Inc.*
Baltaglia, Michael — *Cochran, Cochran & Yale, Inc.*
Baltin, Carrie — *Search West, Inc.*

Barbosa, Frank — *Skott/Edwards Consultants, Inc.*
Barbour, Mary Beth — *Tully/Woodmansee International, Inc.*
Barlow, Ken H. — *The Cherbonnier Group, Inc.*
Barnes, Richard E. — *Barnes Development Group, LLC*
Barnes, Roanne L. — *Barnes Development Group, LLC*
Barthold, James A. — *McNichol Associates*
Bartholdi, Ted — *Bartholdi & Company, Inc.*
Bartholdi, Theodore G. — *Bartholdi & Company, Inc.*
Barton, Gary R. — *Barton Associates, Inc.*
Bason, Maurice L. — *Bason Associates Inc.*
Bass, M. Lynn — *Ray & Berndtson*
Battalia, O. William — *Battalia Winston International*
Bearman, Linda — *Grant Cooper and Associates*
Beaudin, Elizabeth C. — *Callan Associates, Ltd.*
Beaver, Bentley H. — *The Onstott Group, Inc.*
Belfrey, Edward — *Dunhill Professional Search of Irvine, Inc.*
Belin, Jean — *Boyden*
Bender, Alan — *Bender Executive Search*
Bennett, Jo — *Battalia Winston International*
Berkhemer-Credaire, Betsy — *Berkhemer Clayton Incorporated*
Berry, Harold B. — *The Hindman Company*
Biestek, Paul J. — *Paul J. Biestek Associates, Inc.*
Billington, William H. — *Spriggs & Company, Inc.*
Bishop, Susan — *Bishop Partners*
Blackshaw, Brian M. — *Blackshaw, Olmstead, Lynch & Koenig*
Blanton, Julia — *Blanton and Company*
Blanton, Thomas — *Blanton and Company*
Bliley, Jerry — *Spencer Stuart*
Blim, Barbara — *JDG Associates, Ltd.*
Bloomer, James E. — *L.W. Foote Company*
Bluhm, Claudia — *Schweichler Associates, Inc.*
Boel, Werner — *The Dalley Hewitt Company*
Bogansky, Amy — *Conex Incorporated*
Bohn, Steve J. — *MSI International*
Boltrus, Dick — *Sink, Walker, Boltrus International*
Borland, James — *Goodrich & Sherwood Associates, Inc.*
Bormann, Cindy Ann — *MSI International*
Bostic, James E. — *Phillips Resource Group*
Boyd, Lew — *Coastal International Inc.*
Brackman, Janet — *Dahl-Morrow International*
Bradley, Dalena — *Woodworth International Group*
Brady, Robert — *CPS Inc.*
Brandeis, Richard — *CPS Inc.*
Bratches, Howard — *Thorndike Deland Associates*
Brennen, Richard J. — *Spencer Stuart*
Brieger, Steve — *Thorne, Brieger Associates Inc.*
Brooks, Bernard E. — *Mruk & Partners/EMA Partners Int'l*
Brother, Joy — *Charles Luntz & Associates. Inc.*
Brown, Gina — *Strategic Alliance Network, Ltd.*
Brown, Larry C. — *Horton International*
Brown, Steffan — *Woodworth International Group*
Brudno, Robert J. — *Savoy Partners, Ltd.*
Bruno, Deborah F. — *The Hindman Company*

Brunson, Therese — *Kors Montgomery International*
Bryant, Richard D. — *Bryant Associates, Inc.*
Bryant, Shari G. — *Bryant Associates, Inc.*
Bryza, Robert M. — *Robert Lowell International*
Brzezinski, Ronald T. — *Callan Associates, Ltd.*
Buckles, Donna — *Cochran, Cochran & Yale, Inc.*
Budill, Edward — *Professional Search Consultants*
Bueschel, David A. — *Shepherd Bueschel & Provus, Inc.*
Buggy, Linda — *Bonnell Associates Ltd.*
Bullock, Conni — *Earley Kielty and Associates, Inc.*
Burchill, Greg — *BGB Associates*
Burden, Gene — *The Cherbonnier Group, Inc.*
Burfield, Elaine — *Skott/Edwards Consultants, Inc.*
Burke, John — *The Experts*
Burke, Karen A. — *Mazza & Riley, Inc. (a Korn/Ferry International affiliate)*
Burkhill, John — *The Talley Group*
Burns, Alan — *The Enns Partners Inc.*
Busch, Jack — *Busch International*
Button, David R. — *The Button Group*
Cahill, Peter M. — *Peter M. Cahill Associates, Inc.*
Call, David — *Cochran, Cochran & Yale, Inc.*
Callan, Robert M. — *Callan Associates, Ltd.*
Calogeras, Chris — *The Sager Company*
Cameron, James W. — *Cameron Consulting*
Campbell, Patricia A. — *The Onstott Group, Inc.*
Campbell, Robert Scott — *Wellington Management Group*
Campbell, Robert Scott — *Wellington Management Group*
Cannavino, Matthew J. — *Financial Resource Associates, Inc.*
Capizzi, Karen — *Cochran, Cochran & Yale, Inc.*
Carideo, Joseph — *Thorndike Deland Associates*
Caruthers, Robert D. — *James Mead & Company*
Cary, Con — *Cary & Associates*
Cast, Donald — *Dunhill International Search of New Haven*
Caudill, Nancy — *Bishop Partners*
Cavolina, Michael — *Carver Search Consultants*
Celenza, Catherine — *CPS Inc.*
Chappell, Peter — *The Bankers Group*
Chatterjie, Alok — *MSI International*
Chavous, C. Crawford — *Phillips Resource Group*
Cherbonnier, L. Michael — *TCG International, Inc.*
Cherbonnier, L. Michael — *The Cherbonnier Group, Inc.*
Christenson, H. Alan — *Christenson & Hutchison*
Christian, Jeffrey E. — *Christian & Timbers*
Christian, Philip — *Ray & Berndtson*
Christiansen, Amy — *CPS Inc.*
Christiansen, Doug — *CPS Inc.*
Cimino, Ron — *Paul-Tittle Associates, Inc.*
Cizek, John T. — *Cizek Associates, Inc.*
Cizek, Marti J. — *Cizek Associates, Inc.*
Cizynski, Katherine W. — *James Mead & Company*
Clark, James — *CPS Inc.*
Clauhsen, Elizabeth A. — *Savoy Partners, Ltd.*
Clough, Geoff — *Intech Summit Group, Inc.*
Cloutier, Gisella — *Dinte Resources, Inc.*
Cochran, Hale — *Fenwick Partners*
Cochran, Scott P. — *The Badger Group*

Coe, Karen J. — *Coe & Company International Inc.*
Coffman, Brian — *Kossuth & Associates, Inc.*
Cohen, Robert C. — *Intech Summit Group, Inc.*
Colasanto, Frank M. — *W.R. Rosato & Associates, Inc.*
Colling, Douglas — *KPMG Management Consulting*
Colvin, Teresa A. — *Jonas, Walters & Assoc., Inc.*
Combs, Stephen L. — *Juntunen-Combs-Poirier*
Compton, Tonya — *Dunhill Professional Search of Irvine, Inc.*
Conway, Maureen — *Conway & Associates*
Conway, William P. — *Phillips Resource Group*
Cooke, Katherine H. — *Horton International*
Cornehlsen, James H. — *Skott/Edwards Consultants, Inc.*
Corrigan, Gerald F. — *The Corrigan Group*
Cortina Del Valle, Pedro — *Ray & Berndtson*
Costello, Lynda — *Coe & Company International Inc.*
Coulman, Karen — *CPS Inc.*
Crane, Howard C. — *Chartwell Partners International, Inc.*
Crath, Paul F. — *Price Waterhouse*
Critchley, Walter — *Cochran, Cochran & Yale, Inc.*
Crosler, Yvonne — *Paul-Tittle Associates, Inc.*
Crowder, Edward W. — *Crowder & Company*
Cruse, O.D. — *Spencer Stuart*
Cuddihy, Paul — *Dahl-Morrow International*
Cunningham, Lawrence — *Howard Fischer Associates, Inc.*
Cunningham, Robert Y. — *Goodrich & Sherwood Associates, Inc.*
Curci, Donald L. — *A.R.I. International*
Curtis, Ellissa — *Cochran, Cochran & Yale, Inc.*
Czamanske, Paul W. — *Compass Group Ltd.*
Czepiel, Susan — *CPS Inc.*
Daily, John C. — *Handy HRM Corp.*
Dalton, Bret — *Robert W. Dingman Company, Inc.*
Danforth, W. Michael — *Hyde Danforth Wold & Co.*
Daniels, Donna — *Jonas, Walters & Assoc., Inc.*
Danoff, Audrey — *Don Richard Associates of Tidewater, Inc.*
Davis, Bert — *Bert Davis Executive Search, Inc.*
Davis, G. Gordon — *Davis & Company*
Davison, Patricia E. — *Lamalie Amrop International*
De Brun, Thomas P. — *Ray & Berndtson*
de Gury, Glenn — *Taylor-Winfield, Inc.*
Deaver, Henry C. — *Ray & Berndtson*
DeCorrevont, James — *DeCorrevont & Associates*
DeCorrevont, James — *DeCorrevont & Associates*
Delaney, Patrick J. — *Sensible Solutions, Inc.*
DeLong, Art — *Richard Kader & Associates*
Demchak, James P. — *Sandhurst Associates*
Desai, Sushila — *Sink, Walker, Boltrus International*
Desgrosellier, Gary P. — *Personnel Unlimited/Executive Search*
Desmond, Dennis — *Beall & Company, Inc.*
Dezember, Steve — *Ray & Berndtson*
DiCioccio, Carmen — *Cochran, Cochran & Yale, Inc.*

Dickson, Duke — *A.D. & Associates Executive Search, Inc.*
Dietz, David S. — *MSI International*
Dillon, Larry — *Predictor Systems*
DiMarchi, Paul — *DiMarchi Partners, Inc.*
DiMarchi, Paul — *DiMarchi Partners, Inc.*
Dingeldey, Peter E. — *Search Advisors International Corp.*
Dingman, Bruce — *Robert W. Dingman Company, Inc.*
Dingman, Robert W. — *Robert W. Dingman Company, Inc.*
DiSalvo, Fred — *The Cambridge Group Ltd*
Divine, Robert S. — *O'Shea, Divine & Company, Inc.*
Dixon, Aris — *CPS Inc.*
Doele, Donald C. — *Goodrich & Sherwood Associates, Inc.*
Donath, Linda — *Dahl-Morrow International*
Dotson, M. Ileen — *Dotson & Associates*
Dow, Lori — *Davidson, Laird & Associates, Inc.*
Dowell, Mary K. — *Professional Search Associates*
Drew, David R. — *Drew & Associates*
Dromeshauser, Peter — *Dromeshauser Associates*
Drury, James J. — *Spencer Stuart*
Dubbs, William — *Williams Executive Search, Inc.*
Dubrow, Richard M. — *R/K International, Inc.*
Duckworth, Donald R. — *Johnson Smith & Knisely Accord*
Dugan, John H. — *J.H. Dugan and Associates, Inc.*
Duggan, James P. — *Slayton International, Inc./I-I-C Partners*
Duley, Richard I. — *ARJay & Associates*
Dunlop, Eric — *Southwestern Professional Services*
Dunman, Betsy L. — *Crawford & Crofford*
Dussick, Vince — *Dussick Management Associates*
Dwyer, Julie — *CPS Inc.*
Ebeling, John A. — *Gilbert Tweed/INESA*
Edmond, Bruce — *Corporate Recruiters Ltd.*
Edwards, Dorothy — *MSI International*
Edwards, Verba L. — *Wing Tips & Pumps, Inc.*
Eggena, Roger — *Phillips Resource Group*
Eldridge, Charles B. — *Ray & Berndtson*
Ellis, Ted K. — *The Hindman Company*
Ellis, William — *Interspace Interactive Inc.*
Elnaggar, Hani — *Juntunen-Combs-Poirier*
England, Mark — *Austin-McGregor International*
Enns, George — *The Enns Partners Inc.*
Ervin, Darlene — *CPS Inc.*
Esposito, Mark — *Christian & Timbers*
Eustis, Lucy R. — *MSI International*
Evans, David — *Executive Manning Corporation*
Falk, John — *D.S. Allen Associates, Inc.*
Fancher, Robert L. — *Bason Associates Inc.*
Farley, Leon A. — *Leon A. Farley Associates*
Farrow, Jerry M. — *McCormack & Farrow*
Fawkes, Elizabeth — *Paul-Tittle Associates, Inc.*
Federman, Jack R. — *W.R. Rosato & Associates, Inc.*
Feldman, Abe — *A.E. Feldman Associates*
Ferneborg, Jay W. — *Ferneborg & Associates, Inc.*
Ferneborg, John R. — *Ferneborg & Associates, Inc.*
Feyder, Michael — *A.T. Kearney, Inc.*

Fincher, Richard P. — *Phase II Management*
Fini, Ron — *The Sager Company*
Fink, Neil J. — *Neil Fink Associates*
Fischer, Adam — *Howard Fischer Associates, Inc.*
Fischer, Howard M. — *Howard Fischer Associates, Inc.*
Fischer, John C. — *Horton International*
Fishback, Joren — *Derek Associates, Inc.*
Fisher, Neal — *Fisher Personnel Management Services*
Fitzgerald, Diane — *Fitzgerald Associates*
Fitzgerald, Geoffrey — *Fitzgerald Associates*
Flanagan, Robert M. — *Robert M. Flanagan & Associates, Ltd.*
Flannery, Peter F. — *Jonas, Walters & Assoc., Inc.*
Flood, Michael — *Norman Broadbent International, Inc.*
Flora, Dodi — *Crawford & Crofford*
Flynn, Erin — *Neil Fink Associates*
Fogarty, Michael — *CPS Inc.*
Foote, Leland W. — *L.W. Foote Company*
Foreman, David C. — *Koontz, Jeffries & Associates, Inc.*
Forman, Donald R. — *Stanton Chase International*
Foster, Bonnie — *Kirkman & Searing, Inc.*
Fowler, Thomas A. — *The Hindman Company*
Francis, John — *Zwell International*
Frazier, John — *Cochran, Cochran & Yale, Inc.*
Fredericks, Ward A. — *Mixtec Group*
Fulgham MacCarthy, Ann — *Columbia Consulting Group*
Furlong, James W. — *Furlong Search, Inc.*
Furlong, James W. — *Furlong Search, Inc.*
Furlong, James W. — *Furlong Search, Inc.*
Fust, Sheely F. — *Ray & Berndtson*
Gabel, Gregory N. — *Canny, Bowen Inc.*
Gaines, Jay — *Jay Gaines & Company, Inc.*
Galante, Suzanne M. — *Vlcek & Company, Inc.*
Galbraith, Deborah M. — *Stratford Group*
Gale, Rhoda E. — *E.G. Jones Associates, Ltd.*
Gallagher, Terence M. — *Battalia Winston International*
Gantar, Donna — *Howard Fischer Associates, Inc.*
Garcia, Samuel K. — *Southwestern Professional Services*
Garfinkle, Steven M. — *Battalia Winston International*
Garzone, Dolores — *M.A. Churchill & Associates, Inc.*
Gauthier, Robert C. — *Columbia Consulting Group*
George, Delores F. — *Delores F. George Human Resource Management & Consulting Industry*
Gerbasi, Michael — *The Sager Company*
Germain, Valerie — *Jay Gaines & Company, Inc.*
Gestwick, Daniel — *Cochran, Cochran & Yale, Inc.*
Gibbs, John S. — *Spencer Stuart*
Gideon, Mark — *Eagle Search Associates*
Gilbert, Jerry — *Gilbert & Van Campen International*
Gill, Patricia — *Columbia Consulting Group*
Gillespie, Thomas — *Professional Search Consultants*
Gilmore, Connie — *Taylor-Winfield, Inc.*
Giries, Juliet D. — *Barton Associates, Inc.*
Gladstone, Martin J. — *MSI International*

Gloss, Frederick C. — *F. Gloss International*
Goar, Duane R. — *Sandhurst Associates*
Goedtke, Steven — *Southwestern Professional Services*
Gold, Stacey — *Earley Kielty and Associates, Inc.*
Golde, Lisa — *Tully/Woodmansee International, Inc.*
Goldenberg, Susan — *Grant Cooper and Associates*
Goldsmith, Fred J. — *Fred J. Goldsmith Associates*
Gomez, Cristina — *Juntunen-Combs-Poirier*
Goodman, Dawn M. — *Bason Associates Inc.*
Goodman, Victor — *Anderson Sterling Associates*
Gordon, Gerald L. — *E.G. Jones Associates, Ltd.*
Gostyla, Rick — *Spencer Stuart*
Grady, James — *Search West, Inc.*
Graham, Dale — *CPS Inc.*
Grant, Michael — *Zwell International*
Grantham, John — *Grantham & Co., Inc.*
Grantham, Philip H. — *Columbia Consulting Group*
Grasch, Jerry E. — *The Hindman Company*
Grebenstein, Charles R. — *Skott/Edwards Consultants, Inc.*
Green, Jane — *Phillips Resource Group*
Groover, David — *MSI International*
Grotte, Lawrence C. — *Lautz Grotte Engler*
Grzybowski, Jill — *CPS Inc.*
Haas, Margaret P. — *The Haas Associates, Inc.*
Hailey, H.M. — *Damon & Associates, Inc.*
Hall, Peter V. — *Chartwell Partners International, Inc.*
Hallock, Peter B. — *Goodrich & Sherwood Associates, Inc.*
Hamburg, Jennifer Power — *Ledbetter/Davidson International, Inc.*
Hamilton, John R. — *Ray & Berndtson*
Hanes, Leah — *Ray & Berndtson*
Hanley, Alan P. — *Williams, Roth & Krueger Inc.*
Hanley, Maureen E. — *Gilbert Tweed/INESA*
Hanson, Grant M. — *Goodrich & Sherwood Associates, Inc.*
Harris, Joe W. — *Cendea Connection International*
Harris, Seth O. — *Christian & Timbers*
Harrison, Priscilla — *Phillips Resource Group*
Hart, Robert T. — *D.E. Foster Partners Inc.*
Hartle, Larry — *CPS Inc.*
Harvey, Mike — *Advanced Executive Resources*
Haughton, Michael — *DeFrain, Mayer LLC*
Hauswirth, Jeffrey M. — *Spencer Stuart*
Hawksworth, A. Dwight — *A.D. & Associates Executive Search, Inc.*
Hayes, Stacy — *The McCormick Group, Inc.*
Haystead, Steve — *Advanced Executive Resources*
Hazerjian, Cynthia — *CPS Inc.*
Heacock, Burt E. — *Paul-Tittle Associates, Inc.*
Heafey, Bill — *CPS Inc.*
Hechkoff, Robert B. — *Quantex Associates, Inc.*
Heffelfinger, Thomas V. — *Heffelfinger Associates, Inc.*
Heiken, Barbara E. — *Randell-Heiken, Inc.*
Heinze, David — *Heinze & Associates, Inc.*
Helminiak, Audrey — *Gaffney Management Consultants*
Henard, John B. — *Lamalie Amrop International*
Henry, Mary — *Conex Incorporated*

Koenig, Joel S. — *Blackshaw, Olmstead, Lynch & Koenig*
Kohn, Adam P. — *Christian & Timbers*
Koontz, Donald N. — *Koontz, Jeffries & Associates, Inc.*
Kors, R. Paul — *Kors Montgomery International*
Kossuth, David — *Kossuth & Associates, Inc.*
Kossuth, Jane — *Kossuth & Associates, Inc.*
Kotick, Maddy — *The Stevenson Group of New Jersey*
Krejci, Stanley L. — *Boyden Washington, D.C.*
Krieger, Dennis F. — *Seiden Krieger Associates, Inc.*
Kunzer, William J. — *Kunzer Associates, Ltd.*
Kussner, Janice N. — *Herman Smith Executive Initiatives Inc.*
Laba, Marvin — *Marvin Laba & Associates*
Laba, Stuart M. — *Marvin Laba & Associates*
Labrecque, Bernard F. — *Laurendeau Labrecque/Ray & Berndtson, Inc.*
Lache, Shawn E. — *The Arcus Group*
Laird, Cheryl — *CPS Inc.*
Lang, Sharon A. — *Ray & Berndtson*
Langford, Robert W. — *F-O-R-T-U-N-E Personnel Consultants of Huntsville, Inc.*
Lardner, Lucy D. — *Tully/Woodmansee International, Inc.*
Larsen, Jack B. — *Jack B. Larsen & Associates*
Lasher, Charles M. — *Lasher Associates*
Laub, Stuart R. — *Abraham & London, Ltd.*
Lauderback, David R. — *A.T. Kearney, Inc.*
Lautz, Lindsay A. — *Lautz Grotte Engler*
Leahy, Jan — *CPS Inc.*
Ledbetter, Charlene — *Ledbetter/Davidson International, Inc.*
Ledbetter, Steven G. — *Cendea Connection International*
Leininger, Dennis — *Key Employment Services*
Lence, Julie Anne — *MSI International*
Lenkaitis, Lewis F. — *A.T. Kearney, Inc.*
Letcher, Harvey D. — *Sandhurst Associates*
Levitt, Muriel A. — *D.S. Allen Associates, Inc.*
Lewicki, Christopher — *MSI International*
Lewis, Jon A. — *Sandhurst Associates*
Lezama Cohen, Luis — *Ray & Berndtson*
Lindberg, Eric J. — *MSI International*
Linton, Leonard M. — *Byron Leonard International, Inc.*
Lipe, Jerold L. — *Compass Group Ltd.*
Lipson, Harriet — *First Interactive Recruiting Specialists*
Lipson, Howard K. — *First Interactive Recruiting Specialists*
Little, Elizabeth A. — *Financial Resource Associates, Inc.*
Loeb, Stephen H. — *Grant Cooper and Associates*
Lofthouse, Cindy — *CPS Inc.*
Lokken, Karen — *A.E. Feldman Associates*
Long, Helga — *Horton International*
Long, William G. — *McDonald, Long & Associates, Inc.*
Looney, Scott — *A.E. Feldman Associates*
LoPresto, Robert L. — *Rusher, Loscavio & LoPresto*
Lotufo, Donald A. — *D.A.L. Associates, Inc.*
Lovely, Edward — *The Stevenson Group of New Jersey*

Lucarelli, Joan — *The Onstott Group, Inc.*
Lucas, Ronnie L. — *MSI International*
Lucht, John — *The John Lucht Consultancy Inc.*
Luntz, Charles E. — *Charles Luntz & Associates. Inc.*
Lupica, Anthony — *Cochran, Cochran & Yale, Inc.*
Lyon, Jenny — *Marra Peters & Partners*
Lyons, J. David — *Aubin International Inc.*
MacNaughton, Sperry — *McNaughton Associates*
Mader, Stephen P. — *Christian & Timbers*
Maglio, Charles J. — *Maglio and Company, Inc.*
Mallin, Ellen — *Howard Fischer Associates, Inc.*
Manns, Alex — *Crawford & Crofford*
Mansford, Keith — *Howard Fischer Associates, Inc.*
Maphet, Harriet — *The Stevenson Group of New Jersey*
Marcine, John W. — *Keith Bagg & Associates Inc.*
Marino, Chester — *Cochran, Cochran & Yale, Inc.*
Marion, Michael — *S.D. Kelly & Associates, Inc.*
Mark, John L. — *J.L. Mark Associates, Inc.*
Mark, Lynne — *J.L. Mark Associates, Inc.*
Marks, Ira — *Strategic Alternatives*
Marks, Russell E. — *Webb, Johnson Associates, Inc.*
Marra, John — *Marra Peters & Partners*
Marra, John — *Marra Peters & Partners*
Marumoto, William H. — *Boyden Washington, D.C.*
Marye, George — *Damon & Associates, Inc.*
Massey, R. Bruce — *Horton International*
Mather, David R. — *Christian & Timbers*
Mathias, Kathy — *Stone Murphy & Olson*
Matthews, Corwin — *Woodworth International Group*
Matti, Suzy — *Southwestern Professional Services*
May, Peter — *Mixtec Group*
Mazor, Elly — *Howard Fischer Associates, Inc.*
Mazza, David B. — *Mazza & Riley, Inc. (a Korn/Ferry International affiliate)*
McAndrews, Kathy — *CPS Inc.*
McBride, Dee — *Deeco International*
McBride, Jonathan E. — *McBride Associates, Inc.*
McCloskey, Frank D. — *Johnson Smith & Knisely Accord*
McCormick, Brian — *The McCormick Group, Inc.*
McCormick, William J. — *The McCormick Group, Inc.*
McCreary, Charles "Chip" — *Austin-McGregor International*
McDermott, Jeffrey T. — *Vlcek & Company, Inc.*
McDonald, Scott A. — *McDonald Associates International*
McDonald, Stanleigh B. — *McDonald Associates International*
McDonnell, Julie — *Technical Personnel of Minnesota*
McDowell, Robert N. — *Christenson & Hutchison*
McFadden, Ashton S. — *Johnson Smith & Knisely Accord*
McFadzen, Donna — *Holland, McFadzean & Associates, Inc.*
McFadzen, James A. — *Holland, McFadzean & Associates, Inc.*
McGregor, James D. — *John Kurosky & Associates*
McGuire, J. Corey — *Peter W. Ambler Company*

Pickford, Stephen T. — *The Corporate Staff, Inc.*
Pierotazio, John — *CPS Inc.*
Poirier, Roland L. — *Poirier, Hoevel & Co.*
Pomerance, Mark — *CPS Inc.*
Pompeo, Paul — *Search West, Inc.*
Poracky, John W. — *M. Wood Company*
Porter, Albert — *The Experts*
Potter, Douglas C. — *Stanton Chase International*
Provus, Barbara L. — *Shepherd Bueschel & Provus, Inc.*
Pryde, Marcia P. — *A.T. Kearney, Inc.*
Pryor, Bill — *Cendea Connection International*
Raab, Julie — *Dunhill Professional Search of Irvine, Inc.*
Rabe, William — *Sales Executives Inc.*
Rachels, John W. — *Southwestern Professional Services*
Raiber, Laurie Altman — *The IMC Group of Companies Ltd.*
Raines, Bruce R. — *Raines International Inc.*
Ramler, Carolyn S. — *The Corporate Connection, Ltd.*
Ramsey, John H. — *Mark Stanley/EMA Partners International*
Randell, James E. — *Randell-Heiken, Inc.*
Ray, Marianne C. — *Callan Associates, Ltd.*
Raymond, Anne — *Anderson Sterling Associates*
Reddick, David C. — *Horton International*
Reiser, Ellen — *Thorndike Deland Associates*
Remillard, Brad M. — *CJA - The Adler Group*
Renwick, David — *John Kurosky & Associates*
Reuter, Tandom — *CPS Inc.*
Reyman, Susan — *S. Reyman & Associates Ltd.*
Ribeiro, Claudia — *Ledbetter/Davidson International, Inc.*
Rice, Marie — *Jay Gaines & Company, Inc.*
Richards, Paul E. — *Executive Directions*
Richards, R. Glenn — *Executive Directions*
Ridenour, Suzanne S. — *Ridenour & Associates, Ltd.*
Riederer, Larry — *CPS Inc.*
Rimmel, James E. — *The Hindman Company*
Rimmele, Michael — *The Bankers Group*
Rizzo, L. Donald — *R.P. Barone Associates*
Roberts, Carl R. — *Southwestern Professional Services*
Roberts, Mitch — *A.E. Feldman Associates*
Roberts, Scott — *Jonas, Walters & Assoc., Inc.*
Robertson, John A. — *Kaye-Bassman International Corp.*
Robertson, Ronald — *Robertson-Surrette Executive Search*
Robins, Jeri N. — *Nagler, Robins & Poe, Inc.*
Robinson, Bruce — *Bruce Robinson Associates*
Robles Cuellar, Paulina — *Ray & Berndtson*
Roblin, Nancy R. — *Paul-Tittle Associates, Inc.*
Romanello, Daniel P. — *Spencer Stuart*
Romang, Paula — *Agri-Tech Personnel, Inc.*
Rosato, William R. — *W.R. Rosato & Associates, Inc.*
Ross, Curt A. — *Ray & Berndtson*
Ross, H. Lawrence — *Ross & Company*
Ross, Lawrence — *Ray & Berndtson/Lovas Stanley*
Ross, William J. — *Flowers & Associates*
Rossi, Thomas — *Southwestern Professional Services*

Rotella, Marshall W. — *The Corporate Connection, Ltd.*
Roth, Robert J. — *Williams, Roth & Krueger Inc.*
Rudolph, Kenneth — *Kossuth & Associates, Inc.*
Rudzinsky, Howard — *Louis Rudzinsky Associates*
Ruge, Merrill — *William Guy & Associates*
Rurak, Zbigniew T. — *Rurak & Associates, Inc.*
Rush, Michael E. — *D.A.L. Associates, Inc.*
Sacerdote, John — *Raymond Karsan Associates*
Saletra, Andrew — *CPS Inc.*
Salottolo, Al — *Tactical Alternatives*
Salvagno, Michael J. — *The Cambridge Group Ltd*
Sanders, Natalie — *CPS Inc.*
Sanow, Robert — *Cochran, Cochran & Yale, Inc.*
Sarna, Edmund A. — *Jonas, Walters & Assoc., Inc.*
Sausto, Lynne — *Abraham & London, Ltd.*
Savvas, Carol Diane — *Ledbetter/Davidson International, Inc.*
Saxon, Alexa — *Woodworth International Group*
Scalamera, Tom — *CPS Inc.*
Schaefer, Frederic M. — *A.T. Kearney, Inc.*
Schedra, Sharon — *Earley Kielty and Associates, Inc.*
Schene, Philip — *A.E. Feldman Associates*
Schiavone, Mary Rose — *Canny, Bowen Inc.*
Schlpma, Christine — *Advanced Executive Resources*
Schmidt, Peter R. — *Boyden*
Schmidt, William C. — *Christian & Timbers*
Schneiderman, Gerald — *Management Resource Associates, Inc.*
Schueneman, David — *CPS Inc.*
Schultz, Helen — *Predictor Systems*
Schwam, Carol — *A.E. Feldman Associates*
Schweichler, Lee J. — *Schweichler Associates, Inc.*
Scott, Evan — *Howard Fischer Associates, Inc.*
Scott, Gordon S. — *Search Advisors International Corp.*
Searing, James M. — *Kirkman & Searing, Inc.*
Seco, William — *Seco & Zetto Associates, Inc.*
Seiden, Steven A. — *Seiden Krieger Associates, Inc.*
Semyan, John K. — *TNS Partners, Inc.*
Sevilla, Claudio A. — *Crawford & Crofford*
Shamir, Ben — *S.D. Kelly & Associates, Inc.*
Shapiro, Elaine — *CPS Inc.*
Shattuck, Merrill B. — *M.B. Shattuck and Associates, Inc.*
Shepard, Michael J. — *MSI International*
Shepherd, Daniel M. — *Shepherd Bueschel & Provus, Inc.*
Sherwood, Andrew — *Goodrich & Sherwood Associates, Inc.*
Shimp, David J. — *Lamalie Amrop International*
Shufelt, Doug — *Sink, Walker, Boltrus International*
Sickles, Robert — *Dunhill Professional Search of Irvine, Inc.*
Signer, Julie — *CPS Inc.*
Sill, Igor M. — *Geneva Group International*
Silvas, Stephen D. — *Roberson and Company*
Silver, Lee — *L. A. Silver Associates, Inc.*
Simmons, Anneta — *F-O-R-T-U-N-E Personnel Consultants of Huntsville, Inc.*
Simmons, Sandra K. — *MSI International*

Simpson, Scott — *Cendea Connection International*
Sink, Cliff — *Sink, Walker, Boltrus International*
Sitarski, Stan — *Howard Fischer Associates, Inc.*
Skalet, Ira — *A.E. Feldman Associates*
Slosar, John — *Boyden*
Smead, Michelle M. — *A.T. Kearney, Inc.*
Smith, Ana Luz — *Smith Search, S.C.*
Smith, David P. — *HRS, Inc.*
Smith, Grant — *Price Waterhouse*
Smith, Herman M. — *Herman Smith Executive Initiatives Inc.*
Smith, Ian — *International Staffing Consultants, Inc.*
Smith, John E. — *Smith Search, S.C.*
Smith, Lydia — *The Corporate Connection, Ltd.*
Smith, Matt D. — *Ray & Berndtson*
Smith, Ronald V. — *Coe & Company International Inc.*
Snyder, C. Edward — *Horton International*
Snyder, James F. — *Snyder & Company*
Sola, George L. — *A.T. Kearney, Inc.*
Souder, E.G. — *Souder & Associates*
Sowerbutt, Richard S. — *Hite Executive Search*
Spann, Richard E. — *Goodrich & Sherwood Associates, Inc.*
Spiegel, Gayle — *L. A. Silver Associates, Inc.*
Sprau, Collin L. — *Ray & Berndtson*
Spriggs, Robert D. — *Spriggs & Company, Inc.*
St. Clair, Alan — *TNS Partners, Inc.*
Stark, Jeff — *Thorne, Brieger Associates Inc.*
Statson, Dale E. — *Sales Executives Inc.*
Steele, Daniel — *Cochran, Cochran & Yale, Inc.*
Steer, Joe — *CPS Inc.*
Stein, Terry W. — *Stewart, Stein and Scott, Ltd.*
Steinem, Andy — *Dahl-Morrow International*
Steinem, Barbra — *Dahl-Morrow International*
Steinman, Stephen M. — *The Stevenson Group of New Jersey*
Sterling, Jay — *Earley Kielty and Associates, Inc.*
Stern, Stephen — *CPS Inc.*
Sterner, Doug — *CPS Inc.*
Stevens, Craig M. — *Kirkman & Searing, Inc.*
Stevens, Ken — *The Stevens Group*
Stevenson, Jane — *Howard Fischer Associates, Inc.*
Stevenson, Terry — *Bartholdi & Company, Inc.*
Stewart, Jeffrey O. — *Stewart, Stein and Scott, Ltd.*
Stewart, Ross M. — *Human Resources Network Partners Inc.*
Stiles, Judy — *MedQuest Associates*
Stone, Susan L. — *Stone Enterprises Ltd.*
Stranberg, James R. — *Callan Associates, Ltd.*
Stratton, Cary — *Coastal International Inc.*
Strickland, Katie — *Grantham & Co., Inc.*
Strom, Mark N. — *Search Advisors International Corp.*
Sturtz, James W. — *Compass Group Ltd.*
Sullivan, Kay — *Rusher, Loscavio & LoPresto*
Sur, William K. — *Canny, Bowen Inc.*
Surrette, Mark — *Robertson-Surrette Executive Search*
Swanson, Dick — *Raymond Karsan Associates*
Swartz, William K. — *Swartz Executive Search*
Taylor, Conrad G. — *MSI International*
Taylor, James M. — *The HRM Group, Inc.*
Taylor, R.L. (Larry) — *Ray & Berndtson*

Telford, John H. — *Telford, Adams & Alexander/Telford & Co., Inc.*
Tetrick, Tim — *O'Connor, O'Connor, Lordi, Ltd.*
Theobald, David B. — *Theobald & Associates*
Thies, Gary — *S.D. Kelly & Associates, Inc.*
Thomas, Cheryl M. — *CPS Inc.*
Thomas, Kim — *CPS Inc.*
Thomas, Kurt J. — *P.J. Murphy & Associates, Inc.*
Thompson, Dave — *Battalia Winston International*
Thornton, John — *Stratford Group*
Timoney, Laura — *Bishop Partners*
Tincu, John C. — *Ferneborg & Associates, Inc.*
Tipp, George D. — *Intech Summit Group, Inc.*
Tittle, David M. — *Paul-Tittle Associates, Inc.*
Topliff, Marla — *Gaffney Management Consultants*
Tovrog, Dan — *CPS Inc.*
Truemper, Dean — *CPS Inc.*
Tullberg, Tina — *CPS Inc.*
Tully, Margo L. — *Tully/Woodmansee International, Inc.*
Tunney, William — *Grant Cooper and Associates*
Tursi, Deborah J. — *The Corporate Connection, Ltd.*
Tweed, Janet — *Gilbert Tweed/INESA*
Ulrich, Mary Ann — *D.S. Allen Associates, Inc.*
Unger, Paul T. — *A.T. Kearney, Inc.*
Vachon, David A. — *McNichol Associates*
Vairo, Leonard A. — *Christian & Timbers*
Van Campen, Jerry — *Gilbert & Van Campen International*
Vann, Dianne — *The Button Group*
Vaughan, David B. — *Dunhill Professional Search of Irvine, Inc.*
Velten, Mark T. — *Boyden*
Venable, William W. — *Thorndike Deland Associates*
Vernon, Peter C. — *Horton International*
Visnich, L. Christine — *Bason Associates Inc.*
Vlcek, Thomas J. — *Vlcek & Company, Inc.*
Volkman, Arthur — *Cochran, Cochran & Yale, Inc.*
Von Karl, Thomas — *Juntunen-Combs-Poirier*
Vourakis, Zan — *ZanExec LLC*
Vroom, Cynthia D. — *Cyntal International Ltd*
Waldoch, D. Mark — *Barnes Development Group, LLC*
Waldrop, Gary R. — *MSI International*
Walker, Douglas G. — *Sink, Walker, Boltrus International*
Walsh, Kenneth A. — *R/K International, Inc.*
Walsh, Patty — *Abraham & London, Ltd.*
Walters, William F. — *Jonas, Walters & Assoc., Inc.*
Ward, Madeleine — *LTM Associates*
Wasserman, Harvey — *Churchill and Affiliates, Inc.*
Watkinson, Jim W. — *The Badger Group*
Watson, James — *MSI International*
Wayne, Cary S. — *ProSearch Inc.*
Webb, George H. — *Webb, Johnson Associates, Inc.*
Wein, Michael S. — *InterimManagement Solutions, Inc.*
Wein, Michael S. — *Media Management Resources, Inc.*

Wein, William — *InterimManagement Solutions, Inc.*

Wein, William — *Media Management Resources, Inc.*

Weissman-Rosenthal, Abbe — *ALW Research International*

Weisz, Laura — *Anderson Sterling Associates*

Welch, Robert — *Ray & Berndtson*

Weller, Paul S. — *Mark Stanley/EMA Partners International*

Wertheim, Denise — *Paul-Tittle Associates, Inc.*

Westfall, Ed — *Zwell International*

White, William C. — *Venture Resources Inc.*

Whyte, Roger J. — *The Whyte Group, Inc.*

Wilburn, Dan — *Kaye-Bassman International Corp.*

Wilder, Richard B. — *Columbia Consulting Group*

Wilkinson, Barbara — *Beall & Company, Inc.*

Wilkinson, Jr. SPHR

Wilkinson, Charles E. — *The HRM Group, Inc.*

Williams, Dave — *The McCormick Group, Inc.*

Williams, Gary L. — *Barnes Development Group, LLC*

Williams, Roger K. — *Williams, Roth & Krueger Inc.*

Williams, Stephen E. — *Barton Associates, Inc.*

Willner, Leo — *William Guy & Associates*

Wilson, Patricia L. — *Leon A. Farley Associates*

Winitz, Joel — *GSW Consulting Group, Inc.*

Winitz, Marla — *GSW Consulting Group, Inc.*

Winston, Dale — *Battalia Winston International*

Wise, J. Herbert — *Sandhurst Associates*

Witt, Clayton — *Paul-Tittle Associates, Inc.*

Wolf, Stephen M. — *Byron Leonard International, Inc.*

Womack, Joseph — *The Bankers Group*

Wood, Milton M. — *M. Wood Company*

Woodmansee, Bruce J. — *Tully/Woodmansee International, Inc.*

Woodworth, Gail — *Woodworth International Group*

Wooldridge, Jeff — *Ray & Berndtson*

Woollett, James — *Rusher, Loscavio & LoPresto*

Work, Alan — *Quantex Associates, Inc.*

Wren, Jay — *Jay Wren & Associates*

Wright, A. Leo — *The Hindman Company*

Wright, Charles D. — *Goodrich & Sherwood Associates, Inc.*

Wright, Leslie — *The Stevenson Group of New Jersey*

Wyatt, James — *Wyatt & Jaffe*

Yaekle, Gary — *Tully/Woodmansee International, Inc.*

Yen, Maggie Yeh Ching — *Ray & Berndtson*

Young, Lesley — *Search West, Inc.*

Yungerberg, Steven — *Steven Yungerberg Associates Inc.*

Zaffrann, Craig S. — *P.J. Murphy & Associates, Inc.*

Zahradka, James F. — *P.J. Murphy & Associates, Inc.*

Zamborsky, George — *Boyden*

Zaslav, Debra M. — *Telford, Adams & Alexander/Telford & Co., Inc.*

Zatzick, Michael — *Search West, Inc.*

Zetto, Kathryn — *Seco & Zetto Associates, Inc.*

Zinn, Don — *Quantex Associates, Inc.*

Zwell, Michael — *Zwell International*

10. Women/Minorities

Akin, J.R. "Jack" — *J.R. Akin & Company Inc.*

Allen, Scott — *Chrisman & Company, Incorporated*

Allerton, Donald T. — *Allerton Heneghan & O'Neill*

Altreuter, Rose — *ALTCO Temporary Services*

Anderson, Maria H. — *Barton Associates, Inc.*

Anderson, Steve — *CPS Inc.*

Arms, Douglas — *TOPAZ International, Inc.*

Arms, Douglas — *TOPAZ Legal Solutions*

Arnold, David W. — *Christian & Timbers*

Aronin, Michael — *Fisher-Todd Associates*

Ascher, Susan P. — *The Ascher Group*

Atwood, Barrie — *The Abbott Group, Inc.*

Baeder, Jeremy — *Executive Manning Corporation*

Baje, Sarah — *Innovative Search Group, LLC*

Baker, Gary M. — *Cochran, Cochran & Yale, Inc.*

Balbone, Rich — *Executive Manning Corporation*

Balch, Randy — *CPS Inc.*

Baldwin, Keith R. — *The Baldwin Group*

Baltaglia, Michael — *Cochran, Cochran & Yale, Inc.*

Barbour, Mary Beth — *Tully/Woodmansee International, Inc.*

Barnes, Gary — *Brigade Inc.*

Barthold, James A. — *McNichol Associates*

Bass, M. Lynn — *Ray & Berndtson*

Beaudin, Elizabeth C. — *Callan Associates, Ltd.*

Belin, Jean — *Boyden*

Bender, Alan — *Bender Executive Search*

Bennett, Jo — *Battalia Winston International*

Berkhemer-Credaire, Betsy — *Berkhemer Clayton Incorporated*

Blackmon, Sharon — *The Abbott Group, Inc.*

Bongiovanni, Vincent — *ESA Professional Consultants*

Bostic, James E. — *Phillips Resource Group*

Bourrie, Sharon D. — *Chartwell Partners International, Inc.*

Bowden, Otis H. — *BowdenGlobal, Ltd.*

Brady, Dick — *William Guy & Associates*

Brady, Robert — *CPS Inc.*

Brandeis, Richard — *CPS Inc.*

Brooks, Bernard E. — *Mruk & Partners/EMA Partners Int'l*

Brown, Larry C. — *Horton International*

Brudno, Robert J. — *Savoy Partners, Ltd.*

Bruno, Deborah F. — *The Hindman Company*

Bryza, Robert M. — *Robert Lowell International*

Brzezinski, Ronald T. — *Callan Associates, Ltd.*

Buckles, Donna — *Cochran, Cochran & Yale, Inc.*

Buggy, Linda — *Bonnell Associates Ltd.*

Bullock, Conni — *Earley Kielty and Associates, Inc.*

Burchill, Greg — *BGB Associates*

Call, David — *Cochran, Cochran & Yale, Inc.*

Callan, Robert M. — *Callan Associates, Ltd.*

Campbell, Patricia A. — *The Onstott Group, Inc.*

Capizzi, Karen — *Cochran, Cochran & Yale, Inc.*

Cavolina, Michael — *Carver Search Consultants*

Celenza, Catherine — *CPS Inc.*

Chamberlin, Michael A. — *Tower Consultants, Ltd.*

Chappell, Peter — *The Bankers Group*

Chavous, C. Crawford — *Phillips Resource Group*

Hardison, Richard L. — *Hardison & Company*
Hart, Robert T. — *D.E. Foster Partners Inc.*
Hartle, Larry — *CPS Inc.*
Hartzman, Deborah — *Advanced Information Management*
Harvey, Mike — *Advanced Executive Resources*
Hawksworth, A. Dwight — *A.D. & Associates Executive Search, Inc.*
Haystead, Steve — *Advanced Executive Resources*
Hazerjian, Cynthia — *CPS Inc.*
Heacock, Burt E. — *Paul-Tittle Associates, Inc.*
Heafey, Bill — *CPS Inc.*
Heiken, Barbara E. — *Randell-Heiken, Inc.*
Helminiak, Audrey — *Gaffney Management Consultants*
Heneghan, Donald A. — *Allerton Heneghan & O'Neill*
Herman, Eugene J. — *Earley Kielty and Associates, Inc.*
Hicks, Albert M. — *Phillips Resource Group*
Higgins, Donna — *Howard Fischer Associates, Inc.*
Himli, Amy — *Cochran, Cochran & Yale, Inc.*
Hoevel, Michael J. — *Poirier, Hoevel & Co.*
Holland, Kathleen — *TOPAZ International, Inc.*
Holland, Kathleen — *TOPAZ Legal Solutions*
Houchins, William M. — *Christian & Timbers*
Hudson, Reginald M. — *Search Bureau International*
Hughes, Cathy N. — *The Ogdon Partnership*
Hunter, Gabe — *Phillips Resource Group*
Hyde, W. Jerry — *Hyde Danforth Wold & Co.*
Imely, Larry S. — *Stratford Group*
Irish, Alan — *CPS Inc.*
Jacobson, Carolyn — *The Abbott Group, Inc.*
James, Richard — *Criterion Executive Search, Inc.*
Janssen, Don — *Howard Fischer Associates, Inc.*
Januale, Lois — *Cochran, Cochran & Yale, Inc.*
Jaworski, Mary A. — *Tully/Woodmansee International, Inc.*
Jazylo, John V. — *Handy HRM Corp.*
Jeffers, Richard B. — *Dieckmann & Associates, Ltd.*
Johnson, Douglas — *Quality Search*
Johnson, LaDonna — *Gans, Gans & Associates*
Johnson, Robert J. — *Quality Search*
Jones, Amy E. — *The Corporate Connection, Ltd.*
Jones, Barbara — *Kaye-Bassman International Corp.*
Jones, Francis E. — *Earley Kielty and Associates, Inc.*
Jones, Gary — *BGB Associates*
Jordan, Jon — *Cochran, Cochran & Yale, Inc.*
Judge, Alfred L. — *The Cambridge Group Ltd*
Judy, Otto — *CPS Inc.*
Juelis, John J. — *Peeney Associates*
Kane, Karen — *Howard Fischer Associates, Inc.*
Karalis, William — *CPS Inc.*
Kartin, Martin C. — *Martin Kartin and Company, Inc.*
Kehoe, Mike — *CPS Inc.*
Kelly, Elizabeth Ann — *Wellington Management Group*
Kelly, Sheri — *Strategic Associates, Inc.*
Kern, Jerry L. — *ADOW's Executeam*
Kern, Kathleen G. — *ADOW's Executeam*
Kielty, John L. — *Earley Kielty and Associates, Inc.*

Kilcoyne, Pat — *CPS Inc.*
Kinney, Carol — *Dussick Management Associates*
Kip, Luanne S. — *Kip Williams, Inc.*
Kkorzyniewski, Nicole — *CPS Inc.*
Klages, Constance W. — *International Management Advisors, Inc.*
Klavens, Cecile J. — *The Pickwick Group, Inc.*
Klein, Mary Jo — *Cochran, Cochran & Yale, Inc.*
Klopfenstein, Edward L. — *Crowder & Company*
Kohn, Adam P. — *Christian & Timbers*
Koontz, Donald N. — *Koontz, Jeffries & Associates, Inc.*
Kossuth, Jane — *Kossuth & Associates, Inc.*
Krejci, Stanley L. — *Boyden Washington, D.C.*
Kreutz, Gary L. — *Kreutz Consulting Group, Inc.*
Krieger, Dennis F. — *Seiden Krieger Associates, Inc.*
Kurrigan, Geoffrey — *ESA Professional Consultants*
Laird, Cheryl — *CPS Inc.*
Lang, Sharon A. — *Ray & Berndtson*
Lautz, Lindsay A. — *Lautz Grotte Engler*
Leahy, Jan — *CPS Inc.*
Leininger, Dennis — *Key Employment Services*
Lewis, Marc D. — *Handy HRM Corp.*
Lezama Cohen, Luis — *Ray & Berndtson*
Lipe, Jerold L. — *Compass Group Ltd.*
Lofthouse, Cindy — *CPS Inc.*
Long, Helga — *Horton International*
Long, Milt — *William Guy & Associates*
Long, William G. — *McDonald, Long & Associates, Inc.*
Lotz, R. James — *International Management Advisors, Inc.*
Loving, Vikki — *Intersource, Ltd.*
Lucarelli, Joan — *The Onstott Group, Inc.*
Lucht, John — *The John Lucht Consultancy Inc.*
Lumsby, George N. — *International Management Advisors, Inc.*
Luntz, Charles E. — *Charles Luntz & Associates. Inc.*
Lupica, Anthony — *Cochran, Cochran & Yale, Inc.*
MacNaughton, Sperry — *McNaughton Associates*
Mallin, Ellen — *Howard Fischer Associates, Inc.*
Manassero, Henri J.P. — *International Management Advisors, Inc.*
Mansford, Keith — *Howard Fischer Associates, Inc.*
Marino, Chester — *Cochran, Cochran & Yale, Inc.*
Mark, John L. — *J.L. Mark Associates, Inc.*
Mark, Lynne — *J.L. Mark Associates, Inc.*
Marks, Ira — *Strategic Alternatives*
Marlow, William — *Straube Associates*
Marumoto, William H. — *Boyden Washington, D.C.*
Mashakas, Elizabeth — *TOPAZ International, Inc.*
Mashakas, Elizabeth — *TOPAZ Legal Solutions*
Mathias, Kathy — *Stone Murphy & Olson*
Maynard Taylor, Susan — *Chrisman & Company, Incorporated*
Mazor, Elly — *Howard Fischer Associates, Inc.*
McAndrews, Kathy — *CPS Inc.*
McBride, Jonathan E. — *McBride Associates, Inc.*
McCreary, Charles "Chip" — *Austin-McGregor International*
McDermott, Jeffrey T. — *Vlcek & Company, Inc.*

McDonald, Scott A. — *McDonald Associates International*
McDonald, Stanleigh B. — *McDonald Associates International*
McIntyre, Joel — *Phillips Resource Group*
McKell, Linda — *Advanced Information Management*
McKeown, Patricia A. — *DiMarchi Partners, Inc.*
McKnight, Amy E. — *Chartwell Partners International, Inc.*
McManners, Donald E. — *McManners Associates, Inc.*
McNamara, Catherine — *Ray & Berndtson*
McNichol, John — *McNichol Associates*
McSherry, James F. — *Battalia Winston International*
Mercer, Julie — *Columbia Consulting Group*
Michaels, Joseph — *CPS Inc.*
Michaels, Stewart — *TOPAZ International, Inc.*
Michaels, Stewart — *TOPAZ Legal Solutions*
Miller, David — *Cochran, Cochran & Yale, Inc.*
Miller, George N. — *Hite Executive Search*
Misiurewicz, Marc — *Cochran, Cochran & Yale, Inc.*
Mohr, Brian — *CPS Inc.*
Montgomery, James M. — *Houze, Shourds & Montgomery, Inc.*
Moore, T. Wills — *Ray & Berndtson*
Moran, Gayle — *Dussick Management Associates*
Morgan-Christopher, Jeanie — *Kaye-Bassman International Corp.*
Murphy, Erin — *CPS Inc.*
Mydlach, Renee — *CPS Inc.*
Naidicz, Maria — *Ray & Berndtson*
Nees, Eugene C. — *Ray & Berndtson*
Neher, Robert L. — *Intech Summit Group, Inc.*
Nehring, Keith — *Howard Fischer Associates, Inc.*
Nelson, Barbara — *Herman Smith Executive Initiatives Inc.*
Neuberth, Jeffrey G. — *Canny, Bowen Inc.*
Nichols, Gary — *Koontz, Jeffries & Associates, Inc.*
Noebel, Todd R. — *The Noebel Search Group, Inc.*
Norman, Randy — *Austin-McGregor International*
O'Brien, Maggie — *Advanced Information Management*
O'Connell, Mary — *CPS Inc.*
Ogilvie, Kit — *Howard Fischer Associates, Inc.*
Ottenritter, Chris — *CPS Inc.*
Overlock, Craig — *Ray & Berndtson*
Panarese, Pam — *Howard Fischer Associates, Inc.*
Papciak, Dennis J. — *Accounting Personnel Associates, Inc.*
Papoulias, Cathy — *Pendleton James and Associates, Inc.*
Pappas, Timothy C. — *Jonas, Walters & Assoc., Inc.*
Peasback, David R. — *Canny, Bowen Inc.*
Peckenpaugh, Ann D. — *Schweichler Associates, Inc.*
Pedley, Jill — *CPS Inc.*
Peeney, James D. — *Peeney Associates*
Percival, Chris — *Chicago Legal Search, Ltd.*
Pernell, Jeanette — *Norman Broadbent International, Inc.*
Peterson, John — *CPS Inc.*

Phillips, Donald L. — *O'Shea, Divine & Company, Inc.*
Pierotazio, John — *CPS Inc.*
Pigott, Daniel — *ESA Professional Consultants*
Poirier, Roland L. — *Poirier, Hoevel & Co.*
Pomerance, Mark — *CPS Inc.*
Poore, Larry D. — *Ward Howell International, Inc.*
Rabinowitz, Peter A. — *P.A.R. Associates Inc.*
Raines, Bruce R. — *Raines International Inc.*
Ramler, Carolyn S. — *The Corporate Connection, Ltd.*
Randell, James E. — *Randell-Heiken, Inc.*
Ray, Marianne C. — *Callan Associates, Ltd.*
Raymond, Anne — *Anderson Sterling Associates*
Reddick, David C. — *Horton International*
Reece, Christopher S. — *Reece & Mruk Partners*
Regan, Thomas J. — *Tower Consultants, Ltd.*
Reifel, Laurie — *Reifel & Assocaites*
Reuter, Tandom — *CPS Inc.*
Reynolds, Gregory P. — *Roberts Ryan and Bentley*
Rhodes, Bill — *Bench International*
Rice, Raymond D. — *Logue & Rice Inc.*
Riederer, Larry — *CPS Inc.*
Rieger, Louis J. — *Spencer Stuart*
Rimmele, Michael — *The Bankers Group*
Roberts, Norman C. — *Norman Roberts & Associates, Inc.*
Robinson, Bruce — *Bruce Robinson Associates*
Robinson, Eric B. — *Bruce Robinson Associates*
Robles Cuellar, Paulina — *Ray & Berndtson*
Roblin, Nancy R. — *Paul-Tittle Associates, Inc.*
Rose, Robert — *ESA Professional Consultants*
Ross, Curt A. — *Ray & Berndtson*
Rotella, Marshall W. — *The Corporate Connection, Ltd.*
Rubenstein, Alan J. — *Chicago Legal Search, Ltd.*
Rudolph, Kenneth — *Kossuth & Associates, Inc.*
Ruge, Merrill — *William Guy & Associates*
Sacerdote, John — *Raymond Karsan Associates*
Saletra, Andrew — *CPS Inc.*
Salvagno, Michael J. — *The Cambridge Group Ltd*
Sanders, Natalie — *CPS Inc.*
Sanow, Robert — *Cochran, Cochran & Yale, Inc.*
Sawyer, Patricia L. — *Smith & Sawyer Inc.*
Scalamera, Tom — *CPS Inc.*
Schedra, Sharon — *Earley Kielty and Associates, Inc.*
Schlpma, Christine — *Advanced Executive Resources*
Schmidt, Peter R. — *Boyden*
Schueneman, David — *CPS Inc.*
Scott, Evan — *Howard Fischer Associates, Inc.*
Scott, Gordon S. — *Search Advisors International Corp.*
Seco, William — *Seco & Zetto Associates, Inc.*
Seiden, Steven A. — *Seiden Krieger Associates, Inc.*
Shapiro, Elaine — *CPS Inc.*
Sibul, Shelly Remen — *Chicago Legal Search, Ltd.*
Signer, Julie — *CPS Inc.*
Silcott, Marvin L. — *Marvin L. Silcott & Associates, Inc.*
Silcott, Marvin L. — *Marvin L. Silcott & Associates, Inc.*
Sitarski, Stan — *Howard Fischer Associates, Inc.*

Skunda, Donna M. — *Allerton Heneghan & O'Neill*
Slosar, John — *Boyden*
Smith, David P. — *HRS, Inc.*
Smith, Lydia — *The Corporate Connection, Ltd.*
Smith, Matt D. — *Ray & Berndtson*
Snyder, C. Edward — *Horton International*
Steele, Daniel — *Cochran, Cochran & Yale, Inc.*
Steer, Joe — *CPS Inc.*
Sterling, Jay — *Earley Kielty and Associates, Inc.*
Stern, Stephen — *CPS Inc.*
Sterner, Doug — *CPS Inc.*
Stevenson, Jane — *Howard Fischer Associates, Inc.*
Stewart, Ross M. — *Human Resources Network Partners Inc.*
Stranberg, James R. — *Callan Associates, Ltd.*
Stringer, Dann P. — *D.E. Foster Partners Inc.*
Strom, Mark N. — *Search Advisors International Corp.*
Sturtz, James W. — *Compass Group Ltd.*
Sullivan, Kay — *Rusher, Loscavio & LoPresto*
Summerfield-Beall, Dotty — *Summerfield Associates, Inc.*
Sur, William K. — *Canny, Bowen Inc.*
Sussman, Lynda — *Gilbert Tweed/INESA*
Swanson, Dick — *Raymond Karsan Associates*
Taylor, R.L. (Larry) — *Ray & Berndtson*
Thomas, Cheryl M. — *CPS Inc.*
Thomas, Kim — *CPS Inc.*
Tittle, David M. — *Paul-Tittle Associates, Inc.*
Tovrog, Dan — *CPS Inc.*
Truemper, Dean — *CPS Inc.*
Tullberg, Tina — *CPS Inc.*
Tully, Margo L. — *Tully/Woodmansee International, Inc.*
Tursi, Deborah J. — *The Corporate Connection, Ltd.*

Vachon, David A. — *McNichol Associates*
Van Campen, Jerry — *Gilbert & Van Campen International*
Velten, Mark T. — *Boyden*
Vennat, Manon — *Spencer Stuart*
Vlcek, Thomas J. — *Vlcek & Company, Inc.*
Volkman, Arthur — *Cochran, Cochran & Yale, Inc.*
von Baillou, Astrid — *Richard Kinser & Associates*
Vroom, Cynthia D. — *Cyntal International Ltd*
Walker, Ewing J. — *Ward Howell International, Inc.*
Warter, Mark — *Isaacson, Miller*
Watson, Peggy — *Advanced Information Management*
Wein, Michael S. — *Media Management Resources, Inc.*
Wein, William — *Media Management Resources, Inc.*
Weissman-Rosenthal, Abbe — *ALW Research International*
Weisz, Laura — *Anderson Sterling Associates*
Welch, Robert — *Ray & Berndtson*
Willner, Leo — *William Guy & Associates*
Wilson, Patricia L. — *Leon A. Farley Associates*
Winograd, Glenn — *Criterion Executive Search, Inc.*
Winston, Dale — *Battalia Winston International*
Womack, Joseph — *The Bankers Group*
Woodward, Lee — *Search Associates, Inc.*
Wooldridge, Jeff — *Ray & Berndtson*
Yen, Maggie Yeh Ching — *Ray & Berndtson*
Yungerberg, Steven — *Steven Yungerberg Associates Inc.*
Zamborsky, George — *Boyden*
Zetto, Kathryn — *Seco & Zetto Associates, Inc.*

Geographic Index

Alabama
Birmingham
Blanton, Julia — *Blanton and Company*
Blanton, Thomas — *Blanton and Company*
Taylor, James M. — *The HRM Group, Inc.*
Wilkinson, Jr. SPHR
Wilkinson, Charles E. — *The HRM Group, Inc.*
Huntsville
Henry, Patrick — *F-O-R-T-U-N-E Personnel Consultants of Huntsville, Inc.*
Henshaw, Bob — *F-O-R-T-U-N-E Personnel Consultants of Huntsville, Inc.*
Lamb, Lynn M. — *F-O-R-T-U-N-E Personnel Consultants of Huntsville, Inc.*
Langford, Matt — *F-O-R-T-U-N-E Personnel Consultants of Huntsville, Inc.*
Langford, Robert W. — *F-O-R-T-U-N-E Personnel Consultants of Huntsville, Inc.*
Simmons, Anneta — *F-O-R-T-U-N-E Personnel Consultants of Huntsville, Inc.*
Ward, Jim — *F-O-R-T-U-N-E Personnel Consultants of Huntsville, Inc.*
Whitt, Mimi — *F-O-R-T-U-N-E Personnel Consultants of Huntsville, Inc.*

Arizona
Phoenix
Balchumas, Charles — *Source Services Corporation*
Blecker, Jay — *TSS Consulting, Ltd.*
Booth, Ronald — *Source Services Corporation*
Cizek, Marti J. — *Cizek Associates, Inc.*
Collins, Scott — *Source Services Corporation*
Collis, Gerald — *TSS Consulting, Ltd.*
Debus, Wayne — *Source Services Corporation*
Gares, Conrad — *TSS Consulting, Ltd.*
Graff, Jack — *Source Services Corporation*
Green, Marc — *TSS Consulting, Ltd.*
Jones, B.J. — *Intersource, Ltd.*
McDonald, John R. — *TSS Consulting, Ltd.*
McThrall, David — *TSS Consulting, Ltd.*
Nosky, Richard E. — *Ward Howell International, Inc.*
Petersen, Richard — *Source Services Corporation*
Robertson, Sherry — *Source Services Corporation*
Spector, Michael — *Source Services Corporation*
Swick, Jan — *TSS Consulting, Ltd.*
Weeks, Glenn — *Source Services Corporation*
Weis, Theodore — *Source Services Corporation*
Wichansky, Mark — *TSS Consulting, Ltd.*
Scottsdale
Bartholdi, Theodore G. — *Bartholdi & Company, Inc.*
Doyle, Marie — *Spectra International Inc.*
Jacobs, Martin J. — *The Rubicon Group*
James, Bruce — *Roberson and Company*
Nold, Robert — *Roberson and Company*
Reed, Ruthann — *Spectra International Inc.*
Renner, Sandra L. — *Spectra International Inc.*
Silvas, Stephen D. — *Roberson and Company*
Swartz, William K. — *Swartz Executive Search*
Wilder, Richard B. — *Columbia Consulting Group*

California
Agoura Hills
Schmidt, Frank B. — *F.B. Schmidt International*
Shirilla, Robert M. — *F.B. Schmidt International*

Auburn
Norsell, Paul E. — *Paul Norsell & Associates, Inc.*
Beverly Hills
Hensley, Bert — *Morgan Samuels Co., Inc.*
Carmel
Dugan, John H. — *J.H. Dugan and Associates, Inc.*
Clovis
Cavolina, Michael — *Carver Search Consultants*
Corte Madera
Bluhm, Claudia — *Schweichler Associates, Inc.*
Blunt, Peter — *Hernand & Partners*
Gerbosi, Karen — *Hernand & Partners*
Hernand, Warren L. — *Hernand & Partners*
Mikula, Linda — *Schweichler Associates, Inc.*
Peckenpaugh, Ann D. — *Schweichler Associates, Inc.*
Schweichler, Lee J. — *Schweichler Associates, Inc.*
Costa Mesa
Farrow, Jerry M. — *McCormack & Farrow*
Friedman, Helen E. — *McCormack & Farrow*
Phelps, Gene L. — *McCormack & Farrow*
Telford, John H. — *Telford, Adams & Alexander/Telford & Co., Inc.*
Thompson, Kenneth L. — *McCormack & Farrow*
Zaslav, Debra M. — *Telford, Adams & Alexander/Telford & Co., Inc.*
Cupertino
Barnes, Gary — *Brigade Inc.*
King, Margaret — *Christian & Timbers*
Mather, David R. — *Christian & Timbers*
Danville
Badger, Fred H. — *The Badger Group*
Cochran, Scott P. — *The Badger Group*
Watkinson, Jim W. — *The Badger Group*
Del Mar
Clasen, Ryan — *Warren, Morris & Madison*
Cossitt, Chip — *Warren, Morris & Madison*
LoRusso, Steve — *Warren, Morris & Madison*
Morris, Chuck — *Warren, Morris & Madison*
Schnit, David — *Warren, Morris & Madison*
Sweetser, Rob — *Warren, Morris & Madison*
Dublin
Paul, Lisa D. — *Merit Resource Group, Inc.*
Encinitas
Saxon, Alexa — *Woodworth International Group*
Encino
Inguagiato, Gregory — *MSI International*
Fremont
Dillon, Larry — *Predictor Systems*
Schultz, Helen — *Predictor Systems*
Garden Grove
Dowell, Mary K. — *Professional Search Associates*
Greenbrae
Gideon, Mark — *Eagle Search Associates*
Indian Wells
Thomas, Donald — *Mixtec Group*
Irvine
Belfrey, Edward — *Dunhill Professional Search of Irvine, Inc.*
Compton, Tonya — *Dunhill Professional Search of Irvine, Inc.*

De Brun, Thomas P. — *Ray & Berndtson*
Gennawey, Robert — *Source Services Corporation*
Gregory, Gary A. — *John Kurosky & Associates*
Guthrie, Stuart — *Source Services Corporation*
Hart, Crystal — *Source Services Corporation*
Herzog, Sarah — *Source Services Corporation*
Jadulang, Vincent — *Source Services Corporation*
Jeltema, John — *Source Services Corporation*
Jensen, Christine K. — *John Kurosky & Associates*
Kennedy, Paul — *Source Services Corporation*
Ludlow, Michael — *Source Services Corporation*
McGregor, James D. — *John Kurosky & Associates*
Mollichelli, David — *Source Services Corporation*
Noguchi, Yoshi — *Ray & Berndtson*
Paternie, Patrick — *Source Services Corporation*
Pierce, Matthew — *Source Services Corporation*
Raab, Julie — *Dunhill Professional Search of Irvine, Inc.*
Renwick, David — *John Kurosky & Associates*
Sickles, Robert — *Dunhill Professional Search of Irvine, Inc.*
Vaughan, David B. — *Dunhill Professional Search of Irvine, Inc.*
Walker, Rose — *Source Services Corporation*
Ward, Robert — *Source Services Corporation*
Wilson, Joyce — *Source Services Corporation*
Woods, Craig — *Source Services Corporation*
Yen, Maggie Yeh Ching — *Ray & Berndtson*

Laguna Niguel
Levitt, Muriel A. — *D.S. Allen Associates, Inc.*

Long Beach
Curci, Donald L. — *A.R.I. International*
Montgomery, James M. — *Houze, Shourds & Montgomery, Inc.*
Shourds, Mary E. — *Houze, Shourds & Montgomery, Inc.*

Los Altos
Busch, Jack — *Busch International*
Furlong, James W. — *Furlong Search, Inc.*
Hockett, William — *Hockett Associates, Inc.*
Ocon, Olga — *Busch International*

Los Angeles
Ainsworth, Lawrence — *Search West, Inc.*
Allen, Scott — *Chrisman & Company, Incorporated*
Archer, Sandra F. — *Ryan, Miller & Associates Inc.*
Bennett, Ness — *Technical Connections Inc.*
Berkhemer-Credaire, Betsy — *Berkhemer Clayton Incorporated*
Bohle, John B. — *Ray & Berndtson*
Brown, Buzz — *Brown, Bernardy, Van Remmen, Inc.*
Bruce, Michael C. — *Spencer Stuart*
Carter, I. Wayne — *Heidrick & Struggles, Inc.*
Clayton, Fred J. — *Berkhemer Clayton Incorporated*
Connelly, Scott — *Technical Connections Inc.*
Cutka, Matthew — *Source Services Corporation*
Dorsey, Jim — *Ryan, Miller & Associates Inc.*
Dreifus, Donald — *Search West, Inc.*
Dunbar, Geoffrey T. — *Heidrick & Struggles, Inc.*
Feyder, Michael — *A.T. Kearney, Inc.*
Fifield, George C. — *Egon Zehnder International Inc.*
Fishler, Stu — *A.T. Kearney, Inc.*

Flanders, Karen — *Advanced Information Management*
Frank, Valerie S. — *Norman Roberts & Associates, Inc.*
Fulmer, Karen — *Bench International*
Fust, Sheely F. — *Ray & Berndtson*
Gordon, Gloria — *A.T. Kearney, Inc.*
Groban, Jack — *A.T. Kearney, Inc.*
Hanes, Leah — *Ray & Berndtson*
Hanna, Remon — *Source Services Corporation*
Hartzman, Deborah — *Advanced Information Management*
Hoevel, Michael J. — *Poirier, Hoevel & Co.*
Hurtado, Jaime — *Source Services Corporation*
Johnson, Ronald S. — *Ronald S. Johnson Associates, Inc.*
Katz, Cyndi — *Search West, Inc.*
Kerester, Jonathon — *Cadillac Associates*
Koenig, Joel S. — *Blackshaw, Olmstead, Lynch & Koenig*
Laba, Marvin — *Marvin Laba & Associates*
Lin, Felix — *Source Services Corporation*
Lipson, Harriet — *First Interactive Recruiting Specialists*
Lipson, Harriet — *Lipson & Co.*
Lipson, Howard K. — *First Interactive Recruiting Specialists*
Lipson, Howard R. — *Lipson & Co.*
MacKinnon, Helen — *Technical Connections Inc.*
Matueny, Robert — *Ryan, Miller & Associates Inc.*
Maynard Taylor, Susan — *Chrisman & Company, Incorporated*
McHugh, Keith — *Source Services Corporation*
McNamee, Erin — *Technical Connections Inc.*
Milstein, Bonnie — *Marvin Laba & Associates*
Nolen, Shannon — *Source Services Corporation*
O'Brien, Maggie — *Advanced Information Management*
Peters, Kevin — *Source Services Corporation*
Pfannkuche, Anthony V. — *Spencer Stuart*
Poirier, Roland L. — *Poirier, Hoevel & Co.*
Quinn, Nola — *Technical Connections Inc.*
Radden, David B. — *Ray & Berndtson*
Rhodes, Bill — *Bench International*
Roberts, Nick P. — *Spectrum Search Associates, Inc.*
Roberts, Norman C. — *Norman Roberts & Associates, Inc.*
Rubinstein, Walter — *Technical Connections Inc.*
Ryan, Lee — *Ryan, Miller & Associates Inc.*
Santiago, Benefrido — *Source Services Corporation*
Saposhnik, Doron — *Source Services Corporation*
Schoettle, Michael B. — *Heidrick & Struggles, Inc.*
Shanks, Jennifer — *Source Services Corporation*
Shawhan, Heather — *Source Services Corporation*
Siciliano, Gene — *Western Management Associates*
Siegler, Jody Cukiir — *A.T. Kearney, Inc.*
Spencer, John — *Source Services Corporation*
Spencer, John — *Source Services Corporation*
Thompson, Leslie — *Source Services Corporation*
Thrower, Troy — *Source Services Corporation*
Van Remmen, Roger — *Brown, Bernardy, Van Remmen, Inc.*
Vandenbulcke, Cynthia — *Source Services Corporation*

Welch, Robert — *Ray & Berndtson*
Yang, George — *Technical Connections Inc.*
Zatzick, Michael — *Search West, Inc.*
Zilliacus, Patrick W. — *Larsen, Whitney, Blecksmith & Zilliacus*

Los Gatos
Goodere, Greg — *Splaine & Associates, Inc.*
Splaine, Charles — *Splaine & Associates, Inc.*

Malibu
Myers, Thomas — *Careers Plus*

Manhattan Beach
Fisher, Neal — *Fisher Personnel Management Services*

Menlo Park
Champion, Geoffrey — *Korn/Ferry International*
Dean, Mary — *Korn/Ferry International*
Friel, Thomas J. — *Heidrick & Struggles, Inc.*
Gostyla, Rick — *Spencer Stuart*
Kixmiller, David B. — *Heidrick & Struggles, Inc.*
Lewis, Gretchen S. — *Heidrick & Struggles, Inc.*
Lonergan, Mark W. — *Heidrick & Struggles, Inc.*
Mahaney, Joann — *Heidrick & Struggles, Inc.*
Stirn, Bradley A. — *Spencer Stuart*
Strain, Stephen R. — *Spencer Stuart*
Ware, John C. — *Spencer Stuart*

Mill Valley
Block, Randy — *Block & Associates*

Mission Viejo
Miller, Kenneth A. — *Computer Network Resources, Inc.*

Mountain View
McKell, Linda — *Advanced Information Management*
Watson, Peggy — *Advanced Information Management*

Newport Beach
Davis, G. Gordon — *Davis & Company*
Divine, Robert S. — *O'Shea, Divine & Company, Inc.*
Galante, Suzanne M. — *Vlcek & Company, Inc.*
Garrett, James — *International Staffing Consultants, Inc.*
Gettys, James R. — *International Staffing Consultants, Inc.*
Gordon, Elliot — *Korn/Ferry International*
Johnson, Julie M. — *International Staffing Consultants, Inc.*
Kobayashi, Rika — *International Staffing Consultants, Inc.*
McDermott, Jeffrey T. — *Vlcek & Company, Inc.*
Nguyen, John — *International Staffing Consultants, Inc.*
Phillips, Donald L. — *O'Shea, Divine & Company, Inc.*
Reed, Brenda — *International Staffing Consultants, Inc.*
Smith, Ian — *International Staffing Consultants, Inc.*
Thomas, Ian A. — *International Staffing Consultants, Inc.*
Vlcek, Thomas J. — *Vlcek & Company, Inc.*

Northridge
Furlong, James W. — *Furlong Search, Inc.*

Orange
Cooper, William — *Search West, Inc.*
Lindenmuth, Mary — *Search West, Inc.*

Pacific Grove
Cameron, James W. — *Cameron Consulting*

Palm Springs
Hanna, Dwight — *Cadillac Associates*

Palo Alto
LoPresto, Robert L. — *Rusher, Loscavio & LoPresto*
Onstott, Joseph — *The Onstott Group, Inc.*
Sullivan, Kay — *Rusher, Loscavio & LoPresto*
Woollett, James — *Rusher, Loscavio & LoPresto*

Pasadena
Ghurani, Mac — *Gary Kaplan & Associates*
Hansen, David G. — *Ott & Hansen, Inc.*
Harney, Elyane — *Gary Kaplan & Associates*
Herman, Shelli — *Gary Kaplan & Associates*
Kaplan, Gary — *Gary Kaplan & Associates*
Mangum, Maria — *Thomas Mangum Company*
Mangum, William T. — *Thomas Mangum Company*
McNichols, Walter B. — *Gary Kaplan & Associates*
Meyer, Stacey — *Gary Kaplan & Associates*
Ott, George W. — *Ott & Hansen, Inc.*

Portola Valley
Marks, Ira — *Strategic Alternatives*

Redwood City
Keitel, Robert S. — *A.T. Kearney, Inc.*
Olsen, Carl — *A.T. Kearney, Inc.*

Riverside
MacNaughton, Sperry — *McNaughton Associates*

Sacramento
Geiger, Jan — *Wilcox, Bertoux & Miller*
Wilcox, Fred T. — *Wilcox, Bertoux & Miller*
Wren, Jay — *Jay Wren & Associates*

San Bruno
Elder, Tom — *Juntunen-Combs-Poirier*
Gerster, J.P. — *Juntunen-Combs-Poirier*
Poirier, Frank — *Juntunen-Combs-Poirier*

San Diego
Alringer, Marc — *Source Services Corporation*
Anderson, Terry — *Intech Summit Group, Inc.*
Bartels, Fredrick — *Source Services Corporation*
Clough, Geoff — *Intech Summit Group, Inc.*
Cohen, Michael R. — *Intech Summit Group, Inc.*
Cohen, Robert C. — *Intech Summit Group, Inc.*
Dowlatzadch, Homayoun — *Source Services Corporation*
Fagerstrom, Jon — *Source Services Corporation*
Ferrara, David M. — *Intech Summit Group, Inc.*
King, Shannon — *Source Services Corporation*
Kinsey, Joanne — *Eastridge InfoTech*
Levenson, Laurel — *Source Services Corporation*
Lyons, Michael — *Source Services Corporation*
Neher, Robert L. — *Intech Summit Group, Inc.*
Song, Louis — *Source Services Corporation*
Tipp, George D. — *Intech Summit Group, Inc.*
Wenz, Alexander — *Source Services Corporation*
Winitz, Joel — *GSW Consulting Group, Inc.*
Winitz, Marla — *GSW Consulting Group, Inc.*

San Francisco
Adams, Jeffrey C. — *Telford, Adams & Alexander/Jeffrey C. Adams & Co., Inc.*

Gamble, Ira — *Source Services Corporation*
Gray, Russell — *Source Services Corporation*
Hoffman, Stephen — *Source Services Corporation*
Hughes, Barbara — *Source Services Corporation*
Humphrey, Titus — *Source Services Corporation*
Nelson, Hitch — *Source Services Corporation*
Pregeant, David — *Source Services Corporation*
Rosen, Mitchell — *Source Services Corporation*
Schwalbach, Robert — *Source Services Corporation*
Silver, Kit — *Source Services Corporation*

Tarzana
Goodman, Victor — *Anderson Sterling Associates*
Raymond, Anne — *Anderson Sterling Associates*
Weisz, Laura — *Anderson Sterling Associates*

Tiburon
Thomas, Terry — *The Thomas Resource Group*

Tustin
Adler, Louis S. — *CJA - The Adler Group*
Remillard, Brad M. — *CJA - The Adler Group*

Van Nuys
Woodward, Lee — *Search Associates, Inc.*

Walnut Creek
Martin, Lois G. — *The Martin Group*
Martin, Timothy P. — *The Martin Group*

Westlake Village
Baltin, Carrie — *Search West, Inc.*
Dalton, Bret — *Robert W. Dingman Company, Inc.*
Dingman, Bruce — *Robert W. Dingman Company, Inc.*
Dingman, Robert W. — *Robert W. Dingman Company, Inc.*
Diskin, Rochelle — *Search West, Inc.*
Fredericks, Ward A. — *Mixtec Group*
Knotts, Jerry — *Mixtec Group*
Linton, Leonard M. — *Byron Leonard International, Inc.*
May, Peter — *Mixtec Group*
Robinette, Paul — *Hernand & Partners*
Thomas, William — *Mixtec Group*
White, William C. — *Venture Resources Inc.*
Wolf, Stephen M. — *Byron Leonard International, Inc.*
Young, Lesley — *Search West, Inc.*

Canada
Calgary, Alberta
Coe, Karen J. — *Coe & Company International Inc.*
Costello, Lynda — *Coe & Company International Inc.*
Johnson, Valerie — *Coe & Company International Inc.*
Pfeiffer, Irene — *Price Waterhouse*
Smith, Ronald V. — *Coe & Company International Inc.*
Sutton, Robert J. — *The Caldwell Partners Amrop International*

Edmonton, Alberta
Holland, Rose Mary — *Price Waterhouse*

Montreal, Quebec
Krecklo, Brian Douglas — *Krecklo & Associates Inc.*
Labrecque, Bernard F. — *Laurendeau Labrecque/Ray & Berndtson, Inc.*

LeComte, Andre — *Egon Zehnder International Inc.*
Payette, Pierre — *Egon Zehnder International Inc.*
Swidler, J. Robert — *Egon Zehnder International Inc.*
Vennat, Manon — *Spencer Stuart*

North York, Ontario
Nagy, Les — *Source Services Corporation*

Ottawa, Ontario
Morgan, Richard S. — *Ray & Berndtson/Lovas Stanley*

Toronto, Ontario
Baker, Gerry — *A.T. Kearney, Inc.*
Beran, Helena — *Michael J. Cavanagh and Associates*
Bliley, Jerry — *Spencer Stuart*
Britt, Stephen — *Keith Bagg & Associates Inc.*
Burns, Alan — *The Enns Partners Inc.*
Campbell, W. Ross — *Egon Zehnder International Inc.*
Carrott, Gregory T. — *Egon Zehnder International Inc.*
Cavanagh, Michael J. — *Michael J. Cavanagh and Associates*
Colling, Douglas — *KPMG Management Consulting*
Cook, Dennis — *A.T. Kearney, Inc.*
Crath, Paul F. — *Price Waterhouse*
Dunbar, Marilynne — *Ray & Berndtson/Lovas Stanley*
Enns, George — *The Enns Partners Inc.*
Fennell, Patrick — *Korn/Ferry International*
Graham, Craig — *Ward Howell International, Inc.*
Harris, Jack — *A.T. Kearney, Inc.*
Hauswirth, Jeffrey M. — *Spencer Stuart*
Hussey, Wayne — *Krecklo & Associates Inc.*
Kussner, Janice N. — *Herman Smith Executive Initiatives Inc.*
Lennox, Charles — *Price Waterhouse*
Long, Thomas — *Egon Zehnder International Inc.*
Lovas, W. Carl — *Ray & Berndtson/Lovas Stanley*
MacDougall, Andrew J. — *Spencer Stuart*
MacEachern, David — *Spencer Stuart*
Malcolm, Rod — *Korn/Ferry International*
Marcine, John W. — *Keith Bagg & Associates Inc.*
Martin, Jon — *Egon Zehnder International Inc.*
Massey, R. Bruce — *Horton International*
Miller, Roy — *The Enns Partners Inc.*
Murray, Virginia — *A.T. Kearney, Inc.*
Neelin, Sharon — *The Caldwell Partners Amrop International*
Nelson, Barbara — *Herman Smith Executive Initiatives Inc.*
Parr, James A. — *KPMG Management Consulting*
Perry, Glen — *Keith Bagg & Associates Inc.*
Rosin, Jeffrey — *Korn/Ferry International*
Ross, Lawrence — *Ray & Berndtson/Lovas Stanley*
Ross, Mark — *Ray & Berndtson/Lovas Stanley*
Shenfield, Peter — *A.T. Kearney, Inc.*
Shore, Earl L. — *E.L. Shore & Associates Ltd.*
Smith, Herman M. — *Herman Smith Executive Initiatives Inc.*
Stackhouse, P. John — *Heidrick & Struggles, Inc.*
Stanley, Paul R.A. — *Ray & Berndtson/Lovas Stanley*
Stewart, Jan J. — *Egon Zehnder International Inc.*

Kurrigan, Geoffrey — *ESA Professional Consultants*
Moran, Gayle — *Dussick Management Associates*
Pigott, Daniel — *ESA Professional Consultants*
Rose, Robert — *ESA Professional Consultants*

New Haven
Cast, Donald — *Dunhill International Search of New Haven*
Kaiser, Donald J. — *Dunhill International Search of New Haven*
Nemec, Phillip — *Dunhill International Search of New Haven*
Zarnoski, Henry — *Dunhill International Search of New Haven*

Norwalk
Hallock, Peter B. — *Goodrich & Sherwood Associates, Inc.*
Sahagian, John — *The Search Alliance, Inc.*
Spann, Richard E. — *Goodrich & Sherwood Associates, Inc.*
Wright, Charles D. — *Goodrich & Sherwood Associates, Inc.*

Rowayton
Mackenna, Kathy — *Plummer & Associates, Inc.*
Plummer, John — *Plummer & Associates, Inc.*

Shelton
Rios, Vince — *Source Services Corporation*

Southington
Cahill, Peter M. — *Peter M. Cahill Associates, Inc.*

Southport
Buggy, Linda — *Bonnell Associates Ltd.*

Stamford
Broadhurst, Austin — *Lamalie Amrop International*
Emery, Jodie A. — *Lamalie Amrop International*
Hart, Robert T. — *D.E. Foster Partners Inc.*
Howard, Lee Ann — *Lamalie Amrop International*
Jones, Francis E. — *Earley Kielty and Associates, Inc.*
Kanovsky, Gerald — *Career Consulting Group, Inc.*
Kanovsky, Marlene — *Career Consulting Group, Inc.*
Lieberman, Beverly — *Halbrecht Lieberman Associates, Inc.*
Lotufo, Donald A. — *D.A.L. Associates, Inc.*
McMahon, Mark J. — *A.T. Kearney, Inc.*
Mirtz, P. John — *Mirtz Morice, Inc.*
Morice, James L. — *Mirtz Morice, Inc.*
Murphy, Peter — *Korn/Ferry International*
Romanello, Daniel P. — *Spencer Stuart*
Rottblatt, Michael — *Korn/Ferry International*
Rowell, Roger — *Halbrecht Lieberman Associates, Inc.*
Rush, Michael E. — *D.A.L. Associates, Inc.*
Stone, Robert Ryder — *Lamalie Amrop International*
Wasson, Thomas W. — *Spencer Stuart*

Trumbull
Alexander, Karen — *Huntington Group*
Boehmer, John — *Huntington Group*
Tomasco, Ray — *Huntington Group*

West Hartford
Baron, Len — *Industrial Recruiters Associates, Inc.*
Boccella, Ralph — *Susan C. Goldberg Associates*

Girsinger, Linda — *Industrial Recruiters Associates, Inc.*
Goldberg, Susan C. — *Susan C. Goldberg Associates*
Johnston, James R. — *The Stevenson Group of Delaware Inc.*
Mierzwinski, John — *Industrial Recruiters Associates, Inc.*

Westport
Caruthers, Robert D. — *James Mead & Company*
Cizynski, Katherine W. — *James Mead & Company*
Dubrow, Richard M. — *R/K International, Inc.*
Fincher, Richard P. — *Phase II Management*
Jerolman, Gregg — *Masserman & Associates, Inc.*
Judge, Alfred L. — *The Cambridge Group Ltd*
Masserman, Bruce — *Masserman & Associates, Inc.*
Mead, James D. — *James Mead & Company*
Persky, Barry — *Barry Persky & Company, Inc.*
Ross, H. Lawrence — *Ross & Company*
Salvagno, Michael J. — *The Cambridge Group Ltd*
Walsh, Kenneth A. — *R/K International, Inc.*

Wilton
Johnson, Stanley C. — *Johnson & Company*
Knapp, Ronald A. — *Knapp Consultants*
Walsh, Patty — *Abraham & London, Ltd.*

Delaware
Wilmington
Vacca, Domenic — *Romac & Associates*

District of Columbia
Washington
Brudno, Robert J. — *Savoy Partners, Ltd.*
Burch, R. Stuart — *Russell Reynolds Associates, Inc.*
Clauhsen, Elizabeth A. — *Savoy Partners, Ltd.*
Hagerty, Kenneth — *Korn/Ferry International*
Hutchison, Richard H. — *Rurak & Associates, Inc.*
Krejci, Stanley L. — *Boyden Washington, D.C.*
Marumoto, William H. — *Boyden Washington, D.C.*
McBride, Jonathan E. — *McBride Associates, Inc.*
Nye, David S. — *Blake, Hansen & Nye, Limited*
Rurak, Zbigniew T. — *Rurak & Associates, Inc.*
Strassman, Mark — *Don Richard Associates of Washington, D.C., Inc.*
Stringer, Dann P. — *D.E. Foster Partners Inc.*
Vilella, Paul — *Source Services Corporation*
Weller, Paul S. — *Mark Stanley/EMA Partners International*

Florida
Altamonte Springs
Cannavino, Matthew J. — *Financial Resource Associates, Inc.*
Little, Elizabeth A. — *Financial Resource Associates, Inc.*

Boca Raton
Clark, John — *Tate Consulting Inc.*
Marra, John — *Marra Peters & Partners*
Schneiderman, Gerald — *Management Resource Associates, Inc.*

Coral Gables
Park, Dabney G. — *Mark Stanley/EMA Partners International*

Boel, Werner — *The Dalley Hewitt Company*
Campbell, Gary — *Romac & Associates*
Carrington, Timothy — *Korn/Ferry International*
Curren, Camella — *Source Services Corporation*
Dankberg, Iris — *Source Services Corporation*
Dezember, Steve — *Ray & Berndtson*
Dickson, Duke — *A.D. & Associates Executive Search, Inc.*
Dobrow, Samuel — *Source Services Corporation*
Downs, William — *Source Services Corporation*
Duckworth, Donald R. — *Johnson Smith & Knisely Accord*
Duelks, John — *Source Services Corporation*
Edwards, Douglas W. — *Egon Zehnder International Inc.*
Eldridge, Charles B. — *Ray & Berndtson*
Ferguson, Kenneth — *Source Services Corporation*
Freeh, Thomas — *Source Services Corporation*
Gladstone, Martin J. — *MSI International*
Green, Jean — *Broward-Dobbs, Inc.*
Greene, Luke — *Broward-Dobbs, Inc.*
Groover, David — *MSI International*
Hailes, Brian — *Russell Reynolds Associates, Inc.*
Hales, Daphne — *Source Services Corporation*
Hawksworth, A. Dwight — *A.D. & Associates Executive Search, Inc.*
Hewitt, Rives D. — *The Dalley Hewitt Company*
Hewitt, W. Davis — *The Dalley Hewitt Company*
Koblentz, Joel M. — *Egon Zehnder International Inc.*
Koenig, Joel S. — *Blackshaw, Olmstead, Lynch & Koenig*
Lindberg, Eric J. — *MSI International*
Luke, A. Wayne — *Heidrick & Struggles, Inc.*
Mayland, Tina — *Russell Reynolds Associates, Inc.*
McConnell, Greg — *Winter, Wyman & Company*
Miles, Kenneth T. — *MSI International*
Milligan, Dale — *Source Services Corporation*
Moore, Lemuel R. — *MSI International*
Moore, T. Wills — *Ray & Berndtson*
Mouchet, Marcus — *Commonwealth Consultants*
Murphy, James — *Source Services Corporation*
Murphy, Timothy D. — *MSI International*
Neely, Alan S. — *Korn/Ferry International*
Norton, James B. — *Lamalie Amrop International*
Olmstead, George T. — *Blackshaw, Olmstead, Lynch & Koenig*
Panetta, Timothy — *Commonwealth Consultants*
Salet, Michael — *Source Services Corporation*
Savela, Edward — *Source Services Corporation*
Sawyer, Deborah — *Korn/Ferry International*
Semple, David — *Source Services Corporation*
Shepard, Michael J. — *MSI International*
Silkiner, David S. — *Ray & Berndtson*
Simmons, Sandra K. — *MSI International*
St. Martin, Peter — *Source Services Corporation*
Taylor, Charles E. — *Lamalie Amrop International*
Taylor, Conrad G. — *MSI International*
Waldrop, Gary R. — *MSI International*
Watkins, Jeffrey P. — *Lamalie Amrop International*
Watson, James — *MSI International*

Norcross
Patrick, Donald R. — *Sanford Rose Associates*

Roswell
Beall, Charles P. — *Beall & Company, Inc.*
Desmond, Dennis — *Beall & Company, Inc.*

Loving, Vikki — *Intersource, Ltd.*
Palmer, Carlton A. — *Beall & Company, Inc.*
Reddick, David C. — *Horton International*
Smith, R. Michael — *Smith James Group, Inc.*
Soutouras, James — *Smith James Group, Inc.*
Wilkinson, Barbara — *Beall & Company, Inc.*

Snellville
Hubert, David L. — *ARJay & Associates*
Jones, Ronald T. — *ARJay & Associates*

Illinois
Arlington Heights
Baldwin, Keith R. — *The Baldwin Group*
Brindise, Michael J. — *Dynamic Search Systems, Inc.*

Barrington
Bennett, Joan — *Adams & Associates International*
Bryant, Richard D. — *Bryant Associates, Inc.*
Bryant, Shari G. — *Bryant Associates, Inc.*
Cunningham, Sheila — *Adams & Associates International*
Delaney, Patrick J. — *Sensible Solutions, Inc.*

Carol Stream
Bartholomew, Katie — *C. Berger & Company*
Berger, Carol — *C. Berger & Company*
Brill, Pamela — *C. Berger & Company*

Chicago
Allerton, Donald T. — *Allerton Heneghan & O'Neill*
Apostle, George — *Search Dynamics, Inc.*
Arnson, Craig — *Hernand & Partners*
Borenstine, Alvin — *Synergistics Associates Ltd.*
Brennen, Richard J. — *Spencer Stuart*
Bueschel, David A. — *Shepherd Bueschel & Provus, Inc.*
Cesafsky, Barry R. — *Lamalie Amrop International*
Chappell, Peter — *The Bankers Group*
Christoff, Matthew J. — *Spencer Stuart*
Clawson, Robert — *Source Services Corporation*
Cocchiaro, Richard — *Romac & Associates*
Cocconi, Alan — *Source Services Corporation*
Cole, Rosalie — *Source Services Corporation*
Coleman, Patricia — *Korn/Ferry International*
D'Alessio, Gary A. — *Chicago Legal Search, Ltd.*
Deaver, Henry C. — *Ray & Berndtson*
DeCorrevont, James — *DeCorrevont & Associates*
Desmond, Mary — *Source Services Corporation*
Drury, James J. — *Spencer Stuart*
Duggan, James P. — *Slayton International, Inc./ I-I-C Partners*
Grant, Michael — *Zwell International*
Groner, David — *Source Services Corporation*
Gutknecht, Steven — *Jacobson Associates*
Hanley, Alan P. — *Williams, Roth & Krueger Inc.*
Hedlund, David — *Hedlund Corporation*
Heneghan, Donald A. — *Allerton Heneghan & O'Neill*
Himes, Dirk — *A.T. Kearney, Inc.*
Hofner, Andrew — *Source Services Corporation*
Hudson, Reginald M. — *Search Bureau International*
Jeffers, Richard B. — *Dieckmann & Associates, Ltd.*
Johnson, LaDonna — *Gans, Gans & Associates*
Kacyn, Louis J. — *Egon Zehnder International Inc.*
Kleinstein, Scott — *Source Services Corporation*
Lang, Sharon A. — *Ray & Berndtson*

Northbrook
Andrews, J. Douglas — *Clarey & Andrews, Inc.*
Clarey, Jack R. — *Clarey & Andrews, Inc.*

Oak Brook
Beaudin, Elizabeth C. — *Callan Associates, Ltd.*
Brzezinski, Ronald T. — *Callan Associates, Ltd.*
Callan, Robert M. — *Callan Associates, Ltd.*
Cizek, John T. — *Cizek Associates, Inc.*
Kunzer, William J. — *Kunzer Associates, Ltd.*
Ray, Marianne C. — *Callan Associates, Ltd.*
Stranberg, James R. — *Callan Associates, Ltd.*
Walker, Richard — *Bradford & Galt, Inc.*

Oak Park
Cowell, Roy A. — *Cowell & Associates, Ltd.*

Oakbrook Terrace
Lipe, Jerold L. — *Compass Group Ltd.*

Rolling Meadows
Clawson, Bob — *Source Services Corporation*
Fyhrie, David — *Source Services Corporation*
Hayes, Lee — *Source Services Corporation*
Jensen, Robert — *Source Services Corporation*
Power, Michael — *Source Services Corporation*
Price, Carl — *Source Services Corporation*

Rosemont
Biestek, Paul J. — *Paul J. Biestek Associates, Inc.*
Cronin, Richard J. — *Hodge-Cronin & Associates, Inc.*

Schaumburg
Silverman, Paul M. — *The Marshall Group*

Springfield
Cona, Joseph A. — *Cona Personnel Search*

Westchester
Anderson, Steve — *CPS Inc.*
Balch, Randy — *CPS Inc.*
Brady, Robert — *CPS Inc.*
Brandeis, Richard — *CPS Inc.*
Christiansen, Amy — *CPS Inc.*
Christiansen, Doug — *CPS Inc.*
Coulman, Karen — *CPS Inc.*
Dixon, Aris — *CPS Inc.*
Dwyer, Julie — *CPS Inc.*
Ervin, Darlene — *CPS Inc.*
Fogarty, Michael — *CPS Inc.*
Graham, Dale — *CPS Inc.*
Grzybowski, Jill — *CPS Inc.*
Hartle, Larry — *CPS Inc.*
Heafey, Bill — *CPS Inc.*
Irish, Alan — *CPS Inc.*
Judy, Otto — *CPS Inc.*
Karalis, William — *CPS Inc.*
Kehoe, Mike — *CPS Inc.*
Kilcoyne, Pat — *CPS Inc.*
Kkorzyniewski, Nicole — *CPS Inc.*
Laird, Cheryl — *CPS Inc.*
Leahy, Jan — *CPS Inc.*
Lofthouse, Cindy — *CPS Inc.*
McAndrews, Kathy — *CPS Inc.*
Michaels, Joseph — *CPS Inc.*
Mohr, Brian — *CPS Inc.*
Murphy, Erin — *CPS Inc.*
Mydlach, Renee — *CPS Inc.*
Ottenritter, Chris — *CPS Inc.*
Pedley, Jill — *CPS Inc.*
Peterson, John — *CPS Inc.*
Pierotazio, John — *CPS Inc.*

Pomerance, Mark — *CPS Inc.*
Reuter, Tandom — *CPS Inc.*
Riederer, Larry — *CPS Inc.*
Saletra, Andrew — *CPS Inc.*
Sanders, Natalie — *CPS Inc.*
Scalamera, Tom — *CPS Inc.*
Schueneman, David — *CPS Inc.*
Signer, Julie — *CPS Inc.*
Steer, Joe — *CPS Inc.*
Stern, Stephen — *CPS Inc.*
Sterner, Doug — *CPS Inc.*
Thomas, Cheryl M. — *CPS Inc.*
Thomas, Kim — *CPS Inc.*
Tovrog, Dan — *CPS Inc.*
Truemper, Dean — *CPS Inc.*
Tullberg, Tina — *CPS Inc.*

Wilmette
Krueger, Kurt — *Krueger Associates*

Indiana

Indianapolis
Bickett, Nicole — *Source Services Corporation*
Blassaras, Peggy — *Source Services Corporation*
Brassard, Gary — *Source Services Corporation*
Emerson, Randall — *Source Services Corporation*
Houterloot, Tim — *Source Services Corporation*
Long, Mark — *Source Services Corporation*
Necessary, Rick — *Source Services Corporation*
Walker, Ann — *Source Services Corporation*

South Bend
Racht, Janet G. — *Crowe, Chizek and Company, LLP*
Sallows, Jill S. — *Crowe, Chizek and Company, LLP*

Iowa

West Des Moines
Hildebrand, Thomas B. — *Professional Resources Group, Inc.*
Leininger, Dennis — *Key Employment Services*

Kansas

Overland Park
Berger, Jeffrey — *Source Services Corporation*
Blocher, John — *Source Services Corporation*
Fingers, David — *Bradford & Galt, Inc.*
Grossman, James — *Source Services Corporation*
Haselby, James — *Source Services Corporation*
Haughton, Michael — *DeFrain, Mayer LLC*
Heideman, Mary Marren — *DeFrain, Mayer LLC*
Hillyer, Carolyn — *Source Services Corporation*
Jackson, Barry — *Morgan Hunter Corp.*
Johnson, Pete — *Morgan Hunter Corp.*
Msidment, Roger — *Source Services Corporation*
Myers, Kay — *Signature Staffing*
Peternell, Melanie — *Signature Staffing*
Robb, Tammy — *Source Services Corporation*
Rowland, James — *Source Services Corporation*
Ryan, Kathleen — *Source Services Corporation*
Tilley, Kyle — *Source Services Corporation*
Tryon, Katey — *DeFrain, Mayer LLC*
Viviano, Cathleen — *Source Services Corporation*

Shawnee-Mission
Beeson, William B. — *Lawrence-Leiter & Co. Management Conultants*

Czepiel, Susan — *CPS Inc.*
Epstein, Kathy J. — *Lamalie Amrop International*
Feldman, Kimberley — *Atlantic Search Group, Inc.*
Gourley, Timothy — *Source Services Corporation*
Hazerjian, Cynthia — *CPS Inc.*
Hensley, Gayla — *Atlantic Search Group, Inc.*
Holodnak, William A. — *J. Robert Scott*
Howell, Robert B. — *Atlantic Search Group, Inc.*
Howell, Robert B. — *Atlantic Search Group, Inc.*
Jackowitz, Todd — *J. Robert Scott*
Jones, Daniel F. — *Atlantic Search Group, Inc.*
Lapat, Aaron D. — *J. Robert Scott*
Manzo, Renee — *Atlantic Search Group, Inc.*
McClure, James K. — *Korn/Ferry International*
McMahan, Stephen — *Source Services Corporation*
Mead-Fox, David — *Korn/Ferry International*
Nunziata, Peter — *Atlantic Search Group, Inc.*
O'Connell, Mary — *CPS Inc.*
Orr, Stacie — *Source Services Corporation*
Ouellette, Christopher — *Source Services Corporation*
Papoulias, Cathy — *Pendleton James and Associates, Inc.*
Rabinowitz, Peter A. — *P.A.R. Associates Inc.*
Reardon, Joseph — *Source Services Corporation*
Resnic, Alan — *Source Services Corporation*
Reynolds, Catherine — *Winter, Wyman & Company*
Rossi, George A. — *Heidrick & Struggles, Inc.*
Schaad, Carl A. — *Heidrick & Struggles, Inc.*
Serba, Kerri — *Source Services Corporation*
Shapiro, Elaine — *CPS Inc.*
Smith, Timothy — *Source Services Corporation*
Sostilio, Louis — *Source Services Corporation*
Tscelli, Maureen — *Source Services Corporation*
Vande-Water, Katie — *J. Robert Scott*
Walton, Bruce H. — *Heidrick & Struggles, Inc.*
Warter, Mark — *Isaacson, Miller*
Webber, Edward — *Source Services Corporation*
Williams, Walter E. — *Lamalie Amrop International*
Zegel, Gary — *Source Services Corporation*

Burlington
Browne, Michael — *Source Services Corporation*
Cheah, Victor — *Source Services Corporation*
Chronopoulos, Dennis — *Source Services Corporation*
Di Filippo, Thomas — *Source Services Corporation*
Finnerty, James — *Source Services Corporation*
Glickman, Leenie — *Source Services Corporation*
Harris, Seth O. — *Christian & Timbers*
Inger, Barry — *Source Services Corporation*
Lundy, Martin — *Source Services Corporation*
Macrides, Michael — *Source Services Corporation*
Mader, Stephen P. — *Christian & Timbers*
Moore, Craig — *Source Services Corporation*
Murry, John — *Source Services Corporation*
Nephew, Robert — *Christian & Timbers*
Twomey, James — *Source Services Corporation*
Vairo, Leonard A. — *Christian & Timbers*
Winkowski, Stephen — *Source Services Corporation*

Cambridge
Keyser, Anne — *A.T. Kearney, Inc.*
Wacholz, Rick — *A.T. Kearney, Inc.*
Zaleta, Andy R. — *A.T. Kearney, Inc.*
Dedham
Kelly, Susan D. — *S.D. Kelly & Associates, Inc.*
Marion, Michael — *S.D. Kelly & Associates, Inc.*
Nolan, Jean M. — *S.D. Kelly & Associates, Inc.*
Parkin, Myrna — *S.D. Kelly & Associates, Inc.*
Shamir, Ben — *S.D. Kelly & Associates, Inc.*
Thies, Gary — *S.D. Kelly & Associates, Inc.*
Farmingham
Silver, Lee — *L. A. Silver Associates, Inc.*
Spiegel, Gayle — *L. A. Silver Associates, Inc.*
Lexington
Cochran, Hale — *Fenwick Partners*
Fitzgerald, Diane — *Fitzgerald Associates*
Fitzgerald, Geoffrey — *Fitzgerald Associates*
Germaine, Debra — *Fenwick Partners*
Polachi, Charles A. — *Fenwick Partners*
Polachi, Peter V. — *Fenwick Partners*
Rudzinsky, Howard — *Louis Rudzinsky Associates*
Rudzinsky, Jeffrey — *Louis Rudzinsky Associates*
Starner, William S. — *Fenwick Partners*
Manchester-by-the-Sea
Gilreath, James M. — *Gilreath Weatherby, Inc.*
Mendon
Fishback, Joren — *Derek Associates, Inc.*
Natick
Leland, Paul — *McInturff & Associates, Inc.*
McInturff, Robert — *McInturff & Associates, Inc.*
Needham
Burke, John — *The Experts*
Porter, Albert — *The Experts*
Reece, Christopher S. — *Reece & Mruk Partners*
Newbury
Boyd, Lew — *Coastal International Inc.*
Stratton, Cary — *Coastal International Inc.*
North Andover
Marlow, William — *Straube Associates*
Norwood
Heffelfinger, Thomas V. — *Heffelfinger Associates, Inc.*
Kells, John — *Heffelfinger Associates, Inc.*
Sudbury
Travis, Michael — *Travis & Company*
Waltham
Acquaviva, Jay — *Winter, Wyman & Company*
Ahearn, Jennifer — *Logix, Inc.*
Aheran, Jennifer — *Logix Partners*
Aubin, Richard E. — *Aubin International Inc.*
Bell, Lisa — *Winter, Wyman & Company*
Biggins, Joseph — *Winter, Wyman & Company*
Boesel, James — *Logix Partners*
Boesel, Jim — *Logix, Inc.*
Bond, Allan — *Walden Associates*
Brovender, Claire — *Winter, Wyman & Company*
Burmaster, Holly — *Winter, Wyman & Company*
Cashman, Tracy — *Winter, Wyman & Company*
Coffey, Patty — *Winter, Wyman & Company*
Crumpton, Marc — *Logix Partners*
Crumpton, Marc — *Logix, Inc.*
Crumpton, Marc — *Walden Associates*
Fahlin, Kelly — *Winter, Wyman & Company*

Foley, Eileen — *Winter, Wyman & Company*
Fone, Carol — *Walden Associates*
Foreman, Rebecca — *Aubin International Inc.*
Glacy, Kurt — *Winter, Wyman & Company*
Glass, Sharon — *Logix Partners*
Glass, Sharon — *Logix, Inc.*
Gould, Adam — *Logix Partners*
Gould, Adam — *Logix, Inc.*
Gould, Dana — *Logix Partners*
Gould, Dana — *Logix, Inc.*
Hauver, Scott — *Logix Partners*
Hoffman, Brian — *Winter, Wyman & Company*
Houver, Scott — *Logix, Inc.*
Hull, Chuck — *Winter, Wyman & Company*
Hurley, Janeen — *Winter, Wyman & Company*
Ide, Ian — *Winter, Wyman & Company*
Johnson, Peter — *Winter, Wyman & Company*
Kasmouski, Steve — *Winter, Wyman & Company*
Kouble, Tim — *Logix Partners*
Kouble, Tim — *Logix, Inc.*
Langan, Marion — *Logix Partners*
Langan, Marion — *Logix, Inc.*
Lawner, Harvey — *Walden Associates*
Lewis, Susan — *Logix Partners*
Lewis, Susan — *Logix, Inc.*
Louden, Leo — *Winter, Wyman & Company*
Lyons, J. David — *Aubin International Inc.*
McManus, Paul — *Aubin International Inc.*
Miles, Marybeth — *Winter, Wyman & Company*
Morrill, Nancy — *Winter, Wyman & Company*
Newlon, Jay — *Logix, Inc.*
Newton, Jay — *Logix Partners*
Quinlan, Lynne — *Winter, Wyman & Company*
Richard, Ryan — *Logix Partners*
Richard, Ryan — *Logix, Inc.*
Roussel, Vicki — *Logix Partners*
Roussel, Vicki J. — *Logix, Inc.*
Rozentsvayg, Michael — *Logix Partners*
Rozentsvayg, Michael — *Logix, Inc.*
Simankov, Dmitry — *Logix, Inc.*
Steele, Kevin — *Winter, Wyman & Company*
Stenberg, Edward — *Winter, Wyman & Company*
Welch, Dale — *Winter, Wyman & Company*
Williams, Brad — *Winter, Wyman & Company*
Zell, David M. — *Logix Partners*

Wellesley
Beaver, Bentley H. — *The Onstott Group, Inc.*
Boltrus, Dick — *Sink, Walker, Boltrus International*
Bowen, Tad — *Executive Search International*
Burke, Karen A. — *Mazza & Riley, Inc. (a Korn/Ferry International affiliate)*
Campbell, Patricia A. — *The Onstott Group, Inc.*
Desai, Sushila — *Sink, Walker, Boltrus International*
Dromeshauser, Peter — *Dromeshauser Associates*
Gore, Les — *Executive Search International*
Gorfinkle, Gayle — *Executive Search International*
Klavens, Cecile J. — *The Pickwick Group, Inc.*
Lucarelli, Joan — *The Onstott Group, Inc.*
Mazza, David B. — *Mazza & Riley, Inc. (a Korn/Ferry International affiliate)*
Onstott, Joseph E. — *The Onstott Group, Inc.*
Shufelt, Doug — *Sink, Walker, Boltrus International*
Sink, Cliff — *Sink, Walker, Boltrus International*

Walker, Douglas G. — *Sink, Walker, Boltrus International*

Wellesley Hills
Garfinkle, Steven M. — *Battalia Winston International*
Hillen, Skip — *The McCormick Group, Inc.*
Nagler, Leon G. — *Nagler, Robins & Poe, Inc.*
Poe, James B. — *Nagler, Robins & Poe, Inc.*
Robins, Jeri N. — *Nagler, Robins & Poe, Inc.*

Westborough
Chase, James — *Source Services Corporation*
DeMarco, Robert — *Source Services Corporation*
Evans, Timothy — *Source Services Corporation*
Grandinetti, Suzanne — *Source Services Corporation*
Lapointe, Fabien — *Source Services Corporation*
Leighton, Mark — *Source Services Corporation*
Maxwell, John — *Source Services Corporation*
Pototo, Brian — *Source Services Corporation*
Preusse, Eric — *Source Services Corporation*
Rennell, Thomas — *Source Services Corporation*
Sardella, Sharon — *Source Services Corporation*
Yeaton, Robert — *Source Services Corporation*

Woburn
Lamb, Angus K. — *Raymond Karsan Associates*
Sacerdote, John — *Raymond Karsan Associates*
Swanson, Dick — *Raymond Karsan Associates*

Worcester
George, Delores F. — *Delores F. George Human Resource Management & Consulting Industry*

Michigan
Birmingham
Czamanske, Paul W. — *Compass Group Ltd.*
Sturtz, James W. — *Compass Group Ltd.*

Bloomfield Hills
Crowder, Edward W. — *Crowder & Company*
Hokanson, Mark D. — *Crowder & Company*
Klopfenstein, Edward L. — *Crowder & Company*

Center Line
Line, Joseph T. — *Sharrow & Associates*

Grand Rapids
Anderson, Matthew — *Source Services Corporation*
Combs, Thomas — *Source Services Corporation*
Fales, Scott — *Source Services Corporation*
Harvey, Mike — *Advanced Executive Resources*
Haystead, Steve — *Advanced Executive Resources*
Mairn, Todd — *Source Services Corporation*
Peal, Matthew — *Source Services Corporation*
Schlpma, Christine — *Advanced Executive Resources*
Sochacki, Michael — *Source Services Corporation*
Trewhella, Michael — *Source Services Corporation*
Willbrandt, Curt — *Source Services Corporation*

Southfield
Brunner, Terry — *Source Services Corporation*
Buzolits, Patrick — *Source Services Corporation*
Comai, Christine — *Source Services Corporation*
Dow, Lori — *Davidson, Laird & Associates, Inc.*
Foster, Bradley — *Source Services Corporation*
Giles, Joe L. — *Joe L. Giles and Associates, Inc.*
Gluzman, Arthur — *Source Services Corporation*
Guc, Stephen — *Source Services Corporation*

Klusman, Edwin — *Source Services Corporation*
Lewis, Daniel — *Source Services Corporation*
Swanner, William — *Source Services Corporation*
Van Steenkiste, Julie — *Davidson, Laird & Associates, Inc.*

Troy
Brown, Charlene N. — *Accent on Achievement, Inc.*
Edwards, Verba L. — *Wing Tips & Pumps, Inc.*
Gray, Betty — *Accent on Achievement, Inc.*
Rabe, William — *Sales Executives Inc.*
Statson, Dale E. — *Sales Executives Inc.*

Minnesota
Bloomington
Kennedy, Walter — *Source Services Corporation*

Minneapolis
Barnum, Toni M. — *Stone Murphy & Olson*
Cline, Mark — *NYCOR Search, Inc.*
Do, Sonnie — *Whitney & Associates, Inc.*
Dubbs, William — *Williams Executive Search, Inc.*
Heaney, Thomas — *Korn/Ferry International*
Heinze, David — *Heinze & Associates, Inc.*
Herman, Pat — *Whitney & Associates, Inc.*
Hykes, Don A. — *A.T. Kearney, Inc.*
Johnson, Keith — *Romac & Associates*
Kennedy, Walter — *Source Services Corporation*
Mathias, Kathy — *Stone Murphy & Olson*
McDonnell, Julie — *Technical Personnel of Minnesota*
Mertensotto, Chuck H. — *Whitney & Associates, Inc.*
Murphy, Gary J. — *Stone Murphy & Olson*
Nymark, John — *NYCOR Search, Inc.*
Nymark, Paul — *NYCOR Search, Inc.*
Olsen, Kristine — *Williams Executive Search, Inc.*
Pappas, Christina E. — *Williams Executive Search, Inc.*
Stein, Terry W. — *Stewart, Stein and Scott, Ltd.*
Stewart, Jeffrey O. — *Stewart, Stein and Scott, Ltd.*
Whitney, David L. — *Whitney & Associates, Inc.*
Williams, Angie — *Whitney & Associates, Inc.*
Yungerberg, Steven — *Steven Yungerberg Associates Inc.*

Minnetonka
Jaffe, Mark — *Wyatt & Jaffe*
Stephenson, Don L. — *Ells Personnel System Inc.*
Wyatt, James — *Wyatt & Jaffe*

Plymouth
Anderson, Dean C. — *Corporate Resources Professional Placement*
Lanctot, William D. — *Corporate Resources Professional Placement*

Mississippi
Ridgeland
Barlow, Ken H. — *The Cherbonnier Group, Inc.*

Missouri
Chesterfield
Brother, Joy — *Charles Luntz & Associates. Inc.*
Luntz, Charles E. — *Charles Luntz & Associates. Inc.*

Clayton
Bence, Robert J. — *DHR International, Inc.*

Kansas City
Howe, Theodore — *Romac & Associates*
Pickering, Dale — *Agri-Tech Personnel, Inc.*
Pickering, Rita — *Agri-Tech Personnel, Inc.*
Romang, Paula — *Agri-Tech Personnel, Inc.*

St. Louis
Albert, Richard — *Source Services Corporation*
Anderson, Richard — *Grant Cooper and Associates*
Bearman, Linda — *Grant Cooper and Associates*
Deck, Jack — *Source Services Corporation*
Garrett, Mark — *Source Services Corporation*
Goldenberg, Susan — *Grant Cooper and Associates*
Hart, James — *Source Services Corporation*
Issacs, Judith A. — *Grant Cooper and Associates*
Knoll, Robert — *Source Services Corporation*
Loeb, Stephen H. — *Grant Cooper and Associates*
Milner, Carol — *Source Services Corporation*
Paul, Kathleen — *Source Services Corporation*
Ryan, Mark — *Source Services Corporation*
Trieschmann, Daniel — *Source Services Corporation*
Tunney, William — *Grant Cooper and Associates*
Weinberg, Melvin — *Romac & Associates*
Wirtshafter, Linda — *Grant Cooper and Associates*
Zamborsky, George — *Boyden*

Nebraska
Omaha
Moore, Thomas — *Aureus Group*
Ulbert, Nancy — *Aureus Group*

Nevada
Las Vegas
Benson, Edward — *Source Services Corporation*
Bidelman, Richard — *Source Services Corporation*

New Hampshire
Center Harbor
Barger, H. Carter — *Barger & Sargeant, Inc.*

Exeter
Bartholdi, Ted — *Bartholdi & Company, Inc.*

Nashua
Amico, Robert — *Source Services Corporation*
Baranowski, Peter — *Source Services Corporation*
Conard, Rodney J. — *Conard Associates, Inc.*
Hult, Dana — *Source Services Corporation*
McMahan, Stephen — *Source Services Corporation*
Paradise, Malcolm — *Source Services Corporation*
Sapers, Mark — *Source Services Corporation*

Portsmouth
Capra, Jamie — *Warren, Morris & Madison*
Higgins, Dave — *Warren, Morris & Madison*
Scott, Cory — *Warren, Morris & Madison*
Warren, Scott — *Warren, Morris & Madison*

Rye
McDonald, Scott A. — *McDonald Associates International*

New Jersey
Chatham
Christenson, H. Alan — *Christenson & Hutchison*
Hutchison, William K. — *Christenson & Hutchison*
McDowell, Robert N. — *Christenson & Hutchison*

Rutherford
Macdonald, G. William — *The Macdonald Group, Inc.*

Secaucus
Robinson, Bruce — *Bruce Robinson Associates*
Robinson, Eric B. — *Bruce Robinson Associates*

Short Hills
Davis, John J. — *John J. Davis & Associates, Inc.*

Sparta
Lardner, Lucy D. — *Tully/Woodmansee International, Inc.*

Summit
Foreman, David C. — *Koontz, Jeffries & Associates, Inc.*
Koontz, Donald N. — *Koontz, Jeffries & Associates, Inc.*
Nichols, Gary — *Koontz, Jeffries & Associates, Inc.*

Tennent
Porada, Stephen D. — *CAP Inc.*

Upper Saddle River
Tolette, Skip — *The Schmitt Tolette Group*

Verona
Ascher, Susan P. — *The Ascher Group*
Ehrgott, Elizabeth — *The Ascher Group*

West Orange
Arms, Douglas — *TOPAZ International, Inc.*
Arms, Douglas — *TOPAZ Legal Solutions*
Cohen, Pamela — *TOPAZ International, Inc.*
Cohen, Pamela — *TOPAZ Legal Solutions*
Cruz, Catherine — *TOPAZ International, Inc.*
Cruz, Catherine — *TOPAZ Legal Solutions*
Ebeling, John A. — *Gilbert Tweed/INESA*
Gaines, Ronni L. — *TOPAZ International, Inc.*
Gaines, Ronni L. — *TOPAZ Legal Solutions*
Hanley, Maureen E. — *Gilbert Tweed/INESA*
Holland, Kathleen — *TOPAZ International, Inc.*
Holland, Kathleen — *TOPAZ Legal Solutions*
Mashakas, Elizabeth — *TOPAZ International, Inc.*
Mashakas, Elizabeth — *TOPAZ Legal Solutions*
Michaels, Stewart — *TOPAZ International, Inc.*
Michaels, Stewart — *TOPAZ Legal Solutions*
Pinson, Stephanie L. — *Gilbert Tweed/INESA*

Woodbridge
Cram, Noel — *R.P. Barone Associates*
Hughes, James J. — *R.P. Barone Associates*
Rizzo, L. Donald — *R.P. Barone Associates*

New York

Auburn
Jaworski, Mary A. — *Tully/Woodmansee International, Inc.*

Fayetteville
Atkinson, S. Graham — *Raymond Karsan Associates*

Garden City
Portanova, Peter M. — *R.O.I. Associates, Inc.*

Great Neck
Attell, Harold — *A.E. Feldman Associates*
Bender, Alan — *Bender Executive Search*
Feldman, Abe — *A.E. Feldman Associates*
Lokken, Karen — *A.E. Feldman Associates*
Looney, Scott — *A.E. Feldman Associates*
Roberts, Mitch — *A.E. Feldman Associates*

Schene, Philip — *A.E. Feldman Associates*
Schwam, Carol — *A.E. Feldman Associates*
Skalet, Ira — *A.E. Feldman Associates*

Hauppauge
Ames, George C. — *Ames O'Neill Associates*

Jericho
Mogul, Gene — *Mogul Consultants, Inc.*

Mamaroneck
Rozner, Burton L. — *Oliver & Rozner Associates, Inc.*

New York
Adams, Len — *The KPA Group*
Allen, Jean E. — *Lamalie Amrop International*
Alpeyrie, Jean-Louis — *Heidrick & Struggles, Inc.*
Aronin, Michael — *Fisher-Todd Associates*
Atkins, Laurie — *Battalia Winston International*
Bailey, David O. — *Ray & Berndtson*
Bassler, John — *Korn/Ferry International*
Battalia, O. William — *Battalia Winston International*
Bennett, Jo — *Battalia Winston International*
Bigelow, Dennis — *Marshall Consultants, Inc.*
Bishop, Susan — *Bishop Partners*
Blumenthal, Paula — *J.P. Canon Associates*
Bogansky, Amy — *Conex Incorporated*
Borland, James — *Goodrich & Sherwood Associates, Inc.*
Boyle, Russell E. — *Egon Zehnder International Inc.*
Bratches, Howard — *Thorndike Deland Associates*
Brieger, Steve — *Thorne, Brieger Associates Inc.*
Brooks, Bernard E. — *Mruk & Partners/EMA Partners Int'l*
Brophy, Melissa — *Maximum Management Corp.*
Bullock, Conni — *Earley Kielty and Associates, Inc.*
Busterna, Charles — *The KPA Group*
Carideo, Joseph — *Thorndike Deland Associates*
Carro, Carl R. — *Executive Search Consultants International, Inc.*
Caudill, Nancy — *Bishop Partners*
Caudill, Nancy — *Webb, Johnson Associates, Inc.*
Chan, Margaret — *Webb, Johnson Associates, Inc.*
Colasanto, Frank M. — *W.R. Rosato & Associates, Inc.*
Collins, Tom — *J.B. Homer Associates, Inc.*
Cornehlsen, James H. — *Skott/Edwards Consultants, Inc.*
Cunningham, Robert Y. — *Goodrich & Sherwood Associates, Inc.*
Daily, John C. — *Handy HRM Corp.*
Daniel, Beverly — *Foy, Schneid & Daniel, Inc.*
Davis, Bert — *Bert Davis Executive Search, Inc.*
Davis, John — *John J. Davis & Associates, Inc.*
Davis, Steven M. — *Sullivan & Company*
Del Prete, Karen — *Gilbert Tweed/INESA*
DiFilippo, James — *Korn/Ferry International*
Dotson, M. Ileen — *Dotson & Associates*
Doyle, James W. — *Executive Search Consultants International, Inc.*
Edwards, Robert — *J.P. Canon Associates*
Ellis, William — *Interspace Interactive Inc.*
Erder, Debra — *Canny, Bowen Inc.*
Erikson, Theodore J. — *Erikson Consulting Associates, Inc.*

Rios, Vincent — *Source Services Corporation*
Robertson, Bruce J. — *Lamalie Amrop International*
Rohan, James E. — *J.P. Canon Associates*
Rohan, Kevin A. — *J.P. Canon Associates*
Rosato, William R. — *W.R. Rosato & Associates, Inc.*
Runquist, U.W. — *Webb, Johnson Associates, Inc.*
Russo, Karen — *Maximum Management Corp.*
Sarn, Allan G. — *Allan Sarn Associates Inc.*
Savvas, Carol Diane — *Ledbetter/Davidson International, Inc.*
Sawyer, Patricia L. — *Smith & Sawyer Inc.*
Schappell, Marc P. — *Egon Zehnder International Inc.*
Schedra, Sharon — *Earley Kielty and Associates, Inc.*
Schiavone, Mary Rose — *Canny, Bowen Inc.*
Schmidt, Peter R. — *Boyden*
Seiden, Steven A. — *Seiden Krieger Associates, Inc.*
Shapanka, Samuel — *Source Services Corporation*
Shea, Christopher J. — *Ingram & Aydelotte Inc./I-I-C Partners*
Shemin, Grace — *Maximum Management Corp.*
Sherwood, Andrew — *Goodrich & Sherwood Associates, Inc.*
Shield, Nancy — *Maximum Management Corp.*
Simmons, Gerald J. — *Handy HRM Corp.*
Simon, John — *John J. Davis & Associates, Inc.*
Slosar, John — *Boyden*
Smirnov, Tatiana — *Allan Sarn Associates Inc.*
Smith, Robert L. — *Smith & Sawyer Inc.*
Smoller, Howard — *Source Services Corporation*
Sorgen, Jay — *Source Services Corporation*
Spence, Gene L. — *Heidrick & Struggles, Inc.*
Spera, Stefanie — *A.T. Kearney, Inc.*
Stack, Richard — *Source Services Corporation*
Stark, Jeff — *Thorne, Brieger Associates Inc.*
Sterling, Jay — *Earley Kielty and Associates, Inc.*
Stokes, John — *Nordeman Grimm, Inc.*
Sucato, Carolyn — *Jay Gaines & Company, Inc.*
Sur, William K. — *Canny, Bowen Inc.*
Sussman, Lynda — *Gilbert Tweed/INESA*
Tappan, Michael A. — *Ward Howell International, Inc.*
Teger, Stella — *Source Services Corporation*
Thrapp, Mark C. — *Executive Search Consultants International, Inc.*
Timoney, Laura — *Bishop Partners*
Tweed, Janet — *Gilbert Tweed/INESA*
Van Campen, Jerry — *Gilbert & Van Campen International*
Venable, William W. — *Thorndike Deland Associates*
von Baillou, Astrid — *Richard Kinser & Associates*
Vroom, Cynthia D. — *Cyntal International Ltd*
Webb, George H. — *Webb, Johnson Associates, Inc.*
Weber, Fred — *J.B. Homer Associates, Inc.*
Wheatley, William — *Drummond Associates, Inc.*
Winston, Dale — *Battalia Winston International*
Witte, David L. — *Ward Howell International, Inc.*
Wood, John S. — *Egon Zehnder International Inc.*
Work, Alan — *Quantex Associates, Inc.*
Yossem, Sheila — *Bishop Partners*

Zinn, Don — *Quantex Associates, Inc.*
Zucker, Nancy — *Maximum Management Corp.*

North Salem
Flanagan, Robert M. — *Robert M. Flanagan & Associates, Ltd.*
Normann, Amy — *Robert M. Flanagan & Associates, Ltd.*

Port Washington
Janis, Laurence — *Integrated Search Solutions Group, LLC*
Sessa, Vincent J. — *Integrated Search Solutions Group, LLC*

Rochester
Baker, Gary M. — *Cochran, Cochran & Yale, Inc.*
Baltaglia, Michael — *Cochran, Cochran & Yale, Inc.*
Buckles, Donna — *Cochran, Cochran & Yale, Inc.*
Call, David — *Cochran, Cochran & Yale, Inc.*
Capizzi, Karen — *Cochran, Cochran & Yale, Inc.*
Curtis, Ellissa — *Cochran, Cochran & Yale, Inc.*
Frazier, John — *Cochran, Cochran & Yale, Inc.*
Himlin, Amy — *Cochran, Cochran & Yale, Inc.*
Jordan, Jon — *Cochran, Cochran & Yale, Inc.*
Klein, Mary Jo — *Cochran, Cochran & Yale, Inc.*
Miller, David — *Cochran, Cochran & Yale, Inc.*
Misiurewicz, Marc — *Cochran, Cochran & Yale, Inc.*
Murphy, Cornelius J. — *Goodrich & Sherwood Associates, Inc.*
Sanow, Robert — *Cochran, Cochran & Yale, Inc.*

Scarsdale
Long, William G. — *McDonald, Long & Associates, Inc.*
Press, Fred — *Adept Tech Recruiting*

Somers
Gorman, T. Patrick — *Techsearch Services, Inc.*
Taft, David G. — *Techsearch Services, Inc.*

White Plains
Bland, Walter — *Source Services Corporation*
Burch, Donald — *Source Services Corporation*
Devito, Alice — *Source Services Corporation*
Eiseman, Joe — *Source Services Corporation*
Laskin, Sandy — *Source Services Corporation*
Maggio, Mary — *Source Services Corporation*
Occhiboi, Emil — *Source Services Corporation*
Paliwoda, William — *Source Services Corporation*
Parente, James — *Source Services Corporation*
Patel, Shailesh — *Source Services Corporation*
Sirena, Evelyn — *Source Services Corporation*

Williamsville
Critchley, Walter — *Cochran, Cochran & Yale, Inc.*
DiCioccio, Carmen — *Cochran, Cochran & Yale, Inc.*
Gestwick, Daniel — *Cochran, Cochran & Yale, Inc.*
Januale, Lois — *Cochran, Cochran & Yale, Inc.*

North Carolina

Cary
Duley, Richard I. — *ARJay & Associates*
Miller, Russel E. — *ARJay & Associates*

Chapel Hill
Grantham, John — *Grantham & Co., Inc.*
Strickland, Katie — *Grantham & Co., Inc.*

Dublin
Kent, Melvin — *Melvin Kent & Associates, Inc.*
Euclid
Orkin, Ralph — *Sanford Rose Associates*
Orkin, Sheilah — *Sanford Rose Associates*
Fairlawn
Jacobson, Rick — *The Windham Group*
Independence
Banko, Scott — *Source Services Corporation*
Barnaby, Richard — *Source Services Corporation*
Bernas, Sharon — *Source Services Corporation*
Carnal, Rick — *Source Services Corporation*
Fulger, Herbert — *Source Services Corporation*
Gilinsky, David — *Source Services Corporation*
Mayer, Thomas — *Source Services Corporation*
Miller, Timothy — *Source Services Corporation*
Morrow, Melanie — *Source Services Corporation*
Samsel, Randy — *Source Services Corporation*
Seamon, Kenneth — *Source Services Corporation*
Tschan, Stephen — *Source Services Corporation*
Wood, Gary — *Source Services Corporation*
Maumee
Galbraith, Deborah M. — *Stratford Group*
Ross, William J. — *Flowers & Associates*
Miamisburg
O'Reilly, John — *Stratford Group*
Willoughby Hills
Wayne, Cary S. — *ProSearch Inc.*

Oklahoma
Tulsa
Sanitago, Anthony — *TaxSearch, Inc.*

Oregon
Clackamas
Jansen, Douglas L. — *Search Northwest Associates*
Hillsboro
Furlong, James W. — *Furlong Search, Inc.*
Portland
Barnett, Barbara — *D. Brown and Associates, Inc.*
Belden, Jeannette — *Source Services Corporation*
Boehm, Robin — *D. Brown and Associates, Inc.*
Bradley, Dalena — *Woodworth International Group*
Brown, Dennis — *D. Brown and Associates, Inc.*
Brown, Steffan — *Woodworth International Group*
Bryant, Henry — *D. Brown and Associates, Inc.*
Conners, Theresa — *D. Brown and Associates, Inc.*
Diers, Gary — *Source Services Corporation*
Ervin, Russell — *Source Services Corporation*
Hunsaker, Floyd — *Woodworth International Group*
Irwin, Mark — *Source Services Corporation*
Kennedy, Craig — *Source Services Corporation*
Kondra, Vernon J. — *The Douglas Reiter Company, Inc.*
Kopec, Tom — *D. Brown and Associates, Inc.*
Mathias, Douglas — *Source Services Corporation*
Matthews, Corwin — *Woodworth International Group*
Moran, Douglas — *Source Services Corporation*
Papasadero, Kathleen — *Woodworth International Group*
Phipps, Peggy — *Woodworth International Group*

Redding, Denise — *The Douglas Reiter Company, Inc.*
Reiter, Douglas — *The Douglas Reiter Company, Inc.*
Simmons, Deborah — *Source Services Corporation*
Stiles, Jack D. — *Sanford Rose Associates*
Stiles, Timothy — *Sanford Rose Associates*
Stovall, Randal — *D. Brown and Associates, Inc.*
Woodworth, Gail — *Woodworth International Group*

Pennsylvania
Ephrata
Dabich, Thomas M. — *Robert Harkins Associates, Inc.*
Harkins, Robert E. — *Robert Harkins Associates, Inc.*
Erie
Larsen, Jack B. — *Jack B. Larsen & Associates*
Pfister, Shelli — *Jack B. Larsen & Associates*
Feasterville
Wasserman, Harvey — *Churchill and Affiliates, Inc.*
Huntingdon Valley
Vogel, Michael S. — *Vogel Associates*
King of Prussia
Donnelly, Patti — *Source Services Corporation*
Finkel, Leslie — *Source Services Corporation*
Hight, Susan — *Source Services Corporation*
Inskeep, Thomas — *Source Services Corporation*
Januleski, Geoff — *Source Services Corporation*
Moretti, Denise — *Source Services Corporation*
Nolan, Robert — *Source Services Corporation*
Reid, Katherine — *Source Services Corporation*
Selvaggi, Esther — *Source Services Corporation*
Shackleford, David — *Source Services Corporation*
Storm, Deborah — *Source Services Corporation*
Philadelphia
Barthold, James A. — *McNichol Associates*
Battles, Jonathan — *Korn/Ferry International*
Blake, Eileen — *Howard Fischer Associates, Inc.*
Campbell, Robert Scott — *Wellington Management Group*
Cunningham, Lawrence — *Howard Fischer Associates, Inc.*
Fischer, Adam — *Howard Fischer Associates, Inc.*
Fischer, Howard M. — *Howard Fischer Associates, Inc.*
Gantar, Donna — *Howard Fischer Associates, Inc.*
Higgins, Donna — *Howard Fischer Associates, Inc.*
Janssen, Don — *Howard Fischer Associates, Inc.*
Kane, Karen — *Howard Fischer Associates, Inc.*
Kelly, Elizabeth Ann — *Wellington Management Group*
Koehler, Frank R. — *The Koehler Group*
Mallin, Ellen — *Howard Fischer Associates, Inc.*
Mansford, Keith — *Howard Fischer Associates, Inc.*
Mazor, Elly — *Howard Fischer Associates, Inc.*
McCann, Cornelia B. — *Spencer Stuart*
McNichol, John — *McNichol Associates*
Nehring, Keith — *Howard Fischer Associates, Inc.*
Ogilvie, Kit — *Howard Fischer Associates, Inc.*

Bassman, Robert — *Kaye-Bassman International Corp.*
Bassman, Sandy — *Kaye-Bassman International Corp.*
Beal, Richard D. — *A.T. Kearney, Inc.*
Blaydes, James — *Kaye-Bassman International Corp.*
Bloom, Howard C. — *Hernand & Partners*
Bloom, Joyce — *Hernand & Partners*
Brown, Steven — *Source Services Corporation*
Bryza, Robert M. — *Robert Lowell International*
Carter, Linda — *Source Services Corporation*
Cottingham, R.L. — *Marvin L. Silcott & Associates, Inc.*
Cruse, O.D. — *Spencer Stuart*
Danforth, W. Michael — *Hyde Danforth Wold & Co.*
Davison, Patricia E. — *Lamalie Amrop International*
de Gury, Glenn — *Taylor-Winfield, Inc.*
Demchak, James P. — *Sandhurst Associates*
Duncan, Dana — *Source Services Corporation*
Dunlow, Aimee — *Source Services Corporation*
Dupont, Rick — *Source Services Corporation*
England, Mark — *Austin-McGregor International*
Fitzgerald, Brian — *Source Services Corporation*
Forman, Donald R. — *Stanton Chase International*
Gabriel, David L. — *The Arcus Group*
Gilmore, Connie — *Taylor-Winfield, Inc.*
Goar, Duane R. — *Sandhurst Associates*
Grado, Eduardo — *Source Services Corporation*
Grumulaitis, Leo — *Source Services Corporation*
Hailey, H.M. — *Damon & Associates, Inc.*
Hamm, Gary — *Source Services Corporation*
Harrison, Patricia — *Source Services Corporation*
Hicks, Mike — *Damon & Associates, Inc.*
Hinojosa, Oscar — *Source Services Corporation*
Hyde, W. Jerry — *Hyde Danforth Wold & Co.*
Johnson, Rocky — *A.T. Kearney, Inc.*
Jones, Barbara — *Kaye-Bassman International Corp.*
Jones, Barbara J. — *Kaye-Bassman International Corp.*
Kaye, Jeffrey — *Kaye-Bassman International Corp.*
Lache, Shawn E. — *The Arcus Group*
Leblanc, Danny — *Source Services Corporation*
Lee, Everett — *Source Services Corporation*
Letcher, Harvey D. — *Sandhurst Associates*
Lewis, Jon A. — *Sandhurst Associates*
Love, David M. — *Ray & Berndtson*
Marye, George — *Damon & Associates, Inc.*
Mathis, Carrie — *Source Services Corporation*
McCreary, Charles "Chip" — *Austin-McGregor International*
McGinnis, Rita — *Source Services Corporation*
McGuire, J. Corey — *Peter W. Ambler Company*
McIntosh, Arthur — *Source Services Corporation*
McIntosh, Tad — *Source Services Corporation*
McNamara, Catherine — *Ray & Berndtson*
Mitchell, F. Wayne — *Korn/Ferry International*
Mitchell, John — *Romac & Associates*
Moerbe, Ed H. — *Stanton Chase International*
Moodley, Logan — *Austin-McGregor International*
Moore, Mark — *Wheeler, Moore & Elam Co.*
Morgan-Christopher, Jeanie — *Kaye-Bassman International Corp.*
Mott, Greg — *Source Services Corporation*

Mueller, Colleen — *Source Services Corporation*
Neidhart, Craig C. — *TNS Partners, Inc.*
Noebel, Todd R. — *The Noebel Search Group, Inc.*
Norman, Randy — *Austin-McGregor International*
Page, G. Schuyler — *A.T. Kearney, Inc.*
Pearson, Robert L. — *Lamalie Amrop International*
Peters, James N. — *TNS Partners, Inc.*
Pfau, Madelaine — *Heidrick & Struggles, Inc.*
Pillow, Charles — *Source Services Corporation*
Potter, Douglas C. — *Stanton Chase International*
Robertson, John A. — *Kaye-Bassman International Corp.*
Rowe, William D. — *D.E. Foster Partners Inc.*
Semyan, John K. — *TNS Partners, Inc.*
Silcott, Marvin L. — *Marvin L. Silcott & Associates, Inc.*
Silcott, Marvin L. — *Marvin L. Silcott & Associates, Inc.*
St. Clair, Alan — *TNS Partners, Inc.*
Stewart, Ross M. — *Human Resources Network Partners Inc.*
Strander, Dervin — *Source Services Corporation*
Susoreny, Samali — *Source Services Corporation*
Tuttle, Donald E. — *Tuttle Venture Group, Inc.*
Varrichio, Michael — *Source Services Corporation*
Wallace, Toby — *Source Services Corporation*
Ward, Les — *Source Services Corporation*
Watson, Stephen — *Ray & Berndtson*
Weiss, Elizabeth — *Source Services Corporation*
Wilburn, Dan — *Kaye-Bassman International Corp.*
Williams, Jack — *A.T. Kearney, Inc.*
Williams, Scott D. — *Heidrick & Struggles, Inc.*
Wingate, Mary — *Source Services Corporation*
Wise, J. Herbert — *Sandhurst Associates*
Wold, J. Ted W. — *Hyde Danforth Wold & Co.*
Wooldridge, Jeff — *Ray & Berndtson*

Houston
Anderson, Maria H. — *Barton Associates, Inc.*
Baird, John — *Professional Search Consultants*
Barnes, Gregory — *Korn/Ferry International*
Barton, Gary R. — *Barton Associates, Inc.*
Bass, M. Lynn — *Ray & Berndtson*
Batte, Carol — *Source Services Corporation*
Bernard, Bryan — *Source Services Corporation*
Betts, Suzette — *Source Services Corporation*
Brandenburg, David — *Professional Staffing Consultants*
Brunson, Therese — *Kors Montgomery International*
Budill, Edward — *Professional Search Consultants*
Cherbonnier, L. Michael — *TCG International, Inc.*
Cherbonnier, L. Michael — *The Cherbonnier Group, Inc.*
Christian, Philip — *Ray & Berndtson*
Doyle, Bobby — *Richard, Wayne and Roberts*
Edwards, Dorothy — *MSI International*
French, William G. — *Preng & Associates, Inc.*
Gadison, William — *Richard, Wayne and Roberts*
Gates, Lucille C. — *Lamalie Amrop International*
Gillespie, Thomas — *Professional Search Consultants*
Giries, Juliet D. — *Barton Associates, Inc.*
Gobert, Larry — *Professional Search Consultants*
Gray, Heather — *Source Services Corporation*

Richmond

Beck, Michael — *Don Richard Associates of Richmond, Inc.*
Gregory, Stephen — *Don Richard Associates of Richmond, Inc.*
Hall, Marty B. — *Catlin-Wells & White*
Jones, Amy E. — *The Corporate Connection, Ltd.*
Ramler, Carolyn S. — *The Corporate Connection, Ltd.*
Rotella, Marshall W. — *The Corporate Connection, Ltd.*
Smith, Lydia — *The Corporate Connection, Ltd.*
Tursi, Deborah J. — *The Corporate Connection, Ltd.*

Stanton

Burkhill, John — *The Talley Group*
Estes, Susan — *The Talley Group*
Jorgensen, Tom — *The Talley Group*

Vienna

Abell, Vincent W. — *MSI International*
Baglio, Robert — *Source Services Corporation*
Benjamin, Maurita — *Source Services Corporation*
Chatterjie, Alok — *MSI International*
Christy, Michael T. — *Heidrick & Struggles, Inc.*
Coneys, Bridget — *Source Services Corporation*
Dawson, William — *Source Services Corporation*
Dowell, Chris — *The Abbott Group, Inc.*
Elliott, A. Larry — *Heidrick & Struggles, Inc.*
Foster, Bonnie — *Kirkman & Searing, Inc.*
Foster, John — *Source Services Corporation*
Gaffney, Megan — *Source Services Corporation*
Gloss, Frederick C. — *F. Gloss International*
Gnatowski, Bruce — *Source Services Corporation*
Gresia, Paul — *Source Services Corporation*
Hanley, Steven — *Source Services Corporation*
Jacobson, Carolyn — *The Abbott Group, Inc.*
Kaplan, Traci — *Source Services Corporation*
Kasprzyk, Michael — *Source Services Corporation*
Kirkman, J. Michael — *Kirkman & Searing, Inc.*
Lewicki, Christopher — *MSI International*
Ludder, Mark — *Source Services Corporation*
McCarthy, Laura — *Source Services Corporation*
McNerney, Kevin A. — *Heidrick & Struggles, Inc.*
Meehan, John — *Source Services Corporation*
Moore, Suzanne — *Source Services Corporation*
Nelson, Mary — *Source Services Corporation*
Owen, Christopher — *Source Services Corporation*
Powell, Gregory — *Source Services Corporation*
Rice, Raymond D. — *Logue & Rice Inc.*
Searing, James M. — *Kirkman & Searing, Inc.*
Snowden, Charles — *Source Services Corporation*
Stephens, Andrew — *Source Services Corporation*
Stevens, Craig M. — *Kirkman & Searing, Inc.*
Velez, Hector — *Source Services Corporation*
Villella, Paul — *Source Services Corporation*
Vourakis, Zan — *ZanExec LLC*
Zavrel, Mark — *Source Services Corporation*

Virginia Beach

Danoff, Audrey — *Don Richard Associates of Tidewater, Inc.*
Hall, Robert — *Don Richard Associates of Tidewater, Inc.*
Ryan, Annette — *Don Richard Associates of Tidewater, Inc.*

Williamsburg

DiSalvo, Fred — *The Cambridge Group Ltd*

Washington

Bellevue

Bloomer, James E. — *L.W. Foote Company*
Bronger, Patricia — *Source Services Corporation*
Brown, Daniel — *Source Services Corporation*
Burden, Gene — *The Cherbonnier Group, Inc.*
Carlson, Eric — *Source Services Corporation*
Coffman, Brian — *Kossuth & Associates, Inc.*
Farthing, Andrew R. — *Parfitt Recruiting and Consulting*
Foote, Leland W. — *L.W. Foote Company*
Fuhrman, Dennis — *Source Services Corporation*
Heinrich, Scott — *Source Services Corporation*
Henneberry, Ward — *Source Services Corporation*
Kossuth, David — *Kossuth & Associates, Inc.*
Kossuth, Jane — *Kossuth & Associates, Inc.*
Messina, Marco — *Source Services Corporation*
Parfitt, William C. — *Parfitt Recruiting and Consulting*
Rudolph, Kenneth — *Kossuth & Associates, Inc.*
Schrenzel, Benjamin — *Parfitt Recruiting and Consulting*
Schwinden, William — *Source Services Corporation*
Varney, Monique — *Source Services Corporation*
Wert, Marty — *Parfitt Recruiting and Consulting*

Issaquah

Cushman, Judith — *Judith Cushman & Associates*

Seattle

Barbour, Mary Beth — *Tully/Woodmansee International, Inc.*
Fong, Robert — *Korn/Ferry International*

Spokane

Desgrosellier, Gary P. — *Personnel Unlimited/Executive Search*
Hergenrather, Richard A. — *Hergenrather & Company*

Vancouver

Drew, David R. — *Drew & Associates*

Wisconsin

Brookfield

Gibson, Bruce — *Gibson & Company Inc.*
Maglio, Charles J. — *Maglio and Company, Inc.*

Hartland

Mitton, Bill — *Executive Resource, Inc.*

Mequon

Barnes, Richard E. — *Barnes Development Group, LLC*
Barnes, Roanne L. — *Barnes Development Group, LLC*
Kaplan, Alexandra — *J.M. Eagle Partners Ltd.*
Moses, Jerry — *J.M. Eagle Partners Ltd.*
Waldoch, D. Mark — *Barnes Development Group, LLC*
Williams, Gary L. — *Barnes Development Group, LLC*

Milwaukee

Colvin, Teresa A. — *Jonas, Walters & Assoc., Inc.*
Daniels, Donna — *Jonas, Walters & Assoc., Inc.*
Flannery, Peter F. — *Jonas, Walters & Assoc., Inc.*
Hilgenberg, Thomas — *Source Services Corporation*

Appendix: Job-Search Resources

If you would like more information about executive recruiters, or if you would like to order other career strategy guides and subscribe to our online *Job-Seekers Network*, please refer to the following Hunt-Scanlon publications. To learn more about these products and ordering information, please call (800) 477-1199 toll free today!

- Executive Recruiters of North America
- Executive Search Review
- Headhunter News (at www.job-seekers.com)
- The Job-Seekers Network (at www.job-seekers.com)
- The Kingmaker
- The Select Guide to Human Resource Executives
- Silicon Valley Recruiters
- Wall $treet Recruiters
- Workplace America (at www.job-seekers.com)